CRIME IN THE UNITED STATES

2005

Edited by
Daniel Coleman
Shana Hertz

BERNAN PRESS

CRIME IN THE UNITED STATES

2005

Edited by
Daniel Coleman
Shana Hertz

BERNAN PRESS
Lanham, MD

ISBN: 978-1-59888-187-5

Printed by Automated Graphic Systems, Inc., White Plains, MD, on acid-free paper that meets the American National Standards Institute Z39-48 standard.

2008 2007 4 3 2 1

BERNAN PRESS
4611-F Assembly Drive
Lanham, MD 20706
800-274-4447
email: info@bernan.com
www.bernan.com

CONTENTS

PREFACE

Bernan Press's editorial and production departments, under the direction of publisher Kenneth E. Lawrence, completed the data gathering, copyediting, layout, and production of this volume. The data tables and figures were compiled by Daniel Coleman, under the supervision of Bernan Press's managing editor, Katherine DeBrandt. Daniel holds B.A. degrees in English and philosophy from Calvin College. Shana Hertz, who compiled the text and served as the volume's in-house editor, holds a B.S. in journalism and an M.S in education from Northwestern University.

Lateef Padgett, under the direction of production team leader Jo A. Wilson, did the layout and graphics preparation. With support from Automated Graphics Systems, Lateef and Jo assisted the editors tremendously with finalizing this publication.

Finally, special thanks are due to the many federal agency personnel who, as always, responded generously to our frequent need for assistance in obtaining data and background information.

Data included in this volume meet the publication standards established by the Federal Bureau of Investigation, from which they were obtained. Every effort has been made to select data that are accurate, meaningful, and useful. All data from reports, surveys, and administrative records are subject to errors arising from such factors as sampling variability, reporting errors, incomplete coverage, nonresponse, imputations, and processing error. Responsibility of the editors and publishers of this volume is limited to reasonable care in the reproduction and presentation of data obtained from sources believed to be reliable.

SECTION I:
SUMMARY OF THE UCR PROGRAM

SUMMARY OF THE UNIFORM CRIME REPORTING (UCR) PROGRAM

Bernan Press is proud to present its first edition of *Crime in the United States*. This title was formerly published by the Federal Bureau of Investigation (FBI), but is no longer available in printed form from the government.

This section examines the best way of using the publication's data and discusses the history of the UCR Program, which collects the data used in *Crime in the United States*.

About the UCR Program

The UCR Program's primary objective is to generate reliable information for use in law enforcement administration, operation, and management; however, over the course of the program, its data have become one of the country's leading social indicators.

The UCR Program is a nationwide, cooperative statistical effort of more than 17,000 city, university and college, county, state, tribal, and federal law enforcement agencies who voluntarily report data on crimes brought to their attention. During 2005, the law enforcement agencies that were active in the UCR Program represented 94.2 percent of the total population. This coverage included 95.4 percent of the nation's population in metropolitan statistical areas (MSAs), 86.9 percent of the population in cities outside metropolitan areas, and 89.2 percent of the population in nonmetropolitan counties.

Note for Users

It is important for UCR data users to remember that the FBI's primary objective is to generate a reliable set of crime statistics for use in law enforcement administration, operation, and management. The FBI does not provide a ranking of agencies; instead, it provides alphabetical tabulations of states, metropolitan statistical areas, cities with over 10,000 inhabitants, suburban and rural counties, and colleges and universities. Law enforcement officials use these data for their designed purposes. Additionally, the public relies on these data for information about the fluctuations in levels of crime from year to year, while criminologists, sociologists, legislators, city planners, media outlets, and other students of criminal justice use them for a variety of research and planning purposes. Since crime is a sociological phenomenon influenced by a variety of factors, the FBI discourages data users from ranking agencies and using the data as a measurement of the effectiveness of law enforcement.

To ensure that data are uniformly reported, the FBI provides contributing law enforcement agencies with a handbook that explains how to classify and score offenses and provides uniform crime offense definitions. Acknowledging that offense definitions may vary from state to state, the FBI cautions agencies to report offenses according to the guidelines provided in the handbook, rather than by local or state statutes. Most agencies make a good faith effort to comply with established guidelines.

Nearly 17,000 agencies contribute data to the FBI in any given year; however, because of computer problems, changes in record management systems, personnel shortages, or other reasons, some agencies cannot provide data for publication.

The UCR Program publishes the statistics most commonly requested by data users. More information regarding the availability of UCR Program data is available by telephone at (304) 625-4995, by fax at (304) 625-5394, or by e-mail at <cjis_comm@leo.gov>. E-mail data requests cannot be processed without the requester's full name, mailing address, and contact telephone number.

Variables Affecting Crime

Until data users examine all the variables that affect crime in a town, city, county, state, region, or college or university, they can make no meaningful comparisons.

Caution Against Ranking

In each edition of *Crime in the United States*, many entities—including news media, tourism agencies, and other organizations with an interest in crime in the nation—use reported figures to compile rankings of cities and counties. However, these rankings are merely a quick choice made by that data user; they provide no insight into the many variables that mold the crime in a particular town, city, county, state, or region. Consequently, these rankings may lead to simplistic and/or incomplete analyses, which can create misleading perceptions and thus adversely affect cities and counties, along with their residents.

Considering Other Characteristics of a Jurisdiction

To assess criminality and law enforcement's response from jurisdiction to jurisdiction, data users must consider many variables, some of which (despite having significant impact on crime) are not readily measurable or applicable among all locales. Geographic and demographic factors specific to each jurisdiction must be considered and applied in order to make an accurate and complete assessment of crime in that jurisdiction. Several sources of information are available to help the researcher explore the variables that affect crime in a particular locale. U.S. Census Bureau data, for example, can help the user better understand the makeup of a locale's population. The transience of the population, its racial and ethnic makeup, and its composition by age and gender, educational levels, and prevalent family structures are all key factors in assessing and understanding crime.

Local chambers of commerce, planning offices, and similar entities provide information regarding the economic and cultural makeup of cities and counties. Understanding a jurisdiction's industrial/economic base, its dependence upon neighboring jurisdictions, its transportation system, its economic dependence on nonresidents (such as tourists and convention attendees), and its proximity to military installations, correctional institutions, and other types of facilities all contribute to accurately gauging and interpreting the crime known to and reported by law enforcement.

The strength (including personnel and other resources) and aggressiveness of a jurisdiction's law enforcement agency are also key factors in understanding the nature and extent of crime occurring in that area. Although information pertaining to the number of sworn and civilian employees can be found in this publication, it cannot be used alone as an assessment of the emphasis that a community places on enforcing the law. For example, one city may report more crime than another comparable city because its law enforcement agency identifies more offenses. Attitudes of citizens toward crime and their crime reporting practices—especially for minor offenses—also have an impact on the volume of crimes known to police.

Make Valid Assessments of Crime

It is essential for all data users to become as well educated as possible about understanding and quantifying the nature and extent of crime in the United States and in the more than 17,000 jurisdictions represented by law enforcement contributors to the UCR Program. Valid assessments are possible only with careful study and analysis of the various unique conditions that affect each local law enforcement jurisdiction.

Some factors that are known to affect the volume and type of crime occurring from place to place are:

- Population density and degree of urbanization
- Variations in composition of population, particularly in the concentration of youth
- Stability of the population with respect to residents' mobility, commuting patterns, and transient factors
- Modes of transportation and highway systems
- Economic conditions, including median income, poverty level, and job availability
- Cultural factors and educational, recreational, and religious characteristics
- Family conditions, with respect to divorce and family cohesiveness
- Climate
- Effective strength of law enforcement agencies
- Administrative and investigative emphases of law enforcement
- Policies of other components of the criminal justice system (i.e., prosecutorial, judicial, correctional, and probational policies)
- Residents' attitudes toward crime
- Crime reporting practices of residents

Although many of the listed factors equally affect the crime of a particular area, the UCR Program makes no attempt to relate them to the data presented. **The data user is therefore cautioned against comparing statistical data of individual reporting units from cities, counties, metropolitan areas, states, or colleges or universities solely on the basis of their population coverage or student enrollment.** Until data users examine all the variables that affect crime in a town, city, county, state, region, or college or university, they can make no meaningful comparisons.

Historical Background

Since 1930, the FBI has administered the UCR Program; the agency continues to assess and monitor the nature and type of crime in the nation. Data users look to the UCR Program for various research and planning purposes.

Recognizing a need for national crime statistics, the International Association of Chiefs of Police (IACP) formed the Committee on Uniform Crime Records in the 1920s to develop a system of uniform crime statistics. Establishing offenses known to law enforcement as the appropriate measure, the committee evaluated various crimes on the basis of their seriousness, frequency of occurrence, pervasiveness in all geographic areas of the country, and likelihood of being reported to law enforcement. After studying state criminal codes and making an evaluation of the record-keeping practices in use, the committee completed a plan for crime reporting that became the foundation of the UCR Program in 1929.

Seven main offense classifications, known as Part I crimes, were chosen to gauge the state of crime in the nation. These seven offense classifications included the violent crimes of murder and nonnegligent manslaughter, forcible rape, robbery, and aggravated assault; also included were the property crimes of burglary, larceny-theft, and motor vehicle theft. By congressional mandate, arson was added as the eighth Part I offense category. Data collection for arson began in 1979. Agencies classify and score offenses according to a Hierarchy Rule (with the exception of justifiable homicide, motor vehicle theft, and arson) and report their data to the FBI. More information about the Hierarchy Rule is presented in Appendix I.

During the early planning of the program, it was recognized that the differences among criminal codes precluded a mere aggregation of state statistics to arrive at a national total. Also, because of the variances in punishment for the same offenses in different states, no distinction between felony and misdemeanor crimes was possible. To avoid these problems and provide nationwide uniformity in crime reporting, standardized offense definitions were developed. Law enforcement agencies use these to submit data without regard for local statutes. The definitions used by the program can be found in Appendix II.

In January 1930, 400 cities (representing 20 million inhabitants in 43 states) began participating in the UCR Program. Congress enacted Title 28, Section 534, of the United States Code that same year, which authorized the attorney general to gather crime information. The attorney general, in turn, designated the FBI to serve as the national clearinghouse for the collected crime data. Since then, data based on uniform classifications and procedures for reporting have been obtained annually from the nation's law enforcement agencies.

Advisory Groups

Providing vital links between local law enforcement and the FBI for the UCR Program are the Criminal Justice Information Systems Committees of the IACP and the National Sheriffs' Association (NSA). The IACP represents the thousands of police departments nationwide, as it has since the program began. The NSA encourages sheriffs throughout the country to participate fully in the program. Both committees serve the program in advisory capacities.

In 1988, a Data Providers' Advisory Policy Board was established. This board operated until 1993, when it combined with the National Crime Information Center Advisory Policy Board to form a single Advisory Policy Board (APB) to address all FBI criminal justice information services. The current APB works to ensure continuing emphasis on UCR-related issues. The Association of State Uniform Crime Reporting Programs (ASUCRP) focuses on UCR issues within individual state law enforcement associations and also promotes interest in the UCR Program. These organizations foster widespread and responsible use of uniform crime statistics and lend assistance to data contributors.

Redesign of UCR

Although UCR data collection was originally conceived as a tool for law enforcement administration, the data were widely used by other entities involved in various forms of social planning by the 1980s. Recognizing the need for more detailed crime statistics, law enforcement called for a thorough evaluative study to modernize the UCR Program. The FBI formulated a comprehensive three-phase redesign effort. The Bureau of Justice Statistics (BJS), the agency in the Department of Justice responsible for funding criminal justice information projects, agreed to underwrite the first two phases. These phases were conducted by an independent contractor and structured to determine what, if any, changes should be made to the current program. The third phase would involve implementation of the changes identified.

During the first phase, which began in 1982, the historical evolution of the UCR Program was examined. All aspects of the program, including its objectives and intended user audience, data items, reporting mechanisms, quality control issues, publications and user services, and relationships with other criminal justice data systems, were studied.

Early in 1984, a conference on the future of the UCR Program launched the second phase of the study that examined the program's potential and concluded with a set of recommended changes. Phase two ended in early 1985 with the production of a report, *Blueprint for the Future of the Uniform Crime Reporting Program*. The study's Steering Committee reviewed the draft report at a March 1985 meeting and made various recommendations for revision. The committee members, however, endorsed the report's concepts.

In April 1985, the phase two recommendations were presented at the eighth National UCR Conference. Various considerations for the final report were set forth, and the overall concept for the revised UCR Program was unanimously approved. The joint IACP/NSA Committee on UCR also issued a resolution endorsing the *Blueprint*.

The final report, the *Blueprint for the Future of the Uniform Crime Reporting Program*, was released in the summer of 1985. It specifically outlined recommendations for an expanded, improved UCR Program to meet future informational needs. There were three recommended areas of enhancement to the UCR Program:

- Offenses and arrests would be reported using an incident-based system.
- Data would be collected on two levels. Agencies in, level one would report important details about those offenses comprising the Part I crimes, their victims, and arrestees. Level two would consist of law enforcement agencies covering populations of more than 100,000 and a sampling of smaller agencies that would collect expanded detail on all significant offenses.
- A quality assurance program would be introduced.

To begin implementation, the FBI awarded a contract to develop new offense definitions and data elements for the redesigned system. The work involved (a) revising the definitions of certain Part I offenses, (b) identifying additional significant offenses to be reported, (c) refining definitions for both, and (d) developing data elements (incident details) for all UCR Program offenses in order to fulfill the requirements of incident-based reporting versus the current summary system.

Concurrent with the preparation of the data elements, the FBI studied the various state systems to select an experimental site for implementing the redesigned program. In view of its long-standing incident-based program and well-established staff dedicated solely to UCR, the South Carolina Law Enforcement Division (SLED) was chosen. The SLED agreed to adapt its existing system to meet the requirements of the redesigned program and to collect data on both offenses and arrests relating to the newly defined offenses.

Following the completion of the pilot project conducted by the SLED, the FBI produced a draft of guidelines for an enhanced UCR Program. Law enforcement executives from around the country were then invited to a conference where the guidelines were presented for final review.

During the conference, three overall recommendations were passed without dissent: the establishment of a new, incident-based national crime reporting system; the FBI as the managing agency for the program; and the creation of an Advisory Policy Board composed of law enforcement executives to assist in directing and implementing the new program.

Information about the redesigned UCR Program, call the National Incident-Based Reporting System, or NIBRS, is contained in several documents. The *Data Collection Guidelines* publication (August 2000) contains a system overview and descriptions of the offense codes, reports, data elements, and data values used in the system. The *Error Message Manual* (December 1999) contains designations of mandatory and optional data elements, data element edits, and error messages. The *Data Submission Specifications* publication is for the use of local and state systems personnel who are responsible for preparing magnetic media for submission to the FBI. The document is available on the FBI's Web site at <www.fbi.gov/ucr/ucr.htm>. Another publication, the *Handbook for Acquiring a Records Management System (RMS) That Is Compatible with NIBRS*, is also available on that site.

A NIBRS edition of the *UCR Handbook* was published in 1992 to assist law enforcement agency data contributors implementing the NIBRS within their departments. This document is geared toward familiarizing local and state law enforcement personnel with the definitions, policies, and procedures of the NIBRS. It does not contain the technical coding and data transmission requirements presented in the other NIBRS publications.

The NIBRS collects data on each single incident and arrest within 22 crime categories. For each offense known to police within these categories, incident, victim, property, offender, and arrestee information are gathered when available. The goal of the redesign is to modernize crime information by collecting data currently maintained law enforcement records, making the enhanced UCR Program a by-product of current records systems while maintaining the integrity of the program's long-running statistical series.

Implementation of the NIBRS is occurring at a pace commensurate with the resources, abilities, and limitations of the contributing law enforcement agencies. The FBI was able to accept NIBRS data as of January 1989, and to date, the following 29 state programs have been certified for NIBRS participation: Arizona, Arkansas, Colorado, Connecticut, Delaware, Idaho, Iowa, Kansas, Kentucky, Louisiana, Maine, Massachusetts, Michigan, Missouri, Nebraska, New Hampshire, North Dakota, Ohio, Oregon, Rhode Island, South Carolina, South Dakota, Tennessee, Texas, Utah, Vermont, Virginia, West Virginia, and Wisconsin. Among those that submit NIBRS data, 8 states (Delaware, Idaho, Iowa, South Carolina, Tennessee, Virginia, West Virginia, and Vermont) submit all their data via the NIBRS.

Ten state programs are in various stages of testing the NIBRS. Six other state agencies, as well as agencies in the District of Columbia, are in various stages of planning and developing NIBRS.

Suspension of the Crime Index and Modified Crime Index

In June 2004, the Criminal Justice Information Services Advisory Policy Board (CJIS APB) approved discontinuing the use of the Crime Index in the UCR Program and its publications and directed the FBI publish a violent crime total and a property crime total until a more viable index is developed. The Crime Index was first published in *Crime in the United States* in 1960. Congress designated arson as a Part I offense in October 1978, and the UCR Program began collecting arson data in 1979. The FBI adopted the term Modified Crime Index to reflect the addition of arson as a Part I offense. The Modified Crime Index was the number of Crime Index offenses plus arson. However, in recent years, the Crime Index (and subsequently the Modified Crime Index) has not been a true indicator of the degree of criminality. The Crime Index was simply the title used for an aggregation of the seven main offense classifications (Part I offenses) for which data has been collected since the program's implementation.

The Crime Index and the Modified Crime Index were driven upward by the offense with the highest number, creating a bias against a jurisdiction with a high number of larceny-thefts but a low number of other serious crimes such as murder and forcible rape. Thus, the sheer volume of those offenses overshadows more serious but less frequently committed offenses. CJIS studied the appropriateness and usefulness of the Crime Index and Modified Crime Index for several years and brought the matter before many advisory groups affiliated with the UCR Program. The consensus was that the Crime Index and the Modified Crime Index no longer served their original purpose, and that the UCR Program should suspend their use and develop a more robust index of crime.

SECTION II:
OFFENSES REPORTED

VIOLENT CRIME

- Murder
- Forcible Rape
- Robbery
- Aggravated Assault

PROPERTY CRIME

- Burglary
- Larceny-Theft
- Motor Vehicle Theft
- Arson

VIOLENT CRIME

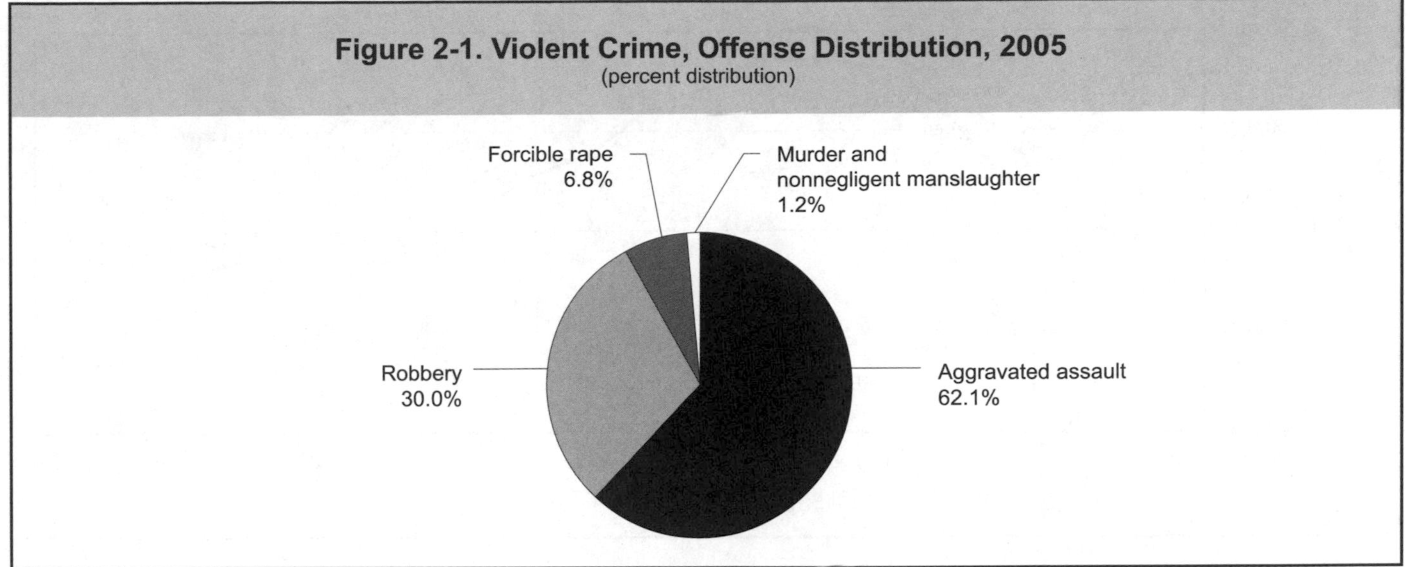

Definition

Violent crime consists of four offenses: murder and nonnegligent manslaughter, forcible rape, robbery, and aggravated assault. According to the Uniform Crime Reporting (UCR) Program, run by the Federal Bureau of Investigation (FBI), violent crimes involve either the use of force or the threat of force.

Data Collection

The data presented in *Crime in the United States* reflect the Hierarchy Rule, which counts only the most serious offense in a multiple-offense criminal incident. In descending order of severity, the violent crimes are murder and nonnegligent manslaughter, forcible rape, robbery, and aggravated assault; these are followed by the property crimes of burglary, larceny-theft, and motor vehicle theft. More information on the expanded violent crime tables (which are available online but not included in this publication) can be found in Appendix I.

National Volume, Trends, and Rate

In 2005, an estimated 1,390,695 violent crimes occurred in the United States. Aggravated assault accounted for 62.1 percent of these crimes, followed by robbery (30.0 percent), forcible rape (6.8 percent), and murder (1.2 percent). (Table 1)

The UCR Program investigates data in 2-year, 5-year, and 10-year increments to formulate trend information. From 2004 to 2005, the estimated volume of violent crime in the United States increased 2.3 percent. (The estimated number of property crimes fell 1.5 percent during the same period.) The 5-year and 10-year trend data showed that the estimated number of violent crimes decreased 3.4 percent between 2001 and 2005 and decreased 17.6 percent between 1996 and 2005. The rate of violent crime in 2005 was 469.2 per 100,000 inhabitants, reversing a 13-year trend of decreasing rates. (Table 1)

An examination of the volume of individual offenses within the violent crime category showed that in a year-to-year comparison of data from 2004 and 2005, the estimated number of aggravated assaults increased 1.8 percent, the estimated number of robberies increased 3.9 percent, and the estimated number of murders increased 3.4 percent. Forcible rape, the only violent crime category to show a decline in the estimated number of incidents from 2004 to 2005, fell 1.2 percent. (Table 1)

In terms of the offense rate for each of the four violent crimes categories, aggravated assault had the highest rate of occurrence. There were an estimated 239.1 aggravated assaults, 140.7 robberies, 31.7 forcible rapes, and 5.6 murders per 100,000 inhabitants in the United States in 2005. (Table 1)

Regional Offense Trends and Rate

The UCR Program divides the United States into four regions: the Northeast, the South, the Midwest, and the West. (More details concerning geographic regions are provided in Appendix III.) The population distribution of the regions is provided in Table 3, and the estimated volume and rate of violent crime by region can be found in Table 4.

The Northeast

The Northeast accounted for an estimated 18.4 percent of the nation's population in 2005 and an estimated 15.5 percent of its violent crimes. (Table 3) Of the four regions, the Northeast, at 0.8 percent, had the smallest increase in the estimated number of violent crimes from 2004 to 2005. The region's population grew by 0.1 percent during this period. In the Northeast, the estimated number of robberies

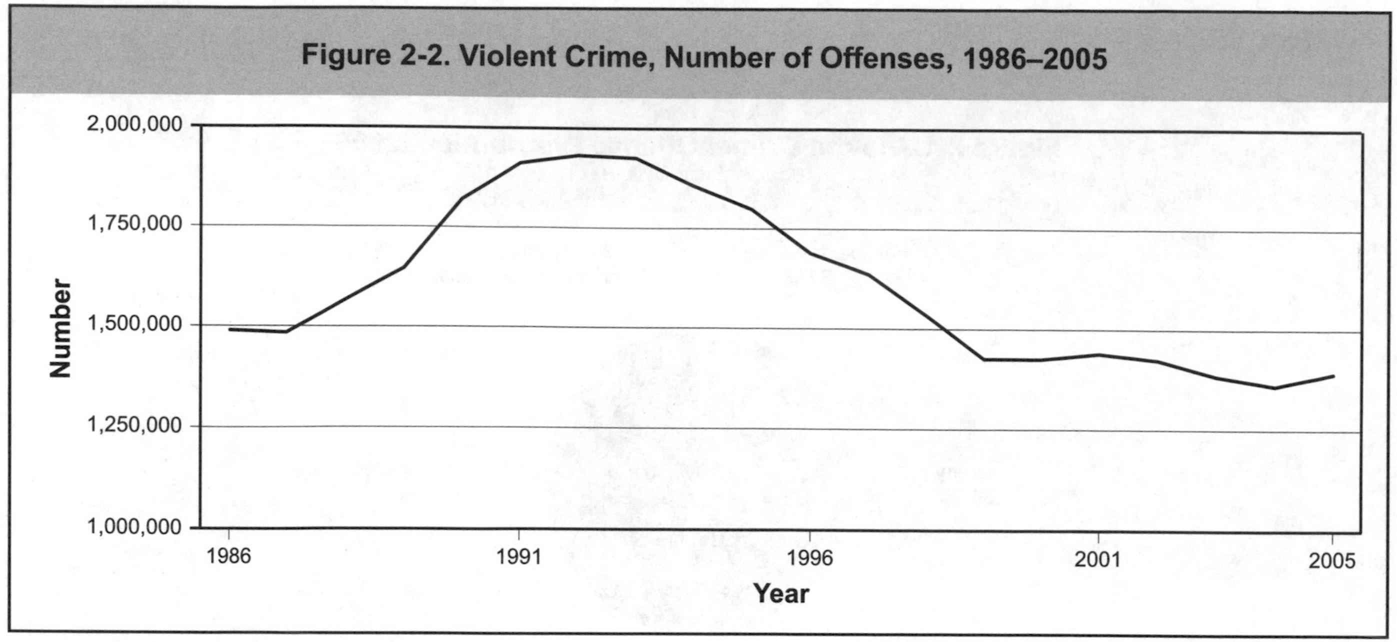

increased 3.1 percent and the estimated number of murders increased 5.4 percent, while the estimated number of aggravated assaults decreased 0.5 percent and the estimated number of forcible rapes decreased 1.8 percent. (Table 4)

In 2005, there were an estimated 393.6 violent crimes per 100,000 inhabitants in the Northeast, a 0.7 percent increase from 2004 figure. By offense, rates were estimated at 219.4 aggravated assaults, 147.7 robberies, 22.1 forcible rapes, and 4.4 murders per 100,000 inhabitants. (Table 4)

The Midwest

With an estimated 22.3 percent of the total population of the United States, the Midwest accounted for 19.6 percent of the nation's estimated number of violent crimes in 2005. (Table 3) The region had a 5.6 percent increase in violent crime and a 0.4 percent growth in population from 2004 to 2005. The estimated number of aggravated assaults in the Midwest increased 5.5 percent, the estimated number of robberies increased 7.7 percent, and the estimated number of murders grew 4.7 percent from 2004 to 2005, while the estimated number of forcible rapes fell 0.6 percent. (Table 4)

The rate of violent crime in the Midwest was estimated at 5.2 incidents per 100,000 inhabitants in 2005, a 5.2 percent increase from the 2004 rate. In 2005, there were 246.2 aggravated assaults, 125.3 robberies, 36.2 forcible rapes, and 4.9 murders per 100,000 inhabitants in the region. The forcible rape rate, with a 1.0 percent decline from the 2004 figure, was the only rate to decrease for the Midwest in 2005. (Table 4)

The South

The South, the nation's most populated region, accounted for an estimated 36.3 percent of the nation's population in 2005. An estimated 41.9 percent of the nation's violent crimes took place in this region in 2005. (Table 3) Violent crime in the South increased 1.7 percent from 2004 to 2005, and the region's population grew 1.4 percent during this period. The estimated number of aggravated assaults increased 1.3 percent from 2004 to 2005, while the estimated number of robberies increased 3.3 percent and the estimated number of murders grew 2.2 percent. The estimated number of forcible rapes showed the region's only decline, dropping 2.0 percent from 2004 to 2005. (Table 4)

The estimated rate of violent crime in the South was 542.6 incidents per 100,000 inhabitants in 2005. There were 354.4 aggravated assaults, 148.4 robberies, 33.1 forcible rapes, and 6.6 murders per 100,000 inhabitants. The forcible rape and aggravated assault rates both showed declines between 2004 and 2005, dropping 3.4 percent and 0.1 percent, respectively. (Table 4)

The West

With an estimated 23.0 percent of the nation's population in 2005, the West also accounted for an estimated 23.0 percent of the nation's violent crime. (Table 3) Violent crime increased 1.6 percent in this region from 2004 to 2005, while its population grew 1.3 percent. Three of the four violent offense categories increased in volume compared to the 2004 data: aggravated assault (1.4 percent), robbery (2.4 percent), and murder (3.1 percent). Only forcible rape showed a decrease, falling 0.3 percent. (Table 4)

The estimated rate of violent crime in the West in 2005 was 468.7 incidents per 100,000 inhabitants, a 0.7 percent increase from the 2004 figure. There were 292.3 aggravated assaults (a rate virtually unchanged from the 2004 rate), 137.9 robberies, 32.7 forcible rapes, and 5.5 murders per 100,000 inhabitants in this region in 2005. Forcible rape was the only rate to post a decline, dropping 1.6 percent from 2004 to 2005. (Table 4)

Community Types

The UCR Program aggregates crime data into three community types: metropolitan statistical areas (MSAs), cities outside MSAs, and nonmetropolitan counties outside MSAs. Appendix III provides additional information regarding community types. Nearly 83 percent of the nation's population lived in MSAs in 2005. Residents of cities outside MSAs accounted for 6.8 percent of the country's population, while 10.3 percent of the population lived in nonmetropolitan counties. (Table 2)

An examination of the volume of violent crime by community type showed that 90.1 percent of the estimated number of violent crimes in the United States occurred in MSAs, 5.4 percent occurred in cities outside MSAs, and 4.6 percent occurred in nonmetropolitan counties. (Table 2) By community type, the violent crime rates were estimated at 509.7 incidents per 100,000 inhabitants in MSAs, 373.5 incidents per 100,000 inhabitants in cities outside MSAs, and 206.8 incidents per 100,000 inhabitants in nonmetropolitan counties. (Table 2)

Population Groups: Trends and Rates

In the UCR Program, data are also aggregated into population groups; these groups are described in more detail in Appendix III. The nation's cities had an overall increase of 2.6 percent in the estimated number of violent crimes from 2004 to 2005. By city population group, cities with 500,000 to 999,999 inhabitants had the greatest percentage increase in the estimated number of violent crimes (9.2 percent), while cities with 10,000 to 24,999 inhabitants posted the smallest increase (0.3 percent). Cities with 1,000,000 or more inhabitants posted the only decrease from 2004 to 2005 in the estimated number of violent crimes, dropping 0.4 percent. (Table 12)

The law enforcement agencies in the nation's cities collectively reported a rate of 580.2 violent crimes per 100,000 inhabitants in 2005. By population group with the *city* label, law enforcement agencies in cities with 250,000 to 499,999 inhabitants reported the highest violent crime rate, 1,015.0 violent crimes per 100,000 inhabitants; the violent crime rate for all cities with 250,000 or more inhabitants was 941.2. Agencies in cities with 10,000 to 24,999 inhabitants reported the lowest violent crime rate (303.1 incidents per 100,000 inhabitants). Law enforcment agencies in the nation's metropolitan counties reported a collective violent crime rate of 338.0 per 100,000 inhabitants, while agencies in nonmetropolitan counties reported a collective rate of 218.8 violent crimes per 100,000 inhabitants. (Table 16)

Weapons Distribution

The UCR Program collects weapons data for murder, robbery, and aggravated assault offenses. An examination of these data indicate that 23.4 percent of violent crimes (for these three categories) involved the use of a firearm; firearms were used in 50.8 percent of all murders in 2005. Approximately 24.3 percent of violent crime offenses involved the use of personal weapons (hands, feet, fists, etc.) or strong-arm methods, 13.0 percent involved the use of knives or cutting instruments, and 22.1 percent involved other dangerous weapons. (Tables 1 and 19 and unpublished Expanded Homicide Table 7)

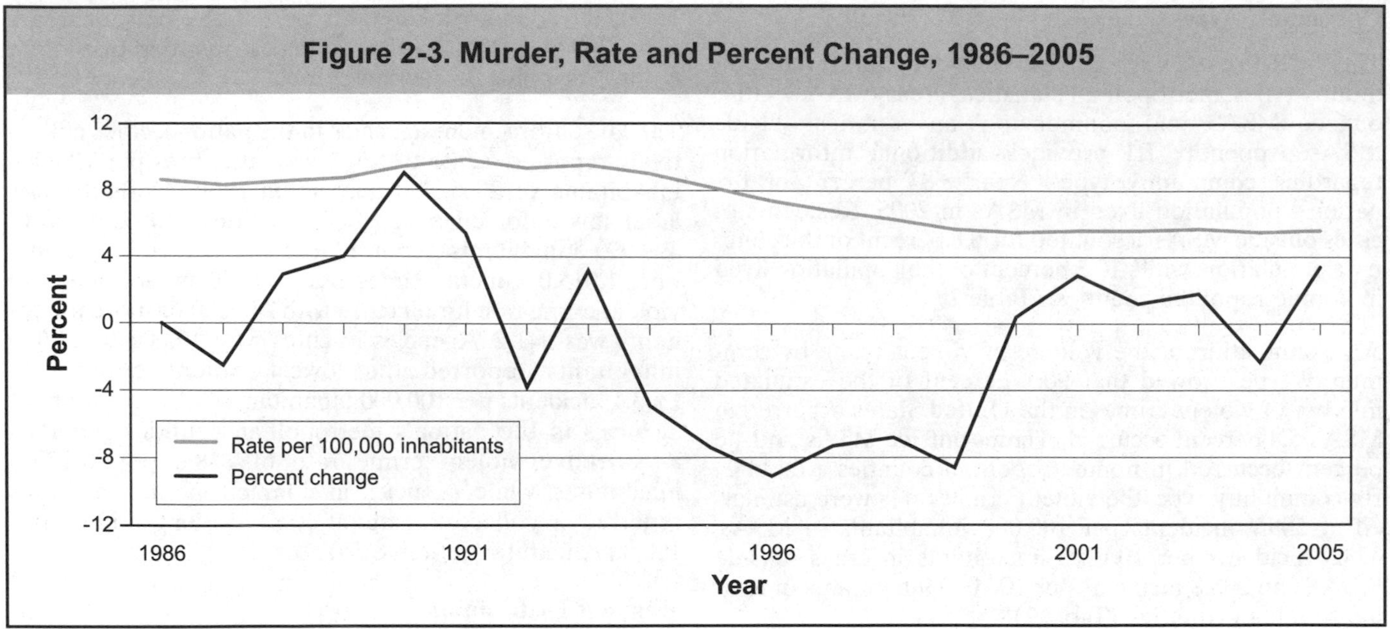

MURDER

Definition

The UCR Program defines murder and nonnegligent manslaughter as the willful (nonnegligent) killing of one human being by another. The classification of this offense is based solely on police investigation, rather than on the determination of a court, medical examiner, coroner, jury, or other judicial body. The UCR Program does not include the following situations under this offense classification: deaths caused by negligence, suicide, or accident; justifiable homicides; and attempts to murder or assaults to murder, which are considered aggravated assaults.

Data Collection

The UCR Program's *Supplementary Homicide Report* (SHR) provides information about murder victims and offenders by age, sex, and race; the types of weapons used in the murders; the relationships of the victims to the offenders; and the circumstances surrounding the incident. Law enforcement agencies are asked to complete an SHR for each murder reported to the UCR Program.

National Volume, Trends, and Rates

The UCR Program's homicide data for 2005 showed that the estimated number of murders in the United States increased, reversing 2004's decline. An estimated 16,692 people were murdered nationwide in 2005, a 3.4 percent increase from the 2004 figure. An analysis of 5-year and 10-year trend data showed that the 2005 estimate increased 4.1 percent from the 2001 (5-year) estimate, but decreased 15.0 percent from the 1996 (10-year) estimate. The number of homicides in 2005 was the seventh lowest over the past twenty years.

The 2005 data yielded an estimated rate of 5.6 murders per 100,000 inhabitants, a 1.8 percent increase from the 2004 rate. The 2005 rate is equal to the rate from 2001, but represents a 21.1 percent decline from the 1996 rate. (Table 1)

Regional Offense Trends and Rates

The UCR Program divides the United States into four regions: the Northeast, the South, the Midwest, and the West. (More details concerning geographic regions are provided in Appendix III.)

The Northeast

In 2005, the Northeast accounted for an estimated 18.4 percent of the nation's population and 14.4 percent of its estimated number of murders. With an estimated 2,403 murders, the Northeast saw a 5.4 percent increase compared with the 2004 figure. The region's population grew 0.1 percent from 2004 to 2005. The offense rate for the Northeast was 4.4 murders per 100,000 inhabitants, up from 4.2 murders per 100,000 inhabitants in 2004. (Tables 3 and 4)

The Midwest

The Midwest accounted for an estimated 22.3 percent of the nation's total population (the region's population having grown 0.4 percent from 2004 to 2005) and 19.4 percent of its estimated number of murders in 2005. There were an estimated 3,243 murders in the Midwest in 2005, a 4.7 percent increase from the estimated figure for 2004. The Midwest experienced a rate of 4.9 murders per 100,000 inhabitants in 2005, an increase from the estimated rate of 4.7 for 2004. (Tables 3 and 4)

The South

The South, the nation's most populated region, experienced a 1.4 percent growth in population from 2004 to 2005. The region accounted for an estimated 36.3 percent of the nation's population in 2005 and the nation's highest proportion of murders (42.6 percent). The estimated 7,112 murders represented a 2.2 percent increase in the estimated number of murders from 2004 to 2005. However, the region's estimated rate of 6.6 murders per 100,000 inhabitants was virtually unchanged from the estimated rate for 2004. (Tables 3 and 4)

The West

The West accounted for an estimated 23.0 percent of the nation's population and 23.6 percent of the estimated number of murders in 2005. Its population grew 1.3 percent from 2004 to 2005. The West experienced an estimated 3,934 murders, a 3.1 percent increase from the 2004 estimate. The region's murder rate was 5.8 per 100,000 inhabitants, an increase from the 2004 rate of 5.7. (Tables 3 and 4)

Community Types

The UCR Program aggregates data for three community types: metropolitan statistical areas (MSAs), cities outside MSAs, and nonmetropolitan counties outside MSAs. (See Appendix III for definitions.) In 2005, MSAs accounted for 82.9 percent of the nation's population and 89.5 percent of the estimated total number of murders. With 14,932 estimated homicides, MSAs experienced a rate of 6.1 murders per 100,000 inhabitants in 2005. Cities outside MSAs accounted for 6.8 percent of the U.S. population and (with an estimated 691 murders), accounted for 4.1 percent of the estimated murders in the nation. The murder rate for cities outside MSAs was 3.4 per 100,000 inhabitants. (Table 2)

In 2005, 10.3 percent of the nation's population lived in nonmetropolitan counties outside MSAs. An estimated 1,069 murders took place in these counties, accounting for 6.4 percent of the nation's estimated total. The murder rate for nonmetropolitan counties outside MSAs was 3.5 murders per 100,000 inhabitants. (Table 2)

Population Groups: Trends and Rates

The UCR Program uses the following population group designations in its data presentations: cities (grouped according to population size) and counties (classified as either metropolitan or nonmetropolitan). A breakdown of these classifications is provided in Appendix III.

From 2004 to 2005, the nation's cities experienced a 5.7 percent increase in homicides. The city group with 10,000 to 24,999 inhabitants was the only group to experience a decrease in homicides from 2004 to 2005 (0.9 percent). Metropolitan and nonmetropolitan counties also experienced decreases in homicides from 2004 to 2005; the decline was 0.5 percent for metropolitan counties and 5.9 percent for nonmetropolitan counties. (Table 12)

In 2005, cities collectively had a rate of 6.9 murders per 100,000 inhabitants. Cities with 500,000 to 999,999 inhabitants had the highest murder rate (14.1 murders per 100,000 inhabitants) among city population groups, while cities with under 10,000 inhabitants had the lowest murder rate (2.5 murders per 100,000 inhabitants). The homicide rates for metropolitan and nonmetropolitan counties were 3.9 and 3.6 per 100,000 inhabitants, respectively. Suburban areas had a homicide rate of 3.2 per 100,000 inhabitants. (Table 16)

Offense Analysis

Supplementary Homicide Report

The UCR Program's *Supplementary Homicide Report* (SHR) provides information regarding the age, sex, and race of both the murder victim and the offender; the type of weapon used in the offense; the relationship of the victim to the offender; and the circumstances surrounding the offense. Of the estimated 16,692 murders that were committed in the United States in 2005, law enforcement agencies contributed data to the UCR Program through SHRs for 14,860 of the incidents. More information on these reports and the expanded homicide tables (which are available online but not included in this publication) can be found in Appendix I. Highlights from these tables have been included below.

Victims

Based on 2005 supplemental homicide data (where the ages, sexes, or races of the murder victims were *known*), 87.8 percent of victims were over 18 years of age, 10.9 percent were under 18 years of age, and the age of 1.3 percent of the victims was unknown. White victims accounted for 52.0 percent of the victims for whom race was known, followed by Black victims (45.2 percent) and victims of other races (2.8 percent). Male victims made up 72.5 percent of victims for whom sex was known; females made up 27.5 percent of these victims. (Expanded Homicide Tables 4 and 5)

Offenders

The data for 2005 concerning murders for which the offenders were known showed that 94.2 percent of offenders were adults and 5.8 percent were juveniles. For offenders for whom the sex was known, 89.9 percent of offenders were male and 10.1 percent were female. Black offenders accounted for 52.6 percent of offenders for whom race was known, followed by White offenders (44.9 percent) and offenders of other races (2.5 percent); 84.8 percent of White victims were murdered by White offenders and 92.6 percent of Black victims were murdered by Black offenders. (Expanded Homicide Tables 4 and 5)

Victim-Offender Relationships

Of the homicides in 2005 for which law enforcement agencies provided supplemental data to the UCR Program, the victim-offender relationship was known for 54.8 percent of the murders. For incidents in which the victim-offender relationship was known, 74.6 percent of victims knew their murderers, while 25.4 percent were killed by strangers. Among the homicides in which the victims knew their killers, 22.4 percent were killed by family members. The 2005 data also showed that 84.7 percent of female victims were killed by their husbands or boyfriends, while 2.6 percent of male victims were slain by their wives or girlfriends. (Expanded Homicide Tables 1 and 9)

Weapons

For incidents in 2005 in which the murder weapon was specified, 68.0 percent were committed with firearms. Of murders committed with firearms, 74.7 percent involved handguns, 5.1 percent involved shotguns, and 4.4 percent involved rifles. Knives or cutting instruments were used in 12.9 percent of the murders; personal weapons, such as hands, fists, and feet, were used in 6.0 percent of the murders. Blunt objects, such as clubs and hammers, were used in 4.0 percent of the incidents. Other weapons, such as poisons, narcotics, explosives, etc., were used in 9.2 percent of the murders. (Expanded Homicide Table 10)

Circumstances

The supplemental homicide data showed that circumstances were unknown for 37.8 percent of the murders that occurred in 2005. For murders for which circumstances were known, 23.4 percent involved another felony, such as forcible rape, robbery, or burglary. Investigators suspected that another 0.5 percent of homicides likely resulted during another felonious activity. Law enforcement agencies cited that arguments—including those over money or property—were the cause of 42.2 percent of murders with no other involved felony. Another 8.2 percent of murders with known circumstances involved juvenile gangland killing. (Expanded Homicide Table 9)

Justifiable Homicide

Certain willful killings must be reported as justifiable, or excusable, homicide. In the UCR Program, justifiable homicide is defined as, and is limited to, the following:

- The killing of a felon by a peace officer in the line of duty.
- The killing of a felon, during the commission of a felony, by a private citizen.

Because these killings are determined by law enforcement investigation to be justifiable, they are tabulated separately from murder and nonnegligent manslaughter.

During 2005, law enforcement agencies provided supplemental data for 533 justifiable homicides. A breakdown of those figures revealed that law enforcement officers justifiably killed 341 felons and private citizens justifiably killed 192 felons. Expanded Homicide Tables 13 and 14 provide further details about justifiable homicide but are not published in this text; see Appendix I for more information.

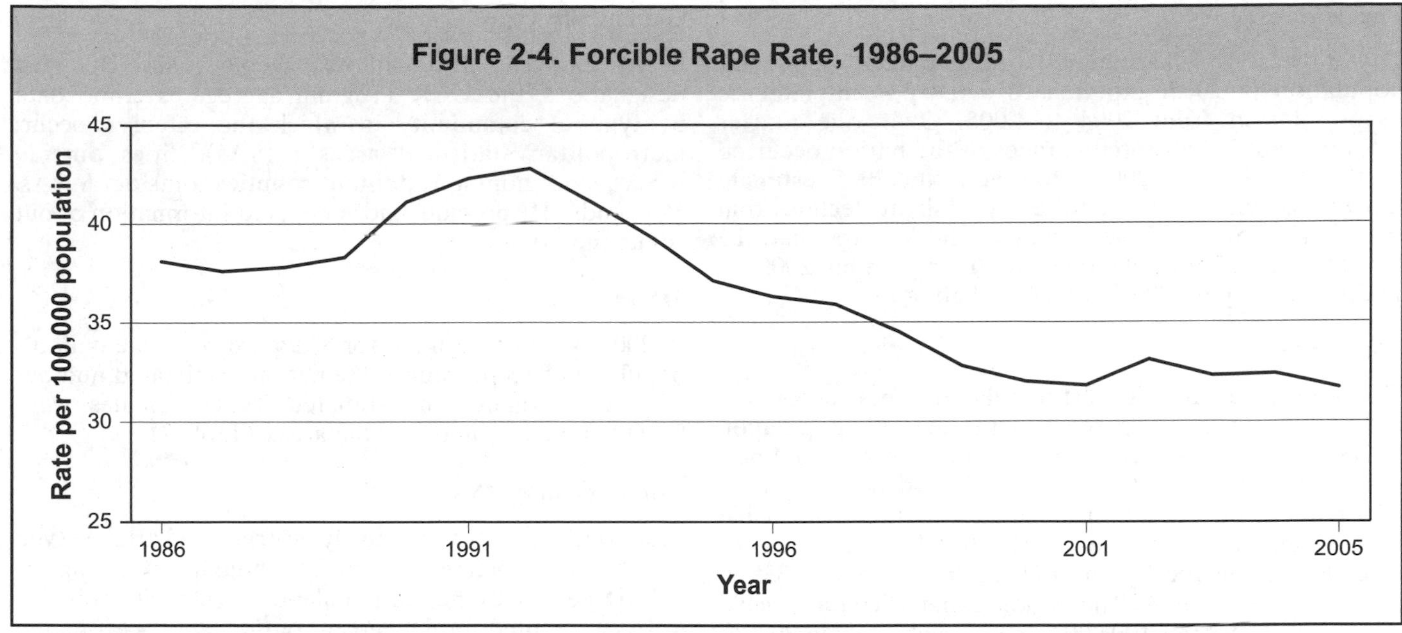

FORCIBLE RAPE

Definition

Forcible rape is the carnal knowledge of a female forcibly and against her will. Assaults and attempts to commit rape by force or threat of force are included; however, statutory rape (without force) and other sex offenses are excluded.

Data Collection

The UCR Program counts one offense for each female victim of a forcible rape, attempted forcible rape, or assault with intent to rape, regardless of the victim's age. The offense of statutory rape, in which no force is used but the female victim is under the age of consent, is included in the arrest total for the sex offenses category. Sexual attacks on males are counted as aggravated assaults or sex offenses, depending on the circumstances and the extent of any injuries.

For this overview only, the FBI deviated from standard procedure and manually calculated the 2005 rate of female rapes based upon the national female population provided by the U.S. Census Bureau (150,410,658 in 2005).

National Volume, Trends, and Rates

During 2005, approximately 93,934 females nationwide were victims of forcible rape. This estimate represents a 1.2 percent decrease from the 2004 figure and a 3.4 percent increase from the 2001 figure. The data also showed a 2.4 percent decrease from the 1996 estimated figure. (Table 1)

In preparing rate tables, the UCR Program's computer system automatically calculates offense rates per 100,000 inhabitants for all Part I crimes, which include murder and nonnegligent manslaughter, forcible rape, robbery, aggravated assault, burglary, larceny-theft, motor vehicle theft, and arson. (See Appendix II for more information.) Thus, the rate data are based upon the total U.S. population. However, for this overview, the 2005 rate of female rapes has been recalculated based upon the national female population provided by the Census Bureau. The recalculation resulted in a rate of 62.5 rape victims per 100,000 females, which was down slightly from the 2004 rate of 63.8. When compared to 2001 data, the number of forcible rapes increased an estimated 3.4 percent, but when compared to 1996 data, the number of forcible rape offenses declined 2.4 percent. (Table 1)

Of the forcible rapes known to law enforcement agencies in 2005, law enforcement agencies reported that 91.8 percent of forcible rapes were completed; the remainder consisted of attempts or assaults to rape. (Table 19)

Regional Offense Trends and Rates

The UCR Program divides the United States into four regions: the Northeast, the South, the Midwest, and the West. (More details concerning geographic regions are provided in Appendix III.) Regional analysis offers estimates of the volume of female rapes, the percent change from the previous year's estimate, and the rate of rape per 100,000 female inhabitants in each region. (Tables 3 and 4)

The Northeast

The Northeast made up 18.4 percent of the U.S. population in 2005 and experienced a 0.1 percent growth in population from 2004 to 2005. In 2005, an estimated 12,061 forcible rapes of females—12.8 percent of the national total—occurred in the Northeast. This was a decline of 1.8 percent from the 2004 estimated figure. (Tables 3 and 4) The Northeast had a forcible rape rate of 42.9 incidents per 100,000 female inhabitants in 2005, the lowest in the nation.

The Midwest

The Midwest, which accounted for 22.3 percent of the U.S. population in 2005, experienced a 0.4 percent increase in population from 2004 to 2005. Over one-quarter (25.4 percent) of all forcible rapes in the nation occurred in the Midwest in 2005. However, the 2005 estimate (23,905 forcible rapes) represented a slight decline from the 2004 estimate. (Tables 3 and 4) The Midwest had the highest rate of forcible rape in the nation in 2005, at 71.3 incidents per 100,000 female inhabitants.

The South

The South, the nation's most populated region, accounted for an estimated 36.3 percent of the nation's population in 2005 (and experienced a population growth of 1.4 percent from 2004 to 2005); the region also accounted for 37.9 percent of the nation's estimated number offorcible rapes. There were an estimated 35,606 female victims of forcible rape in the South in 2005, down from 36,335 in 2004. (Tables 3 and 4) The region experienced a forcible rape rate of 65.2 per 100,000 female inhabitants in 2005.

The West

The West, which experienced a population growth of 1.3 percent from 2004 to 2005, accounted for 23.0 percent of the nation's population in 2005. The region also accounted for 23.8 percent of the nation's total number of estimated forcible rapes with an estimated 22,362 offenses. The West saw a decline in forcible rapes from 2004 to 2005. (Tables 3 and 4) The region's rate of forcible rape in 2005 was 65.5 incidents per 100,000 female inhabitants.

Community Types

Using the U.S. Office of Management and Budget's designations, the UCR Program aggregates crime data by type of community in which the offenses occur: metropolitan statistical areas (MSAs), cities outside MSAs, and nonmetropolitan counties outside MSAs. (Appendix III provides more detailed information about community types.)

MSAs

In 2005, MSAs accounted for 82.9 percent of the nation's population 83.3 percent of the nation's estimated number of forcible rapes. An estimated 78,264 females were forcibly raped in metropolitan areas. (Table 2)

Cities Outside MSAs

Cities outside MSAs are mostly incorporated areas served by city law enforcement agencies. Though accounting for only 6.8 percent of the U.S. population in 2005, cities outside MSAs accounted for 8.4 percent of the nation's estimated forcible rapes (7,893 offenses). (Table 2)

Nonmetropolitan Counties

In 2005, approximately 10.3 percent of the nation's population lived in nonmetropolitan counties outside MSAs (counties made up of mostly nonincorporated areas served by noncity law enforcement agencies). Collectively, these areas had approximately 7,777 forcible rapes of females, representing 8.3 percent of the nation's estimated total. (Table 2)

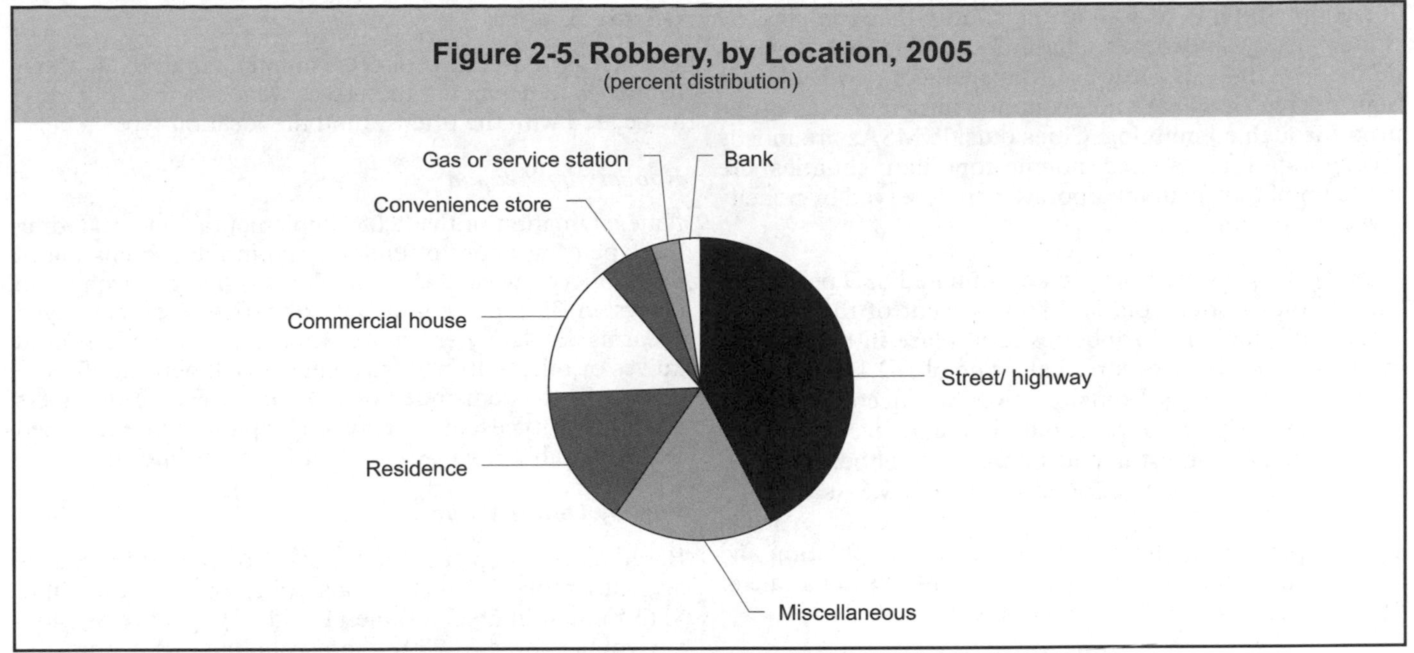

ROBBERY

Definition

The UCR Program defines robbery as the taking or attempting to take anything of value from the care, custody, or control of a person or persons by force or threat of force or violence and/or by putting the victim in fear.

National Volume, Trends, and Rates

Reversing its 3-year trend of decline, the number of robberies nationwide increased in 2005. Estimated offenses totaled 417,122 in 2005, a 3.9 percent increase from the 2004 estimate. However, the 2005 total was below the totals from 2001 (5 years before) and 1996 (10 years before) by 1.5 percent and 22.1 percent, respectively.

Regional Offense Trends and Rates

The UCR Program divides the United States into four regions: the Northeast, the South, the Midwest, and the West. (More details concerning geographic regions are provided in Appendix III.)

The Northeast

The Northeast, with an estimated 18.4 percent of the nation's population in 2005 (and a 0.1 percent growth in population from 2004 to 2005), accounted for 19.4 percent of its estimated number of robberies. (Table 3) The estimated number of robberies increased 3.1 percent from the 2004 estimate. The rate for this region was 147.7 robberies per 100,000 inhabitants, a 2.9 percent increase from the 2004 rate. (Table 4)

The Midwest

The Midwest accounted for 22.3 percent of the total population of the United States, and 19.8 percent of its estimated number of robberies, in 2005. The region experienced a 0.4 percent growth in population from 2004 to 2005. (Table 3) There were an estimated 82,682 robberies in the Midwest in 2005, a 7.7 percent increase from the estimated figure from 2004. Of all four regions, the Midwest experienced the highest increase in robberies from 2004 to 2005. The region's robbery rate was 125.3 robberies per 100,000 inhabitants in 2005, a 7.3 percent increase from the estimated rate for 2004. (Table 4)

The South

The South, the nation's most highly populated region, experienced a 1.4 percent growth in population from 2004 to 2005; in 2005, it accounted for an estimated 36.3 percent of the nation's population in 2005 and 38.2 percent of the nation's estimated number of robberies. (Table 3) This figure represented a 3.3 percent increase from the 2004 figure. The region experienced the highest rate of robberies per 100,000 inhabitants (148.4), a 1.9 percent increase from the 2004 rate. (Table 4)

The West

The West, having experienced a population growth of 1.3 percent from 2004 to 2005, was home to an estimated 23.0 percent of the nation's population and accounted for 22.6 percent of the nation's estimated number of robberies in 2005. (Table 3) The estimated number of robberies in the region in 2005 represented a 2.4 percent increase from the 2004 figure. The rate of robberies per 100,000 inhabitants in the West was 137.9, a 1.0 percent increase from the 2004 rate. This was the lowest rate among all four regions. (Table 4)

Community Types

The UCR Program aggregates data for three community types: metropolitan statistical areas (MSAs), cities outside MSAs, and nonmetropolitan counties outside MSAs. MSAs include a central city or urbanized area with at least

50,000 inhabitants, as well as the county that contains the principal city and other adjacent counties that have, as defined by the U.S. Office of Management and Budget, a high degree of social and economic integration as measured through commuting. Cities outside MSAs are mostly incorporated areas, and nonmetropolitan counties are made up of mostly unincorporated areas served by noncity law enforcement.

In 2005, MSAs were home to an estimated 82.9 percent of the nation's population, and 96.1 percent of the nation's estimated number of robberies took place in these areas. Robberies in MSAs occurred at a rate of 163.1 per 100,000 inhabitants. Cities outside MSAs accounted for 6.8 percent of the U.S. population and accounted for 2.8 percent of the estimated number of robberies in the nation. The robbery rate for cities outside MSAs was 57.5 per 100,000 inhabitants. Nonmetropolitan counties made up 10.3 percent of the nation's estimated population and 1.2 percent of the nation's estimated robberies, at a rate of 15.7 robberies per 100,000 inhabitants. (Table 2)

Population Groups: Trends and Rates

The national UCR Program aggregates data by various population groups, which include cities, metropolitan counties, and nonmetropolitan counties. A definition of these groups can be found in Appendix III. Most of the population groups experienced increases in the estimated number of robberies in 2005, compared with the figure for 2004. Robberies in cities as a whole increased 4.0 percent. Among the population groups labeled *city*, those cities with 500,000 to 999,999 inhabitants had the greatest increase in the number of robberies (10.2 percent), while cities with 1,000,000 or more inhabitants had the smallest increase in number of robberies (1.3 percent). Nonmetropolitan counties had a 0.8 percent increase in the estimated number of robberies, and metropolitan counties showed a 7.7 percent increase. The number of robberies in suburban areas increased 5.3 percent. (Table 12)

Among the population groups, the nation's cities collectively had a rate of 196.1 robberies per 100,000 inhabitants. Of the population groups designated *city*, those with 1,000,000 or more inhabitants had the highest rate (379.0 per 100,000 inhabitants), while those with fewer than 10,000 inhabitants had the lowest rate (52.8 per 100,000 inhabitants). Of the two county groups, metropolitan counties had a rate of 72.8 robberies per 100,000 inhabitants, while nonmetropolitan counties had a rate of 16.2 robberies per 100,000 inhabitants. Suburban areas had a robbery rate of 73.2. (Table 16)

Offense Analysis

The UCR Program collects supplemental data about robberies to document the use of weapons, the dollar loss associated with the offense, and the location types.

Robbery by Weapon

An examination of the 2005 supplemental data regarding the type of weapons offenders used in the commission of the robbery revealed that assailants relied on strong-arm tactics in 39.7 percent of all robberies; they employed firearms in 42.1 percent of robberies. Offenders used knives or other cutting instruments in 8.8 percent of these crimes. In the remainder of the robberies, the offenders used other types of weapons. (Unpublished Expanded Robbery Table 3; see Appendix I for more information)

Loss by Dollar Value

Based on the supplemental reports from law enforcement agencies, robberies cost victims, collectively, an estimated $513 million in 2005. (Tables 1 and 23) The average loss per robbery was $1,230. Average dollar losses were the highest for banks, which suffered an average loss of $4,169 per offense. Gas and service stations lost an average $1,104 per offense. Commercial houses, which include supermarkets, department stores, and restaurants, had average losses of $1,670. An average of $1,335 was taken from residences; individuals lost $1,005, on average, from street and highway robberies. An average of $625 was lost in each offense against convenience stores. An average of $1,217 was taken in all other types of robberies. (Table 23)

Robbery Trends by Location

Among the location types, robberies from banks decreased 8.9 percent from 2004 to 2005. Robberies that occurred at residences increased 9.7 percent, and those at commercial houses rose 3.5 percent. The number of robberies on streets and highways increased 5.8 percent, and robberies at convenience stores fell 0.3 percent. The cumulative total of robberies that took place in all other locations increased 1.3 percent from 2004 to 2005. (Table 23)

Percent Distribution

By location type, the greatest proportion of robberies in 2005 occurred on streets and highways (44.1 percent). Robbers targeted commercial houses in 14.3 percent of offenses and residences in 14.2 percent of offenses. Convenience stores accounted for 5.7 percent of robberies, followed by gas and service stations (2.8 percent) and banks (2.1 percent). Robberies in all other places, cumulatively, represented 16.7 percent of offenses. (Table 23)

Figure 2-6. Violent Crime and Aggravated Assault Rates, 1986–2005

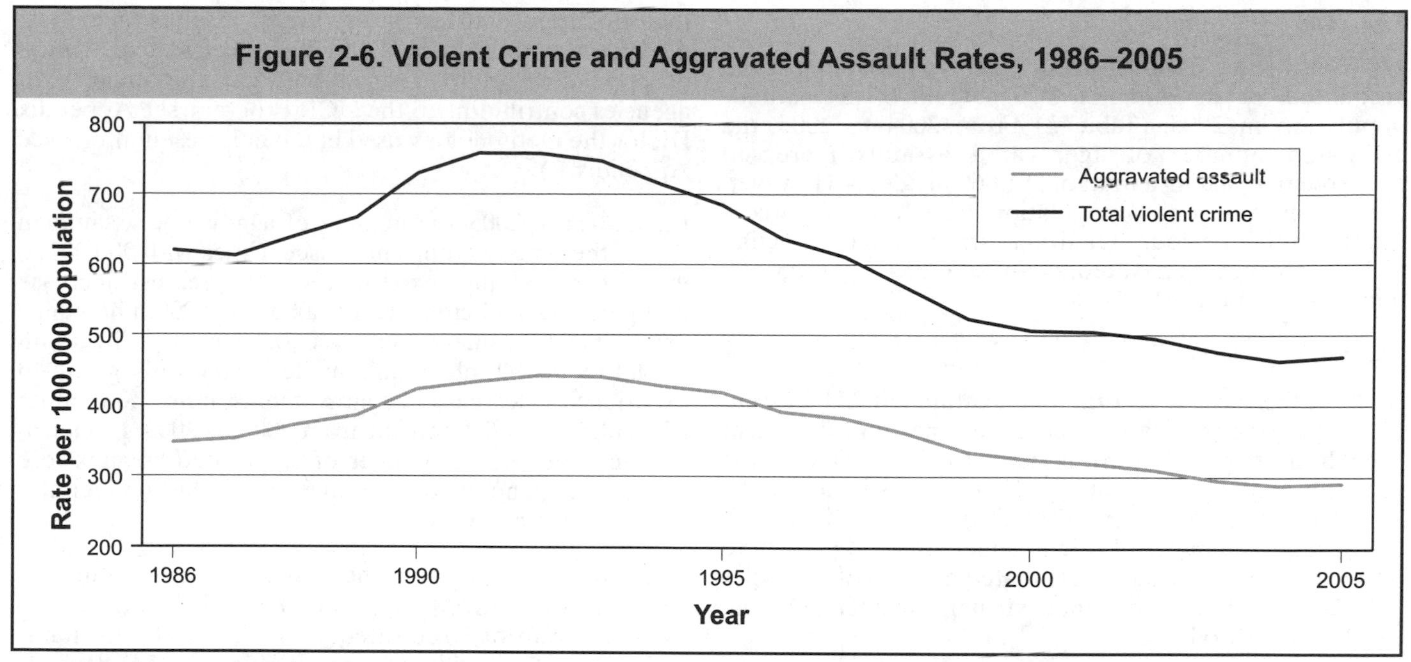

AGGRAVATED ASSAULT

Definition

The UCR Program defines aggravated assault as an unlawful attack by one person upon another for the purpose of inflicting severe or aggravated bodily injury. This type of assault is usually accompanied by the use of a weapon or by other means likely to produce death or great bodily harm. Attempted aggravated assaults that involve the display or threat of a gun, knife, or other weapon are included in this crime category because serious personal injury would likely result if these assaults were completed. When aggravated assault and larceny-theft occur together, the offense falls under the category of robbery.

National Volume, Trends, and Rates

The estimated number of aggravated assaults in the United States increased in 2005, reversing an 11-year trend of decline. In 2005, estimated occurrences of aggravated assault totaled 862,947, a 1.8 percent increase from the 2004 figure. The 5-year and 10-year trend data show a 5.1 percent decrease and a 16.8 percent decrease, respectively. The 2005 data also show an increase in the rate of aggravated assault per 100,000 U.S. inhabitants. This rate, estimated at 291.1, represents a 0.9 percent increase from the 2004 rate. However, it also represents an 8.6 percent decrease from the 2001 (5-year trend) rate and a 25.5 percent decrease from the 1996 (10-year trend) rate. (Table 1)

Among the four types of violent crime offenses (murder, forcible rape, robbery, and aggravated assault), aggravated assault typically has the highest rate of occurrence. This trend continued in 2005 with aggravated assault accounting for 62.1 percent of all violent crime. (Table 4)

Regional Offense Trends and Rates

The UCR Program divides the United States into four regions: the Northeast, the South, the Midwest, and the West. (More details concerning geographic regions are provided in Appendix III.) In the Midwest, South, and West, the estimated number of aggravated assaults increased from 2004 to 2005; the Northeast, however, saw a 0.5 percent decline in its estimated number of aggravated assaults. (Table 4)

The Northeast

The region with the smallest proportion of the nation's population (an estimated 18.4 percent in 2005, representing a 0.1 percent population growth from 2004 to 2005) also accounted for the smallest proportion of the nation's estimated number of aggravated assaults (13.9 percent). (Table 3) Occurrences of aggravated assault decreased 0.5 percent from 2004 to 2005, down to an estimated 119,868. The region also had the lowest aggravated assault rate in the nation, at 219.4 incidents per 100,000 inhabitants, a 0.6 percent decline from the 2004 rate. (Table 4)

The Midwest

With 22.3 percent of the nation's total population in 2005—and with a 0.4 percent growth in population from 2004 to 2005—the Midwest accounted for approximately 18.8 percent of the nation's estimated number of aggravated assaults. (Table 3) Occurrences of this offense increased 5.5 percent from the estimated total for 2004, rising to an estimated 162,417 incidents. The region's aggravated assault rate, at 246.2 incidents per 100,000 inhabitants, represented a 5.1 percent increase from the 2004 rate. (Table 4)

The South

The South, the nation's most highly populated region, accounted for an estimated 36.3 percent of the nation's population in 2005. (Table 3) From 2004 to 2005, the estimated number of aggravated assaults increased 1.3 percent, reaching a total of 381,060 incidents. However, the region experienced population growth of 1.4 percent during this period, resulting in a slight decline (0.1 percent) in aggravated assaults, to 354.5 per 100,000 inhabitants. (Table 4)

The West

In 2005, the West was home to an estimated 23.0 percent of the nation's population and experienced a 1.3 percent growth in population from 2004 to 2005. The region accounted for 23.1 percent of the nation's estimated number of aggravated assaults. (Table 3) From 2004 to 2005, the estimated number of offenses increased 1.4 percent to 199,602 incidents. The rate, estimated at 292.3 offenses per 100,000 inhabitants, remained virtually unchanged from the 2004 rate. (Table 4)

Community Types

The UCR Program aggregates data for three community types: metropolitan statistical areas (MSAs), cities outside MSAs, and nonmetropolitan counties outside MSAs. MSAs include a central city or urbanized area with at least 50,000 inhabitants, as well as the county that contains the principal city and other adjacent counties that have a high degree of social and economic integration as measured through commuting. Cities outside MSAs are mostly incorporated areas, and nonmetropolitan counties are made up of mostly unincorporated areas. (For additional information about community types, see Appendix III.)

In 2005, 82.9 percent of the nation's population lived in MSAs, where the rate of aggravated assault was an estimated 308.6 per 100,000 inhabitants. Cities outside MSAs (with 6.8 percent of the U.S. population) had the next-highest rate of aggravated assault at 273.2 offenses per 100,000 inhabitants. Nonmetropolitan counties accounted for 10.3 percent of the U.S. population and had an offense rate of 162.2 aggravated assaults per 100,000 inhabitants. (Table 2)

Population Groups: Trends and Rates

To calculate 2-year trend data for population groups, the UCR Program staff reviewed reports from all agencies that submitted statistics on aggravated assaults for at least 6 common months in 2004 and 2005. (For an explanation of population-group designations and the number of agencies contributing to the UCR Program, see Appendix III; for the methodology used in tabular presentations, see Appendix I.)

From 2004 to 2005, the number of aggravated assaults in five of the six city groups increased. Cities with 500,000 to 999,999 inhabitants experienced the greatest increase (9.6 percent), and cities with 50,000 to 99,999 inhabitants experienced the smallest increase (0.3 percent). Cities with 10,000 to 24,999 inhabitants made up the only group to experience a decrease in aggravated assaults; the number of incidents fell 0.4 percent from 2004 to 2005. In metropolitan counties, the number of aggravated assaults rose 1.4 percent; in nonmetropolitan counties, this number also rose 1.4 percent. (Table 12)

Based on reports from agencies submitting 12 months of complete data for 2005, aggravated assault occurred at an estimated rate of 301.6 offenses per 100,000 inhabitants nationwide. The collective rate for cities was 341.8 aggravated assaults per 100,000 inhabitants. Among city population groups, rates ranged from a high of 513.7 offenses per 100,000 inhabitants (in cities with 250,000 or more inhabitants) to a low of 200.4 offenses per 100,000 inhabitants (in cities with 10,000 to 24,999 inhabitants). The aggravated assault rate was 236.0 in metropolitan counties and 172.8 in nonmetropolitan counties.

Offense Analysis

Aggravated Assault by Weapon

The UCR Program collects data about the type of weapons used in aggravated assaults. In 2005, personal weapons (such as hands, feet, fists, etc.) were used in 25.0 percent of aggravated assaults for which weapons information was known, firearms were used in 21.0 percent of aggravated assaults, and knives and other cutting instruments were used in 18.9 percent of aggravated assaults. Weapons classified in the "other" category were used in the remaining 35.1 percent of offenses. (Table 19)

An analysis by weapon type showed that the rate of aggravated assaults per 100,000 inhabitants was 73.4 with personal weapons, 61.5 with firearms, 55.6 with knives and other cutting instruments, and 102.9 with weapons in the "other" category. (Table 19)

PROPERTY CRIME

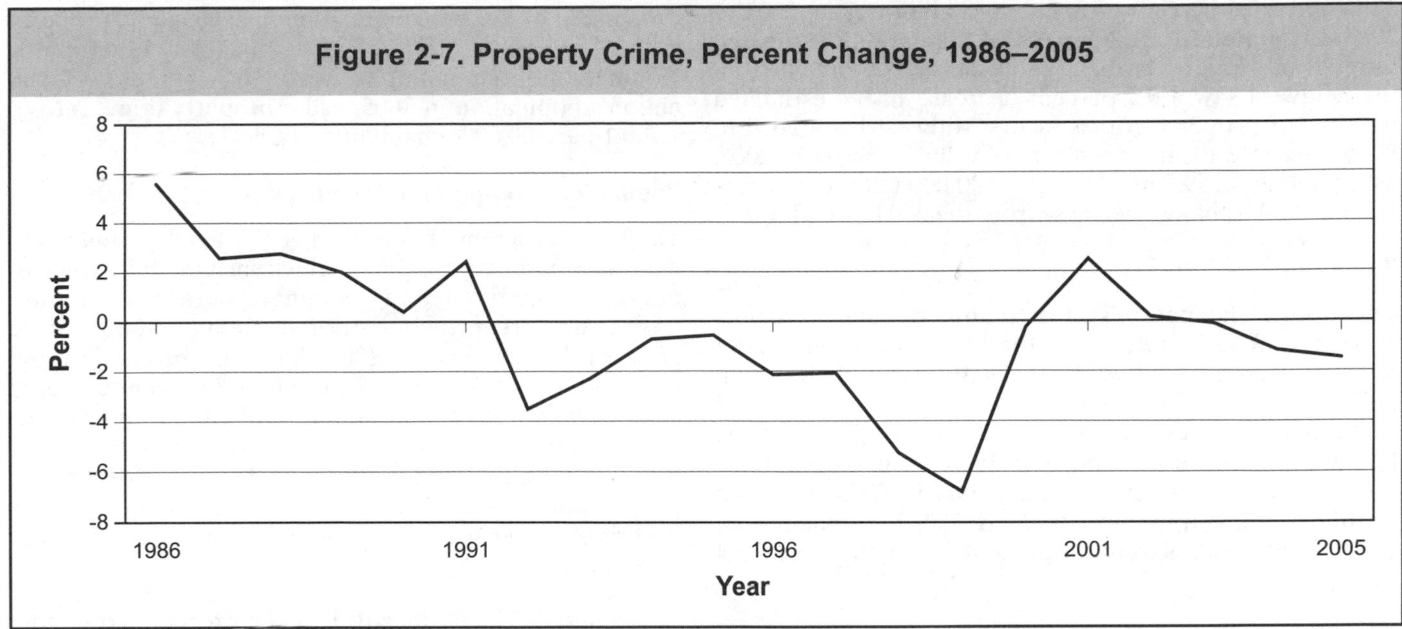

Definition

The Uniform Crime Reporting (UCR) Program's definition of property crime includes the offenses of burglary, larceny-theft, motor vehicle theft, and arson. The object of theft-type offenses is the taking of money or property without the use of force or threat of force against the victims. Property crime includes arson because the offense involves the destruction of property; however, arson victims may be subjected to force. Because of limited participation and the varying collection procedures conducted by local law enforcement agencies, only limited data are available for arson. Arson statistics are included in the trend, clearance, and arrest tables in *Crime in the United States*, but they are not included in any estimated volume data. More information on the expanded arson tables (which are available online but not included in this publication) can be found in Appendix I.

Data Collection

The data presented in *Crime in the United States* reflect the Hierarchy Rule, which counts only the most serious offense in a multiple-offense criminal incident. In descending order of severity, the violent crimes are murder and nonnegligent manslaughter, forcible rape, robbery, aggravated assault; these are followed by the property crimes of burglary, larceny-theft, and motor vehicle theft.

National Volume, Trends, and Rates

An estimated 10,166,159 property crimes were committed in the United States in 2005, representing a 1.5 percent decrease from the 2004 (2-year trend) estimate, a 2.6 percent decrease from the 2001 (5-year trend) estimate, and a 13.9 percent decrease from the 1996 (10-year trend) estimate. (Table 1)

In 2005, larceny-theft and motor vehicle theft incidents showed a decline from their 2004 estimates; however, the number of estimated incidents of burglary showed an increase during this period. The number of larceny-thefts was down 2.3 percent and the number of motor vehicle thefts was down 0.2 percent. The number of burglaries was up 0.5 percent. (Table 1)

The estimated property crime rate per 100,000 inhabitants in 2005 was 3,429.8, a 2.4 percent decrease from the 2004 rate, a 6.2 percent decrease from the 2001 rate, and a 22.9 percent decrease from the 1996 rate. (Table 1)

Regional Offense Trends and Rates

The UCR Program separates the United States into four regions: the Northeast, the Midwest, the South, and the West. (Geographic breakdowns can be found in Appendix III.) Property crime data collected by the UCR Program and aggregated by region reflected the following results.

The Northeast

The Northeast region accounted for 18.4 percent of the nation's population and experienced a 0.1 percent growth in population from 2004 to 2005. The region also accounted for 12.3 of the nation's estimated number of property crimes in 2005. (Table 3) Law enforcement in the Northeast saw a 3.1 percent decrease in the estimated number of property crimes from 2004 to 2005. The property crime rate for the Northeast, estimated at 2,287.2 incidents per 100,000 inhabitants, was 3.2 percent lower than the 2004 rate. (Table 4)

The Midwest

The Midwest, with 22.3 percent of the U.S. population in 2005 and a 0.4 percent growth in population from 2004 to 2005, accounted for 21.2 percent of the nation's estimated number of property crimes. (Table 3) Law enforcement in the Midwest saw a 0.2 percent decrease in the estimated number of property crimes in the Midwest from 2004 to 2005. The rate of property crime in the Midwest in 2005, estimated at 3,259.9 incidents per 100,000 inhabitants, represented a 0.6 percent decrease from the 2004 rate. (Table 4)

The South

The South, the nation's most highly populated region, accounted for 36.3 percent of the U.S. population in 2005 and experienced a 1.4 percent growth in population from 2004 to 2005. The region also accounted for an estimated 41.1 percent of the nation's property crimes. (Table 3) The South experienced a 2.2 percent decrease in its estimated number of property crimes from 2004 to 2005. The 2005 property crime rate, an estimated 3,883.1 incidents per 100,000 inhabitants, was 3.5 percent lower than the 2004 rate. (Table 4)

The West

In 2005, the West accounted for 23.0 percent of the nation's population; the region experienced a 1.3 percent growth in population from 2004 to 2005. The West also accounted for 25.5 percent of the nation's estimated number of property crimes. (Table 3) From 2004 to 2005, the estimated number of property crimes in this region decreased 0.6 percent. The estimated property crime rate in the West in 2005, 3,794.5 incidents per 100,000 inhabitants, was 1.9 percent lower than the 2004 rate. (Table 4)

Community Types

The UCR Program aggregates data by three community types: metropolitan statistical areas (MSAs), cities outside metropolitan areas, and nonmetropolitan counties. (Additional in-depth information regarding community types can be found in Appendix III.) In 2005, 82.9 percent of the U.S. population lived in MSAs. The property crime rate for MSAs was 3,598.8 per 100,000 inhabitants. Cities outside metropolitan areas, which accounted for 6.8 percent of the total population in 2005, had a property crime rate of 3,998.1 per 100,000 inhabitants. Nonmetropolitan counties, with 10.3 percent of the nation's population in 2005, had a property crime rate of 1,700.1 per 100,000 inhabitants. (Table 2)

Population Groups: Trends and Rates

The UCR Program organizes the agencies that contribute data into population groups, which include cities, metropolitan counties, and nonmetropolitan counties. (Appendix III provides further details about these groups.) From 2004 to 2005, law enforcement in the nation's cities collectively reported a 1.7 percent decrease in the number of property crimes. All city groups experienced decreased in the number of property crimes; cities with over 1,000,000 inhabitants had the largest declines at 3.3 percent. Metropolitan and nonmetropolitan counties experienced declines of 0.9 or 0.7 percent, respectively. (Table 12)

The country's cities collectively had a property crime rate of 4,133.9 incidents per 100,000 inhabitants in 2005. Nonmetropolitan counties had a rate of 1,743.4 incidents per 100,000 inhabitants, and metropolitan counties had a rate of 2,509.4 incidents per 100,000 inhabitants. Property crime rates for each population group can be found in Table 16.

Offense Analysis

The estimated dollar loss attributing to property crimes (excluding arson) in 2005 was $16.5 billion, representing a 2.5 percent increase from the 2004 figure. Among the individual property crime categories, the dollar losses were an estimated $2.8 billion for burglary, $3.8 billion for larceny-theft, and $6.0 billion for motor vehicle theft. (Tables 1 and 23) Arson had an average dollar loss of $14,910 for the 59,540 incidents for which monetary figures were reported. (Unpublished Expanded Arson Table 2)

Figure 2-8. Burglary, by Location, 2005
(percent distribution)

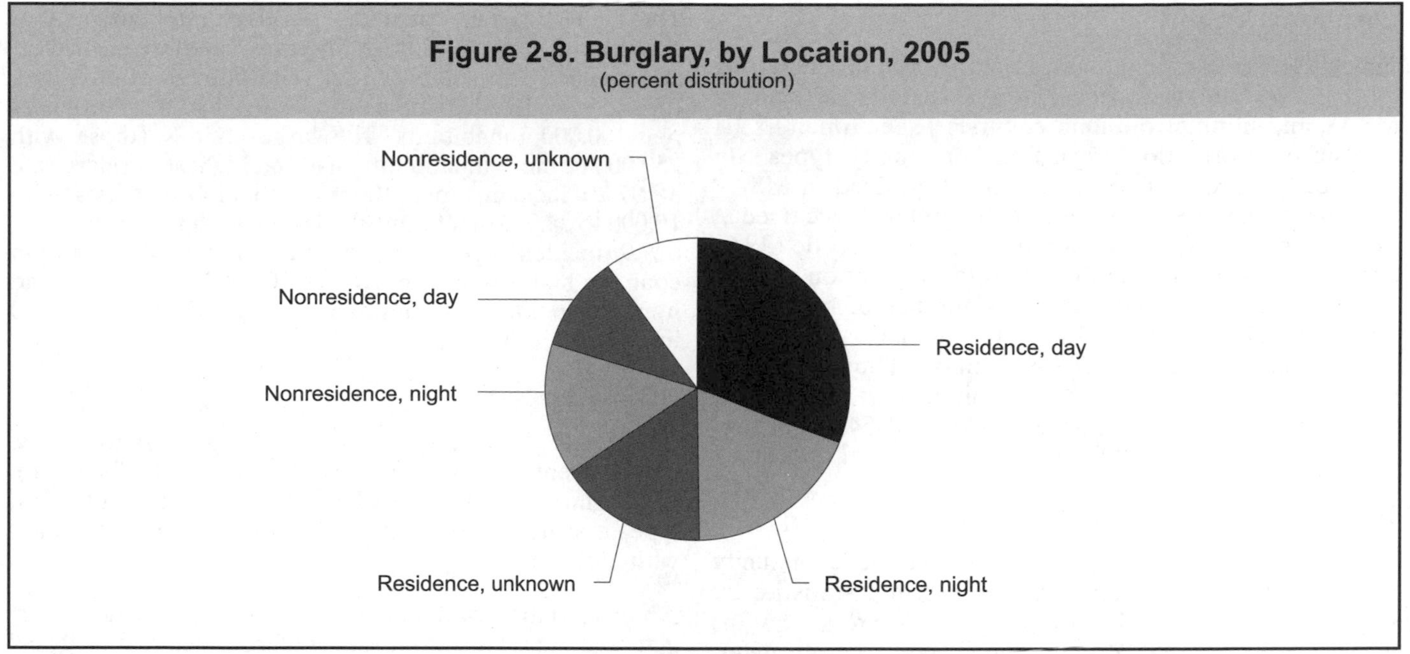

BURGLARY

Definition

The UCR Program defines burglary as the unlawful entry of a structure to commit a felony or theft. To classify an offense as a burglary, the use of force to gain entry need not have occurred. The program has three subclassifications for burglary: forcible entry, unlawful entry where no force is used, and attempted forcible entry. The UCR definition of "structure" includes, but is not limited to, apartments, barns, house trailers or houseboats (when used as permanent dwellings), offices, railroad cars (but not automobiles), stables, and vessels (i.e., ships).

National Volume, Trends, and Rate

In 2005, an estimated 2,154,126 burglary offenses occurred in the United States. This figure represented a 0.5 percent increase from the 2004 figure. An examination of 5-year and 10-year trends demonstrated a 1.8 percent increase from the 2001 estimate and a 14.1 percent decrease from 1996 estimate. However, the burglary rate for the United States in 2005 was 726.7 incidents per 100,000 inhabitants, a 0.5 percent decrease from the 2004 rate. The 2005 rate was 2.0 percent lower than the 2001 rate and 23.1 percent lower than the 1996 rate. (Table 1)

Regional Offense Trends and Rates

The UCR Program divides the United States into four regions: the Northeast, the Midwest, the South, and the West. (Details regarding these regions can be found in Appendix III.) An analysis of burglary data by region showed the following details.

The Northeast

In 2005, 18.4 percent of the nation's population lived in the Northeast, which experienced a 0.1 percent growth in population from 2004 to 2005. This region accounted for 10.8 percent of the estimated total number of burglary offenses in the nation. This figure represented a 2.1 percent decrease from the 2004 estimate. The region's burglary rate, an estimated 424.5 offenses per 100,000 inhabitants, represented a decrease of 2.2 percent from the 2004 rate. (Tables 3 and 4)

The Midwest

The Midwest accounted for 22.3 percent of the nation's population in 2005 and experienced a 0.4 percent growth in population from 2004 to 2005. This region also accounted for 20.4 percent of the nation's estimated number of burglaries. The estimated number of burglaries in this region increased 3.5 percent from 2004 to 2005. The Midwest had a burglary rate of 666.2 offenses per 100,000 inhabitants, a 3.1 percent increase from the 2004 rate. (Tables 3 and 4)

The South

The South, the nation's most highly populated region, had the most burglaries in 2005 (an estimated 965,476). With 36.3 percent of the nation's population (and having experienced a 1.4 percent growth in population from 2004 to 2005), this region accounted for 44.8 percent of all burglaries in the United States. The estimated rate of burglary in the South was 898.1 incidents per 100,000 inhabitants, a 1.8 percent decrease from the 2004 rate. (Tables 3 and 4)

The West

The West accounted for 23.0 percent of the nation's population in 2005 and experienced a 1.3 percent growth in population from 2004 to 2005. In 2005, this region also accounted for an estimated 24.0 percent of the nation's burglaries. The region's burglary rate was 757.3, a 0.6 percent decrease from the 2004 rate. However, the total number of burglaries (517,163) represented a 0.7 percent increase from the 2004 figure. (Tables 3 and 4)

Community Types

The UCR Program aggregates data by three community types: metropolitan statistical areas (MSAs), cities outside MSAs, and nonmetropolitan counties. (See Appendix III for more information regarding community types.) In 2005, 82.9 percent of the U.S. population lived in MSAs, and an estimated 84.8 percent of all burglaries occurred in this type of community. Inhabitants of cities outside MSAs accounted for 6.8 percent of the total population in 2005 and 7.5 percent of the estimated number of burglaries; nonmetropolitan counties, with 10.3 percent of the U.S. population, accounted for 7.7 percent of all burglaries. The burglary rates per 100,000 inhabitants were 743.7 in MSAs, 800.9 in cities outside MSAs, and 542.3 in nonmetropolitan counties. (Table 2)

Population Groups: Trends and Rates

In addition to analyzing data by region and community type, the UCR Program aggregates crime statistics by population groups. Cities are categorized into six groups based on the number of inhabitants; counties are categorized into two groups, metropolitan and nonmetropolitan. (Appendix III offers further details regarding these population groups.)

An examination of data from law enforcement agencies that provided statistics for at least 6 common months in 2004 and 2005 showed that the nation's cities experienced a collective 0.9 percent increase in burglaries from 2004 to 2005. Burglaries increased in every city group. Cities with 25,000 to 49,999 inhabitants experienced the largest increase (1.6 percent) and cities with 100,000 to 249,999 inhabitants experienced the smallest increase (0.5 percent). However, cities with 1,000,000 inhabitants or more—a subset of the city group of cities with 250,000 inhabitants or more—experienced a 1.5 percent decline in the number of burglaries, though the number for the overall group increased 0.8 percent. The volume of burglaries increased 0.5 percent in metropolitan counties, but decreased 2.4 percent in nonmetropolitan counties. (Table 12)

The UCR Program calculates burglary rates for population groups from the information provided by participating agencies that submitted all 12 months of offense data for the year. In 2005, the nation's cities had 821.4 offenses per 100,000 inhabitants. The largest cities (those with 250,000 or more inhabitants) had the highest burglary rate at 974.0 incidents per 100,000 inhabitants. Cities with 10,000 to 24,999 inhabitants had the lowest burglary rate—629.9 incidents per 100,000 inhabitants. Metropolitan counties had a rate of 619.1 per 100,000 inhabitants, and nonmetropolitan counties had a rate of 559.5 per 100,000 inhabitants. (Table 16)

Offense Analysis

The UCR Program requests that participating law enforcement agencies provide details regarding the nature of burglaries in their jurisdictions, such as type of entry, type of structure, time of day, and dollar loss associated with each offense.

An examination of data from agencies that provided burglary data for all 12 months of 2005 revealed that 60.9 percent of all burglaries involved forcible entry. Unlawful entry accounted for 32.7 percent of offenses, and attempted forcible entry accounted for 6.4 percent of burglaries reported to the UCR Program in 2005. (Table 19)

As in the past, burglars targeted residences more often than nonresidential structures. An analysis of data from agencies that provided supplemental burglary data for at least 6 months of 2005 showed that 65.8 percent of burglaries occurred at residences, while 34.2 percent of burglaries occurred at nonresidential structures. (Table 23)

Law enforcement agencies were unable to determine the time of day for 25.8 percent of all reported burglaries. However, of the burglaries for which time of day could be established, most burglaries of residences (62.4 percent) occurred during the day (between 6 a.m. and 6 p.m.). Nonresidential structures were targeted more often at night, with 58.0 percent of all nonresidential burglaries occurring between 6 p.m. and 6 a.m. The average dollar loss per burglary was $1,725. (Table 23)

Figure 2-9. Larceny-Theft Rate, 1986–2005

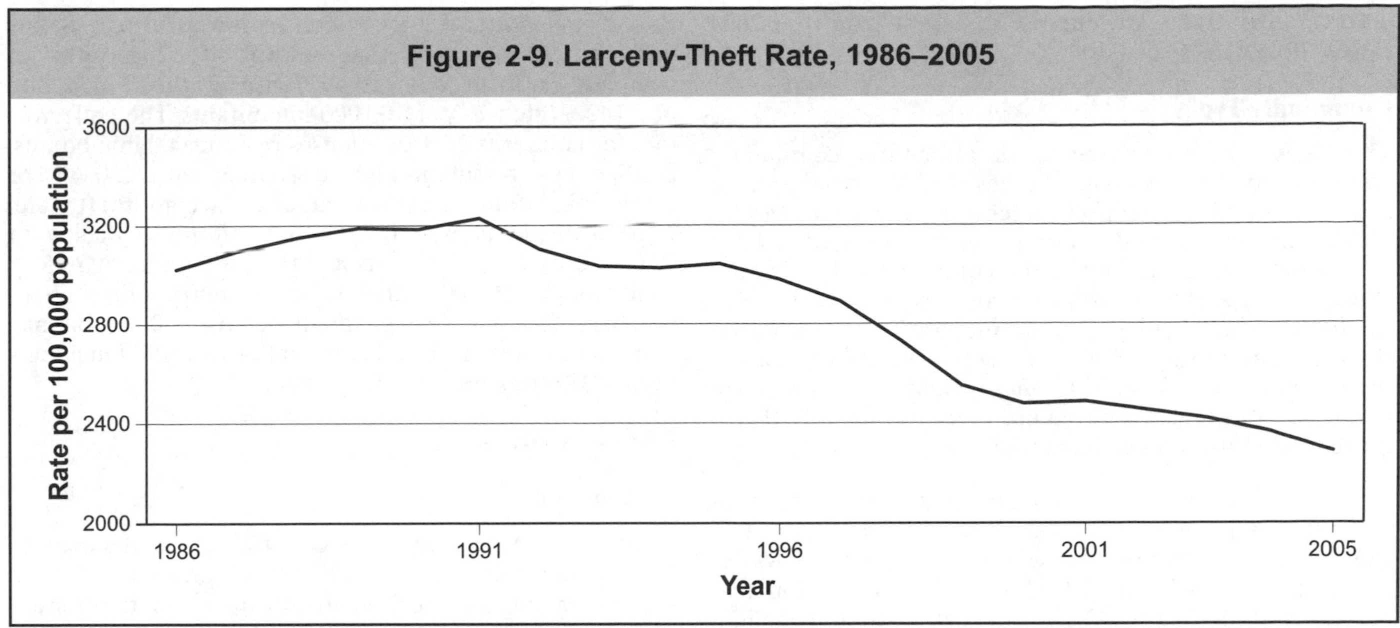

LARCENY-THEFT

Definition

The UCR Program defines larceny-theft as the unlawful taking, carrying, leading, or riding away of property from the possession or constructive possession of another. Examples are thefts of bicycles, motor vehicle parts and accessories, shoplifting, pocket picking, or the stealing of any property or article not taken by force and violence or by fraud. Attempted larcenies are included. Embezzlement, confidence games, forgery, check fraud, etc., are excluded from this category.

National Volume, Trends, and Rates

In 2005, larceny-theft accounted for an estimated 66.7 percent of the nation's property crimes. (Table 1) Trend data showed that the number of larceny-thefts decreased 2.3 percent from 2004 to 2005 (2-year trend data), decreased 4.4 percent from 2001 to 2005 (5-year trend data), and decreased 14.3 percent from 1996 to 2005 (10-year trend data). The trend data also showed decreases in the larceny-theft rates per 100,000 inhabitants during these periods. The larceny-theft rate decreased 3.2 percent between 2004 and 2005, 8.0 percent between 2001 and 2005, and 23.3 percent between 1996 and 2005. (Table 1)

Regional Offense Trends and Rates

The UCR Program defines four regions within the United States: the Northeast, the Midwest, the South, and the West. (See Appendix III for a geographical description of each region.) A comparison of 2004 and 2005 data showed that both the estimated number and the estimate rate of larceny-theft declined across all regions. (Tables 3 and 4) The following paragraphs provide a region overview of larceny-theft.

The Northeast

The region with the smallest proportion (18.4 percent) of the U.S. population in 2005, the Northeast experienced the smallest growth in population in the nation from 2004 to 2005 (0.1 percent). The region also experienced the fewest larceny-thefts in the country, accounting for only 13.1 percent of all larceny-thefts. (Table 3) The estimated number of offenses in 2005—887,943—represented a 2.4 percent decline from 2004, and the estimated rate—1,625.0 incidents per 100,000 inhabitants—represented a 2.5 percent decline. (Table 4)

The Midwest

With 22.3 percent of the U.S. population in 2005, and a 0.4 percent growth in population from 2004 to 2005, the Midwest accounted for an estimated 21.9 percent of the nation's larceny-thefts. (Table 3) The estimated number of offenses (1,485,603) declined 1.4 percent compared with the 2004 data, and the estimated rate of occurrences (2,251.9 incidents per 100,000 inhabitants) declined 1.8 percent. (Table 4)

The South

With more than one-third of the U.S. population in 2005 (36.3 percent), the South experienced a 1.4 percent growth in population from 2004 to 2005. The region had the nation's highest percentage of larceny-theft offenses: an estimated 41.3 percent. (Table 3) Estimated offenses in this region totaled 2,796,990, a 2.7 percent decrease from the 2004 estimate. The South's larceny-theft rate—estimated at 2,601.7 offenses per 100,000 inhabitants—decreased 4.1 percent from the 2004 estimate. (Table 4)

The West

In 2005, an estimated 23.0 percent of the U.S. population lived in the West, which experienced a 1.3 percent growth in population from 2004 to 2005. This region was also where 23.7 percent of the nation's estimated number of larceny-thefts took place. (Table 3) Occurrences of larceny-theft declined 2.4 percent from 2004 to 2005, dropping to an estimated total of 1,606,271 offenses. The region's larceny-theft rate, estimated at 2,352.1 offenses per

100,000 inhabitants, declined 3.7 percent from the 2004 rate. (Table 4)

Community Types

The UCR Program aggregates data for three community types: metropolitan statistical areas (MSAs), cities outside MSAs, and nonmetropolitan counties outside MSAs. MSAs include a central city or urbanized area with at least 50,000 inhabitants, as well as the county that contains the principal city and other adjacent counties that share a high degree of social and economic integration as measured through commuting. Cities outside MSAs are mostly incorporated areas, and nonmetropolitan counties are composed of unincorporated areas. (See Appendix III for more information regarding community types.)

In 2005, MSAs were home to an estimated 82.9 percent of the nation's population and experienced 86.5 percent of the nation's larceny-theft incidents. Cities outside MSAs accounted for 6.8 percent of the U.S. population and 8.9 percent of larceny-theft offenses. Nonmetropolitan counties, which were home to 10.3 percent of the nation's population, accounted for 4.6 percent of the estimated number of larceny-theft offenses. (Table 2)

Population Groups: Trends and Rates

To calculate 2-year trend data for population groups, the UCR Program reviewed reports from all agencies that submitted statistics on larceny-theft offenses for at least 6 common months in 2004 and 2005. (For an explanation of population groups and the number of agencies contributing to the UCR Program, see Appendix III; for the methodology used in tabular presentations, see Appendix I.)

In cities, collectively, occurrences of larceny-theft declined 2.7 percent between 2004 and 2005; all city groups, along with both metropolitan and nonmetropolitan counties, experienced declines in occurrences of larceny-theft during this time period. Among the city groups, cities with 250,000 or more inhabitants and cities with 100,000 to 249,999 inhabitants both experienced the greatest decrease (3.7 percent). Cities with 25,000 to 49,999 inhabitants had the smallest decrease (1.2 percent). In metropolitan and nonmetropolitan counties, the declines were 1.8 percent and 0.4 percent, respectively. (Table 12)

Based on reports of larceny-theft offenses from U.S. law enforcement agencies that submitted 12 months of complete data for 2005, this offense occurred at a rate of 2,342.6 offenses per 100,000 inhabitants. The collective rate for cities was 2,784.9 offenses per 100,000 inhabitants. Among city population groups, cities with 250,000 or more inhabitants had the highest larceny-theft rate, 2,953.3 incidents per 100,000 inhabitants. Cities with 10,000 to 24,999 inhabitants had the lowest rate at 2,450.2 incidents per 100,000 inhabitants. In metropolitan counties, the rate was 1,576.6 incidents per 100,000 inhabitants; in nonmetropolitan counties, the rate was 1,037.4 incidents per 100,000 inhabitants. (Table 16)

Offense Analysis

Distribution

Thefts from motor vehicles accounted for the majority of larceny-theft offenses in 2005 (25.8 percent). Table 23 provides a further breakdown of larceny-theft offenses, including shoplifting, thefts from buildings, thefts of motor vehicle accessories, thefts of bicycles, thefts from coin-operated machines, purse snatching, and pocket picking. The "all other" category, which includes the less-defined types of larceny-theft, accounted for 32.2 percent of all offenses. (Table 23)

Loss by Dollar Value

Larceny-theft offenses cost victims an estimated $5.2 billion dollars in 2005, up from $5.1 billion in 2004. (Tables 1 and 23) The average value of property stolen was $764 per offense, up 5.1 percent from the 2004 estimate. Larceny-theft from buildings had the highest average dollar loss per offense at $1,155. Thefts from motor vehicles had an average dollar loss of $691 per offense; thefts of motor vehicle accessories, $457; purse snatching, $377; pocket picking, $346; thefts from coin-operated machines, $233; thefts of bicycles, $268; and shoplifting, $163. (Table 23)

Offenses in which the stolen property was valued at more than $200 accounted for 40.0 percent of all larceny-thefts. Table 23 provides further analysis, including the average dollar value per offense, of all offenses in the overall category of property crime. (Table 23)

Figure 2-10. Motor Vehicle Theft, Number of Offenses, 1986–2005

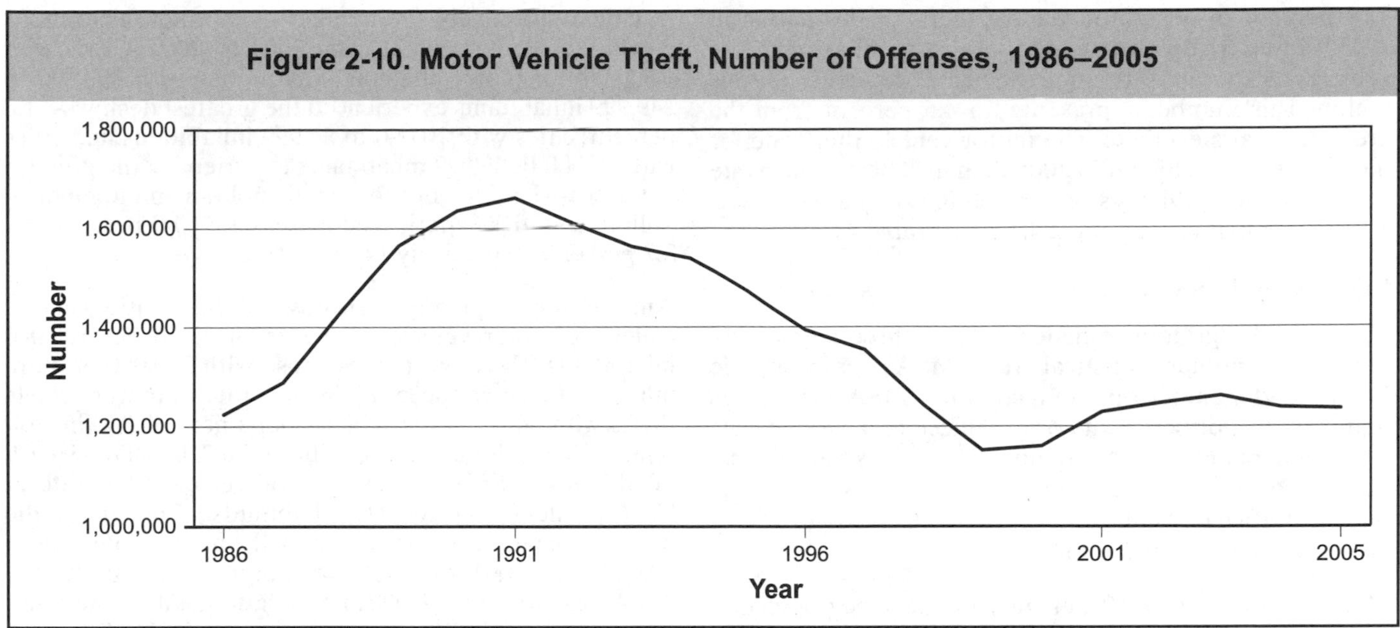

MOTOR VEHICLE THEFT

Definition

The UCR Program defines motor vehicle theft as the theft or attempted theft of a motor vehicle. The offense includes the stealing of automobiles, trucks, buses, motorcycles, snowmobiles, etc. The taking of a motor vehicle for temporary use by a person or persons with lawful access is excluded.

National Volume, Trends, and Rates

In 2005, an estimated 1,235,226 motor vehicle thefts took place in the United States. The 2-year, 5-year, and 10-year trend data showed some volatility: the number of motor vehicles estimated to have been stolen decreased 0.2 percent between 2004 and 2005, increased 0.6 percent between 2001 and 2005, and decreased 11.4 percent between 1996 and 2005. (Table 1)

The estimated rate of motor vehicle theft in 2005 was 416.7 incidents per 100,000 inhabitants. In the 2-year, 5-year, and 10-year trend data, this rate showed decline: the 2005 rate was 1.1 percent lower than the 2004 rate, 3.2 percent lower than the 2001 rate, and 20.7 percent lower than the 1996 rate. (Table 1)

Regional Offense Trends and Rates

In order to analyze crime by geographic area, the UCR Program divides the United States into four regions: the Northeast, the Midwest, the South, and the West. (Appendix III provides a map delineating the regions.) This section provides a regional overview of motor vehicle theft.

The Northeast

The Northeast accounted for an estimated 18.4 percent of the nation's population in 2005 and experienced a 0.1 percent growth in population from 2004 to 2005. The region also accounted for an estimated 10.5 percent of its motor vehicle thefts. (Table 3) An estimated 129,835 motor vehicle thefts occurred in the Northeast in 2005, representing a 9.5 percent decrease from the 2004 estimate. This was the largest decline among the regions. The estimated rate of 237.6 motor vehicle thefts per 100,000 inhabitants in thc Northeast in 2005 represented a 9.6 percent decline from the 2004 rate. (Table 4)

The Midwest

An estimated 22.3 percent of the country's population resided in the Midwest in 2005, and the region experienced a 0.4 growth in population from 2004 to 2005. The region accounted for 18.3 percent of the nation's motor vehicle thefts. (Table 3) The Midwest had an estimated 225,519 motor vehicle thefts in 2005, a 0.4 percent increase from the previous year's volume. The motor vehicle theft rate was estimated at 341.8 motor vehicles stolen per 100,000 inhabitants, a 0.1 percent decrease from the 2004 rate. (Table 4)

The South

The South, the nation's most highly populated region, was home to an estimated 36.3 percent of the U.S. population in 2005 and experienced a 1.4 percent growth in population from 2004 to 2005. This region accounted for over one-third (33.4 percent) of the Nation's motor vehicle thefts. (Table 3) The estimated 412,033 motor vehicle thefts in the South decreased 2.3 percent from the 2004 estimate. Motor vehicles in the South were stolen at an estimated rate of 383.3 per 100,000 inhabitants in 2005, a rate that was 3.7 percent lower than the 2004 rate. (Table 4)

The West

With approximately 23.0 percent of the U.S. population in 2005, the West experienced a 1.3 percent growth in population from 2004 to 2005. This region accounted for

37.9 percent of all motor vehicle thefts in the nation in 2005. (Table 3) By volume, the largest number of motor vehicle thefts, an estimated 467,839, occurred in this region. This number represented a 4.5 percent from the previous year's estimate. The motor vehicle theft rate for the West was also higher in 2005 than in 2004: the 2005 rate of 685.1 motor vehicles stolen per 100,000 inhabitants was 3.1 percent higher than the 2004 rate. (Table 4)

Community Types

The UCR Program aggregates data by three community types: metropolitan statistical areas (MSAs), cities outside MSAs, and nonmetropolitan counties. MSAs are areas that include a principal city or urbanized area with at least 50,000 inhabitants and the county that contains the principal city and other adjacent counties that have, as defined by the U.S. Office of Management and Budget, a high degree of economic and social integration.

The vast majority (82.9 percent) of the U.S. population resided in MSAs during 2005, where approximately 93.3 percent of motor vehicle thefts occurred. For 2005, the UCR Program estimated an overall rate of 469.1 motor vehicles stolen per 100,000 MSA inhabitants. Cities outside MSAs and nonmetropolitan counties comprised 6.8 and 10.3 percent of the nation's population, respectively. Cities outside MSAs accounted for 3.2 percent of motor vehicle thefts, and nonmetropolitan counties accounted for 3.5 percent of motor vehicle thefts. The UCR Program estimated a 2005 rate of 195.4 motor vehicles stolen for every 100,000 inhabitants in cities outside MSAs and a rate of 141.0 motor vehicles stolen per 100,000 inhabitants in nonmetropolitan counties. (Table 2)

Population Groups: Trends and Rates

The UCR Program aggregates data by various population groups, which include cities, metropolitan counties, and nonmetropolitan counties. (A definition of these groups can be found in Appendix III.)

In cities, collectively, the number of motor vehicle thefts decreased 0.3 percent in from 2004 to 2005. Cities with 1,000,000 or more inhabitants and cities with 100,000 to 249,999 inhabitants experienced the greatest declines—1.8 percent; cities with 10,000 to 24,999 inhabitants and cities with 25,000 to 49,999 inhabitants experienced the greatest increases—1.8 percent. Both metropolitan and nonmetropolitan counties experienced increases, at 1.3 percent and 3.7 percent, respectively. (Table 12)

Among the population groups, in 2005 cities had a collective motor vehicle theft rate of 527.6 per 100,000 inhabitants. The largest cities, those with 250,000 or more inhabitants, experienced the highest rate of motor vehicle thefts with 866.8 motor vehicle thefts per 100,000 inhabitants. (Within this city group, cities with 250,000 to 499,999 inhabitants had the highest motor vehicle theft rate at 997.6 incidents per 100,000 inhabitants.) Conversely, the nation's smallest cities, those with populations under 10,000, had the lowest rate of motor vehicle theft with 217.4 incidents per 100,000 in population. Within the county groups, metropolitan counties had a rate of 313.8 motor vehicles stolen per 100,000 inhabitants, while nonmetropolitan counties had a rate of 146.4 incident per 100,000 inhabitants. (Table 16)

Offense Analysis

Based on the reports of law enforcement agencies, the UCR Program estimated the combined value of motor vehicles stolen nationwide in 2005 at approximately $7.6 billion. (Tables 1 and 23) Automobiles were, by far, the most frequently stolen vehicle, accounting for 73.4 percent of all vehicles stolen. Trucks and buses accounted for 17.7 percent of stolen vehicles, and other vehicles accounted for 9.0 percent of stolen vehicles. (Table 19)

By type of vehicle, automobiles were stolen at a rate of 323.2 cars per 100,000 inhabitants in 2005. Trucks and buses were stolen at a rate of 77.8 vehicles per 100,000 in population, and other types of vehicles were stolen at a rate of 39.5 vehicles per 100,000 inhabitants. (Table 19)

ARSON

Definition

The UCR Program defines arson as any willful or malicious burning or attempt to burn (with or without intent to defraud) a dwelling house, public building, motor vehicle, aircraft, personal property of another, etc.

Data Collection

Only fires that investigators determined were willfully set (not fires labeled as "suspicious" or "of unknown origin") are included in this arson data collection. Points to consider regarding arson statistics include:

National offense rates per 100,000 inhabitants (found in Tables 1 through 4) do not include arson data; the FBI presents rates for arson separately. Arson rates are calculated based upon data received from all law enforcement agencies that provide the UCR Program with data for 12 complete months.

Arson data collection does not include estimates for arson, because the degree of reporting arson offenses varies from agency to agency. Because of this unevenness of reporting, arson offenses are excluded from Tables 1 through 7, all of which contain offense estimations.

The number of arsons reported by individual law enforcement agencies is available in Tables 8 through 11. Arson trend data (which indicate year-to-year changes) can be found in Tables 12 through 15, and arson clearance data (crimes solved) can be found in Tables 25 through 28.

National Coverage

In 2005, 13,868 agencies (providing 1 to 12 months of data) reported 67,504 arson offenses. Supplemental data, such as the type of structure burned and the estimated dollar loss, were received for 59,540 arsons. (Unpublished Expanded Arson Table 2; see Appendix I for more information) The UCR Program received 12 complete months of arson data from 10,629 agencies, representing 77.7 percent of the U.S. population. (Expanded Arson Table 1)

Population Groups: Trends and Rates

Law enforcement agencies in the nation's cities collectively reported a 2.1 percent decline in the number of arsons from the 2004 figure. Among the population groups labeled *city*, those with 500,000 to 999,999 inhabitants had the largest year-to-year decrease in reported arsons, 10.5 percent (the overarching group of cities with 250,000 or more inhabitants experienced a 4.2 percent decline); cities with 10,000 to 24,999 inhabitants had the smallest decrease in reported arsons, 1.0 percent. Cities with 100,000 to 249,999 inhabitants and cities with 1,000,000 or more inhabitants experienced increases in reported arsons (2.2 percent and 3.5 percent, respectively). Agencies in the nation's metropolitan counties reported a 4.2 percent decrease in the number of arsons, and those in nonmetropolitan counties reported a 5.4 percent decline. (Table 12)

Arson rates were based on information received from 10,629 agencies that provided 12 months of complete arson data to the UCR Program. An examination of data from those agencies indicated that in 2005, the highest rate—50.7 arsons per 100,000 inhabitants—was reported in cities with 250,000 to 499,999 inhabitants; cities with 250,000 or more inhabitants had a collective arson rate of 46.3. Cities with 10,000 to 24,999 residents had the lowest arson rate of all the city groups, 18.3 per 100,000 inhabitants. Metropolitan counties had 22.8 arsons per 100,000 inhabitants, and nonmetropolitan counties had 17.2 arsons per 100,000 inhabitants, the lowest of all the population groups. (Unpublished Expanded Arson Table 1; see Appendix I for more information)

Offense Analysis

The UCR Program breaks down arson offenses into three property categories: structural, mobile, and other. In addition, the structural property type is broken down into seven types of structures, and the mobile property type consists of two subgroupings. The program also collects information on the estimated dollar value of the damaged property.

Property Type

The number of arsons decreased for structural and mobile property types in 2005, but increased for other property types. Arsons for the structural property type decreased 1.5 percent, while arsons for the mobile property type dropped 5.6 percent. Arsons of other property types increased 4.8 percent. (Table 15)

Distributions by Property Type

In 2005, arsons of structures accounted for 43.6 percent of all arsons. Of these arsons, 61.7 percent involved residential properties. Of the residential arsons, most (71.8 percent) were single-occupancy residences, such as houses, townhouses, duplexes, etc. Mobile arsons accounted for 29.0 percent of all arsons. Within this category, 94.4 percent of offenses involved the burning of motor vehicles. Other types of property, such as crops, timber, fences, etc., accounted for 27.4 percent of reported arson offenses. (Expanded Arson Table 2)

Dollar Loss

In monetary terms, the average dollar loss in 2005 for an arson was $14,910. The average dollar loss for a structural arson was $28,964. Mobile property had an average dollar loss of $6,147. Other property types had an average dollar loss of $1,831. (Expanded Arson Table 2)

Within the structural arson category, the industrial/manufacturing subcategory had the highest average dollar loss at $356,324. Within that same category, single-occupancy dwellings had an average dollar loss of $24,512. Other residential dwellings had an average dollar loss of $27,552. (Expanded Arson Table 2)

Table 1. Crime in the United States, 1986–2005

(Number, rate per 100,000 population, percent.)

Year	Population[1]	Violent crime		Murder and nonnegligent manslaughter		Forcible rape		Robbery	
		Number	Rate	Number	Rate	Number	Rate	Number	Rate
1986	240 132 887	1 489 169	620.1	20 613	8.6	91 459	38.1	542 775	226.0
1987	242 288 918	1 483 999	612.5	20 096	8.3	91 111	37.6	517 704	213.7
1988	244 498 982	1 566 221	640.6	20 675	8.5	92 486	37.8	542 968	222.1
1989	246 819 230	1 646 037	666.9	21 500	8.7	94 504	38.3	578 326	234.3
1990	249 464 396	1 820 127	729.6	23 438	9.4	102 555	41.1	639 271	256.3
1991	252 153 092	1 911 767	758.2	24 703	9.8	106 593	42.3	687 732	272.7
1992	255 029 699	1 932 274	757.7	23 760	9.3	109 062	42.8	672 478	263.7
1993	257 782 608	1 926 017	747.1	24 526	9.5	106 014	41.1	659 870	256.0
1994	260 327 021	1 857 670	713.6	23 326	9.0	102 216	39.3	618 949	237.8
1995	262 803 276	1 798 792	684.5	21 606	8.2	97 470	37.1	580 509	220.9
1996	265 228 572	1 688 540	636.6	19 645	7.4	96 252	36.3	535 594	201.9
1997	267 783 607	1 636 096	611.0	18 208	6.8	96 153	35.9	498 534	186.2
1998	270 248 003	1 533 887	567.6	16 974	6.3	93 144	34.5	447 186	165.5
1999	272 690 813	1 426 044	523.0	15 522	5.7	89 411	32.8	409 371	150.1
2000	281 421 906	1 425 486	506.5	15 586	5.5	90 178	32.0	408 016	145.0
2001[2]	285 317 559	1 439 480	504.5	16 037	5.6	90 863	31.8	423 557	148.5
2002	287 973 924	1 423 677	494.4	16 229	5.6	95 235	33.1	420 806	146.1
2003	290 788 976	1 383 676	475.8	16 528	5.7	93 883	32.3	414 235	142.5
2004[3]	293 656 842	1 360 088	463.2	16 148	5.5	95 089	32.4	401 470	136.7
2005	296 410 404	1 390 695	469.2	16 692	5.6	93 934	31.7	417 122	140.7
Percent Change									
1996–2005	X	-17.6	-26.3	-15.0	-24.0	-2.4	-12.7	-22.1	-30.3
2001–2005	X	-3.4	-7.0	4.1	0.2	3.4	-0.5	-1.5	-5.2
2004–2005	X	2.3	1.3	3.4	2.4	-1.2	-2.1	4	2.9

Year	Aggravated assault		Property crime		Burglary		Larceny-theft		Motor vehicle theft	
	Number	Rate	Number	Rate	Number	Rate	Number	Rate	Number	Rate
1986	834 322	347.4	11 722 700	4 881.8	3 241 410	1 349.8	7 257 153	3 022.1	1 224 137	509.8
1987	855 088	352.9	12 024 709	4 963.0	3 236 184	1 335.7	7 499 851	3 095.4	1 288 674	531.9
1988	910 092	372.2	12 356 865	5 054.0	3 218 077	1 316.2	7 705 872	3 151.7	1 432 916	586.1
1989	951 707	385.6	12 605 412	5 107.1	3 168 170	1 283.6	7 872 442	3 189.6	1 564 800	634.0
1990	1 054 863	422.9	12 655 486	5 073.1	3 073 909	1 232.2	7 945 670	3 185.1	1 635 907	655.8
1991	1 092 739	433.4	12 961 116	5 140.2	3 157 150	1 252.1	8 142 228	3 229.1	1 661 738	659.0
1992	1 126 974	441.9	12 505 917	4 903.7	2 979 884	1 168.4	7 915 199	3 103.6	1 610 834	631.6
1993	1 135 607	440.5	12 218 777	4 740.0	2 834 808	1 099.7	7 820 909	3 033.9	1 563 060	606.3
1994	1 113 179	427.6	12 131 873	4 660.2	2 712 774	1 042.1	7 879 812	3 026.9	1 539 287	591.3
1995	1 099 207	418.3	12 063 935	4 590.5	2 593 784	987.0	7 997 710	3 043.2	1 472 441	560.3
1996	1 037 049	391.0	11 805 323	4 451.0	2 506 400	945.0	7 904 685	2 980.3	1 394 238	525.7
1997	1 023 201	382.1	11 558 475	4 316.3	2 460 526	918.8	7 743 760	2 891.8	1 354 189	505.7
1998	976 583	361.4	10 951 827	4 052.5	2 332 735	863.2	7 376 311	2 729.5	1 242 781	459.9
1999	911 740	334.3	10 208 334	3 743.6	2 100 739	770.4	6 955 520	2 550.7	1 152 075	422.5
2000	911 706	324.0	10 182 584	3 618.3	2 050 992	728.8	6 971 590	2 477.3	1 160 002	412.2
2001[2]	909 023	318.6	10 437 189	3 658.1	2 116 531	741.8	7 092 267	2 485.7	1 228 391	430.5
2002	891 407	309.5	10 455 277	3 630.6	2 151 252	747.0	7 057 379	2 450.7	1 246 646	432.9
2003	859 030	295.4	10 442 862	3 591.2	2 154 834	741.0	7 026 802	2 416.5	1 261 226	433.7
2004[3]	847 381	288.6	10 319 386	3 514.1	2 144 446	730.3	6 937 089	2 362.3	1 237 851	421.5
2005	862 947	291.1	10 166 159	3 429.8	2 154 126	726.7	6 776 807	2 286.3	1 235 226	416.7
Percent Change										
1996–2005	-16.8	-25.5	-13.9	-22.9	-14.1	-23.1	-14.3	-23.3	-11.4	-20.7
2001–2005	-5.1	-8.6	-2.6	-6.2	1.8	-2.0	-4.4	-8.0	0.6	-3.2
2004–2005	1.8	0.9	-1.5	-2.4	0.5	-0.5	-2.3	-3.2	-0.2	-1.1

Note: Although arson data are included in the trend and clearance tables, sufficient data are not available to estimate totals for this offense. Thus, arson data are not published in this table.

[1]Populations are Census Bureau provisional estimates as of July 1 for each year except 1990 and 2000, whose populations are decennial census counts.
[2]Murder and nonnegligent homicides that occurred as a result of the September 11, 2001, terrorist attacks are not included in this table.
[3]Crime figures for 2004 have been adjusted.
X = Not applicable.

Table 2. Crime, by Community Type, 2005

(Number, percent, rate per 100,000 population.)

Area	Population[1]	Violent crime	Murder and nonnegligent manslaughter	Forcible rape	Robbery	Aggravated assault	Property crime	Burglary	Larceny-theft	Motor vehicle theft
United States Total	296 410 404	1 390 695	16 692	93 934	417 122	862 947	10 166 159	2 154 126	6 776 807	1 235 226
Rate		469.2	5.6	31.7	140.7	291.1	3 429.8	726.7	2 286.3	416.7
Metropolitan Statistical Areas	245 756 143									
Area actually reporting[2]	95.4%	1 173 673	14 081	73 628	375 063	710 901	8 359 242	1 732 265	5 523 323	1 103 654
Estimated total	100.0%	1 252 512	14 932	78 264	400 792	758 524	8 844 369	1 827 587	5 863 902	1 152 880
Rate		509.7	6.1	31.8	163.1	308.6	3 598.8	743.7	2 386.1	469.1
Cities Outside Metropolitan Areas	20 044 706									
Area actually reporting[2]	86.8%	66 509	609	6 901	10 122	48 877	703 885	141 386	527 186	35 313
Estimated total	100.0%	74 868	691	7 893	11 516	54 768	801 411	160 537	601 701	39 173
Rate		373.5	3.4	39.4	57.5	273.2	3 998.1	800.9	3 001.8	195.4
Nonmetropolitan Counties	30 609 555									
Area actually reporting[2]	88.1%	57 685	943	6 812	4 253	45 677	461 562	147 548	275 389	38 625
Estimated total	100.0%	63 315	1 069	7 777	4 814	49 655	520 379	166 002	311 204	43 173
Rate		206.8	3.5	25.4	15.7	162.2	1 700.1	542.3	1 016.7	141.0

Note: Percentages may not add to 100 because of rounding. Although arson data are included in the trend and clearance tables, sufficient data are not available to estimate totals for this offense. Thus, arson data are not published in this table.

[1]Populations are Census Bureau provisional estimates as of July 1, 2005.
[2]Area actually reporting is based on the population covered by agencies providing 3 months or more of crime reports to the FBI.

Table 3. Population and Offense Distribution, by Region, 2005

(Percent distribution.)

Region	Population	Violent crime	Murder and nonnegligent manslaughter	Forcible rape	Robbery	Aggravated assault	Property crime	Burglary	Larceny-theft	Motor vehicle theft
United States Total	100.0	100.0	100.0	100.0	100.0	100.0	100.0	100.0	100.0	100.0
Northeast	18.4	15.5	14.4	12.8	19.4	13.9	12.3	10.8	13.1	10.5
Midwest	22.3	19.6	19.4	25.4	19.8	18.8	21.2	20.4	21.9	18.3
South	36.3	41.9	42.6	37.9	38.2	44.2	41.1	44.8	41.3	33.4
West	23.0	23.0	23.6	23.8	22.6	23.1	25.5	24.0	23.7	37.9

Note: Percentages may not add to 100 because of rounding. Although arson data are included in the trend and clearance tables, sufficient data are not available to estimate totals for this offense. Thus, arson data are not published in this table.

Table 4. Crime, by Region, Geographic Division, State, and Territory, 2004–2005

(Number, rate per 100,000 population, percent.)

Region and State	Population[1]	Violent crime		Murder and nonnegligent manslaughter		Forcible rape		Robbery	
		Number	Rate	Number	Rate	Number	Rate	Number	Rate
United States Total[2,3,4]									
2004	293 656 842	1 360 088	463.2	16 148	5.5	95 089	32.4	401 470	136.7
2005	296 410 404	1 390 695	469.2	16 692	5.6	93 934	31.7	417 122	140.7
Percent change		2.3	1.3	3.4	2.4	-1.2	-2.1	3.9	2.9
Northeast[2]									
2004	54 582 015	213 409	391.0	2 279	4.2	12 284	22.5	78 326	143.5
2005	54 641 895	215 052	393.6	2 403	4.4	12 061	22.1	80 720	147.7
Percent change		0.8	0.7	5.4	5.3	-1.8	-1.9	3.1	2.9
New England[2]									
2004	14 221 651	46 554	327.3	348	2.4	3 810	26.8	13 270	93.3
2005	14 239 724	45 533	319.8	356	2.5	3 631	25.5	13 112	92.1
Percent change		-2.2	-2.3	2.3	2.2	-4.7	-4.8	-1.2	-1.3
Connecticut[2]									
2004	3 498 966	10 113	289.0	100	2.9	755	21.6	4 188	119.7
2005	3 510 297	9 635	274.5	102	2.9	702	20.0	3 966	113.0
Percent change		-4.7	-5.0	2.0	1.7	-7.0	-7.3	-5.3	-5.6
Maine									
2004	1 314 985	1 364	103.7	18	1.4	315	24.0	289	22.0
2005	1 321 505	1 483	112.2	19	1.4	326	24.7	323	24.4
Percent change		8.7	8.2	5.6	5.0	3.5	3.0	11.8	11.2
Massachusetts[2]									
2004	6 407 382	29 489	460.2	171	2.7	1 794	28.0	7 484	116.8
2005	6 398 743	29 237	456.9	175	2.7	1 732	27.1	7 615	119.0
Percent change		-0.9	-0.7	2.3	2.5	-3.5	-3.3	1.8	1.9
New Hampshire[2]									
2004	1 299 169	2 202	169.5	17	1.3	466	35.9	500	38.5
2005	1 309 940	1 729	132.0	18	1.4	405	30.9	359	27.4
Percent change		-21.5	-22.1	5.9	5.0	-13.1	-13.8	-28.2	-28.8
Rhode Island									
2004	1 079 916	2 673	247.5	26	2.4	320	29.6	731	67.7
2005	1 076 189	2 703	251.2	34	3.2	321	29.8	776	72.1
Percent change		1.1	1.5	30.8	31.2	0.3	0.7	6.2	6.5
Vermont[2]									
2004	621 233	713	114.8	16	2.6	160	25.8	78	12.6
2005	623 050	746	119.7	8	1.3	145	23.3	73	11.7
Percent change		4.6	4.3	-50.0	-50.1	-9.4	-9.6	-6.4	-6.7
Middle Atlantic									
2004	40 360 364	166 855	413.4	1 931	4.8	8 474	21.0	65 056	161.2
2005	40 402 171	169 519	419.6	2 047	5.1	8 430	20.9	67 608	167.3
Percent change		1.6	1.5	6.0	5.9	-0.5	-0.6	3.9	3.8
New Jersey									
2004	8 685 166	30 943	356.3	392	4.5	1 331	15.3	13 076	150.6
2005	8 717 925	30 919	354.7	417	4.8	1 208	13.9	13 215	151.6
Percent change		-0.1	-0.5	6.4	6.0	-9.2	-9.6	1.1	0.7
New York									
2004	19 280 727	84 914	440.4	889	4.6	3 608	18.7	33 506	173.8
2005	19 254 630	85 839	445.8	874	4.5	3 636	18.9	35 179	182.7
Percent change		1.1	1.2	-1.7	-1.6	0.8	0.9	5.0	5.1
Pennsylvania									
2004	12 394 471	50 998	411.5	650	5.2	3 535	28.5	18 474	149.1
2005	12 429 616	52 761	424.5	756	6.1	3 586	28.9	19 214	154.6
Percent change		3.5	3.2	16.3	16.0	1.4	1.2	4.0	3.7
Midwest[2,3]									
2004	65 693 747	257 807	392.4	3 097	4.7	24 044	36.6	76 752	116.8
2005	65 971 974	272 247	412.7	3 243	4.9	23 905	36.2	82 682	125.3
Percent change		5.6	5.2	4.7	4.3	-0.6	-1.0	7.7	7.3
East North Central[2,3]									
2004	45 996 435	189 731	412.5	2 399	5.2	17 385	37.8	61 787	134.3
2005	46 156 447	200 215	433.8	2 517	5.5	17 045	36.9	66 584	144.3
Percent change		5.5	5.2	4.9	4.6	-2.0	-2.3	7.8	7.4
Illinois[2,3]									
2004	12 712 016	69 365	545.7	780	6.1	4 220	33.2	22 582	177.6
2005	12 763 371	70 392	551.5	766	6.0	4 297	33.7	23 187	181.7
Percent change		1.5	1.1	-1.8	-2.2	1.8	1.4	2.7	2.3
Indiana									
2004	6 226 537	20 294	325.9	316	5.1	1 803	29.0	6 373	102.4
2005	6 271 973	20 302	323.7	356	5.7	1 856	29.6	6 809	108.6
Percent change		0.0	-0.7	12.7	11.8	2.9	2.2	6.8	6.1
Michigan[2]									
2004	10 104 206	49 737	492.2	643	6.4	5 482	54.3	11 336	112.2
2005	10 120 860	55 877	552.1	616	6.1	5 193	51.3	13 342	131.8
Percent change		12.3	12.2	-4.2	-4.4	-5.3	-5.4	17.7	17.5

Note: Although arson data are included in the trend and clearance tables, sufficient data are not available to estimate totals for this offense. Thus, arson data are not published in this table.

[1]Populations are U.S. Census Bureau provisional estimates as of July 1, 2005, and July 1, 2004.
[2]The 2004 crime figures have been adjusted.
[3]Limited data for 2005 were available for Illinois.
[4]Includes offenses reported by the Zoological Police and the Metro Transit Police.

Table 4. Crime, by Region, Geographic Division, State, and Territory, 2004–2005—*Continued*

(Number, rate per 100,000 population, percent.)

Region and State	Aggravated assault		Property crime		Burglary		Larceny-theft		Motor vehicle theft	
	Number	Rate	Number	Rate	Number	Rate	Number	Rate	Number	Rate
United States Total[2,3,4]										
2004	847 381	288.6	10 319 386	3 514.1	2 144 446	730.3	6 937 089	2 362.3	1 237 851	421.5
2005	862 947	291.1	10 166 159	3 429.8	2 154 126	726.7	6 776 807	2 286.3	1 235 226	416.7
Percent change	1.8	0.9	-1.5	-2.4	0.5	-0.5	-2.3	-3.2	-0.2	-1.1
Northeast[2]										
2004	120 520	220.8	1 289 873	2 363.2	236 845	433.9	909 566	1 666.4	143 462	262.8
2005	119 868	219.4	1 249 751	2 287.2	231 973	424.5	887 943	1 625.0	129 835	237.6
Percent change	-0.5	-0.6	-3.1	-3.2	-2.1	-2.2	-2.4	-2.5	-9.5	-9.6
New England[2]										
2004	29 126	204.8	356 215	2 504.7	70 676	497.0	244 354	1 718.2	41 185	289.6
2005	28 434	199.7	339 926	2 387.2	68 825	483.3	234 079	1 643.8	37 022	260.0
Percent change	-2.4	-2.5	-4.6	-4.7	-2.6	-2.7	-4.2	-4.3	-10.1	-10.2
Connecticut[2]										
2004	5 070	144.9	93 942	2 684.9	15 959	456.1	66 770	1 908.3	11 213	320.5
2005	4 865	138.6	89 794	2 558.0	15 343	437.1	64 033	1 824.1	10 418	296.8
Percent change	-4.0	-4.4	-4.4	-4.7	-3.9	-4.2	-4.1	-4.4	-7.1	-7.4
Maine										
2004	742	56.4	31 740	2 413.7	6 341	482.2	24 096	1 832.4	1 303	99.1
2005	815	61.7	31 889	2 413.1	6 323	478.5	24 218	1 832.6	1 348	102.0
Percent change	9.8	9.3	0.5	0.0	-0.3	-0.8	0.5	0.0	3.5	2.9
Massachusetts[2]										
2004	20 040	312.8	158 150	2 468.2	34 497	538.4	101 605	1 585.7	22 048	344.1
2005	19 715	308.1	151 241	2 363.6	34 624	541.1	97 737	1 527.4	18 880	295.1
Percent change	-1.6	-1.5	-4.4	-4.2	0.4	0.5	-3.8	-3.7	-14.4	-14.3
New Hampshire[2]										
2004	1 219	93.8	26 658	2 051.9	4 979	383.2	19 723	1 518.1	1 956	150.6
2005	947	72.3	23 532	1 796.4	4 153	317.0	18 042	1 377.3	1 337	102.1
Percent change	-22.3	-23.0	-11.7	-12.5	-16.6	-17.3	-8.5	-9.3	-31.6	-32.2
Rhode Island										
2004	1 596	147.8	31 166	2 886.0	5 465	506.1	21 623	2 002.3	4 078	377.6
2005	1 572	146.1	29 260	2 718.9	5 318	494.2	19 544	1 816.0	4 398	408.7
Percent change	-1.5	-1.2	-6.1	-5.8	-2.7	-2.4	-9.6	-9.3	7.8	8.2
Vermont[2]										
2004	459	73.9	14 559	2 343.6	3 435	552.9	10 537	1 696.1	587	94.5
2005	520	83.5	14 210	2 280.7	3 064	401.8	10 505	1 686.1	641	102.9
Percent change	13.3	13.0	-2.4	-2.7	-10.8	-11.1	-0.3	-0.6	9.2	8.9
Middle Atlantic										
2004	91 394	226.4	933 658	2 313.3	166 169	411.7	665 212	1 648.2	102 277	253.4
2005	91 434	226.3	909 825	2 251.9	163 148	403.8	653 864	1 618.4	92 813	229.7
Percent change	0.0	-0.1	-2.6	-2.7	-1.8	-1.9	-1.7	-1.8	-9.3	-9.3
New Jersey										
2004	16 144	185.9	211 313	2 433.0	41 030	472.4	139 977	1 611.7	30 306	348.9
2005	16 079	184.4	203 391	2 333.0	38 980	447.1	136 728	1 568.4	27 683	317.5
Percent change	-0.4	-0.8	-3.7	-4.1	-5.0	-5.4	-2.3	-2.7	-8.7	-9.0
New York										
2004	46 911	243.3	422 734	2 192.5	70 696	366.7	311 036	1 613.2	41 002	212.7
2005	46 150	239.7	405 990	2 108.5	68 034	353.3	302 220	1 569.6	35 736	185.6
Percent change	-1.6	-1.5	-4.0	-3.8	-3.8	-3.6	-2.8	-2.7	-12.8	-12.7
Pennsylvania										
2004	28 339	228.6	299 611	2 417.3	54 443	439.3	214 199	1 728.2	30 969	249.9
2005	29 205	235.0	300 444	2 417.2	56 134	451.6	214 916	1 729.1	29 394	236.5
Percent change	3.1	2.8	0.3	0.0	3.1	2.8	0.3	0.1	-5.1	-5.4
Midwest[2,3]										
2004	153 914	234.3	2 155 351	3 280.9	424 469	646.1	1 506 184	2 292.7	224 698	342.0
2005	162 417	246.2	2 150 636	3 259.9	439 514	666.2	1 485 603	2 251.9	225 519	341.8
Percent change	5.5	5.1	-0.2	-0.6	3.5	3.1	-1.4	-1.8	0.4	-0.1
East North Central[2,3]										
2004	108 160	235.1	1 491 267	3 242.1	302 861	658.4	1 024 333	2 227.0	164 073	356.7
2005	114 069	247.1	1 489 943	3 228.0	316 206	685.1	1 010 460	2 189.2	163 277	353.7
Percent change	5.5	5.1	-0.1	-0.4	4.4	4.0	-1.4	-1.7	-0.5	-0.8
Illinois[2,3]										
2004	41 783	328.7	403 486	3 174.1	76 088	598.6	287 025	2 257.9	40 373	317.6
2005	42 142	330.2	393 148	3 080.3	77 462	606.9	276 301	2 164.8	39 385	308.6
Percent change	0.9	0.5	-2.6	-3.0	1.8	1.4	-3.7	-4.1	-2.4	-2.8
Indiana										
2004	11 802	189.5	211 929	3 403.6	42 168	677.2	148 670	2 387.7	21 091	338.7
2005	11 281	179.9	216 778	3 456.3	43 756	697.6	151 278	2 412.0	21 744	346.7
Percent change	-4.4	-5.1	2.3	1.5	3.8	3.0	1.8	1.0	3.1	2.3
Michigan[2]										
2004	32 276	319.4	309 805	3 066.1	64 233	635.7	194 988	1 929.8	50 584	500.6
2005	36 726	362.9	312 843	3 091.1	70 519	696.8	194 101	1 917.8	48 223	476.5
Percent change	13.8	13.6	1.0	0.8	9.8	9.6	-0.5	-0.6	-4.7	-4.8

Note: Although arson data are included in the trend and clearance tables, sufficient data are not available to estimate totals for this offense. Thus, arson data are not published in this table.

[2]The 2004 crime figures have been adjusted.
[3]Limited data for 2005 were available for Illinois.
[4]Includes offenses reported by the Zoological Police and the Metro Transit Police.

Table 4. Crime, by Region, Geographic Division, State, and Territory, 2004–2005—*Continued*

(Number, rate per 100,000 population, percent.)

Region and State	Population[1]	Violent crime		Murder and nonnegligent manslaughter		Forcible rape		Robbery	
		Number	Rate	Number	Rate	Number	Rate	Number	Rate
Ohio[2]									
2004	11 450 143	38 787	338.7	506	4.4	4 744	41.4	17 429	152.2
2005	11 464 042	40 273	351.3	585	5.1	4 557	39.8	18 696	163.1
Percent change		3.8	3.7	15.6	15.5	-3.9	-4.1	7.3	7.1
Wisconsin									
2004	5 503 533	11 548	209.8	154	2.8	1 136	20.6	4 067	73.9
2005	5 536 201	13 371	241.5	194	3.5	1 142	20.6	4 550	82.2
Percent change		15.8	15.1	26.0	25.2	0.5	-0.1	11.9	11.2
West North Central[2]									
2004	19 697 312	68 076	345.6	698	3.5	6 659	33.8	14 965	76.0
2005	19 815 527	72 032	363.5	726	3.7	6 860	34.6	16 098	81.2
Percent change		5.8	5.2	4.0	3.4	3.0	2.4	7.6	6.9
Iowa[2]									
2004	2 952 904	8 499	287.8	44	1.5	782	26.5	1 160	39.3
2005	2 966 334	8 642	291.3	38	1.3	827	27.9	1 154	38.9
Percent change		1.7	1.2	-13.6	-14.0	5.8	5.3	-0.5	-1.0
Kansas[2]									
2004	2 733 697	10 330	377.9	122	4.5	1 142	41.8	1 812	66.3
2005	2 744 687	10 634	387.4	102	3.7	1 055	38.4	1 793	65.3
Percent change		2.9	2.5	-16.4	-16.7	-7.6	-8.0	-1.0	-1.4
Minnesota									
2004	5 096 546	13 751	269.8	113	2.2	2 123	41.7	4 070	79.9
2005	5 132 799	15 243	297.0	115	2.2	2 258	44.0	4 724	92.0
Percent change		10.9	10.1	1.8	1.1	6.4	5.6	16.1	15.2
Missouri									
2004	5 759 532	28 226	490.1	354	6.1	1 479	25.7	6 630	115.1
2005	5 800 310	30 477	525.4	402	6.9	1 625	28.0	7 196	124.1
Percent change		8.0	7.2	13.6	12.8	9.9	9.1	8.5	7.8
Nebraska									
2004	1 747 704	5 393	308.6	40	2.3	620	35.5	1 138	65.1
2005	1 758 787	5 048	287.0	44	2.5	579	32.9	1 040	59.1
Percent change		-6.4	-7.0	10.0	9.3	-6.6	-7.2	-8.6	-9.2
North Dakota[2]									
2004	636 308	558	87.7	8	1.3	177	27.8	43	6.8
2005	636 677	625	98.2	7	1.1	154	24.2	47	7.4
Percent change		12.0	11.9	-12.5	-12.6	-13.0	-13.0	9.3	9.2
South Dakota[2]									
2004	770 621	1 319	171.2	17	2.2	336	43.6	112	14.5
2005	775 933	1 363	175.7	18	2.3	362	46.7	144	18.6
Percent change		3.3	2.6	5.9	5.2	7.7	7.0	28.6	27.7
South[2,4]									
2004	105 994 495	573 753	541.3	6 956	6.6	36 335	34.3	154 412	145.7
2005	107 505 413	583 323	542.6	7 112	6.6	35 606	33.1	159 545	148.4
Percent change		1.7	0.2	2.2	0.8	-2.0	-3.4	3.3	1.9
South Atlantic[2,4]									
2004	55 281 439	312 749	565.7	3 582	6.5	17 168	31.1	85 893	155.4
2005	56 179 519	318 806	567.5	3 672	6.5	16 697	29.7	90 141	160.5
Percent change		1.9	0.3	2.5	0.9	-2.7	-4.3	4.9	3.3
Delaware[2]									
2004	830 069	5 105	615.0	28	3.4	357	43.0	1 343	161.8
2005	843 524	5 332	632.1	37	4.4	377	44.7	1 306	154.8
Percent change		4.4	2.8	32.1	30.0	5.6	3.9	-2.8	-4.3
District of Columbia[4]									
2004	554 239	7 590	1 369.4	198	35.7	222	40.1	3 202	577.7
2005	550 521	8 032	1 459.0	195	35.4	166	30.2	3 700	672.1
Percent change		5.8	6.5	-1.5	-0.9	-25.2	-24.7	15.6	16.3
Florida									
2004	17 385 430	123 754	711.8	946	5.4	6 612	38.0	29 997	172.5
2005	17 789 864	125 957	708.0	883	5.0	6 592	37.1	30 141	169.4
Percent change		1.8	-0.5	-6.7	-8.8	-0.3	-2.6	0.5	-1.8
Georgia									
2004	8 918 129	40 217	451.0	613	6.9	2 387	26.8	13 656	153.1
2005	9 072 576	40 725	448.9	564	6.2	2 143	23.6	14 041	154.8
Percent change		1.3	-0.5	-8.0	-9.6	-10.2	-11.8	2.8	1.1
Maryland[2]									
2004	5 561 332	38 961	700.6	521	9.4	1 317	23.7	12 772	229.7
2005	5 600 388	39 369	703.0	552	9.9	1 266	22.6	14 378	256.7
Percent change		1.0	0.3	6.0	5.2	-3.9	-4.5	12.6	11.8
North Carolina									
2004	8 540 468	38 244	447.8	532	6.2	2 339	27.4	11 782	138.0
2005	8 683 242	40 650	468.1	585	6.7	2 302	26.5	12 635	145.5
Percent change		6.3	4.5	10.0	8.2	-1.6	-3.2	7.2	5.5

Note: Although arson data are included in the trend and clearance tables, sufficient data are not available to estimate totals for this offense. Thus, arson data are not published in this table.

[1]Populations are U.S. Census Bureau provisional estimates as of July 1, 2005, and July 1, 2004.
[2]The 2004 crime figures have been adjusted.
[4]Includes offenses reported by the Zoological Police and the Metro Transit Police.

Table 4. Crime, by Region, Geographic Division, State, and Territory, 2004–2005—*Continued*

(Number, rate per 100,000 population, percent.)

Region and State	Aggravated assault		Property crime		Burglary		Larceny-theft		Motor vehicle theft	
	Number	Rate	Number	Rate	Number	Rate	Number	Rate	Number	Rate
Ohio[2]										
2004	16 108	140.7	419 337	3 662.3	96 518	842.9	282 168	2 464.3	40 651	355.0
2005	16 435	143.4	419 899	3 662.7	100 063	872.8	278 457	2 429.0	41 379	360.9
Percent change	2.0	1.9	0.1	0.0	3.7	3.5	-1.3	-1.4	1.8	1.7
Wisconsin										
2004	6 191	112.5	146 710	2 665.7	23 854	433.4	111 482	2 025.6	11 374	206.7
2005	7 485	135.2	147 275	2 660.2	24 406	440.8	110 323	1 992.8	12 546	226.6
Percent change	20.9	20.2	0.4	-0.2	2.3	1.7	-1.0	-1.6	10.3	9.7
West North Central[2]										
2004	45 754	232.3	664 084	3 371.4	121 608	617.4	481 851	2 446.3	60 625	307.8
2005	48 348	244.0	660 693	3 334.2	123 308	622.3	475 143	2 397.8	62 242	314.1
Percent change	5.7	5.0	-0.5	-1.1	1.4	0.8	-1.4	-2.0	2.7	2.1
Iowa[2]										
2004	6 513	220.6	85 775	2 904.8	17 928	607.1	62 214	2 106.9	5 633	190.8
2005	6 623	223.3	84 056	2 833.7	17 987	606.4	60 594	2 042.7	5 475	184.6
Percent change	1.7	1.2	-2.0	-2.4	0.3	-0.1	-2.6	-3.0	-2.8	-3.2
Kansas[2]										
2004	7 254	265.4	109 771	4 015.5	20 146	737.0	81 115	2 967.2	8 510	311.3
2005	7 684	280.0	103 941	3 787.0	18 917	689.2	75 702	2 758.1	9 322	339.6
Percent change	5.9	5.5	-5.3	-5.7	-6.1	-6.5	-6.7	-7.0	9.5	9.1
Minnesota										
2004	7 445	146.1	155 019	3 041.6	28 048	550.3	113 453	2 226.1	13 518	265.2
2005	8 146	158.7	158 301	3 084.1	29 716	578.9	114 304	2 226.9	14 281	278.2
Percent change	9.4	8.6	2.1	1.4	5.9	5.2	0.8	0.0	5.6	4.9
Missouri										
2004	19 763	343.1	224 629	3 900.1	40 472	702.7	158 264	2 747.9	25 893	449.6
2005	21 254	366.4	227 809	3 927.5	42 822	738.3	159 288	2 746.2	25 699	443.1
Percent change	7.5	6.8	1.4	0.7	5.8	5.1	0.6	-0.1	-0.7	-1.4
Nebraska										
2004	3 595	205.7	61 512	3 519.6	9 826	562.2	46 399	2 654.9	5 287	302.5
2005	3 385	192.5	60 207	3 423.2	9 363	532.4	45 277	2 574.3	5 567	316.5
Percent change	-5.8	-6.4	-2.1	-2.7	-4.7	-5.3	-2.4	-3.0	5.3	4.6
North Dakota[2]										
2004	330	51.9	12 493	1 963.4	2 040	320.6	9 516	1 495.5	937	147.3
2005	417	65.5	12 595	1 978.2	1 986	311.9	9 552	1 500.3	1 057	166.0
Percent change	26.4	26.3	0.8	0.8	-2.6	-2.7	0.4	0.3	12.8	12.7
South Dakota[2]										
2004	854	110.8	14 885	1 931.6	3 148	408.5	10 890	1 413.1	847	109.9
2005	839	108.1	13 784	1 776.4	2 517	324.4	10 426	1 343.7	841	108.4
Percent change	-1.8	-2.4	-7.4	-8.0	-20.0	-20.6	-4.3	-4.9	-0.7	-1.4
South[2,4]										
2004	376 050	354.8	4 266 659	4 025.4	969 815	915.0	2 875 036	2 712.4	421 808	398.0
2005	381 060	354.5	4 174 499	3 883.1	965 476	898.1	2 796 990	2 601.7	412 033	383.3
Percent change	1.3	-0.1	-2.2	-3.5	-0.4	-1.8	-2.7	-4.1	-2.3	-3.7
South Atlantic[2,4]										
2004	206 106	372.8	2 152 901	3 894.4	480 328	868.9	1 439 483	2 603.9	233 090	421.6
2005	208 296	370.8	2 128 234	3 788.3	482 401	858.7	1 417 302	2 522.8	228 531	406.8
Percent change	1.1	-0.6	-1.1	-2.7	0.4	-1.2	-1.5	-3.1	-2.0	-3.5
Delaware[2]										
2004	3 377	406.8	27 256	3 283.6	5 669	683.0	19 285	2 323.3	2 302	277.3
2005	3 612	428.2	26 245	3 111.4	5 811	688.9	18 085	2 144.0	2 349	278.5
Percent change	7.0	5.3	-3.7	-5.2	2.5	0.9	-6.2	-7.7	2.0	0.4
District of Columbia[4]										
2004	3 968	715.9	26 896	4 852.8	3 946	712.0	14 542	2 623.8	8 408	1 517.0
2005	3 971	721.3	26 133	4 747.0	3 577	649.7	14 836	2 694.9	7 720	1 402.3
Percent change	0.1	0.8	-2.8	-2.2	-9.4	-8.7	2.0	2.7	-8.2	-7.6
Florida										
2004	86 199	495.8	727 141	4 182.5	166 332	956.7	482 484	2 775.2	78 325	450.5
2005	88 341	496.6	712 998	4 007.9	164 783	926.3	472 912	2 658.3	75 303	423.3
Percent change	2.5	0.2	-1.9	-4.2	-0.9	-3.2	-2.0	-4.2	-3.9	-6.0
Georgia										
2004	23 561	264.2	376 656	4 223.5	82 992	930.6	249 426	2 796.8	44 238	496.0
2005	23 977	264.3	378 534	4 172.3	84 463	931.0	249 594	2 751.1	44 477	490.2
Percent change	1.8	0.0	0.5	-1.2	1.8	0.0	0.1	-1.6	0.5	-1.2
Maryland[2]										
2004	24 351	437.9	202 474	3 640.7	36 704	660.0	129 888	2 335.6	35 882	645.2
2005	23 173	413.8	198 483	3 544.1	35 922	641.4	128 491	2 294.3	34 070	608.4
Percent change	-4.8	-5.5	-2.0	-2.7	-2.1	-2.8	-1.1	-1.8	-5.0	-5.7
North Carolina										
2004	23 591	276.2	355 328	4 160.5	101 193	1 184.9	227 147	2 659.7	26 988	316.0
2005	25 128	289.4	353 855	4 075.1	104 298	1 201.1	221 091	2 546.2	28 466	327.8
Percent change	6.5	4.8	-0.4	-2.1	3.1	1.4	-2.7	-4.3	5.5	3.7

Note: Although arson data are included in the trend and clearance tables, sufficient data are not available to estimate totals for this offense. Thus, arson data are not published in this table.

[2]The 2004 crime figures have been adjusted.
[4]Includes offenses reported by the Zoological Police and the Metro Transit Police.

Table 4. Crime, by Region, Geographic Division, State, and Territory, 2004–2005—*Continued*

(Number, rate per 100,000 population, percent.)

Region and State	Population[1]	Violent crime		Murder and nonnegligent manslaughter		Forcible rape		Robbery	
		Number	Rate	Number	Rate	Number	Rate	Number	Rate
South Carolina[2]									
2004	4 197 892	33 160	789.9	286	6.8	1 772	42.2	5 468	130.3
2005	4 255 083	32 384	761.1	315	7.4	1 809	42.5	5 622	132.1
Percent change		-2.3	-3.7	10.1	8.7	2.1	0.7	2.8	1.4
Virginia[2]									
2004	7 481 332	20 608	275.5	390	5.2	1 816	24.3	6 899	92.2
2005	7 567 465	21 400	282.8	461	6.1	1 721	22.7	7 507	99.2
Percent change		3.8	2.7	18.2	16.9	-5.2	-6.3	8.8	7.6
West Virginia[2]									
2004	1 812 548	5 110	281.9	68	3.8	346	19.1	774	42.7
2005	1 816 856	4 957	272.8	80	4.4	321	17.7	811	44.6
Percent change		-3.0	-3.2	17.6	17.4	-7.2	-7.4	4.8	4.5
East South Central[2]									
2004	17 461 276	79 157	453.3	1 074	6.2	6 423	36.8	20 676	118.4
2005	17 615 260	83 834	475.9	1 210	6.9	6 303	35.8	22 516	127.8
Percent change		5.9	5.0	12.7	11.7	-1.9	-2.7	8.9	7.9
Alabama									
2004	4 525 375	19 324	427.0	254	5.6	1 742	38.5	6 042	133.5
2005	4 557 808	19 678	431.7	374	8.2	1 564	34.3	6 447	141.4
Percent change		1.8	1.1	47.2	46.2	-10.2	-10.9	6.7	5.9
Kentucky									
2004	4 141 835	10 152	245.1	236	5.7	1 238	29.9	3 268	78.9
2005	4 173 405	11 134	266.8	190	4.6	1 421	34.0	3 690	88.4
Percent change		9.7	8.8	-19.5	-20.1	14.8	13.9	12.9	12.1
Mississippi									
2004	2 900 768	8 568	295.4	227	7.8	1 161	40.0	2 503	86.3
2005	2 921 088	8 131	278.4	214	7.3	1 147	39.3	2 405	82.3
Percent change		-5.1	-5.8	-5.7	-6.4	-1.2	-1.9	-3.9	-4.6
Tennessee[2]									
2004	5 893 298	41 113	697.6	357	6.1	2 282	38.7	8 863	150.4
2005	5 962 959	44 891	752.8	432	7.2	2 171	36.4	9 974	167.3
Percent change		9.2	7.9	21.0	19.6	-4.9	-6.0	12.5	11.2
West South Central[2]									
2004	33 251 780	181 847	546.9	2 300	6.9	12 744	38.3	47 843	143.9
2005	33 710 634	180 683	536.0	2 230	6.6	12 606	37.4	46 888	139.1
Percent change		-0.6	-2.0	-3.0	-4.4	-1.1	-2.4	-2.0	-3.3
Arkansas[2]									
2004	2 750 000	13 814	502.3	176	6.4	1 183	43.0	2 372	86.3
2005	2 779 154	14 659	527.5	186	6.7	1 193	42.9	2 531	91.1
Percent change		6.1	5.0	5.7	4.6	0.8	-0.2	6.7	5.6
Louisiana									
2004	4 506 685	28 844	640.0	574	12.7	1 616	35.9	6 564	145.7
2005	4 523 628	26 889	594.4	450	9.9	1 421	31.4	5 337	118.0
Percent change		-6.8	-7.1	-21.6	-21.9	-12.1	-12.4	-18.7	-19.0
Oklahoma									
2004	3 523 546	17 635	500.5	186	5.3	1 557	44.2	3 090	87.7
2005	3 547 884	18 044	508.6	187	5.3	1 481	41.7	3 230	91.0
Percent change		2.3	1.6	0.5	-0.2	-4.9	-5.5	4.5	3.8
Texas									
2004	22 471 549	121 554	540.9	1 364	6.1	8 388	37.3	35 817	159.4
2005	22 859 968	121 091	529.7	1 407	6.2	8 511	37.2	35 790	156.6
Percent change		-0.4	-2.1	3.2	1.4	1.5	-0.3	-0.1	-1.8
West[2]									
2004	67 386 585	315 119	467.6	3 816	5.7	22 426	33.3	91 980	136.5
2005	68 291 122	320 073	468.7	3 934	5.8	22 362	32.7	94 175	137.9
Percent change		1.6	0.2	3.1	1.7	-0.3	-1.6	2.4	1.0
Mountain[2]									
2004	19 826 259	86 518	436.4	1 074	5.4	7 780	39.2	20 204	101.9
2005	20 291 305	90 259	444.8	1 090	5.4	8 012	39.5	20 749	102.3
Percent change		4.3	1.9	1.5	-0.8	3.0	0.6	2.7	0.3
Arizona[2]									
2004	5 739 879	28 952	504.4	414	7.2	1 896	33.0	7 721	134.5
2005	5 939 292	30 478	513.2	445	7.5	2 006	33.8	8 579	144.4
Percent change		5.3	1.7	7.5	3.9	5.8	2.2	11.1	7.4
Colorado[2]									
2004	4 601 821	17 121	372.0	201	4.4	1 945	42.3	3 739	81.3
2005	4 665 177	18 498	396.5	173	3.7	2 026	43.4	3 948	84.6
Percent change		8.0	6.6	-13.9	-15.1	4.2	2.7	5.6	4.2
Idaho[2]									
2004	1 395 140	3 452	247.4	31	2.2	594	42.6	241	17.3
2005	1 429 096	3 670	256.8	35	2.4	577	40.4	266	18.6
Percent change		6.3	3.8	12.9	10.2	-2.9	-5.2	10.4	7.8

Note: Although arson data are included in the trend and clearance tables, sufficient data are not available to estimate totals for this offense. Thus, arson data are not published in this table.

[1]Populations are U.S. Census Bureau provisional estimates as of July 1, 2005, and July 1, 2004.
[2]The 2004 crime figures have been adjusted.

Table 4. Crime, by Region, Geographic Division, State, and Territory, 2004–2005—*Continued*

(Number, rate per 100,000 population, percent.)

Region and State	Aggravated assault		Property crime		Burglary		Larceny-theft		Motor vehicle theft	
	Number	Rate	Number	Rate	Number	Rate	Number	Rate	Number	Rate
South Carolina[2]										
2004	25 634	610.6	190 456	4 536.9	43 739	1 041.9	130 991	3 120.4	15 726	374.6
2005	24 638	579.0	184 646	4 339.4	42 589	1 000.9	125 699	2 954.1	16 358	384.4
Percent change	-3.9	-5.2	-3.1	-4.4	-2.6	-3.9	-4.0	-5.3	4.0	2.6
Virginia[2]										
2004	11 503	153.8	200 368	2 678.2	28 759	384.4	154 154	2 060.5	17 455	233.3
2005	11 711	154.8	199 644	2 638.2	29 672	392.1	154 000	2 035.0	15 972	211.1
Percent change	1.8	0.6	-0.4	-1.5	3.2	2.0	-0.1	-1.2	-8.5	-9.5
West Virginia[2]										
2004	3 922	216.4	46 326	2 555.8	10 994	606.5	31 566	1 741.5	3 766	207.8
2005	3 745	206.1	47 696	2 625.2	11 286	621.2	32 594	1 794.0	3 816	210.0
Percent change	-4.5	-4.7	3.0	2.7	2.7	2.4	3.3	3.0	1.3	1.1
East South Central[2]										
2004	50 984	292.0	643 520	3 685.4	158 615	908.4	429 453	2 459.5	55 452	317.6
2005	53 805	305.4	633 180	3 594.5	158 030	897.1	420 644	2 388.0	54 506	309.4
Percent change	5.5	4.6	-1.6	-2.5	-0.4	-1.2	-2.1	-2.9	-1.7	-2.6
Alabama										
2004	11 286	249.4	182 340	4 029.3	44 666	987.0	123 650	2 732.4	14 024	309.9
2005	11 293	247.8	177 393	3 892.1	43 473	953.8	120 780	2 650.0	13 140	288.3
Percent change	0.1	-0.7	-2.7	-3.4	-2.7	-3.4	-2.3	-3.0	-6.3	-7.0
Kentucky										
2004	5 410	130.6	105 209	2 540.2	25 902	625.4	70 535	1 703.0	8 772	211.8
2005	5 833	139.8	105 608	2 530.5	26 458	634.0	70 354	1 685.8	8 796	210.8
Percent change	7.8	7.0	0.4	-0.4	2.1	1.4	-0.3	-1.0	0.3	-0.5
Mississippi										
2004	4 677	161.2	100 980	3 481.1	27 661	953.6	65 440	2 256.0	7 879	271.6
2005	4 365	149.4	95 231	3 260.1	26 866	919.7	60 873	2 083.9	7 492	256.5
Percent change	-6.7	-7.3	-5.7	-6.3	-2.9	-3.5	-7.0	-7.6	-4.9	-5.6
Tennessee[2]										
2004	29 611	502.5	254 991	4 326.8	60 386	1 024.7	169 828	2 881.7	24 777	420.4
2005	32 314	541.9	254 948	4 275.5	61 233	1 026.9	168 637	2 828.1	25 078	420.6
Percent change	9.1	7.9	0.0	-1.2	1.4	0.2	-0.7	-1.9	1.2	0.0
West South Central[2]										
2004	118 960	357.8	1 470 238	4 421.5	330 872	995.1	1 006 100	3 025.7	133 266	400.8
2005	118 959	352.9	1 413 085	4 191.8	325 045	964.2	959 044	2 844.9	128 996	382.7
Percent change	0.0	-1.4	-3.9	-5.2	-1.8	-3.1	-4.7	-6.0	-3.2	-4.5
Arkansas[2]										
2004	10 083	366.7	110 911	4 033.1	30 151	1 096.4	74 242	2 699.7	6 518	237.0
2005	10 749	386.8	112 775	4 057.9	30 143	1 084.6	75 348	2 711.2	7 284	262.1
Percent change	6.6	5.5	1.7	0.6	0.0	-1.1	1.5	0.4	11.8	10.6
Louisiana										
2004	20 090	445.8	199 153	4 419.1	45 359	1 006.5	134 080	2 975.1	19 714	437.4
2005	19 681	435.1	166 611	3 683.1	39 382	870.6	112 840	2 494.5	14 389	318.1
Percent change	-2.0	-2.4	-16.3	-16.7	-13.2	-13.5	-15.8	-16.2	-27.0	-27.3
Oklahoma										
2004	12 802	363.3	149 472	4 242.1	35 244	1 000.2	101 271	2 874.1	12 957	367.7
2005	13 146	370.5	143 406	4 042.0	35 692	1 006.0	93 814	2 644.2	13 900	391.8
Percent change	2.7	2.0	-4.1	-4.7	1.3	0.6	-7.4	-8.0	7.3	6.5
Texas										
2004	75 985	338.1	1 010 702	4 497.7	220 118	979.5	696 507	3 099.5	94 077	418.6
2005	75 383	329.8	990 293	4 332.0	219 828	961.6	677 042	2 961.7	93 423	408.7
Percent change	-0.8	-2.5	-2.0	-3.7	-0.1	-1.8	-2.8	-4.4	-0.7	-2.4
West[2]										
2004	196 897	292.2	2 607 503	3 869.5	513 317	761.7	1 646 303	2 443.1	447 883	664.6
2005	199 602	292.3	2 591 273	3 794.5	517 163	757.3	1 606 271	2 352.1	467 839	685.1
Percent change	1.4	0.0	-0.6	-1.9	0.7	-0.6	-2.4	-3.7	4.5	3.1
Mountain[2]										
2004	57 460	289.8	830 300	4 187.9	162 110	817.7	545 539	2 751.6	122 651	618.6
2005	60 408	297.7	837 792	4 128.8	164 755	811.9	543 020	2 676.1	130 017	640.8
Percent change	5.1	2.7	0.9	-1.4	1.6	-0.7	-0.5	-2.7	6.0	3.6
Arizona[2]										
2004	18 921	329.6	291 203	5 073.3	56 885	991.0	179 012	3 118.7	55 306	963.5
2005	19 448	327.4	287 345	4 838.0	56 328	948.4	176 112	2 965.2	54 905	924.4
Percent change	2.8	-0.7	-1.3	-4.6	-1.0	-4.3	-1.6	-4.9	-0.7	-4.1
Colorado[2]										
2004	11 236	244.2	180 322	3 918.5	33 010	717.3	123 308	2 679.5	24 004	521.6
2005	12 351	264.7	188 449	4 039.5	34 746	744.8	127 602	2 735.2	26 101	559.5
Percent change	9.9	8.4	4.5	3.1	5.3	3.8	3.5	2.1	8.7	7.3
Idaho[2]										
2004	2 586	185.4	38 799	2 781.0	7 671	549.8	28 389	2 034.8	2 739	196.3
2005	2 792	195.4	38 556	2 697.9	8 066	564.4	27 606	1 931.7	2 884	201.8
Percent change	8.0	5.4	-0.6	-3.0	5.1	2.7	-2.8	-5.1	5.3	2.8

Note: Although arson data are included in the trend and clearance tables, sufficient data are not available to estimate totals for this offense. Thus, arson data are not published in this table.

[2]The 2004 crime figures have been adjusted.

Table 4. Crime, by Region, Geographic Division, State, and Territory, 2004–2005—*Continued*

(Number, rate per 100,000 population, percent.)

Region and State	Population[1]	Violent crime		Murder and nonnegligent manslaughter		Forcible rape		Robbery	
		Number	Rate	Number	Rate	Number	Rate	Number	Rate
Montana									
2004	926 920	2 723	293.8	30	3.2	273	29.5	233	25.1
2005	935 670	2 634	281.5	18	1.9	301	32.2	177	18.9
Percent change		-3.3	-4.2	-40.0	-40.6	10.3	9.2	-24.0	-24.7
Nevada									
2004	2 332 898	14 379	616.4	172	7.4	954	40.9	4 905	210.3
2005	2 414 807	14 654	606.8	206	8.5	1 016	42.1	4 702	194.7
Percent change		1.9	-1.5	19.8	15.7	6.5	2.9	-4.1	-7.4
New Mexico									
2004	1 903 006	13 081	687.4	169	8.9	1 039	54.6	2 062	108.4
2005	1 928 384	13 541	702.2	143	7.4	1 044	54.1	1 904	98.7
Percent change		3.5	2.2	-15.4	-16.5	0.5	-0.8	-7.7	-8.9
Utah[2]									
2004	2 420 708	5 647	233.3	46	1.9	967	39.9	1 236	51.1
2005	2 469 585	5 612	227.2	56	2.3	920	37.3	1 095	44.3
Percent change		-0.6	-2.6	21.7	19.3	-4.9	-6.7	-11.4	-13.2
Wyoming									
2004	505 887	1 163	229.9	11	2.2	112	22.1	67	13.2
2005	509 294	1 172	230.1	14	2.7	122	24.0	78	15.3
Percent change		0.8	0.1	27.3	26.4	8.9	8.2	16.4	15.6
Pacific[2]									
2004	47 560 326	228 601	480.7	2 742	5.8	14 646	30.8	71 776	150.9
2005	47 999 817	229 814	478.8	2 844	5.9	14 350	29.9	73 426	153.0
Percent change		0.5	-0.4	3.7	2.8	-2.0	-2.9	2.3	1.4
Alaska									
2004	657 755	4 159	632.3	37	5.6	558	84.8	447	68.0
2005	663 661	4 194	631.9	32	4.8	538	81.1	537	80.9
Percent change		0.8	-0.1	-13.5	-14.3	-3.6	-4.4	20.1	19.1
California[2]									
2004	35 842 038	189 175	527.8	2 392	6.7	9 615	26.8	61 768	172.3
2005	36 132 147	190 178	526.3	2 503	6.9	9 392	26.0	63 622	176.1
Percent change		0.5	-0.3	4.6	3.8	-2.3	-3.1	3.0	2.2
Hawaii									
2004	1 262 124	3 213	254.6	33	2.6	333	26.4	944	74.8
2005	1 275 194	3 253	255.1	24	1.9	343	26.9	1 001	78.5
Percent change		1.2	0.2	-27.3	-28.0	3.0	1.9	6.0	5.0
Oregon									
2004	3 591 363	10 724	298.6	90	2.5	1 283	35.7	2 751	76.6
2005	3 641 056	10 444	286.8	80	2.2	1 266	34.8	2 478	68.1
Percent change		-2.6	-3.9	-11.1	-12.3	-1.3	-2.7	-9.9	-11.2
Washington									
2004	6 207 046	21 330	343.6	190	3.1	2 857	46.0	5 866	94.5
2005	6 287 759	21 745	345.8	205	3.3	2 811	44.7	5 788	92.1
Percent change		1.9	0.6	7.9	6.5	-1.6	-2.9	-1.3	-2.6
Puerto Rico									
2004	3 895 107	10 045	257.9	793	20.4	199	5.1	6 030	154.8
2005	3 912 054	9 579	244.9	766	19.6	169	4.3	5 550	141.9
Percent change		-4.6	-5.1	-3.4	-3.8	-15.1	-15.4	-8.0	-8.4

Note: Although arson data are included in the trend and clearance tables, sufficient data are not available to estimate totals for this offense. Thus, arson data are not published in this table.

[1]Populations are U.S. Census Bureau provisional estimates as of July 1, 2005, and July 1, 2004.
[2]The 2004 crime figures have been adjusted.

Table 4. Crime, by Region, Geographic Division, State, and Territory, 2004–2005—*Continued*

(Number, rate per 100,000 population, percent.)

Region and State	Aggravated assault		Property crime		Burglary		Larceny-theft		Motor vehicle theft	
	Number	Rate	Number	Rate	Number	Rate	Number	Rate	Number	Rate
Montana										
2004	2 187	235.9	27 215	2 936.1	3 515	379.2	22 082	2 382.3	1 618	174.6
2005	2 138	228.5	29 407	3 142.9	3 642	389.2	23 794	2 543.0	1 971	210.7
Percent change	-2.2	-3.2	8.1	7.0	3.6	2.6	7.8	6.7	21.8	20.7
Nevada										
2004	8 348	357.8	98 215	4 210.0	23 142	992.0	52 438	2 247.8	22 635	970.3
2005	8 730	361.5	102 424	4 241.5	23 481	972.4	52 012	2 153.9	26 931	1 115.2
Percent change	4.6	1.0	4.3	0.7	1.5	-2.0	-0.8	-4.2	19.0	14.9
New Mexico										
2004	9 811	515.6	79 895	4 198.4	19 924	1 047.0	52 069	2 736.1	7 902	415.2
2005	10 450	541.9	79 995	4 148.3	21 095	1 093.9	50 907	2 639.9	7 993	414.5
Percent change	6.5	5.1	0.1	-1.2	5.9	4.5	-2.2	-3.5	1.2	-0.2
Utah[2]										
2004	3 398	140.4	97 762	4 038.6	15 225	628.9	74 889	3 093.7	7 648	315.9
2005	3 541	143.4	95 546	3 868.9	14 971	606.2	72 082	2 918.8	8 493	343.9
Percent change	4.2	2.1	-2.3	-4.2	-1.7	-3.6	-3.7	-5.7	11.0	8.9
Wyoming										
2004	973	192.3	16 889	3 338.5	2 738	541.2	13 352	2 639.3	799	157.9
2005	958	188.1	16 070	3 155.3	2 426	476.3	12 905	2 533.9	739	145.1
Percent change	-1.5	-2.2	-4.8	-5.5	-11.4	-12.0	-3.3	-4.0	-7.5	-8.1
Pacific[2]										
2004	139 437	293.2	1 777 203	3 736.7	351 207	738.4	1 100 764	2 314.5	325 232	683.8
2005	139 194	290.0	1 753 481	3 653.1	352 408	734.2	1 063 251	2 215.1	337 822	703.8
Percent change	-0.2	-1.1	-1.3	-2.2	0.3	-0.6	-3.4	-4.3	3.9	2.9
Alaska										
2004	3 117	473.9	22 172	3 370.9	3 773	573.6	16 159	2 456.7	2 240	340.6
2005	3 087	465.1	23 975	3 612.5	4 131	622.5	17 249	2 599.1	2 595	391.0
Percent change	-1.0	-1.8	8.1	7.2	9.5	8.5	6.7	5.8	15.8	14.8
California[2]										
2004	115 400	322.0	1 227 194	3 423.9	245 903	686.1	728 687	2 033.1	252 604	704.8
2005	114 661	317.3	1 200 531	3 322.6	250 521	693.3	692 467	1 916.5	257 543	712.8
Percent change	-0.6	-1.4	-2.2	-3.0	1.9	1.1	-5.0	-5.7	2.0	1.1
Hawaii										
2004	1 903	150.8	60 525	4 795.5	10 827	857.8	41 078	3 254.7	8 620	683.0
2005	1 885	147.8	61 115	4 792.6	9 792	767.9	42 188	3 308.4	9 135	716.4
Percent change	-0.9	-2.0	1.0	-0.1	-9.6	-10.5	2.7	1.6	6.0	4.9
Oregon										
2004	6 600	183.8	166 475	4 635.4	30 072	837.3	117 868	3 282.0	18 535	516.1
2005	6 620	181.8	160 199	4 399.8	27 621	758.6	113 316	3 112.2	19 262	529.0
Percent change	0.3	-1.1	-3.8	-5.1	-8.2	-9.4	-3.9	-5.2	3.9	2.5
Washington										
2004	12 417	200.0	300 837	4 846.7	60 632	976.8	196 972	3 173.4	43 233	696.5
2005	12 941	205.8	307 661	4 893.0	60 343	959.7	198 031	3 149.5	49 287	783.9
Percent change	4.2	2.9	2.3	1.0	-0.5	-1.8	0.5	-0.8	14.0	12.5
Puerto Rico										
2004	3 023	77.6	60 073	1 542.3	18 264	468.9	31 681	813.4	10 128	260.0
2005	3 094	79.1	55 466	1 417.8	17 191	439.4	28 976	740.7	9 299	237.7
Percent change	2.3	1.9	-7.7	-8.1	-5.9	-6.3	-8.5	-8.9	-8.2	-8.6

Note: Although arson data are included in the trend and clearance tables, sufficient data are not available to estimate totals for this offense. Thus, arson data are not published in this table.

[2]The 2004 crime figures have been adjusted.

Table 5. Crime, by State and Territory, 2005

(Number, percent, rate per 100,000 population.)

Area	Population	Violent crime	Murder and nonnegligent manslaughter	Forcible rape	Robbery	Aggravated assault	Property crime	Burglary	Larceny-theft	Motor vehicle theft
Alabama										
State total	4 557 808	19 678	374	1 564	6 447	11 293	177 393	43 473	120 780	13 140
Rate		431.7	8.2	34.3	141.4	247.8	3 892.1	953.8	2 650.0	288.3
Metropolitan statistical areas	3 225 901									
Area actually reporting	86.9%	14 466	292	1 145	5 467	7 562	128 757	32 178	86 479	10 100
Estimated total	100.0%	15 745	311	1 254	5 832	8 348	142 137	35 463	95 594	11 080
Cities outside metropolitan areas	578 770									
Area actually reporting	77.8%	2 208	30	152	383	1 643	20 668	3 934	15 689	1 045
Estimated total	100.0%	2 825	39	193	487	2 106	26 409	5 025	20 051	1 333
Nonmetropolitan counties	753 137									
Area actually reporting	84.6%	937	20	99	108	710	7 486	2 526	4 345	615
Estimated total	100.0%	1 108	24	117	128	839	8 847	2 985	5 135	727
Alaska										
State total	663 661	4 194	32	538	537	3 087	23 975	4 131	17 249	2 595
Rate		631.9	4.8	81.1	80.9	465.1	3 612.5	622.5	2 599.1	391.0
Metropolitan statistical areas	324 121									
Area actually reporting	100.0%	2 510	18	276	462	1 754	14 276	2 132	10 491	1 653
Cities outside metropolitan areas	123 801									
Area actually reporting	89.5%	571	4	93	30	444	4 372	603	3 472	297
Estimated total	100.0%	638	4	104	34	496	4 887	674	3 881	332
Nonmetropolitan counties	215 739									
Area actually reporting	100.0%	1 046	10	158	41	837	4 812	1 325	2 877	610
Arizona										
State total	5 939 292	30 478	445	2 006	8 579	19 448	287 345	56 328	176 112	54 905
Rate		513.2	7.5	33.8	144.4	327.4	4 838.0	948.4	2 965.2	924.4
Metropolitan statistical areas	5 285 836									
Area actually reporting	92.6%	27 028	401	1 827	8 250	16 550	254 833	47 985	155 870	50 978
Estimated total	100.0%	27 940	419	1 876	8 393	17 252	265 089	50 575	161 845	52 669
Cities outside metropolitan areas	321 912									
Area actually reporting	98.7%	1 314	10	89	139	1 076	14 527	2 991	10 218	1 318
Estimated total	100.0%	1 331	10	90	141	1 090	14 721	3 031	10 354	1 336
Nonmetropolitan counties	331 544									
Area actually reporting	88.4%	1 066	14	35	40	977	6 657	2 405	3 457	795
Estimated total	100.0%	1 207	16	40	45	1 106	7 535	2 722	3 913	900
Arkansas										
State total	2 779 154	14 659	186	1 193	2 531	10 749	112 775	30 143	75 348	7 284
Rate		527.5	6.7	42.9	91.1	386.8	4 057.9	1 084.6	2 711.2	262.1
Metropolitan statistical areas	1 616 500									
Area actually reporting	97.5%	11 060	124	835	2 110	7 991	79 343	19 874	54 194	5 275
Estimated total	100.0%	11 197	126	848	2 125	8 098	80 480	20 239	54 886	5 355
Cities outside metropolitan areas	490 978									
Area actually reporting	93.3%	2 133	36	193	329	1 575	20 798	6 095	13 741	962
Estimated total	100.0%	2 288	39	207	353	1 689	22 299	6 535	14 733	1 031
Nonmetropolitan counties	671 676									
Area actually reporting	85.0%	997	18	117	45	817	8 492	2 862	4 867	763
Estimated total	100.0%	1 174	21	138	53	962	9 996	3 369	5 729	898
California										
State total	36 132 147	190 178	2 503	9 392	63 622	114 661	1 200 531	250 521	692 467	257 543
Rate		526.3	6.9	26.0	176.1	317.3	3 322.6	693.3	1 916.5	712.8
Metropolitan statistical areas	35 292 558									
Area actually reporting	100.0%	186 982	2 475	9 087	63 325	112 095	1 178 603	243 735	679 817	255 051
Cities outside metropolitan areas	267 741									
Area actually reporting	100.0%	1 240	4	137	179	920	11 322	3 008	7 156	1 158
Nonmetropolitan counties	571 848									
Area actually reporting	100.0%	1 956	24	168	118	1 646	10 606	3 778	5 494	1 334
Colorado										
State total	4 665 177	18 498	173	2 026	3 948	12 351	188 449	34 746	127 602	26 101
Rate		396.5	3.7	43.4	84.6	264.7	4 039.5	744.8	2 735.2	559.5
Metropolitan statistical areas	4 005 624									
Area actually reporting	97.2%	16 376	161	1 741	3 795	10 679	166 744	31 296	110 900	24 548
Estimated total	100.0%	16 712	163	1 779	3 866	10 904	171 737	32 056	114 419	25 262
Cities outside metropolitan areas	297 857									
Area actually reporting	92.5%	1 109	8	156	63	882	11 419	1 613	9 300	506
Estimated total	100.0%	1 200	9	169	68	954	12 348	1 744	10 057	547
Nonmetropolitan counties	361 696									
Area actually reporting	96.9%	569	1	76	14	478	4 230	917	3 030	283
Estimated total	100.0%	586	1	78	14	493	4 364	946	3 126	292
Connecticut										
State total	3 510 297	9 635	102	702	3 966	4 865	89 794	15 343	64 033	10 418
Rate		274.5	2.9	20.0	113.0	138.6	2 558.0	437.1	1 824.1	296.8
Metropolitan statistical areas	2 826 978									
Area actually reporting	97.9%	8 841	89	550	3 802	4 400	80 250	13 252	57 333	9 665
Estimated total	100.0%	8 923	90	558	3 836	4 439	81 641	13 486	58 371	9 784
Cities outside metropolitan areas	158 760									
Area actually reporting	100.0%	274	0	26	68	180	3 395	697	2 483	215
Nonmetropolitan counties	524 559									
Area actually reporting	100.0%	438	12	118	62	246	4 758	1 160	3 179	419
Delaware										
State total	843 524	5 332	37	377	1 306	3 612	26 245	5 811	18 085	2 349
Rate		632.1	4.4	44.7	154.8	428.2	3 111.4	688.9	2 144.0	278.5
Metropolitan statistical areas	668 579									
Area actually reporting	100.0%	4 266	28	272	1 183	2 783	21 192	4 485	14 622	2 085
Cities outside metropolitan areas	39 833									
Area actually reporting	100.0%	379	1	38	71	269	1 991	393	1 533	65
Nonmetropolitan counties	135 112									
Area actually reporting	100.0%	687	8	67	52	560	3 062	933	1 930	199

Note: Although arson data are included in the trend and clearance tables, sufficient data are not available to estimate totals for this offense. Thus, arson data are not published in this table.

Table 5. Crime, by State and Territory, 2005—*Continued*

(Number, percent, rate per 100,000 population.)

Area	Population	Violent crime	Murder and nonnegligent manslaughter	Forcible rape	Robbery	Aggravated assault	Property crime	Burglary	Larceny-theft	Motor vehicle theft
District of Columbia[1]										
City total	550 521	8 032	195	166	3 700	3 971	26 133	3 577	14 836	7 720
Rate		1 459.0	35.4	30.2	672.1	721.3	4 747.0	649.7	2 694.9	1 402.3
Metropolitan statistical areas	550 521									
Area actually reporting	100.0%	8 032	195	166	3 700	3 971	26 133	3 577	14 836	7 720
Cities outside metropolitan areas	X									
Nonmetropolitan counties	X									
Florida										
State total	17 789 864	125 957	883	6 592	30 141	88 341	712 998	164 783	472 912	75 303
Rate		708.0	5.0	37.1	169.4	496.6	4 007.9	926.3	2 658.3	423.3
Metropolitan statistical areas	16 674 801									
Area actually reporting	99.9%	119 621	833	6 143	29 542	83 103	682 668	156 216	453 234	73 218
Estimated total	100.0%	119 632	833	6 144	29 545	83 110	682 738	156 231	453 282	73 225
Cities outside metropolitan areas	192 797									
Area actually reporting	96.7%	1 993	12	101	281	1 599	10 061	2 210	7 226	625
Estimated total	100.0%	2 061	12	104	291	1 654	10 410	2 287	7 476	647
Nonmetropolitan counties	922 266									
Area actually reporting	100.0%	4 264	38	344	305	3 577	19 850	6 265	12 154	1 431
Georgia										
State total	9 072 576	40 725	564	2 143	14 041	23 977	378 534	84 463	249 594	44 477
Rate		448.9	6.2	23.6	154.8	264.3	4 172.3	931.0	2 751.1	490.2
Metropolitan statistical areas	7 292 348									
Area actually reporting	98.3%	33 585	475	1 768	12 752	18 590	308 620	69 012	199 676	39 932
Estimated total	100.0%	34 133	478	1 795	12 948	18 912	314 494	70 115	203 819	40 560
Cities outside metropolitan areas	666 985									
Area actually reporting	79.1%	3 208	38	148	688	2 334	30 392	5 796	23 177	1 419
Estimated total	100.0%	4 055	48	187	870	2 950	38 403	7 323	29 287	1 793
Nonmetropolitan counties	1 113 243									
Area actually reporting	79.4%	2 015	30	128	177	1 680	20 364	5 580	13 097	1 687
Estimated total	100.0%	2 537	38	161	223	2 115	25 637	7 025	16 488	2 124
Hawaii										
State total	1 275 194	3 253	24	343	1 001	1 885	61 115	9 792	42 188	9 135
Rate		255.1	1.9	26.9	78.5	147.8	4 792.6	767.9	3 308.4	716.4
Metropolitan statistical areas	908 521									
Area actually reporting	100.0%	2 570	15	234	841	1 480	42 383	6 209	29 376	6 798
Cities outside metropolitan areas										
Nonmetropolitan counties	366 673									
Area actually reporting	55.1%	376	5	60	88	223	10 325	1 975	7 062	1 288
Estimated total	100.0%	683	9	109	160	405	18 732	3 583	12 812	2 337
Idaho										
State total	1 429 096	3 670	35	577	266	2 792	38 556	8 066	27 606	2 884
Rate		256.8	2.4	40.4	18.6	195.4	2 697.9	564.4	1 931.7	201.8
Metropolitan statistical areas	913 756									
Area actually reporting	99.6%	2 666	23	457	212	1 974	28 437	5 759	20 504	2 174
Estimated total	100.0%	2 677	23	458	212	1 984	28 565	5 786	20 595	2 184
Cities outside metropolitan areas	225 726									
Area actually reporting	98.1%	523	7	72	41	403	6 250	1 148	4 706	396
Estimated total	100.0%	533	7	73	42	411	6 368	1 170	4 795	403
Nonmetropolitan counties	289 614									
Area actually reporting	100.0%	460	5	46	12	397	3 623	1 110	2 216	297
Illinois[2]										
State total	12 763 371	70 392	766	4 297	23 187	42 142	393 148	77 462	276 301	39 385
Rate		551.5	6.0	33.7	181.7	330.2	3 080.3	606.9	2 164.8	308.6
Indiana										
State total	6 271 973	20 302	356	1 856	6 809	11 281	216 778	43 756	151 278	21 744
Rate		323.7	5.7	29.6	108.6	179.9	3 456.3	697.6	2 412.0	346.7
Metropolitan statistical areas	4 863 320									
Area actually reporting	88.6%	17 518	303	1 492	6 280	9 443	170 388	34 663	116 894	18 831
Estimated total	100.0%	18 416	311	1 572	6 458	10 075	181 437	36 873	124 785	19 779
Cities outside metropolitan areas	507 774									
Area actually reporting	83.9%	794	9	101	215	469	19 429	3 179	15 288	962
Estimated total	100.0%	946	11	120	256	559	23 146	3 787	18 213	1 146
Nonmetropolitan counties	900 879									
Area actually reporting	54.8%	516	19	90	52	355	6 688	1 698	4 541	449
Estimated total	100.0%	940	34	164	95	647	12 195	3 096	8 280	819
Iowa										
State total	2 966 334	8 642	38	827	1 154	6 623	84 056	17 987	60 594	5 475
Rate		291.3	1.3	27.9	38.9	223.3	2 833.7	606.4	2 042.7	184.6
Metropolitan statistical areas	1 616 968									
Area actually reporting	98.8%	6 322	21	597	1 035	4 669	59 286	12 115	43 193	3 978
Estimated total	100.0%	6 354	21	602	1 037	4 694	59 783	12 198	43 586	3 999
Cities outside metropolitan areas	596 078									
Area actually reporting	96.5%	1 731	14	164	106	1 447	18 013	3 710	13 378	925
Estimated total	100.0%	1 793	14	170	110	1 499	18 658	3 843	13 857	958
Nonmetropolitan counties	753 288									
Area actually reporting	97.1%	480	3	53	7	417	5 451	1 889	3 059	503
Estimated total	100.0%	495	3	55	7	430	5 615	1 946	3 151	518

Note: Although arson data are included in the trend and clearance tables, sufficient data are not available to estimate totals for this offense. Thus, arson data are not published in this table.

[1]Includes offenses reported by the Zoological Police and the Metro Transit Police.
[2]Limited data for 2005 were available for Illinois.
X = Not applicable.

Table 5. Crime, by State and Territory, 2005—*Continued*

(Number, percent, rate per 100,000 population.)

Area	Population	Violent crime	Murder and nonnegligent manslaughter	Forcible rape	Robbery	Aggravated assault	Property crime	Burglary	Larceny-theft	Motor vehicle theft
Kansas										
State total	2 744 687	10 634	102	1 055	1 793	7 684	103 941	18 917	75 702	9 322
Rate		387.4	3.7	38.4	65.3	280.0	3 787.0	689.2	2 758.1	339.6
Metropolitan statistical areas	1 720 248									
Area actually reporting	99.8%	7 686	77	683	1 582	5 344	72 131	12 583	51 769	7 779
Estimated total	100.0%	7 694	77	684	1 583	5 350	72 229	12 597	51 847	7 785
Cities outside metropolitan areas	606 739									
Area actually reporting	92.3%	1 941	16	253	166	1 506	23 199	4 120	18 084	995
Estimated total	100.0%	2 102	17	274	180	1 631	25 129	4 463	19 588	1 078
Nonmetropolitan counties	417 700									
Area actually reporting	98.5%	826	8	96	30	692	6 483	1 829	4 202	452
Estimated total	100.0%	838	8	97	30	703	6 583	1 857	4 267	459
Kentucky										
State total	4 173 405	11 134	190	1 421	3 690	5 833	105 608	26 458	70 354	8 796
Rate		266.8	4.6	34.0	88.4	139.8	2 530.5	634.0	1 685.8	210.8
Metropolitan statistical areas	2 362 333									
Area actually reporting	92.6%	7 559	90	657	3 028	3 784	66 799	15 358	45 670	5 771
Estimated total	100.0%	7 945	91	705	3 155	3 994	72 087	16 335	49 629	6 123
Cities outside metropolitan areas	517 744									
Area actually reporting	89.3%	1 158	4	142	279	733	15 107	3 205	10 989	913
Estimated total	100.0%	1 297	4	159	313	821	16 922	3 590	12 309	1 023
Nonmetropolitan counties	1 293 328									
Area actually reporting	86.1%	1 629	82	480	191	876	14 292	5 625	7 246	1 421
Estimated total	100.0%	1 892	95	557	222	1 018	16 599	6 533	8 416	1 650
Louisiana										
State total	4 523 628	26 889	450	1 421	5 337	19 681	166 611	39 382	112 840	14 389
Rate		594.4	9.9	31.4	118.0	435.1	3 683.1	870.6	2 494.5	318.1
Metropolitan statistical areas	3 393 914									
Area actually reporting	96.2%	20 467	393	1 121	4 685	14 268	128 449	29 466	86 630	12 353
Estimated total	100.0%	21 117	401	1 155	4 797	14 764	134 053	30 521	90 770	12 762
Cities outside metropolitan areas	385 173									
Area actually reporting	53.5%	1 320	11	68	170	1 071	9 243	2 318	6 536	389
Estimated total	100.0%	2 466	20	127	318	2 001	17 271	4 331	12 213	727
Nonmetropolitan counties	744 541									
Area actually reporting	79.6%	2 632	23	111	177	2 321	12 166	3 605	7 845	716
Estimated total	100.0%	3 306	29	139	222	2 916	15 287	4 530	9 857	900
Maine										
State total	1 321 505	1 483	19	326	323	815	31 889	6 323	24 218	1 348
Rate		112.2	1.4	24.7	24.4	61.7	2 413.1	478.5	1 832.6	102.0
Metropolitan statistical areas	768 481									
Area actually reporting	100.0%	969	10	191	264	504	19 662	3 654	15 130	878
Cities outside metropolitan areas	275 707									
Area actually reporting	99.0%	353	3	93	39	218	8 062	1 342	6 489	231
Estimated total	100.0%	356	3	94	39	220	8 141	1 355	6 553	233
Nonmetropolitan counties	277 317									
Area actually reporting	95.8%	151	6	39	19	87	3 914	1 259	2 428	227
Estimated total	100.0%	158	6	41	20	91	4 086	1 314	2 535	237
Maryland										
State total	5 600 388	39 369	552	1 266	14 378	23 173	198 483	35 922	128 491	34 070
Rate		703.0	9.9	22.6	256.7	413.8	3 544.1	641.4	2 294.3	608.4
Metropolitan statistical areas	5 307 587									
Area actually reporting	100.0%	37 983	544	1 183	14 171	22 085	190 814	34 211	122 973	33 630
Cities outside metropolitan areas	74 501									
Area actually reporting	100.0%	681	3	44	146	488	3 988	744	3 102	142
Nonmetropolitan counties	218 300									
Area actually reporting	100.0%	705	5	39	61	600	3 681	967	2 416	298
Massachusetts										
State total	6 398 743	29 237	175	1 732	7 615	19 715	151 241	34 624	97 737	18 880
Rate		456.9	2.7	27.1	119.0	308.1	2 363.6	541.1	1 527.4	295.1
Metropolitan statistical areas	6 365 624									
Area actually reporting	97.4%	28 676	174	1 691	7 515	19 296	147 421	33 700	95 211	18 510
Estimated total	100.0%	29 142	175	1 724	7 613	19 630	150 695	34 484	97 367	18 844
Cities outside metropolitan areas	32 100									
Area actually reporting	92.0%	87	0	7	2	78	502	129	340	33
Estimated total	100.0%	95	0	8	2	85	546	140	370	36
Nonmetropolitan counties	1 019									
Area actually reporting	100.0%	0	0	0	0	0	0	0	0	0
Michigan										
State total	10 120 860	55 877	616	5 193	13 342	36 726	312 843	70 519	194 101	48 223
Rate		552.1	6.1	51.3	131.8	362.9	3 091.1	696.8	1 917.8	476.5
Metropolitan statistical areas	8 240 515									
Area actually reporting	99.2%	51 662	589	3 970	13 128	33 975	270 813	60 252	164 472	46 089
Estimated total	100.0%	51 860	590	3 995	13 175	34 100	272 836	60 605	165 908	46 323
Cities outside metropolitan areas	645 965									
Area actually reporting	91.5%	1 443	7	379	85	972	17 425	2 590	14 210	625
Estimated total	100.0%	1 544	8	403	91	1 042	18 761	2 781	15 306	674
Nonmetropolitan counties	1 234 380									
Area actually reporting	98.4%	2 434	18	782	75	1 559	20 906	7 019	12 681	1 206
Estimated total	100.0%	2 473	18	795	76	1 584	21 246	7 133	12 887	1 226
Minnesota										
State total	5 132 799	15 243	115	2 258	4 724	8 146	158 301	29 716	114 304	14 281
Rate		297.0	2.2	44.0	92.0	158.7	3 084.1	578.9	2 226.9	278.2
Metropolitan statistical areas	3 716 276									
Area actually reporting	99.3%	13 059	100	1 602	4 581	6 776	125 270	23 028	89 984	12 258
Estimated total	100.0%	13 103	100	1 611	4 592	6 800	126 094	23 145	90 635	12 314
Cities outside metropolitan areas	560 554									
Area actually reporting	99.5%	1 171	3	332	96	740	19 025	2 653	15 544	828
Estimated total	100.0%	1 178	3	334	97	744	19 124	2 667	15 625	832
Nonmetropolitan counties	855 969									
Area actually reporting	100.0%	962	12	313	35	602	13 083	3 904	8 044	1 135

Note: Although arson data are included in the trend and clearance tables, sufficient data are not available to estimate totals for this offense. Thus, arson data are not published in this table.

Table 5. Crime, by State and Territory, 2005—*Continued*

(Number, percent, rate per 100,000 population.)

Area	Population	Violent crime	Murder and nonnegligent manslaughter	Forcible rape	Robbery	Aggravated assault	Property crime	Burglary	Larceny-theft	Motor vehicle theft
Mississippi										
State total	2 921 088	8 131	214	1 147	2 405	4 365	95 231	26 866	60 873	7 492
Rate		278.4	7.3	39.3	82.3	149.4	3 260.1	919.7	2 083.9	256.5
Metropolitan statistical areas	1 266 425									
Area actually reporting	87.6%	3 439	94	517	1 269	1 559	44 147	11 376	28 114	4 657
Estimated total	100.0%	3 730	102	568	1 331	1 729	48 045	12 360	30 631	5 054
Cities outside metropolitan areas	599 896									
Area actually reporting	79.7%	2 028	40	268	635	1 085	24 908	6 203	17 605	1 100
Estimated total	100.0%	2 545	50	336	797	1 362	31 264	7 786	22 097	1 381
Nonmetropolitan counties	1 054 767									
Area actually reporting	46.9%	871	29	114	130	598	7 473	3 154	3 823	496
Estimated total	100.0%	1 856	62	243	277	1 274	15 922	6 720	8 145	1 057
Missouri										
State total	5 800 310	30 477	402	1 625	7 196	21 254	227 809	42 822	159 288	25 699
Rate		525.4	6.9	28.0	124.1	366.4	3 927.5	738.3	2 746.2	443.1
Metropolitan statistical areas	4 233 869									
Area actually reporting	99.9%	25 633	353	1 276	6 853	17 151	187 518	33 420	130 586	23 512
Estimated total	100.0%	25 644	353	1 276	6 856	17 159	187 636	33 437	130 677	23 522
Cities outside metropolitan areas	679 565									
Area actually reporting	98.9%	2 653	22	198	279	2 154	26 926	4 833	20 940	1 153
Estimated total	100.0%	2 682	22	200	282	2 178	27 226	4 887	21 173	1 166
Nonmetropolitan counties	886 876									
Area actually reporting	100.0%	2 151	27	149	58	1 917	12 947	4 498	7 438	1 011
Montana										
State total	935 670	2 634	18	301	177	2 138	29 407	3 642	23 794	1 971
Rate		281.5	1.9	32.2	18.9	228.5	3 142.9	389.2	2 543.0	210.7
Metropolitan statistical areas	326 409									
Area actually reporting	99.8%	845	10	118	119	598	15 020	1 628	12 522	870
Estimated total	100.0%	847	10	118	119	600	15 044	1 631	12 542	871
Cities outside metropolitan areas	195 669									
Area actually reporting	89.4%	651	3	80	32	536	7 004	743	5 814	447
Estimated total	100.0%	727	3	89	36	599	7 833	831	6 502	500
Nonmetropolitan counties	413 592									
Area actually reporting	95.8%	1 016	5	90	21	900	6 258	1 131	4 552	575
Estimated total	100.0%	1 060	5	94	22	939	6 530	1 180	4 750	600
Nebraska										
State total	1 758 787	5 048	44	579	1 040	3 385	60 207	9 363	45 277	5 567
Rate		287.0	2.5	32.9	59.1	192.5	3 423.2	532.4	2 574.3	316.5
Metropolitan statistical areas	995 173									
Area actually reporting	98.0%	4 078	36	374	964	2 704	41 074	6 155	30 199	4 720
Estimated total	100.0%	4 101	36	377	967	2 721	41 367	6 219	30 404	4 744
Cities outside metropolitan areas	395 904									
Area actually reporting	91.7%	621	4	134	59	424	13 541	2 018	11 020	503
Estimated total	100.0%	676	4	146	64	462	14 761	2 200	12 013	548
Nonmetropolitan counties	367 710									
Area actually reporting	89.7%	243	4	50	8	181	3 657	846	2 564	247
Estimated total	100.0%	271	4	56	9	202	4 079	944	2 860	275
Nevada										
State total	2 414 807	14 654	206	1 016	4 702	8 730	102 424	23 481	52 012	26 931
Rate		606.8	8.5	42.1	194.7	361.5	4 241.5	972.4	2 153.9	1 115.2
Metropolitan statistical areas	2 162 821									
Area actually reporting	100.0%	13 934	191	902	4 639	8 202	96 515	21 935	48 161	26 419
Cities outside metropolitan areas	45 470									
Area actually reporting	100.0%	155	5	30	20	100	1 686	348	1 221	117
Nonmetropolitan counties	206 516									
Area actually reporting	100.0%	565	10	84	43	428	4 223	1 198	2 630	395
New Hampshire										
State total	1 309 940	1 729	18	405	359	947	23 532	4 153	18 042	1 337
Rate		132.0	1.4	30.9	27.4	72.3	1 796.4	317.0	1 377.3	102.1
Metropolitan statistical areas	815 819									
Area actually reporting	87.3%	1 016	11	237	264	504	13 485	2 261	10 400	824
Estimated total	100.0%	1 106	12	261	280	553	14 802	2 472	11 434	896
Cities outside metropolitan areas	438 230									
Area actually reporting	85.5%	494	5	107	68	314	7 235	1 316	5 552	367
Estimated total	100.0%	577	6	125	79	367	8 457	1 538	6 490	429
Nonmetropolitan counties	55 891									
Area actually reporting	2.7%	17	0	10	0	7	59	18	37	4
Estimated total	100.0%	46	0	19	0	27	273	143	118	12
New Jersey										
State total	8 717 925	30 919	417	1 208	13 215	16 079	203 391	38 980	136 728	27 683
Rate		354.7	4.8	13.9	151.6	184.4	2 333.0	447.1	1 568.4	317.5
Metropolitan statistical areas	8 717 925									
Area actually reporting	100.0%	30 919	417	1 208	13 215	16 079	203 391	38 980	136 728	27 683
Cities outside metropolitan areas	X									
Nonmetropolitan counties	X									
New Mexico										
State total	1 928 384	13 541	143	1 044	1 904	10 450	79 995	21 095	50 907	7 993
Rate		702.2	7.4	54.1	98.7	541.9	4 148.3	1 093.9	2 639.9	414.5
Metropolitan statistical areas	1 246 636									
Area actually reporting	99.5%	9 595	92	710	1 583	7 210	53 240	13 317	33 682	6 241
Estimated total	100.0%	9 646	92	712	1 587	7 255	53 493	13 379	33 847	6 267
Cities outside metropolitan areas	402 633									
Area actually reporting	89.2%	2 638	22	173	219	2 224	18 474	4 497	13 030	947
Estimated total	100.0%	2 956	25	194	245	2 492	20 704	5 040	14 603	1 061
Nonmetropolitan counties	279 115									
Area actually reporting	73.9%	693	19	102	53	519	4 283	1 977	1 815	491
Estimated total	100.0%	939	26	138	72	703	5 798	2 676	2 457	665

Note: Although arson data are included in the trend and clearance tables, sufficient data are not available to estimate totals for this offense. Thus, arson data are not published in this table.

X = Not applicable.

Table 5. Crime, by State and Territory, 2005—*Continued*

(Number, percent, rate per 100,000 population.)

Area	Population	Violent crime	Murder and nonnegligent manslaughter	Forcible rape	Robbery	Aggravated assault	Property crime	Burglary	Larceny-theft	Motor vehicle theft
New York										
State total	19 254 630	85 839	874	3 636	35 179	46 150	405 990	68 034	302 220	35 736
Rate		445.8	4.5	18.9	182.7	239.7	2 108.5	353.3	1 569.6	185.6
Metropolitan statistical areas	17 687 934	0								
Area actually reporting	99.0%	82 052	839	3 127	34 735	43 351	369 485	60 172	274 688	34 625
Estimated total	100.0%	82 387	841	3 149	34 850	43 547	372 815	60 672	277 326	34 817
Cities outside metropolitan areas	582 615									
Area actually reporting	95.0%	1 518	11	171	239	1 097	16 717	3 067	13 227	423
Estimated total	100.0%	1 599	12	180	252	1 155	17 604	3 230	13 929	445
Nonmetropolitan counties	984 081									
Area actually reporting	95.7%	1 773	20	294	74	1 385	14 895	3 953	10 489	453
Estimated total	100.0%	1 853	21	307	77	1 448	15 571	4 132	10 965	474
North Carolina										
State total	8 683 242	40 650	585	2 302	12 635	25 128	353 855	104 298	221 091	28 466
Rate		468.1	6.7	26.5	145.5	289.4	4 075.1	1 201.1	2 546.2	327.8
Metropolitan statistical areas	5 990 267									
Area actually reporting	98.2%	30 298	385	1 643	10 403	17 867	254 799	72 224	160 599	21 976
Estimated total	100.0%	30 593	388	1 663	10 459	18 083	258 045	73 233	162 631	22 181
Cities outside metropolitan areas	835 748									
Area actually reporting	94.9%	5 237	81	286	1 458	3 412	49 304	12 987	33 820	2 497
Estimated total	100.0%	5 510	85	301	1 533	3 591	51 865	13 655	35 586	2 624
Nonmetropolitan counties	1 857 227									
Area actually reporting	93.9%	4 270	105	317	604	3 244	41 272	16 351	21 483	3 438
Estimated total	100.0%	4 547	112	338	643	3 454	43 945	17 410	22 874	3 661
North Dakota										
State total	636 677	625	7	154	47	417	12 595	1 986	9 552	1 057
Rate		98.2	1.1	24.2	7.4	65.5	1 978.2	311.9	1 500.3	166.0
Metropolitan statistical areas	292 524									
Area actually reporting	99.5%	330	3	78	31	218	7 599	1 156	5 792	651
Estimated total	100.0%	332	3	78	31	220	7 638	1 161	5 824	653
Cities outside metropolitan areas	137 205									
Area actually reporting	87.6%	201	1	60	12	128	3 098	423	2 448	227
Estimated total	100.0%	229	1	68	14	146	3 536	483	2 794	259
Nonmetropolitan counties	206 948									
Area actually reporting	89.1%	57	3	7	2	45	1 266	305	832	129
Estimated total	100.0%	64	3	8	2	51	1 421	342	934	145
Ohio										
State total	11 464 042	40 273	585	4 557	18 696	16 435	419 899	100 063	278 457	41 379
Rate		351.3	5.1	39.8	163.1	143.4	3 662.7	872.8	2 429.0	360.9
Metropolitan statistical areas	9 227 978									
Area actually reporting	89.1%	35 480	517	3 679	17 414	13 870	332 999	80 892	215 369	36 738
Estimated total	100.0%	37 086	529	3 946	17 981	14 630	360 003	86 247	235 290	38 466
Cities outside metropolitan areas	864 829									
Area actually reporting	75.0%	1 464	14	270	418	762	27 990	5 130	21 859	1 001
Estimated total	100.0%	1 951	19	360	557	1 015	37 298	6 836	29 128	1 334
Nonmetropolitan counties	1 371 235									
Area actually reporting	75.6%	934	28	190	119	597	17 075	5 274	10 608	1 193
Estimated total	100.0%	1 236	37	251	158	790	22 598	6 980	14 039	1 579
Oklahoma										
State total	3 547 884	18 044	187	1 481	3 230	13 146	143 406	35 692	93 814	13 900
Rate		508.6	5.3	41.7	91.0	370.5	4 042.0	1 006.0	2 644.2	391.8
Metropolitan statistical areas	2 241 767									
Area actually reporting	100.0%	13 487	146	1 019	2 825	9 497	105 218	24 874	68 966	11 378
Cities outside metropolitan areas	694 861									
Area actually reporting	100.0%	3 066	21	316	359	2 370	29 704	7 571	20 505	1 628
Nonmetropolitan counties	611 256									
Area actually reporting	100.0%	1 491	20	146	46	1 279	8 484	3 247	4 343	894
Oregon										
State total	3 641 056	10 444	80	1 266	2 478	6 620	160 199	27 621	113 316	19 262
Rate		286.8	2.2	34.8	68.1	181.8	4 399.8	758.6	3 112.2	529.0
Metropolitan statistical areas	2 805 013									
Area actually reporting	99.9%	8 843	69	1 034	2 212	5 528	129 294	21 219	91 395	16 680
Estimated total	100.0%	8 850	69	1 035	2 214	5 532	129 424	21 239	91 490	16 695
Cities outside metropolitan areas	382 878									
Area actually reporting	96.3%	863	7	119	196	541	20 031	3 372	15 224	1 435
Estimated total	100.0%	897	7	124	204	562	20 798	3 501	15 807	1 490
Nonmetropolitan counties	453 165									
Area actually reporting	93.7%	653	4	100	56	493	9 347	2 699	5 639	1 009
Estimated total	100.0%	697	4	107	60	526	9 977	2 881	6 019	1 077
Pennsylvania										
State total	12 429 616	52 761	756	3 586	19 214	29 205	300 444	56 134	214 916	29 394
Rate		424.5	6.1	28.9	154.6	235.0	2 417.2	451.6	1 729.1	236.5
Metropolitan statistical areas	10 440 725	0								
Area actually reporting	92.8%	46 753	698	2 868	18 221	24 966	249 000	45 285	177 476	26 239
Estimated total	100.0%	48 602	715	2 992	18 709	26 186	265 028	47 659	190 064	27 305
Cities outside metropolitan areas	880 169									
Area actually reporting	79.4%	2 016	18	206	280	1 512	15 723	2 806	12 217	700
Estimated total	100.0%	2 541	23	260	353	1 905	19 810	3 535	15 393	882
Nonmetropolitan counties	1 108 722									
Area actually reporting	100.0%	1 618	18	334	152	1 114	15 606	4 940	9 459	1 207
Puerto Rico										
Teritotry total	3 912 054	9 579	766	169	5 550	3 094	55 466	17 191	28 976	9 299
Rate		244.9	19.6	4.3	141.9	79.1	1 417.8	439.4	740.7	237.7
Metropolitan statistical areas	3 715 706									
Area actually reporting	100.0%	9 202	745	160	5 379	2 918	53 369	16 213	28 076	9 080
Cities outside metropolitan areas	196 348									
Area actually reporting	100.0%	377	21	9	171	176	2 097	978	900	219
Nonmetropolitan counties	X									

Note: Although arson data are included in the trend and clearance tables, sufficient data are not available to estimate totals for this offense. Thus, arson data are not published in this table.

X = Not applicable.

Table 5. Crime, by State and Territory, 2005—*Continued*

(Number, percent, rate per 100,000 population.)

Area	Population	Violent crime	Murder and nonnegligent manslaughter	Forcible rape	Robbery	Aggravated assault	Property crime	Burglary	Larceny-theft	Motor vehicle theft
Rhode Island										
State total	1 076 189	2 703	34	321	776	1 572	29 260	5 318	19 544	4 398
Rate		251.2	3.2	29.8	72.1	146.1	2 718.9	494.2	1 816.0	408.7
Metropolitan statistical areas	1 076 189									
Area actually reporting	100.0%	2 685	32	316	774	1 563	29 187	5 316	19 516	4 355
Cities outside metropolitan areas	X									
Nonmetropolitan counties	X									
Area actually reporting	100.0%	18	2	5	2	9	73	2	28	43
South Carolina										
State total	4 255 083	32 384	315	1 809	5 622	24 638	184 646	42 589	125 699	16 358
Rate		761.1	7.4	42.5	132.1	579.0	4 339.4	1 000.9	2 954.1	384.4
Metropolitan statistical areas	3 205 817									
Area actually reporting	99.9%	24 723	240	1 368	4 627	18 488	142 152	31 893	97 158	13 101
Estimated total	100.0%	24 725	240	1 368	4 627	18 490	142 168	31 896	97 170	13 102
Cities outside metropolitan areas	273 133									
Area actually reporting	99.7%	3 152	17	136	483	2 516	17 177	3 595	12 760	822
Estimated total	100.0%	3 160	17	136	484	2 523	17 221	3 604	12 793	824
Nonmetropolitan counties	776 133									
Area actually reporting	100.0%	4 499	58	305	511	3 625	25 257	7 089	15 736	2 432
South Dakota										
State total	775 933	1 363	18	362	144	839	13 784	2 517	10 426	841
Rate		175.7	2.3	46.7	18.6	108.1	1 776.4	324.4	1 343.7	108.4
Metropolitan statistical areas	336 356									
Area actually reporting	96.6%	909	9	267	115	518	8 311	1 521	6 256	534
Estimated total	100.0%	920	9	268	116	527	8 459	1 552	6 361	546
Cities outside metropolitan areas	210 074									
Area actually reporting	81.5%	263	1	65	19	178	3 552	562	2 815	175
Estimated total	100.0%	322	1	80	23	218	4 357	689	3 453	215
Nonmetropolitan counties	229 503									
Area actually reporting	77.4%	94	6	11	4	73	750	214	474	62
Estimated total	100.0%	121	8	14	5	94	968	276	612	80
Tennessee										
State total	5 962 959	44 891	432	2 171	9 974	32 314	254 948	61 233	168 637	25 078
Rate		752.8	7.2	36.4	167.3	541.9	4 275.5	1 026.9	2 828.1	420.6
Metropolitan statistical areas	4 332 089									
Area actually reporting	100.0%	37 540	367	1 786	9 335	26 052	202 571	47 018	134 771	20 782
Cities outside metropolitan areas	591 225									
Area actually reporting	100.0%	3 989	21	218	498	3 252	31 016	6 692	22 348	1 076
Nonmetropolitan counties	1 039 645									
Area actually reporting	100.0%	3 362	44	167	141	3 010	21 361	7 523	11 518	2 320
Texas										
State total	22 859 968	121 091	1 407	8 511	35 790	75 383	990 293	219 828	677 042	93 423
Rate		529.7	6.2	37.2	156.6	329.8	4 332.0	961.6	2 961.7	408.7
Metropolitan statistical areas	19 838 854									
Area actually reporting	99.9%	111 852	1 280	7 617	34 886	68 069	910 695	197 615	623 991	89 089
Estimated total	100.0%	111 867	1 280	7 618	34 889	68 080	910 919	197 658	624 156	89 105
Cities outside metropolitan areas	1 392 423									
Area actually reporting	98.9%	5 481	50	605	718	4 108	53 885	12 451	39 017	2 417
Estimated total	100.0%	5 526	51	611	723	4 141	54 396	12 570	39 393	2 433
Nonmetropolitan counties	1 628 691									
Area actually reporting	100.0%	3 698	76	282	178	3 162	24 978	9 600	13 493	1 885
Utah										
State total	2 469 585	5 612	56	920	1 095	3 541	95 546	14 971	72 082	8 493
Rate		227.2	2.3	37.3	44.3	143.4	3 868.9	606.2	2 918.8	343.9
Metropolitan statistical areas	2 187 374									
Area actually reporting	99.7%	5 175	53	839	1 067	3 216	88 688	13 597	66 993	8 098
Estimated total	100.0%	5 186	53	841	1 069	3 223	88 912	13 635	67 159	8 118
Cities outside metropolitan areas	132 036									
Area actually reporting	88.9%	192	1	39	19	133	3 698	629	2 904	165
Estimated total	100.0%	216	1	44	21	150	4 158	707	3 265	186
Nonmetropolitan counties	150 175									
Area actually reporting	94.3%	198	2	33	5	158	2 334	593	1 563	178
Estimated total	100.0%	210	2	35	5	168	2 476	629	1 658	189
Vermont										
State total	623 050	746	8	145	73	520	14 210	3 064	10 505	641
Rate		119.7	1.3	23.3	11.7	83.5	2 280.7	491.8	1 686.1	102.9
Metropolitan statistical areas	205 030									
Area actually reporting	100.0%	362	5	71	38	248	6 658	1 460	4 956	242
Cities outside metropolitan areas	199 547									
Area actually reporting	93.6%	222	1	33	27	161	4 498	620	3 690	188
Estimated total	100.0%	237	1	35	29	172	4 808	663	3 944	201
Nonmetropolitan counties	218 473									
Area actually reporting	96.9%	143	2	38	6	97	2 660	912	1 556	192
Estimated total	100.0%	147	2	39	6	100	2 744	941	1 605	198
Virginia										
State total	7 567 465	21 400	461	1 721	7 507	11 711	199 644	29 672	154 000	15 972
Rate		282.8	6.1	22.7	99.2	154.8	2 638.2	392.1	2 035.0	211.1
Metropolitan statistical areas	6 460 729									
Area actually reporting	99.4%	19 234	394	1 475	7 130	10 235	177 912	25 498	137 840	14 574
Estimated total	100.0%	19 413	396	1 490	7 183	10 344	179 512	25 740	139 085	14 687
Cities outside metropolitan areas	269 213									
Area actually reporting	99.0%	779	16	75	172	516	8 431	1 152	6 905	374
Estimated total	100.0%	787	16	76	174	521	8 513	1 163	6 972	378
Nonmetropolitan counties	837 523									
Area actually reporting	99.1%	1 190	49	154	149	838	11 514	2 744	7 871	899
Estimated total	100.0%	1 200	49	155	150	846	11 619	2 769	7 943	907

Note: Although arson data are included in the trend and clearance tables, sufficient data are not available to estimate totals for this offense. Thus, arson data are not published in this table.

X = Not applicable.

Table 5. Crime, by State and Territory, 2005—*Continued*

(Number, percent, rate per 100,000 population.)

Area	Population	Violent crime	Murder and nonnegligent manslaughter	Forcible rape	Robbery	Aggravated assault	Property crime	Burglary	Larceny-theft	Motor vehicle theft
Washington										
State total	6 287 759	21 745	205	2 811	5 788	12 941	307 661	60 343	198 031	49 287
Rate		345.8	3.3	44.7	92.1	205.8	4 893.0	959.7	3 149.5	783.9
Metropolitan statistical areas	5 498 893									
Area actually reporting	99.9%	19 916	180	2 321	5 565	11 850	274 338	52 053	175 593	46 692
Estimated total	100.0%	19 937	180	2 324	5 571	11 862	274 742	52 119	175 865	46 758
Cities outside metropolitan areas	329 882									
Area actually reporting	95.3%	995	4	277	137	577	18 630	3 431	13 920	1 279
Estimated total	100.0%	1 045	4	291	144	606	19 559	3 602	14 614	1 343
Nonmetropolitan counties	458 984									
Area actually reporting	100.0%	763	21	196	73	473	13 360	4 622	7 552	1 186
West Virginia										
State total	1 816 856	4 957	80	321	811	3 745	47 696	11 286	32 594	3 816
Rate		272.8	4.4	17.7	44.6	206.1	2 625.2	621.2	1 794.0	210.0
Metropolitan statistical areas	997 999									
Area actually reporting	94.5%	2 959	49	192	596	2 122	29 784	7 026	20 362	2 396
Estimated total	100.0%	3 075	50	197	609	2 219	31 238	7 340	21 386	2 512
Cities outside metropolitan areas	225 283									
Area actually reporting	83.4%	600	8	40	98	454	5 926	1 167	4 438	321
Estimated total	100.0%	719	10	48	117	544	7 104	1 399	5 320	385
Nonmetropolitan counties	593 574									
Area actually reporting	95.8%	1 114	19	73	81	941	8 964	2 441	5 642	881
Estimated total	100.0%	1 163	20	76	85	982	9 354	2 547	5 888	919
Wisconsin										
State total	5 536 201	13 371	194	1 142	4 550	7 485	147 275	24 406	110 323	12 546
Rate		241.5	3.5	20.6	82.2	135.2	2 660.2	440.8	1 992.8	226.6
Metropolitan statistical areas	4 002 856									
Area actually reporting	98.6%	11 396	174	864	4 435	5 923	116 440	18 570	86 831	11 039
Estimated total	100.0%	11 466	174	874	4 457	5 961	117 947	18 775	88 065	11 107
Cities outside metropolitan areas	619 782									
Area actually reporting	96.5%	1 045	11	146	69	819	18 263	2 330	15 249	684
Estimated total	100.0%	1 083	11	151	72	849	18 935	2 416	15 810	709
Nonmetropolitan counties	913 563									
Area actually reporting	100.0%	822	9	117	21	675	10 393	3 215	6 448	730
Wyoming										
State total	509 294	1 172	14	122	78	958	16 070	2 426	12 905	739
Rate		230.1	2.7	24.0	15.3	188.1	3 155.3	476.3	2 533.9	145.1
Metropolitan statistical areas	155 151									
Area actually reporting	100.0%	316	7	34	38	237	6 450	1 064	5 121	265
Cities outside metropolitan areas	210 170									
Area actually reporting	97.4%	555	5	61	32	457	7 280	965	5 997	318
Estimated total	100.0%	570	5	63	33	469	7 476	991	6 158	327
Nonmetropolitan counties	143 973									
Area actually reporting	100.0%	286	2	25	7	252	2 144	371	1 626	147

Note: Although arson data are included in the trend and clearance tables, sufficient data are not available to estimate totals for this offense. Thus, arson data are not published in this table.

Table 6. Crime, by Metropolitan Statistical Area, 2005

(Number, percent, rate per 100,000 inhabitants.)

Metropolitan statistical area	Population	Violent crime	Murder and non-negligent man-slaughter	Forcible rape	Robbery	Aggravated assault	Property crime	Burglary	Larceny-theft	Motor vehicle theft
Abilene, TX MSA										
Callahan, Jones, and Taylor Counties	161 123									
City of Abilene	116 695	576	5	78	146	347	5 504	1 521	3 685	298
Actually reporting	100.0%	640	7	82	156	395	6 196	1 769	4 076	351
Rate		397.2	4.3	50.9	96.8	245.2	3 845.5	1 097.9	2 529.7	217.8
Akron, OH MSA										
Portage and Summit Counties	702 386									
City of Akron	212 272	1 265	27	183	625	430	12 040	3 409	7 253	1 378
Actually reporting	1.0%	1 827	38	325	803	661	25 011	5 873	17 053	2 085
Estimated total	100.0%	1 871	38	332	819	682	25 722	6 002	17 589	2 131
Rate		266.4	5.4	47.3	116.6	97.1	3 662.1	854.5	2 504.2	303.4
Albany, GA MSA										
Baker, Dougherty, Lee, Terrell, and Worth Counties	167 284									
City of Albany	78 353	516	8	40	216	252	4 991	1 704	2 958	329
Actually reporting	1.0%	622	8	51	231	332	6 735	2 177	4 148	410
Estimated total	100.0%	627	8	51	233	335	6 787	2 186	4 186	415
Rate		374.8	4.8	30.5	139.3	200.3	4 057.2	1 306.8	2 502.3	248.1
Albany-Schenectady-Troy, NY MSA										
Albany, Rensselaer, Saratoga, Schenectady, and Schoharie Counties	846 480									
City of Albany	94 361	1 275	8	68	439	760	4 883	1 328	3 186	369
City of Schenectady	61 213	609	8	41	252	308	3 049	795	1 975	279
City of Troy	48 231	309	4	18	78	209	2 053	517	1 333	203
Actually reporting	100.0%	3 096	25	225	906	1 940	22 534	4 511	16 693	1 330
Rate		365.7	3.0	26.6	107.0	229.2	2 662.1	532.9	1 972.0	157.1
Albuquerque, NM MSA										
Bernalillo, Sandoval, Torrance, and Valencia Counties	791 750									
City of Albuquerque	490 631	4 670	53	285	1 150	3 182	30 243	5 744	20 703	3 796
Actually reporting	1.0%	6 630	74	377	1 336	4 843	38 850	8 678	25 055	5 117
Estimated total	100.0%	6 642	74	377	1 337	4 854	38 910	8 693	25 094	5 123
Rate		838.9	9.3	47.6	168.9	613.1	4 914.4	1 097.9	3 169.4	647.0
Alexandria, LA MSA										
Grant and Rapides Parishes	147 408									
City of Alexandria	46 051	1 022	9	21	147	845	3 787	948	2 629	210
Actually reporting	0.9%	1 398	10	51	160	1 177	6 596	1 792	4 332	472
Estimated total	100.0%	1 449	11	53	169	1 216	7 056	1 873	4 680	503
Rate		983.0	7.5	36.0	114.6	824.9	4 786.7	1 270.6	3 174.9	341.2
Allentown-Bethlehem-Easton, PA-NJ MSA										
Warren County, NJ; and Carbon, Lehigh, and Northampton Counties, PA	781 316									
City of Allentown, PA	106 933	863	21	45	512	285	5 771	1 393	3 905	473
City of Bethlehem, PA	72 577	268	2	17	114	135	2 301	409	1 700	192
Actually reporting	0.9%	2 200	31	139	810	1 220	18 764	3 279	14 264	1 221
Estimated total	100.0%	2 335	32	148	846	1 309	19 938	3 453	15 186	1 299
Rate		298.9	4.1	18.9	108.3	167.5	2 551.8	441.9	1 943.6	166.3
Altoona, PA MSA										
Blair County	127 708									
City of Altoona	47 922	186	5	26	69	86	1 653	463	1 117	73
Actually reporting	0.9%	310	7	39	88	176	2 860	727	2 000	133
Estimated total	100.0%	339	7	41	96	195	3 111	764	2 197	150
Rate		265.4	5.5	32.1	75.2	152.7	2 436.0	598.2	1 720.3	117.5
Amarillo, TX MSA										
Armstrong, Carson, Potter, and Randall Counties	239 998									
City of Amarillo	183 765	1 537	10	88	347	1 092	11 850	2 549	8 245	1 056
Actually reporting	100.0%	1 623	11	96	352	1 164	12 839	2 811	8 894	1 134
Rate		676.3	4.6	40.0	146.7	485.0	5 349.6	1 171.3	3 705.9	472.5
Ames, IA MSA										
Story County	80 727									
City of Ames	52 529	98	0	14	14	70	1 537	465	1 028	44
Actually reporting	100.0%	151	0	30	18	103	2 220	634	1 520	66
Rate		187.1	0.0	37.2	22.3	127.6	2 750.0	785.4	1 882.9	81.8
Anchorage, AK MSA										
Anchorage Municipality and Matanuska-Susitna Borough	291 624									
City of Anchorage	276 109	2 031	16	224	384	1 407	11 365	1 783	8 248	1 334
Actually reporting	100.0%	2 198	16	228	397	1 557	12 470	1 882	9 165	1 423
Rate		753.7	5.5	78.2	136.1	533.9	4 276.1	645.4	3 142.7	488.0
Anderson, IN MSA										
Madison County	131 322									
City of Anderson	58 262	150	2	19	63	66	2 688	611	1 886	191
Actually reporting	100.0%	200	3	22	76	99	4 189	851	3 106	232
Rate		152.3	2.3	16.8	57.9	75.4	3 189.9	648.0	2 365.2	176.7
Anderson, SC MSA										
Anderson County	175 907									
City of Anderson	26 064	166	2	10	32	122	1 614	334	1 145	135
Actually reporting	100.0%	1 093	16	68	160	849	8 785	2 083	5 889	813
Rate		621.4	9.1	38.7	91.0	482.6	4 994.1	1 184.1	3 347.8	462.2

Note: Although arson data are included in the trend and clearance tables, sufficient data are not available to estimate totals for this offense.

Table 6. Crime, by Metropolitan Statistical Area, 2005—*Continued*

(Number, percent, rate per 100,000 inhabitants.)

Metropolitan statistical area	Population	Violent crime	Murder and non-negligent man-slaughter	Forcible rape	Robbery	Aggravated assault	Property crime	Burglary	Larceny-theft	Motor vehicle theft
Ann Arbor, MI MSA										
Washtenaw County	339 467									
City of Ann Arbor	113 660	358	0	37	102	219	3 379	859	2 282	238
Actually reporting	100.0%	1 169	8	145	273	743	10 160	2 311	6 913	936
Rate		344.4	2.4	42.7	80.4	218.9	2 992.9	680.8	2 036.4	275.7
Appleton, WI MSA										
Calumet and Outagamie Counties	214 153									
City of Appleton	70 640	173	0	27	16	130	2 083	403	1 635	45
Actually reporting	100.0%	239	2	38	21	178	4 588	694	3 750	144
Rate		111.6	0.9	17.7	9.8	83.1	2 142.4	324.1	1 751.1	67.2
Asheville, NC MSA										
Buncombe, Haywood, Henderson, and Madison Counties	393 687									
City of Asheville	71 571	434	2	16	229	187	5 266	991	3 642	633
Actually reporting	1.0%	1 006	14	80	320	592	12 798	3 371	8 162	1 265
Estimated total	100.0%	1 012	14	80	322	596	12 867	3 387	8 211	1 269
Rate		257.1	3.6	20.3	81.8	151.4	3 268.3	860.3	2 085.7	322.3
Athens-Clarke County, GA MSA										
Clarke, Madison, Oconee, and Oglethorpe Counties	178 545									
City of Athens-Clarke County	105 727	357	5	41	135	176	5 593	1 047	4 185	361
Actually reporting	1.0%	497	5	46	152	294	7 420	1 322	5 610	488
Estimated total	100.0%	500	5	46	153	296	7 449	1 327	5 631	491
Rate		280.0	2.8	25.8	85.7	165.8	4 172.1	743.2	3 153.8	275.0
Atlanta-Sandy Springs-Marietta, GA MSA										
Barrow, Bartow, Butts, Carroll, Cherokee, Clayton, Cobb, Coweta, Dawson, DeKalb, Douglas, Fayette, Forsyth, Fulton, Gwinnett, Haralson, Heard, Henry, Jasper, Lamar, Meriwether, Newton, Paulding, Pickens, Pike, Rockdale, Spalding, and Walton Counties	4 837 981									
City of Atlanta	430 666	7 213	90	223	2 861	4 039	31 397	6 648	18 993	5 756
City of Marietta	62 215	331	6	11	194	120	2 371	426	1 548	397
Actually reporting	1.0%	23 445	331	1 056	9 348	12 710	195 237	44 603	121 644	28 990
Estimated total	100.0%	23 803	334	1 073	9 476	12 920	199 092	45 325	124 367	29 400
Rate		492.0	6.9	22.2	195.9	267.1	4 115.2	936.9	2 570.6	607.7
Atlantic City, NJ MSA										
Atlantic County	269 281									
City of Atlantic City	40 669	753	9	44	374	326	4 514	522	3 838	154
Actually reporting	100.0%	1 390	16	84	562	728	10 756	1 821	8 472	463
Rate		516.2	5.9	31.2	208.7	270.3	3 994.3	676.2	3 146.2	171.9
Auburn-Opelika, AL MSA										
Lee County	121 450									
City of Auburn	48 643	154	1	18	52	83	2 172	464	1 639	69
City of Opelika	23 626	272	5	17	41	209	1 727	319	1 347	61
Actually reporting	100.0%	484	6	43	115	320	5 254	1 199	3 811	244
Rate		398.5	4.9	35.4	94.7	263.5	4 326.1	987.2	3 137.9	200.9
Augusta-Richmond County, GA-SC MSA										
Burke, Columbia, McDuffie, and Richmond Counties, GA; and Aiken and Edgefield Counties, SC	527 083									
Actually reporting	1.0%	2 050	27	250	793	980	23 620	4 737	16 261	2 622
Estimated total	100.0%	2 068	27	251	799	991	23 816	4 770	16 405	2 641
Rate		392.3	5.1	47.6	151.6	188.0	4 518.5	905.0	3 112.4	501.1
Austin-Round Rock, TX MSA										
Bastrop, Caldwell, Hays, Travis, and Williamson Counties	1 435 502									
City of Austin	693 019	3 393	26	312	1 182	1 873	41 668	7 285	31 835	2 548
City of Round Rock	83 390	121	0	21	24	76	2 205	281	1 873	51
Actually reporting	100.0%	4 970	42	503	1 387	3 038	59 347	11 246	44 647	3 454
Rate		346.2	2.9	35.0	96.6	211.6	4 134.2	783.4	3 110.2	240.6
Bakersfield, CA MSA										
Kern County	739 726									
City of Bakersfield	285 821	1 706	32	45	530	1 099	16 438	3 746	10 034	2 658
Actually reporting	100.0%	3 899	69	205	952	2 673	33 979	8 472	19 612	5 895
Rate		527.1	9.3	27.7	128.7	361.4	4 593.5	1 145.3	2 651.3	796.9
Baltimore-Towson, MD MSA										
Anne Arundel, Baltimore, Carroll, Harford, Howard, and Queen Anne's Counties and Baltimore City	2 659 312									
City of Baltimore	641 097	11 248	269	162	3 910	6 907	33 241	7 338	19 691	6 212
Actually reporting	100.0%	22 262	338	545	7 077	14 302	92 213	18 067	62 167	11 979
Rate		837.1	12.7	20.5	266.1	537.8	3 467.6	679.4	2 337.7	450.5
Bangor, ME MSA										
Penobscot County	148 674									
City of Bangor	31 697	65	0	6	26	33	1 568	219	1 304	45
Actually reporting	100.0%	123	0	15	33	75	4 244	780	3 326	138
Rate		82.7	0.0	10.1	22.2	50.4	2 854.6	524.6	2 237.1	92.8
Barnstable Town, MA MSA										
Barnstable County	228 050									
City of Barnstable	48 403	346	2	34	25	285	1 238	429	724	85
Actually reporting	1.0%	911	3	73	67	768	5 234	1 830	3 102	302
Estimated total	100.0%	926	3	74	70	779	5 343	1 856	3 174	313
Rate		406.1	1.3	32.4	30.7	341.6	2 342.9	813.9	1 391.8	137.3

Note: Although arson data are included in the trend and clearance tables, sufficient data are not available to estimate totals for this offense.

Table 6. Crime, by Metropolitan Statistical Area, 2005—*Continued*

(Number, percent, rate per 100,000 inhabitants.)

Metropolitan statistical area	Population	Violent crime	Murder and non-negligent man-slaughter	Forcible rape	Robbery	Aggravated assault	Property crime	Burglary	Larceny-theft	Motor vehicle theft
Baton Rouge, LA MSA										
Ascension, East Baton Rouge, East Feliciana, Iberville, Livingston, Pointe Coupee, St. Helena, West Baton Rouge, and West Feliciana Parishes	729 999									
City of Baton Rouge	224 487	2 698	49	83	993	1 573	14 378	3 940	8 949	1 489
Actually reporting	1.0%	5 119	85	215	1 386	3 433	33 382	7 383	23 288	2 711
Estimated total	100.0%	5 250	87	222	1 409	3 532	34 480	7 597	24 089	2 794
Rate		719.2	11.9	30.4	193.0	483.8	4 723.3	1 040.7	3 299.9	382.7
Battle Creek, MI MSA										
Calhoun County	139 180									
City of Battle Creek	63 054	755	6	61	109	579	3 472	691	2 594	187
Actually reporting	100.0%	1 068	7	105	143	813	5 705	1 146	4 253	306
Rate		767.4	5.0	75.4	102.7	584.1	4 099.0	823.4	3 055.8	219.9
Bay City, MI MSA										
Bay County	109 569									
City of Bay City	35 346	168	0	30	31	107	1 155	292	789	74
Actually reporting	100.0%	307	1	75	50	181	2 942	654	2 098	190
Rate		280.2	0.9	68.5	45.6	165.2	2 685.1	596.9	1 914.8	173.4
Beaumont-Port Arthur, TX MSA										
Hardin, Jefferson, and Orange Counties	389 750									
City of Beaumont	114 141	1 130	11	97	337	685	8 320	2 057	5 735	528
City of Port Arthur	57 660	370	11	26	118	215	2 809	938	1 632	239
Actually reporting	100.0%	2 132	30	176	561	1 365	17 531	4 848	11 400	1 283
Rate		547.0	7.7	45.2	143.9	350.2	4 498.0	1 243.9	2 925.0	329.2
Bellingham, WA MSA										
Whatcom County	182 606									
City of Bellingham	73 980	174	3	28	53	90	5 573	709	4 555	309
Actually reporting	100.0%	419	5	72	82	260	9 524	1 754	7 174	596
Rate		229.5	2.7	39.4	44.9	142.4	5 215.6	960.5	3 928.7	326.4
Bend, OR MSA										
Deschutes County	136 218									
City of Bend	63 751	133	2	21	19	91	3 159	509	2 401	249
Actually reporting	100.0%	291	4	53	34	200	5 973	1 111	4 387	475
Rate		213.6	2.9	38.9	25.0	146.8	4 384.9	815.6	3 220.6	348.7
Billings, MT MSA[1]										
Carbon and Yellowstone Counties	145 842									
City of Billings	97 898	201	5	34	50	112	5 520	598	4 563	359
Actually reporting	1.0%	317	5	43	54	215	6 690	797	5 467	426
Estimated total	100.0%	319	5	43	54	217	6 714	800	5 487	427
Rate		218.7	3.4	29.5	37.0	148.8	4 603.6	548.5	3 762.3	292.8
Binghamton, NY MSA										
Broome and Tioga Counties	249 588									
City of Binghamton	45 930	177	3	19	61	94	1 902	236	1 646	20
Actually reporting	100.0%	432	8	56	98	270	6 240	869	5 244	127
Rate		173.1	3.2	22.4	39.3	108.2	2 500.1	348.2	2 101.1	50.9
Bismarck, ND MSA										
Burleigh and Morton Counties	98 280									
City of Bismarck	56 825	51	0	8	8	35	1 488	197	1 164	127
Actually reporting	100.0%	108	0	19	11	78	2 165	275	1 697	193
Rate		109.9	0.0	19.3	11.2	79.4	2 202.9	279.8	1 726.7	196.4
Blacksburg-Christiansburg-Radford, VA MSA										
Giles, Montgomery, and Pulaski Counties and Radford City	153 046									
City of Blacksburg	39 778	55	0	8	13	34	562	105	435	22
City of Christiansburg	17 747	28	0	5	5	18	638	76	518	44
City of Radford	14 983	50	0	10	8	32	517	129	357	31
Actually reporting	100.0%	299	2	50	53	194	4 095	745	3 160	190
Rate		195.4	1.3	32.7	34.6	126.8	2 675.7	486.8	2 064.7	124.1
Bloomington, IN MSA										
Greene, Monroe, and Owen Counties	178 566									
City of Bloomington	69 158	171	0	25	54	92	2 683	566	1 969	148
Actually reporting	0.8%	278	3	52	63	160	4 154	903	3 005	246
Estimated total	100.0%	331	3	57	74	197	4 810	1 032	3 476	302
Rate		185.4	1.7	31.9	41.4	110.3	2 693.7	577.9	1 946.6	169.1

Note: Although arson data are included in the trend and clearance tables, sufficient data are not available to estimate totals for this offense.

[1]Because of changes in the state/local agency's reporting practices, figures are not comparable to previous years' data.

Table 6. Crime, by Metropolitan Statistical Area, 2005—*Continued*

(Number, percent, rate per 100,000 inhabitants.)

Metropolitan statistical area	Population	Violent crime	Murder and non-negligent man-slaughter	Forcible rape	Robbery	Aggravated assault	Property crime	Burglary	Larceny-theft	Motor vehicle theft
Boston-Cambridge-Quincy, MA-NH MSA										
Metropolitan divisions of Boston-Quincy, MA; Cambridge-Newton-Framingham, MA; and Essex County, MA; and Rockingham County-Strafford County, NH	4 416 837									
City of Boston, MA	567 589	7 479	73	268	2 649	4 489	25 205	4 531	15 957	4 717
City of Cambridge, MA	100 492	494	3	18	239	234	3 309	623	2 396	290
City of Quincy, MA	89 661	339	2	26	92	219	1 422	387	883	152
City of Newton, MA	83 570	114	1	6	15	92	1 098	269	783	46
City of Framingham, MA	65 416	184	0	12	48	124	1 556	312	1 025	219
City of Waltham, MA	59 068	77	0	7	15	55	661	85	498	78
Actually reporting	1.0%	17 189	117	938	5 174	10 960	95 152	19 855	63 075	12 222
Estimated total	100.0%	17 587	119	980	5 256	11 232	98 492	20 570	65 409	12 513
Rate		398.2	2.7	22.2	119.0	254.3	2 229.9	465.7	1 480.9	283.3
Boston-Quincy, MA M.D.										
Norfolk, Plymouth, and Suffolk Counties	1 805 283									
Actually reporting	1.0%	10 463	91	503	3 446	6 423	46 916	9 007	30 737	7 172
Estimated total	100.0%	10 700	92	520	3 496	6 592	48 572	9 403	31 828	7 341
Rate		592.7	5.1	28.8	193.7	365.2	2 690.5	520.9	1 763.0	406.6
Cambridge-Newton-Framingham, MA M.D.										
Middlesex County	1 460 573									
Actually reporting	1.0%	3 456	13	206	1 002	2 235	27 476	6 045	18 583	2 848
Estimated total	100.0%	3 503	13	209	1 012	2 269	27 810	6 125	18 803	2 882
Rate		239.8	0.9	14.3	69.3	155.3	1 904.0	419.4	1 287.4	197.3
Essex County, MA M.D.										
Essex County	736 938									
Actually reporting	1.0%	2 854	9	109	659	2 077	15 195	3 919	9 388	1 888
Estimated total	100.0%	2 896	9	112	668	2 107	15 488	3 989	9 581	1 918
Rate		393.0	1.2	15.2	90.6	285.9	2 101.7	541.3	1 300.1	260.3
Rockingham County-Strafford County, NH M.D.										
Rockingham and Strafford Counties	414 043									
Actually reporting	0.8%	416	4	120	67	225	5 565	884	4 367	314
Estimated total	100.0%	488	5	139	80	264	6 622	1 053	5 197	372
Rate		117.9	1.2	33.6	19.3	63.8	1 599.4	254.3	1 255.2	89.8
Bowling Green, KY MSA										
Edmonson and Warren Counties	109 812									
City of Bowling Green	51 634	328	3	47	88	190	3 020	584	2 282	154
Actually reporting	100.0%	345	3	47	90	205	3 771	755	2 817	199
Rate		314.2	2.7	42.8	82.0	186.7	3 434.1	687.5	2 565.3	181.2
Bremerton-Silverdale, WA MSA										
Kitsap County	242 375									
City of Bremerton	36 454	402	2	80	73	247	1 890	425	1 267	198
Actually reporting	100.0%	1 019	7	211	119	682	6 977	1 819	4 572	586
Rate		420.4	2.9	87.1	49.1	281.4	2 878.6	750.5	1 886.3	241.8
Bridgeport-Stamford-Norwalk, CT MSA[1]										
Fairfield County	886 621									
City of Bridgeport	140 177	1 508	19	65	648	776	7 118	1 383	4 452	1 283
City of Stamford[1]	120 456	355	1	18	157	179	2 390	427	1 740	223
City of Norwalk	84 562	308	7	9	92	200	2 578	365	1 889	324
City of Danbury	78 413	128	1	22	58	47	1 579	223	1 220	136
City of Stratford	50 352	116	1	12	49	54	1 497	212	1 067	218
Actually reporting	100.0%	2 540	31	139	1 034	1 336	19 910	3 397	13 977	2 536
Rate		286.5	3.5	15.7	116.6	150.7	2 245.6	383.1	1 576.4	286.0
Brownsville-Harlingen, TX MSA										
Cameron County	377 941									
City of Brownsville	163 877	903	4	53	128	718	8 313	1 236	6 647	430
City of Harlingen	62 602	330	0	24	63	243	4 959	1 128	3 598	233
Actually reporting	100.0%	1 813	13	143	261	1 396	18 996	3 741	14 297	958
Rate		479.7	3.4	37.8	69.1	369.4	5 026.2	989.8	3 782.9	253.5
Brunswick, GA MSA										
Brantley, Glynn, and McIntosh Counties	100 737									
City of Brunswick	16 418	388	0	15	64	309	1 331	331	935	65
Actually reporting	1.0%	703	3	36	119	545	4 490	1 042	3 192	256
Estimated total	100.0%	708	3	36	121	548	4 549	1 052	3 235	262
Rate		702.8	3.0	35.7	120.1	544.0	4 515.7	1 044.3	3 211.3	260.1
Buffalo-Niagara Falls, NY MSA										
Erie and Niagara Counties	1 156 031									
City of Buffalo	283 269	3 938	56	184	1 667	2 031	16 730	4 240	10 089	2 401
City of Cheektowaga Town	81 793	239	0	11	91	137	2 517	406	1 929	182
City of Tonawanda	15 537	40	0	3	6	31	368	56	295	17
City of Niagara Falls	53 785	685	4	24	242	415	2 687	703	1 728	256
Actually reporting	100.0%	5 962	66	340	2 273	3 283	34 832	7 554	23 926	3 352
Rate		515.7	5.7	29.4	196.6	284.0	3 013.1	653.4	2 069.7	290.0
Burlington, NC MSA										
Alamance County	140 764									
City of Burlington	47 421	420	4	13	91	312	3 207	719	2 352	136
Actually reporting	1.0%	702	8	29	127	538	5 521	1 443	3 805	273
Estimated total	100.0%	711	8	30	129	544	5 623	1 467	3 878	278
Rate		505.1	5.7	21.3	91.6	386.5	3 994.6	1 042.2	2 755.0	197.5

Note: Although arson data are included in the trend and clearance tables, sufficient data are not available to estimate totals for this offense.

[1]Because of changes in the state/local agency's reporting practices, figures are not comparable to previous years' data.

Table 6. Crime, by Metropolitan Statistical Area, 2005—*Continued*

(Number, percent, rate per 100,000 inhabitants.)

Metropolitan statistical area	Population	Violent crime	Murder and non-negligent man-slaughter	Forcible rape	Robbery	Aggravated assault	Property crime	Burglary	Larceny-theft	Motor vehicle theft
Cape Coral-Fort Myers, FL MSA										
Lee County	525 904									
City of Cape Coral	130 874	361	5	45	74	237	3 900	1 026	2 567	307
City of Fort Myers	54 095	964	13	32	309	610	3 059	592	1 848	619
Actually reporting	100.0%	2 986	33	187	823	1 943	18 579	4 875	11 341	2 363
Rate		567.8	6.3	35.6	156.5	369.5	3 532.8	927.0	2 156.5	449.3
Carson City, NV MSA										
Carson City	57 893									
Actually reporting	100.0%	294	2	2	27	263	1 449	386	948	115
Rate		507.8	3.5	3.5	46.6	454.3	2 502.9	666.7	1 637.5	198.6
Casper, WY MSA										
Natrona County	69 387									
City of Casper	51 520	135	2	7	14	112	2 699	525	2 077	97
Actually reporting	100.0%	163	2	7	16	138	3 315	687	2 497	131
Rate		234.9	2.9	10.1	23.1	198.9	4 777.6	990.1	3 598.7	188.8
Cedar Rapids, IA MSA										
Benton, Jones, and Linn Counties	245 529									
City of Cedar Rapids	122 698	417	1	45	121	250	6 391	1 067	5 022	302
Actually reporting	1.0%	553	1	63	124	365	7 549	1 370	5 799	380
Estimated total	100.0%	568	1	65	125	377	7 788	1 410	5 988	390
Rate		231.3	0.4	26.5	50.9	153.5	3 171.9	574.3	2 438.8	158.8
Charleston, WV MSA										
Boone, Clay, Kanawha, Lincoln, and Putnam Counties	308 017									
City of Charleston	51 728	555	7	16	128	404	3 836	818	2 712	306
Actually reporting	0.9%	1 088	19	51	187	831	11 640	2 736	7 809	1 095
Estimated total	100.0%	1 179	20	56	197	906	12 672	2 979	8 510	1 183
Rate		382.8	6.5	18.2	64.0	294.1	4 114.1	967.2	2 762.8	384.1
Charleston-North Charleston, SC MSA										
Berkeley, Charleston, and Dorchester Counties	591 358									
City of Charleston	106 307	1 003	10	49	290	654	4 756	810	3 464	482
City of North Charleston	85 416	1 473	11	82	519	861	7 328	1 365	5 033	930
Actually reporting	100.0%	4 989	40	291	1 189	3 469	25 986	5 334	17 656	2 996
Rate		843.7	6.8	49.2	201.1	586.6	4 394.3	902.0	2 985.7	506.6
Charlotte-Gastonia-Concord, NC-SC MSA										
Anson, Cabarrus, Gaston, Mecklenburg, and Union Counties, NC; and York County, SC	1 498 697									
City of Charlotte-Mecklenburg, NC	677 122	7 933	85	323	3 649	3 876	46 589	12 783	26 708	7 098
City of Gastonia, NC	69 428	670	5	36	257	372	6 190	1 268	4 389	533
City of Concord, NC	60 957	221	5	15	74	127	2 995	505	2 245	245
City of Rock Hill, SC	58 688	709	4	41	85	579	2 770	464	2 111	195
Actually reporting	1.0%	12 521	118	559	4 501	7 343	77 089	20 183	47 403	9 503
Estimated total	100.0%	12 554	118	561	4 510	7 365	77 492	20 277	47 691	9 524
Rate		837.7	7.9	37.4	300.9	491.4	5 170.6	1 353.0	3 182.2	635.5
Charlottesville, VA MSA										
Albemarle, Fluvanna, Greene, and Nelson Counties and Charlottesville City	183 511									
City of Charlottesville	37 133	307	2	35	72	198	1 875	264	1 442	169
Actually reporting	100.0%	529	6	78	101	344	4 892	672	3 895	325
Rate		288.3	3.3	42.5	55.0	187.5	2 665.8	366.2	2 122.5	177.1
Chattanooga, TN-GA MSA										
Catoosa, Dade, and Walker Counties, GA; and Hamilton, Marion, and Sequatchie Counties, TN	497 125									
City of Chattanooga, TN	156 480	1 754	23	116	442	1 173	12 606	2 190	9 365	1 051
Actually reporting	100.0%	2 929	31	184	543	2 171	22 981	4 476	16 508	1 997
Rate		589.2	6.2	37.0	109.2	436.7	4 622.8	900.4	3 320.7	401.7
Cheyenne, WY MSA										
Laramie County	85 764									
City of Cheyenne	55 664	97	4	12	17	64	2 585	272	2 222	91
Actually reporting	100.0%	153	5	27	22	99	3 135	377	2 624	134
Rate		178.4	5.8	31.5	25.7	115.4	3 655.4	439.6	3 059.6	156.2
Chico, CA MSA										
Butte County	214 382									
City of Chico	70 670	253	3	32	79	139	2 671	719	1 462	490
Actually reporting	100.0%	752	10	98	166	478	7 335	2 235	3 756	1 344
Rate		350.8	4.7	45.7	77.4	223.0	3 421.5	1 042.5	1 752.0	626.9
Cincinnati-Middletown, OH-KY-IN MSA										
Dearborn, Franklin, and Ohio Counties, IN; Boone, Bracken, Campbell, Gallatin, Grant, Kenton, and Pendleton Counties, KY; and Brown, Butler, Clermont, Hamilton, and Warren Counties, OH	2 061 977									
City of Cincinnati, OH	314 292	3 723	79	315	2 319	1 010	22 411	5 430	14 029	2 952
City of Middletown, OH	51 827	237	2	44	110	81	3 540	721	2 657	162
Actually reporting	0.9%	7 098	111	845	3 500	2 642	68 766	13 868	48 775	6 123
Estimated total	100.0%	7 566	115	910	3 651	2 890	75 796	15 224	53 977	6 595
Rate		366.9	5.6	44.1	177.1	140.2	3 675.9	738.3	2 617.7	319.8

Note: Although arson data are included in the trend and clearance tables, sufficient data are not available to estimate totals for this offense.

Table 6. Crime, by Metropolitan Statistical Area, 2005—*Continued*

(Number, percent, rate per 100,000 inhabitants.)

Metropolitan statistical area	Population	Violent crime	Murder and non-negligent man-slaughter	Forcible rape	Robbery	Aggravated assault	Property crime	Burglary	Larceny-theft	Motor vehicle theft
Clarksville, TN-KY MSA										
Christian and Trigg Counties, KY; and Montgomery and Stewart Counties, TN	241 081									
City of Clarksville, TN	110 117	881	5	52	138	686	4 129	1 071	2 802	256
Actually reporting	1.0%	1 256	8	99	216	933	7 389	1 939	5 017	433
Estimated total	100.0%	1 258	8	99	217	934	7 416	1 944	5 037	435
Rate		521.8	3.3	41.1	90.0	387.4	3 076.1	806.4	2 089.3	180.4
Coeur d'Alene, ID MSA										
Kootenai County	125 497									
City of Coeur d'Alene	39 375	215	1	32	18	164	2 133	365	1 587	181
Actually reporting	100.0%	407	5	66	27	309	4 249	887	3 012	350
Rate		324.3	4.0	52.6	21.5	246.2	3 385.7	706.8	2 400.1	278.9
College Station-Bryan, TX MSA										
Brazos, Burleson, and Robertson Counties	192 585									
City of College Station	73 373	206	2	38	38	128	2 929	555	2 292	82
City of Bryan	67 407	617	6	45	93	473	4 216	1 207	2 784	225
Actually reporting	100.0%	979	9	106	146	718	8 854	2 265	6 213	376
Rate		508.3	4.7	55.0	75.8	372.8	4 597.5	1 176.1	3 226.1	195.2
Colorado Springs, CO MSA										
El Paso and Teller Counties	584 237									
City of Colorado Springs	374 482	1 792	12	251	439	1 090	19 619	3 676	14 164	1 779
Actually reporting	1.0%	2 787	17	317	474	1 979	23 949	4 646	17 088	2 215
Estimated total	100.0%	2 790	17	317	475	1 981	23 990	4 652	17 117	2 221
Rate		477.5	2.9	54.3	81.3	339.1	4 106.2	796.3	2 929.8	380.2
Columbia, MO MSA										
Boone and Howard Counties	152 508									
City of Columbia	90 304	477	7	19	114	337	3 065	506	2 386	173
Actually reporting	1.0%	639	9	29	127	474	4 595	823	3 503	269
Estimated total	100.0%	643	9	29	128	477	4 635	829	3 534	272
Rate		421.6	5.9	19.0	83.9	312.8	3 039.2	543.6	2 317.3	178.4
Columbia, SC MSA										
Calhoun, Fairfield, Kershaw, Lexington, Richland, and Saluda Counties	688 684									
City of Columbia	117 911	1 311	15	56	381	859	7 682	1 332	5 513	837
Actually reporting	1.0%	4 997	49	284	973	3 691	27 636	5 531	19 540	2 565
Estimated total	100.0%	4 999	49	284	973	3 693	27 652	5 534	19 552	2 566
Rate		725.9	7.1	41.2	141.3	536.2	4 015.2	803.6	2 839.0	372.6
Columbus, GA-AL MSA										
Russell County, AL; and Chattahoochee, Harris, Marion, and Muscogee Counties, GA	286 160									
City of Columbus, GA	187 886	992	22	24	446	500	13 125	2 681	8 763	1 681
Actually reporting	0.9%	1 129	26	32	484	587	14 800	3 012	9 999	1 789
Estimated total	100.0%	1 208	27	39	507	635	15 649	3 250	10 525	1 874
Rate		422.1	9.4	13.6	177.2	221.9	5 468.6	1 135.7	3 678.0	654.9
Columbus, IN MSA										
Bartholomew County	73 390									
City of Columbus	39 467	81	0	7	18	56	2 488	247	2 115	126
Actually reporting	1.0%	105	0	10	19	76	2 888	333	2 425	130
Estimated total	100.0%	106	0	10	19	77	2 900	335	2 434	131
Rate		144.4	0.0	13.6	25.9	104.9	3 951.5	456.5	3 316.5	178.5
Columbus, OH MSA										
Delaware, Fairfield, Franklin, Licking, Madison, Morrow, Pickaway, and Union Counties	1 694 651									
City of Columbus	730 329	6 111	102	518	3 777	1 714	54 141	14 604	31 724	7 813
Actually reporting	0.9%	7 341	110	793	4 301	2 137	79 122	20 405	49 514	9 203
Estimated total	100.0%	7 482	111	820	4 346	2 205	81 790	21 044	51 373	9 373
Rate		441.5	6.6	48.4	256.5	130.1	4 826.4	1 241.8	3 031.5	553.1
Corpus Christi, TX MSA										
Aransas, Nueces, and San Patricio Counties	416 481									
City of Corpus Christi	285 821	2 048	8	217	481	1 342	20 133	3 357	15 870	906
Actually reporting	100.0%	2 506	12	286	539	1 669	26 222	4 818	20 227	1 177
Rate		601.7	2.9	68.7	129.4	400.7	6 296.1	1 156.8	4 856.6	282.6
Corvallis, OR MSA										
Benton County	80 383									
City of Corvallis	51 031	69	1	11	18	39	1 994	247	1 656	91
Actually reporting	100.0%	108	1	14	23	70	3 018	417	2 439	162
Rate		134.4	1.2	17.4	28.6	87.1	3 754.5	518.8	3 034.2	201.5
Cumberland, MD-WV MSA										
Allegany County, MD; and Mineral County, WV	101 601									
City of Cumberland, MD	21 117	154	1	20	11	122	1 120	246	846	28
Actually reporting	1.0%	341	1	33	26	281	2 454	567	1 799	88
Estimated total	100.0%	344	1	33	26	284	2 509	576	1 841	92
Rate		338.6	1.0	32.5	25.6	279.5	2 469.5	566.9	1 812.0	90.6

Note: Although arson data are included in the trend and clearance tables, sufficient data are not available to estimate totals for this offense.

Table 6. Crime, by Metropolitan Statistical Area, 2005—*Continued*

(Number, percent, rate per 100,000 inhabitants.)

Metropolitan statistical area	Population	Violent crime	Murder and non-negligent man-slaughter	Forcible rape	Robbery	Aggravated assault	Property crime	Burglary	Larceny-theft	Motor vehicle theft
Dallas-Fort Worth-Arlington, TX MSA										
Metropolitan divisions of Dallas-Plano-Irving and Fort Worth-Arlington	5 794 020									
City of Dallas	1 230 303	15 429	202	562	6 882	7 783	88 955	22 363	52 315	14 277
City of Fort Worth	613 261	3 920	60	311	1 379	2 170	37 210	8 684	24 811	3 715
City of Arlington	365 380	2 369	24	178	768	1 399	20 403	3 984	14 609	1 810
City of Plano	249 448	721	2	54	119	546	8 677	1 365	6 723	589
City of Irving	197 747	910	2	66	270	572	9 548	1 730	6 658	1 160
City of Carrollton	119 761	300	5	12	95	188	4 090	916	2 675	499
City of Richardson	100 896	261	2	12	98	149	3 478	764	2 437	277
City of Denton	99 905	378	5	72	76	225	4 110	684	3 180	246
City of McKinney	89 863	228	1	44	41	142	2 059	451	1 469	139
Actually reporting	1.0%	31 914	392	1 984	11 307	18 231	273 907	60 898	181 663	31 346
Estimated total	100.0%	31 915	392	1 984	11 307	18 232	273 926	60 902	181 677	31 347
Rate		550.8	6.8	34.2	195.1	314.7	4 727.7	1 051.1	3 135.6	541.0
Dallas-Plano-Irving, TX M.D.										
Collin, Dallas, Delta, Denton, Ellis, Hunt, Kaufman, and Rockwall Counties	3 875 593									
Actually reporting	1.0%	22 902	284	1 232	8 693	12 693	182 666	41 419	118 146	23 101
Estimated total	100.0%	22 903	284	1 232	8 693	12 694	182 685	41 423	118 160	23 102
Rate		591.0	7.3	31.8	224.3	327.5	4 713.7	1 068.8	3 048.8	596.1
Fort Worth-Arlington, TX M.D.										
Johnson, Parker, Tarrant, and Wise Counties	1 918 427									
Actually reporting	100.0%	9 012	108	752	2 614	5 538	91 241	19 479	63 517	8 245
Rate		469.8	5.6	39.2	136.3	288.7	4 756.0	1 015.4	3 310.9	429.8
Danville, VA MSA										
Pittsylvania County and Danville City	109 683									
City of Danville	47 040	248	8	12	88	140	2 178	322	1 745	111
Actually reporting	100.0%	320	11	25	104	180	2 749	482	2 093	174
Rate		291.7	10.0	22.8	94.8	164.1	2 506.3	439.4	1 908.2	158.6
Dayton, OH MSA										
Greene, Miami, Montgomery, and Preble Counties	846 018									
City of Dayton	160 363	1 533	32	140	851	510	11 471	3 229	6 031	2 211
Actually reporting	0.8%	2 323	39	327	1 093	864	27 447	6 169	17 937	3 341
Estimated total	100.0%	2 581	41	372	1 181	987	31 956	7 129	21 198	3 629
Rate		305.1	4.8	44.0	139.6	116.7	3 777.2	842.7	2 505.6	429.0
Decatur, AL MSA										
Lawrence and Morgan	148 529									
City of Decatur	54 861	200	1	12	62	125	3 994	742	3 035	217
Actually reporting	1.0%	287	2	26	72	187	5 168	1 138	3 751	279
Estimated total	100.0%	310	2	28	79	201	5 404	1 185	3 924	295
Rate		208.7	1.3	18.9	53.2	135.3	3 638.3	797.8	2 641.9	198.6
Deltona-Daytona Beach-Ormond Beach, FL MSA										
Volusia County	489 475									
City of Daytona Beach	65 876	1 079	8	65	342	664	4 827	1 399	2 698	730
City of Ormond Beach	38 785	88	0	4	17	67	1 065	181	834	50
Actually reporting	100.0%	2 781	28	189	623	1 941	17 196	4 316	11 055	1 825
Rate		568.2	5.7	38.6	127.3	396.5	3 513.2	881.8	2 258.5	372.8
Denver-Aurora, CO MSA[1]										
Adams, Arapahoe, Broomfield, Clear Creek, Denver, Douglas, Elbert, Gilpin, Jefferson, and Park Counties	2 362 441									
City of Denver	564 552	4 492	59	328	1 432	2 673	33 902	7 360	18 518	8 024
City of Aurora	295 888	1 836	28	223	644	941	14 718	2 474	9 502	2 742
Actually reporting	1.0%	10 494	117	1 079	2 904	6 394	105 272	19 108	66 830	19 334
Estimated total	100.0%	10 497	117	1 079	2 905	6 396	105 311	19 114	66 857	19 340
Rate		444.3	5.0	45.7	123.0	270.7	4 457.7	809.1	2 830.0	818.6
Des Moines-West Des Moines, IA MSA[1]										
Dallas, Guthrie, Madison, Polk, and Warren Counties	513 940									
City of Des Moines1	195 093	1 228	5	110	294	819	13 799	2 630	10 045	1 124
City of West Des Moines	51 570	88	0	14	11	63	1 807	279	1 459	69
Actually reporting	100.0%	1 708	6	159	334	1 209	21 530	4 099	15 873	1 558
Rate		332.3	1.2	30.9	65.0	235.2	4 189.2	797.6	3 088.5	303.1

Note: Although arson data are included in the trend and clearance tables, sufficient data are not available to estimate totals for this offense.

[1]Because of changes in the state/local agency's reporting practices, figures are not comparable to previous years' data.

Table 6. Crime, by Metropolitan Statistical Area, 2005—*Continued*

(Number, percent, rate per 100,000 inhabitants.)

Metropolitan statistical area	Population	Violent crime	Murder and non-negligent man-slaughter	Forcible rape	Robbery	Aggravated assault	Property crime	Burglary	Larceny-theft	Motor vehicle theft
Detroit-Warren-Livonia, MI MSA[1,2]										
Metropolitan divisions of Detroit-Livonia-Dearborn and Warren-Troy-Farmington Hills Counties	4 496 826									
City of Detroit[1]	900 932	21 240	354	589	6 820	13 477	53 972	15 304	17 383	21 285
City of Warren[2]	136 229	862	5	67	223	567	. . .	812	2 251	. . .
City of Livonia	99 017	170	3	13	62	92	2 301	444	1 574	283
City of Dearborn	95 548	571	3	30	223	315	4 924	651	3 191	1 082
City of Troy	81 498	72	1	8	19	44	1 991	277	1 578	136
City of Farmington Hills	80 853	178	3	23	38	114	1 642	403	1 086	153
City of Southfield	77 554	939	4	22	159	754	3 747	748	2 149	850
City of Pontiac	67 637	1 255	9	82	253	911	2 799	1 117	1 194	488
City of Taylor	65 436	233	1	26	67	139	3 043	455	2 117	471
City of Novi	51 976	61	0	2	11	48	1 259	197	993	69
Actually reporting	1.0%	33 003	439	1 757	9 633	21 174	. . .	32 849	81 135	. . .
Estimated total	100.0%	33 111	440	1 771	9 658	21 242	. . .	33 039	81 907	. . .
Rate		736.3	9.8	39.4	214.8	472.4	. . .	734.7	1 821.4	. . .
Detroit-Livonia-Dearborn, MI M.D.[1]										
Wayne County	2 017 845									
Actually reporting	1.0%	25 144	392	979	8 070	15 703	90 140	21 891	39 976	28 273
Estimated total	100.0%	25 238	393	991	8 092	15 762	91 090	22 057	40 650	28 383
Rate		1 250.7	19.5	49.1	401.0	781.1	4 514.2	1 093.1	2 014.5	1 406.6
Warren-Troy-Farmington Hills, MI M.D.[2]										
Lapeer, Livingston, Macomb, Oakland, and St. Clair Counties	2 478 981									
Actually reporting	1.0%	7 859	47	778	1 563	5 471	. . .	10 958	41 159	. . .
Estimated total	100.0%	7 873	47	780	1 566	5 480	. . .	10 982	41 257	. . .
Rate		317.6	1.9	31.5	63.2	221.1	. . .	443.0	1 664.3	. . .
Dothan, AL MSA										
Geneva, Henry, and Houston Counties	136 070									
City of Dothan	60 844	329	8	56	154	111	3 486	750	2 583	153
Actually reporting	0.9%	465	9	71	165	220	4 882	1 117	3 498	267
Estimated total	100.0%	503	10	74	177	242	5 269	1 194	3 782	293
Rate		369.7	7.3	54.4	130.1	177.8	3 872.3	877.5	2 779.5	215.3
Dover, DE MSA										
Kent County	140 951									
City of Dover	34 151	207	2	13	40	152	1 642	93	1 434	115
Actually reporting	100.0%	853	4	73	97	679	4 240	775	3 182	283
Rate		605.2	2.8	51.8	68.8	481.7	3 008.1	549.8	2 257.5	200.8
Dubuque, IA MSA										
Dubuque County	91 366									
City of Dubuque	57 735	315	1	16	10	288	1 770	398	1 306	66
Actually reporting	100.0%	371	1	22	10	338	2 089	495	1 488	106
Rate		406.1	1.1	24.1	10.9	369.9	2 286.4	541.8	1 628.6	116.0
Durham, NC MSA										
Chatham, Durham, Orange, and Person Counties	458 714									
City of Durham	205 080	1 477	35	89	627	726	12 037	3 157	7 944	936
Actually reporting	100.0%	2 283	48	127	824	1 284	20 607	5 300	13 939	1 368
Rate		497.7	10.5	27.7	179.6	279.9	4 492.3	1 155.4	3 038.7	298.2
Eau Claire, WI MSA										
Chippewa and Eau Claire Counties	153 906									
City of Eau Claire	62 885	116	0	7	24	85	1 929	329	1 522	78
Actually reporting	100.0%	193	1	16	30	146	3 508	591	2 757	160
Rate		125.4	0.6	10.4	19.5	94.9	2 279.3	384.0	1 791.4	104.0
El Centro, CA MSA										
Imperial County	153 460									
City of El Centro	38 605	348	0	18	43	287	2 115	758	1 097	260
Actually reporting	100.0%	785	0	37	111	637	6 229	2 217	2 944	1 068
Rate		511.5	0.0	24.1	72.3	415.1	4 059.0	1 444.7	1 918.4	695.9
El Paso, TX MSA[1]										
El Paso County	724 856									
City of El Paso[1]	601 839	2 614	14	295	448	1 857	19 675	2 151	14 925	2 599
Actually reporting	100.0%	2 964	18	337	477	2 132	22 489	2 617	17 031	2 841
Rate		408.9	2.5	46.5	65.8	294.1	3 102.5	361.0	2 349.6	391.9
Elizabethtown, KY MSA										
Hardin and Larue Counties	110 277									
City of Elizabethtown	23 344	76	0	14	23	39	1 087	182	847	58
Actually reporting	1.0%	177	1	29	50	97	2 051	388	1 557	106
Rate		160.5	0.9	26.3	45.3	88.0	1 859.9	351.8	1 411.9	96.1
Elkhart-Goshen, IN MSA										
Elkhart County	192 826									
City of Elkhart	52 164	200	5	39	146	10	3 761	775	2 724	262
City of Goshen	30 724	73	1	0	7	65	1 366	142	1 188	36
Actually reporting	100.0%	343	6	60	174	103	7 217	1 381	5 326	510
Rate		177.9	3.1	31.1	90.2	53.4	3 742.8	716.2	2 762.1	264.5

Note: Although arson data are included in the trend and clearance tables, sufficient data are not available to estimate totals for this offense.

[1]Because of changes in the state/local agency's reporting practices, figures are not comparable to previous years' data.
[2]After examining the data and making inquiries, the FBI determined that the agency's offense count was inflated. Consequently, this figure is not included in this table.
. . . = Not available.

Table 6. Crime, by Metropolitan Statistical Area, 2005—*Continued*

(Number, percent, rate per 100,000 inhabitants.)

Metropolitan statistical area	Population	Violent crime	Murder and non-negligent man-slaughter	Forcible rape	Robbery	Aggravated assault	Property crime	Burglary	Larceny-theft	Motor vehicle theft
Elmira, NY MSA										
Chemung County	90 113									
City of Elmira	30 116	121	2	14	39	66	1 621	282	1 295	44
Actually reporting	100.0%	209	4	28	46	131	2 631	429	2 138	64
Rate		231.9	4.4	31.1	51.0	145.4	2 919.7	476.1	2 372.6	71.0
Erie, PA MSA										
Erie County	282 886									
City of Erie	104 120	472	6	75	200	191	2 867	632	2 129	106
Actually reporting	1.0%	733	8	117	246	362	5 664	1 247	4 143	274
Estimated total	100.0%	737	8	117	247	365	5 697	1 252	4 169	276
Rate		260.5	2.8	41.4	87.3	129.0	2 013.9	442.6	1 473.7	97.6
Eugene-Springfield, OR MSA										
Lane County	335 881									
City of Eugene	144 526	328	5	54	119	150	9 902	1 603	6 639	1 660
City of Springfield	55 760	195	0	10	36	149	4 859	814	3 207	838
Actually reporting	100.0%	831	8	105	190	528	18 478	3 560	11 864	3 054
Rate		247.4	2.4	31.3	56.6	157.2	5 501.4	1 059.9	3 532.2	909.3
Evansville, IN-KY MSA										
Gibson, Posey, Vanderburgh, and Warrick Counties, IN; and Henderson and Webster Counties, KY	350 443									
City of Evansville, IN	117 802	478	8	59	176	235	6 008	1 255	4 469	284
Actually reporting	0.8%	699	10	79	190	420	8 432	1 570	6 487	375
Estimated total	100.0%	815	10	93	222	490	10 010	1 886	7 635	489
Rate		232.6	2.9	26.5	63.3	139.8	2 856.4	538.2	2 178.7	139.5
Fairbanks, AK MSA										
Fairbanks North Star Borough	32 497									
City of Fairbanks	30 817	306	2	47	65	192	1 587	227	1 155	205
Actually reporting	100.0%	312	2	48	65	197	1 806	250	1 326	230
Rate		960.1	6.2	147.7	200.0	606.2	5 557.4	769.3	4 080.4	707.8
Fargo, ND-MN MSA										
Clay County, MN; and Cass County, ND	182 319									
City of Fargo, ND	91 380	104	2	42	11	49	2 348	438	1 697	213
Actually reporting	100.0%	220	3	70	20	127	4 074	686	3 061	327
Rate		120.7	1.6	38.4	11.0	69.7	2 234.5	376.3	1 678.9	179.4
Farmington, NM MSA[2]										
San Juan County	125 803									
City of Farmington	42 980	. . .	3	66	27	. . .	1 523	412	918	193
Actually reporting	100.0%	. . .	4	118	48	. . .	3 333	766	2 207	360
Rate		. . .	3	94	38	. . .	2 649	609	1 754	286
Fayetteville, NC MSA										
Cumberland and Hoke Counties	353 533									
City of Fayetteville	127 323	1 152	14	47	429	662	10 551	2 531	7 234	786
Actually reporting	100.0%	2 057	23	90	651	1 293	19 658	6 034	12 336	1 288
Rate		581.8	6.5	25.5	184.1	365.7	5 560.4	1 706.8	3 489.3	364.3
Fayetteville-Springdale-Rogers, AR-MO MSA										
Benton, Madison, and Washington Counties, AR; and McDonald County, MO	394 610									
City of Fayetteville, AR	64 809	313	2	51	33	227	2 945	458	2 338	149
City of Springdale, AR	56 510	198	0	57	15	126	2 398	267	1 984	147
City of Rogers, AR	45 318	95	1	36	24	34	2 633	257	2 278	98
City of Bentonville, AR	28 033	93	1	21	4	67	957	122	776	59
Actually reporting	100.0%	1 156	11	220	90	835	12 183	1 999	9 421	763
Rate		292.9	2.8	55.8	22.8	211.6	3 087.4	506.6	2 387.4	193.4
Flagstaff, AZ MSA										
Coconino County	126 931									
City of Flagstaff	58 979	529	1	48	62	418	4 277	511	3 560	206
Actually reporting	100.0%	747	1	76	74	596	6 047	895	4 877	275
Rate		588.5	0.8	59.9	58.3	469.5	4 764.0	705.1	3 842.2	216.7
Flint, MI MSA[1]										
Genesee County	444 309									
City of Flint[1]	119 814	2 708	48	105	566	1 989	7 709	2 634	3 492	1 583
Actually reporting	1.0%	3 816	57	310	773	2 676	18 073	5 019	10 353	2 701
Estimated total	100.0%	3 817	57	310	773	2 677	18 084	5 021	10 361	2 702
Rate		859.1	12.8	69.8	174.0	602.5	4 070.1	1 130.1	2 331.9	608.1
Florence, SC MSA										
Darlington and Florence Counties	199 935									
City of Florence	31 302	555	4	18	201	332	3 387	592	2 582	213
Actually reporting	100.0%	2 572	16	102	445	2 009	11 463	2 811	7 825	827
Rate		1 286.4	8.0	51.0	222.6	1 004.8	5 733.4	1 406.0	3 913.8	413.6
Fond du Lac, WI MSA										
Fond du Lac County	99 150									
City of Fond du Lac	42 617	75	0	3	11	61	1 195	138	1 015	42
Actually reporting	100.0%	125	0	9	11	105	1 809	248	1 498	63
Rate		126.1	0.0	9.1	11.1	105.9	1 824.5	250.1	1 510.8	63.5

Note: Although arson data are included in the trend and clearance tables, sufficient data are not available to estimate totals for this offense.

[1]Because of changes in the state/local agency's reporting practices, figures are not comparable to previous years' data.
[2]After examining the data and making inquiries, the FBI determined that the agency's offense count was inflated. Consequently, this figure is not included in this table.
. . . = Not available.

Table 6. Crime, by Metropolitan Statistical Area, 2005—*Continued*

(Number, percent, rate per 100,000 inhabitants.)

Metropolitan statistical area	Population	Violent crime	Murder and non-negligent man-slaughter	Forcible rape	Robbery	Aggravated assault	Property crime	Burglary	Larceny-theft	Motor vehicle theft
Fort Collins-Loveland, CO MSA										
Larimer County	272 598									
City of Fort Collins	128 727	442	2	118	57	265	4 434	764	3 239	431
City of Loveland	58 585	108	2	21	17	68	1 790	271	1 418	101
Actually reporting	100.0%	658	5	165	83	405	8 195	1 369	6 167	659
Rate		241.4	1.8	60.5	30.4	148.6	3 006.3	502.2	2 262.3	241.7
Fort Smith, AR-OK MSA										
Crawford, Franklin, and Sebastian Counties, AR; and Le Flore and Sequoyah Counties, OK	284 640									
City of Fort Smith, AR	82 638	865	5	95	117	648	5 459	971	4 146	342
Actually reporting	0.9%	1 452	10	129	138	1 175	8 779	1 963	6 294	522
Estimated total	100.0%	1 568	12	140	149	1 267	9 723	2 278	6 854	591
Rate		550.9	4.2	49.2	52.3	445.1	3 415.9	800.3	2 408.0	207.6
Fort Walton Beach-Crestview-Destin, FL MSA										
Okaloosa County	185 556									
City of Fort Walton Beach	20 443	106	1	8	28	69	833	155	608	70
City of Crestview	17 206	76	0	10	16	50	698	130	524	44
Actually reporting	100.0%	589	3	45	106	435	5 378	1 081	3 909	388
Rate		317.4	1.6	24.3	57.1	234.4	2 898.3	582.6	2 106.6	209.1
Fort Wayne, IN MSA										
Allen, Wells, and Whitley Counties	404 303									
City of Fort Wayne	220 561	732	25	84	375	248	10 732	2 233	7 841	658
Actually reporting	0.9%	851	26	101	403	321	12 450	2 614	9 036	800
Estimated total	100.0%	924	27	107	419	371	13 300	2 772	9 654	874
Rate		228.5	6.7	26.5	103.6	91.8	3 289.6	685.6	2 387.8	216.2
Fresno, CA MSA										
Fresno County	872 528									
City of Fresno	460 758	3 897	49	149	1 275	2 424	25 546	4 170	16 088	5 288
Actually reporting	100.0%	5 574	77	255	1 606	3 636	41 890	7 590	26 165	8 135
Rate		638.8	8.8	29.2	184.1	416.7	4 801.0	869.9	2 998.8	932.3
Gadsden, AL MSA										
Etowah County	103 880									
City of Gadsden	37 870	315	6	46	146	117	3 120	663	2 243	214
Actually reporting	0.9%	375	6	47	152	170	4 064	825	2 956	283
Estimated total	100.0%	434	7	51	171	205	4 677	946	3 406	325
Rate		417.8	6.7	49.1	164.6	197.3	4 502.3	910.7	3 278.8	312.9
Gainesville, FL MSA										
Alachua and Gilchrist Counties	244 512									
City of Gainesville	111 313	973	5	99	168	701	4 870	1 178	3 262	430
Actually reporting	100.0%	2 121	7	177	294	1 643	10 076	2 549	6 738	789
Rate		867.4	2.9	72.4	120.2	672.0	4 120.9	1 042.5	2 755.7	322.7
Gainesville, GA MSA										
Hall County	165 357									
City of Gainesville	31 964	149	1	15	31	102	2 191	235	1 790	166
Actually reporting	1.0%	386	6	48	58	274	5 752	1 094	3 998	660
Estimated total	100.0%	404	6	49	64	285	5 947	1 127	4 141	679
Rate		244.3	3.6	29.6	38.7	172.4	3 596.5	681.6	2 504.3	410.6
Goldsboro, NC MSA										
Wayne County	116 145									
City of Goldsboro	39 419	325	7	3	109	206	2 694	594	1 956	144
Actually reporting	1.0%	522	13	8	145	356	4 943	1 329	3 359	255
Estimated total	100.0%	525	13	8	146	358	4 980	1 338	3 385	257
Rate		452.0	11.2	6.9	125.7	308.2	4 287.7	1 152.0	2 914.5	221.3
Grand Forks, ND-MN MSA										
Polk County, MN; and Grand Forks County, ND	96 477									
City of Grand Forks, ND	49 162	65	1	9	6	49	2 074	271	1 628	175
Actually reporting	0.9%	126	3	26	7	90	2 927	427	2 287	213
Estimated total	100.0%	143	3	29	11	100	3 234	470	2 531	233
Rate		148.2	3.1	30.1	11.4	103.7	3 352.1	487.2	2 623.4	241.5
Grand Junction, CO MSA										
Mesa County	129 017									
City of Grand Junction	45 312	299	0	23	32	244	3 360	542	2 583	235
Actually reporting	1.0%	347	0	26	40	281	5 272	998	3 846	428
Estimated total	100.0%	350	0	26	41	283	5 312	1 004	3 874	434
Rate		271.3	0.0	20.2	31.8	219.4	4 117.3	778.2	3 002.7	336.4
Grand Rapids-Wyoming, MI MSA[1]										
Barry, Ionia, Kent, and Newaygo Counties	768 164									
City of Grand Rapids[1]	195 274	1 962	8	66	674	1 214	9 766	2 038	7 050	678
City of Wyoming	70 357	295	0	32	72	191	1 997	568	1 218	211
Actually reporting	1.0%	3 408	12	379	879	2 138	23 726	5 187	17 080	1 459
Estimated total	100.0%	3 434	12	382	885	2 155	24 001	5 235	17 275	1 491
Rate		447.0	1.6	49.7	115.2	280.5	3 124.5	681.5	2 248.9	194.1
Great Falls, MT MSA[1]										
Cascade County	80 608									
City of Great Falls	57 040	171	2	20	25	124	3 394	297	2 959	138
Actually reporting	100.0%	207	2	20	25	160	3 781	306	3 277	198
Rate		256.8	2.5	24.8	31.0	198.5	4 690.6	379.6	4 065.4	245.6

Note: Although arson data are included in the trend and clearance tables, sufficient data are not available to estimate totals for this offense.

[1]Because of changes in the state/local agency's reporting practices, figures are not comparable to previous years' data.

Table 6. Crime, by Metropolitan Statistical Area, 2005—*Continued*

(Number, percent, rate per 100,000 inhabitants.)

Metropolitan statistical area	Population	Violent crime	Murder and non-negligent man-slaughter	Forcible rape	Robbery	Aggravated assault	Property crime	Burglary	Larceny-theft	Motor vehicle theft
Greeley, CO MSA										
Weld County	222 296									
City of Greeley	85 991	556	2	48	60	446	5 475	1 149	3 878	448
Actually reporting	1.0%	956	7	72	85	792	9 512	2 230	6 340	942
Estimated total	100.0%	979	7	75	90	807	9 856	2 282	6 583	991
Rate		440.4	3.1	33.7	40.5	363.0	4 433.7	1 026.6	2 961.4	445.8
Green Bay, WI MSA										
Brown, Kewaunee, and Oconto Counties	296 931									
City of Green Bay	101 599	495	5	58	72	360	2 931	605	2 099	227
Actually reporting	100.0%	590	10	84	74	422	6 950	1 292	5 250	408
Rate		198.7	3.4	28.3	24.9	142.1	2 340.6	435.1	1 768.1	137.4
Greensboro-High Point, NC MSA										
Guilford, Randolph, and Rockingham Counties	678 641									
City of Greensboro	235 393	1 941	30	85	787	1 039	14 360	3 954	9 198	1 208
City of High Point	92 982	608	8	27	214	359	5 867	1 940	3 456	471
Actually reporting	1.0%	3 257	54	150	1 177	1 876	31 270	9 073	19 911	2 286
Estimated total	100.0%	3 261	54	150	1 178	1 879	31 334	9 088	19 957	2 289
Rate		480.5	8.0	22.1	173.6	276.9	4 617.2	1 339.1	2 940.7	337.3
Greenville, NC MSA										
Greene and Pitt Counties	163 480									
City of Greenville	69 829	509	6	12	177	314	4 321	1 505	2 617	199
Actually reporting	100.0%	914	15	41	236	622	7 242	2 378	4 519	345
Rate		559.1	9.2	25.1	144.4	380.5	4 429.9	1 454.6	2 764.3	211.0
Greenville, SC MSA										
Greenville, Laurens, and Pickens Counties	591 797									
City of Greenville	57 056	656	5	32	161	458	3 794	776	2 710	308
Actually reporting	100.0%	4 176	37	245	690	3 204	23 934	5 949	15 831	2 154
Rate		705.6	6.3	41.4	116.6	541.4	4 044.3	1 005.2	2 675.1	364.0
Hagerstown-Martinsburg, MD-WV MSA										
Washington County, MD; and Berkeley and Morgan Counties, WV	245 946									
City of Hagerstown, MD	37 822	279	2	4	84	189	1 487	328	1 024	135
City of Martinsburg, WV	15 648	87	0	1	30	56	982	98	840	44
Actually reporting	1.0%	742	7	22	159	554	5 526	1 071	4 027	428
Estimated total	100.0%	744	7	22	159	556	5 567	1 078	4 058	431
Rate		302.5	2.8	8.9	64.6	226.1	2 263.5	438.3	1 650.0	175.2
Hanford-Corcoran, CA MSA										
Kings County	143 508									
City of Hanford	47 131	185	0	17	51	117	1 855	224	1 407	224
City of Corcoran	22 583	65	1	2	4	58	243	103	119	21
Actually reporting	100.0%	547	4	44	84	415	3 976	835	2 508	633
Rate		381.2	2.8	30.7	58.5	289.2	2 770.6	581.8	1 747.6	441.1
Harrisburg-Carlisle, PA MSA										
Cumberland, Dauphin, and Perry Counties	520 307									
City of Harrisburg	47 725	805	12	52	480	261	2 336	600	1 583	153
City of Carlisle	18 108	38	0	8	17	13	533	75	449	9
Actually reporting	0.9%	1 662	17	174	716	755	11 200	2 057	8 616	527
Estimated total	100.0%	1 824	19	185	759	861	12 597	2 264	9 713	620
Rate		350.6	3.7	35.6	145.9	165.5	2 421.1	435.1	1 866.8	119.2
Harrisonburg, VA MSA										
Rockingham County and Harrisonburg City	112 890									
City of Harrisonburg	41 659	98	2	14	35	47	1 164	205	883	76
Actually reporting	100.0%	133	2	25	38	68	1 760	348	1 312	100
Rate		117.8	1.8	22.1	33.7	60.2	1 559.0	308.3	1 162.2	88.6
Hartford-West Hartford-East Hartford, CT MSA										
Hartford, Middlesex, and Tolland Counties	1 002 799									
City of Hartford	125 086	1 442	25	46	692	679	9 513	1 398	6 255	1 860
City of West Hartford	61 371	120	1	0	68	51	1 640	219	1 309	112
City of East Hartford	49 456	176	2	20	66	88	1 612	236	1 148	228
City of Middletown	47 247	59	2	1	25	31	1 588	195	1 245	148
Actually reporting	0.9%	2 875	40	176	1 288	1 371	30 824	4 921	22 159	3 744
Estimated total	100.0%	2 957	41	184	1 322	1 410	32 215	5 155	23 197	3 863
Rate		294.9	4.1	18.3	131.8	140.6	3 212.5	514.1	2 313.2	385.2
Hickory-Lenoir-Morganton, NC MSA										
Alexander, Burke, Caldwell, and Catawba Counties	358 599									
City of Hickory	40 779	368	2	28	112	226	3 435	773	2 381	281
City of Lenoir	18 241	47	0	0	14	33	685	172	454	59
City of Morganton	17 462	64	1	5	13	45	724	161	526	37
Actually reporting	1.0%	1 005	19	77	212	697	12 861	4 080	7 792	989
Estimated total	100.0%	1 016	19	78	215	704	12 986	4 109	7 882	995
Rate		283.3	5.3	21.8	60.0	196.3	3 621.3	1 145.8	2 198.0	277.5
Hinesville-Fort Stewart, GA MSA										
Liberty and Long Counties	74 678									
City of Hinesville	31 408	172	0	14	55	103	1 899	414	1 425	60
Actually reporting	1.0%	264	1	19	69	175	2 706	653	1 942	111
Estimated total	100.0%	278	1	20	74	183	2 851	678	2 048	125
Rate		372.3	1.3	26.8	99.1	245.1	3 817.7	907.9	2 742.4	167.4

Note: Although arson data are included in the trend and clearance tables, sufficient data are not available to estimate totals for this offense.

Table 6. Crime, by Metropolitan Statistical Area, 2005—*Continued*

(Number, percent, rate per 100,000 inhabitants.)

Metropolitan statistical area	Population	Violent crime	Murder and non-negligent man-slaughter	Forcible rape	Robbery	Aggravated assault	Property crime	Burglary	Larceny-theft	Motor vehicle theft
Holland-Grand Haven, MI MSA										
Ottawa County	252 557									
City of Holland	27 207	109	0	36	6	67	925	160	734	31
City of Grand Haven	10 742	24	0	6	5	13	377	43	318	16
Actually reporting	100.0%	491	2	199	38	252	4 816	1 010	3 597	209
Rate		194.4	0.8	78.8	15.0	99.8	1 906.9	399.9	1 424.2	82.8
Honolulu, HI MSA										
Honolulu County	908 521									
City of Honolulu	908 521	2 570	15	234	841	1 480	42 383	6 209	29 376	6 798
Actually reporting	100.0%	2 570	15	234	841	1 480	42 383	6 209	29 376	6 798
Rate		282.9	1.7	25.8	92.6	162.9	4 665.1	683.4	3 233.4	748.2
Hot Springs, AR MSA										
Garland County	93 029									
City of Hot Springs	37 604	496	4	26	87	379	4 528	894	3 348	286
Actually reporting	1.0%	613	8	52	103	450	7 033	1 794	4 735	504
Estimated total	100.0%	617	8	52	104	453	7 072	1 804	4 762	506
Rate		663.2	8.6	55.9	111.8	486.9	7 601.9	1 939.2	5 118.8	543.9
Houma-Bayou Cane-Thibodaux, LA MSA										
Lafourche and Terrebonne Parishes	199 025									
City of Houma	32 078	319	6	14	67	232	1 725	290	1 379	56
City of Thibodaux	14 526	105	0	12	18	75	586	118	459	9
Actually reporting	1.0%	901	11	69	140	681	7 188	1 416	5 412	360
Estimated total	100.0%	914	11	70	142	691	7 303	1 436	5 499	368
Rate		459.2	5.5	35.2	71.3	347.2	3 669.4	721.5	2 763.0	184.9
Houston-Sugar Land-Baytown, TX MSA										
Austin, Brazoria, Chambers, Fort Bend, Galveston, Harris, Liberty, Montgomery, San Jacinto, and Waller Counties	5 265 657									
City of Houston	2 045 732	23 987	334	872	11 128	11 653	120 425	27 541	72 476	20 408
City of Sugar Land	74 934	117	1	4	62	50	1 829	285	1 434	110
City of Baytown	68 428	291	4	32	112	143	3 042	705	2 100	237
City of Galveston	58 298	530	8	87	172	263	3 580	687	2 530	363
Actually reporting	1.0%	37 520	477	1 885	14 615	20 543	222 215	52 887	139 290	30 038
Estimated total	100.0%	37 521	477	1 885	14 615	20 544	222 236	52 891	139 305	30 040
Rate		712.6	9.1	35.8	277.6	390.2	4 220.5	1 004.5	2 645.5	570.5
Huntington-Ashland, WV-KY-OH MSA										
Boyd and Greenup Counties, KY; Lawrence County, OH; and Cabell and Wayne Counties, WV	287 756									
City of Huntington, WV	49 932	325	11	36	164	114	3 677	1 071	2 296	310
City of Ashland, KY	21 729	87	2	11	20	54	1 103	202	840	61
Actually reporting	1.0%	568	16	59	219	274	8 167	1 991	5 553	623
Estimated total	100.0%	599	16	63	230	290	8 655	2 079	5 922	654
Rate		208.2	5.6	21.9	79.9	100.8	3 007.8	722.5	2 058.0	227.3
Huntsville, AL MSA										
Limestone and Madison Counties	364 669									
City of Huntsville	165 147	1 220	22	88	500	610	11 513	2 446	7 979	1 088
Actually reporting	0.8%	1 601	29	121	602	849	15 749	3 550	10 799	1 400
Estimated total	100.0%	1 782	32	138	650	962	17 645	4 066	12 035	1 544
Rate		488.7	8.8	37.8	178.2	263.8	4 838.6	1 115.0	3 300.3	423.4
Idaho Falls, ID MSA										
Bonneville and Jefferson Counties	113 276									
City of Idaho Falls	53 489	156	0	27	9	120	1 923	339	1 454	130
Actually reporting	100.0%	240	0	44	13	183	2 970	561	2 214	195
Rate		211.9	0.0	38.8	11.5	161.6	2 621.9	495.3	1 954.5	172.1
Indianapolis-Carmel, IN MSA										
Boone, Brown, Hamilton, Hancock, Hendricks, Johnson,[1] Marion, Morgan, Putnam, and Shelby Counties	1 630 558									
City of Indianapolis	800 304	7 948	108	527	3 274	4 039	50 081	11 548	29 541	8 992
City of Carmel	58 519	24	0	8	6	10	989	134	814	41
Actually reporting	0.9%	9 028	118	619	3 533	4 758	64 763	13 982	40 829	9 952
Estimated total	100.0%	9 366	122	648	3 601	4 995	68 888	14 802	43 780	10 306
Rate		574.4	7.5	39.7	220.8	306.3	4 224.8	907.8	2 685.0	632.1
Iowa City, IA MSA										
Johnson and Washington Counties	137 950									
City of Iowa City	63 280	184	0	32	37	115	1 480	326	1 082	72
Actually reporting	1.0%	322	1	56	44	221	2 806	566	2 126	114
Estimated total	100.0%	334	1	58	45	230	2 987	596	2 269	122
Rate		242.1	0.7	42.0	32.6	166.7	2 165.3	432.0	1 644.8	88.4
Jackson, MI MSA										
Jackson County	163 106									
City of Jackson	35 162	297	3	47	66	181	2 272	413	1 706	153
Actually reporting	1.0%	630	6	115	97	412	4 725	1 076	3 302	347
Estimated total	100.0%	637	6	116	99	416	4 794	1 088	3 351	355
Rate		390.5	3.7	71.1	60.7	255.0	2 939.2	667.1	2 054.5	217.6
Jackson, MS MSA										
Copiah, Hinds, Madison, Rankin, and Simpson Counties	520 502									
City of Jackson	180 417	1 225	38	158	612	417	12 008	3 139	6 960	1 909
Actually reporting	0.9%	1 754	51	229	719	755	17 905	4 685	10 891	2 329
Estimated total	100.0%	1 889	55	250	755	829	20 022	5 153	12 369	2 500
Rate		362.9	10.6	48.0	145.1	159.3	3 846.7	990.0	2 376.4	480.3

Note: Although arson data are included in the trend and clearance tables, sufficient data are not available to estimate totals for this offense.

[1]Because of changes in the state/local agency's reporting practices, figures are not comparable to previous years' data.

Table 6. Crime, by Metropolitan Statistical Area, 2005—*Continued*

(Number, percent, rate per 100,000 inhabitants.)

Metropolitan statistical area	Population	Violent crime	Murder and non-negligent man-slaughter	Forcible rape	Robbery	Aggravated assault	Property crime	Burglary	Larceny-theft	Motor vehicle theft
Jackson, TN MSA										
Chester and Madison Counties	111 328									
City of Jackson	62 421	836	5	49	177	605	4 885	1 269	3 141	475
Actually reporting	100.0%	1 101	8	69	194	830	6 243	1 635	3 989	619
Rate		989.0	7.2	62.0	174.3	745.5	5 607.8	1 468.6	3 583.1	556.0
Jacksonville, FL MSA										
Baker, Clay, Duval, Nassau, and St. Johns Counties	1 253 042									
City of Jacksonville	795 259	6 600	91	189	2 253	4 067	43 517	8 998	29 583	4 936
Actually reporting	1.0%	9 285	104	314	2 519	6 348	56 466	11 931	38 635	5 900
Estimated total	100.0%	9 296	104	315	2 522	6 355	56 536	11 946	38 683	5 907
Rate		741.9	8.3	25.1	201.3	507.2	4 511.9	953.4	3 087.1	471.4
Janesville, WI MSA										
Rock County	157 284									
City of Janesville	61 908	170	0	34	64	72	2 968	515	2 317	136
Actually reporting	100.0%	437	4	61	113	259	5 731	1 072	4 371	288
Rate		277.8	2.5	38.8	71.8	164.7	3 643.7	681.6	2 779.0	183.1
Jefferson City, MO MSA										
Callaway, Cole, Moniteau, and Osage Counties	143 579									
City of Jefferson City	38 978	312	8	25	34	245	1 733	310	1 344	79
Actually reporting	100.0%	492	11	34	55	392	3 811	856	2 748	207
Rate		342.7	7.7	23.7	38.3	273.0	2 654.3	596.2	1 913.9	144.2
Johnson City, TN MSA										
Carter, Unicoi, and Washington Counties	189 289									
City of Johnson City	58 419	375	5	20	73	277	3 697	692	2 797	208
Actually reporting	100.0%	817	10	40	91	676	7 104	1 585	5 125	394
Rate		431.6	5.3	21.1	48.1	357.1	3 753.0	837.3	2 707.5	208.1
Jonesboro, AR MSA										
Craighead and Poinsett Counties	112 605									
City of Jonesboro	59 366	481	2	27	101	351	3 719	1 397	2 154	168
Actually reporting	1.0%	674	2	51	108	513	5 445	2 030	3 173	242
Estimated total	100.0%	681	2	52	109	518	5 511	2 047	3 218	246
Rate		604.8	1.8	46.2	96.8	460.0	4 894.1	1 817.9	2 857.8	218.5
Joplin, MO MSA										
Jasper and Newton Counties	165 539									
City of Joplin	47 202	323	2	34	87	200	4 206	656	3 146	404
Actually reporting	100.0%	643	8	69	107	459	8 022	1 423	5 958	641
Rate		388.4	4.8	41.7	64.6	277.3	4 846.0	859.6	3 599.2	387.2
Kalamazoo-Portage, MI MSA										
Kalamazoo and Van Buren Counties	319 525									
City of Kalamazoo	74 020	596	3	55	178	360	4 541	1 106	3 116	319
City of Portage	45 247	127	1	15	28	83	1 955	287	1 604	64
Actually reporting	1.0%	1 293	9	176	271	837	11 538	2 627	8 199	712
Estimated total	100.0%	1 301	9	177	273	842	11 624	2 642	8 260	722
Rate		407.2	2.8	55.4	85.4	263.5	3 637.9	826.9	2 585.1	226.0
Kansas City, MO-KS MSA										
Franklin, Johnson, Leavenworth, Linn, Miami, and Wyandotte Counties, KS; and Bates, Caldwell, Cass, Clay, Clinton, Jackson, Lafayette, Platte, and Ray Counties, MO	1 936 981									
City of Kansas City, MO	447 915	6 536	126	295	2 000	4 115	34 822	7 429	21 603	5 790
City of Overland Park, KS	163 274	494	2	30	63	399	4 559	488	3 661	410
City of Kansas City, KS	145 491	1 166	37	100	416	613	10 678	1 842	5 924	2 912
Actually reporting	1.0%	11 904	190	752	3 072	7 890	90 547	16 606	61 336	12 605
Estimated total	100.0%	11 907	190	752	3 073	7 892	90 587	16 612	61 367	12 608
Rate		614.7	9.8	38.8	158.6	407.4	4 676.7	857.6	3 168.2	650.9
Kennewick-Richland-Pasco, WA MSA										
Benton and Franklin Counties	218 379									
City of Kennewick	60 932	215	4	26	35	150	3 150	523	2 410	217
City of Richland	44 015	120	0	17	11	92	1 467	240	1 140	87
City of Pasco	42 862	98	0	19	29	50	2 015	413	1 389	213
Actually reporting	100.0%	520	7	69	82	362	8 135	1 526	5 917	692
Rate		238.1	3.2	31.6	37.5	165.8	3 725.2	698.8	2 709.5	316.9
Killeen-Temple-Fort Hood, TX MSA										
Bell, Coryell, and Lampasas Counties	351 810									
City of Killeen	98 538	806	8	85	224	489	5 862	2 071	3 644	147
City of Temple	55 402	175	3	5	57	110	2 546	502	1 893	151
Actually reporting	100.0%	1 341	16	172	337	816	12 949	3 782	8 676	491
Rate		381.2	4.5	48.9	95.8	231.9	3 680.7	1 075.0	2 466.1	139.6
Kingsport-Bristol-Bristol, TN-VA MSA										
Hawkins and Sullivan Counties, TN; and Scott and Washington Counties and Bristol City, VA	304 191									
City of Kingsport, TN	44 533	403	3	32	71	297	3 253	521	2 553	179
City of Bristol, TN	25 195	139	0	9	12	118	1 394	234	1 088	72
City of Bristol, VA	17 558	89	2	8	16	63	789	108	640	41
Actually reporting	100.0%	1 361	13	125	143	1 080	10 613	2 191	7 726	696
Rate		447.4	4.3	41.1	47.0	355.0	3 488.9	720.3	2 539.9	228.8

Note: Although arson data are included in the trend and clearance tables, sufficient data are not available to estimate totals for this offense.

Table 6. Crime, by Metropolitan Statistical Area, 2005—*Continued*

(Number, percent, rate per 100,000 inhabitants.)

Metropolitan statistical area	Population	Violent crime	Murder and non-negligent man-slaughter	Forcible rape	Robbery	Aggravated assault	Property crime	Burglary	Larceny-theft	Motor vehicle theft
Kingston, NY MSA										
Ulster County	182 039									
City of Kingston	23 252	117	0	11	72	34	1 091	114	928	49
Actually reporting	1.0%	561	3	65	105	388	3 502	565	2 768	169
Estimated total	100.0%	570	3	66	108	393	3 594	578	2 842	174
Rate		313.1	1.6	36.3	59.3	215.9	1 974.3	317.5	1 561.2	95.6
Knoxville, TN MSA										
Anderson, Blount, Knox, Loudon, and Union Counties	653 969									
City of Knoxville	179 989	1 728	25	99	545	1 059	11 062	2 471	7 370	1 221
Actually reporting	100.0%	3 158	39	194	731	2 194	24 892	6 033	16 514	2 345
Rate		482.9	6.0	29.7	111.8	335.5	3 806.3	922.5	2 525.2	358.6
Kokomo, IN MSA										
Howard and Tipton Counties	101 779									
City of Kokomo	46 324	196	11	24	71	90	2 990	666	2 181	143
Actually reporting	100.0%	300	12	33	80	175	4 285	1 109	2 967	209
Rate		294.8	11.8	32.4	78.6	171.9	4 210.1	1 089.6	2 915.1	205.3
La Crosse, WI-MN MSA										
Houston County, MN; and La Crosse County, WI	129 304									
City of La Crosse, WI	50 945	99	1	16	20	62	1 627	213	1 348	66
Actually reporting	1.0%	182	1	23	27	131	2 834	403	2 323	108
Estimated total	100.0%	191	1	25	29	136	3 005	427	2 458	120
Rate		147.7	0.8	19.3	22.4	105.2	2 324.0	330.2	1 900.9	92.8
Lafayette, IN MSA										
Benton, Carroll, and Tippecanoe Counties	182 513									
City of Lafayette	60 083	258	4	35	70	149	3 267	649	2 394	224
Actually reporting	0.8%	352	4	51	86	211	5 267	1 059	3 893	315
Estimated total	100.0%	385	4	55	91	235	5 708	1 156	4 200	352
Rate		210.9	2.2	30.1	49.9	128.8	3 127.4	633.4	2 301.2	192.9
Lafayette, LA MSA										
Lafayette and St. Martin Parishes	246 589									
City of Lafayette	112 161	991	8	91	141	751	6 342	1 233	4 691	418
Actually reporting	0.8%	1 307	13	116	187	991	8 325	1 773	5 943	609
Estimated total	100.0%	1 564	16	131	232	1 185	10 451	2 196	7 481	774
Rate		634.3	6.5	53.1	94.1	480.6	4 238.2	890.6	3 033.8	313.9
Lake Charles, LA MSA										
Calcasieu and Cameron Parishes	194 981									
City of Lake Charles	70 942	562	6	44	153	359	3 638	1 720	1 678	240
Actually reporting	0.9%	999	10	111	220	658	7 654	2 762	4 388	504
Estimated total	100.0%	1 154	12	118	246	778	9 056	3 008	5 449	599
Rate		591.9	6.2	60.5	126.2	399.0	4 644.6	1 542.7	2 794.6	307.2
Lakeland, FL MSA										
Polk County	536 226									
City of Lakeland	90 351	437	6	26	140	265	5 045	912	3 755	378
Actually reporting	100.0%	2 646	19	199	533	1 895	21 814	5 169	14 822	1 823
Rate		493.4	3.5	37.1	99.4	353.4	4 068.1	964.0	2 764.1	340.0
Lancaster, PA MSA										
Lancaster County	488 248									
City of Lancaster	55 286	420	1	32	189	198	3 025	549	2 271	205
Actually reporting	1.0%	792	6	82	305	399	10 416	2 015	7 796	605
Estimated total	100.0%	841	6	85	318	432	10 855	2 080	8 141	634
Rate		172.2	1.2	17.4	65.1	88.5	2 223.3	426.0	1 667.4	129.9
Lansing-East Lansing, MI MSA										
Clinton, Eaton, and Ingham Counties	456 300									
City of Lansing	117 036	1 407	8	115	254	1 030	4 745	1 129	3 204	412
City of East Lansing	46 716	175	0	20	40	115	1 129	202	874	53
Actually reporting	1.0%	2 159	16	264	376	1 503	13 418	2 720	9 872	826
Estimated total	100.0%	2 175	16	266	380	1 513	13 580	2 748	9 987	845
Rate		476.7	3.5	58.3	83.3	331.6	2 976.1	602.2	2 188.7	185.2
Laredo, TX MSA										
Webb County	223 074									
City of Laredo	206 555	1 054	18	64	246	726	12 462	1 552	9 953	957
Actually reporting	100.0%	1 121	23	71	253	774	12 866	1 660	10 219	987
Rate		502.5	10.3	31.8	113.4	347.0	5 767.6	744.1	4 581.0	442.5
Las Cruces, NM MSA										
Dona Ana County	188 549									
City of Las Cruces	80 573	465	5	96	101	263	3 949	750	2 954	245
Actually reporting	1.0%	785	8	149	120	508	5 960	1 382	4 140	438
Estimated total	100.0%	802	8	150	121	523	6 046	1 403	4 196	447
Rate		425.4	4.2	79.6	64.2	277.4	3 206.6	744.1	2 225.4	237.1
Las Vegas-Paradise, NV MSA										
Clark County	1 707 257									
City of Las Vegas Metropolitan Police Department	1 281 698	9 530	145	616	3 494	5 275	62 013	14 368	27 695	19 950
Actually reporting	100.0%	11 523	175	724	4 073	6 551	78 757	18 304	36 392	24 061
Rate		674.9	10.3	42.4	238.6	383.7	4 613.1	1 072.1	2 131.6	1 409.3
Lawrence, KS MSA										
Douglas County	103 131									
City of Lawrence	82 148	276	2	30	41	203	3 493	545	2 797	151
Actually reporting	100.0%	320	2	30	41	247	4 167	709	3 276	182
Rate		310.3	1.9	29.1	39.8	239.5	4 040.5	687.5	3 176.5	176.5

Note: Although arson data are included in the trend and clearance tables, sufficient data are not available to estimate totals for this offense.

Table 6. Crime, by Metropolitan Statistical Area, 2005—*Continued*

(Number, percent, rate per 100,000 inhabitants.)

Metropolitan statistical area	Population	Violent crime	Murder and non-negligent man-slaughter	Forcible rape	Robbery	Aggravated assault	Property crime	Burglary	Larceny-theft	Motor vehicle theft
Lawton, OK MSA										
Comanche County	111 277									
City of Lawton	88 823	669	6	41	135	487	4 653	1 362	3 078	213
Actually reporting	100.0%	721	6	45	138	532	4 976	1 452	3 276	248
Rate		647.9	5.4	40.4	124.0	478.1	4 471.7	1 304.9	2 944.0	222.9
Lebanon, PA MSA										
Lebanon County	124 723									
City of Lebanon	23 970	168	0	8	59	101	949	194	676	79
Actually reporting	0.9%	385	1	30	82	272	2 398	441	1 792	165
Estimated total	100.0%	414	1	32	90	291	2 648	478	1 988	182
Rate		331.9	0.8	25.7	72.2	233.3	2 123.1	383.2	1 593.9	145.9
Lewiston, ID-WA MSA										
Nez Perce County, ID; and Asotin County, WA	59 909									
City of Lewiston, ID	31 826	38	0	9	4	25	1 394	251	1 072	71
Actually reporting	1.0%	85	2	15	11	57	2 138	346	1 670	122
Estimated total	100.0%	88	2	15	11	60	2 180	355	1 700	125
Rate		146.9	3.3	25.0	18.4	100.2	3 638.9	592.6	2 837.6	208.6
Lewiston-Auburn, ME MSA										
Androscoggin County	107 367									
City of Lewiston	35 891	91	2	22	35	32	1 250	241	967	42
City of Auburn	23 627	17	0	3	6	8	821	103	683	35
Actually reporting	100.0%	131	3	30	44	54	2 882	506	2 241	135
Rate		122.0	2.8	27.9	41.0	50.3	2 684.3	471.3	2 087.2	125.7
Lexington-Fayette, KY MSA										
Bourbon, Clark, Fayette, Jessamine, Scott, and Woodford Counties	427 476									
City of Lexington	268 124	1 476	15	147	575	739	10 308	2 172	7 391	745
Actually reporting	1.0%	1 668	15	173	619	861	14 460	2 949	10 549	962
Estimated total	100.0%	1 725	15	180	638	892	15 238	3 089	11 136	1 013
Rate		403.5	3.5	42.1	149.2	208.7	3 564.6	722.6	2 605.1	237.0
Lima, OH MSA										
Allen County	106 920									
City of Lima	39 350	453	5	92	126	230	2 678	839	1 687	152
Actually reporting	0.8%	506	5	103	140	258	4 143	1 108	2 832	203
Estimated total	100.0%	536	5	108	151	272	4 637	1 198	3 204	235
Rate		501.3	4.7	101.0	141.2	254.4	4 336.9	1 120.5	2 996.6	219.8
Lincoln, NE MSA										
Lancaster and Seward Counties	280 043									
City of Lincoln	237 710	1 364	4	112	225	1 023	12 703	1 893	10 388	422
Actually reporting	100.0%	1 403	4	128	228	1 043	13 690	2 090	11 144	456
Rate		501.0	1.4	45.7	81.4	372.4	4 888.5	746.3	3 979.4	162.8
Little Rock-North Little Rock, AR MSA										
Faulkner, Grant, Lonoke, Perry, Pulaski, and Saline Counties	642 769									
City of Little Rock	185 855	3 293	41	116	860	2 276	16 322	3 803	11 409	1 110
City of North Little Rock	60 047	794	4	60	205	525	5 638	1 121	3 979	538
Actually reporting	1.0%	5 540	57	305	1 266	3 912	36 982	8 644	25 725	2 613
Estimated total	100.0%	5 550	57	306	1 268	3 919	37 070	8 667	25 785	2 618
Rate		863.5	8.9	47.6	197.3	609.7	5 767.2	1 348.4	4 011.6	407.3
Logan, UT-ID MSA										
Franklin County, ID; and Cache County, UT	113 266									
City of Logan, UT	47 052	38	1	16	5	16	1 044	162	842	40
Actually reporting	100.0%	76	2	34	7	33	2 101	338	1 690	73
Rate		67.1	1.8	30.0	6.2	29.1	1 854.9	298.4	1 492.1	64.5
Longview, TX MSA										
Gregg, Rusk, and Upshur Counties	203 701									
City of Longview	74 879	828	8	66	124	630	4 818	1 063	3 200	555
Actually reporting	1.0%	1 347	18	99	171	1 059	9 656	2 168	6 584	904
Estimated total	100.0%	1 350	18	99	172	1 061	9 702	2 177	6 618	907
Rate		662.7	8.8	48.6	84.4	520.9	4 762.9	1 068.7	3 248.9	445.3
Longview, WA MSA										
Cowlitz County	97 491									
City of Longview	36 430	147	3	24	32	88	3 136	748	2 076	312
Actually reporting	100.0%	308	3	66	55	184	5 935	1 464	3 873	598
Rate		315.9	3.1	67.7	56.4	188.7	6 087.7	1 501.7	3 972.7	613.4

Note: Although arson data are included in the trend and clearance tables, sufficient data are not available to estimate totals for this offense.

Table 6. Crime, by Metropolitan Statistical Area, 2005—*Continued*

(Number, percent, rate per 100,000 inhabitants.)

Metropolitan statistical area	Population	Violent crime	Murder and non-negligent man-slaughter	Forcible rape	Robbery	Aggravated assault	Property crime	Burglary	Larceny-theft	Motor vehicle theft
Los Angeles-Long Beach-Santa Ana, CA MSA[1]										
Metropolitan divisions of Los Angeles-Long Beach-Glendale and Santa Ana-Anaheim-Irvine	13 011 161									
City of Los Angeles[1]	3 871 077	31 767	489	1 105	13 797	16 376	117 285	22 592	65 972	28 721
City of Long Beach	479 729	3 399	42	104	1 403	1 850	13 506	2 955	6 808	3 743
City of Santa Ana	344 991	1 845	17	74	644	1 110	10 292	1 194	5 515	3 583
City of Anaheim	335 992	1 616	10	81	554	971	9 512	1 929	5 537	2 046
City of Glendale	202 663	350	19	14	136	181	3 790	723	2 453	614
City of Irvine	179 501	151	2	17	42	90	3 225	709	2 211	305
City of Pomona	156 480	1 235	21	44	385	785	5 308	997	2 775	1 536
City of Torrance	143 790	320	1	20	211	88	3 290	641	2 144	505
City of Pasadena	145 025	803	6	23	285	489	4 389	788	3 041	560
City of Orange	134 708	225	2	2	100	121	3 419	537	2 301	581
City of Fullerton	134 325	390	0	37	149	204	4 584	805	3 152	627
City of Costa Mesa	111 144	306	3	30	119	154	3 843	596	2 692	555
City of Burbank	104 805	246	3	13	67	163	2 771	586	1 690	495
City of Compton	96 874	1 731	65	40	474	1 152	2 615	638	971	1 006
City of Carson	94 355	646	7	19	221	399	2 402	543	1 270	589
City of Santa Monica	88 406	551	4	21	241	285	3 496	788	2 286	422
City of Newport Beach	80 488	122	3	12	26	81	2 496	589	1 715	192
City of Tustin	69 068	228	2	10	60	156	1 926	438	1 146	342
City of Montebello	64 123	282	5	18	125	134	2 143	300	1 094	749
City of Monterey Park	62 812	149	2	4	89	54	1 395	274	707	414
City of Gardena	60 124	496	3	16	295	182	1 594	453	715	426
City of Paramount	57 277	452	10	4	221	217	2 082	358	956	768
City of Fountain Valley	56 726	72	1	6	30	35	1 383	303	884	196
City of Arcadia	56 364	136	2	7	61	66	1 849	433	1 254	162
City of Cerritos	53 249	175	1	5	97	72	2 020	453	1 287	280
Actually reporting	100.0%	74 880	1 145	2 822	29 445	41 468	358 169	72 263	202 208	83 698
Rate		575.5	8.8	21.7	226.3	318.7	2 752.8	555.4	1 554.1	643.3
Los Angeles-Long Beach-Glendale, CA M.D.[1]										
Los Angeles County	10 003 731									
Actually reporting	100.0%	66 351	1 069	2 384	26 694	36 204	286 163	58 861	156 681	70 621
Rate		663.3	10.7	23.8	266.8	361.9	2 860.6	588.4	1 566.2	705.9
Santa Ana-Anaheim-Irvine, CA M.D.										
Orange County	3 007 430									
Actually reporting	100.0%	8 529	76	438	2 751	5 264	72 006	13 402	45 527	13 077
Rate		283.6	2.5	14.6	91.5	175.0	2 394.3	445.6	1 513.8	434.8
Louisville-Jefferson County, KY-IN MSA[1]										
Clark, Floyd, Harrison, and Washington Counties, IN; and Bullitt, Henry, Jefferson, Meade, Nelson, Oldham, Shelby, Spencer, and Trimble Counties, KY	1 208 545									
City of Louisville Metro, KY[1]	623 735	3 896	55	209	1 822	1 810	27 446	7 146	17 150	3 150
Actually reporting	1.0%	4 871	65	298	2 136	2 372	40 640	10 064	26 316	4 260
Estimated total	100.0%	4 987	65	311	2 169	2 442	42 168	10 350	27 446	4 372
Rate		412.6	5.4	25.7	179.5	202.1	3 489.2	856.4	2 271.0	361.8
Lubbock, TX MSA										
Crosby and Lubbock Counties	261 901									
City of Lubbock	211 271	2 222	11	105	309	1 797	12 786	2 697	9 312	777
Actually reporting	100.0%	2 369	14	125	323	1 907	14 430	3 249	10 264	917
Rate		904.5	5.3	47.7	123.3	728.1	5 509.7	1 240.5	3 919.0	350.1
Lynchburg, VA MSA										
Amherst, Appomattox, Bedford, and Campbell Counties and Bedford and Lynchburg Cities	235 893									
City of Lynchburg	65 869	257	6	23	73	155	2 390	412	1 805	173
Actually reporting	100.0%	477	10	53	107	307	4 724	825	3 574	325
Rate		202.2	4.2	22.5	45.4	130.1	2 002.6	349.7	1 515.1	137.8
Macon, GA MSA										
Bibb, Crawford, Jones, Monroe, and Twiggs Counties	234 455									
City of Macon	97 606	816	20	58	332	406	9 217	2 028	6 124	1 065
Actually reporting	1.0%	1 156	28	76	383	669	14 279	3 207	9 473	1 599
Estimated total	100.0%	1 176	28	77	390	681	14 491	3 243	9 629	1 619
Rate		501.6	11.9	32.8	166.3	290.5	6 180.7	1 383.2	4 107.0	690.5
Madera, CA MSA										
Madera County	139 874									
City of Madera	50 375	399	4	22	88	285	1 808	367	1 085	356
Actually reporting	100.0%	731	10	44	113	564	4 116	1 133	2 170	813
Rate		522.6	7.1	31.5	80.8	403.2	2 942.6	810.0	1 551.4	581.2
Madison, WI MSA										
Columbia, Dane, and Iowa Counties	534 388									
City of Madison	221 419	839	2	80	329	428	7 737	1 449	5 682	606
Actually reporting	1.0%	1 223	2	135	416	670	15 125	2 430	11 827	868
Estimated total	100.0%	1 226	2	135	417	672	15 196	2 440	11 885	871
Rate		229.4	0.4	25.3	78.0	125.8	2 843.6	456.6	2 224.0	163.0
Manchester-Nashua, NH MSA										
Hillsborough County	401 776									
City of Manchester	110 188	308	4	73	140	91	3 518	693	2 570	255
City of Nashua	88 113	164	2	20	28	114	2 061	308	1 622	131
Actually reporting	0.9%	600	7	117	197	279	7 920	1 377	6 033	510
Estimated total	100.0%	618	7	122	200	289	8 180	1 419	6 237	524
Rate		153.8	1.7	30.4	49.8	71.9	2 036.0	353.2	1 552.4	130.4

Note: Although arson data are included in the trend and clearance tables, sufficient data are not available to estimate totals for this offense.

[1]Because of changes in the state/local agency's reporting practices, figures are not comparable to previous years' data.

Table 6. Crime, by Metropolitan Statistical Area, 2005—*Continued*

(Number, percent, rate per 100,000 inhabitants.)

Metropolitan statistical area	Population	Violent crime	Murder and non-negligent man-slaughter	Forcible rape	Robbery	Aggravated assault	Property crime	Burglary	Larceny-theft	Motor vehicle theft
Mansfield, OH MSA										
Richland County	128 152									
City of Mansfield	50 579	161	0	31	94	36	3 343	906	2 217	220
Actually reporting	1.0%	227	2	50	115	60	5 720	1 377	4 056	287
Estimated total	100.0%	231	2	51	116	62	5 779	1 388	4 100	291
Rate		180.3	1.6	39.8	90.5	48.4	4 509.5	1 083.1	3 199.3	227.1
McAllen-Edinburg-Mission, TX MSA										
Hidalgo County	669 076									
City of McAllen	122 729	421	8	34	129	250	8 187	734	6 877	576
City of Edinburg	59 409	442	1	31	67	343	4 945	712	3 887	346
City of Mission	58 763	72	4	5	20	43	3 437	619	2 497	321
City of Pharr	57 774	198	4	17	52	125	2 912	573	2 183	156
Actually reporting	1.0%	3 099	37	232	515	2 315	35 082	6 816	25 855	2 411
Estimated total	100.0%	3 103	37	232	516	2 318	35 140	6 827	25 898	2 415
Rate		463.8	5.5	34.7	77.1	346.4	5 252.0	1 020.4	3 870.7	360.9
Medford, OR MSA										
Jackson County	195 487									
City of Medford	68 979	325	1	28	53	243	4 290	556	3 455	279
Actually reporting	1.0%	591	5	65	76	445	7 578	1 233	5 861	484
Estimated total	100.0%	592	5	65	76	446	7 596	1 236	5 874	486
Rate		302.8	2.6	33.3	38.9	228.1	3 885.7	632.3	3 004.8	248.6
Memphis, TN-MS-AR MSA										
Crittenden County, AR; DeSoto, Marshall, Tate, and Tunica Counties, MS; and Fayette, Shelby, and Tipton Counties, TN	1 262 520									
City of Memphis	678 988	12 629	137	400	4 464	7 628	56 780	15 844	32 632	8 304
Actually reporting	1.0%	15 063	174	563	4 913	9 413	76 271	21 057	45 083	10 131
Estimated total	100.0%	15 110	175	572	4 921	9 442	76 835	21 216	45 419	10 200
Rate		1 196.8	13.9	45.3	389.8	747.9	6 085.8	1 680.4	3 597.5	807.9
Merced, CA MSA										
Merced County	238 579									
City of Merced	72 968	572	10	24	167	371	4 189	697	2 957	535
Actually reporting	100.0%	1 496	22	82	249	1 143	9 451	2 308	5 730	1 413
Rate		627.0	9.2	34.4	104.4	479.1	3 961.4	967.4	2 401.7	592.3
Miami-Fort Lauderdale-Miami Beach, FL MSA										
Metropolitan divisions of Fort Lauderdale-Pompano Beach-Deerfield Beach, Miami-Miami Beach-Kendall, and West Palm Beach-Boca Raton-Boynton Beach	5 482 749									
City of Miami	388 295	6 134	54	62	2 019	3 999	23 321	5 377	13 930	4 014
City of Fort Lauderdale	168 293	1 503	15	67	741	680	11 216	2 555	7 564	1 097
City of Miami Beach	91 115	1 173	3	62	515	593	8 121	1 463	5 681	977
City of West Palm Beach	97 496	1 221	22	71	528	600	7 182	1 605	4 610	967
City of Pompano Beach	90 880	1 382	5	57	420	900	5 248	958	3 676	614
City of Boca Raton	79 831	241	0	15	53	173	2 844	591	2 071	182
City of Deerfield Beach	67 683	593	2	35	144	412	2 517	485	1 767	265
City of Boynton Beach	66 237	497	1	4	139	353	3 408	720	2 381	307
City of Delray Beach	65 598	658	6	26	132	494	3 207	595	2 293	319
Actually reporting	100.0%	43 013	303	1 799	13 209	27 702	247 192	51 778	164 776	30 638
Rate		784.5	5.5	32.8	240.9	505.3	4 508.5	944.4	3 005.4	558.8
Fort Lauderdale-Pompano Beach-Deerfield Beach, FL M.D.										
Broward County	1 794 506									
Actually reporting	100.0%	10 596	63	541	3 372	6 620	65 530	13 414	44 903	7 213
Rate		590.5	3.5	30.1	187.9	368.9	3 651.7	747.5	2 502.2	401.9
Miami-Miami Beach-Kendall, FL M.D.										
Miami-Dade County	2 416 950									
Actually reporting	100.0%	23 907	171	778	7 385	15 573	127 115	25 588	84 253	17 274
Rate		989.1	7.1	32.2	305.6	644.3	5 259.3	1 058.7	3 485.9	714.7
West Palm Beach-Boca Raton-Boynton Beach, FL M.D.										
Palm Beach County	1 271 293									
Actually reporting	100.0%	8 510	69	480	2 452	5 509	54 547	12 776	35 620	6 151
Rate		669.4	5.4	37.8	192.9	433.3	4 290.7	1 005.0	2 801.9	483.8
Michigan City-La Porte, IN MSA										
La Porte County	110 360									
City of Michigan City	32 356	136	4	14	70	48	1 883	213	1 515	155
City of La Porte	21 098	25	0	4	7	14	1 433	137	1 235	61
Actually reporting	0.9%	194	7	23	83	81	3 934	505	3 152	277
Estimated total	100.0%	224	7	25	91	101	4 268	557	3 404	307
Rate		203.0	6.3	22.7	82.5	91.5	3 867.3	504.7	3 084.5	278.2
Midland, TX MSA										
Midland County	122 324									
City of Midland	99 695	408	1	80	50	277	3 765	779	2 808	178
Actually reporting	100.0%	451	1	80	56	314	4 224	893	3 126	205
Rate		368.7	0.8	65.4	45.8	256.7	3 453.1	730.0	2 555.5	167.6

Note: Although arson data are included in the trend and clearance tables, sufficient data are not available to estimate totals for this offense.

Table 6. Crime, by Metropolitan Statistical Area, 2005—*Continued*

(Number, percent, rate per 100,000 inhabitants.)

Metropolitan statistical area	Population	Violent crime	Murder and non-negligent man-slaughter	Forcible rape	Robbery	Aggravated assault	Property crime	Burglary	Larceny-theft	Motor vehicle theft
Milwaukee-Waukesha-West Allis, WI MSA[1]										
Milwaukee, Ozaukee, Washington, and Waukesha Counties	1 523 217									
City of Milwaukee[1]	586 500	6 010	121	158	2 927	2 804	32 812	4 570	21 611	6 631
City of Waukesha	67 590	95	0	27	19	49	1 322	266	959	97
City of West Allis	59 802	190	4	18	81	87	2 659	476	1 960	223
Actually reporting	1.0%	6 914	131	301	3 268	3 214	52 330	7 359	37 252	7 719
Estimated total	100.0%	6 975	131	310	3 287	3 247	53 640	7 537	38 325	7 778
Rate		457.9	8.6	20.4	215.8	213.2	3 521.5	494.8	2 516.1	510.6
Missoula, MT MSA[1]										
Missoula County	99 959									
City of Missoula	62 377	254	1	40	40	173	3 629	395	3 046	188
Actually reporting	100.0%	321	3	55	40	223	4 549	525	3 778	246
Rate		321.1	3.0	55.0	40.0	223.1	4 550.9	525.2	3 779.5	246.1
Mobile, AL MSA										
Mobile County	402 968									
City of Mobile[3]	249 798	1 165	35	74	597	459	14 349	3 832	9 396	1 121
Actually reporting	1.0%	1 585	50	105	703	727	18 602	5 071	11 979	1 552
Estimated total	100.0%	1 600	50	106	708	736	18 763	5 103	12 097	1 563
Rate		397.1	12.4	26.3	175.7	182.6	4 656.2	1 266.4	3 002.0	387.9
Modesto, CA MSA										
Stanislaus County	501 664									
City of Modesto	208 142	1 316	8	65	388	855	13 046	1 742	8 290	3 014
Actually reporting	100.0%	3 080	30	129	663	2 258	27 180	4 836	15 988	6 356
Rate		614.0	6.0	25.7	132.2	450.1	5 418.0	964.0	3 187.0	1 267.0
Monroe, LA MSA										
Ouachita and Union Parishes	171 547									
City of Monroe	52 232	607	3	33	61	510	4 685	988	3 575	122
Actually reporting	1.0%	1 014	7	61	109	837	8 480	2 000	6 199	281
Estimated total	100.0%	1 033	7	62	112	852	8 660	2 032	6 335	293
Rate		602.2	4.1	36.1	65.3	496.7	5 048.2	1 184.5	3 692.9	170.8
Monroe, MI MSA										
Monroe County	152 676									
City of Monroe	21 708	73	0	9	13	51	663	119	497	47
Actually reporting	100.0%	323	2	62	49	210	3 613	831	2 433	349
Rate		211.6	1.3	40.6	32.1	137.5	2 366.4	544.3	1 593.6	228.6
Montgomery, AL MSA										
Autauga, Elmore, Lowndes, and Montgomery	357 347									
City of Montgomery	202 209	1 641	29	109	847	656	12 997	3 528	8 449	1 020
Actually reporting	0.9%	1 894	32	146	907	809	15 879	4 325	10 363	1 191
Estimated total	100.0%	2 019	33	157	943	886	17 186	4 649	11 250	1 287
Rate		565.0	9.2	43.9	263.9	247.9	4 809.3	1 301.0	3 148.2	360.2
Morgantown, WV MSA										
Monongalia and Preston Counties	113 868									
City of Morgantown	28 183	109	0	21	30	58	1 030	251	758	21
Actually reporting	1.0%	283	2	28	52	201	2 623	662	1 848	113
Estimated total	100.0%	289	2	28	53	206	2 711	677	1 915	119
Rate		253.8	1.8	24.6	46.5	180.9	2 380.8	594.5	1 681.8	104.5
Morristown, TN MSA										
Grainger, Hamblen, and Jefferson	130 365									
City of Morristown	25 730	248	2	11	37	198	1 788	204	1 441	143
Actually reporting	100.0%	546	2	31	63	450	4 434	835	3 177	422
Rate		418.8	1.5	23.8	48.3	345.2	3 401.2	640.5	2 437.0	323.7
Mount Vernon-Anacortes, WA MSA										
Skagit County	112 567									
City of Mount Vernon	29 211	76	0	23	17	36	2 618	330	2 107	181
City of Anacortes	15 977	22	0	4	4	14	780	135	596	49
Actually reporting	100.0%	241	3	60	52	126	8 408	1 592	6 229	587
Rate		214.1	2.7	53.3	46.2	111.9	7 469.3	1 414.3	5 533.6	521.5
Muncie, IN MSA										
Delaware County	118 424									
City of Muncie	67 536	314	1	74	65	174	2 783	552	2 059	172
Actually reporting	100.0%	346	2	79	71	194	3 748	699	2 820	229
Rate		292.2	1.7	66.7	60.0	163.8	3 164.9	590.3	2 381.3	193.4
Muskegon-Norton Shores, MI MSA										
Muskegon County	174 543									
City of Muskegon	39 987	464	3	57	99	305	2 817	523	2 056	238
City of Norton Shores	23 306	35	0	5	5	25	1 013	129	854	30
Actually reporting	100.0%	982	4	141	170	667	8 352	1 404	6 380	568
Rate		562.6	2.3	80.8	97.4	382.1	4 785.1	804.4	3 655.3	325.4
Myrtle Beach-Conway-North Myrtle Beach, SC MSA										
Horry County	220 563									
City of Myrtle Beach	25 755	501	3	54	193	251	5 141	851	3 834	456
City of Conway	13 474	137	4	4	35	94	1 071	175	843	53
City of North Myrtle Beach	13 339	61	2	6	16	37	1 461	258	1 136	67
Actually reporting	100.0%	1 898	29	116	413	1 340	15 135	2 986	10 712	1 437
Rate		860.5	13.1	52.6	187.2	607.5	6 862.0	1 353.8	4 856.7	651.5

Note: Although arson data are included in the trend and clearance tables, sufficient data are not available to estimate totals for this offense.

[1]Because of changes in the state/local agency's reporting practices, figures are not comparable to previous years' data.
[3]The population for the city of Mobile, Alabama, includes 55,864 inhabitants from the jurisdiction of the Mobile County Sheriff's Department.

Table 6. Crime, by Metropolitan Statistical Area, 2005—*Continued*

(Number, percent, rate per 100,000 inhabitants.)

Metropolitan statistical area	Population	Violent crime	Murder and non-negligent man-slaughter	Forcible rape	Robbery	Aggravated assault	Property crime	Burglary	Larceny-theft	Motor vehicle theft
Napa, CA MSA										
Napa County	133 218									
City of Napa	75 966	384	0	19	34	331	2 080	359	1 553	168
Actually reporting	100.0%	477	1	36	44	396	3 272	652	2 272	348
Rate		358.1	0.8	27.0	33.0	297.3	2 456.1	489.4	1 705.5	261.2
Naples-Marco Island, FL MSA										
Collier County	303 375									
City of Naples	21 965	40	0	4	4	32	732	101	615	16
City of Marco Island	16 185	22	0	2	0	20	229	37	188	4
Actually reporting	100.0%	1 343	9	95	218	1 021	6 404	1 413	4 569	422
Rate		442.7	3.0	31.3	71.9	336.5	2 110.9	465.8	1 506.1	139.1
Nashville-Davidson–Murfreesboro, TN MSA										
Cannon, Cheatham, Davidson, Dickson, Hickman, Macon, Robertson, Rutherford, Smith, Sumner, Trousdale, Williamson, and Wilson Counties	1 410 545									
City of Nashville	557 034	8 974	95	336	2 440	6 103	35 796	6 448	25 900	3 448
City of Murfreesboro	82 367	641	2	35	113	491	4 021	790	2 994	237
Actually reporting	100.0%	12 611	114	632	2 831	9 034	58 333	10 936	42 211	5 186
Rate		894.1	8.1	44.8	200.7	640.5	4 135.5	775.3	2 992.5	367.7
New York-Northern New Jersey-Long Island, NY-NJ-PA MSA										
Metropolitan divisions of Edison, NJ; Nassau-Suffolk County, NY; Newark-Union, NJ-PA; and New York-Wayne-White Plains, NY-NJ	18 741 475									
City of New York, NY	8 115 690	54 623	539	1 412	24 722	27 950	162 509	23 210	120 918	18 381
City of Newark, NJ	281 063	2 821	97	83	1 250	1 391	12 720	2 056	4 974	5 690
City of Edison Township, NJ	100 361	231	0	6	71	154	2 456	470	1 715	271
City of White Plains, NY	56 590	177	1	7	46	123	1 267	69	1 142	56
City of Union Township, NJ	55 758	170	1	14	88	67	1 589	199	1 139	251
City of Wayne Township, NJ	55 523	58	1	0	19	38	1 246	110	1 043	93
Actually reporting	1.0%	84 875	928	2 484	38 034	43 429	369 355	59 308	263 173	46 874
Estimated total	100.0%	84 967	929	2 489	38 066	43 483	370 274	59 442	263 908	46 924
Rate		453.4	5.0	13.3	203.1	232.0	1 975.7	317.2	1 408.1	250.4
Edison, NJ M.D.										
Middlesex, Monmouth, Ocean, and Somerset Counties	2 296 411									
Actually reporting	100.0%	3 960	26	243	1 382	2 309	43 073	7 713	32 374	2 986
Rate		172.4	1.1	10.6	60.2	100.5	1 875.7	335.9	1 409.8	130.0
Nassau-Suffolk, NY M.D.										
Nassau and Suffolk Counties	2 819 162									
Actually reporting	1.0%	5 678	55	209	2 357	3 057	47 291	7 114	35 795	4 382
Estimated total	100.0%	5 685	55	209	2 360	3 061	47 367	7 125	35 856	4 386
Rate		201.7	2.0	7.4	83.7	108.6	1 680.2	252.7	1 271.9	155.6
Newark-Union, NJ-PA M.D.										
Essex, Hunterdon, Morris, Sussex, and Union Counties, NJ; and Pike County, PA	2 157 592									
Actually reporting	1.0%	9 237	194	303	4 437	4 303	54 035	9 907	30 724	13 404
Estimated total	100.0%	9 250	194	304	4 440	4 312	54 147	9 924	30 812	13 411
Rate		428.7	9.0	14.1	205.8	199.9	2 509.6	460.0	1 428.1	621.6
New York-White Plains-Wayne, NY-NJ M.D.										
Bergen, Hudson, and Passaic Counties, NJ; and Bronx, Kings, New York, Putnam, Queens, Richmond, Rockland, and Westchester Counties, NY	11 468 310									
Actually reporting	1.0%	66 000	653	1 729	29 858	33 760	224 956	34 574	164 280	26 102
Estimated total	100.0%	66 072	654	1 733	29 884	33 801	225 687	34 680	164 866	26 141
Rate		576.1	5.7	15.1	260.6	294.7	1 967.9	302.4	1 437.6	227.9
Niles-Benton Harbor, MI MSA										
Berrien County	163 258									
City of Niles	11 886	113	0	14	27	72	493	67	395	31
City of Benton Harbor	10 860	238	0	13	10	215	395	137	213	45
Actually reporting	1.0%	787	5	109	80	593	5 101	892	3 916	293
Estimated total	100.0%	795	5	110	82	598	5 180	906	3 972	302
Rate		487.0	3.1	67.4	50.2	366.3	3 172.9	554.9	2 433.0	185.0
Norwich-New London, CT MSA										
New London County	141 228									
City of Norwich	36 715	185	0	27	51	107	1 048	224	748	76
City of New London	26 369	178	1	27	63	87	936	195	627	114
Actually reporting	100.0%	468	2	77	132	257	3 642	661	2 721	260
Rate		331.4	1.4	54.5	93.5	182.0	2 578.8	468.0	1 926.7	184.1
Ocala, FL MSA										
Marion County	297 898									
City of Ocala	50 005	587	4	43	157	383	3 416	804	2 408	204
Actually reporting	100.0%	2 097	16	155	251	1 675	8 582	2 500	5 469	613
Rate		703.9	5.4	52.0	84.3	562.3	2 880.9	839.2	1 835.9	205.8
Ocean City, NJ MSA										
Cape May County	100 979									
City of Ocean City	15 540	28	0	0	13	15	971	152	805	14
Actually reporting	100.0%	310	2	14	76	218	4 482	899	3 429	154
Rate		307.0	2.0	13.9	75.3	215.9	4 438.5	890.3	3 395.8	152.5

Note: Although arson data are included in the trend and clearance tables, sufficient data are not available to estimate totals for this offense.

Table 6. Crime, by Metropolitan Statistical Area, 2005—*Continued*

(Number, percent, rate per 100,000 inhabitants.)

Metropolitan statistical area	Population	Violent crime	Murder and non-negligent man-slaughter	Forcible rape	Robbery	Aggravated assault	Property crime	Burglary	Larceny-theft	Motor vehicle theft
Odessa, TX MSA										
Ector County	126 536									
City of Odessa	94 371	590	3	12	72	503	3 720	756	2 785	179
Actually reporting	100.0%	632	6	15	76	535	5 023	969	3 815	239
Rate		499.5	4.7	11.9	60.1	422.8	3 969.6	765.8	3 015.0	188.9
Ogden-Clearfield, UT MSA										
Davis, Morgan, and Weber Counties	493 553									
City of Ogden	81 166	383	5	40	121	217	4 931	797	3 723	411
City of Clearfield	28 145	37	0	14	6	17	891	120	714	57
Actually reporting	100.0%	860	10	165	202	483	15 443	2 432	11 974	1 037
Rate		174.2	2.0	33.4	40.9	97.9	3 128.9	492.8	2 426.1	210.1
Oklahoma City, OK MSA										
Canadian, Cleveland, Grady, Lincoln, Logan, McClain, and Oklahoma Counties	1 152 229									
City of Oklahoma City	531 688	4 538	54	358	1 193	2 933	42 145	8 925	28 635	4 585
Actually reporting	100.0%	6 138	64	551	1 450	4 073	61 591	13 426	42 038	6 127
Rate		532.7	5.6	47.8	125.8	353.5	5 345.4	1 165.2	3 648.4	531.8
Olympia, WA MSA										
Thurston County	227 714									
City of Olympia	44 577	115	0	24	26	65	2 549	467	1 849	233
Actually reporting	100.0%	596	2	65	101	428	8 590	1 793	5 983	814
Rate		261.7	0.9	28.5	44.4	188.0	3 772.3	787.4	2 627.4	357.5
Omaha-Council Bluffs, NE-IA MSA										
Harrison, Mills, and Pottawattamie Counties, IA; and Cass, Douglas, Sarpy, Saunders, and Washington Counties, NE	808 810									
City of Omaha, NE	412 128	2 327	31	199	682	1 415	22 056	3 164	15 079	3 813
City of Council Bluffs, IA	59 586	725	0	61	79	585	5 145	1 034	3 435	676
Actually reporting	1.0%	3 458	33	327	817	2 281	33 498	5 358	23 102	5 038
Estimated total	100.0%	3 481	33	330	820	2 298	33 774	5 420	23 293	5 061
Rate		430.4	4.1	40.8	101.4	284.1	4 175.8	670.1	2 879.9	625.7
Orlando-Kissimmee, FL MSA										
Lake, Orange, Osceola, and Seminole Counties	1 903 731									
City of Orlando	210 290	3 801	22	165	1 204	2 410	18 226	3 882	12 175	2 169
City of Kissimmee	57 421	541	1	30	131	379	2 652	716	1 732	204
Actually reporting	100.0%	15 637	103	807	3 954	10 773	82 127	20 743	52 158	9 226
Rate		821.4	5.4	42.4	207.7	565.9	4 314.0	1 089.6	2 739.8	484.6
Oshkosh-Neenah, WI MSA										
Winnebago County	159 792									
City of Oshkosh	63 828	183	0	12	17	154	1 853	297	1 496	60
City of Neenah	24 678	28	0	6	2	20	411	79	324	8
Actually reporting	100.0%	305	1	28	21	255	3 391	640	2 623	128
Rate		190.9	0.6	17.5	13.1	159.6	2 122.1	400.5	1 641.5	80.1
Owensboro, KY MSA										
Daviess, Hancock, and McLean Counties	111 764									
City of Owensboro	55 264	148	4	16	50	78	2 072	438	1 564	70
Actually reporting	1.0%	191	5	20	56	110	2 581	602	1 894	85
Estimated total	100.0%	193	5	20	57	111	2 614	608	1 919	87
Rate		172.7	4.5	17.9	51.0	99.3	2 338.9	544.0	1 717.0	77.8
Oxnard-Thousand Oaks-Ventura, CA MSA										
Ventura County	802 996									
City of Oxnard	184 806	830	19	47	386	378	4 384	941	2 681	762
City of Thousand Oaks	125 884	174	2	13	56	103	1 784	379	1 289	116
City of Ventura	104 759	297	1	19	107	170	3 911	815	2 695	401
City of Camarillo	61 294	94	1	15	30	48	1 046	259	710	77
Actually reporting	100.0%	2 083	32	146	729	1 176	16 727	3 773	10 966	1 988
Rate		259.4	4.0	18.2	90.8	146.5	2 083.1	469.9	1 365.6	247.6
Palm Bay-Melbourne-Titusville, FL MSA										
Brevard County	531 111									
City of Palm Bay	90 762	482	2	42	79	359	3 269	1 032	1 999	238
City of Melbourne	77 067	684	1	30	124	529	3 657	884	2 557	216
City of Titusville	43 576	346	4	21	79	242	1 512	417	909	186
Actually reporting	100.0%	3 311	18	218	499	2 576	17 035	4 348	11 499	1 188
Rate		623.4	3.4	41.0	94.0	485.0	3 207.4	818.7	2 165.1	223.7
Panama City-Lynn Haven, FL MSA										
Bay County	161 514									
City of Panama City	37 916	336	2	19	76	239	2 074	363	1 607	104
City of Lynn Haven	14 994	38	0	1	4	33	368	76	265	27
Actually reporting	100.0%	1 068	4	93	164	807	6 754	1 373	5 001	380
Rate		661.2	2.5	57.6	101.5	499.6	4 181.7	850.1	3 096.3	235.3
Parkersburg-Marietta-Vienna, WV-OH MSA										
Washington County, OH; and Pleasants, Wirt, and Wood Counties, WV	163 063									
City of Parkersburg, WV	32 186	140	3	12	30	95	1 645	347	1 191	107
City of Marietta, OH	14 301	28	0	13	5	10	535	107	402	26
City of Vienna, WV	10 776	18	0	0	3	15	339	20	312	7
Actually reporting	1.0%	438	5	45	54	334	4 054	889	2 927	238
Estimated total	100.0%	440	5	45	55	335	4 102	898	2 963	241
Rate		269.8	3.1	27.6	33.7	205.4	2 515.6	550.7	1 817.1	147.8

Note: Although arson data are included in the trend and clearance tables, sufficient data are not available to estimate totals for this offense.

Table 6. Crime, by Metropolitan Statistical Area, 2005—*Continued*

(Number, percent, rate per 100,000 inhabitants.)

Metropolitan statistical area	Population	Violent crime	Murder and non-negligent man-slaughter	Forcible rape	Robbery	Aggravated assault	Property crime	Burglary	Larceny-theft	Motor vehicle theft
Pascagoula, MS MSA										
George and Jackson Counties	157 249									
City of Pascagoula	26 035	139	3	38	54	44	2 019	703	1 133	183
Actually reporting	100.0%	383	12	74	119	178	5 813	1 828	3 333	652
Rate		243.6	7.6	47.1	75.7	113.2	3 696.7	1 162.5	2 119.6	414.6
Pensacola-Ferry Pass-Brent, FL MSA										
Escambia and Santa Rosa Counties	447 002									
City of Pensacola	55 970	448	1	37	89	321	2 424	423	1 824	177
Actually reporting	100.0%	2 723	12	187	479	2 045	14 157	3 363	9 622	1 172
Rate		609.2	2.7	41.8	107.2	457.5	3 167.1	752.3	2 152.6	262.2
Philadelphia-Camden-Wilmington, PA-NJ-DE-MD MSA										
Metropolitan divisions of Camden, NJ; Philadelphia, PA; and Wilmington, DE-MD-NJ	5 819 726									
City of Philadelphia, PA	1 472 915	21 609	377	1 024	10 069	10 139	60 419	10 960	38 039	11 420
City of Camden, NJ	80 125	1 680	33	47	702	898	4 307	1 020	2 332	955
City of Wilmington, DE	73 938	1 049	12	27	433	577	3 434	817	2 104	513
Actually reporting	1.0%	36 286	535	1 862	14 655	19 234	157 580	28 843	108 727	20 010
Estimated total	100.0%	36 462	537	1 874	14 701	19 350	159 104	29 069	109 924	20 111
Rate		626.5	9.2	32.2	252.6	332.5	2 733.9	499.5	1 888.8	345.6
Camden, NJ M.D.										
Burlington, Camden, and Gloucester Counties	1 240 483									
Actually reporting	100.0%	4 358	48	261	1 549	2 500	31 255	6 310	22 149	2 796
Rate		351.3	3.9	21.0	124.9	201.5	2 519.6	508.7	1 785.5	225.4
Philadelphia, PA M.D.										
Bucks, Chester, Delaware, Montgomery, and Philadelphia Counties	3 889 872									
Actually reporting	1.0%	27 844	454	1 384	11 885	14 121	104 847	17 545	72 267	15 035
Estimated total	100.0%	28 020	456	1 396	11 931	14 237	106 371	17 771	73 464	15 136
Rate		720.3	11.7	35.9	306.7	366.0	2 734.6	456.9	1 888.6	389.1
Wilmington, DE-MD-NJ M.D.										
New Castle County, DE; Cecil County, MD; and Salem County, NJ	689 371									
Actually reporting	100.0%	4 084	33	217	1 221	2 613	21 478	4 988	14 311	2 179
Rate		592.4	4.8	31.5	177.1	379.0	3 115.6	723.6	2 076.0	316.1
Phoenix-Mesa-Scottsdale, AZ MSA										
Maricopa and Pinal Counties	3 841 790									
City of Phoenix	1 466 296	10 691	220	533	4 237	5 701	93 328	16 255	52 537	24 536
City of Mesa	452 340	2 280	29	194	460	1 597	24 071	3 560	16 263	4 248
City of Scottsdale	229 339	465	4	51	125	285	7 733	1 869	4 703	1 161
City of Tempe	166 144	1 060	4	72	326	658	12 400	1 835	8 260	2 305
Actually reporting	0.9%	18 684	307	1 193	6 071	11 113	188 136	36 383	110 812	40 941
Estimated total	100.0%	19 709	324	1 284	6 254	11 847	201 158	39 226	119 274	42 658
Rate		513.0	8.4	33.4	162.8	308.4	5 236.0	1 021.0	3 104.6	1 110.4
Pine Bluff, AR MSA										
Cleveland, Jefferson, and Lincoln Counties	106 885									
City of Pine Bluff	53 934	725	16	41	209	459	4 820	1 681	2 727	412
Actually reporting	100.0%	855	21	53	221	560	5 898	2 174	3 254	470
Rate		799.9	19.6	49.6	206.8	523.9	5 518.1	2 034.0	3 044.4	439.7
Pittsburgh, PA MSA										
Allegheny, Armstrong, Beaver, Butler, Fayette, Washington, and Westmoreland Counties	2 406 001									
City of Pittsburgh	330 780	3 385	63	117	1 617	1 588	15 628	3 018	10 337	2 273
Actually reporting	0.9%	7 856	108	396	2 698	4 654	51 478	9 547	36 981	4 950
Estimated total	100.0%	8 674	116	451	2 914	5 193	58 560	10 596	42 543	5 421
Rate		360.5	4.8	18.7	121.1	215.8	2 433.8	440.4	1 768.1	225.3
Pittsfield, MA MSA										
Berkshire County	132 119									
City of Pittsfield	44 162	352	2	32	36	282	1 041	309	668	64
Actually reporting	0.9%	545	3	53	47	442	2 432	704	1 588	140
Estimated total	100.0%	569	3	55	52	459	2 602	745	1 700	157
Rate		430.7	2.3	41.6	39.4	347.4	1 969.4	563.9	1 286.7	118.8
Pocatello, ID MSA										
Bannock and Power Counties	85 293									
City of Pocatello	52 028	159	1	35	7	116	1 763	283	1 416	64
Actually reporting	100.0%	259	1	43	9	206	2 646	488	2 057	101
Rate		303.7	1.2	50.4	10.6	241.5	3 102.2	572.1	2 411.7	118.4
Port St. Lucie-Fort Pierce, FL MSA										
Martin and St. Lucie Counties	373 006									
City of Port St. Lucie	121 069	287	1	17	27	242	2 697	770	1 783	144
City of Fort Pierce	38 816	736	10	36	195	495	2 877	872	1 629	376
Actually reporting	1.0%	2 006	14	95	400	1 497	11 008	2 896	7 090	1 022
Rate		537.8	3.8	25.5	107.2	401.3	2 951.2	776.4	1 900.8	274.0
Portland-South Portland-Biddeford, ME MSA										
Cumberland, Sagadahoc, and York Counties	512 440.0									
City of Portland	64 111	267	3	39	100	125	2 970	536	2 261	173
City of South Portland	23 589	38	0	1	13	24	1 091	72	986	33
City of Biddeford	21 913	46	0	19	9	18	864	95	744	25
Actually reporting	1.0%	715	7	146	187	375	12 536	2 368	9 563	605
Rate		139.5	1.4	28.5	36.5	73.2	2 446.3	462.1	1 866.2	118.1

Note: Although arson data are included in the trend and clearance tables, sufficient data are not available to estimate totals for this offense.

Table 6. Crime, by Metropolitan Statistical Area, 2005—*Continued*

(Number, percent, rate per 100,000 inhabitants.)

Metropolitan statistical area	Population	Violent crime	Murder and non-negligent man-slaughter	Forcible rape	Robbery	Aggravated assault	Property crime	Burglary	Larceny-theft	Motor vehicle theft
Portland-Vancouver-Beaverton, OR-WA MSA										
Clackamas, Columbia, Multnomah, Washington, and Yamhill Counties, OR; and Clark and Skamania Counties, WA	2091269.0									
City of Portland, OR	540 389	3 858	20	325	1 137	2 376	37 645	6 121	25 794	5 730
City of Vancouver, WA	157 152	626	8	111	161	346	7 943	1 218	5 573	1 152
City of Beaverton, OR	83 979	189	1	32	43	113	2 957	340	2 301	316
City of Hillsboro, OR	82 912	163	2	30	63	68	3 647	473	2 807	367
Actually reporting	1.0%	6 841	55	902	1 921	3 963	92 104	14 936	64 764	12 404
Estimated total	100.0%	6 845	55	903	1 922	3 965	92 175	14 947	64 816	12 412
Rate		327.3	2.6	43.2	91.9	189.6	4 407.6	714.7	3 099.4	593.5
Poughkeepsie-Newburgh-Middletown, NY MSA										
Dutchess and Orange Counties	664 698									
City of Poughkeepsie	30 391	371	2	16	149	204	1 108	234	787	87
City of Newburgh	28 592	432	3	12	174	243	1 077	294	707	76
City of Middletown	26 154	122	2	12	58	50	810	114	657	39
Actually reporting	1.0%	1 756	13	149	541	1 053	11 807	1 928	9 253	626
Estimated total	100.0%	1 823	13	153	565	1 092	12 497	2 028	9 806	663
Rate		274.3	2.0	23.0	85.0	164.3	1 880.1	305.1	1 475.3	99.7
Prescott, AZ MSA										
Yavapai County	197 115									
City of Prescott	40 255	143	0	12	22	109	1 878	386	1 365	127
Actually reporting	1.0%	695	4	44	42	605	5 868	1 314	4 114	440
Estimated total	100.0%	696	4	44	42	606	5 884	1 318	4 124	442
Rate		353.1	2.0	22.3	21.3	307.4	2 985.1	668.6	2 092.2	224.2
Provo-Orem, UT MSA										
Juab and Utah Counties	426 264									
City of Provo	102 983	182	3	55	17	107	3 298	673	2 417	208
City of Orem	91 607	65	0	16	13	36	3 483	392	2 909	182
Actually reporting	1.0%	466	5	136	51	274	12 995	2 309	9 965	721
Estimated total	100.0%	472	5	137	52	278	13 121	2 332	10 056	733
Rate		110.7	1.2	32.1	12.2	65.2	3 078.1	547.1	2 359.1	172.0
Pueblo, CO MSA										
Pueblo County	152 252									
City of Pueblo	105 057	686	13	22	162	489	6 981	1 525	4 978	478
Actually reporting	100.0%	736	13	24	168	531	8 640	1 909	6 184	547
Rate		483.4	8.5	15.8	110.3	348.8	5 674.8	1 253.8	4 061.7	359.3
Punta Gorda, FL MSA										
Charlotte County	160 681									
City of Punta Gorda	17 604	51	1	3	3	44	436	139	273	24
Actually reporting	100.0%	734	2	44	64	624	4 949	1 200	3 437	312
Rate		456.8	1.2	27.4	39.8	388.3	3 080.0	746.8	2 139.0	194.2
Racine, WI MSA										
Racine County	195 146									
City of Racine	80 503	391	16	31	242	102	4 557	982	3 235	340
Actually reporting	100.0%	448	16	41	267	124	6 851	1 377	5 004	470
Rate		229.6	8.2	21.0	136.8	63.5	3 510.7	705.6	2 564.2	240.8
Raleigh-Cary, NC MSA										
Franklin, Johnston, and Wake Counties	929 889									
City of Raleigh	332 084	2 051	20	88	762	1 181	12 528	3 040	8 480	1 008
City of Cary	102 949	133	0	13	50	70	1 963	432	1 428	103
Actually reporting	1.0%	3 052	31	192	1 035	1 794	26 839	7 169	17 771	1 899
Estimated total	100.0%	3 077	31	194	1 042	1 810	27 136	7 238	17 984	1 914
Rate		330.9	3.3	20.9	112.1	194.6	2 918.2	778.4	1 934.0	205.8
Rapid City, SD MSA										
Meade and Pennington Counties	118 257									
City of Rapid City	61 862	257	1	58	38	160	2 551	459	1 980	112
Actually reporting	100.0%	378	3	107	42	226	3 581	677	2 736	168
Rate		319.6	2.5	90.5	35.5	191.1	3 028.2	572.5	2 313.6	142.1
Reading, PA MSA										
Berks County	392 376									
City of Reading	80 879	936	22	51	372	491	5 093	1 512	2 520	1 061
Actually reporting	1.0%	1 365	23	82	465	795	10 600	2 360	6 706	1 534
Estimated total	100.0%	1 418	23	86	479	830	11 053	2 427	7 062	1 564
Rate		361.4	5.9	21.9	122.1	211.5	2 816.9	618.5	1 799.8	398.6
Redding, CA MSA										
Shasta County	178 997									
City of Redding	89 161	550	2	80	75	393	4 102	943	2 665	494
Actually reporting	100.0%	851	4	119	96	632	6 025	1 578	3 590	857
Rate		475.4	2.2	66.5	53.6	353.1	3 366.0	881.6	2 005.6	478.8
Reno-Sparks, NV MSA										
Storey and Washoe Counties	397 671									
City of Reno	204 749	1 518	8	110	421	979	10 989	1 916	7 547	1 526
City of Sparks	83 791	359	5	56	96	202	3 235	740	2 045	450
Actually reporting	100.0%	2 117	14	176	539	1 388	16 309	3 245	10 821	2 243
Rate		532.3	3.5	44.3	135.5	349.0	4 101.1	816.0	2 721.1	564.0

Note: Although arson data are included in the trend and clearance tables, sufficient data are not available to estimate totals for this offense.

Table 6. Crime, by Metropolitan Statistical Area, 2005—*Continued*

(Number, percent, rate per 100,000 inhabitants.)

Metropolitan statistical area	Population	Violent crime	Murder and non-negligent man-slaughter	Forcible rape	Robbery	Aggravated assault	Property crime	Burglary	Larceny-theft	Motor vehicle theft
Richmond, VA MSA[2]										
Amelia,[2] Caroline, Charles City, Chesterfield, Cumberland, Dinwiddie, Goochland, Hanover, Henrico, King and Queen, King William, Louisa, New Kent, Powhatan, Prince George, and Sussex Counties; and Colonial Heights, Hopewell, Petersburg, and Richmond Cities	1 170 973									
City of Richmond	195 271	2 385	84	80	1 196	1 025	12 898	2 529	8 168	2 201
Actually reporting	1.0%	4 747	137	264	2 023	2 323	. . .	7 203	29 087	. . .
Estimated total	100.0%	4 754	137	265	2 025	2 327	. . .	7 212	29 133	. . .
Rate		406.0	11.7	22.6	172.9	198.7	. . .	615.9	2 487.9	. . .
Riverside-San Bernardino-Ontario, CA MSA										
Riverside and San Bernardino Counties	3 818 268									
City of Riverside	290 299	1 954	10	113	675	1 156	13 425	2 498	8 157	2 770
City of San Bernardino	199 723	2 510	58	72	912	1 468	11 226	2 525	5 527	3 174
City of Ontario	171 186	866	12	56	294	504	6 744	991	3 714	2 039
City of Temecula	82 628	269	4	16	73	176	2 808	684	1 725	399
City of Victorville	83 340	435	12	30	153	240	4 229	865	2 536	828
City of Chino	76 547	210	2	9	75	124	2 539	521	1 576	442
City of Redlands	70 145	310	1	19	92	198	2 799	553	1 799	447
City of Hemet	67 005	381	3	19	141	218	3 419	910	1 943	566
City of Colton	51 723	267	5	17	105	140	1 941	472	983	486
Actually reporting	100.0%	18 397	283	1 080	5 514	11 520	140 651	32 668	77 116	30 867
Rate		481.8	7.4	28.3	144.4	301.7	3 683.6	855.6	2 019.7	808.4
Roanoke, VA MSA										
Botetourt, Craig, Franklin, and Roanoke Counties and Roanoke and Salem Cities	295 336									
City of Roanoke	93 685	895	16	55	228	596	6 369	1 011	4 912	446
Actually reporting	100.0%	1 245	20	94	266	865	9 736	1 531	7 545	660
Rate		421.6	6.8	31.8	90.1	292.9	3 296.6	518.4	2 554.7	223.5
Rochester, MN MSA										
Dodge, Olmsted, and Wabasha Counties	175 945									
City of Rochester	93 866	261	0	51	71	139	2 465	421	1 917	127
Actually reporting	100.0%	319	0	62	75	182	3 460	652	2 609	199
Rate		181.3	0.0	35.2	42.6	103.4	1 966.5	370.6	1 482.8	113.1
Rochester, NY MSA										
Livingston, Monroe, Ontario, Orleans, and Wayne Counties	1 042 990									
City of Rochester	212 785	1 974	53	100	1 026	795	13 828	2 758	8 826	2 244
Actually reporting	1.0%	2 975	62	230	1 282	1 401	31 155	5 573	22 526	3 056
Estimated total	100.0%	3 006	62	232	1 293	1 419	31 483	5 621	22 789	3 073
Rate		288.2	5.9	22.2	124.0	136.1	3 018.5	538.9	2 185.0	294.6
Rocky Mount, NC MSA										
Edgecombe and Nash Counties	147 841									
City of Rocky Mount	57 288	497	8	22	197	270	4 876	1 380	3 264	232
Actually reporting	100.0%	763	14	41	246	462	7 100	2 127	4 595	378
Rate		516.1	9.5	27.7	166.4	312.5	4 802.5	1 438.7	3 108.1	255.7
Rome, GA MSA										
Floyd County	96 598									
City of Rome	36 530	269	2	17	76	174	2 652	597	1 908	147
Actually reporting	100.0%	344	2	17	86	239	4 776	1 167	3 290	319
Rate		356.1	2.1	17.6	89.0	247.4	4 944.2	1 208.1	3 405.9	330.2
Sacramento–Arden-Arcade–Roseville, CA MSA										
El Dorado, Placer, Sacramento, and Yolo Counties	2 030 094									
City of Sacramento	457 347	5 265	52	170	2 018	3 025	26 083	5 841	13 320	6 922
City of Roseville	104 297	363	0	28	87	248	4 750	852	3 188	710
City of Folsom	64 385	89	0	11	18	60	1 716	305	1 238	173
City of Woodland	52 036	142	1	14	34	93	1 794	307	1 182	305
Actually reporting	100.0%	11 580	124	553	3 643	7 260	82 500	18 540	45 159	18 801
Rate		570.4	6.1	27.2	179.4	357.6	4 063.9	913.3	2 224.5	926.1
Saginaw-Saginaw Township North, MI MSA										
Saginaw County	209 232									
City of Saginaw	59 093	1 606	17	44	212	1 333	2 610	1 286	948	376
Actually reporting	1.0%	2 164	21	110	292	1 741	7 081	2 186	4 216	679
Estimated total	100.0%	2 171	21	111	294	1 745	7 151	2 198	4 266	687
Rate		1 037.6	10.0	53.1	140.5	834.0	3 417.7	1 050.5	2 038.9	328.3
Salem, OR MSA										
Marion and Polk Counties	374 181									
City of Salem	148 009	706	3	53	134	516	9 004	1 170	6 752	1 082
Actually reporting	1.0%	1 199	10	118	209	862	17 191	2 772	12 393	2 026
Estimated total	100.0%	1 201	10	118	210	863	17 232	2 778	12 423	2 031
Rate		321.0	2.7	31.5	56.1	230.6	4 605.3	742.4	3 320.1	542.8
Salinas, CA MSA										
Monterey County	417 382									
City of Salinas	149 167	1 030	7	43	335	645	6 778	935	4 339	1 504
Actually reporting	100.0%	1 858	14	118	569	1 157	14 618	2 809	9 490	2 319
Rate		445.2	3.4	28.3	136.3	277.2	3 502.3	673.0	2 273.7	555.6

Note: Although arson data are included in the trend and clearance tables, sufficient data are not available to estimate totals for this offense.

[2]After examining the data and making inquiries, the FBI determined that the agency's offense count was inflated. Consequently, this figure is not included in this table.
. . . = Not available.

Table 6. Crime, by Metropolitan Statistical Area, 2005—*Continued*

(Number, percent, rate per 100,000 inhabitants.)

Metropolitan statistical area	Population	Violent crime	Murder and non-negligent man-slaughter	Forcible rape	Robbery	Aggravated assault	Property crime	Burglary	Larceny-theft	Motor vehicle theft
Salisbury, MD MSA										
Somerset and Wicomico Counties	115 518									
City of Salisbury	26 347	490	1	14	160	315	2 501	623	1 766	112
Actually reporting	100.0%	1 047	5	37	239	766	4 880	1 302	3 346	232
Rate		906.4	4.3	32.0	206.9	663.1	4 224.4	1 127.1	2 896.5	200.8
Salt Lake City, UT MSA										
Salt Lake, Summit, and Tooele Counties	1 053 174									
City of Salt Lake City	184 627	1 283	10	72	417	784	15 859	2 172	11 608	2 079
Actually reporting	1.0%	3 496	34	478	794	2 190	55 610	7 989	41 652	5 969
Estimated total	100.0%	3 500	34	479	795	2 192	55 683	8 000	41 708	5 975
Rate		332.3	3.2	45.5	75.5	208.1	5 287.2	759.6	3 960.2	567.3
San Angelo, TX MSA										
Irion and Tom Green Counties	107 246									
City of San Angelo	89 561	373	3	55	40	275	5 358	1 137	3 941	280
Actually reporting	100.0%	401	4	60	40	297	5 714	1 224	4 195	295
Rate		373.9	3.7	55.9	37.3	276.9	5 327.9	1 141.3	3 911.6	275.1
San Antonio, TX MSA										
Atascosa, Bandera, Bexar, Comal, Guadalupe, Kendall, Medina, and Wilson Counties	1 884 548									
City of San Antonio	1 256 584	8 007	86	593	2 154	5 174	80 987	14 365	60 649	5 973
Actually reporting	100.0%	9 697	107	791	2 385	6 414	100 765	18 791	75 013	6 961
Rate		514.6	5.7	42.0	126.6	340.3	5 346.9	997.1	3 980.4	369.4
San Diego-Carlsbad-San Marcos, CA MSA										
San Diego County	2 951 182									
City of San Diego	1 272 148	6 603	51	376	1 862	4 314	46 213	7 462	24 613	14 138
City of Carlsbad	89 633	256	2	11	79	164	2 411	517	1 648	246
City of San Marcos	68 801	237	0	15	57	165	1 630	359	989	282
City of National City	54 934	456	4	16	182	254	2 726	376	1 409	941
Actually reporting	100.0%	13 849	98	814	3 941	8 996	97 623	17 666	54 207	25 750
Rate		469.3	3.3	27.6	133.5	304.8	3 307.9	598.6	1 836.8	872.5
Sandusky, OH MSA										
Erie County	79 027									
City of Sandusky	26 989	189	1	7	49	132	1 831	385	1 379	67
Actually reporting	1.0%	233	1	16	57	159	2 900	593	2 215	92
Estimated total	100.0%	233	1	16	57	159	2 912	595	2 224	93
Rate		294.8	1.3	20.2	72.1	201.2	3 684.8	752.9	2 814.2	117.7
San Francisco-Oakland-Fremont, CA MSA										
Metropolitan divisions of Oakland-Fremont-Hayward and San Francisco-San Mateo-Redwood City	4 181 453									
City of San Francisco	749 172	5 985	96	172	3 078	2 639	34 269	6 208	19 887	8 174
City of Oakland	400 619	5 692	93	306	2 672	2 621	23 027	5 783	8 227	9 017
City of Fremont	203 717	521	1	40	188	292	4 803	1 009	3 035	759
City of Hayward	141 730	641	9	37	301	294	5 473	1 147	2 338	1 988
City of Berkeley	102 191	570	3	18	354	195	7 976	1 229	5 503	1 244
City of San Mateo	91 881	403	4	22	117	260	2 780	355	2 205	220
City of San Leandro	79 709	465	4	23	237	201	4 069	701	2 328	1 040
City of Redwood City	73 833	388	3	22	103	260	2 553	354	1 831	368
City of Pleasanton	66 389	96	0	10	24	62	1 555	260	1 152	143
City of Walnut Creek	65 252	130	1	8	38	83	2 919	507	2 142	270
City of South San Francisco	60 295	175	3	8	46	118	1 541	609	640	292
City of San Rafael	55 929	172	2	22	65	83	2 052	427	1 247	378
Actually reporting	100.0%	23 234	335	1 123	10 252	11 524	162 102	31 805	91 906	38 391
Rate		555.6	8.0	26.9	245.2	275.6	3 876.7	760.6	2 197.9	918.1
Oakland-Fremont-Hayward, CA M.D.										
Alameda and Contra Costa Counties	2 480 743									
Actually reporting	100.0%	14 262	206	739	6 288	7 029	102 181	20 685	54 896	26 600
Rate		574.9	8.3	29.8	253.5	283.3	4 119.0	833.8	2 212.9	1 072.3
San Francisco-San Mateo-Redwood City, CA M.D.										
Marin, San Francisco, and San Mateo Counties	1 700 710									
Actually reporting	100.0%	8 972	129	384	3 964	4 495	59 921	11 120	37 010	11 791
Rate		527.5	7.6	22.6	233.1	264.3	3 523.3	653.8	2 176.1	693.3
San Jose-Sunnyvale-Santa Clara, CA MSA										
San Benito and Santa Clara Counties	1 752 994									
City of San Jose	910 528	3 492	26	263	884	2 319	22 930	4 049	13 374	5 507
City of Sunnyvale	128 862	232	3	27	73	129	2 661	495	1 794	372
City of Santa Clara	104 692	190	5	18	49	118	3 420	553	2 470	397
City of Mountain View	69 469	302	1	5	63	233	2 176	253	1 660	263
City of Milpitas	63 114	195	2	17	36	140	2 168	315	1 575	278
City of Palo Alto	57 240	91	1	5	46	39	2 043	371	1 548	124
City of Cupertino	51 746	56	0	0	10	46	933	250	632	51
Actually reporting	100.0%	5 543	44	415	1 341	3 743	46 417	8 370	29 919	8 128
Rate		316.2	2.5	23.7	76.5	213.5	2 647.9	477.5	1 706.7	463.7
San Luis Obispo-Paso Robles, CA MSA										
San Luis Obispo County	256 256									
City of San Luis Obispo	44 324	170	2	23	35	110	1 793	361	1 335	97
City of Paso Robles	27 066	110	0	14	11	85	667	194	388	85
Actually reporting	100.0%	760	4	76	90	590	6 427	1 469	4 434	524
Rate		296.6	1.6	29.7	35.1	230.2	2 508.0	573.3	1 730.3	204.5

Note: Although arson data are included in the trend and clearance tables, sufficient data are not available to estimate totals for this offense.

Table 6. Crime, by Metropolitan Statistical Area, 2005—*Continued*

(Number, percent, rate per 100,000 inhabitants.)

Metropolitan statistical area	Population	Violent crime	Murder and non-negligent man-slaughter	Forcible rape	Robbery	Aggravated assault	Property crime	Burglary	Larceny-theft	Motor vehicle theft
Santa Barbara-Santa Maria, CA MSA										
Santa Barbara County	404 519									
City of Santa Barbara	87 950	560	0	31	76	453	2 944	680	2 060	204
City of Santa Maria	84 312	601	3	36	92	470	2 354	383	1 342	629
Actually reporting	100.0%	1 668	9	119	252	1 288	9 737	2 084	6 541	1 112
Rate		412.3	2.2	29.4	62.3	318.4	2 407.1	515.2	1 617.0	274.9
Santa Cruz-Watsonville, CA MSA										
Santa Cruz County	252 297									
City of Santa Cruz	54 573	503	2	49	96	356	3 137	573	2 316	248
City of Watsonville	47 465	237	2	17	81	137	2 043	284	1 481	278
Actually reporting	100.0%	1 155	5	112	232	806	10 255	1 940	7 256	1 059
Rate		457.8	2.0	44.4	92.0	319.5	4 064.7	768.9	2 876.0	419.7
Santa Fe, NM MSA										
Santa Fe County	140 534									
City of Santa Fe	68 938	379	5	44	70	260	4 022	1 837	1 978	207
Actually reporting	1.0%	971	6	66	79	820	5 097	2 491	2 280	326
Estimated total	100.0%	993	6	67	81	839	5 204	2 517	2 350	337
Rate		706.6	4.3	47.7	57.6	597.0	3 703.0	1 791.0	1 672.2	239.8
Santa Rosa-Petaluma, CA MSA										
Sonoma County	471 561									
City of Santa Rosa	154 656	1 021	2	61	168	790	4 900	803	3 508	589
City of Petaluma	55 727	215	0	34	24	157	1 300	128	1 036	136
Actually reporting	100.0%	2 407	5	168	288	1 946	12 067	2 340	8 417	1 310
Rate		510.4	1.1	35.6	61.1	412.7	2 558.9	496.2	1 784.9	277.8
Sarasota-Bradenton-Venice, FL MSA										
Manatee and Sarasota Counties	666 576									
City of Sarasota	54 553	522	5	37	154	326	3 562	769	2 535	258
City of Bradenton	54 335	318	3	18	111	186	2 832	597	1 944	291
City of Venice	20 441	31	0	3	2	26	481	153	308	20
Actually reporting	100.0%	4 213	23	201	808	3 181	27 030	6 242	18 794	1 994
Rate		632.0	3.5	30.2	121.2	477.2	4 055.1	936.4	2 819.5	299.1
Savannah, GA MSA										
Bryan, Chatham, and Effingham Counties	319 272									
City of Savannah-Chatham Metropolitan[4]	213 587	1 390	30	83	704	573	11 671	2 530	7 603	1 538
Actually reporting	1.0%	1 836	33	97	786	920	14 860	3 218	9 893	1 749
Estimated total	100.0%	1 861	33	98	795	935	15 126	3 263	10 088	1 775
Rate		582.9	10.3	30.7	249.0	292.9	4 737.7	1 022.0	3 159.7	556.0
Scranton–Wilkes-Barre, PA MSA										
Lackawanna, Luzerne, and Wyoming Counties	552 568									
City of Scranton	74 067	452	1	47	89	315	2 371	630	1 569	172
City of Wilkes-Barre	41 637	207	3	30	112	62	1 602	338	1 143	121
Actually reporting	0.9%	1 605	15	178	350	1 062	11 588	2 377	8 448	763
Estimated total	100.0%	1 787	17	190	398	1 182	13 171	2 612	9 691	868
Rate		323.4	3.1	34.4	72.0	213.9	2 383.6	472.7	1 753.8	157.1
Seattle-Tacoma-Bellevue, WA MSA										
Metropolitan divisions of Seattle-Bellevue-Everett and Tacoma	3 209 692									
City of Seattle	579 215	4 109	25	138	1 607	2 339	43 471	6 761	27 147	9 563
City of Tacoma	198 748	2 014	13	120	690	1 191	16 802	3 255	9 989	3 558
City of Bellevue	118 496	172	2	29	49	92	4 665	595	3 503	567
City of Everett	97 402	537	3	48	173	313	7 600	1 272	4 243	2 085
City of Kent	82 736	479	3	57	165	254	6 153	1 187	3 492	1 474
City of Renton	55 549	223	2	24	95	102	5 311	680	3 670	961
Actually reporting	1.0%	12 998	98	1 243	4 218	7 439	171 367	30 697	104 931	35 739
Estimated total	100.0%	13 013	98	1 245	4 222	7 448	171 656	30 744	105 126	35 786
Rate		405.4	3.1	38.8	131.5	232.0	5 348.1	957.8	3 275.3	1 114.9
Seattle-Bellevue-Everett, WA M.D.										
King and Snohomish Counties	2 454 192									
Actually reporting	100.0%	8 908	70	913	3 096	4 829	131 522	22 340	80 869	28 313
Rate		363.0	2.9	37.2	126.2	196.8	5 359.1	910.3	3 295.1	1 153.7
Tacoma, WA M.D.										
Pierce County	755 500									
Actually reporting	1.0%	4 090	28	330	1 122	2 610	39 845	8 357	24 062	7 426
Estimated total	100.0%	4 105	28	332	1 126	2 619	40 134	8 404	24 257	7 473
Rate		543.3	3.7	43.9	149.0	346.7	5 312.2	1 112.4	3 210.7	989.1
Sebastian-Vero Beach, FL MSA										
Indian River County	126 916									
City of Sebastian	19 092	45	0	4	3	38	481	125	330	26
City of Vero Beach	17 597	86	0	6	16	64	740	145	551	44
Actually reporting	100.0%	447	2	33	85	327	4 293	986	3 035	272
Rate		352.2	1.6	26.0	67.0	257.7	3 382.6	776.9	2 391.3	214.3
Sheboygan, WI MSA										
Sheboygan County	114 520									
City of Sheboygan	49 262	68	0	25	10	33	2 098	266	1 746	86
Actually reporting	100.0%	123	0	29	12	82	2 958	366	2 485	107
Rate		107.4	0.0	25.3	10.5	71.6	2 583.0	319.6	2 169.9	93.4

Note: Although arson data are included in the trend and clearance tables, sufficient data are not available to estimate totals for this offense.

[4]Savannah-Chatham Metropolitan is a city-county government that includes the Savannah city and Chatham County police departments.

Table 6. Crime, by Metropolitan Statistical Area, 2005—*Continued*

(Number, percent, rate per 100,000 inhabitants.)

Metropolitan statistical area	Population	Violent crime	Murder and non-negligent man-slaughter	Forcible rape	Robbery	Aggravated assault	Property crime	Burglary	Larceny-theft	Motor vehicle theft
Sherman-Denison, TX MSA										
Grayson County	117 840									
City of Sherman	37 180	159	3	6	19	131	1 932	439	1 405	88
City of Denison	23 764	83	0	4	20	59	1 290	260	933	97
Actually reporting	100.0%	332	3	14	51	264	4 402	1 057	3 078	267
Rate		281.7	2.5	11.9	43.3	224.0	3 735.6	897.0	2 612.0	226.6
Shreveport-Bossier City, LA MSA										
Bossier, Caddo, and De Soto Parishes	382 482									
City of Shreveport	199 021	2 249	39	151	628	1 431	12 878	2 969	8 893	1 016
City of Bossier City	59 715	1 247	0	32	89	1 126	3 131	627	2 241	263
Actually reporting	100.0%	4 125	41	218	755	3 111	18 722	4 097	13 105	1 520
Rate		1 078.5	10.7	57.0	197.4	813.4	4 894.9	1 071.2	3 426.3	397.4
Sioux City, IA-NE-SD MSA										
Woodbury County, IA; Dakota and Dixon Counties, NE; and Union County, SD	143 872									
City of Sioux City, IA	84 017	400	2	54	52	292	3 590	797	2 562	231
Actually reporting	1.0%	468	2	57	56	353	4 160	952	2 949	259
Estimated total	100.0%	470	2	57	56	355	4 210	961	2 986	263
Rate		326.7	1.4	39.6	38.9	246.7	2 926.2	668.0	2 075.5	182.8
Sioux Falls, SD MSA[1]										
Lincoln, McCook, Minnehaha, and Turner Counties	204 654									
City of Sioux Falls[1]	137 590	473	4	145	71	253	4 264	682	3 253	329
Actually reporting	1.0%	526	6	158	73	289	4 709	836	3 507	366
Estimated total	100.0%	535	6	159	74	296	4 824	860	3 589	375
Rate		261.4	2.9	77.7	36.2	144.6	2 357.1	420.2	1 753.7	183.2
South Bend-Mishawaka, IN-MI MSA[1]										
St. Joseph County, IN; and Cass County, MI	319 704									
City of South Bend, IN	106 076	794	12	69	348	365	6 612	1 678	4 366	568
City of Mishawaka, IN[1]	48 652	189	1	24	52	112	3 317	346	2 804	167
Actually reporting	1.0%	1 149	14	133	434	568	12 965	2 672	9 363	930
Estimated total	100.0%	1 166	14	135	438	579	13 148	2 704	9 493	951
Rate		364.7	4.4	42.2	137.0	181.1	4 112.6	845.8	2 969.3	297.5
Spartanburg, SC MSA										
Spartanburg County	267 819									
City of Spartanburg	39 123	692	11	28	149	504	4 097	939	2 866	292
Actually reporting	100.0%	1 739	28	85	306	1 320	12 024	2 818	8 266	940
Rate		649.3	10.5	31.7	114.3	492.9	4 489.6	1 052.2	3 086.4	351.0
Spokane, WA MSA										
Spokane County	441 541									
City of Spokane	199 384	1 120	13	78	286	743	12 170	2 436	7 932	1 802
Actually reporting	100.0%	1 776	16	133	362	1 265	19 309	3 952	12 660	2 697
Rate		402.2	3.6	30.1	82.0	286.5	4 373.1	895.0	2 867.2	610.8
Springfield, MA MSA										
Franklin, Hampden, and Hampshire Counties	678 672									
City of Springfield	151 670	2 689	16	109	771	1 793	8 703	2 141	4 974	1 588
Actually reporting	1.0%	4 330	32	296	1 024	2 978	20 607	5 242	12 532	2 833
Estimated total	100.0%	4 373	32	299	1 033	3 009	20 907	5 314	12 729	2 864
Rate		644.3	4.7	44.1	152.2	443.4	3 080.6	783.0	1 875.6	422.0
Springfield, MO MSA										
Christian, Dallas, Greene, Polk, and Webster Counties	394 091									
City of Springfield	151 901	892	5	85	203	599	12 723	1 759	10 060	904
Actually reporting	100.0%	1 402	9	108	226	1 059	17 448	2 780	13 458	1 210
Rate		355.8	2.3	27.4	57.3	268.7	4 427.4	705.4	3 414.9	307.0
Springfield, OH MSA										
Clark County	142 676									
City of Springfield	63 637	548	7	70	280	191	6 321	1 832	4 027	462
Actually reporting	1.0%	625	9	85	301	230	8 540	2 371	5 566	603
Estimated total	100.0%	629	9	86	302	232	8 605	2 383	5 615	607
Rate		440.9	6.3	60.3	211.7	162.6	6 031.1	1 670.2	3 935.5	425.4
St. Cloud, MN MSA										
Benton and Stearns Counties	180 272									
City of St. Cloud	64 739	251	2	59	34	156	2 780	398	2 245	137
Actually reporting	1.0%	351	5	95	37	214	4 604	725	3 657	222
Rate		194.7	2.8	52.7	20.5	118.7	2 553.9	402.2	2 028.6	123.1
St. George, UT MSA										
Washington County	113 630.0									
City of St. George	61 795	224	1	13	12	198	1 865	385	1 249	231
Actually reporting	1.0%	282	2	27	13	240	2 673	551	1 823	299
Estimated total	100.0%	283	2	27	13	241	2 698	555	1 842	301
Rate		249.1	1.8	23.8	11.4	212.1	2 374.4	488.4	1 621.1	264.9
St. Joseph, MO-KS MSA[1]										
Doniphan County, KS; and Andrew, Buchanan, and De Kalb Counties, MO	123 143									
City of St. Joseph, MO[1]	73 205	216	2	22	60	132	4 204	763	3 079	362
Actually reporting	1.0%	297	3	28	66	200	5 061	976	3 658	427
Estimated total	100.0%	301	3	28	67	203	5 104	982	3 691	431
Rate		244.4	2.4	22.7	54.4	164.8	4 144.8	797.4	2 997.3	350.0

Note: Although arson data are included in the trend and clearance tables, sufficient data are not available to estimate totals for this offense.

[1]Because of changes in the state/local agency's reporting practices, figures are not comparable to previous years' data.

Table 6. Crime, by Metropolitan Statistical Area, 2005—*Continued*

(Number, percent, rate per 100,000 inhabitants.)

Metropolitan statistical area	Population	Violent crime	Murder and non-negligent man-slaughter	Forcible rape	Robbery	Aggravated assault	Property crime	Burglary	Larceny-theft	Motor vehicle theft
St. Louis, MO-IL MSA[1]										
Bond, Calhoun, Clinton, Jersey, Macoupin, Madison, Monroe, and St. Clair Counties, IL; and Franklin, Jefferson, Lincoln, St. Charles, St. Louis, Warren, and Washington Counties and St. Louis City, MO	2 784 658									
City of St. Louis, MO	346 005	8 323	131	276	2 965	4 951	38 245	7 213	22 886	8 146
City of St. Charles, MO[1]	61 899	146	1	10	21	114	1 996	267	1 593	136
Actually reporting	0.8%	13 240	168	548	3 892	8 632	87 614	14 475	60 600	12 539
Estimated total	100.0%	15 159	208	548	4 396	10 007	101 454	17 004	71 032	13 418
Rate		544.4	7.5	19.7	157.9	359.4	3 643.3	610.6	2 550.8	481.9
State College, PA MSA										
Centre County	140 740									
City of State College	52 843	32	0	4	6	22	884	138	726	20
Actually reporting	1.0%	145	1	20	15	109	2 753	435	2 226	92
Estimated total	100.0%	152	1	20	17	114	2 816	444	2 276	96
Rate		108.0	0.7	14.2	12.1	81.0	2 000.9	315.5	1 617.2	68.2
Stockton, CA MSA										
San Joaquin County	654 183									
City of Stockton	281 747	4 202	41	109	1 357	2 695	18 861	3 434	11 487	3 940
Actually reporting	100.0%	5 949	56	181	1 750	3 962	36 552	7 088	22 292	7 172
Rate		909.4	8.6	27.7	267.5	605.6	5 587.4	1 083.5	3 407.6	1 096.3
Sumter, SC MSA										
Sumter County	107 382									
City of Sumter	40 210	602	3	8	117	474	2 324	616	1 580	128
Actually reporting	100.0%	1 009	8	25	171	805	4 916	1 707	2 877	332
Rate		939.6	7.5	23.3	159.2	749.7	4 578.0	1 589.7	2 679.2	309.2
Syracuse, NY MSA										
Madison, Onondaga, and Oswego Counties	654 925									
City of Syracuse	143 306	1 570	19	73	554	924	6 486	1 867	3 639	980
Actually reporting	1.0%	2 242	21	165	690	1 366	15 642	3 550	10 872	1 220
Estimated total	100.0%	2 251	21	166	693	1 371	15 731	3 563	10 943	1 225
Rate		343.7	3.2	25.3	105.8	209.3	2 402.0	544.0	1 670.9	187.0
Tallahassee, FL MSA										
Gadsden, Jefferson, Leon, and Wakulla Counties	339 142									
City of Tallahassee	160 147	1 646	9	132	386	1 119	8 519	2 614	5 191	714
Actually reporting	100.0%	2 780	20	213	526	2 021	13 459	4 236	8 171	1 052
Rate		819.7	5.9	62.8	155.1	595.9	3 968.5	1 249.0	2 409.3	310.2
Tampa-St. Petersburg-Clearwater, FL MSA										
Hernando, Hillsborough, Pasco, and Pinellas Counties	2 646 385									
City of Tampa	329 035	4 707	20	210	1 160	3 317	20 271	4 914	12 564	2 793
City of St. Petersburg	254 713	3 937	30	101	959	2 847	16 323	3 534	10 395	2 394
City of Clearwater	111 058	993	9	48	210	726	5 077	949	3 695	433
City of Largo	73 323	349	4	26	77	242	2 556	468	1 860	228
Actually reporting	100.0%	19 841	113	1 092	3 987	14 649	110 169	25 217	73 113	11 839
Rate		749.7	4.3	41.3	150.7	553.5	4 163.0	952.9	2 762.7	447.4
Texarkana, TX-Texarkana, AR MSA										
Miller County, AR; and Bowie County, TX	134 610									
Texarkana County, TX	36 076	500	3	31	69	397	2 646	556	1 926	164
Texarkana County, AR	29 778	455	1	6	45	403	1 732	357	1 264	111
Actually reporting	100.0%	1 141	8	53	124	956	5 705	1 256	4 035	414
Rate		847.6	5.9	39.4	92.1	710.2	4 238.2	933.1	2 997.5	307.6
Toledo, OH MSA										
Fulton, Lucas, Ottawa, and Wood Counties	658 525									
City of Toledo	305 107	3 725	28	179	1 356	2 162	23 630	7 101	13 331	3 198
Actually reporting	0.9%	3 919	32	223	1 398	2 266	30 528	8 091	19 046	3 391
Estimated total	100.0%	3 965	32	232	1 413	2 288	31 386	8 290	19 650	3 446
Rate		602.1	4.9	35.2	214.6	347.4	4 766.1	1 258.9	2 983.9	523.3
Topeka, KS MSA										
Jackson, Jefferson, Osage, Shawnee, and Wabaunsee Counties	228 584									
City of Topeka	122 218	682	7	50	275	350	9 662	1 719	7 244	699
Actually reporting	1.0%	907	10	76	278	543	12 420	2 310	9 255	855
Estimated total	100.0%	914	10	77	279	548	12 497	2 321	9 316	860
Rate		399.9	4.4	33.7	122.1	239.7	5 467.1	1 015.4	4 075.5	376.2
Trenton-Ewing, NJ MSA										
Mercer County	366 071									
City of Trenton	85 566	1 515	31	21	805	658	3 574	962	1 940	672
City of Ewing Township	37 138	121	1	9	52	59	910	165	670	75
Actually reporting	100.0%	1 988	34	56	1 009	889	9 237	1 978	6 183	1 076
Rate		543.1	9.3	15.3	275.6	242.8	2 523.3	540.3	1 689.0	293.9
Tucson, AZ MSA[1]										
Pima County	937 925									
City of Tucson[1]	529 447	5 048	55	378	1 685	2 930	31 299	5 130	19 642	6 527
Actually reporting	100.0%	6 094	78	478	1 962	3 576	49 052	8 080	32 523	8 449
Rate		649.7	8.3	51.0	209.2	381.3	5 229.8	861.5	3 467.5	900.8

Note: Although arson data are included in the trend and clearance tables, sufficient data are not available to estimate totals for this offense.

[1]Because of changes in the state/local agency's reporting practices, figures are not comparable to previous years' data.

Table 6. Crime, by Metropolitan Statistical Area, 2005—*Continued*

(Number, percent, rate per 100,000 inhabitants.)

Metropolitan statistical area	Population	Violent crime	Murder and non-negligent man-slaughter	Forcible rape	Robbery	Aggravated assault	Property crime	Burglary	Larceny-theft	Motor vehicle theft
Tulsa, OK MSA										
Creek, Okmulgee, Osage, Pawnee, Rogers, Tulsa, and Wagoner Counties	887 903									
City of Tulsa	386 414	4 995	58	303	1 096	3 538	25 169	6 592	14 847	3 730
Actually reporting	100.0%	6 228	72	405	1 224	4 527	36 941	9 541	22 523	4 877
Rate		701.4	8.1	45.6	137.9	509.9	4 160.5	1 074.6	2 536.7	549.3
Tyler, TX MSA										
Smith County	189 480									
City of Tyler	91 025	574	6	52	172	344	4 728	1 119	3 412	197
Actually reporting	1.0%	935	11	109	201	614	7 416	1 981	5 024	411
Estimated total	100.0%	941	11	110	202	618	7 496	1 996	5 083	417
Rate		496.6	5.8	58.1	106.6	326.2	3 956.1	1 053.4	2 682.6	220.1
Utica-Rome, NY MSA										
Herkimer and Oneida Counties	299 248									
City of Utica	59 769	268	8	18	133	109	2 672	619	1 967	86
City of Rome	34 600	49	0	8	10	31	627	164	428	35
Actually reporting	0.9%	718	10	80	169	459	6 190	1 358	4 619	213
Estimated total	100.0%	768	10	83	187	488	6 714	1 434	5 039	241
Rate		256.6	3.3	27.7	62.5	163.1	2 243.6	479.2	1 683.9	80.5
Valdosta, GA MSA										
Brooks, Echols, Lanier, and Lowndes Counties	126 064									
City of Valdosta	46 623	312	7	29	106	170	3 461	666	2 602	193
Actually reporting	0.9%	524	10	45	137	332	5 599	1 076	4 212	311
Estimated total	100.0%	568	10	48	153	357	6 055	1 177	4 509	369
Rate		450.6	7.9	38.1	121.4	283.2	4 803.1	933.7	3 576.8	292.7
Victoria, TX MSA										
Calhoun, Goliad, and Victoria Counties	115 316									
City of Victoria	62 692	300	2	34	58	206	3 654	829	2 670	155
Actually reporting	100.0%	407	4	43	63	297	4 787	1 139	3 415	233
Rate		352.9	3.5	37.3	54.6	257.6	4 151.2	987.7	2 961.4	202.1
Vineland-Millville-Bridgeton, NJ MSA										
Cumberland County	151 514									
City of Vineland	58 136	721	2	15	198	506	2 845	591	2 084	170
City of Millville	27 671	241	1	18	80	142	1 494	315	1 108	71
City of Bridgeton	22 777	322	5	18	125	174	973	227	671	75
Actually reporting	100.0%	1 363	8	51	411	893	5 975	1 336	4 259	380
Rate		899.6	5.3	33.7	271.3	589.4	3 943.5	881.8	2 811.0	250.8
Virginia Beach-Norfolk-Newport News, VA-NC MSA										
Currituck County, NC; and Gloucester, Isle of Wight, James City, Mathews, Surry, and York Counties, VA; and Chesapeake, Hampton, Newport News, Norfolk, Poquoson, Portsmouth, Suffolk, Virginia Beach, and Williamsburg Cities, VA	1 668 025									
City of Virginia Beach, VA	446 448	1 140	20	96	622	402	13 342	2 213	10 376	753
City of Norfolk, VA	241 267	1 841	59	92	886	804	13 061	1 769	10 153	1 139
City of Newport News, VA	184 538	1 439	20	103	542	774	8 216	1 470	5 887	859
City of Hampton, VA	148 057	595	11	47	276	261	5 388	887	3 941	560
City of Portsmouth, VA	100 724	901	22	41	366	472	5 164	1 049	3 708	407
Actually reporting	100.0%	7 844	159	505	3 197	3 983	61 434	10 072	46 694	4 668
Rate		470.3	9.5	30.3	191.7	238.8	3 683.0	603.8	2 799.4	279.9
Visalia-Porterville, CA MSA										
Tulare County	404 168									
City of Visalia	105 350	1 055	10	39	192	814	6 765	1 216	4 347	1 202
City of Porterville	44 303	257	2	18	48	189	2 287	506	1 351	430
Actually reporting	100.0%	2 760	54	117	465	2 124	. . .	4 655	11 733	. . .
Rate		682.9	13.4	28.9	115.1	525.5	. . .	1 151.7	2 903.0	. . .
Waco, TX MSA										
McLennan County	226 098									
City of Waco	120 036	895	12	60	257	566	8 845	2 413	5 740	692
Actually reporting	100.0%	1 248	14	118	290	826	12 489	3 178	8 397	914
Rate		552.0	6.2	52.2	128.3	365.3	5 523.7	1 405.6	3 713.9	404.2
Warner Robins, GA MSA										
Houston County	127 162									
City of Warner Robins	57 729	253	1	12	94	146	3 100	832	2 100	168
Actually reporting	100.0%	420	2	19	125	274	4 723	1 143	3 270	310
Rate		330.3	1.6	14.9	98.3	215.5	3 714.2	898.9	2 571.5	243.8

Note: Although arson data are included in the trend and clearance tables, sufficient data are not available to estimate totals for this offense.

. . . = Not available.

Table 6. Crime, by Metropolitan Statistical Area, 2005—*Continued*

(Number, percent, rate per 100,000 inhabitants.)

Metropolitan statistical area	Population	Violent crime	Murder and non-negligent man-slaughter	Forcible rape	Robbery	Aggravated assault	Property crime	Burglary	Larceny-theft	Motor vehicle theft
Washington-Arlington-Alexandria, DC-VA-MD-WV MSA										
Metropolitan divisions of Bethesda-Frederick-Gaithersburg, MD and Washington-Arlington-Alexandria, DC-VA-MD-WV	5 187 049									
City of Washington, DC	550 521	7 716	195	165	3 502	3 854	25 200	3 571	14 162	7 467
City of Alexandria, VA	130 056	462	3	22	199	238	3 331	294	2 570	467
City of Frederick, MD	57 443	490	0	11	118	361	1 575	256	1 244	75
Actually reporting	1.0%	24 827	429	1 037	11 528	11 833	155 910	19 727	103 882	32 301
Estimated total	100.0%	25 001	431	1 051	11 579	11 940	157 488	19 966	105 110	32 412
Rate		482.0	8.3	20.3	223.2	230.2	3 036.2	384.9	2 026.4	624.9
Bethesda-Gaithersburg-Frederick, MD M.D.										
Frederick and Montgomery Counties	1 148 021									
Actually reporting	100.0%	2 932	22	187	1 257	1 466	26 430	4 401	19 161	2 868
Rate		255.4	1.9	16.3	109.5	127.7	2 302.2	383.4	1 669.0	249.8
Washington-Arlington-Alexandria, DC-VA-MD-WV M.D.										
District of Columbia; Calvert, Charles, and Prince George's Counties, MD; Arlington, Clarke, Fairfax, Fauquier, Loudoun, Prince William, Spotsylvania, Stafford, and Warren Counties and Alexandria, Fairfax, Falls Church, Fredericksburg, Manassas, and Manassas Park Cities, VA; and Jefferson County, WV	4 039 028									
Actually reporting	1.0%	21 895	407	850	10 271	10 367	129 480	15 326	84 721	29 433
Estimated total	100.0%	22 069	409	864	10 322	10 474	131 058	15 565	85 949	29 544
Rate		546.4	10.1	21.4	255.6	259.3	3 244.8	385.4	2 128.0	731.5
Waterloo-Cedar Falls, IA MSA										
Black Hawk, Bremer, and Grundy Counties	162 564									
City of Waterloo	67 036	360	1	36	80	243	3 251	825	2 242	184
City of Cedar Falls	36 489	70	0	12	4	54	662	88	540	34
Actually reporting	100.0%	523	1	68	85	369	4 624	1 118	3 261	245
Rate		321.7	0.6	41.8	52.3	227.0	2 844.4	687.7	2 006.0	150.7
Wausau, WI MSA										
Marathon County	128 363									
City of Wausau	37 356	117	0	23	21	73	1 125	251	826	48
Actually reporting	1.0%	185	0	30	27	128	2 288	475	1 723	90
Estimated total	100.0%	191	0	31	29	131	2 414	492	1 826	96
Rate		148.8	0.0	24.2	22.6	102.1	1 880.6	383.3	1 422.5	74.8
Wenatchee, WA MSA										
Chelan and Douglas Counties	104 814									
City of Wenatchee	29 415	105	1	19	16	69	1 751	287	1 348	116
Actually reporting	100.0%	218	2	44	28	144	4 254	762	3 258	234
Rate		208.0	1.9	42.0	26.7	137.4	4 058.6	727.0	3 108.4	223.3
Wheeling, WV-OH MSA										
Belmont County, OH; and Marshall and Ohio Counties, WV	149 595									
City of Wheeling, WV	29 916	138	0	20	32	86	961	227	645	89
Actually reporting	0.9%	245	1	32	40	172	2 428	624	1 619	185
Estimated total	100.0%	264	1	35	46	182	2 748	682	1 860	206
Rate		176.5	0.7	23.4	30.7	121.7	1 837.0	455.9	1 243.4	137.7
Wichita Falls, TX MSA										
Archer, Clay, and Wichita Counties	150 258									
City of Wichita Falls	102 589	733	6	43	239	445	7 641	1 703	5 386	552
Actually reporting	100.0%	787	8	48	246	485	8 600	2 006	5 982	612
Rate		523.8	5.3	31.9	163.7	322.8	5 723.5	1 335.0	3 981.2	407.3
Williamsport, PA MSA										
Lycoming County	118 765									
City of Williamsport	30 232	134	3	16	64	51	1 202	219	917	66
Actually reporting	0.9%	206	4	27	69	106	2 327	483	1 711	133
Estimated total	100.0%	230	4	29	75	122	2 532	513	1 872	147
Rate		193.7	3.4	24.4	63.1	102.7	2 131.9	431.9	1 576.2	123.8
Wilmington, NC MSA										
Brunswick, New Hanover, and Pender Counties	308 288									
City of Wilmington	94 843	794	8	57	292	437	6 558	1 855	4 000	703
Actually reporting	1.0%	1 371	13	133	396	829	14 678	4 695	8 792	1 191
Estimated total	100.0%	1 389	13	134	401	841	14 901	4 747	8 952	1 202
Rate		450.6	4.2	43.5	130.1	272.8	4 833.5	1 539.8	2 903.8	389.9
Winchester, VA-WV MSA										
Frederick County and Winchester City, VA; and Hampshire County, WV	114 269									
City of Winchester, VA	25 137	118	1	6	34	77	1 373	135	1 177	61
Actually reporting	1.0%	237	2	32	42	161	2 857	428	2 220	209
Estimated total	100.0%	237	2	32	42	161	2 863	429	2 225	209
Rate		207.4	1.8	28.0	36.8	140.9	2 505.5	375.4	1 947.2	182.9
Winston-Salem, NC MSA										
Davie, Forsyth, Stokes, and Yadkin Counties	448 950									
City of Winston-Salem	194 708	1 639	16	118	608	897	12 118	4 016	7 146	956
Actually reporting	1.0%	2 378	23	172	682	1 501	19 394	6 093	11 920	1 381
Estimated total	100.0%	2 390	23	173	685	1 509	19 534	6 126	12 020	1 388
Rate		532.4	5.1	38.5	152.6	336.1	4 351.0	1 364.5	2 677.4	309.2

Note: Although arson data are included in the trend and clearance tables, sufficient data are not available to estimate totals for this offense.

Table 6. Crime, by Metropolitan Statistical Area, 2005—*Continued*

(Number, percent, rate per 100,000 inhabitants.)

Metropolitan statistical area	Population	Violent crime	Murder and non-negligent man-slaughter	Forcible rape	Robbery	Aggravated assault	Property crime	Burglary	Larceny-theft	Motor vehicle theft
Worcester, MA MSA										
Worcester County	777 330									
City of Worcester	175 479	1 390	6	143	389	852	6 078	1 248	3 673	1 157
Actually reporting	1.0%	2 870	9	310	586	1 965	15 298	3 622	9 800	1 876
Estimated total	100.0%	2 910	9	313	594	1 994	15 581	3 690	9 986	1 905
Rate		374.4	1.2	40.3	76.4	256.5	2 004.4	474.7	1 284.7	245.1
Yakima, WA MSA										
Yakima County	232 195									
City of Yakima	81 986	452	10	62	149	231	7 532	1 451	5 021	1 060
Actually reporting	1.0%	759	22	129	218	390	16 179	3 824	10 179	2 176
Estimated total	100.0%	765	22	130	220	393	16 294	3 843	10 256	2 195
Rate		329.5	9.5	56.0	94.7	169.3	7 017.4	1 655.1	4 417.0	945.3
York-Hanover, PA MSA										
York County	402 368									
City of York	40 118	413	13	39	242	119	2 314	400	1 703	211
City of Hanover	14 944	25	0	6	9	10	567	62	483	22
Actually reporting	1.0%	1 101	18	144	393	546	9 764	1 561	7 647	556
Estimated total	100.0%	1 121	18	145	398	560	9 945	1 588	7 789	568
Rate		278.6	4.5	36.0	98.9	139.2	2 471.6	394.7	1 935.8	141.2
Yuba City, CA MSA										
Sutter and Yuba Counties	152 396									
City of Yuba City	52 470	188	3	17	48	120	2 304	453	1 604	247
Actually reporting	100.0%	671	11	53	107	500	5 876	1 551	3 453	872
Rate		440.3	7.2	34.8	70.2	328.1	3 855.7	1 017.7	2 265.8	572.2
Yuma, AZ MSA										
Yuma County	182 075									
City of Yuma	86 157	565	10	30	76	449	3 863	749	2 523	591
Actually reporting	0.9%	808	11	36	101	660	5 730	1 313	3 544	873
Estimated total	100.0%	888	12	42	118	716	6 684	1 543	4 118	1 023
Rate		487.7	6.6	23.1	64.8	393.2	3 671.0	847.5	2 261.7	561.9
Aguadilla-Isabela-San Sebastian, Puerto Rico MSA										
Aguada, Aguadilla, Anasco, Isabela, Lares, Moca, Rincon, and San Sebastian Municipios	324 095									
Actually reporting	100.0%	216	3	1	119	93	1 917	817	953	147
Rate		66.6	0.9	0.3	36.7	28.7	591.5	252.1	294.0	45.4
Fajardo, Puerto Rico MSA										
Ceiba, Fajardo, and Luquillo Municipios	80 724									
Actually reporting	100.0%	191	25	4	76	86	1 019	391	547	81
Rate		236.6	31.0	5.0	94.1	106.5	1 262.3	484.4	677.6	100.3
Guayama, Puerto Rico MSA										
Arroyo, Guayama, and Patillas Municipios	85 296									
Actually reporting	100.0%	129	11	7	63	48	497	336	101	60
Rate		151.2	12.9	8.2	73.9	56.3	582.7	393.9	118.4	70.3
Mayaguez, Puerto Rico MSA										
Hormigueros and Mayaguez Municipios	116 303									
Actually reporting	100.0%	187	7	4	110	66	2 581	742	1 722	117
Rate		160.8	6.0	3.4	94.6	56.7	2 219.2	638.0	1 480.6	100.6
Ponce, Puerto Rico MSA										
Juana Diaz, Ponce, and Villalba Municipios	269 900									
Actually reporting	100.0%	798	117	21	333	327	4 332	1 108	2 826	398
Rate		295.7	43.3	7.8	123.4	121.2	1 605.0	410.5	1 047.1	147.5
San German-Cabo Rojo, Puerto Rico MSA										
Cabo Rojo, Lajas, Sabana Grande, and San German Municipios	141 085									
Actually reporting	100.0%	108	4	5	66	33	866	389	414	63
Rate		76.5	2.8	3.5	46.8	23.4	613.8	275.7	293.4	44.7
San Juan-Caguas-Guaynabo, Puerto Rico MSA										
Aguas Buenas, Aibonito, Arecibo, Barceloneta, Barranquitas, Bayamon, Caguas, Camuy, Canovanas, Carolina, Catano, Cayey, Ciales, Cidra, Comerio, Corozal, Dorado, Florida, Guaynabo, Gurabo, Hatillo, Humacao, Juncos, Las Piedras, Loiza, Manati, Maunabo, Morovis, Naguabo, Naranjito, Orocovis, Quebradillas, Rio Grande, San Juan, San Lorenzo, Toa Alta, Toa Baja, Trujillo Alto, Vega Alta, Vega Baja, and Yabucoa Municipios	2 576 510									
Actually reporting	100.0%	7 373	560	110	4 547	2 156	41 018	12 022	20 845	8 151
Rate		286.2	21.7	4.3	176.5	83.7	1 592.0	466.6	809.0	316.4
Yauco, Puerto Rico MSA										
Guanica, Guayanilla, Penuelas, and Yauco Municipios	121 793									
Actually reporting	100.0%	200	18	8	65	109	1 139	408	668	63
Rate		164.2	14.8	6.6	53.4	89.5	935.2	335.0	548.5	51.7

Note: Although arson data are included in the trend and clearance tables, sufficient data are not available to estimate totals for this offense.

Table 7. Offense Analysis, 2001–2005

(Number.)

Classification	2001[1]	2002	2003	2004[2]	2005
Murder	16 037	16 229	16 528	16 148	16 692
Forcible Rape	90 863	95 235	93 883	95 089	93 934
Robbery					
Total[3]	423 557	420 806	414 235	401 470	417 122
Robbery by location					
Street/highway	187 571	180 058	179 657	171 812	184 049
Commercial house	61 152	61 312	60 615	59 006	59 649
Gas or service station	12 084	11 254	11 385	10 893	11 880
Convenience store	27 783	27 183	25 826	24 653	23 804
Residence	53 268	56 723	56 755	55 525	59 163
Bank	10 262	9 693	9 523	9 775	8 759
Miscellaneous	71 436	74 584	70 474	69 806	69 818
Burglary					
Total[3]	2 116 531	2 151 252	2 154 834	2 144 446	2 154 126
Burglary by location					
Residence (dwelling)	1 380 472	1 415 561	1 418 423	1 409 253	1 416 570
Residence, night	410 071	418 094	409 188	405 556	402 634
Residence, day	642 264	673 781	668 759	666 345	669 169
Residence, unknown	328 137	323 687	340 477	337 351	344 768
Nonresidence (store, office, etc.)	736 059	735 691	736 411	735 193	737 556
Nonresidence, night	310 596	312 516	310 187	307 702	305 541
Nonresidence, day	224 538	228 698	221 240	223 012	221 048
Nonresidence, unknown	200 925	194 477	204 984	204 479	210 967
Larceny-Theft (Except Motor Vehicle Theft)					
Total[3]	7 092 267	7 057 379	7 026 802	6 937 089	6 776 807
Larceny-theft by type					
Pocket-picking	33 346	32 451	31 966	29 840	29 193
Purse-snatching	38 550	38 896	42 181	42 345	41 999
Shoplifting	978 802	986 296	1 013 265	1 009 214	939 491
Items from motor vehicles (except accessories)	1 832 934	1 866 922	1 857 619	1 758 241	1 750 564
Motor vehicle accessories	723 419	756 250	781 279	749 173	692 546
Bicycles	291 203	277 003	271 801	249 813	248 548
Items from buildings	943 631	883 847	868 621	861 197	851 628
Items from coin-operated machines	52 039	52 374	52 373	45 927	40 845
All others	2 198 344	2 163 340	2 107 696	2 191 338	2 181 993
Larceny-theft by value					
Under $50	2 669 469	2 668 084	2 678 377	2 662 857	2 542 150
$50 to $200	1 630 567	1 592 830	1 586 672	1 562 672	1 521 319
Over $200	2 792 231	2 796 465	2 761 752	2 711 560	2 713 338
Motor Vehicle Theft	1 228 391	1 246 646	1 261 226	1 237 851	1 235 226

[1]Murder and nonnegligent homicides that occurred as a result of the September 11, 2001, terrorist attacks are not included in this table.
[2]Crime figures for 2004 have been adjusted.
[3]Number of offenses may not add to total because of rounding.

Table 8. Offenses Known to Law Enforcement, by State and City, 2005

(Number.)

City	Population	Violent crime	Murder and non-negligent man-slaughter	Forcible rape	Robbery	Aggravated assault	Property crime	Burglary	Larceny-theft	Motor vehicle theft	Arson[1]
Alabama											
Abbeville	3 004	17	0	3	1	13	141	35	99	7	. . .
Adamsville	4 929	40	0	3	12	25	386	51	307	28	. . .
Alexander City	15 062	142	1	8	21	112	859	190	643	26	. . .
Aliceville	2 499	23	0	0	3	20	95	25	64	6	. . .
Andalusia	8 645	51	0	7	10	34	488	125	340	23	. . .
Anniston	23 967	494	5	14	148	327	2 955	870	1 879	206	15
Ardmore	1 094	2	0	0	1	1	42	13	27	2	. . .
Ariton	763	4	0	0	0	4	4	0	4	0	. . .
Ashford	1 924	3	0	0	1	2	47	10	34	3	. . .
Ashland	1 916	0	0	0	0	0	11	4	6	1	. . .
Ashville	2 404	6	0	0	0	6	56	20	30	6	. . .
Atmore	7 618	82	2	2	24	54	542	106	413	23	. . .
Attalla	6 434	46	0	0	4	42	420	54	354	12	. . .
Auburn	48 643	154	1	18	52	83	2 172	464	1 639	69	. . .
Autaugaville	861	6	0	1	1	4	25	9	15	1	. . .
Bay Minette	7 867	44	0	1	11	32	343	59	270	14	. . .
Bayou La Batre	2 758	20	0	1	3	16	218	54	143	21	. . .
Berry	1 234	0	0	0	0	0	2	0	2	0	. . .
Bessemer	28 902	555	3	24	234	294	3 531	903	2 336	292	. . .
Birmingham	234 571	3 449	104	241	1 429	1 675	18 923	4 933	11 962	2 028	136
Blountsville	1 914	2	0	0	0	2	23	3	19	1	. . .
Boaz	7 786	11	0	2	1	8	589	99	460	30	. . .
Brantley	905	5	0	1	0	4	19	5	14	0	. . .
Brent	4 116	5	0	2	1	2	14	3	9	2	. . .
Brewton	5 433	129	0	1	17	111	406	65	332	9	. . .
Brilliant	739	1	0	0	0	1	15	3	11	1	. . .
Brundidge	2 330	7	0	0	2	5	64	17	46	1	. . .
Butler	1 840	3	0	0	1	2	12	8	3	1	. . .
Camden	2 236	6	1	0	3	2	42	9	32	1	. . .
Carbon Hill	2 055	4	0	0	0	4	68	15	48	5	. . .
Cedar Bluff	1 528	0	0	0	0	0	2	1	1	0	. . .
Centre	3 322	3	0	0	1	2	25	2	23	0	. . .
Centreville	2 494	10	0	0	0	10	58	20	34	4	. . .
Chatom	1 188	5	0	0	1	4	24	6	16	2	. . .
Cherokee	1 194	2	0	0	0	2	11	3	6	2	. . .
Chickasaw	6 100	36	1	2	7	26	337	75	244	18	. . .
Clanton	8 267	56	0	1	9	46	241	25	200	16	. . .
Clayton	1 419	2	0	0	0	2	16	2	14	0	. . .
Cleveland	1 352	1	0	0	0	1	18	7	10	1	0
Clio	2 233	1	0	0	0	1	1	1	0	0	. . .
Collinsville	1 668	2	0	0	1	1	75	16	52	7	. . .
Columbiana	3 634	9	0	2	3	4	141	16	122	3	. . .
Coosada	1 455	0	0	0	0	0	21	7	14	0	. . .
Cordova	2 354	10	0	0	1	9	123	36	72	15	. . .
Cottonwood	1 180	4	0	1	0	3	47	4	40	3	. . .
Courtland	763	2	0	0	0	2	14	2	10	2	. . .
Creola	2 065	10	0	1	1	8	76	12	52	12	. . .
Crossville	1 449	0	0	0	0	0	2	1	1	0	. . .
Cullman	14 633	21	0	3	7	11	945	130	757	58	. . .
Dadeville	3 168	19	0	2	4	13	255	44	194	17	. . .
Daleville	4 595	16	0	6	3	7	74	24	45	5	. . .
Daphne	18 225	26	1	4	10	11	524	71	417	36	. . .
Dauphin Island	1 512	3	0	0	1	2	23	11	8	4	. . .
Decatur	54 861	200	1	12	62	125	3 994	742	3 035	217	. . .
Demopolis	7 346	81	1	3	8	69	514	125	373	16	. . .
Dora	2 360	1	0	0	1	0	95	19	67	9	. . .
Dothan	61 661	333	8	57	156	112	3 532	760	2 617	155	. . .
Double Springs	989	4	0	0	0	4	20	3	16	1	. . .
East Brewton	2 459	4	0	0	0	4	86	12	63	11	. . .
Eclectic	1 092	11	0	1	2	8	67	15	52	0	. . .
Elba	4 221	15	0	2	3	10	148	50	91	7	2
Elberta	580	8	0	0	3	5	110	28	74	8	. . .
Enterprise	22 367	38	0	5	18	15	347	100	211	36	. . .
Evergreen	3 512	24	0	1	6	17	174	37	130	7	. . .
Fairfield	11 938	135	4	6	83	42	1 121	236	794	91	. . .
Fairhope	14 691	21	3	6	5	7	505	90	397	18	. . .
Falkville	1 187	0	0	0	0	0	4	0	4	0	. . .
Fayette	4 793	13	0	4	1	8	147	24	113	10	. . .
Flomaton	1 576	7	0	1	3	3	48	10	30	8	. . .
Florence	36 479	223	5	23	63	132	1 763	410	1 297	56	8
Fultondale	6 854	27	0	4	7	16	357	66	262	29	. . .
Gadsden	37 870	315	6	46	146	117	3 120	663	2 243	214	. . .
Geneva	4 376	37	0	0	3	34	98	17	75	6	. . .
Geraldine	816	0	0	0	0	0	1	0	0	1	. . .
Gordo	1 620	10	0	0	2	8	49	16	30	3	. . .
Grant	683	1	0	0	1	0	4	1	3	0	. . .
Graysville	2 344	6	0	0	0	6	75	10	63	2	. . .
Greenville	7 121	60	2	1	12	45	592	163	411	18	. . .
Grove Hill	1 396	0	0	0	0	0	21	12	6	3	. . .
Guin	2 271	10	0	0	0	10	49	10	35	4	. . .

[1]The FBI does not publish arson data unless it receives data from either the agency or the state for all 12 months of the calendar year.
. . . = Not available.

Table 8. Offenses Known to Law Enforcement, by State and City, 2005—*Continued*

(Number.)

City	Population	Violent crime	Murder and non-negligent man-slaughter	Forcible rape	Robbery	Aggravated assault	Property crime	Burglary	Larceny-theft	Motor vehicle theft	Arson[1]
Gulf Shores	6 333	41	1	2	5	33	429	94	318	17	. . .
Guntersville	7 688	65	2	7	12	44	838	156	635	47	. . .
Hackleburg	1 488	4	0	0	0	4	31	6	24	1	. . .
Hamilton	6 543	5	0	1	0	4	291	70	211	10	. . .
Hammondville	518	0	0	0	0	0	7	1	6	0	. . .
Hanceville	3 043	7	0	0	0	7	50	8	42	0	. . .
Harpersville	1 643	1	0	0	1	0	5	1	4	0	. . .
Hartford	2 363	6	1	0	0	5	115	31	82	2	. . .
Hartselle	12 944	27	0	4	2	21	350	45	290	15	. . .
Hayneville	1 153	11	0	1	0	10	33	11	18	4	. . .
Helena	12 509	16	0	0	0	16	153	22	129	2	. . .
Henagar	2 506	3	0	0	0	3	81	12	59	10	. . .
Hillsboro	589	0	0	0	0	0	3	2	1	0	. . .
Hobson City	866	5	0	0	1	4	15	1	13	1	. . .
Hodges	260	0	0	0	0	0	3	2	1	0	0
Hokes Bluff	4 297	4	0	0	1	3	45	11	32	2	. . .
Hollywood	938	0	0	0	0	0	14	0	14	0	. . .
Huntsville	165 147	1 220	22	88	500	610	11 513	2 446	7 979	1 088	. . .
Ider	687	0	0	0	0	0	1	1	0	0	. . .
Jackson	5 341	21	0	2	3	16	230	55	160	15	. . .
Jasper	13 992	73	2	7	19	45	1 135	197	867	71	. . .
Jemison	2 359	5	0	0	0	5	59	14	38	7	. . .
Killen	1 122	1	0	0	0	1	71	5	66	0	. . .
Kinston	617	0	0	0	0	0	2	1	1	0	. . .
Lafayette	3 119	45	2	0	3	40	196	48	137	11	. . .
Lake View	1 565	1	0	0	1	0	64	14	48	2	. . .
Leeds	11 087	29	0	9	6	14	554	123	406	25	. . .
Lexington	833	0	0	0	0	0	3	3	0	0	. . .
Lineville	2 364	37	0	1	1	35	33	4	26	3	0
Lipscomb	2 368	0	0	0	0	0	1	0	1	0	. . .
Littleville	959	1	0	0	1	0	32	13	17	2	. . .
Livingston	3 132	18	0	1	6	11	130	19	107	4	. . .
Louisville	586	2	0	0	0	2	8	2	5	1	. . .
Loxley	1 413	0	0	0	0	0	145	23	104	18	. . .
Luverne	2 659	3	0	0	1	2	72	18	51	3	. . .
Maplesville	691	0	0	0	0	0	7	3	3	1	. . .
Marion	3 487	51	0	2	3	46	244	37	195	12	. . .
McIntosh	240	3	1	0	0	2	29	6	22	1	. . .
McKenzie	625	2	0	0	1	1	7	2	5	0	. . .
Millry	610	0	0	0	0	0	1	0	1	0	. . .
Mobile[2]	249 798	1 165	35	74	597	459	14 349	3 832	9 396	1 121	92
Monroeville	6 727	104	0	7	4	93	420	77	293	50	0
Montevallo	5 113	27	0	0	6	21	227	43	168	16	. . .
Montgomery	202 209	1 641	29	109	847	656	12 997	3 528	8 449	1 020	41
Moody	9 877	9	1	2	5	1	277	49	203	25	. . .
Morris	1 881	1	0	1	0	0	36	14	21	1	. . .
Mosses	1 092	3	0	0	0	3	6	0	5	1	. . .
Moundville	2 060	11	0	0	1	10	47	18	28	1	. . .
Mountain Brook	20 874	15	1	1	3	10	311	44	257	10	. . .
Mount Vernon	829	13	0	0	0	13	13	3	10	0	. . .
Napier Field	406	1	0	0	1	0	3	0	3	0	. . .
New Brockton	1 251	0	0	0	0	0	5	1	4	0	. . .
New Hope	2 737	0	0	0	0	0	29	5	23	1	. . .
North Courtland	796	2	0	1	0	1	6	1	4	1	. . .
Notasulga	872	1	0	0	0	1	22	7	15	0	0
Odenville	1 192	6	0	1	0	5	50	16	32	2	0
Ohatchee	1 217	8	0	2	0	6	103	21	65	17	. . .
Opelika	23 626	272	5	17	41	209	1 727	319	1 347	61	. . .
Opp	6 692	25	0	2	2	21	269	50	215	4	1
Orange Beach	4 721	12	0	1	2	9	353	40	302	11	. . .
Ozark	15 044	112	2	7	15	88	689	136	493	60	2
Pelham	18 223	41	1	3	19	18	664	43	592	29	1
Pell City	10 667	77	0	6	11	60	533	94	415	24	. . .
Pennington	343	1	0	0	0	1	0	0	0	0	. . .
Phil Campbell	1 058	0	0	0	0	0	9	4	3	2	. . .
Pickensville	655	6	0	0	0	6	14	7	6	1	. . .
Piedmont	5 024	7	0	1	4	2	265	49	212	4	. . .
Pine Hill	931	16	0	0	2	14	31	9	21	1	. . .
Pisgah	706	0	0	0	0	0	1	0	0	1	. . .
Pleasant Grove	10 440	22	1	0	3	18	230	57	145	28	. . .
Powell	960	0	0	0	0	0	1	0	0	1	. . .
Prattville	27 668	87	0	9	22	56	1 276	226	978	72	. . .
Priceville	2 164	1	0	0	1	0	36	10	23	3	1
Prichard	27 790	103	8	7	37	51	737	193	407	137	. . .
Ragland	2 009	8	0	1	0	7	57	19	31	7	. . .
Rainsville	4 757	8	0	4	0	4	131	22	103	6	. . .
Ranburne	472	2	0	0	1	1	29	4	20	5	. . .
Red Bay	3 307	8	0	1	0	7	116	27	74	15	. . .
Red Level	551	0	0	0	0	0	4	3	0	1	. . .
Reform	1 894	7	0	6	0	1	22	1	20	1	. . .

[1]The FBI does not publish arson data unless it receives data from either the agency or the state for all 12 months of the calendar year.
[2]The population for the city of Mobile, Alabama, includes 55,864 inhabitants from the jurisdiction of the Mobile County Sheriff's Department.
. . . = Not available.

Table 8. Offenses Known to Law Enforcement, by State and City, 2005—*Continued*

(Number.)

City	Population	Violent crime	Murder and non-negligent man-slaughter	Forcible rape	Robbery	Aggravated assault	Property crime	Burglary	Larceny-theft	Motor vehicle theft	Arson[1]
Riverside	1 688	3	0	0	0	3	35	7	26	2	. . .
Roanoke	6 639	18	0	3	4	11	226	30	183	13	. . .
Rockford	413	1	0	0	0	1	0	0	0	0	. . .
Rogersville	1 190	2	0	0	0	2	21	4	15	2	. . .
Russellville	8 851	45	1	3	5	36	219	36	159	24	. . .
Samson	2 030	10	0	1	0	9	75	30	42	3	. . .
Saraland	12 680	17	0	1	9	7	420	73	329	18	. . .
Sardis City	1 838	3	0	0	1	2	59	7	42	10	. . .
Satsuma	5 966	10	0	0	0	10	70	8	39	23	. . .
Scottsboro	14 896	35	0	6	11	18	1 043	94	925	24	. . .
Section	769	0	0	0	0	0	0	0	0	0	. . .
Sheffield	9 357	30	2	2	10	16	536	107	420	9	. . .
Shorter	336	2	0	0	2	0	16	1	15	0	. . .
Silverhill	690	2	0	0	0	2	38	5	27	6	. . .
Skyline	845	2	0	0	0	2	8	3	5	0	. . .
Slocomb	2 032	1	0	0	0	1	34	12	21	1	. . .
Snead	811	0	0	0	0	0	55	6	41	8	. . .
Southside	7 680	4	0	1	0	3	119	18	93	8	. . .
Springville	2 942	4	0	1	1	2	61	5	52	4	. . .
Stevenson	1 750	50	0	1	3	46	120	26	81	13	. . .
St. Florian	409	3	0	0	0	3	12	3	9	0	. . .
Sulligent	2 039	2	0	0	0	2	12	3	9	0	. . .
Sumiton	2 590	8	0	2	3	3	260	35	198	27	. . .
Summerdale	674	9	0	1	1	7	90	17	64	9	. . .
Sylacauga	12 962	37	0	1	17	19	786	129	641	16	. . .
Sylvania	1 238	4	0	0	0	4	14	2	9	3	. . .
Tallassee	5 019	33	1	2	4	26	410	76	319	15	. . .
Tarrant City	6 833	70	3	5	44	18	592	145	387	60	1
Thomasville	4 587	20	0	1	2	17	179	34	145	0	. . .
Thorsby	1 975	0	0	0	0	0	8	3	5	0	. . .
Town Creek	1 205	0	0	0	0	0	35	19	16	0	0
Troy	13 821	64	0	5	24	35	1 082	210	843	29	. . .
Trussville	15 840	32	0	7	14	11	795	70	689	36	. . .
Tuscaloosa	80 670	504	7	39	200	258	5 033	1 191	3 582	260	. . .
Tuscumbia	8 222	7	0	0	6	1	345	51	280	14	. . .
Uniontown	1 543	37	0	1	2	34	85	34	43	8	. . .
Vernon	1 993	1	0	0	0	1	13	3	10	0	. . .
Vestavia Hills	31 201	31	0	4	11	16	267	93	151	23	. . .
Weaver	2 573	15	0	1	0	14	66	17	46	3	. . .
West Blocton	1 410	0	0	0	0	0	4	0	4	0	. . .
Winfield	4 677	3	0	0	0	3	156	36	109	11	. . .
Woodstock	913	5	0	1	2	2	160	51	97	12	. . .
York	2 699	28	0	0	7	21	89	22	62	5	. . .
Alaska											
Anchorage	276 109	2 031	16	224	384	1 407	11 365	1 783	8 248	1 334	76
Bethel	6 183	43	1	0	4	38	135	41	49	45	1
Bristol Bay Borough	1 117	16	0	0	1	15	51	11	28	12	0
Cordova	2 378	13	0	0	0	13	39	9	27	3	1
Craig	1 268	14	0	0	0	14	31	7	21	3	2
Dillingham	2 490	29	0	9	0	20	80	15	55	10	0
Fairbanks	30 817	306	2	47	65	192	1 587	227	1 155	205	10
Haines	1 813	0	0	0	0	0	54	9	42	3	0
Homer	5 318	35	0	0	1	34	255	31	212	12	2
Houston	1 440	10	0	1	0	9	17	3	13	1	0
Juneau	31 509	135	0	30	14	91	1 296	125	1 124	47	5
Kenai	7 472	31	0	3	0	28	284	46	226	12	0
Ketchikan	7 516	44	1	15	2	26	536	58	445	33	3
Kodiak	6 343	36	0	0	0	36	271	16	238	17	3
Kotzebue	3 245	18	0	1	1	16	45	18	22	5	1
North Pole	1 680	3	0	1	0	2	96	16	60	20	1
North Slope Borough	7 090	66	0	20	3	43	154	61	71	22	2
Palmer	6 240	57	0	0	4	53	213	16	183	14	0
Petersburg	3 058	10	1	0	1	8	98	22	73	3	0
Seward	3 024	6	0	0	0	6	168	31	122	15	1
Sitka	8 960	31	0	10	2	19	362	39	298	25	2
Skagway	846	1	0	0	0	1	18	2	15	1	0
Soldotna	4 068	20	1	4	1	14	318	43	259	16	1
St. Paul	488	0	0	0	0	0	2	0	2	0	0
Unalaska	4 379	15	0	1	0	14	52	7	41	4	0
Wasilla	7 835	94	0	3	7	84	626	60	516	50	2
Wrangell	2 176	8	0	0	0	8	123	12	102	9	1
Arizona											
Apache Junction	34 596	114	1	14	6	93	1 605	385	986	234	6
Benson	5 076	7	0	2	0	5	240	57	157	26	0
Bisbee	6 250	10	0	0	0	10	324	62	251	11	0
Buckeye	9 586	26	0	5	7	14	956	461	236	259	2
Bullhead City	38 846	172	0	4	30	138	2 211	498	1 454	259	19
Casa Grande	32 253	266	3	4	53	206	3 337	1 208	1 761	368	16
Chandler	231 613	826	8	54	200	564	8 323	1 439	5 684	1 200	65
Chino Valley	9 472	25	1	3	0	21	227	57	156	14	3
Clarkdale	3 826	14	0	1	0	13	76	39	29	8	0
Clifton	2 339	6	0	0	1	5	28	11	14	3	0

[1]The FBI does not publish arson data unless it receives data from either the agency or the state for all 12 months of the calendar year.
. . . = Not available.

Table 8. Offenses Known to Law Enforcement, by State and City, 2005—*Continued*

(Number.)

City	Population	Violent crime	Murder and non-negligent man-slaughter	Forcible rape	Robbery	Aggravated assault	Property crime	Burglary	Larceny-theft	Motor vehicle theft	Arson[1]
Coolidge	8 518	82	0	3	17	62	591	153	353	85	24
Cottonwood	10 779	43	1	4	3	35	671	100	530	41	5
Douglas	17 274	44	0	1	6	37	696	102	525	69	0
Eagar	4 200	15	0	1	0	14	142	43	90	9	0
El Mirage	21 626	135	3	17	20	95	764	226	401	137	5
Eloy	11 059	106	1	7	18	80	766	294	402	70	15
Flagstaff	58 979	529	1	48	62	418	4 277	511	3 560	206	59
Florence	17 783	51	0	1	1	49	231	90	130	11	0
Fredonia	1 082	4	0	0	0	4	15	6	9	0	0
Gilbert	162 257	215	0	27	35	153	4 455	975	3 057	423	18
Glendale	243 608	1 409	19	84	393	913	12 413	3 332	5 980	3 101	73
Globe	7 449	68	1	4	7	56	514	142	346	26	5
Goodyear	38 772	105	0	18	24	63	2 041	1 048	608	385	13
Holbrook	5 275	115	0	9	6	100	468	81	374	13	6
Huachuca City	1 944	4	1	1	0	2	29	14	13	2	0
Kearny	2 677	26	0	0	0	26	57	16	41	0	0
Kingman	24 997	95	0	13	15	67	2 245	415	1 624	206	9
Lake Havasu City	55 014	142	3	17	11	111	1 842	315	1 345	182	8
Mammoth	2 100	0	0	0	0	0	48	20	22	6	1
Marana	23 885	66	2	2	11	51	1 217	176	878	163	2
Mesa	452 340	2 280	29	194	460	1 597	24 071	3 560	16 263	4 248	52
Miami	1 914	22	0	1	1	20	113	50	55	8	4
Nogales	21 321	74	0	3	11	60	713	114	453	146	0
Oro Valley	38 934	24	0	3	4	17	847	134	644	69	8
Page	7 050	42	0	5	3	34	491	84	392	15	1
Paradise Valley	14 818	12	0	2	3	7	392	233	143	16	4
Parker	3 275	8	0	0	2	6	205	58	123	24	4
Payson	14 966	17	0	4	2	11	410	56	344	10	1
Peoria	136 995	289	1	38	69	181	5 984	1 127	3 710	1 147	20
Phoenix	1 466 296	10 691	220	533	4 237	5 701	93 328	16 255	52 537	24 536	472
Prescott	40 255	143	0	12	22	109	1 878	386	1 365	127	19
Prescott Valley	31 260	145	2	10	7	126	801	137	604	60	3
Quartzsite	3 469	11	0	0	2	9	134	31	93	10	0
Sahuarita	4 987	15	0	1	2	12	238	35	178	25	0
Scottsdale	229 339	465	4	51	125	285	7 733	1 869	4 703	1 161	30
Sedona	11 444	22	0	6	1	15	324	78	236	10	1
Show Low	9 775	118	0	6	5	107	553	146	367	40	3
Sierra Vista	42 209	123	4	11	33	75	1 482	240	1 116	126	9
Snowflake-Taylor	8 782	47	0	0	1	46	256	65	176	15	4
Somerton	9 350	27	0	0	9	18	210	47	143	20	0
South Tucson	5 753	157	1	4	52	100	825	112	630	83	12
Springerville	2 012	21	1	1	0	19	142	30	101	11	0
St. Johns	3 632	10	0	0	0	10	176	68	97	11	3
Surprise	62 751	84	1	12	15	56	1 863	290	1 332	241	11
Tempe	166 144	1 060	4	72	326	658	12 400	1 835	8 260	2 305	57
Thatcher	4 216	13	0	0	0	13	209	35	172	2	0
Tolleson	6 150	57	2	2	11	42	829	283	395	151	7
Tucson[3]	529 447	5 048	55	378	1 685	2 930	31 299	5 130	19 642	6 527	307
Wellton	1 927	7	0	3	0	4	21	6	15	0	0
Wickenburg	5 739	15	0	2	1	12	229	82	116	31	0
Willcox	3 888	15	0	8	2	5	236	61	145	30	0
Williams	3 070	30	0	3	0	27	142	28	109	5	4
Winslow	10 238	135	0	3	4	128	750	160	539	51	14
Youngtown	3 462	30	0	1	2	27	136	42	71	23	2
Yuma	86 157	565	10	30	76	449	3 863	749	2 523	591	40
Arkansas											
Arkadelphia	10 768	45	0	5	4	36	307	99	196	12	6
Ashdown	4 652	9	0	2	2	5	181	24	146	11	1
Augusta	2 492	14	0	1	1	12	83	14	65	4	1
Barling	4 376	8	0	2	0	6	108	38	68	2	2
Bay	1 966	1	0	1	0	0	60	28	32	0	0
Bearden	1 067	6	0	2	2	2	44	22	20	2	0
Benton	24 933	106	4	8	23	71	1 633	282	1 272	79	4
Bentonville	28 033	93	1	21	4	67	957	122	776	59	1
Berryville	4 791	14	0	7	0	7	241	59	169	13	1
Blytheville	17 031	89	0	11	26	52	1 474	435	947	92	13
Booneville	4 185	12	0	0	4	8	195	85	108	2	1
Bradford	831	1	0	0	0	1	33	11	19	3	0
Bryant	12 664	9	0	4	0	5	547	65	444	38	1
Bull Shoals	2 025	0	0	0	0	0	8	3	5	0	0
Camden	12 461	62	1	8	24	29	639	177	435	27	5
Carlisle	2 426	8	0	0	1	7	84	17	63	4	0
Cave Springs	1 331	3	0	0	0	3	17	4	12	1	0
Centerton	3 774	13	0	3	1	9	79	20	55	4	0
Charleston	3 028	3	0	0	0	3	39	12	25	2	0
Cherokee Village	4 716	8	0	1	0	7	65	12	46	7	1
Clinton	2 496	3	0	1	0	2	73	11	56	6	1
Conway	50 843	135	0	25	41	69	2 748	425	2 154	169	4
Crossett	5 992	23	0	3	1	19	300	87	209	4	1
Decatur	1 364	2	0	0	1	1	18	8	10	0	0
De Witt	3 459	18	1	1	0	16	122	34	86	2	1
Dover	1 366	4	0	2	0	2	40	25	15	0	0
Dumas	5 013	52	3	1	8	40	226	46	162	18	0
Earle	2 942	86	0	0	7	79	157	76	76	5	0
El Dorado	20 881	162	5	6	37	114	1 363	569	717	77	11
England	3 041	23	0	1	1	21	48	25	13	10	4

[1]The FBI does not publish arson data unless it receives data from either the agency or the state for all 12 months of the calendar year.
[3]Because of changes in the state/local agency's reporting practices, figures are not comparable to previous years' data.

Table 8. Offenses Known to Law Enforcement, by State and City, 2005—*Continued*

(Number.)

City	Population	Violent crime	Murder and non-negligent man-slaughter	Forcible rape	Robbery	Aggravated assault	Property crime	Burglary	Larceny-theft	Motor vehicle theft	Arson[1]
Eureka Springs	2 352	4	0	1	0	3	62	12	48	2	0
Fairfield Bay	2 532	0	0	0	0	0	41	12	28	1	0
Farmington	4 162	6	0	1	2	3	61	25	33	3	0
Fayetteville	64 809	313	2	51	33	227	2 945	458	2 338	149	6
Flippin	1 380	5	0	0	0	5	59	16	43	0	1
Fordyce	4 528	35	4	1	10	20	241	82	148	11	1
Forrest City	14 379	114	3	5	35	71	1 185	238	915	32	7
Fort Smith	82 638	865	5	95	117	648	5 459	971	4 146	342	24
Gassville	1 918	3	0	0	0	3	43	12	31	0	0
Gentry	2 602	8	0	0	0	8	37	7	30	0	0
Glenwood	2 065	7	0	0	1	6	56	20	29	7	1
Gosnell	3 746	34	0	1	0	33	115	46	66	3	3
Gould	1 228	10	1	1	0	8	44	17	25	2	0
Greenbrier	3 490	4	0	0	0	4	2	0	2	0	0
Greenland	1 033	2	0	0	0	2	21	6	14	1	0
Greenwood	7 731	24	0	3	0	21	146	63	83	0	0
Greers Ferry	965	1	0	0	0	1	18	7	10	1	1
Gurdon	2 274	10	0	1	0	9	40	14	25	1	0
Hamburg	2 937	13	1	2	1	9	74	28	46	0	0
Hampton	1 516	2	0	1	0	1	22	7	12	3	0
Harrisburg	2 192	3	0	0	0	3	122	42	62	18	0
Harrison	12 684	40	1	3	3	33	566	175	362	29	6
Hazen	1 589	9	0	1	0	8	26	11	14	1	0
Highland	1 032	3	0	0	1	2	49	27	22	0	0
Hope	10 563	100	1	12	15	72	944	212	684	48	12
Horseshoe Bend	2 293	2	0	0	0	2	32	9	21	2	0
Hot Springs	37 604	496	4	26	87	379	4 528	894	3 348	286	13
Hoxie	2 786	4	0	0	2	2	29	7	22	0	0
Huntsville	2 110	0	0	0	0	0	35	15	18	2	0
Jacksonville	30 895	223	1	8	58	156	1 961	431	1 427	103	2
Jonesboro	59 366	481	2	27	101	351	3 719	1 397	2 154	168	6
Kensett	1 719	5	0	0	2	3	32	14	18	0	0
Lake City	2 015	1	0	0	0	1	20	11	9	0	0
Lake Village	2 684	7	0	0	3	4	63	26	37	0	0
Leachville	1 884	5	0	1	0	4	21	13	5	3	0
Lepanto	2 104	10	0	1	0	9	104	54	46	4	1
Lincoln	1 915	3	0	0	0	3	28	13	14	1	0
Little Rock	185 855	3 293	41	116	860	2 276	16 322	3 803	11 409	1 110	134
Lonoke	4 549	45	1	1	7	36	216	47	159	10	0
Lowell	6 738	12	0	4	0	8	263	95	132	36	0
Magnolia	10 559	55	2	6	23	24	635	295	316	24	0
Marianna	4 910	30	1	1	5	23	256	104	151	1	3
Marion	9 500	52	0	1	2	49	415	152	255	8	0
Marked Tree	2 756	9	0	1	3	5	94	13	78	3	1
Marmaduke	1 175	6	0	1	0	5	31	9	21	1	2
Marvell	1 276	2	0	1	1	0	46	9	37	0	0
Maumelle	13 401	18	1	1	8	8	318	145	146	27	2
McGehee	4 376	22	1	1	0	20	75	19	55	1	2
Mena	5 640	2	0	0	0	2	127	21	93	13	0
Mountain Home	11 822	12	0	2	0	10	462	17	431	14	3
Murfreesboro	1 720	4	0	0	1	3	35	12	23	0	0
North Little Rock	60 047	794	4	60	205	525	5 638	1 121	3 979	538	28
Osceola	8 305	120	2	5	9	104	386	131	237	18	3
Ozark	3 590	14	0	1	0	13	73	15	54	4	0
Paragould	23 622	103	1	8	17	77	1 838	451	1 248	139	8
Paris	3 753	21	0	2	0	19	126	61	53	12	1
Pea Ridge	2 939	3	0	1	0	2	67	27	37	3	0
Piggott	3 728	6	0	1	0	5	20	14	6	0	0
Pine Bluff	53 934	725	16	41	209	459	4 820	1 681	2 727	412	76
Plummerville	874	7	0	1	0	6	34	16	13	5	0
Prairie Grove	2 889	7	0	1	0	6	54	15	37	2	0
Prescott	4 074	28	0	0	1	27	139	39	94	6	0
Quitman	740	0	0	0	0	0	17	4	12	1	0
Redfield	1 194	1	0	0	0	1	16	7	8	1	1
Rogers	45 318	95	1	36	24	34	2 633	257	2 278	98	1
Russellville	25 422	97	1	13	6	77	1 326	245	1 025	56	1
Searcy	20 626	147	1	8	13	125	844	130	665	49	0
Sherwood	22 781	111	0	3	15	93	824	154	594	76	2
Siloam Springs	13 374	38	0	9	2	27	423	66	325	32	1
Smackover	1 968	4	0	0	0	4	23	4	16	3	0
Springdale	56 510	198	0	57	15	126	2 398	267	1 984	147	14
Stuttgart	9 467	49	0	1	5	43	544	188	351	5	0
Texarkana	29 778	455	1	6	45	403	1 732	357	1 264	111	8
Van Buren	20 836	83	0	8	6	69	842	230	579	33	4
Waldron	3 531	41	0	2	0	39	73	42	30	1	1
Walnut Ridge	4 843	8	0	1	1	6	71	23	41	7	1
Ward	3 048	33	0	1	0	32	101	41	54	6	0
Warren	6 403	41	2	3	7	29	125	71	49	5	0
West Fork	2 192	14	0	0	0	14	32	15	17	0	0
West Helena	8 008	84	1	7	13	63	626	256	339	31	7
West Memphis	28 388	523	11	32	131	349	2 251	1 043	1 038	170	20
White Hall	5 138	3	0	0	1	2	180	33	140	7	0
Wynne	8 545	29	1	5	4	19	290	114	168	8	3

[1]The FBI does not publish arson data unless it receives data from either the agency or the state for all 12 months of the calendar year.

Table 8. Offenses Known to Law Enforcement, by State and City, 2005—*Continued*

(Number.)

City	Population	Violent crime	Murder and non-negligent man-slaughter	Forcible rape	Robbery	Aggravated assault	Property crime	Burglary	Larceny-theft	Motor vehicle theft	Arson[1]
California											
Adelanto	21 786	99	1	7	23	68	639	263	260	116	15
Agoura Hills	23 015	47	0	7	9	31	337	83	230	24	2
Alameda	71 608	232	0	11	88	133	1 959	367	1 285	307	21
Albany	16 324	55	0	1	36	18	776	136	497	143	3
Alhambra	88 579	321	1	12	154	154	2 607	575	1 472	560	16
Aliso Viejo	41 743	32	2	3	8	19	553	115	394	44	7
Alturas	2 948	9	0	5	0	4	61	17	42	2	3
American Canyon	13 979	32	0	2	9	21	341	91	201	49	4
Anaheim	335 992	1 616	10	81	554	971	9 512	1 929	5 537	2 046	79
Anderson	10 444	61	0	9	5	47	429	167	231	31	0
Antioch	101 593	553	10	28	232	283	2 920	733	1 269	918	44
Apple Valley	63 055	253	4	20	43	186	2 224	603	1 227	394	11
Arcadia	56 364	136	2	7	61	66	1 849	433	1 254	162	5
Arcata	17 041	48	0	6	11	31	854	252	519	83	4
Arroyo Grande	16 290	43	0	3	6	34	415	86	300	29	1
Artesia	16 893	118	1	4	33	80	338	98	173	67	7
Arvin	14 500	44	2	4	6	32	783	189	482	112	12
Atascadero	27 338	113	0	12	10	91	607	118	431	58	2
Atherton	7 174	22	0	2	8	12	219	50	164	5	0
Atwater	26 545	108	5	6	13	84	1 086	255	694	137	7
Auburn	12 860	55	0	3	2	50	385	88	249	48	2
Avalon	3 382	20	0	1	3	16	159	33	68	58	0
Avenal	16 792	46	0	0	3	43	166	66	92	8	3
Azusa	47 703	198	0	15	47	136	1 297	269	738	290	5
Bakersfield	285 821	1 706	32	45	530	1 099	16 438	3 746	10 034	2 658	182
Baldwin Park	79 411	353	5	14	100	234	2 103	439	1 036	628	13
Banning	28 876	192	0	11	40	141	1 169	510	520	139	0
Barstow	23 684	290	1	21	69	199	1 051	305	493	253	11
Bear Valley	4 514	1	0	1	0	0	20	5	13	2	0
Beaumont	18 235	53	1	4	17	31	637	123	405	109	1
Bell	38 030	166	5	7	65	89	458	132	133	193	0
Bellflower	75 462	537	9	14	247	267	2 500	477	1 170	853	14
Bell Gardens	45 673	284	5	25	73	181	944	251	316	377	4
Belmont	24 611	10	0	1	9	0	636	94	478	64	0
Belvedere	2 101	1	0	0	0	1	39	22	16	1	0
Benicia	27 006	53	0	3	14	36	550	160	303	87	3
Berkeley	102 191	570	3	18	354	195	7 976	1 229	5 503	1 244	25
Beverly Hills	35 321	134	1	10	58	65	1 052	314	700	38	5
Biggs	1 827	3	0	0	0	3	46	18	21	7	0
Bishop	3 645	23	0	1	4	18	172	31	135	6	0
Blue Lake	1 146	6	0	2	1	3	94	29	50	15	0
Blythe	22 577	142	2	4	14	122	691	175	441	75	27
Bradbury	991	0	0	0	0	0	11	6	4	1	0
Brawley	22 403	86	0	6	18	62	999	395	448	156	19
Brea	38 778	87	1	2	40	44	1 622	277	1 179	166	6
Brentwood	40 091	100	0	14	24	62	985	186	679	120	9
Brisbane	3 583	11	0	1	2	8	136	19	92	25	4
Broadmoor	4 295	10	0	0	2	8	80	23	31	26	1
Buellton	3 773	6	1	1	2	2	75	19	52	4	0
Buena Park	79 884	306	2	14	124	166	1 926	449	1 042	435	23
Burbank	104 805	246	3	13	67	163	2 771	586	1 690	495	5
Burlingame	27 602	68	0	3	28	37	939	145	697	97	8
Calabasas	21 773	16	0	2	5	9	285	81	172	32	1
Calexico	34 554	138	0	4	25	109	1 313	396	504	413	31
California City	11 498	57	1	2	4	50	263	93	151	19	2
Calimesa	7 547	18	1	1	6	10	186	50	109	27	1
Calipatria	7 729	2	0	0	0	2	32	13	19	0	0
Calistoga	5 242	16	0	2	0	14	118	17	80	21	0
Camarillo	61 294	94	1	15	30	48	1 046	259	710	77	12
Campbell	37 259	71	0	5	13	53	1 217	225	872	120	17
Canyon Lake	11 235	12	0	4	1	7	136	39	69	28	1
Capitola	9 704	70	0	7	9	54	987	110	835	42	0
Carlsbad	89 633	256	2	11	79	164	2 411	517	1 648	246	11
Carmel	4 095	8	0	2	2	4	131	32	95	4	0
Carpinteria	13 921	28	2	2	3	21	179	33	127	19	1
Carson	94 355	646	7	19	221	399	2 402	543	1 270	589	23
Cathedral City	51 093	252	3	10	44	195	2 079	559	1 023	497	0
Ceres	38 802	170	2	8	38	122	2 229	280	1 294	655	21
Cerritos	53 249	175	1	5	97	72	2 020	453	1 287	280	20
Chico	70 670	253	3	32	79	139	2 671	719	1 462	490	62
Chino	76 547	210	2	9	75	124	2 539	521	1 576	442	12
Chino Hills	76 124	100	3	8	18	71	1 092	259	705	128	5
Chowchilla	15 797	47	0	2	6	39	408	121	234	53	10
Chula Vista	206 239	927	5	66	338	518	7 489	1 235	3 758	2 496	23
City of Angels	3 725	21	0	1	0	20	55	21	30	4	1
Claremont	35 330	60	3	2	30	25	1 116	310	731	75	0
Clayton	11 200	10	0	0	4	6	176	31	132	13	1
Clearlake	14 609	52	0	0	5	47	524	159	305	60	12
Cloverdale	7 896	40	0	0	2	38	177	38	120	19	1
Clovis	82 921	151	4	21	47	79	3 286	642	2 222	422	15

[1]The FBI does not publish arson data unless it receives data from either the agency or the state for all 12 months of the calendar year.

Table 8. Offenses Known to Law Enforcement, by State and City, 2005—*Continued*

(Number.)

City	Population	Violent crime	Murder and non-negligent man-slaughter	Forcible rape	Robbery	Aggravated assault	Property crime	Burglary	Larceny-theft	Motor vehicle theft	Arson[1]
Coachella	30 394	155	1	13	51	90	1 393	342	727	324	8
Coalinga	17 216	33	0	6	4	23	428	123	261	44	2
Colma	1 419	16	0	0	5	11	308	12	275	21	0
Colton	51 723	267	5	17	105	140	1 941	472	983	486	6
Colusa	5 894	7	0	2	0	5	183	62	106	15	0
Commerce	13 494	147	2	4	64	77	1 118	116	559	443	23
Compton	96 874	1 731	65	40	474	1 152	2 615	638	971	1 006	91
Concord	125 154	508	1	14	197	296	6 248	1 114	3 972	1 162	11
Corcoran	22 583	65	1	2	4	58	243	103	119	21	5
Corning	7 126	47	0	2	4	41	445	140	264	41	3
Corona	146 363	321	4	33	140	144	4 448	926	2 587	935	37
Coronado	23 932	22	0	6	6	10	527	90	349	88	5
Costa Mesa	111 144	306	3	30	119	154	3 843	596	2 692	555	12
Cotati	7 136	44	0	4	3	37	237	50	175	12	2
Covina	48 410	213	0	9	85	119	2 136	468	1 359	309	25
Crescent City	7 473	41	1	6	8	26	367	86	250	31	0
Cudahy	25 358	132	4	3	44	81	456	82	153	221	2
Culver City	40 161	183	1	9	130	43	1 282	246	898	138	2
Cupertino	51 746	56	0	0	10	46	933	250	632	51	12
Cypress	47 930	67	1	5	28	33	1 003	174	707	122	9
Daly City	101 288	286	2	20	122	142	2 158	251	1 439	468	15
Dana Point	36 258	61	0	7	9	45	529	120	371	38	6
Danville	42 479	41	0	1	9	31	621	119	477	25	3
Davis	64 145	232	0	26	45	161	1 909	483	1 239	187	18
Delano	44 280	209	5	5	48	151	2 121	669	845	607	61
Del Mar	4 455	10	0	0	1	9	266	50	179	37	0
Del Rey Oaks	1 625	0	0	0	0	0	45	21	24	0	0
Desert Hot Springs	19 401	256	3	22	47	184	1 703	752	670	281	0
Diamond Bar	58 713	107	2	3	38	64	899	282	463	154	8
Dinuba	18 602	152	2	4	23	123	1 089	225	668	196	6
Dixon	16 821	81	2	6	19	54	639	107	457	75	7
Dorris	883	6	0	2	2	2	18	8	10	0	0
Dos Palos	4 985	37	0	3	0	34	123	42	68	13	1
Downey	111 051	448	7	30	250	161	3 532	579	1 851	1 102	28
Duarte	22 421	77	0	0	20	57	502	128	265	109	6
Dublin	37 241	79	0	1	15	63	807	170	499	138	9
Dunsmuir	1 897	4	0	1	0	3	66	21	41	4	0
East Palo Alto	32 255	429	15	21	108	285	1 125	387	432	306	0
El Cajon	94 611	518	2	40	171	305	4 045	769	2 140	1 136	36
El Centro	38 605	348	0	18	43	287	2 115	758	1 097	260	2
El Cerrito	23 292	180	3	2	120	55	1 443	241	878	324	5
El Monte	122 934	711	4	21	241	445	3 487	702	1 650	1 135	22
El Segundo	16 602	42	0	7	17	18	692	177	445	70	5
Emeryville	8 076	94	1	3	60	30	1 187	134	836	217	0
Encinitas	60 456	171	3	11	45	112	1 234	324	724	186	7
Escalon	6 983	25	0	2	2	21	325	58	226	41	2
Escondido	136 362	692	2	31	186	473	4 911	801	3 031	1 079	37
Etna	796	0	0	0	0	0	18	8	10	0	0
Eureka	25 974	170	1	25	63	81	1 851	503	1 000	348	18
Exeter	9 907	55	0	2	5	48	565	135	361	69	1
Fairfax	7 207	7	0	0	0	7	129	29	88	12	0
Fairfield	104 639	585	9	38	218	320	4 460	748	2 876	836	34
Farmersville	9 647	42	1	1	11	29	340	65	219	56	1
Ferndale	1 415	0	0	0	0	0	22	12	10	0	3
Fillmore	15 066	63	0	0	14	49	332	72	239	21	6
Firebaugh	6 983	15	0	1	0	14	257	15	227	15	0
Folsom	64 385	89	0	11	18	60	1 716	305	1 238	173	19
Fontana	159 769	734	10	50	232	442	3 681	782	1 496	1 403	20
Fort Bragg	6 924	44	0	3	2	39	347	92	245	10	5
Fort Jones	669	2	0	0	0	2	15	7	7	1	0
Fortuna	11 068	21	0	7	2	12	453	95	316	42	4
Foster City	29 039	29	0	0	7	22	421	80	308	33	5
Fountain Valley	56 726	72	1	6	30	35	1 383	303	884	196	10
Fowler	4 568	28	0	1	6	21	259	34	183	42	0
Fremont	203 717	521	1	40	188	292	4 803	1 009	3 035	759	20
Fresno[3]	460 758	3 897	49	149	1 275	2 424	25 546	4 170	16 088	5 288	248
Fullerton	134 325	390	0	37	149	204	4 584	805	3 152	627	44
Galt	23 117	83	1	7	22	53	930	324	446	160	6
Gardena	60 124	496	3	16	295	182	1 594	453	715	426	5
Garden Grove	168 458	745	6	22	229	488	4 505	803	2 591	1 111	56
Gilroy	44 651	203	0	13	67	123	1 735	246	1 309	180	13
Glendale	202 663	350	19	14	136	181	3 790	723	2 453	614	29
Glendora	51 227	56	0	5	24	27	1 265	183	954	128	8
Goleta	28 368	43	0	7	12	24	486	141	325	20	2
Gonzales	8 538	40	0	2	11	27	260	89	130	41	3
Grand Terrace	12 431	20	0	3	9	8	371	103	216	52	1
Grass Valley	12 066	72	0	2	12	58	433	82	300	51	4
Greenfield	12 930	42	1	7	24	10	598	159	393	46	2
Gridley	5 686	39	0	2	1	36	250	108	119	23	0
Grover Beach	13 123	36	0	2	8	26	286	66	188	32	0

[1]The FBI does not publish arson data unless it receives data from either the agency or the state for all 12 months of the calendar year.
[3]Because of changes in the state/local agency's reporting practices, figures are not comparable to previous years' data.

Table 8. Offenses Known to Law Enforcement, by State and City, 2005—*Continued*

(Number.)

City	Population	Violent crime	Murder and non-negligent man-slaughter	Forcible rape	Robbery	Aggravated assault	Property crime	Burglary	Larceny-theft	Motor vehicle theft	Arson[1]
Guadalupe	6 029	17	0	0	1	16	105	24	70	11	4
Gustine	5 375	22	0	1	0	21	112	24	77	11	0
Half Moon Bay	12 289	20	0	6	0	14	253	44	198	11	4
Hanford	47 131	185	0	17	51	117	1 855	224	1 407	224	11
Hawaiian Gardens	15 508	142	3	3	70	66	499	101	272	126	4
Hawthorne	86 852	520	10	18	225	267	2 196	785	841	570	5
Hayward	141 730	641	9	37	301	294	5 473	1 147	2 338	1 988	52
Healdsburg	11 204	22	0	3	4	15	381	148	208	25	5
Hemet	67 005	381	3	19	141	218	3 419	910	1 943	566	14
Hercules	23 581	56	0	2	25	29	600	113	331	156	1
Hermosa Beach	19 667	48	1	5	10	32	561	184	336	41	2
Hesperia	73 863	223	4	14	81	124	2 032	484	945	603	12
Hidden Hills	2 006	1	0	0	0	1	19	5	11	3	0
Highland	50 570	204	7	10	77	110	1 403	316	705	382	14
Hillsborough	10 670	5	0	2	0	3	99	43	49	7	0
Hollister	36 571	155	0	8	29	118	1 033	214	659	160	15
Holtville	5 542	0	0	0	0	0	139	47	66	26	1
Hughson	5 946	8	0	0	2	6	208	84	96	28	0
Huntington Beach	196 602	466	1	32	92	341	4 103	789	2 783	531	24
Huntington Park	63 397	577	2	18	357	200	2 671	287	1 336	1 048	16
Huron	7 043	61	0	2	18	41	279	73	178	28	3
Imperial	9 676	10	0	3	2	5	188	38	130	20	2
Imperial Beach	26 887	132	0	3	41	88	790	188	335	267	4
Indian Wells	4 761	7	0	2	2	3	249	53	183	13	0
Indio	63 747	299	6	28	96	169	2 924	802	1 479	643	1
Industry	840	140	3	4	63	70	1 728	223	1 124	381	7
Inglewood	116 079	1 057	26	42	555	434	3 091	822	1 347	922	16
Ione	7 627	19	0	5	0	14	122	32	80	10	0
Irvine	179 501	151	2	17	42	90	3 225	709	2 211	305	30
Irwindale	1 488	23	0	1	5	17	197	91	57	49	7
Isleton	840	8	0	0	2	6	45	13	28	4	1
Jackson	4 201	41	0	3	1	37	202	70	118	14	2
Kensington	5 266	1	0	0	0	1	135	24	82	29	0
Kerman	10 306	36	0	5	5	26	410	97	244	69	4
King City	11 236	37	1	3	12	21	596	184	378	34	8
Kingsburg	11 122	19	0	0	4	15	421	85	247	89	4
La Canada Flintridge	21 203	28	0	1	9	18	274	94	160	20	3
Lafayette	24 829	30	2	6	7	15	489	112	322	55	1
Laguna Beach	24 411	45	0	6	9	30	579	151	381	47	0
Laguna Hills	32 595	53	0	4	16	33	703	160	486	57	7
Laguna Niguel	65 377	62	2	2	15	43	780	143	600	37	14
Laguna Woods	18 428	4	0	0	4	0	110	14	93	3	1
La Habra	60 200	190	4	6	77	103	1 614	284	1 014	316	17
La Habra Heights	6 028	6	0	0	0	6	120	24	87	9	1
Lake Elsinore	37 255	172	4	11	32	125	1 511	319	883	309	4
Lake Forest	77 523	121	2	8	33	78	971	198	675	98	8
Lakeport	5 265	14	0	1	2	11	132	26	97	9	0
Lake Shastina	2 337	1	0	0	0	1	23	9	13	1	0
Lakewood	81 626	371	0	13	193	165	2 788	418	1 880	490	16
La Mesa	54 213	201	2	10	107	82	2 229	328	1 345	556	6
La Mirada	49 966	125	1	3	41	80	1 258	307	741	210	4
Lancaster	129 784	1 186	16	54	347	769	4 707	1 260	2 436	1 011	70
La Palma	16 041	23	1	2	12	8	320	114	175	31	2
La Puente	42 337	237	4	8	57	168	827	165	404	258	4
La Quinta	35 598	128	0	9	21	98	2 075	621	1 290	164	1
La Verne	33 366	67	0	7	23	37	889	159	658	72	1
Lawndale	32 651	208	1	12	80	115	622	154	316	152	8
Lemon Grove	24 700	156	1	6	59	90	805	208	339	258	6
Lemoore	22 379	78	0	9	9	60	760	144	516	100	5
Lincoln	28 321	47	0	2	8	37	678	174	422	82	11
Lindsay	10 805	96	0	1	8	87	483	127	231	125	6
Livermore	78 501	141	1	27	27	86	1 659	422	1 006	231	52
Livingston	12 173	58	0	7	7	44	284	104	120	60	21
Lodi	62 372	260	1	17	74	168	2 974	538	1 900	536	12
Loma Linda	20 467	35	2	4	16	13	626	139	350	137	3
Lomita	20 685	104	0	8	28	68	415	104	253	58	2
Lompoc	41 180	228	1	14	40	173	1 191	155	948	88	14
Long Beach	479 729	3 399	42	104	1 403	1 850	13 506	2 955	6 808	3 743	123
Los Alamitos	11 858	29	1	1	10	17	341	108	199	34	5
Los Altos	27 171	10	0	2	4	4	325	130	181	14	2
Los Altos Hills	8 176	2	0	2	0	0	82	38	44	0	1
Los Angeles[3]	3 871 077	31 767	489	1 105	13 797	16 376	117 285	22 592	65 972	28 721	2 229
Los Banos	32 041	227	0	13	23	191	1 092	268	699	125	8
Los Gatos	28 115	37	0	5	15	17	580	145	393	42	10
Lynwood	72 108	676	21	23	258	374	1 910	295	578	1 037	52
Madera	50 375	399	4	22	88	285	1 808	367	1 085	356	0
Malibu	13 393	23	1	3	3	16	269	92	141	36	2
Mammoth Lakes	7 307	44	0	8	4	32	354	80	248	26	0
Manhattan Beach	36 562	73	1	5	32	35	818	216	535	67	4
Manteca	61 815	283	2	15	71	195	3 362	553	2 147	662	8

[1]The FBI does not publish arson data unless it receives data from either the agency or the state for all 12 months of the calendar year.
[3]Because of changes in the state/local agency's reporting practices, figures are not comparable to previous years' data.

Table 8. Offenses Known to Law Enforcement, by State and City, 2005—*Continued*

(Number.)

City	Population	Violent crime	Murder and non-negligent man-slaughter	Forcible rape	Robbery	Aggravated assault	Property crime	Burglary	Larceny-theft	Motor vehicle theft	Arson[1]
Marina	19 452	90	0	9	28	53	518	113	355	50	2
Martinez	36 546	115	0	9	28	78	1 424	235	979	210	0
Marysville	12 601	110	1	9	10	90	733	123	444	166	5
Maywood	29 007	158	4	5	70	79	447	77	138	232	6
Menlo Park	29 957	88	0	9	43	36	747	159	497	91	4
Merced	72 968	572	10	24	167	371	4 189	697	2 957	535	39
Millbrae	20 555	31	1	3	14	13	364	95	228	41	7
Mill Valley	13 448	15	0	0	8	7	268	70	167	31	1
Milpitas	63 114	195	2	17	36	140	2 168	315	1 575	278	16
Mission Viejo	96 892	110	2	3	36	69	1 259	225	953	81	14
Modesto	208 142	1 316	8	65	388	855	13 046	1 742	8 290	3 014	95
Monrovia	38 427	118	0	11	54	53	1 167	149	851	167	4
Montague	1 498	5	0	1	1	3	42	12	19	11	0
Montclair	35 479	222	5	12	89	116	2 047	253	1 339	455	7
Montebello	64 123	282	5	18	125	134	2 143	300	1 094	749	30
Monterey	29 866	172	0	16	31	125	1 295	245	977	73	1
Monterey Park	62 812	149	2	4	89	54	1 395	274	707	414	1
Monte Sereno	3 459	0	0	0	0	0	52	10	42	0	0
Moorpark	36 132	45	2	2	9	32	357	91	238	28	4
Moraga	16 909	18	0	3	2	13	167	31	120	16	2
Moreno Valley	167 394	757	11	57	344	345	6 260	1 522	3 274	1 464	15
Morgan Hill	35 117	60	1	11	16	32	1 058	244	728	86	21
Morro Bay	10 377	16	0	1	0	15	177	32	132	13	3
Mountain View	69 469	302	1	5	63	233	2 176	253	1 660	263	8
Mount Shasta	3 653	7	1	1	0	5	126	23	98	5	0
Murrieta	75 008	122	1	9	36	76	1 815	489	1 058	268	8
Napa	75 966	384	0	19	34	331	2 080	359	1 553	168	16
National City	54 934	456	4	16	182	254	2 726	376	1 409	941	15
Needles	5 381	32	0	2	5	25	227	57	144	26	5
Nevada City	3 061	7	0	1	1	5	100	19	70	11	0
Newark	42 793	175	2	17	71	85	1 977	331	1 321	325	12
Newman	8 609	16	0	0	3	13	192	50	118	24	3
Newport Beach	80 488	122	3	12	26	81	2 496	589	1 715	192	8
Norco	26 845	90	1	3	17	69	1 079	216	714	149	2
Norwalk	107 391	473	11	17	189	256	2 831	558	1 399	874	24
Novato	49 565	88	1	13	22	52	1 233	334	754	145	18
Oakdale	17 796	52	2	4	15	31	1 223	351	729	143	4
Oakland	400 619	5 692	93	306	2 672	2 621	23 027	5 783	8 227	9 017	266
Oakley	26 996	72	0	3	17	52	686	117	441	128	4
Oceanside	168 550	983	7	78	264	634	5 657	1 065	3 846	746	33
Ojai	8 099	18	0	0	3	15	203	32	160	11	1
Ontario	171 186	866	12	56	294	504	6 744	991	3 714	2 039	84
Orange	134 708	225	2	2	100	121	3 419	537	2 301	581	45
Orinda	18 297	10	0	2	6	2	261	51	186	24	0
Orland	6 645	30	0	6	2	22	316	119	157	40	4
Oroville	13 297	164	2	22	37	103	935	285	449	201	1
Oxnard	184 806	830	19	47	386	378	4 384	941	2 681	762	63
Pacifica	37 429	67	0	7	12	48	794	122	567	105	2
Pacific Grove	15 381	18	0	0	5	13	325	75	243	7	0
Palmdale	132 024	1 042	15	48	318	661	4 115	967	2 384	764	62
Palm Desert	46 925	145	2	6	38	99	2 662	714	1 691	257	4
Palm Springs	46 744	347	4	23	112	208	3 102	872	1 659	571	39
Palo Alto	57 240	91	1	5	46	39	2 043	371	1 548	124	19
Palos Verdes Estates	13 960	9	0	1	1	7	103	36	64	3	0
Paradise	26 848	33	0	6	7	20	796	249	463	84	4
Paramount	57 277	452	10	4	221	217	2 082	358	956	768	22
Parlier	13 067	82	2	1	8	71	650	110	376	164	5
Pasadena	145 025	803	6	23	285	489	4 389	788	3 041	560	29
Paso Robles	27 066	110	0	14	11	85	667	194	388	85	6
Patterson	14 891	33	2	3	6	22	511	117	306	88	1
Perris	46 097	229	4	12	80	133	2 104	368	1 137	599	4
Petaluma	55 727	215	0	34	24	157	1 300	128	1 036	136	15
Pico Rivera	65 631	373	15	17	117	224	1 535	264	773	498	25
Piedmont	10 784	11	0	0	10	1	306	67	178	61	4
Pinole	19 400	127	2	3	52	70	1 294	200	797	297	7
Pismo Beach	8 529	33	0	3	5	25	379	90	272	17	1
Pittsburg	63 016	248	5	7	114	122	2 604	458	1 516	630	5
Placentia	50 281	124	3	8	30	83	1 043	231	668	144	45
Placerville	10 218	26	1	2	4	19	362	80	212	70	1
Pleasant Hill	33 752	127	1	10	47	69	1 874	334	1 304	236	13
Pleasanton	66 389	96	0	10	24	62	1 555	260	1 152	143	11
Pomona	156 480	1 235	21	44	385	785	5 308	997	2 775	1 536	25
Porterville	44 303	257	2	18	48	189	2 287	506	1 351	430	1
Port Hueneme	22 187	96	4	3	20	69	477	122	283	72	2
Poway	49 302	95	1	11	20	63	815	172	551	92	7
Rancho Cucamonga	160 404	372	2	35	134	201	4 393	768	2 921	704	30
Rancho Mirage	16 338	42	1	0	4	37	1 051	253	688	110	2
Rancho Palos Verdes	42 591	45	2	3	4	36	387	116	247	24	5
Rancho Santa Margarita	50 336	32	0	0	7	25	453	80	342	31	7
Red Bluff	14 003	170	1	10	14	145	862	215	587	60	5

[1]The FBI does not publish arson data unless it receives data from either the agency or the state for all 12 months of the calendar year.

Table 8. Offenses Known to Law Enforcement, by State and City, 2005—*Continued*

(Number.)

City	Population	Violent crime	Murder and non-negligent man-slaughter	Forcible rape	Robbery	Aggravated assault	Property crime	Burglary	Larceny-theft	Motor vehicle theft	Arson[1]
Redding	89 161	550	2	80	75	393	4 102	943	2 665	494	23
Redlands	70 145	310	1	19	92	198	2 799	553	1 799	447	24
Redondo Beach	67 126	178	0	9	68	101	1 599	319	1 080	200	0
Redwood City	73 833	388	3	22	103	260	2 553	354	1 831	368	29
Reedley	22 412	164	2	9	21	132	664	132	351	181	7
Rialto	100 321	804	11	33	214	546	3 490	715	1 602	1 173	23
Richmond	102 997	1 174	40	35	526	573	5 808	1 062	2 350	2 396	46
Ridgecrest	26 026	101	0	6	14	81	696	217	414	65	13
Rio Dell	3 178	18	0	2	0	16	73	16	50	7	0
Rio Vista	6 600	3	0	0	2	1	125	19	77	29	0
Ripon	13 066	23	0	3	6	14	411	34	286	91	2
Riverbank	20 341	47	0	0	13	34	810	133	539	138	14
Riverside	290 299	1 954	10	113	675	1 156	13 425	2 498	8 157	2 770	208
Rocklin	48 960	70	0	6	15	49	1 304	254	900	150	16
Rohnert Park	42 245	277	0	12	21	244	1 045	156	811	78	5
Rolling Hills	1 944	1	0	0	0	1	14	3	11	0	0
Rolling Hills Estates	8 043	16	0	1	4	11	130	31	91	8	1
Rosemead	55 663	195	3	8	75	109	1 540	403	662	475	8
Roseville	104 297	363	0	28	87	248	4 750	852	3 188	710	8
Ross	2 309	0	0	0	0	0	49	9	38	2	0
Sacramento	457 347	5 265	52	170	2 018	3 025	26 083	5 841	13 320	6 922	352
Salinas	149 167	1 030	7	43	335	645	6 778	935	4 339	1 504	35
San Anselmo	12 190	33	0	3	2	28	273	59	201	13	3
San Bernardino	199 723	2 510	58	72	912	1 468	11 226	2 525	5 527	3 174	87
San Bruno	39 924	141	1	8	33	99	947	127	654	166	8
San Carlos	27 094	31	0	3	10	18	580	105	419	56	7
San Clemente	59 945	80	1	5	15	59	853	200	579	74	10
Sand City	309	8	0	0	3	5	145	2	141	2	0
San Diego	1 272 148	6 603	51	376	1 862	4 314	46 213	7 462	24 613	14 138	233
San Dimas	36 306	74	1	3	23	47	880	202	552	126	3
San Fernando	24 517	123	0	8	54	61	517	139	252	126	8
San Francisco	749 172	5 985	96	172	3 078	2 639	34 269	6 208	19 887	8 174	188
San Gabriel	41 534	202	4	9	99	90	1 089	327	584	178	5
Sanger	21 180	102	0	9	16	77	912	167	585	160	2
San Jacinto	28 229	132	4	8	40	80	1 222	329	654	239	0
San Jose	910 528	3 492	26	263	884	2 319	22 930	4 049	13 374	5 507	388
San Juan Capistrano	35 114	59	0	2	21	36	465	105	303	57	9
San Leandro	79 709	465	4	23	237	201	4 069	701	2 328	1 040	18
San Luis Obispo	44 324	170	2	23	35	110	1 793	361	1 335	97	38
San Marcos	68 801	237	0	15	57	165	1 630	359	989	282	10
San Marino	13 360	9	0	0	7	2	263	66	181	16	0
San Mateo	91 881	403	4	22	117	260	2 780	355	2 205	220	24
San Pablo	31 247	269	3	5	160	101	1 831	316	874	641	6
San Rafael	55 929	172	2	22	65	83	2 052	427	1 247	378	12
San Ramon	45 919	66	1	5	14	46	972	146	733	93	4
Santa Ana	344 991	1 845	17	74	644	1 110	10 292	1 194	5 515	3 583	156
Santa Barbara	87 950	560	0	31	76	453	2 944	680	2 060	204	43
Santa Clara	104 692	190	5	18	49	118	3 420	553	2 470	397	10
Santa Clarita	165 894	336	3	17	106	210	3 552	838	2 200	514	27
Santa Cruz	54 573	503	2	49	96	356	3 137	573	2 316	248	25
Santa Fe Springs	17 173	174	1	3	77	93	1 709	300	1 005	404	4
Santa Maria	84 312	601	3	36	92	470	2 354	383	1 342	629	19
Santa Monica	88 406	551	4	21	241	285	3 496	788	2 286	422	16
Santa Paula	28 923	100	0	8	29	63	641	140	407	94	1
Santa Rosa	154 656	1 021	2	61	168	790	4 900	803	3 508	589	26
Santee	52 926	163	1	16	30	116	1 316	281	800	235	9
Saratoga	29 830	21	1	3	2	15	377	115	249	13	1
Sausalito	7 276	8	0	1	3	4	209	44	147	18	1
Scotts Valley	11 279	16	1	2	2	11	351	79	257	15	1
Seal Beach	24 621	49	0	1	9	39	497	105	340	52	3
Seaside	34 357	171	0	10	42	119	738	129	545	64	9
Sebastopol	7 736	19	0	1	4	14	187	41	130	16	4
Selma	22 065	103	0	4	35	64	1 396	176	938	282	1
Shafter	14 249	53	1	6	5	41	688	193	413	82	12
Sierra Madre	11 096	5	0	1	0	4	210	64	134	12	0
Signal Hill	10 769	57	0	4	30	23	583	121	360	102	7
Simi Valley	119 682	172	0	17	47	108	2 315	583	1 515	217	22
Solana Beach	12 945	24	0	1	12	11	312	87	179	46	1
Soledad	26 500	33	1	5	21	6	497	206	251	40	0
Solvang	5 260	12	0	5	6	1	96	23	73	0	3
Sonoma	9 744	31	0	1	2	28	387	132	238	17	12
Sonora	4 649	22	0	2	6	14	496	151	312	33	3
South El Monte	21 946	130	3	5	41	81	750	147	313	290	5
South Gate	100 289	527	6	19	305	197	2 897	444	1 164	1 289	18
South Lake Tahoe	24 085	131	1	8	21	101	553	189	301	63	1
South Pasadena	25 214	42	0	1	28	13	655	148	409	98	3
South San Francisco	60 295	175	3	8	46	118	1 541	609	640	292	25
Stallion Springs	1 624	0	0	0	0	0	43	16	26	1	0
Stanton	38 175	149	3	6	63	77	937	201	526	210	15
St. Helena	6 066	5	0	1	0	4	129	39	81	9	0

[1]The FBI does not publish arson data unless it receives data from either the agency or the state for all 12 months of the calendar year.

Table 8. Offenses Known to Law Enforcement, by State and City, 2005—*Continued*

(Number.)

City	Population	Violent crime	Murder and non-negligent man-slaughter	Forcible rape	Robbery	Aggravated assault	Property crime	Burglary	Larceny-theft	Motor vehicle theft	Arson[1]
Stockton	281 747	4 202	41	109	1 357	2 695	18 861	3 434	11 487	3 940	60
Suisun City	27 124	127	0	13	39	75	576	124	304	148	5
Sunnyvale	128 862	232	3	27	73	129	2 661	495	1 794	372	16
Susanville	18 163	45	0	5	1	39	295	76	208	11	6
Sutter Creek	2 443	12	0	3	2	7	93	31	58	4	3
Taft	9 136	34	0	2	6	26	275	61	198	16	18
Temecula	82 628	269	4	16	73	176	2 808	684	1 725	399	4
Temple City	37 156	76	0	3	31	42	557	181	296	80	2
Thousand Oaks	125 884	174	2	13	56	103	1 784	379	1 289	116	18
Tiburon	8 749	5	0	1	0	4	100	21	70	9	4
Torrance	143 790	320	1	20	211	88	3 290	641	2 144	505	24
Tracy	77 411	149	0	7	60	82	3 301	473	2 366	462	20
Trinidad	312	0	0	0	0	0	46	10	33	3	1
Truckee	15 554	26	0	4	4	18	352	99	207	46	2
Tulare	49 020	497	8	17	85	387	3 187	904	1 809	474	60
Tulelake	1 015	2	0	0	0	2	17	6	11	0	0
Turlock	65 919	411	2	18	97	294	3 705	637	2 014	1 054	22
Tustin	69 068	228	2	10	60	156	1 926	438	1 146	342	14
Twentynine Palms	30 281	105	0	11	5	89	530	194	270	66	8
Twin Cities	21 113	13	0	3	6	4	672	222	385	65	3
Ukiah	15 683	74	0	5	11	58	542	189	291	62	10
Union City	69 396	416	3	15	167	231	2 507	603	1 325	579	11
Upland	74 014	282	4	21	104	153	3 025	466	2 107	452	11
Vacaville	94 929	262	2	23	69	168	2 518	353	1 899	266	33
Ventura	104 759	297	1	19	107	170	3 911	815	2 695	401	18
Vernon	94	48	0	0	28	20	544	52	260	232	9
Victorville	83 340	435	12	30	153	240	4 229	865	2 536	828	10
Villa Park	6 109	4	0	0	0	4	118	25	87	6	0
Visalia	105 350	1 055	10	39	192	814	6 765	1 216	4 347	1 202	31
Vista	92 193	530	4	21	190	315	2 971	771	1 621	579	29
Walnut	31 817	45	0	1	21	23	492	178	236	78	6
Walnut Creek	65 252	130	1	8	38	83	2 919	507	2 142	270	14
Waterford	8 173	41	0	2	2	37	317	98	172	47	0
Watsonville	47 465	237	2	17	81	137	2 043	284	1 481	278	7
Weed	3 097	15	0	5	1	9	137	39	83	15	2
West Covina	109 390	350	6	19	150	175	4 050	744	2 398	908	5
West Hollywood	37 178	342	2	19	167	154	1 647	312	1 073	262	5
Westlake Village	8 641	16	0	0	3	13	150	39	99	12	0
Westminster	90 452	351	3	14	96	238	2 866	561	1 769	536	27
Westmorland	2 105	1	0	0	0	1	25	14	10	1	0
West Sacramento	39 612	361	2	23	60	276	1 433	563	480	390	27
Wheatland	3 360	9	0	2	0	7	98	24	59	15	0
Whittier	86 077	307	5	15	125	162	2 592	429	1 655	508	14
Williams	4 064	15	0	3	1	11	71	14	42	15	1
Willits	5 132	34	0	1	9	24	148	41	92	15	4
Willows	6 341	34	0	1	4	29	303	60	220	23	0
Windsor	24 915	87	0	5	5	77	354	61	264	29	2
Winters	6 883	6	0	0	0	6	131	27	92	12	6
Woodlake	7 129	42	1	5	3	33	375	98	206	71	2
Woodland	52 036	142	1	14	34	93	1 794	307	1 182	305	24
Yorba Linda	64 083	49	0	2	5	42	797	169	553	75	9
Yountville	3 350	3	0	1	0	2	54	11	39	4	0
Yreka	7 214	27	0	2	1	24	323	36	264	23	1
Yuba City	52 470	188	3	17	48	120	2 304	453	1 604	247	15
Yucaipa	48 182	71	3	3	12	53	855	208	468	179	15
Yucca Valley	19 157	71	0	7	9	55	478	129	254	95	7
Colorado											
Alamosa	8 663	83	0	5	5	73	317	55	245	17	0
Arvada	103 983	196	2	23	52	119	3 877	524	2 772	581	46
Aspen	5 796	22	0	6	0	16	402	32	359	11	4
Ault	1 429	13	0	2	0	11	62	19	40	3	3
Aurora	295 888	1 836	28	223	644	941	14 718	2 474	9 502	2 742	90
Avon	6 451	27	0	3	2	22	219	27	174	18	3
Basalt	3 015	0	0	0	0	0	51	8	34	9	0
Bayfield	1 619	8	0	1	0	7	63	10	53	0	0
Berthoud	5 125	0	0	0	0	0	54	5	49	0	0
Boulder	93 474	216	0	42	34	140	3 624	551	2 821	252	61
Bow Mar	815	0	0	0	0	0	25	10	13	2	0
Breckenridge	2 700	41	0	1	1	39	440	51	378	11	0
Brighton	27 300	59	0	4	10	45	1 424	204	1 038	182	19
Broomfield	43 496	42	0	9	11	22	1 697	124	1 403	170	17
Brush	5 291	6	0	1	0	5	161	19	134	8	2
Buena Vista	2 214	3	0	0	0	3	26	5	21	0	0
Burlington	3 587	10	0	5	0	5	107	25	77	5	3
Canon City	16 032	108	0	31	4	73	693	87	579	27	7
Carbondale	5 785	28	0	7	1	20	158	23	130	5	0
Castle Rock	33 162	43	0	0	2	41	660	114	487	59	4
Cedaredge	2 128	2	0	0	0	2	47	12	32	3	1
Centennial	99 607	217	3	33	38	143	2 022	422	1 400	200	28
Center	2 593	4	0	2	0	2	28	11	12	5	0
Central City	493	16	0	0	0	16	45	0	43	2	0
Cherry Hills Village	6 176	4	0	1	1	2	168	40	116	12	0
Colorado Springs	374 482	1 792	12	251	439	1 090	19 619	3 676	14 164	1 779	107
Columbine Valley	1 177	2	0	0	0	2	29	14	13	2	0
Commerce City	30 146	127	5	5	19	98	2 027	403	1 254	370	4
Cortez	8 366	17	1	0	0	16	380	47	319	14	0
Craig	9 348	37	0	8	9	20	342	50	272	20	1

[1]The FBI does not publish arson data unless it receives data from either the agency or the state for all 12 months of the calendar year.

Table 8. Offenses Known to Law Enforcement, by State and City, 2005—*Continued*

(Number.)

City	Population	Violent crime	Murder and non-negligent man-slaughter	Forcible rape	Robbery	Aggravated assault	Property crime	Burglary	Larceny-theft	Motor vehicle theft	Arson[1]
Cripple Creek	1 089	10	0	0	0	10	83	11	66	6	0
Dacono	3 420	20	0	1	0	19	89	20	60	9	0
Del Norte	1 626	0	0	0	0	0	13	3	10	0	0
Delta	8 176	34	1	7	1	25	272	68	193	11	8
Denver[3]	564 552	4 492	59	328	1 432	2 673	33 902	7 360	18 518	8 024	256
Dillon	793	11	0	1	0	10	72	7	62	3	0
Durango	15 228	75	2	18	8	47	1 413	151	1 189	73	5
Eaton	3 846	1	0	0	0	1	52	10	37	5	0
Edgewater	5 346	28	0	2	7	19	404	35	319	50	3
Elizabeth	1 539	6	0	3	0	3	44	6	35	3	0
Empire	346	2	0	0	0	2	14	6	6	2	0
Englewood	32 881	185	0	27	35	123	2 229	431	1 382	416	19
Erie	10 203	8	0	1	0	7	186	63	99	24	8
Estes Park	5 870	9	0	0	1	8	149	32	111	6	1
Evans	16 540	47	0	0	11	36	864	178	564	122	7
Federal Heights	11 973	78	0	20	16	42	622	105	390	127	2
Firestone	5 836	20	0	0	0	20	170	36	122	12	0
Florence	3 736	19	0	4	1	14	52	6	43	3	0
Fort Collins	128 727	442	2	118	57	265	4 434	764	3 239	431	21
Fort Lupton	7 187	27	0	4	3	20	246	40	177	29	4
Fort Morgan	11 144	26	0	4	7	15	377	55	305	17	1
Fountain	15 880	24	0	5	5	14	555	80	419	56	2
Fowler	1 159	5	0	0	0	5	23	5	18	0	2
Frisco	2 467	8	0	1	0	7	134	12	106	16	0
Fruita	6 910	2	0	0	2	0	271	43	215	13	3
Georgetown	1 089	1	0	0	0	1	21	6	15	0	0
Glendale	4 847	22	0	0	14	8	456	44	355	57	0
Glenwood Springs	8 592	43	0	6	1	36	537	76	430	31	2
Golden	17 678	34	0	5	3	26	727	117	525	85	2
Grand Junction	45 312	299	0	23	32	244	3 360	542	2 583	235	21
Greeley	85 991	556	2	48	60	446	5 475	1 149	3 878	448	19
Greenwood Village	12 854	25	0	3	14	8	821	118	635	68	2
Gunnison	5 393	32	0	8	0	24	330	36	282	12	0
Haxtun	1 011	1	0	0	0	1	6	1	5	0	0
Holyoke	2 324	1	0	0	0	1	6	1	5	0	0
Idaho Springs	1 828	32	0	1	0	31	121	11	95	15	1
Ignacio	696	8	0	1	0	7	10	6	3	1	0
Johnstown	6 495	17	0	0	0	17	178	30	133	15	2
Kersey	1 390	1	0	0	1	0	45	10	29	6	0
Kiowa	607	3	0	0	0	3	21	10	11	0	0
Lafayette	24 091	50	0	1	2	47	669	119	495	55	8
La Junta	7 408	25	0	10	4	11	385	87	288	10	10
Lakeside	20	2	0	0	2	0	93	1	82	10	0
Lakewood	143 259	671	5	93	187	386	8 331	1 259	5 650	1 422	27
Lamar	8 649	11	0	0	0	11	426	67	349	10	0
La Salle	1 846	10	0	1	0	9	66	12	42	12	0
Las Animas	2 607	14	0	1	0	13	76	33	40	3	1
Leadville	2 741	9	0	0	0	9	64	10	53	1	0
Limon	1 958	13	0	0	1	12	16	1	15	0	0
Littleton	41 017	66	0	6	33	27	1 796	306	1 184	306	23
Lochbuie	3 429	19	0	1	0	18	78	20	47	11	2
Lone Tree	7 972	18	0	0	1	17	400	68	292	40	1
Loveland	58 585	108	2	21	17	68	1 790	271	1 418	101	5
Manitou Springs	5 108	22	0	1	0	21	198	29	159	10	6
Meeker	2 297	24	0	0	0	24	60	2	55	3	2
Milliken	5 274	7	0	0	1	6	100	24	69	7	1
Monte Vista	4 402	12	0	1	0	11	136	30	104	2	0
Montrose	14 976	32	1	7	7	17	656	77	562	17	5
Monument	2 535	19	0	0	3	16	134	16	110	8	1
Morrison	423	1	0	0	0	1	28	5	21	2	0
Mountain View	543	2	0	0	1	1	19	4	11	4	1
Mount Crested Butte	757	4	0	0	0	4	33	1	31	1	0
New Castle	2 858	6	0	2	0	4	84	14	56	14	1
Northglenn	33 695	138	0	2	28	108	1 959	258	1 390	311	15
Oak Creek	818	13	0	0	0	13	4	2	2	0	0
Olathe	1 689	0	0	0	0	0	20	7	12	1	0
Ouray	866	0	0	0	0	0	20	1	17	2	0
Pagosa Springs	1 629	13	0	0	1	12	95	13	78	4	0
Palisade	2 703	6	0	1	0	5	21	3	17	1	0
Palmer Lake	2 295	6	0	3	0	3	37	18	16	3	0
Parachute	1 084	8	0	1	1	6	73	18	48	7	0
Parker	37 474	61	0	7	19	35	872	172	634	66	12
Platteville	2 603	3	0	0	0	3	83	21	53	9	0
Pueblo	105 057	686	13	22	162	489	6 981	1 525	4 978	478	54
Rangely	2 120	0	0	0	0	0	29	1	26	2	0
Rocky Ford	4 210	37	1	2	1	33	132	31	96	5	0
Salida	5 567	36	0	0	0	36	216	24	185	7	0
Sheridan	5 573	24	0	3	8	13	545	48	406	91	2
Silt	2 192	10	0	1	0	9	57	3	48	6	1
Silverthorne	3 659	7	0	0	0	7	106	16	83	7	0

[1]The FBI does not publish arson data unless it receives data from either the agency or the state for all 12 months of the calendar year.
[3]Because of changes in the state/local agency's reporting practices, figures are not comparable to previous years' data.

Table 8. Offenses Known to Law Enforcement, by State and City, 2005—*Continued*

(Number.)

City	Population	Violent crime	Murder and non-negligent man-slaughter	Forcible rape	Robbery	Aggravated assault	Property crime	Burglary	Larceny-theft	Motor vehicle theft	Arson[1]
Snowmass Village	1 778	2	1	0	0	1	86	6	80	0	0
Springfield	1 408	2	0	0	0	2	8	3	5	0	0
Steamboat Springs	9 474	51	0	3	1	47	440	39	382	19	3
Sterling	12 906	44	0	4	4	36	375	77	277	21	5
Stratton	646	5	0	0	0	5	27	4	22	1	0
Telluride	2 329	3	0	0	0	3	190	10	179	1	0
Thornton	103 487	368	1	69	61	237	4 825	672	3 402	751	48
Trinidad	9 172	19	0	0	0	19	191	45	138	8	1
Vail	4 681	15	0	2	3	10	399	31	356	12	3
Walsenburg	4 004	15	1	0	0	14	100	18	78	4	1
Walsh	692	0	0	0	0	0	1	1	0	0	0
Westminster	106 211	318	2	25	72	219	5 109	701	3 453	955	12
Wheat Ridge	31 846	162	1	17	27	117	2 076	308	1 462	306	13
Windsor	14 024	2	0	0	0	2	118	49	48	21	0
Woodland Park	6 737	13	0	0	2	11	215	39	160	16	4
Wray	2 179	0	0	0	0	0	8	0	8	0	0
Yuma	3 284	3	0	2	0	1	81	12	64	5	1
Connecticut											
Ansonia	18 880	15	0	3	8	4	405	59	296	50	3
Avon	17 074	5	0	0	3	2	184	20	160	4	0
Berlin	19 517	18	0	1	7	10	408	47	331	30	1
Bethel	18 798	2	0	1	0	1	144	22	116	6	0
Bloomfield	20 473	57	0	4	20	33	584	72	464	48	1
Branford	29 247	36	0	16	12	8	735	49	634	52	2
Bridgeport	140 177	1 508	19	65	648	776	7 118	1 383	4 452	1 283	80
Bristol	61 122	133	2	14	52	65	1 588	425	1 059	104	5
Brookfield	16 267	2	0	0	1	1	136	21	105	10	0
Canton	9 624	5	0	0	0	5	116	18	96	2	0
Clinton	13 662	21	0	7	3	11	272	38	218	16	2
Coventry	12 185	10	0	3	0	7	146	37	101	8	0
Cromwell	13 560	10	0	1	8	1	322	31	273	18	0
Danbury	78 413	128	1	22	58	47	1 579	223	1 220	136	3
Darien	20 547	1	0	0	0	1	160	32	121	7	0
Derby	12 632	3	0	1	2	0	368	65	252	51	0
East Hampton	11 948	6	1	3	0	2	91	20	65	6	3
East Hartford	49 456	176	2	20	66	88	1 612	236	1 148	228	9
East Haven	28 880	31	0	0	21	10	690	93	470	127	4
Easton	7 510	1	0	0	0	1	28	12	10	6	0
East Windsor	10 287	23	2	4	6	11	358	56	261	41	2
Enfield	45 660	61	0	7	24	30	1 044	180	753	111	8
Fairfield	57 919	37	2	4	4	27	1 246	202	952	92	2
Farmington	24 784	9	0	2	3	4	614	73	508	33	2
Glastonbury	32 982	14	0	0	3	11	372	61	297	14	0
Granby	11 028	2	0	0	0	2	135	21	104	10	0
Greenwich	62 359	18	0	1	6	11	556	101	422	33	8
Groton	9 734	25	0	6	2	17	219	44	156	19	3
Groton Long Point	684	1	0	0	0	1	5	0	5	0	0
Guilford	22 331	19	0	2	2	15	326	64	249	13	1
Hamden	58 521	76	0	4	50	22	1 235	100	1 008	127	1
Hartford	125 086	1 442	25	46	692	679	9 513	1 398	6 255	1 860	76
Madison	18 851	6	0	1	2	3	145	35	104	6	0
Manchester	55 650	141	1	11	40	89	2 223	260	1 761	202	0
Meriden	59 249	186	1	14	93	78	2 298	504	1 617	177	13
Middlebury	6 860	2	0	1	0	1	110	14	88	8	0
Middletown	47 247	59	2	1	25	31	1 588	195	1 245	148	0
Milford	54 586	57	0	6	20	31	1 628	144	1 331	153	8
Monroe	19 747	5	0	1	2	2	183	32	130	21	0
Naugatuck	31 866	21	0	3	11	7	584	73	448	63	2
New Britain	71 836	359	2	10	189	158	3 330	782	2 171	377	1
New Canaan	20 003	3	0	0	0	3	151	21	125	5	2
Newington	29 732	24	0	9	14	1	817	128	615	74	8
New London	26 369	178	1	27	63	87	936	195	627	114	10
New Milford	28 581	16	0	3	8	5	307	66	224	17	2
Newtown	26 854	5	0	1	0	4	213	53	154	6	4
North Branford	14 347	15	0	0	1	14	182	24	148	10	1
North Haven	23 767	13	0	0	7	6	562	71	457	34	1
Norwalk	84 562	308	7	9	92	200	2 578	365	1 889	324	7
Norwich	36 715	185	0	27	51	107	1 048	224	748	76	15
Old Saybrook	10 536	0	0	0	0	0	218	13	201	4	0
Orange	13 617	6	0	2	2	2	427	35	368	24	0
Plainfield	15 378	13	0	4	5	4	145	40	85	20	2
Plainville	17 405	21	0	3	9	9	520	70	408	42	0
Plymouth	12 134	17	0	1	0	16	212	47	157	8	0
Portland	9 345	5	0	1	1	3	97	17	75	5	0
Putnam	9 242	20	0	3	6	11	204	39	151	14	3
Redding	8 672	5	0	0	0	5	78	14	60	4	0
Ridgefield	24 281	0	0	0	0	0	74	10	63	1	2
Seymour	16 171	38	0	0	5	33	211	37	155	19	1
Shelton	39 396	15	0	1	7	7	448	97	277	74	2
Simsbury	23 549	6	0	0	4	2	212	31	176	5	0
South Windsor	25 700	15	0	4	5	6	407	89	299	19	0
Stamford[3]	120 456	355	1	18	157	179	2 390	427	1 740	223	4
Stonington	18 401	4	0	0	1	3	376	69	292	15	0
Stratford	50 352	116	1	12	49	54	1 497	212	1 067	218	2
Suffield	14 577	5	0	0	0	5	210	49	141	20	6
Torrington	35 999	114	0	3	13	98	1 042	213	776	53	3
Trumbull	35 392	13	0	2	6	5	684	76	547	61	2
Vernon	29 366	47	0	12	15	20	385	79	243	63	8

[1]The FBI does not publish arson data unless it receives data from either the agency or the state for all 12 months of the calendar year.
[3]Because of changes in the state/local agency's reporting practices, figures are not comparable to previous years' data.

Table 8. Offenses Known to Law Enforcement, by State and City, 2005—*Continued*

(Number.)

City	Population	Violent crime	Murder and non-negligent man-slaughter	Forcible rape	Robbery	Aggravated assault	Property crime	Burglary	Larceny-theft	Motor vehicle theft	Arson[1]
Wallingford	44 715	35	0	12	14	9	838	112	679	47	7
Waterbury	108 636	434	6	32	214	182	6 027	1 198	4 212	617	0
Waterford	19 126	45	1	4	8	32	678	69	583	26	3
Watertown	22 316	7	0	0	1	6	345	59	267	19	0
West Hartford	61 371	120	1	0	68	51	1 640	219	1 309	112	0
West Haven	53 188	152	0	4	67	81	1 661	251	1 209	201	3
Weston	10 298	5	0	0	0	5	75	12	62	1	1
Westport	26 595	11	0	2	3	6	386	48	317	21	0
Wethersfield	26 408	34	0	3	17	14	574	87	435	52	4
Willimantic	16 309	59	0	6	33	20	773	170	548	55	4
Wilton	18 023	0	0	0	0	0	126	26	96	4	0
Winchester	10 888	24	0	2	2	20	257	59	170	28	4
Windsor	28 729	29	0	7	14	8	567	56	461	50	5
Windsor Locks	12 351	11	1	1	0	9	243	37	174	32	2
Wolcott	16 198	1	0	0	0	1	207	40	157	10	1
Woodbridge	9 313	4	0	0	4	0	121	18	88	15	0
Delaware											
Bethany Beach	951	1	0	0	0	1	134	17	116	1	1
Blades	1 007	4	0	0	0	4	25	4	20	1	0
Bridgeville	1 585	12	0	0	2	10	12	4	7	1	0
Camden	2 240	15	0	2	3	10	130	14	114	2	0
Cheswold	340	4	0	1	0	3	18	7	11	0	0
Clayton	1 360	4	0	0	0	4	18	7	10	1	0
Dagsboro	557	0	0	0	0	0	1	0	1	0	0
Delaware City	1 529	5	0	0	0	5	26	4	21	1	0
Delmar	1 492	5	0	0	1	4	60	12	46	2	0
Dewey Beach	314	17	0	4	3	10	46	3	42	1	0
Dover	34 151	207	2	13	40	152	1 642	93	1 434	115	8
Ellendale	346	0	0	0	0	0	7	2	5	0	1
Elsmere	5 813	37	0	1	7	29	180	52	109	19	0
Felton	830	8	0	1	1	6	25	10	12	3	0
Fenwick Island	361	1	0	0	0	1	2	0	1	1	0
Georgetown	4 928	95	0	10	28	57	246	61	176	9	0
Greenwood	890	0	0	0	0	0	34	5	24	5	0
Harrington	3 229	22	0	1	4	17	133	30	93	10	0
Laurel	3 854	39	0	7	8	24	180	53	124	3	0
Lewes	3 141	7	0	2	4	1	70	16	51	3	0
Milford	7 200	115	0	7	12	96	491	74	396	21	2
Millsboro	2 520	28	0	4	2	22	130	29	94	7	0
Milton	1 804	18	0	2	0	16	86	34	52	0	1
Newark	30 294	160	1	18	48	93	1 088	197	806	85	9
New Castle	4 917	38	0	2	14	22	279	33	231	15	1
Newport	1 129	6	0	1	2	3	72	17	44	11	1
Ocean View	1 098	3	0	0	0	3	34	14	19	1	1
Rehoboth Beach	1 568	15	0	1	7	7	215	32	180	3	1
Seaford	7 049	60	1	4	8	47	384	61	308	15	1
Selbyville	1 751	6	0	0	1	5	39	4	35	0	1
Smyrna	6 916	37	0	4	7	26	251	41	189	21	0
South Bethany	518	2	0	0	0	2	7	0	7	0	0
Wilmington	73 938	1 049	12	27	433	577	3 434	817	2 104	513	8
Wyoming	1 164	6	0	0	0	6	29	5	24	0	1
District of Columbia											
Washington	550 521	7 716	195	165	3 502	3 854	25 200	3 571	14 162	7 467	61
Florida											
Alachua	7 178	55	0	1	3	51	307	51	221	35	1
Altamonte Springs	41 707	199	1	14	51	133	1 808	283	1 319	206	1
Altha	518	0	0	0	0	0	4	2	2	0	0
Apalachicola	2 373	1	0	0	0	1	139	54	80	5	1
Apopka	32 786	369	2	19	105	243	1 695	389	1 196	110	7
Arcadia	7 275	46	0	1	4	41	310	78	195	37	0
Astatula	1 586	13	0	0	0	13	18	5	10	3	0
Atlantic Beach	13 859	81	1	9	23	48	376	69	281	26	1
Atlantis	2 193	16	0	0	0	16	49	9	36	4	0
Auburndale	12 428	75	0	6	25	44	964	125	798	41	5
Aventura	27 851	35	0	1	26	8	1 611	139	1 416	56	2
Bal Harbour Village	3 409	2	0	0	0	2	73	18	55	0	0
Bartow	16 181	112	1	7	25	79	1 157	238	847	72	2
Belleair	4 167	4	0	2	0	2	56	9	45	2	0
Belleair Beach	1 673	0	0	0	0	0	25	5	19	1	0
Belleair Bluffs	2 287	5	0	1	1	3	62	11	49	2	1
Belle Glade	15 664	373	2	9	77	285	1 374	357	935	82	10
Biscayne Park	3 263	8	0	0	0	8	62	27	26	9	0
Blountstown	2 478	7	0	0	0	7	46	10	30	6	0
Boca Raton	79 831	241	0	15	53	173	2 844	591	2 071	182	16
Bonifay	2 742	0	0	0	0	0	26	11	10	5	0
Bowling Green	2 985	22	0	2	4	16	54	12	35	7	0
Boynton Beach	66 237	497	1	4	139	353	3 408	720	2 381	307	4
Bradenton	54 335	318	3	18	111	186	2 832	597	1 944	291	0
Bradenton Beach	1 571	5	0	0	0	5	89	23	62	4	1
Brooksville	7 656	48	0	0	4	44	517	77	412	28	2
Bunnell	2 227	89	0	1	19	69	176	45	99	32	0
Bushnell	2 127	17	0	2	1	14	93	13	75	5	1
Cape Coral	130 874	361	5	45	74	237	3 900	1 026	2 567	307	41
Carrabelle	1 321	11	0	0	2	9	46	3	36	7	3

[1]The FBI does not publish arson data unless it receives data from either the agency or the state for all 12 months of the calendar year.

Table 8. Offenses Known to Law Enforcement, by State and City, 2005—*Continued*

(Number.)

City	Population	Violent crime	Murder and non-negligent man-slaughter	Forcible rape	Robbery	Aggravated assault	Property crime	Burglary	Larceny-theft	Motor vehicle theft	Arson[1]
Casselberry	24 687	126	0	18	31	77	981	211	673	97	2
Cedar Grove	5 472	16	0	0	4	12	215	74	115	26	0
Center Hill	954	10	0	0	0	10	19	11	6	2	0
Chattahoochee	3 806	54	0	3	3	48	92	14	70	8	0
Chiefland	2 132	40	0	1	0	39	320	59	259	2	0
Chipley	3 727	11	1	1	0	9	153	32	119	2	0
Clearwater	111 058	993	9	48	210	726	5 077	949	3 695	433	42
Clermont	11 376	124	0	9	18	97	522	150	340	32	3
Clewiston	7 129	96	1	0	29	66	452	105	330	17	0
Cocoa	17 070	415	0	28	70	317	1 139	346	692	101	0
Cocoa Beach	12 872	131	0	15	29	87	828	98	695	35	2
Coconut Creek	49 993	119	0	17	28	74	1 151	201	831	119	1
Coleman	676	1	0	1	0	0	4	0	4	0	0
Cooper City	30 111	101	0	2	17	82	598	107	467	24	4
Coral Gables	43 417	152	0	4	40	108	2 208	471	1 613	124	6
Coral Springs	131 252	224	0	9	58	157	2 642	424	1 975	243	7
Crescent City	1 843	26	0	3	6	17	167	56	107	4	0
Crestview	17 206	76	0	10	16	50	698	130	524	44	0
Cross City	1 841	13	0	1	3	9	100	20	79	1	1
Crystal River	3 685	42	0	1	8	33	321	39	262	20	1
Dade City	6 764	56	0	4	12	40	411	159	224	28	1
Dania	29 122	291	2	10	85	194	1 623	362	1 053	208	3
Davenport	2 040	4	0	0	2	2	115	37	61	17	0
Davie	84 443	298	2	19	71	206	3 160	556	2 293	311	14
Daytona Beach	65 876	1 079	8	65	342	664	4 827	1 399	2 698	730	12
Daytona Beach Shores	4 690	26	0	3	0	23	291	117	145	29	0
Deerfield Beach	67 683	593	2	35	144	412	2 517	485	1 767	265	6
De Funiak Springs	5 257	130	0	3	6	121	346	71	248	27	2
Deland	23 373	185	3	11	48	123	1 467	305	1 061	101	3
Delray Beach	65 598	658	6	26	132	494	3 207	595	2 293	319	10
Doral	30 969	165	1	29	39	96	2 584	246	2 086	252	3
Dundee	3 076	17	2	1	0	14	250	20	211	19	0
Dunedin	37 459	135	0	15	16	104	1 069	222	788	59	4
Dunnellon	1 995	22	0	1	5	16	65	25	40	0	0
Eagle Lake	2 549	5	0	0	1	4	78	19	44	15	0
Eatonville	2 441	47	0	13	2	32	85	31	30	24	1
Edgewater	21 189	67	0	5	9	53	653	174	423	56	2
Edgewood	2 143	5	0	0	1	4	109	40	64	5	0
El Portal	2 524	10	0	0	3	7	143	58	73	12	0
Eustis	17 624	71	1	7	22	41	419	88	301	30	3
Fellsmere	4 763	16	0	1	1	14	101	49	41	11	1
Fernandina Beach	11 495	55	0	8	6	41	355	73	270	12	1
Flagler Beach	5 346	14	0	0	3	11	126	30	90	6	0
Florida City	8 552	274	0	5	61	208	1 193	155	955	83	2
Fort Lauderdale	168 293	1 503	15	67	741	680	11 216	2 555	7 564	1 097	48
Fort Meade	5 891	31	0	0	6	25	222	50	160	12	0
Fort Myers	54 095	964	13	32	309	610	3 059	592	1 848	619	21
Fort Pierce	38 816	736	10	36	195	495	2 877	872	1 629	376	13
Fort Walton Beach	20 443	106	1	8	28	69	833	155	608	70	2
Frostproof	3 021	7	0	0	0	7	107	18	78	11	0
Fruitland Park	3 646	18	0	0	0	18	111	15	85	11	0
Gainesville	111 313	973	5	99	168	701	4 870	1 178	3 262	430	6
Golden Beach	942	1	0	0	0	1	17	10	6	1	0
Graceville	2 446	2	0	0	0	2	111	25	80	6	0
Greenacres City	32 742	256	1	14	41	200	1 136	242	811	83	2
Green Cove Springs	6 125	56	0	1	6	49	261	101	144	16	2
Greensboro	629	7	0	0	4	3	15	15	0	0	0
Gretna	1 739	19	0	0	4	15	38	20	12	6	0
Groveland	4 693	10	0	0	0	10	102	33	61	8	0
Gulf Breeze	6 476	10	0	0	1	9	141	28	108	5	0
Gulfport	13 028	90	0	5	27	58	555	144	348	63	0
Gulf Stream	763	0	0	0	0	0	28	3	24	1	0
Haines City	14 858	112	2	7	37	66	996	201	704	91	1
Hallandale	37 169	367	1	9	99	258	1 472	349	963	160	2
Havana	1 741	20	0	0	2	18	63	29	31	3	0
Hialeah	229 590	1 348	8	38	387	915	8 772	1 542	5 698	1 532	31
Hialeah Gardens	20 420	52	0	0	18	34	883	161	608	114	1
Highland Beach	4 219	2	0	0	0	2	30	8	22	0	0
Hillsboro Beach	2 365	2	0	1	0	1	23	6	16	1	0
Holly Hill	12 870	88	0	7	36	45	750	184	456	110	1
Hollywood	147 798	773	6	60	330	377	6 498	1 314	4 366	818	23
Holmes Beach	5 215	11	0	0	0	11	158	33	120	5	0
Homestead	38 814	818	5	8	328	477	3 055	782	1 980	293	3
Howey-in-the-Hills	1 176	1	0	0	0	1	6	0	5	1	0
Hypoluxo	2 658	2	0	2	0	0	71	16	46	9	0
Indialantic	3 038	5	0	0	0	5	126	25	90	11	0
Indian Creek Village	39	0	0	0	0	0	0	0	0	0	0
Indian Harbour Beach	8 695	15	0	2	2	11	106	26	72	8	0
Indian River Shores	3 661	0	0	0	0	0	32	7	25	0	0
Indian Rocks Beach	5 374	14	0	2	2	10	148	33	106	9	3

[1]The FBI does not publish arson data unless it receives data from either the agency or the state for all 12 months of the calendar year.

Table 8. Offenses Known to Law Enforcement, by State and City, 2005—*Continued*

(Number.)

City	Population	Violent crime	Murder and non-negligent man-slaughter	Forcible rape	Robbery	Aggravated assault	Property crime	Burglary	Larceny-theft	Motor vehicle theft	Arson[1]
Indian Shores	3 909	2	0	0	1	1	70	35	27	8	0
Inglis	1 626	10	0	1	0	9	40	13	22	5	1
Jacksonville	795 259	6 600	91	189	2 253	4 067	43 517	8 998	29 583	4 936	182
Jacksonville Beach	21 835	148	3	8	45	92	1 278	184	980	114	6
Jennings	862	8	0	0	1	7	18	8	6	4	0
Juno Beach	3 468	1	0	0	0	1	84	16	60	8	0
Jupiter	47 807	162	1	8	59	94	1 352	316	963	73	5
Jupiter Inlet Colony	397	0	0	0	0	0	3	1	2	0	1
Jupiter Island	668	0	0	0	0	0	15	7	6	2	0
Kenneth City	4 520	14	0	0	3	11	191	39	143	9	0
Key Biscayne	10 557	10	0	0	3	7	296	22	255	19	0
Key Colony Beach	831	1	0	0	0	1	17	0	17	0	0
Key West	25 327	153	1	27	48	77	1 454	250	1 044	160	0
Kissimmee	57 421	541	1	30	131	379	2 652	716	1 732	204	8
Lady Lake	13 336	30	0	4	1	25	264	69	186	9	0
Lake Alfred	4 033	3	0	0	1	2	138	54	74	10	0
Lake City	10 941	184	1	10	31	142	858	107	710	41	4
Lake Clarke Shores	3 553	1	0	0	1	0	42	15	15	12	0
Lake Hamilton	1 438	11	0	0	0	11	84	30	40	14	0
Lake Helen	2 871	4	0	0	0	4	77	27	44	6	0
Lakeland	90 351	437	6	26	140	265	5 045	912	3 755	378	12
Lake Mary	14 232	27	1	1	7	18	267	76	170	21	0
Lake Park	9 285	101	0	12	40	49	837	205	463	169	6
Lake Placid	1 792	20	0	1	3	16	137	22	108	7	0
Lake Worth	36 286	540	4	14	276	246	3 083	919	1 843	321	8
Lantana	10 624	91	1	11	31	48	545	95	394	56	0
Largo	73 323	349	4	26	77	242	2 556	468	1 860	228	6
Lauderdale-by-the-Sea	6 103	13	0	0	4	9	208	48	143	17	0
Lauderdale Lakes	32 353	415	4	17	113	281	1 388	399	773	216	7
Lauderhill	60 886	561	3	30	157	371	2 027	608	1 072	347	9
Lawtey	688	0	0	0	0	0	9	3	6	0	0
Leesburg	18 487	257	2	5	55	195	1 306	372	874	60	4
Lighthouse Point	11 465	15	0	5	4	6	249	39	189	21	0
Live Oak	6 982	48	0	2	6	40	312	136	163	13	1
Longboat Key	7 794	0	0	0	0	0	100	12	84	4	0
Longwood	13 877	100	0	3	13	84	587	137	409	41	2
Lynn Haven	14 994	38	0	1	4	33	368	76	265	27	0
Madeira Beach	4 593	38	0	5	8	25	376	62	296	18	1
Madison	3 267	42	2	2	11	27	295	90	198	7	0
Maitland	14 417	33	0	0	4	29	448	118	285	45	0
Manalapan	348	0	0	0	0	0	24	8	16	0	0
Mangonia Park	1 318	106	2	2	35	67	361	66	228	67	3
Marco Island	16 185	22	0	2	0	20	229	37	188	4	0
Margate	56 397	192	0	4	39	149	1 115	209	799	107	2
Marianna	6 340	83	4	10	5	64	266	50	195	21	2
Mascotte	4 461	15	1	1	0	13	62	27	29	6	0
Medley	1 100	15	1	0	4	10	259	76	157	26	1
Melbourne	77 067	684	1	30	124	529	3 657	884	2 557	216	15
Melbourne Beach	3 430	3	0	0	0	3	34	17	13	4	0
Melbourne Village	723	1	0	0	0	1	20	0	20	0	0
Mexico Beach	1 056	4	0	0	1	3	50	17	31	2	0
Miami	388 295	6 134	54	62	2 019	3 999	23 321	5 377	13 930	4 014	143
Miami Beach	91 115	1 173	3	62	515	593	8 121	1 463	5 681	977	12
Miami Gardens	103 164	1 913	11	57	540	1 305	6 598	1 395	4 235	968	21
Miami Lakes	23 200	96	1	5	17	73	1 034	149	772	113	4
Miami Shores	10 425	79	1	4	33	41	718	272	375	71	1
Miami Springs	13 725	66	0	2	36	28	518	108	355	55	0
Milton	8 226	54	0	1	4	49	386	68	299	19	2
Miramar	103 777	486	3	35	152	296	3 212	939	1 831	442	14
Monticello	2 630	22	0	1	1	20	38	22	12	4	0
Mount Dora	10 899	92	1	14	14	63	432	84	317	31	2
Mulberry	3 301	22	0	7	5	10	224	54	157	13	3
Naples	21 965	40	0	4	4	32	732	101	615	16	0
Neptune Beach	7 281	11	0	2	3	6	214	51	153	10	0
New Port Richey	17 051	162	1	8	27	126	879	283	534	62	2
New Smyrna Beach	21 949	97	0	8	21	68	746	168	523	55	5
Niceville	12 797	13	0	3	0	10	124	20	90	14	0
North Bay Village	6 973	15	0	0	8	7	244	52	152	40	0
North Lauderdale	35 180	321	0	17	68	236	1 110	226	758	126	1
North Miami	60 076	687	6	25	339	317	4 091	1 025	2 538	528	12
North Miami Beach	40 822	493	1	26	201	265	2 328	593	1 412	323	12
North Palm Beach	12 930	33	0	1	12	20	312	92	189	31	0
North Port	36 068	149	0	11	18	120	1 097	248	789	60	5
North Redington Beach	1 560	3	0	2	0	1	37	7	29	1	0
Oak Hill	1 487	15	0	0	0	15	25	15	8	2	0
Oakland	1 081	15	0	0	2	13	56	30	15	11	0
Oakland Park	32 223	476	3	23	139	311	2 047	451	1 357	239	6
Ocala	50 005	587	4	43	157	383	3 416	804	2 408	204	9
Ocean Ridge	1 740	0	0	0	0	0	40	7	31	2	0
Ocoee	28 886	166	0	6	39	121	1 493	294	1 091	108	2

[1]The FBI does not publish arson data unless it receives data from either the agency or the state for all 12 months of the calendar year.

Table 8. Offenses Known to Law Enforcement, by State and City, 2005—*Continued*

(Number.)

City	Population	Violent crime	Murder and non-negligent man-slaughter	Forcible rape	Robbery	Aggravated assault	Property crime	Burglary	Larceny-theft	Motor vehicle theft	Arson[1]
Okeechobee	5 915	42	0	1	7	34	344	57	265	22	0
Oldsmar	14 015	52	1	7	1	43	540	123	388	29	6
Opa Locka	15 673	352	8	4	176	164	1 529	703	626	200	0
Orange City	7 334	91	0	5	18	68	634	102	485	47	0
Orange Park	9 452	40	0	2	9	29	239	45	180	14	2
Orlando	210 290	3 801	22	165	1 204	2 410	18 226	3 882	12 175	2 169	42
Ormond Beach	38 785	88	0	4	17	67	1 065	181	834	50	1
Oviedo	29 452	104	0	8	9	87	567	94	445	28	6
Pahokee	6 605	47	0	2	15	30	259	94	160	5	0
Palatka	11 040	247	1	15	12	219	1 090	180	841	69	1
Palm Bay	90 762	482	2	42	79	359	3 269	1 032	1 999	238	13
Palm Beach	10 083	10	0	0	3	7	185	19	151	15	0
Palm Beach Gardens	45 315	113	1	10	37	65	1 879	377	1 319	183	4
Palm Beach Shores	1 545	6	0	0	4	2	95	11	65	19	0
Palmetto	13 428	218	0	5	44	169	775	159	559	57	3
Palmetto Bay	25 465	112	1	2	42	67	954	144	707	103	2
Palm Springs	15 022	116	2	7	45	62	880	206	535	139	2
Panama City	37 916	336	2	19	76	239	2 074	363	1 607	104	6
Panama City Beach	10 429	101	1	8	32	60	806	155	640	11	0
Parker	4 794	14	0	0	6	8	98	22	53	23	0
Parkland	21 020	21	0	1	2	18	251	38	202	11	1
Pembroke Park	5 537	80	0	3	22	55	354	79	215	60	3
Pembroke Pines	153 492	353	6	25	95	227	4 471	743	3 295	433	14
Pensacola	55 970	448	1	37	89	321	2 424	423	1 824	177	16
Perry	6 854	105	0	4	6	95	330	136	183	11	2
Pinellas Park	48 231	296	1	26	46	223	2 784	483	2 153	148	12
Plantation	87 427	226	4	15	114	93	3 508	587	2 586	335	5
Plant City	31 604	262	3	13	96	150	1 540	231	1 118	191	2
Pompano Beach	90 880	1 382	5	57	420	900	5 248	958	3 676	614	17
Ponce Inlet	3 250	1	0	0	0	1	40	19	15	6	0
Port Orange	53 985	35	4	2	9	20	1 084	181	849	54	5
Port Richey	3 368	33	0	0	10	23	446	51	380	15	0
Port St. Joe	3 720	20	0	1	3	16	75	32	42	1	0
Port St. Lucie	121 069	287	1	17	27	242	2 697	770	1 783	144	11
Punta Gorda	17 604	51	1	3	3	44	436	139	273	24	1
Quincy	7 132	122	0	8	13	101	524	218	303	3	3
Redington Beaches	1 569	5	0	0	0	5	54	5	46	3	1
Riviera Beach	33 256	655	12	11	240	392	2 902	891	1 435	576	20
Rockledge	23 821	70	0	1	12	57	716	141	539	36	1
Royal Palm Beach	31 057	86	0	5	23	58	1 180	211	867	102	2
Safety Harbor	17 946	43	0	6	2	35	312	68	231	13	1
Sanford	46 486	316	5	25	130	156	3 601	759	2 393	449	0
Sanibel	6 240	3	0	0	0	3	122	60	57	5	0
Sarasota	54 553	522	5	37	154	326	3 562	769	2 535	258	15
Satellite Beach	10 062	38	0	5	4	29	248	68	176	4	1
Sea Ranch Lakes	778	1	0	0	1	0	12	0	11	1	0
Sebastian	19 092	45	0	4	3	38	481	125	330	26	3
Sebring	10 303	119	1	5	31	82	630	159	444	27	6
Seminole	18 637	77	0	10	16	51	672	80	551	41	1
Sewall's Point	2 099	0	0	0	0	0	28	6	21	1	0
Shalimar	755	4	0	1	1	2	11	5	6	0	0
South Bay	4 128	79	1	2	13	63	180	70	103	7	1
South Miami	11 528	62	0	2	23	37	766	126	596	44	0
South Palm Beach	1 571	0	0	0	0	0	13	3	9	1	0
South Pasadena	5 875	11	0	1	2	8	217	35	175	7	0
Southwest Ranches	7 508	14	0	1	2	11	166	23	126	17	2
Springfield	9 193	131	0	1	14	116	377	128	230	19	2
Starke	5 899	52	0	1	2	49	159	4	140	15	0
St. Augustine	12 431	102	0	8	21	73	948	123	778	47	0
St. Augustine Beach	5 778	13	0	1	0	12	153	25	118	10	0
St. Cloud	22 890	170	0	17	22	131	1 129	278	787	64	7
St. Pete Beach	10 253	35	0	1	11	23	603	238	353	12	0
St. Petersburg	254 713	3 937	30	101	959	2 847	16 323	3 534	10 395	2 394	84
Stuart	16 083	111	1	5	20	85	740	119	563	58	1
Sunny Isles Beach	15 747	47	0	2	15	30	520	145	319	56	0
Sunrise	92 264	381	1	22	128	230	3 148	554	2 288	306	4
Surfside	4 910	24	0	0	4	20	167	24	129	14	1
Sweetwater	14 308	37	0	3	11	23	260	57	166	37	1
Tallahassee	160 147	1 646	9	132	386	1 119	8 519	2 614	5 191	714	11
Tamarac	60 616	194	1	4	65	124	1 229	268	818	143	1
Tampa	329 035	4 707	20	210	1 160	3 317	20 271	4 914	12 564	2 793	49
Tarpon Springs	23 063	248	0	4	13	231	695	164	498	33	4
Tavares	11 625	28	0	2	1	25	250	47	186	17	0
Temple Terrace	22 184	89	0	7	26	56	931	164	633	134	1
Tequesta	5 960	12	0	1	0	11	91	15	70	6	0
Titusville	43 576	346	4	21	79	242	1 512	417	909	186	11
Treasure Island	7 691	17	1	1	4	11	294	35	241	18	3
Umatilla	2 558	27	0	2	0	25	119	26	79	14	0
Valparaiso	6 479	2	0	0	0	2	151	17	134	0	0
Venice	20 441	31	0	3	2	26	481	153	308	20	2

[1]The FBI does not publish arson data unless it receives data from either the agency or the state for all 12 months of the calendar year.

Table 8. Offenses Known to Law Enforcement, by State and City, 2005—*Continued*

(Number.)

City	Population	Violent crime	Murder and non-negligent man-slaughter	Forcible rape	Robbery	Aggravated assault	Property crime	Burglary	Larceny-theft	Motor vehicle theft	Arson[1]
Vero Beach	17 597	86	0	6	16	64	740	145	551	44	1
Village of Pinecrest	19 871	67	0	2	14	51	659	113	502	44	0
Waldo	802	1	0	0	0	1	4	2	2	0	0
Wauchula	4 541	43	0	1	5	37	194	57	131	6	0
Webster	837	4	0	0	2	2	31	6	24	1	0
Welaka	618	0	0	0	0	0	7	3	4	0	0
Wellington	51 104	148	2	24	18	104	1 472	326	1 019	127	8
West Melbourne	14 108	56	1	1	8	46	608	90	489	29	2
West Miami	6 059	16	0	0	2	14	154	40	102	12	0
Weston	64 968	131	0	4	18	109	773	141	599	33	10
West Palm Beach	97 496	1 221	22	71	528	600	7 182	1 605	4 610	967	23
White Springs	847	4	0	0	1	3	23	5	16	2	0
Wildwood	3 679	47	0	3	2	42	180	56	119	5	2
Williston	2 523	77	0	0	2	75	164	29	125	10	0
Wilton Manors	13 134	75	0	2	32	41	649	160	417	72	1
Windermere	2 002	0	0	0	0	0	34	13	21	0	0
Winter Garden	22 568	218	0	1	43	174	1 006	323	603	80	4
Winter Haven	28 484	222	2	21	54	145	2 057	392	1 514	151	4
Winter Park	27 209	47	0	6	20	21	841	194	545	102	3
Winter Springs	32 694	58	0	5	4	49	639	139	472	28	2
Zephyrhills	12 122	54	2	3	15	34	674	148	490	36	1
Georgia											
Adairsville	3 122	8	0	2	3	3	333	55	250	28	0
Albany	78 353	516	8	40	216	252	4 991	1 704	2 958	329	21
Alpharetta	35 188	84	1	4	19	60	1 469	182	1 198	89	3
Americus	17 198	81	0	0	15	66	1 122	332	765	25	10
Aragon	1 085	2	0	0	2	0	40	5	35	0	0
Athens-Clarke County	105 727	357	5	41	135	176	5 593	1 047	4 185	361	30
Atlanta	430 666	7 213	90	223	2 861	4 039	31 397	6 648	18 993	5 756	198
Attapulgus	498	0	0	0	0	0	7	3	4	0	0
Auburn	7 128	21	0	1	10	10	200	64	119	17	0
Austell	6 697	78	0	3	5	70	407	65	304	38	1
Avondale Estates	2 699	1	0	0	1	0	79	19	52	8	. . .
Bainbridge	12 439	165	1	5	24	135	968	147	798	23	2
Baldwin	2 759	4	0	0	0	4	96	13	75	8	0
Baxley	4 577	63	0	1	3	59	270	68	188	14	0
Blackshear	3 447	21	0	0	5	16	558	44	498	16	0
Blairsville	738	0	0	0	0	0	0	0	0	0	0
Blythe	809	0	0	0	0	0	6	2	3	1	0
Broxton	1 504	16	0	0	0	16	148	14	127	7	0
Brunswick	16 418	388	0	15	64	309	1 331	331	935	65	3
Buchanan	1 029	5	0	1	0	4	91	14	67	10	0
Cairo	9 621	51	0	2	16	33	475	133	317	25	4
Calhoun	13 464	51	0	5	21	25	1 155	177	940	38	1
Cartersville	17 882	84	1	5	21	57	1 212	252	801	159	5
Cave Spring	1 022	3	0	0	0	3	24	4	18	2	0
Chamblee	9 363	109	0	0	85	24	743	127	512	104	1
Clarkston	7 303	66	0	1	26	39	318	99	140	79	0
Clayton	2 138	16	0	0	1	15	95	7	80	8	0
Cochran	4 750	13	1	0	4	8	231	52	177	2	1
College Park	18 859	312	2	21	137	152	1 753	517	932	304	11
Columbus	187 886	992	22	24	446	500	13 125	2 681	8 763	1 681	80
Comer	1 172	0	0	0	0	0	14	1	13	0	0
Conyers	12 482	62	0	7	37	18	1 081	195	742	144	0
Coolidge	572	0	0	0	0	0	6	1	5	0	0
Cordele	11 875	77	2	4	31	40	1 041	199	816	26	3
Danielsville	514	4	0	0	1	3	51	2	46	3	0
Dawson	5 120	13	0	0	1	12	139	27	111	1	0
Decatur	18 754	64	1	3	36	24	620	141	419	60	2
Donalsonville	2 808	15	0	0	1	14	105	18	80	7	0
Doraville	10 308	84	1	1	40	42	540	75	401	64	0
Douglasville	27 190	187	1	10	65	111	2 909	297	2 378	234	10
Dublin	17 149	94	3	3	18	70	1 159	190	928	41	0
Duluth	24 923	100	0	4	13	83	565	121	390	54	0
East Dublin	2 675	18	0	0	2	16	95	12	75	8	0
East Point	36 434	346	4	15	159	168	2 393	682	1 364	347	1
Elberton	4 863	52	0	1	8	43	469	86	364	19	0
Ellaville	1 768	5	0	0	0	5	34	7	20	7	0
Enigma	913	0	0	0	0	0	11	11	0	0	0
Fairburn	7 198	36	0	1	17	18	666	155	424	87	1
Fayetteville	14 240	20	0	1	9	10	726	31	657	38	0
Folkston	3 331	23	0	0	0	23	66	24	39	3	. . .
Forest Park	21 767	177	2	8	113	54	1 542	276	1 026	240	. . .
Fort Oglethorpe	8 663	43	0	0	8	35	789	68	670	51	. . .
Fort Valley	8 461	84	0	6	12	66	462	173	272	17	0
Gainesville	31 964	149	1	15	31	102	2 191	235	1 790	166	2
Garden City	10 042	128	3	3	26	96	631	125	441	65	. . .
Gordon	2 185	4	0	0	0	4	51	9	38	4	0
Griffin	24 041	188	1	4	62	121	1 445	410	953	82	. . .
Grovetown	7 110	12	0	2	1	9	179	40	133	6	0
Hahira	1 852	1	0	0	1	0	88	4	83	1	. . .
Helen	641	4	0	0	0	4	72	6	55	11	0

[1]The FBI does not publish arson data unless it receives data from either the agency or the state for all 12 months of the calendar year.
. . . = Not available.

Table 8. Offenses Known to Law Enforcement, by State and City, 2005—*Continued*

(Number.)

City	Population	Violent crime	Murder and non-negligent man-slaughter	Forcible rape	Robbery	Aggravated assault	Property crime	Burglary	Larceny-theft	Motor vehicle theft	Arson[1]
Helena	2 383	3	0	0	1	2	18	14	3	1	0
Hephzibah	4 278	3	0	0	0	3	115	29	78	8	0
Hinesville	31 408	172	0	14	55	103	1 899	414	1 425	60	. . .
Hoschton	1 480	0	0	0	0	0	14	1	11	2	0
Jackson	4 442	0	0	0	0	0	115	0	114	1	. . .
Jasper	2 830	5	1	0	0	4	180	13	151	16	1
Kennesaw	28 189	34	0	0	7	27	545	91	398	56	0
Kingsland	11 907	52	1	8	13	30	459	89	342	28	. . .
Lafayette	6 988	16	0	0	2	14	397	59	324	14	. . .
LaGrange	27 697	184	2	9	83	90	2 233	379	1 685	169	. . .
Lake City	2 899	18	0	2	14	2	330	46	228	56	. . .
Lookout Mountain	1 622	0	0	0	0	0	14	6	8	0	0
Luthersville	852	6	0	0	3	3	43	11	31	1	0
Macon	97 606	816	20	58	332	406	9 217	2 028	6 124	1 065	81
Madison	3 885	11	0	0	5	6	227	45	168	14	0
Manchester	3 857	22	0	0	6	16	255	55	171	29	0
Marietta	62 215	331	6	11	194	120	2 371	426	1 548	397	0
McCaysville	1 019	2	0	0	1	1	26	7	18	1	0
McDonough	13 997	169	0	4	18	147	890	172	648	70	0
McIntyre	740	3	0	0	0	3	18	6	12	0	0
McRae	3 983	56	1	3	3	49	146	40	98	8	0
Milledgeville	19 799	57	2	6	14	35	803	136	639	28	0
Molena	502	0	0	0	0	0	0	0	0	0	0
Monroe	12 231	72	0	1	8	63	730	129	567	34	. . .
Montezuma	4 123	22	0	1	0	21	126	42	73	11	0
Morrow	5 240	75	0	2	33	40	1 173	52	985	136	. . .
Moultrie	15 199	176	3	6	69	98	1 357	326	944	87	4
Mount Airy	679	0	0	0	0	0	0	0	0	0	0
Newnan	23 140	115	0	0	20	95	1 093	181	851	61	0
Norcross	9 780	117	0	6	63	48	701	187	364	150	3
Norman Park	892	0	0	0	0	0	46	10	34	2	0
Ocilla	3 293	19	1	2	3	13	155	30	115	10	. . .
Omega	1 396	5	0	0	2	3	6	3	1	2	0
Oxford	2 215	2	0	0	0	2	21	8	11	2	1
Peachtree City	34 741	11	0	3	3	5	335	26	258	51	6
Pearson	1 948	10	0	0	1	9	116	21	89	6	1
Perry	10 954	49	0	2	9	38	344	49	258	37	0
Pine Mountain	1 238	2	0	0	1	1	88	20	64	4	0
Porterdale	1 558	9	0	0	1	8	71	15	52	4	1
Port Wentworth	3 202	3	0	0	1	2	103	24	67	12	0
Powder Springs	14 694	27	0	1	12	14	363	84	253	26	0
Remerton	859	0	0	0	0	0	31	4	26	1	0
Richmond Hill	9 040	29	0	2	19	8	211	26	163	22	0
Ringgold	2 819	17	0	0	5	12	275	39	219	17	2
Riverdale	16 041	85	3	2	48	32	1 216	212	851	153	0
Rome	36 530	269	2	17	76	174	2 652	597	1 908	147	12
Roswell	87 386	146	0	7	71	68	2 340	442	1 724	174	4
Savannah-Chatham Metropolitan[4]	213 587	1 390	30	83	704	573	11 671	2 530	7 603	1 538	41
Smyrna	47 015	227	6	14	127	80	2 144	461	1 387	296	2
Snellville	19 299	50	0	2	25	23	896	105	752	39	1
Springfield	2 065	5	0	0	2	3	80	5	68	7	0
Suwanee	11 258	19	0	1	9	9	330	65	235	30	0
Tallapoosa	3 102	10	0	0	0	10	130	46	70	14	0
Tallulah Falls	166	0	0	0	0	0	5	0	5	0	0
Thomasville	19 036	48	0	4	19	25	1 034	230	769	35	8
Trenton	2 190	3	0	1	1	1	35	7	23	5	0
Tunnel Hill	1 261	8	0	0	0	8	111	14	90	7	0
Tyrone	5 372	6	0	2	2	2	101	30	70	1	3
Union City	13 723	124	2	5	60	57	1 403	239	867	297	5
Valdosta	46 623	312	7	29	106	170	3 461	666	2 602	193	. . .
Varnell	1 568	6	0	0	0	6	141	28	106	7	0
Vidalia	11 167	90	1	2	29	58	672	153	482	37	0
Vienna	3 023	26	0	0	1	25	80	16	58	6	0
Villa Rica	9 176	50	0	3	3	44	864	114	684	66	0
Warm Springs	491	0	0	0	0	0	11	11	0	0	0
Warner Robins	57 856	253	1	12	94	146	3 106	834	2 104	168	13
Watkinsville	2 463	3	0	0	0	3	74	9	64	1	1
Waverly Hall	776	2	0	0	0	2	12	6	4	2	0
Waycross	15 605	126	5	4	29	88	1 295	196	1 051	48	8
Waynesboro	6 082	41	2	1	13	25	479	65	375	39	2
West Point	3 422	32	0	1	5	26	430	44	380	6	2
Whitesburg	603	1	0	0	0	1	29	8	20	1	0
Willacoochee	1 543	3	0	0	0	3	43	9	34	0	0
Winder	12 416	104	1	5	17	81	767	108	599	60	0
Woodbury	1 132	2	0	1	1	0	3	0	1	2	0
Woodstock	17 688	29	0	5	7	17	667	65	555	47	0
Wrens	2 298	29	0	3	6	20	128	26	99	3	0
Zebulon	1 265	2	0	1	1	0	27	7	20	0	0
Hawaii											
Honolulu	908 521	2 570	15	234	841	1 480	42 383	6 209	29 376	6 798	547

[1]The FBI does not publish arson data unless it receives data from either the agency or the state for all 12 months of the calendar year.
[4]Savannah-Chatham Metropolitan is a city-county government that includes the Savannah city and Chatham County police departments.
. . . = Not available.

Table 8. Offenses Known to Law Enforcement, by State and City, 2005—*Continued*

(Number.)

City	Population	Violent crime	Murder and non-negligent man-slaughter	Forcible rape	Robbery	Aggravated assault	Property crime	Burglary	Larceny-theft	Motor vehicle theft	Arson[1]
Idaho											
Aberdeen	1 874	1	0	0	0	1	16	2	12	2	0
American Falls	4 087	8	0	5	1	2	96	23	69	4	0
Bellevue	2 258	2	0	0	0	2	22	3	12	7	0
Blackfoot	10 982	44	1	7	5	31	496	92	380	24	1
Boise	195 012	748	5	120	86	537	7 484	1 358	5 627	499	73
Bonners Ferry	2 767	5	0	0	0	5	56	12	40	4	0
Buhl	4 068	10	0	1	0	9	93	16	68	9	0
Caldwell	33 559	170	3	14	9	144	1 907	462	1 259	186	14
Cascade	1 002	1	0	0	0	1	16	1	11	4	0
Coeur d'Alene	39 375	215	1	32	18	164	2 133	365	1 587	181	24
Cottonwood	1 054	1	0	1	0	0	5	1	4	0	1
Emmett	6 135	24	0	0	0	24	115	16	93	6	1
Filer	1 763	4	0	0	0	4	12	5	5	2	0
Fruitland	4 289	19	0	3	0	16	101	21	78	2	2
Garden City	11 460	57	0	3	6	48	480	108	315	57	6
Gooding	3 398	7	0	5	1	1	45	1	38	6	0
Grangeville	3 237	10	0	2	0	8	113	11	89	13	1
Hagerman	864	0	0	0	0	0	6	5	1	0	0
Hailey	7 654	8	0	1	0	7	44	2	37	5	0
Heyburn	2 853	3	0	0	0	3	16	8	8	0	0
Idaho Falls	53 489	156	0	27	9	120	1 923	339	1 454	130	9
Jerome	8 592	46	1	1	2	42	408	61	308	39	2
Kellogg	2 276	5	0	0	0	5	47	5	41	1	0
Ketchum	3 223	12	0	2	2	8	148	27	113	8	0
Kimberly	2 743	3	0	0	0	3	36	11	21	4	0
Lewiston	31 826	38	0	9	4	25	1 394	251	1 072	71	4
McCall	2 363	28	0	6	2	20	157	33	117	7	1
Meridian	46 118	87	1	12	7	67	1 253	254	931	68	10
Montpelier	2 667	0	0	0	0	0	20	18	2	0	0
Moscow	22 463	18	0	3	2	13	524	76	431	17	1
Mountain Home	11 721	50	0	5	1	44	380	54	302	24	3
Orofino	3 232	3	0	0	0	3	53	17	36	0	0
Payette	7 609	14	0	2	0	12	199	51	141	7	1
Pinehurst	1 599	0	0	0	0	0	49	15	32	2	1
Pocatello	52 028	159	1	35	7	116	1 763	283	1 416	64	6
Ponderay	704	2	0	0	1	1	94	14	78	2	0
Post Falls	21 900	56	0	16	1	39	784	145	591	48	2
Preston	5 090	3	0	1	0	2	92	21	71	0	0
Rathdrum	5 749	15	0	2	1	12	160	25	118	17	5
Rexburg	25 369	13	0	4	1	8	234	30	194	10	1
Rigby	3 089	7	0	3	0	4	60	6	50	4	0
Rupert	5 439	6	0	1	0	5	162	29	129	4	0
Salmon	3 135	4	0	2	0	2	47	10	34	3	0
Sandpoint	7 844	11	1	1	0	9	339	82	242	15	2
Shelley	4 058	4	0	3	0	1	104	21	76	7	1
Soda Springs	3 384	5	0	0	1	4	31	9	21	1	0
St. Anthony	3 502	11	0	1	0	10	39	4	33	2	0
St. Maries	2 635	8	0	0	1	7	24	7	16	1	0
Sun Valley	1 490	3	0	0	0	3	36	4	28	4	0
Twin Falls	38 587	138	4	20	22	92	1 968	368	1 448	152	22
Wendell	2 412	9	0	1	0	8	33	4	25	4	0
Wilder	1 495	3	0	1	0	2	50	22	22	6	0
Illinois[5]											
Aurora	167 266	. . .	14	. . .	176	480	4 832	883	3 642	307	31
Chicago	2 873 441	. . .	448	. . .	15 964	17 943	131 183	25 314	83 373	22 496	682
Joliet	130 026	. . .	11	. . .	145	309	4 228	745	3 312	171	63
Naperville	140 654	. . .	3	. . .	25	45	2 472	290	2 108	74	7
Peoria	113 161	. . .	14	. . .	380	528	7 470	1 839	4 848	783	68
Rockford	153 048	. . .	19	. . .	537	764	10 106	2 371	6 758	977	. . .
Springfield	115 187	. . .	5	. . .	258	1 306	7 345	1 719	5 288	338	51
Indiana											
Alexandria	6 010	18	1	0	6	11	320	46	269	5	2
Anderson	58 262	150	2	19	63	66	2 688	611	1 886	191	26
Angola	7 838	4	0	0	0	4	490	39	440	11	0
Attica	3 460	3	0	0	1	2	124	30	88	6	1
Auburn	12 731	17	0	1	9	7	459	65	374	20	1
Bargersville	2 382	0	0	0	0	0	0	0	0	0	0
Bedford	13 645	9	0	1	1	7	416	47	331	38	1
Beech Grove	14 315	27	0	4	18	5	462	99	309	54	1
Berne	4 191	5	0	1	1	3	66	16	47	3	0
Bloomington	69 158	171	0	25	54	92	2 683	566	1 969	148	13
Bluffton	9 509	4	0	0	2	2	200	32	164	4	0
Boonville	6 868	0	0	0	0	0	158	6	151	1	0
Brazil	8 289	4	0	0	1	3	173	37	121	15	1
Bremen	4 666	2	0	1	0	1	75	10	62	3	1
Brownsburg	17 719	2	0	0	0	2	304	37	253	14	1
Burns Harbor	781	0	0	0	0	0	30	6	20	4	0
Carmel	58 519	24	0	8	6	10	989	134	814	41	4
Charlestown	8 015	11	0	1	0	10	260	65	177	18	0
Chesterfield	2 844	1	0	0	1	0	142	19	119	4	0
Chesterton	11 634	12	0	0	5	7	320	66	228	26	3

[1]The FBI does not publish arson data unless it receives data from either the agency or the state for all 12 months of the calendar year.
[5]Limited data for 2005 were available for Illinois.
. . . = Not available.

Table 8. Offenses Known to Law Enforcement, by State and City, 2005—*Continued*

(Number.)

City	Population	Violent crime	Murder and non-negligent man-slaughter	Forcible rape	Robbery	Aggravated assault	Property crime	Burglary	Larceny-theft	Motor vehicle theft	Arson[1]
Clarks Hill	666	0	0	0	0	0	10	8	2	0	2
Clarksville	21 253	77	0	12	42	23	1 890	250	1 473	167	1
Clinton	4 938	7	0	0	0	7	83	11	59	13	5
Columbia City	7 807	15	0	1	0	14	78	12	57	9	0
Columbus	39 467	81	0	7	18	56	2 488	247	2 115	126	19
Connersville	14 525	44	3	4	9	28	1 036	158	827	51	1
Corydon	2 788	1	0	0	1	0	61	12	44	5	0
Crawfordsville	15 171	17	0	6	1	10	914	190	704	20	0
Crown Point	21 942	17	1	2	4	10	417	53	314	50	2
Culver	1 532	5	0	0	1	4	16	2	13	1	0
Decatur	9 558	4	0	0	0	4	107	20	79	8	1
Delphi	2 999	9	0	0	0	9	23	4	19	0	0
Dyer	14 875	16	2	4	8	2	315	37	250	28	0
East Chicago	31 409	714	12	12	125	565	1 860	397	1 124	339	15
Elkhart	52 164	200	5	39	146	10	3 761	775	2 724	262	20
Elwood	9 314	5	0	0	1	4	428	72	341	15	0
Evansville	117 802	478	8	59	176	235	6 008	1 255	4 469	284	72
Fairmount	2 882	6	0	1	1	4	72	14	57	1	1
Fishers	54 630	30	0	7	9	14	599	61	511	27	0
Fort Wayne	220 561	732	25	84	375	248	10 732	2 233	7 841	658	131
Frankfort	16 532	31	0	7	3	21	897	140	711	46	9
Franklin	21 318	113	0	7	10	96	1 229	113	1 100	16	0
Gary	100 065	718	58	70	306	284	5 310	1 593	2 556	1 161	. . .
Gas City	5 900	2	0	0	0	2	203	33	166	4	1
Georgetown	2 575	2	0	0	0	2	6	2	2	2	0
Goshen	30 724	73	1	0	7	65	1 366	142	1 188	36	0
Greendale	4 369	8	0	3	0	5	177	18	153	6	3
Greenfield	16 137	21	0	7	6	8	410	53	328	29	1
Greensburg	10 520	11	0	0	3	8	371	84	277	10	0
Greenwood	41 038	144	1	1	15	127	2 049	207	1 753	89	8
Griffith	16 899	43	0	5	19	19	659	70	508	81	4
Hagerstown	1 710	2	0	0	0	2	50	14	35	1	0
Hammond	80 426	712	9	30	279	394	4 554	1 047	2 728	779	56
Hartford City	6 739	4	0	0	2	2	230	41	177	12	0
Hebron	3 566	7	0	0	0	7	24	9	12	3	1
Highland	23 418	55	1	6	32	16	970	103	772	95	2
Hobart	27 662	186	3	11	13	159	1 484	165	1 199	120	7
Huntingburg	5 922	0	0	0	0	0	75	9	63	3	0
Indianapolis	800 304	7 948	108	527	3 274	4 039	50 081	11 548	29 541	8 992	374
Jasper	13 608	6	0	1	0	5	213	28	174	11	0
Jeffersonville	28 798	95	2	5	32	56	1 086	234	709	143	4
Kokomo	46 324	196	11	24	71	90	2 990	666	2 181	143	18
Kouts	1 756	0	0	0	0	0	76	4	72	0	0
Lafayette	60 083	258	4	35	70	149	3 267	649	2 394	224	13
La Porte	21 098	25	0	4	7	14	1 433	137	1 235	61	0
Lawrence	41 103	145	1	13	76	55	1 119	305	616	198	15
Ligonier	4 431	6	0	1	0	5	96	9	78	9	0
Logansport	19 457	16	0	7	6	3	764	119	600	45	2
Long Beach	1 544	0	0	0	0	0	24	3	19	2	0
Lowell	7 940	16	0	0	1	15	168	11	142	15	1
Madison	12 403	16	0	5	1	10	454	134	293	27	0
Marion	31 000	113	1	18	50	44	1 786	302	1 388	96	8
Martinsville	11 804	44	0	4	3	37	907	86	799	22	1
Merrillville	31 430	89	0	4	18	67	990	82	754	154	1
Michigan City	32 356	136	4	14	70	48	1 883	213	1 515	155	20
Mishawaka[3]	48 652	189	1	24	52	112	3 317	346	2 804	167	19
Monticello	5 580	2	0	0	0	2	126	8	117	1	1
Mooresville	10 886	16	0	0	6	10	346	40	292	14	0
Mount Vernon	7 360	0	0	0	0	0	129	47	67	15	0
Muncie	67 536	314	1	74	65	174	2 783	552	2 059	172	38
Munster	22 363	37	0	0	11	26	483	39	420	24	2
Nappanee	6 878	3	0	3	0	0	164	21	133	10	1
New Albany	37 080	166	0	11	62	93	2 331	486	1 678	167	35
New Castle	19 048	11	0	5	3	3	1 955	385	1 508	62	1
New Whiteland	4 483	8	0	0	0	8	96	11	83	2	1
Noblesville	35 633	36	2	6	4	24	760	152	567	41	3
North Liberty	1 378	12	0	0	0	12	10	1	6	3	0
North Manchester	6 079	6	0	2	0	4	199	27	165	7	0
North Vernon	6 490	10	1	1	2	6	325	41	268	16	0
Plainfield	22 688	33	2	1	8	22	939	154	734	51	3
Plymouth	10 787	10	0	3	6	1	469	55	389	25	2
Portage	35 464	57	0	7	7	43	1 279	204	970	105	5
Portland	6 283	5	0	0	2	3	278	34	240	4	0
Princeton	8 707	10	0	5	2	3	299	13	278	8	0
Rensselaer	6 243	22	0	3	0	19	175	33	132	10	1
Richmond	38 152	154	0	6	77	71	1 879	366	1 355	158	61
Rushville	5 817	8	0	0	2	6	120	13	99	8	1
Salem	6 452	12	0	0	0	12	24	10	14	0	0
Schererville	27 602	13	0	1	9	3	707	45	596	66	0
Scottsburg	6 067	43	0	1	2	40	451	62	379	10	0

[1]The FBI does not publish arson data unless it receives data from either the agency or the state for all 12 months of the calendar year.
[3]Because of changes in the state/local agency's reporting practices, figures are not comparable to previous years' data.
. . . = Not available.

Table 8. Offenses Known to Law Enforcement, by State and City, 2005—*Continued*

(Number.)

City	Population	Violent crime	Murder and non-negligent man-slaughter	Forcible rape	Robbery	Aggravated assault	Property crime	Burglary	Larceny-theft	Motor vehicle theft	Arson[1]
Seymour	18 807	122	1	15	11	95	1 281	105	1 102	74	6
South Bend	106 076	794	12	69	348	365	6 612	1 678	4 366	568	87
South Whitley	1 804	6	0	0	0	6	57	8	48	1	0
Speedway	12 639	97	2	4	54	37	506	68	372	66	2
St. John	10 030	5	0	0	0	5	142	8	123	11	0
Tell City	7 740	13	1	1	0	11	211	33	166	12	0
Terre Haute	57 540	152	1	31	63	57	5 155	934	3 718	503	43
Tipton	5 366	5	0	0	1	4	168	32	134	2	0
Valparaiso	28 909	73	1	4	2	66	886	86	758	42	3
Vincennes	18 205	27	0	6	8	13	1 319	255	995	69	10
Wabash	11 405	3	0	0	3	0	168	65	88	15	1
Warsaw	12 742	19	0	4	9	6	747	101	619	27	3
Waterloo	2 221	1	0	1	0	0	58	3	55	0	0
Westfield	11 977	18	0	1	8	9	400	71	319	10	1
West Lafayette	28 767	49	0	8	7	34	539	93	425	21	0
West Terre Haute	2 298	34	0	2	0	32	73	8	58	7	3
Whiting	4 963	10	0	3	5	2	263	50	185	28	1
Winchester	4 883	9	0	2	1	6	174	17	147	10	0
Iowa											
Adel	3 900	8	0	1	1	6	94	12	77	5	1
Albia	3 709	17	0	2	0	15	62	11	46	5	0
Algona	5 584	8	0	0	0	8	77	32	40	5	1
Altoona	12 156	16	1	2	4	9	542	68	462	12	3
Ames	52 529	98	0	14	14	70	1 537	465	1 028	44	1
Anamosa	5 657	4	0	2	0	2	74	12	60	2	0
Ankeny	34 578	36	0	1	3	32	872	157	670	45	2
Audubon	2 273	2	0	0	0	2	41	16	23	2	3
Belmond	2 472	4	0	0	0	4	4	3	1	0	1
Bettendorf	31 742	95	0	7	11	77	692	96	566	30	6
Bloomfield	2 614	8	0	0	0	8	10	1	9	0	0
Boone	12 908	10	0	5	1	4	395	69	311	15	5
Burlington	25 682	137	1	10	18	108	1 086	312	723	51	5
Camanche	4 276	2	0	0	0	2	98	6	91	1	1
Carlisle	3 496	1	0	0	0	1	20	6	13	1	1
Carter Lake	3 320	5	0	0	0	5	216	36	162	18	3
Cedar Falls	36 489	70	0	12	4	54	662	88	540	34	6
Cedar Rapids	122 608	417	1	45	121	250	6 391	1 067	5 022	302	18
Centerville	5 821	19	0	3	3	13	333	64	252	17	1
Chariton	4 663	14	1	1	0	12	192	31	152	9	0
Charles City	7 672	13	0	2	0	11	131	29	99	3	1
Cherokee	5 142	4	0	1	0	3	141	27	110	4	0
Clarinda	5 515	11	0	1	0	10	162	34	108	20	2
Clarion	2 859	6	0	0	0	6	50	18	29	3	0
Clinton	27 429	147	3	6	18	120	1 439	275	1 093	71	7
Clive	13 653	23	0	1	4	18	397	54	327	16	2
Coralville	17 598	19	0	6	6	7	715	82	622	11	3
Council Bluffs	59 586	725	0	61	79	585	5 145	1 034	3 435	676	34
Cresco	3 839	0	0	0	0	0	59	10	46	3	1
Davenport	98 751	1 323	7	54	272	990	7 080	1 451	5 213	416	51
Decorah	8 102	11	0	1	0	10	66	20	43	3	0
Denison	7 416	9	0	2	0	7	111	17	86	8	0
Des Moines[3]	195 093	1 228	5	110	294	819	13 799	2 630	10 045	1 124	52
De Witt	5 197	7	0	0	1	6	104	36	66	2	0
Dubuque	57 735	315	1	16	10	288	1 770	398	1 306	66	36
Dyersville	4 059	0	0	0	0	0	45	4	39	2	0
Eldora	2 904	3	1	1	0	1	43	7	32	4	1
Eldridge	4 619	5	0	1	0	4	206	15	183	8	0
Emmetsburg	3 751	8	0	3	0	5	39	9	19	11	0
Estherville	6 427	17	0	0	0	17	150	50	85	15	0
Evansdale	4 539	6	0	4	0	2	104	26	75	3	0
Fairfield	9 497	23	0	1	2	20	296	78	204	14	1
Forest City	4 265	6	0	1	0	5	17	10	7	0	0
Fort Dodge	25 826	151	2	17	15	117	1 718	375	1 221	122	18
Fort Madison	10 988	7	0	1	2	4	439	65	355	19	2
Glenwood	5 558	11	1	7	1	2	113	15	86	12	1
Grinnell	9 349	26	0	5	0	21	232	59	164	9	8
Grundy Center	2 605	4	0	1	0	3	18	1	16	1	0
Hampton	4 203	6	0	0	0	6	24	6	17	1	0
Hawarden	2 440	2	0	0	0	2	20	6	13	1	1
Humboldt	4 385	1	0	0	0	1	34	6	25	3	0
Independence	6 038	3	0	0	1	2	186	46	129	11	1
Indianola	13 769	24	0	2	1	21	332	43	274	15	5
Iowa City	63 280	184	0	32	37	115	1 480	326	1 082	72	9
Iowa Falls	5 111	7	1	2	1	3	169	16	141	12	1
Jefferson	4 469	0	0	0	0	0	58	5	53	0	1
Johnston	11 817	16	0	0	0	16	202	40	153	9	0
Keokuk	10 889	132	0	2	3	127	533	74	421	38	5
Le Mars	9 355	19	0	7	0	12	287	41	235	11	1
Leon	1 944	10	0	0	0	10	35	3	29	3	0

[1]The FBI does not publish arson data unless it receives data from either the agency or the state for all 12 months of the calendar year.
[3]Because of changes in the state/local agency's reporting practices, figures are not comparable to previous years' data.

Table 8. Offenses Known to Law Enforcement, by State and City, 2005—*Continued*

(Number.)

City	Population	Violent crime	Murder and non-negligent man-slaughter	Forcible rape	Robbery	Aggravated assault	Property crime	Burglary	Larceny-theft	Motor vehicle theft	Arson[1]
Manchester	5 105	11	0	0	0	11	81	20	54	7	1
Maquoketa	6 072	10	0	7	1	2	189	53	125	11	0
Marion	29 945	24	0	10	2	12	430	115	288	27	7
Marshalltown	26 162	182	1	5	4	172	1 097	177	847	73	1
Mason City	28 290	72	0	12	12	48	1 594	306	1 227	61	9
Monticello	3 755	8	0	0	0	8	40	4	31	5	0
Mount Pleasant	8 805	35	0	5	1	29	236	45	178	13	2
Mount Vernon	4 026	0	0	0	0	0	78	12	64	2	0
Muscatine	22 804	127	3	24	2	98	665	145	499	21	14
Nevada	6 274	14	0	4	1	9	157	49	99	9	1
Newton	15 759	9	0	0	2	7	477	66	395	16	0
North Liberty	7 669	17	0	3	0	14	43	11	24	8	0
Norwalk	7 754	15	0	4	0	11	129	12	111	6	2
Oelwein	6 378	15	1	4	1	9	167	87	73	7	2
Orange City	5 736	2	0	0	0	2	65	13	51	1	0
Osage	3 506	1	0	0	0	1	49	10	36	3	0
Osceola	4 816	9	0	0	1	8	177	28	147	2	3
Oskaloosa	10 989	27	0	4	2	21	374	61	294	19	3
Ottumwa	24 779	182	0	11	6	165	1 286	328	897	61	9
Pella	10 223	28	0	3	0	25	199	42	148	9	3
Perry	8 677	34	0	1	0	33	209	41	156	12	2
Pleasant Hill	6 015	10	0	0	1	9	140	54	79	7	1
Red Oak	6 000	11	0	1	2	8	217	48	159	10	4
Sac City	2 219	1	0	0	0	1	28	8	19	1	0
Sergeant Bluff	3 792	6	0	0	0	6	71	6	65	0	0
Sheldon	4 952	7	0	0	0	7	66	18	41	7	0
Shenandoah	5 277	3	0	1	0	2	132	13	110	9	1
Sioux City	84 017	400	2	54	52	292	3 590	797	2 562	231	17
Spencer	11 107	0	0	0	0	0	327	58	258	11	0
Spirit Lake	4 511	5	0	0	0	5	139	23	114	2	0
Storm Lake	10 021	32	0	2	2	28	324	64	251	9	4
Story City	3 201	2	0	0	1	1	38	11	26	1	0
Tama	2 669	6	0	0	0	6	40	9	26	5	1
Urbandale	33 513	39	0	7	7	25	582	130	417	35	12
Vinton	5 220	7	0	1	0	6	66	20	44	2	2
Waterloo	67 036	360	1	36	80	243	3 251	825	2 242	184	21
Waukee	8 501	4	0	1	0	3	216	59	149	8	5
Waverly	9 129	32	0	3	0	29	140	29	106	5	0
Webster City	8 138	32	0	4	1	27	202	35	149	18	0
West Burlington	3 163	5	0	1	1	3	216	6	203	7	0
West Des Moines	51 570	88	0	14	11	63	1 807	279	1 459	69	9
Williamsburg	2 738	5	0	0	0	5	28	4	23	1	0
Wilton	2 869	7	0	2	0	5	36	15	20	1	1
Windsor Heights	4 655	10	0	0	3	7	280	36	232	12	2
Winterset	4 897	8	0	0	0	8	104	26	75	3	0
Kansas											
Abilene	6 418	12	0	3	0	9	160	19	136	5	2
Alta Vista	432	0	0	0	0	0	0	0	0	0	0
Andover	8 646	8	0	3	0	5	163	41	111	11	2
Anthony	2 315	7	0	1	0	6	42	10	30	2	0
Arkansas City	11 792	69	1	9	2	57	531	112	390	29	5
Arma	1 499	4	0	0	0	4	27	4	21	2	2
Atchison	10 219	20	0	2	2	16	378	47	304	27	1
Auburn	1 129	0	0	0	0	0	2	0	2	0	0
Augusta	8 589	14	0	4	2	8	403	45	343	15	1
Baldwin City	3 676	3	0	0	0	3	101	21	71	9	1
Basehor	3 009	11	0	3	0	8	49	13	29	7	0
Baxter Springs	4 361	19	0	6	0	13	145	29	109	7	2
Bel Aire	6 552	3	0	0	0	3	18	2	11	5	1
Belle Plaine	1 655	3	0	1	0	2	29	13	14	2	3
Belleville	1 991	0	0	0	0	0	24	8	14	2	0
Bonner Springs	6 915	24	1	1	0	22	420	56	318	46	2
Buhler	1 341	0	0	0	0	0	20	6	14	0	0
Burrton	922	2	0	0	0	2	16	3	9	4	0
Bushton	301	0	0	0	0	0	0	0	0	0	0
Chanute	9 073	21	0	3	1	17	363	122	224	17	3
Chapman	1 243	2	0	0	0	2	36	3	33	0	0
Cheney	1 850	1	0	0	0	1	25	3	19	3	0
Chetopa	1 241	15	0	0	0	15	38	7	30	1	0
Clay Center	4 396	14	0	5	1	8	141	47	90	4	0
Coffeyville	10 539	66	1	7	11	47	761	173	554	34	7
Colby	5 162	10	0	2	0	8	171	20	145	6	2
Colony	392	0	0	0	0	0	0	0	0	0	0
Columbus	3 322	4	0	0	0	4	102	10	87	5	2
Concordia	5 410	10	0	3	0	7	151	47	93	11	0
Council Grove	2 261	3	0	0	0	3	42	9	29	4	0
Derby	20 394	24	0	5	4	15	567	81	464	22	6
Edwardsville	4 510	8	0	1	0	7	122	33	81	8	1
El Dorado	12 760	30	0	4	1	25	618	73	519	26	2
Elkhart	2 088	12	0	1	0	11	36	14	17	5	0
Ellsworth	2 893	2	0	2	0	0	39	5	33	1	0
Emporia	26 728	64	1	14	9	40	1 478	189	1 248	41	7
Eskridge	581	2	0	0	0	2	5	4	1	0	0
Eudora	5 136	18	0	0	0	18	113	19	89	5	0
Fairway	3 862	1	0	0	1	0	25	5	16	4	1
Fort Scott	8 075	41	0	2	6	33	447	95	335	17	4

[1]The FBI does not publish arson data unless it receives data from either the agency or the state for all 12 months of the calendar year.

Table 8. Offenses Known to Law Enforcement, by State and City, 2005—*Continued*

(Number.)

City	Population	Violent crime	Murder and non-negligent man-slaughter	Forcible rape	Robbery	Aggravated assault	Property crime	Burglary	Larceny-theft	Motor vehicle theft	Arson[1]
Fredonia	2 496	6	0	0	0	6	85	17	65	3	1
Frontenac	3 089	6	0	0	0	6	83	16	61	6	4
Galena	3 221	20	0	3	0	17	148	23	101	24	1
Garden City	27 404	137	1	22	8	106	1 189	160	980	49	8
Gardner	12 980	42	0	8	3	31	358	54	282	22	3
Garnett	3 374	16	0	0	1	15	110	27	75	8	4
Girard	2 696	7	0	1	0	6	86	8	72	6	1
Goddard	3 207	2	0	1	0	1	156	87	68	1	0
Goodland	4 549	16	0	2	0	14	133	26	101	6	0
Grandview Plaza	1 075	3	0	0	0	3	64	10	54	0	0
Haven	1 179	0	0	0	0	0	11	3	6	2	0
Hays	19 908	49	0	4	2	43	594	75	490	29	4
Haysville	9 659	20	1	2	2	15	364	51	295	18	0
Herington	2 477	8	0	0	0	8	76	19	50	7	0
Hesston	3 637	5	0	1	0	4	55	10	44	1	0
Hiawatha	3 298	10	1	0	1	8	144	39	95	10	0
Hill City	1 474	4	0	1	0	3	14	3	11	0	0
Hillsboro	2 759	1	0	0	0	1	60	14	45	1	0
Hoisington	2 979	2	0	0	0	2	48	9	39	0	0
Holcomb	1 950	0	0	0	0	0	35	4	30	1	0
Holton	3 356	4	0	1	0	3	104	15	83	6	0
Horton	1 875	11	0	3	0	8	31	7	22	2	0
Hugoton	3 734	5	0	1	0	4	49	12	37	0	1
Hutchinson	41 185	158	1	21	16	120	2 539	426	2 025	88	23
Iola	6 103	43	0	2	0	41	266	34	224	8	1
Kansas City	145 491	1 166	37	100	416	613	10 678	1 842	5 924	2 912	60
Kechi	1 214	0	0	0	0	0	18	1	15	2	0
Kingman	3 286	2	0	0	0	2	52	11	38	3	0
La Cygne	1 127	11	0	5	0	6	55	11	38	6	0
Lansing	10 151	16	0	3	1	12	213	44	162	7	4
Larned	3 928	27	0	3	1	23	225	45	171	9	1
Lawrence	82 148	276	2	30	41	203	3 493	545	2 797	151	6
Leavenworth	35 408	294	0	23	51	220	1 410	300	1 024	86	12
Leawood	29 603	17	0	5	3	9	463	85	360	18	3
Lenexa	42 758	96	4	10	23	59	2 044	536	1 417	91	8
Liberal	20 286	106	6	15	16	69	1 073	220	796	57	2
Lindsborg	3 316	1	0	0	0	1	55	14	39	2	2
Little River	532	0	0	0	0	0	4	0	3	1	0
Louisburg	3 008	10	0	1	0	9	67	9	54	4	0
Lyndon	1 047	0	0	0	0	0	18	1	16	1	0
Lyons	3 588	10	0	2	0	8	79	16	58	5	0
Maize	2 125	3	0	0	0	3	49	13	31	5	0
Maple Hill	493	0	0	0	0	0	2	0	2	0	0
Marysville	3 075	7	0	0	0	7	33	2	29	2	0
McPherson	13 727	30	0	9	3	18	309	88	207	14	6
Merriam	10 810	58	1	8	20	29	739	56	586	97	6
Minneapolis	2 044	1	0	0	0	1	16	4	10	2	0
Mission	9 805	49	0	2	16	31	602	47	480	75	0
Mission Hills	3 536	6	0	0	2	4	17	1	15	1	0
Mulvane	5 594	7	0	2	0	5	106	12	86	8	1
Neodesha	2 699	9	0	1	0	8	100	39	59	2	0
Newton	18 215	85	0	12	7	66	658	86	546	26	3
Norton	2 899	1	0	0	0	1	21	11	10	0	0
Oakley	2 013	2	0	0	0	2	30	6	23	1	0
Olathe	108 754	336	1	45	29	261	3 328	249	2 818	261	18
Osage City	3 002	12	0	0	0	12	64	14	43	7	0
Osawatomie	4 615	21	0	1	1	19	132	24	98	10	0
Oswego	2 009	1	0	0	0	1	39	4	33	2	0
Ottawa	12 541	77	0	11	6	60	719	95	592	32	6
Overland Park	163 274	494	2	30	63	399	4 559	488	3 661	410	28
Paola	5 178	9	0	1	0	8	204	17	180	7	2
Park City	7 024	15	0	3	0	12	187	36	137	14	1
Parsons	11 329	78	0	5	10	63	626	121	486	19	11
Peabody	1 325	3	0	1	0	2	11	0	9	2	0
Pittsburg	19 216	119	0	19	10	90	1 161	226	888	47	12
Pleasanton	1 375	4	0	1	0	3	22	9	11	2	0
Prairie Village	21 583	23	0	2	8	13	288	51	215	22	3
Pratt	6 418	9	0	0	1	8	143	29	109	5	3
Roeland Park	7 020	22	0	1	12	9	425	22	369	34	4
Rolla	455	0	0	0	0	0	0	0	0	0	0
Rose Hill	3 870	6	0	0	0	6	63	16	45	2	0
Rossville	996	1	0	0	0	1	5	1	3	1	0
Russell	4 446	6	0	0	0	6	99	33	60	6	1
Scott City	3 557	18	0	2	0	16	97	21	74	2	0
Shawnee	56 367	87	0	10	30	47	1 233	156	964	113	17
South Hutchinson	2 496	3	0	1	0	2	85	8	74	3	0
Spring Hill	4 173	10	0	0	1	9	124	14	103	7	1
Sterling	2 596	2	0	0	0	2	27	4	22	1	3
St. Marys	2 254	2	0	0	0	2	22	5	17	0	0
Topeka	122 218	682	7	50	275	350	9 662	1 719	7 244	699	10

[1]The FBI does not publish arson data unless it receives data from either the agency or the state for all 12 months of the calendar year.

Table 8. Offenses Known to Law Enforcement, by State and City, 2005—*Continued*

(Number.)

City	Population	Violent crime	Murder and non-negligent man-slaughter	Forcible rape	Robbery	Aggravated assault	Property crime	Burglary	Larceny-theft	Motor vehicle theft	Arson[1]
Towanda	1 347	2	0	0	0	2	15	8	7	0	0
Ulysses	5 788	15	0	1	0	14	81	12	64	5	0
Valley Center	5 387	11	0	3	0	8	141	20	118	3	2
Wa Keeney	1 827	3	0	0	0	3	32	8	21	3	0
Wakefield	871	0	0	0	0	0	13	3	8	2	0
Wamego	4 238	7	0	2	0	5	77	12	61	4	2
Wathena	1 332	4	0	0	0	4	24	5	17	2	0
Wellington	8 305	28	2	6	1	19	366	54	299	13	0
Westwood	1 860	0	0	0	0	0	81	10	63	8	0
Winchester	577	0	0	0	0	0	2	0	2	0	0
Yates Center	1 493	1	0	0	0	1	27	10	17	0	0
Kentucky											
Adairville	933	0	0	0	0	0	11	6	4	1	0
Albany	2 280	2	0	0	1	1	13	5	7	1	0
Anchorage	2 517	0	0	0	0	0	48	8	38	2	0
Ashland	21 729	87	2	11	20	54	1 103	202	840	61	5
Auburn	1 493	1	0	0	1	0	10	3	6	1	0
Audubon Park	1 553	3	0	0	2	1	37	16	19	2	0
Barbourville	3 538	1	0	1	0	0	40	10	24	6	1
Bardstown	10 969	17	0	3	6	8	208	60	137	11	0
Beattyville	1 172	0	0	0	0	0	7	3	4	0	0
Benham	569	0	0	0	0	0	1	1	0	0	0
Bloomfield	874	0	0	0	0	0	4	0	3	1	0
Bowling Green	51 634	328	3	47	88	190	3 020	584	2 282	154	1
Brandenburg	2 208	1	0	0	1	0	34	8	25	1	0
Brownsville	942	1	0	0	0	1	19	1	16	2	0
Burkesville	1 779	0	0	0	0	0	2	1	0	1	0
Burnside	674	0	0	0	0	0	17	4	13	0	0
Cadiz	2 533	19	0	1	5	13	99	13	84	2	0
Campbellsville	10 823	32	0	5	13	14	414	91	304	19	3
Campton	416	0	0	0	0	0	3	0	2	1	0
Carlisle	2 059	2	0	1	0	1	25	8	14	3	0
Carrollton	3 855	41	0	3	3	35	96	13	79	4	0
Catlettsburg	1 946	4	0	1	1	2	78	20	54	4	2
Cave City	1 936	5	0	0	1	4	67	33	29	5	0
Central City	5 862	7	0	2	0	5	99	18	77	4	0
Clarkson	825	0	0	0	0	0	1	0	1	0	0
Clay City	1 346	6	0	0	1	5	52	16	34	2	0
Clinton	1 398	2	1	1	0	0	22	15	6	1	0
Columbia	4 204	3	0	0	1	2	84	26	52	6	0
Corbin	8 165	20	0	2	1	17	346	73	257	16	4
Crescent Springs	3 989	5	1	0	2	2	131	14	109	8	0
Crofton	840	0	0	0	0	0	11	2	9	0	0
Cumberland	2 371	3	0	1	0	2	22	11	11	0	0
Cynthiana	6 284	19	0	4	3	12	314	59	233	22	0
Danville	15 530	42	0	4	17	21	475	105	352	18	1
Dawson Springs	2 992	3	0	1	0	2	33	18	14	1	3
Earlington	1 623	2	0	0	0	2	37	11	26	0	1
Eddyville	2 394	4	0	2	0	2	38	7	28	3	0
Edgewood	9 072	2	0	0	2	0	143	22	112	9	0
Edmonton	1 606	0	0	0	0	0	5	1	3	1	0
Elizabethtown	23 344	76	0	14	23	39	1 087	182	847	58	5
Elkton	1 946	9	0	0	4	5	34	16	17	1	0
Elsmere	8 107	15	0	0	6	9	130	32	83	15	0
Eminence	2 267	11	0	6	3	2	25	8	15	2	0
Erlanger	16 857	24	0	5	8	11	461	68	360	33	2
Evarts	1 070	2	0	0	1	1	6	1	4	1	0
Falmouth	2 112	1	0	0	0	1	64	17	44	3	0
Flatwoods	7 710	8	0	2	0	6	30	11	16	3	0
Fleming-Neon	821	2	0	0	1	1	6	2	4	0	0
Flemingsburg	3 107	3	0	1	1	1	23	4	18	1	0
Florence	25 618	91	1	6	32	52	1 413	148	1 175	90	5
Fort Mitchell	7 744	4	0	1	2	1	152	36	110	6	0
Fort Wright	5 529	17	0	0	14	3	308	41	243	24	0
Frankfort	27 462	81	0	13	25	43	1 190	255	844	91	9
Franklin	8 125	23	0	2	7	14	319	66	234	19	0
Fulton	2 634	10	0	1	1	8	173	27	139	7	2
Georgetown	19 863	35	0	2	9	24	1 043	159	823	61	2
Glasgow	13 921	22	0	4	7	11	302	97	183	22	1
Glencoe	251	1	0	0	0	1	6	4	2	0	0
Graymoor-Devondale	2 965	0	0	0	0	0	37	2	32	3	0
Grayson	4 044	4	0	2	0	2	103	39	61	3	5
Greenville	4 343	2	0	0	1	1	24	4	15	5	0
Guthrie	1 433	0	0	0	0	0	0	0	0	0	0
Hardinsburg	2 445	1	0	0	1	0	14	2	5	7	0
Harlan	1 946	15	0	1	7	7	172	20	145	7	1
Harrodsburg	8 094	28	1	3	5	19	124	46	69	9	0
Hartford	2 658	3	0	0	0	3	47	13	31	3	0
Hazard	4 879	27	1	5	7	14	460	150	299	11	5
Hickman	2 426	0	0	0	0	0	39	9	26	4	0
Hillview	7 301	12	0	0	4	8	129	28	90	11	0
Hodgenville	2 797	6	1	1	2	2	19	7	9	3	0

[1]The FBI does not publish arson data unless it receives data from either the agency or the state for all 12 months of the calendar year.

Table 8. Offenses Known to Law Enforcement, by State and City, 2005—*Continued*

(Number.)

City	Population	Violent crime	Murder and non-negligent man-slaughter	Forcible rape	Robbery	Aggravated assault	Property crime	Burglary	Larceny-theft	Motor vehicle theft	Arson[1]
Hopkinsville	29 145	146	1	26	52	67	1 732	409	1 253	70	8
Horse Cave	2 326	4	0	0	1	3	25	8	16	1	0
Indian Hills	2 991	2	0	0	1	1	24	6	18	0	0
Irvine	2 756	3	0	1	0	2	87	18	66	3	0
Jackson	2 428	3	0	0	2	1	91	32	57	2	1
Jamestown	1 706	3	0	0	0	3	49	17	31	1	0
Jeffersontown	26 406	49	0	3	28	18	603	111	422	70	1
Jenkins	2 337	1	0	0	0	1	25	5	19	1	0
La Center	1 043	0	0	0	0	0	2	0	0	2	0
Lakeside Park-Crestview Hills	6 057	3	0	0	2	1	92	14	74	4	0
Lancaster	4 118	7	0	1	1	5	121	40	72	9	1
Lawrenceburg	9 458	9	0	0	0	9	263	56	198	9	0
Lebanon Junction	1 910	1	0	0	0	1	26	4	18	4	0
Leitchfield	6 462	1	0	1	0	0	199	67	123	9	1
Lewisburg	919	0	0	0	0	0	5	3	2	0	0
Lewisport	1 638	0	0	0	0	0	12	3	9	0	0
Lexington	268 124	1 476	15	147	575	739	10 308	2 172	7 391	745	22
Liberty	1 884	0	0	0	0	0	11	3	6	2	0
Livermore	1 492	0	0	0	0	0	12	4	8	0	0
London	7 818	14	0	0	7	7	373	55	276	42	2
Lone Oak	446	0	0	0	0	0	13	6	6	1	1
Louisa	2 052	0	0	0	0	0	29	6	20	3	2
Louisville Metro[3]	623 735	3 896	55	209	1 822	1 810	27 446	7 146	17 150	3 150	281
Lynch	860	3	0	1	0	2	18	15	3	0	0
Lynnview	971	0	0	0	0	0	5	1	4	0	0
Manchester	1 980	5	0	0	2	3	39	5	30	4	1
Marion	3 067	4	0	0	0	4	48	10	35	3	0
Maysville	9 071	27	0	2	7	18	457	124	311	22	0
Millersburg	838	0	0	0	0	0	14	4	10	0	0
Minor Lane Heights	1 526	1	0	0	0	1	24	13	7	4	0
Morganfield	3 484	19	0	2	4	13	145	22	120	3	0
Mortons Gap	968	0	0	0	0	0	2	2	0	0	0
Mount Sterling	6 163	10	0	1	4	5	365	31	317	17	1
Mount Vernon	2 627	6	0	1	0	5	52	7	39	6	2
Mount Washington	8 776	9	0	1	3	5	155	43	101	11	0
Muldraugh	1 367	2	0	0	0	2	19	5	9	5	0
Munfordville	1 616	7	0	0	1	6	17	5	10	2	0
New Castle	933	0	0	0	0	0	3	0	2	1	0
Nortonville	1 268	0	0	0	0	0	8	4	4	0	0
Oak Grove	7 651	28	0	5	7	16	262	91	147	24	6
Olive Hill	1 832	1	0	0	0	1	11	2	3	6	0
Owensboro	55 264	148	4	16	50	78	2 072	438	1 564	70	3
Owenton	1 476	1	0	0	0	1	7	3	4	0	0
Owingsville	1 553	2	0	0	1	1	34	7	22	5	0
Paducah	25 714	200	0	21	44	135	1 782	253	1 386	143	5
Paintsville	4 124	4	0	0	2	2	145	9	127	9	0
Paris	9 346	25	0	2	8	15	230	61	157	12	2
Pikeville	6 346	16	0	0	6	10	489	62	386	41	0
Pineville	2 028	0	0	0	0	0	89	14	74	1	0
Pioneer Village	2 615	1	0	0	1	0	21	7	14	0	0
Prestonsburg	3 739	4	0	2	1	1	75	12	56	7	0
Princeton	6 455	23	0	3	3	17	194	49	136	9	1
Providence	3 578	7	0	1	1	5	26	9	12	5	0
Raceland	2 459	1	0	0	0	1	32	5	26	1	0
Radcliff	21 760	85	0	14	23	48	738	137	572	29	0
Ravenna	685	0	0	0	0	0	10	2	7	1	0
Richmond	30 207	106	0	8	22	76	1 124	203	862	59	7
Russell	3 639	6	0	0	5	1	74	1	69	4	0
Russell Springs	2 514	2	0	0	0	2	9	3	6	0	0
Russellville	7 283	27	1	2	4	20	332	93	230	9	1
Sadieville	291	0	0	0	0	0	1	1	0	0	0
Science Hill	653	0	0	0	0	0	3	3	0	0	0
Scottsville	4 498	4	0	2	0	2	44	15	23	6	1
Shelbyville	10 692	46	0	6	20	20	335	81	227	27	1
Shepherdsville	8 795	17	0	5	4	8	414	79	310	25	0
Shively	15 359	107	1	8	57	41	698	162	450	86	3
Silver Grove	1 179	1	0	0	1	0	10	1	9	0	0
Somerset	12 051	47	0	4	18	25	665	117	515	33	4
Southgate	3 413	4	0	0	0	4	46	15	25	6	0
Stanford	3 466	2	0	0	0	2	29	12	13	4	0
Stanton	3 115	5	0	0	3	2	142	39	97	6	0
Sturgis	2 040	4	0	0	3	1	42	5	36	1	0
Taylor Mill	6 831	6	0	0	4	2	53	9	37	7	0
Taylorsville	1 132	4	0	1	0	3	18	6	11	1	0
Tompkinsville	2 651	2	0	0	0	2	20	12	7	1	0
Uniontown	1 079	1	0	0	1	0	5	2	2	1	0
Vanceburg	1 700	7	0	0	1	6	38	14	23	1	0
Villa Hills	7 861	1	0	1	0	0	57	8	49	0	0
Vine Grove	4 015	2	0	0	0	2	66	14	50	2	3
Wallins	244	2	0	0	0	2	8	1	6	1	0

[1]The FBI does not publish arson data unless it receives data from either the agency or the state for all 12 months of the calendar year.
[3]Because of changes in the state/local agency's reporting practices, figures are not comparable to previous years' data.

Table 8. Offenses Known to Law Enforcement, by State and City, 2005—*Continued*

(Number.)

City	Population	Violent crime	Murder and non-negligent man-slaughter	Forcible rape	Robbery	Aggravated assault	Property crime	Burglary	Larceny-theft	Motor vehicle theft	Arson[1]
Warsaw	1 852	3	0	0	0	3	21	7	11	3	0
West Buechel	1 333	12	0	0	11	1	241	13	211	17	0
West Liberty	3 376	0	0	0	0	0	4	0	2	2	0
West Point	1 052	1	0	0	0	1	7	1	4	2	0
Wilder	2 899	0	0	0	0	0	21	2	17	2	0
Williamsburg	5 141	6	0	0	3	3	79	28	41	10	0
Williamstown	3 419	7	0	0	0	7	60	22	34	4	0
Wilmore	5 884	1	0	1	0	0	47	8	38	1	0
Winchester	16 521	43	0	7	15	21	865	160	660	45	2
Louisiana											
Addis	2 455	11	0	0	0	11	1	0	1	0	0
Alexandria	46 051	1 022	9	21	147	845	3 787	948	2 629	210	16
Baker	13 409	51	3	3	10	35	769	149	559	61	0
Basile	2 387	7	0	0	0	7	16	3	12	1	0
Baton Rouge	224 487	2 698	49	83	993	1 573	14 378	3 940	8 949	1 489	183
Bernice	1 765	10	0	0	1	9	34	12	22	0	0
Blanchard	2 280	2	0	0	1	1	40	4	32	4	0
Bogalusa	12 930	161	2	10	24	125	645	232	364	49	6
Bossier City	59 715	1 247	0	32	89	1 126	3 131	627	2 241	263	16
Broussard	6 549	26	0	3	3	20	308	60	221	27	0
Church Point	4 673	12	0	0	6	6	62	22	37	3	0
Clinton	1 938	22	0	0	2	20	84	30	49	5	0
Coushatta	2 249	20	0	0	4	16	62	21	40	1	0
Covington	8 897	30	0	2	11	17	243	54	179	10	1
Denham Springs	10 124	155	0	7	32	116	1 238	174	1 004	60	2
De Ridder	9 864	39	0	1	3	35	211	46	162	3	0
Elton	1 253	5	0	0	0	5	41	7	32	2	0
Erath	2 181	5	0	0	0	5	75	23	50	2	0
Eunice	11 589	26	0	5	7	14	918	329	541	48	1
Farmerville	3 732	44	0	0	5	39	226	57	160	9	1
Folsom	602	3	0	0	0	3	11	1	10	0	0
Franklin	7 998	81	3	0	15	63	543	68	462	13	1
Franklinton	3 672	24	0	5	4	15	268	40	221	7	2
French Settlement	1 044	6	0	0	0	6	15	4	11	0	0
Gonzales	8 414	57	0	1	8	48	304	48	210	46	0
Gramercy	6 762	26	0	0	3	23	132	27	96	9	0
Gretna	17 208	121	3	11	40	67	791	262	397	132	0
Harahan	9 791	35	0	0	4	31	157	26	121	10	0
Haughton	2 801	8	0	1	1	6	44	7	35	2	0
Homer	3 571	42	0	0	9	33	172	69	96	7	0
Houma	32 078	319	6	14	67	232	1 725	290	1 379	56	8
Independence	1 727	20	0	2	3	15	77	9	68	0	0
Iowa	2 620	16	0	0	3	13	142	36	96	10	0
Jackson	3 873	24	0	0	2	22	57	10	44	3	0
Jeanerette	6 016	10	0	2	1	7	131	33	90	8	0
Kaplan	5 141	37	0	0	4	33	267	48	208	11	0
Kenner	70 374	253	4	19	68	162	2 799	716	1 734	349	20
Kentwood	2 177	17	0	0	1	16	199	23	170	6	0
Kinder	2 131	21	0	0	2	19	48	4	42	2	0
Lafayette	112 161	991	8	91	141	751	6 342	1 233	4 691	418	30
Lake Arthur	2 924	19	1	2	1	15	148	30	114	4	0
Lake Charles	70 942	562	6	44	153	359	3 638	1 720	1 678	240	3
Lake Providence	4 712	37	1	2	2	32	53	21	30	2	0
Leesville	6 270	62	0	6	6	50	408	66	335	7	0
Mamou	3 440	55	0	0	1	54	192	43	144	5	1
Mandeville	11 531	47	2	0	5	40	399	60	319	20	0
Mansfield	5 506	31	0	1	5	25	330	65	243	22	0
Minden	13 304	33	2	1	4	26	277	55	208	14	0
Monroe	52 232	607	3	33	61	510	4 685	988	3 575	122	0
Morgan City	12 174	69	0	6	16	47	475	126	326	23	0
Olla	1 373	3	0	0	0	3	54	14	36	4	1
Pineville	13 808	39	0	3	5	31	701	124	529	48	0
Plaquemine	6 760	88	0	1	5	82	392	49	329	14	0
Pollock	373	0	0	0	0	0	3	0	3	0	0
Ponchatoula	5 601	87	0	4	9	74	590	165	401	24	0
Port Allen	5 163	23	4	0	4	15	227	58	158	11	0
Ruston	20 701	112	0	2	22	88	1 004	133	815	56	0
Shreveport	199 021	2 249	39	151	628	1 431	12 878	2 969	8 893	1 016	186
Slidell	26 892	143	1	8	28	106	1 923	352	1 422	149	0
St. Gabriel	5 486	31	1	1	0	29	63	8	53	2	0
Thibodaux	14 526	105	0	12	18	75	586	118	459	9	1
Tickfaw	630	2	0	0	0	2	6	0	6	0	1
Vidalia	4 343	18	0	2	2	14	194	30	159	5	0
Washington	1 062	0	0	0	0	0	1	0	1	0	0
West Monroe	13 013	81	0	6	11	64	1 097	176	861	60	3
Westwego	10 555	27	0	0	10	17	259	65	165	29	0
Zachary	12 091	39	0	1	7	31	323	42	257	24	0
Maine											
Ashland	1 471	3	0	0	1	2	18	11	6	1	0
Auburn	23 627	17	0	3	6	8	821	103	683	35	3
Augusta	18 691	41	0	16	7	18	1 181	206	953	22	8
Baileyville	1 641	4	0	1	0	3	44	13	30	1	0
Bangor	31 697	65	0	6	26	33	1 568	219	1 304	45	2
Bar Harbor	5 087	14	0	1	0	13	64	10	50	4	0
Bath	9 424	3	0	0	2	1	309	18	283	8	2
Belfast	6 862	14	0	3	0	11	253	34	211	8	0
Berwick	7 162	9	0	2	2	5	111	19	80	12	3
Bethel	2 544	0	0	0	0	0	39	7	29	3	0

[1]The FBI does not publish arson data unless it receives data from either the agency or the state for all 12 months of the calendar year.

Table 8. Offenses Known to Law Enforcement, by State and City, 2005—*Continued*

(Number.)

City	Population	Violent crime	Murder and non-negligent man-slaughter	Forcible rape	Robbery	Aggravated assault	Property crime	Burglary	Larceny-theft	Motor vehicle theft	Arson[1]
Biddeford	21 913	46	0	19	9	18	864	95	744	25	11
Boothbay Harbor	2 380	4	0	1	0	3	51	9	39	3	0
Brewer	9 139	8	0	1	3	4	439	57	376	6	1
Bridgton	5 154	3	0	0	1	2	164	16	144	4	0
Brownville	1 266	0	0	0	0	0	7	1	6	0	0
Brunswick	21 849	16	0	4	5	7	482	102	361	19	1
Bucksport	4 984	12	0	1	0	11	93	13	76	4	0
Buxton	8 088	8	0	3	0	5	116	19	87	10	0
Calais	3 348	27	0	2	1	24	163	12	143	8	0
Camden	5 372	0	0	0	0	0	77	11	64	2	0
Cape Elizabeth	9 021	1	0	0	0	1	103	18	83	2	0
Caribou	8 306	2	1	0	1	0	240	49	186	5	0
Carrabassett Valley	429	1	0	0	0	1	81	3	76	2	0
Clinton	3 430	2	0	0	0	2	82	18	63	1	0
Cumberland	7 576	1	0	0	0	1	65	15	47	3	0
Damariscotta	2 069	0	0	0	0	0	33	5	26	2	0
Dexter	3 836	7	0	0	0	7	118	23	89	6	0
Dixfield	2 547	1	0	1	0	0	37	14	21	2	0
Dover-Foxcroft	4 369	17	0	1	0	16	110	20	86	4	0
East Millinocket	3 264	2	0	0	0	2	23	7	16	0	0
Eastport	1 608	4	0	1	1	2	27	7	19	1	0
Eliot	6 410	4	0	0	1	3	45	6	37	2	0
Ellsworth	6 959	3	0	0	0	3	328	57	263	8	0
Fairfield	6 679	4	0	2	1	1	265	35	221	9	0
Falmouth	10 662	0	0	0	0	0	120	20	94	6	0
Farmington	7 416	18	0	12	4	2	243	31	206	6	0
Fort Fairfield	3 548	10	0	0	0	10	32	3	26	3	0
Fort Kent	4 219	0	0	0	0	0	34	2	29	3	0
Freeport	8 054	4	0	0	3	1	186	31	151	4	0
Fryeburg	3 303	6	0	1	3	2	46	20	24	2	2
Gardiner	6 252	8	0	0	1	7	155	10	141	4	0
Gorham	15 194	17	0	6	4	7	235	76	146	13	1
Gouldsboro	2 023	0	0	0	0	0	8	7	1	0	0
Greenville	1 697	6	0	0	0	6	54	15	36	3	0
Hallowell	2 532	1	0	0	0	1	70	4	61	5	0
Hampden	6 727	0	0	0	0	0	88	16	70	2	0
Holden	2 942	2	0	0	0	2	41	17	22	2	1
Houlton	6 370	6	1	2	0	3	144	24	112	8	0
Jay	4 952	1	0	1	0	0	93	18	68	7	0
Kennebunk	11 501	5	0	2	0	3	220	39	175	6	0
Kennebunkport	4 024	2	0	1	0	1	55	4	50	1	0
Kittery	10 174	10	0	1	2	7	121	11	107	3	0
Lewiston	35 891	91	2	22	35	32	1 250	241	967	42	6
Lincoln	5 274	1	0	1	0	0	54	11	41	2	0
Lisbon	9 373	3	0	1	1	1	130	23	96	11	0
Livermore Falls	3 253	6	0	0	0	6	124	18	103	3	1
Machias	2 342	3	0	0	0	3	65	10	55	0	0
Madawaska	4 524	1	0	0	1	0	55	7	44	4	0
Madison	4 598	12	0	0	1	11	129	27	101	1	0
Mechanic Falls	3 222	0	0	0	0	0	37	8	29	0	1
Mexico	2 979	5	0	1	0	4	126	30	94	2	0
Milbridge	1 310	0	0	0	0	0	32	10	21	1	0
Millinocket	5 100	1	0	1	0	0	67	15	50	2	0
Milo	2 415	0	0	0	0	0	12	1	10	1	0
Monmouth	3 814	3	0	0	0	3	20	6	13	1	0
Mount Desert	2 192	1	0	0	1	0	38	7	30	1	0
Newport	3 084	2	0	0	0	2	104	14	84	6	2
North Berwick	4 761	0	0	0	0	0	3	0	3	0	0
Norway	4 806	7	0	2	0	5	62	20	40	2	0
Oakland	6 152	3	0	2	0	1	93	24	68	1	0
Ogunquit	1 285	1	0	1	0	0	71	17	53	1	0
Old Orchard Beach	9 356	21	0	7	6	8	296	71	207	18	1
Old Town	8 092	6	0	2	0	4	164	19	137	8	0
Orono	10 281	5	0	1	1	3	199	22	172	5	1
Oxford	3 991	0	0	0	0	0	143	15	125	3	0
Paris	5 010	6	0	2	3	1	81	10	67	4	0
Phippsburg	2 220	0	0	0	0	0	23	8	15	0	0
Pittsfield	4 270	2	0	0	0	2	119	13	102	4	0
Portland	64 111	267	3	39	100	125	2 970	536	2 261	173	12
Presque Isle	9 432	7	0	3	1	3	381	64	309	8	0
Rangeley	1 117	2	0	0	0	2	53	9	39	5	0
Richmond	3 424	0	0	0	0	0	14	2	12	0	0
Rockland	7 691	11	1	8	2	0	486	37	437	12	0
Rockport	3 447	0	0	0	0	0	41	8	32	1	0
Rumford	6 487	15	0	7	1	7	247	47	196	4	0
Sabattus	4 657	6	1	1	2	2	72	13	50	9	0
Saco	18 148	20	0	9	6	5	610	119	451	40	0
Sanford	21 785	64	0	25	12	27	685	138	511	36	6
Scarborough	18 815	11	0	2	1	8	375	60	299	16	1
Skowhegan	8 891	19	0	13	1	5	350	67	279	4	3

[1]The FBI does not publish arson data unless it receives data from either the agency or the state for all 12 months of the calendar year.

Table 8. Offenses Known to Law Enforcement, by State and City, 2005—*Continued*

(Number.)

City	Population	Violent crime	Murder and non-negligent man-slaughter	Forcible rape	Robbery	Aggravated assault	Property crime	Burglary	Larceny-theft	Motor vehicle theft	Arson[1]
South Berwick	7 286	2	0	1	0	1	88	17	69	2	3
South Portland	23 589	38	0	1	13	24	1 091	72	986	33	1
Southwest Harbor	1 997	1	0	0	0	1	92	21	68	3	1
Swan's Island	322	0	0	0	0	0	4	4	0	0	0
Thomaston	4 167	1	0	0	0	1	58	9	47	2	0
Topsham	9 863	4	0	1	1	2	156	26	126	4	2
Van Buren	2 581	0	0	0	0	0	18	5	13	0	0
Veazie	1 854	0	0	0	0	0	27	5	19	3	0
Waldoboro	5 108	1	0	0	1	0	107	26	76	5	0
Washburn	1 620	1	0	1	0	0	39	18	21	0	0
Waterville	15 948	27	0	6	6	15	644	86	545	13	1
Wells	10 062	5	0	1	0	4	195	30	163	2	0
Westbrook	16 056	23	2	2	7	12	518	120	368	30	7
Wilton	4 219	7	0	0	0	7	132	20	110	2	0
Windham	16 260	11	0	0	3	8	368	75	258	35	0
Winslow	7 974	6	0	2	0	4	187	33	143	11	0
Winter Harbor	975	0	0	0	0	0	13	9	4	0	0
Winthrop	6 469	2	0	0	1	1	81	18	62	1	0
Wiscasset	3 814	0	0	0	0	0	55	7	44	4	0
Yarmouth	8 304	7	1	1	1	4	112	24	88	0	0
York	13 582	3	0	0	2	1	187	25	154	8	0
Maryland											
Aberdeen	14 312	159	0	6	42	111	802	131	604	67	6
Annapolis	36 493	445	4	11	186	244	1 652	314	1 188	150	23
Baltimore	641 097	11 248	269	162	3 910	6 907	33 241	7 338	19 691	6 212	422
Baltimore City Sheriff	. . .	0	0	0	0	0	0	0	0	0	0
Bel Air	9 957	67	0	1	12	54	535	54	458	23	2
Berlin	3 715	8	0	1	3	4	115	22	91	2	0
Berwyn Heights	3 072	16	0	0	7	9	96	9	68	19	0
Bladensburg	7 980	179	2	3	112	62	790	130	385	275	0
Brunswick	5 265	13	0	1	0	12	70	21	46	3	0
Cambridge	10 908	135	0	6	42	87	717	112	582	23	6
Capitol Heights	4 329	16	0	0	13	3	91	14	39	38	0
Centreville	2 553	7	0	2	2	3	130	25	95	10	1
Chestertown	4 509	57	0	3	12	42	142	25	106	11	0
Cheverly	6 712	46	0	0	32	14	283	44	145	94	0
Cottage City	1 184	6	2	0	3	1	48	5	26	17	0
Crisfield	2 837	10	0	0	3	7	172	32	135	5	1
Cumberland	21 117	154	1	20	11	122	1 120	246	846	28	12
Delmar	2 049	21	0	1	3	17	101	27	70	4	0
Denton	3 122	15	0	0	7	8	138	28	104	6	2
District Heights	6 344	38	0	1	28	9	339	44	117	178	0
Easton	12 943	94	2	8	22	62	600	105	490	5	2
Edmonston	1 397	7	0	0	1	6	172	21	114	37	0
Elkton	14 174	135	0	3	36	96	913	174	673	66	11
Fairmount Heights	1 574	8	0	0	2	6	68	13	40	15	2
Federalsburg	2 610	24	0	2	5	17	147	46	96	5	0
Forest Heights	2 693	6	0	0	3	3	91	43	42	6	0
Frederick	57 443	490	0	11	118	361	1 575	256	1 244	75	32
Frostburg	8 201	27	0	1	1	25	197	67	125	5	0
Fruitland	3 814	70	0	1	6	63	253	26	218	9	1
Glenarden	6 618	6	0	0	3	3	58	13	31	14	0
Greenbelt	22 345	241	2	11	139	89	1 231	126	809	296	0
Greensboro	1 765	12	0	1	0	11	61	19	39	3	0
Hagerstown	37 822	279	2	4	84	189	1 487	328	1 024	135	39
Hampstead	5 458	2	0	0	0	2	95	8	80	7	3
Hancock	1 726	14	0	0	1	13	55	14	39	2	1
Havre de Grace	11 693	84	0	0	23	61	473	87	367	19	6
Hurlock	1 928	3	0	0	0	3	122	37	73	12	1
Hyattsville	15 302	115	0	1	81	33	780	103	478	199	0
Landover Hills	1 598	2	0	0	2	0	39	14	14	11	0
La Plata	8 171	37	0	0	6	31	190	17	154	19	4
Laurel	21 208	194	2	9	95	88	1 199	170	753	276	1
Lonaconing	1 187	0	0	0	0	0	2	0	2	0	0
Luke	78	0	0	0	0	0	0	0	0	0	0
Manchester	3 564	18	0	0	0	18	58	18	38	2	1
Morningside	1 360	4	0	0	3	1	55	8	33	14	0
Mount Rainier	8 806	76	1	2	50	23	482	63	205	214	1
North East	2 813	12	0	0	5	7	158	23	113	22	1
Oakland	1 938	3	0	0	0	3	58	8	48	2	1
Ocean City	7 191	277	1	15	49	212	1 269	232	978	59	12
Ocean Pines	11 099	7	0	0	1	6	94	17	77	0	0
Oxford	757	1	0	0	0	1	4	2	2	0	0
Perryville	3 776	17	0	0	1	16	124	29	90	5	0
Pocomoke City	4 020	22	0	5	4	13	222	32	184	6	1
Preston	577	1	0	0	0	1	14	4	10	0	0
Princess Anne	2 641	42	0	1	17	24	144	45	95	4	1
Ridgely	1 352	9	0	1	1	7	63	10	50	3	0
Rising Sun	1 789	1	0	0	0	1	83	20	61	2	1
Riverdale Park	6 662	94	1	2	68	23	348	44	188	116	0
Rock Hall	2 591	1	0	1	0	0	27	6	19	2	0
Salisbury	26 347	490	1	14	160	315	2 501	623	1 766	112	28

[1]The FBI does not publish arson data unless it receives data from either the agency or the state for all 12 months of the calendar year.
. . . = Not available.

Table 8. Offenses Known to Law Enforcement, by State and City, 2005—*Continued*

(Number.)

City	Population	Violent crime	Murder and non-negligent man-slaughter	Forcible rape	Robbery	Aggravated assault	Property crime	Burglary	Larceny-theft	Motor vehicle theft	Arson[1]
Seat Pleasant	5 090	56	3	0	29	24	169	23	102	44	0
Smithsburg	2 752	6	0	1	0	5	38	7	30	1	. . .
Snow Hill	2 339	6	0	0	0	6	42	11	30	1	0
St. Michaels	1 137	4	0	0	0	4	66	22	44	0	1
Sykesville	4 450	8	0	0	0	8	28	5	23	0	8
Takoma Park	17 725	96	0	5	66	25	782	144	462	176	0
Taneytown	5 462	4	0	0	0	4	105	5	98	2	2
Thurmont	6 041	29	0	1	5	23	76	13	55	8	1
University Park	2 410	5	0	0	0	5	66	10	38	18	0
Upper Marlboro	685	1	0	0	1	0	14	5	5	4	0
Westernport	2 063	11	0	1	0	10	41	14	26	1	2
Westminster	17 696	100	1	0	17	82	783	105	640	38	3
Massachusetts											
Abington	16 219	54	0	5	8	41	233	68	134	31	0
Acton	20 603	3	0	2	1	0	251	40	203	8	1
Acushnet	10 553	34	0	2	3	29	131	55	67	9	1
Adams	8 484	42	0	0	0	42	220	85	119	16	6
Agawam	28 537	43	0	5	4	34	521	206	239	76	4
Amesbury	16 691	50	0	4	1	45	214	36	167	11	5
Amherst	34 160	75	0	17	4	54	369	176	168	25	7
Andover	32 052	30	0	6	3	21	468	63	382	23	4
Arlington	41 431	40	0	4	9	27	501	157	313	31	5
Ashburnham	5 885	17	0	2	1	14	84	35	40	9	0
Ashfield	1 815	2	0	0	0	2	2	2	0	0	0
Ashland	15 485	21	0	7	1	13	69	17	48	4	2
Athol	11 641	49	1	4	2	42	153	52	91	10	1
Attleboro	43 386	114	0	9	12	93	919	176	654	89	7
Auburn	16 336	(6)	0	9	5	(6)	586	142	406	38	3
Avon	4 373	21	0	1	1	19	178	42	120	16	0
Ayer	7 192	25	1	4	2	18	118	51	62	5	2
Barnstable	48 403	346	2	34	25	285	1 238	429	724	85	12
Barre	5 342	17	0	3	0	14	68	25	35	8	1
Becket	1 770	3	0	0	0	3	18	11	6	1	0
Bedford	12 484	0	0	0	0	0	47	2	45	0	0
Belchertown	13 808	17	0	3	0	14	103	56	88	19	1
Bellingham	15 718	22	0	3	2	17	290	65	208	17	1
Belmont	23 539	32	0	5	6	21	220	69	140	11	7
Berkley	6 333	6	0	0	0	6	40	8	28	4	0
Berlin	2 670	0	0	0	0	0	31	1	26	4	0
Bevorly	40 055	93	0	8	17	68	635	145	445	45	0
Billerica	39 840	37	0	0	3	34	435	55	347	33	1
Blackstone	9 030	21	0	2	1	18	166	69	85	12	0
Bolton	4 377	2	0	0	0	2	42	12	26	4	0
Boston	567 589	7 479	73	268	2 649	4 489	25 205	4 531	15 957	4 717	. . .
Bourne	19 462	(6)	0	7	8	(6)	627	256	330	41	7
Boylston	4 169	3	0	0	0	3	46	7	36	3	0
Braintree	33 779	96	0	6	13	77	1 019	112	808	99	1
Bridgewater	25 652	24	0	3	3	18	284	66	196	22	1
Brimfield	3 590	0	0	0	0	0	17	0	15	2	0
Brockton	94 746	(6)	10	47	211	(6)	3 707	687	2 282	738	17
Brookline	56 032	(6)	0	7	59	(6)	1 013	219	749	45	. . .
Buckland	1 981	1	0	0	0	1	21	9	12	0	0
Burlington	23 159	45	0	0	10	35	718	125	550	43	1
Cambridge	100 492	494	3	18	239	234	3 309	623	2 396	290	. . .
Canton	21 445	(6)	0	0	4	(6)	210	45	148	17	4
Carver	11 460	9	0	2	0	7	79	44	32	3	0
Charlemont	1 392	0	0	0	0	0	10	1	7	2	0
Charlton	12 261	16	0	2	1	13	87	30	49	8	1
Chelmsford	33 676	34	0	2	5	27	589	78	481	30	1
Chelsea	33 135	(6)	4	21	151	(6)	1 195	286	627	282	7
Cheshire	3 346	0	0	0	0	0	7	5	1	1	0
Chicopee	54 686	343	2	27	46	268	1 750	479	1 048	223	12
Clinton	13 852	3	0	0	1	2	46	18	26	2	0
Cohasset	7 254	3	0	0	0	3	107	22	78	7	1
Concord	16 872	20	0	1	0	19	217	38	174	5	0
Cummington	991	5	0	0	0	5	11	7	4	0	0
Dalton	6 717	(6)	0	3	1	(6)	64	27	35	2	1
Danvers	25 588	52	0	6	11	35	788	72	659	57	1
Dartmouth	31 230	104	0	2	20	82	1 037	199	759	79	3
Dedham	23 161	16	0	1	9	6	472	43	378	51	0
Deerfield	4 785	15	2	1	1	11	84	35	42	7	0
Dennis	16 078	81	0	5	7	69	456	147	281	28	5
Douglas	7 741	11	0	3	2	6	43	23	15	5	0
Dracut	28 602	36	0	7	2	27	384	115	232	37	2
Dudley	10 745	17	1	2	1	13	63	32	26	5	2
East Bridgewater	13 654	9	0	2	3	4	125	14	103	8	0
East Brookfield	2 115	4	0	0	0	4	21	3	17	1	0
Easthampton	16 044	43	2	2	1	38	193	67	113	13	0
East Longmeadow	14 770	19	0	2	3	14	334	66	249	19	3
Easton	22 997	10	0	0	7	3	124	32	85	7	0
Edgartown	3 929	6	0	0	0	6	92	16	75	1	0
Egremont	1 344	1	0	0	0	1	26	2	24	0	0
Erving	1 526	4	0	1	0	3	19	10	6	3	0

[1]The FBI does not publish arson data unless it receives data from either the agency or the state for all 12 months of the calendar year.
[6]The data collection methodology for the offense of aggravated assault used by these agencies does not comply with national UCR guidelines. Consequently, their figures for aggravated assault and violent crime (of which aggravated assault is a part) are not included in this table.
. . . = Not available.

Table 8. Offenses Known to Law Enforcement, by State and City, 2005—*Continued*

(Number.)

City	Population	Violent crime	Murder and non-negligent man-slaughter	Forcible rape	Robbery	Aggravated assault	Property crime	Burglary	Larceny-theft	Motor vehicle theft	Arson[1]
Everett	37 092	116	0	6	40	70	1 186	292	709	185	7
Fairhaven	16 290	69	0	3	10	56	441	148	264	29	1
Falmouth	33 712	(6)	1	7	15	(6)	1 006	432	523	51	7
Fitchburg	39 800	(6)	1	25	47	(6)	1 080	340	658	82	7
Foxborough	16 309	48	0	9	1	38	157	56	83	18	0
Framingham	65 416	184	0	12	48	124	1 556	312	1 025	219	. . .
Franklin	30 108	7	0	2	0	5	130	43	72	15	0
Freetown	8 946	18	0	3	2	13	121	47	63	11	1
Gardner	20 909	116	0	11	9	96	532	173	308	51	7
Georgetown	7 939	2	0	0	2	0	51	18	30	3	. . .
Gloucester	30 732	47	0	6	8	33	591	100	456	35	1
Goshen	955	0	0	0	0	0	7	7	0	0	0
Grafton	16 252	16	0	1	1	14	92	21	60	11	1
Granby	6 321	18	0	2	1	15	93	27	60	6	0
Great Barrington	7 413	27	0	1	1	25	88	20	65	3	0
Greenfield	17 876	(6)	0	21	5	(6)	546	250	260	36	5
Groton	10 340	0	0	0	0	0	51	13	37	1	0
Groveland	6 454	2	0	1	0	1	52	7	44	1	0
Hadley	4 847	13	0	2	3	8	142	30	98	14	0
Hamilton	8 403	8	1	0	0	7	111	40	59	12	0
Hampden	5 301	6	0	1	0	5	51	18	31	2	0
Hanover	13 815	3	0	0	2	1	247	27	214	6	0
Hanson	9 871	(6)	0	1	1	(6)	127	26	93	8	2
Hardwick	2 658	(6)	0	1	1	(6)	29	13	12	4	0
Harvard	6 066	7	0	0	0	7	52	14	37	1	1
Harwich	12 774	24	0	1	0	23	223	77	133	13	1
Hatfield	3 302	0	0	0	0	0	12	2	5	5	0
Haverhill	60 315	296	0	13	52	231	1 417	593	708	116	14
Hingham	21 139	34	0	0	1	33	219	33	180	6	0
Hinsdale	1 820	(6)	0	0	0	(6)	6	2	2	2	0
Holbrook	10 802	18	0	0	5	13	182	50	117	15	0
Holden	16 549	18	0	3	2	13	92	17	71	4	2
Holliston	13 880	8	0	0	0	8	41	20	19	2	0
Holyoke	39 947	(6)	3	30	92	(6)	2 213	356	1 560	297	16
Hopedale	6 205	6	0	0	0	6	35	10	21	4	2
Hubbardston	4 261	9	0	2	0	7	37	11	22	4	1
Hudson	18 674	3	0	1	1	1	190	25	147	18	1
Hull	11 289	41	0	2	2	37	112	47	53	12	1
Ipswich	13 337	8	0	0	1	7	150	40	103	7	2
Lakeville	10 504	10	0	3	2	5	76	25	46	5	0
Lawrence	71 659	584	0	17	159	408	1 711	601	577	533	. . .
Lee	5 872	15	0	1	4	10	26	4	20	2	0
Leicester	10 874	25	0	1	2	22	122	30	77	15	1
Lenox	5 148	6	0	0	0	6	75	18	52	5	0
Lexington	30 335	12	0	3	1	8	275	50	210	15	4
Lincoln	7 978	5	0	0	1	4	35	11	21	3	0
Littleton	8 554	15	0	2	2	11	84	25	52	7	1
Longmeadow	15 588	14	0	1	4	9	198	83	112	3	1
Lowell	103 370	1 009	2	41	213	753	3 295	664	1 942	689	. . .
Ludlow	21 873	35	0	1	7	27	300	64	199	37	1
Lunenburg	9 952	6	0	0	1	5	156	16	132	8	0
Lynn	89 234	1 070	5	12	270	783	2 925	816	1 527	582	. . .
Malden	55 187	213	2	9	78	124	1 293	366	782	145	4
Manchester-by-the-Sea	5 355	0	0	0	0	0	74	0	70	4	0
Mansfield	22 934	49	0	3	5	41	377	121	226	30	3
Marblehead	20 315	2	0	0	0	2	239	29	193	17	1
Marion	5 295	10	0	1	0	9	98	20	76	2	1
Marlborough	37 595	38	0	8	11	19	616	126	442	48	1
Marshfield	24 748	31	0	2	5	24	274	50	204	20	0
Mashpee	14 261	49	0	5	2	42	249	63	164	22	1
Mattapoisett	6 449	11	0	0	1	10	87	9	74	4	1
Maynard	10 293	7	0	1	0	6	24	3	18	3	0
Medford	54 047	71	1	8	47	15	1 460	327	944	189	. . .
Medway	12 850	1	0	0	0	1	56	12	43	1	0
Melrose	26 460	50	0	4	14	32	352	89	229	34	3
Mendon	5 745	14	0	2	2	10	61	21	38	2	1
Merrimac	6 304	3	0	0	0	3	33	12	17	4	1
Methuen	44 721	83	1	3	27	52	1 000	205	709	86	2
Middleboro	21 063	69	0	11	11	47	386	104	240	42	2
Middleton	9 082	7	0	0	1	6	119	7	104	8	0
Milford	27 334	75	0	6	13	56	298	50	231	17	. . .
Millville	2 928	5	0	0	0	5	30	2	22	6	1
Milton	25 783	13	0	1	5	7	241	47	179	15	. . .
Monson	8 660	24	0	3	0	21	99	38	43	18	3
Monterey	951	1	0	0	0	1	2	1	1	0	0
Nahant	3 610	20	0	3	0	17	50	8	42	0	0
Nantucket	10 096	41	0	4	0	37	144	42	90	12	0
Natick	32 024	67	0	8	13	46	692	88	568	36	1
Needham	28 942	7	0	0	2	5	275	76	192	7	0
New Bedford	93 720	1 024	8	52	257	707	3 116	877	1 924	315	20

[1]The FBI does not publish arson data unless it receives data from either the agency or the state for all 12 months of the calendar year.
[6]The data collection methodology for the offense of aggravated assault used by these agencies does not comply with national UCR guidelines. Consequently, their figures for aggravated assault and violent crime (of which aggravated assault is a part) are not included in this table.
. . . = Not available.

Table 8. Offenses Known to Law Enforcement, by State and City, 2005—*Continued*

(Number.)

City	Population	Violent crime	Murder and non-negligent man-slaughter	Forcible rape	Robbery	Aggravated assault	Property crime	Burglary	Larceny-theft	Motor vehicle theft	Arson[1]
Newbury	6 867	14	0	1	1	12	43	14	27	2	0
Newburyport	17 503	16	0	0	6	10	211	71	133	7	2
New Salem	985	0	0	0	0	0	5	0	4	1	0
Newton	83 570	114	1	6	15	92	1 098	269	783	46	3
Norfolk	10 463	12	0	3	0	9	50	15	35	0	0
North Adams	14 128	(6)	0	14	5	(6)	462	162	274	26	4
Northampton	28 850	114	0	9	9	96	805	122	626	57	4
North Attleboro	28 098	45	0	2	8	35	741	88	603	50	4
Northborough	14 280	5	0	0	1	4	119	14	103	2	1
Northbridge	13 844	38	0	8	1	29	149	41	103	5	2
North Brookfield	4 802	(6)	0	1	0	(6)	41	11	26	4	2
Northfield	3 164	3	0	0	0	3	41	16	24	1	0
Norton	19 104	4	0	1	0	3	148	36	104	8	0
Norwell	10 361	12	0	0	2	10	87	22	58	7	3
Norwood	28 469	27	0	5	14	8	501	68	376	57	1
Oak Bluffs	3 817	27	0	2	2	23	91	31	53	7	0
Orange	7 542	33	0	4	1	28	171	56	102	13	6
Oxford	13 697	36	0	2	4	30	90	44	38	8	3
Palmer	12 866	44	0	4	5	35	217	60	128	29	8
Paxton	4 528	5	0	1	0	4	21	4	16	1	0
Peabody	50 231	165	1	8	24	132	1 142	199	829	114	4
Pembroke	17 666	40	0	2	2	36	223	36	169	18	5
Pepperell	11 402	16	0	1	1	14	106	28	73	5	2
Pittsfield	44 162	352	2	32	36	282	1 041	309	668	64	12
Plainville	7 904	14	0	2	3	9	105	30	69	6	2
Plymouth	54 453	76	0	3	10	63	710	193	479	38	3
Princeton	3 489	1	0	1	0	0	35	19	16	0	0
Provincetown	3 440	21	0	1	0	20	165	13	143	9	0
Quincy	89 661	339	2	26	92	219	1 422	387	883	152	6
Randolph	30 663	127	1	7	24	95	666	122	465	79	0
Raynham	13 287	(6)	0	1	7	(6)	584	48	499	37	. . .
Reading	23 297	17	0	1	4	12	215	44	154	17	0
Rehoboth	11 106	10	0	0	1	9	111	35	69	7	1
Revere	46 041	302	1	16	72	213	1 806	347	1 139	320	9
Rochester	5 188	2	0	0	0	2	39	18	13	8	2
Rockland	17 812	26	0	4	10	12	268	40	192	36	. . .
Rowley	5 704	4	0	1	0	3	26	5	18	3	1
Royalston	1 350	6	0	0	0	6	9	4	4	1	0
Rutland	7 225	14	0	0	0	14	53	25	26	2	0
Salem	41 796	98	0	2	27	69	973	171	735	67	0
Salisbury	8 136	49	0	6	4	39	168	63	88	17	3
Sandwich	20 768	51	0	1	2	48	212	83	119	10	6
Saugus	26 688	(6)	0	5	39	(6)	1 071	321	654	96	4
Scituate	18 145	20	0	0	0	20	158	32	114	12	1
Seekonk	13 692	50	0	3	9	38	589	77	480	32	1
Sharon	17 299	4	0	1	1	2	90	17	69	4	0
Shelburne	2 055	0	0	0	0	0	9	2	6	1	0
Sherborn	4 218	2	0	0	0	2	40	28	12	0	0
Shirley	7 580	4	0	0	0	4	22	7	15	0	0
Shrewsbury	33 069	21	0	4	7	10	480	73	376	31	1
Somerset	18 640	70	0	6	5	59	328	46	263	19	4
Somerville	75 412	262	1	7	139	115	1 673	521	833	319	3
Southampton	5 756	17	0	3	0	14	30	7	19	4	0
Southborough	9 523	3	0	0	0	3	39	8	29	2	0
Southbridge	17 266	83	0	9	10	64	270	117	137	16	5
South Hadley	17 133	19	0	1	2	16	220	41	161	18	1
Southwick	9 402	16	0	1	2	13	145	38	99	8	2
Spencer	11 981	40	0	5	2	33	180	53	115	12	1
Springfield	151 670	2 691	18	109	771	1 793	8 703	2 141	4 974	1 588	59
Sterling	7 721	10	0	4	0	6	56	18	30	8	1
Stockbridge	2 244	7	1	0	0	6	83	20	58	5	0
Stoneham	21 721	45	0	0	18	27	405	94	293	18	. . .
Stow	6 102	11	0	0	0	11	40	15	20	5	0
Sturbridge	8 668	20	0	4	2	14	166	33	122	11	1
Sudbury	17 116	2	0	0	1	1	96	14	82	0	0
Sunderland	3 793	7	0	1	1	5	32	7	25	0	0
Sutton	8 853	16	0	2	1	13	91	32	49	10	0
Swampscott	14 393	7	0	0	4	3	277	40	230	7	0
Swansea	16 272	69	1	2	9	57	273	49	202	22	2
Taunton	56 491	280	2	12	59	207	1 237	322	748	167	6
Templeton	7 302	14	0	0	3	11	62	23	26	13	1
Tewksbury	29 049	14	0	1	6	7	401	70	298	33	0
Tisbury	3 840	9	0	0	0	9	135	27	97	11	0
Topsfield	6 211	1	0	0	1	0	32	5	24	3	0
Townsend	9 300	8	0	4	1	3	57	17	39	1	0
Truro	2 174	1	0	0	0	1	19	0	19	0	0
Tyngsboro	11 355	30	1	3	1	25	195	30	154	11	1
Upton	6 245	4	0	1	0	3	28	8	17	3	2
Uxbridge	12 209	23	0	4	2	17	104	35	59	10	2
Wales	1 793	0	0	0	0	0	3	0	3	0	0

[1]The FBI does not publish arson data unless it receives data from either the agency or the state for all 12 months of the calendar year.
[6]The data collection methodology for the offense of aggravated assault used by these agencies does not comply with national UCR guidelines. Consequently, their figures for aggravated assault and violent crime (of which aggravated assault is a part) are not included in this table.
. . . = Not available.

Table 8. Offenses Known to Law Enforcement, by State and City, 2005—*Continued*

(Number.)

City	Population	Violent crime	Murder and non-negligent man-slaughter	Forcible rape	Robbery	Aggravated assault	Property crime	Burglary	Larceny-theft	Motor vehicle theft	Arson[1]
Walpole	22 456	13	0	4	1	8	273	27	223	23	1
Waltham	59 068	77	0	7	15	55	661	85	498	78	4
Ware	9 994	45	1	5	3	36	119	26	78	15	3
Wareham	21 165	(6)	0	10	12	(6)	583	194	341	48	. . .
Watertown	32 513	62	0	1	15	46	669	116	518	35	0
Wayland	13 027	4	0	0	0	4	96	14	75	7	2
Webster	16 833	69	0	3	8	58	329	106	188	35	5
Wellesley	26 442	20	0	0	1	19	239	61	174	4	0
Wellfleet	2 833	4	0	0	0	4	56	9	47	0	0
Wenham	4 441	3	0	0	1	2	27	7	16	4	0
Westborough	18 685	24	0	6	2	16	264	70	177	17	3
West Boylston	7 595	13	0	1	3	9	162	6	147	9	2
West Bridgewater	6 825	8	0	1	3	4	148	26	110	12	0
West Brookfield	3 887	11	0	1	2	8	40	10	27	3	0
Westfield	40 447	(6)	2	16	13	(6)	646	243	333	70	7
Westford	21 416	2	0	0	1	1	150	11	137	2	0
Westhampton	1 559	3	0	0	0	3	12	5	5	2	0
West Newbury	4 285	3	0	0	0	3	23	5	18	0	1
Westport	14 700	46	0	3	0	43	196	68	106	22	1
West Springfield	27 970	125	2	4	32	87	1 259	195	934	130	3
West Tisbury	2 663	1	0	1	0	0	7	1	6	0	0
Westwood	13 981	11	0	2	2	7	131	19	106	6	0
Weymouth	54 052	109	0	6	26	77	907	202	637	68	. . .
Whately	1 582	6	0	0	0	6	26	5	15	6	1
Wilbraham	13 899	22	0	3	4	15	214	35	165	14	2
Williamsburg	2 436	3	0	0	0	3	24	10	13	1	0
Williamstown	8 249	6	0	2	0	4	198	5	191	2	0
Wilmington	21 508	43	0	5	3	35	382	67	284	31	. . .
Winchendon	10 009	72	0	6	2	64	198	64	117	17	2
Winchester	21 108	14	0	1	7	6	230	45	169	16	0
Woburn	37 344	64	1	3	16	44	842	116	622	104	4
Worcester	175 479	1 390	6	143	389	852	6 078	1 248	3 673	1 157	11
Wrentham	11 055	8	0	2	2	4	98	12	85	1	0
Yarmouth	24 903	157	0	10	8	139	587	237	320	30	2
Michigan											
Adrian	21 995	87	0	26	11	50	947	175	722	50	12
Algonac	4 619	7	0	0	0	7	63	7	53	3	2
Allegan	4 963	55	0	3	0	52	119	10	103	6	3
Allen Park	28 504	66	0	12	15	39	666	112	428	126	1
Alma	9 316	13	0	6	0	7	86	43	42	1	0
Almont	2 881	14	0	3	0	11	88	20	63	5	2
Alpena	10 948	51	0	15	2	34	348	55	281	12	3
Ann Arbor	113 660	358	0	37	102	219	3 379	859	2 282	238	21
Argentine Township	7 121	5	0	2	1	2	95	30	55	10	1
Armada	1 639	3	0	1	0	2	17	2	13	2	0
Auburn	2 060	1	0	1	0	0	20	5	15	0	0
Auburn Hills	20 754	86	0	8	28	50	1 189	120	992	77	4
Bad Axe	3 287	8	0	6	0	2	155	20	131	4	1
Bangor	1 898	12	0	1	2	9	109	18	85	6	0
Bath Township	10 124	10	1	1	1	7	118	18	96	4	1
Battle Creek	63 054	755	6	61	109	579	3 472	691	2 594	187	20
Bay City	35 346	168	0	30	31	107	1 155	292	789	74	14
Belding	5 875	23	0	5	0	18	223	23	194	6	0
Belleville	3 903	5	0	1	2	2	175	20	136	19	1
Benton Harbor	10 860	238	0	13	10	215	395	137	213	45	2
Benton Township	16 115	131	1	11	21	98	1 432	198	1 144	90	6
Berkley	15 248	20	0	1	9	10	249	53	180	16	0
Berrien Springs-Oronoko Township	9 763	10	0	3	2	5	166	29	130	7	3
Beverly Hills	10 194	8	0	1	1	6	142	13	126	3	0
Big Rapids	10 861	33	0	8	6	19	278	47	224	7	1
Birch Run	1 731	8	0	0	1	7	253	17	232	4	0
Birmingham	19 233	25	0	0	10	15	405	63	319	23	0
Blackman Township	24 857	67	2	15	14	36	447	72	338	37	4
Blissfield	3 265	3	0	0	1	2	62	5	51	6	0
Bloomfield Hills	3 863	0	0	0	0	0	76	6	68	2	0
Bloomfield Township	42 098	30	0	1	11	18	764	121	604	39	8
Bloomingdale	516	0	0	0	0	0	14	2	12	0	1
Boyne City	3 335	12	0	2	0	10	116	7	103	6	0
Breckenridge	1 323	2	0	1	0	1	9	5	3	1	0
Bridgeport Township	11 442	48	0	5	4	39	310	71	207	32	2
Bridgman	2 454	3	0	1	0	2	104	7	97	0	1
Brighton	7 122	10	0	2	4	4	279	26	250	3	2
Brooklyn/Columbia	7 587	12	0	1	0	11	98	24	71	3	1
Brown City	1 320	1	0	0	1	0	37	1	33	3	0
Brownstown Township	28 064	67	0	7	9	51	714	182	426	106	8
Buchanan	4 579	23	0	3	3	17	181	21	159	1	2
Buena Vista Township	9 969	140	2	7	20	111	480	175	259	46	9
Burton	30 951	163	2	22	35	104	1 473	334	970	169	11
Cadillac	10 143	39	0	13	0	26	468	64	385	19	8
Calumet	816	4	0	3	0	1	15	4	10	1	0
Cambridge Township	5 796	1	0	1	0	0	11	2	9	0	0
Canton Township	84 723	146	2	31	23	90	1 604	346	1 113	145	17
Capac	2 234	5	0	2	0	3	55	13	41	1	1
Carleton	2 835	3	0	0	0	3	37	9	25	3	1
Caro	4 211	9	0	1	4	4	191	20	169	2	2

[1]The FBI does not publish arson data unless it receives data from either the agency or the state for all 12 months of the calendar year.
[6]The data collection methodology for the offense of aggravated assault used by these agencies does not comply with national UCR guidelines. Consequently, their figures for aggravated assault and violent crime (of which aggravated assault is a part) are not included in this table.
. . . = Not available.

Table 8. Offenses Known to Law Enforcement, by State and City, 2005—*Continued*

(Number.)

City	Population	Violent crime	Murder and non-negligent man-slaughter	Forcible rape	Robbery	Aggravated assault	Property crime	Burglary	Larceny-theft	Motor vehicle theft	Arson[1]
Carrollton Township	6 354	19	0	1	4	14	256	36	205	15	1
Caspian	2 146	0	0	0	0	0	7	0	6	1	1
Cass City	2 617	2	0	2	0	0	52	6	44	2	0
Cedar Springs	3 230	19	0	2	1	16	104	12	86	6	1
Center Line	8 369	30	0	2	10	18	336	37	204	95	2
Central Lake	999	3	0	0	0	3	18	3	15	0	0
Charlotte	9 053	32	0	14	1	17	274	44	221	9	0
Cheboygan	5 212	12	0	6	0	6	217	37	171	9	0
Chelsea	4 722	11	0	2	1	8	149	15	126	8	1
Chesterfield Township	42 595	112	0	7	14	91	979	127	779	73	5
Chikaming Township	3 708	1	0	0	0	1	77	18	54	5	0
Chocolay Township	6 090	1	0	0	0	1	79	7	69	3	0
Clare	3 241	15	0	4	0	11	195	20	171	4	0
Clawson	12 453	22	0	2	4	16	200	36	146	18	0
Clayton Township	7 735	3	0	2	0	1	127	59	67	1	0
Clay Township	9 915	3	0	0	1	2	127	28	85	14	0
Clinton	2 377	0	0	0	0	0	30	6	23	1	0
Clinton Township	96 028	360	0	20	64	276	2 265	406	1 561	298	18
Clio	2 655	9	0	2	0	7	76	14	56	6	2
Coldwater	10 830	51	0	16	2	33	488	60	405	23	6
Coleman	1 284	4	0	1	0	3	50	9	38	3	0
Coloma Township	6 803	23	0	3	1	19	178	54	118	6	2
Colon	1 197	7	0	4	1	2	44	3	41	0	0
Constantine	2 147	6	0	2	0	4	91	2	87	2	0
Corunna	3 407	10	0	2	1	7	95	16	67	12	1
Croswell	2 460	2	0	1	0	1	70	13	55	2	0
Davison	5 414	13	0	2	1	10	107	32	71	4	0
Davison Township	18 447	26	0	6	2	18	322	99	169	54	1
Dearborn	95 548	571	3	30	223	315	4 924	651	3 191	1 082	49
Dearborn Heights	56 874	206	0	25	82	99	1 808	424	967	417	16
Decatur	1 933	13	1	1	0	11	169	10	155	4	1
Denton Township	5 757	7	0	0	1	6	105	33	64	8	1
Detroit[3]	900 932	21 240	354	589	6 820	13 477	53 972	15 304	17 383	21 285	936
Dewitt	4 441	2	0	0	0	2	41	8	30	3	0
Dewitt Township	13 076	30	0	5	3	22	215	42	155	18	0
Douglas	2 265	11	0	1	1	9	96	16	79	1	0
Dryden Township	4 743	2	0	0	1	1	42	12	28	2	0
Durand	3 904	4	0	0	0	4	5	4	1	0	0
East Grand Rapids	10 491	6	0	1	0	5	155	40	110	5	0
East Jordan	2 369	6	0	2	0	4	84	14	69	1	0
East Lansing	46 716	175	0	20	40	115	1 129	202	874	53	21
Eastpointe	33 411	198	2	22	74	100	1 361	238	736	387	18
East Tawas	2 849	12	0	3	0	9	126	27	94	5	3
Eaton Rapids	5 283	11	0	4	0	7	215	38	164	13	2
Eau Claire	647	1	0	0	0	1	22	5	16	1	0
Edmore	1 259	5	0	0	0	5	17	3	14	0	1
Elk Rapids	1 729	0	0	0	0	0	43	2	39	2	0
Elkton	816	0	0	0	0	0	18	5	12	1	1
Emmett Township	12 125	69	1	7	9	52	596	72	502	22	0
Erie Township	4 791	6	0	1	0	5	90	25	46	19	1
Essexville	3 630	8	0	3	1	4	109	7	100	2	0
Evart	1 747	6	0	0	0	6	84	16	64	4	0
Farmington	10 154	16	2	1	3	10	223	43	164	16	0
Farmington Hills	80 853	178	3	23	38	114	1 642	403	1 086	153	14
Fenton	11 921	21	0	4	2	15	298	45	231	22	1
Ferndale	21 684	90	1	10	35	44	758	180	424	154	3
Flint[3]	119 814	2 708	48	105	566	1 989	7 709	2 634	3 492	1 583	188
Flint Township	33 292	176	2	24	66	84	2 296	382	1 627	287	8
Flushing	8 187	16	0	0	0	16	136	13	112	11	1
Flushing Township	10 494	10	0	3	1	6	117	41	60	16	0
Forsyth Township	4 860	5	0	1	0	4	94	16	75	3	0
Fowlerville	3 134	6	0	2	0	4	61	11	45	5	0
Frankenmuth	4 808	2	0	0	1	1	72	14	58	0	0
Frankfort	1 503	0	0	0	0	0	36	6	30	0	0
Franklin	2 960	1	0	0	1	0	33	6	25	2	0
Fraser	15 142	25	2	4	2	17	427	50	333	44	1
Fremont	4 274	4	0	0	0	4	133	6	123	4	1
Frost Township	1 180	4	0	0	0	4	6	3	3	0	0
Fruitport	1 091	33	0	3	1	29	681	62	600	19	1
Garden City	29 334	100	0	8	22	70	760	174	475	111	5
Gaylord	3 730	13	0	2	1	10	228	53	163	12	2
Genesee Township	24 222	114	0	20	19	75	873	261	520	92	9
Gerrish Township	3 173	3	0	1	0	2	42	6	35	1	1
Gibraltar	5 099	5	0	1	0	4	116	10	94	12	0
Gladstone	5 270	9	0	4	0	5	197	15	178	4	1
Gladwin	3 030	12	0	0	1	11	129	30	98	1	1
Grand Beach	236	1	0	0	0	1	24	0	24	0	0
Grand Blanc	7 991	25	0	5	4	16	218	44	164	10	3
Grand Blanc Township	34 702	65	1	11	7	46	691	120	506	65	4
Grand Haven	10 742	24	0	6	5	13	377	43	318	16	7

[1]The FBI does not publish arson data unless it receives data from either the agency or the state for all 12 months of the calendar year.
[3]Because of changes in the state/local agency's reporting practices, figures are not comparable to previous years' data.

Table 8. Offenses Known to Law Enforcement, by State and City, 2005—*Continued*

(Number.)

City	Population	Violent crime	Murder and non-negligent man-slaughter	Forcible rape	Robbery	Aggravated assault	Property crime	Burglary	Larceny-theft	Motor vehicle theft	Arson[1]
Grand Ledge	7 814	11	0	1	0	10	182	21	158	3	4
Grand Rapids[3]	195 274	1 962	8	66	674	1 214	9 766	2 038	7 050	678	134
Grandville	16 694	38	1	10	11	16	903	88	797	18	3
Grayling	1 957	3	0	0	2	1	56	8	46	2	0
Green Oak Township	17 229	20	0	3	4	13	271	62	182	27	0
Greenville	8 289	30	0	8	2	20	413	70	328	15	2
Grosse Ile Township	10 756	5	0	0	1	4	79	13	64	2	2
Grosse Pointe	5 508	11	1	0	8	2	184	13	139	32	1
Grosse Pointe Farms	9 476	7	0	0	5	2	171	11	137	23	0
Grosse Pointe Park	12 074	20	0	1	13	6	339	34	222	83	0
Grosse Pointe Shores	2 745	0	0	0	0	0	3	1	2	0	0
Grosse Pointe Woods	16 559	8	0	0	4	4	254	22	199	33	0
Hamburg Township	21 769	11	0	4	1	6	211	61	131	19	5
Hampton Township	9 935	17	0	3	2	12	375	55	304	16	0
Hamtramck	22 259	308	2	13	165	128	1 524	438	442	644	11
Hancock	4 226	3	0	2	0	1	96	17	71	8	0
Harbor Beach	1 741	3	0	2	0	1	29	6	23	0	0
Harbor Springs	1 593	0	0	0	0	0	52	16	36	0	0
Harper Woods	13 826	98	1	5	60	32	1 396	130	919	347	5
Hart	2 007	7	0	2	1	4	116	12	102	2	1
Hartford	2 452	10	0	1	1	8	99	23	69	7	1
Hastings	7 157	15	0	4	0	11	233	14	216	3	3
Hazel Park	18 568	115	0	17	47	51	701	108	340	253	4
Hillsdale	8 033	8	0	3	0	5	189	28	150	11	0
Holland	34 634	139	0	46	8	85	1 177	204	934	39	9
Holly	6 352	14	0	3	2	9	129	26	97	6	1
Homer	1 831	4	0	0	0	4	16	4	11	1	0
Houghton	7 016	5	0	1	1	3	111	18	90	3	1
Howard City	1 619	15	0	9	1	5	69	9	58	2	0
Howell	9 742	17	0	7	0	10	291	36	241	14	2
Hudson	2 440	6	0	3	0	3	48	4	43	1	0
Hudsonville	7 097	10	0	0	2	8	108	23	82	3	1
Huntington Woods	6 003	2	0	0	1	1	79	8	62	9	0
Huron Township	14 980	38	0	5	4	29	353	87	203	63	1
Imlay City	3 858	9	0	2	1	6	119	11	106	2	2
Inkster	29 263	259	13	22	75	149	1 047	320	461	266	17
Ionia	12 369	27	0	11	1	15	236	36	192	8	0
Iron Mountain	8 002	12	0	5	0	7	199	18	178	3	6
Iron River	3 199	9	0	3	0	6	89	16	68	5	0
Ironwood	5 813	6	0	2	0	4	80	15	60	5	0
Ishpeming	6 549	15	2	5	0	8	170	12	143	15	1
Jackson	35 162	297	3	47	66	181	2 272	413	1 706	153	26
Jonesville	2 326	10	0	3	1	6	102	16	86	0	1
Kalamazoo	74 020	596	3	55	178	360	4 541	1 106	3 116	319	35
Kalamazoo Township	21 657	63	2	9	8	44	663	180	428	55	8
Kalkaska	2 224	1	0	1	0	0	149	15	130	4	4
Keego Harbor	2 729	10	0	0	4	6	56	3	50	3	1
Kentwood	46 576	166	0	36	40	90	1 759	368	1 303	88	8
Kinross Township	8 075	6	0	3	0	3	51	10	41	0	0
Laingsburg	1 241	4	0	0	0	4	35	4	30	1	1
Lake Orion	2 764	19	0	5	1	13	78	8	63	7	0
Lakeview	1 124	3	0	1	0	2	64	15	47	2	0
Lansing	117 036	1 407	8	115	254	1 030	4 745	1 129	3 204	412	43
Lansing Township	8 124	48	0	5	13	30	348	66	266	16	2
Lapeer	9 370	44	0	5	4	35	430	37	368	25	0
Lapeer Township	5 195	1	0	0	0	1	18	3	11	4	0
Lathrup Village	4 205	13	0	0	8	5	88	25	54	9	1
Laurium	2 053	2	0	2	0	0	44	6	36	2	1
Lawton	1 858	4	0	0	0	4	61	10	50	1	1
Lennon	511	1	0	0	0	1	9	5	3	1	0
Leoni Township	13 677	34	0	1	3	30	311	106	184	21	1
Leslie	1 984	4	0	0	0	4	48	7	39	2	0
Lincoln Park	38 776	146	4	8	47	87	1 919	361	1 155	403	4
Lincoln Township	14 352	18	0	5	3	10	292	41	243	8	0
Linden	3 342	3	0	0	0	3	25	1	24	0	0
Litchfield	1 448	3	0	0	0	3	83	21	60	2	0
Livonia	99 017	170	3	13	62	92	2 301	444	1 574	283	10
Lowell	4 131	12	0	2	1	9	58	9	40	9	0
Ludington	8 356	29	1	12	0	16	371	57	300	14	7
Luna Pier	1 446	6	0	3	0	3	41	8	31	2	0
Mackinac Island	497	9	0	2	0	7	321	3	317	1	0
Mackinaw City	864	0	0	0	0	0	27	0	27	0	0
Madison Heights	30 535	80	0	13	36	31	1 300	175	822	303	5
Madison Township	7 877	1	0	0	0	1	42	5	36	1	0
Manistee	6 719	17	0	6	0	11	173	21	146	6	1
Marlette	2 085	12	0	2	0	10	44	4	36	4	0
Marquette	20 681	15	0	7	1	7	396	42	336	18	3
Marysville	9 990	8	0	2	1	5	244	28	210	6	2
Mason	7 876	19	0	4	2	13	201	17	181	3	0
Mattawan	2 789	1	0	0	0	1	41	2	38	1	0

[1]The FBI does not publish arson data unless it receives data from either the agency or the state for all 12 months of the calendar year.
[3]Because of changes in the state/local agency's reporting practices, figures are not comparable to previous years' data.

Table 8. Offenses Known to Law Enforcement, by State and City, 2005—*Continued*

(Number.)

City	Population	Violent crime	Murder and non-negligent man-slaughter	Forcible rape	Robbery	Aggravated assault	Property crime	Burglary	Larceny-theft	Motor vehicle theft	Arson[1]
Mayville	1 039	0	0	0	0	0	15	6	9	0	0
Memphis	1 130	2	0	0	0	2	25	2	23	0	0
Menominee	8 873	15	0	1	2	12	312	74	229	9	0
Meridian Township	38 706	68	0	9	11	48	1 150	196	924	30	6
Metamora Township	4 551	6	0	1	1	4	63	16	35	12	0
Midland	42 179	50	0	13	1	36	1 045	199	814	32	12
Milan	5 153	5	0	0	0	5	146	12	127	7	2
Milford	15 784	11	0	4	1	6	200	33	141	26	3
Monroe	21 708	73	0	9	13	51	663	119	497	47	3
Montague	2 347	3	0	0	1	2	58	7	50	1	0
Montrose Township	7 996	20	0	3	1	16	167	43	114	10	5
Morenci	2 366	5	0	2	0	3	70	10	60	0	0
Mount Morris	3 360	17	0	5	1	11	174	38	121	15	0
Mount Morris Township	23 574	226	3	41	40	142	1 200	423	592	185	17
Mount Pleasant	25 672	63	1	12	7	43	637	92	528	17	3
Mundy Township	13 668	40	1	2	13	24	547	61	449	37	0
Munising	2 444	2	0	1	0	1	26	6	19	1	0
Muskegon	39 987	464	3	57	99	305	2 817	523	2 056	238	22
Muskegon Heights	11 817	223	0	21	43	159	1 158	231	806	121	10
Muskegon Township	18 515	76	1	15	7	53	1 050	123	859	68	7
Napoleon Township	7 085	6	0	2	0	4	94	21	61	12	0
Nashville	1 703	7	0	0	0	7	39	5	31	3	0
Negaunee	4 498	4	0	2	0	2	113	14	90	9	1
Newaygo	1 691	18	0	6	0	12	119	12	102	5	0
New Baltimore	10 866	13	0	3	1	9	168	15	140	13	1
New Buffalo	2 270	0	0	0	0	0	43	2	38	3	0
New Haven	4 425	5	0	1	0	4	1	0	0	1	0
Niles	11 886	113	0	14	27	72	493	67	395	31	4
North Branch	1 015	6	0	0	0	6	39	3	35	1	0
Northfield Township	8 462	27	0	1	0	26	205	49	136	20	2
North Muskegon	4 012	1	0	1	0	0	65	5	60	0	0
Northville	6 389	1	0	0	0	1	75	17	57	1	0
Northville Township	24 449	24	0	2	9	13	470	111	327	32	1
Norton Shores	23 306	35	0	5	5	25	1 013	129	854	30	7
Norvell Township	3 040	0	0	0	0	0	20	11	8	1	0
Norway	2 908	2	0	0	0	2	67	10	56	1	0
Novi	51 976	61	0	2	11	48	1 259	197	993	69	3
Oakley-Brady	2 335	2	0	0	0	2	2	1	0	1	1
Oak Park	29 098	173	0	18	71	84	1 257	300	655	302	19
Orchard Lake	2 262	2	0	0	0	2	52	8	44	0	0
Oscoda Township	7 090	17	0	7	2	8	225	71	142	12	1
Otsego	3 987	23	0	9	1	13	151	22	125	4	0
Ovid	1 454	2	0	0	0	2	5	0	5	0	0
Owosso	15 545	82	0	17	8	57	681	118	525	38	14
Oxford	3 564	2	0	1	0	1	71	14	55	2	0
Parchment	1 833	4	0	1	0	3	52	2	50	0	0
Parma-Sandstone	6 831	2	0	0	0	2	59	9	47	3	0
Paw Paw	3 353	13	0	4	0	9	129	16	107	6	0
Peck	591	0	0	0	0	0	5	1	4	0	0
Perry	2 062	2	0	1	0	1	19	4	15	0	0
Petoskey	6 232	5	1	0	0	4	182	19	158	5	2
Pinckney	2 436	4	0	0	1	3	70	7	62	1	0
Pinconning	1 367	1	0	1	0	0	81	14	65	2	0
Pittsfield Township	32 482	86	0	12	15	59	1 091	158	822	111	6
Plainwell	4 014	5	0	3	2	0	109	3	102	4	0
Pleasant Ridge	2 526	4	0	0	1	3	36	4	29	3	0
Plymouth	8 884	8	0	1	0	7	176	32	125	19	0
Plymouth Township	28 221	29	0	4	9	16	401	85	278	38	3
Pontiac	67 637	1 255	9	82	253	911	2 799	1 117	1 194	488	39
Portage	45 247	127	1	15	28	83	1 955	287	1 604	64	14
Port Austin	701	0	0	0	0	0	13	2	11	0	0
Port Huron	31 736	199	2	24	34	139	1 344	275	976	93	13
Portland	3 809	7	0	2	1	4	108	21	81	6	1
Prairieville Township	3 458	0	0	0	0	0	20	6	14	0	0
Raisin Township	7 063	3	0	0	0	3	21	5	15	1	0
Reading	1 121	1	0	0	0	1	6	0	5	1	0
Redford Township	50 205	200	2	5	90	103	2 171	443	1 193	535	7
Richfield Township, Genesee County	8 661	9	0	4	0	5	129	59	58	12	1
Richfield Township, Roscommon County	4 239	7	0	1	0	6	60	7	49	4	2
Richmond	5 543	36	0	3	0	33	156	25	123	8	2
Riverview	12 920	10	0	1	0	9	252	25	205	22	1
Rochester	11 226	8	0	1	2	5	134	20	105	9	1
Rockford	4 958	8	0	3	1	4	133	21	110	2	0
Rockwood	3 460	7	0	0	2	5	39	4	31	4	1
Rogers City	3 214	2	0	1	0	1	58	7	51	0	2
Romeo	3 845	4	0	0	0	4	93	16	62	15	0
Romulus	23 628	163	2	20	28	113	1 142	290	685	167	6
Roosevelt Park	3 822	11	0	2	8	1	170	10	154	6	0
Roseville	47 999	153	3	21	35	94	2 302	237	1 722	343	5
Rothbury	445	1	0	0	0	1	4	0	4	0	0

[1]The FBI does not publish arson data unless it receives data from either the agency or the state for all 12 months of the calendar year.

Table 8. Offenses Known to Law Enforcement, by State and City, 2005—*Continued*

(Number.)

City	Population	Violent crime	Murder and non-negligent man-slaughter	Forcible rape	Robbery	Aggravated assault	Property crime	Burglary	Larceny-theft	Motor vehicle theft	Arson[1]
Royal Oak	58 621	127	1	20	34	72	1 421	278	954	189	8
Saginaw	59 093	1 606	17	44	212	1 333	2 610	1 286	948	376	91
Saginaw Township	40 147	89	0	4	27	58	1 171	214	886	71	7
Saline	8 866	10	0	3	3	4	141	17	122	2	2
Sand Lake	510	4	0	1	0	3	12	2	9	1	0
Sandusky	2 710	3	0	1	0	2	159	25	130	4	0
Sault Ste. Marie	14 169	34	0	4	4	26	539	77	432	30	0
Scottville	1 274	7	0	3	0	4	36	4	31	1	0
Shelby Township	68 390	143	0	23	19	101	1 249	214	937	98	7
Somerset Township	4 585	2	0	1	0	1	58	6	51	1	1
Southfield	77 554	939	4	22	159	754	3 747	748	2 149	850	8
Southgate	29 943	104	0	8	27	69	1 388	161	1 000	227	10
South Haven	5 148	35	2	2	6	25	277	33	237	7	1
South Lyon	11 026	14	0	1	2	11	130	20	101	9	1
Sparta	4 076	4	0	2	0	2	116	13	97	6	2
Spring Arbor Township	8 058	2	0	0	0	2	71	25	44	2	0
Springfield	5 241	28	0	7	4	17	222	39	166	17	1
Spring Lake-Ferrysburg	5 419	6	0	2	0	4	121	15	104	2	1
St. Charles	2 163	11	0	0	0	11	102	12	86	4	0
St. Clair Shores	61 914	161	0	11	35	115	1 455	266	942	247	13
St. Ignace	2 488	2	0	0	0	2	58	6	51	1	0
St. Johns	7 499	6	0	1	2	3	160	18	131	11	0
St. Joseph	8 708	35	0	4	3	28	436	48	377	11	5
St. Joseph Township	10 030	13	0	0	2	11	181	25	149	7	1
St. Louis	5 430	1	1	0	0	0	62	7	52	3	0
Sterling Heights	127 580	282	0	19	46	217	2 840	314	2 287	239	7
Sturgis	11 129	38	0	9	4	25	383	71	303	9	3
Summit Township	22 061	25	0	2	4	19	297	55	208	34	1
Sumpter Township	11 979	46	1	7	3	35	252	71	151	30	2
Swartz Creek	5 304	14	0	2	1	11	164	42	113	9	1
Taylor	65 436	233	1	26	67	139	3 043	455	2 117	471	16
Tecumseh	8 780	9	0	3	0	6	111	21	87	3	0
Thomas Township	12 509	43	0	5	3	35	386	42	335	9	0
Three Rivers	7 132	98	1	12	4	81	492	82	390	20	3
Tittabawassee Township	8 781	7	0	1	1	5	161	43	104	14	0
Traverse City	14 520	59	0	13	2	44	421	39	365	17	4
Trenton	19 484	9	0	1	1	7	137	12	115	10	1
Troy	81 498	72	1	8	19	44	1 991	277	1 578	136	5
Tuscarora Township	3 155	12	0	2	0	10	122	13	101	8	0
Unadilla Township	3 366	7	0	2	0	5	74	29	43	2	1
Utica	4 698	9	0	0	3	6	282	35	223	24	1
Van Buren Township	26 467	34	0	4	14	16	512	78	357	77	4
Vassar	2 788	4	0	1	0	3	49	5	42	2	3
Vernon	830	1	0	0	0	1	4	1	3	0	1
Vicksburg	2 209	5	0	0	0	5	19	6	13	0	0
Walker	23 334	58	0	14	24	20	1 007	123	852	32	3
Walled Lake	6 883	16	0	1	0	15	160	25	122	13	0
Warren	136 229	862	5	67	223	567	(7)	812	2 251	(7)	37
Waterford Township	72 066	181	3	27	47	104	1 966	481	1 314	171	12
Waterloo Township	3 035	3	0	0	0	3	39	19	20	0	1
Wayland	3 993	0	0	0	0	0	80	5	72	3	0
Wayne	18 795	121	0	26	31	64	673	127	447	99	18
West Bloomfield Township	65 546	22	0	2	11	9	807	125	648	34	6
West Branch	1 914	4	0	0	1	3	70	9	61	0	0
Westland	86 386	303	0	54	72	177	2 619	533	1 621	465	44
White Cloud	1 437	7	0	1	0	6	86	16	69	1	0
Whitehall	2 830	5	0	0	1	4	164	23	134	7	0
White Lake Township	29 655	40	0	5	5	30	677	139	509	29	2
White Pigeon	1 612	2	0	2	0	0	55	6	49	0	0
Williamston	3 787	5	0	2	0	3	55	12	41	2	0
Wixom	13 525	28	0	3	4	21	445	53	354	38	1
Wolverine Lake	4 310	4	0	2	0	2	53	13	37	3	0
Wyandotte	27 269	46	0	9	8	29	786	107	592	87	3
Wyoming	70 357	295	0	32	72	191	1 997	568	1 218	211	20
Yale	2 009	2	0	1	0	1	38	11	25	2	0
Ypsilanti	22 232	247	5	18	64	160	1 233	279	799	155	6
Zeeland	5 593	7	0	4	0	3	79	8	69	2	0
Minnesota											
Albany	1 951	0	0	0	0	0	0	0	0	0	0
Albert Lea	17 930	21	1	3	1	16	449	37	394	18	1
Alexandria	10 295	20	0	6	0	14	288	23	255	10	0
Andover	29 634	43	0	12	5	26	758	117	606	35	6
Annandale	2 872	2	0	0	0	2	130	13	107	10	1
Anoka	17 908	43	0	18	11	14	(8)	122	(8)	62	4
Appleton	2 914	4	0	3	0	1	34	9	23	2	0
Apple Valley	49 916	57	0	16	11	30	1 582	255	1 290	37	9
Arden Hills	9 627	7	0	3	1	3	223	20	180	23	3
Aurora	1 787	1	0	0	0	1	7	2	5	0	0

[1]The FBI does not publish arson data unless it receives data from either the agency or the state for all 12 months of the calendar year.
[7]After examining the data and making inquiries, the FBI determined that the agency's offense count was inflated. Consequently, this figure is not included in this table.
[8]After examining the data and making inquiries, the FBI determined that the agency's offense count was underreported. Consequently, this figure is not included in this table.

Table 8. Offenses Known to Law Enforcement, by State and City, 2005—*Continued*

(Number.)

City	Population	Violent crime	Murder and non-negligent man-slaughter	Forcible rape	Robbery	Aggravated assault	Property crime	Burglary	Larceny-theft	Motor vehicle theft	Arson[1]
Austin	23 654	95	0	34	11	50	1 162	138	973	51	10
Avon	1 303	0	0	0	0	0	24	3	20	1	0
Babbitt	1 638	0	0	0	0	0	1	1	0	0	0
Baxter	7 111	5	0	1	1	3	377	27	336	14	0
Bayport	3 181	4	0	0	1	3	39	7	29	3	0
Becker	3 649	4	0	0	0	4	9	1	8	0	5
Belgrade	735	0	0	0	0	0	0	0	0	0	0
Bemidji	13 097	57	1	11	7	38	1 084	77	956	51	10
Benson	3 257	2	0	1	0	1	58	14	35	9	0
Big Lake	8 475	19	0	4	2	13	272	25	237	10	0
Biwabik	940	4	0	2	0	2	4	2	2	0	0
Blaine	52 462	94	0	5	17	72	2 387	242	2 042	103	9
Blooming Prairie	1 963	4	0	0	0	4	39	19	13	7	0
Blue Earth	3 510	2	0	0	0	2	81	15	63	3	3
Brainerd	13 832	69	0	18	8	43	868	123	691	54	8
Breckenridge	3 387	4	0	0	0	4	122	18	95	9	2
Brooklyn Center	28 025	168	0	21	59	88	1 927	180	1 512	235	9
Brooklyn Park	68 351	309	1	47	81	180	2 932	594	2 036	302	11
Browns Valley	645	2	0	0	1	1	6	2	3	1	0
Brownton	805	0	0	0	0	0	5	3	2	0	0
Buffalo	12 881	22	0	10	2	10	477	42	404	31	3
Burnsville	59 755	114	3	18	32	61	1 693	249	1 355	89	14
Caledonia	2 955	9	0	3	1	5	72	15	49	8	0
Cambridge	6 804	15	0	6	1	8	479	72	384	23	3
Cannon Falls	3 964	3	0	0	1	2	204	13	178	13	0
Centennial Lakes	10 916	8	0	2	2	4	170	28	132	10	1
Champlin	23 438	21	1	6	3	11	626	65	535	26	. . .
Chaska	21 829	26	0	8	2	16	380	72	300	8	9
Cold Spring	3 666	7	0	4	0	3	49	12	35	2	0
Columbia Heights	18 372	115	2	11	53	49	1 082	247	723	112	5
Coon Rapids	63 113	108	1	26	24	57	3 071	227	2 709	135	18
Corcoran	5 736	2	0	0	0	2	47	9	32	6	0
Cottage Grove	32 347	43	0	15	5	23	864	148	670	46	6
Crosby	2 273	10	0	1	1	8	164	15	138	11	3
Crystal	22 020	34	0	1	19	14	873	129	667	77	7
Dayton	4 676	3	0	1	0	2	36	9	7	20	1
Deephaven-Woodland	4 241	3	0	1	1	1	31	7	22	2	0
Detroit Lakes	7 913	16	0	3	1	12	453	33	408	12	2
Dilworth	3 210	5	0	1	0	4	92	8	78	6	0
Eagan	64 505	45	0	8	13	24	1 595	266	1 270	59	12
Eagle Lake	1 977	2	0	1	0	1	29	8	18	3	0
East Bethel	11 930	21	0	7	1	13	445	89	310	46	2
East Grand Forks	7 724	19	1	5	0	13	306	57	244	5	3
Eden Prairie	60 807	57	0	13	21	23	1 177	182	955	40	19
Edina	46 369	25	0	4	12	9	1 046	172	843	31	4
Elk River	20 350	38	0	8	6	24	759	121	614	24	12
Elmore	708	3	0	1	0	2	12	6	5	1	0
Ely	3 701	8	0	4	1	3	143	39	94	10	0
Eveleth	3 732	14	0	3	1	10	228	55	152	21	2
Fairmont	10 614	17	0	1	2	14	376	60	310	6	0
Falcon Heights	5 466	3	0	0	2	1	101	19	78	4	0
Faribault	22 061	83	0	28	7	48	945	176	724	45	7
Farmington	17 452	10	0	2	1	7	214	29	172	13	1
Fergus Falls	13 801	35	0	14	2	19	482	86	381	15	6
Floodwood	490	0	0	0	0	0	10	0	8	2	0
Forest Lake	17 054	15	0	4	1	10	474	60	352	62	3
Fridley	27 110	121	0	10	43	68	1 523	124	1 259	140	4
Gilbert	1 793	6	0	0	0	6	44	5	36	3	0
Glencoe	5 569	8	0	2	0	6	107	14	87	6	0
Glenwood	2 586	3	0	0	0	3	29	0	28	1	0
Golden Valley	20 326	51	0	8	17	26	666	112	476	78	6
Goodview	3 355	4	0	0	1	3	71	9	60	2	0
Grand Rapids	8 096	12	0	3	1	8	33	9	23	1	1
Granite Falls	3 022	2	0	0	0	2	34	12	20	2	0
Hallock	1 097	0	0	0	0	0	0	0	0	0	0
Ham Lake	14 650	21	0	2	1	18	704	106	551	47	4
Hastings	20 480	22	2	7	1	12	536	59	445	32	4
Hermantown	8 428	9	0	2	1	6	396	61	318	17	1
Hibbing	16 810	9	0	0	1	8	160	45	107	8	1
Hilltop	777	21	0	2	6	13	104	19	70	15	0
Hokah	601	0	0	0	0	0	12	4	7	1	0
Houston	1 008	0	0	0	0	0	26	4	22	0	0
Hoyt Lakes	2 037	0	0	0	0	0	8	3	5	0	0
Hutchinson	13 605	36	0	15	2	19	389	57	322	10	3
International Falls	6 378	34	0	16	2	16	256	47	193	16	1
Inver Grove Heights	32 540	56	0	13	10	33	1 080	144	859	77	16
Jackson	3 488	12	0	5	0	7	88	16	70	2	1
Janesville	2 128	0	0	0	0	0	9	2	7	0	0
Kimball	650	1	0	0	0	1	19	7	12	0	0
Lake City	5 346	7	0	1	0	6	143	14	118	11	1

[1] The FBI does not publish arson data unless it receives data from either the agency or the state for all 12 months of the calendar year.
. . . = Not available.

Table 8. Offenses Known to Law Enforcement, by State and City, 2005—*Continued*

(Number.)

City	Population	Violent crime	Murder and non-negligent man-slaughter	Forcible rape	Robbery	Aggravated assault	Property crime	Burglary	Larceny-theft	Motor vehicle theft	Arson[1]
Lake Crystal	2 489	1	0	1	0	0	29	14	15	0	0
Lakefield	1 715	0	0	0	0	0	9	5	2	2	0
Lakes Area	6 854	13	0	3	0	10	178	21	148	9	2
Lakeville	49 749	38	0	9	7	22	984	177	784	23	2
Lauderdale	2 256	2	0	1	0	1	51	16	33	2	0
Lester Prairie	1 474	2	0	0	1	1	36	4	32	0	0
Lewiston	1 503	1	0	0	0	1	1	0	1	0	0
Litchfield	6 707	15	0	10	1	4	227	37	175	15	0
Little Canada	9 740	19	0	3	3	13	412	55	303	54	5
Little Falls	8 242	16	0	7	1	8	408	40	357	11	0
Long Prairie	2 990	8	0	0	0	8	89	5	81	3	1
Madison	1 701	0	0	0	0	0	0	0	0	0	0
Mankato	34 678	118	0	41	15	62	1 730	256	1 403	71	3
Maple Grove	58 994	63	0	20	16	27	1 384	190	1 144	50	17
Maplewood	35 750	90	0	4	32	54	2 496	312	1 934	250	9
Marshall	12 486	19	0	7	0	12	385	38	336	11	1
Medina	4 680	1	0	0	0	1	118	29	84	5	0
Melrose	3 205	1	0	1	0	0	25	4	21	0	0
Minneapolis	376 277	5 472	47	402	2 584	2 439	22 417	5 535	12 988	3 894	220
Minnetonka	50 390	44	0	12	13	19	1 123	219	848	56	9
Minnetrista	7 591	5	0	0	0	5	67	22	39	6	0
Montevideo	5 333	2	0	0	0	2	193	28	157	8	1
Montgomery	2 925	6	0	1	1	4	99	13	84	2	0
Moorhead	33 598	59	1	16	5	37	839	94	694	51	4
Moose Lake	2 461	3	0	1	0	2	87	12	73	2	0
Mora	3 474	18	0	5	0	13	180	16	161	3	0
Morris	5 227	16	0	4	0	12	65	8	53	4	0
Mound	9 470	11	1	4	0	6	126	21	96	9	1
Mounds View	12 437	32	0	5	2	25	514	53	419	42	5
Mountain Lake	2 045	4	0	3	0	1	36	13	22	1	1
New Brighton	21 277	18	0	0	9	9	640	89	497	54	5
New Hope	20 108	42	0	9	13	20	731	82	617	32	2
Newport	3 714	9	0	1	2	6	181	38	129	14	3
New Prague	6 153	6	0	3	1	2	93	14	76	3	3
New Richland	1 153	1	0	1	0	0	24	12	12	0	0
New Ulm	13 791	9	0	0	0	9	302	60	230	12	0
North Branch	10 079	10	0	4	0	6	367	41	306	20	0
Northfield	18 683	8	0	1	1	6	505	76	405	24	0
North Mankato	12 210	5	0	4	0	1	203	2	189	12	16
North Oaks	4 154	0	0	0	0	0	54	7	44	3	0
North St. Paul	11 672	33	0	9	7	17	545	63	417	65	5
Oakdale	27 743	63	0	12	21	30	1 124	148	875	101	8
Oak Park Heights	4 045	8	0	2	1	5	265	21	230	14	0
Olivia	2 513	4	0	0	0	4	81	19	60	2	0
Orono	11 894	8	0	1	1	6	120	17	94	9	0
Ortonville	2 072	3	0	0	0	3	15	4	7	4	0
Osseo	2 596	1	0	0	0	1	10	3	4	3	0
Owatonna	23 855	41	0	7	4	30	795	141	621	33	2
Park Rapids	3 432	9	0	2	0	7	240	48	172	20	2
Paynesville	2 270	1	0	0	0	1	45	8	36	1	0
Plymouth	70 233	65	0	14	17	34	1 629	336	1 230	63	17
Princeton	4 650	8	0	2	0	6	219	28	184	7	0
Prior Lake	21 419	32	0	7	6	19	507	90	373	44	1
Proctor	2 796	5	0	0	2	3	122	18	101	3	0
Ramsey	20 864	24	0	9	3	12	662	58	570	34	15
Red Wing	16 006	32	1	9	4	18	708	93	578	37	13
Redwood Falls	5 365	23	0	2	1	20	252	36	203	13	1
Richfield	34 123	143	0	23	63	57	1 430	266	1 047	117	14
Richmond	1 284	0	0	0	0	0	0	0	0	0	0
Robbinsdale	13 574	40	0	1	22	17	591	107	398	86	2
Rochester	93 866	261	0	51	71	139	2 465	421	1 917	127	29
Roseau	2 797	0	0	0	0	0	76	3	71	2	0
Rosemount	18 109	20	0	7	2	11	466	83	367	16	2
Roseville	32 899	44	2	6	16	20	1 523	164	1 210	149	2
Sartell	12 380	5	0	1	0	4	156	9	141	6	0
Sauk Centre	3 981	4	0	1	0	3	134	13	120	1	0
Sauk Rapids	11 452	9	1	1	0	7	222	32	170	20	1
Savage	25 875	42	0	4	5	33	666	122	519	25	3
Scanlon	844	0	0	0	0	0	0	0	0	0	0
Shakopee	29 504	55	1	10	7	37	1 019	171	800	48	4
Shoreview	27 159	8	0	2	1	5	389	47	321	21	4
Silver Bay	2 024	2	0	1	0	1	7	3	3	1	0
Silver Lake	792	1	0	0	0	1	17	7	9	1	0
Slayton	2 007	1	0	0	0	1	28	4	22	2	0
Sleepy Eye	3 547	0	0	0	0	0	26	8	15	3	0
South Eastern Faribault County	1 209	0	0	0	0	0	4	1	3	0	0
South Lake Minnetonka	12 201	12	0	2	1	9	191	33	151	7	3
Spring Grove	1 289	1	0	0	0	1	24	8	15	1	0
Spring Lake Park	6 852	28	0	2	10	16	384	76	263	45	0
Staples	3 108	4	0	1	1	2	130	17	109	4	0

[1]The FBI does not publish arson data unless it receives data from either the agency or the state for all 12 months of the calendar year.

Table 8. Offenses Known to Law Enforcement, by State and City, 2005—*Continued*

(Number.)

City	Population	Violent crime	Murder and non-negligent man-slaughter	Forcible rape	Robbery	Aggravated assault	Property crime	Burglary	Larceny-theft	Motor vehicle theft	Arson[1]
St. Charles	3 473	1	0	0	0	1	31	3	26	2	0
St. Cloud	64 739	251	2	59	34	156	2 780	398	2 245	137	27
St. Francis	6 972	20	0	9	0	11	223	46	159	18	0
St. James	4 528	12	0	3	0	9	126	8	111	7	0
St. Joseph	5 420	3	0	0	0	3	17	4	12	1	0
St. Louis Park	43 879	88	0	13	35	40	1 506	299	1 106	101	10
St. Paul	278 692	2 443	24	220	778	1 421	13 693	3 484	7 761	2 448	153
St. Paul Park	5 052	10	0	1	1	8	212	35	158	19	3
St. Peter	10 423	24	0	9	0	15	321	48	256	17	3
Stewart	555	1	0	0	0	1	6	1	2	3	0
Stillwater	17 278	17	0	4	4	9	513	89	389	35	7
Thief River Falls	8 401	18	0	6	2	10	293	38	247	8	0
Vadnais Heights	12 949	13	0	1	6	6	302	29	233	40	7
Virginia	8 838	47	0	19	3	25	602	102	474	26	1
Wabasha	2 589	6	0	3	0	3	76	9	67	0	0
Wadena	4 154	10	0	2	0	8	153	13	135	5	0
Waite Park	6 900	20	0	4	6	10	500	44	437	19	3
Warroad	1 686	0	0	0	0	0	67	3	61	3	0
Waseca	9 526	21	0	5	0	16	318	45	258	15	0
Wayzata	4 001	0	0	0	0	0	152	27	120	5	0
Wells	2 430	0	0	0	0	0	26	8	17	1	0
West Hennepin	5 569	7	0	1	0	6	66	10	47	9	2
West St. Paul	19 303	65	0	13	25	27	1 247	109	1 056	82	3
Wheaton	1 521	3	0	0	0	3	22	5	17	0	0
White Bear Lake	24 201	29	0	2	11	16	870	215	589	66	3
Willmar	18 319	64	0	23	7	34	900	123	749	28	5
Windom	4 488	9	0	0	0	9	89	18	63	8	0
Winnebago	1 444	1	0	0	0	1	29	11	16	2	2
Winona	26 616	29	0	3	4	22	677	124	535	18	2
Winsted	2 363	0	0	0	0	0	47	12	34	1	2
Woodbury	50 332	33	2	7	5	19	1 237	157	1 022	58	5
Worthington	11 156	19	0	2	4	13	251	53	183	15	0
Wyoming	3 849	1	0	0	0	1	85	18	66	1	0
Zumbrota	2 964	4	0	0	0	4	102	14	80	8	3
Mississippi											
Aberdeen	6 313	14	0	2	4	8	144	40	99	5	1
Amory[3]	6 872	19	1	4	4	10	495	97	387	11	2
Batesville	7 722	12	0	1	3	8	386	98	267	21	0
Bay St. Louis	8 345	11	0	1	4	6	434	67	342	25	1
Belzoni	2 591	16	0	2	6	8	147	51	96	0	0
Booneville	8 759	13	1	5	0	7	338	102	234	2	2
Brandon	18 747	6	0	1	4	1	263	78	171	14	1
Brookhaven	9 916	20	0	2	5	13	288	30	246	12	2
Bruce	2 081	0	0	0	0	0	14	2	12	0	0
Byhalia	720	5	0	0	0	5	72	14	51	7	0
Canton	12 906	122	4	11	25	82	385	181	194	10	0
Charleston	2 090	30	0	1	0	29	142	44	91	7	0
Cleveland	12 978	46	3	0	6	37	1 044	243	795	6	1
Collins	2 770	5	0	2	3	0	167	44	113	10	0
Columbus	24 946	79	1	4	33	41	1 295	195	1 045	55	1
Edwards	1 328	2	0	0	1	1	8	5	3	0	0
Eupora	2 271	7	0	0	1	6	31	27	1	3	0
Fulton	4 114	3	0	0	1	2	88	24	59	5	0
Gloster	1 069	1	0	0	1	0	15	13	0	2	0
Greenville	39 222	245	6	45	90	104	2 859	925	1 793	141	91
Greenwood	17 548	116	2	5	59	50	1 103	353	699	51	5
Grenada	14 582	80	1	4	24	51	826	246	513	67	4
Gulfport	72 300	227	6	34	110	77	4 597	1 164	3 108	325	29
Hattiesburg	46 732	175	5	21	75	74	2 818	747	1 889	182	13
Heidelberg	808	7	0	0	2	5	10	8	2	0	0
Hollandale	3 222	5	0	0	3	2	70	41	26	3	0
Holly Springs[3]	8 059	55	0	7	12	36	329	82	222	25	4
Horn Lake[3]	21 900	32	1	1	19	11	1 321	139	1 073	109	1
Houston	4 034	0	0	0	0	0	0	0	0	0	0
Indianola	11 520	71	2	6	20	43	825	315	490	20	7
Iuka	2 988	12	0	3	2	7	57	30	24	3	0
Jackson	180 417	1 225	38	158	612	417	12 008	3 139	6 960	1 909	59
Kosciusko	7 405	22	0	2	13	7	174	73	100	1	0
Laurel	18 300	108	1	21	52	34	1 724	218	1 436	70	6
Leakesville	1 024	0	0	0	0	0	0	0	0	0	0
Leland	5 216	13	0	1	4	8	189	71	112	6	1
Lexington	1 960	6	1	0	2	3	23	14	8	1	0
Long Beach	17 366	12	0	0	6	6	375	40	323	12	1
Louisville	6 816	8	0	0	4	4	85	51	34	0	0
Lucedale	2 840	11	0	0	2	9	96	26	62	8	0
Madison	16 565	10	0	2	0	8	186	9	175	2	0
Magee	4 245	11	1	1	4	5	173	20	139	14	0
McComb	13 295	81	2	6	25	48	791	168	566	57	0
Meridian	39 075	198	6	29	79	84	2 030	744	1 181	105	15
Morton	3 458	13	0	3	3	7	48	33	13	2	0
Moss Point	15 414	84	5	12	38	29	1 164	465	577	122	7
Natchez	17 380	34	0	3	16	15	1 116	153	943	20	7
Newton	3 699	9	0	1	0	8	80	40	36	4	0
Ocean Springs	17 808	26	0	6	9	11	679	165	478	36	3
Olive Branch	26 682	61	1	13	20	27	1 219	315	808	96	4

[1]The FBI does not publish arson data unless it receives data from either the agency or the state for all 12 months of the calendar year.
[3]Because of changes in the state/local agency's reporting practices, figures are not comparable to previous years' data.

Table 8. Offenses Known to Law Enforcement, by State and City, 2005—*Continued*

(Number.)

City	Population	Violent crime	Murder and non-negligent man-slaughter	Forcible rape	Robbery	Aggravated assault	Property crime	Burglary	Larceny-theft	Motor vehicle theft	Arson[1]
Oxford	13 384	37	2	6	5	24	390	75	279	36	0
Pascagoula	26 035	139	3	38	54	44	2 019	703	1 133	183	3
Pearl	23 183	90	1	23	15	51	805	258	475	72	1
Pelahatchie	1 498	1	0	0	1	0	3	2	0	1	0
Petal	7 809	6	0	1	2	3	156	40	109	7	1
Picayune	10 817	37	1	4	10	22	600	95	482	23	2
Poplarville	2 683	9	0	0	4	5	96	18	74	4	0
Port Gibson	1 781	1	0	0	1	0	19	3	15	1	0
Richland	7 037	19	1	7	4	7	251	56	181	14	0
Ridgeland	21 712	33	1	0	12	20	743	74	636	33	0
Ripley	5 571	5	0	0	1	4	67	25	38	4	0
Roxie	568	0	0	0	0	0	0	0	0	0	0
Senatobia	6 793	13	0	0	10	3	386	115	256	15	0
Southaven	36 470	64	3	10	29	22	1 699	196	1 319	184	2
Starkville	22 101	73	1	7	17	48	755	150	582	23	1
Summit	1 428	0	0	0	0	0	67	15	49	3	0
Tupelo	35 639	126	1	33	38	54	1 809	342	1 338	129	1
Vaiden	846	1	0	0	0	1	0	0	0	0	0
Verona	3 392	5	0	1	3	1	170	109	58	3	0
Vicksburg	25 937	261	6	53	39	163	1 937	376	1 439	122	19
West Point	11 883	43	1	4	11	27	428	148	280	0	0
Wiggins	4 330	26	2	10	2	12	348	79	268	1	0
Winona	4 982	14	0	1	2	11	45	8	35	2	0
Missouri											
Adrian	1 824	11	0	0	0	11	8	3	1	4	1
Advance	1 230	1	0	0	1	0	21	2	19	0	0
Alma	387	0	0	0	0	0	2	1	1	0	0
Alton	656	1	0	0	0	1	2	2	0	0	0
Anderson	1 880	2	0	0	1	1	86	11	70	5	1
Annapolis	300	2	0	0	0	2	4	2	2	0	0
Appleton City	1 304	12	0	0	0	12	43	10	31	2	0
Arbyrd	510	3	0	2	0	1	2	0	1	1	0
Archie	934	0	0	0	0	0	21	3	18	0	0
Arnold	20 306	28	0	3	9	16	1 451	65	1 344	42	4
Ash Grove	1 483	4	0	0	0	4	16	6	9	1	0
Ashland	2 207	9	0	0	1	8	78	12	64	2	0
Aurora	7 202	18	0	0	1	17	386	79	283	24	0
Auxvasse	940	7	1	0	0	6	15	6	9	0	0
Ava	3 087	33	0	0	2	31	120	19	94	7	0
Ballwin[3]	31 022	38	0	1	3	34	291	53	227	11	0
Bates City	245	6	0	0	1	5	26	4	20	2	0
Battlefield	3 196	2	0	0	0	2	33	4	27	2	0
Bella Villa	668	2	0	0	0	2	7	1	4	2	0
Bellefontaine Neighbors	10 817	64	0	3	13	48	504	102	312	90	2
Bellerive	261	0	0	0	0	0	5	3	1	1	0
Bellflower	417	0	0	0	0	0	0	0	0	0	0
Bel-Nor	1 556	0	0	0	0	0	40	1	30	9	0
Bel-Ridge	3 004	35	1	1	8	25	201	54	116	31	2
Belton	23 982	38	0	7	6	25	745	114	579	52	3
Berkeley	9 817	95	0	8	19	68	569	116	325	128	4
Bernie	1 824	5	0	0	0	5	16	7	7	2	0
Bethany	3 065	17	1	0	0	16	72	16	49	7	1
Beverly Hills	587	4	0	0	0	4	10	2	6	2	0
Billings	1 151	6	0	0	0	6	27	5	21	1	1
Bismarck	1 553	2	0	0	2	0	9	6	0	3	1
Blackburn	279	0	0	0	0	0	2	2	0	0	0
Bloomfield	1 910	3	0	0	0	3	23	13	7	3	0
Blue Springs	49 860	76	0	13	22	41	2 022	293	1 589	140	4
Bolivar	9 836	25	0	8	0	17	437	40	389	8	2
Boonville	8 676	10	0	0	1	9	287	25	255	7	3
Bourbon	1 395	16	0	1	0	15	42	2	40	0	1
Bowling Green	5 143	23	0	1	0	22	133	34	91	8	0
Branson	6 365	66	0	6	8	52	1 003	126	835	42	4
Branson West	491	1	0	0	0	1	64	1	60	3	0
Breckenridge Hills[3]	4 692	26	0	4	4	18	262	34	198	30	5
Brentwood	7 502	11	1	4	4	2	280	22	241	17	0
Bridgeton	15 504	93	2	5	26	60	1 126	104	893	129	4
Brookfield	4 596	9	0	2	0	7	81	22	55	4	1
Bucklin	504	0	0	0	0	0	3	2	1	0	0
Buckner	2 739	16	0	2	1	13	64	11	50	3	0
Buffalo	2 921	17	0	1	0	16	155	25	126	4	2
Butler	4 237	5	0	0	0	5	213	51	157	5	1
Byrnes Mill	2 725	1	0	0	0	1	14	3	10	1	0
Cabool	2 148	2	0	0	0	2	51	9	40	2	0
California	4 139	5	0	0	0	5	95	28	60	7	0
Camden Point	549	1	0	0	0	1	2	0	0	2	0
Camdenton	2 987	12	0	1	1	10	222	24	193	5	2
Cameron	9 396	29	1	1	1	26	221	28	186	7	4
Campbell	1 875	0	0	0	0	0	29	4	21	4	0
Canton	2 519	24	0	1	0	23	49	4	44	1	0
Cape Girardeau	36 279	187	0	13	32	142	2 125	324	1 750	51	16
Cardwell	758	0	0	0	0	0	1	1	0	0	0
Carl Junction	6 188	4	0	2	1	1	114	26	85	3	1
Carterville	1 922	16	0	2	0	14	62	9	49	4	1

[1]The FBI does not publish arson data unless it receives data from either the agency or the state for all 12 months of the calendar year.
[3]Because of changes in the state/local agency's reporting practices, figures are not comparable to previous years' data.

Table 8. Offenses Known to Law Enforcement, by State and City, 2005—*Continued*

(Number.)

City	Population	Violent crime	Murder and non-negligent man-slaughter	Forcible rape	Robbery	Aggravated assault	Property crime	Burglary	Larceny-theft	Motor vehicle theft	Arson[1]
Carthage	13 106	33	3	5	4	21	499	70	411	18	2
Caruthersville	6 557	18	1	1	7	9	352	113	228	11	1
Cassville	3 085	3	0	0	0	3	146	23	109	14	0
Centralia	3 720	18	0	1	0	17	144	15	124	5	0
Chaffee	3 015	9	0	1	0	8	60	10	43	7	0
Charlack	1 400	6	0	1	0	5	104	8	94	2	0
Charleston	5 207	36	0	2	8	26	140	46	86	8	0
Chesterfield	47 484	40	1	1	6	32	755	92	649	14	1
Chillicothe	8 766	35	0	9	3	23	281	57	206	18	3
Clarkson Valley	2 644	4	0	0	0	4	37	2	34	1	0
Clarkton	1 281	12	0	0	0	12	15	7	6	2	0
Claycomo	1 278	2	0	0	1	1	53	7	38	8	0
Clayton	16 071	10	1	0	2	7	415	55	330	30	2
Cleveland	666	0	0	0	0	0	3	1	2	0	0
Clinton	9 518	33	2	3	5	23	580	100	453	27	0
Cole Camp	1 072	0	0	0	0	0	9	3	6	0	0
Columbia	90 304	477	7	19	114	337	3 065	506	2 386	173	28
Concordia	2 419	4	0	0	0	4	31	6	23	2	0
Cool Valley	1 053	12	0	2	5	5	83	8	61	14	0
Cooter	442	1	0	0	0	1	0	0	0	0	1
Corder	431	0	0	0	0	0	3	0	3	0	0
Country Club Hills	1 344	4	0	0	0	4	44	8	27	9	1
Country Club Village	1 902	2	0	0	0	2	10	1	9	0	0
Crane	1 472	2	0	0	0	2	7	0	7	0	0
Crestwood	11 850	10	0	1	3	6	594	13	575	6	5
Creve Coeur	16 774	31	0	5	6	20	318	23	273	22	0
Crocker	1 026	1	0	0	0	1	17	2	14	1	1
Crystal City	4 526	23	0	4	3	16	172	19	144	9	1
Cuba	3 411	18	0	2	5	11	307	21	276	10	1
Dellwood	5 124	24	1	1	12	10	162	42	83	37	0
Desloge	5 077	8	0	2	1	5	160	18	136	6	1
De Soto	6 593	86	0	0	1	85	219	20	184	15	0
Des Peres	8 675	7	0	1	4	2	341	27	309	5	0
Dexter	7 607	60	2	2	3	53	283	66	204	13	0
Diamond	841	6	0	0	0	6	7	3	4	0	0
Dixon	1 579	5	1	0	0	4	22	3	19	0	0
Doniphan	1 937	3	0	1	1	1	116	25	83	8	2
Drexel	1 118	3	0	0	0	3	24	5	17	2	1
Duenweg	1 056	2	0	0	0	2	55	11	41	3	0
Duquesne	1 702	3	0	1	0	2	10	5	5	0	0
East Prairie	3 160	1	0	0	0	1	117	6	101	10	1
Edgerton	550	1	0	0	0	1	6	3	3	0	0
Edmundson	818	7	0	1	1	5	62	8	37	17	0
Eldon	4 962	9	0	1	2	6	208	40	156	12	0
Ellington	1 024	0	0	0	0	0	7	1	5	1	0
Ellisville	9 464	8	0	1	2	5	155	24	124	7	0
Elsberry	2 346	15	0	1	1	13	34	3	31	0	0
Eureka	8 864	14	0	3	0	11	278	17	243	18	0
Excelsior Springs	11 414	81	0	2	4	75	479	118	321	40	7
Exeter	735	1	0	0	0	1	4	0	2	2	0
Fair Grove	1 287	0	0	0	0	0	12	4	7	1	0
Fair Play	436	0	0	0	0	0	15	6	9	0	0
Farmington	14 925	87	0	5	6	76	503	38	443	22	1
Fayette	2 720	9	0	0	3	6	13	3	10	0	0
Ferguson	21 849	108	1	8	40	59	1 109	213	718	178	1
Ferrelview	599	4	0	1	1	2	17	6	10	1	0
Festus	10 521	129	0	6	10	113	310	43	255	12	1
Flordell Hills	905	19	0	0	4	15	75	28	33	14	0
Florissant	51 993	98	0	4	60	34	1 147	182	871	94	0
Foley	197	0	0	0	0	0	0	0	0	0	0
Fordland	740	1	0	0	0	1	7	2	4	1	0
Forsyth	1 685	4	0	3	0	1	57	10	42	5	1
Fredericktown	3 961	4	1	0	0	3	142	26	112	4	0
Freeman	566	0	0	0	0	0	2	1	1	0	0
Frontenac	3 526	0	0	0	0	0	54	2	48	4	0
Fulton[3]	11 973	45	1	3	4	37	589	95	471	23	2
Gainesville	605	2	0	1	0	1	27	2	25	0	0
Gallatin	1 794	2	0	0	0	2	25	8	17	0	0
Garden City	1 665	5	0	0	0	5	30	5	22	3	0
Gerald	1 221	2	0	0	0	2	11	4	7	0	0
Gideon	1 049	0	0	0	0	0	0	0	0	0	0
Gladstone	27 398	58	0	1	17	40	884	129	646	109	2
Glasgow	1 212	11	0	0	0	11	26	8	17	1	0
Glendale	5 688	5	0	0	0	5	32	3	28	1	1
Goodman	1 210	1	0	0	0	1	6	4	2	0	0
Gower	1 456	1	0	0	0	1	6	0	6	0	1
Grain Valley	8 049	19	0	5	0	14	221	50	160	11	2
Granby	2 211	17	0	0	1	16	53	9	39	5	0
Grandin	239	0	0	0	0	0	0	0	0	0	0
Grandview	25 045	182	1	10	58	113	714	273	294	147	10

[1]The FBI does not publish arson data unless it receives data from either the agency or the state for all 12 months of the calendar year.
[3]Because of changes in the state/local agency's reporting practices, figures are not comparable to previous years' data.

Table 8. Offenses Known to Law Enforcement, by State and City, 2005—*Continued*

(Number.)

City	Population	Violent crime	Murder and non-negligent man-slaughter	Forcible rape	Robbery	Aggravated assault	Property crime	Burglary	Larceny-theft	Motor vehicle theft	Arson[1]
Greendale	719	0	0	0	0	0	11	1	10	0	0
Greenfield	1 312	10	0	0	0	10	30	11	17	2	0
Greenwood	4 490	1	0	0	0	1	41	10	30	1	0
Hallsville	971	1	0	0	0	1	13	2	10	1	0
Hamilton	1 825	15	0	1	0	14	23	7	15	1	0
Hannibal	17 860	118	0	18	26	74	1 246	176	1 062	8	4
Harrisonville	9 668	37	1	2	0	34	864	61	769	34	2
Hartville	605	1	0	0	0	1	0	0	0	0	0
Hayti	3 116	10	2	0	3	5	173	32	137	4	0
Hayti Heights	785	2	0	0	0	2	5	2	3	0	0
Hazelwood	25 855	119	0	5	25	89	1 060	144	819	97	0
Henrietta	458	1	0	0	0	1	8	0	7	1	0
Herculaneum	3 199	2	0	0	0	2	194	12	177	5	0
Hermann	2 720	21	0	0	1	20	63	12	48	3	1
Higginsville	4 696	26	0	0	1	25	166	24	133	9	1
High Hill	228	0	0	0	0	0	12	2	8	2	0
Highlandville	925	0	0	0	0	0	8	1	6	1	0
Hillsboro	1 703	52	0	0	0	52	212	4	199	9	0
Hillsdale	1 437	11	0	0	1	10	10	8	0	2	0
Holcomb	696	0	0	0	0	0	1	1	0	0	0
Hollister	3 800	13	0	1	0	12	157	41	103	13	0
Holt	437	0	0	0	0	0	35	2	33	0	2
Holts Summit	3 302	([9])	0	0	([9])	17	([9])	([9])	36	1	0
Houston	2 011	2	0	0	0	2	67	6	60	1	0
Humansville	981	7	0	2	0	5	10	2	8	0	1
Huntsville	1 624	7	0	2	0	5	25	10	13	2	0
Independence	111 905	796	6	45	123	622	8 190	1 304	5 956	930	34
Indian Point	626	0	0	0	0	0	9	2	6	1	0
Ironton	1 385	1	0	1	0	0	39	4	35	0	0
Jackson	12 852	21	0	1	2	18	286	55	226	5	0
JASCO Metropolitan	2 202	7	0	0	0	7	42	6	34	2	1
Jefferson City	38 978	312	8	25	34	245	1 733	310	1 344	79	6
Jennings	15 176	170	3	3	47	117	1 155	332	542	281	7
Jonesburg	694	3	0	2	0	1	23	9	13	1	0
Joplin	47 202	323	2	34	87	200	4 206	656	3 146	404	25
Kahoka	2 208	7	0	0	0	7	28	4	24	0	0
Kansas City	447 915	6 536	126	295	2 000	4 115	34 822	7 429	21 603	5 790	395
Kearney	6 992	7	1	0	2	4	157	8	133	16	0
Kennett	11 092	60	0	7	10	43	758	189	534	35	0
Keytesville	520	0	0	0	0	0	0	0	0	0	0
Kimberling City	2 477	7	0	0	0	7	44	11	28	5	0
Kimmswick	94	0	0	0	0	0	2	0	1	1	0
Kirksville	17 192	74	0	5	2	67	458	74	373	11	3
Kirkwood	27 372	70	1	1	8	60	758	54	677	27	6
Knob Noster	2 718	19	0	4	0	15	88	21	65	2	0
Ladue	8 371	14	0	0	10	4	147	24	119	4	0
La Grange	969	6	0	0	0	6	7	4	3	0	0
Lake Lafayette	365	4	0	0	0	4	12	7	4	1	0
Lake Lotawana	1 903	0	0	0	0	0	21	4	17	0	1
Lake Ozark	1 835	11	0	1	0	10	72	14	53	5	0
Lakeshire	1 343	2	0	0	0	2	18	1	16	1	0
Lake St. Louis	12 995	14	0	4	2	8	176	20	147	9	2
Lake Tapawingo	817	0	0	0	0	0	3	0	2	1	0
Lake Waukomis	923	0	0	0	0	0	16	0	14	2	0
Lake Winnebago	1 045	0	0	0	0	0	5	0	5	0	0
Lamar	4 638	39	1	1	0	37	253	67	173	13	0
La Monte	1 056	10	0	1	1	8	32	12	18	2	0
La Plata	1 448	3	0	0	0	3	21	5	16	0	0
Lathrop	2 320	4	0	0	0	4	29	14	8	7	0
Laurie	700	5	0	0	1	4	51	1	48	2	0
Lawson	2 416	2	0	0	0	2	50	5	41	4	0
Leadwood	1 174	8	0	1	0	7	3	1	1	1	1
Lebanon	12 967	60	1	3	4	52	651	94	527	30	1
Lee's Summit	79 284	134	1	12	32	89	2 237	350	1 770	117	8
Leeton	631	1	0	0	0	1	15	2	13	0	0
Lexington	4 721	13	0	0	0	13	171	35	121	15	0
Liberal	816	0	0	0	0	0	0	0	0	0	0
Liberty	28 755	58	0	11	6	41	788	103	623	62	14
Licking	2 742	1	0	1	0	0	52	8	39	5	1
Lilbourn	1 272	4	0	0	3	1	16	13	3	0	0
Lincoln	1 092	2	0	0	0	2	32	11	20	1	0
Linn[3]	1 412	11	0	0	1	10	31	14	16	1	1
Linn Creek	291	2	0	0	0	2	9	2	7	0	0
Lockwood	968	0	0	0	0	0	7	2	5	0	0
Lone Jack	601	0	0	0	0	0	26	9	17	0	0
Louisiana	3 817	23	0	0	0	23	57	18	38	1	0
Macon	5 442	15	0	2	2	11	146	28	107	11	2
Malden	4 672	20	0	0	1	19	140	37	97	6	1
Manchester	19 210	9	0	0	4	5	281	31	239	11	0
Mansfield	1 345	4	0	0	0	4	20	6	13	1	0

[1]The FBI does not publish arson data unless it receives data from either the agency or the state for all 12 months of the calendar year.
[3]Because of changes in the state/local agency's reporting practices, figures are not comparable to previous years' data.
[9]After examining the data and making inquiries, the FBI determined that the agency's offense count was misclassified. Consequently, this figure is not included in this table.

Table 8. Offenses Known to Law Enforcement, by State and City, 2005—*Continued*

(Number.)

City	Population	Violent crime	Murder and non-negligent man-slaughter	Forcible rape	Robbery	Aggravated assault	Property crime	Burglary	Larceny-theft	Motor vehicle theft	Arson[1]
Maplewood	8 982	34	0	1	7	26	382	57	297	28	1
Marble Hill	1 525	11	0	0	0	11	32	7	25	0	0
Marionville	2 163	5	0	1	0	4	83	23	58	2	0
Marquand	256	0	0	0	0	0	1	1	0	0	0
Marshall	12 199	9	0	1	1	7	230	47	181	2	0
Marshfield	6 605	8	0	1	1	6	178	31	145	2	2
Marston	584	0	0	0	0	0	0	0	0	0	0
Marthasville	866	1	0	0	0	1	5	1	4	0	0
Martinsburg	330	1	0	1	0	0	7	4	3	0	0
Maryland Heights	25 609	29	0	0	13	16	1 005	107	800	98	3
Maryville	10 594	16	0	0	0	16	272	29	236	7	1
Matthews	566	4	0	0	1	3	13	7	6	0	0
Memphis	2 010	3	0	0	0	3	14	4	8	2	0
Merriam Woods	1 140	1	0	0	0	1	0	0	0	0	0
Mexico	11 052	17	0	2	6	9	267	50	209	8	2
Milan	1 878	6	0	0	0	6	38	12	25	1	1
Miller	791	0	0	0	0	0	6	3	2	1	0
Miner	1 248	8	0	0	0	8	69	12	55	2	2
Moberly	13 854	19	0	0	7	12	602	116	469	17	3
Moline Acres	2 596	27	0	1	7	19	131	38	75	18	1
Monett	8 202	3	0	0	0	3	435	103	310	22	1
Montgomery City	2 501	16	0	0	0	16	52	14	35	3	0
Montrose	435	0	0	0	0	0	3	2	1	0	0
Morehouse	988	3	0	0	0	3	14	4	9	1	1
Mosby	244	0	0	0	0	0	44	0	44	0	0
Mound City	1 122	0	0	0	0	0	17	3	14	0	0
Mountain Grove	4 591	2	0	0	0	2	142	28	112	2	2
Mountain View	2 520	12	0	1	0	11	145	23	102	20	1
Mount Vernon	4 334	22	0	3	0	19	213	23	181	9	2
Napoleon	207	2	0	0	0	2	4	0	0	4	0
Naylor	614	0	0	0	0	0	6	2	3	1	0
Neosho	11 048	10	0	1	0	9	505	84	398	23	2
Nevada	8 501	22	0	0	3	19	621	93	486	42	5
New Bloomfield	672	0	0	0	0	0	5	3	2	0	0
New Haven	1 947	3	0	1	0	2	19	4	11	4	0
New Madrid	3 213	3	0	2	0	1	61	13	48	0	0
New Melle	287	2	0	0	0	2	10	8	1	1	0
Nixa	14 733	17	0	1	1	15	273	42	216	15	0
Noel	1 488	19	0	2	0	17	34	12	19	3	1
Norborne	794	1	0	0	0	1	0	0	0	0	0
Normandy	5 125	47	1	1	6	39	231	50	134	47	0
North Kansas City	4 956	42	0	3	14	25	575	50	456	69	0
Northmoor	413	2	0	0	1	1	17	11	2	4	1
Northwoods	4 522	13	0	3	6	4	104	25	43	36	3
Oak Grove	6 707	6	0	2	2	2	177	37	126	14	2
Oakland	1 601	1	0	0	1	0	41	3	38	0	0
Oakview Village	389	1	0	0	1	0	6	4	1	1	0
Odessa	4 905	9	2	2	2	3	141	28	98	15	2
O'Fallon	67 541	59	1	6	9	43	1 827	187	1 587	53	2
Olivette	7 517	30	0	0	6	24	164	32	119	13	0
Olympian Village	686	0	0	0	0	0	2	0	2	0	0
Oran	1 259	3	0	0	0	3	8	4	4	0	0
Orrick	877	7	0	0	0	7	15	5	10	0	1
Osage Beach	4 115	29	0	2	3	24	458	56	389	13	0
Overland	16 401	51	1	8	16	26	740	95	586	59	1
Owensville	2 536	1	0	0	0	1	93	8	82	3	0
Ozark	14 572	9	0	0	1	8	416	51	347	18	0
Pacific	5 851	66	0	1	1	64	130	16	109	5	1
Pagedale	3 518	45	0	5	10	30	241	46	156	39	4
Palmyra	3 481	12	0	0	0	12	46	3	40	3	0
Park Hills	8 486	12	0	2	1	9	157	9	134	14	0
Parkville	5 073	7	0	2	3	2	193	22	160	11	0
Parma	829	2	0	0	0	2	22	10	8	4	1
Peculiar	3 610	6	1	0	1	4	186	32	146	8	0
Perry	657	2	0	0	0	2	5	3	2	0	0
Perryville	7 865	17	0	2	0	15	242	25	201	16	2
Pevely	4 158	10	0	1	0	9	132	19	107	6	0
Piedmont	1 982	4	0	2	0	2	47	8	36	3	0
Pierce City	1 433	3	0	2	0	1	34	16	17	1	0
Pilot Grove	743	0	0	0	0	0	16	0	16	0	0
Pilot Knob	675	0	0	0	0	0	8	4	3	1	0
Pineville	795	6	0	0	0	6	4	2	1	1	0
Platte City	4 952	4	0	1	0	3	87	16	65	6	0
Platte Woods	471	3	0	0	1	2	30	2	28	0	0
Plattsburg	2 489	2	0	1	0	1	38	9	28	1	2
Pleasant Hill	6 543	6	0	1	0	5	136	17	110	9	0
Pleasant Hope	570	0	0	0	0	0	4	1	3	0	0
Pleasant Valley	3 398	9	0	2	2	5	108	15	84	9	0
Polo	602	1	0	0	0	1	7	3	2	2	0
Poplar Bluff	16 810	84	6	6	26	46	1 313	186	1 056	71	12

[1]The FBI does not publish arson data unless it receives data from either the agency or the state for all 12 months of the calendar year.

Table 8. Offenses Known to Law Enforcement, by State and City, 2005—*Continued*

(Number.)

City	Population	Violent crime	Murder and non-negligent man-slaughter	Forcible rape	Robbery	Aggravated assault	Property crime	Burglary	Larceny-theft	Motor vehicle theft	Arson[1]
Portageville	3 166	8	0	2	0	6	30	12	18	0	1
Potosi	2 713	13	0	0	0	13	79	8	70	1	0
Puxico	1 157	1	0	0	0	1	9	3	3	3	0
Randolph	49	1	0	0	1	0	5	1	3	1	0
Raymore	14 528	9	0	1	4	4	392	46	334	12	0
Raytown	29 581	77	1	2	41	33	1 321	243	952	126	8
Reeds Spring	653	4	0	0	0	4	28	16	8	4	0
Republic	10 015	51	0	2	0	49	358	43	295	20	1
Richland	1 802	3	0	0	0	3	45	12	29	4	1
Richmond	6 091	22	0	3	2	17	249	50	193	6	2
Richmond Heights	9 450	41	0	2	15	24	561	46	487	28	1
Risco	377	2	0	0	0	2	1	0	1	0	0
Riverside	2 979	21	0	2	10	9	305	26	254	25	0
Riverview	3 054	31	0	0	6	25	123	38	51	34	0
Rockaway Beach	598	1	0	0	0	1	11	1	9	1	1
Rock Hill	4 755	3	0	0	1	2	101	19	75	7	0
Rogersville	2 099	9	0	2	1	6	66	14	52	0	0
Rolla	17 549	86	0	12	14	60	982	135	797	50	13
Salem	4 815	33	0	0	0	33	203	36	167	0	1
Salisbury	1 648	1	0	0	0	1	20	3	16	1	0
Savannah	4 925	2	0	0	0	2	57	9	43	5	0
Scott City	4 600	7	0	4	0	3	9	5	2	2	0
Sedalia	20 356	192	0	4	18	170	1 565	288	1 217	60	9
Seligman	901	0	0	0	0	0	3	1	2	0	0
Senath	1 645	0	0	0	0	0	0	0	0	0	0
Seneca	2 209	1	0	0	0	1	66	11	51	4	0
Seymour	1 936	1	0	0	0	1	66	15	46	5	0
Shelbina	1 894	1	0	0	0	1	26	13	12	1	0
Shrewsbury	6 510	3	0	1	0	2	134	18	107	9	0
Sikeston[3]	17 192	210	0	10	15	185	804	183	583	38	7
Silex	228	0	0	0	0	0	1	0	0	1	0
Slater	1 973	2	0	0	0	2	41	5	34	2	0
Smithville	6 658	6	0	1	0	5	78	10	58	10	1
Southwest City	903	7	0	1	0	6	28	15	12	1	0
Springfield	151 901	892	5	85	203	599	12 723	1 759	10 060	904	60
St. Ann	13 340	69	1	5	12	51	763	73	626	64	1
St. Charles[3]	61 899	146	1	10	21	114	1 996	267	1 593	136	7
St. Clair	4 461	27	0	3	1	23	293	46	232	15	1
St. George	1 261	3	0	1	0	2	13	2	9	2	0
St. James	4 028	24	1	0	0	23	194	36	149	9	0
St. John	6 688	22	0	3	4	15	253	25	205	23	4
St. Joseph[3]	73 205	216	2	22	60	132	4 204	763	3 079	362	18
St. Louis	346 005	8 323	131	276	2 965	4 951	38 245	7 213	22 886	8 146	535
St. Marys	382	4	0	0	0	4	13	4	9	0	1
St. Peters	54 335	92	0	11	11	70	1 264	108	1 116	40	2
St. Robert	3 041	34	2	4	8	20	243	25	205	13	1
Steele	2 203	3	1	0	0	2	71	20	49	2	0
Steelville	1 451	16	0	3	0	13	30	8	21	1	0
Stover	1 017	2	0	0	0	2	17	9	6	2	0
Strafford	1 936	8	0	0	1	7	119	5	110	4	0
Sturgeon	929	2	0	0	0	2	41	7	33	1	0
Sugar Creek	3 682	16	1	0	3	12	166	33	115	18	2
Sullivan	6 631	9	0	0	3	6	303	55	230	18	0
Summersville	553	5	0	0	0	5	32	16	11	5	2
Sunset Hills	8 444	26	0	1	2	23	335	39	269	27	0
Sweet Springs	1 565	5	0	1	0	4	(8)	(8)	(8)	1	0
Thayer	2 179	1	0	0	0	1	6	2	4	0	0
Theodosia	248	1	0	0	0	1	4	0	4	0	0
Tipton	3 162	0	0	0	0	0	30	5	23	2	0
Town and Country	10 937	21	2	0	2	17	112	6	104	2	1
Tracy	215	0	0	0	0	0	14	0	13	1	0
Trenton	6 081	11	0	2	3	6	217	47	166	4	0
Troy	9 022	32	0	0	0	32	397	34	347	16	0
Truesdale	477	0	0	0	0	0	12	2	8	2	0
Union	8 694	22	0	2	0	20	421	53	351	17	1
Unionville	1 961	4	0	0	0	4	9	3	6	0	0
University City	37 791	180	0	10	66	104	1 850	330	1 360	160	10
Van Buren	832	2	0	0	0	2	31	10	18	3	0
Vandalia	4 083	1	0	0	0	1	35	9	24	2	1
Velda City	1 572	4	0	0	0	4	33	9	15	9	1
Verona	724	2	0	0	0	2	6	3	3	0	0
Versailles	2 660	3	0	0	1	2	152	19	132	1	0
Viburnum	817	3	0	0	0	3	11	5	6	0	0
Vienna	630	0	0	0	0	0	11	3	7	1	0
Vinita Park	1 873	8	0	0	4	4	65	17	43	5	0
Walnut Grove	633	1	0	0	0	1	16	5	10	1	2
Wardell	267	0	0	0	0	0	6	1	4	1	0
Warrensburg	17 591	41	0	4	7	30	551	119	404	28	0
Warrenton	6 331	18	0	1	0	17	274	32	231	11	0
Warsaw	2 194	20	0	0	0	20	92	19	67	6	0

[1]The FBI does not publish arson data unless it receives data from either the agency or the state for all 12 months of the calendar year.
[3]Because of changes in the state/local agency's reporting practices, figures are not comparable to previous years' data.
[8]After examining the data and making inquiries, the FBI determined that the agency's offense count was underreported. Consequently, this figure is not included in this table.

Table 8. Offenses Known to Law Enforcement, by State and City, 2005—*Continued*

(Number.)

City	Population	Violent crime	Murder and non-negligent man-slaughter	Forcible rape	Robbery	Aggravated assault	Property crime	Burglary	Larceny-theft	Motor vehicle theft	Arson[1]
Warson Woods	1 933	0	0	0	0	0	23	0	23	0	0
Washburn	467	0	0	0	0	0	2	1	1	0	0
Washington	14 066	25	0	1	2	22	358	46	301	11	0
Waverly	817	2	0	0	0	2	6	2	3	1	0
Waynesville	3 533	18	0	2	4	12	84	16	59	9	0
Weatherby Lake	1 898	4	0	0	0	4	22	3	19	0	0
Webb City	10 637	27	0	5	1	21	347	37	287	23	1
Webster Groves	23 259	15	0	1	4	10	335	62	252	21	0
Wellington	793	0	0	0	0	0	0	0	0	0	1
Wellsville	1 409	2	0	0	0	2	21	3	16	2	0
Wentzville	14 717	30	1	7	5	17	447	34	392	21	0
Weston	1 665	1	0	0	0	1	35	1	32	2	0
West Plains	11 200	22	0	5	7	10	779	153	573	53	3
Westwood	296	0	0	0	0	0	1	0	1	0	0
Wheaton	733	0	0	0	0	0	0	0	0	0	0
Willard	3 314	38	0	0	0	38	29	7	20	2	0
Willow Springs	2 119	5	0	1	0	4	8	1	6	1	0
Winfield	830	2	0	0	0	2	6	2	3	1	2
Winona	1 325	2	0	0	0	2	7	7	0	0	2
Wood Heights	778	0	0	0	0	0	7	1	5	1	0
Woodson Terrace	4 171	15	0	4	8	3	177	39	111	27	0
Wright City	2 212	15	1	0	0	14	76	22	48	6	0
Montana[3]											
Belgrade	7 113	15	0	3	0	12	242	35	189	18	3
Billings	97 898	201	5	34	50	112	5 520	598	4 563	359	18
Boulder	1 411	10	0	1	0	9	24	2	18	4	0
Bozeman	32 722	71	0	17	10	44	1 577	207	1 249	121	7
Chinook	1 327	4	0	2	0	2	15	1	14	0	0
Colstrip	2 377	2	0	0	0	2	51	1	49	1	0
Columbia Falls	4 220	8	0	0	2	6	235	14	210	11	0
Columbus	1 900	5	0	1	0	4	82	7	73	2	0
Conrad	2 663	2	0	0	0	2	25	3	22	0	0
Cut Bank	3 185	50	1	0	0	49	154	19	132	3	0
Dillon	4 048	16	0	3	0	13	90	6	78	6	0
Fort Benton	1 520	0	0	0	0	0	45	7	37	1	0
Glasgow	3 113	11	0	4	0	7	72	10	55	7	0
Glendive	4 702	11	0	0	0	11	135	8	122	5	1
Great Falls	57 040	171	2	20	25	124	3 394	297	2 959	138	25
Helena	27 454	99	2	14	10	73	1 046	119	862	65	3
Kalispell	17 546	70	0	9	6	55	1 009	85	864	60	6
Laurel	6 399	14	0	1	1	12	229	28	196	5	2
Lewistown	6 174	22	0	13	0	9	107	7	99	1	3
Libby	2 678	51	0	0	1	50	143	13	125	5	0
Livingston	7 129	25	0	2	0	23	196	35	141	20	0
Manhattan	1 498	1	0	0	0	1	45	2	41	2	0
Missoula	62 377	254	1	40	40	173	3 629	395	3 046	188	13
Plains	1 249	4	0	0	1	3	13	4	9	0	0
Red Lodge	2 350	13	0	1	0	12	69	13	51	5	2
Ronan City	1 968	31	0	3	0	28	90	13	61	16	1
Stevensville	1 846	9	0	1	0	8	30	6	22	2	0
St. Ignatius	820	2	0	0	0	2	30	4	23	3	0
Thompson Falls	1 392	8	0	0	0	8	43	4	35	4	1
Three Forks	1 892	3	0	0	0	3	38	4	27	7	2
Troy	985	4	0	0	0	4	61	2	56	3	0
West Yellowstone	1 246	3	0	0	0	3	43	3	32	8	0
Whitefish	6 209	24	0	3	0	21	266	19	228	19	0
Nebraska											
Alliance	8 406	26	0	0	1	25	135	32	91	12	6
Ashland	2 460	1	0	0	0	1	18	1	16	1	0
Auburn	3 124	0	0	0	0	0	106	17	82	7	1
Bayard	1 188	0	0	0	0	0	25	1	20	4	0
Beatrice	13 049	43	1	8	4	30	719	106	590	23	5
Bellevue	47 661	57	1	10	10	36	1 481	152	1 188	141	7
Blair	7 757	6	0	4	0	2	158	20	123	15	1
Bridgeport	1 526	0	0	0	0	0	5	0	5	0	0
Broken Bow	3 372	2	0	2	0	0	61	8	52	1	0
Central City	2 938	2	0	0	0	2	86	6	73	7	1
Chadron	5 438	7	0	3	0	4	66	8	50	8	0
Columbus	21 019	11	0	4	5	2	577	97	463	17	0
Cozad	4 235	7	0	5	1	1	129	8	119	2	0
Crete	6 374	11	0	1	2	8	227	25	196	6	1
David City	2 598	2	0	0	0	2	43	9	34	0	1
Elkhorn	8 093	1	0	0	0	1	96	13	81	2	1
Falls City	4 324	4	0	3	0	1	87	14	67	6	0
Fremont	25 439	34	0	12	2	20	832	122	676	34	9
Gering	7 791	11	1	0	1	9	201	31	152	18	2
Gothenburg	3 705	3	0	1	0	2	109	12	93	4	1
Grand Island	44 580	99	1	17	13	68	2 545	384	2 057	104	4
Hastings	23 559	50	0	20	4	26	882	164	697	21	6
Holdrege	5 517	8	0	5	0	3	157	17	128	12	1
Imperial	1 934	1	0	0	0	1	11	6	5	0	0
Kearney	28 830	57	0	13	4	40	876	127	722	27	5
La Vista	14 782	19	0	3	3	13	384	41	317	26	7
Lexington	10 123	18	0	5	1	12	491	110	362	19	1
Lincoln	237 710	1 364	4	112	225	1 023	12 703	1 893	10 388	422	20
Lyons	921	0	0	0	0	0	4	2	2	0	0
Madison	2 351	6	0	0	0	6	29	3	23	3	0

[1]The FBI does not publish arson data unless it receives data from either the agency or the state for all 12 months of the calendar year.
[3]Because of changes in the state/local agency's reporting practices, figures are not comparable to previous years' data.

Table 8. Offenses Known to Law Enforcement, by State and City, 2005—*Continued*

(Number.)

City	Population	Violent crime	Murder and non-negligent man-slaughter	Forcible rape	Robbery	Aggravated assault	Property crime	Burglary	Larceny-theft	Motor vehicle theft	Arson[1]
McCook	7 793	7	0	4	0	3	273	26	238	9	4
Milford	2 078	0	0	0	0	0	24	2	22	0	0
Minden	2 985	1	0	0	0	1	60	6	54	0	0
Mitchell	1 808	1	0	0	0	1	22	1	18	3	0
Nebraska City	7 114	8	0	2	0	6	250	35	209	6	0
Norfolk	24 231	25	0	11	7	7	931	141	760	30	1
North Platte	24 103	109	1	4	7	97	1 594	242	1 297	55	3
Ogallala	4 759	1	0	0	0	1	207	13	189	5	0
Omaha	412 128	2 327	31	199	682	1 415	22 056	3 164	15 079	3 813	138
O'Neill	3 536	3	0	0	0	3	51	11	38	2	0
Ord	2 202	2	0	0	0	2	8	0	6	2	1
Papillion	19 626	20	0	5	1	14	318	49	256	13	5
Plainview	1 313	2	0	1	0	1	22	4	15	3	0
Plattsmouth	7 122	10	0	6	0	4	128	21	94	13	0
Ralston	6 261	12	0	0	2	10	171	38	117	16	1
Schuyler	5 400	5	0	2	0	3	97	13	83	1	0
Scottsbluff	14 865	39	0	5	4	30	944	140	775	29	1
Seward	6 708	0	0	0	0	0	94	6	83	5	0
Sidney	6 423	8	0	1	3	4	201	27	165	9	0
South Sioux City	12 222	16	0	0	4	12	239	66	159	14	0
St. Paul	2 291	0	0	0	0	0	19	4	15	0	0
Superior	1 943	2	0	1	0	1	2	1	1	0	0
Valley	1 841	3	0	1	0	2	38	3	33	2	0
Wahoo	4 062	3	0	0	0	3	68	7	58	3	0
West Point	3 532	0	0	0	0	0	22	0	20	2	0
Wymore	1 640	2	0	1	0	1	34	7	27	0	0
York	7 848	1	0	1	0	0	214	9	198	7	0
Nevada											
Boulder City	15 769	19	1	2	2	14	309	124	138	47	2
Carlin	2 140	23	0	1	0	22	57	32	24	1	0
Elko	16 786	36	1	16	7	12	597	118	438	41	8
Fallon	8 232	27	2	0	4	21	543	61	453	29	0
Henderson	232 536	432	9	40	133	250	6 654	1 556	3 645	1 453	98
Las Vegas Metropolitan Police Department	1 281 698	9 530	145	616	3 494	5 275	62 013	14 368	27 695	19 950	441
Lovelock	1 961	10	0	2	0	8	51	18	29	4	0
Mesquite	13 064	28	0	1	4	23	358	18	287	53	0
North Las Vegas	164 190	1 356	20	56	408	872	7 581	1 866	3 249	2 466	42
Reno	204 749	1 518	8	110	421	979	10 989	1 916	7 547	1 526	. . .
Sparks	83 791	359	5	56	96	202	3 235	740	2 045	450	8
West Wendover	5 090	34	0	8	5	21	222	51	155	16	7
Winnemucca	7 853	22	1	2	4	15	164	41	99	24	0
Yerington	3 408	2	0	1	0	1	52	27	23	2	0
New Hampshire											
Alton	5 002	8	0	0	2	6	36	13	21	2	2
Amherst	11 659	7	0	1	3	3	309	26	280	3	5
Antrim	2 566	4	0	1	1	2	26	7	18	1	1
Ashland	2 003	3	0	1	0	2	45	6	37	2	0
Auburn	5 077	3	0	0	0	3	45	14	28	3	1
Barrington	8 136	3	0	1	0	2	88	23	61	4	3
Bartlett	2 907	3	1	0	1	1	41	6	33	2	0
Bedford	20 645	19	0	0	10	9	222	45	170	7	5
Belmont	7 288	6	0	1	1	4	134	35	92	7	3
Bennington	1 462	4	0	1	0	3	45	4	40	1	1
Berlin	10 568	14	0	2	3	9	140	39	96	5	5
Bethlehem	2 351	2	0	1	0	1	30	12	18	0	2
Boscawen	3 844	4	0	3	0	1	22	13	5	4	1
Bow	8 025	3	1	0	1	1	78	11	65	2	1
Brentwood	3 716	2	1	0	0	1	19	9	8	2	0
Bristol	3 118	2	0	1	0	1	63	10	48	5	0
Campton	2 864	2	0	0	0	2	66	28	36	2	1
Candia	4 176	1	0	0	0	1	36	9	26	1	0
Carroll	731	2	0	1	0	1	35	2	32	1	0
Charlestown	4 969	12	0	3	0	9	24	6	13	5	0
Chester	4 602	2	0	0	0	2	38	9	24	5	1
Claremont	13 451	28	0	7	1	20	366	49	290	27	5
Colebrook	2 396	1	1	0	0	0	23	10	12	1	0
Concord	42 685	69	0	18	16	35	949	160	747	42	14
Conway	9 166	13	0	2	3	8	372	46	308	18	2
Danville	4 362	6	0	1	0	5	33	5	23	5	0
Deerfield	4 051	6	0	3	0	3	37	4	31	2	1
Deering	2 001	4	0	2	0	2	20	5	13	2	0
Derry	34 647	62	0	12	6	44	739	149	541	49	31
Dover	28 724	29	1	8	5	15	492	44	432	16	5
Dublin	1 564	0	0	0	0	0	9	2	7	0	1
Dunbarton	2 504	2	0	1	0	1	18	4	10	4	0
Enfield	4 839	5	0	0	0	5	44	5	39	0	0
Epping	6 071	5	1	1	0	3	107	28	71	8	1
Epsom	4 457	1	0	0	0	1	64	6	54	4	3
Exeter	14 827	7	1	4	1	1	174	43	124	7	1
Farmington	6 347	15	0	4	2	9	184	45	130	9	3
Fitzwilliam	2 296	0	0	0	0	0	13	5	5	3	1
Franconia	998	3	0	0	0	3	21	4	15	2	0
Freedom	1 429	2	0	0	0	2	11	4	5	2	0

[1]The FBI does not publish arson data unless it receives data from either the agency or the state for all 12 months of the calendar year.
. . . = Not available.

Table 8. Offenses Known to Law Enforcement, by State and City, 2005—*Continued*

(Number.)

City	Population	Violent crime	Murder and non-negligent man-slaughter	Forcible rape	Robbery	Aggravated assault	Property crime	Burglary	Larceny-theft	Motor vehicle theft	Arson[1]
Fremont	3 906	4	0	0	0	4	20	5	11	4	3
Gilford	7 496	7	0	0	0	7	122	10	105	7	0
Gilmanton	3 483	6	0	0	0	6	20	9	7	4	0
Goffstown	17 677	18	1	3	2	12	361	50	301	10	4
Gorham	2 941	0	0	0	0	0	37	10	25	2	0
Grantham	2 462	1	1	0	0	0	0	0	0	0	0
Greenland	3 417	6	0	2	1	3	44	13	30	1	0
Hampstead	8 770	0	0	0	0	0	82	13	65	4	1
Hampton	15 486	32	0	8	14	10	368	56	284	28	3
Hancock	1 816	0	0	0	0	0	6	1	3	2	0
Hanover	11 213	1	0	1	0	0	192	7	183	2	0
Haverhill	4 531	15	1	6	0	8	35	21	11	3	0
Henniker	4 856	2	0	1	0	1	135	11	122	2	1
Hinsdale	4 253	4	0	0	0	4	70	10	55	5	4
Hooksett	13 169	18	0	9	2	7	281	35	230	16	2
Hopkinton	5 647	2	0	1	0	1	31	6	23	2	0
Hudson	24 505	23	0	4	4	15	370	57	275	38	5
Jaffrey	5 779	9	0	3	2	4	58	20	33	5	0
Keene	23 139	42	0	4	16	22	359	100	235	24	6
Kingston	6 266	6	0	0	1	5	46	12	30	4	0
Laconia	17 271	51	0	10	6	35	674	98	547	29	7
Lancaster	3 365	6	0	0	0	6	53	11	39	3	0
Lebanon	12 757	24	0	8	0	16	407	38	365	4	4
Lee	4 434	1	0	0	1	0	70	15	49	6	1
Lincoln	1 290	1	0	0	0	1	101	3	98	0	1
Lisbon	1 647	2	0	0	0	2	26	10	15	1	0
Litchfield	8 195	4	0	1	0	3	60	12	42	6	1
Littleton	6 165	9	0	1	1	7	113	32	75	6	0
Londonderry	24 602	19	0	4	6	9	244	55	163	26	6
Loudon	5 037	2	0	2	0	0	86	9	71	6	0
Madison	2 223	2	0	0	0	2	13	9	4	0	0
Manchester	110 188	308	4	73	140	91	3 518	693	2 570	255	68
Meredith	6 545	5	0	2	1	2	185	27	150	8	1
Merrimack	26 791	2	0	0	1	1	252	31	210	11	0
Middleton	1 622	4	0	0	0	4	20	0	18	2	0
Milford	14 675	20	0	3	4	13	218	48	158	12	1
Milton	4 333	5	0	1	0	4	42	14	25	3	0
Mont Vernon	2 322	0	0	0	0	0	11	1	9	1	0
Moultonborough	4 931	2	0	0	0	2	56	12	40	4	1
Nashua	88 113	164	2	20	28	114	2 061	300	1 622	131	47
New Boston	4 815	2	0	1	0	1	22	9	9	4	0
New Durham	2 437	1	0	0	0	1	36	6	28	2	0
Newfields	1 610	0	0	0	0	0	14	0	13	1	0
New Hampton	2 202	5	0	3	0	2	15	3	10	2	0
Newington	803	3	0	0	1	2	190	5	183	2	1
New Ipswich	5 016	1	0	0	1	0	50	3	41	6	2
Newmarket	8 951	17	0	6	2	9	33	9	22	2	1
Newport	6 524	18	0	2	3	13	264	42	211	11	4
Newton	4 500	5	0	1	0	4	34	9	24	1	1
Northfield	4 962	6	0	1	1	4	81	14	55	12	0
Northumberland	2 431	4	0	0	0	4	24	6	15	3	1
Northwood	3 921	3	0	1	0	2	20	7	12	1	0
Nottingham	4 202	0	0	0	0	0	34	3	29	2	0
Ossipee	4 559	1	0	0	1	0	90	24	56	10	0
Pelham	12 409	10	0	3	1	6	178	36	127	15	7
Pembroke	7 318	3	0	0	1	2	102	30	65	7	7
Peterborough	6 118	4	0	2	1	1	99	13	85	1	1
Pittsfield	4 354	7	0	0	0	7	95	11	79	5	0
Plaistow	7 872	3	0	0	1	2	165	24	128	13	0
Plymouth	6 275	15	0	3	4	8	250	68	179	3	2
Portsmouth	20 953	32	0	8	7	17	572	61	483	28	3
Raymond	10 108	23	0	6	2	15	128	18	98	12	3
Rindge	6 186	5	0	1	1	3	76	23	48	5	0
Rochester	29 996	75	0	43	10	22	916	96	789	31	7
Rollinsford	2 669	3	0	0	1	2	7	1	5	1	1
Rye	5 290	2	0	1	0	1	42	13	29	0	1
Sandown	5 686	4	0	1	0	3	21	4	15	2	1
Sandwich	1 350	0	0	0	0	0	34	8	26	0	0
Seabrook	8 443	12	0	1	3	8	203	31	158	14	2
Strafford	3 985	1	0	1	0	0	13	3	9	1	1
Stratham	6 947	1	0	0	1	0	39	6	33	0	0
Sugar Hill	591	0	0	0	0	0	4	3	1	0	0
Thornton	1 965	2	0	0	0	2	13	2	11	0	1
Tilton	3 634	10	0	1	1	8	117	14	94	9	0
Troy	2 067	0	0	0	0	0	34	13	18	3	0
Wakefield	5 298	6	0	2	0	4	102	20	80	2	1
Walpole	3 734	3	0	0	0	3	19	6	9	4	0
Warner	2 973	1	0	1	0	0	25	2	22	1	0
Waterville Valley	270	0	0	0	0	0	51	2	49	0	0
Weare	8 611	1	0	0	1	0	30	7	20	3	0
Webster	1 791	2	0	1	0	1	20	6	6	8	0
Wilton	3 872	5	0	2	0	3	62	21	40	1	2
Windham	12 552	6	0	2	2	2	147	23	115	9	1
Wolfeboro	6 625	8	0	3	0	5	59	19	32	8	2
Woodstock	1 174	2	0	0	0	2	18	6	11	1	1

[1]The FBI does not publish arson data unless it receives data from either the agency or the state for all 12 months of the calendar year.

Table 8. Offenses Known to Law Enforcement, by State and City, 2005—*Continued*

(Number.)

City	Population	Violent crime	Murder and non-negligent man-slaughter	Forcible rape	Robbery	Aggravated assault	Property crime	Burglary	Larceny-theft	Motor vehicle theft	Arson[1]
New Jersey											
Aberdeen Township	18 507	23	0	2	4	17	234	33	185	16	2
Absecon	7 922	38	0	1	10	27	342	61	253	28	0
Allendale	6 814	0	0	0	0	0	59	6	52	1	2
Allenhurst	716	2	0	1	0	1	22	1	21	0	0
Allentown	1 879	0	0	0	0	0	15	1	13	1	0
Alpha	2 485	9	0	0	0	9	40	7	31	2	0
Alpine	2 345	1	0	0	0	1	14	8	5	1	0
Andover Township	6 500	1	0	0	0	1	79	5	68	6	0
Asbury Park	16 856	346	3	10	148	185	967	288	547	132	4
Atlantic City	40 669	753	9	44	374	326	4 514	522	3 838	154	15
Atlantic Highlands	4 695	6	0	0	0	6	72	14	57	1	1
Audubon	9 090	12	0	0	4	8	227	32	190	5	2
Audubon Park	1 087	1	0	0	0	1	14	5	9	0	0
Avalon	2 169	2	0	0	0	2	215	31	183	1	0
Avon-by-the-Sea	2 236	3	0	0	2	1	60	13	47	0	1
Barnegat Light	817	1	0	1	0	0	21	1	20	0	0
Barnegat Township	19 219	41	0	1	4	36	206	55	149	2	3
Barrington	7 051	11	0	0	0	11	81	24	50	7	0
Bay Head	1 267	0	0	0	0	0	46	6	38	2	0
Bayonne	60 881	220	2	7	79	132	933	191	602	140	1
Beach Haven	1 328	4	0	0	0	4	128	8	119	1	0
Beachwood	10 764	16	0	0	5	11	194	30	155	9	2
Bedminster Township	8 410	1	0	0	0	1	68	14	52	2	0
Belleville	35 477	125	1	7	48	69	926	164	500	262	4
Bellmawr	11 208	11	0	0	6	5	251	55	177	19	0
Belmar	6 046	29	0	0	5	24	404	77	314	13	1
Belvidere	2 767	4	0	0	0	4	9	3	5	1	0
Bergenfield	26 267	20	0	0	12	8	192	22	153	17	1
Berkeley Heights Township	13 649	4	0	0	0	4	61	4	51	6	1
Berkeley Township	42 620	62	0	2	12	48	703	143	535	25	14
Berlin	7 612	5	0	0	4	1	193	25	157	11	1
Berlin Township	5 384	21	1	6	4	10	211	22	178	11	2
Bernards Township	26 963	1	0	0	0	1	163	34	123	6	2
Bernardsville	7 614	1	0	0	0	1	73	15	57	1	0
Beverly	2 695	13	0	2	3	8	54	20	28	6	0
Blairstown Township	6 013	2	0	0	0	2	32	6	26	0	0
Bloomfield	46 895	133	0	3	84	46	1 645	226	993	426	8
Bloomingdale	7 716	3	0	0	0	3	47	6	39	2	0
Bogota	8 226	7	0	0	3	4	90	20	57	13	0
Boonton	8 487	11	0	0	2	9	86	18	64	4	2
Boonton Township	4 369	4	0	1	0	3	28	7	20	1	0
Bordentown	4 019	4	0	2	1	1	67	11	50	6	0
Bordentown Township	9 995	15	0	1	8	6	167	31	120	16	0
Bound Brook	10 196	27	0	3	13	11	223	54	150	19	0
Bradley Beach	4 815	11	0	0	5	6	220	76	141	3	1
Branchburg Township	14 976	1	0	0	0	1	120	30	84	6	0
Brick Township	78 646	44	0	0	6	38	1 336	192	1 099	45	2
Bridgeton	22 777	322	5	18	125	174	973	227	671	75	2
Bridgewater Township	44 467	19	0	2	6	11	593	85	477	31	6
Brielle	4 924	6	0	0	1	5	47	15	28	4	0
Brigantine	12 797	12	1	1	4	6	204	30	166	8	1
Brooklawn	2 330	27	0	4	15	8	177	14	150	13	0
Buena	3 870	25	0	4	0	21	135	43	90	2	0
Burlington	9 855	48	0	4	16	28	161	40	93	28	1
Burlington Township	22 042	21	0	4	14	3	448	52	363	33	2
Butler	8 136	5	0	2	0	3	100	43	56	1	3
Byram Township	8 681	1	0	0	0	1	96	10	84	2	1
Caldwell	7 611	1	0	0	1	0	69	23	43	3	0
Califon	1 058	1	0	0	0	1	8	1	7	0	0
Camden	80 125	1 680	33	47	702	898	4 307	1 020	2 332	955	142
Cape May	3 864	4	0	0	0	4	210	21	187	2	1
Cape May Point	240	0	0	0	0	0	16	8	8	0	0
Carlstadt	6 032	8	0	0	3	5	200	19	149	32	0
Carney's Point Township	7 829	23	1	0	6	16	189	47	130	12	1
Carteret	21 570	56	1	7	20	28	375	61	256	58	4
Cedar Grove Township	12 593	11	0	2	1	8	178	24	143	11	0
Chatham	8 446	3	0	1	0	2	72	16	46	10	0
Chatham Township	10 184	2	0	1	0	1	37	3	31	3	1
Cherry Hill Township	72 086	100	1	5	46	48	2 030	265	1 656	109	0
Chesilhurst	1 815	7	0	0	3	4	37	10	24	3	0
Chester	1 659	0	0	0	0	0	21	2	19	0	0
Chesterfield Township	6 123	0	0	0	0	0	28	4	24	0	0
Chester Township	7 782	1	0	0	0	1	48	2	46	0	0
Cinnaminson Township	15 162	32	0	2	12	18	299	44	228	27	2
Clark Township	14 741	3	0	0	1	2	215	13	187	15	0
Clayton	7 440	25	0	2	12	11	234	44	172	18	0
Clementon	4 963	41	0	2	13	26	231	49	152	30	3
Cliffside Park	23 062	27	0	0	4	23	233	47	173	13	0
Clifton	80 119	169	2	9	85	73	1 889	305	1 285	299	3
Clinton	2 645	2	0	1	1	0	20	4	15	1	0

[1]The FBI does not publish arson data unless it receives data from either the agency or the state for all 12 months of the calendar year.

Table 8. Offenses Known to Law Enforcement, by State and City, 2005—*Continued*

(Number.)

City	Population	Violent crime	Murder and non-negligent man-slaughter	Forcible rape	Robbery	Aggravated assault	Property crime	Burglary	Larceny-theft	Motor vehicle theft	Arson[1]
Clinton Township	13 892	4	0	0	0	4	64	12	47	5	1
Closter	8 642	1	0	0	0	1	62	13	46	3	0
Collingswood	14 169	29	0	1	7	21	415	110	273	32	2
Colts Neck Township	11 727	9	0	0	0	9	123	19	102	2	1
Cranbury Township	2 730	1	0	0	0	1	50	13	23	14	0
Cranford Township	22 667	13	0	2	4	7	318	45	256	17	0
Cresskill	8 230	1	0	0	0	1	54	4	50	0	2
Deal	1 057	2	0	0	1	1	33	6	27	0	0
Delanco Township	3 709	4	0	0	1	3	59	12	42	5	0
Delaware Township	4 711	0	0	0	0	0	32	13	17	2	0
Delran Township	17 347	39	0	2	18	19	254	46	198	10	3
Demarest	4 949	1	0	0	0	1	41	3	38	0	0
Denville Township	16 223	6	0	1	1	4	199	28	159	12	1
Deptford Township	29 006	98	1	1	30	66	1 368	230	1 062	76	12
Dover	18 503	62	0	4	25	33	441	163	248	30	0
Dover Township	94 527	133	2	9	42	80	1 849	316	1 461	72	12
Dumont	17 609	7	0	0	1	6	149	15	133	1	0
Dunellen	7 010	20	0	0	6	14	141	19	109	13	0
Eastampton Township	6 760	11	0	2	1	8	100	12	78	10	0
East Brunswick Township	48 423	51	0	7	12	32	817	112	664	41	6
East Greenwich Township	6 127	10	0	1	2	7	84	17	60	7	1
East Hanover Township	11 560	10	0	0	2	8	230	15	197	18	1
East Newark	2 312	7	0	0	1	6	31	4	11	16	0
East Orange	69 081	1 061	14	31	551	465	3 503	876	1 637	990	41
East Rutherford	8 773	10	0	0	2	8	313	42	216	55	0
East Windsor Township	26 931	32	0	3	9	20	356	63	266	27	4
Eatontown	14 170	23	0	4	8	11	522	32	473	17	2
Edgewater	9 378	8	0	0	4	4	158	16	125	17	0
Edgewater Park Township	8 087	16	0	3	6	7	202	26	152	24	0
Edison Township	100 361	231	0	6	71	154	2 456	470	1 715	271	18
Egg Harbor City	4 510	15	1	0	5	9	92	19	70	3	0
Egg Harbor Township	36 958	71	3	2	27	39	1 164	230	889	45	20
Elizabeth	124 997	823	17	18	541	247	4 996	647	2 903	1 446	5
Elk Township	3 687	3	0	0	0	3	71	17	45	9	5
Elmer	1 374	0	0	0	0	0	14	4	10	0	0
Elmwood Park	19 047	25	1	0	10	14	395	62	282	51	0
Elsinboro Township	1 079	0	0	0	0	0	21	8	12	1	0
Emerson	7 355	4	0	0	2	2	50	10	38	2	0
Englewood	26 411	74	1	5	26	42	577	141	368	68	1
Englewood Cliffs	5 667	2	0	1	0	1	92	17	71	4	0
Englishtown	1 818	1	0	0	0	1	18	0	18	0	1
Essex Fells	2 135	1	0	0	0	1	15	5	10	0	0
Evesham Township	46 961	47	1	9	8	29	648	98	528	22	10
Ewing Township	37 138	121	1	9	52	59	910	165	670	75	9
Fairfield Township	7 844	16	0	0	2	14	309	34	255	20	0
Fair Haven	5 974	0	0	0	0	0	47	5	42	0	0
Fair Lawn	31 682	35	0	2	19	14	363	48	290	25	2
Fairview	13 591	57	0	3	28	26	278	127	133	18	8
Fanwood	7 271	5	1	0	2	2	82	17	54	11	1
Far Hills	921	0	0	0	0	0	10	4	5	1	0
Flemington	4 215	5	0	0	0	5	122	18	96	8	0
Florence Township	11 287	10	1	1	0	8	127	43	71	13	2
Florham Park	12 583	1	0	0	0	1	113	12	97	4	2
Fort Lee	37 392	25	0	1	12	12	373	67	273	33	2
Franklin	5 244	2	0	0	0	2	116	13	99	4	0
Franklin Lakes	11 285	1	0	0	0	1	109	17	91	1	1
Franklin Township (Gloucester County)	16 414	22	1	2	7	12	329	119	190	20	4
Franklin Township (Hunterdon County)	3 140	1	0	0	0	1	32	5	24	3	0
Franklin Township (Somerset County)	56 988	93	1	9	44	39	861	218	573	70	14
Freehold	11 552	30	0	0	11	19	310	59	234	17	3
Freehold Township	33 927	56	0	18	12	26	979	89	854	36	2
Frenchtown	1 515	1	1	0	0	0	22	4	18	0	0
Galloway Township	35 135	82	0	5	26	51	692	173	487	32	5
Garfield	29 898	73	1	0	40	32	592	140	381	71	0
Garwood	4 175	4	0	2	1	1	61	10	48	3	0
Gibbsboro	2 478	3	0	0	1	2	46	15	29	2	1
Glassboro	19 219	67	0	12	30	25	722	152	540	30	4
Glen Ridge	7 139	16	1	2	2	11	244	46	163	35	3
Glen Rock	11 550	2	0	1	0	1	59	8	51	0	0
Gloucester City	11 633	27	1	5	9	12	267	49	195	23	0
Gloucester Township	66 431	195	0	18	52	125	1 580	355	1 112	113	12
Green Brook Township	6 688	7	0	1	2	4	148	23	115	10	1
Greenwich Township (Gloucester County)	5 005	5	0	1	0	4	135	33	97	5	0
Greenwich Township (Warren County)	5 234	3	0	1	1	1	93	8	84	1	1
Guttenberg	11 035	57	0	0	25	32	180	72	87	21	2
Hackensack	43 777	134	0	5	39	90	1 060	59	874	127	0
Hackettstown	9 359	9	0	1	1	7	133	11	115	7	0
Haddonfield	11 621	9	0	0	0	9	237	39	197	1	4
Haddon Heights	7 469	3	0	1	0	2	117	13	101	3	0
Haddon Township	14 624	24	0	0	12	12	291	42	237	12	4

[1]The FBI does not publish arson data unless it receives data from either the agency or the state for all 12 months of the calendar year.

Table 8. Offenses Known to Law Enforcement, by State and City, 2005—*Continued*

(Number.)

City	Population	Violent crime	Murder and non-negligent man-slaughter	Forcible rape	Robbery	Aggravated assault	Property crime	Burglary	Larceny-theft	Motor vehicle theft	Arson[1]
Haledon	8 458	12	0	0	6	6	113	36	56	21	1
Hamburg	3 536	1	0	0	0	1	38	9	29	0	0
Hamilton Township (Atlantic County)	23 751	77	1	7	18	51	1 036	124	857	55	18
Hamilton Township (Mercer County)	90 255	170	2	9	92	67	1 688	387	1 122	179	3
Hammonton	13 309	32	0	1	8	23	236	62	161	13	3
Hanover Township	13 586	7	0	0	2	5	176	27	137	12	1
Harding Township	3 299	0	0	0	0	0	28	2	26	0	1
Hardyston Township	7 608	2	0	1	0	1	77	19	52	6	0
Harrington Park	4 906	0	0	0	0	0	22	2	20	0	0
Harrison	14 195	67	1	1	29	36	384	56	225	103	1
Harrison Township	10 927	10	0	0	0	10	234	35	195	4	5
Harvey Cedars	381	0	0	0	0	0	15	2	13	0	0
Hasbrouck Heights	11 705	4	0	0	4	0	190	22	148	20	1
Haworth	3 426	1	0	0	0	1	3	1	2	0	0
Hawthorne	18 418	10	0	0	1	9	279	54	207	18	0
Hazlet Township	21 272	7	0	0	3	4	235	30	187	18	2
Helmetta	2 027	3	0	0	0	3	6	1	3	2	0
High Bridge	3 801	1	0	1	0	0	40	15	21	4	1
Highland Park	14 203	15	1	1	9	4	207	30	172	5	2
Highlands	5 083	8	1	1	1	5	86	14	70	2	0
Hightstown	5 338	14	0	0	6	8	98	17	79	2	2
Hillsborough Township	37 934	18	0	1	4	13	350	60	274	16	9
Hillsdale	10 160	2	0	0	0	2	57	7	50	0	0
Hillside Township	21 939	108	0	11	62	35	791	152	468	171	4
Hi-Nella	1 021	6	0	0	1	5	37	11	23	3	0
Hoboken	40 263	114	1	2	54	57	1 370	390	815	165	5
Ho-Ho-Kus	4 104	1	0	0	0	1	30	5	25	0	0
Holland Township	5 320	1	0	0	0	1	18	7	11	0	0
Holmdel Township	16 993	6	1	0	2	3	218	29	187	2	1
Hopatcong	16 070	7	0	2	0	5	129	26	98	5	1
Hopewell	2 055	0	0	0	0	0	26	7	18	1	0
Hopewell Township	17 620	14	0	3	0	11	93	19	67	7	0
Howell Township	50 430	46	1	6	5	34	621	116	467	38	4
Independence Township	5 809	2	0	0	0	2	51	10	40	1	0
Interlaken	897	0	0	0	0	0	9	6	3	0	0
Irvington	59 820	1 393	28	23	726	616	3 307	1 018	1 249	1 040	3
Island Heights	1 853	0	0	0	0	0	17	2	10	5	1
Jackson Township	51 720	43	0	6	11	26	532	122	372	38	8
Jamesburg	6 538	11	0	2	1	8	53	13	36	4	0
Jefferson Township	21 327	22	0	3	0	19	261	77	181	3	2
Jersey City	239 603	3 136	38	43	1 642	1 413	8 729	2 216	4 658	1 855	73
Keansburg	10 763	40	0	4	7	29	269	40	212	17	1
Kearny	39 582	113	0	6	39	68	1 068	151	653	264	10
Kenilworth	7 781	5	0	0	2	3	157	7	129	21	0
Keyport	7 587	12	0	3	4	5	131	15	106	10	3
Kinnelon	9 563	2	0	0	0	2	73	22	48	3	0
Lacey Township	26 278	18	0	0	3	15	493	58	422	13	1
Lake Como	1 800	2	0	0	1	1	34	9	24	1	0
Lakehurst	2 696	9	0	3	2	4	35	2	27	6	0
Lakewood Township	66 807	164	0	13	81	70	1 471	345	1 004	122	20
Lambertville	3 880	8	0	0	0	8	81	5	73	3	1
Laurel Springs	1 951	17	1	2	2	12	54	12	37	5	0
Lavallette	2 749	0	0	0	0	0	29	2	27	0	0
Lawnside	2 754	16	0	0	8	8	109	7	96	6	0
Lawrence Township	31 460	57	0	2	18	37	1 062	117	889	56	3
Lebanon Township	6 297	3	0	1	1	1	84	11	69	4	0
Leonia	8 931	9	0	0	1	8	72	18	48	6	0
Lincoln Park	10 918	5	0	1	0	4	125	28	93	4	2
Linden	40 092	104	0	2	60	42	1 465	172	924	369	3
Lindenwold	17 335	124	2	8	48	66	622	251	308	63	5
Linwood	7 431	4	0	0	0	4	106	39	64	3	0
Little Egg Harbor Township	19 376	27	0	2	0	25	431	74	345	12	2
Little Falls Township	11 972	26	0	6	3	17	334	53	252	29	0
Little Ferry	10 864	10	0	2	3	5	95	8	67	20	1
Little Silver	6 205	2	0	1	0	1	88	9	78	1	0
Livingston Township	27 922	15	0	1	3	11	583	46	504	33	2
Loch Arbour	280	2	0	0	0	2	8	2	6	0	0
Lodi	24 389	52	2	0	20	30	396	78	251	67	1
Logan Township	6 120	5	0	2	1	2	107	19	82	6	0
Long Beach Township	3 458	6	0	4	1	1	227	18	205	4	0
Long Branch	31 595	138	0	1	51	86	816	186	591	39	3
Long Hill Township	8 806	6	0	2	0	4	59	1	58	0	0
Longport	1 085	0	0	0	0	0	11	2	9	0	0
Lopatcong Township	8 060	3	0	0	0	3	100	21	73	6	0
Lower Alloways Creek Township	1 908	3	0	0	0	3	10	4	6	0	0
Lower Township	22 067	34	0	3	8	23	521	146	352	23	1
Lumberton Township	12 324	24	0	1	4	19	339	54	272	13	5
Lyndhurst Township	19 583	22	0	1	11	10	296	41	210	45	1
Madison	16 040	12	0	1	1	10	173	58	106	9	1
Magnolia	4 402	16	0	0	5	11	121	33	72	16	1

[1]The FBI does not publish arson data unless it receives data from either the agency or the state for all 12 months of the calendar year.

Table 8. Offenses Known to Law Enforcement, by State and City, 2005—*Continued*

(Number.)

City	Population	Violent crime	Murder and non-negligent man-slaughter	Forcible rape	Robbery	Aggravated assault	Property crime	Burglary	Larceny-theft	Motor vehicle theft	Arson[1]
Mahwah Township	24 736	13	0	0	2	11	176	12	150	14	1
Manalapan Township	37 069	11	0	2	3	6	337	58	263	16	0
Manasquan	6 300	6	1	1	0	4	166	24	140	2	0
Manchester Township	42 204	14	0	2	0	12	347	69	261	17	6
Mansfield Township (Burlington County)	7 817	9	1	0	0	8	116	11	92	13	0
Mansfield Township (Warren County)	8 340	5	0	1	0	4	105	11	93	1	0
Mantoloking	452	0	0	0	0	0	13	1	12	0	0
Mantua Township	14 321	11	0	1	3	7	320	51	258	11	2
Manville	10 439	8	1	0	3	4	257	15	219	23	1
Maple Shade Township	19 372	38	1	3	16	18	421	115	266	40	2
Maplewood Township	23 501	84	0	2	47	35	689	87	468	134	16
Margate City	8 646	7	0	1	0	6	127	34	86	7	1
Marlboro Township	39 867	17	1	0	6	10	345	65	268	12	3
Matawan	8 939	17	0	1	7	9	130	14	103	13	0
Maywood	9 526	1	0	0	0	1	73	20	47	6	0
Medford Lakes	4 211	4	0	0	0	4	21	0	18	3	0
Medford Township	23 620	20	0	1	8	11	312	50	251	11	1
Mendham	5 171	0	0	0	0	0	43	9	34	0	0
Mendham Township	5 637	4	0	0	0	4	43	4	37	2	0
Merchantville	3 824	4	0	0	1	3	105	21	79	5	0
Metuchen	13 364	13	0	1	4	8	245	64	167	14	0
Middlesex	13 998	7	0	0	2	5	102	15	80	7	2
Middle Township	16 761	84	0	3	13	68	622	139	445	38	13
Middletown Township	68 334	38	0	1	5	32	702	105	554	43	4
Midland Park	6 968	3	0	0	0	3	48	9	38	1	0
Millburn Township	19 628	22	0	0	14	8	622	43	538	41	0
Milltown	7 164	6	0	2	1	3	153	15	130	8	1
Millville	27 671	241	1	18	80	142	1 494	315	1 108	71	1
Mine Hill Township	3 691	0	0	0	0	0	55	18	31	6	1
Monmouth Beach	3 642	0	0	0	0	0	42	4	37	1	0
Monroe Township (Gloucester County)	31 028	65	0	2	18	45	669	204	432	33	0
Monroe Township (Middlesex County)	32 692	11	0	1	2	8	230	38	185	7	1
Montclair	38 382	119	0	2	47	70	954	214	602	138	5
Montgomery Township	22 336	4	0	0	0	4	214	49	157	8	4
Montvale	7 337	2	0	0	0	2	39	0	37	2	0
Montville Township	21 415	10	0	0	1	9	227	27	174	26	1
Moonachie	2 822	3	0	0	0	3	93	11	72	10	0
Moorestown Township	20 085	21	0	1	13	7	521	61	436	24	1
Morris Plains	5 575	3	0	0	1	2	90	10	79	1	0
Morristown	18 883	142	0	4	66	72	827	196	574	57	4
Morris Township	21 459	22	0	0	1	21	151	25	111	15	2
Mountain Lakes	4 333	1	0	1	0	0	69	23	46	0	1
Mountainside	6 675	5	0	0	1	4	67	5	53	9	0
Mount Arlington	5 150	2	0	0	1	1	59	4	54	1	0
Mount Ephraim	4 480	7	0	0	3	4	188	26	146	16	1
Mount Holly Township	10 762	41	0	0	18	23	359	48	286	25	0
Mount Laurel Township	40 771	46	1	10	18	17	636	88	516	32	1
Mount Olive Township	25 774	13	1	0	1	11	305	65	227	13	0
Mullica Township	6 083	17	0	0	0	17	51	8	35	8	1
National Park	3 215	10	0	0	2	8	56	12	41	3	1
Neptune City	5 385	19	0	1	7	11	173	35	137	1	0
Neptune Township	32 679	151	0	4	76	71	1 447	264	1 077	106	8
Netcong	3 303	2	0	1	0	1	89	20	60	9	1
Newark	281 063	2 821	97	83	1 250	1 391	12 720	2 056	4 974	5 690	179
New Brunswick	50 119	343	3	17	204	119	1 825	519	1 106	200	8
Newfield	1 657	1	0	0	0	1	23	12	9	2	0
New Hanover Township	9 836	0	0	0	0	0	8	0	8	0	0
New Milford	16 433	15	0	2	5	8	122	22	97	3	0
New Providence	12 007	5	1	1	0	3	92	8	77	7	1
Newton	8 400	13	0	0	2	11	181	16	160	5	1
North Arlington	15 287	13	0	1	5	7	255	41	180	34	3
North Bergen Township	58 131	131	0	12	71	48	1 209	189	790	230	5
North Brunswick Township	39 957	88	1	6	44	37	977	237	642	98	6
North Caldwell	7 370	5	0	0	0	5	56	7	47	2	0
Northfield	8 072	4	0	2	2	0	169	58	105	6	0
North Haledon	8 831	2	0	0	0	2	50	14	35	1	1
North Hanover Township	7 599	11	0	2	2	7	75	16	50	9	1
North Plainfield	21 181	59	1	1	41	16	521	121	342	58	0
Northvale	4 581	0	0	0	0	0	30	5	24	1	0
North Wildwood	4 812	26	0	2	7	17	316	42	272	2	1
Norwood	6 237	3	0	1	0	2	46	5	41	0	0
Nutley Township	27 936	23	1	0	6	16	376	102	255	19	1
Oakland	13 737	9	0	1	1	7	106	15	89	2	0
Oaklyn	4 138	9	0	3	3	3	115	25	87	3	2
Ocean City	15 540	28	0	0	13	15	971	152	805	14	3
Ocean Gate	2 122	6	0	0	0	6	32	8	24	0	0
Oceanport	5 845	5	0	0	0	5	104	11	92	1	2
Ocean Township (Monmouth County)	27 439	35	0	6	13	16	727	102	597	28	1
Ocean Township (Ocean County)	7 508	3	0	0	0	3	78	16	61	1	1
Ogdensburg	2 649	1	0	0	0	1	4	0	3	1	0

[1]The FBI does not publish arson data unless it receives data from either the agency or the state for all 12 months of the calendar year.

Table 8. Offenses Known to Law Enforcement, by State and City, 2005—*Continued*

(Number.)

City	Population	Violent crime	Murder and non-negligent man-slaughter	Forcible rape	Robbery	Aggravated assault	Property crime	Burglary	Larceny-theft	Motor vehicle theft	Arson[1]
Old Bridge Township	64 291	64	1	6	27	30	1 024	181	751	92	9
Old Tappan	5 882	0	0	0	0	0	39	4	35	0	0
Oradell	8 059	2	0	0	1	1	61	20	41	0	0
Orange	32 459	354	4	8	214	128	1 579	363	630	586	3
Oxford Township	2 631	1	0	0	0	1	18	9	9	0	0
Palisades Park	18 341	25	0	2	11	12	108	31	69	8	0
Palmyra	7 689	10	0	3	4	3	166	51	100	15	1
Paramus	26 682	66	1	1	28	36	1 491	68	1 349	74	5
Park Ridge	8 990	5	0	0	1	4	38	1	35	2	0
Parsippany-Troy Hills Township	51 752	39	0	6	6	27	707	183	475	49	4
Passaic	68 812	684	4	6	331	343	1 619	363	977	279	12
Paterson	151 200	1 444	20	32	588	804	4 433	1 413	2 107	913	13
Paulsboro	6 123	43	0	1	18	24	286	60	208	18	5
Peapack and Gladstone	2 473	0	0	0	0	0	9	3	6	0	0
Pemberton	1 328	3	0	0	1	2	44	10	33	1	0
Pemberton Township	29 030	109	1	17	26	65	668	190	422	56	11
Pennington	2 719	1	0	0	0	1	25	7	18	0	0
Pennsauken Township	35 703	172	0	7	73	92	1 307	263	884	160	10
Penns Grove	4 818	66	0	4	22	40	242	49	171	22	1
Pennsville Township	13 223	19	0	0	2	17	389	65	309	15	2
Pequannock Township	15 225	4	0	0	2	2	178	46	125	7	0
Perth Amboy	48 930	168	2	3	59	104	1 200	270	778	152	1
Phillipsburg	15 103	21	0	0	8	13	274	86	159	29	3
Pine Beach	2 024	0	0	0	0	0	32	3	29	0	0
Pine Hill	11 246	44	1	5	6	32	255	60	180	15	4
Pine Valley	22	0	0	0	0	0	0	0	0	0	0
Piscataway Township	52 527	60	0	5	21	34	800	154	576	70	7
Pitman	9 291	5	0	0	0	5	123	5	111	7	0
Plainfield	48 092	517	15	16	244	242	1 577	371	853	353	16
Plainsboro Township	21 347	9	0	1	3	5	226	38	178	10	3
Pleasantville	19 155	143	1	8	56	78	604	191	360	53	5
Plumsted Township	8 063	8	0	0	0	8	56	17	34	5	0
Pohatcong Township	3 435	19	0	0	0	19	162	13	145	4	0
Point Pleasant	19 864	10	0	0	2	8	300	46	247	7	0
Point Pleasant Beach	5 420	7	0	0	3	4	204	22	174	8	0
Pompton Lakes	11 414	8	1	0	1	6	106	19	82	5	0
Princeton	13 620	20	0	0	10	10	422	76	333	13	0
Princeton Township	17 387	16	0	4	8	4	175	57	106	12	1
Prospect Park	5 815	19	0	0	6	13	112	19	84	9	0
Rahway	27 638	87	0	2	44	41	551	95	376	80	5
Ramsey	14 633	9	0	0	2	7	145	11	121	13	0
Randolph Township	25 790	13	1	0	2	10	201	28	168	5	1
Raritan	6 415	7	0	1	2	4	131	23	104	4	0
Raritan Township	22 411	27	5	0	2	20	196	37	149	10	1
Readington Township	16 437	5	0	0	1	4	135	28	105	2	1
Red Bank	11 966	29	0	2	13	14	263	16	233	14	0
Ridgefield	11 029	5	0	0	2	3	84	18	55	11	0
Ridgefield Park	12 850	12	0	0	2	10	138	20	104	14	2
Ridgewood	24 971	11	0	1	2	8	249	54	189	6	1
Ringwood	12 797	8	0	0	1	7	72	17	53	2	1
Riverdale	2 639	3	0	0	0	3	78	18	58	2	0
River Edge	10 990	4	0	2	0	2	117	35	79	3	1
Riverside Township	8 025	18	0	0	5	13	133	23	100	10	0
Riverton	2 760	8	0	1	2	5	49	6	42	1	0
River Vale Township	9 833	3	0	0	0	3	59	5	54	0	0
Rochelle Park Township	5 747	5	0	0	3	2	104	14	85	5	0
Rockaway	6 451	4	0	0	1	3	74	10	57	7	0
Rockaway Township	25 299	19	0	1	8	10	413	35	363	15	3
Rockleigh	397	1	0	0	0	1	7	1	6	0	0
Roseland	5 353	2	0	0	1	1	59	15	38	6	1
Roselle	21 462	76	0	2	42	32	547	147	289	111	2
Roselle Park	13 325	24	1	0	15	8	205	36	140	29	2
Roxbury Township	23 906	19	0	0	5	14	321	56	250	15	2
Rumson	7 287	4	0	0	0	4	65	17	47	1	0
Runnemede	8 530	22	0	0	4	18	287	38	233	16	1
Rutherford	18 124	14	0	0	6	8	250	50	170	30	1
Saddle Brook Township	13 265	8	0	0	0	8	418	45	351	22	1
Saddle River	3 751	1	0	0	0	1	17	4	13	0	0
Salem	5 800	64	2	1	22	39	288	106	165	17	6
Sayreville	42 756	57	1	7	18	31	688	103	519	66	8
Scotch Plains Township	23 077	18	0	2	7	9	262	69	176	17	0
Sea Bright	1 823	0	0	0	0	0	41	1	40	0	0
Sea Girt	2 102	3	0	0	1	2	32	7	25	0	0
Sea Isle City	2 983	17	0	0	1	16	297	24	270	3	0
Seaside Heights	3 201	86	0	5	15	66	249	62	168	19	1
Seaside Park	2 307	4	0	0	1	3	71	11	55	5	0
Secaucus	15 697	17	0	0	7	10	664	43	536	85	1
Ship Bottom	1 421	8	0	0	0	8	87	14	71	2	2
Shrewsbury	3 739	3	0	0	0	3	94	16	70	8	0
Somerdale	5 173	20	0	1	7	12	142	26	105	11	0

[1]The FBI does not publish arson data unless it receives data from either the agency or the state for all 12 months of the calendar year.

Table 8. Offenses Known to Law Enforcement, by State and City, 2005—*Continued*

(Number.)

City	Population	Violent crime	Murder and non-negligent man-slaughter	Forcible rape	Robbery	Aggravated assault	Property crime	Burglary	Larceny-theft	Motor vehicle theft	Arson[1]
Somers Point	11 757	44	0	3	14	27	327	72	250	5	1
Somerville	12 461	25	0	2	14	9	245	40	196	9	0
South Amboy	8 026	17	0	0	1	16	133	28	90	15	3
South Bound Brook	4 517	2	0	0	2	0	4	1	2	1	0
South Brunswick Township	40 406	31	0	1	15	15	514	112	357	45	1
South Hackensack Township	2 330	13	0	7	1	5	58	14	33	11	0
South Harrison Township	2 851	2	0	0	0	2	24	13	11	0	0
South Orange	16 825	80	0	2	42	36	554	87	353	114	1
South Plainfield	23 084	38	1	0	18	19	465	77	348	40	2
South River	16 060	32	0	2	10	20	179	46	127	6	3
South Toms River	3 707	7	0	0	1	6	102	27	67	8	1
Sparta Township	19 298	4	0	0	1	3	94	8	85	1	1
Spotswood	8 233	7	0	0	2	5	91	11	79	1	0
Springfield	14 820	12	0	1	6	5	252	26	172	54	0
Springfield Township	3 551	3	0	0	2	1	39	13	16	10	0
Spring Lake	3 565	1	0	0	0	1	88	11	77	0	0
Spring Lake Heights	5 201	5	0	1	0	4	29	6	23	0	0
Stafford Township	24 999	41	0	2	1	38	529	76	430	23	4
Stanhope	3 717	3	0	0	1	2	50	8	38	4	0
Stillwater Township	4 394	2	0	1	0	1	44	3	40	1	0
Stone Harbor	1 089	4	0	0	0	4	61	7	54	0	0
Stratford	7 217	16	0	1	6	9	187	20	158	9	2
Summit	21 314	13	0	2	2	9	358	32	290	36	1
Surf City	1 520	4	0	0	0	4	44	5	38	1	0
Swedesboro	2 058	5	0	0	0	5	49	8	38	3	0
Tavistock	30	0	0	0	0	0	2	0	2	0	0
Teaneck Township	39 940	73	1	3	37	32	614	114	446	54	6
Tenafly	14 245	7	0	0	2	5	104	20	77	7	2
Teterboro	18	0	0	0	0	0	17	2	7	8	0
Tewksbury Township	6 011	1	0	0	0	1	27	5	22	0	0
Tinton Falls	16 241	11	0	1	4	6	283	53	203	27	1
Totowa	10 383	8	1	0	1	6	260	27	207	26	0
Trenton	85 566	1 515	31	21	805	658	3 574	962	1 940	672	27
Tuckerton	3 608	3	0	0	1	2	78	15	60	3	0
Union Beach	6 765	10	0	1	5	4	70	10	57	3	0
Union City	66 312	326	3	10	178	134	1 499	396	836	267	3
Union Township	55 758	170	1	14	88	67	1 589	199	1 139	251	9
Upper Saddle River	8 380	8	0	1	1	6	38	7	28	3	0
Ventnor City	12 859	15	0	3	6	6	290	85	202	3	0
Vernon Township	25 609	12	1	0	1	10	314	27	281	6	0
Verona	13 344	4	0	0	2	2	200	28	154	18	1
Vineland	58 136	721	2	15	198	506	2 845	591	2 084	170	21
Voorhees Township	28 805	44	0	5	12	27	853	124	705	24	4
Waldwick	9 685	0	0	0	0	0	104	7	95	2	0
Wallington	11 583	11	0	0	5	6	191	23	136	32	3
Wall Township	26 325	29	0	1	0	28	385	81	288	16	1
Wanaque	10 463	9	0	0	4	5	112	12	95	5	0
Warren Township	15 565	5	0	3	0	2	103	9	90	4	0
Washington	6 900	8	0	0	1	7	129	29	98	2	0
Washington Township (Bergen County)	9 644	1	0	0	0	1	40	7	33	0	0
Washington Township (Gloucester County)	50 991	77	0	5	26	46	1 056	194	802	60	17
Washington Township (Mercer County)	11 470	8	0	0	3	5	125	25	89	11	0
Washington Township (Morris County)	18 525	7	0	0	0	7	152	28	122	2	0
Washington Township (Warren County)	6 824	5	0	0	0	5	63	18	44	1	0
Watchung	5 802	7	0	2	5	0	426	9	400	17	0
Waterford Township	10 702	28	0	3	3	22	162	43	104	15	1
Wayne Township	55 523	58	1	0	19	38	1 246	110	1 043	93	1
Weehawken Township	13 224	22	0	2	11	9	329	87	188	54	1
Wenonah	2 326	1	0	0	1	0	13	2	10	1	0
Westampton Township	8 447	21	0	3	6	12	191	25	148	18	0
West Amwell Township	2 853	1	0	0	0	1	38	5	33	0	0
West Caldwell Township	11 120	8	0	0	3	5	106	13	85	8	1
West Cape May	1 069	0	0	0	0	0	49	9	40	0	0
West Deptford Township	20 509	33	0	6	9	18	469	113	320	36	5
Westfield	30 128	17	0	1	5	11	328	53	266	9	2
West Long Branch	8 259	9	0	2	2	5	292	33	252	7	0
West Milford Township	28 279	24	0	5	1	18	432	171	247	14	3
West New York	46 332	168	3	8	89	68	861	227	508	126	0
West Orange	44 930	91	0	0	55	36	1 071	191	640	240	2
West Paterson	11 323	22	0	3	3	16	311	84	206	21	0
Westville	4 481	12	0	1	1	10	120	40	70	10	2
West Wildwood	421	2	1	0	0	1	35	9	25	1	0
West Windsor Township	24 512	13	0	4	4	5	521	74	432	15	1
Westwood	11 075	9	0	2	2	5	117	22	92	3	1
Wharton	6 253	9	0	1	4	4	95	28	64	3	1
Wildwood	5 222	75	1	4	31	39	541	142	366	33	0
Wildwood Crest	3 870	2	0	0	1	1	218	53	162	3	0
Willingboro Township	33 187	121	0	10	49	62	626	146	428	52	15
Winfield Township	1 514	1	0	0	0	1	28	4	23	1	0
Winslow Township	36 140	200	0	7	37	156	792	238	476	78	13

[1]The FBI does not publish arson data unless it receives data from either the agency or the state for all 12 months of the calendar year.

Table 8. Offenses Known to Law Enforcement, by State and City, 2005—*Continued*

(Number.)

City	Population	Violent crime	Murder and non-negligent man-slaughter	Forcible rape	Robbery	Aggravated assault	Property crime	Burglary	Larceny-theft	Motor vehicle theft	Arson[1]
Woodbine	2 622	1	0	0	0	1	30	0	30	0	0
Woodbridge Township	100 998	303	2	17	81	203	2 809	347	2 168	294	19
Woodbury	10 460	42	0	7	12	23	555	75	450	30	0
Woodbury Heights	3 017	10	0	0	4	6	94	21	68	5	0
Woodcliff Lake	5 899	3	0	1	0	2	40	1	39	0	0
Woodland Township	1 367	0	0	0	0	0	22	2	19	1	0
Woodlynne	2 763	13	0	0	4	9	95	16	66	13	1
Wood-Ridge	7 674	4	0	0	2	2	55	8	37	10	1
Woodstown	3 280	1	0	0	0	1	56	7	44	5	1
Woolwich Township	6 128	7	0	0	2	5	102	31	65	6	2
Wyckoff Township	17 244	11	0	0	2	9	97	12	83	2	1
New Mexico											
Alamogordo	36 688	111	0	25	9	77	1 019	121	860	38	5
Albuquerque	490 631	4 670	53	285	1 150	3 182	30 243	5 744	20 703	3 796	60
Angel Fire	1 061	0	0	0	0	0	20	4	16	0	0
Bayard	2 406	11	0	0	0	11	31	7	23	1	0
Belen	7 038	120	1	3	22	94	1 070	377	521	172	0
Bloomfield	7 335	106	0	2	5	99	298	55	208	35	2
Bosque Farms	3 938	9	0	2	1	6	59	10	41	8	1
Carrizozo	1 067	7	0	0	0	7	24	10	12	2	0
Clovis	33 499	240	2	21	34	183	2 031	624	1 285	122	24
Corrales	7 716	3	0	0	0	3	93	35	54	4	1
Deming	14 840	53	0	2	6	45	618	186	331	101	6
Dexter	1 241	7	0	0	0	7	37	16	19	2	1
Eunice	2 622	3	0	0	0	3	57	22	31	4	1
Farmington	42 980	([7])	3	66	27	([7])	1 523	412	918	193	6
Gallup	19 975	339	1	20	50	268	1 875	266	1 487	122	4
Grants	9 160	62	1	0	11	50	384	160	184	40	4
Hobbs	29 087	333	4	22	20	287	2 478	324	2 088	66	5
Jal	2 037	2	0	0	0	2	9	1	7	1	0
Las Cruces	80 573	465	5	96	101	263	3 949	750	2 954	245	15
Las Vegas	14 216	199	1	10	14	174	656	159	450	47	8
Los Alamos	19 044	19	0	0	0	19	261	65	178	18	0
Los Lunas	11 903	215	1	6	4	204	462	100	291	71	0
Lovington	9 679	44	0	1	2	41	334	147	177	10	0
Milan	2 560	20	0	1	1	18	122	45	73	4	0
Moriarty	1 836	11	0	2	1	8	102	45	52	5	. . .
Red River	501	4	0	0	0	4	18	3	13	2	0
Rio Rancho	62 770	204	3	9	15	177	1 395	404	870	121	13
Roswell	45 668	438	10	30	24	374	3 192	745	2 317	130	24
Ruidoso Downs	1 946	31	0	3	1	27	171	23	141	7	1
Santa Fe	68 938	379	5	44	70	260	4 022	1 837	1 978	207	3
Silver City	10 042	66	1	5	9	51	722	160	511	51	2
Socorro	8 839	123	0	0	1	122	379	67	304	8	2
Tatum	699	2	0	0	0	2	13	8	5	0	0
Truth or Consequences	7 257	61	0	0	3	58	283	55	213	15	. . .
New York											
Adams Village	1 601	0	0	0	0	0	12	5	7	0	. . .
Addison Town and Village	2 604	3	0	0	0	3	15	6	9	0	. . .
Akron Village	3 100	7	0	1	0	6	19	4	15	0	. . .
Albany	94 361	1 275	8	68	439	760	4 883	1 328	3 186	369	. . .
Albion Village	5 844	41	0	3	4	34	344	56	279	9	. . .
Alexandria Bay Village	1 074	8	0	0	0	8	26	8	16	2	. . .
Alfred Village	4 685	3	0	1	0	2	68	10	57	1	. . .
Allegany Village	1 838	7	0	0	0	7	95	7	88	0	. . .
Altamont Village	1 738	0	0	0	0	0	5	1	3	1	. . .
Amherst Town	111 178	102	1	7	43	51	1 915	196	1 681	38	5
Amity Town and Belmont Village	2 204	0	0	0	0	0	1	0	1	0	. . .
Amityville Village	9 571	13	0	1	8	4	177	24	146	7	. . .
Amsterdam	17 954	71	0	0	3	68	244	66	177	1	. . .
Angola Village	2 216	6	0	1	0	5	62	12	49	1	. . .
Asharoken Village	648	1	0	0	0	1	3	1	2	0	. . .
Attica Village	2 527	0	0	0	0	0	36	2	33	1	. . .
Avon Village	3 004	3	0	0	1	2	75	8	62	5	. . .
Bainbridge Village	1 363	0	0	0	0	0	13	0	13	0	. . .
Baldwinsville Village	7 183	12	0	0	0	12	225	23	199	3	. . .
Ballston Spa Village	5 595	2	0	1	0	1	111	13	94	4	. . .
Batavia	15 853	31	0	2	4	25	742	94	646	2	. . .
Bath Village	5 630	12	1	5	1	5	194	43	147	4	. . .
Beacon	14 783	59	0	5	15	39	329	80	223	26	. . .
Bedford Town	18 627	3	0	0	0	3	185	17	160	8	. . .
Bethlehem Town	32 905	23	0	3	3	17	502	85	397	20	. . .
Binghamton	45 930	177	3	19	61	94	1 902	236	1 646	20	. . .
Blooming Grove Town	12 170	6	0	0	0	6	109	24	79	6	. . .
Bolivar Village	1 153	1	0	0	0	1	12	1	11	0	. . .
Boonville Village	2 112	3	0	1	0	2	39	4	30	5	. . .
Brant Town	1 890	0	0	0	0	0	9	2	6	1	. . .
Briarcliff Manor Village	7 911	1	0	0	0	1	12	1	10	1	. . .
Brighton Town	34 651	36	0	3	17	16	1 033	200	770	63	. . .
Brockport Village	8 148	16	0	3	4	9	142	18	121	3	. . .
Bronxville Village	6 512	1	0	0	0	1	28	8	18	2	. . .
Buffalo	283 269	3 938	56	184	1 667	2 031	16 730	4 240	10 089	2 401	368
Cairo Town	6 586	5	0	0	1	4	25	6	19	0	. . .
Caledonia Village	2 258	5	0	0	0	5	101	3	97	1	. . .
Cambridge Village	1 929	1	0	0	1	0	46	4	37	5	. . .
Camillus Town and Village	23 287	7	0	0	2	5	225	18	200	7	. . .
Canisteo Village	2 297	5	0	0	0	5	74	18	55	1	. . .

[1]The FBI does not publish arson data unless it receives data from either the agency or the state for all 12 months of the calendar year.
[7]After examining the data and making inquiries, the FBI determined that the agency's offense count was inflated. Consequently, this figure is not included in this table.
. . . = Not available.

Table 8. Offenses Known to Law Enforcement, by State and City, 2005—*Continued*

(Number.)

City	Population	Violent crime	Murder and non-negligent man-slaughter	Forcible rape	Robbery	Aggravated assault	Property crime	Burglary	Larceny-theft	Motor vehicle theft	Arson[1]
Canton Village	6 110	3	0	1	0	2	153	14	138	1	. . .
Cape Vincent Village	751	0	0	0	0	0	9	2	7	0	. . .
Carmel Town	34 754	18	0	0	9	9	258	62	176	20	. . .
Carroll Town	3 569	2	0	0	0	2	12	2	8	2	. . .
Carthage Village	3 650	4	1	0	0	3	104	19	85	0	. . .
Catskill Village	4 346	8	0	0	1	7	151	14	131	6	. . .
Cattaraugus Village	1 044	3	0	0	0	3	4	2	2	0	. . .
Cayuga Heights Village	3 714	1	0	0	0	1	63	9	54	0	. . .
Chatham Village	1 785	9	0	0	2	7	60	11	45	4	. . .
Cheektowaga Town	81 793	239	0	11	91	137	2 517	406	1 929	182	. . .
Chester Town	9 602	3	0	0	1	2	35	6	27	2	. . .
Chester Village	3 615	13	0	2	7	4	180	14	161	5	. . .
Chittenango Village	4 892	8	0	0	1	7	112	9	100	3	. . .
Cicero Town	27 732	11	0	1	2	8	541	50	485	6	. . .
Clayton Village	1 798	2	0	0	0	2	39	12	23	4	. . .
Clay Town	54 493	20	0	1	7	12	382	89	270	23	. . .
Clifton Springs Village	2 201	1	0	0	0	1	14	1	11	2	. . .
Clyde Village	2 203	6	0	0	1	5	86	15	69	2	. . .
Cobleskill Village	4 719	4	0	1	0	3	155	18	132	5	. . .
Coeymans Town	4 757	8	0	0	1	7	79	19	55	5	. . .
Cohoes	15 233	64	1	1	4	58	157	44	100	13	. . .
Colchester Town	2 051	1	0	0	0	1	7	5	2	0	. . .
Colonie Town	77 048	78	0	9	33	36	2 898	326	2 454	118	. . .
Cooperstown Village	1 944	5	0	1	0	4	35	6	29	0	. . .
Corfu Village	774	0	0	0	0	0	0	0	0	0	. . .
Corinth Village	2 486	10	0	0	0	10	66	11	54	1	. . .
Corning	10 623	49	0	4	6	39	555	62	483	10	. . .
Cornwall-on-Hudson Village	3 132	0	0	0	0	0	14	1	13	0	. . .
Cornwall Town	9 681	7	0	0	1	6	7	4	2	1	. . .
Cortland	18 740	85	0	14	11	60	488	135	327	26	. . .
Coxsackie Village	2 869	11	0	0	1	10	13	4	9	0	. . .
Croton-on-Hudson Village	7 873	2	0	0	1	1	104	15	86	3	. . .
Cuba Town	3 404	16	0	2	0	14	49	12	34	3	. . .
Dansville Village	4 715	8	0	1	2	5	240	17	221	2	. . .
Deerpark Town	8 294	16	0	1	0	15	201	45	149	7	. . .
Delhi Village	2 542	2	0	0	0	2	10	4	6	0	. . .
Depew Village	16 026	19	0	4	3	12	391	69	318	4	. . .
Deposit Village	1 648	5	0	0	2	3	3	3	0	0	. . .
Dewitt Town	22 056	38	0	0	18	20	558	72	475	11	. . .
Dobbs Ferry Village	11 152	4	0	1	2	1	136	16	111	9	. . .
Dolgeville Village	2 109	4	0	1	0	3	71	8	61	2	. . .
Dryden Village	1 838	2	0	0	0	2	63	5	57	1	. . .
Dunkirk	12 645	57	1	2	15	39	398	73	315	10	. . .
Durham Town	2 677	0	0	0	0	0	1	1	0	0	. . .
East Aurora-Aurora Town	13 844	8	0	2	3	3	200	28	170	2	. . .
Eastchester Town	18 784	9	0	0	4	5	170	26	139	5	. . .
East Fishkill Town	28 328	68	0	0	3	65	331	48	261	22	. . .
East Greenbush Town	16 186	19	0	2	2	15	452	71	369	12	. . .
East Hampton Town	18 825	20	0	0	0	20	466	114	336	16	. . .
East Rochester Village	6 450	16	0	0	2	14	156	41	111	4	. . .
East Syracuse Village	3 098	10	0	0	1	9	172	21	142	9	. . .
Eden Town	7 980	0	0	0	0	0	69	21	46	2	. . .
Ellenville Village	4 097	15	0	3	7	5	177	36	132	9	. . .
Ellicott Town	5 426	6	0	2	0	4	299	37	252	10	. . .
Ellicottville	1 808	3	0	0	0	3	168	13	154	1	. . .
Elmira	30 116	121	2	14	39	66	1 621	282	1 295	44	. . .
Elmira Heights Village	4 052	8	0	2	1	5	167	13	152	2	. . .
Elmira Town	6 067	1	0	0	0	1	21	3	18	0	. . .
Elmsford Village	4 742	11	1	2	3	5	92	8	66	18	. . .
Endicott Village	12 767	37	1	9	6	21	553	87	454	12	. . .
Evans Town	15 154	26	0	4	4	18	252	50	187	15	. . .
Fairport Village	5 648	4	0	0	3	1	55	17	37	1	. . .
Fallsburg Town	11 740	32	0	4	5	23	281	95	179	7	. . .
Fishkill Village	1 760	9	0	0	1	8	59	4	53	2	. . .
Floral Park Village	15 873	12	0	1	7	4	71	13	53	5	. . .
Florida Village	2 801	1	0	0	0	1	41	3	38	0	. . .
Fort Edward Village	3 145	9	0	2	0	7	55	5	48	2	. . .
Fort Plain Village	2 238	12	0	0	0	12	11	3	7	1	. . .
Frankfort Town	4 946	1	0	1	0	0	27	5	21	1	. . .
Fredonia Village	10 720	15	0	1	4	10	230	26	196	8	. . .
Freeport Village	43 789	157	2	8	66	81	885	142	603	140	. . .
Freeville Village	508	0	0	0	0	0	8	3	4	1	. . .
Friendship Town	1 901	1	0	0	0	1	12	3	9	0	. . .
Fulton City	11 660	30	0	5	6	19	616	79	525	12	. . .
Garden City Village	21 879	9	0	0	5	4	265	35	213	17	. . .
Gates Town	28 790	46	0	3	32	11	1 057	109	887	61	. . .
Geddes Town	10 770	9	0	0	5	4	194	34	154	6	. . .
Geneseo Village	7 857	5	0	4	0	1	218	14	204	0	. . .
Geneva	13 577	35	0	9	9	17	439	107	325	7	. . .
Germantown Town	2 045	0	0	0	0	0	1	0	1	0	. . .

[1]The FBI does not publish arson data unless it receives data from either the agency or the state for all 12 months of the calendar year.
. . . = Not available.

Table 8. Offenses Known to Law Enforcement, by State and City, 2005—*Continued*

(Number.)

City	Population	Violent crime	Murder and non-negligent man-slaughter	Forcible rape	Robbery	Aggravated assault	Property crime	Burglary	Larceny-theft	Motor vehicle theft	Arson[1]
Glen Park Village	480	0	0	0	0	0	0	0	0	0	. . .
Glens Falls	14 186	20	2	0	5	13	367	55	304	8	. . .
Glenville Town	20 669	13	0	0	6	7	367	43	306	18	. . .
Gloversville	15 299	54	0	3	4	47	628	129	477	22	. . .
Goshen Town	8 279	7	0	1	1	5	81	12	65	4	. . .
Gouverneur Village	4 154	7	0	3	0	4	185	23	158	4	. . .
Gowanda Village	2 759	5	0	0	0	5	133	16	117	0	. . .
Granville Village	2 645	5	0	2	0	3	48	15	33	0	. . .
Great Neck Estates Village	2 756	3	0	0	1	2	10	3	7	0	. . .
Greece Town	94 688	67	2	12	39	14	1 988	241	1 614	133	. . .
Greenburgh Town	43 545	62	0	4	17	41	820	76	685	59	. . .
Greene Village	1 701	0	0	0	0	0	0	0	0	0	. . .
Green Island Village	2 606	5	0	0	1	4	49	13	32	4	. . .
Greenport Town	4 164	0	0	0	0	0	36	2	33	1	. . .
Greenwich Village	1 903	3	0	0	1	2	52	14	33	5	. . .
Greenwood Lake Village	3 484	11	0	3	0	8	17	0	17	0	. . .
Groton Village	2 448	1	0	0	0	1	50	4	45	1	. . .
Guilderland Town	33 129	45	1	3	10	31	1 006	80	921	5	. . .
Hamburg Town	44 357	7	0	0	2	5	320	32	268	20	. . .
Hamburg Village	9 755	7	0	1	4	2	205	28	173	4	. . .
Hamilton Village	3 512	1	0	0	0	1	22	5	17	0	. . .
Hancock Village	1 147	4	0	0	0	4	8	0	7	1	. . .
Harriman Village	2 301	1	0	0	1	0	43	2	36	5	. . .
Harrison Town	25 590	16	0	2	5	9	282	37	231	14	. . .
Haverstraw Town	24 563	32	0	2	9	21	326	53	263	10	. . .
Haverstraw Village	10 151	75	0	0	11	64	213	32	167	14	. . .
Hempstead Village	53 221	395	4	16	210	165	1 085	204	565	316	. . .
Herkimer Village	7 305	91	0	11	10	70	531	68	459	4	. . .
Highland Falls Village	3 792	8	0	0	2	6	45	8	34	3	. . .
Highlands Town	9 149	3	0	0	1	2	12	1	11	0	. . .
Homer Village	3 351	1	0	1	0	0	46	19	26	1	. . .
Hornell	8 813	50	0	9	1	40	277	33	240	4	. . .
Horseheads Village	6 434	10	0	3	3	4	176	24	152	0	. . .
Hudson Falls Village	6 919	14	0	3	0	11	106	19	81	6	. . .
Huntington Bay Village	1 502	0	0	0	0	0	6	1	5	0	. . .
Ilion Village	8 386	30	0	3	2	25	145	34	107	4	. . .
Irondequoit Town	51 714	91	0	5	50	36	1 746	269	1 369	108	. . .
Irvington Village	6 665	0	0	0	0	0	8	4	3	1	. . .
Jamestown	30 739	213	1	23	46	143	1 132	364	728	40	. . .
Johnson City Village	15 106	63	0	5	12	46	686	93	584	9	. . .
Johnstown	8 569	5	0	2	3	0	307	31	263	13	. . .
Jordan Village	1 360	0	0	0	0	0	7	0	7	0	. . .
Kenmore Village	15 772	26	0	4	10	12	284	44	231	9	. . .
Kensington Village	1 205	0	0	0	0	0	1	1	0	0	. . .
Kent Town	14 491	2	0	0	0	2	135	28	105	2	. . .
Kings Point Village	5 207	0	0	0	0	0	21	3	17	1	. . .
Kingston	23 252	117	0	11	72	34	1 091	114	928	49	. . .
Kirkland Town	8 263	4	0	0	0	4	116	23	88	5	. . .
Lackawanna	18 420	111	0	10	23	78	509	134	343	32	. . .
Lake Placid Village	2 715	7	0	1	1	5	62	11	50	1	. . .
Lake Success Village	2 841	5	0	0	1	4	51	9	37	5	. . .
Lakewood-Busti	7 630	3	0	1	1	1	71	12	59	0	. . .
Lancaster Town	23 116	16	0	1	10	5	446	60	379	7	. . .
Le Roy Village	4 342	3	0	1	1	1	150	14	133	3	. . .
Lewisboro Town	12 550	2	0	0	0	2	1	0	1	0	. . .
Lewiston Town and Village	16 443	11	2	2	1	6	164	19	124	21	. . .
Liberty Village	3 950	15	0	0	4	11	158	26	128	4	. . .
Liverpool Village	2 439	1	0	0	0	1	47	6	35	6	. . .
Lloyd Harbor Village	3 744	0	0	0	0	0	30	4	26	0	. . .
Lloyd Town	10 340	11	0	5	1	5	152	21	131	0	. . .
Lockport	21 535	70	0	12	22	36	967	183	745	39	. . .
Long Beach	35 604	94	0	1	30	63	355	30	281	44	. . .
Lowville Village	3 282	9	0	0	1	8	73	16	56	1	. . .
Lynbrook Village	19 823	28	0	2	16	10	169	25	127	17	. . .
Lyons Village	3 590	29	0	2	2	25	211	45	158	8	. . .
Macedon Town and Village	8 984	2	0	0	0	2	61	7	53	1	. . .
Malone Village	5 967	13	0	5	1	7	180	17	163	0	. . .
Malverne Village	8 879	0	0	0	0	0	4	2	1	1	. . .
Mamaroneck Town	11 441	2	0	0	0	2	123	12	99	12	. . .
Manchester Village	1 464	0	0	0	0	0	0	0	0	0	. . .
Manlius Town	25 089	26	0	0	4	22	407	49	348	10	. . .
Marlborough Town	8 381	12	0	1	0	11	86	19	58	9	. . .
Massena Village	10 927	10	0	3	0	7	192	25	166	1	. . .
Maybrook Village	4 086	3	0	0	1	2	34	7	25	2	. . .
McGraw Village	989	0	0	0	0	0	2	2	0	0	. . .
Mechanicville	5 026	40	0	0	0	40	67	19	44	4	. . .
Medina Village	6 321	27	0	0	0	27	84	15	68	1	. . .
Menands Village	3 865	12	0	1	2	9	115	16	92	7	. . .
Middleport Village	1 851	0	0	0	0	0	41	5	36	0	. . .
Middletown	26 154	122	2	12	58	50	810	114	657	39	. . .

[1]The FBI does not publish arson data unless it receives data from either the agency or the state for all 12 months of the calendar year.
. . . = Not available.

Table 8. Offenses Known to Law Enforcement, by State and City, 2005—*Continued*

(Number.)

City	Population	Violent crime	Murder and non-negligent man-slaughter	Forcible rape	Robbery	Aggravated assault	Property crime	Burglary	Larceny-theft	Motor vehicle theft	Arson[1]
Millbrook Village	1 553	1	0	0	0	1	12	2	10	0	. . .
Mohawk Village	2 590	9	0	2	0	7	55	8	45	2	. . .
Monroe Village	8 141	9	0	0	4	5	360	27	320	13	. . .
Montgomery Town	8 759	11	0	1	2	8	129	10	114	5	. . .
Montgomery Village	4 138	0	0	0	0	0	13	0	12	1	. . .
Monticello Village	6 574	69	0	2	23	44	259	98	144	17	. . .
Moravia Village	1 338	0	0	0	0	0	8	0	7	1	. . .
Moriah Town	3 702	1	0	0	0	1	0	0	0	0	. . .
Mount Hope Town	7 274	3	0	0	1	2	37	13	21	3	. . .
Mount Kisco Village	10 071	17	0	2	2	13	77	13	60	4	. . .
Mount Morris Village	3 027	6	0	2	0	4	84	11	73	0	. . .
Mount Pleasant Town	26 567	4	0	0	2	2	92	17	73	2	. . .
Mount Vernon	68 419	631	5	9	334	283	1 677	344	1 084	249	. . .
Newark Village	9 495	27	0	2	3	22	409	51	345	13	. . .
New Berlin Town	1 694	2	0	0	0	2	22	0	22	0	. . .
Newburgh	28 592	432	3	12	174	243	1 077	294	707	76	. . .
Newburgh Town	30 333	26	0	3	13	10	824	69	707	48	. . .
New Castle Town	17 746	5	0	0	0	5	103	11	87	5	. . .
New Paltz Town and Village	13 488	70	1	8	6	55	265	22	237	6	. . .
New Rochelle	73 090	260	3	4	146	107	1 428	177	1 147	104	. . .
New Windsor Town	24 763	55	1	2	10	42	525	87	410	28	. . .
New York	8 115 690	54 623	539	1 412	24 722	27 950	162 509	23 210	120 918	18 381	. . .
New York Mills Village	3 171	7	0	0	0	7	79	14	63	2	. . .
Niagara Falls	53 785	685	4	24	242	415	2 687	703	1 728	256	. . .
Niagara Town	8 750	15	0	1	8	6	261	55	190	16	. . .
Niskayuna Town	21 257	23	0	2	7	14	585	53	506	26	. . .
Nissequogue Village	1 581	0	0	0	0	0	3	1	2	0	. . .
Norfolk Town	4 526	8	0	0	0	8	14	5	6	3	. . .
North Castle Town	11 838	8	0	0	0	8	87	10	75	2	. . .
North Greenbush Town	11 563	28	0	2	2	24	149	29	115	5	. . .
Northport Village	7 675	5	0	0	2	3	51	9	37	5	. . .
North Syracuse Village	6 803	13	0	1	5	7	82	11	71	0	. . .
North Tonawanda	32 234	47	1	3	12	31	568	126	415	27	. . .
Northville Village	1 153	0	0	0	0	0	8	2	6	0	. . .
Norwich	7 306	9	0	5	2	2	335	42	288	5	. . .
Norwood Village	1 636	0	0	0	0	0	16	2	14	0	. . .
Nunda Town and Village	3 026	0	0	0	0	0	69	11	58	0	. . .
Ogdensburg	11 502	13	1	0	4	8	651	142	490	19	. . .
Ogden Town	19 190	7	0	1	3	3	341	60	253	28	. . .
Old Brookville Village	2 227	3	0	0	0	3	115	35	77	3	. . .
Old Westbury Village	4 565	0	0	0	0	0	50	24	26	0	. . .
Olean	14 993	25	1	12	5	7	668	88	576	4	. . .
Oneida	10 993	31	1	6	8	16	498	72	423	3	. . .
Oneonta City	13 118	41	1	1	11	28	317	70	233	14	. . .
Orangetown Town	35 947	40	0	1	16	23	563	95	449	19	. . .
Orchard Park Town	27 906	15	0	1	6	8	482	59	407	16	. . .
Oriskany Village	1 441	2	0	0	1	1	11	0	10	1	. . .
Ossining Town	5 674	1	0	0	0	1	50	10	38	2	. . .
Ossining Village	23 690	61	0	2	26	33	278	48	199	31	. . .
Oswego City	18 433	50	1	6	12	31	600	96	479	25	. . .
Owego Village	3 816	3	0	0	0	3	16	8	8	0	. . .
Oxford Village	1 582	0	0	0	0	0	31	5	23	3	. . .
Oyster Bay Cove Village	2 286	0	0	0	0	0	6	2	4	0	. . .
Painted Post Village	1 804	2	0	0	1	1	21	1	19	1	. . .
Palmyra Village	3 450	3	0	0	1	2	82	15	65	2	. . .
Pelham Manor Village	5 442	3	0	0	3	0	123	18	96	9	. . .
Pelham Village	6 412	14	0	1	10	3	115	14	92	9	. . .
Penn Yan Village	5 126	2	0	1	1	0	122	24	98	0	. . .
Perry Village	3 838	4	0	1	0	3	119	26	87	6	. . .
Phelps Village	1 937	0	0	0	0	0	1	0	1	0	. . .
Phoenix Village	2 222	19	0	1	1	17	45	2	41	2	. . .
Piermont Village	2 621	1	0	0	0	1	23	1	20	2	. . .
Plattekill Town	10 651	0	0	0	0	0	17	2	15	0	. . .
Plattsburgh City	19 246	22	0	6	8	8	558	144	403	11	. . .
Port Byron Village	1 275	1	0	0	0	1	2	0	2	0	. . .
Port Chester Village	27 942	84	0	4	63	17	851	92	724	35	. . .
Port Dickinson Village	1 642	0	0	0	0	0	35	5	30	0	. . .
Port Jervis	9 174	16	0	0	5	11	198	30	156	12	. . .
Portville Village	1 007	0	0	0	0	0	34	8	23	3	. . .
Poughkeepsie	30 391	371	2	16	149	204	1 108	234	787	87	. . .
Poughkeepsie Town	43 820	80	1	14	17	48	1 171	130	1 003	38	. . .
Pound Ridge Town	4 925	0	0	0	0	0	18	5	13	0	. . .
Quogue Village	1 102	2	0	0	0	2	18	2	16	0	. . .
Ramapo Town	74 388	63	0	2	11	50	686	125	538	23	. . .
Ravena Village	3 345	4	0	0	0	4	41	12	29	0	. . .
Rensselaer City	7 795	21	0	3	5	13	292	62	210	20	. . .
Rhinebeck Village	3 136	1	0	0	0	1	55	3	52	0	. . .
Riverhead Town	33 171	153	3	8	62	80	1 354	187	1 142	25	. . .
Rochester	212 785	1 974	53	100	1 026	795	13 828	2 758	8 826	2 244	265
Rockville Centre Village	24 427	11	0	0	11	0	238	52	173	13	. . .

[1]The FBI does not publish arson data unless it receives data from either the agency or the state for all 12 months of the calendar year.
. . . = Not available.

Table 8. Offenses Known to Law Enforcement, by State and City, 2005—*Continued*

(Number.)

City	Population	Violent crime	Murder and non-negligent man-slaughter	Forcible rape	Robbery	Aggravated assault	Property crime	Burglary	Larceny-theft	Motor vehicle theft	Arson[1]
Rome	34 600	49	0	8	10	31	627	164	428	35	. . .
Rosendale Town	6 374	5	0	1	0	4	70	10	55	5	. . .
Rotterdam Town	28 945	29	0	1	11	17	769	64	686	19	. . .
Rouses Point Village	2 391	5	0	0	0	5	15	3	12	0	. . .
Rushford Town	1 262	0	0	0	0	0	0	0	0	0	. . .
Rye	15 089	5	0	0	0	5	215	17	183	15	. . .
Rye Brook Village	9 408	9	0	0	3	6	97	6	84	7	. . .
Sackets Harbor Village	1 369	1	0	0	0	1	10	2	7	1	. . .
Saranac Lake Village	4 957	20	0	4	1	15	49	13	34	2	. . .
Saratoga Springs	27 726	34	0	3	4	27	577	98	457	22	. . .
Saugerties Town	15 370	9	0	4	2	3	263	55	187	21	. . .
Scarsdale Village	17 914	3	0	0	1	2	163	24	133	6	. . .
Schenectady	61 213	609	8	41	252	308	3 049	795	1 975	279	. . .
Schoharie Village	988	0	0	0	0	0	7	1	5	1	. . .
Scotia Village	7 893	4	0	0	1	3	207	22	178	7	. . .
Seneca Falls Village	6 907	8	0	0	0	8	35	9	26	0	. . .
Shawangunk Town	12 694	5	0	1	0	4	59	22	35	2	. . .
Shelter Island Town	2 423	1	0	0	0	1	77	19	56	2	. . .
Sherburne Village	1 456	0	0	0	0	0	38	8	30	0	. . .
Sherrill	3 130	3	0	0	1	2	28	5	22	1	. . .
Shortsville Village	1 302	5	0	0	0	5	0	0	0	0	. . .
Sidney Village	3 931	12	0	1	2	9	186	16	168	2	. . .
Silver Creek Village	2 864	12	0	0	2	10	75	13	61	1	. . .
Skaneateles Village	2 592	0	0	0	0	0	49	2	47	0	. . .
Sodus Village	1 690	1	0	0	1	0	45	9	36	0	. . .
Solvay Village	6 686	16	0	0	2	14	168	52	107	9	. . .
South Glens Falls Village	3 447	9	0	0	1	8	102	18	80	4	. . .
South Nyack Village	3 470	2	0	0	1	1	61	8	51	2	. . .
Southold Town	19 622	33	0	4	9	20	432	88	323	21	. . .
Spring Valley Village	25 579	180	4	7	49	120	462	84	335	43	. . .
Stillwater Town	6 261	2	0	0	1	1	23	5	18	0	. . .
Stockport Town	2 965	0	0	0	0	0	1	0	1	0	. . .
Stony Point Town	14 985	4	0	0	0	4	78	12	66	0	. . .
Suffern Village	11 000	7	0	0	2	5	84	6	72	6	. . .
Syracuse	143 306	1 570	19	73	554	924	6 486	1 867	3 639	980	53
Tarrytown Village	11 418	11	0	2	5	4	122	21	92	9	. . .
Ticonderoga Town	5 157	6	0	0	0	6	106	24	76	6	. . .
Tonawanda	15 537	40	0	3	6	31	368	56	295	17	. . .
Tonawanda Town	59 435	159	1	13	46	99	1 265	242	946	77	. . .
Troy	48 231	309	4	18	78	209	2 053	517	1 333	203	. . .
Tuckahoe Village	6 266	5	0	0	1	4	21	4	12	5	. . .
Tupper Lake Village	3 876	6	0	0	0	6	138	36	97	5	. . .
Tuxedo Town	2 961	2	0	0	0	2	16	3	13	0	. . .
Ulster Town	12 885	13	0	0	6	7	215	18	183	14	. . .
Utica	59 769	268	8	18	133	109	2 672	619	1 967	86	. . .
Vernon Village	1 180	1	0	0	0	1	32	2	30	0	. . .
Vestal Town	27 094	13	0	3	2	8	649	29	609	11	. . .
Walden Village	6 772	9	0	0	0	9	140	6	129	5	. . .
Wallkill Town	26 919	19	0	1	14	4	534	47	466	21	. . .
Walton Village	2 965	12	0	1	0	11	72	19	52	1	. . .
Wappingers Falls Village	5 039	24	0	1	7	16	130	18	108	4	. . .
Warsaw Village	3 732	7	0	3	1	3	88	12	70	6	. . .
Warwick Town	19 761	3	1	1	1	0	157	39	113	5	. . .
Washingtonville Village	6 280	2	0	0	0	2	105	15	86	4	. . .
Waterford Town and Village	8 735	2	0	1	0	1	76	18	49	9	. . .
Waterloo Village	5 149	6	0	0	1	5	221	34	177	10	. . .
Watertown	26 278	129	3	14	28	84	1 441	227	1 143	71	. . .
Watervliet	10 006	37	0	4	11	22	194	38	144	12	. . .
Watkins Glen Village	2 129	5	0	1	0	4	147	7	138	2	. . .
Waverly Village	4 524	4	0	0	0	4	116	16	98	2	. . .
Wayland Village	1 854	0	0	0	0	0	24	1	22	1	. . .
Webster Town and Village	40 479	20	0	4	2	14	561	116	416	29	. . .
Weedsport Village	1 980	0	0	0	0	0	27	1	26	0	. . .
Wellsville Village	4 823	26	0	0	0	26	177	30	145	2	. . .
Westhampton Beach Village	1 957	2	0	0	1	1	42	4	35	3	. . .
West Seneca Town	45 097	61	1	7	18	35	1 063	147	857	59	. . .
Whitehall Village	2 671	6	0	3	0	3	38	3	33	2	. . .
White Plains	56 590	177	1	7	46	123	1 267	69	1 142	56	. . .
Whitesboro Village	3 890	6	0	0	1	5	44	8	35	1	. . .
Whitestown Town	9 193	1	0	0	0	1	67	14	50	3	. . .
Windham Town	1 778	0	0	0	0	0	48	8	40	0	. . .
Woodbury Town	10 151	4	0	1	1	2	263	20	236	7	. . .
Woodridge Village	992	6	0	0	0	6	12	2	9	1	. . .
Woodstock Town	6 274	5	0	0	1	4	91	20	70	1	. . .
Yonkers	197 408	970	9	21	518	422	3 406	641	2 277	488	34
North Carolina											
Aberdeen	4 645	34	1	1	13	19	285	34	238	13	1
Albemarle	15 646	111	1	8	29	73	880	210	609	61	8
Andrews	1 724	3	0	0	0	3	80	34	46	0	2
Angier	4 106	32	0	1	5	26	182	62	111	9	0
Apex	27 966	46	1	2	7	36	517	93	399	25	1
Archdale	9 426	26	0	2	10	14	412	111	280	21	2
Asheboro	23 601	49	0	4	22	23	1 471	309	1 072	90	1
Asheville	71 571	434	2	16	229	187	5 266	991	3 642	633	40
Atlantic Beach	1 835	19	0	1	2	16	163	29	126	8	0
Aulander	912	1	0	0	1	0	54	35	18	1	0

[1]The FBI does not publish arson data unless it receives data from either the agency or the state for all 12 months of the calendar year.
. . . = Not available.

Table 8. Offenses Known to Law Enforcement, by State and City, 2005—*Continued*

(Number.)

City	Population	Violent crime	Murder and non-negligent man-slaughter	Forcible rape	Robbery	Aggravated assault	Property crime	Burglary	Larceny-theft	Motor vehicle theft	Arson[1]
Ayden	4 666	30	6	1	6	17	213	63	143	7	0
Bailey	685	3	0	0	2	1	36	4	28	4	1
Bald Head Islands	250	0	0	0	0	0	13	3	9	1	0
Banner Elk	946	4	0	2	0	2	26	8	15	3	0
Beaufort	4 061	25	1	1	4	19	166	37	125	4	3
Beech Mountain	310	0	0	0	0	0	24	8	16	0	2
Belhaven	1 963	14	0	0	1	13	59	21	38	0	0
Belmont	8 932	56	1	5	19	31	384	100	245	39	3
Bethel	1 713	16	0	1	1	14	31	6	24	1	0
Beulaville	1 111	2	0	0	0	2	61	9	50	2	0
Biltmore Forest	1 503	0	0	0	0	0	18	5	11	2	0
Biscoe	1 746	3	0	0	2	1	216	22	185	9	0
Black Mountain	7 724	6	1	2	0	3	168	64	95	9	1
Bladenboro	1 751	41	0	1	2	38	139	43	94	2	0
Boiling Spring Lakes	3 931	3	0	0	0	3	68	30	34	4	0
Boiling Springs	3 915	4	0	1	1	2	48	8	33	7	0
Boone	13 507	18	1	4	2	11	429	87	327	15	0
Brevard	6 761	17	0	1	2	14	239	65	165	9	3
Bryson City	1 405	34	0	2	0	32	93	0	88	5	1
Burgaw	3 800	11	0	2	0	9	128	29	90	9	0
Burlington	47 421	420	4	13	91	312	3 207	719	2 352	136	9
Burnsville	1 663	0	0	0	0	0	44	9	33	2	0
Butner	6 248	39	0	2	6	31	287	58	221	8	2
Cameron	158	1	0	0	1	0	13	8	4	1	0
Candor	843	2	0	0	1	1	44	10	28	6	0
Canton	4 076	13	0	1	3	9	222	53	155	14	0
Cape Carteret	1 429	1	0	0	0	1	36	2	33	1	0
Carolina Beach	5 278	29	0	4	9	16	342	95	224	23	3
Carrboro	16 702	94	0	5	39	50	851	207	605	39	4
Carthage	1 944	13	0	1	3	9	46	13	30	3	0
Cary	102 949	133	0	13	50	70	1 963	432	1 428	103	14
Chadbourn	2 142	33	1	2	6	24	203	79	113	11	3
Chapel Hill	50 189	219	2	13	59	145	2 080	425	1 571	84	3
Charlotte-Mecklenburg	677 122	7 933	85	323	3 649	3 876	46 589	12 783	26 708	7 098	317
Cherryville	5 520	18	0	0	4	14	202	57	138	7	0
China Grove	3 755	14	0	1	4	9	130	26	99	5	1
Chocowinity	743	1	0	1	0	0	18	4	13	1	0
Claremont	1 106	3	0	0	0	3	88	22	62	4	0
Clayton	12 375	30	0	2	14	14	434	136	270	28	5
Cleveland	833	1	0	0	1	0	100	5	92	3	0
Clinton	8 840	70	2	6	15	47	614	164	409	41	3
Coats	2 012	9	0	2	2	5	52	18	32	2	0
Concord	60 957	221	5	15	74	127	2 995	505	2 245	245	3
Cornelius	18 172	33	0	2	6	25	326	63	237	26	0
Creedmoor	3 090	13	0	3	1	9	101	16	83	2	3
Davidson	8 482	5	0	0	1	4	81	29	35	17	0
Dobson	1 481	1	0	0	1	0	48	27	20	1	0
Drexel	1 940	2	0	1	1	0	28	6	22	0	0
Dunn	9 953	108	3	10	51	44	817	206	564	47	5
Durham	205 080	1 477	35	89	627	726	12 037	3 157	7 944	936	43
East Spencer	1 788	40	0	3	5	32	121	51	57	13	2
Eden	16 016	75	2	5	19	49	1 040	308	702	30	7
Elizabeth City	18 107	145	2	5	39	99	1 109	280	754	75	15
Elkin	4 163	20	0	2	3	15	198	36	152	10	1
Elon	7 195	7	0	0	0	7	94	25	67	2	0
Emerald Isle	3 709	2	0	0	0	2	190	91	93	6	0
Enfield	2 346	16	1	1	2	12	117	47	65	5	3
Erwin	4 827	7	0	2	0	5	191	60	119	12	0
Fairmont	2 641	62	0	2	14	46	258	93	143	22	1
Faison	782	2	0	0	1	1	24	0	23	1	0
Farmville	4 664	35	1	1	7	26	214	64	142	8	1
Fayetteville	127 323	1 152	14	47	429	662	10 551	2 531	7 234	786	46
Fletcher	4 459	9	1	0	3	5	199	32	153	14	2
Forest City	7 436	45	1	4	17	23	648	133	478	37	7
Franklin	3 615	8	0	1	0	7	158	63	82	13	1
Franklinton	1 916	2	0	0	1	1	111	19	92	0	1
Fremont	1 466	5	1	1	2	1	99	33	61	5	0
Fuquay-Varina	11 295	47	0	7	14	26	523	141	353	29	5
Garland	841	1	0	0	0	1	36	14	20	2	0
Garner	22 134	76	2	1	35	38	1 266	226	978	62	4
Garysburg	1 233	0	0	0	0	0	57	27	23	7	0
Gastonia	69 428	670	5	36	257	372	6 190	1 268	4 389	533	52
Gibsonville	4 601	6	0	0	2	4	73	18	52	3	0
Goldsboro	39 419	325	7	3	109	206	2 694	594	1 956	144	3
Graham	13 718	95	1	4	19	71	716	190	484	42	2
Granite Quarry	2 261	6	0	2	1	3	59	17	33	9	0
Greensboro	235 393	1 941	30	85	787	1 039	14 360	3 954	9 198	1 208	163
Greenville	69 829	509	6	12	177	314	4 321	1 505	2 617	199	8
Grifton	2 083	4	0	0	3	1	69	13	53	3	0
Hamlet	5 931	47	2	4	10	31	337	92	229	16	2

[1]The FBI does not publish arson data unless it receives data from either the agency or the state for all 12 months of the calendar year.

Table 8. Offenses Known to Law Enforcement, by State and City, 2005—*Continued*

(Number.)

City	Population	Violent crime	Murder and non-negligent man-slaughter	Forcible rape	Robbery	Aggravated assault	Property crime	Burglary	Larceny-theft	Motor vehicle theft	Arson[1]
Havelock	22 741	51	0	4	14	33	520	112	388	20	2
Henderson	16 513	130	2	3	67	58	1 511	324	1 126	61	11
Hendersonville	11 419	106	1	10	29	66	1 093	145	890	58	2
Hertford	2 110	17	2	1	10	4	112	36	70	6	0
Hickory	40 779	368	2	28	112	226	3 435	773	2 381	281	15
High Point	94 401	616	8	27	217	364	5 957	1 970	3 509	478	36
Hillsborough	5 390	40	0	0	6	34	239	72	156	11	1
Holly Ridge	804	2	0	0	0	2	95	13	78	4	1
Holly Springs	13 968	17	0	4	1	12	180	49	124	7	2
Hope Mills	12 737	52	0	0	27	25	801	222	544	35	3
Hudson	3 115	2	0	0	0	2	123	32	85	6	0
Huntersville	34 903	72	1	4	20	47	1 204	258	871	75	8
Indian Beach	98	0	0	0	0	0	8	3	5	0	0
Jacksonville	73 538	105	0	21	23	61	799	128	635	36	4
Jefferson	1 448	1	0	0	0	1	8	0	8	0	0
Jonesville	2 295	11	0	2	2	7	156	46	103	7	0
Kenansville	893	3	0	0	2	1	50	7	43	0	0
Kenly	1 827	9	0	1	2	6	171	77	83	11	1
Kernersville	20 827	122	1	9	19	93	1 072	193	825	54	5
Kill Devil Hills	6 532	41	0	4	5	32	509	150	346	13	0
King	6 360	26	0	2	2	22	268	47	212	9	1
Kings Mountain	10 811	47	0	3	18	26	577	138	407	32	3
Kinston	23 298	288	2	8	60	218	2 315	526	1 689	100	10
Kitty Hawk	3 368	7	0	1	1	5	159	68	86	5	2
La Grange	2 866	29	1	0	8	20	135	38	93	4	1
Lake Lure	1 038	1	0	0	0	1	49	22	26	1	0
Lake Royale	. . .	0	0	0	0	0	37	21	16	0	0
Landis	3 098	0	0	0	0	0	160	43	110	7	2
Laurel Park	2 102	2	0	0	1	1	16	5	10	1	1
Laurinburg	16 055	111	1	9	46	55	1 033	401	579	53	10
Leland	4 363	19	1	2	4	12	383	139	242	2	1
Lenoir	18 241	47	0	0	14	33	685	172	454	59	1
Lexington	20 812	148	0	12	32	104	1 236	321	821	94	4
Liberty	2 727	7	0	0	1	6	75	24	51	0	1
Lillington	3 198	15	0	0	2	13	124	24	95	5	1
Lincolnton	10 364	36	0	0	16	20	713	118	555	40	6
Longview	4 874	24	0	2	11	11	321	126	159	36	3
Louisburg	3 335	12	1	1	5	5	211	48	155	8	2
Lumberton	21 668	281	8	9	128	136	3 013	1 008	1 779	226	8
Madison	2 284	13	0	0	4	9	139	52	87	0	0
Maggie Valley	716	6	0	3	0	3	79	11	62	6	0
Maiden	3 281	9	0	0	1	8	117	24	88	5	0
Manteo	1 284	2	0	0	1	1	69	15	51	3	0
Mars Hill	1 764	2	0	0	0	2	58	14	43	1	0
Marshville	2 735	18	0	0	6	12	116	39	67	10	1
Matthews	24 294	61	0	5	28	28	1 084	174	815	95	8
Mayodan	2 421	9	0	0	1	8	88	23	60	5	0
Maysville	1 018	5	0	0	0	5	36	12	22	2	0
Middlesex	865	6	0	3	1	2	26	2	23	1	0
Mint Hill	17 771	74	1	2	22	49	407	181	192	34	. . .
Mocksville	4 431	20	0	4	1	15	321	50	258	13	2
Monroe	28 895	218	5	13	54	146	2 005	401	1 482	122	6
Mooresville	20 457	39	0	3	10	26	515	59	424	32	1
Morehead City	8 626	73	0	6	11	56	645	96	529	20	2
Morganton	17 462	64	1	5	13	45	724	161	526	37	0
Morrisville	11 788	12	0	2	4	6	284	54	211	19	4
Mount Airy	8 560	84	0	6	8	70	655	163	463	29	5
Mount Holly	9 799	44	0	2	9	33	284	93	164	27	2
Mount Olive	4 548	68	3	1	9	55	401	67	315	19	0
Murfreesboro	2 321	20	0	0	6	14	172	53	119	0	0
Murphy	1 581	12	1	3	0	8	129	20	105	4	0
Nags Head	3 118	12	0	4	1	7	367	104	260	3	0
Nashville	4 528	19	0	1	6	12	84	31	46	7	0
New Bern	23 757	154	2	13	45	94	1 495	341	1 113	41	3
Newland	711	1	0	0	0	1	22	1	20	1	0
Newport	3 859	9	0	0	1	8	64	24	37	3	0
Newton	13 095	42	1	7	12	22	813	231	539	43	2
North Topsail Beach	858	4	0	0	0	4	71	35	35	1	0
North Wilkesboro	4 183	21	0	1	3	17	270	54	206	10	7
Norwood	2 210	7	0	0	1	6	97	17	74	6	0
Oak Island	7 402	28	0	0	1	27	361	151	201	9	1
Ocean Isle Beach	491	1	0	0	0	1	167	24	140	3	0
Old Fort	991	2	0	0	0	2	44	9	32	3	0
Oxford	8 647	95	1	2	34	58	677	229	413	35	2
Pembroke	2 741	23	2	0	7	14	279	172	94	13	0
Pilot Mountain	1 295	4	1	1	0	2	107	6	99	2	0
Pinebluff	1 197	6	0	0	0	6	20	6	13	1	0
Pinehurst	11 181	7	0	0	3	4	123	4	118	1	1
Pinetops	1 357	14	1	1	0	12	49	11	36	2	0
Pineville	3 704	86	1	3	39	43	992	83	820	89	1

[1]The FBI does not publish arson data unless it receives data from either the agency or the state for all 12 months of the calendar year.
. . . = Not available.

Table 8. Offenses Known to Law Enforcement, by State and City, 2005—*Continued*

(Number.)

City	Population	Violent crime	Murder and non-negligent man-slaughter	Forcible rape	Robbery	Aggravated assault	Property crime	Burglary	Larceny-theft	Motor vehicle theft	Arson[1]
Pittsboro	2 482	7	0	0	4	3	71	6	62	3	0
Plymouth	4 052	75	1	0	2	72	242	88	144	10	1
Raeford	3 591	22	0	3	10	9	244	75	157	12	0
Raleigh	332 084	2 051	20	88	762	1 181	12 528	3 040	8 480	1 008	78
Ramseur	1 625	8	0	1	1	6	119	32	87	0	1
Randleman	3 673	9	1	0	0	8	333	55	267	11	2
Red Springs	3 514	26	2	3	9	12	296	158	106	32	4
Reidsville	15 026	74	1	3	22	48	1 155	362	746	47	8
Richlands	882	1	0	1	0	0	28	9	18	1	1
River Bend	2 866	1	0	0	1	0	3	1	2	0	0
Roanoke Rapids	16 670	116	0	5	40	71	1 129	292	781	56	7
Robbins	1 228	1	0	0	0	1	38	5	27	6	0
Robersonville	1 675	23	1	0	8	14	127	29	94	4	0
Rockingham	9 478	62	0	2	10	50	906	208	664	34	8
Rockwell	2 009	6	0	0	1	5	56	8	48	0	0
Rocky Mount	57 288	497	8	22	197	270	4 876	1 380	3 264	232	19
Rowland	1 158	19	0	1	14	4	121	75	38	8	0
Roxboro	8 906	80	0	4	21	55	496	165	308	23	1
Salisbury	26 960	251	5	12	83	151	2 025	406	1 500	119	8
Sanford	23 859	147	6	9	62	70	1 763	397	1 254	112	11
Scotland Neck	2 291	23	0	0	3	20	269	97	168	4	2
Selma	6 610	52	0	3	23	26	456	187	242	27	1
Sharpsburg	2 491	15	0	1	3	11	118	72	44	2	0
Shelby	21 629	198	5	10	69	114	1 650	465	1 086	99	16
Siler City	8 212	30	2	1	11	16	297	43	236	18	0
Smithfield	11 897	128	2	10	40	76	907	186	675	46	1
Southern Pines	11 748	86	0	5	24	57	642	181	427	34	0
Southern Shores	2 638	3	0	0	1	2	63	24	37	2	0
Southport	2 655	11	0	0	2	9	177	60	112	5	2
Sparta	1 824	1	0	0	0	1	43	17	24	2	0
Spencer	3 400	18	0	5	8	5	187	72	110	5	0
Spring Hope	1 291	3	0	0	2	1	58	20	38	0	0
Stanley	3 136	13	0	1	5	7	123	44	75	4	0
Star	824	1	0	0	0	1	29	7	20	2	0
Statesville	24 896	264	4	8	72	180	2 027	616	1 318	93	7
St. Pauls	2 284	5	1	0	1	3	122	27	81	14	0
Sunset Beach	2 130	3	0	0	1	2	59	19	40	0	0
Surf City	1 668	15	0	0	3	12	140	55	84	1	0
Swansboro	1 420	5	0	1	1	3	62	15	46	1	0
Sylva	2 452	25	0	1	1	23	253	65	179	9	1
Tabor City	2 666	25	0	3	6	16	172	69	95	8	1
Tarboro	10 759	49	0	1	9	39	456	95	356	5	2
Thomasville	26 180	191	0	5	56	130	1 310	318	921	71	3
Topsail Beach	532	0	0	0	0	0	16	3	13	0	1
Trent Woods	4 125	1	1	0	0	0	34	7	27	0	0
Troutman	1 705	9	0	0	1	8	95	30	62	3	0
Troy	3 519	13	1	2	2	8	160	33	123	4	0
Tryon	1 775	5	0	0	3	2	50	25	23	2	0
Valdese	4 625	9	0	0	0	9	100	30	60	10	1
Vass	776	0	0	0	0	0	30	5	22	3	0
Wadesboro	5 417	62	0	3	17	42	502	180	291	31	6
Wake Forest	17 679	27	0	0	8	19	505	112	381	12	4
Wallace	3 580	19	2	0	6	11	196	103	74	19	1
Walnut Creek	865	0	0	0	0	0	3	2	1	0	0
Warsaw	3 136	17	1	2	7	7	315	26	268	21	1
Washington	9 926	45	1	5	17	22	449	145	281	23	3
Waxhaw	3 097	8	0	2	0	6	111	34	73	4	0
Waynesville	9 572	28	1	4	5	18	282	103	158	21	1
Weaverville	2 496	2	0	1	1	0	92	11	81	0	0
Weldon	1 344	9	0	0	3	6	123	23	92	8	1
Wendell	4 461	12	0	0	1	11	118	45	65	8	0
West Jefferson	1 088	4	1	0	0	3	33	5	27	1	0
Whitakers	790	3	0	1	1	1	31	12	17	2	0
White Lake	545	9	0	0	0	9	85	33	49	3	0
Whiteville	5 236	77	1	2	23	51	839	144	660	35	1
Wilkesboro	3 254	19	0	1	7	11	391	73	309	9	0
Williamston	5 772	65	1	3	8	53	506	138	349	19	0
Wilmington	94 843	794	8	57	292	437	6 558	1 855	4 000	703	16
Wilson	47 280	233	4	8	55	166	1 927	561	1 271	95	8
Windsor	2 288	7	0	1	4	2	134	33	92	9	1
Wingate	2 773	25	0	0	3	22	68	18	46	4	0
Winston-Salem	194 708	1 639	16	118	608	897	12 118	4 016	7 146	956	29
Winterville	4 747	14	0	1	2	11	179	22	148	9	2
Winton	933	2	0	0	0	2	31	5	26	0	0
Woodland	814	13	1	1	0	11	30	14	15	1	0
Wrightsville Beach	2 581	8	0	1	1	6	258	110	140	8	0
Yadkinville	2 891	20	0	0	4	16	138	19	116	3	0
Yanceyville	2 162	14	0	1	1	12	104	37	58	9	0
Youngsville	718	2	0	1	1	0	25	7	17	1	0
Zebulon	4 204	46	0	1	14	31	243	32	203	8	1

[1]The FBI does not publish arson data unless it receives data from either the agency or the state for all 12 months of the calendar year.

Table 8. Offenses Known to Law Enforcement, by State and City, 2005—*Continued*

(Number.)

City	Population	Violent crime	Murder and non-negligent man-slaughter	Forcible rape	Robbery	Aggravated assault	Property crime	Burglary	Larceny-theft	Motor vehicle theft	Arson[1]
North Dakota											
Beulah	3 071	4	0	1	0	3	36	7	25	4	1
Bismarck	56 825	51	0	8	8	35	1 488	197	1 164	127	12
Devils Lake	6 867	26	0	0	3	23	319	40	261	18	1
Dickinson	15 743	11	0	2	3	6	545	118	406	21	0
Emerado	498	0	0	0	0	0	16	3	10	3	0
Fargo	91 380	104	2	42	11	49	2 348	438	1 697	213	10
Grafton	4 283	1	0	0	0	1	134	15	113	6	0
Grand Forks	49 162	65	1	9	6	49	2 074	271	1 628	175	5
Harvey	1 801	3	0	2	0	1	21	1	18	2	0
Jamestown	14 979	34	0	13	1	20	337	60	265	12	5
Lincoln	2 155	0	0	0	0	0	16	3	13	0	0
Mandan	17 031	29	0	3	3	23	401	26	341	34	5
Mayville	1 936	4	0	4	0	0	11	3	6	2	0
Minot	35 277	81	1	28	4	48	1 041	108	855	78	6
Northwood	907	0	0	0	0	0	4	0	4	0	0
Portland	590	0	0	0	0	0	0	0	0	0	0
Rolla	1 449	2	0	0	0	2	105	11	86	8	1
Rugby	2 738	2	0	1	0	1	37	5	29	3	0
Steele	717	1	0	0	0	1	3	0	2	1	0
Valley City	6 469	3	0	1	0	2	78	4	66	8	1
Wahpeton	8 442	9	0	3	0	6	184	16	154	14	0
Watford City	1 345	2	0	0	0	2	9	3	6	0	0
Williston	12 235	15	0	3	1	11	186	26	118	42	0
Ohio											
Akron	212 272	1 265	27	183	625	430	12 040	3 409	7 253	1 378	92
Alliance	23 278	86	1	13	26	46	1 086	247	799	40	11
Amberley Village	3 311	3	0	0	0	3	26	2	22	2	0
Amherst	11 810	19	0	1	12	6	210	31	176	3	1
Arcanum	2 049	1	0	0	0	1	32	9	23	0	0
Archbold	4 502	2	0	1	0	1	74	15	57	2	0
Ashland	21 636	23	0	7	9	7	606	82	514	10	2
Athens	21 834	35	1	9	4	21	502	88	401	13	1
Aurora	14 363	6	1	0	1	4	210	45	159	6	0
Avon	14 887	13	0	1	1	11	205	55	138	12	2
Bainbridge Township	11 237	13	0	0	0	13	313	47	262	4	1
Barberton	27 374	62	0	22	21	19	1 295	225	1 002	68	5
Bath Township (Summit County)	10 100	22	0	0	7	15	251	29	209	13	0
Bay Village	15 446	3	0	0	0	3	5	3	1	1	0
Beavercreek	39 438	45	0	4	11	30	1 181	106	1 013	62	3
Beaver Township	6 181	3	0	1	1	1	221	77	127	17	0
Bedford	13 589	27	0	6	7	14	434	33	348	53	1
Bedford Heights	11 020	28	0	1	9	18	272	56	177	39	2
Bellaire	4 776	5	0	1	3	1	216	38	170	8	3
Bellbrook	7 013	5	0	1	0	4	122	10	110	2	0
Bellefontaine	13 040	88	2	5	12	69	662	146	496	20	0
Bellville	1 750	3	0	0	0	3	74	10	62	2	0
Belpre	6 588	8	0	1	3	4	124	16	103	5	0
Berea[3]	18 284	15	0	3	5	7	388	36	338	14	2
Bexley	12 416	34	0	1	24	9	468	159	294	15	0
Blue Ash	11 922	19	1	1	7	10	310	48	255	7	2
Boardman	41 172	76	0	12	53	11	2 172	303	1 727	142	9
Bowling Green	29 467	34	0	7	13	14	930	95	813	22	0
Bradford	1 893	0	0	0	0	0	11	6	5	0	0
Brecksville	13 383	1	0	0	0	1	68	6	59	3	0
Brimfield Township	7 936	6	3	1	0	2	210	41	162	7	0
Broadview Heights	17 231	12	0	0	0	12	96	23	59	14	1
Brooklyn	11 056	46	0	1	30	15	647	70	497	80	0
Brooklyn Heights	1 530	0	0	0	0	0	25	5	17	3	1
Brook Park	20 305	22	0	3	3	16	222	16	141	65	0
Brookville	5 307	3	0	3	0	0	97	26	66	5	0
Bryan	8 393	7	0	5	1	1	228	39	179	10	0
Buckeye Lake[3]	3 052	11	0	10	1	0	64	33	20	11	2
Cadiz	3 386	1	0	0	1	0	89	16	69	4	0
Cambridge	11 662	105	0	11	10	84	1 307	132	1 110	65	0
Campbell	8 995	21	1	3	13	4	207	85	101	21	0
Canal Fulton	5 071	0	0	0	0	0	143	35	105	3	0
Canfield	7 194	2	0	1	1	0	130	13	113	4	0
Canton[3]	79 940	668	4	57	381	226	6 051	1 566	3 939	546	40
Cardington	2 024	4	0	1	0	3	12	2	9	1	0
Carlisle	5 623	2	0	0	1	1	73	20	47	6	1
Celina	10 273	26	0	7	2	17	418	74	331	13	4
Centerville	23 132	23	0	4	7	12	496	84	387	25	0
Chardon	5 285	10	0	0	1	9	65	2	59	4	0
Cheviot	8 403	7	0	0	6	1	143	23	115	5	0
Chillicothe	22 049	60	2	12	30	16	2 242	300	1 852	90	14
Cincinnati	314 292	3 723	79	315	2 319	1 010	22 411	5 430	14 029	2 952	240
Circleville	13 371	44	1	13	6	24	959	232	685	42	5
Cleveland	458 885	6 416	109	478	3 743	2 086	28 543	8 598	13 145	6 800	505
Cleveland Heights	48 664	21	0	0	21	0	618	78	453	87	0
Clinton Township	4 057	42	0	1	35	6	449	57	346	46	2
Clyde	6 104	7	0	1	1	5	187	25	156	6	2
Coitsville Township	1 647	2	0	0	1	1	47	19	24	4	0
Coldwater	4 446	2	0	0	0	2	84	19	61	4	0
Columbus	730 329	6 111	102	518	3 777	1 714	54 141	14 604	31 724	7 813	465

[1]The FBI does not publish arson data unless it receives data from either the agency or the state for all 12 months of the calendar year.
[3]Because of changes in the state/local agency's reporting practices, figures are not comparable to previous years' data.

Table 8. Offenses Known to Law Enforcement, by State and City, 2005—*Continued*

(Number.)

City	Population	Violent crime	Murder and non-negligent man-slaughter	Forcible rape	Robbery	Aggravated assault	Property crime	Burglary	Larceny-theft	Motor vehicle theft	Arson[1]
Conneaut	12 699	35	0	1	1	33	574	127	414	33	0
Copley Township	14 041	6	0	5	0	1	297	50	231	16	0
Covington	2 564	2	0	2	0	0	46	12	34	0	0
Crestline	4 999	11	1	0	2	8	66	13	40	13	0
Creston	2 147	2	0	1	0	1	84	9	73	2	0
Cuyahoga Falls	50 537	67	0	19	18	30	1 879	194	1 553	132	1
Dayton	160 363	1 533	32	140	851	510	11 471	3 229	6 031	2 211	143
Deer Park	5 683	7	0	1	4	2	110	19	87	4	0
Defiance	16 083	31	0	8	3	20	635	102	524	9	2
Delaware	30 025	84	1	41	19	23	1 115	243	830	42	12
Delhi Township	30 702	29	0	4	9	16	453	49	387	17	1
Delta	2 949	4	0	0	1	3	118	19	97	2	0
Dover	12 503	2	0	1	0	1	203	42	152	9	1
Dublin	34 316	9	0	2	7	0	574	141	402	31	5
Eastlake	19 910	20	0	2	15	3	448	37	370	41	3
East Liverpool	12 545	17	0	1	7	9	497	133	342	22	0
Eaton	8 219	14	0	1	2	11	365	39	311	15	2
Englewood	12 604	25	1	6	10	8	443	51	371	21	1
Euclid	50 420	176	3	14	104	55	1 612	342	1 075	195	10
Fairborn	32 425	163	1	39	46	77	1 425	312	1 033	80	14
Fairfield	42 398	164	0	19	33	112	1 658	250	1 292	116	9
Fairfield Township	16 640	171	0	6	5	160	526	83	411	32	0
Fairlawn	7 241	4	0	1	3	0	398	17	365	16	0
Fairport Harbor	3 228	8	0	2	2	4	161	36	120	5	2
Fayette	1 339	3	0	1	0	2	26	4	21	1	0
Findlay	40 193	98	0	23	24	51	1 871	375	1 457	39	10
Forest	1 475	3	0	0	1	2	45	12	30	3	0
Forest Park	18 389	46	0	8	29	9	814	124	647	43	2
Fort Recovery	1 319	1	0	0	0	1	33	16	17	0	0
Franklin	12 251	25	0	2	7	16	698	151	492	55	2
Franklin Township	14 940	14	0	4	4	6	177	68	91	18	4
Fredericktown	2 538	2	0	2	0	0	88	16	71	1	0
Fremont	17 189	55	0	1	32	22	1 230	213	993	24	5
Gahanna	32 805	43	0	5	27	11	887	179	647	61	9
Galion	11 428	29	0	6	3	20	524	87	419	18	1
Garfield Heights	29 458	136	2	20	34	80	918	234	620	64	4
Gates Mills	2 399	0	0	0	0	0	14	2	12	0	0
Geneva-on-the-Lake	1 542	2	0	2	0	0	17	7	9	1	0
Genoa Township	12 806	5	1	2	2	0	191	39	150	2	0
Georgetown	3 821	11	0	1	3	7	123	17	105	1	0
German Township (Montgomery County)	3 183	4	0	1	0	3	66	15	45	6	1
Gibsonburg	2 473	5	0	0	1	4	121	27	89	5	0
Glendale	2 164	3	0	1	2	0	24	4	15	5	0
Goshen Township (Clermont County)	15 604	32	0	1	6	25	359	78	258	23	5
Grandview Heights	6 334	6	0	2	4	0	193	51	137	5	0
Granville	5 243	1	0	0	0	1	66	13	52	1	0
Greenfield	5 134	17	0	4	2	11	673	124	500	49	3
Greenville	13 273	44	0	6	6	32	521	121	370	30	5
Groveport	4 578	5	0	1	1	3	158	23	123	12	1
Hamilton	61 023	500	3	84	220	193	4 449	1 013	2 966	470	22
Harrison	7 587	9	0	3	4	2	355	33	307	15	1
Hartville	2 291	0	0	0	0	0	55	10	42	3	0
Heath	8 765	24	0	4	9	11	(7)	61	450	(7)	2
Hebron	2 119	3	0	0	1	2	140	34	102	4	1
Highland Heights	8 567	0	0	0	0	0	104	13	80	11	0
Highland Hills	1 595	0	0	0	0	0	0	0	0	0	0
Hilliard	26 461	33	0	2	19	12	781	148	602	31	12
Howland Township	17 128	9	0	0	6	3	533	120	386	27	0
Hubbard Township	5 927	13	0	0	5	8	240	45	166	29	2
Hudson	23 064	8	0	3	0	5	248	59	178	11	6
Hunting Valley	710	0	0	0	0	0	0	0	0	0	0
Huron	7 695	3	0	1	1	1	167	32	133	2	0
Indian Hill	5 655	2	0	1	0	1	51	7	40	4	0
Jackson Township (Stark County)	40 078	47	0	2	25	20	1 245	150	1 042	53	3
Johnstown	3 757	3	0	2	1	0	114	15	93	6	2
Kent	27 613	74	0	11	19	44	834	201	571	62	67
Kettering	55 928	73	3	30	32	8	1 910	347	1 428	135	9
Kirtland	7 109	4	0	0	1	3	53	14	39	0	0
Kirtland Hills	702	0	0	0	0	0	9	1	8	0	0
Lakemore	2 536	8	1	3	2	2	143	21	118	4	4
Lake Township	7 343	12	0	4	6	2	532	57	460	15	0
Lakewood	53 995	114	2	5	37	70	1 334	237	961	136	9
Lancaster	35 949	102	0	24	32	46	1 952	339	1 509	104	5
Lawrence Township	8 436	10	1	0	0	9	101	25	70	6	0
Lebanon[3]	19 379	42	1	13	9	19	552	99	422	31	1
Lexington	4 106	1	0	0	0	1	70	25	44	1	0
Liberty Township	12 379	16	0	0	15	1	543	118	373	52	1
Lima	39 350	453	5	92	126	230	2 678	839	1 687	152	30
Lockland	3 453	24	1	0	15	8	185	51	104	30	1
Logan	7 090	5	0	2	2	1	438	69	356	13	1

[1]The FBI does not publish arson data unless it receives data from either the agency or the state for all 12 months of the calendar year.
[3]Because of changes in the state/local agency's reporting practices, figures are not comparable to previous years' data.
[7]After examining the data and making inquiries, the FBI determined that the agency's offense count was inflated. Consequently, this figure is not included in this table.

Table 8. Offenses Known to Law Enforcement, by State and City, 2005—*Continued*

(Number.)

City	Population	Violent crime	Murder and non-negligent man-slaughter	Forcible rape	Robbery	Aggravated assault	Property crime	Burglary	Larceny-theft	Motor vehicle theft	Arson[1]
London	9 332	14	0	4	4	6	303	52	247	4	1
Lorain	67 945	341	6	14	119	202	2 321	661	1 499	161	3
Lordstown	3 642	1	0	0	0	1	45	14	30	1	1
Loudonville	2 992	4	0	0	0	4	105	10	93	2	0
Lyndhurst	14 606	2	0	0	0	2	5	1	3	1	0
Madeira	8 468	1	0	0	0	1	75	9	61	5	1
Madison Township (Lake County)[3]	16 503	15	0	5	2	8	374	58	299	17	1
Malvern	1 233	0	0	0	0	0	43	13	30	0	0
Manchester	2 085	3	0	0	1	2	15	6	8	1	0
Mansfield	50 579	161	0	31	94	36	3 343	906	2 217	220	28
Marietta	14 301	28	0	13	5	10	535	107	402	26	1
Marion	37 152	83	1	24	26	32	1 493	345	1 115	33	5
Marysville	16 794	19	0	5	8	6	572	119	434	19	3
Maumee	14 478	8	0	3	3	2	556	80	456	20	2
Mayfield Heights	18 546	7	0	0	2	5	370	26	316	28	0
Mayfield Village	3 285	2	0	0	1	1	81	10	69	2	0
McComb	1 729	4	0	1	1	2	47	8	39	0	0
Medina Township	8 400	0	0	0	0	0	128	20	100	8	0
Mentor	51 355	57	0	12	29	16	1 385	159	1 133	93	12
Mentor-on-the-Lake	8 297	5	0	0	4	1	91	6	76	9	0
Miamisburg	19 818	49	0	8	19	22	892	211	559	122	6
Miami Township	38 976	34	0	9	8	17	714	95	585	34	5
Middlefield	2 412	3	0	0	0	3	63	2	58	3	0
Middletown	51 827	237	2	44	110	81	3 540	721	2 657	162	20
Milford	6 369	10	0	5	4	1	217	19	193	5	0
Millersburg	3 567	4	0	0	0	4	85	13	67	5	0
Milton Township	2 892	3	0	1	0	2	73	22	44	7	0
Minerva	3 993	7	0	1	1	5	161	27	128	6	0
Mingo Junction	3 474	16	0	0	2	14	77	26	44	7	0
Mogadore	3 959	0	0	0	0	0	80	12	67	1	0
Monroe[3]	11 849	49	0	14	4	31	624	105	499	20	4
Montgomery	10 151	2	0	1	0	1	233	23	202	8	3
Montpelier	4 189	7	0	4	1	2	221	49	167	5	4
Montville Township	6 574	3	0	0	1	2	89	13	72	4	0
Mount Gilead	3 594	3	0	1	0	2	118	24	85	9	0
Mount Healthy	6 816	29	0	1	21	7	225	23	180	22	2
Mount Sterling	1 843	2	1	0	0	1	68	9	56	3	0
Munroe Falls	5 329	3	0	0	0	3	56	11	43	2	1
Napoleon	9 177	10	0	6	1	3	418	79	328	11	3
Navarre	1 442	0	0	0	0	0	8	1	7	0	0
New Albany	5 335	3	0	1	0	2	92	21	69	2	0
Newark	46 766	114	0	29	56	29	2 495	570	1 801	124	43
Newcomerstown	3 988	6	0	0	0	6	134	11	111	12	0
New Concord	2 680	1	0	0	0	1	5	3	1	1	0
New Lexington	4 656	7	2	0	3	2	158	22	128	8	1
New Middletown	1 631	0	0	0	0	0	29	9	20	0	0
Newtown	2 357	3	0	0	0	3	65	6	55	4	0
North Baltimore	3 342	1	0	0	0	1	5	0	4	1	0
North Canton	16 803	11	0	3	6	2	327	63	254	10	2
North College Hill	9 532	80	0	5	39	36	549	108	379	62	1
North Olmsted	33 120	45	1	8	16	20	543	85	396	62	5
North Ridgeville	25 215	22	0	7	4	11	415	88	306	21	4
Northwood	5 495	11	0	1	8	2	432	51	363	18	2
Norton	11 601	12	3	1	3	5	58	11	45	2	2
Norwalk	16 464	0	0	0	0	0	363	74	277	12	0
Oakwood	8 821	5	0	1	0	4	145	28	116	1	0
Olmsted Falls	8 504	5	0	2	1	2	127	13	108	6	2
Ontario	5 264	9	0	3	3	3	524	28	481	15	0
Oregon	19 277	9	0	0	0	9	284	12	272	0	0
Orrville	8 506	11	0	6	1	4	196	30	164	2	4
Ottawa Hills	4 588	1	0	1	0	0	31	9	19	3	0
Oxford	22 327	93	0	10	14	69	721	150	550	21	3
Parma	82 708	146	0	12	63	71	1 966	573	1 216	177	12
Parma Heights	20 963	19	0	4	8	7	468	91	332	45	5
Pataskala	12 353	15	0	7	2	6	354	107	222	25	5
Peninsula	669	0	0	0	0	0	39	7	29	3	0
Perkins Township	12 697	15	0	2	5	8	351	11	339	1	0
Perrysburg	16 954	13	0	1	2	10	454	69	373	12	0
Perry Township (Franklin County)	3 623	2	0	0	1	1	75	9	59	7	0
Piqua	20 783	44	1	16	16	11	1 545	266	1 225	54	11
Plain City	3 257	3	0	3	0	0	41	4	31	6	0
Poland Township	11 579	0	0	0	0	0	43	10	32	1	0
Poland Village	2 769	4	0	0	0	4	29	4	23	2	0
Port Clinton	6 332	5	0	5	0	0	221	37	179	5	0
Portsmouth	20 109	193	0	21	107	65	2 391	557	1 660	174	1
Powell	9 720	3	0	1	1	1	116	28	87	1	0
Powhatan Point	1 711	0	0	0	0	0	6	2	4	0	0
Ravenna[3]	11 508	7	0	0	5	2	601	109	453	39	0
Reading	10 526	44	0	13	16	15	356	61	253	42	0
Reminderville	2 432	1	0	0	0	1	22	4	18	0	0

[1]The FBI does not publish arson data unless it receives data from either the agency or the state for all 12 months of the calendar year.
[3]Because of changes in the state/local agency's reporting practices, figures are not comparable to previous years' data.

Table 8. Offenses Known to Law Enforcement, by State and City, 2005—*Continued*

(Number.)

City	Population	Violent crime	Murder and non-negligent man-slaughter	Forcible rape	Robbery	Aggravated assault	Property crime	Burglary	Larceny-theft	Motor vehicle theft	Arson[1]
Reynoldsburg	32 957	84	0	13	44	27	1 158	204	862	92	6
Richland Township	8 679	0	0	0	0	0	21	1	17	3	0
Rittman	6 315	12	0	0	2	10	79	11	63	5	4
Riverside	22 879	59	0	4	27	28	1 037	255	624	158	10
Salem	12 068	2	0	0	1	1	77	3	69	5	0
Sandusky	26 989	189	1	7	49	132	1 831	385	1 379	67	3
Sebring	4 755	6	0	0	0	6	212	44	154	14	0
Seven Hills	12 007	8	0	1	1	6	81	35	40	6	0
Seville	2 445	4	0	0	0	4	64	14	47	3	0
Shadyside	3 584	2	0	0	0	2	66	16	47	3	0
Sharon Township	2 344	0	0	0	0	0	46	12	31	3	0
Sharonville	13 305	26	1	1	16	8	665	87	535	43	2
Sheffield Lake	9 175	8	0	0	3	5	217	38	169	10	1
Shelby	9 484	12	0	2	7	3	497	53	434	10	1
Silverton	4 830	12	0	2	6	4	174	21	120	33	3
Smith Township	4 966	15	0	2	3	10	109	24	74	11	0
Solon	22 319	14	1	4	1	8	277	44	232	1	0
South Euclid	22 514	46	0	0	24	22	490	107	328	55	1
South Russell	4 017	2	0	0	0	2	25	6	19	0	0
South Solon	392	0	0	0	0	0	0	0	0	0	0
Spencerville	2 219	2	0	0	0	2	60	10	49	1	0
Springboro	15 787	11	0	3	3	5	262	32	216	14	0
Springdale	9 954	41	2	7	26	6	903	49	812	42	1
Springfield	63 637	548	7	70	280	191	6 321	1 832	4 027	462	13
Springfield Township (Hamilton County)	36 222	129	2	13	55	59	837	175	594	68	2
Springfield Township (Summit County)	15 461	34	0	7	9	18	854	166	655	33	3
St. Bernard	4 585	22	0	0	18	4	186	30	142	14	0
St. Henry	2 324	1	0	0	0	1	13	3	10	0	0
Steubenville	19 521	80	1	9	36	34	1 015	136	836	43	0
St. Paris	1 994	0	0	0	0	0	56	8	47	1	0
Stow	34 409	27	0	12	7	8	659	83	555	21	5
Streetsboro	13 906	13	0	4	6	3	475	58	407	10	7
Strongsville[3]	44 334	38	0	5	13	20	805	116	659	30	2
Sugarcreek Township	6 771	9	0	2	1	6	187	17	166	4	1
Swanton	3 386	3	0	0	0	3	105	20	79	6	0
Sylvania	18 913	9	1	5	0	3	292	46	233	13	3
Sylvania Township	25 936	1	0	0	0	1	299	8	291	0	0
Tiffin	17 517	22	0	10	4	8	749	172	561	16	0
Tipp City	9 305	10	0	4	3	3	282	32	245	5	1
Toledo	305 107	3 725	28	179	1 356	2 162	23 630	7 101	13 331	3 198	421
Toronto	5 489	5	0	0	0	5	93	16	73	4	0
Trenton	10 299	2	1	0	1	0	125	39	84	2	0
Twinsburg	17 294	18	1	1	7	9	186	42	138	6	4
University Heights	13 559	26	0	10	11	5	250	42	199	9	2
Upper Arlington	31 874	22	0	3	11	8	421	85	327	9	7
Urbana	11 620	28	1	7	5	15	457	91	353	13	3
Vandalia	14 310	11	0	4	4	3	387	77	287	23	6
Van Wert	10 538	23	0	4	5	14	500	90	393	17	7
Vermilion	10 976	11	0	3	0	8	314	63	241	10	2
Wadsworth	19 716	13	0	5	1	7	422	76	322	24	7
Waite Hill	510	1	0	0	0	1	1	1	0	0	0
Walbridge	3 095	1	0	1	0	0	41	6	33	2	0
Walton Hills	2 371	2	0	0	1	1	31	9	22	0	0
Wapakoneta	9 535	8	0	1	3	4	190	40	143	7	0
Warrensville Heights	14 450	28	0	3	23	2	336	99	163	74	0
Warren Township	6 304	65	0	1	5	59	306	80	200	26	3
Washington Court House	13 308	42	1	7	9	25	562	117	421	24	2
Waterville Township	5 162	0	0	0	0	0	26	6	20	0	0
Wauseon	7 306	4	0	1	2	1	155	14	136	5	1
Waverly	4 464	1	0	0	0	1	326	29	291	6	0
Waynesville	2 930	2	0	0	0	2	22	1	15	6	0
Wellsville	4 067	22	0	0	2	20	50	11	27	12	0
West Carrollton	13 305	43	0	8	8	27	595	141	338	116	11
West Chester Township	53 742	66	0	21	20	25	1 635	294	1 278	63	15
Westerville	34 861	32	0	2	17	13	958	151	784	23	18
West Jefferson	4 299	0	0	0	0	0	149	30	111	8	1
Whitehall	18 266	146	0	18	98	30	1 664	411	1 086	167	6
Willard	6 854	4	0	0	2	2	184	27	156	1	0
Willoughby	22 503	22	0	6	6	10	476	92	344	40	7
Willowick	14 181	10	0	3	2	5	239	27	183	29	0
Wilmington	12 361	43	1	6	13	23	612	79	531	2	3
Windham	2 763	11	0	4	3	4	182	33	138	11	0
Wintersville	3 805	4	0	2	0	2	82	10	69	3	0
Woodlawn	2 634	12	1	2	6	3	215	31	162	22	1
Worthington	13 341	13	0	1	10	2	389	64	298	27	4
Wyoming	7 859	6	0	0	5	1	115	22	85	8	0
Xenia	23 778	28	0	11	13	4	1 224	178	1 005	41	7
Youngstown	77 747	917	34	60	347	476	4 698	1 718	2 216	764	107

[1]The FBI does not publish arson data unless it receives data from either the agency or the state for all 12 months of the calendar year.
[3]Because of changes in the state/local agency's reporting practices, figures are not comparable to previous years' data.

Table 8. Offenses Known to Law Enforcement, by State and City, 2005—*Continued*

(Number.)

City	Population	Violent crime	Murder and non-negligent man-slaughter	Forcible rape	Robbery	Aggravated assault	Property crime	Burglary	Larceny-theft	Motor vehicle theft	Arson[1]
Oklahoma											
Achille	524	5	0	0	0	5	23	7	14	2	2
Ada	15 949	127	1	14	12	100	902	253	597	52	13
Agra	361	0	0	0	0	0	0	0	0	0	0
Altus	20 534	55	1	10	12	32	872	225	615	32	10
Alva	4 968	4	0	0	0	4	136	32	99	5	2
Anadarko	6 608	56	1	1	7	47	493	151	309	33	19
Antlers	2 537	27	1	1	0	25	102	29	70	3	1
Apache	1 605	10	1	0	2	7	33	12	18	3	1
Ardmore	24 509	260	0	11	27	222	1 423	320	1 046	57	6
Arkoma	2 197	1	0	0	0	1	21	1	18	2	0
Atoka	3 045	12	0	1	2	9	123	37	81	5	2
Barnsdall	1 299	1	0	0	0	1	3	1	1	1	0
Bartlesville	34 877	123	2	16	10	95	1 339	303	965	71	13
Beaver	1 453	5	0	0	0	5	34	6	26	2	0
Beggs	1 392	3	0	1	0	2	47	8	35	4	1
Bethany	20 008	75	0	12	20	43	785	135	565	85	2
Bixby	17 851	31	0	3	6	22	353	91	227	35	0
Blackwell	7 408	17	0	4	3	10	223	79	132	12	8
Blanchard	3 394	6	0	3	1	2	98	21	62	15	1
Boise City	1 364	0	0	0	0	0	10	0	10	0	0
Boley	1 111	2	0	0	0	2	16	6	8	2	0
Bristow	4 354	16	0	2	2	12	193	43	136	14	1
Broken Arrow	84 982	188	0	11	22	155	2 070	415	1 484	171	21
Broken Bow	4 194	36	0	1	2	33	391	103	259	29	8
Buffalo	1 139	1	0	0	0	1	7	3	3	1	0
Caddo	971	4	0	0	1	3	22	10	9	3	1
Calera	1 795	8	0	2	0	6	62	18	40	4	1
Carnegie	1 612	8	0	0	1	7	46	28	14	4	2
Catoosa	6 062	17	0	1	4	12	279	85	152	42	1
Chandler	2 878	6	0	0	2	4	89	19	65	5	0
Checotah	3 532	14	0	3	2	9	139	38	90	11	1
Chelsea	2 262	3	0	1	0	2	44	22	19	3	0
Cherokee	1 525	0	0	0	0	0	9	6	3	0	0
Chickasha	16 577	134	1	11	7	115	878	239	589	50	11
Choctaw	10 347	18	2	1	4	11	260	69	177	14	1
Chouteau	1 989	11	0	1	0	10	84	17	60	7	1
Claremore	17 111	39	0	9	5	25	594	131	416	47	3
Clayton	730	4	0	1	0	3	15	3	10	2	0
Cleveland	3 264	4	0	1	0	3	81	17	57	7	1
Clinton	8 426	32	1	1	6	24	280	68	197	15	8
Coalgate	1 957	7	0	1	1	5	27	5	22	0	0
Colbert	1 101	8	0	0	0	8	32	10	20	2	0
Collinsville	4 326	13	0	1	1	11	110	28	70	12	2
Comanche	1 530	8	0	0	0	8	95	23	63	9	2
Cordell	2 928	4	0	0	0	4	48	0	48	0	0
Coweta	8 191	23	0	2	3	18	222	58	144	20	4
Crescent	1 329	2	0	0	0	2	16	4	11	1	0
Cushing	8 382	22	0	3	2	17	366	80	261	25	3
Davenport	892	2	0	0	0	2	8	2	5	1	0
Davis	2 616	14	0	1	1	12	59	22	37	0	0
Del City	22 181	96	3	8	31	54	1 114	290	703	121	11
Dewey	3 312	12	0	1	2	9	156	38	115	3	1
Drumright	2 905	0	0	0	0	0	88	12	68	8	2
Duncan	22 360	52	0	7	8	37	960	191	738	31	3
Durant	14 882	64	0	12	8	44	1 179	324	757	98	3
Edmond	73 585	111	1	26	18	66	1 922	389	1 453	80	22
Elk City	10 514	6	0	0	1	5	221	31	172	18	0
El Reno	16 062	47	0	6	8	33	489	142	314	33	13
Enid	46 948	199	0	25	32	142	2 706	785	1 820	101	6
Erick	1 024	1	0	0	0	1	7	1	6	0	0
Eufaula	2 811	17	0	0	1	16	148	56	82	10	0
Fairfax	1 527	8	0	0	0	8	61	11	41	9	1
Fairview	2 652	6	0	2	0	4	95	23	64	8	0
Fort Gibson	4 267	5	0	0	1	4	63	25	36	2	0
Frederick	4 372	14	0	0	6	8	142	36	98	8	1
Geary	1 299	12	0	1	0	11	47	13	32	2	1
Glenpool	8 601	15	0	1	0	14	162	38	108	16	0
Goodwell	1 166	0	0	0	0	0	21	7	13	1	0
Granite	1 803	6	1	2	0	3	10	4	5	1	0
Grove	5 707	9	1	0	0	8	226	40	180	6	1
Guthrie	10 578	35	0	3	7	25	259	68	178	13	3
Guymon	10 804	25	1	7	5	12	325	59	252	14	2
Harrah	4 995	8	0	0	0	8	122	45	73	4	0
Hartshorne	2 065	9	0	2	0	7	34	10	23	1	0
Haskell	1 788	1	0	0	0	1	6	2	4	0	0
Healdton	2 806	5	0	0	0	5	39	19	20	0	0
Heavener	3 262	9	0	1	0	8	134	67	64	3	1
Henryetta	6 118	23	0	0	0	23	133	38	82	13	0
Hinton	2 195	0	0	0	0	0	23	10	10	3	1
Hobart	3 849	12	0	0	2	10	45	15	28	2	0

[1]The FBI does not publish arson data unless it receives data from either the agency or the state for all 12 months of the calendar year.

Table 8. Offenses Known to Law Enforcement, by State and City, 2005—*Continued*

(Number.)

City	Population	Violent crime	Murder and non-negligent man-slaughter	Forcible rape	Robbery	Aggravated assault	Property crime	Burglary	Larceny-theft	Motor vehicle theft	Arson[1]
Holdenville	5 658	17	0	0	1	16	174	42	118	14	4
Hollis	2 079	2	0	0	1	1	61	13	47	1	1
Hominy	3 770	57	1	0	0	56	65	23	39	3	0
Hooker	1 752	3	0	0	0	3	24	11	13	0	0
Hugo	5 606	42	2	1	8	31	273	99	165	9	1
Hulbert	536	0	0	0	0	0	1	0	1	0	0
Hydro	1 050	1	0	0	0	1	27	17	10	0	0
Idabel	6 992	52	1	10	4	37	257	50	187	20	0
Inola	1 717	2	0	0	0	2	51	21	28	2	0
Jay	2 798	6	0	1	0	5	79	24	52	3	0
Jenks	12 162	14	0	0	2	12	233	58	166	9	0
Jones	2 627	6	0	1	1	4	31	13	11	7	0
Kingfisher	4 500	4	0	0	0	4	100	10	84	6	0
Kingston	1 472	5	0	0	0	5	39	18	20	1	0
Konawa	1 438	4	0	0	0	4	7	2	4	1	0
Krebs	2 103	4	0	0	1	3	33	15	15	3	1
Lawton	88 823	669	6	41	135	487	4 653	1 362	3 078	213	33
Lexington	2 121	6	0	0	0	6	54	14	37	3	0
Lindsay	2 901	9	0	0	3	6	64	17	41	6	0
Locust Grove	1 421	21	0	0	0	21	57	15	33	9	0
Lone Grove	5 013	9	0	1	0	8	120	25	89	6	2
Luther	498	3	0	0	0	3	30	14	15	1	0
Madill	3 575	9	0	1	0	8	126	43	78	5	1
Mangum	2 751	4	0	0	0	4	53	1	51	1	1
Mannford	2 241	3	0	0	1	2	65	10	48	7	1
Marietta	2 536	12	0	0	0	12	126	37	84	5	3
Marlow	4 550	30	0	6	0	24	74	22	47	5	1
Maysville	1 304	5	1	0	1	3	27	5	20	2	0
McAlester	17 906	43	0	2	10	31	701	166	512	23	6
McLoud	3 114	18	0	0	1	17	21	6	7	8	0
Meeker	991	3	0	0	1	2	38	15	21	2	0
Miami	13 557	109	0	15	10	84	774	155	589	30	10
Midwest City	55 201	147	0	19	37	91	2 428	553	1 616	259	9
Minco	1 745	0	0	0	0	0	7	5	2	0	0
Moore	46 527	123	0	21	23	79	1 635	353	1 149	133	6
Mooreland	1 224	2	0	1	0	1	38	12	24	2	1
Morris	1 343	5	0	1	0	4	20	3	13	4	0
Mountain View	845	2	0	0	0	2	7	0	5	2	0
Muldrow	3 172	6	0	1	1	4	80	26	52	2	1
Muskogee	39 114	272	3	30	52	187	2 052	720	1 210	122	20
Mustang	15 273	57	0	4	4	49	454	90	349	15	1
Newcastle	5 998	12	0	0	3	9	178	44	118	16	1
Newkirk	2 183	24	0	0	1	23	136	28	97	11	0
Nichols Hills	4 027	0	0	0	0	0	52	7	39	6	0
Nicoma Park	2 411	8	1	2	1	4	62	14	38	10	0
Noble	5 418	8	0	1	0	7	107	26	74	7	4
Norman	101 620	229	0	34	40	155	3 213	654	2 299	260	10
Nowata	4 009	6	0	2	0	4	82	20	57	5	0
Oilton	1 121	3	0	0	0	3	30	5	25	0	2
Okemah	3 029	17	1	3	2	11	167	32	122	13	1
Oklahoma City	531 688	4 538	54	358	1 193	2 933	42 145	8 925	28 635	4 585	180
Okmulgee	12 943	55	1	2	11	41	431	118	278	35	0
Oologah	1 120	2	0	0	0	2	54	9	42	3	0
Owasso	22 738	52	3	7	2	40	733	96	582	55	4
Pauls Valley	6 238	42	0	4	2	36	465	79	366	20	3
Pawhuska	3 582	54	0	1	2	51	123	31	78	14	0
Pawnee	2 222	15	0	2	0	13	28	18	9	1	0
Perkins	2 271	4	0	0	0	4	35	3	28	4	0
Perry	5 160	9	0	1	2	6	188	28	145	15	0
Piedmont	4 388	4	0	0	0	4	49	8	37	4	1
Pocola	4 340	4	0	1	0	3	43	16	22	5	0
Ponca City	25 398	156	1	23	13	119	1 306	264	968	74	15
Porum	741	1	0	0	0	1	12	1	9	2	0
Poteau	8 079	99	0	7	2	90	443	56	354	33	7
Prague	2 136	9	0	3	0	6	6	2	3	1	0
Pryor	9 236	65	0	3	1	61	352	65	254	33	1
Purcell	5 752	17	0	1	1	15	236	97	123	16	0
Ringling	1 087	1	0	0	1	0	7	3	2	2	0
Roland	3 074	2	0	0	0	2	53	23	27	3	1
Rush Springs	1 315	0	0	0	0	0	29	10	19	0	0
Sallisaw	8 595	140	0	2	5	133	270	35	221	14	3
Sand Springs	17 764	49	0	5	16	28	598	92	422	84	1
Sapulpa	19 940	45	1	7	11	26	752	165	507	80	11
Sayre	3 776	7	0	0	1	6	68	14	49	5	2
Seiling	848	4	1	0	0	3	12	4	5	3	0
Seminole	6 943	25	0	0	4	21	513	122	364	27	12
Shawnee	29 951	167	0	15	30	122	1 702	454	1 063	185	16
Skiatook	6 129	11	0	2	0	9	312	63	229	20	0
Snyder	1 466	12	0	0	0	12	32	14	16	2	0
Spencer	3 808	14	0	2	2	10	98	26	61	11	0

[1]The FBI does not publish arson data unless it receives data from either the agency or the state for all 12 months of the calendar year.

Table 8. Offenses Known to Law Enforcement, by State and City, 2005—*Continued*

(Number.)

City	Population	Violent crime	Murder and non-negligent man-slaughter	Forcible rape	Robbery	Aggravated assault	Property crime	Burglary	Larceny-theft	Motor vehicle theft	Arson[1]
Spiro	2 279	8	1	0	0	7	28	9	15	4	0
Stigler	2 811	14	0	0	0	14	31	0	29	2	0
Stillwater	41 012	123	0	30	10	83	1 519	317	1 147	55	14
Stratford	1 493	5	0	0	0	5	34	11	21	2	0
Stringtown	411	6	0	1	0	5	9	3	6	0	0
Stroud	2 784	9	0	0	1	8	58	6	48	4	0
Sulphur	4 830	8	0	0	1	7	133	32	95	6	2
Tahlequah	15 818	29	0	12	12	5	831	210	564	57	0
Talihina	1 234	19	1	0	1	17	64	8	47	9	0
Tecumseh	6 533	58	0	3	4	51	240	69	151	20	5
The Village	9 975	51	0	1	6	44	401	88	281	32	7
Tishomingo	3 180	7	0	0	0	7	60	24	33	3	0
Tonkawa	3 176	8	0	0	3	5	105	33	69	3	0
Tulsa	386 414	4 995	58	303	1 096	3 538	25 169	6 592	14 847	3 730	308
Tushka	360	1	0	0	1	0	12	10	2	0	0
Tuttle	5 105	6	0	0	1	5	156	59	92	5	0
Valliant	769	3	0	0	0	3	41	5	35	1	0
Vian	1 469	11	0	1	1	9	9	6	1	2	0
Vinita	5 990	13	0	0	1	12	167	51	106	10	2
Wagoner	7 920	36	1	2	2	31	342	79	249	14	1
Walters	2 601	15	0	0	1	14	32	12	19	1	0
Warner	1 457	10	0	0	1	9	29	11	16	2	0
Warr Acres	9 617	58	0	2	23	33	918	131	737	50	4
Watonga	4 061	7	0	0	0	7	80	14	58	8	0
Waukomis	1 227	1	0	0	0	1	23	1	21	1	0
Waurika	1 875	11	0	0	1	10	26	13	12	1	0
Waynoka	938	0	0	0	0	0	14	6	5	3	0
Weatherford	9 803	35	0	6	2	27	392	71	304	17	0
Westville	1 640	23	0	2	0	21	121	25	87	9	1
Wetumka	1 447	3	0	0	0	3	41	10	27	4	3
Wewoka	3 456	48	0	1	6	41	102	43	52	7	0
Wilburton	2 960	1	0	0	1	0	39	12	22	5	0
Wilson	1 636	12	0	0	0	12	41	12	25	4	0
Woodward	11 946	22	0	8	1	13	595	188	398	9	2
Wright City	823	4	0	0	0	4	29	7	21	1	2
Wynnewood	2 337	3	0	0	2	1	20	9	11	0	2
Yale	1 302	3	0	0	0	3	21	5	15	1	0
Yukon	21 745	33	0	4	4	25	606	96	472	38	2
Oregon											
Albany	44 456	63	0	8	22	33	3 114	337	2 446	331	14
Amity	1 478	1	0	0	0	1	70	11	57	2	1
Ashland	21 023	35	0	16	5	14	807	121	658	28	7
Astoria	9 884	18	0	3	5	10	556	124	401	31	3
Athena	1 237	0	0	0	0	0	13	5	5	3	0
Aumsville	3 209	8	0	0	0	8	64	13	45	6	0
Aurora	733	3	0	0	1	2	33	4	26	3	1
Baker City	9 872	8	0	2	3	3	288	59	215	14	1
Bandon	2 908	2	0	2	0	0	58	15	41	2	1
Beaverton	83 979	189	1	32	43	113	2 957	340	2 301	316	19
Bend	63 751	133	2	21	19	91	3 159	509	2 401	249	23
Black Butte	. . .	0	0	0	0	0	3	0	2	1	0
Brookings	6 200	3	0	0	3	0	216	23	175	18	2
Burns	2 891	7	0	2	1	4	97	29	62	6	0
Canby	14 905	22	0	5	3	14	454	56	374	24	6
Cannon Beach	1 680	0	0	0	0	0	43	7	35	1	0
Central Point	15 348	3	0	0	1	2	438	76	338	24	0
Clatskanie	1 636	0	0	0	0	0	39	8	30	1	0
Coburg	1 009	2	0	0	1	1	38	8	25	5	0
Columbia City	1 785	0	0	0	0	0	13	0	13	0	0
Condon	728	2	0	0	2	0	1	0	1	0	0
Coos Bay	15 766	29	1	6	8	14	714	158	514	42	6
Coquille	4 258	8	0	1	1	6	71	11	55	5	0
Cornelius	10 480	9	0	4	1	4	310	59	223	28	3
Corvallis	51 031	69	1	11	18	39	1 994	247	1 656	91	18
Cottage Grove	8 743	23	0	4	6	13	547	85	373	89	14
Creswell	4 302	15	0	3	2	10	178	51	102	25	0
Dallas	13 635	24	1	3	2	18	430	67	324	39	5
Eagle Point	7 049	6	2	3	0	1	173	16	142	15	0
Elgin	1 655	1	0	1	0	0	28	10	16	2	1
Enterprise	1 818	10	0	0	1	9	45	11	32	2	0
Estacada	2 447	12	0	1	5	6	227	50	146	31	1
Eugene	144 526	328	5	54	119	150	9 902	1 603	6 639	1 660	72
Fairview	9 375	17	0	1	6	10	437	69	276	92	0
Florence	7 763	9	0	3	1	5	411	67	317	27	3
Forest Grove	19 510	22	1	3	10	8	926	129	707	90	6
Gaston	770	0	0	0	0	0	21	3	14	4	0
Gearhart	1 030	0	0	0	0	0	26	8	18	0	0
Gervais	2 216	6	0	0	3	3	130	34	65	31	2
Gladstone	12 288	19	0	6	8	5	471	66	341	64	7

[1]The FBI does not publish arson data unless it receives data from either the agency or the state for all 12 months of the calendar year.
. . . = Not available.

Table 8. Offenses Known to Law Enforcement, by State and City, 2005—*Continued*

(Number.)

City	Population	Violent crime	Murder and non-negligent man-slaughter	Forcible rape	Robbery	Aggravated assault	Property crime	Burglary	Larceny-theft	Motor vehicle theft	Arson[1]
Gold Beach	1 940	7	0	0	0	7	50	13	30	7	0
Grants Pass	27 547	37	2	10	14	11	1 742	140	1 459	143	9
Gresham	96 609	500	3	69	148	280	5 347	882	3 216	1 249	37
Hermiston	14 626	19	0	4	9	6	1 051	179	771	101	1
Hillsboro	82 912	163	2	30	63	68	3 647	473	2 807	367	13
Hines	1 567	2	0	0	0	2	9	5	4	0	0
Hubbard	2 580	7	0	1	1	5	46	6	33	7	0
Independence	7 650	16	0	3	1	12	248	35	197	16	0
Jacksonville	2 271	3	0	0	0	3	31	3	27	1	0
John Day	1 650	0	0	0	0	0	39	13	24	2	0
Junction City	5 297	4	0	0	1	3	69	15	50	4	0
Keizer	34 859	86	1	9	12	64	999	164	717	118	13
King City	2 053	0	0	0	0	0	63	9	51	3	1
Klamath Falls	19 949	47	2	9	29	7	895	224	584	87	3
La Grande	12 531	21	0	3	5	13	300	67	214	19	2
Lake Oswego	36 838	8	0	1	1	6	551	124	397	30	14
Lakeview	2 451	10	0	1	0	9	107	31	68	8	0
Lebanon	13 690	34	0	6	13	15	1 092	181	860	51	8
Lincoln City	7 623	32	0	3	4	25	536	90	420	26	4
Madras	5 213	26	0	1	2	23	312	64	220	28	2
Manzanita	605	1	0	0	0	1	36	6	28	2	0
McMinnville	29 348	46	1	8	16	21	985	125	800	60	10
Medford	68 979	325	1	28	53	243	4 290	556	3 455	279	37
Milton-Freewater	6 546	13	0	3	2	8	306	69	223	14	2
Milwaukie	21 023	30	1	5	9	15	891	90	685	116	6
Molalla	6 397	15	0	4	1	10	270	32	220	18	2
Monmouth	8 497	9	1	2	1	5	278	58	210	10	1
Mount Angel	3 382	10	0	1	0	9	134	31	96	7	2
Myrtle Point	2 510	2	0	1	1	0	24	7	16	1	0
Newberg	23 504	31	1	10	5	15	755	133	576	46	7
Newport	9 751	57	0	7	5	45	827	133	633	61	13
North Bend	9 783	7	0	1	5	1	432	103	299	30	9
Oakridge	3 176	1	0	0	1	0	126	37	83	6	0
Ontario	11 296	48	0	4	8	36	768	80	643	45	5
Oregon City	30 152	29	0	7	12	10	1 329	186	1 024	119	6
Pendleton	16 820	64	0	14	10	40	1 029	167	795	67	2
Philomath	4 265	6	0	1	0	5	145	26	117	2	1
Phoenix	4 436	2	0	1	0	1	172	17	148	7	2
Pilot Rock	1 550	0	0	0	0	0	20	10	7	3	0
Portland	540 389	3 858	20	325	1 137	2 376	37 645	6 121	25 794	5 730	375
Prineville	8 686	113	0	7	0	106	391	59	315	17	6
Rainier	1 822	1	0	0	0	1	53	18	31	4	0
Redmond	18 250	47	0	10	11	26	1 362	243	1 015	104	11
Reedsport	4 405	2	0	0	0	2	170	38	119	13	1
Rockaway Beach	1 297	3	0	0	0	3	63	18	43	2	0
Rogue River	1 940	1	0	1	0	0	88	11	71	6	0
Roseburg	20 711	46	0	6	16	24	1 220	185	962	73	23
Salem	148 009	706	3	53	134	516	9 004	1 170	6 752	1 082	32
Sandy	7 642	5	0	1	1	3	315	31	256	28	0
Scappoose	5 780	4	0	3	1	0	170	18	142	10	2
Seaside	6 101	20	0	5	7	8	661	99	545	17	2
Shady Cove	2 344	1	0	0	0	1	71	19	46	6	1
Sherwood	14 728	5	0	3	2	0	273	47	210	16	3
Silverton	8 221	11	0	1	2	8	311	73	221	17	1
Springfield	55 760	195	0	10	36	149	4 859	814	3 207	838	33
Stayton	7 217	24	0	6	3	15	391	71	295	25	4
St. Helens	11 580	19	0	3	0	16	367	60	290	17	6
Sunriver	. . .	1	0	0	0	1	97	13	82	2	. . .
Sutherlin	7 350	14	0	2	2	10	297	76	204	17	1
Sweet Home	8 404	45	0	3	5	37	823	194	591	38	1
The Dalles	12 102	26	1	3	6	16	734	126	566	42	5
Tigard	47 466	103	0	16	29	58	2 289	307	1 824	158	16
Tillamook	4 534	2	0	0	1	1	296	41	242	13	0
Toledo	3 468	3	0	0	3	0	181	36	134	11	1
Troutdale	14 901	20	0	3	11	6	543	72	398	73	6
Tualatin	25 595	35	0	7	11	17	841	119	636	86	0
Turner	1 559	1	0	0	0	1	47	14	29	4	0
Umatilla	6 132	12	1	0	2	9	141	26	96	19	0
Veneta	3 227	44	0	8	2	34	273	114	114	45	9
Vernonia	2 293	0	0	0	0	0	27	7	19	1	3
Warrenton	4 322	2	0	1	1	0	120	42	69	9	1
West Linn	25 375	19	0	1	3	15	329	52	247	30	7
Weston	725	2	0	1	1	0	69	14	48	7	0
Wilsonville	15 715	18	0	3	6	9	730	78	582	70	2
Winston	4 810	2	0	0	2	0	197	38	139	20	2
Woodburn	22 433	69	0	7	21	41	1 319	234	900	185	5
Yamhill	820	0	0	0	0	0	10	3	5	2	0

[1]The FBI does not publish arson data unless it receives data from either the agency or the state for all 12 months of the calendar year.
. . . = Not available.

Table 8. Offenses Known to Law Enforcement, by State and City, 2005—*Continued*

(Number.)

City	Population	Violent crime	Murder and non-negligent man-slaughter	Forcible rape	Robbery	Aggravated assault	Property crime	Burglary	Larceny-theft	Motor vehicle theft	Arson[1]
Pennsylvania											
Abington Township	55 804	62	0	4	30	28	1 118	146	923	49	9
Adamstown	1 290	0	0	0	0	0	18	3	15	0	1
Adams Township (Butler County)	7 863	2	0	1	0	1	83	13	69	1	0
Akron	4 034	0	0	0	0	0	32	5	22	5	0
Alburtis	2 125	4	0	1	0	3	23	2	21	0	0
Aldan	4 315	13	0	0	4	9	81	8	65	8	0
Aliquippa	11 291	77	1	2	25	49	322	82	193	47	0
Allegheny Township (Blair County)	6 943	34	0	1	5	28	165	25	134	6	2
Allegheny Township (Westmoreland County)	8 128	2	0	0	0	2	88	27	56	5	0
Allentown	106 933	863	21	45	512	285	5 771	1 393	3 905	473	56
Altoona	47 922	186	5	26	69	86	1 653	463	1 117	73	24
Ambler	6 398	9	0	1	3	5	120	11	101	8	0
Amity Township	10 839	2	0	0	0	2	113	19	83	11	3
Annville Township	4 684	8	0	0	3	5	79	21	53	5	0
Arnold	5 473	22	1	0	10	11	103	24	57	22	0
Ashland	3 182	6	0	0	0	6	66	22	42	2	4
Ashley	2 755	3	0	1	1	1	21	3	16	2	0
Ashville	269	0	0	0	0	0	2	1	1	0	0
Aspinwall	2 841	3	0	0	2	1	40	2	35	3	0
Aston Township	16 749	27	1	1	12	13	190	26	149	15	4
Avalon	5 053	11	0	0	5	6	133	8	109	16	1
Baldwin Borough	19 174	21	0	1	5	15	156	29	103	24	0
Bally	1 100	0	0	0	0	0	4	0	4	0	0
Bangor	5 292	29	0	2	0	27	173	15	139	19	1
Barrett Township	4 202	9	0	1	0	8	57	14	42	1	0
Beaver	4 600	5	0	0	3	2	104	8	87	9	0
Beaver Falls	9 543	91	0	8	29	54	468	47	378	43	2
Bedford	3 079	4	1	2	0	1	45	6	36	3	1
Bedminster Township	4 949	3	0	0	1	2	29	4	25	0	0
Bell Acres	1 402	0	0	0	0	0	3	3	0	0	0
Bellwood	1 949	6	0	0	0	6	10	3	6	1	0
Bensalem Township	58 685	134	3	7	61	63	2 097	331	1 578	188	21
Berks-Lehigh Regional	23 833	22	0	2	7	13	340	51	255	34	0
Bern Township	7 042	8	0	0	0	8	55	11	39	5	1
Berwick	10 513	44	0	19	1	24	382	68	301	13	6
Bessemer	1 140	1	0	0	0	1	5	0	4	1	0
Bethel Park	32 731	18	0	0	4	14	316	46	261	9	2
Bethel Township (Berks County)	4 383	1	0	0	1	0	45	11	32	2	0
Bethlehem	72 577	268	2	17	114	135	2 301	409	1 700	192	6
Bethlehem Township	23 177	36	0	3	11	22	459	30	415	14	1
Biglerville	1 147	0	0	0	0	0	9	0	9	0	0
Birdsboro	5 194	7	0	1	3	3	105	16	83	6	1
Birmingham Township	4 274	3	0	0	0	3	38	6	26	6	0
Blairsville	3 478	6	0	1	1	4	106	19	84	3	0
Blakely	6 854	4	0	2	1	1	107	7	96	4	3
Blawnox	1 497	2	0	0	0	2	5	1	3	1	0
Bloomsburg Town	12 829	16	0	6	2	8	253	36	208	9	1
Brackenridge	3 383	3	0	0	1	2	98	15	78	5	0
Bradford Township	4 801	17	0	1	0	16	53	12	40	1	0
Brandywine Regional	9 663	21	0	2	0	19	52	6	42	4	2
Brecknock Township (Berks County)	4 747	1	0	0	0	1	29	6	20	3	0
Brecknock Township (Lancaster County)	11 525	0	0	0	0	0	34	10	24	0	0
Brentwood	9 983	31	0	3	9	19	224	23	177	24	0
Bridgeport	4 414	7	0	0	0	7	131	22	96	13	0
Bridgeville	5 104	8	0	0	2	6	91	10	72	9	0
Brighton Township	8 046	8	0	1	1	6	49	4	40	5	0
Bristol	9 888	39	0	4	20	15	445	58	341	46	2
Bristol Township	54 919	142	1	16	70	55	1 650	247	1 201	202	5
Brockway	2 138	1	0	0	0	1	19	3	13	3	0
Brookhaven	7 881	13	0	0	4	9	173	15	150	8	0
Brookville	4 149	13	1	3	1	8	101	8	91	2	0
Brownsville	2 720	17	0	3	2	12	72	19	42	11	0
Bryn Athyn	1 365	1	0	0	0	1	16	2	14	0	0
Buckingham Township	18 118	4	0	0	0	4	120	5	111	4	1
Buffalo Township	7 059	25	0	0	0	25	82	12	66	4	1
Bushkill Township	7 657	1	0	0	0	1	62	7	54	1	0
Butler	14 653	155	0	7	15	133	596	126	460	10	0
Butler Township (Butler County)	17 075	30	0	1	6	23	481	38	431	12	2
Butler Township (Luzerne County)	8 172	36	0	1	0	35	150	15	128	7	4
California	5 718	19	0	1	2	16	80	24	54	2	0
Caln Township	12 198	59	0	0	8	51	311	32	254	25	0
Cambria Township	6 191	9	0	1	2	6	146	21	121	4	0
Cambridge Springs	2 309	0	0	0	0	0	44	5	39	0	1
Camp Hill	7 479	6	0	2	1	3	97	15	78	4	0
Carbondale	9 441	28	1	1	9	17	194	22	153	19	2
Carlisle	18 108	38	0	8	17	13	533	75	449	9	1
Carnegie	8 235	21	2	0	12	7	191	35	128	28	1
Carrolltown	1 007	3	0	0	0	3	11	1	9	1	0
Carroll Township (Washington County)	5 626	15	0	0	0	15	74	11	58	5	2
Carroll Township (York County)	5 039	19	0	1	4	14	129	33	92	4	0

[1] The FBI does not publish arson data unless it receives data from either the agency or the state for all 12 months of the calendar year.

Table 8. Offenses Known to Law Enforcement, by State and City, 2005—*Continued*

(Number.)

City	Population	Violent crime	Murder and non-negligent man-slaughter	Forcible rape	Robbery	Aggravated assault	Property crime	Burglary	Larceny-theft	Motor vehicle theft	Arson[1]
Carroll Valley	3 988	2	0	0	0	2	84	6	77	1	1
Castle Shannon	8 411	24	0	0	0	24	156	19	135	2	0
Catawissa	1 572	3	0	1	0	2	45	7	36	2	0
Center Township	11 740	39	0	0	10	29	385	30	351	4	1
Centerville	3 314	5	0	0	1	4	16	4	10	2	1
Chalfont	4 188	2	0	0	0	2	23	0	22	1	0
Chambersburg	18 060	208	0	11	29	168	614	101	476	37	6
Chartiers Township	7 186	3	0	2	0	1	55	13	40	2	0
Cheltenham Township	36 874	116	0	6	81	29	982	139	740	103	1
Chester	36 991	934	15	34	229	656	1 480	480	710	290	36
Cheswick	1 823	0	0	0	0	0	23	4	17	2	0
Chippewa Township	11 000	3	0	1	2	0	209	17	187	5	0
Clairton	8 189	33	0	0	13	20	304	44	218	42	0
Claysville	701	1	0	0	0	1	16	0	16	0	0
Clearfield	6 399	20	1	0	1	18	147	25	106	16	0
Cleona	2 122	0	0	0	0	0	18	4	14	0	0
Coal Township	10 544	40	1	2	0	37	227	31	184	12	2
Coatesville	11 407	102	4	2	46	50	431	91	258	82	1
Cochranton	1 114	0	0	0	0	0	10	0	10	0	0
Collier Township	5 807	10	0	0	4	6	233	17	211	5	2
Collingdale	8 540	113	0	3	19	91	300	32	230	38	0
Colonial Regional	18 255	46	0	5	8	33	591	34	544	13	0
Columbia	10 178	35	0	0	15	20	301	64	218	19	2
Colwyn	2 408	13	0	0	2	11	44	9	30	5	0
Conemaugh Township (Cambria County)	2 553	3	0	0	0	3	4	2	2	0	0
Conewango Township	3 769	16	0	3	1	12	85	5	77	3	0
Conneaut Lake Regional	3 602	3	0	0	0	3	83	16	59	8	0
Connellsville	8 755	32	1	4	10	17	470	76	362	32	5
Conshohocken	7 760	30	1	5	4	20	171	0	152	19	2
Coopersburg	2 572	10	0	2	2	6	38	6	32	0	0
Coraopolis	5 859	40	0	1	3	36	176	31	132	13	2
Cornwall	3 470	0	0	0	0	0	28	7	20	1	0
Corry	6 650	42	0	7	2	33	80	17	61	2	0
Covington Township	2 078	2	0	1	0	1	47	16	24	7	1
Crafton	6 399	11	0	0	2	9	119	13	95	11	0
Cranberry Township	26 647	37	0	2	5	30	400	42	348	10	1
Croyle Township	2 235	0	0	0	0	0	16	2	13	1	0
Cumru Township	17 157	27	0	1	15	11	459	74	329	56	1
Dallas	2 513	0	0	0	0	0	42	6	35	1	1
Dallas Township	8 324	6	0	1	1	4	53	15	32	6	1
Darby	10 104	313	1	8	31	273	400	100	232	68	3
Decatur Township	3 071	2	0	0	0	2	37	5	32	0	0
Delmont	2 525	1	0	1	0	0	55	9	44	2	2
Denver	3 568	2	0	0	0	2	99	5	90	4	0
Derry Township (Dauphin County)	21 754	51	0	4	9	38	610	89	501	20	0
Dickson City	6 018	10	0	0	4	6	388	13	364	11	1
Donegal Township	2 413	2	0	0	0	2	20	1	19	0	0
Dormont	8 862	62	0	5	9	48	129	15	107	7	1
Douglass Township (Montgomery County)	10 278	13	0	0	1	12	147	5	131	11	0
Downingtown	7 874	26	0	1	8	17	346	36	293	17	0
Doylestown	8 237	13	0	3	2	8	179	26	144	9	2
Doylestown Township	17 822	32	0	3	3	26	238	35	194	9	0
Duboistown	1 244	0	0	0	0	0	1	0	1	0	0
Duquesne	7 001	91	0	3	29	59	378	118	229	31	8
Earl Township	6 683	2	0	0	0	2	67	24	31	12	0
East Bethlehem Township	2 444	12	0	0	0	12	3	0	3	0	0
East Cocalico Township	10 241	1	0	1	0	0	151	23	117	11	4
East Conemaugh	1 229	6	0	0	0	6	5	1	3	1	0
East Coventry Township	4 892	2	0	0	0	2	57	9	41	7	0
East Fallowfield Township	6 531	20	0	1	0	19	75	18	54	3	0
East Franklin Township	4 027	3	0	1	0	2	33	2	31	0	0
East Hempfield Township	22 475	22	0	3	12	7	565	100	446	19	1
East Lampeter Township	14 508	38	0	5	14	19	838	115	706	17	0
East McKeesport	2 939	13	0	0	3	10	28	6	21	1	0
East Norriton Township	13 593	6	0	0	4	2	305	12	279	14	0
Easton	26 316	176	3	16	47	110	1 078	189	745	144	17
East Pennsboro Township	19 471	24	0	4	16	4	407	62	331	14	5
East Petersburg	4 385	7	0	1	2	4	58	10	46	2	4
East Pikeland Township	6 846	2	0	0	0	2	122	18	97	7	2
East Taylor Township	2 641	1	0	0	0	1	1	1	0	0	0
Easttown Township	10 403	3	0	0	3	0	119	25	92	2	0
East Vincent Township	6 367	2	0	0	1	1	43	5	33	5	0
East Washington	1 868	5	0	0	0	5	29	5	23	1	0
East Whiteland Township	10 223	4	0	0	1	3	143	18	114	11	0
Ebensburg	2 972	2	0	0	1	1	42	3	39	0	1
Edgewood	3 156	11	0	0	7	4	274	26	239	9	0
Edgeworth	1 651	0	0	0	0	0	1	1	0	0	0
Edinboro	6 892	10	0	1	0	9	100	21	75	4	0
Edwardsville	4 787	22	1	2	6	13	203	23	151	29	0
Elizabethtown	11 942	7	0	3	1	3	173	32	137	4	1

[1]The FBI does not publish arson data unless it receives data from either the agency or the state for all 12 months of the calendar year.

Table 8. Offenses Known to Law Enforcement, by State and City, 2005—*Continued*

(Number.)

City	Population	Violent crime	Murder and non-negligent man-slaughter	Forcible rape	Robbery	Aggravated assault	Property crime	Burglary	Larceny-theft	Motor vehicle theft	Arson[1]
Elizabeth Township	13 324	28	0	1	0	27	138	27	102	9	2
Ellwood City	8 382	33	0	4	4	25	178	36	134	8	2
Emmaus	11 346	33	0	5	6	22	345	26	308	11	2
Emporium	2 371	0	0	0	0	0	62	7	54	1	0
Emsworth	2 486	15	0	0	0	15	35	0	35	0	0
Ephrata	13 205	17	0	4	3	10	282	48	218	16	6
Ephrata Township	8 757	6	0	0	1	5	127	24	95	8	0
Erie	104 120	472	6	75	200	191	2 867	632	2 129	106	35
Etna	3 740	25	0	0	1	24	49	12	24	13	0
Evans City	1 970	1	0	0	0	1	20	6	14	0	0
Exeter	6 047	23	0	1	0	22	128	30	93	5	1
Exeter Township (Berks County)	25 715	20	0	1	4	15	500	68	384	48	4
Fairview Township (York County)	15 528	23	0	6	0	17	285	54	224	7	0
Falls Township (Bucks County)	34 314	68	1	3	29	35	891	143	652	96	4
Ferguson Township	15 568	7	0	0	1	6	196	28	165	3	2
Findlay Township	5 191	5	0	0	0	5	85	14	61	10	0
Fleetwood	4 004	5	0	0	0	5	82	9	71	2	1
Ford City	3 326	17	0	1	2	14	78	12	61	5	0
Forest City	1 806	3	0	0	0	3	18	8	9	1	2
Forest Hills	6 538	6	0	0	6	0	90	20	62	8	0
Forks Township	12 187	17	0	1	0	16	148	12	133	3	0
Forty Fort	4 375	7	0	1	0	6	91	21	67	3	1
Foster Township	4 421	7	0	1	0	6	30	1	28	1	0
Fountain Hill	4 601	26	0	0	2	24	166	24	123	19	1
Fox Chapel	5 317	2	0	1	0	1	15	3	12	0	0
Frackville	5 073	2	0	0	1	1	31	6	22	3	0
Franconia Township	12 076	11	0	0	0	11	90	11	77	2	2
Franklin	6 960	15	0	1	2	12	187	45	135	7	0
Franklin Park	11 730	4	0	0	0	4	105	15	88	2	1
Franklin Township (Carbon County)	4 630	11	0	0	1	10	49	8	38	3	0
Gallitzin	1 967	6	0	0	1	5	35	11	22	2	0
Gettysburg	7 906	9	0	3	4	2	109	14	94	1	2
Gilpin Township	2 558	11	0	0	0	11	1	0	1	0	0
Girard	3 068	9	0	0	2	7	30	3	26	1	0
Glenolden	7 350	30	0	1	12	17	179	25	140	14	2
Greencastle	3 767	8	0	0	3	5	119	13	97	9	0
Greensburg	15 608	35	0	4	9	22	559	83	447	29	0
Greenwood Township	1 998	0	0	0	0	0	0	0	0	0	0
Grove City	7 815	4	0	2	0	2	106	12	93	1	1
Halifax	852	1	0	0	0	1	11	4	6	1	0
Hamburg	4 161	18	0	3	0	15	88	14	67	7	2
Hamiltonban Township	2 538	2	0	0	0	2	0	0	0	0	0
Hanover	14 944	25	0	6	9	10	567	62	483	22	0
Harmar Township	3 119	10	0	0	4	6	90	11	74	5	0
Harmony Township	3 240	4	1	0	1	2	98	19	74	5	0
Harrisburg	47 725	805	12	52	480	261	2 336	600	1 583	153	22
Harrison Township	10 454	14	0	0	6	8	369	52	298	19	0
Hatboro	7 343	14	0	3	3	8	79	14	59	6	5
Hatfield Township	20 217	23	0	3	5	15	324	38	277	9	4
Haverford Township	48 997	22	1	1	9	11	470	53	389	28	4
Hawley	1 298	0	0	0	0	0	1	0	1	0	0
Heidelberg	1 169	2	0	0	2	0	6	2	3	1	0
Hellam Township	8 410	26	0	7	9	10	192	41	135	16	1
Hemlock Township	2 089	1	0	1	0	0	175	9	166	0	0
Hempfield Township (Mercer County)	3 973	4	0	0	1	3	135	19	100	16	2
Hermitage	16 580	20	0	0	9	11	578	38	529	11	0
Highspire	2 647	21	0	1	8	12	94	14	72	8	1
Hilltown Township	12 375	33	1	2	7	23	207	17	177	13	0
Homestead	3 600	62	0	7	28	27	342	47	246	49	0
Honesdale	4 874	12	0	3	3	6	166	26	130	10	0
Hooversville	744	0	0	0	0	0	0	0	0	0	0
Horsham Township	25 207	19	0	1	4	14	259	21	218	20	3
Huntingdon	6 892	13	0	0	0	13	80	6	72	2	1
Indiana	14 953	80	2	6	11	61	354	54	287	13	1
Indiana Township	6 907	4	0	0	0	4	57	22	33	2	0
Ingram	3 543	17	0	1	2	14	28	7	17	4	1
Irwin	4 232	17	0	0	1	16	121	29	89	3	0
Jackson Township (Butler County)	3 832	26	0	1	0	25	100	12	83	5	1
Jackson Township (Cambria County)	4 842	11	0	2	0	9	103	24	72	7	3
Jackson Township (Luzerne County)	4 717	12	0	1	1	10	42	18	20	4	0
Jefferson Hills Borough	9 697	8	0	1	1	6	76	8	60	8	1
Jenkins Township	4 795	2	0	0	2	0	134	25	104	5	1
Jermyn	2 258	9	0	0	0	9	11	5	4	2	1
Jersey Shore	4 470	7	0	0	1	6	147	20	111	16	0
Jim Thorpe	4 884	14	0	0	0	14	92	17	72	3	0
Johnstown	27 322	164	2	7	45	110	1 052	351	640	61	11
Juniata Valley Regional	440	0	0	0	0	0	4	1	3	0	0
Kane	3 946	3	0	0	1	2	32	9	22	1	3
Kennedy Township	8 270	16	0	1	3	12	212	8	200	4	0
Kidder Township	1 298	8	0	1	1	6	121	27	90	4	1

[1]The FBI does not publish arson data unless it receives data from either the agency or the state for all 12 months of the calendar year.

Table 8. Offenses Known to Law Enforcement, by State and City, 2005—*Continued*

(Number.)

City	Population	Violent crime	Murder and non-negligent man-slaughter	Forcible rape	Robbery	Aggravated assault	Property crime	Burglary	Larceny-theft	Motor vehicle theft	Arson[1]
Kingston	13 309	68	0	3	10	55	314	60	236	18	2
Kingston Township	7 071	8	0	0	0	8	83	24	56	3	0
Kline Township	1 519	1	0	0	1	0	17	4	11	2	0
Koppel	822	5	0	0	1	4	34	2	28	4	1
Kutztown	5 154	9	0	0	5	4	212	51	143	18	3
Laflin Borough	1 512	5	0	0	1	4	23	3	18	2	0
Lake City	2 995	4	0	0	0	4	37	9	26	2	0
Lancaster	55 286	420	1	32	189	198	3 025	549	2 271	205	19
Lancaster Township (Butler County)	2 560	1	0	0	0	1	11	5	6	0	0
Lansdale	16 044	17	1	4	5	7	371	62	293	16	20
Lansdowne	10 847	51	1	1	9	40	254	57	181	16	3
Lawrence Park Township	3 906	5	0	0	1	4	61	3	56	2	0
Lawrence Township	7 639	45	1	1	3	40	299	35	254	10	1
Lebanon	23 970	168	0	8	59	101	949	194	676	79	13
Leetsdale	1 174	0	0	0	0	0	0	0	0	0	0
Leet Township	1 546	0	0	0	0	0	0	0	0	0	0
Lehighton	5 546	14	0	3	0	11	175	23	144	8	2
Lehman Township	3 255	16	0	0	0	16	30	5	25	0	2
Lilly	907	0	0	0	0	0	4	1	3	0	0
Limerick Township	16 313	7	0	0	4	3	288	45	219	24	1
Lincoln	1 169	1	0	0	0	1	8	3	4	1	0
Lititz	9 039	7	0	1	1	5	109	11	96	2	2
Littlestown	4 115	29	0	0	1	28	123	18	98	7	1
Lock Haven	9 000	18	0	3	2	13	336	49	277	10	3
Locust Township	2 521	5	0	0	0	5	20	6	13	1	1
Logan Township	11 934	26	0	3	5	18	299	58	228	13	3
Lower Burrell	12 545	12	0	0	3	9	201	35	149	17	1
Lower Gwynedd Township	11 141	11	0	1	1	9	170	22	143	5	1
Lower Heidelberg Township	4 770	5	0	0	1	4	43	5	35	3	0
Lower Makefield Township	32 835	31	0	4	6	21	344	40	295	9	0
Lower Merion Township	58 596	66	0	6	41	19	978	147	796	35	0
Lower Moreland Township	11 754	16	0	0	2	14	154	26	122	6	2
Lower Paxton Township	44 896	83	0	9	29	45	1 155	177	949	29	13
Lower Pottsgrove Township	11 907	21	0	5	3	13	300	36	245	19	0
Lower Providence Township	24 070	15	0	0	7	8	289	61	210	18	0
Lower Saucon Township	10 864	26	0	2	2	22	101	15	81	5	0
Lower Southampton Township	19 105	58	0	3	4	51	409	41	333	35	2
Lower Swatara Township	8 323	4	0	0	1	3	127	32	89	6	0
Lower Windsor Township	7 639	9	0	2	0	7	104	35	65	4	2
Luzerne Township	4 595	3	0	0	1	2	33	7	23	3	1
Madison Township	1 616	0	0	0	0	0	0	0	0	0	0
Malvern	3 105	8	0	0	0	8	30	10	20	0	0
Manheim	4 710	2	0	0	0	2	75	8	61	6	0
Manheim Township	35 319	48	0	8	16	24	908	168	705	35	10
Mansfield	3 470	4	0	0	2	2	6	1	3	2	0
Marion Township	920	0	0	0	0	0	9	2	7	0	0
Marlborough Township	3 262	3	0	0	0	3	35	6	23	6	0
Marple Township	23 662	12	1	2	4	5	221	19	192	10	0
Martinsburg	2 186	0	0	0	0	0	63	14	47	2	1
Masontown	3 507	49	0	2	3	44	106	26	62	18	1
Mayfield	1 730	0	0	0	0	0	0	0	0	0	0
McCandless	28 253	10	0	0	3	7	512	48	455	9	3
McKeesport	23 096	355	1	14	71	269	909	287	542	80	35
McKees Rocks	6 317	42	0	0	26	16	230	55	149	26	0
McSherrystown	2 794	6	0	0	0	6	52	6	43	3	0
Meadville	13 385	43	1	10	9	23	423	76	329	18	0
Mechanicsburg	8 860	39	0	3	5	31	270	49	214	7	2
Media	5 479	16	1	0	3	12	24	14	9	1	2
Mercer	2 302	5	0	0	0	5	25	8	16	1	0
Meyersdale	2 376	2	0	0	0	2	23	1	22	0	0
Middlesex Township (Cumberland County)	6 775	10	0	1	3	6	245	13	219	13	1
Middletown	9 018	33	0	5	6	22	190	36	151	3	2
Middletown Township	47 711	76	1	2	35	38	1 249	147	1 017	85	7
Midland	3 014	12	0	1	4	7	151	42	99	10	0
Mifflin County Regional	19 256	67	0	4	14	49	647	114	504	29	1
Millcreek Township	52 861	39	1	4	17	17	784	177	569	38	0
Millersburg	2 498	24	0	1	1	22	95	16	79	0	1
Millersville	7 507	5	0	2	0	3	109	12	93	4	0
Milton	6 519	15	1	1	1	12	65	12	48	5	0
Mohnton	3 052	9	0	0	1	8	22	7	15	0	0
Monaca	6 070	19	0	0	0	19	102	16	78	8	0
Monessen	8 413	82	0	0	12	70	269	46	200	23	3
Monroeville	28 540	93	2	5	29	57	837	114	636	87	6
Montgomery Township	24 219	14	0	0	8	6	573	18	544	11	1
Montrose	1 607	8	0	0	0	8	20	7	13	0	2
Moon Township	22 778	21	0	2	6	13	347	61	259	27	1
Moore Township	9 182	10	1	2	0	7	73	8	63	2	0
Moosic	5 717	40	0	3	5	32	209	30	169	10	3
Morrisville	9 883	29	1	0	14	14	368	59	263	46	0
Morton	2 678	4	0	1	0	3	94	9	83	2	0

[1]The FBI does not publish arson data unless it receives data from either the agency or the state for all 12 months of the calendar year.

Table 8. Offenses Known to Law Enforcement, by State and City, 2005—*Continued*

(Number.)

City	Population	Violent crime	Murder and non-negligent man-slaughter	Forcible rape	Robbery	Aggravated assault	Property crime	Burglary	Larceny-theft	Motor vehicle theft	Arson[1]
Moscow	1 911	2	0	0	0	2	32	6	26	0	0
Mount Carmel	6 115	17	0	1	2	14	89	14	68	7	0
Mount Gretna Borough	235	0	0	0	0	0	1	0	1	0	0
Mount Joy	6 919	6	0	0	1	5	144	22	114	8	0
Mount Lebanon	31 791	68	1	1	11	55	237	51	177	9	4
Mount Oliver	3 843	52	0	2	33	17	231	53	119	59	1
Mount Union	2 428	10	0	0	0	10	61	8	53	0	0
Muhlenberg Township	17 426	28	0	0	18	10	752	109	567	76	3
Munhall	11 719	5	0	0	1	4	197	52	128	17	0
Nanticoke	10 491	36	1	4	9	22	345	84	241	20	5
Narberth	4 192	7	0	0	3	4	50	11	38	1	0
Neshannock Township	9 372	9	0	0	5	4	146	26	118	2	0
Nether Providence Township	13 358	28	0	0	3	25	142	22	113	7	0
Neville Township	1 182	2	0	0	1	1	46	0	45	1	0
Newberry Township	15 126	40	0	16	5	19	325	55	243	27	3
New Bethlehem	1 014	2	0	1	0	1	39	8	30	1	0
New Britain	3 092	21	0	2	1	18	45	5	36	4	1
New Britain Township	10 709	4	0	1	1	2	83	12	66	5	2
New Cumberland	7 175	6	0	2	2	2	106	22	82	2	0
New Hanover Township	8 516	5	0	0	0	5	106	5	94	7	0
New Holland	5 191	4	0	0	3	1	101	22	73	6	0
New Hope	2 270	12	0	0	1	11	71	6	64	1	0
New Kensington	14 272	81	0	6	18	57	472	102	324	46	6
Newport	1 474	9	0	2	0	7	52	6	46	0	1
Newport Township	4 846	6	1	1	1	3	89	15	68	6	2
New Sewickley Township	7 434	17	0	1	1	15	112	25	81	6	0
Newtown	2 273	1	0	0	0	1	27	2	25	0	0
Newtown Township (Bucks County)	19 081	37	0	0	2	35	232	22	205	5	1
Newtown Township (Delaware County)	11 838	9	0	0	2	7	93	8	77	8	2
Newville	1 333	3	0	0	0	3	52	17	33	2	0
New Wilmington	2 486	2	0	0	1	1	32	3	27	2	0
Northampton	9 665	18	0	1	1	16	182	27	150	5	0
Northampton Township	40 906	15	0	0	3	12	291	28	253	10	0
North Catasauqua	2 858	2	0	1	0	1	142	16	120	6	1
North Cornwall Township	6 490	31	0	0	2	29	117	9	104	4	1
North Coventry Township	7 617	14	0	0	2	12	312	28	268	16	0
North East	4 446	11	0	2	1	8	94	14	78	2	0
Northeastern Regional	9 870	10	0	2	3	5	153	30	107	16	1
Northern Berks Regional	11 040	13	0	1	2	10	122	20	95	7	0
Northern York Regional	54 691	63	0	2	22	39	1 155	153	942	60	2
North Fayette Township	12 834	4	0	0	1	3	231	16	206	9	0
North Huntingdon Township	29 400	19	0	2	7	10	411	85	300	26	1
North Lebanon Township	10 833	23	0	4	5	14	390	48	331	11	0
North Londonderry Township	6 893	12	0	0	0	12	122	10	108	4	1
North Strabane Township	11 415	36	0	1	1	34	253	24	221	8	1
Northumberland	3 614	2	0	1	0	1	104	24	75	5	0
North Versailles Town	12 773	60	0	1	14	45	338	50	261	27	3
North Wales	3 326	3	0	0	2	1	58	11	44	3	3
Northwest Lawrence Regional	6 953	10	0	1	0	9	76	35	38	3	0
Northwest Regional	16 531	2	0	1	0	1	179	11	165	3	1
Norwood	5 884	7	0	0	1	6	132	9	116	7	1
O'Hara Township	9 266	15	0	0	1	14	119	11	102	6	0
Ohio Township	3 556	0	0	0	0	0	5	0	5	0	0
Ohioville	3 708	9	0	1	1	7	32	3	26	3	0
Oil City	11 081	17	0	2	3	12	218	33	166	19	3
Old Lycoming Township	5 409	5	1	0	1	3	103	24	74	5	0
Orwigsburg	3 017	1	0	1	0	0	26	4	20	2	0
Paint Township	3 271	6	0	1	1	4	19	3	16	0	0
Palmerton	5 299	15	0	0	1	14	119	18	97	4	1
Palmyra	7 011	38	0	1	1	36	117	19	89	9	2
Parkesburg	3 441	10	0	3	1	6	45	6	38	1	2
Patton Township	12 389	6	0	3	3	0	217	27	183	7	1
Paxtang	1 519	6	0	0	3	3	32	5	22	5	0
Pen Argyl	3 642	5	0	1	2	2	54	16	38	0	3
Penbrook	2 954	16	0	2	7	7	52	17	32	3	1
Penn Hills	45 535	141	8	11	54	68	1 200	239	810	151	10
Pennridge Regional	14 848	22	1	3	0	18	119	21	95	3	2
Penn Township (Butler County)	5 246	2	0	0	0	2	37	3	31	3	2
Penn Township (Lancaster County)	7 765	7	0	0	0	7	145	24	96	25	1
Penn Township (Westmoreland County)	20 161	21	0	1	0	20	64	24	40	0	0
Penn Township (York County)	15 444	10	1	3	2	4	273	33	234	6	0
Pequea Township	4 439	4	0	0	0	4	57	13	40	4	0
Perkasie	8 787	7	0	4	2	1	175	23	147	5	2
Peters Township	19 285	17	0	1	6	10	246	56	175	15	5
Philadelphia	1 472 915	21 609	377	1 024	10 069	10 139	60 419	10 960	38 039	11 420	. . .
Phoenixville	15 004	51	1	3	4	43	397	39	342	16	1
Pine-Marshall-Bradford Woods	16 899	3	1	0	2	0	318	34	277	7	0
Pittsburgh	330 780	3 385	63	117	1 617	1 588	15 628	3 018	10 337	2 273	55
Plainfield Township	5 992	0	0	0	0	0	68	16	49	3	0
Pleasant Hills	8 080	5	0	0	2	3	103	11	80	12	0

[1]The FBI does not publish arson data unless it receives data from either the agency or the state for all 12 months of the calendar year.
. . . = Not available.

Table 8. Offenses Known to Law Enforcement, by State and City, 2005—*Continued*

(Number.)

City	Population	Violent crime	Murder and non-negligent man-slaughter	Forcible rape	Robbery	Aggravated assault	Property crime	Burglary	Larceny-theft	Motor vehicle theft	Arson[1]
Plum	26 734	5	0	4	1	0	232	52	165	15	5
Plumstead Township	11 871	6	0	1	1	4	140	22	105	13	3
Plymouth Township (Montgomery County)	16 151	16	0	2	12	2	698	78	586	34	4
Pocono Township	10 822	20	0	0	13	7	295	37	244	14	1
Point Township	3 822	4	0	1	0	3	32	11	20	1	0
Portage	2 719	1	0	0	0	1	21	3	15	3	0
Port Allegany	2 290	0	0	0	0	0	0	0	0	0	0
Pottstown	21 706	164	2	23	43	96	1 141	123	916	102	14
Pottsville	14 909	44	0	3	6	35	262	42	200	20	8
Prospect Park	6 478	29	0	0	4	25	155	24	120	11	0
Punxsutawney	6 142	32	1	5	2	24	96	4	89	3	2
Pymatuning Township	3 728	3	0	0	1	2	119	35	78	6	0
Radnor Township	31 174	28	0	2	11	15	332	45	275	12	1
Reading	80 879	936	22	51	372	491	5 093	1 512	2 520	1 061	45
Reynoldsville	2 656	1	0	0	0	1	13	2	11	0	0
Rice Township	2 599	2	0	0	0	2	19	6	11	2	0
Richland Township (Bucks County)	12 058	14	0	1	5	8	230	16	201	13	0
Richland Township (Cambria County)	12 593	17	0	3	2	12	376	51	322	3	1
Ridgway	4 390	34	0	0	1	33	153	18	129	6	1
Ridley Park	7 082	3	0	0	0	3	64	9	48	7	1
Ridley Township	30 373	84	0	2	15	67	481	77	356	48	1
Riverside	1 832	1	0	0	0	1	13	6	6	1	0
Roaring Spring	2 345	4	0	0	2	2	43	5	37	1	0
Robesonia	2 056	2	0	0	0	2	18	0	17	1	0
Robeson Township	7 339	6	1	0	1	4	48	9	37	2	5
Robinson Township (Allegheny County)	13 678	32	0	2	4	26	404	35	358	11	1
Rochester	3 867	16	2	2	6	6	242	25	206	11	0
Rockledge	2 557	3	0	0	0	3	30	7	23	0	1
Rosslyn Farms	443	0	0	0	0	0	3	1	2	0	0
Ross Township	31 495	42	0	1	14	27	948	81	831	36	0
Royersford	4 333	8	0	0	0	8	103	13	82	8	0
Salisbury Township	13 759	8	1	2	2	3	332	39	286	7	0
Sandy Township	11 547	9	0	0	2	7	262	24	229	9	1
Sayre	5 653	18	0	6	2	10	108	6	100	2	1
Schuylkill Haven	5 346	3	1	1	0	1	148	15	127	6	3
Schuylkill Township (Chester County)	7 801	4	0	0	0	4	102	11	89	2	2
Scottdale	4 625	12	0	3	4	5	115	11	101	3	2
Scranton	74 067	452	1	47	89	315	2 371	630	1 569	172	19
Selinsgrove	5 384	61	0	9	1	51	250	37	208	5	1
Seward	471	0	0	0	0	0	0	0	0	0	0
Sewickley	3 743	6	0	0	1	5	101	6	92	3	1
Shaler Township	29 075	17	0	0	5	12	321	60	233	28	0
Shamokin	7 666	49	2	3	2	42	28	13	6	9	0
Sharon Hill	5 369	32	0	2	18	12	162	20	129	13	0
Sharpsburg	3 428	4	0	0	3	1	46	16	15	15	0
Shenandoah	5 364	17	0	0	3	14	192	54	128	10	1
Shenango Township (Lawrence County)	7 721	8	0	0	4	4	237	43	189	5	0
Shippingport	231	1	0	0	0	1	3	0	3	0	0
Shiremanstown	1 491	0	0	0	0	0	1	1	0	0	0
Shohola Township	2 338	0	0	0	0	0	14	9	5	0	0
Silver Lake Township	1 758	1	0	0	0	1	17	2	14	1	0
Sinking Spring	3 345	2	0	0	0	2	118	23	86	9	0
Slatington	4 416	0	0	0	0	0	22	0	22	0	0
Slippery Rock	3 136	0	0	0	0	0	60	11	49	0	0
Smethport	1 639	1	0	0	0	1	47	6	40	1	1
Solebury Township	8 835	5	1	0	0	4	59	7	50	2	1
South Buffalo Township	2 834	0	0	0	0	0	7	2	5	0	0
South Coatesville	1 011	5	0	0	0	5	11	6	4	1	1
Southern Regional (Lancaster County)	3 811	2	0	0	0	2	52	11	38	3	0
Southern Regional (York County)	9 429	18	0	4	6	8	237	42	190	5	0
South Fayette Township	13 001	52	0	1	2	49	101	16	76	9	0
South Fork	1 084	2	0	1	0	1	8	4	4	0	1
South Greensburg	2 284	9	0	0	2	7	59	10	44	5	0
South Heidelberg Township	6 480	5	0	0	0	5	57	11	42	4	0
South Lebanon Township	8 580	4	0	1	0	3	128	36	88	4	0
South Londonderry Township	6 347	4	0	0	2	2	59	3	52	4	0
South Park Township	14 364	8	0	1	1	6	52	11	31	10	0
South Pymatuning Township	2 858	3	0	0	0	3	21	5	16	0	0
South Strabane Township	8 293	16	0	3	7	6	454	19	419	16	0
Southwest Greensburg	2 315	13	0	1	1	11	43	9	28	6	0
Southwest Mercer County Regional	7 694	30	0	1	11	18	349	81	241	27	0
South Whitehall Township	18 711	67	0	6	10	51	667	35	616	16	6
South Williamsport	6 240	13	0	0	1	12	127	23	97	7	1
Spring City	3 294	8	0	1	1	6	73	21	52	0	0
Springdale	3 661	6	0	0	1	5	63	13	48	2	0
Springettsbury Township	24 014	46	0	4	28	14	1 042	66	954	22	8
Springfield Township (Bucks County)	5 033	8	0	0	0	8	42	7	33	2	0
Springfield Township (Delaware County)	23 206	25	1	5	8	11	697	37	615	45	0
Springfield Township (Montgomery County)	19 449	19	0	1	5	13	204	31	166	7	0
Spring Garden Township	12 201	27	0	5	8	14	401	53	323	25	0

[1]The FBI does not publish arson data unless it receives data from either the agency or the state for all 12 months of the calendar year.

Table 8. Offenses Known to Law Enforcement, by State and City, 2005—*Continued*

(Number.)

City	Population	Violent crime	Murder and non-negligent man-slaughter	Forcible rape	Robbery	Aggravated assault	Property crime	Burglary	Larceny-theft	Motor vehicle theft	Arson[1]
Spring Township (Berks County)	23 371	13	0	3	6	4	435	53	353	29	0
Spring Township, Centre County	6 484	1	0	0	0	1	74	9	63	2	0
St. Clair Boro	3 103	14	0	0	0	14	117	7	109	1	0
State College	52 843	32	0	4	6	22	884	138	726	20	4
Steelton	5 718	32	0	2	19	11	223	54	148	21	1
Stewartstown	2 013	0	0	0	0	0	25	3	18	4	0
Stowe Township	6 394	31	0	5	6	20	142	40	85	17	0
Strasburg	2 767	2	0	0	1	1	31	3	27	1	0
Stroud Area Regional	33 532	93	0	9	37	47	965	133	772	60	12
Sugarcreek	5 177	22	0	4	3	15	118	14	103	1	2
Sugarloaf Township (Luzerne County)	3 813	5	0	0	1	4	146	5	138	3	0
Summerhill Township	2 653	7	0	0	1	6	34	9	24	1	0
Sunbury	10 190	68	0	7	6	55	314	53	246	15	11
Susquehanna Township (Dauphin County)	22 672	58	0	5	26	27	499	89	388	22	3
Swarthmore	6 184	11	0	0	1	10	70	13	55	2	0
Swatara Township	22 486	55	3	5	29	18	1 064	117	902	45	8
Swissvale	9 209	41	0	1	12	28	220	48	138	34	2
Swoyersville	4 980	31	0	1	2	28	144	45	98	1	0
Sykesville	1 221	1	0	0	0	1	13	1	12	0	0
Tamaqua	6 840	23	0	6	4	13	205	27	170	8	0
Tatamy	1 024	0	0	0	0	0	9	0	9	0	0
Telford	4 654	14	0	1	2	11	71	7	61	3	0
Tidioute	761	0	0	0	0	0	7	2	5	0	0
Tinicum Township (Bucks County)	4 247	2	0	0	0	2	35	8	27	0	0
Tinicum Township (Delaware County)	4 275	20	0	2	1	17	226	14	177	35	0
Titusville	5 906	6	0	0	1	5	149	18	121	10	0
Towamencin Township	18 043	22	0	1	3	18	242	38	192	12	1
Towanda	2 941	5	0	1	3	1	25	7	17	1	0
Trainer	1 870	25	0	3	3	19	94	20	61	13	0
Tredyffrin Township	29 115	29	0	1	4	24	428	31	381	16	0
Troy	1 486	2	0	1	0	1	19	3	15	1	1
Tullytown	2 005	2	0	0	1	1	66	7	56	3	0
Tunkhannock	1 852	10	0	1	0	9	41	8	30	3	0
Tunkhannock Township (Wyoming County)	4 351	3	0	1	0	2	76	13	56	7	1
Union City	3 396	4	0	0	0	4	24	11	13	0	2
Uniontown	12 088	52	0	2	25	25	500	100	344	56	0
Union Township (Lawrence County)	5 222	2	0	0	0	2	194	18	172	4	0
Upper Chichester Township	17 049	70	1	1	27	41	519	63	409	47	9
Upper Darby Township	80 104	278	5	16	168	89	2 033	286	1 467	280	2
Upper Dublin Township	26 600	63	1	0	6	56	414	54	340	20	0
Upper Gwynedd Township	14 576	18	0	0	2	16	206	35	170	1	6
Upper Leacock Township	8 327	13	0	2	7	4	173	28	128	17	1
Upper Makefield Township	8 208	7	1	1	1	4	65	13	50	2	1
Upper Merion Township	27 083	46	4	0	18	24	1 397	82	1 255	60	1
Upper Moreland Township	24 958	32	0	4	9	19	403	70	316	17	3
Upper Nazareth Township	5 131	7	0	0	0	7	81	3	77	1	0
Upper Perkiomen	8 761	25	0	1	7	17	106	17	78	11	1
Upper Pottsgrove Township	4 798	10	0	1	1	8	49	11	36	2	0
Upper Providence Township (Delaware County)	11 186	3	0	1	1	1	36	18	18	0	0
Upper Providence Township (Montgomery County)	17 873	4	1	1	0	2	191	30	154	7	0
Upper Saucon Township	13 527	7	0	2	1	4	133	20	110	3	0
Upper Southampton Township	15 620	9	0	0	3	6	171	14	150	7	2
Upper St. Clair Township	19 540	2	0	0	1	1	114	22	81	11	0
Upper Uwchlan Township	7 648	1	0	0	0	1	97	21	72	4	0
Uwchlan Township	18 311	21	0	1	2	18	216	36	177	3	4
Vandergrift	5 260	26	0	1	1	24	42	14	25	3	3
Vandling	712	0	0	0	0	0	5	1	3	1	0
Vernon Township	5 430	0	0	0	0	0	85	2	79	4	0
Walnutport	2 119	5	0	1	0	4	75	5	67	3	0
Warminster Township	32 356	51	3	8	16	24	565	71	452	42	2
Warren	9 798	70	2	3	1	64	133	17	115	1	1
Warwick Township (Bucks County)	14 371	7	0	0	0	7	78	15	61	2	2
Warwick Township (Lancaster County)	17 024	6	2	1	1	2	85	11	72	2	0
Washington Township (Fayette County)	4 296	9	0	1	1	7	47	19	25	3	1
Washington Township (Franklin County)	11 919	12	0	3	2	7	273	45	216	12	4
Washington Township (Westmoreland County)	7 508	8	0	1	2	5	55	12	39	4	0
Watsontown	2 170	15	0	1	0	14	46	11	32	3	1
Waynesboro	9 706	23	0	4	6	13	257	22	218	17	0
Waynesburg	4 103	5	0	0	2	3	99	22	72	5	2
Weatherly	2 631	8	0	0	0	8	46	14	30	2	1
Weissport	434	1	0	0	0	1	8	2	6	0	0
Wellsboro	3 381	1	0	0	0	1	63	8	52	3	1
Wernersville	2 282	1	0	0	1	0	48	8	39	1	0
West Alexander	313	1	0	0	0	1	4	0	4	0	0
West Chester	17 734	139	1	22	44	72	505	90	373	42	6
West Cocalico Township	7 111	3	0	0	0	3	50	7	40	3	0
West Conshohocken	1 454	6	0	0	0	6	45	3	40	2	1
West Cornwall Township	1 963	23	0	2	2	19	21	1	19	1	0
West Earl Township	7 020	2	0	0	2	0	105	18	79	8	0
West Fallowfield Township	2 585	0	0	0	0	0	11	2	9	0	0

[1]The FBI does not publish arson data unless it receives data from either the agency or the state for all 12 months of the calendar year.

Table 8. Offenses Known to Law Enforcement, by State and City, 2005—*Continued*

(Number.)

City	Population	Violent crime	Murder and non-negligent man-slaughter	Forcible rape	Robbery	Aggravated assault	Property crime	Burglary	Larceny-theft	Motor vehicle theft	Arson[1]
Westfall Township	2 778	2	0	0	1	1	140	20	114	6	2
West Goshen Township	21 214	44	0	4	9	31	511	69	422	20	2
West Hempfield Township	15 779	10	0	0	4	6	274	43	212	19	2
West Hills Regional	8 304	6	0	2	1	3	102	16	81	5	0
West Kittanning	1 516	0	0	0	0	0	22	0	21	1	0
West Lampeter Township	14 839	6	0	1	3	2	181	27	143	11	1
West Lebanon Township	841	9	0	0	1	8	39	1	35	3	0
West Manchester Township	17 583	39	1	7	18	13	736	47	679	10	3
West Manheim Township	6 359	0	0	0	0	0	51	15	34	2	0
West Norriton Township	14 904	33	1	3	4	25	305	36	258	11	2
West Pikeland Township	3 919	0	0	0	0	0	11	2	8	1	1
West Pittston	4 886	5	0	0	0	5	100	19	76	5	0
West Pottsgrove Township	3 813	43	0	0	4	39	92	6	76	10	0
West Reading	4 012	27	0	3	6	18	227	35	168	24	1
West Sadsbury Township	2 499	7	0	2	1	4	113	0	111	2	0
West Shore Regional	6 630	49	0	5	10	34	109	29	66	14	2
West View	6 982	5	0	0	3	2	187	10	171	6	1
West Whiteland Township	18 252	15	0	1	8	6	564	39	507	18	1
West York	4 240	17	0	4	7	6	120	15	101	4	1
Whitehall	13 949	12	0	1	1	10	68	6	59	3	0
Whitehall Township	25 696	67	0	7	38	22	1 236	128	1 069	39	5
White Haven Borough	1 164	2	0	0	0	2	11	2	9	0	0
Wilkes-Barre	41 637	207	3	30	112	62	1 602	338	1 143	121	20
Wilkes-Barre Township	3 115	12	0	0	7	5	433	18	402	13	2
Wilkins Township	6 739	9	1	0	3	5	166	13	146	7	3
Williamsport	30 232	134	3	16	64	51	1 202	219	917	66	13
Willistown Township	10 766	5	0	0	0	5	60	13	44	3	0
Windber	4 184	2	0	1	0	1	32	11	19	2	0
Yardley	2 537	0	0	0	0	0	16	1	15	0	0
Yeadon	11 557	96	2	4	27	63	342	38	250	54	5
York	40 118	413	13	39	242	119	2 314	400	1 703	211	10
York Area Regional	53 927	100	2	12	13	73	766	180	557	29	6
York Springs-Latimore Township	3 369	4	0	0	0	4	41	5	36	0	0
Youngsville	1 758	7	0	0	0	7	15	2	13	0	0
Zelienople	4 033	9	0	1	0	8	133	14	115	4	1
Rhode Island[3]											
Barrington	16 767	4	0	2	1	1	200	26	169	5	6
Bristol	24 639	20	0	3	0	17	340	43	279	18	4
Burrillville	16 425	13	0	4	0	9	155	40	106	9	2
Central Falls	19 213	105	1	13	30	61	625	147	310	168	6
Charlestown	8 232	4	0	0	0	4	117	25	83	9	0
Coventry	34 928	36	0	7	4	25	374	94	247	33	14
Cranston	81 649	137	0	12	48	77	2 073	322	1 480	271	23
Cumberland	33 655	24	0	3	6	15	565	78	450	37	2
East Greenwich	13 538	4	0	1	0	3	139	31	98	10	3
East Providence	49 560	64	0	10	18	36	761	149	530	82	11
Foster	4 476	2	0	0	0	2	32	11	20	1	0
Glocester	10 508	5	1	1	0	3	59	17	36	6	1
Hopkinton	8 087	6	0	3	0	3	100	22	65	13	1
Jamestown	5 674	3	1	0	0	2	124	23	99	2	4
Johnston	29 179	41	0	4	4	33	734	99	555	80	13
Lincoln	22 097	25	1	2	11	11	488	57	394	37	2
Little Compton	3 607	0	0	0	0	0	44	9	30	5	0
Middletown	16 962	20	0	2	4	14	333	43	288	2	3
Narragansett	16 875	9	0	2	0	7	295	57	229	9	0
Newport	25 773	110	0	16	13	81	1 157	241	861	55	19
New Shoreham	1 042	0	0	0	0	0	76	4	70	2	0
North Providence	33 192	41	0	7	8	26	563	99	384	80	6
North Smithfield	10 981	10	0	3	0	7	157	31	113	13	5
Pawtucket	73 949	261	3	24	106	128	2 763	512	1 815	436	22
Portsmouth	17 238	7	0	1	2	4	255	64	172	19	3
Providence	177 392	1 207	20	106	424	657	9 124	1 835	5 025	2 264	. . .
Richmond	7 696	2	0	1	0	1	95	5	87	3	0
Scituate	10 896	5	0	1	2	2	128	27	93	8	2
South Kingstown	29 155	24	0	3	1	20	328	74	242	12	2
Tiverton	15 400	10	0	0	2	8	250	65	174	11	1
Warren	11 365	20	0	3	3	14	226	38	175	13	3
Warwick	87 322	122	4	18	24	76	2 614	277	2 021	316	25
Westerly	23 649	27	1	7	3	16	523	80	415	28	4
West Greenwich	5 634	4	0	0	0	4	81	18	56	7	0
West Warwick	29 990	62	0	13	11	38	602	116	422	64	8
South Carolina											
Abbeville	5 855	104	0	3	3	98	204	36	162	6	0
Aiken	27 670	105	1	6	23	75	1 356	192	1 102	62	5
Allendale	4 003	63	0	0	5	58	245	86	149	10	2
Anderson	26 064	166	2	10	32	122	1 614	334	1 145	135	4
Andrews	3 108	34	0	1	1	32	194	36	140	18	0
Atlantic Beach	369	12	0	0	2	10	24	4	16	4	0
Aynor	594	39	0	0	0	39	63	3	54	6	0
Bamberg	3 616	20	0	1	2	17	130	32	95	3	1
Barnwell	4 952	62	0	3	4	55	276	56	211	9	1
Batesburg-Leesville	5 622	30	0	5	4	21	260	62	188	10	0

[1]The FBI does not publish arson data unless it receives data from either the agency or the state for all 12 months of the calendar year.
[3]Because of changes in the state/local agency's reporting practices, figures are not comparable to previous years' data.
. . . = Not available.

Table 8. Offenses Known to Law Enforcement, by State and City, 2005—*Continued*

(Number.)

City	Population	Violent crime	Murder and non-negligent man-slaughter	Forcible rape	Robbery	Aggravated assault	Property crime	Burglary	Larceny-theft	Motor vehicle theft	Arson[1]
Beaufort	12 456	186	0	13	50	123	787	180	559	48	6
Belton	4 603	18	0	3	1	14	213	43	152	18	0
Bennettsville	9 386	182	2	7	19	154	529	118	395	16	2
Bethune	363	0	0	0	0	0	0	0	0	0	0
Blacksburg	1 926	29	0	1	1	27	146	15	121	10	2
Blackville	2 975	5	0	0	1	4	46	11	35	0	0
Bluffton	2 290	17	0	1	4	12	152	36	106	10	1
Bonneau	351	2	0	0	1	1	12	4	8	0	0
Bowman	1 188	13	0	0	0	13	37	13	18	6	1
Branchville	1 071	5	0	0	0	5	32	7	24	1	1
Burnettown	2 822	6	0	1	0	5	33	8	17	8	0
Calhoun Falls	2 316	11	1	1	0	9	80	19	55	6	1
Camden	7 070	122	3	2	21	96	510	67	411	32	0
Cameron	436	0	0	0	0	0	0	0	0	0	0
Campobello	467	1	0	0	1	0	6	2	3	1	0
Cayce	12 587	121	0	6	33	82	786	105	629	52	2
Central	3 671	12	0	1	0	11	85	19	53	13	0
Chapin	674	6	0	0	1	5	69	7	62	0	0
Charleston	106 307	1 003	10	49	290	654	4 756	810	3 464	482	11
Cheraw	5 502	54	1	0	13	40	351	40	303	8	0
Chesnee	1 033	7	0	0	1	6	52	10	35	7	0
Chester	6 358	111	0	5	7	99	413	118	271	24	6
Chesterfield	1 362	8	0	1	0	7	102	38	62	2	2
Clemson	12 238	23	0	3	2	18	303	49	217	37	0
Clinton	9 107	102	0	3	11	88	549	89	439	21	3
Clio	769	8	0	0	2	6	27	4	20	3	0
Clover	4 109	119	1	5	3	110	150	39	106	5	1
Columbia	117 911	1 311	15	56	381	859	7 682	1 332	5 513	837	26
Conway	13 474	137	4	4	35	94	1 071	175	843	53	4
Coward	673	0	0	0	0	0	7	1	6	0	1
Cowpens	2 354	9	0	1	1	7	169	36	132	1	0
Darlington	6 664	169	0	7	21	141	571	97	440	34	1
Denmark	3 191	40	1	3	4	32	134	52	76	6	0
Dillon	6 524	181	0	4	26	151	622	174	413	35	1
Duncan	2 991	14	0	2	6	6	107	19	81	7	0
Easley	18 896	73	0	10	14	49	1 096	184	845	67	2
Eastover	803	5	0	0	0	5	19	8	10	1	0
Edgefield	4 571	10	0	2	0	8	61	12	44	5	1
Edisto Beach	704	1	0	1	0	0	41	11	25	5	0
Ehrhardt	586	2	0	0	0	2	21	4	16	1	0
Elgin	898	12	0	1	4	7	43	4	37	2	0
Estill	2 424	21	2	1	0	18	60	23	34	3	0
Eutawville	340	0	0	0	0	0	19	4	14	1	0
Fairfax	3 248	11	0	0	0	11	17	10	6	1	0
Florence	31 302	555	4	18	201	332	3 387	592	2 582	213	31
Folly Beach	2 291	19	0	5	3	11	163	28	130	5	0
Forest Acres	10 265	85	0	5	21	59	751	117	585	49	2
Fort Lawn	855	17	0	2	1	14	50	11	30	9	0
Fort Mill	8 150	56	0	2	8	46	229	38	178	13	3
Fountain Inn	6 673	30	0	2	3	25	192	51	117	24	0
Gaffney	13 145	126	2	12	25	87	937	131	758	48	3
Gaston	1 409	6	0	0	0	6	35	1	30	4	0
Georgetown	9 047	119	0	2	18	99	549	93	434	22	2
Goose Creek	32 688	77	1	5	19	52	762	125	579	58	7
Great Falls	2 150	14	0	0	2	12	112	13	96	3	1
Greeleyville	431	2	0	1	0	1	4	1	3	0	0
Greenville	57 056	656	5	32	161	458	3 794	776	2 710	308	11
Greenwood	22 544	394	2	10	51	331	1 824	345	1 395	84	5
Greer	20 693	107	1	7	34	65	778	121	604	53	3
Hampton	2 833	19	0	2	7	10	247	98	135	14	0
Hanahan	13 558	89	0	6	36	47	554	110	387	57	1
Hardeeville	1 863	30	0	6	4	20	452	52	386	14	0
Harleyville	693	12	0	0	0	12	16	3	11	2	0
Hartsville	7 530	218	1	7	32	178	977	144	797	36	3
Hemingway	538	1	0	0	1	0	37	5	31	1	0
Holly Hill	1 392	4	0	0	0	4	34	3	27	4	0
Honea Path	3 626	53	0	1	4	48	196	43	141	12	1
Inman	1 930	13	0	1	1	11	58	15	39	4	0
Irmo	11 333	54	0	5	12	37	373	66	301	6	0
Isle of Palms	4 665	5	0	0	0	5	147	9	131	7	0
Iva	1 190	2	0	0	1	1	32	8	21	3	0
Jackson	1 666	7	0	0	2	5	55	20	23	12	0
Jamestown	97	0	0	0	0	0	5	0	5	0	0
Johnsonville	1 464	17	0	1	3	13	52	4	48	0	0
Johnston	2 374	15	0	0	3	12	105	19	76	10	3
Jonesville	954	13	0	0	1	12	23	3	20	0	0
Kingstree	3 444	26	0	0	11	15	246	57	171	18	1
Lake City	6 708	122	0	10	29	83	671	151	480	40	5
Lake View	810	4	0	0	1	3	22	9	13	0	0
Lamar	1 024	4	0	1	0	3	32	11	16	5	0

[1]The FBI does not publish arson data unless it receives data from either the agency or the state for all 12 months of the calendar year.

Table 8. Offenses Known to Law Enforcement, by State and City, 2005—*Continued*

(Number.)

City	Population	Violent crime	Murder and non-negligent man-slaughter	Forcible rape	Robbery	Aggravated assault	Property crime	Burglary	Larceny-theft	Motor vehicle theft	Arson[1]
Lancaster	8 587	211	0	11	27	173	796	181	588	27	3
Landrum	2 543	6	0	0	1	5	98	20	70	8	0
Lane	559	5	0	2	1	2	10	3	4	3	1
Latta	1 479	2	0	0	2	0	26	9	16	1	1
Laurens	9 968	152	1	3	14	134	646	131	492	23	11
Lexington	12 781	29	0	2	5	22	520	40	451	29	1
Liberty	3 036	15	0	0	0	15	135	29	99	7	1
Lincolnville	882	0	0	0	0	0	0	0	0	0	0
Loris	2 234	11	0	0	4	7	105	22	75	8	0
Lyman	2 788	5	0	1	3	1	102	24	68	10	0
Lynchburg	603	6	0	0	1	5	43	21	19	3	1
Manning	4 059	42	0	1	14	27	343	151	180	12	0
Marion	7 124	66	1	4	8	53	546	130	393	23	5
Mauldin	18 857	79	0	1	10	68	525	87	397	41	4
McColl	2 470	29	0	0	6	23	187	50	134	3	2
McCormick	2 698	17	0	1	2	14	61	15	42	4	0
Moncks Corner	6 434	48	1	3	10	34	358	43	263	52	4
Mount Pleasant	57 115	194	0	12	36	146	1 295	181	1 006	108	2
Mullins	4 937	61	0	3	19	39	626	159	449	18	2
Myrtle Beach	25 755	501	3	54	193	251	5 141	851	3 834	456	16
Newberry	10 845	46	0	5	7	34	505	56	438	11	3
New Ellenton	2 304	8	0	1	0	7	76	19	48	9	1
Nichols	409	0	0	0	0	0	10	3	6	1	0
Ninety Six	1 952	5	0	0	0	5	53	14	36	3	1
North	803	8	0	0	0	8	50	6	41	3	1
North Augusta	19 354	33	1	3	14	15	663	103	500	60	4
North Charleston	85 416	1 473	11	82	519	861	7 328	1 365	5 033	930	32
North Myrtle Beach	13 339	61	2	6	16	37	1 461	258	1 136	67	1
Norway	384	0	0	0	0	0	7	3	3	1	0
Orangeburg	13 070	105	1	3	35	66	868	229	569	70	5
Pacolet	2 754	5	0	0	0	5	75	11	60	4	1
Pageland	2 567	52	0	1	2	49	150	22	123	5	0
Pamplico	1 162	17	0	1	2	14	35	15	19	1	0
Pawleys Island	142	0	0	0	0	0	18	2	16	0	0
Pendleton	3 071	13	0	0	1	12	131	26	98	7	0
Pickens	3 035	20	0	1	2	17	180	37	135	8	3
Pine Ridge	1 706	14	0	1	1	12	27	7	19	1	0
Port Royal	9 313	34	0	0	9	25	269	49	197	23	2
Prosperity	1 116	7	0	1	0	6	46	6	40	0	0
Ridgeland	2 647	22	0	3	10	9	135	27	95	13	0
Ridge Spring	808	0	0	0	0	0	0	0	0	0	0
Rock Hill	58 688	709	4	41	85	579	2 770	464	2 111	195	19
Salem	131	1	0	0	0	1	2	0	2	0	0
Salley	419	0	0	0	0	0	0	0	0	0	0
Saluda	3 011	38	0	1	5	32	128	12	113	3	0
Santee	734	23	0	1	6	16	393	14	369	10	0
Scranton	1 005	0	0	0	0	0	27	2	25	0	0
Seneca	8 066	98	0	5	14	79	539	95	410	34	0
Simpsonville	15 127	96	2	8	11	75	755	122	589	44	4
Society Hill	712	1	0	0	0	1	19	7	9	3	1
South Congaree	2 354	6	0	2	0	4	74	14	55	5	0
Spartanburg	39 123	692	11	28	149	504	4 097	939	2 866	292	34
Springdale	2 934	5	0	1	1	3	105	12	85	8	0
St. George	2 124	27	0	0	2	25	121	39	69	13	2
St. Matthews	2 083	33	0	0	1	32	102	20	77	5	0
St. Stephen	1 778	21	0	2	9	10	98	30	60	8	0
Sullivans Island	1 920	0	0	0	0	0	47	10	32	5	0
Summerton	1 062	12	1	0	4	7	87	15	70	2	0
Summerville	34 706	133	1	10	34	88	1 342	185	1 059	98	5
Sumter	40 210	602	3	8	117	474	2 324	616	1 580	128	18
Surfside Beach	4 724	14	0	0	4	10	275	53	201	21	0
Swansea	551	7	0	0	1	6	72	5	65	2	1
Tega Cay	4 322	3	0	0	0	3	50	3	45	2	0
Timmonsville	2 393	37	0	0	4	33	206	76	120	10	2
Travelers Rest	4 216	2	0	0	1	1	168	19	130	19	0
Turbeville	732	8	0	0	2	6	30	7	23	0	0
Union	8 491	121	0	4	11	106	405	68	324	13	6
Vance	206	2	0	0	0	2	2	0	2	0	0
Wagener	884	2	0	0	0	2	32	8	18	6	0
Walhalla	3 818	27	0	2	3	22	127	20	98	9	2
Walterboro	5 591	71	0	5	14	52	534	77	424	33	2
Ware Shoals	2 414	13	0	0	0	13	125	16	102	7	2
Wellford	2 305	4	0	0	1	3	74	25	40	9	0
West Columbia	13 206	289	1	12	51	225	904	172	667	65	0
Westminster	2 737	11	0	0	0	11	73	13	57	3	1
West Pelzer	906	5	1	1	0	3	30	5	20	5	0
West Union	305	0	0	0	0	0	4	0	3	1	0
Whitmire	1 548	5	0	1	0	4	36	6	30	0	0
Williamston	3 906	18	0	2	3	13	142	17	110	15	2
Williston	3 315	10	1	2	2	5	143	23	115	5	1
Winnsboro	3 676	54	1	3	4	46	216	23	184	9	3
Woodruff	4 203	36	0	1	3	32	195	45	139	11	2
Yemassee	841	11	0	0	1	10	18	5	10	3	0
York	7 123	143	0	4	18	121	472	109	346	17	1

[1]The FBI does not publish arson data unless it receives data from either the agency or the state for all 12 months of the calendar year.

Table 8. Offenses Known to Law Enforcement, by State and City, 2005—*Continued*

(Number.)

City	Population	Violent crime	Murder and non-negligent man-slaughter	Forcible rape	Robbery	Aggravated assault	Property crime	Burglary	Larceny-theft	Motor vehicle theft	Arson[1]
South Dakota											
Armour	742	0	0	0	0	0	0	0	0	0	0
Belle Fourche	4 683	3	0	0	0	3	15	3	10	2	0
Burke	616	0	0	0	0	0	0	0	0	0	0
Canton	3 093	0	0	0	0	0	30	7	19	4	0
Colman	565	0	0	0	0	0	2	1	1	0	0
Eagle Butte	671	0	0	0	0	0	24	6	17	1	0
Elk Point	1 848	1	0	1	0	0	9	0	9	0	0
Gettysburg	1 255	0	0	0	0	0	0	0	0	0	0
Hermosa	334	0	0	0	0	0	0	0	0	0	0
Hot Springs	4 128	6	0	1	0	5	24	10	11	3	0
Jefferson	596	0	0	0	0	0	0	0	0	0	0
Kadoka	682	3	0	1	0	2	8	7	0	1	1
Leola	434	0	0	0	0	0	0	0	0	0	0
Madison	6 203	3	0	0	0	3	113	15	93	5	0
McLaughlin	791	2	0	0	0	2	13	5	8	0	1
Mitchell	14 985	33	0	10	1	22	358	34	309	15	0
Mobridge	3 306	12	0	3	0	9	114	19	85	10	0
Parkston	1 588	1	0	0	0	1	30	19	10	1	0
Rapid City	61 862	257	1	58	38	160	2 551	459	1 980	112	6
Salem	1 403	2	1	0	0	1	11	1	9	1	0
Sioux Falls[3]	137 590	473	4	145	71	253	4 264	682	3 253	329	. . .
Spearfish	9 265	15	1	3	1	10	240	28	196	16	2
Sturgis	6 421	14	0	1	3	10	177	16	143	18	2
Tripp	682	0	0	0	0	0	0	0	0	0	0
Wagner	1 602	7	0	0	0	7	36	15	20	1	0
Wilmot	534	0	0	0	0	0	0	0	0	0	0
Yankton	13 579	29	0	13	2	14	375	59	308	8	0
Tennessee											
Adamsville	2 066	0	0	0	0	0	17	3	12	2	0
Alamo	2 402	22	0	1	2	19	46	12	31	3	1
Alcoa	8 453	101	0	7	11	83	656	94	523	39	5
Alexandria	861	2	0	0	0	2	23	6	16	1	1
Algood	3 117	2	0	0	0	2	124	3	114	7	0
Athens	13 863	212	1	12	23	176	1 370	282	1 016	72	8
Atoka	5 037	7	0	0	1	6	167	30	128	9	0
Baileyton	508	1	0	0	0	1	24	1	20	3	0
Bartlett	43 315	60	0	7	21	32	1 069	161	844	64	4
Baxter	1 343	3	0	0	0	3	19	8	10	1	0
Bean Station	2 720	26	0	0	1	25	143	43	82	18	0
Belle Meade	3 089	1	0	0	0	1	25	3	18	4	0
Bells	2 323	22	0	1	1	20	66	26	36	4	1
Benton	1 133	3	0	0	0	3	26	8	18	0	0
Berry Hill	688	13	0	0	6	7	91	9	69	13	0
Bethel Springs	773	0	0	0	0	0	0	0	0	0	0
Big Sandy	524	5	0	0	0	5	9	2	6	1	0
Bluff City	1 594	7	0	0	0	7	36	9	24	3	0
Bolivar	5 726	52	2	4	8	38	354	102	228	24	2
Bradford	1 092	3	0	0	0	3	27	7	18	2	0
Brentwood	30 907	21	0	1	7	13	550	73	461	16	3
Brighton	2 254	5	0	1	0	4	46	9	30	7	0
Bristol	25 195	139	0	9	12	118	1 394	234	1 088	72	2
Brownsville	10 817	173	0	11	15	147	636	173	447	16	2
Bruceton	1 521	12	0	0	1	11	7	0	7	0	0
Burns	1 417	4	0	0	0	4	22	5	13	4	0
Calhoun	516	2	0	0	0	2	13	1	11	1	0
Camden	3 787	14	0	3	1	10	150	43	93	14	0
Carthage	2 273	20	0	2	1	17	107	18	84	5	0
Caryville	2 391	10	0	1	3	6	66	9	47	10	0
Celina	1 386	3	0	0	1	2	42	13	26	3	0
Centerville	4 021	4	0	1	0	3	101	35	57	9	0
Chapel Hill	987	1	0	0	1	0	20	6	13	1	0
Charleston	649	0	0	0	0	0	17	3	13	1	0
Chattanooga	156 480	1 754	23	116	442	1 173	12 606	2 190	9 365	1 051	23
Church Hill	6 287	17	0	0	0	17	166	42	115	9	0
Clarksburg	379	0	0	0	0	0	6	1	4	1	0
Clarksville	110 117	881	5	52	138	686	4 129	1 071	2 802	256	25
Clinton	9 446	43	2	1	8	32	391	91	262	38	3
Collegedale	7 241	11	0	2	2	7	218	42	173	3	0
Collierville	36 946	64	3	2	11	48	614	98	460	56	5
Collinwood	1 045	1	0	0	0	1	7	1	5	1	0
Columbia	33 952	433	3	22	72	336	1 796	347	1 341	108	6
Coopertown	3 209	15	0	0	1	14	50	11	36	3	0
Copperhill	498	1	0	0	0	1	9	5	3	1	0
Cornersville	948	0	0	0	0	0	5	2	3	0	0
Covington	9 083	98	0	1	10	87	549	170	349	30	1
Cowan	1 780	11	0	0	0	11	77	12	55	10	4
Cross Plains	1 514	6	0	0	0	6	24	6	17	1	1
Crossville	10 060	66	0	4	10	52	938	150	718	70	3

[1]The FBI does not publish arson data unless it receives data from either the agency or the state for all 12 months of the calendar year.
[3]Because of changes in the state/local agency's reporting practices, figures are not comparable to previous years' data.
. . . = Not available.

Table 8. Offenses Known to Law Enforcement, by State and City, 2005—*Continued*

(Number.)

City	Population	Violent crime	Murder and non-negligent man-slaughter	Forcible rape	Robbery	Aggravated assault	Property crime	Burglary	Larceny-theft	Motor vehicle theft	Arson[1]
Crump	1 556	6	0	0	0	6	91	32	43	16	0
Cumberland City	322	2	0	0	1	1	14	5	9	0	0
Cumberland Gap	203	0	0	0	0	0	14	6	8	0	1
Dayton	6 507	28	0	2	5	21	394	39	345	10	0
Decatur	1 445	7	0	0	0	7	49	15	29	5	0
Decaturville	853	0	0	0	0	0	6	1	3	2	0
Decherd	2 225	20	0	1	0	19	77	32	40	5	2
Dickson	12 894	125	1	19	12	93	811	121	620	70	5
Dover	1 479	0	0	0	0	0	31	4	26	1	0
Dresden	2 739	7	0	0	0	7	81	25	53	3	0
Dunlap	4 588	33	0	4	0	29	120	23	81	16	1
Dyer	2 435	3	0	0	0	3	35	8	26	1	0
Dyersburg	17 589	157	0	12	20	125	1 361	294	954	113	8
Eagleville	467	0	0	0	0	0	2	0	2	0	0
East Ridge	20 220	145	0	7	17	121	1 392	322	959	111	5
Elizabethton	14 140	64	0	2	5	57	692	113	556	23	3
Elkton	512	0	0	0	0	0	5	2	3	0	0
Englewood	1 659	1	0	0	0	1	53	6	42	5	0
Erin	1 458	4	0	1	0	3	48	6	37	5	2
Erwin	5 901	18	3	0	0	15	422	35	382	5	1
Estill Springs	2 193	1	0	0	0	1	43	13	27	3	0
Ethridge	558	4	0	0	0	4	8	0	8	0	1
Etowah	3 746	9	0	0	1	8	229	43	179	7	2
Fairview	6 842	24	0	4	0	20	192	23	155	14	0
Fayetteville	7 070	72	0	1	8	63	378	63	298	17	3
Franklin	48 697	115	2	7	14	92	906	97	751	58	5
Friendship	616	3	0	0	0	3	15	5	10	0	0
Gadsden	562	3	0	0	2	1	7	3	4	0	0
Gainesboro	874	5	0	0	0	5	59	15	43	1	0
Gallatin	25 923	132	0	5	20	107	746	125	579	42	3
Gallaway	735	3	0	0	0	3	8	2	4	2	0
Gates	879	0	0	0	0	0	11	6	5	0	0
Gatlinburg	4 221	28	0	4	1	23	462	106	327	29	2
Germantown	37 950	37	0	3	13	21	690	120	533	37	6
Gibson	415	0	0	0	0	0	10	3	6	1	0
Gleason	1 448	11	0	2	0	9	37	13	23	1	1
Goodlettsville	15 270	87	0	3	26	58	876	111	705	60	2
Grand Junction	321	8	0	1	0	7	18	4	10	4	0
Graysville	1 453	6	0	0	0	6	57	4	50	3	2
Greenbrier	5 990	26	1	1	1	23	113	26	76	11	0
Greeneville	15 463	106	0	9	24	73	1 384	226	1 083	75	1
Greenfield	2 121	7	0	1	0	6	26	6	20	0	0
Halls	2 284	12	0	1	0	11	110	46	59	5	7
Harriman	6 828	57	1	2	11	43	500	119	343	38	1
Henderson	6 027	35	1	2	8	24	266	58	198	10	2
Hendersonville	44 327	143	1	7	14	121	950	162	714	74	11
Henning	1 282	20	0	0	0	20	40	14	24	2	1
Henry	535	2	0	0	0	2	8	1	7	0	0
Hohenwald	3 828	25	1	0	1	23	61	15	42	4	1
Hollow Rock	968	7	0	0	0	7	10	3	4	3	0
Hornbeak	432	0	0	0	0	0	3	1	2	0	0
Humboldt	9 430	124	0	3	9	112	556	148	368	40	9
Huntingdon	4 272	13	0	1	3	9	93	31	55	7	2
Huntland	901	1	0	0	0	1	6	3	2	1	0
Jacksboro	1 998	11	0	0	0	11	170	11	150	9	0
Jackson	62 421	836	5	49	177	605	4 885	1 269	3 141	475	28
Jamestown	1 872	18	0	0	2	16	179	50	126	3	0
Jasper	3 112	13	0	0	0	13	118	23	86	9	0
Jefferson City	8 008	29	0	1	6	22	404	49	324	31	4
Johnson City	58 419	375	5	20	73	277	3 697	692	2 797	208	12
Jonesborough	4 531	9	0	2	0	7	218	40	172	6	1
Kimball	1 358	11	0	2	0	9	85	10	66	9	0
Kingsport	44 533	403	3	32	71	297	3 253	521	2 553	179	19
Kingston	5 496	13	0	3	5	5	143	21	112	10	2
Kingston Springs	2 887	3	0	1	0	2	34	2	26	6	0
Knoxville	179 989	1 728	25	99	545	1 059	11 062	2 471	7 370	1 221	137
Lafayette	4 131	11	0	0	0	11	80	29	48	3	0
La Follette	8 241	103	1	3	7	92	473	168	278	27	0
La Grange	150	0	0	0	0	0	0	0	0	0	0
Lake City	1 873	11	0	1	2	8	134	28	86	20	9
Lakewood	2 409	9	0	0	0	9	45	15	24	6	1
La Vergne	25 072	166	2	10	9	145	708	177	455	76	10
Lawrenceburg	10 979	142	0	7	9	126	817	189	572	56	1
Lebanon	22 688	162	1	4	19	138	921	61	785	75	0
Lenoir City	7 481	51	2	2	4	43	572	75	470	27	4
Lewisburg	10 895	76	0	6	15	55	374	76	285	13	3
Lexington	7 685	66	1	4	12	49	530	121	380	29	3
Livingston	3 501	15	0	2	0	13	151	46	98	7	0
Lookout Mountain	1 936	0	0	0	0	0	11	1	10	0	0
Loretto	1 718	7	1	0	0	6	28	4	21	3	0

[1]The FBI does not publish arson data unless it receives data from either the agency or the state for all 12 months of the calendar year.

Table 8. Offenses Known to Law Enforcement, by State and City, 2005—*Continued*

(Number.)

City	Population	Violent crime	Murder and non-negligent man-slaughter	Forcible rape	Robbery	Aggravated assault	Property crime	Burglary	Larceny-theft	Motor vehicle theft	Arson[1]
Loudon	4 717	19	0	1	0	18	254	62	183	9	0
Lynnville	344	1	0	0	0	1	1	1	0	0	0
Madisonville	4 272	46	0	0	2	44	368	29	307	32	3
Manchester	9 239	47	0	0	1	46	533	152	349	32	2
Martin	10 204	37	0	3	4	30	303	26	262	15	1
Maryville	25 838	51	0	11	9	31	667	100	516	51	11
Mason	1 146	26	0	1	2	23	26	4	19	3	0
Maury City	722	2	0	0	1	1	17	7	9	1	0
Maynardville	1 912	5	0	0	0	5	51	9	36	6	0
McEwen	1 681	5	0	3	0	2	27	8	19	0	2
McKenzie	5 533	23	0	4	1	18	207	53	143	11	1
McMinnville	13 246	60	0	6	10	44	730	130	541	59	3
Medina	1 116	4	0	0	0	4	31	12	17	2	0
Memphis	678 988	12 629	137	400	4 464	7 628	56 780	15 844	32 632	8 304	225
Middleton	629	2	0	0	0	2	31	6	22	3	1
Milan	7 878	50	1	6	2	41	373	76	271	26	3
Millersville	6 149	24	0	2	2	20	150	28	106	16	1
Millington	10 508	87	1	3	19	64	599	109	431	59	0
Minor Hill	434	2	0	0	0	2	13	4	6	3	0
Monteagle	1 228	7	0	1	0	6	21	7	8	6	0
Monterey	2 812	14	0	0	3	11	93	15	70	8	0
Morristown	25 730	248	2	11	37	198	1 788	204	1 441	143	16
Moscow	551	0	0	0	0	0	18	4	13	1	0
Mountain City	2 463	4	0	1	0	3	16	5	4	7	0
Mount Carmel	5 273	8	0	0	0	8	69	12	54	3	0
Mount Juliet	17 478	43	0	4	8	31	509	108	377	24	1
Mount Pleasant	4 525	28	0	0	1	27	208	47	147	14	3
Munford	5 475	46	0	1	1	44	197	56	120	21	1
Murfreesboro	82 367	641	2	35	113	491	4 021	790	2 994	237	15
Nashville	557 034	8 974	95	336	2 440	6 103	35 796	6 448	25 900	3 448	135
Newbern	3 086	17	0	1	1	15	101	30	65	6	1
New Hope	1 030	4	0	0	0	4	3	2	1	0	0
New Johnsonville	1 977	10	0	0	2	8	43	14	27	2	2
New Market	1 331	0	0	0	0	0	9	2	7	0	0
Newport	7 344	69	0	1	18	50	581	73	459	49	0
New Tazewell	2 896	23	0	3	3	17	185	33	145	7	0
Niota	803	2	0	0	0	2	20	8	12	0	1
Nolensville	2 567	4	0	0	0	4	21	5	13	3	0
Norris	1 445	3	1	0	0	2	18	4	14	0	0
Oakland	1 710	3	0	0	0	3	63	7	54	2	0
Oak Ridge	27 585	169	1	11	51	106	1 880	383	1 350	147	6
Obion	1 129	10	0	0	0	10	40	2	38	0	1
Oliver Springs	3 324	8	0	0	2	6	98	12	75	11	0
Oneida	3 732	19	0	0	1	18	217	41	166	10	2
Paris	9 964	61	0	1	10	50	654	156	465	33	1
Parsons	2 461	2	0	1	1	0	63	5	56	2	0
Petersburg	599	1	0	0	0	1	16	0	16	0	0
Pigeon Forge	5 619	63	0	5	10	48	765	206	498	61	4
Pikeville	1 860	5	0	0	0	5	41	11	26	4	1
Pittman Center	519	0	0	0	0	0	7	4	2	1	0
Portland	10 193	76	0	7	0	69	302	78	199	25	1
Powells Crossroads	1 237	5	0	0	0	5	7	1	4	2	1
Pulaski	7 927	66	0	6	5	55	378	68	287	23	0
Puryear	678	2	0	0	1	1	13	1	11	1	0
Red Bank	11 990	76	0	10	11	55	586	113	432	41	2
Red Boiling Springs	1 068	6	0	2	0	4	19	4	13	2	0
Ridgely	1 634	7	0	0	0	7	19	5	12	2	0
Ridgetop	1 679	0	0	0	0	0	21	8	9	4	0
Ripley	7 854	152	1	4	14	133	612	196	378	38	0
Rockwood	5 497	13	0	3	5	5	381	67	299	15	0
Rogersville	4 327	30	0	0	0	30	286	49	226	11	1
Rutherford	1 268	1	0	0	0	1	21	9	12	0	0
Rutledge	1 257	1	0	1	0	0	23	5	18	0	0
Savannah	7 206	43	0	4	8	31	529	135	373	21	1
Scotts Hill	920	3	0	0	1	2	15	5	9	1	0
Selmer	4 636	34	0	0	3	31	256	49	187	20	0
Sevierville	14 249	45	0	4	10	31	959	131	758	70	3
Sewanee	2 475	1	0	0	0	1	44	17	26	1	0
Sharon	951	2	0	0	0	2	14	7	6	1	0
Shelbyville	18 170	120	3	4	36	77	741	227	459	55	2
Signal Mountain	7 283	6	0	1	1	4	75	19	55	1	1
Smithville	4 176	21	0	1	1	19	194	43	130	21	1
Smyrna	32 260	190	0	8	17	165	1 112	192	861	59	8
Sneedville	1 323	4	0	0	0	4	68	16	49	3	0
Soddy-Daisy	12 096	64	0	4	5	55	371	76	269	26	2
Somerville	2 967	21	0	0	3	18	121	23	88	10	0
South Carthage	1 318	5	0	0	0	5	33	6	25	2	0
South Fulton	2 500	4	0	0	0	4	65	17	44	4	1
South Pittsburg	3 160	13	0	0	0	13	120	24	83	13	0
Sparta	4 747	14	0	3	1	10	445	97	313	35	11

[1]The FBI does not publish arson data unless it receives data from either the agency or the state for all 12 months of the calendar year.

Table 8. Offenses Known to Law Enforcement, by State and City, 2005—*Continued*

(Number.)

City	Population	Violent crime	Murder and non-negligent man-slaughter	Forcible rape	Robbery	Aggravated assault	Property crime	Burglary	Larceny-theft	Motor vehicle theft	Arson[1]
Spencer	1 712	1	0	0	0	1	19	5	13	1	0
Spring City	2 044	4	0	0	0	4	47	8	39	0	0
Springfield	15 848	263	2	16	53	192	1 014	121	834	59	1
Spring Hill	14 583	36	0	4	4	28	183	51	121	11	2
St. Joseph	862	3	0	0	0	3	15	7	6	2	1
Surgoinsville	1 742	3	0	0	0	3	26	10	15	1	0
Tazewell	2 161	13	0	1	0	12	114	27	76	11	0
Tellico Plains	924	10	0	0	0	10	55	13	38	4	2
Tiptonville	4 167	9	0	2	1	6	70	19	48	3	5
Toone	363	1	0	0	0	1	0	0	0	0	0
Townsend	257	1	0	0	0	1	10	3	7	0	0
Trenton	4 560	33	0	2	6	25	214	59	151	4	0
Trezevant	910	4	0	0	0	4	23	5	13	5	0
Trimble	733	3	0	0	0	3	23	6	16	1	0
Troy	1 273	1	0	0	0	1	48	3	43	2	0
Tullahoma	18 873	64	0	2	25	37	1 011	269	677	65	7
Tusculum	2 208	2	0	1	0	1	30	9	21	0	0
Union City	10 938	91	0	3	10	78	714	140	517	57	8
Vonore	1 337	15	0	0	1	14	77	10	62	5	4
Wartburg	926	0	0	0	0	0	3	0	3	0	0
Wartrace	574	2	0	0	0	2	5	2	3	0	1
Watertown	1 409	1	0	0	0	1	30	5	25	0	0
Waverly	4 144	7	0	0	0	7	66	15	45	6	1
Waynesboro	2 176	17	0	0	1	16	46	12	31	3	1
Westmoreland	2 167	15	0	0	3	12	56	16	38	2	0
White Bluff	2 344	11	0	0	0	11	62	24	35	3	0
White House	8 517	10	0	3	0	7	144	22	114	8	0
White Pine	2 066	4	0	2	1	1	102	13	84	5	1
Whiteville	4 537	7	0	0	0	7	49	14	33	2	0
Whitwell	1 629	12	0	0	0	12	62	14	40	8	1
Winchester	7 749	80	0	3	4	73	406	107	280	19	5
Winfield	951	16	0	0	0	16	34	14	15	5	1
Woodbury	2 550	8	0	0	0	8	58	13	37	8	0
Texas											
Abernathy	2 824	5	0	2	0	3	23	7	16	0	0
Abilene	116 695	576	5	78	146	347	5 504	1 521	3 685	298	24
Addison	14 005	95	0	11	24	60	1 186	161	828	197	2
Alamo	16 190	60	0	0	14	46	1 345	136	1 117	92	3
Alamo Heights	7 427	3	0	0	1	2	272	26	240	6	0
Alice	19 765	164	1	10	11	142	1 768	308	1 392	68	14
Allen	67 432	53	0	9	14	30	1 528	286	1 188	54	3
Alpine	6 179	28	0	2	0	26	92	30	60	2	0
Alto	1 159	5	0	0	1	4	55	35	19	1	0
Alton	6 898	24	0	0	9	15	382	77	259	46	0
Alvarado	3 967	20	0	2	3	15	151	44	102	5	1
Alvin	22 506	53	0	2	12	39	848	191	612	45	1
Amarillo	183 765	1 537	10	88	347	1 092	11 850	2 549	8 245	1 056	62
Andrews	9 619	33	1	14	1	17	249	48	191	10	2
Angleton	19 012	78	0	3	8	67	525	99	388	38	2
Anson	2 411	1	0	0	0	1	12	7	4	1	0
Anthony	4 108	8	0	0	3	5	105	18	83	4	0
Aransas Pass	8 962	53	1	9	14	29	708	134	527	47	2
Arcola	1 214	2	0	0	0	2	24	15	7	2	6
Argyle	2 869	5	0	2	1	2	48	12	35	1	0
Arlington	365 380	2 369	24	178	768	1 399	20 403	3 984	14 609	1 810	52
Arp	936	1	0	0	0	1	10	4	5	1	0
Athens	12 567	53	0	17	11	25	500	129	335	36	0
Atlanta	5 708	49	1	9	8	31	241	49	182	10	0
Austin	693 019	3 393	26	312	1 182	1 873	41 668	7 285	31 835	2 548	115
Azle	10 470	36	0	0	3	33	512	91	392	29	12
Balch Springs	19 661	146	2	20	25	99	1 211	206	899	106	5
Balcones Heights	3 064	29	0	1	9	19	598	96	472	30	0
Ballinger	4 068	3	0	0	0	3	111	19	88	4	0
Bangs	1 649	3	0	0	0	3	57	8	48	1	1
Bartlett	1 715	9	0	1	0	8	33	8	24	1	0
Bastrop	7 121	20	0	3	8	9	394	34	341	19	6
Bay City	18 683	103	2	0	38	63	868	213	635	20	1
Bayou Vista	1 695	1	0	1	0	0	3	3	0	0	0
Baytown	68 428	291	4	32	112	143	3 042	705	2 100	237	15
Beaumont	114 141	1 130	11	97	337	685	8 320	2 057	5 735	528	47
Bedford	49 213	240	2	14	35	189	1 825	342	1 344	139	11
Beeville	13 809	48	1	2	2	43	486	108	363	15	1
Bellaire	17 227	38	0	3	20	15	454	83	355	16	0
Bellmead	9 795	137	0	10	13	114	946	131	770	45	2
Bellville	4 323	27	1	0	1	25	128	29	93	6	1
Belton	15 082	32	0	0	7	25	560	139	396	25	3
Benbrook	22 002	36	0	12	5	19	530	123	363	44	4
Bertram	1 305	6	0	0	0	6	16	2	13	1	0
Beverly Hills	2 129	9	0	2	1	6	151	25	109	17	0
Big Sandy	1 357	3	0	0	0	3	40	22	17	1	0
Big Spring	24 927	87	1	18	13	55	872	346	483	43	4
Bishop	3 296	5	0	1	0	4	200	13	184	3	0
Bloomburg	376	0	0	0	0	0	2	1	1	0	0
Blue Mound	2 414	1	0	0	0	1	53	9	39	5	0

[1]The FBI does not publish arson data unless it receives data from either the agency or the state for all 12 months of the calendar year.

Table 8. Offenses Known to Law Enforcement, by State and City, 2005—*Continued*

(Number.)

City	Population	Violent crime	Murder and non-negligent man-slaughter	Forcible rape	Robbery	Aggravated assault	Property crime	Burglary	Larceny-theft	Motor vehicle theft	Arson[1]
Boerne	7 517	10	0	2	1	7	238	42	189	7	2
Bogata	1 336	3	0	0	0	3	22	3	17	2	2
Bonham	10 611	51	1	1	3	46	477	137	316	24	0
Borger	13 620	69	0	13	6	50	926	178	705	43	5
Bovina	1 874	1	0	0	0	1	9	4	3	2	2
Bowie	5 560	12	0	4	6	2	507	90	393	24	2
Brady	5 536	32	0	1	1	30	185	77	105	3	0
Brazoria	2 934	11	0	0	2	9	69	22	44	3	1
Breckenridge	5 721	0	0	0	0	0	128	55	69	4	5
Bremond	909	5	0	0	0	5	18	9	6	3	0
Brenham	14 275	83	1	4	10	68	554	176	345	33	2
Bridge City	8 873	19	1	1	2	15	196	55	127	14	2
Bridgeport	5 493	23	1	0	1	21	221	66	140	15	0
Brookshire	3 631	17	1	1	7	8	101	27	67	7	1
Brookside Village	2 062	9	0	0	1	8	23	5	15	3	. . .
Brownfield	9 455	26	0	2	4	20	225	59	154	12	1
Brownsville	163 877	903	4	53	128	718	8 313	1 236	6 647	430	8
Brownwood	19 787	82	1	8	12	61	1 145	206	890	49	4
Bruceville-Eddy	1 569	0	0	0	0	0	21	4	16	1	0
Bryan	67 407	617	6	45	93	473	4 216	1 207	2 784	225	16
Bullard	1 490	2	0	0	0	2	75	15	55	5	1
Bulverde	4 290	8	0	0	0	8	84	13	71	0	0
Burkburnett	10 686	5	0	0	2	3	188	70	118	0	2
Burleson	28 391	49	0	6	16	27	1 377	169	1 117	91	4
Burnet	5 504	17	0	2	0	15	95	32	59	4	0
Caddo Mills	1 230	2	0	0	0	2	10	4	6	0	0
Caldwell	3 867	11	0	0	2	9	32	18	14	0	0
Calvert	1 425	8	0	0	0	8	42	24	15	3	1
Cameron	5 959	8	0	0	3	5	310	82	222	6	0
Caney City	262	3	0	0	0	3	10	4	5	1	0
Canton	3 601	16	0	4	3	9	122	20	95	7	0
Canyon	13 275	3	0	1	0	2	203	29	169	5	0
Carrollton	119 761	300	5	12	95	188	4 090	916	2 675	499	29
Carthage	6 823	26	0	0	5	21	240	41	180	19	1
Castle Hills	4 260	10	1	1	4	4	346	62	278	6	0
Castroville	2 948	11	3	1	3	4	89	10	79	0	0
Cedar Hill	40 881	123	0	9	37	77	1 427	311	972	144	1
Cedar Park	46 106	85	1	14	10	60	686	157	499	30	6
Celina	3 028	8	0	0	0	8	104	9	95	0	1
Center	5 807	35	1	1	4	29	444	79	337	28	1
Childress	6 683	30	0	0	3	27	158	58	94	6	1
Chillicothe	759	1	0	0	0	1	47	7	40	0	0
Cibolo	5 943	17	0	1	0	16	130	20	104	6	1
Cisco	3 860	5	0	0	3	2	175	41	127	7	1
Clarksville	3 712	8	0	3	0	5	83	50	31	2	2
Cleburne	29 277	151	1	22	16	112	1 529	278	1 142	109	2
Cleveland	8 185	56	3	4	8	41	650	126	485	39	2
Clifton	3 699	6	0	0	0	6	47	23	19	5	0
Clint	998	0	0	0	0	0	2	0	1	1	0
Clute	10 940	71	0	5	15	51	441	118	291	32	1
Clyde	3 665	7	0	0	0	7	79	16	63	0	0
Cockrell Hill	4 388	20	0	2	8	10	143	45	43	55	0
Coffee City	207	1	0	0	0	1	4	2	1	1	0
Coleman	4 960	6	0	0	0	6	207	76	114	17	2
College Station	73 373	206	2	38	38	128	2 929	555	2 292	82	1
Colleyville	22 077	10	0	1	1	8	299	52	234	13	0
Collinsville	1 442	10	0	0	0	10	20	3	15	2	0
Colorado City	4 029	16	0	1	1	14	153	23	121	9	1
Columbus	3 983	27	0	6	1	20	136	27	96	13	2
Comanche	4 344	5	0	0	0	5	113	23	88	2	1
Commerce	8 812	44	2	6	13	23	395	87	294	14	0
Conroe	44 116	340	2	24	101	213	2 638	569	1 897	172	12
Converse	12 212	8	0	2	4	2	245	66	169	10	1
Coppell	39 580	22	1	2	3	16	930	206	666	58	1
Copperas Cove	30 490	107	1	22	24	60	1 037	245	769	23	12
Corinth	17 495	3	0	0	1	2	267	39	203	25	0
Corpus Christi	285 821	2 048	8	217	481	1 342	20 133	3 357	15 870	906	112
Corrigan	1 959	4	0	0	1	3	21	8	12	1	0
Corsicana	26 283	86	0	20	19	47	1 555	376	1 085	94	8
Cottonwood Shores	1 065	0	0	0	0	0	10	3	6	1	0
Crane	3 106	5	0	2	0	3	37	6	30	1	0
Crockett	7 170	34	0	3	3	28	295	53	228	14	0
Crowell	1 105	0	0	0	0	0	8	4	4	0	0
Crowley	9 491	22	0	6	3	13	283	74	195	14	0
Crystal City	7 291	9	0	0	2	7	237	56	165	16	1
Cuero	6 836	37	1	10	2	24	225	54	167	4	0
Daingerfield	2 542	8	0	1	1	6	57	22	31	4	2
Dalhart	7 244	39	0	2	1	36	276	61	205	10	2
Dallas	1 230 303	15 429	202	562	6 882	7 783	88 955	22 363	52 315	14 277	984
Dalworthington Gardens	2 386	4	0	0	2	2	53	18	28	7	0

[1]The FBI does not publish arson data unless it receives data from either the agency or the state for all 12 months of the calendar year.
. . . = Not available.

Table 8. Offenses Known to Law Enforcement, by State and City, 2005—*Continued*

(Number.)

City	Population	Violent crime	Murder and non-negligent man-slaughter	Forcible rape	Robbery	Aggravated assault	Property crime	Burglary	Larceny-theft	Motor vehicle theft	Arson[1]
Danbury	1 685	8	0	1	0	7	21	6	15	0	0
Dayton	6 636	15	1	3	4	7	242	56	171	15	1
Decatur	6 004	9	1	2	0	6	257	22	208	27	0
Deer Park	29 118	43	1	9	9	24	629	126	456	47	4
De Kalb	1 822	3	0	0	0	3	14	6	8	0	0
De Leon	2 406	3	0	0	0	3	60	17	38	5	0
Del Rio	36 405	58	1	1	10	46	1 245	211	973	61	5
Denison	23 764	83	0	4	20	59	1 290	260	933	97	5
Denton	99 905	378	5	72	76	225	4 110	684	3 180	246	22
Denver City	4 032	2	0	0	0	2	63	1	62	0	0
DeSoto	43 758	141	1	6	35	99	1 762	552	1 072	138	5
Devine	4 407	8	1	0	0	7	142	36	100	6	0
Diboll	5 551	10	0	6	0	4	145	37	99	9	1
Dickinson	18 041	43	1	10	10	22	470	121	315	34	1
Dilley	4 273	17	0	0	0	17	48	14	34	0	1
Dimmitt	4 082	9	0	0	0	9	242	55	175	12	0
Donna	15 868	85	2	7	9	67	989	177	747	65	3
Double Oak	2 684	0	0	0	0	0	12	5	7	0	0
Driscoll	842	3	0	0	1	2	199	11	188	0	0
Dublin	3 768	17	0	2	8	7	66	19	45	2	0
Dumas	14 046	33	0	5	0	28	469	88	357	24	4
Duncanville	35 927	169	1	7	53	108	1 422	346	905	171	4
Eagle Lake	3 779	33	0	0	2	31	105	25	78	2	2
Eagle Pass	25 256	72	0	1	9	62	818	76	704	38	0
Early	2 787	10	0	3	0	7	100	18	79	3	0
Eastland	3 894	7	0	1	0	6	133	28	97	8	0
East Mountain	624	1	0	1	0	0	7	1	3	3	0
Edcouch	4 520	19	0	0	3	16	153	42	100	11	2
Eden	2 488	2	0	0	1	1	25	5	20	0	0
Edinburg	59 409	442	1	31	67	343	4 945	712	3 887	346	. . .
Edna	5 984	18	3	10	0	5	120	32	81	7	0
El Campo	11 108	39	0	1	9	29	402	87	289	26	3
Electra	3 050	5	0	0	0	5	149	52	84	13	2
Elgin	8 139	30	0	3	9	18	303	97	193	13	1
El Paso[3]	601 839	2 614	14	295	448	1 857	19 675	2 151	14 925	2 599	161
Elsa	6 474	49	0	4	5	40	368	81	259	28	5
Ennis	18 856	50	0	15	14	21	867	161	652	54	4
Euless	51 407	162	3	7	49	103	1 892	371	1 379	142	8
Everman	5 889	29	0	3	11	15	136	30	88	18	2
Fairfield	3 490	6	0	0	1	5	73	16	49	8	0
Fair Oaks Ranch	5 618	2	0	2	0	0	61	31	30	0	0
Falfurrias	5 185	29	0	4	8	17	177	64	110	3	16
Farmers Branch	27 145	57	3	5	22	27	1 249	244	795	210	3
Farmersville	3 379	1	0	0	0	1	79	25	51	3	1
Farwell	1 358	0	0	0	0	0	13	6	7	0	0
Ferris	2 343	7	0	0	2	5	73	17	54	2	0
Flatonia	1 443	1	0	0	0	1	13	5	7	1	2
Florence	1 133	9	0	0	2	7	25	8	16	1	0
Floresville	6 855	31	0	2	2	27	238	37	191	10	1
Flower Mound	63 232	31	1	1	5	24	673	104	524	45	2
Floydada	3 424	8	0	0	0	8	54	23	29	2	1
Forest Hill	13 493	87	0	6	25	56	487	120	310	57	0
Forney	8 919	11	0	1	3	7	283	65	194	24	1
Fort Stockton	7 440	20	0	0	2	18	238	96	136	6	1
Fort Worth	613 261	3 920	60	311	1 379	2 170	37 210	8 684	24 811	3 715	283
Frankston	1 239	2	0	0	0	2	67	14	46	7	1
Fredericksburg	10 253	2	0	0	1	1	217	31	180	6	0
Freeport	12 969	83	1	34	7	41	515	166	320	29	7
Freer	3 157	6	0	0	0	6	95	24	69	2	1
Friendswood	33 255	42	0	6	5	31	433	103	308	22	3
Friona	3 869	7	0	1	2	4	51	18	31	2	0
Frisco	63 398	74	1	15	10	48	2 542	608	1 850	84	4
Gainesville	16 630	74	1	8	17	48	1 114	299	748	67	2
Galena Park	10 511	33	0	6	5	22	278	88	166	24	2
Galveston	58 298	530	8	87	172	263	3 580	687	2 530	363	10
Ganado	1 928	1	0	0	0	1	14	7	6	1	2
Garland	220 748	655	7	41	239	368	8 206	2 011	5 445	750	37
Gatesville	15 991	26	0	4	2	20	214	55	149	10	0
Georgetown	37 062	44	0	10	5	29	695	105	546	44	5
Giddings	5 525	37	0	3	4	30	201	34	161	6	0
Gilmer	5 154	22	1	0	9	12	483	89	376	18	0
Gladewater	6 364	13	0	0	3	10	253	63	178	12	0
Glenn Heights	8 789	41	0	5	9	27	340	94	206	40	4
Godley	989	3	0	1	0	2	11	2	8	1	0
Gonzales	7 522	77	0	4	5	68	341	54	286	1	1
Gorman	1 290	0	0	0	0	0	14	4	8	2	0
Graham	8 823	18	0	6	0	12	345	70	266	9	0
Granbury	6 926	0	0	0	0	0	436	1	410	25	3
Grand Prairie	142 628	449	9	56	170	214	7 468	1 439	4 979	1 050	24
Grand Saline	3 242	8	0	1	0	7	72	12	58	2	0

[1]The FBI does not publish arson data unless it receives data from either the agency or the state for all 12 months of the calendar year.
[3]Because of changes in the state/local agency's reporting practices, figures are not comparable to previous years' data.
. . . = Not available.

Table 8. Offenses Known to Law Enforcement, by State and City, 2005—*Continued*

(Number.)

City	Population	Violent crime	Murder and non-negligent man-slaughter	Forcible rape	Robbery	Aggravated assault	Property crime	Burglary	Larceny-theft	Motor vehicle theft	Arson[1]
Granger	1 336	6	0	0	0	6	32	6	24	2	0
Granite Shoals	2 324	8	1	0	0	7	24	10	11	3	0
Grapeland	1 450	5	0	0	1	4	32	16	16	0	0
Grapevine	48 042	91	2	9	25	55	1 457	238	1 095	124	8
Greenville	25 563	212	2	4	35	171	1 531	331	1 091	109	5
Gregory	2 311	6	0	2	0	4	151	12	137	2	0
Groesbeck	4 424	12	0	3	1	8	78	23	49	6	1
Groves	15 396	22	0	0	8	14	575	140	379	56	0
Gruver	1 136	0	0	0	0	0	6	4	1	1	0
Gun Barrel City	5 998	52	0	8	5	39	361	67	285	9	1
Hale Center	2 221	4	0	0	0	4	5	1	3	1	0
Hallettsville	2 523	15	0	3	0	12	94	13	78	3	0
Hallsville	2 887	3	0	0	1	2	47	18	24	5	0
Haltom City	40 792	164	1	17	36	110	2 272	511	1 453	308	14
Hamlin	2 105	0	0	0	0	0	24	6	15	3	0
Harker Heights	20 588	34	1	6	15	12	1 026	261	720	45	1
Harlingen	62 602	330	0	24	63	243	4 959	1 128	3 598	233	32
Hart	1 126	2	0	0	0	2	14	4	8	2	0
Haskell	2 858	3	0	0	0	3	63	20	43	0	1
Hawk Cove	504	2	0	0	0	2	14	2	10	2	0
Hawkins	1 465	4	0	0	0	4	29	3	24	2	2
Hawley	627	0	0	0	0	0	4	1	3	0	0
Hearne	4 764	19	0	5	4	10	201	54	142	5	3
Heath	6 216	11	0	2	0	9	79	7	69	3	0
Hedwig Village	2 346	9	0	1	3	5	246	37	193	16	0
Helotes	5 948	0	0	0	0	0	128	23	100	5	2
Hemphill	1 090	4	0	0	1	3	33	7	24	2	0
Hempstead	6 367	32	0	1	10	21	228	79	126	23	1
Henderson	11 605	143	1	4	8	130	786	114	638	34	0
Hereford	14 696	65	0	0	2	63	518	127	376	15	2
Hewitt	12 888	11	0	2	0	9	237	55	167	15	2
Hickory Creek	2 896	1	0	0	0	1	107	14	93	0	0
Hidalgo	10 239	33	0	4	8	21	265	98	127	40	0
Highland Park	8 955	11	0	1	2	8	325	73	234	18	1
Highland Village	14 829	6	0	3	0	3	113	32	75	6	3
Hill Country Village	1 093	0	0	0	0	0	56	9	44	3	0
Hillsboro	9 051	38	0	6	11	21	331	53	260	18	0
Hitchcock	7 265	21	0	9	1	11	252	90	142	20	0
Holland	1 102	2	0	0	0	2	29	14	14	1	0
Holliday	1 739	0	0	0	0	0	17	2	15	0	0
Hollywood Park	3 231	2	0	0	1	1	88	18	67	3	0
Hondo	8 621	47	1	6	2	38	286	58	222	6	4
Hooks	2 979	5	0	0	0	5	24	5	16	3	0
Horizon City	7 925	5	0	2	1	2	161	30	120	11	0
Horseshoe Bay	3 656	4	2	0	0	2	45	18	27	0	0
Houston	2 045 732	23 987	334	872	11 128	11 653	120 425	27 541	72 476	20 408	1 262
Howe	2 723	13	0	0	0	13	25	6	16	3	0
Hubbard	1 709	12	0	0	1	11	26	6	17	3	0
Hudson	4 030	1	0	0	0	1	32	19	12	1	0
Hudson Oaks	1 836	7	0	1	1	5	113	2	106	5	0
Humble	15 000	127	2	14	55	56	1 533	129	1 203	201	3
Huntington	2 108	0	0	0	0	0	20	11	8	1	0
Huntsville	36 430	135	0	7	29	99	1 404	269	1 058	77	3
Hurst	38 516	169	0	16	27	126	2 080	268	1 686	126	0
Hutchins	2 899	20	2	1	5	12	131	26	86	19	1
Hutto	5 680	10	1	2	0	7	91	17	70	4	1
Idalou	2 131	7	0	1	1	5	43	8	33	2	0
Ingleside	9 307	15	0	8	2	5	211	56	144	11	3
Ingram	1 847	3	0	0	1	2	56	5	47	4	3
Iowa Park	6 324	12	0	1	1	10	113	27	79	7	0
Irving	197 747	910	2	66	270	572	9 548	1 730	6 658	1 160	61
Italy	2 126	13	0	2	0	11	66	13	50	3	0
Itasca	1 629	6	0	0	1	5	44	9	32	3	0
Jacinto City	10 213	33	0	0	15	18	347	64	247	36	0
Jacksboro	4 645	5	0	0	0	5	13	3	9	1	0
Jacksonville	14 371	78	0	12	13	53	682	140	500	42	2
Jamaica Beach	1 123	5	1	0	0	4	11	3	8	0	0
Jasper	7 664	76	0	9	21	46	676	110	556	10	0
Jefferson	2 044	13	0	3	2	8	105	26	77	2	1
Jersey Village	7 280	26	0	1	4	21	315	53	221	41	0
Johnson City	1 461	2	0	0	0	2	53	4	48	1	0
Jones Creek	2 188	4	0	0	0	4	0	0	0	0	1
Jonestown	1 799	12	0	1	3	8	52	10	39	3	0
Jourdanton	4 234	11	0	0	0	11	58	22	32	4	0
Junction	2 684	10	0	0	1	9	56	3	51	2	0
Karnes City	3 496	5	1	0	0	4	48	16	29	3	0
Katy	13 226	99	0	2	10	87	570	76	467	27	1
Kaufman	7 897	23	0	6	6	11	293	71	196	26	0
Keene	5 825	7	0	1	2	4	133	43	80	10	0
Keller	35 489	35	1	8	5	21	601	95	483	23	0

[1]The FBI does not publish arson data unless it receives data from either the agency or the state for all 12 months of the calendar year.

Table 8. Offenses Known to Law Enforcement, by State and City, 2005—*Continued*

(Number.)

City	Population	Violent crime	Murder and non-negligent man-slaughter	Forcible rape	Robbery	Aggravated assault	Property crime	Burglary	Larceny-theft	Motor vehicle theft	Arson[1]
Kemah	2 416	7	1	2	0	4	71	6	61	4	1
Kemp	1 253	3	0	0	0	3	49	8	39	2	0
Kenedy	3 510	13	0	1	0	12	62	21	40	1	0
Kennedale	6 602	30	0	4	5	21	314	76	203	35	2
Kermit	5 395	9	0	0	0	9	47	4	40	3	0
Kerrville	21 830	66	0	20	18	28	785	136	631	18	6
Kilgore	11 810	52	0	7	7	38	1 040	131	860	49	0
Killeen	98 538	806	8	85	224	489	5 862	2 071	3 644	147	34
Kingsville	25 672	182	1	9	16	156	1 593	477	1 080	36	5
Kirby	8 818	19	0	2	5	12	146	35	97	14	3
Kirbyville	2 061	3	0	0	0	3	38	20	13	5	0
Knox City	1 131	2	0	1	0	1	21	12	8	1	0
Kountze	2 172	4	0	0	1	3	63	25	28	10	1
Kress	795	2	0	0	0	2	12	7	4	1	1
Kyle	14 284	14	0	1	2	11	195	39	147	9	0
Lacy-Lakeview	5 923	26	0	9	4	13	317	60	225	32	0
Lago Vista	5 514	14	0	2	0	12	131	29	93	9	4
La Grange	4 646	5	0	0	1	4	96	22	69	5	0
Laguna Vista	2 447	7	0	2	0	5	33	3	27	3	0
La Joya	4 426	13	0	2	0	11	80	25	50	5	1
Lake Dallas	7 007	10	0	1	4	5	189	21	153	15	0
Lake Jackson	27 466	34	0	3	12	19	809	111	670	28	1
Lakeside	1 154	2	0	0	0	2	32	5	20	7	0
Lakeview	6 688	11	0	0	0	11	70	14	51	5	0
Lakeway	8 542	5	0	3	0	2	137	21	109	7	0
Lake Worth	4 724	61	1	0	13	47	1 037	70	946	21	1
La Marque	13 959	101	1	27	23	50	728	206	454	68	11
Lamesa	9 537	57	1	4	0	52	227	73	145	9	1
Lampasas	8 013	32	0	18	0	14	271	31	226	14	1
Lancaster	30 802	158	3	6	24	125	1 691	520	974	197	0
La Porte	33 812	32	0	6	4	22	574	138	365	71	13
Laredo	206 555	1 054	18	64	246	726	12 462	1 552	9 953	957	117
La Vernia	1 075	1	0	0	0	1	24	3	18	3	0
Lavon	426	1	0	0	0	1	14	4	9	1	0
League City	58 935	42	1	11	9	21	1 537	365	1 088	84	4
Leander	16 135	30	0	0	2	28	243	52	178	13	4
Leon Valley	9 530	38	2	4	12	20	771	80	654	37	0
Levelland	12 981	53	0	8	5	40	502	144	339	19	9
Lewisville	90 608	199	2	23	55	119	3 772	510	2 913	349	11
Lexington	1 271	7	0	1	0	6	61	14	46	1	1
Liberty	8 441	9	0	0	3	6	257	75	168	14	1
Lindale	3 877	3	0	3	0	0	146	17	125	4	3
Linden	2 230	10	0	4	1	5	80	21	50	9	0
Little Elm	15 129	20	0	1	2	17	191	40	144	7	1
Littlefield	6 465	30	0	12	0	18	163	52	109	2	0
Live Oak	10 188	32	0	3	4	25	559	45	481	33	5
Livingston	6 486	19	0	5	1	13	363	87	265	11	0
Llano	3 438	1	0	1	0	0	70	18	47	5	0
Lockhart	13 745	58	0	2	3	53	437	73	350	14	0
Lockney	1 953	3	0	1	0	2	37	14	23	0	0
Lone Star	1 633	10	0	1	0	9	86	30	51	5	0
Longview	76 545	846	8	67	127	644	4 926	1 087	3 272	567	28
Lorena	1 566	2	0	0	1	1	29	4	24	1	0
Los Fresnos	5 181	3	0	1	0	2	103	17	83	3	4
Lubbock	211 271	2 222	11	105	309	1 797	12 786	2 697	9 312	777	77
Lufkin	34 051	188	2	22	39	125	1 165	341	744	80	8
Luling	5 507	23	0	1	2	20	309	44	253	12	3
Lumberton	9 535	9	0	0	1	8	268	52	202	14	0
Lytle	2 665	3	0	0	1	2	68	11	56	1	0
Madisonville	4 324	43	0	7	5	31	217	62	139	16	0
Magnolia	1 255	9	0	2	1	6	60	9	44	7	0
Malakoff	2 397	12	0	4	1	7	100	28	63	9	0
Manor	1 184	17	0	1	1	15	105	17	80	8	0
Mansfield	35 306	108	0	7	19	82	1 124	261	776	87	4
Manvel	3 320	2	0	0	1	1	102	30	66	6	0
Marble Falls	6 159	8	0	5	2	1	355	39	286	30	3
Marfa	2 038	6	0	0	0	6	33	11	21	1	0
Marion	1 146	0	0	0	0	0	30	9	20	1	1
Marlin	6 402	27	1	3	4	19	157	41	105	11	2
Marshall	24 060	127	3	26	22	76	1 206	344	797	65	14
Mart	2 471	5	0	0	1	4	39	10	26	3	0
Martindale	1 029	0	0	0	0	0	6	3	2	1	0
Mathis	5 434	34	1	0	5	28	153	72	78	3	2
McAllen	122 729	421	8	34	129	250	8 187	734	6 877	576	19
McGregor	4 855	19	0	3	1	15	130	25	102	3	0
McKinney	89 863	228	1	44	41	142	2 059	451	1 469	139	26
Meadows Place	5 865	8	0	0	6	2	81	6	67	8	0
Melissa	2 099	4	0	0	1	3	66	19	44	3	0
Memorial Villages	11 801	10	0	1	5	4	172	49	115	8	0
Memphis	2 466	3	0	0	0	3	57	29	23	5	0

[1]The FBI does not publish arson data unless it receives data from either the agency or the state for all 12 months of the calendar year.

Table 8. Offenses Known to Law Enforcement, by State and City, 2005—*Continued*

(Number.)

City	Population	Violent crime	Murder and non-negligent man-slaughter	Forcible rape	Robbery	Aggravated assault	Property crime	Burglary	Larceny-theft	Motor vehicle theft	Arson[1]
Mercedes	14 397	52	0	3	5	44	668	159	438	71	4
Meridian	1 542	5	0	0	0	5	9	2	6	1	0
Merkel	2 652	2	0	0	2	0	44	18	24	2	0
Mesquite	131 844	530	7	15	169	339	5 510	837	3 964	709	. . .
Mexia	6 854	43	0	4	9	30	502	117	362	23	2
Midland	99 695	408	1	80	50	277	3 765	779	2 808	178	9
Midlothian	11 790	15	0	5	2	8	331	71	232	28	2
Milford	728	2	0	0	0	2	6	2	4	0	0
Mineral Wells	17 131	66	1	22	8	35	910	163	701	46	3
Mission	58 763	72	4	5	20	43	3 437	619	2 497	321	3
Missouri City	67 682	167	2	13	73	79	1 288	345	826	117	8
Monahans	6 508	25	1	1	0	23	136	36	98	2	1
Mont Belvieu	2 530	9	1	0	4	4	162	16	141	5	0
Montgomery	544	1	0	0	1	0	11	3	8	0	0
Morgans Point Resort	3 796	3	0	0	1	2	46	17	28	1	0
Mount Pleasant	14 850	51	1	0	10	40	537	87	416	34	4
Muleshoe	4 615	10	0	5	0	5	167	51	110	6	2
Munday	1 418	1	0	0	0	1	17	4	13	0	0
Mustang Ridge	912	1	0	0	0	1	22	7	14	1	0
Nacogdoches	31 151	111	0	13	33	65	1 173	221	914	38	1
Nash	2 330	5	0	0	0	5	47	11	34	2	0
Nassau Bay	4 175	8	1	0	1	6	126	28	92	6	0
Navasota	7 407	37	0	2	11	24	422	81	328	13	2
Nederland	17 114	39	0	6	7	26	668	154	479	35	3
Needville	3 199	6	0	0	0	6	30	15	13	2	0
New Boston	4 720	16	0	0	1	15	258	25	223	10	1
New Braunfels	45 670	122	0	8	19	95	2 028	295	1 643	90	6
New Deal	721	0	0	0	0	0	5	1	4	0	0
Nocona	3 283	9	0	3	0	6	87	25	56	6	0
Nolanville	2 158	8	0	1	1	6	127	50	70	7	1
Northlake	1 037	2	0	0	0	2	24	10	9	5	0
North Richland Hills	61 478	158	0	21	37	100	2 144	416	1 599	129	2
Oak Ridge	259	0	0	0	0	0	3	0	2	1	0
Oak Ridge North	3 356	9	0	3	2	4	48	11	33	4	0
Odessa	94 371	590	3	12	72	503	3 720	756	2 785	179	33
Olmos Park	2 364	1	0	0	0	1	54	7	46	1	0
Olney	3 392	4	0	1	1	2	67	13	53	1	0
Orange	18 438	206	1	27	40	138	1 224	331	806	87	6
Orange Grove	1 404	9	0	1	1	7	27	21	4	2	0
Overton	2 354	3	0	0	0	3	34	14	20	0	0
Ovilla	3 796	2	0	0	0	2	64	6	51	7	0
Oyster Creek	1 258	12	0	1	0	11	47	25	19	3	0
Paducah	1 388	0	0	0	0	0	16	11	4	1	4
Palacios	5 320	39	1	2	2	34	185	84	90	11	0
Palestine	18 163	80	0	4	9	67	737	147	547	43	5
Palmer	2 049	4	0	0	1	3	50	4	45	1	0
Pampa	16 977	81	0	11	4	66	881	192	640	49	0
Panhandle	2 607	7	0	2	0	5	11	4	7	0	0
Pantego	2 375	14	0	1	3	10	179	34	139	6	0
Paris	27 015	250	1	55	41	153	2 555	432	2 036	87	1
Parker	1 998	0	0	0	0	0	32	2	30	0	0
Pasadena	146 546	632	5	51	146	430	4 914	1 063	3 397	454	50
Pearland	53 264	86	1	34	22	29	1 373	364	921	88	3
Pearsall	7 811	25	3	0	1	21	334	105	223	6	1
Pecos	8 557	16	0	0	1	15	155	31	122	2	0
Pelican Bay	1 618	15	0	0	0	15	36	14	20	2	4
Penitas	1 212	5	0	0	3	2	39	14	22	3	0
Perryton	8 014	12	0	1	0	11	67	8	56	3	1
Pflugerville	26 337	27	1	7	7	12	438	74	346	18	5
Pharr	57 774	198	4	17	52	125	2 912	573	2 183	156	17
Pilot Point	4 039	8	0	1	0	7	91	24	61	6	. . .
Pinehurst	2 276	8	0	0	2	6	115	27	85	3	0
Pineland	932	0	0	0	0	0	19	5	13	1	0
Pittsburg	4 533	37	0	2	6	29	177	54	120	3	0
Plainview	22 357	72	0	8	21	43	1 353	263	1 053	37	6
Plano	249 448	721	2	54	119	546	8 677	1 365	6 723	589	29
Pleasanton	9 372	24	0	11	2	11	234	38	187	9	3
Point Comfort	756	0	0	0	0	0	8	1	6	1	0
Ponder	722	2	0	0	0	2	13	2	10	1	0
Port Aransas	3 684	26	0	3	4	19	299	39	242	18	2
Port Arthur	57 660	370	11	26	118	215	2 809	938	1 632	239	40
Port Isabel	5 480	42	0	13	2	27	383	72	303	8	0
Portland	15 840	15	0	5	3	7	365	50	290	25	0
Port Lavaca	11 952	33	0	5	2	26	385	83	272	30	0
Port Neches	13 442	30	2	2	4	22	556	160	368	28	4
Poteet	3 636	5	0	1	0	4	113	37	71	5	1
Pottsboro	1 826	3	0	0	0	3	60	17	38	5	1
Premont	2 881	9	0	0	0	9	66	21	45	0	0
Presidio	4 729	6	0	0	0	6	29	5	19	5	0
Primera	3 153	0	0	0	0	0	63	15	41	7	2

[1]The FBI does not publish arson data unless it receives data from either the agency or the state for all 12 months of the calendar year.
. . . = Not available.

Table 8. Offenses Known to Law Enforcement, by State and City, 2005—*Continued*

(Number.)

City	Population	Violent crime	Murder and non-negligent man-slaughter	Forcible rape	Robbery	Aggravated assault	Property crime	Burglary	Larceny-theft	Motor vehicle theft	Arson[1]
Princeton	4 008	16	0	6	2	8	142	24	104	14	0
Progreso	5 132	19	0	0	0	19	106	34	70	2	2
Prosper	3 557	2	0	0	0	2	95	22	72	1	1
Queen City	1 612	7	0	0	2	5	101	19	82	0	0
Quinlan	1 475	1	0	0	0	1	56	11	36	9	0
Quitman	2 186	3	0	0	0	3	33	11	22	0	0
Ransom Canyon	1 080	0	0	0	0	0	9	1	8	0	0
Raymondville	9 612	131	0	11	8	112	841	184	649	8	2
Red Oak	6 550	21	0	1	1	19	244	61	164	19	0
Refugio	2 850	4	0	0	0	4	74	20	53	1	1
Reno	2 967	0	0	0	0	0	49	16	32	1	0
Richardson	100 896	261	2	12	98	149	3 478	764	2 437	277	6
Richland Hills	8 234	21	0	4	3	14	278	76	165	37	1
Richmond	13 215	68	3	6	11	48	412	112	270	30	10
Richwood	3 277	2	0	0	0	2	72	14	56	2	0
Riesel	1 016	3	0	0	0	3	9	2	7	0	0
Rio Grande City	13 623	50	2	0	4	44	501	128	319	54	1
River Oaks	7 058	9	0	1	2	6	183	51	110	22	1
Roanoke	3 530	13	0	1	1	11	133	23	105	5	2
Robinson	8 854	20	2	2	1	15	242	24	209	9	1
Robstown	12 821	83	0	3	9	71	698	322	350	26	4
Rockdale	6 126	21	0	3	1	17	165	47	108	10	0
Rockport	8 837	29	0	11	3	15	834	170	630	34	1
Rockwall	27 135	52	0	6	12	34	747	112	569	66	19
Rollingwood	1 386	1	0	1	0	0	42	22	19	1	0
Roma	10 874	30	2	1	9	18	212	55	109	48	2
Roman Forest	2 686	0	0	0	0	0	12	3	7	2	0
Ropesville	535	0	0	0	0	0	3	1	1	1	0
Roscoe	1 321	1	0	0	0	1	5	2	3	0	0
Rosebud	1 433	0	0	0	0	0	24	17	6	1	0
Rose City	530	0	0	0	0	0	0	0	0	0	0
Rosenberg	29 955	123	0	30	30	63	759	186	515	58	17
Round Rock	83 390	121	0	21	24	76	2 205	281	1 873	51	14
Rowlett	53 647	69	0	3	17	49	1 011	185	747	79	7
Royse City	4 953	4	0	1	0	3	100	14	78	8	1
Runaway Bay	1 317	4	0	0	1	3	24	7	17	0	0
Rusk	5 320	22	0	0	2	20	87	21	64	2	1
Sabinal	1 662	4	0	1	1	2	54	16	38	0	0
Sachse	16 341	21	1	4	1	15	157	30	115	12	0
Saginaw	17 152	37	0	3	12	22	555	86	422	47	2
Salado	1 977	0	0	0	0	0	41	13	28	0	0
San Angelo	89 561	373	3	55	40	275	5 358	1 137	3 941	280	13
San Antonio	1 256 584	8 007	86	593	2 154	5 174	80 987	14 365	60 649	5 973	424
San Augustine	2 507	8	0	0	1	7	61	19	37	5	0
San Benito	24 788	93	0	14	23	56	1 631	203	1 375	53	4
San Diego	4 703	32	1	1	3	27	118	46	65	7	3
Sanger	5 943	10	1	4	0	5	189	53	116	20	0
San Juan	30 230	149	1	6	14	128	1 893	385	1 399	109	7
San Marcos	45 362	157	3	24	25	105	1 406	208	1 071	127	2
San Saba	2 661	2	0	0	0	2	31	9	17	5	0
Sansom Park Village	4 222	12	1	1	1	9	160	45	91	24	0
Santa Anna	1 049	3	0	1	0	2	8	2	5	1	0
Santa Fe	10 542	7	0	4	1	2	398	150	207	41	0
Santa Rosa	3 003	11	0	0	0	11	54	13	40	1	1
Schertz	25 386	36	0	12	11	13	514	89	394	31	2
Seabrook	11 035	25	0	7	4	14	236	53	167	16	2
Seadrift	1 405	3	0	0	1	2	33	8	24	1	0
Seagoville	11 253	56	0	4	10	42	704	169	436	99	1
Seagraves	2 343	9	0	1	1	7	61	30	28	3	1
Sealy	6 034	12	1	1	1	9	174	64	101	9	1
Seguin	24 610	75	1	12	13	49	1 207	166	1 008	33	2
Selma	2 223	11	0	0	3	8	215	16	193	6	1
Seminole	5 978	4	0	1	0	3	90	18	69	3	0
Seven Points	1 268	14	0	0	0	14	116	13	89	14	0
Seymour	2 811	15	0	3	0	12	60	21	39	0	0
Shallowater	2 192	3	0	2	1	0	72	12	58	2	0
Shamrock	1 851	0	0	0	0	0	53	30	21	2	2
Shavano Park	2 221	0	0	0	0	0	64	16	48	0	0
Shenandoah	1 582	1	0	0	1	0	236	16	201	19	0
Sherman	37 180	159	3	6	19	131	1 932	439	1 405	88	4
Silsbee	6 729	8	0	0	4	4	169	59	103	7	1
Sinton	5 608	22	0	1	4	17	208	48	151	9	0
Slaton	5 970	13	0	0	2	11	171	44	110	17	3
Smithville	4 410	23	0	5	1	17	182	31	148	3	1
Snyder	10 715	57	0	5	5	47	243	71	163	9	1
Socorro	28 490	82	0	8	8	66	505	77	371	57	10
Somerset	1 811	0	0	0	0	0	32	5	26	1	0
Somerville	1 771	12	0	1	1	10	17	8	9	0	0
Sonora	2 978	19	0	1	0	18	40	7	31	2	1
Sour Lake	1 751	1	0	0	0	1	38	8	29	1	0

[1]The FBI does not publish arson data unless it receives data from either the agency or the state for all 12 months of the calendar year.

Table 8. Offenses Known to Law Enforcement, by State and City, 2005—*Continued*

(Number.)

City	Population	Violent crime	Murder and non-negligent man-slaughter	Forcible rape	Robbery	Aggravated assault	Property crime	Burglary	Larceny-theft	Motor vehicle theft	Arson[1]
South Houston	16 619	111	1	11	48	51	716	161	429	126	0
Southlake	24 893	10	0	4	0	6	536	114	411	11	3
South Padre Island	2 621	66	0	16	10	40	576	79	481	16	0
Southside Place	1 622	0	0	0	0	0	10	1	5	4	0
Spearman	2 962	1	0	0	0	1	16	5	10	1	0
Springtown	2 604	13	0	2	1	10	69	16	49	4	1
Spring Valley	3 674	1	0	0	1	0	77	15	59	3	0
Spur	1 076	0	0	0	0	0	5	2	3	0	1
Stafford	19 103	103	1	14	48	40	959	174	680	105	1
Stamford	3 398	10	1	2	4	3	97	34	57	6	0
Stanton	2 356	1	0	0	0	1	30	6	24	0	0
Stephenville	15 670	50	0	3	6	41	531	68	445	18	2
Stratford	2 003	7	0	0	0	7	28	16	8	4	1
Sugar Land	74 934	117	1	4	62	50	1 829	285	1 434	110	11
Sullivan City	4 363	14	0	0	3	11	74	32	33	9	1
Sulphur Springs	15 329	40	1	2	3	34	355	93	234	28	2
Sunset Valley	480	2	0	0	2	0	152	2	148	2	0
Surfside Beach	831	4	0	1	1	2	25	8	12	5	0
Sweeny	3 695	4	0	0	1	3	117	34	77	6	0
Sweetwater	11 061	41	3	2	10	26	380	133	231	16	5
Taft	3 482	5	0	0	2	3	168	29	135	4	0
Tahoka	2 745	2	0	0	0	2	51	18	31	2	0
Tatum	1 208	0	0	0	0	0	47	2	44	1	0
Taylor	14 877	19	2	2	3	12	446	74	342	30	6
Teague	4 684	8	0	0	3	5	14	4	2	8	0
Temple	55 402	175	3	5	57	110	2 546	502	1 893	151	2
Terrell	17 192	140	1	10	29	100	907	240	554	113	12
Terrell Hills	5 172	3	0	0	2	1	128	26	96	6	0
Texarkana	36 076	500	3	31	69	397	2 646	556	1 926	164	21
Texas City	44 251	191	2	19	87	83	2 812	859	1 735	218	10
The Colony	36 913	29	0	4	7	18	862	165	631	66	13
Thorndale	1 334	5	0	1	1	3	13	3	9	1	0
Thrall	853	3	0	0	0	3	28	9	18	1	0
Three Rivers	1 764	9	0	0	0	9	38	10	27	1	1
Tioga	894	0	0	0	0	0	15	6	9	0	0
Tomball	10 015	29	1	5	9	14	473	61	387	25	1
Tool	2 463	19	0	0	0	19	82	33	44	5	1
Trinity	2 810	4	0	0	1	3	82	11	67	4	0
Trophy Club	7 389	5	0	0	0	5	52	10	39	3	0
Tulia	4 824	24	0	4	2	18	207	45	151	11	1
Tye	1 166	4	0	2	0	2	29	5	20	4	0
Tyler	91 025	574	6	52	172	344	4 728	1 119	3 412	197	14
Universal City	16 081	35	1	1	10	23	389	58	305	26	2
University Park	24 076	17	3	0	7	7	556	103	432	21	1
Uvalde	16 500	104	3	4	6	91	1 084	251	816	17	8
Van	2 587	2	0	0	0	2	64	21	41	2	0
Van Alstyne	2 676	18	0	0	2	16	51	7	42	2	1
Vernon	11 349	91	0	7	5	79	620	128	469	23	0
Victoria	62 692	300	2	34	58	206	3 654	829	2 670	155	9
Vidor	11 479	22	0	2	5	15	466	179	241	46	6
Waco	120 036	895	12	60	257	566	8 845	2 413	5 740	692	41
Waelder	1 008	1	0	0	0	1	5	3	1	1	0
Wake Village	5 263	3	0	0	0	3	78	16	50	12	1
Waller	2 065	7	0	0	3	4	137	36	92	9	1
Wallis	1 284	4	0	2	0	2	71	9	59	3	0
Watauga	24 038	55	0	9	7	39	655	115	494	46	5
Waxahachie	25 060	113	1	14	17	81	1 238	256	912	70	5
Weatherford	22 711	48	1	10	8	29	927	122	749	56	1
Webster	9 051	70	1	16	14	39	912	95	738	79	10
Weimar	2 036	2	0	0	0	2	34	2	29	3	0
Wells	797	6	0	0	0	6	7	2	4	1	0
Weslaco	31 592	144	1	8	36	99	2 447	468	1 811	168	1
West	2 779	2	0	1	0	1	32	3	28	1	0
West Columbia	4 352	12	1	0	3	8	102	24	75	3	0
West Lake Hills	3 063	0	0	0	0	0	81	18	63	0	0
West Orange	4 081	15	0	0	7	8	291	42	240	9	0
Westover Hills	694	0	0	0	0	0	7	1	6	0	0
West Tawakoni	1 681	16	0	1	0	15	72	28	37	7	0
West University Place	15 064	13	0	1	8	4	207	47	152	8	0
Westworth	2 142	2	0	0	1	1	61	11	48	2	0
Wharton	9 567	62	0	12	13	37	520	126	369	25	0
Whitehouse	6 932	14	0	4	0	10	72	10	58	4	1
White Oak	6 122	12	0	4	5	3	167	43	98	26	0
Whitesboro	4 029	3	0	0	2	1	93	2	86	5	0
White Settlement	15 909	64	1	0	12	51	1 054	217	710	127	5
Whitney	2 056	2	0	0	0	2	75	8	65	2	0
Wichita Falls	102 589	733	6	43	239	445	7 641	1 703	5 386	552	115
Willis	4 267	44	1	5	4	34	205	42	150	13	0
Willow Park	3 403	1	0	0	0	1	26	14	10	2	0
Wills Point	3 843	5	0	0	0	5	65	21	42	2	0

[1]The FBI does not publish arson data unless it receives data from either the agency or the state for all 12 months of the calendar year.

Table 8. Offenses Known to Law Enforcement, by State and City, 2005—*Continued*

(Number.)

City	Population	Violent crime	Murder and non-negligent man-slaughter	Forcible rape	Robbery	Aggravated assault	Property crime	Burglary	Larceny-theft	Motor vehicle theft	Arson[1]
Wilmer	3 652	10	1	1	0	8	127	45	71	11	2
Windcrest	5 184	14	0	3	8	3	347	70	262	15	2
Wink	894	0	0	0	0	0	9	1	8	0	0
Winnsboro	3 841	8	0	0	0	8	48	10	32	6	0
Winters	2 780	19	0	0	0	19	85	29	48	8	1
Wolfforth	2 748	5	0	1	0	4	56	14	34	8	0
Woodville	2 346	4	0	0	1	3	22	11	10	1	0
Woodway	8 894	10	0	0	2	8	133	40	85	8	0
Wortham	1 099	2	0	0	0	2	11	8	2	1	1
Wylie	26 166	35	2	7	2	24	586	110	444	32	3
Yoakum	5 814	7	1	0	2	4	153	47	104	2	0
Yorktown	2 293	3	0	0	0	3	64	14	47	3	0
Utah											
American Fork	23 142	29	1	10	1	17	970	144	755	71	2
Big Water	431	2	0	0	0	2	4	4	0	0	0
Blanding	3 159	6	0	3	0	3	35	13	20	2	3
Bountiful	42 561	69	1	19	11	38	1 045	175	798	72	5
Brian Head	119	0	0	0	0	0	14	3	11	0	0
Brigham City	17 727	37	0	8	5	24	525	106	390	29	1
Cedar City	22 973	28	0	5	4	19	691	120	525	46	4
Centerville	15 165	11	0	3	3	5	369	66	277	26	7
Clearfield	28 145	37	0	14	6	17	891	120	714	57	5
Clinton	17 002	16	0	2	2	12	224	36	178	10	1
Draper	34 156	33	1	8	4	20	1 144	182	897	65	1
Ephraim	4 926	3	0	3	0	0	188	48	133	7	1
Grantsville	7 316	9	0	2	2	5	147	28	106	13	0
Harrisville	4 941	13	0	1	9	3	328	35	282	11	0
Helper	1 973	7	0	0	0	7	41	15	22	4	0
Hurricane	10 077	13	0	6	0	7	249	52	179	18	0
Kanab	3 647	6	0	0	0	6	48	10	38	0	0
Kaysville	22 482	16	0	6	3	7	481	100	363	18	4
La Verkin	3 976	9	0	4	0	5	71	17	49	5	0
Layton	63 269	95	2	32	17	44	1 897	289	1 500	108	8
Lehi	26 530	28	0	10	1	17	706	243	408	55	2
Logan	47 052	38	1	16	5	16	1 044	162	842	40	1
Mapleton	6 336	1	0	0	0	1	77	12	62	3	0
Midvale	27 930	111	0	28	17	66	1 605	178	1 232	195	1
Moab	4 988	24	0	4	3	17	212	37	165	10	0
Monticello	1 976	4	0	0	0	4	32	2	28	2	1
Murray	44 789	164	0	22	40	102	3 903	472	3 069	362	7
Nephi	5 204	19	0	6	0	13	62	10	51	1	0
North Ogden	16 878	3	0	1	0	2	248	45	191	12	0
North Park	9 973	5	0	2	1	2	196	38	151	7	0
North Salt Lake	9 877	8	0	0	2	6	462	68	350	44	1
Ogden	81 166	383	5	40	121	217	4 931	797	3 723	411	0
Orem	91 607	65	0	16	13	36	3 483	392	2 909	182	1
Park City	8 148	15	0	4	4	7	485	63	399	23	0
Payson	15 032	16	0	1	3	12	601	166	398	37	1
Perry	3 014	5	0	2	1	2	42	8	32	2	1
Pleasant View	6 252	4	0	1	0	3	177	26	144	7	0
Price	8 473	14	1	3	1	9	379	56	312	11	4
Provo	102 983	182	3	55	17	107	3 298	673	2 417	208	11
Richfield	7 286	8	0	0	0	8	297	36	254	7	0
Riverdale	8 162	12	0	2	4	6	518	41	450	27	1
Roosevelt	4 587	6	0	3	0	3	171	9	153	9	1
Roy	36 498	53	0	17	7	29	764	113	603	48	4
Salem	5 001	2	0	0	0	2	128	16	101	11	0
Salina	2 487	7	0	0	0	7	174	17	151	6	0
Salt Lake City	184 627	1 283	10	72	417	784	15 859	2 172	11 608	2 079	60
Sandy	93 013	161	1	14	27	119	3 240	474	2 530	236	14
Santaquin/Genola	7 209	4	0	0	0	4	134	30	97	7	0
Smithfield	8 064	3	1	2	0	0	92	9	76	7	0
South Jordan	38 031	30	0	6	3	21	889	116	724	49	6
South Ogden	15 640	20	2	5	9	4	503	70	410	23	5
South Salt Lake	22 235	195	1	44	38	112	2 197	284	1 559	354	5
Spanish Fork	23 609	16	0	4	2	10	816	142	643	31	4
Springville	22 232	30	0	9	6	15	855	138	689	28	2
St. George	61 795	224	1	13	12	198	1 865	385	1 249	231	4
Stockton	592	2	0	1	0	1	11	3	8	0	0
Sunset	5 169	10	0	4	1	5	131	28	100	3	0
Syracuse	16 703	17	0	4	0	13	224	50	164	10	2
Tooele	28 844	47	2	9	4	32	905	144	697	64	12
Tremonton	6 414	7	0	1	0	6	259	31	224	4	0
Vernal	8 207	21	0	5	5	11	304	56	224	24	3
Wendover	1 680	5	0	0	0	5	43	11	29	3	0
West Bountiful	4 915	7	0	0	0	7	179	10	164	5	0
West Valley	116 477	519	10	89	93	327	7 086	1 039	5 233	814	28
Willard	1 706	5	0	0	0	5	69	4	65	0	0
Woods Cross	8 124	9	0	2	2	5	251	47	180	24	3

[1]The FBI does not publish arson data unless it receives data from either the agency or the state for all 12 months of the calendar year.

Table 8. Offenses Known to Law Enforcement, by State and City, 2005—*Continued*

(Number.)

City	Population	Violent crime	Murder and non-negligent man-slaughter	Forcible rape	Robbery	Aggravated assault	Property crime	Burglary	Larceny-theft	Motor vehicle theft	Arson[1]
Vermont											
Barre	9 165	14	0	4	3	7	304	43	244	17	1
Barre Town	7 926	1	0	0	0	1	50	7	38	5	0
Bellows Falls	3 062	8	0	0	0	8	48	13	34	1	0
Bennington	15 768	29	0	5	4	20	379	57	296	26	5
Berlin	2 894	5	0	0	0	5	144	4	138	2	0
Brandon	3 953	1	0	0	0	1	113	27	82	4	0
Brattleboro	11 976	24	0	3	3	18	331	33	281	17	1
Castleton	4 367	0	0	0	0	0	32	8	24	0	0
Chester	3 130	6	0	1	1	4	41	15	25	1	0
Colchester	17 223	23	0	7	2	14	600	118	461	21	0
Dover	1 449	3	0	0	0	3	180	12	165	3	0
Essex	19 116	16	0	2	3	11	476	110	351	15	1
Hardwick	3 242	6	0	1	0	5	89	13	70	6	0
Hartford	10 727	5	0	1	1	3	146	26	114	6	0
Hinesburg	4 439	2	0	1	0	1	69	14	53	2	0
Ludlow	2 644	0	0	0	0	0	40	7	33	0	0
Manchester	4 961	2	0	0	0	2	93	24	67	2	0
Milton	10 092	11	0	1	2	8	303	56	241	6	0
Morristown	5 517	6	0	1	0	5	114	14	92	8	0
Newport	5 132	4	0	2	0	2	146	10	134	2	0
Northfield	5 802	7	0	0	0	7	83	7	74	2	0
Randolph	5 044	3	0	0	1	2	38	8	27	3	0
Richmond	4 131	4	0	0	0	4	48	16	28	4	1
Rutland	17 126	39	1	4	9	25	892	124	728	40	9
Shelburne	7 003	2	0	0	1	1	109	21	83	5	1
South Burlington	16 504	20	1	8	1	10	693	71	606	16	4
Springfield	8 981	19	0	4	3	12	255	35	211	9	2
St. Albans	7 568	14	0	0	3	11	348	68	271	9	0
St. Johnsbury	7 580	6	0	0	1	5	62	10	48	4	0
Stowe	4 715	1	0	0	0	1	169	16	149	4	0
Swanton	6 440	0	0	0	0	0	31	10	20	1	0
Thetford	2 768	0	0	0	0	0	11	2	9	0	0
Vergennes	2 790	1	0	1	0	0	46	14	32	0	0
Waterbury	5 178	1	0	0	0	1	34	2	32	0	0
Weathersfield	2 847	0	0	0	0	0	19	6	11	2	0
Williston	8 246	11	0	1	1	9	290	50	235	5	0
Wilmington	2 276	0	0	0	0	0	48	6	40	2	0
Windsor	3 769	8	0	2	0	6	73	15	52	6	0
Winhall	750	3	0	1	0	2	96	21	71	4	0
Winooski	6 382	21	0	1	5	15	323	86	229	8	0
Woodstock	3 244	0	0	0	0	0	24	0	24	0	0
Virginia											
Abingdon	8 053	17	1	4	3	9	376	35	318	23	0
Alexandria	130 056	462	3	22	199	238	3 331	294	2 570	467	11
Altavista	3 415	7	0	0	3	4	133	15	108	10	0
Amherst	2 253	4	0	0	0	4	31	7	23	1	0
Appalachia	1 800	0	0	0	0	0	36	0	34	2	0
Ashland	7 043	28	0	6	14	8	290	31	242	17	1
Bedford	6 319	21	1	1	8	11	165	16	146	3	0
Berryville	3 155	10	0	1	2	7	94	20	73	1	1
Big Stone Gap	5 917	12	2	1	1	8	178	27	147	4	0
Blacksburg	39 778	55	0	8	13	34	562	105	435	22	4
Blackstone	3 644	25	0	2	4	19	156	26	120	10	2
Bluefield	5 103	5	0	0	1	4	202	26	173	3	1
Boykins	612	2	0	0	0	2	10	1	9	0	0
Bridgewater	5 377	1	0	0	0	1	42	11	29	2	1
Bristol	17 558	89	2	8	16	63	789	108	640	41	4
Broadway	2 464	2	0	0	0	2	10	3	7	0	0
Brookneal	1 262	5	0	0	1	4	11	4	7	0	1
Cedar Bluff	1 092	3	0	0	0	3	15	5	8	2	0
Charlottesville	37 133	307	2	35	72	198	1 875	264	1 442	169	11
Chase City	2 428	5	1	0	0	4	81	6	75	0	1
Chesapeake	217 823	1 117	14	51	298	754	7 870	1 426	5 905	539	26
Chilhowie	1 810	5	0	0	0	5	34	8	24	2	0
Chincoteague	4 480	8	0	0	2	6	74	14	55	5	1
Christiansburg	17 747	28	0	5	5	18	638	76	518	44	3
Clarksville	1 314	2	0	0	1	1	17	1	16	0	1
Clifton Forge	4 726	8	0	0	0	8	91	28	61	2	1
Clinchco	418	0	0	0	0	0	0	0	0	0	0
Clintwood	1 533	2	0	0	0	2	39	10	29	0	1
Coeburn	2 014	5	1	1	1	2	25	8	13	4	1
Colonial Beach	3 349	3	0	0	0	3	64	6	50	8	0
Colonial Heights	17 764	37	1	3	11	22	797	69	685	43	16
Courtland	1 261	0	0	0	0	0	0	0	0	0	0
Covington	6 346	13	0	2	1	10	173	28	140	5	3
Crewe	2 348	5	0	1	1	3	49	0	47	2	1
Culpeper	11 230	42	0	7	13	22	493	43	436	14	2
Danville	47 040	248	8	12	88	140	2 178	322	1 745	111	13
Dayton	1 364	1	0	1	0	0	13	0	10	3	0
Dublin	2 259	1	0	0	1	0	89	5	82	2	1
Dumfries	4 918	14	0	0	7	7	131	26	79	26	0
Elkton	2 067	3	0	0	1	2	19	10	6	3	0

[1]The FBI does not publish arson data unless it receives data from either the agency or the state for all 12 months of the calendar year.

Table 8. Offenses Known to Law Enforcement, by State and City, 2005—*Continued*

(Number.)

City	Population	Violent crime	Murder and non-negligent man-slaughter	Forcible rape	Robbery	Aggravated assault	Property crime	Burglary	Larceny-theft	Motor vehicle theft	Arson[1]
Emporia	5 756	53	0	7	17	29	441	52	374	15	2
Exmore	1 425	3	0	0	2	1	21	11	10	0	0
Falls Church	10 937	23	0	2	12	9	319	34	243	42	9
Farmville	7 112	3	1	0	1	1	104	22	78	4	0
Franklin	8 593	52	0	2	27	23	300	42	239	19	0
Fredericksburg	20 753	109	0	14	41	54	974	77	835	62	6
Front Royal	14 415	29	0	5	7	17	451	46	357	48	3
Galax	6 753	41	0	8	4	29	299	33	252	14	1
Gate City	2 110	6	0	0	0	6	60	8	47	5	0
Gordonsville	1 600	1	0	0	0	1	51	2	45	4	0
Grottoes	2 197	0	0	0	0	0	16	2	13	1	0
Grundy	1 037	0	0	0	0	0	18	1	16	1	0
Hampton	148 057	595	11	47	276	261	5 388	887	3 941	560	50
Harrisonburg	41 659	98	2	14	35	47	1 164	205	883	76	5
Herndon	21 979	46	0	6	10	30	394	39	328	27	3
Hillsville	2 782	14	0	3	0	11	86	11	67	8	0
Honaker	935	1	0	0	0	1	22	7	13	2	3
Hopewell	22 692	174	0	11	56	107	1 168	265	765	138	16
Hurt	1 266	0	0	0	0	0	2	0	2	0	0
Independence	943	1	0	0	0	1	11	2	8	1	0
Jonesville	1 004	0	0	0	0	0	6	1	5	0	0
Kenbridge	1 331	4	0	1	1	2	15	8	5	2	0
La Crosse	615	0	0	0	0	0	7	0	6	1	0
Lawrenceville	1 252	7	0	0	1	6	23	6	16	1	0
Lebanon	3 274	10	0	1	2	7	147	16	128	3	0
Leesburg	35 331	84	0	8	22	54	720	40	631	49	1
Lexington	7 010	7	0	0	5	2	102	14	82	6	1
Louisa	1 498	1	0	0	0	1	35	6	28	1	0
Luray	4 948	6	1	2	0	3	140	13	121	6	1
Lynchburg	65 869	257	6	23	73	155	2 390	412	1 805	173	15
Manassas	38 158	188	0	21	64	103	1 196	137	937	122	12
Marion	6 257	30	2	2	0	26	278	25	240	13	2
Martinsville	15 256	55	0	3	21	31	509	74	410	25	8
Middleburg	854	0	0	0	0	0	34	5	28	1	0
Mount Jackson	1 757	2	0	0	0	2	27	4	22	1	0
Narrows	2 176	1	0	0	0	1	28	7	19	2	0
New Market	1 824	1	0	0	0	1	12	3	8	1	0
Newport News	184 538	1 439	20	103	542	774	8 216	1 470	5 887	859	75
Norfolk	241 267	1 841	59	92	886	804	13 061	1 769	10 153	1 139	43
Norton	3 807	11	0	2	0	9	233	20	204	9	0
Onancock	1 515	2	0	0	1	1	65	6	55	4	0
Onley	505	2	0	0	1	1	35	0	33	2	0
Orange	4 389	11	1	2	1	7	159	12	143	4	1
Pearisburg	2 809	3	0	0	1	2	74	7	63	4	0
Petersburg	33 230	364	9	25	149	181	2 625	803	1 534	288	25
Pocahontas	439	0	0	0	0	0	2	1	1	0	0
Poquoson	11 869	4	0	0	0	4	166	21	136	9	1
Portsmouth	100 724	901	22	41	366	472	5 164	1 049	3 708	407	15
Pound	1 100	5	0	0	1	4	42	7	32	3	1
Pulaski	9 301	35	0	3	9	23	448	103	325	20	3
Purcellville	4 544	7	0	4	1	2	142	10	128	4	0
Quantico	621	1	0	1	0	0	17	6	11	0	0
Radford	14 983	50	0	10	8	32	517	129	357	31	9
Richlands	4 179	8	0	1	4	3	210	40	166	4	2
Richmond	195 271	2 385	84	80	1 196	1 025	12 898	2 529	8 168	2 201	83
Roanoke	93 685	895	16	55	228	596	6 369	1 011	4 912	446	37
Rocky Mount	4 621	13	0	2	1	10	145	6	135	4	0
Rural Retreat	1 360	0	0	0	0	0	0	0	0	0	0
Salem	24 698	31	0	5	13	13	636	78	521	37	1
Saltville	2 304	4	0	3	0	1	59	24	34	1	2
Shenandoah	1 904	0	0	0	0	0	43	13	29	1	0
South Boston	8 269	34	0	1	9	24	391	63	313	15	3
South Hill	4 648	33	1	0	6	26	204	27	165	12	1
Stanley	1 354	0	0	0	0	0	10	0	10	0	1
Stephens City	1 240	2	0	1	0	1	42	6	35	1	0
St. Paul	981	0	0	0	0	0	1	1	0	0	0
Strasburg	4 248	6	0	0	0	6	123	9	112	2	1
Suffolk	77 691	466	9	34	119	304	2 743	434	2 192	117	43
Tappahannock	2 175	20	2	1	5	12	217	29	181	7	3
Tazewell	4 219	9	0	2	1	6	134	24	103	7	0
Timberville	1 728	3	0	0	0	3	11	2	8	1	0
Victoria	1 802	1	0	1	0	0	24	3	17	4	0
Vinton	7 854	11	0	2	3	6	291	35	237	19	1
Virginia Beach	446 448	1 140	20	96	622	402	13 342	2 213	10 376	753	116
Warrenton	8 415	25	0	2	6	17	186	21	162	3	1
Warsaw	1 387	0	0	0	0	0	12	0	12	0	0
Waverly	2 231	8	0	1	0	7	36	8	26	2	0
Waynesboro	21 054	97	2	9	16	70	722	116	566	40	10
Weber City	1 307	1	0	0	0	1	35	7	28	0	0
West Point	3 029	3	0	0	1	2	49	5	41	3	1
Williamsburg	11 630	23	1	3	13	6	307	26	259	22	0
Winchester	25 137	118	1	6	34	77	1 373	135	1 177	61	8
Wise	3 280	2	0	1	0	1	128	11	109	8	1
Woodstock	4 213	0	0	0	0	0	21	1	20	0	0
Wytheville	8 031	12	0	3	4	5	311	35	263	13	2

[1] The FBI does not publish arson data unless it receives data from either the agency or the state for all 12 months of the calendar year.

Table 8. Offenses Known to Law Enforcement, by State and City, 2005—*Continued*

(Number.)

City	Population	Violent crime	Murder and non-negligent man-slaughter	Forcible rape	Robbery	Aggravated assault	Property crime	Burglary	Larceny-theft	Motor vehicle theft	Arson[1]
Washington											
Aberdeen	16 585	55	0	13	20	22	1 788	218	1 399	171	6
Airway Heights	4 604	19	0	1	1	17	158	34	110	14	0
Algona	2 669	2	0	0	1	1	47	18	18	11	0
Anacortes	15 977	22	0	4	4	14	780	135	596	49	5
Arlington	14 687	24	0	3	4	17	1 130	144	846	140	1
Asotin	1 127	0	0	0	0	0	21	2	17	2	0
Auburn	45 589	268	1	14	85	168	4 001	623	2 509	869	34
Bainbridge Island	22 207	24	0	6	0	18	419	90	311	18	10
Battle Ground	13 177	24	0	11	3	10	500	87	393	20	6
Bellevue	118 496	172	2	29	49	92	4 665	595	3 503	567	46
Bellingham	73 980	174	3	28	53	90	5 573	709	4 555	309	24
Bingen	693	2	0	0	0	2	64	23	33	8	0
Black Diamond	3 989	10	0	2	2	6	88	35	49	4	1
Blaine	4 177	7	0	1	0	6	263	32	222	9	0
Bonney Lake	14 333	42	0	3	6	33	593	94	430	69	3
Bothell	31 086	47	0	11	13	23	838	180	503	155	10
Bremerton	36 454	402	2	80	73	247	1 890	425	1 267	198	18
Brewster	2 171	13	0	2	0	11	119	33	86	0	2
Brier	6 405	4	0	1	1	2	98	23	66	9	1
Buckley	4 545	4	0	0	1	3	111	13	82	16	0
Burien	31 305	160	2	24	52	82	2 037	340	1 090	607	26
Burlington	7 943	33	0	7	9	17	1 479	186	1 203	90	7
Camas	16 307	13	0	8	3	2	542	112	403	27	11
Carnation	1 864	0	0	0	0	0	13	2	8	3	0
Castle Rock	2 127	15	0	5	3	7	129	22	85	22	3
Centralia	15 456	72	0	15	14	43	1 370	260	967	143	10
Chehalis	7 278	44	0	21	3	20	772	101	613	58	1
Cheney	10 212	15	0	3	4	8	289	47	225	17	1
Chewelah	2 276	3	0	1	1	1	115	31	77	7	0
Clarkston	7 364	26	0	5	4	17	410	23	357	30	4
Cle Elum	1 819	5	0	1	0	4	219	49	150	20	1
Clyde Hill	2 957	2	0	0	1	1	46	10	31	5	0
Colfax	2 785	10	0	1	1	8	89	22	65	2	0
College Place	8 898	6	0	2	0	4	163	16	138	9	3
Colton	377	0	0	0	0	0	1	1	0	0	0
Colville	5 057	7	0	1	1	5	313	65	241	7	0
Connell	3 207	1	0	1	0	0	72	6	65	1	0
Cosmopolis	1 654	2	0	0	1	1	21	2	18	1	0
Coulee City	639	3	0	0	0	3	28	10	15	3	0
Coulee Dam	1 097	2	0	0	1	1	37	12	24	1	0
Coupeville	1 841	2	0	2	0	0	96	27	61	8	0
Covington	16 424	46	2	10	16	18	657	120	433	104	5
Des Moines	29 237	116	1	18	45	52	1 403	244	741	418	4
Dupont	4 096	4	0	0	0	4	40	6	25	9	1
Duvall	5 732	5	0	0	2	3	47	9	34	4	0
East Wenatchee	8 839	34	0	6	8	20	654	85	537	32	0
Eatonville	2 265	4	0	1	0	3	41	10	29	2	1
Edgewood	9 728	24	0	1	6	17	301	124	149	28	2
Edmonds	40 137	55	0	5	29	21	1 384	235	903	246	10
Ellensburg	16 607	42	0	18	4	20	1 205	191	964	50	2
Elma	3 197	4	0	1	1	2	307	67	211	29	1
Elmer City	259	0	0	0	0	0	0	0	0	0	0
Enumclaw	11 088	8	0	4	3	1	394	69	252	73	5
Ephrata	7 192	10	0	2	0	8	659	208	429	22	1
Everett	97 402	537	3	48	173	313	7 600	1 272	4 243	2 085	14
Everson	2 096	6	0	2	1	3	65	17	44	4	0
Federal Way	82 457	315	6	55	153	101	6 159	800	3 786	1 573	25
Ferndale	9 868	29	0	8	5	16	666	104	532	30	5
Fife	5 037	42	0	8	6	28	699	117	459	123	0
Fircrest	6 097	14	0	2	4	8	205	41	136	28	0
Forks	3 203	10	0	2	0	8	207	51	149	7	0
Garfield	652	1	0	0	0	1	22	4	14	4	0
Gig Harbor	6 686	19	0	1	4	14	495	70	368	57	2
Goldendale	3 816	4	0	1	0	3	171	47	112	12	0
Grand Coulee	926	13	0	2	1	10	43	16	21	6	1
Grandview	8 736	10	0	1	2	7	658	166	438	54	0
Granger	2 777	5	0	1	0	4	158	44	106	8	0
Granite Falls	2 789	3	0	0	2	1	143	38	96	9	3
Hoquiam	9 158	16	0	2	4	10	659	142	448	69	2
Ilwaco	965	0	0	0	0	0	58	9	48	1	2
Issaquah	15 781	12	0	2	2	8	1 092	143	767	182	2
Kalama	1 922	5	0	0	0	5	150	19	123	8	1
Kelso	11 980	73	0	17	15	41	1 195	214	859	122	7
Kenmore	19 615	23	1	4	6	12	594	153	359	82	10
Kennewick	60 932	215	4	26	35	150	3 150	523	2 410	217	27
Kent	82 736	479	3	57	165	254	6 153	1 187	3 492	1 474	42
Kettle Falls	1 587	1	0	0	0	1	79	15	61	3	0
Kirkland	46 174	74	0	21	20	33	1 757	297	1 215	245	8
Kittitas	1 092	2	0	1	0	1	55	5	46	4	0
La Center	1 856	2	0	1	0	1	32	3	25	4	0

[1]The FBI does not publish arson data unless it receives data from either the agency or the state for all 12 months of the calendar year.

Table 8. Offenses Known to Law Enforcement, by State and City, 2005—*Continued*

(Number.)

City	Population	Violent crime	Murder and non-negligent man-slaughter	Forcible rape	Robbery	Aggravated assault	Property crime	Burglary	Larceny-theft	Motor vehicle theft	Arson[1]
Lacey	33 427	91	1	6	33	51	1 756	235	1 405	116	10
Lake Forest Park	12 643	11	0	2	2	7	362	84	230	48	1
Lake Stevens	7 336	8	0	1	0	7	227	39	165	23	2
Lakewood	58 856	491	3	61	124	303	3 918	872	2 488	558	27
Langley	1 042	1	0	0	0	1	53	10	36	7	0
Liberty Lake	5 029	2	0	0	0	2	110	16	86	8	0
Long Beach	1 378	8	0	1	2	5	121	30	84	7	1
Longview	36 430	147	3	24	32	88	3 136	748	2 076	312	20
Lynden	10 598	6	0	2	1	3	227	34	183	10	1
Lynnwood	33 870	93	1	7	45	40	2 856	308	2 028	520	8
Maple Valley	14 479	21	0	6	4	11	389	108	209	72	3
Marysville	29 194	57	1	16	16	24	1 283	244	725	314	5
McCleary	1 497	11	0	1	1	9	39	18	16	5	0
Medical Lake	4 140	14	0	5	3	6	75	9	59	7	3
Medina	3 055	0	0	0	0	0	77	25	48	4	0
Mercer Island	22 482	7	0	0	2	5	451	70	343	38	2
Mill Creek	13 689	21	0	2	3	16	684	80	470	134	5
Milton	6 322	27	1	6	6	14	382	64	246	72	2
Monroe	15 383	26	0	7	3	16	615	69	460	86	3
Montesano	3 412	5	0	2	0	3	211	21	182	8	0
Morton	1 090	4	0	1	0	3	68	9	58	1	0
Moses Lake	16 676	77	0	20	13	44	1 420	263	1 075	82	8
Mountlake Terrace	20 585	27	0	3	8	16	867	116	518	233	12
Mount Vernon	29 211	76	0	23	17	36	2 618	330	2 107	181	10
Moxee	915	0	0	0	0	0	39	10	23	6	1
Mukilteo	19 697	17	0	4	6	7	549	109	356	84	7
Napavine	1 456	7	0	1	1	5	68	5	62	1	0
Newcastle	9 137	6	0	1	3	2	289	69	176	44	3
Newport	2 157	9	0	0	1	8	140	23	114	3	2
Normandy Park	6 284	3	0	0	0	3	168	39	112	17	0
North Bend	4 664	11	0	1	1	9	229	52	144	33	1
North Bonneville	663	2	1	0	0	1	19	7	11	1	0
Oakesdale	409	0	0	0	0	0	9	6	2	1	0
Oak Harbor	21 953	36	0	12	3	21	497	89	385	23	4
Oakville	683	4	0	0	1	3	43	9	31	3	0
Ocean Shores	4 372	2	1	0	1	0	231	61	158	12	0
Odessa	965	5	0	1	0	4	19	5	13	1	0
Olympia	44 577	115	0	24	26	65	2 549	467	1 849	233	4
Omak	4 783	20	0	1	3	16	313	77	224	12	3
Oroville	1 621	8	0	2	0	6	83	14	66	3	1
Othello	6 189	21	0	8	7	6	373	55	289	29	4
Pacific	5 725	20	0	6	8	6	221	43	101	77	3
Pasco	42 862	98	0	19	29	50	2 015	413	1 389	213	6
Pe Ell	684	0	0	0	0	0	2	0	2	0	1
Port Angeles	18 887	63	0	23	7	33	1 010	178	747	85	28
Port Orchard	8 091	60	0	13	2	45	453	79	321	53	3
Port Townsend	8 929	19	0	4	3	12	492	67	415	10	2
Poulsbo	7 536	31	1	6	3	21	241	45	187	9	1
Pullman	25 361	38	2	13	3	20	549	102	431	16	3
Puyallup	35 976	128	0	17	39	72	3 188	362	2 288	538	8
Quincy	5 417	29	0	8	6	15	340	84	232	24	0
Rainier	1 659	1	0	0	0	1	41	6	23	12	0
Raymond	3 005	4	0	1	0	3	58	5	51	2	0
Reardan	622	2	0	2	0	0	20	4	14	2	0
Redmond	47 601	86	0	21	16	49	1 788	203	1 393	192	4
Renton	55 549	223	2	24	95	102	5 311	680	3 670	961	19
Republic	1 010	3	0	1	0	2	10	0	8	2	0
Richland	44 015	120	0	17	11	92	1 467	240	1 140	87	10
Ridgefield	2 321	1	0	0	0	1	92	17	66	9	0
Ritzville	1 730	1	0	0	0	1	71	17	49	5	0
Rosalia	621	0	0	0	0	0	2	2	0	0	0
Royal City	1 955	6	0	0	1	5	57	13	34	10	0
Ruston	755	0	0	0	0	0	18	1	14	3	0
Sammamish	34 733	16	0	8	1	7	537	96	404	37	4
SeaTac	25 495	130	1	22	42	65	2 206	346	1 172	688	9
Seattle	579 215	4 109	25	138	1 607	2 339	43 471	6 761	27 147	9 563	217
Sedro Woolley	9 990	24	0	9	10	5	964	166	713	85	12
Selah	6 807	2	0	1	1	0	312	51	231	30	0
Sequim	4 995	12	0	2	1	9	289	43	235	11	4
Shelton	9 067	63	1	12	13	37	1 218	189	876	153	5
Shoreline	52 653	124	0	21	42	61	2 354	468	1 358	528	28
Snohomish	8 712	23	0	3	6	14	445	56	323	66	6
Snoqualmie	5 328	8	0	2	0	6	170	26	105	39	1
Soap Lake	1 848	3	0	0	0	3	78	36	42	0	0
South Bend	1 836	4	0	1	0	3	78	15	50	13	0
Spokane	199 384	1 120	13	78	286	743	12 170	2 436	7 932	1 802	94
Spokane Valley	82 288	331	1	33	55	242	3 900	629	2 708	563	34
Stanwood	4 851	6	0	0	0	6	323	57	239	27	4
Steilacoom	6 227	14	0	2	1	11	142	28	99	15	1
Sultan	3 839	5	0	1	0	4	148	33	96	19	1

[1]The FBI does not publish arson data unless it receives data from either the agency or the state for all 12 months of the calendar year.

Table 8. Offenses Known to Law Enforcement, by State and City, 2005—*Continued*

(Number.)

City	Population	Violent crime	Murder and non-negligent man-slaughter	Forcible rape	Robbery	Aggravated assault	Property crime	Burglary	Larceny-theft	Motor vehicle theft	Arson[1]
Sumas	1 063	4	0	0	1	3	68	13	51	4	0
Sumner	9 244	53	0	2	6	45	633	145	358	130	9
Sunnyside	14 408	31	5	1	6	19	1 197	305	729	163	13
Tacoma	198 748	2 014	13	120	690	1 191	16 802	3 255	9 989	3 558	101
Tenino	1 568	6	0	1	0	5	84	21	58	5	0
Tieton	1 188	3	0	1	0	2	17	5	9	3	0
Toledo	681	6	0	1	2	3	45	16	25	4	0
Tonasket	976	1	0	0	0	1	80	5	74	1	0
Toppenish	9 329	57	1	9	10	37	976	261	565	150	5
Tukwila	17 222	197	2	22	89	84	3 662	342	2 504	816	13
Tumwater	13 360	49	0	12	15	22	534	109	353	72	4
Union Gap	5 781	29	0	10	10	9	1 087	129	892	66	1
University Place	30 810	97	0	12	26	59	1 128	235	737	156	5
Vader	616	2	0	1	0	1	8	3	4	1	0
Vancouver	157 152	626	8	111	161	346	7 943	1 218	5 573	1 152	25
Walla Walla	30 682	175	0	64	13	98	1 370	237	1 064	69	9
Wapato	4 668	32	0	9	11	12	365	96	179	90	7
Warden	2 636	4	0	2	0	2	94	18	67	9	0
Washougal	10 271	24	0	2	3	19	408	80	290	38	9
Wenatchee	29 415	105	1	19	16	69	1 751	287	1 348	116	9
Westport	2 312	7	0	2	1	4	95	17	72	6	1
West Richland	9 639	9	0	2	0	7	169	41	114	14	2
White Salmon	2 308	1	0	0	1	0	94	32	53	9	0
Wilbur	923	0	0	0	0	0	3	1	2	0	0
Wilkeson	404	5	0	1	2	2	32	12	12	8	0
Winthrop	356	2	0	1	1	0	15	8	7	0	0
Woodinville	9 720	19	0	7	5	7	587	129	379	79	8
Woodland	4 315	15	0	3	4	8	255	64	169	22	4
Woodway	1 206	0	0	0	0	0	37	8	28	1	0
Yakima	81 986	452	10	62	149	231	7 532	1 451	5 021	1 060	77
Yarrow Point	1 023	1	0	0	0	1	17	4	13	0	0
Yelm	4 469	10	1	4	1	4	256	46	193	17	0
Zillah	2 579	4	0	1	0	3	249	45	182	22	2
West Virginia											
Albright	248	0	0	0	0	0	0	0	0	0	0
Alderson	1 097	2	0	0	1	1	3	3	0	0	0
Athens	1 092	0	0	0	0	0	0	0	0	0	0
Barboursville	3 201	6	0	0	1	5	358	35	313	10	0
Beckley	17 008	120	0	2	20	98	1 262	163	1 023	76	4
Belington	1 792	2	0	0	0	2	5	1	4	0	0
Benwood	1 513	4	0	0	0	4	3	2	1	0	0
Bethany	992	0	0	0	0	0	0	0	0	0	0
Bethlehem	2 558	0	0	0	0	0	8	1	6	1	0
Bluefield	11 231	50	1	0	12	37	321	101	191	29	5
Bradshaw	267	0	0	0	0	0	1	0	1	0	0
Bramwell	416	0	0	0	0	0	1	1	0	0	0
Bridgeport	7 468	2	0	0	0	2	279	25	248	6	0
Buckhannon	5 871	6	0	0	0	6	90	20	59	11	0
Cameron	1 161	4	0	0	0	4	9	1	7	1	0
Ceredo	1 647	5	0	0	0	5	28	7	18	3	0
Chapmanville	1 154	14	0	0	2	12	84	9	65	10	0
Charleston	51 728	555	7	16	128	404	3 836	818	2 712	306	28
Chesapeake	1 582	0	0	0	0	0	7	1	4	2	0
Chester	2 458	0	0	0	0	0	37	7	28	2	1
Clarksburg	16 536	87	3	9	12	63	804	163	595	46	10
Clearview	568	0	0	0	0	0	0	0	0	0	0
Dunbar	7 843	26	0	2	2	22	378	97	240	41	6
East Bank	905	0	0	0	0	0	5	1	4	0	0
Elkins	7 026	26	1	6	3	16	216	48	152	16	2
Fairmont	19 008	54	0	12	19	23	480	127	316	37	13
Fairview	436	1	0	0	0	1	0	0	0	0	0
Fayetteville	2 672	0	0	0	0	0	30	3	26	1	0
Follansbee	3 014	3	0	0	2	1	12	3	9	0	0
Glasgow	754	0	0	0	0	0	3	1	2	0	0
Glen Dale	1 491	0	0	0	0	0	42	9	33	0	1
Glenville	1 476	2	0	1	0	1	20	8	11	1	0
Grafton	5 393	5	0	0	0	5	40	22	16	2	0
Handley	348	0	0	0	0	0	0	0	0	0	0
Harpers Ferry/Bolivar	1 379	0	0	0	0	0	4	1	3	0	0
Hartford City	520	0	0	0	0	0	0	0	0	0	0
Henderson	318	0	0	0	0	0	0	0	0	0	0
Hundred	333	0	0	0	0	0	0	0	0	0	0
Huntington	49 932	325	11	36	164	114	3 677	1 071	2 296	310	28
Hurricane	5 793	8	0	0	1	7	139	8	116	15	1
Kenova	3 426	11	0	0	1	10	183	16	151	16	0
Kermit	228	0	0	0	0	0	0	0	0	0	0
Keyser	5 507	17	0	1	4	12	171	23	139	9	0
Kimball	366	0	0	0	0	0	0	0	0	0	0
Kingwood	2 916	0	0	0	0	0	0	0	0	0	0
Lewisburg	3 592	2	0	2	0	0	76	6	68	2	0
Logan	1 560	16	1	0	7	8	317	42	268	7	3
Mabscott	1 370	3	0	0	0	3	21	1	17	3	0
Man	726	0	0	0	0	0	2	1	1	0	0
Mannington	2 090	1	0	0	0	1	8	2	6	0	0

[1]The FBI does not publish arson data unless it receives data from either the agency or the state for all 12 months of the calendar year.

Table 8. Offenses Known to Law Enforcement, by State and City, 2005—*Continued*

(Number.)

City	Population	Violent crime	Murder and non-negligent man-slaughter	Forcible rape	Robbery	Aggravated assault	Property crime	Burglary	Larceny-theft	Motor vehicle theft	Arson[1]
Marlinton	1 272	2	0	0	0	2	12	3	8	1	0
Marmet	1 640	0	0	0	0	0	5	0	5	0	0
Martinsburg	15 648	87	0	1	30	56	982	98	840	44	3
Masontown	645	0	0	0	0	0	2	0	2	0	0
Matoaka	309	0	0	0	0	0	2	0	2	0	0
McMechen	1 858	0	0	0	0	0	11	2	9	0	0
Milton	2 279	1	0	0	1	0	36	8	26	2	0
Monongah	916	1	0	0	0	1	13	4	9	0	0
Montgomery	2 025	0	0	0	0	0	49	7	41	1	0
Moorefield	2 413	12	0	2	1	9	40	6	32	2	0
Morgantown	28 183	109	0	21	30	58	1 030	251	758	21	6
Moundsville	9 703	13	1	2	1	9	269	72	180	17	2
Mullens	1 679	1	0	0	0	1	9	1	7	1	0
New Cumberland	1 051	0	0	0	0	0	3	1	2	0	0
New Haven	1 538	0	0	0	0	0	7	3	4	0	0
New Martinsville	5 765	3	0	1	0	2	64	14	45	5	1
Northfork	463	0	0	0	0	0	0	0	0	0	0
Nutter Fort	1 653	4	0	0	0	4	18	5	11	2	0
Oceana	1 493	5	0	0	0	5	81	11	67	3	1
Paden City	2 738	1	0	0	0	1	2	0	2	0	0
Parkersburg	32 186	140	3	12	30	95	1 645	347	1 191	107	25
Pennsboro	1 195	0	0	0	0	0	3	3	0	0	0
Philippi	2 783	10	0	1	1	8	92	31	56	5	1
Poca	1 025	0	0	0	0	0	7	1	6	0	0
Point Pleasant	4 539	8	0	0	2	6	263	74	180	9	3
Princeton	6 248	70	1	1	14	54	419	100	300	19	3
Rainelle	1 511	0	0	0	0	0	0	0	0	0	0
Ranson	3 435	6	0	1	0	5	16	4	9	3	0
Ravenswood	4 016	7	1	0	0	6	29	5	21	3	0
Ripley	3 282	9	0	0	2	7	86	11	73	2	0
Rivesville	914	1	0	0	0	1	0	0	0	0	0
Romney	1 962	1	0	0	0	1	12	3	8	1	1
Ronceverte	1 547	4	0	0	0	4	17	3	14	0	1
Rowlesburg	616	4	0	0	0	4	1	0	1	0	0
Smithers	864	4	0	0	2	2	34	5	29	0	0
South Charleston	12 880	55	2	7	10	36	606	87	471	48	5
Spencer	2 279	4	0	0	0	4	86	14	70	2	0
St. Albans	11 182	20	0	0	0	20	407	89	268	50	4
St. Marys	1 977	3	0	0	0	3	7	1	5	1	0
Stonewood	1 844	3	0	0	0	3	8	2	5	1	0
Terra Alta	1 484	2	0	0	0	2	14	3	10	1	0
Triadelphia	785	0	0	0	0	0	0	0	0	0	0
Vienna	10 776	18	0	0	3	15	339	20	312	7	0
Wardensville	247	0	0	0	0	0	0	0	0	0	0
Welch	2 417	16	0	0	0	16	153	31	116	6	0
West Logan	400	0	0	0	0	0	2	1	1	0	0
West Milford	645	0	0	0	0	0	0	0	0	0	0
Weston	4 230	2	0	0	0	2	3	0	3	0	0
Westover	3 925	20	0	0	3	17	98	27	66	5	0
West Union	804	0	0	0	0	0	11	7	3	1	0
Wheeling	29 916	138	0	20	32	86	961	227	645	89	5
White Sulphur Springs	2 378	5	0	0	0	5	1	1	0	0	0
Williamson	3 218	13	0	0	0	13	70	16	46	8	2
Williamstown	2 949	1	0	0	0	1	55	7	48	0	0
Winfield	1 979	4	0	0	0	4	27	1	26	0	0
Wisconsin											
Algoma	3 234	0	0	0	0	0	127	7	115	5	1
Altoona	6 501	8	0	2	1	5	138	31	102	5	0
Amery	2 876	13	0	0	0	13	68	13	50	5	0
Antigo	8 385	45	0	0	0	45	465	62	387	16	0
Appleton	70 640	173	0	27	16	130	2 083	403	1 635	45	10
Arcadia	2 344	4	0	0	2	2	61	3	51	7	0
Ashland	8 423	36	1	4	0	31	444	41	389	14	5
Ashwaubenon	17 134	7	0	1	2	4	898	78	796	24	0
Bangor	1 395	4	0	0	0	4	16	3	13	0	0
Baraboo	10 824	31	0	5	0	26	447	49	378	20	0
Barron	3 201	6	0	3	0	3	70	9	51	10	1
Bayfield	610	4	0	0	0	4	9	0	9	0	0
Bayside	4 444	0	0	0	0	0	46	8	35	3	0
Beaver Dam	15 089	5	0	0	1	4	428	37	386	5	2
Belleville	2 022	5	0	0	5	0	39	1	36	2	0
Beloit	35 980	150	4	13	48	85	1 859	306	1 444	109	10
Beloit Town	7 427	13	0	3	1	9	181	52	121	8	4
Berlin	5 291	7	0	2	0	5	153	16	133	4	0
Black River Falls	3 581	4	0	0	1	3	91	24	66	1	0
Blair	1 278	4	0	0	0	4	23	4	19	0	1
Bloomer	3 330	0	0	0	0	0	63	7	55	1	0
Bloomfield	5 691	3	0	2	0	1	59	21	37	1	0
Boscobel	3 370	4	0	0	0	4	14	3	11	0	0
Brillion	2 920	2	0	0	0	2	24	8	16	0	0
Brodhead	3 101	5	0	0	0	5	25	4	21	0	0
Brookfield Township	6 370	6	0	0	5	1	193	20	161	12	0
Brown Deer	11 954	22	0	2	11	9	532	34	481	17	0
Burlington	11 097	2	0	2	0	0	378	48	313	17	4
Burlington Town	6 656	6	0	0	1	5	99	12	81	6	0
Butler	1 850	4	0	0	1	3	63	12	46	5	0

[1]The FBI does not publish arson data unless it receives data from either the agency or the state for all 12 months of the calendar year.

Table 8. Offenses Known to Law Enforcement, by State and City, 2005—*Continued*

(Number.)

City	Population	Violent crime	Murder and non-negligent man-slaughter	Forcible rape	Robbery	Aggravated assault	Property crime	Burglary	Larceny-theft	Motor vehicle theft	Arson[1]
Caledonia	24 339	12	0	1	8	3	305	69	211	25	2
Campbellsport	1 933	0	0	0	0	0	25	7	18	0	1
Campbell Township	4 499	9	0	0	2	7	61	17	43	1	0
Cedarburg	11 359	5	0	2	0	3	155	12	139	4	1
Chenequa	595	0	0	0	0	0	3	2	1	0	0
Chetek	2 158	6	0	1	0	5	66	20	42	4	0
Chilton	3 626	7	0	1	0	6	56	7	48	1	0
Chippewa Falls	12 784	11	0	3	0	8	290	36	242	12	0
Cleveland	1 403	1	0	0	0	1	17	1	16	0	0
Clinton	3 020	2	0	0	0	2	48	2	45	1	0
Colby-Abbotsford	3 608	5	0	2	0	3	60	7	52	1	0
Columbus	5 014	7	0	0	0	7	99	7	92	0	0
Cornell	1 411	3	0	0	1	2	25	1	23	1	0
Cottage Grove	8 811	9	0	1	1	7	119	20	96	3	0
Crandon	1 866	2	0	0	0	2	76	10	56	10	0
Cross Plains	3 368	1	0	0	1	0	37	4	33	0	0
Cuba City	2 130	2	0	0	0	2	56	13	42	1	0
Cudahy	18 201	41	1	5	18	17	625	116	473	36	11
Cumberland	2 270	6	0	0	3	3	105	21	82	2	0
Dane	878	0	0	0	0	0	0	0	0	0	0
Darlington	2 370	3	0	0	0	3	35	4	29	2	0
Deerfield	2 077	2	0	1	0	1	44	10	34	0	0
Deforest	8 223	4	0	1	2	1	192	22	167	3	0
Delafield	6 773	1	0	0	0	1	104	20	83	1	1
Delavan	8 356	6	1	1	0	4	482	45	417	20	0
Delavan Town	4 594	7	2	1	3	1	118	42	71	5	0
Denmark	1 994	1	0	0	0	1	26	4	22	0	0
De Pere	22 988	6	0	3	0	3	415	63	334	18	1
Dodgeville	4 765	2	0	0	0	2	132	6	121	5	0
Durand	1 930	2	0	2	0	0	16	2	13	1	0
Eagle River	1 588	2	0	0	2	0	111	6	101	4	0
East Troy	4 207	2	0	0	1	1	152	10	122	20	0
Eau Claire	62 885	116	0	7	24	85	1 929	329	1 522	78	10
Edgerton	5 049	0	0	0	0	0	48	15	30	3	0
Eleva	647	0	0	0	0	0	15	1	13	1	0
Elkhart Lake	1 060	0	0	0	0	0	32	1	31	0	0
Elkhorn	8 582	8	0	1	1	6	210	26	180	4	1
Ellsworth	3 040	1	0	0	0	1	61	10	49	2	0
Elm Grove	6 266	1	0	0	1	0	94	18	76	0	0
Elroy	1 544	1	0	0	0	1	56	9	47	0	0
Evansville	4 481	18	0	0	0	18	58	15	42	1	0
Everest	14 996	16	0	0	4	12	331	64	254	13	1
Fennimore	2 369	1	0	0	1	0	50	10	39	1	0
Fitchburg	21 929	75	0	5	22	48	561	74	455	32	4
Fond du Lac	42 617	75	0	3	11	61	1 195	138	1 015	42	1
Fontana	1 965	1	0	0	0	1	34	3	30	1	0
Fort Atkinson	11 929	9	0	2	2	5	359	36	311	12	0
Fox Lake	1 467	1	0	0	1	0	16	5	9	2	0
Fox Point	6 847	2	0	2	0	0	80	6	68	6	0
Fox Valley	17 137	7	1	4	1	1	506	46	452	8	1
Franklin	32 565	24	0	3	5	16	589	99	464	26	2
Frederic	1 257	2	0	0	0	2	15	3	12	0	0
Geneva Town	4 161	3	0	0	0	3	118	13	104	1	0
Genoa City	2 613	0	0	0	0	0	48	10	36	2	0
Germantown	19 198	9	0	5	4	0	390	58	313	19	4
Glendale	13 072	23	0	1	16	6	605	30	533	42	0
Grafton	11 645	3	0	0	1	2	165	6	154	5	0
Grand Chute	20 135	11	0	2	4	5	819	71	707	41	1
Grantsburg	1 427	2	0	0	0	2	35	11	23	1	0
Green Bay	101 599	495	5	58	72	360	2 931	605	2 099	227	12
Greendale	14 064	9	0	0	4	5	514	26	481	7	3
Greenfield	36 042	34	0	3	21	10	1 120	159	893	68	3
Green Lake	1 125	1	0	1	0	0	29	2	27	0	1
Hales Corners	7 617	11	0	2	5	4	188	14	172	2	1
Hartford	12 687	25	0	0	0	25	350	34	292	24	0
Hartland	8 637	1	0	0	1	0	125	22	101	2	0
Hayward	2 285	6	0	2	0	4	161	26	129	6	0
Hazel Green	1 204	0	0	0	0	0	9	7	1	1	0
Hobart-Lawrence	7 688	0	0	0	0	0	72	15	49	8	0
Holmen	7 115	3	0	0	0	3	136	25	108	3	0
Horicon	3 690	2	0	1	0	1	48	9	38	1	1
Hudson	10 807	15	1	2	3	9	599	59	524	16	0
Hurley	1 714	9	1	0	1	7	72	10	53	9	0
Iron Ridge	990	0	0	0	0	0	8	1	7	0	0
Jackson	5 913	10	0	1	1	8	37	7	27	3	0
Janesville	61 908	170	0	34	64	72	2 968	515	2 317	136	10
Jefferson	7 546	19	0	0	3	16	228	11	204	13	0
Juneau	2 701	0	0	0	0	0	60	6	51	3	0
Kaukauna	14 534	8	0	1	0	7	270	16	244	10	0
Kenosha	94 261	249	3	35	124	87	2 899	575	2 130	194	9

[1]The FBI does not publish arson data unless it receives data from either the agency or the state for all 12 months of the calendar year.

Table 8. Offenses Known to Law Enforcement, by State and City, 2005—*Continued*

(Number.)

City	Population	Violent crime	Murder and non-negligent man-slaughter	Forcible rape	Robbery	Aggravated assault	Property crime	Burglary	Larceny-theft	Motor vehicle theft	Arson[1]
Kewaskum	3 519	1	0	1	0	0	82	6	71	5	1
Kewaunee	2 879	1	0	0	0	1	37	4	32	1	0
Kiel	3 498	1	0	0	0	1	73	2	69	2	0
Kohler	1 987	1	0	0	1	0	54	2	52	0	0
La Crosse	50 945	99	1	16	20	62	1 627	213	1 348	66	6
Ladysmith	3 853	3	0	0	1	2	141	13	128	0	0
Lake Delton	2 990	18	0	3	5	10	477	29	439	9	1
Lake Hallie	4 523	3	0	1	0	2	159	24	130	5	0
Lake Mills	4 993	3	0	2	0	1	55	9	46	0	0
Lancaster	4 000	0	0	0	0	0	25	5	20	0	0
Lodi	3 010	2	0	0	0	2	97	3	92	2	0
Luxemburg	2 154	1	0	0	0	1	20	1	19	0	0
Madison	221 419	839	2	80	329	428	7 737	1 449	5 682	606	65
Maple Bluff	1 320	0	0	0	0	0	17	4	13	0	0
Marinette	11 430	12	1	2	2	7	404	57	339	8	1
Markesan	1 370	0	0	0	0	0	28	1	27	0	0
Marshfield	18 736	9	0	5	1	3	582	89	463	30	4
Mauston	4 332	34	0	3	2	29	248	44	191	13	2
Mayville	4 986	0	0	0	0	0	43	4	39	0	2
McFarland	7 290	6	0	0	0	6	177	13	162	2	0
Medford	4 245	5	0	2	0	3	142	16	123	3	0
Menasha	16 444	39	1	2	2	34	410	86	305	19	4
Menomonee Falls	34 044	17	0	6	7	4	487	60	399	28	0
Menomonie	15 270	19	0	3	1	15	431	65	349	17	0
Mequon	23 910	4	0	1	0	3	198	47	150	1	0
Merrill	10 203	10	0	1	1	8	338	52	279	7	1
Middleton	16 035	17	0	6	5	6	498	94	386	18	0
Milwaukee[3]	586 500	6 010	121	158	2 927	2 804	32 812	4 570	21 611	6 631	254
Mineral Point	2 509	2	0	0	0	2	44	5	38	1	0
Minocqua	4 925	8	0	0	0	8	147	20	127	0	0
Mondovi	2 643	0	0	0	0	0	40	6	33	1	0
Monona	7 856	10	0	2	6	2	336	26	302	8	0
Monroe	10 635	3	0	0	0	3	230	19	199	12	1
Mosinee	4 025	1	0	0	0	1	134	22	109	3	0
Mount Horeb	6 141	10	0	0	0	10	183	14	165	4	3
Mount Pleasant	25 514	25	0	2	12	11	727	137	559	31	2
Mukwonago	6 733	2	0	0	1	1	160	34	118	8	1
Muskego	22 711	2	1	1	0	0	239	46	187	6	2
Neenah	24 678	28	0	6	2	20	411	79	324	8	2
Neillsville	2 715	0	0	0	0	0	87	18	67	2	1
New Berlin	38 910	16	0	0	5	11	547	90	437	20	11
New Glarus	2 060	0	0	0	0	0	70	6	64	0	0
New Holstein	3 224	4	0	0	0	4	73	8	62	3	0
New Lisbon	1 429	4	0	0	0	4	59	3	56	0	0
New London	7 059	6	1	3	0	2	194	22	166	6	0
Niagara	1 814	3	0	0	0	3	9	2	7	0	0
North Fond du Lac	4 877	7	0	2	0	5	96	4	85	7	0
North Hudson	3 692	1	0	0	0	1	21	4	16	1	0
Oak Creek	32 314	30	1	10	9	10	1 018	127	855	36	2
Oconomowoc	13 595	11	0	3	1	7	162	27	130	5	0
Oconto	4 714	16	0	4	0	12	205	17	177	11	0
Oconto Falls	2 826	2	0	0	0	2	64	9	54	1	0
Omro	3 267	10	0	0	0	10	9	7	0	2	0
Onalaska	15 699	35	0	0	3	32	447	39	402	6	0
Oregon	8 278	3	0	1	0	2	264	12	243	9	0
Osceola	2 695	10	0	0	1	9	67	10	57	0	0
Oshkosh	63 828	183	0	12	17	154	1 853	297	1 496	60	1
Osseo	1 660	1	0	0	1	0	63	5	52	6	. . .
Palmyra	1 775	5	0	0	1	4	57	6	48	3	0
Park Falls	2 560	0	0	0	0	0	56	6	49	1	0
Pepin	928	0	0	0	0	0	13	4	8	1	0
Peshtigo	3 376	3	0	0	0	3	63	8	51	4	0
Pewaukee	12 772	9	0	1	0	8	152	42	108	2	0
Pewaukee Village	8 968	5	0	1	1	3	153	20	132	1	0
Platteville	9 899	9	0	3	0	6	192	7	178	7	0
Pleasant Prairie	18 574	14	0	4	3	7	296	34	250	12	0
Plover	11 210	37	0	9	0	28	240	44	191	5	0
Plymouth	8 191	2	0	2	0	0	188	10	171	7	0
Portage	10 059	26	0	6	1	19	384	56	322	6	0
Port Washington	10 944	2	0	0	0	2	159	11	143	5	0
Prescott	3 879	2	0	0	1	1	152	38	110	4	0
Princeton	1 482	2	0	0	1	1	27	5	19	3	0
Pulaski	3 524	11	0	0	0	11	64	16	45	3	0
Racine	80 503	391	16	31	242	102	4 557	982	3 235	340	25
Reedsburg	8 409	12	0	5	1	6	237	17	212	8	3
Rice Lake	8 395	7	0	0	0	7	211	13	184	14	1
Richland Center	5 234	24	1	4	0	19	57	9	47	1	0
Ripon	7 323	9	0	1	0	8	121	13	107	1	0
River Falls	13 083	12	0	0	3	9	514	85	409	20	0
River Hills	1 639	1	0	1	0	0	20	1	17	2	0

[1]The FBI does not publish arson data unless it receives data from either the agency or the state for all 12 months of the calendar year.
[3]Because of changes in the state/local agency's reporting practices, figures are not comparable to previous years' data.
. . . = Not available.

Table 8. Offenses Known to Law Enforcement, by State and City, 2005—*Continued*

(Number.)

City	Population	Violent crime	Murder and non-negligent man-slaughter	Forcible rape	Robbery	Aggravated assault	Property crime	Burglary	Larceny-theft	Motor vehicle theft	Arson[1]
Rothschild	5 059	2	0	0	1	1	137	4	132	1	0
Sauk Prairie	4 140	0	0	0	0	0	268	17	249	2	1
Saukville	4 210	1	0	0	1	0	119	10	106	3	0
Shawano	8 413	18	0	7	1	10	528	49	466	13	1
Sheboygan	49 262	68	0	25	10	33	2 098	266	1 746	86	11
Sheboygan Falls	7 251	3	0	1	1	1	57	6	49	2	0
Shorewood	13 417	17	0	1	16	0	352	36	303	13	0
Shorewood Hills	1 679	1	0	0	1	0	91	2	89	0	0
Silver Lake	2 482	9	0	2	0	7	16	2	14	0	0
Siren	1 024	13	0	0	1	12	44	4	36	4	0
Slinger	4 195	3	0	2	0	1	118	9	100	9	0
Somerset	2 414	1	0	1	0	0	30	2	24	4	0
South Milwaukee	21 155	36	1	7	14	14	488	68	384	36	3
Sparta	8 836	19	0	6	3	10	315	30	250	35	2
Spooner	2 719	3	0	2	1	0	93	10	83	0	0
St. Croix Falls	2 111	2	0	0	0	2	77	4	70	3	0
St. Francis	9 419	14	0	1	10	3	273	31	229	13	1
Stanley	3 325	1	0	0	0	1	38	6	32	0	0
Stevens Point	24 403	86	1	14	4	67	879	150	707	22	1
Stoughton	12 755	5	0	0	2	3	302	34	264	4	0
Strum	980	0	0	0	0	0	11	5	6	0	0
Sturgeon Bay	9 336	4	0	0	0	4	171	32	136	3	0
Sturtevant	5 734	1	0	0	1	0	99	19	70	10	0
Summit	5 119	1	0	0	0	1	26	1	23	2	0
Sun Prairie	24 585	22	0	1	5	16	599	82	500	17	0
Superior	27 080	64	0	16	12	36	1 565	299	1 177	89	6
Theresa	1 268	6	0	0	0	6	33	9	21	3	0
Thiensville	3 713	3	0	0	0	3	21	3	18	0	0
Tomah	8 656	33	1	2	0	30	442	32	399	11	0
Tomahawk	3 847	10	0	1	0	9	126	15	107	4	0
Town of East Troy	3 916	0	0	0	0	0	26	12	13	1	0
Town of Madison	6 358	48	0	9	14	25	347	46	277	24	0
Town of Menasha	15 724	11	0	4	0	7	207	54	138	15	1
Trempealeau	1 449	1	0	1	0	0	1	0	1	0	0
Twin Lakes	5 447	2	0	1	0	1	138	21	110	7	3
Two Rivers	12 223	35	0	2	1	32	252	34	211	7	0
Valders	1 002	0	0	0	0	0	0	0	0	0	0
Verona	9 987	19	0	0	3	16	185	12	169	4	0
Viroqua	4 403	3	0	0	1	2	89	14	73	2	0
Walworth	2 589	7	0	1	0	6	64	7	57	0	0
Washburn	2 309	11	0	1	0	10	49	2	45	2	0
Waterloo	3 315	0	0	0	0	0	44	7	37	0	0
Watertown	22 937	47	0	7	5	35	453	67	363	23	5
Waukesha	67 590	95	0	27	19	49	1 322	266	959	97	5
Waunakee	10 032	5	0	1	0	4	119	30	84	5	0
Waupaca	5 866	18	0	1	1	16	245	23	211	11	0
Waupun	10 604	8	0	2	0	6	196	17	175	4	0
Wausau	37 356	117	0	23	21	73	1 125	251	826	48	9
Wautoma	2 165	2	0	0	1	1	57	5	50	2	0
Wauwatosa	45 827	101	0	15	57	29	2 152	275	1 722	155	1
West Allis	59 802	190	4	18	81	87	2 659	476	1 960	223	30
West Bend	29 447	24	0	2	8	14	713	57	637	19	4
Westby	2 158	1	0	0	0	1	36	7	24	5	0
West Milwaukee	4 081	16	1	2	7	6	174	28	110	36	0
West Salem	4 789	2	0	1	0	1	71	7	63	1	0
Whitefish Bay	13 739	3	0	0	1	2	135	18	113	4	0
Whitehall	1 636	1	0	0	0	1	38	2	36	0	0
Whitewater	14 285	17	0	3	3	11	285	33	245	7	1
Wisconsin Dells	2 483	15	0	2	1	12	359	40	303	16	0
Wisconsin Rapids	17 933	14	0	5	1	8	848	141	678	29	2
Woodruff	1 984	5	0	0	1	4	46	6	39	1	0
Wyoming											
Afton	1 807	10	1	0	0	9	31	10	21	0	0
Baggs	356	0	0	0	0	0	2	0	2	0	4
Basin	1 222	4	0	1	0	3	26	9	14	3	0
Buffalo	4 279	21	0	0	1	20	118	10	101	7	0
Casper	51 520	135	2	7	14	112	2 699	525	2 077	97	21
Cheyenne	55 664	97	4	12	17	64	2 585	272	2 222	91	7
Cody	9 099	21	0	5	0	16	259	34	218	7	0
Diamondville	702	1	0	0	0	1	21	15	5	1	0
Douglas	5 519	11	0	1	0	10	143	23	114	6	1
Evanston	11 469	7	0	0	3	4	505	54	420	31	0
Evansville	2 319	3	0	0	1	2	142	24	103	15	0
Gillette	22 382	39	0	3	5	31	933	79	822	32	7
Glenrock	2 313	4	0	0	0	4	36	8	26	2	1
Green River	11 871	34	0	1	0	33	396	68	309	19	1
Guernsey	1 127	4	0	1	0	3	22	6	10	6	1
Hanna	871	2	0	0	0	2	6	3	3	0	0
Jackson	9 015	44	0	12	2	30	362	59	282	21	1
Kemmerer	2 575	3	0	0	0	3	39	4	35	0	0
La Barge	421	0	0	0	0	0	4	0	2	2	0
Lander	6 926	15	0	0	0	15	266	31	228	7	0

[1]The FBI does not publish arson data unless it receives data from either the agency or the state for all 12 months of the calendar year.

Table 8. Offenses Known to Law Enforcement, by State and City, 2005—*Continued*

(Number.)

City	Population	Violent crime	Murder and non-negligent man-slaughter	Forcible rape	Robbery	Aggravated assault	Property crime	Burglary	Larceny-theft	Motor vehicle theft	Arson[1]
Laramie	26 585	26	2	0	1	23	824	91	700	33	2
Lovell	2 323	6	0	3	0	3	41	5	35	1	0
Lusk	1 348	3	0	0	0	3	15	8	7	0	0
Mills	2 891	9	0	0	0	9	132	23	102	7	0
Moorcroft	821	0	0	0	0	0	5	3	2	0	0
Newcastle	3 225	9	0	1	1	7	106	30	76	0	0
Pine Bluffs	1 187	4	0	0	1	3	41	8	31	2	0
Powell	5 279	14	0	5	0	9	233	37	193	3	1
Rawlins	8 680	34	0	3	4	27	422	57	332	33	1
Riverton	9 440	30	1	6	6	17	542	61	462	19	0
Rock Springs	18 848	110	1	10	7	92	800	151	600	49	5
Saratoga	1 719	13	0	0	0	13	59	3	56	0	0
Sheridan	16 206	22	0	2	1	19	450	40	392	18	0
Sundance	1 168	5	0	0	0	5	29	4	24	1	0
Thermopolis	2 969	4	0	1	0	3	95	5	89	1	0
Torrington	5 590	33	0	2	1	30	191	33	149	9	0
Wheatland	3 519	9	0	4	0	5	93	9	81	3	0
Worland	5 007	17	0	0	0	17	40	10	29	1	0

[1]The FBI does not publish arson data unless it receives data from either the agency or the state for all 12 months of the calendar year.

Table 9. Offenses Known to Law Enforcement, by State and University or College, 2005

(Number.)

School	Student enrollment[1]	Violent crime	Murder and non-negligent man-slaughter	Forcible rape	Robbery	Aggravated assault	Property crime	Burglary	Larceny-theft	Motor vehicle theft	Arson[2]
Alabama											
Alabama A&M University	6 323	1	0	0	0	1	84	35	47	2	. . .
Auburn University, Montgomery	5 123	0	0	0	0	0	2	0	2	0	. . .
Jacksonville State University	8 930	1	0	0	0	1	78	15	63	0	. . .
Troy University	20 855	2	0	1	1	0	158	4	153	1	1
University of Alabama											
Huntsville	7 036	0	0	0	0	0	106	4	101	1	. . .
Tuscaloosa	20 929	4	0	1	1	2	335	17	313	5	1
University of Montevallo	3 061	0	0	0	0	0	26	4	22	0	. . .
University of South Alabama	13 340	12	0	0	6	6	145	28	113	4	. . .
Alaska											
University of Alaska											
Anchorage	16 261	6	0	0	2	4	132	13	117	2	0
Fairbanks	8 693	3	0	0	0	3	86	4	80	2	0
Arizona											
Arizona State University, Main Campus	49 171	39	0	9	6	24	1 358	166	1 110	82	2
Central Arizona College	6 525	2	0	1	0	1	48	27	20	1	0
Northern Arizona University	19 137	22	0	5	2	15	442	60	373	9	3
Pima Community College	31 545	2	0	0	1	1	219	4	200	15	0
University of Arizona	36 932	14	0	4	4	6	1 142	121	916	105	3
Yavapai College	7 375	3	0	1	0	2	53	8	44	1	0
Arkansas											
Arkansas State University, Jonesboro	10 508	0	0	0	0	0	154	20	131	3	0
Arkansas Tech University	6 483	2	0	2	0	0	55	24	31	0	0
Henderson State University	3 569	1	0	0	1	0	28	11	17	0	0
Northwest Arkansas Community College	5 266	0	0	0	0	0	10	2	7	1	0
University of Arkansas											
Fayetteville	17 269	4	0	0	0	4	240	64	163	13	0
Little Rock	11 806	10	0	2	1	7	161	73	74	14	0
Medical Sciences	2 225	2	0	0	0	2	282	18	253	11	1
University of Central Arkansas	10 071	5	0	1	0	4	252	84	159	9	1
California											
Allan Hancock College	12 595	0	0	0	0	0	26	6	20	0	0
California State Polytechnic University											
Pomona	19 003	4	0	0	3	1	267	53	182	32	3
San Luis Obispo	17 582	1	0	0	0	1	211	10	192	9	0
California State University											
Bakersfield	7 755	2	0	0	0	2	66	10	55	1	0
Channel Islands	2 021	2	0	0	0	2	13	0	12	1	0
Chico	15 734	21	0	2	6	13	339	61	269	9	0
Dominguez Hills	12 613	4	0	1	2	1	124	22	85	17	0
East Bay	13 061	4	0	1	1	2	151	18	128	5	0
Fresno	19 781	8	0	1	3	4	328	49	268	11	1
Fullerton	32 744	6	0	2	1	3	219	44	158	17	0
Long Beach	33 479	7	0	2	1	4	276	22	172	82	0
Los Angeles	20 307	6	0	0	3	3	360	23	309	28	3
Monterey Bay	3 945	7	0	5	0	2	145	42	100	3	8
Northridge	31 341	18	0	2	8	8	253	103	124	26	0
Sacramento	27 972	7	0	2	3	2	282	31	237	14	0
San Bernardino	16 194	5	0	2	0	3	198	40	133	25	0
San Jose[3]	. . .	9	0	3	4	2	536	36	493	7	5
San Marcos	7 365	3	0	1	0	2	62	8	52	2	0
Stanislaus	7 858	2	0	2	0	0	72	6	51	15	0
College of the Sequoias	10 710	5	0	0	3	2	110	51	43	16	0
Contra Costa Community College	6 937	21	0	0	16	5	327	26	268	33	0
Cuesta College	10 114	0	0	0	0	0	32	4	27	1	0
El Camino College	24 732	7	0	0	7	0	158	17	127	14	0
Foothill-De Anza College	39 401	5	0	1	2	2	138	58	80	0	0
Fresno Community College	21 540	1	0	0	0	1	222	20	176	26	0
Humboldt State University	7 550	5	0	3	0	2	169	10	158	1	3
Marin Community College	6 883	0	0	0	0	0	37	4	31	2	0
Pasadena Community College	27 584	3	0	0	0	3	226	5	183	38	0
Reedley College	11 082	1	0	1	0	0	45	2	40	3	0
Riverside Community College	30 101	3	0	0	1	2	132	7	113	12	0
San Bernardino Community College	12 904	0	0	0	0	0	46	9	32	5	0
San Francisco State University	28 804	19	0	1	13	5	325	41	240	44	1
San Jose/Evergreen Community College	19 422	1	0	0	0	1	76	12	61	3	0
Santa Rosa Junior College	24 176	1	0	0	0	1	85	12	70	3	0
Solano Community College	11 471	1	0	1	0	0	42	1	39	2	0
Sonoma State University	7 977	2	0	2	0	0	125	26	90	9	1

Note: Caution should be exercised in making any intercampus comparisons or ranking schools, because school crime statistics are affected by a variety of factors. These include demographic characteristics of the surrounding community, the ratio of male to female students, the number of on-campus residents, the accessibility of outside visitors, the size of enrollment, etc.

[1]The student enrollment figures provided by the Department of Education are for the 2004 school year, the most recent available. Enrollment figures include full-time and part-time students.
[2]The FBI does not publish arson data unless it receives data from either the agency or the state for all 12 months of the calendar year.
[3]Student enrollment figures were not available.
. . . = Not available.

Table 9. Offenses Known to Law Enforcement, by State and University or College, 2005—*Continued*

(Number.)

School	Student enrollment[1]	Violent crime	Murder and non-negligent man-slaughter	Forcible rape	Robbery	Aggravated assault	Property crime	Burglary	Larceny-theft	Motor vehicle theft	Arson[2]
University of California											
Berkeley	32 803	25	0	3	15	7	864	74	767	23	4
Davis	29 210	4	0	1	2	1	564	53	494	17	0
Hastings College of Law	1 269	2	0	0	2	0	22	7	15	0	0
Irvine	24 344	5	0	2	0	3	536	67	441	28	1
Lawrence-Livermore Laboratory[3]	. . .	0	0	0	0	0	3	0	3	0	0
Los Angeles	35 966	37	0	7	13	17	1 133	297	790	46	1
Medical Center, Sacramento[3]	. . .	3	0	0	0	3	213	15	180	18	0
Riverside	17 104	13	0	1	2	10	355	29	303	23	0
San Diego	24 663	12	0	1	4	7	742	55	619	68	1
San Francisco	2 754	8	0	1	4	3	502	53	433	16	0
Santa Barbara	21 026	12	0	5	0	7	427	51	374	2	0
Santa Cruz	15 036	7	0	2	0	5	293	48	240	5	1
West Valley-Mission College	19 295	1	0	0	0	1	88	6	79	3	0
Colorado											
Arapahoe Community College	7 560	0	0	0	0	0	28	0	25	3	1
Auraria Higher Education Center[3]	. . .	3	0	0	0	3	228	15	205	8	1
Colorado School of Mines	4 101	7	0	2	1	4	62	2	57	3	2
Colorado State University											
Fort Collins	27 973	3	0	1	0	2	481	17	455	9	5
Pueblo	5 741	1	0	1	0	0	50	2	48	0	0
Fort Lewis College	4 194	4	0	0	0	4	84	27	55	2	2
Pikes Peak Community College	10 917	1	0	0	0	1	32	0	32	0	0
University of Colorado											
Boulder	32 362	18	0	4	4	10	668	107	536	25	20
Colorado Springs	9 039	0	0	0	0	0	82	4	77	1	0
Health Sciences Center	3 165	0	0	0	0	0	52	5	45	2	0
Health Sciences Center, Fitzsimons Campus[3]	. . .	0	0	0	0	0	33	0	31	2	0
University of Northern Colorado	13 156	9	0	1	0	8	304	24	275	5	3
Connecticut											
Central Connecticut State University	12 320	0	0	0	0	0	101	17	83	1	0
Eastern Connecticut State University	5 156	4	0	4	0	0	94	4	89	1	0
Southern Connecticut State University	12 177	2	0	2	0	0	115	18	95	2	0
University of Connecticut											
Health Center[3]	. . .	1	0	0	0	1	58	2	56	0	0
Storrs, Avery Point, and Hartford[3]	. . .	5	0	2	0	3	268	56	207	5	0
Western Connecticut State University	5 884	2	0	0	1	1	60	8	52	0	2
Yale University	11 441	11	0	5	5	1	398	71	322	5	0
Delaware											
Delaware State University	3 270	6	0	1	2	3	44	11	33	0	0
University of Delaware	21 238	18	0	2	10	6	349	38	307	4	5
Florida											
Florida A&M University	13 067	23	0	1	15	7	406	44	354	8	9
Florida Atlantic University	25 319	4	0	2	0	2	280	52	197	31	3
Florida Gulf Coast University	5 955	5	0	3	0	2	33	6	27	0	0
Florida International University	34 865	5	0	0	1	4	418	112	289	17	1
Florida State University											
Panama City[3]	. . .	0	0	0	0	0	3	0	3	0	0
Tallahassee	38 431	29	0	7	9	13	529	30	479	20	0
New College of Florida	692	1	0	0	1	0	50	3	45	2	0
Pensacola Junior College	10 879	2	0	0	0	2	42	4	38	0	0
Santa Fe Community College	13 888	3	0	0	1	2	88	2	84	2	0
Tallahassee Community College	12 775	0	0	0	0	0	95	1	90	4	0
University of Central Florida	42 465	19	1	5	4	9	482	84	373	25	0
University of Florida	47 993	17	0	2	4	11	681	44	616	21	1
University of North Florida	14 533	6	0	0	0	6	161	6	155	0	1
University of South Florida											
St. Petersburg[3]	. . .	0	0	0	0	0	37	0	33	4	0
Tampa	42 238	19	0	2	2	15	549	204	296	49	2
University of West Florida	9 518	1	0	0	0	1	81	9	70	2	0
Georgia											
Abraham Baldwin Agricultural College	3 362	4	0	0	0	4	65	8	54	3	0
Albany State University	3 668	0	0	0	0	0	91	14	76	1	0
Armstrong Atlantic State University	7 009	4	0	1	2	1	33	5	27	1	1
Augusta State University	6 353	0	0	0	0	0	27	0	27	0	0
Berry College	2 008	0	0	0	0	0	51	19	32	0	0
Clark Atlanta University	4 588	23	0	0	17	6	177	44	120	13	0
Coastal Georgia Community College	2 879	0	0	0	0	0	9	0	9	0	0
Dalton State College	4 250	0	0	0	0	0	7	2	5	0	0
Emory University	11 781	10	0	3	0	7	420	35	380	5	2
Fort Valley State University	2 558	0	0	0	0	0	102	6	95	1	. . .

Note: Caution should be exercised in making any intercampus comparisons or ranking schools, because school crime statistics are affected by a variety of factors. These include demographic characteristics of the surrounding community, the ratio of male to female students, the number of on-campus residents, the accessibility of outside visitors, the size of enrollment, etc.

[1]The student enrollment figures provided by the Department of Education are for the 2004 school year, the most recent available. Enrollment figures include full-time and part-time students.
[2]The FBI does not publish arson data unless it receives data from either the agency or the state for all 12 months of the calendar year.
[3]Student enrollment figures were not available.
. . . = Not available.

Table 9. Offenses Known to Law Enforcement, by State and University or College, 2005—*Continued*

(Number.)

School	Student enrollment[1]	Violent crime	Murder and non-negligent man-slaughter	Forcible rape	Robbery	Aggravated assault	Property crime	Burglary	Larceny-theft	Motor vehicle theft	Arson[2]
Georgia College and State University	5 531	1	0	1	0	0	48	4	42	2	. . .
Georgia Institute of Technology	16 841	17	0	0	9	8	605	106	471	28	1
Georgia Perimeter College	20 316	4	0	0	0	4	170	2	149	19	0
Georgia Southern University	16 100	3	0	1	2	0	198	0	196	2	0
Georgia Southwestern State University	2 323	3	0	0	1	2	58	3	53	2	0
Georgia State University	27 261	17	0	0	14	3	488	27	457	4	. . .
Kennesaw State University	17 955	4	0	1	1	2	142	14	122	6	0
Medical College of Georgia	2 127	4	0	0	2	2	119	0	107	12	0
Mercer University	7 180	3	0	1	1	1	74	4	69	1	0
Middle Georgia College	2 626	0	0	0	0	0	40	2	38	0	0
Morris-Brown College[3]	. . .	0	0	0	0	0	6	1	5	0	0
North Georgia College	4 552	0	0	0	0	0	41	6	35	0	0
Southern Polytechnic State University	3 801	0	0	0	0	0	64	8	55	1	0
South Georgia College	1 443	0	0	0	0	0	11	4	7	0	0
University of Georgia	33 405	6	0	1	3	2	449	22	417	10	3
Valdosta State University	10 400	0	0	0	0	0	149	2	145	2	0
Wesleyan College	654	0	0	0	0	0	14	0	13	1	0
Young Harris College	605	0	0	0	0	0	0	0	0	0	0
Indiana											
Ball State University	20 507	7	0	0	2	5	368	53	312	3	0
Indiana State University	11 200	2	0	0	0	2	260	31	223	6	0
Indiana University											
Bloomington	37 821	35	0	16	2	17	564	52	501	11	1
Gary	5 138	4	0	0	2	2	36	2	34	0	0
Indianapolis[3]	. . .	10	0	3	7	0	377	47	319	11	0
New Albany	6 238	0	0	0	0	0	34	7	27	0	0
Marian College	1 685	2	0	0	0	2	4	0	3	1	0
Purdue University	40 108	5	0	2	0	3	513	17	492	4	0
Iowa											
Iowa State University	26 380	13	0	4	2	7	309	36	271	2	9
University of Iowa	28 442	12	0	2	0	10	271	32	234	5	2
University of Northern Iowa	12 927	2	0	1	0	1	89	4	85	0	3
Kansas											
Emporia State University	6 194	1	0	0	0	1	49	18	31	0	0
Fort Hays State University	8 500	0	0	0	0	0	21	7	14	0	0
Kansas State University	23 151	4	0	1	0	3	203	52	150	1	3
Pittsburg State University	6 537	1	0	1	0	0	74	10	63	1	3
University of Kansas											
Main Campus	26 980	4	0	0	0	4	234	81	147	6	0
Medical Center	1 925	5	0	0	1	4	219	2	182	35	0
Washburn University	7 251	1	0	1	0	0	95	19	75	1	0
Kentucky											
Eastern Kentucky University	16 183	1	0	0	0	1	203	22	180	1	16
Kentucky State University	2 335	1	0	0	1	0	29	10	18	1	0
Morehead State University	9 278	2	0	2	0	0	61	5	53	3	0
Murray State University	10 120	4	0	1	2	1	114	19	93	2	2
Northern Kentucky University	13 903	2	0	1	0	1	165	5	160	0	0
University of Kentucky	25 686	21	0	8	6	7	681	36	638	7	7
University of Louisville	20 729	2	0	0	2	0	339	11	313	15	2
Western Kentucky University	18 485	3	0	0	2	1	220	30	183	7	2
Louisiana											
Delgado Community College	16 669	0	0	0	0	0	44	3	41	0	0
Grambling State University	5 039	4	0	1	0	3	159	88	66	5	1
Louisiana State University											
Baton Rouge[3]	. . .	14	0	0	3	11	497	42	432	23	0
Health Sciences Center, Shreveport	688	5	0	3	1	1	104	1	101	2	0
Shreveport	4 401	4	0	0	0	4	29	2	27	0	0
Louisiana Tech University	11 691	2	0	0	0	2	177	42	127	8	2
McNeese State University	8 785	5	0	0	0	5	113	13	99	1	0
Nicholls State University	7 473	5	0	0	0	5	41	3	38	0	1
Northwestern State University	10 546	6	0	3	2	1	102	50	46	6	0
Southeastern Louisiana University	15 465	12	0	1	1	10	241	45	188	8	4
Southern University and A&M College											
Baton Rouge	9 438	10	0	2	3	5	43	4	36	3	0
New Orleans	3 647	1	0	0	0	1	11	0	11	0	0
Tulane University	12 667	8	0	3	1	4	180	26	149	5	0
University of Louisiana, Monroe	8 831	8	0	0	1	7	138	15	121	2	0
University of New Orleans	17 350	2	0	0	1	1	144	9	129	6	0
Maine											
University of Maine											
Farmington	2 347	1	0	0	0	1	27	5	22	0	2
Orono	11 358	3	0	2	0	1	276	14	261	1	31
University of Southern Maine	11 089	1	0	0	0	1	100	17	82	1	0

Note: Caution should be exercised in making any intercampus comparisons or ranking schools, because school crime statistics are affected by a variety of factors. These include demographic characteristics of the surrounding community, the ratio of male to female students, the number of on-campus residents, the accessibility of outside visitors, the size of enrollment, etc.

[1]The student enrollment figures provided by the Department of Education are for the 2004 school year, the most recent available. Enrollment figures include full-time and part-time students.
[2]The FBI does not publish arson data unless it receives data from either the agency or the state for all 12 months of the calendar year.
[3]Student enrollment figures were not available.
. . . = Not available.

Table 9. Offenses Known to Law Enforcement, by State and University or College, 2005—*Continued*

(Number.)

School	Student enrollment[1]	Violent crime	Murder and non-negligent man-slaughter	Forcible rape	Robbery	Aggravated assault	Property crime	Burglary	Larceny-theft	Motor vehicle theft	Arson[2]
Maryland											
Bowie State University	5 415	7	0	0	2	5	94	43	44	7	0
Coppin State University	3 875	12	0	0	4	8	49	6	41	2	0
Frostburg State University	5 327	8	0	0	0	8	104	20	82	2	1
Morgan State University	6 891	15	0	0	15	0	144	37	102	5	0
Salisbury University	6 942	5	0	1	2	2	124	4	120	0	0
St. Mary's College	1 935	2	0	1	0	1	87	6	79	2	0
Towson University	17 667	7	0	0	1	6	136	26	109	1	4
University of Baltimore	5 045	0	0	0	0	0	84	7	66	11	0
University of Maryland											
Baltimore City	5 602	16	0	0	5	11	166	0	165	1	0
Baltimore County	11 852	1	0	0	1	0	154	14	138	2	0
College Park	34 933	38	0	2	18	18	661	107	511	43	3
Eastern Shore	3 775	5	0	0	3	2	170	42	127	1	2
Massachusetts											
Bentley College	5 582	11	0	3	0	8	113	25	86	2	0
Boston College	14 561	13	0	3	3	7	189	57	132	0	0
Boston University	29 596	14	0	1	3	10	538	104	428	6	. . .
Brandeis University	5 072	5	0	2	0	3	81	39	42	0	0
Bristol Community College	6 864	2	0	0	1	1	14	2	12	0	0
Clark University	3 115	12	0	0	7	5	50	12	38	0	0
Emerson College	4 398	6	0	2	0	4	39	8	31	0	0
Fitchburg State College	5 201	3	0	0	0	3	103	2	100	1	0
Framingham State College	6 016	4	0	0	0	4	22	6	16	0	0
Harvard University	24 648	7	0	1	1	5	603	387	214	2	0
Holyoke Community College	6 298	3	0	0	2	1	35	0	34	1	0
Lasell College	1 196	0	0	0	0	0	19	6	13	0	0
Massachusetts College of Art	2 047	4	0	1	3	0	35	4	31	0	0
Massachusetts College of Liberal Arts	1 831	5	0	0	0	5	35	1	34	0	0
Massachusetts Institute of Technology	10 320	4	0	0	1	3	520	68	449	3	0
Massasoit Community College	6 908	0	0	0	0	0	36	2	33	1	0
Merrimack College	2 352	15	0	3	0	12	65	26	39	0	0
Mount Holyoke College	2 145	4	0	3	0	1	91	8	82	1	0
Northeastern University	22 932	10	0	3	4	3	358	25	331	2	0
North Shore Community College	6 690	0	0	0	0	0	11	1	9	1	0
Quinsigamond Community College	5 794	0	0	0	0	0	19	0	19	0	0
Salem State College	9 347	6	0	3	0	3	108	41	65	2	0
Springfield College	5 062	12	0	5	1	6	80	22	49	9	0
Tufts University											
Medford	9 690	3	0	1	1	1	120	22	95	3	0
Suffolk[3]	. . .	2	0	0	2	0	54	1	53	0	0
Worcester[3]	. . .	0	0	0	0	0	5	0	5	0	0
University of Massachusetts											
Amherst	24 646	20	0	5	3	12	253	120	126	7	4
Dartmouth	8 299	14	0	0	0	14	141	29	109	3	0
Harbor Campus, Boston	11 682	1	0	0	0	1	103	4	99	0	0
Medical Center, Worcester	871	11	0	1	0	10	130	2	123	5	0
Wellesley College	2 289	0	0	0	0	0	56	26	30	0	0
Westfield State College	4 914	0	0	0	0	0	44	10	34	0	0
Michigan											
Central Michigan University	27 683	4	0	3	0	1	219	4	215	0	0
Delta College	10 459	0	0	0	0	0	36	1	35	0	0
Eastern Michigan University	23 862	14	0	5	4	5	402	39	349	14	6
Ferris State University	11 803	4	0	1	0	3	135	3	131	1	0
Grand Rapids Community College	14 144	1	0	0	0	1	138	3	134	1	3
Grand Valley State University	22 063	4	0	2	1	1	134	5	129	0	1
Lansing Community College	19 471	3	1	0	1	1	121	1	120	0	0
Michigan State University	44 836	30	0	3	9	18	900	116	773	11	4
Michigan Technological University	6 527	0	0	0	0	0	83	1	82	0	0
Mott Community College	10 328	2	0	0	0	2	103	0	98	5	1
Northern Michigan University	9 331	5	0	1	0	4	159	2	154	3	0
Oakland Community College	24 296	0	0	0	0	0	105	0	102	3	0
Oakland University	16 902	4	0	2	0	2	126	9	114	3	1
Saginaw Valley State University	9 448	3	0	2	0	1	98	8	89	1	0
University of Michigan											
Ann Arbor	39 533	18	0	1	6	11	928	45	866	17	11
Dearborn	8 420	0	0	0	0	0	57	1	48	8	0
Flint	6 188	0	0	0	0	0	77	6	69	2	0
Minnesota											
University of Minnesota											
Duluth	10 366	0	0	0	0	0	77	5	72	0	1
Twin Cities	50 954	33	0	4	20	9	788	48	716	24	1

Note: Caution should be exercised in making any intercampus comparisons or ranking schools, because school crime statistics are affected by a variety of factors. These include demographic characteristics of the surrounding community, the ratio of male to female students, the number of on-campus residents, the accessibility of outside visitors, the size of enrollment, etc.

[1]The student enrollment figures provided by the Department of Education are for the 2004 school year, the most recent available. Enrollment figures include full-time and part-time students.
[2]The FBI does not publish arson data unless it receives data from either the agency or the state for all 12 months of the calendar year.
[3]Student enrollment figures were not available.
. . . = Not available.

Table 9. Offenses Known to Law Enforcement, by State and University or College, 2005—*Continued*

(Number.)

School	Student enrollment[1]	Violent crime	Murder and non-negligent man-slaughter	Forcible rape	Robbery	Aggravated assault	Property crime	Burglary	Larceny-theft	Motor vehicle theft	Arson[2]
Mississippi											
Coahoma Community College	1 961	0	0	0	0	0	9	8	1	0	0
Hinds Community College	9 822	3	0	0	0	3	69	17	50	2	0
Jackson State University	8 351	14	0	0	1	13	174	37	124	13	0
Mississippi State University	15 934	4	0	2	1	1	143	9	133	1	0
University of Mississippi, Oxford	14 497	0	0	0	0	0	134	4	128	2	0
Missouri											
Central Missouri State University	10 051	10	0	0	0	10	170	52	114	4	1
Lincoln University	3 275	3	0	0	0	3	63	33	30	0	0
Mineral Area College	2 820	0	0	0	0	0	6	2	4	0	0
Missouri Western State University	5 065	3	0	1	0	2	98	19	77	2	0
Northwest Missouri State University	6 230	5	0	2	0	3	39	1	38	0	1
Southeast Missouri State University	9 615	3	0	1	1	1	84	4	80	0	0
St. Louis Community College, Meramec	12 120	0	0	0	0	0	25	1	23	1	0
Truman State University	5 948	2	0	1	0	1	75	9	65	1	0
University of Missouri											
Columbia	27 003	12	1	0	3	8	340	26	309	5	4
Kansas City	14 256	3	0	0	3	0	196	43	145	8	0
Rolla	5 404	3	0	0	1	2	63	20	43	0	1
St. Louis	15 498	7	0	1	1	5	149	14	130	5	0
Washington University	13 210	3	0	0	0	3	213	14	191	8	2
Nebraska											
University of Nebraska											
Kearney	6 382	1	0	1	0	0	72	19	53	0	0
Lincoln	21 792	6	0	2	3	1	371	68	297	6	1
Nevada											
Truckee Meadows Community College	11 174	0	0	0	0	0	23	11	12	0	0
University of Nevada											
Las Vegas	27 339	13	0	3	4	6	389	95	258	36	2
Reno	15 950	21	0	8	3	10	187	29	150	8	4
New Jersey											
Brookdale Community College	13 083	2	0	0	0	2	41	1	40	0	0
Essex County College	11 268	3	0	0	1	2	97	0	90	7	0
Kean University of New Jersey	12 897	7	0	3	0	4	159	13	142	4	2
Middlesex County College	12 984	0	0	0	0	0	57	1	56	0	0
Monmouth University	6 329	3	0	2	1	0	83	9	74	0	0
Montclair State University	15 637	12	0	6	2	4	228	30	194	4	0
New Jersey Institute of Technology	8 249	10	0	1	8	1	161	8	125	28	0
Richard Stockton College	7 002	2	0	0	0	2	72	12	60	0	0
Rowan University	9 688	7	0	5	2	0	179	17	159	3	0
Rutgers University											
Camden	5 563	3	0	0	1	2	88	15	71	2	0
Newark	10 293	6	0	0	3	3	176	16	142	18	0
New Brunswick	34 696	13	0	6	4	3	581	159	410	12	3
Stevens Institute of Technology	4 638	1	0	0	0	1	54	11	43	0	2
The College of New Jersey	6 812	4	0	3	0	1	117	28	85	4	0
University of Medicine and Dentistry											
Camden[3]	. . .	0	0	0	0	0	0	0	0	0	0
Newark	5 329	58	0	0	30	28	418	17	358	43	0
New Brunswick[3]	. . .	3	0	0	0	3	52	2	50	0	0
Piscataway[3]	. . .	1	0	0	0	1	8	0	8	0	0
William Paterson University	11 409	3	0	0	1	2	103	18	84	1	0
New Mexico											
Eastern New Mexico University	3 939	0	0	0	0	0	46	8	36	2	0
New Mexico State University	16 428	15	0	2	1	12	397	51	332	14	5
University of New Mexico	26 242	24	0	1	7	16	798	49	682	67	5
New York											
Cornell University	19 518	4	0	2	1	1	442	59	375	8	. . .
Ithaca College	6 337	1	0	0	0	1	120	9	111	0	. . .
Rensselaer Polytechnic Institute	6 696	2	0	0	1	1	132	21	110	1	. . .
State University of New York											
Albany	16 293	2	0	0	2	0	172	12	160	0	. . .
Maritime College	1 201	0	0	0	0	0	52	20	32	0	. . .
Stony Brook	21 685	11	0	0	2	9	541	54	480	7	. . .
State University of New York Agricultural and Technical College											
Alfred	3 597	8	0	2	1	5	134	14	117	3	. . .
Canton	2 518	1	0	0	0	1	63	1	62	0	. . .
Cobleskill	2 514	2	0	1	0	1	68	16	52	0	. . .
Farmingdale[3]	. . .	0	0	0	0	0	65	0	59	6	. . .
Morrisville[3]	. . .	1	0	0	1	0	101	8	93	0	. . .

Note: Caution should be exercised in making any intercampus comparisons or ranking schools, because school crime statistics are affected by a variety of factors. These include demographic characteristics of the surrounding community, the ratio of male to female students, the number of on-campus residents, the accessibility of outside visitors, the size of enrollment, etc.

[1]The student enrollment figures provided by the Department of Education are for the 2004 school year, the most recent available. Enrollment figures include full-time and part-time students.
[2]The FBI does not publish arson data unless it receives data from either the agency or the state for all 12 months of the calendar year.
[3]Student enrollment figures were not available.
. . . = Not available.

Table 9. Offenses Known to Law Enforcement, by State and University or College, 2005—*Continued*

(Number.)

School	Student enrollment[1]	Violent crime	Murder and non-negligent man-slaughter	Forcible rape	Robbery	Aggravated assault	Property crime	Burglary	Larceny-theft	Motor vehicle theft	Arson[2]
State University of New York College											
Cortland	7 350	2	0	1	1	0	133	34	98	1	. . .
Fredonia	5 359	2	0	0	1	1	134	14	119	1	. . .
Geneseo	5 573	1	0	1	0	0	129	6	121	2	. . .
New Paltz	7 603	2	0	1	1	0	101	14	87	0	. . .
Old Westbury	3 359	0	0	0	0	0	67	7	59	1	. . .
Oneonta	5 806	4	0	3	0	1	85	9	75	1	. . .
Oswego	8 289	1	0	1	0	0	119	29	87	3	. . .
Plattsburgh	5 909	1	0	0	1	0	120	27	93	0	. . .
Potsdam	4 311	0	0	0	0	0	83	17	65	1	. . .
Purchase	3 832	7	0	2	4	1	169	38	130	1	. . .
Utica-Rome[3]	. . .	0	0	0	0	0	28	2	26	0	. . .
United States Merchant Marine Academy	962	0	0	0	0	0	36	17	19	0	. . .
North Carolina											
Appalachian State University	14 653	3	0	3	0	0	143	12	130	1	2
Duke University	12 770	12	0	1	5	6	690	41	636	13	4
East Carolina University	22 767	5	0	2	0	3	226	17	207	2	2
Elizabeth City State University	2 470	3	0	0	1	2	92	51	38	3	0
Elon University	4 796	0	0	0	0	0	71	20	51	0	0
Fayetteville State University	5 441	5	0	0	1	4	128	2	122	4	0
North Carolina Agricultural and Technical State University	10 383	19	0	2	9	8	320	40	279	1	3
North Carolina Central University	7 727	12	0	1	4	7	292	28	251	13	1
North Carolina School of the Arts	788	0	0	0	0	0	47	2	45	0	0
North Carolina State University, Raleigh	29 957	11	0	3	2	6	418	59	356	3	0
University of North Carolina											
Asheville	3 574	0	0	0	0	0	29	4	25	0	1
Chapel Hill	26 878	7	0	2	2	3	468	38	426	4	0
Charlotte	19 846	9	0	1	2	6	248	36	195	17	1
Greensboro	15 329	6	0	0	3	3	65	0	63	2	0
Pembroke	5 027	3	0	0	2	1	92	12	77	3	0
Wilmington	11 574	6	0	5	1	0	226	32	193	1	1
Wake Forest University	6 504	6	0	3	1	2	121	38	83	0	0
Western Carolina University	8 396	4	0	1	0	3	157	31	126	0	6
Winston-Salem State University	4 805	3	0	0	1	2	100	4	93	3	0
North Dakota											
North Dakota State College of Science	2 481	3	0	2	0	1	32	2	30	0	0
North Dakota State University	12 026	2	0	0	0	2	135	17	118	0	0
University of North Dakota	13 187	5	0	0	0	5	197	21	171	5	0
Ohio											
Bowling Green State University	18 989	6	0	2	1	3	253	19	234	0	1
Cleveland State University	15 664	8	0	0	8	0	246	6	218	22	2
Cuyahoga Community College	24 664	7	0	0	2	5	143	6	135	2	0
Kent State University	24 347	7	0	0	3	4	237	28	209	0	0
Lakeland Community College	8 605	0	0	0	0	0	19	0	19	0	0
Marietta College	1 480	2	0	2	0	0	45	26	19	0	0
Miami University	17 161	3	0	1	0	2	195	27	168	0	0
Muskingum College	2 176	0	0	0	0	0	19	9	10	0	0
Ohio State University	50 995	17	0	5	9	3	1 151	349	779	23	7
Ohio University	20 143	8	0	4	0	4	304	58	246	0	0
University of Cincinnati	27 178	15	0	4	6	5	643	45	595	3	3
University of Toledo	19 480	7	0	0	1	6	434	100	325	9	2
Wright State University	15 985	5	0	2	1	2	194	2	186	6	0
Youngstown State University	13 157	0	0	0	0	0	271	20	243	8	1
Oklahoma											
Cameron University	5 933	0	0	0	0	0	26	2	24	0	0
East Central University	4 651	0	0	0	0	0	18	3	15	0	0
Murray State College	2 045	0	0	0	0	0	3	0	3	0	0
Northeastern Oklahoma A&M College	2 032	8	0	2	4	2	37	17	20	0	1
Northeastern State University	9 455	5	0	0	0	5	94	12	80	2	0
Oklahoma State University											
Main Campus	23 819	5	0	1	1	3	267	60	204	3	2
Okmulgee	2 677	3	0	0	0	3	36	11	23	2	0
Tulsa[3]	. . .	0	0	0	0	0	12	5	6	1	0
Rogers State University	3 754	0	0	0	0	0	24	3	21	0	0
Seminole State College	2 178	0	0	0	0	0	19	0	19	0	0
Southeastern Oklahoma State University	3 983	0	0	0	0	0	34	4	28	2	2
Southwestern Oklahoma State University	5 310	0	0	0	0	0	49	14	35	0	0
Tulsa Community College	17 143	0	0	0	0	0	31	4	26	1	0
University of Central Oklahoma	14 598	6	0	4	0	2	115	6	105	4	0
University of Oklahoma											
Health Sciences Center	3 398	3	0	0	2	1	240	24	209	7	0
Norman	27 483	10	0	2	5	3	304	47	245	12	0

Note: Caution should be exercised in making any intercampus comparisons or ranking schools, because school crime statistics are affected by a variety of factors. These include demographic characteristics of the surrounding community, the ratio of male to female students, the number of on-campus residents, the accessibility of outside visitors, the size of enrollment, etc.

[1]The student enrollment figures provided by the Department of Education are for the 2004 school year, the most recent available. Enrollment figures include full-time and part-time students.
[2]The FBI does not publish arson data unless it receives data from either the agency or the state for all 12 months of the calendar year.
[3]Student enrollment figures were not available.
. . . = Not available.

Table 9. Offenses Known to Law Enforcement, by State and University or College, 2005—*Continued*

(Number.)

School	Student enrollment[1]	Violent crime	Murder and non-negligent man-slaughter	Forcible rape	Robbery	Aggravated assault	Property crime	Burglary	Larceny-theft	Motor vehicle theft	Arson[2]
Pennsylvania											
Bloomsburg University	8 304	1	0	0	0	1	73	2	71	0	0
California University	6 640	0	0	0	0	0	47	1	45	1	0
Cheyney University	1 545	12	0	1	4	7	52	13	39	0	1
Clarion University	6 421	1	0	0	0	1	50	22	28	0	0
Community College of Beaver County	2 490	0	0	0	0	0	0	0	0	0	0
Edinboro University	7 773	5	0	1	1	3	83	5	78	0	1
Elizabethtown College	2 125	0	0	0	0	0	18	1	17	0	0
Indiana University	13 998	19	0	4	0	15	158	26	129	3	0
Kutztown University	9 585	13	0	8	1	4	149	8	138	3	0
Lehigh University	6 641	2	0	0	2	0	73	2	69	2	0
Lock Haven University	5 126	0	0	0	0	0	47	5	42	0	0
Mansfield University	3 556	0	0	0	0	0	23	0	23	0	0
Millersville University	7 998	5	0	0	0	5	83	5	78	0	0
Moravian College	2 043	1	0	1	0	0	34	2	32	0	0
Pennsylvania State University											
Altoona	3 766	0	0	0	0	0	48	3	45	0	0
Beaver	666	0	0	0	0	0	9	0	9	0	0
Behrend	3 593	0	0	0	0	0	36	5	31	0	3
Berks	2 416	0	0	0	0	0	31	0	28	3	0
Harrisburg	3 729	0	0	0	0	0	14	0	14	0	0
Hazelton	1 114	0	0	0	0	0	23	1	21	1	0
Mont Alto	1 028	1	0	0	0	1	16	0	16	0	0
University Park	41 289	8	0	0	3	5	566	45	517	4	2
Shippensburg University	7 653	3	0	0	0	3	66	2	64	0	0
Slippery Rock University	7 928	0	0	0	0	0	121	2	119	0	0
University of Pittsburgh, Pittsburgh	26 731	11	0	1	6	4	473	25	440	8	1
West Chester University	12 822	7	0	0	0	7	153	70	82	1	0
Rhode Island[4]											
Brown University	8 004	2	0	1	0	1	230	15	215	0	0
University of Rhode Island	14 749	2	0	1	0	1	199	22	176	1	1
South Carolina											
Benedict College	2 769	12	0	0	6	6	257	104	146	7	1
Bob Jones University	. . .	0	0	0	0	0	0	0	0	0	0
Clemson University	17 110	4	0	2	0	2	246	37	190	19	0
Coastal Carolina University	7 021	7	0	1	1	5	108	37	67	4	0
College of Charleston	11 607	3	0	0	2	1	193	33	159	1	1
Columbia College	1 453	1	0	1	0	0	4	1	2	1	0
Denmark Technical College	1 423	2	0	0	0	2	3	1	1	1	0
Francis Marion University	3 698	1	0	0	0	1	59	4	52	3	0
Lander University	2 918	1	0	0	0	1	40	9	30	1	0
Medical University of South Carolina	2 433	5	0	0	1	4	176	2	172	2	0
Midlands Technical College	10 710	0	0	0	0	0	68	2	66	0	0
South Carolina State University	4 294	16	0	0	10	6	280	66	211	3	1
The Citadel	3 351	0	0	0	0	0	27	0	26	1	0
Trident Technical College	11 795	0	0	0	0	0	43	1	40	2	0
University of South Carolina											
Aiken	3 382	1	0	1	0	0	14	1	12	1	0
Columbia	25 596	22	0	3	7	12	573	30	529	14	3
Upstate	4 370	2	0	0	0	2	26	0	26	0	0
Winthrop University	6 447	2	0	0	0	2	100	24	74	2	0
Tennessee											
Austin Peay State University	8 650	5	0	0	2	3	73	2	63	8	0
East Tennessee State University	11 869	3	0	1	0	2	150	35	109	6	2
Middle Tennessee State University	22 322	6	0	0	2	4	284	39	239	6	1
Southwest Tennessee Community College	11 791	1	0	0	0	1	86	21	58	7	0
Tennessee State University	9 100	12	1	0	3	8	165	22	120	23	1
Tennessee Technological University	9 217	3	0	3	0	0	110	18	90	2	3
University of Memphis	20 668	8	0	0	4	4	265	44	204	17	1
University of Tennessee											
Chattanooga	8 689	8	0	2	2	4	261	88	171	2	3
Knoxville	27 792	8	0	2	2	4	414	13	388	13	5
Martin	6 098	1	0	0	0	1	52	7	43	2	0
Vanderbilt University	11 294	20	0	6	4	10	662	104	541	17	2
Volunteer State Community College	7 044	0	0	0	0	0	27	0	26	1	0

Note: Caution should be exercised in making any intercampus comparisons or ranking schools, because school crime statistics are affected by a variety of factors. These include demographic characteristics of the surrounding community, the ratio of male to female students, the number of on-campus residents, the accessibility of outside visitors, the size of enrollment, etc.

[1]The student enrollment figures provided by the Department of Education are for the 2004 school year, the most recent available. Enrollment figures include full-time and part-time students.
[2]The FBI does not publish arson data unless it receives data from either the agency or the state for all 12 months of the calendar year.
[4]Because of changes in the state/local agency's reporting practices, figures are not comparable to previous years' data.
. . . = Not available.

Table 9. Offenses Known to Law Enforcement, by State and University or College, 2005—*Continued*

(Number.)

School	Student enrollment[1]	Violent crime	Murder and non-negligent man-slaughter	Forcible rape	Robbery	Aggravated assault	Property crime	Burglary	Larceny-theft	Motor vehicle theft	Arson[2]
Texas											
Abilene Christian University	4 761	1	0	0	0	1	93	28	62	3	0
Alamo Community College District	. . .	3	0	1	0	2	328	1	319	8	0
Alvin Community College	3 932	1	0	0	1	0	11	0	9	2	0
Amarillo College	10 701	0	0	0	0	0	56	2	52	2	0
Angelo State University	6 137	2	0	0	0	2	78	6	71	1	0
Austin College	1 323	1	0	0	0	1	36	3	33	0	0
Baylor Health Care System	. . .	3	0	0	1	2	521	16	486	19	0
Baylor University, Waco	13 799	6	0	0	0	6	275	36	228	11	0
Central Texas College	18 351	1	0	0	0	1	23	1	22	0	0
College of the Mainland	3 948	0	0	0	0	0	38	0	36	2	0
Eastfield College	11 690	2	0	1	1	0	86	3	79	4	0
El Paso Community College	26 078	0	0	0	0	0	117	1	114	2	0
Grayson County College	3 918	0	0	0	0	0	19	3	16	0	1
Hardin-Simmons University	2 392	0	0	0	0	0	52	8	43	1	0
Houston Baptist University	2 227	1	0	0	0	1	16	8	8	0	0
Lamar University, Beaumont	10 804	4	0	3	0	1	139	8	127	4	0
Laredo Community College	9 032	0	0	0	0	0	24	1	21	2	0
McLennan Community College	7 531	0	0	0	0	0	60	0	58	2	0
Midwestern State University	6 348	5	0	2	1	2	46	6	40	0	0
Mountain View College	6 480	0	0	0	0	0	28	0	26	2	0
North Lake College	8 779	1	0	0	0	1	49	6	42	1	0
Paris Junior College	4 212	0	0	0	0	0	22	7	15	0	0
Prairie View A&M University	8 350	19	0	0	3	16	278	112	153	13	1
Rice University	4 855	0	0	0	0	0	194	51	143	0	0
Richland College	13 922	2	0	1	0	1	122	0	112	10	0
Southern Methodist University	10 901	3	0	0	0	3	239	20	211	8	1
South Plains College	9 476	0	0	0	0	0	15	1	14	0	0
Southwestern University	1 277	2	0	2	0	0	41	2	36	3	0
Stephen F. Austin State University	11 374	5	0	1	0	4	201	40	160	1	1
St. Mary's University	4 110	0	0	0	0	0	102	7	91	4	0
Sul Ross State University	2 993	0	0	0	0	0	44	9	35	0	0
Tarleton State University	9 033	0	0	0	0	0	52	5	47	0	0
Texas A&M International University	4 269	5	0	1	0	4	29	7	22	0	0
Texas A&M University											
College Station	44 435	8	0	4	3	1	659	67	585	7	0
Commerce	8 620	7	0	0	1	6	123	31	89	3	1
Corpus Christi	8 227	3	0	1	0	2	71	9	60	2	0
Galveston	1 615	1	0	0	0	1	46	9	37	0	0
Kingsville	7 126	1	0	0	0	1	118	26	92	0	2
Texas Christian University	8 632	0	0	0	0	0	166	5	154	7	3
Texas Southern University	11 635	18	0	0	9	9	281	68	195	18	2
Texas State Technical College											
Harlingen	4 456	0	0	0	0	0	46	7	38	1	0
Waco	4 418	13	0	1	2	10	178	43	130	5	2
Texas State University, San Marcos	26 783	1	0	0	0	1	258	38	217	3	0
Texas Technological University, Lubbock	28 325	8	0	1	1	6	362	39	323	0	1
Texas Woman's University	10 750	2	0	0	2	0	41	2	38	1	0
Trinity University	2 640	1	0	1	0	0	157	38	113	6	0
Tyler Junior College	9 528	0	0	0	0	0	80	4	73	3	0
University of Houston											
Central Campus	35 180	15	0	3	8	4	514	27	450	37	3
Clearlake	7 785	0	0	0	0	0	25	0	25	0	0
Downtown Campus	11 408	5	0	0	3	2	72	1	66	5	0
University of Mary Hardin-Baylor	2 694	0	0	0	0	0	47	14	33	0	0
University of North Texas											
Denton	31 155	6	0	2	2	2	227	32	187	8	1
Health Science Center	1 021	0	0	0	0	0	15	0	15	0	0
University of Texas											
Arlington	25 297	19	0	0	4	15	403	49	334	20	0
Austin	50 377	14	0	0	2	12	516	35	470	11	5
Brownsville	11 560	3	0	0	0	3	72	1	60	11	0
Dallas	14 092	1	0	0	0	1	160	10	140	10	0
El Paso	18 918	8	0	2	0	6	178	8	165	5	0
Health Science Center, San Antonio	2 837	0	0	0	0	0	44	3	41	0	0
Health Science Center, Tyler[3]	. . .	1	0	0	0	1	10	0	10	0	0
Houston[3]	. . .	4	0	0	1	3	301	3	294	4	0
Medical Branch	2 051	1	0	0	0	1	205	5	197	3	0
Pan American	17 030	1	0	0	0	1	148	16	124	8	0
Permian Basin	3 291	2	0	1	0	1	35	8	27	0	0
San Antonio	26 175	4	0	2	1	1	182	54	119	9	0
Southwestern Medical School	2 282	2	0	1	1	0	240	2	230	8	0
Tyler	5 303	0	0	0	0	0	32	0	32	0	0
West Texas A&M University	7 299	1	0	1	0	0	61	10	51	0	0

Note: Caution should be exercised in making any intercampus comparisons or ranking schools, because school crime statistics are affected by a variety of factors. These include demographic characteristics of the surrounding community, the ratio of male to female students, the number of on-campus residents, the accessibility of outside visitors, the size of enrollment, etc.

[1]The student enrollment figures provided by the Department of Education are for the 2004 school year, the most recent available. Enrollment figures include full-time and part-time students.
[2]The FBI does not publish arson data unless it receives data from either the agency or the state for all 12 months of the calendar year.
[3]Student enrollment figures were not available.
. . . = Not available.

Table 9. Offenses Known to Law Enforcement, by State and University or College, 2005—*Continued*

(Number.)

School	Student enrollment[1]	Violent crime	Murder and non-negligent man-slaughter	Forcible rape	Robbery	Aggravated assault	Property crime	Burglary	Larceny-theft	Motor vehicle theft	Arson[2]
Utah											
Brigham Young University	34 347	2	0	0	0	2	330	13	313	4	0
College of Eastern Utah	2 471	1	0	1	0	0	17	2	15	0	0
University of Utah	28 933	10	0	2	1	7	532	33	475	24	0
Utah State University	16 130	2	0	1	1	0	160	12	148	0	0
Utah Valley State College	24 149	3	0	1	1	1	98	5	93	0	0
Weber State University	18 498	2	0	1	1	0	93	9	84	0	0
Virginia											
Christopher Newport University	4 681	6	0	2	0	4	105	4	101	0	0
College of William and Mary	7 575	6	0	4	0	2	196	14	179	3	1
Emory and Henry College	1 028	0	0	0	0	0	2	1	1	0	0
George Mason University	28 874	8	0	1	3	4	328	9	296	23	1
Hampton University	6 154	1	0	0	0	1	166	48	115	3	0
James Madison University	16 108	1	0	0	1	0	153	5	145	3	0
Longwood College	4 289	6	0	4	2	0	55	1	54	0	1
Norfolk State University	6 165	15	0	0	10	5	237	52	180	5	2
Northern Virginia Community College	37 392	4	0	0	1	3	110	0	109	1	1
Old Dominion University	20 595	4	0	1	3	0	79	1	72	6	0
Radford University	9 329	6	0	1	0	5	122	9	113	0	5
Thomas Nelson Community College	8 515	0	0	0	0	0	33	1	32	0	0
University of Richmond	4 475	4	0	0	0	4	167	6	158	3	2
University of Virginia	23 341	12	0	3	1	8	336	13	320	3	9
University of Virginia, College at Wise	. . .	0	0	0	0	0	4	0	2	2	0
Virginia Commonwealth University	28 303	28	1	1	12	14	580	22	542	16	3
Virginia Polytechnic Institute and State University	27 619	4	0	3	0	1	256	18	234	4	9
Virginia State University	4 859	6	0	1	2	3	142	8	133	1	0
Virginia Western Community College	8 361	0	0	0	0	0	17	0	17	0	0
Washington											
Central Washington University	9 912	3	0	1	0	2	210	21	185	4	0
Eastern Washington University	10 706	3	0	2	1	0	89	22	63	4	0
Evergreen State College	4 410	1	0	0	0	1	130	17	109	4	0
University of Washington	39 199	10	0	5	2	3	738	89	604	45	3
Washington State University, Vancouver	. . .	0	0	0	0	0	21	0	21	0	0
Western Washington University	14 190	0	0	0	0	0	222	13	203	6	1
West Virginia											
Concord University	2 820	1	0	0	0	1	19	4	15	0	0
Fairmont State University	4 071	0	0	0	0	0	66	31	35	0	0
Glenville State College	1 313	0	0	0	0	0	0	0	0	0	0
Marshall University	13 920	6	0	0	1	5	137	10	126	1	0
Potomac State College	1 304	1	0	0	0	1	12	8	4	0	0
Shepherd University	5 206	0	0	0	0	0	20	0	20	0	1
West Virginia State University	3 344	3	0	1	0	2	78	10	66	2	0
West Virginia Tech	1 692	2	0	0	0	2	27	3	24	0	0
West Virginia University	25 255	9	0	1	5	3	241	29	210	2	3
Wisconsin											
University of Wisconsin											
Eau Claire	10 648	0	0	0	0	0	102	0	94	8	0
Green Bay	5 557	0	0	0	0	0	34	0	34	0	0
La Crosse	9 019	0	0	0	0	0	76	14	62	0	0
Madison	40 455	10	0	3	4	3	460	20	425	15	8
Milwaukee	26 832	3	0	1	1	1	278	27	250	1	4
Oshkosh	11 532	3	0	1	0	2	89	14	75	0	1
Parkside	4 977	2	0	0	1	1	56	1	53	2	0
Platteville	6 177	5	0	1	0	4	80	4	75	1	0
Stevens Point	8 942	0	0	0	0	0	113	7	106	0	2
Stout	7 750	3	0	1	0	2	140	35	104	1	0
Superior	2 858	1	0	1	0	0	35	15	20	0	0
Whitewater	10 938	3	0	0	0	3	160	39	121	0	0
Wyoming											
Sheridan College	2 718	0	0	0	0	0	0	0	0	0	0
University of Wyoming	13 207	0	0	0	0	0	166	5	158	3	0

Note: Caution should be exercised in making any intercampus comparisons or ranking schools, because school crime statistics are affected by a variety of factors. These include demographic characteristics of the surrounding community, the ratio of male to female students, the number of on-campus residents, the accessibility of outside visitors, the size of enrollment, etc.

[1]The student enrollment figures provided by the Department of Education are for the 2004 school year, the most recent available. Enrollment figures include full-time and part-time students.
[2]The FBI does not publish arson data unless it receives data from either the agency or the state for all 12 months of the calendar year.
. . . = Not available.

Table 10. Offenses Known to Law Enforcement, by State Metropolitan and Nonmetropolitan Counties, 2005

(Number.)

County	Violent crime	Murder and nonnegligent manslaughter	Forcible rape	Robbery	Aggravated assault	Property crime	Burglary	Larceny-theft	Motor vehicle theft	Arson[1]
ALABAMA										
Metropolitan Counties										
Autauga	21	0	5	6	10	373	131	200	42	. . .
Blount	103	0	14	6	83	1 012	400	488	124	3
Calhoun	37	0	13	6	18	886	280	595	11	. . .
Colbert	123	0	3	3	117	205	66	138	1	. . .
Elmore	31	1	14	10	6	644	214	400	30	. . .
Etowah	2	0	0	0	2	249	63	152	34	. . .
Geneva	23	0	7	0	16	209	62	113	34	. . .
Greene	31	0	0	1	30	124	59	54	11	. . .
Hale	46	1	1	6	38	188	66	104	18	. . .
Henry	18	0	2	1	15	154	48	92	14	. . .
Houston	17	0	1	5	11	469	117	312	40	. . .
Jefferson	457	4	43	149	261	5 278	1 833	2 927	518	. . .
Lauderdale	29	0	6	8	15	187	52	129	6	. . .
Lawrence	27	1	6	3	17	382	115	239	28	. . .
Lee	49	0	7	19	23	1 266	398	760	108	. . .
Lowndes	57	1	4	16	36	156	133	13	10	. . .
Madison	230	4	23	54	149	2 444	744	1 498	202	. . .
Mobile	196	6	19	42	129	2 214	782	1 238	194	4
Morgan	28	0	3	4	21	356	204	138	14	. . .
Shelby	120	1	29	18	72	1 057	437	537	83	. . .
St. Clair	53	0	7	1	45	437	116	298	23	. . .
Nonmetropolitan Counties										
Barbour	18	0	3	1	14	80	29	45	6	. . .
Bullock	36	0	3	3	30	115	61	54	0	. . .
Butler	9	0	2	2	5	84	33	47	4	. . .
Chambers	27	0	0	5	22	200	63	130	7	. . .
Clay	37	0	0	0	37	101	30	71	0	. . .
Cleburne	20	1	1	5	13	275	88	147	40	. . .
Coffee	18	1	2	4	11	176	48	116	12	. . .
Conecuh	4	0	0	0	4	16	2	13	1	. . .
Coosa	25	0	1	6	18	127	29	91	7	. . .
Covington	60	0	5	0	55	222	88	121	13	. . .
Crenshaw	18	0	4	1	13	192	44	136	12	. . .
Cullman	101	2	19	11	69	1 569	511	924	134	. . .
Dale	10	0	0	2	8	75	17	50	8	. . .
Dallas	23	0	4	7	12	215	135	69	11	. . .
Franklin	18	1	4	3	10	100	39	53	8	. . .
Jackson	71	3	15	5	48	644	201	348	95	. . .
Lamar	1	0	0	0	1	43	16	22	5	. . .
Marengo	9	1	0	0	8	117	54	53	10	. . .
Marion	18	0	0	1	17	215	78	131	6	. . .
Marshall	0	0	0	0	0	1	0	1	0	. . .
Monroe	49	1	0	1	47	69	17	41	11	. . .
Perry	8	0	1	1	6	95	38	49	8	. . .
Pickens	23	2	1	11	9	78	37	38	3	. . .
Pike	7	0	0	1	6	71	21	48	2	. . .
Talladega	65	0	6	4	55	597	165	383	49	. . .
Tallapoosa	32	0	4	8	20	197	75	109	13	. . .
Wilcox	2	0	0	0	2	14	0	11	3	. . .
ARIZONA										
Metropolitan Counties										
Coconino	114	0	13	7	94	587	184	366	37	9
Pima	768	20	86	203	459	13 265	2 368	9 435	1 462	105
Pinal	289	11	42	40	196	4 122	966	2 439	717	26
Yavapai	260	0	7	9	244	1 590	462	967	161	7
Yuma	209	1	3	16	189	1 636	511	863	262	1
Nonmetropolitan Counties										
Cochise	593	2	17	16	558	1 279	362	704	213	23
Gila	96	0	8	2	86	692	331	281	80	5
Greenlee	9	0	0	0	9	40	8	32	0	0
La Paz	66	0	1	4	61	471	79	353	39	1
Mohave	198	11	2	11	174	3 399	1 182	1 807	410	28
ARKANSAS										
Metropolitan Counties										
Benton	44	0	16	4	24	498	93	365	40	13
Cleveland	4	0	0	0	4	83	43	33	7	4
Craighead	42	0	4	2	36	394	155	213	26	5
Crittenden	97	5	7	15	70	501	166	292	43	17
Faulkner	47	0	14	2	31	755	204	490	61	5
Franklin	0	0	0	0	0	83	30	51	2	0
Garland	117	4	26	16	71	2 505	900	1 387	218	34
Grant	33	1	4	3	25	134	45	76	13	4
Jefferson	69	2	3	6	58	601	298	269	34	8
Lonoke	72	1	9	5	57	371	219	128	24	7

Note: The data shown in this table do not reflect county totals but are the number of offenses reported by the sheriff's office or county police department.

[1]The FBI does not publish arson data unless it receives data from either the agency or the state for all 12 months of the calendar year.
. . . = Not available.

Table 10. Offenses Known to Law Enforcement, by State Metropolitan and Nonmetropolitan Counties, 2005—*Continued*

(Number.)

County	Violent crime	Murder and nonnegligent manslaughter	Forcible rape	Robbery	Aggravated assault	Property crime	Burglary	Larceny-theft	Motor vehicle theft	Arson[1]
Madison	20	0	1	0	19	62	28	26	8	0
Perry	36	1	1	0	34	67	46	17	4	0
Poinsett	78	0	4	0	74	115	95	9	11	4
Pulaski	405	2	18	32	353	2 250	785	1 233	232	24
Saline	74	0	20	3	51	1 164	384	737	43	0
Sebastian	55	1	2	2	50	319	149	159	11	2
Washington	171	5	10	0	156	680	223	367	90	2
Nonmetropolitan Counties										
Arkansas	2	0	0	0	2	69	21	33	15	0
Ashley	41	0	4	2	35	222	77	126	19	1
Baxter	35	0	3	0	32	535	79	426	30	1
Boone	53	2	1	0	50	299	147	112	40	4
Calhoun	7	1	0	0	6	27	10	15	2	0
Carroll	2	0	1	0	1	150	35	97	18	0
Chicot	2	0	0	0	2	91	21	63	7	0
Clark	24	0	2	1	21	156	56	88	12	0
Clay	24	0	4	0	20	87	40	42	5	1
Cleburne	31	0	8	0	23	308	144	138	26	5
Columbia	58	3	2	1	52	265	96	159	10	8
Cross	42	2	5	1	34	128	32	75	21	6
Dallas	6	0	0	1	5	24	9	14	1	0
Drew	11	0	5	1	5	77	29	40	8	1
Fulton	10	0	0	0	10	63	36	22	5	2
Greene	20	0	6	0	14	136	68	60	8	1
Hempstead	33	0	4	1	28	170	52	106	12	4
Hot Spring	42	0	6	0	36	347	131	195	21	1
Howard	15	1	3	1	10	99	30	64	5	1
Independence	21	0	4	5	12	1 136	127	912	97	0
Jackson	29	0	1	3	25	191	58	104	29	7
Lee	4	0	2	0	2	10	5	4	1	0
Logan	17	2	4	0	11	226	100	106	20	2
Marion	16	0	1	0	15	105	31	71	3	0
Mississippi	50	0	7	4	39	366	126	203	37	4
Monroe	3	0	1	0	2	52	5	30	17	0
Nevada	10	0	3	1	6	32	19	13	0	0
Ouachita	32	2	3	3	24	151	83	63	5	4
Pike	17	0	6	0	11	68	22	43	3	3
Polk	5	0	0	1	4	74	46	25	3	2
Prairie	6	0	2	1	3	66	32	19	15	0
Scott	10	0	2	0	8	77	26	45	6	2
Sharp	19	0	4	0	15	156	85	58	13	2
St. Francis	68	0	11	5	52	351	123	228	0	2
Union	40	2	3	7	28	431	105	280	46	1
Van Buren	13	1	1	1	10	88	37	35	16	0
White	45	0	2	3	40	896	360	411	125	15
Yell	54	1	4	0	49	127	79	42	6	5
CALIFORNIA										
Metropolitan Counties										
Alameda	505	9	26	209	261	3 160	692	1 480	988	34
Butte	235	5	33	36	161	1 711	787	881	43	69
Contra Costa	637	11	38	159	429	3 737	1 019	2 690	28	19
El Dorado	325	3	11	17	294	2 276	741	1 520	15	11
Fresno	872	20	45	163	644	6 441	1 683	3 752	1 006	260
Imperial	199	0	6	23	170	1 127	415	657	55	38
Kern	1 691	28	134	339	1 190	12 195	3 260	6 926	2 009	240
Kings	160	3	16	16	125	671	296	361	14	9
Los Angeles	7 459	168	233	1 910	5 148	20 433	5 024	8 682	6 727	420
Madera	285	6	20	19	240	1 452	644	781	27	11
Marin	169	0	12	46	111	961	231	726	4	7
Merced	471	7	28	39	397	1 957	917	1 026	14	12
Monterey	201	4	16	54	127	2 030	576	1 421	33	23
Napa	35	1	9	1	24	430	135	282	13	2
Orange	242	1	10	38	193	1 514	371	919	224	15
Placer	127	5	17	8	97	2 171	789	1 325	57	8
Riverside	2 147	39	115	416	1 577	15 954	3 829	8 215	3 910	69
Sacramento	4 134	57	219	1 262	2 596	26 191	7 159	16 855	2 177	247
San Benito	38	1	1	0	36	351	142	190	19	0
San Bernardino	1 057	27	71	177	782	6 774	2 063	2 997	1 714	124
San Diego	1 589	13	86	270	1 220	9 179	2 469	4 626	2 084	43
San Joaquin	879	12	28	165	674	4 928	1 522	3 141	265	34
San Luis Obispo	210	2	16	15	177	1 558	507	1 045	6	11
San Mateo	220	1	17	46	156	1 906	259	1 354	293	8
Santa Barbara	159	2	18	20	119	1 687	569	1 107	11	15
Santa Clara	355	3	24	20	308	2 222	453	1 404	365	3
Santa Cruz	315	0	34	44	237	2 806	844	1 947	15	15
Shasta	234	2	30	15	187	1 165	467	652	46	33
Solano	150	1	9	20	120	421	209	194	18	36
Sonoma	646	3	45	54	544	2 303	744	1 531	28	13

Note: The data shown in this table do not reflect county totals but are the number of offenses reported by the sheriff's office or county police department.

[1]The FBI does not publish arson data unless it receives data from either the agency or the state for all 12 months of the calendar year.

Table 10. Offenses Known to Law Enforcement, by State Metropolitan and Nonmetropolitan Counties, 2005—*Continued*

(Number.)

County	Violent crime	Murder and nonnegligent manslaughter	Forcible rape	Robbery	Aggravated assault	Property crime	Burglary	Larceny-theft	Motor vehicle theft	Arson[1]
Stanislaus	980	14	27	99	840	4 243	1 337	2 347	559	290
Sutter	151	0	10	13	128	1 096	372	635	89	7
Tulare[2]	558	30	30	87	411	. . .	1 328	2 117	. . .	535
Ventura	185	3	22	28	132	1 153	332	680	141	23
Yolo	28	1	2	6	19	331	122	193	16	8
Yuba	208	7	14	36	151	1 260	576	670	14	20
Nonmetropolitan Counties										
Alpine	7	0	0	0	7	97	18	79	0	0
Amador	66	0	10	7	49	553	240	309	4	2
Calaveras	132	2	17	7	106	715	287	425	3	8
Colusa	29	0	2	3	24	285	110	169	6	1
Del Norte	79	0	30	3	46	368	180	183	5	1
Glenn	9	0	1	0	8	175	74	101	0	0
Humboldt	124	2	9	21	92	940	354	569	17	4
Inyo	62	1	7	3	51	229	67	160	2	3
Lake	186	1	11	7	167	918	422	491	5	5
Lassen	56	3	6	3	44	143	50	93	0	5
Mariposa	75	0	3	0	72	378	121	256	1	3
Mendocino	313	4	20	24	265	705	285	410	10	19
Modoc	10	0	0	1	9	51	16	35	0	0
Mono	15	0	1	0	14	73	22	50	1	0
Nevada	184	2	15	7	160	703	250	447	6	4
Plumas	37	0	5	3	29	569	227	338	4	0
Sierra	7	0	0	0	7	49	17	32	0	1
Siskiyou	67	3	7	1	56	331	115	208	8	2
Tehama	308	2	5	11	290	478	290	187	1	24
Trinity	36	1	6	5	24	121	86	35	0	0
COLORADO										
Metropolitan Counties										
Adams	434	4	23	81	326	4 155	835	2 309	1 011	44
Arapahoe	300	3	40	43	214	1 748	417	1 044	287	32
Boulder	109	2	10	1	96	827	220	531	76	17
Clear Creek	13	0	2	0	11	119	28	88	3	1
Douglas	169	2	63	15	89	2 839	620	2 069	150	34
Elbert	10	0	2	0	8	112	39	60	13	1
El Paso	873	3	57	24	789	2 858	721	1 807	330	26
Gilpin	9	0	1	0	8	37	12	25	0	0
Jefferson	249	2	37	26	184	3 698	721	2 564	413	20
Larimer	96	1	25	8	62	1 281	277	893	111	13
Mesa	40	0	2	6	32	1 620	410	1 031	179	25
Park	21	0	0	1	20	75	40	24	11	0
Pueblo	49	0	1	6	42	1 607	381	1 157	69	5
Teller	14	2	0	0	12	102	40	60	2	0
Weld	199	5	14	9	171	1 477	561	701	215	14
Nonmetropolitan Counties										
Alamosa	11	0	0	0	11	57	8	49	0	0
Archuleta	36	0	4	1	31	143	57	77	9	2
Baca	0	0	0	0	0	6	5	1	0	0
Bent	2	0	1	0	1	30	10	16	4	0
Chaffee	13	0	5	1	7	119	30	80	9	0
Cheyenne	0	0	0	0	0	20	2	17	1	0
Crowley	1	0	0	0	1	0	0	0	0	0
Custer	8	0	1	0	7	39	14	23	2	0
Delta	19	0	1	1	17	141	42	79	20	3
Dolores	0	0	0	0	0	22	8	11	3	0
Eagle	33	1	6	3	23	580	48	532	0	7
Fremont	42	0	2	1	39	213	41	162	10	5
Garfield	82	0	8	1	73	357	92	202	63	10
Grand	41	0	0	0	41	265	54	204	7	0
Gunnison	16	0	0	0	16	30	6	19	5	0
Hinsdale	0	0	0	0	0	10	5	5	0	1
Huerfano	1	0	0	0	1	42	9	27	6	0
Jackson	4	0	0	0	4	16	7	5	4	0
Kit Carson	1	0	0	0	1	26	8	18	0	0
Lake	6	0	0	0	6	26	9	14	3	0
La Plata	28	0	11	0	17	345	110	207	28	0
Las Animas	8	0	0	0	8	5	4	1	0	1
Logan	9	0	2	0	7	78	19	53	6	0
Moffat	5	0	0	0	5	38	11	26	1	1
Montezuma	36	0	4	0	32	253	80	157	16	1
Montrose	5	0	1	0	4	21	3	17	1	1
Morgan	2	0	1	0	1	72	23	48	1	0
Phillips	0	0	0	0	0	8	3	5	0	0
Pitkin	10	0	6	0	4	134	16	109	9	0
Prowers	10	0	4	0	6	42	14	23	5	0

Note: The data shown in this table do not reflect county totals but are the number of offenses reported by the sheriff's office or county police department.

[1]The FBI does not publish arson data unless it receives data from either the agency or the state for all 12 months of the calendar year.
[2]The motor vehicle thefts for this county are collected by the Tulare County Highway Patrol. These data can be found in Table 11.
. . . = Not available.

Table 10. Offenses Known to Law Enforcement, by State Metropolitan and Nonmetropolitan Counties, 2005—*Continued*

(Number.)

County	Violent crime	Murder and nonnegligent manslaughter	Forcible rape	Robbery	Aggravated assault	Property crime	Burglary	Larceny-theft	Motor vehicle theft	Arson[1]
Rio Grande	11	0	1	0	10	21	10	10	1	0
Routt	15	0	1	0	14	24	5	16	3	0
Saguache	5	0	0	0	5	33	8	23	2	1
San Juan	6	0	0	0	6	15	5	10	0	1
San Miguel	7	0	0	0	7	37	8	27	2	0
Sedgwick	7	0	3	0	4	11	3	5	3	1
Summit	19	0	2	2	15	723	60	645	18	0
Washington	15	0	2	0	13	56	19	33	4	0
DELAWARE										
Metropolitan Counties										
New Castle County Police Department	1 380	8	127	267	978	5 970	1 719	3 536	715	20
FLORIDA										
Metropolitan Counties										
Alachua	1 027	2	72	113	840	3 634	1 147	2 234	253	12
Baker	152	0	5	10	137	484	78	383	23	4
Bay	428	1	64	27	336	2 760	537	2 055	168	8
Brevard	1 064	10	73	92	889	4 768	1 204	3 245	319	28
Broward	691	3	34	164	490	2 028	422	1 419	187	3
Charlotte	680	1	41	61	577	4 512	1 061	3 163	288	11
Clay	703	5	57	55	586	3 633	873	2 449	311	19
Collier	1 279	9	89	214	967	5 442	1 274	3 766	402	39
Escambia	1 963	9	119	374	1 461	9 304	2 351	6 142	811	40
Gadsden	255	6	4	29	216	756	304	399	53	3
Gilchrist	22	0	0	0	22	240	75	136	29	0
Hernando	641	0	66	52	523	4 372	1 154	2 917	301	13
Hillsborough	4 991	23	272	895	3 801	28 089	5 965	19 072	3 052	86
Indian River	300	2	22	65	211	2 930	660	2 079	191	10
Jefferson	58	0	10	4	44	169	47	108	14	0
Lake	905	8	38	32	827	3 706	1 346	1 995	365	22
Lee	1 645	15	107	440	1 083	11 206	3 185	6 614	1 407	100
Leon	411	1	33	51	326	1 674	696	788	190	20
Manatee	2 228	11	75	382	1 760	10 473	2 377	7 307	789	20
Marion	1 468	11	111	89	1 257	4 864	1 635	2 835	394	3
Martin	496	2	9	124	361	2 631	578	1 865	188	6
Miami-Dade	9 263	70	432	2 341	6 420	50 208	9 381	33 802	7 025	179
Nassau	711	0	9	15	687	1 115	334	673	108	1
Okaloosa	388	2	23	61	302	3 559	754	2 545	260	6
Orange	6 351	49	283	1 790	4 229	28 749	7 337	17 366	4 046	3
Osceola	677	8	53	118	498	5 524	2 130	2 980	414	4
Palm Beach	2 794	11	221	612	1 950	18 371	4 423	11 720	2 228	100
Pasco	1 236	12	118	149	957	10 853	3 231	6 712	910	31
Pinellas	1 130	5	126	139	860	7 643	1 883	5 103	657	55
Polk	1 480	6	120	191	1 163	9 319	2 839	5 599	881	0
Santa Rosa	240	2	30	11	197	1 777	480	1 140	157	4
Sarasota	725	4	52	95	574	7 407	1 867	5 036	504	12
Seminole	623	0	53	80	490	3 815	923	2 532	360	4
St. Johns	494	3	10	48	433	2 850	825	1 833	192	7
St. Lucie	366	0	28	34	304	1 998	544	1 203	251	9
Volusia	935	13	78	100	744	4 903	1 326	3 069	508	27
Wakulla	103	3	13	5	82	513	182	306	25	13
Nonmetropolitan Counties										
Bradford	79	1	8	4	66	269	114	135	20	4
Calhoun	20	1	2	0	17	73	29	35	9	0
Citrus	325	6	23	20	276	2 162	506	1 536	120	18
Columbia	265	4	35	15	211	1 169	382	686	101	8
DeSoto	156	1	12	13	130	855	321	510	24	0
Dixie	85	1	12	3	69	318	110	187	21	1
Flagler	197	1	11	23	162	1 381	320	964	97	2
Glades	44	1	1	11	31	268	93	147	28	3
Gulf	89	1	5	2	81	158	50	96	12	0
Hamilton	53	1	4	4	44	182	59	104	19	1
Hardee	127	2	13	4	108	495	106	348	41	3
Hendry	246	2	8	49	187	1 025	355	573	97	5
Highlands	192	2	24	20	146	1 717	564	1 029	124	4
Holmes	67	0	3	0	64	198	46	133	19	0
Jackson	152	1	9	7	135	623	236	354	33	0
Lafayette	10	0	0	0	10	43	10	31	2	0
Levy	156	3	19	6	128	729	248	440	41	9
Liberty	18	0	3	1	14	38	15	18	5	0
Madison	88	1	4	14	69	323	115	198	10	3
Monroe	200	0	18	21	161	1 960	387	1 476	97	10
Okeechobee	303	2	13	14	274	801	374	361	66	1
Putnam	655	1	29	40	585	2 164	962	989	213	7
Sumter	181	0	34	8	139	734	240	438	56	6
Suwannee	171	1	21	8	141	538	136	363	39	0
Taylor	92	0	5	0	87	182	101	73	8	0
Union	66	0	10	4	52	244	80	131	33	2
Walton	144	3	8	7	126	787	193	544	50	3
Washington	34	1	4	0	29	239	80	123	36	1

Note: The data shown in this table do not reflect county totals but are the number of offenses reported by the sheriff's office or county police department.

[1]The FBI does not publish arson data unless it receives data from either the agency or the state for all 12 months of the calendar year.

Table 10. Offenses Known to Law Enforcement, by State Metropolitan and Nonmetropolitan Counties, 2005—*Continued*

(Number.)

County	Violent crime	Murder and nonnegligent manslaughter	Forcible rape	Robbery	Aggravated assault	Property crime	Burglary	Larceny-theft	Motor vehicle theft	Arson[1]
GEORGIA										
Metropolitan Counties										
Augusta-Richmond	1 019	14	155	626	224	13 934	2 799	9 295	1 840	94
Bartow	170	0	17	18	135	2 900	790	1 849	261	0
Bibb	208	8	12	34	154	2 972	627	2 005	340	5
Brantley	30	1	2	1	26	392	125	233	34	0
Brooks	63	0	0	3	60	267	57	185	25	3
Bryan	16	0	1	7	8	287	62	214	11	0
Burke	261	1	2	11	247	524	145	345	34	0
Butts	33	2	2	5	24	504	94	346	64	1
Carroll	108	1	12	20	75	2 249	708	1 337	204	5
Catoosa	76	3	6	13	54	955	189	594	172	2
Chattahoochee	5	0	1	0	4	64	20	37	7	4
Cherokee	93	5	10	12	66	1 904	532	1 196	176	5
Clayton County Police Department	1 023	22	33	443	525	8 759	2 824	4 236	1 699	36
Cobb County Police Department	1 227	21	113	467	626	13 631	2 820	9 086	1 725	61
Columbia	89	1	15	28	45	2 005	270	1 613	122	3
Coweta	42	1	2	10	29	1 349	371	803	175	12
Crawford	16	0	1	2	13	375	129	210	36	0
Dawson	19	1	3	1	14	690	146	439	105	2
DeKalb County Police Department	3 518	75	126	1 943	1 374	28 442	7 309	14 531	6 602	119
Dougherty	1	0	0	0	1	69	10	57	2	0
Douglas	200	2	9	73	116	2 535	544	1 724	267	7
Effingham	51	0	3	5	43	532	171	309	52	0
Fayette	31	1	3	11	16	636	150	431	55	0
Forsyth	209	0	14	18	177	2 898	695	1 993	210	2
Fulton County Police Department	959	27	61	485	386	9 856	2 829	5 502	1 525	25
Glynn County Police Department	228	2	18	52	156	2 478	519	1 832	127	. . .
Gwinnett County Police Department	1 748	29	135	882	702	19 077	5 247	11 194	2 636	121
Hall	237	5	33	27	172	3 439	822	2 131	486	12
Haralson	26	2	0	4	20	671	139	442	90	. . .
Heard	25	0	0	4	21	260	70	149	41	1
Houston	94	1	3	18	72	1 050	230	727	93	. . .
Jones	18	0	0	3	15	607	166	372	69	1
Lee	20	0	2	2	16	499	113	373	13	0
Liberty	61	1	3	12	45	637	158	437	42	. . .
Long	31	0	2	2	27	170	81	80	9	1
Lowndes	96	3	15	19	59	1 238	266	900	72	. . .
Madison	61	0	0	9	52	564	65	460	39	. . .
Meriwether	17	0	0	1	16	449	117	216	116	. . .
Newton	144	0	10	19	115	1 526	489	848	189	7
Paulding	200	1	15	12	172	2 772	615	1 769	388	24
Rockdale	351	3	11	51	286	2 496	586	1 635	275	13
Spalding	129	0	13	15	101	1 499	384	956	159	6
Walker	201	2	5	5	189	1 529	326	1 046	157	17
Walton	23	0	3	7	13	921	134	641	146	0
Worth	5	0	2	0	3	161	64	86	11	0
Nonmetropolitan Counties										
Bacon	0	0	0	0	0	71	31	27	13	0
Baldwin	99	2	5	8	84	790	201	552	37	2
Bleckley	8	1	1	0	6	95	27	63	5	0
Bulloch	57	2	0	10	45	861	227	589	45	2
Camden	43	0	3	5	35	393	103	268	22	. . .
Candler	6	0	0	6	0	90	30	56	4	0
Clay	2	0	0	0	2	3	0	2	1	0
Colquitt	90	2	5	6	77	869	264	534	71	1
Decatur	14	0	0	4	10	277	76	181	20	0
Dooly	12	0	1	4	7	51	10	39	2	0
Early	34	0	1	5	28	170	52	100	18	. . .
Habersham	32	1	3	3	25	551	209	277	65	0
Hancock County Police Department	0	0	0	0	0	0	0	0	0	0
Irwin	7	0	1	0	6	89	22	56	11	0
Jackson	61	0	7	2	52	892	279	527	86	. . .
Jefferson	31	1	0	0	30	156	54	84	18	1
Johnson	16	0	1	1	14	51	23	25	3	. . .
Laurens	52	0	8	5	39	634	197	379	58	1
Lumpkin	50	1	2	4	43	561	127	390	44	. . .
Polk	0	0	0	0	0	0	0	0	0	0
Polk County Police Department	111	0	11	10	90	914	263	583	68	0
Pulaski	8	0	0	1	7	111	31	68	12	0
Putnam	38	1	2	1	34	266	94	161	11	0
Schley	0	0	0	0	0	19	2	16	1	0
Seminole	8	0	0	0	8	44	30	9	5	0
Stephens	33	0	9	5	19	400	81	262	57	1
Tattnall	18	0	2	3	13	188	58	111	19	0
Taylor	8	1	0	0	7	73	39	28	6	0
Tift	110	5	11	24	70	968	273	626	69	2
Towns	12	0	1	2	9	158	45	101	12	1

Note: The data shown in this table do not reflect county totals but are the number of offenses reported by the sheriff's office or county police department.

[1]The FBI does not publish arson data unless it receives data from either the agency or the state for all 12 months of the calendar year.
. . . = Not available.

Table 10. Offenses Known to Law Enforcement, by State Metropolitan and Nonmetropolitan Counties, 2005—*Continued*

(Number.)

County	Violent crime	Murder and nonnegligent manslaughter	Forcible rape	Robbery	Aggravated assault	Property crime	Burglary	Larceny-theft	Motor vehicle theft	Arson[1]
Treutlen	8	0	0	0	8	106	26	72	8	0
Troup	17	0	1	2	14	1 177	194	931	52	0
Ware	42	0	5	7	30	439	135	248	56	1
Wheeler	4	0	0	0	4	55	22	26	7	0
Wilkes	5	0	1	0	4	13	6	4	3	0
Wilkinson	12	0	0	1	11	78	29	42	7	1
Nonmetropolitan Counties										
Maui Police Department	252	3	26	74	149	8 363	1 523	5 678	1 162	73
IDAHO										
Metropolitan Counties										
Bannock	19	0	2	1	16	187	48	132	7	2
Boise	11	0	1	0	10	99	39	56	4	0
Canyon	74	0	10	5	59	941	314	495	132	10
Franklin	2	0	0	0	2	42	1	40	1	0
Gem	12	0	2	0	10	20	6	11	3	0
Kootenai	118	4	16	7	91	1 148	350	700	98	4
Nez Perce	3	1	0	0	2	132	35	94	3	0
Power	4	0	1	0	3	53	13	37	3	0
Nonmetropolitan Counties										
Adams	9	0	0	0	9	20	1	16	3	0
Benewah	8	0	0	0	8	18	5	13	0	1
Bingham	32	3	6	0	23	363	88	234	41	4
Blaine	8	0	1	0	7	38	8	29	1	1
Bonner	41	0	7	2	32	605	195	360	50	1
Boundary	3	0	0	0	3	93	40	48	5	0
Butte	2	0	0	0	2	4	1	3	0	0
Camas	0	0	0	0	0	10	3	4	3	0
Caribou	5	0	0	0	5	26	15	10	1	0
Cassia	53	0	5	1	47	604	160	406	38	4
Clearwater	16	0	0	1	15	99	21	77	1	1
Elmore	19	0	2	1	16	158	37	98	23	2
Fremont	9	1	2	0	6	86	15	58	13	0
Idaho	16	0	0	0	16	62	16	41	5	1
Jerome	17	0	3	2	12	149	42	97	10	0
Latah	10	0	0	0	10	86	34	47	5	2
Lemhi	8	0	1	0	7	20	7	11	2	0
Lewis	8	0	0	0	8	63	18	39	6	1
Lincoln	6	1	0	0	5	0	0	0	0	0
Madison	20	0	2	1	17	50	10	38	2	0
Minidoka	10	0	3	0	7	165	50	102	13	2
Oneida	8	0	0	0	8	23	8	14	1	0
Payette	11	0	1	0	10	70	27	29	14	0
Shoshone	43	0	3	1	39	128	45	71	12	2
Teton	8	0	1	0	7	111	14	90	7	0
Twin Falls	51	0	4	2	45	357	185	150	22	5
Valley	14	0	2	0	12	99	33	65	1	1
Washington	5	0	0	0	5	29	20	8	1	0
INDIANA										
Metropolitan Counties										
Allen	75	1	16	23	35	1 205	275	811	119	4
Bartholomew	23	0	3	0	20	392	86	304	2	0
Brown	4	0	0	2	2	55	19	34	2	0
Clark	67	2	2	3	60	630	188	411	31	2
Delaware	23	1	4	3	15	576	91	431	54	2
Elkhart	60	0	18	21	21	1 899	442	1 257	200	9
Floyd	7	1	1	0	5	688	128	520	40	0
Franklin	5	0	1	0	4	229	88	94	47	1
Greene	13	0	1	1	11	225	74	130	21	2
Hancock	17	0	1	7	9	356	95	227	34	1
Hendricks	54	2	10	7	35	817	239	489	89	4
Howard	81	0	8	5	68	753	258	449	46	3
Johnson[3]	18	0	6	6	6	809	135	664	10	1
Lake	45	0	5	9	31	589	100	323	166	3
La Porte	22	1	5	4	12	457	152	263	42	0
Madison	9	0	3	5	1	587	100	473	14	0
Monroe	37	1	9	6	21	562	178	328	56	4
Newton	8	0	0	0	8	188	75	92	21	1
Porter	53	1	3	5	44	910	178	640	92	0
Putnam	125	0	5	2	118	399	161	191	47	3
Shelby	22	0	0	0	22	225	97	115	13	1
St. Joseph	84	1	16	29	38	1 712	295	1 314	103	11
Tippecanoe	23	0	3	9	11	844	273	510	61	6
Vanderburgh	59	1	5	5	48	1 136	140	961	35	6
Warrick	118	0	4	1	113	560	90	456	14	7
Wells	2	0	0	1	1	102	43	53	6	1

Note: The data shown in this table do not reflect county totals but are the number of offenses reported by the sheriff's office or county police department.

[1]The FBI does not publish arson data unless it receives data from either the agency or the state for all 12 months of the calendar year.
[3]Because of changes in the state/local agency's reporting practices, figures are not comparable to previous years' data.

Table 10. Offenses Known to Law Enforcement, by State Metropolitan and Nonmetropolitan Counties, 2005—*Continued*

(Number.)

County	Violent crime	Murder and nonnegligent manslaughter	Forcible rape	Robbery	Aggravated assault	Property crime	Burglary	Larceny-theft	Motor vehicle theft	Arson[1]
Nonmetropolitan Counties										
Blackford	0	0	0	0	0	66	11	49	6	0
Cass	29	0	3	0	26	198	61	131	6	. . .
Daviess	10	1	0	0	9	140	24	101	15	0
Fayette	2	0	0	1	1	241	86	142	13	0
Grant	4	0	0	2	2	385	89	269	27	3
Henry	10	2	4	3	1	724	178	500	46	0
Huntington	5	0	2	0	3	136	34	93	9	0
Knox	27	0	1	11	15	83	12	70	1	0
Kosciusko	20	1	4	5	10	864	145	673	46	3
LaGrange	5	2	0	2	1	201	74	123	4	0
Lawrence	15	0	8	0	7	259	100	135	24	6
Martin	3	0	0	1	2	48	13	27	8	0
Randolph[4]	. . .	0	5	0	. . .	125	53	71	1	0
Ripley	31	0	2	5	24	178	57	111	10	1
Starke	13	1	2	0	10	545	108	350	87	2
Steuben	17	0	4	0	13	539	99	415	25	1
Union	4	0	0	3	1	50	17	30	3	1
Wabash	6	0	1	0	5	160	24	130	6	2
Wayne	0	0	0	0	0	105	26	76	3	0
White	0	0	0	0	0	27	27	0	0	0
IOWA										
Metropolitan Counties										
Benton	8	0	0	0	8	51	10	40	1	0
Black Hawk	35	0	9	1	25	273	121	138	14	2
Bremer	13	0	2	0	11	48	11	37	0	0
Dallas	6	0	0	1	5	150	46	90	14	3
Dubuque	56	0	6	0	50	275	93	144	38	2
Grundy	1	0	0	0	1	39	13	22	4	0
Guthrie	0	0	0	0	0	66	19	43	4	0
Harrison	12	0	1	1	10	141	50	75	16	1
Johnson	64	1	5	1	57	237	79	143	15	3
Jones	1	0	0	0	1	59	19	33	7	1
Linn	84	0	5	1	78	360	111	217	32	2
Mills	12	0	3	0	9	180	74	86	20	6
Polk	102	0	5	3	94	1 149	258	754	137	9
Pottawattamie	29	0	7	4	18	554	161	350	43	2
Scott	25	1	1	0	23	237	34	181	22	0
Story	24	0	8	0	16	179	73	96	10	1
Warren	35	0	7	1	27	331	113	203	15	1
Washington	26	0	8	0	18	60	36	21	3	0
Woodbury	35	0	1	0	34	142	46	87	9	6
Nonmetropolitan Counties										
Adair	3	0	0	0	3	35	11	20	4	1
Adams	6	0	0	0	6	57	19	34	4	1
Appanoose	4	0	0	0	4	136	32	91	13	7
Boone	15	0	4	0	11	46	14	25	7	0
Buchanan	7	0	3	0	4	184	98	70	16	3
Buena Vista	6	0	0	0	6	92	33	54	5	2
Butler	8	0	0	0	8	53	20	29	4	0
Calhoun	3	0	0	1	2	111	32	71	8	1
Carroll	4	0	0	0	4	27	11	14	2	0
Cedar	4	0	0	0	4	90	23	60	7	2
Cerro Gordo	15	0	0	0	15	147	61	77	9	1
Cherokee	0	0	0	0	0	46	15	29	2	0
Chickasaw	6	0	2	0	4	45	22	19	4	0
Clarke	9	1	1	0	7	99	35	55	9	1
Clay	1	0	0	0	1	85	33	42	10	0
Clayton	5	0	2	0	3	80	29	44	7	1
Clinton	3	0	0	0	3	109	24	83	2	12
Davis	8	0	2	0	6	33	12	20	1	0
Delaware	7	0	0	0	7	22	14	8	0	0
Des Moines	15	1	2	0	12	194	60	114	20	3
Fayette	10	0	0	0	10	48	16	29	3	0
Floyd	2	1	0	0	1	38	20	16	2	0
Franklin	0	0	0	0	0	15	1	9	5	0
Greene	2	0	0	0	2	60	22	36	2	0
Hamilton	6	0	0	0	6	113	32	69	12	1
Hancock	2	0	0	0	2	52	22	25	5	1
Hardin	5	0	2	0	3	102	37	56	9	3
Henry	10	0	0	0	10	79	29	39	11	0
Howard	0	0	0	0	0	70	8	55	7	0
Humboldt	0	0	0	0	0	51	20	25	6	2

Note: The data shown in this table do not reflect county totals but are the number of offenses reported by the sheriff's office or county police department.

[1]The FBI does not publish arson data unless it receives data from either the agency or the state for all 12 months of the calendar year.
[4]After examining the data and making inquiries, the FBI determined that the agency was unable to report aggravated assaults according to the UCR definition. Consequently, this figure is not included in this table.
. . . = Not available.

Table 10. Offenses Known to Law Enforcement, by State Metropolitan and Nonmetropolitan Counties, 2005—*Continued*

(Number.)

County	Violent crime	Murder and nonnegligent manslaughter	Forcible rape	Robbery	Aggravated assault	Property crime	Burglary	Larceny-theft	Motor vehicle theft	Arson[1]
Ida	1	0	0	0	1	41	1	38	2	0
Iowa	7	0	2	0	5	92	14	71	7	1
Jasper	7	0	0	0	7	145	59	62	24	4
Jefferson	5	0	0	1	4	76	22	47	7	0
Keokuk	0	0	0	0	0	29	4	24	1	0
Kossuth	10	0	1	1	8	40	23	11	6	1
Lee	16	0	0	0	16	167	67	89	11	1
Louisa	10	0	2	0	8	128	45	68	15	0
Lucas	10	0	2	0	8	81	24	47	10	4
Lyon	14	0	7	0	7	50	13	33	4	0
Mahaska	15	0	1	0	14	81	27	44	10	7
Marion	5	0	0	0	5	90	47	39	4	1
Marshall	12	0	1	0	11	95	41	46	8	2
Mitchell	1	0	0	0	1	30	17	13	0	0
Monroe	3	0	1	0	2	28	6	19	3	2
Muscatine	12	0	6	0	6	152	64	72	16	4
O'Brien	5	0	1	0	4	101	46	54	1	1
Osceola	3	0	0	0	3	110	30	76	4	0
Page	6	0	0	0	6	71	14	46	11	1
Palo Alto	4	0	0	0	4	50	23	23	4	1
Plymouth	12	0	4	2	6	61	22	36	3	2
Pocahontas	3	0	0	0	3	35	15	18	2	1
Poweshiek	2	0	1	0	1	146	29	81	36	1
Sac	6	0	0	0	6	37	20	17	0	0
Sioux	4	0	1	0	3	88	36	47	5	1
Tama	56	0	2	0	54	105	34	58	13	7
Taylor	0	0	0	0	0	19	5	14	0	1
Union	10	0	1	1	8	43	14	26	3	0
Van Buren	7	0	0	0	7	74	26	43	5	1
Wapello	4	0	0	0	4	51	24	22	5	1
Wayne	3	0	0	0	3	59	16	40	3	0
Webster	41	0	0	1	40	324	108	177	39	4
Winneshiek	2	0	0	0	2	37	11	20	6	0
Worth	4	0	1	0	3	115	30	71	14	0
Wright	2	0	0	0	2	50	27	20	3	1
KANSAS										
Metropolitan Counties										
Butler	41	0	7	2	32	444	128	298	18	3
Doniphan	3	0	1	0	2	49	16	26	7	0
Douglas	19	0	0	0	19	226	43	172	11	6
Franklin	37	0	3	3	31	245	119	114	12	2
Harvey	9	0	1	0	8	76	32	40	4	2
Jackson	27	0	2	0	25	211	55	146	10	0
Jefferson	27	0	4	2	21	375	67	276	32	4
Johnson	45	0	9	3	33	418	75	308	35	8
Leavenworth	24	0	3	1	20	174	48	101	25	16
Linn	9	0	1	1	7	102	57	34	11	1
Miami	34	1	9	0	24	180	68	91	21	17
Osage	31	1	5	1	24	186	62	105	19	2
Shawnee	76	1	8	0	67	1 307	285	968	54	8
Sumner	7	0	4	0	3	114	40	66	8	6
Wabaunsee	13	0	3	0	10	105	23	69	13	2
Nonmetropolitan Counties										
Allen	9	1	0	1	7	59	20	31	8	0
Anderson	6	1	0	0	5	65	21	36	8	0
Atchison	11	0	1	0	10	64	21	35	8	7
Barber	4	0	0	0	4	24	12	10	2	0
Barton	7	0	1	0	6	185	56	127	2	0
Bourbon	13	0	3	1	9	151	61	78	12	5
Brown	5	0	0	0	5	58	21	31	6	2
Chase	1	0	0	0	1	20	10	7	3	0
Chautauqua	5	1	0	0	4	36	6	27	3	4
Cherokee	27	0	1	0	26	163	48	90	25	13
Cheyenne	3	0	0	0	3	17	6	11	0	0
Clay	6	0	2	0	4	34	17	16	1	0
Cloud	1	0	0	0	1	65	16	48	1	2
Coffey	10	0	5	0	5	83	23	53	7	12
Cowley	35	1	4	2	28	205	80	109	16	8
Crawford	32	0	5	0	27	241	80	147	14	9
Dickinson	3	0	2	0	1	89	30	54	5	1
Elk	15	0	2	0	13	60	10	45	5	1
Ellis	7	1	2	0	4	51	13	34	4	2
Ellsworth	2	0	0	0	2	42	8	29	5	3

Note: The data shown in this table do not reflect county totals but are the number of offenses reported by the sheriff's office or county police department.

[1]The FBI does not publish arson data unless it receives data from either the agency or the state for all 12 months of the calendar year.

Table 10. Offenses Known to Law Enforcement, by State Metropolitan and Nonmetropolitan Counties, 2005—*Continued*

(Number.)

County	Violent crime	Murder and nonnegligent manslaughter	Forcible rape	Robbery	Aggravated assault	Property crime	Burglary	Larceny-theft	Motor vehicle theft	Arson[1]
Finney	35	0	8	1	26	220	54	151	15	2
Ford	5	0	0	0	5	42	25	13	4	0
Geary	5	0	0	1	4	40	12	27	1	1
Gove	0	0	0	0	0	38	15	21	2	0
Graham	0	0	0	0	0	11	2	8	1	0
Gray	6	0	1	0	5	36	18	15	3	1
Greenwood	11	1	0	1	9	70	28	36	6	0
Haskell	5	0	2	0	3	47	25	20	2	0
Hodgeman	5	0	0	0	5	74	20	52	2	0
Kearny	9	0	3	0	6	90	17	70	3	1
Kingman	5	0	1	0	4	67	22	39	6	2
Kiowa	4	0	2	0	2	17	3	11	3	0
Labette	14	0	1	0	13	95	34	52	9	5
Lane	2	0	1	0	1	22	3	19	0	0
Lincoln	7	0	0	0	7	47	16	29	2	1
Lyon	8	0	2	0	6	98	33	61	4	7
Marion	6	0	0	0	6	58	19	35	4	3
Marshall	3	0	0	0	3	26	5	19	2	1
McPherson	4	0	1	1	2	55	20	26	9	1
Meade	1	0	1	0	0	13	2	6	5	0
Morris	6	0	2	0	4	48	24	21	3	1
Morton	9	0	1	0	8	39	16	22	1	0
Nemaha	4	0	0	0	4	48	13	31	4	2
Neosho	9	0	0	0	9	96	29	54	13	1
Norton	3	0	0	0	3	14	6	7	1	0
Ottawa	1	0	0	0	1	95	22	67	6	0
Pawnee	6	0	0	0	6	52	15	36	1	1
Phillips	8	0	2	0	6	22	7	14	1	1
Pottawatomie	21	0	5	0	16	322	88	219	15	1
Pratt	3	0	0	0	3	45	11	30	4	0
Rawlins	2	0	1	0	1	14	4	10	0	0
Reno	29	0	2	1	26	276	95	163	18	13
Republic	6	0	0	1	5	59	24	35	0	0
Rice	5	0	1	0	4	65	15	43	7	0
Riley County Police Department	225	0	25	19	181	1 418	241	1 130	47	24
Rush	3	0	0	0	3	47	22	19	6	0
Russell	4	0	0	0	4	75	29	38	8	1
Saline	6	0	1	0	5	139	42	86	11	4
Scott	4	0	0	0	4	20	6	13	1	1
Seward	9	0	1	0	8	82	23	55	4	1
Sherman	4	0	1	0	3	19	6	11	2	0
Smith	7	1	2	0	4	21	4	17	0	0
Stafford	2	0	0	0	2	30	7	21	2	3
Stevens	17	0	1	0	16	65	29	33	3	0
Thomas	0	0	0	0	0	28	8	19	1	0
Washington	3	0	0	0	3	16	6	9	1	0
Wichita	5	0	0	0	5	39	7	29	3	1
Wilson	5	0	0	0	5	40	14	19	7	0
Woodson	3	0	0	0	3	41	16	22	3	3
KENTUCKY										
Metropolitan Counties										
Boone	105	1	14	18	72	1 150	256	801	93	5
Bourbon	1	0	0	0	1	12	8	4	0	0
Boyd	17	0	4	4	9	224	64	125	35	0
Boyd County Police Department	2	0	0	0	2	72	11	58	3	0
Bullitt	16	0	4	6	6	481	151	273	57	0
Campbell County Police Department	37	2	25	1	9	279	77	175	27	3
Christian	14	1	2	7	4	253	108	133	12	3
Christian County Police Department	13	0	0	0	13	11	1	10	0	0
Clark	17	0	4	1	12	236	75	147	14	2
Daviess	42	1	4	6	31	449	143	295	11	5
Edmonson	3	0	0	0	3	46	21	23	2	0
Gallatin	1	0	0	0	1	16	4	11	1	0
Grant	5	1	2	1	1	96	29	54	13	0
Greenup	1	0	0	1	0	25	9	11	5	0
Hancock	0	0	0	0	0	19	5	12	2	0
Hardin	3	0	0	0	3	90	32	52	6	5
Henry	0	0	0	0	0	2	2	0	0	0
Jefferson	2	0	0	2	0	18	1	6	11	0
Jessamine	11	0	0	2	9	283	111	155	17	0
Kenton	3	0	0	0	3	7	0	4	3	0
Larue	2	0	0	1	1	42	15	21	6	0
McLean	1	0	0	0	1	15	9	4	2	0
Meade	5	0	1	1	3	106	53	42	11	0
Nelson	14	0	1	1	12	217	80	123	14	3
Oldham County Police Department	15	0	4	4	7	393	108	268	17	0
Pendleton	2	0	1	1	0	75	32	36	7	2
Scott	8	0	2	0	6	221	69	124	28	1
Shelby	26	0	1	6	19	399	82	276	41	1
Spencer	4	0	0	1	3	26	12	11	3	0
Trigg	1	0	0	0	1	100	50	44	6	0

Note: The data shown in this table do not reflect county totals but are the number of offenses reported by the sheriff's office or county police department.

[1]The FBI does not publish arson data unless it receives data from either the agency or the state for all 12 months of the calendar year.

Table 10. Offenses Known to Law Enforcement, by State Metropolitan and Nonmetropolitan Counties, 2005—*Continued*

(Number.)

County	Violent crime	Murder and nonnegligent manslaughter	Forcible rape	Robbery	Aggravated assault	Property crime	Burglary	Larceny-theft	Motor vehicle theft	Arson[1]
Trimble	2	0	1	0	1	17	7	8	2	0
Webster	0	0	0	0	0	3	0	3	0	0
Nonmetropolitan Counties										
Allen	4	0	3	0	1	69	30	35	4	0
Anderson	8	0	5	1	2	80	31	48	1	0
Ballard	4	2	0	1	1	86	34	46	6	0
Barren	0	0	0	0	0	167	34	122	11	0
Bell	7	0	0	2	5	128	45	69	14	1
Boyle	3	0	0	0	3	53	26	22	5	1
Breckinridge	1	0	1	0	0	58	38	13	7	0
Butler	1	0	0	0	1	13	6	5	2	0
Caldwell	6	0	0	0	6	44	16	23	5	1
Calloway	14	0	4	3	7	306	123	165	18	0
Carlisle	0	0	0	0	0	17	13	4	0	0
Carter	5	0	1	1	3	18	8	8	2	0
Casey	0	0	0	0	0	39	20	16	3	0
Clay	7	0	0	1	6	116	37	56	23	1
Clinton	0	0	0	0	0	2	2	0	0	0
Crittenden	1	0	0	0	1	81	28	48	5	0
Estill	3	0	0	1	2	52	23	22	7	0
Fleming	2	0	0	0	2	25	4	20	1	0
Floyd	7	0	1	0	6	141	34	91	16	1
Franklin	16	0	2	4	10	159	53	86	20	0
Fulton	2	0	1	1	0	31	8	20	3	1
Garrard	0	0	0	0	0	86	11	65	10	0
Graves	13	0	4	0	9	193	86	95	12	1
Grayson	12	0	4	0	8	133	67	51	15	1
Harlan	16	0	0	1	15	75	23	43	9	5
Harrison	0	0	0	0	0	32	13	18	1	0
Hart	0	0	0	0	0	39	9	24	6	0
Hopkins	10	0	0	1	9	217	68	126	23	2
Jackson	0	0	0	0	0	15	4	8	3	0
Johnson	5	0	0	2	3	59	13	23	23	0
Knott	1	0	0	0	1	62	12	46	4	0
Laurel	12	1	1	1	9	691	226	385	80	1
Lewis	3	0	0	0	3	66	31	27	8	1
Lincoln	1	0	0	0	1	97	36	56	5	0
Livingston	9	0	4	2	3	177	67	101	9	0
Logan	17	0	0	3	14	151	68	74	9	0
Madison	5	0	0	1	4	346	116	211	19	0
Magoffin	0	0	0	0	0	2	0	2	0	0
Marion	6	0	0	2	4	38	19	15	4	0
Marshall	26	2	2	1	21	278	103	155	20	0
Martin	3	0	0	2	1	75	27	36	12	0
Mason	3	0	1	0	2	102	35	58	9	1
McCreary	0	0	0	0	0	64	15	41	8	0
Menifee	0	0	0	0	0	23	11	12	0	0
Mercer	8	0	0	3	5	91	46	41	4	0
Metcalfe	3	0	0	0	3	36	5	22	9	1
Montgomery	8	0	0	0	8	393	142	220	31	1
Morgan	0	0	0	0	0	5	3	0	2	0
Muhlenberg	3	0	0	1	2	45	19	19	7	1
Ohio	8	0	0	0	8	138	51	77	10	1
Owen	1	0	0	1	0	53	31	17	5	0
Owsley	2	0	0	1	1	35	16	16	3	0
Perry	10	0	2	3	5	81	55	20	6	0
Pike	1	0	0	1	0	28	6	22	0	0
Powell	0	0	0	0	0	73	24	47	2	0
Pulaski	27	2	7	6	12	814	247	505	62	7
Rockcastle	11	0	1	3	7	67	26	27	14	2
Russell	0	0	0	0	0	16	5	11	0	0
Simpson	6	0	0	2	4	82	21	56	5	0
Taylor	11	0	3	0	8	129	64	58	7	3
Todd	0	0	0	0	0	4	1	2	1	0
Union	2	0	0	1	1	48	8	34	6	0
Wayne	10	2	1	0	7	69	36	24	9	0
Wolfe	0	0	0	0	0	35	9	22	4	0
LOUISIANA										
Metropolitan Counties										
Ascension	384	5	24	28	327	2 981	592	2 090	299	6
Bossier	275	0	4	3	268	581	74	447	60	1
Caddo	197	1	22	22	152	1 104	272	711	121	12
Calcasieu	337	4	67	63	203	3 408	910	2 264	234	15
Cameron	69	0	0	1	68	233	57	163	13	1
East Baton Rouge	776	10	40	245	481	9 270	1 445	7 336	489	47
Grant	46	0	2	0	44	269	104	138	27	1
Lafayette	240	5	22	33	180	1 481	442	879	160	15
Lafourche	170	2	10	20	138	1 828	391	1 356	81	2
Livingston	276	6	24	10	236	930	485	355	90	1

Note: The data shown in this table do not reflect county totals but are the number of offenses reported by the sheriff's office or county police department.

[1]The FBI does not publish arson data unless it receives data from either the agency or the state for all 12 months of the calendar year.

Table 10. Offenses Known to Law Enforcement, by State Metropolitan and Nonmetropolitan Counties, 2005—*Continued*

(Number.)

County	Violent crime	Murder and nonnegligent manslaughter	Forcible rape	Robbery	Aggravated assault	Property crime	Burglary	Larceny-theft	Motor vehicle theft	Arson[1]
Ouachita	223	4	21	30	168	2 253	740	1 425	88	8
Plaquemines	74	1	0	6	67	381	103	254	24	1
Pointe Coupee	69	2	4	2	61	283	59	221	3	0
St. Charles	96	5	8	24	59	1 463	437	874	152	14
St. Helena	42	1	1	1	39	151	44	94	13	1
St. John the Baptist	146	5	19	45	77	1 338	303	911	124	0
St. Tammany	424	8	24	43	349	2 906	782	1 884	240	14
Terrebonne	302	3	33	35	231	3 008	614	2 180	214	26
West Baton Rouge	102	0	4	12	86	655	51	563	41	0
West Feliciana	72	2	3	7	60	144	41	90	13	3
Nonmetropolitan Counties										
Acadia	20	2	2	6	10	565	93	428	44	0
Assumption	202	0	0	3	199	382	35	317	30	0
Beauregard	28	0	4	0	24	345	117	196	32	3
Bienville	25	0	4	0	21	128	36	87	5	0
Caldwell	32	0	0	2	30	151	53	91	7	0
Concordia	21	1	2	2	16	157	37	110	10	1
East Carroll	20	1	2	2	15	61	28	30	3	1
Evangeline	44	0	7	2	35	394	113	249	32	0
Franklin	23	1	0	1	21	240	71	163	6	3
Jackson	8	0	0	1	7	93	23	68	2	0
Lincoln	22	0	2	0	20	300	80	212	8	0
Madison	66	0	2	3	61	135	32	91	12	1
Morehouse	41	0	2	5	34	321	57	258	6	0
Natchitoches	147	2	5	4	136	466	176	254	36	0
Richland	10	0	3	2	5	184	60	108	16	0
St. James	86	1	2	7	76	522	134	363	25	2
St. Landry	151	3	5	8	135	898	254	567	77	9
Tangipahoa	962	2	25	66	869	3 288	1 322	1 854	112	0
Vermilion	90	0	2	1	87	168	23	136	9	1
Vernon	95	0	11	3	81	574	102	450	22	2
Washington	44	2	2	13	27	352	113	216	23	0
Webster	58	3	3	5	47	256	86	151	19	1
West Carroll	31	0	1	0	30	277	88	157	32	0
MAINE										
Metropolitan Counties										
Androscoggin	6	0	3	0	3	298	55	228	15	0
Cumberland	42	0	9	5	28	580	234	301	45	1
Penobscot	8	0	0	0	8	758	228	495	35	0
Sagadahoc	12	0	2	0	10	209	56	142	11	1
York	40	0	4	1	35	363	146	207	10	1
Nonmetropolitan Counties										
Aroostook	5	0	0	2	3	133	46	84	3	0
Hancock	3	0	0	1	2	202	40	150	12	0
Kennebec	19	0	9	1	9	293	109	171	13	0
Knox	15	0	6	3	6	207	64	132	11	0
Lincoln	9	0	5	2	2	242	61	173	8	0
Oxford	5	0	2	0	3	253	104	135	14	0
Piscataquis	3	0	1	1	1	97	32	61	4	0
Somerset	15	0	4	1	10	288	85	185	18	1
Waldo	20	0	1	2	17	263	68	177	18	0
Washington	1	0	0	0	1	119	52	62	5	0
MARYLAND										
Metropolitan Counties										
Allegany	13	0	0	0	13	117	26	90	1	0
Anne Arundel	0	0	0	0	0	0	0	0	0	0
Anne Arundel County Police Department	2 705	12	75	679	1 939	15 187	2 805	11 031	1 351	133
Baltimore County	0	0	0	0	0	0	0	0	0	0
Baltimore County Police Department	5 609	40	177	1 765	3 627	24 937	4 589	17 324	3 024	312
Calvert	153	1	11	20	121	1 217	253	899	65	0
Carroll	35	0	2	2	31	225	55	163	7	1
Cecil	55	1	0	8	46	761	252	412	97	0
Charles	715	4	35	188	488	4 024	636	2 785	603	0
Frederick	143	1	13	13	116	1 279	286	909	84	6
Harford	374	2	17	95	260	2 602	572	1 854	176	7
Howard	2	0	0	0	2	0	0	0	0	0
Howard County Police Department	609	4	42	262	301	7 146	1 225	5 385	536	172
Montgomery	0	0	0	0	0	0	0	0	0	0
Montgomery County Police Department	2 079	19	150	1 035	875	21 925	3 570	15 869	2 486	315
Prince George's	27	0	0	0	27	0	0	0	0	0
Prince George's County Police Department	8 232	150	266	4 447	3 369	45 563	6 372	24 003	15 188	471
Queen Anne's	43	1	5	10	27	558	138	399	21	2
Somerset	5	0	0	0	5	23	4	19	0	0
Washington	163	2	8	15	138	1 239	275	878	86	0
Wicomico	199	2	16	24	157	815	274	495	46	5

Note: The data shown in this table do not reflect county totals but are the number of offenses reported by the sheriff's office or county police department.

[1]The FBI does not publish arson data unless it receives data from either the agency or the state for all 12 months of the calendar year.

Table 10. Offenses Known to Law Enforcement, by State Metropolitan and Nonmetropolitan Counties, 2005—*Continued*

(Number.)

County	Violent crime	Murder and nonnegligent manslaughter	Forcible rape	Robbery	Aggravated assault	Property crime	Burglary	Larceny-theft	Motor vehicle theft	Arson[1]
Nonmetropolitan Counties										
Caroline	63	0	2	1	60	274	114	143	17	1
Dorchester	25	0	2	1	22	225	56	145	24	2
Garrett	25	0	1	0	24	239	63	166	10	0
Kent	17	0	0	1	16	93	40	47	6	0
St. Mary's	262	1	19	34	208	1 596	348	1 149	99	8
Talbot	13	0	0	4	9	124	27	87	10	0
Worcester	75	1	3	0	71	145	42	91	12	0
MICHIGAN										
Metropolitan Counties										
Barry	21	0	2	1	18	218	45	157	16	2
Bay	41	0	8	9	24	695	148	500	47	3
Berrien	93	4	20	5	64	583	130	416	37	5
Calhoun	86	0	11	7	68	532	156	332	44	5
Cass	44	0	16	3	25	752	252	455	45	4
Clinton	22	2	8	0	12	284	85	181	18	2
Eaton	132	2	23	23	84	1 705	314	1 285	106	6
Genesee	48	0	20	2	26	633	138	432	63	2
Ingham[3]	95	2	19	16	58	1 186	283	819	84	13
Ionia	57	1	15	1	40	341	96	211	34	2
Jackson	92	1	18	5	68	500	153	306	41	7
Kalamazoo	204	0	31	40	133	1 881	502	1 256	123	21
Kent	353	0	44	48	261	4 128	1 062	2 872	194	35
Lapeer	65	0	10	1	54	495	102	361	32	2
Livingston	68	0	10	7	51	923	191	651	81	9
Macomb[3]	281	1	24	33	223	2 571	349	1 966	256	10
Monroe	189	2	39	29	119	2 463	591	1 631	241	48
Muskegon	73	0	19	2	52	805	163	590	52	8
Newaygo	75	1	38	1	35	421	174	230	17	0
Oakland	512	3	82	54	373	4 721	805	3 655	261	61
Ottawa	318	2	140	24	152	2 990	733	2 107	150	24
Saginaw	102	2	14	10	76	895	191	630	74	5
St. Clair	218	2	37	15	164	1 845	457	1 206	182	9
Van Buren	56	0	12	2	42	672	198	421	53	7
Washtenaw	362	3	57	77	225	2 239	691	1 210	338	19
Wayne	225	2	13	59	151	678	150	189	339	21
Nonmetropolitan Counties										
Alcona	7	1	0	0	6	254	101	150	3	1
Alger	1	0	0	0	1	3	1	2	0	0
Allegan	86	1	19	6	60	675	196	434	45	5
Antrim	12	0	0	0	12	276	109	155	12	3
Arenac	24	0	5	1	18	181	58	112	11	0
Baraga	1	0	0	0	1	19	1	16	2	0
Benzie	20	0	8	0	12	207	63	131	13	0
Branch	19	0	9	0	10	241	61	170	10	0
Charlevoix	18	1	8	0	9	218	55	148	15	0
Cheboygan	9	0	2	0	7	97	25	67	5	0
Chippewa	9	0	0	0	9	66	18	40	8	0
Clare	69	0	13	2	54	836	373	419	44	6
Crawford	14	0	8	1	5	151	44	88	19	0
Delta	4	0	1	0	3	99	35	60	4	0
Dickinson	0	0	0	0	0	79	13	62	4	0
Emmet	12	1	0	1	10	233	48	173	12	1
Gladwin	17	0	6	3	8	152	67	71	14	1
Grand Traverse	121	0	36	2	83	1 041	195	816	30	3
Gratiot	11	0	3	3	5	205	55	137	13	3
Hillsdale	50	0	17	1	32	218	84	122	12	1
Houghton	5	0	2	1	2	114	28	75	11	0
Huron	13	0	1	1	11	201	66	126	9	3
Iosco	0	0	0	0	0	34	12	22	0	0
Iron	3	0	1	0	2	28	8	19	1	0
Isabella	47	0	12	4	31	427	117	287	23	5
Kalkaska	14	0	5	0	9	271	112	151	8	2
Keweenaw	3	0	0	0	3	79	32	46	1	0
Lake	23	0	3	1	19	317	169	138	10	4
Lenawee	33	0	10	1	22	430	158	246	26	2
Luce	2	0	0	0	2	15	5	10	0	0
Mackinac	4	0	1	0	3	57	29	27	1	1
Manistee	10	1	4	0	5	86	19	60	7	2
Marquette	8	0	1	0	7	96	20	70	6	1
Mason	29	0	5	0	24	560	136	406	18	2
Mecosta	44	1	7	5	31	667	217	427	23	9
Menominee	11	0	5	2	4	93	43	45	5	3
Midland	54	0	19	4	31	493	118	351	24	3
Missaukee	14	0	1	2	11	227	86	129	12	1
Montcalm	77	0	39	2	36	689	248	394	47	5
Montmorency	9	1	0	0	8	78	39	36	3	1

Note: The data shown in this table do not reflect county totals but are the number of offenses reported by the sheriff's office or county police department.

[1]The FBI does not publish arson data unless it receives data from either the agency or the state for all 12 months of the calendar year.
[3]Because of changes in the state/local agency's reporting practices, figures are not comparable to previous years' data.

Table 10. Offenses Known to Law Enforcement, by State Metropolitan and Nonmetropolitan Counties, 2005—*Continued*

(Number.)

County	Violent crime	Murder and nonnegligent manslaughter	Forcible rape	Robbery	Aggravated assault	Property crime	Burglary	Larceny-theft	Motor vehicle theft	Arson[1]
Oceana	31	3	4	2	22	267	82	171	14	2
Ogemaw	19	0	7	1	11	178	68	105	5	7
Ontonagon	5	0	0	0	5	21	6	12	3	1
Osceola	34	0	8	0	26	205	91	105	9	1
Oscoda	13	0	3	0	10	221	41	164	16	2
Otsego	4	0	0	0	4	93	29	59	5	2
Roscommon	28	0	6	1	21	289	59	183	47	1
Sanilac	25	0	5	0	20	220	63	138	19	0
Schoolcraft	0	0	0	0	0	0	0	0	0	0
Shiawassee	55	0	5	1	49	451	141	280	30	1
St. Joseph	18	0	4	1	13	289	98	177	14	4
Tuscola	40	1	3	1	35	325	124	170	31	0
Wexford	28	0	5	1	22	356	97	250	9	2
MINNESOTA										
Metropolitan Counties										
Anoka	36	0	7	1	28	637	124	475	38	3
Benton	27	0	15	0	12	350	78	250	22	0
Carlton	25	0	11	0	14	348	103	218	27	2
Carver	44	0	7	2	35	774	145	580	49	6
Chisago	30	0	6	1	23	671	130	464	77	0
Clay	12	0	4	1	7	109	26	75	8	0
Dakota	17	0	2	0	15	197	50	129	18	0
Dodge	9	0	0	3	6	175	48	120	7	4
Hennepin	31	0	2	3	26	168	34	119	15	1
Houston	4	0	1	0	3	80	24	53	3	0
Isanti	17	0	7	0	10	402	122	223	57	2
Olmsted	23	0	5	1	17	409	115	252	42	2
Polk	29	1	11	1	16	221	47	162	12	10
Ramsey	17	0	3	3	11	224	25	172	27	8
Scott	9	0	5	0	4	169	32	109	28	0
Sherburne	46	0	8	1	37	670	123	496	51	5
Stearns	45	2	14	0	29	542	150	367	25	5
St. Louis	72	0	37	3	32	1 106	499	504	103	11
Washington	60	0	14	3	43	1 232	242	896	94	7
Wright	50	0	7	7	36	2 006	241	1 628	137	9
Nonmetropolitan Counties										
Aitkin	27	0	11	0	16	459	179	247	33	0
Becker	24	0	2	3	19	255	83	128	44	0
Beltrami	50	2	8	3	37	436	105	263	68	13
Big Stone	1	0	1	0	0	73	38	30	5	0
Blue Earth	18	0	11	0	7	296	123	155	18	2
Brown	1	0	0	0	1	17	3	13	1	0
Cass	122	4	64	9	45	1 020	246	673	101	1
Clearwater	12	1	5	1	5	154	45	101	8	0
Cottonwood	4	0	2	0	2	40	14	25	1	0
Crow Wing	33	1	11	2	19	658	239	377	42	0
Douglas	22	1	4	1	16	387	124	239	24	2
Faribault	4	0	1	0	3	75	33	31	11	1
Fillmore	15	0	9	0	6	120	35	75	10	1
Freeborn	8	0	2	0	6	155	50	91	14	0
Goodhue	17	0	7	0	10	272	74	171	27	0
Grant	2	0	0	0	2	89	26	62	1	1
Hubbard	17	0	5	1	11	325	117	183	25	1
Itasca	50	0	9	2	39	525	200	273	52	3
Jackson	6	0	2	0	4	33	11	20	2	0
Kanabec	20	0	9	0	11	254	98	123	33	1
Kandiyohi	22	0	12	0	10	355	78	257	20	2
Kittson	5	0	1	0	4	79	18	58	3	1
Koochiching	12	0	4	0	8	143	66	73	4	1
Lac Qui Parle	2	0	2	0	0	50	17	30	3	0
Lake	1	0	1	0	0	101	42	48	11	0
Lake of the Woods	6	0	1	0	5	85	15	60	10	0
Le Sueur	10	0	2	0	8	159	9	132	18	0
Lincoln	11	0	0	0	11	11	0	11	0	0
Lyon	6	0	4	0	2	70	34	31	5	0
Mahnomen	35	0	1	1	33	203	50	139	14	3
Marshall	6	0	0	0	6	109	7	98	4	0
Martin	2	0	1	0	1	58	22	28	8	0
McLeod	8	0	5	0	3	135	50	64	21	1
Meeker	23	0	14	2	7	348	97	231	20	1
Mille Lacs	34	1	7	1	25	649	132	440	77	3
Morrison	18	0	5	0	13	424	84	310	30	1
Mower	16	0	5	0	11	270	77	171	22	0
Murray	5	0	1	0	4	85	38	38	9	0
Nicollet	5	0	3	0	2	112	27	76	9	0
Nobles	1	0	1	0	0	63	25	36	2	0

Note: The data shown in this table do not reflect county totals but are the number of offenses reported by the sheriff's office or county police department.

[1]The FBI does not publish arson data unless it receives data from either the agency or the state for all 12 months of the calendar year.

Table 10. Offenses Known to Law Enforcement, by State Metropolitan and Nonmetropolitan Counties, 2005—*Continued*

(Number.)

County	Violent crime	Murder and nonnegligent manslaughter	Forcible rape	Robbery	Aggravated assault	Property crime	Burglary	Larceny-theft	Motor vehicle theft	Arson[1]
Norman	4	0	0	0	4	57	21	33	3	0
Otter Tail	35	1	12	1	21	572	170	359	43	5
Pennington	1	0	0	0	1	53	23	26	4	0
Pope	5	0	0	0	5	48	7	33	8	0
Red Lake	1	0	0	0	1	15	1	13	1	0
Redwood	13	0	8	0	5	90	26	53	11	1
Renville	25	0	6	2	17	247	67	142	38	2
Rice	14	1	6	1	6	276	88	159	29	13
Rock	18	0	0	0	18	55	10	36	9	0
Roseau	3	0	1	0	2	105	22	78	5	1
Steele	14	0	3	1	10	199	56	125	18	5
Stevens	3	0	1	0	2	30	7	21	2	0
Swift	1	0	0	0	1	22	8	11	3	0
Todd	22	0	10	0	12	267	89	155	23	1
Traverse	5	0	2	0	3	27	9	18	0	0
Wadena	10	0	4	0	6	76	26	41	9	2
Waseca	7	0	4	0	3	103	47	49	7	1
Watonwan	3	0	2	0	1	88	27	57	4	0
Wilkin	5	0	1	0	4	46	7	38	1	1
Winona	10	0	0	0	10	95	17	64	14	1
Yellow Medicine	1	0	0	0	1	98	35	59	4	0
MISSISSIPPI										
Metropolitan Counties										
Desoto	42	0	6	11	25	664	152	380	132	3
George[3]	22	0	1	0	21	223	81	124	18	3
Harrison	111	8	49	11	43	1 451	343	979	129	4
Hinds	55	1	12	17	25	748	260	378	110	1
Jackson	101	4	17	16	64	1 632	388	959	285	0
Lamar	40	1	15	7	17	678	261	388	29	1
Madison	60	2	5	10	43	434	112	293	29	2
Rankin	41	1	2	5	33	687	261	371	55	12
Stone	35	0	5	3	27	112	15	85	12	0
Tate	8	0	2	3	3	244	103	99	42	3
Nonmetropolitan Counties										
Adams	38	2	4	4	28	556	196	327	33	3
Chickasaw	23	1	0	5	17	59	35	24	0	1
Claiborne	19	4	1	1	13	108	67	39	2	2
Coahoma	12	0	1	2	9	154	76	54	24	0
Grenada	20	2	3	0	15	163	59	85	19	0
Issaquena	0	0	0	0	0	0	0	0	0	0
Itawamba[3]	10	2	2	3	3	209	102	92	15	2
Jefferson	41	1	1	0	39	25	8	17	0	0
Lauderdale	26	1	4	11	10	497	244	218	35	2
Lee	91	0	12	15	64	731	312	378	41	28
Leflore	133	1	4	11	117	479	178	266	35	1
Lincoln	22	0	1	1	20	296	87	191	18	1
Lowndes	55	1	13	9	32	526	149	345	32	2
Marion	58	2	10	3	43	375	173	178	24	0
Oktibbeha	3	0	0	0	3	31	8	23	0	0
Panola	77	4	4	10	59	601	280	290	31	1
Pike	28	1	2	5	20	384	171	202	11	. . .
Scott	49	1	14	5	29	341	138	173	30	. . .
Sharkey	17	1	0	1	15	20	19	1	0	0
Tippah	28	1	0	5	22	34	27	2	5	0
Tishomingo	27	0	3	21	3	59	52	2	5	0
Union	11	1	0	3	7	193	109	72	12	3
Warren	9	0	3	0	6	366	143	198	25	0
Washington	18	1	7	4	6	433	158	238	37	6
MISSOURI										
Metropolitan Counties										
Andrew	4	0	1	0	3	139	36	89	14	2
Bates	29	1	1	1	26	189	86	90	13	4
Boone	95	1	5	6	83	832	211	542	79	9
Buchanan	28	0	2	5	21	233	64	155	14	2
Caldwell	35	0	1	0	34	77	26	39	12	3
Callaway	19	0	2	0	17	566	142	375	49	1
Cass	102	0	3	0	99	538	162	314	62	0
Christian	143	1	2	5	135	356	122	179	55	5
Clay	46	0	0	1	45	209	63	121	25	7
Clinton[3]	24	1	3	1	19	99	29	58	12	2

Note: The data shown in this table do not reflect county totals but are the number of offenses reported by the sheriff's office or county police department.

[1]The FBI does not publish arson data unless it receives data from either the agency or the state for all 12 months of the calendar year.
[3]Because of changes in the state/local agency's reporting practices, figures are not comparable to previous years' data.
. . . = Not available.

Table 10. Offenses Known to Law Enforcement, by State Metropolitan and Nonmetropolitan Counties, 2005—*Continued*

(Number.)

County	Violent crime	Murder and nonnegligent manslaughter	Forcible rape	Robbery	Aggravated assault	Property crime	Burglary	Larceny-theft	Motor vehicle theft	Arson[1]
Cole	41	0	4	3	34	432	125	279	28	5
Dallas	54	0	0	1	53	225	94	105	26	2
De Kalb	15	0	0	0	15	67	16	36	15	0
Franklin	51	4	3	2	42	762	152	560	50	5
Greene	40	3	0	8	29	1 289	287	901	101	0
Howard	5	0	4	0	1	43	33	8	2	1
Jackson	91	0	7	6	78	649	182	396	71	4
Jasper	100	3	9	12	76	837	210	619	8	0
Jefferson	375	1	33	11	330	3 321	532	2 512	277	28
Lafayette	12	0	4	0	8	232	103	111	18	0
Lincoln	69	1	0	1	67	282	85	157	40	2
McDonald	70	2	5	3	60	442	122	261	59	4
Moniteau	12	1	0	0	11	71	28	37	6	0
Newton	90	0	10	1	79	1 179	276	763	140	11
Osage	6	0	0	0	6	126	49	66	11	3
Platte	30	0	2	1	27	315	51	236	28	7
Polk	30	0	4	2	24	298	107	166	25	0
Ray	14	0	1	0	13	175	56	91	28	0
St. Charles	222	0	8	15	199	1 593	342	1 143	108	24
St. Louis County Police Department	1 111	9	49	274	779	10 260	1 681	7 410	1 169	80
Warren	54	0	3	1	50	277	85	170	22	5
Washington	50	1	0	1	48	271	86	161	24	0
Webster	38	0	0	2	36	290	97	181	12	3
Nonmetropolitan Counties										
Adair	10	0	0	0	10	38	12	21	5	0
Atchison	4	0	1	0	3	14	8	4	2	0
Audrain	17	0	0	2	15	167	53	104	10	2
Barry	21	2	8	1	10	524	201	292	31	3
Barton	25	1	3	1	20	133	38	90	5	4
Benton	33	0	1	1	31	335	127	187	21	0
Bollinger	25	0	5	0	20	74	29	42	3	0
Butler	61	3	0	9	49	518	147	303	68	5
Camden	35	1	5	4	25	619	241	354	24	0
Cape Girardeau	76	0	4	1	71	211	77	124	10	4
Carroll	5	2	0	0	3	61	16	39	6	1
Carter	19	1	2	0	16	28	8	18	2	1
Cedar	0	0	0	0	0	104	37	62	5	2
Clark	7	0	1	0	6	58	27	28	3	1
Cooper	29	0	1	1	27	143	15	121	7	0
Crawford	23	1	2	1	19	267	93	164	10	1
Dade	5	0	0	0	5	23	6	13	4	0
Daviess	5	0	1	1	3	82	36	39	7	1
Dent	24	0	6	0	18	105	58	37	10	2
Douglas	40	1	2	0	37	137	42	64	31	0
Dunklin	18	1	1	1	15	153	52	94	7	0
Gasconade	27	0	0	4	23	71	19	41	11	1
Grundy	6	0	0	0	6	57	38	19	0	0
Henry	35	1	3	0	31	316	135	171	10	6
Hickory	3	0	0	0	3	147	55	83	9	1
Holt	6	0	0	0	6	91	35	46	10	1
Howell	60	0	3	0	57	354	118	194	42	1
Iron	14	0	2	0	12	63	31	27	5	1
Johnson	37	1	8	0	28	328	105	199	24	0
Knox	6	0	0	0	6	92	17	75	0	0
Laclede	51	0	2	0	49	367	132	222	13	0
Lawrence	13	0	1	3	9	216	92	101	23	3
Lewis	1	0	0	0	1	77	19	52	6	0
Linn	1	0	0	0	1	72	22	44	6	8
Livingston	2	0	0	0	2	49	23	22	4	0
Madison	13	1	0	0	12	54	20	22	12	1
Maries	15	0	0	0	15	50	26	24	0	0
Marion	7	0	0	0	7	92	24	67	1	1
Mercer	7	0	0	0	7	27	22	1	4	0
Miller	60	0	8	0	52	163	50	87	26	1
Mississippi	18	0	1	1	16	85	29	46	10	1
Monroe	1	0	0	0	1	51	14	33	4	2
Montgomery	4	0	0	0	4	92	27	60	5	0
New Madrid	20	0	2	0	18	57	21	31	5	2
Nodaway	16	0	1	0	15	118	48	63	7	2
Oregon	4	1	0	0	3	7	1	0	6	0
Ozark	12	0	1	1	10	74	33	37	4	3
Pemiscot	17	1	0	2	14	122	47	74	1	0
Perry	9	1	0	0	8	45	12	27	6	0
Pettis	29	0	5	2	22	276	83	177	16	1

Note: The data shown in this table do not reflect county totals but are the number of offenses reported by the sheriff's office or county police department.

[1]The FBI does not publish arson data unless it receives data from either the agency or the state for all 12 months of the calendar year.

Table 10. Offenses Known to Law Enforcement, by State Metropolitan and Nonmetropolitan Counties, 2005—*Continued*

(Number.)

County	Violent crime	Murder and nonnegligent manslaughter	Forcible rape	Robbery	Aggravated assault	Property crime	Burglary	Larceny-theft	Motor vehicle theft	Arson[1]
Phelps	160	0	11	3	146	543	155	351	37	1
Pike	5	0	1	0	4	61	36	17	8	4
Pulaski	104	2	12	6	84	260	96	143	21	0
Putnam	2	0	0	0	2	11	6	3	2	0
Ralls	17	0	0	0	17	86	31	43	12	0
Randolph	18	0	1	1	16	153	78	64	11	0
Reynolds	6	1	1	0	4	30	19	5	6	0
Ripley	22	0	0	0	22	220	68	134	18	2
Saline	14	0	4	0	10	130	50	74	6	0
Schuyler	1	0	0	0	1	18	10	4	4	3
Scotland	0	0	0	0	0	39	18	21	0	0
Scott	16	0	1	1	14	133	54	76	3	0
Shannon	10	0	1	0	9	59	11	30	18	3
Shelby	1	0	0	0	1	41	13	27	1	0
St. Clair	12	0	0	0	12	200	84	116	0	1
Ste. Genevieve	14	0	0	1	13	157	42	104	11	0
St. Francois	57	0	7	3	47	526	161	308	57	1
Stoddard	20	1	2	0	17	136	57	65	14	4
Stone	320	1	2	2	315	670	213	397	60	7
Sullivan	13	0	0	0	13	47	19	21	7	0
Taney	134	2	9	2	121	641	157	427	57	0
Texas	38	0	6	1	31	218	69	121	28	8
Vernon	21	0	1	1	19	270	87	162	21	5
Wayne	20	1	2	0	17	105	35	62	8	1
Worth	9	0	0	0	9	31	18	11	2	0
Wright	11	0	1	0	10	76	18	41	17	1
MONTANA										
Metropolitan Counties[3]										
Carbon	2	0	0	0	2	26	1	22	3	0
Yellowstone	86	0	7	3	76	843	157	632	54	5
Nonmetropolitan Counties										
Beaverhead	9	0	1	0	8	54	5	39	10	0
Big Horn	46	0	0	2	44	372	26	319	27	1
Blaine	10	0	0	1	9	52	10	39	3	0
Broadwater	44	0	3	0	41	182	14	160	8	2
Chouteau	5	0	1	0	4	20	6	13	1	0
Dawson	6	1	0	0	5	41	9	30	2	0
Deer Lodge	20	0	0	0	20	151	11	132	8	0
Fergus	9	0	5	0	4	20	5	11	4	0
Gallatin	44	0	11	1	32	501	99	355	47	10
Glacier	36	0	1	0	35	44	9	30	5	1
Granite	3	0	0	0	3	61	13	47	1	0
Hill	21	0	1	0	20	140	20	99	21	0
Jefferson	12	0	2	0	10	41	13	22	6	1
Lake	58	2	4	1	51	369	100	225	44	1
Lewis and Clark	63	0	12	1	50	356	71	235	50	5
Lincoln	78	0	1	0	77	271	58	186	27	0
Madison	6	0	0	0	6	54	13	35	6	0
Meagher	5	0	0	0	5	33	6	26	1	0
Mineral	31	1	1	0	29	22	2	17	3	0
Musselshell	19	0	0	0	19	125	7	112	6	3
Park	27	0	2	0	25	111	33	69	9	3
Phillips	18	0	3	0	15	55	13	41	1	0
Ravalli	45	0	13	0	32	286	46	227	13	5
Rosebud	13	0	0	0	13	48	18	24	6	0
Sanders	32	0	1	0	31	122	24	93	5	2
Sheridan	1	0	0	0	1	24	3	19	2	0
Silver Bow	144	0	12	12	120	1 398	270	976	152	5
Stillwater	13	0	1	0	12	45	17	24	4	1
Sweet Grass	8	0	0	0	8	51	7	32	12	0
Teton	15	0	2	0	13	79	19	56	4	0
Toole	12	0	0	0	12	67	10	47	10	1
Valley	10	0	0	0	10	22	5	15	2	1
NEBRASKA										
Metropolitan Counties										
Dakota	2	0	0	0	2	38	10	27	1	0
Dixon	4	0	0	0	4	59	19	36	4	1
Douglas	124	0	3	25	96	1 175	330	755	90	0
Lancaster	22	0	9	0	13	427	102	308	17	4
Sarpy	54	0	13	5	36	791	94	612	85	7
Saunders	9	0	0	2	7	62	16	35	11	3
Seward	6	0	3	0	3	62	17	42	3	0
Washington	2	0	0	0	2	91	18	66	7	0

Note: The data shown in this table do not reflect county totals but are the number of offenses reported by the sheriff's office or county police department.

[1]The FBI does not publish arson data unless it receives data from either the agency or the state for all 12 months of the calendar year.
[3]Because of changes in the state/local agency's reporting practices, figures are not comparable to previous years' data.

Table 10. Offenses Known to Law Enforcement, by State Metropolitan and Nonmetropolitan Counties, 2005—*Continued*

(Number.)

County	Violent crime	Murder and nonnegligent manslaughter	Forcible rape	Robbery	Aggravated assault	Property crime	Burglary	Larceny-theft	Motor vehicle theft	Arson[1]
Nonmetropolitan Counties										
Adams	2	0	1	1	0	132	55	74	3	0
Antelope	2	0	1	0	1	13	0	13	0	0
Arthur	0	0	0	0	0	0	0	0	0	0
Box Butte	1	0	0	0	1	3	0	3	0	0
Boyd	0	0	0	0	0	11	1	9	1	0
Brown	2	0	0	0	2	48	4	43	1	0
Buffalo	9	0	2	0	7	247	42	185	20	3
Burt	1	0	0	0	1	28	7	21	0	1
Butler	0	0	0	0	0	36	3	33	0	1
Chase	1	0	0	0	1	9	0	7	2	0
Colfax	3	0	0	0	3	41	3	37	1	1
Cuming	1	0	1	0	0	15	6	8	1	0
Custer	1	0	1	0	0	76	14	61	1	0
Dawson	11	0	3	0	8	96	22	70	4	0
Deuel	1	0	0	0	1	35	9	19	7	0
Dodge	4	0	1	0	3	180	24	136	20	2
Franklin	2	0	0	0	2	21	1	16	4	0
Frontier	0	0	0	0	0	36	5	30	1	1
Furnas	1	0	0	0	1	38	4	32	2	1
Gage	7	0	2	0	5	183	41	126	16	0
Garden	1	0	0	0	1	4	1	3	0	0
Gosper	2	0	0	0	2	40	10	28	2	0
Hall	5	0	0	2	3	316	53	245	18	0
Hamilton	5	0	0	0	5	62	21	38	3	1
Harlan	1	0	1	0	0	1	0	1	0	0
Hitchcock	1	0	0	0	1	11	5	5	1	0
Hooker	1	0	0	0	1	1	1	0	0	0
Jefferson	6	0	2	0	4	48	11	35	2	0
Kearney	5	0	4	0	1	36	7	28	1	0
Keith	1	0	1	0	0	78	21	52	5	0
Kimball	3	0	0	0	3	20	1	17	2	0
Knox	8	0	0	1	7	32	6	25	1	0
Lincoln	11	0	1	1	9	150	45	97	8	0
Madison	10	0	2	0	8	92	28	58	6	0
Merrick	0	0	0	0	0	68	21	42	5	0
Morrill	1	0	0	0	1	18	5	12	1	0
Nance	0	0	0	0	0	30	10	14	6	0
Nemaha	2	0	0	0	2	29	12	15	2	1
Pawnee	0	0	0	0	0	61	6	50	5	0
Perkins	3	0	0	0	3	26	6	19	1	0
Phelps	1	0	0	0	1	36	14	19	3	0
Platte	5	0	2	1	2	219	52	148	19	0
Red Willow	1	0	0	0	1	47	12	33	2	0
Rock	1	0	0	0	1	20	3	16	1	0
Saline	5	1	0	0	4	62	13	46	3	0
Scotts Bluff	9	0	3	0	6	103	25	66	12	1
Sheridan	4	1	0	0	3	50	13	32	5	0
Sioux	0	0	0	0	0	0	0	0	0	0
Stanton	4	1	1	0	2	76	30	46	0	1
Thayer	1	0	0	0	1	120	34	79	7	1
Thurston	1	0	0	0	1	0	0	0	0	1
Wayne	2	0	1	0	1	19	3	15	1	0
Webster	7	0	1	0	6	52	14	35	3	2
Wheeler	0	0	0	0	0	4	0	2	2	0
York	1	0	0	1	0	70	11	58	1	1
NEVADA										
Metropolitan Counties										
Carson City	294	2	2	27	263	1 449	386	948	115	19
Washoe	205	1	2	14	188	1 482	488	744	250	8
Nonmetropolitan Counties										
Churchill	51	1	11	1	38	286	106	151	29	3
Douglas	82	1	23	15	43	1 109	259	785	65	5
Elko	30	1	6	4	19	236	103	105	28	1
Esmeralda	2	0	0	0	2	7	2	4	1	0
Eureka	4	0	0	0	4	14	7	7	0	0
Humboldt	54	0	0	1	53	70	20	44	6	2
Lander	22	0	10	3	9	137	52	81	4	0
Lincoln	4	0	1	0	3	44	16	22	6	1
Lyon	114	1	10	8	95	840	243	522	75	7
Mineral	8	0	1	0	7	65	37	21	7	2
Nye	110	4	12	9	85	1 128	257	720	151	27
Pershing	51	0	7	1	43	80	32	44	4	0
White Pine	33	2	3	1	27	207	64	124	19	0

Note: The data shown in this table do not reflect county totals but are the number of offenses reported by the sheriff's office or county police department.

[1] The FBI does not publish arson data unless it receives data from either the agency or the state for all 12 months of the calendar year.

Table 10. Offenses Known to Law Enforcement, by State Metropolitan and Nonmetropolitan Counties, 2005—*Continued*

(Number.)

County	Violent crime	Murder and nonnegligent manslaughter	Forcible rape	Robbery	Aggravated assault	Property crime	Burglary	Larceny-theft	Motor vehicle theft	Arson[1]
NEW HAMPSHIRE										
Metropolitan Counties										
Rockingham	7	0	0	0	7	23	0	20	3	0
Nonmetropolitan Counties										
Carroll	5	0	4	0	1	49	16	29	4	2
Cheshire	4	0	2	0	2	3	1	2	0	0
Merrimack	7	0	4	0	3	2	0	2	0	0
NEW JERSEY										
Metropolitan Counties										
Essex County Police Department	90	1	7	55	27	96	7	73	16	0
NEW MEXICO										
Metropolitan Counties										
Bernalillo	866	11	35	116	704	2 601	841	1 298	462	75
Sandoval	51	0	9	0	42	199	99	87	13	0
San Juan	255	1	42	10	202	1 239	246	886	107	10
Santa Fe	592	1	22	9	560	1 075	654	302	119	10
Valencia[3]	157	5	13	8	131	1 516	842	320	354	13
Nonmetropolitan Counties										
Catron	4	0	2	1	1	1	1	0	0	0
Chaves	60	2	13	5	40	492	288	161	43	0
Cibola	9	0	1	0	8	55	33	15	7	0
Colfax	1	0	0	0	1	14	6	6	2	0
Grant	13	0	0	2	11	101	48	53	0	0
Lea	31	1	10	1	19	465	135	300	30	0
McKinley	101	0	14	8	79	306	122	155	29	5
Mora	4	0	0	1	3	16	12	2	2	0
Otero	41	0	0	0	41	253	98	151	4	0
Roosevelt	6	1	0	0	5	62	29	25	8	. . .
Sierra	12	0	1	2	9	47	16	24	7	0
Socorro	9	0	1	0	8	22	7	5	10	0
NEW YORK										
Metropolitan Counties										
Albany	24	1	2	0	21	92	24	56	12	. . .
Broome	55	0	4	8	43	984	146	801	37	. . .
Chemung	30	0	2	3	25	292	51	230	11	. . .
Dutchess	66	1	7	6	52	741	151	551	39	4
Erie	136	0	12	13	111	887	218	648	21	11
Herkimer	0	0	0	0	0	24	0	24	0	. . .
Livingston	22	1	2	1	18	798	136	644	18	. . .
Madison	12	0	4	1	7	241	85	148	8	. . .
Monroe	216	2	27	53	134	4 089	602	3 308	179	17
Nassau	1 793	16	76	833	868	14 421	2 153	10 836	1 432	137
Niagara	112	0	21	26	65	1 291	318	906	67	. . .
Oneida	88	1	19	4	64	513	90	394	29	. . .
Onondaga	174	0	29	44	101	1 689	330	1 312	47	24
Ontario	50	0	5	14	31	887	192	650	45	. . .
Orleans	16	2	1	0	13	122	31	79	12	. . .
Oswego	22	0	8	3	11	317	96	205	16	. . .
Putman	39	0	8	7	24	447	97	318	32	. . .
Rensselaer	33	0	2	0	31	158	40	109	9	. . .
Rockland	13	0	0	1	12	32	0	32	0	. . .
Saratoga	48	1	6	6	35	867	140	702	25	6
Schenectady	3	0	0	1	2	9	1	5	3	. . .
Schoharie	2	0	0	0	2	81	14	64	3	. . .
Suffolk	291	0	0	1	290	17	4	7	6	. . .
Suffolk County Police Department	2 446	28	82	1 037	1 299	24 096	3 509	18 372	2 215	245
Tioga	10	1	0	0	9	182	51	115	16	. . .
Tompkins	27	0	12	8	7	488	128	335	25	. . .
Ulster	47	0	5	2	40	328	58	254	16	. . .
Washington	37	1	4	2	30	310	69	233	8	. . .
Wayne	40	1	8	5	26	649	158	460	31	. . .
Westchester Public Safety	57	1	2	6	48	269	17	238	14	. . .
Nonmetropolitan Counties										
Allegany	1	0	0	0	1	3	0	3	0	. . .
Cattaraugus	57	0	8	1	48	464	147	285	32	. . .
Cayuga	19	1	3	1	14	338	90	240	8	. . .
Chautauqua	51	0	8	7	36	997	232	737	28	. . .
Clinton	0	0	0	0	0	2	2	0	0	. . .
Delaware	13	1	3	0	9	112	41	70	1	. . .
Franklin	0	0	0	0	0	0	0	0	0	. . .
Fulton	18	1	0	1	16	422	107	291	24	. . .
Genesee	48	1	17	5	25	601	84	496	21	. . .
Greene	3	0	0	0	3	43	19	24	0	. . .

Note: The data shown in this table do not reflect county totals but are the number of offenses reported by the sheriff's office or county police department.

[1]The FBI does not publish arson data unless it receives data from either the agency or the state for all 12 months of the calendar year.
[3]Because of changes in the state/local agency's reporting practices, figures are not comparable to previous years' data.
. . . = Not available.

Table 10. Offenses Known to Law Enforcement, by State Metropolitan and Nonmetropolitan Counties, 2005—*Continued*

(Number.)

County	Violent crime	Murder and nonnegligent manslaughter	Forcible rape	Robbery	Aggravated assault	Property crime	Burglary	Larceny-theft	Motor vehicle theft	Arson[1]
Hamilton	1	1	0	0	0	22	8	14	0	. . .
Jefferson	44	0	11	2	31	506	97	398	11	. . .
Lewis	0	0	0	0	0	185	105	70	10	. . .
Otsego	17	1	4	1	11	164	54	100	10	. . .
Seneca	12	0	2	1	9	155	27	125	3	. . .
St. Lawrence	28	0	2	1	25	419	113	287	19	. . .
Sullivan	46	0	6	7	33	696	125	555	16	. . .
Wyoming	41	0	2	0	39	300	66	223	11	. . .
Yates	12	0	0	1	11	140	52	86	2	. . .
NORTH CAROLINA										
Metropolitan Counties										
Alamance	146	3	11	9	123	1 153	423	639	91	5
Alexander	69	2	6	7	54	730	281	385	64	11
Brunswick	127	4	17	24	82	2 150	1 004	955	191	9
Buncombe	165	4	12	30	119	2 610	980	1 369	261	9
Burke	106	5	5	11	85	1 553	647	783	123	9
Cabarrus	54	0	5	11	38	1 048	596	389	63	3
Caldwell	81	4	6	6	65	1 358	588	686	84	20
Catawba	136	4	14	15	103	1 816	715	923	178	9
Cumberland	644	8	29	133	474	5 997	2 310	3 384	303	79
Currituck	49	0	5	3	41	578	163	396	19	1
Davie	61	0	8	6	47	552	222	290	40	3
Durham	127	2	0	23	102	968	240	656	72	1
Edgecombe	61	2	2	10	47	628	259	320	49	4
Forsyth	291	1	22	25	243	2 929	834	1 928	167	52
Franklin	24	1	1	9	13	806	397	348	61	4
Gaston County Police Department	216	5	12	32	167	1 785	640	914	231	37
Greene	54	0	7	12	35	410	163	221	26	2
Guilford	206	2	11	45	148	1 853	705	999	149	38
Haywood	103	1	6	2	94	985	366	547	72	5
Henderson	96	2	20	16	58	1 372	471	766	135	3
Hoke	99	1	5	18	75	1 215	674	456	85	21
Johnston	153	4	10	15	124	2 298	867	1 223	208	8
Madison	24	1	3	0	20	186	74	88	24	3
Nash	99	3	9	16	71	787	271	441	75	12
New Hanover	255	0	39	44	172	2 617	778	1 713	126	8
Orange	30	3	1	13	13	672	309	303	60	2
Pender	52	0	5	9	38	762	260	410	92	3
Person	85	2	6	4	73	531	239	277	15	2
Pitt	247	2	16	28	201	1 585	526	969	90	9
Randolph	121	9	3	22	87	2 568	686	1 727	155	9
Rockingham	83	1	7	16	59	1 370	463	812	95	4
Stokes	95	4	3	9	79	969	383	501	85	11
Union	677	0	21	10	646	1 675	622	984	69	17
Wake	133	0	38	26	69	2 342	868	1 284	190	17
Wayne	124	2	3	25	94	1 747	633	1 027	87	3
Yadkin	82	1	1	4	76	562	236	282	44	5
Nonmetropolitan Counties										
Beaufort	89	1	5	15	68	845	280	514	51	8
Bertie	20	0	3	1	16	346	154	167	25	2
Bladen	166	1	4	7	154	882	288	533	61	2
Camden	12	0	0	1	11	50	19	28	3	1
Carteret	70	3	4	7	56	445	148	251	46	3
Caswell	72	3	2	8	59	379	144	205	30	0
Cherokee	68	1	8	1	58	431	147	250	34	7
Chowan	10	0	1	1	8	133	63	58	12	0
Clay	4	1	0	0	3	142	52	69	21	4
Cleveland	46	0	9	34	3	1 588	559	912	117	5
Columbus	250	6	9	33	202	1 618	685	792	141	4
Craven	164	0	5	12	147	1 401	413	892	96	1
Dare	43	1	3	1	38	569	146	408	15	1
Davidson	173	1	3	23	146	2 201	166	1 783	252	16
Duplin	107	2	2	8	95	794	446	271	77	4
Granville	63	1	2	14	46	752	300	408	44	4
Halifax	100	8	5	23	64	1 084	551	437	96	9
Harnett	252	3	24	27	198	2 396	1 058	1 120	218	24
Hertford	29	0	5	11	13	370	160	179	31	4
Iredell	189	6	20	18	145	2 088	782	1 119	187	22
Jackson	78	1	9	4	64	601	215	341	45	4
Lee	17	0	5	6	6	444	196	189	59	6
Lenoir	106	6	6	8	86	955	312	597	46	6
Macon	20	1	3	1	15	465	163	276	26	2
Martin	95	1	1	2	91	459	195	230	34	2
McDowell	32	2	5	8	17	685	296	320	69	8
Montgomery	56	1	6	5	44	335	115	188	32	0
Moore	85	1	6	11	67	907	421	406	80	28
Pasquotank	20	0	2	2	16	385	147	209	29	16
Perquimans	6	0	1	3	2	183	99	65	19	5

Note: The data shown in this table do not reflect county totals but are the number of offenses reported by the sheriff's office or county police department.

[1]The FBI does not publish arson data unless it receives data from either the agency or the state for all 12 months of the calendar year.
. . . = Not available.

Table 10. Offenses Known to Law Enforcement, by State Metropolitan and Nonmetropolitan Counties, 2005—*Continued*

(Number.)

County	Violent crime	Murder and nonnegligent manslaughter	Forcible rape	Robbery	Aggravated assault	Property crime	Burglary	Larceny-theft	Motor vehicle theft	Arson[1]
Polk	21	2	2	0	17	251	77	146	28	3
Richmond	102	1	9	24	68	1 130	456	625	49	5
Robeson	508	17	24	108	359	3 618	1 955	1 263	400	38
Rowan	137	2	20	19	96	1 430	489	810	131	19
Rutherford	110	6	8	18	78	1 036	469	483	84	8
Sampson	108	2	12	26	68	1 441	770	567	104	12
Scotland	54	3	11	16	24	585	302	244	39	20
Stanly	36	1	19	2	14	340	139	180	21	2
Surry	153	1	5	12	135	1 374	560	659	155	17
Swain	34	3	2	0	29	227	58	150	19	2
Transylvania	31	0	2	1	28	272	108	141	23	7
Tyrrell	17	1	1	6	9	60	12	43	5	0
Vance	70	2	4	19	45	1 354	674	608	72	10
Warren	42	3	4	9	26	568	233	300	35	8
Watauga	25	1	5	1	18	506	241	224	41	1
Wilkes	135	1	7	15	112	1 082	355	643	84	5
Wilson	85	3	3	6	73	773	282	428	63	. . .
Yancey	15	0	3	0	12	86	45	38	3	1
NORTH DAKOTA										
Metropolitan Counties										
Burleigh	17	0	4	0	13	162	36	103	23	1
Cass	10	0	2	0	8	217	45	147	25	1
Grand Forks	8	0	1	0	7	103	26	64	13	0
Morton	11	0	4	0	7	98	13	76	9	2
Nonmetropolitan Counties										
Adams	0	0	0	0	0	17	5	11	1	0
Barnes	5	0	0	0	5	35	11	21	3	0
Bottineau	0	0	0	0	0	65	14	47	4	0
Cavalier	0	0	0	0	0	10	2	8	0	0
Dickey	0	0	0	0	0	45	3	40	2	1
Dunn	0	0	0	0	0	0	0	0	0	0
Eddy	3	1	0	0	2	14	2	12	0	0
Emmons	0	0	0	0	0	30	11	18	1	0
Foster	0	0	0	0	0	4	1	3	0	0
Grant	0	0	0	0	0	5	0	5	0	0
Griggs	0	0	0	0	0	3	1	2	0	0
Kidder	1	0	0	0	1	5	5	0	0	0
McHenry	5	0	0	0	5	47	19	23	5	0
McKenzie	0	0	0	0	0	10	5	3	2	0
McLean	1	0	0	0	1	47	3	42	2	0
Mercer	2	0	0	0	2	24	9	14	1	0
Oliver	0	0	0	0	0	6	0	5	1	0
Pembina	1	0	0	0	1	45	3	30	12	0
Pierce	0	0	0	0	0	11	4	7	0	0
Ramsey	3	0	0	0	3	23	4	14	5	0
Ransom	0	0	0	0	0	20	9	7	4	0
Richland	7	1	0	0	6	126	35	77	14	0
Sargent	0	0	0	0	0	31	5	23	3	0
Sheridan	1	0	0	0	1	12	1	11	0	0
Stark	3	0	0	0	3	55	4	46	5	1
Stutsman	6	0	2	1	3	60	15	44	1	2
Towner	0	0	0	0	0	16	1	10	5	0
Traill	2	0	0	0	2	26	4	16	6	4
Walsh	3	0	2	0	1	105	31	61	13	1
Ward	7	0	0	1	6	156	36	102	18	3
Wells	0	0	0	0	0	14	4	9	1	1
Williams	2	0	2	0	0	73	23	42	8	0
OHIO										
Metropolitan Counties										
Allen	47	0	11	13	23	1 220	211	966	43	2
Belmont	15	0	7	2	6	460	146	275	39	11
Clark	67	2	15	17	33	1 979	520	1 330	129	17
Clermont	72	0	45	12	15	1 670	363	1 204	103	30
Erie	21	0	5	2	14	413	137	258	18	7
Greene	12	0	7	2	3	471	114	318	39	4
Hamilton	283	7	40	173	63	7 230	1 172	5 667	391	42
Lake	17	0	1	6	10	668	99	526	43	4
Lawrence	9	0	0	0	9	107	32	63	12	0
Licking	15	0	1	5	9	709	228	412	69	3
Lorain	58	0	17	21	20	1 165	626	504	35	20
Lucas	20	1	0	1	18	458	69	389	0	0
Miami	35	0	4	3	28	524	184	305	35	10
Pickaway	58	0	4	5	49	1 057	394	616	47	15
Portage	51	2	18	21	10	1 687	534	1 028	125	7
Preble	24	1	4	4	15	513	160	320	33	2
Richland	41	2	14	11	14	1 212	355	818	39	6
Stark	166	0	24	48	94	2 662	769	1 707	186	15
Summit	83	0	22	31	30	1 479	308	1 085	86	9
Trumbull	28	0	5	2	21	307	107	160	40	2

Note: The data shown in this table do not reflect county totals but are the number of offenses reported by the sheriff's office or county police department.

[1]The FBI does not publish arson data unless it receives data from either the agency or the state for all 12 months of the calendar year.
. . . = Not available.

Table 10. Offenses Known to Law Enforcement, by State Metropolitan and Nonmetropolitan Counties, 2005—*Continued*

(Number.)

County	Violent crime	Murder and nonnegligent manslaughter	Forcible rape	Robbery	Aggravated assault	Property crime	Burglary	Larceny-theft	Motor vehicle theft	Arson[1]
Washington	21	0	10	1	10	470	154	289	27	4
Wood	15	1	2	1	11	585	134	416	35	3
Nonmetropolitan Counties										
Adams	25	4	2	3	16	384	135	218	31	19
Ashland	13	1	6	1	5	311	100	201	10	1
Auglaize	2	0	0	1	1	62	27	31	4	0
Champaign	6	0	4	1	1	369	107	240	22	3
Clinton	24	1	7	0	16	275	64	194	17	3
Crawford	10	1	4	0	5	176	42	131	3	0
Defiance	20	0	11	1	8	278	75	193	10	1
Fayette	17	0	5	4	8	723	179	516	28	3
Gallia	25	0	6	5	14	839	319	460	60	14
Guernsey	27	1	7	2	17	502	156	304	42	7
Hancock	21	0	3	1	17	428	109	298	21	6
Hardin	5	0	0	3	2	223	95	119	9	0
Harrison	14	0	3	2	9	182	66	91	25	0
Henry	1	0	1	0	0	93	32	57	4	2
Highland	16	1	0	1	14	394	181	183	30	2
Hocking	19	3	5	3	8	324	114	179	31	8
Holmes	12	0	3	0	9	240	68	161	11	2
Logan	17	5	0	3	9	285	120	137	28	0
Marion	12	0	1	7	4	717	211	477	29	5
Meigs	15	0	6	1	8	287	130	136	21	6
Mercer	8	0	4	0	4	268	53	196	19	0
Morgan	2	0	1	0	1	131	29	80	22	2
Muskingum	35	1	17	12	5	1 023	209	730	84	7
Paulding	16	0	2	1	13	172	35	137	0	0
Putnam	4	1	0	0	3	69	20	48	1	1
Ross	55	1	25	11	18	1 911	485	1 269	157	14
Scioto	76	0	6	23	47	2 310	742	1 499	69	0
Van Wert	8	2	5	0	1	233	63	166	4	1
Vinton	18	2	4	2	10	329	131	178	20	1
Wayne	28	0	11	3	14	601	269	302	30	7
Williams	16	0	12	0	4	299	60	227	12	1
OKLAHOMA										
Metropolitan Counties										
Canadian	22	0	2	1	19	93	40	39	14	1
Cleveland	42	1	11	1	29	371	150	182	39	5
Creek	85	0	11	3	71	574	226	315	33	14
Grady	45	0	1	1	43	294	112	154	28	4
Lincoln	21	0	1	0	20	274	122	113	39	0
Logan	28	0	4	1	23	285	105	165	15	2
McClain	24	1	2	0	21	116	39	57	20	4
Oklahoma	49	0	1	0	48	302	96	147	59	2
Okmulgee	26	1	4	4	17	281	121	132	28	10
Osage	29	3	6	0	20	514	176	288	50	6
Pawnee	45	0	6	1	38	187	67	92	28	9
Rogers	2	0	0	0	2	297	88	162	47	0
Sequoyah	66	1	3	1	61	365	132	212	21	2
Tulsa	225	3	11	28	183	1 171	328	687	156	9
Wagoner	31	0	2	2	27	348	125	155	68	5
Nonmetropolitan Counties										
Adair	21	0	7	0	14	205	74	94	37	14
Alfalfa	1	0	1	0	0	41	14	25	2	0
Atoka	6	0	0	1	5	101	32	59	10	3
Beaver	7	0	3	0	4	62	23	32	7	2
Beckham	13	0	1	1	11	67	27	32	8	2
Blaine	8	1	2	0	5	25	8	16	1	1
Bryan	69	1	14	3	51	338	162	138	38	0
Caddo	131	0	2	0	129	309	106	160	43	6
Carter	40	3	4	3	30	187	57	112	18	1
Cherokee	187	2	11	1	173	542	233	243	66	4
Choctaw	30	1	2	1	26	128	53	61	14	4
Cimarron	0	0	0	0	0	8	3	3	2	0
Coal	4	0	0	0	4	79	36	39	4	1
Cotton	4	0	0	1	3	25	11	12	2	1
Craig	17	0	1	1	15	130	60	61	9	2
Custer	9	0	0	0	9	61	21	39	1	0
Delaware	95	0	10	1	84	521	244	219	58	2
Dewey	2	0	0	0	2	25	5	15	5	1
Ellis	2	0	0	0	2	30	18	7	5	0
Garfield	12	0	4	0	8	77	27	43	7	1

Note: The data shown in this table do not reflect county totals but are the number of offenses reported by the sheriff's office or county police department.

[1]The FBI does not publish arson data unless it receives data from either the agency or the state for all 12 months of the calendar year.

Table 10. Offenses Known to Law Enforcement, by State Metropolitan and Nonmetropolitan Counties, 2005—*Continued*

(Number.)

County	Violent crime	Murder and nonnegligent manslaughter	Forcible rape	Robbery	Aggravated assault	Property crime	Burglary	Larceny-theft	Motor vehicle theft	Arson[1]
Garvin	23	0	3	2	18	142	41	80	21	6
Grant	4	0	0	1	3	34	15	19	0	0
Greer	0	0	0	0	0	15	9	6	0	1
Harmon	2	0	0	0	2	6	1	5	0	0
Harper	0	0	0	0	0	9	2	5	2	0
Haskell	51	0	0	0	51	92	26	45	21	1
Hughes	6	0	2	1	3	91	25	51	15	2
Jackson	10	1	1	0	8	101	46	42	13	4
Jefferson	8	1	0	0	7	31	12	14	5	1
Johnston	35	0	3	0	32	69	41	19	9	0
Kay	17	0	3	1	13	189	64	115	10	5
Kingfisher	3	0	0	0	3	66	20	35	11	0
Kiowa	17	0	1	1	15	69	18	38	13	1
Latimer	48	0	3	0	45	69	27	36	6	1
Love	7	0	1	0	6	89	27	55	7	0
Major	3	0	1	0	2	8	5	2	1	0
Marshall	25	0	3	1	21	113	47	54	12	0
Mayes	31	2	3	5	21	291	91	178	22	0
McCurtain	122	1	10	2	109	450	185	187	78	6
McIntosh	10	0	2	3	5	307	111	165	31	7
Murray	5	0	0	0	5	57	25	27	5	0
Muskogee	42	0	7	1	34	248	110	104	34	19
Noble	2	0	0	0	2	89	30	54	5	2
Nowata	13	0	0	0	13	94	31	58	5	4
Okfuskee	4	1	0	0	3	67	23	28	16	4
Ottawa	36	1	3	2	30	203	88	76	39	2
Payne	31	0	12	0	19	217	89	117	11	17
Pittsburg	23	1	3	5	14	397	144	234	19	2
Pontotoc	19	1	2	1	15	144	47	85	12	5
Pottawatomie	71	0	7	4	60	615	226	329	60	14
Pushmataha	9	0	0	1	8	132	66	55	11	2
Roger Mills	5	0	0	0	5	57	9	48	0	1
Seminole	56	2	3	0	51	297	97	182	18	4
Stephens	44	0	3	1	40	158	54	97	7	0
Texas	12	0	1	0	11	50	22	25	3	0
Tillman	2	0	0	0	2	38	6	28	4	0
Washington	25	0	4	1	20	226	85	131	10	9
Washita	5	0	1	0	4	52	18	23	11	1
Woods	2	0	2	0	0	40	9	26	5	1
Woodward	5	1	0	0	4	101	41	55	5	1
OREGON										
Metropolitan Counties										
Benton	21	0	1	0	20	272	75	183	14	8
Clackamas	253	5	54	95	99	7 271	1 219	5 150	902	18
Columbia	29	0	1	0	28	49	25	16	8	0
Deschutes	99	2	15	4	78	1 341	345	880	116	15
Jackson	204	1	10	16	177	1 300	381	816	103	4
Lane	190	3	18	21	148	1 986	757	886	343	12
Marion	93	4	19	23	47	3 239	664	2 176	399	7
Multnomah	56	1	7	5	43	865	142	603	120	3
Polk	30	0	4	2	24	410	131	239	40	2
Washington	216	2	56	42	116	4 271	791	3 054	426	35
Yamhill	31	3	3	3	22	703	139	494	70	14
Nonmetropolitan Counties										
Baker	2	0	0	0	2	53	16	28	9	0
Clatsop	11	0	2	0	9	219	79	118	22	0
Crook	24	0	1	0	23	171	83	79	9	4
Curry	8	0	3	2	3	131	36	86	9	1
Douglas	59	0	15	8	36	1 594	442	985	167	12
Gilliam	1	0	0	0	1	26	11	12	3	0
Grant	0	0	0	0	0	63	15	41	7	0
Harney	1	0	1	0	0	22	7	14	1	0
Hood River	19	0	4	1	14	202	58	121	23	4
Jefferson	66	0	2	0	64	221	48	133	40	2
Josephine	59	0	6	12	41	1 149	294	682	173	7
Klamath	111	0	18	15	78	1 111	324	690	97	11
Lake	3	0	1	0	2	58	20	32	6	1
Lincoln	49	1	10	1	37	588	197	348	43	3
Linn	19	1	2	5	11	1 516	428	965	123	19
Malheur	9	0	5	0	4	232	82	127	23	3
Morrow	29	0	4	1	24	248	54	168	26	0
Sherman	0	0	0	0	0	38	8	29	1	1
Tillamook	21	0	4	3	14	548	166	336	46	2
Umatilla	30	0	7	2	21	437	147	210	80	1
Union	2	0	0	0	2	105	36	59	10	1
Wallowa	3	1	0	0	2	64	30	31	3	0
Wasco	2	0	0	0	2	269	75	157	37	1
Wheeler	2	0	0	0	2	16	5	8	3	0

Note: The data shown in this table do not reflect county totals but are the number of offenses reported by the sheriff's office or county police department.

[1]The FBI does not publish arson data unless it receives data from either the agency or the state for all 12 months of the calendar year.

Table 10. Offenses Known to Law Enforcement, by State Metropolitan and Nonmetropolitan Counties, 2005—*Continued*

(Number.)

County	Violent crime	Murder and nonnegligent manslaughter	Forcible rape	Robbery	Aggravated assault	Property crime	Burglary	Larceny-theft	Motor vehicle theft	Arson[1]
PENNSYLVANIA										
Metropolitan Counties										
Allegheny	10	0	0	0	10	0	0	0	0	0
Allegheny County Police Department	62	0	10	16	36	445	55	363	27	139
Beaver	8	0	0	0	8	5	0	5	0	0
Centre	2	0	0	0	2	5	0	4	1	0
Cumberland	1	0	0	0	1	0	0	0	0	0
Lancaster	3	0	0	0	3	0	0	0	0	0
Pike	0	0	0	0	0	0	0	0	0	0
Washington	0	0	0	0	0	0	0	0	0	0
York	1	0	0	0	1	0	0	0	0	0
Nonmetropolitan Counties										
Adams	0	0	0	0	0	0	0	0	0	0
Clarion	0	0	0	0	0	0	0	0	0	0
Elk	0	0	0	0	0	0	0	0	0	0
Franklin	4	0	0	0	4	3	0	3	0	0
Greene	0	0	0	0	0	1	0	1	0	0
Jefferson	0	0	0	0	0	0	0	0	0	0
Snyder	0	0	0	0	0	0	0	0	0	0
Union	0	0	0	0	0	1	0	1	0	0
Warren	2	0	0	0	2	11	3	8	0	0
SOUTH CAROLINA										
Metropolitan Counties										
Aiken	327	7	53	59	208	2 646	778	1 540	328	4
Anderson	813	13	51	114	635	6 387	1 607	4 169	611	31
Berkeley	635	8	55	92	480	3 256	1 018	1 763	475	25
Calhoun	51	0	3	2	46	243	61	139	43	1
Charleston	865	6	39	98	722	3 013	817	1 756	440	9
Darlington	819	3	30	41	745	2 240	770	1 250	220	19
Edgefield	34	0	1	2	31	343	90	224	29	2
Fairfield	217	2	7	12	196	559	222	293	44	6
Florence	612	8	27	112	465	3 175	937	1 976	262	8
Greenville	2 303	24	136	413	1 730	11 179	3 102	6 928	1 149	49
Horry	1	0	0	0	1	39	1	38	0	0
Horry County Police Department	1 114	20	51	158	885	6 848	1 582	4 448	818	19
Kershaw	180	0	14	20	155	1 070	265	691	114	2
Laurens	306	2	22	18	264	1 561	516	865	180	5
Lexington	565	8	45	104	408	4 084	1 071	2 570	443	4
Pickens	233	2	17	8	206	2 008	623	1 226	159	11
Richland	1 668	19	103	275	1 271	7 869	1 657	5 452	760	33
Saluda	30	0	2	1	27	145	32	104	9	1
Spartanburg	905	16	48	127	714	6 668	1 628	4 479	561	31
Sumter	407	5	17	54	331	2 591	1 091	1 296	204	39
York	670	3	32	63	572	3 088	747	2 068	273	16
Nonmetropolitan Counties										
Abbeville	54	0	4	3	47	286	83	198	5	3
Bamberg	69	1	5	4	59	199	71	95	33	3
Barnwell	115	1	3	5	106	318	80	217	21	5
Beaufort	650	5	31	149	465	4 135	1 066	2 778	291	19
Cherokee	247	3	25	17	202	1 580	390	1 069	121	9
Chester	202	2	9	11	180	850	184	617	49	7
Chesterfield	133	2	11	8	112	686	237	378	71	10
Clarendon	243	2	7	17	217	798	231	464	103	2
Colleton	253	6	14	26	207	1 019	224	668	127	18
Dillon	190	5	5	27	153	906	341	467	98	5
Georgetown	207	1	24	29	153	1 240	340	785	115	8
Hampton	46	2	0	5	39	282	97	165	20	1
Jasper	166	2	10	24	130	659	244	357	58	3
Lancaster	237	2	27	32	176	1 708	472	1 140	96	6
Lee	106	1	9	9	87	457	156	260	41	1
Marion	110	0	6	2	102	777	229	479	69	15
Marlboro	185	3	4	10	168	614	191	348	75	7
McCormick	43	0	3	2	38	113	28	49	36	0
Newberry	80	0	5	2	73	563	78	458	27	3
Oconee	229	1	20	7	201	1 453	479	859	115	9
Orangeburg	386	13	53	80	240	3 444	1 055	1 809	580	8
Union	128	1	5	8	114	529	146	339	44	9
Williamsburg	148	4	13	23	108	1 003	364	500	139	27
SOUTH DAKOTA										
Metropolitan Counties										
Lincoln	5	1	1	0	3	66	19	41	6	0
McCook	15	0	5	0	10	31	0	31	0	0
Meade	28	1	4	0	23	156	31	118	7	0
Minnehaha	21	0	6	1	14	220	97	99	24	2
Pennington	75	1	44	1	29	633	137	469	27	2
Turner	6	0	1	1	4	26	14	11	1	0
Union	1	0	0	0	1	9	8	1	0	0

Note: The data shown in this table do not reflect county totals but are the number of offenses reported by the sheriff's office or county police department.

[1]The FBI does not publish arson data unless it receives data from either the agency or the state for all 12 months of the calendar year.

Table 10. Offenses Known to Law Enforcement, by State Metropolitan and Nonmetropolitan Counties, 2005—*Continued*

(Number.)

County	Violent crime	Murder and nonnegligent manslaughter	Forcible rape	Robbery	Aggravated assault	Property crime	Burglary	Larceny-theft	Motor vehicle theft	Arson[1]
Nonmetropolitan Counties										
Aurora	0	0	0	0	0	8	2	6	0	0
Beadle	1	0	0	0	1	11	4	7	0	0
Butte	2	0	1	0	1	10	3	6	1	0
Campbell	0	0	0	0	0	5	3	2	0	0
Charles Mix	14	0	2	1	11	36	6	28	2	0
Clay	1	1	0	0	0	19	1	18	0	0
Codington	1	0	1	0	0	39	17	20	2	0
Hamlin	1	0	1	0	0	18	10	8	0	0
Kingsbury	1	0	0	0	1	36	12	21	3	0
Lawrence	2	0	1	1	0	69	21	47	1	1
Lyman	1	0	0	0	1	13	1	9	3	0
McPherson	0	0	0	0	0	0	0	0	0	0
Perkins	1	0	1	0	0	14	8	6	0	0
Potter	0	0	0	0	0	10	1	8	1	0
Roberts	10	1	1	0	8	15	7	4	4	0
Spink	4	0	0	1	3	35	7	27	1	2
Todd	0	0	0	0	0	13	1	6	6	0
Ziebach	1	0	0	0	1	6	2	1	3	0
TENNESSEE										
Metropolitan Counties										
Anderson	66	1	2	9	54	819	277	442	100	6
Blount	290	2	38	21	229	1 733	587	983	163	8
Bradley	317	0	7	4	306	1 095	315	680	100	6
Cannon	25	0	0	1	24	115	40	49	26	1
Carter	60	1	4	3	52	691	239	395	57	16
Cheatham	87	0	6	5	76	505	109	322	74	6
Chester	32	1	1	0	30	161	51	96	14	2
Dickson	164	0	41	7	116	638	215	360	63	3
Fayette	104	1	3	6	94	548	190	282	76	6
Grainger	28	0	0	1	27	358	90	237	31	0
Hamblen	114	0	4	13	97	565	183	336	46	7
Hamilton	284	3	19	12	250	1 867	550	1 175	142	5
Hartsville-Trousdale	31	0	1	3	27	146	49	89	8	3
Hawkins	64	1	15	0	48	897	339	474	84	7
Hickman	54	1	7	6	40	396	158	208	30	1
Jefferson	91	0	11	4	76	792	224	425	143	7
Knox	523	5	15	66	437	5 394	1 575	3 377	442	36
Loudon	67	0	4	4	59	676	194	429	53	1
Macon	38	0	1	3	34	215	47	138	30	4
Madison	198	1	17	9	171	929	257	552	120	3
Marion	59	0	0	1	58	316	97	162	57	2
Montgomery	116	1	12	4	99	516	148	335	33	4
Robertson	118	1	10	4	103	489	128	324	37	1
Rutherford	254	1	39	7	207	1 205	354	702	149	9
Sequatchie	32	1	2	0	29	161	47	80	34	7
Shelby	480	5	34	54	387	3 255	1 098	1 828	329	24
Smith	42	1	2	2	37	85	25	46	14	0
Stewart	31	0	1	0	30	155	35	99	21	1
Sullivan	466	5	30	30	401	1 816	578	1 065	173	28
Sumner	127	0	24	3	100	647	174	403	70	8
Tipton	203	5	16	10	172	764	285	391	88	7
Unicoi	16	1	0	0	15	163	34	120	9	2
Union	35	0	1	4	30	272	99	151	22	1
Washington	273	0	11	10	252	1 086	400	605	81	10
Williamson	75	0	9	0	66	520	104	370	46	9
Wilson	115	1	3	9	102	839	282	475	82	3
Nonmetropolitan Counties										
Bedford	52	0	2	3	47	409	170	188	51	1
Benton	38	0	1	0	37	240	133	86	21	1
Campbell	84	1	2	0	81	655	174	427	54	0
Carroll	50	0	1	3	46	214	72	108	34	0
Claiborne	74	4	3	2	65	453	123	291	39	2
Clay	8	0	0	0	8	49	25	17	7	0
Coffee	44	0	0	1	43	464	132	278	54	0
Crockett	19	0	0	1	18	140	35	88	17	0
Cumberland	74	0	4	1	69	973	254	572	147	8
Decatur	13	0	1	2	10	159	72	77	10	0
DeKalb	47	4	2	0	41	419	129	247	43	2
Dyer	35	1	5	2	27	352	131	194	27	0
Franklin	70	0	3	4	63	288	122	127	39	10
Gibson	61	0	4	2	55	265	110	114	41	3
Giles	100	0	7	6	87	235	90	122	23	2
Greene	266	3	11	12	240	1 379	492	779	108	34
Hancock	8	0	1	1	6	101	41	58	2	0
Hardeman	91	1	2	7	81	391	170	170	51	1
Hardin	92	2	2	4	84	496	179	275	42	3
Haywood	35	2	1	8	24	215	76	112	27	1

Note: The data shown in this table do not reflect county totals but are the number of offenses reported by the sheriff's office or county police department.

[1]The FBI does not publish arson data unless it receives data from either the agency or the state for all 12 months of the calendar year.

Table 10. Offenses Known to Law Enforcement, by State Metropolitan and Nonmetropolitan Counties, 2005—*Continued*

(Number.)

County	Violent crime	Murder and nonnegligent manslaughter	Forcible rape	Robbery	Aggravated assault	Property crime	Burglary	Larceny-theft	Motor vehicle theft	Arson[1]
Henderson	47	0	6	4	37	384	171	165	48	0
Henry	71	0	6	2	63	487	169	276	42	7
Houston	27	0	0	0	27	88	18	59	11	1
Humphreys	29	0	0	1	28	154	55	84	15	1
Jackson	39	1	1	1	36	259	60	179	20	1
Johnson	76	1	1	0	74	167	82	67	18	2
Lake	11	0	1	0	10	34	7	24	3	0
Lawrence	147	0	8	2	137	615	260	296	59	5
Lewis	17	1	1	1	14	133	52	68	13	2
Lincoln	99	0	2	5	92	407	177	194	36	3
Marshall	13	0	1	0	12	181	63	104	14	1
Maury	133	2	10	9	112	718	182	461	75	6
McMinn	137	0	7	5	125	804	294	429	81	2
McNairy	58	0	1	2	55	437	126	255	56	0
Meigs	34	0	1	6	27	223	86	113	24	2
Monroe	160	0	7	4	149	735	220	444	71	8
Moore	6	0	0	1	5	72	34	36	2	0
Morgan	14	2	1	0	11	225	107	90	28	0
Obion	46	1	2	2	41	233	45	153	35	7
Overton	17	2	0	1	14	162	62	82	18	2
Perry	20	3	2	2	13	143	61	73	9	6
Pickett	2	1	0	0	1	15	4	11	0	0
Putnam	77	1	13	5	58	517	84	384	49	2
Rhea	40	0	7	0	33	320	53	235	32	0
Roane	86	2	6	5	73	910	357	466	87	6
Scott	146	1	5	1	139	450	153	261	36	4
Sevier	105	2	12	5	86	1 646	620	885	141	4
Van Buren	8	1	0	0	7	63	14	39	10	0
Warren	49	1	1	3	44	379	100	213	66	2
Wayne	25	0	0	0	25	215	104	71	40	1
Weakley	57	0	0	1	56	223	100	101	22	2
White	67	2	2	4	59	423	181	193	49	7
TEXAS										
Metropolitan Counties										
Aransas	31	1	2	2	26	800	221	539	40	2
Archer	13	0	1	0	12	94	30	57	7	2
Armstrong	3	0	0	0	3	19	9	7	3	0
Atascosa	27	0	1	10	16	316	120	170	26	1
Austin	21	0	4	3	14	218	77	133	8	0
Bandera	18	0	7	0	11	274	110	154	10	0
Bastrop	137	2	1	12	122	1 150	559	491	100	4
Bell	77	3	29	5	40	794	268	471	55	0
Bexar	610	7	66	84	453	5 586	1 675	3 554	357	100
Bowie	92	0	11	8	73	629	183	353	93	1
Brazoria	68	5	5	20	38	1 797	773	940	84	3
Brazos	63	1	4	2	56	479	179	268	32	5
Burleson	11	0	4	1	6	99	49	36	14	5
Caldwell	55	0	5	1	49	210	94	111	5	4
Calhoun	13	0	1	0	12	154	53	90	11	3
Callahan	7	0	0	1	6	33	16	12	5	1
Cameron	293	9	16	26	242	1 774	801	800	173	10
Carson	2	0	0	0	2	1	1	0	0	0
Chambers	54	0	1	4	49	549	249	269	31	7
Clay	9	2	1	2	4	184	58	116	10	1
Collin	73	3	26	2	42	725	220	349	156	0
Comal	133	0	19	7	107	863	272	545	46	11
Coryell	20	0	2	0	18	117	54	53	10	0
Crosby	7	2	1	0	4	14	4	10	0	0
Dallas	43	1	0	2	40	245	79	142	24	10
Delta	9	0	2	0	7	121	43	71	7	2
Denton	90	3	18	5	64	971	315	628	28	8
Ector	47	3	2	5	37	1 061	214	785	62	3
Ellis	146	0	3	10	133	1 100	394	582	124	8
El Paso	210	4	30	16	160	1 140	304	675	161	14
Fort Bend	662	8	42	110	502	3 339	1 136	1 959	244	33
Galveston	189	0	21	19	149	881	345	467	69	17
Goliad	5	0	0	0	5	34	13	21	0	0
Grayson	42	0	4	8	30	861	311	485	65	4
Gregg	63	2	12	8	41	837	191	578	68	6
Guadalupe	126	1	14	5	106	833	273	496	64	5
Hardin	47	3	0	0	44	434	161	202	71	3
Harris	6 952	66	327	1 912	4 647	41 087	10 840	25 364	4 883	403
Hays	104	0	5	9	90	774	207	492	75	0
Hidalgo	1 293	16	111	138	1 028	6 593	2 416	3 822	355	. . .

Note: The data shown in this table do not reflect county totals but are the number of offenses reported by the sheriff's office or county police department.

[1]The FBI does not publish arson data unless it receives data from either the agency or the state for all 12 months of the calendar year.
. . . = Not available.

Table 10. Offenses Known to Law Enforcement, by State Metropolitan and Nonmetropolitan Counties, 2005—*Continued*

(Number.)

County	Violent crime	Murder and nonnegligent manslaughter	Forcible rape	Robbery	Aggravated assault	Property crime	Burglary	Larceny-theft	Motor vehicle theft	Arson[1]
Hunt	47	3	0	11	33	945	285	528	132	4
Irion	3	0	0	0	3	18	7	9	2	0
Jefferson	40	1	5	10	24	500	190	263	47	1
Johnson	239	2	0	5	232	1 586	530	864	192	28
Jones	7	0	0	0	7	36	22	10	4	1
Kaufman	176	2	13	7	154	1 540	532	838	170	17
Kendall	37	1	3	2	31	221	53	153	15	0
Lampasas	9	0	0	1	8	76	33	41	2	2
Liberty	113	4	13	6	90	823	318	396	109	6
Lubbock	103	1	14	9	79	902	426	367	109	10
McLennan	90	0	28	7	55	845	303	473	69	22
Medina	47	1	7	3	36	256	128	116	12	0
Midland	36	0	0	5	31	365	94	246	25	2
Montgomery	941	7	48	121	765	6 238	1 670	3 979	589	29
Nueces	57	0	19	5	33	332	121	188	23	0
Orange	158	0	7	15	136	700	262	354	84	7
Parker	60	3	16	6	35	1 164	404	670	90	0
Potter	16	0	2	3	11	252	77	153	22	4
Randall	54	1	2	2	49	382	129	207	46	7
Robertson	19	0	5	2	12	162	95	62	5	1
Rockwall	55	1	4	3	47	259	84	151	24	3
Rusk	134	4	4	4	122	599	214	318	67	5
San Jacinto	55	1	0	6	48	516	186	268	62	1
San Patricio	27	1	4	1	21	374	131	221	22	1
Smith	337	5	50	27	255	2 044	788	1 060	196	49
Tarrant	119	1	24	15	79	1 571	470	960	141	0
Taylor	23	1	0	3	19	179	85	72	22	0
Tom Green	23	1	5	0	17	260	74	174	12	1
Travis	323	4	45	51	223	3 555	1 130	2 248	177	5
Upshur	73	2	1	3	67	555	222	263	70	3
Victoria	53	2	3	2	46	519	152	332	35	4
Waller	19	0	1	1	17	288	122	134	32	0
Webb	58	5	6	7	40	219	91	103	25	5
Wichita	5	0	0	1	4	168	58	87	23	6
Williamson	163	2	27	13	121	1 634	404	1 131	99	19
Wilson	23	1	2	1	19	234	94	123	17	1
Wise	141	0	7	3	131	693	267	408	18	1
Nonmetropolitan Counties										
Anderson	84	0	7	1	76	460	201	235	24	5
Andrews	5	0	0	0	5	64	23	37	4	1
Angelina	259	1	7	8	243	707	317	319	71	0
Bailey	6	0	0	0	6	23	8	12	3	0
Baylor	2	0	1	0	1	25	12	8	5	0
Bee	24	1	3	1	19	197	67	121	9	3
Blanco	2	0	0	0	2	48	19	28	1	0
Borden	3	0	0	0	3	11	2	9	0	0
Bosque	21	0	3	2	16	148	54	77	17	4
Brewster	5	0	0	0	5	22	7	13	2	0
Briscoe	0	0	0	0	0	11	3	5	3	0
Brooks	0	0	0	0	0	18	4	13	1	0
Brown	51	0	0	0	51	251	97	144	10	1
Burnet	35	1	4	2	28	258	104	138	16	3
Camp	15	0	3	1	11	118	64	48	6	2
Cass	25	0	7	3	15	264	112	115	37	1
Castro	8	0	1	0	7	37	11	22	4	0
Cherokee	101	0	27	9	65	484	199	232	53	1
Childress	4	0	2	0	2	58	16	40	2	0
Cochran	9	0	2	1	6	79	32	38	9	0
Coke	0	0	0	0	0	11	10	0	1	0
Coleman	3	0	0	0	3	38	20	16	2	0
Collingsworth	1	0	0	1	0	15	14	0	1	0
Colorado	13	0	3	2	8	163	44	103	16	0
Comanche	6	0	1	0	5	104	38	64	2	1
Concho	4	0	0	0	4	24	10	14	0	0
Cooke	47	2	1	0	44	305	116	140	49	0
Cottle	0	0	0	0	0	1	1	0	0	0
Crane	1	0	0	0	1	41	11	28	2	0
Crockett	9	0	3	2	4	56	17	37	2	1
Culberson	1	0	0	0	1	3	3	0	0	1
Dallam	5	0	0	0	5	22	9	12	1	0
Dawson	1	0	0	0	1	55	21	26	8	0
Deaf Smith	7	1	1	0	5	43	20	23	0	1
Dewitt	17	1	0	0	16	59	31	25	3	1
Dickens	0	0	0	0	0	0	0	0	0	0
Dimmit	38	0	0	3	35	363	158	174	31	0
Donley	9	0	0	0	9	44	18	25	1	0
Duval	14	0	1	2	11	115	35	63	17	0
Eastland	7	0	0	0	7	109	30	71	8	0

Note: The data shown in this table do not reflect county totals but are the number of offenses reported by the sheriff's office or county police department.

[1]The FBI does not publish arson data unless it receives data from either the agency or the state for all 12 months of the calendar year.

Table 10. Offenses Known to Law Enforcement, by State Metropolitan and Nonmetropolitan Counties, 2005—*Continued*

(Number.)

County	Violent crime	Murder and nonnegligent manslaughter	Forcible rape	Robbery	Aggravated assault	Property crime	Burglary	Larceny-theft	Motor vehicle theft	Arson[1]
Edwards	8	0	0	0	8	41	20	14	7	4
Erath	15	0	4	1	10	162	48	97	17	1
Falls	18	0	0	0	18	114	64	37	13	0
Fannin	32	4	2	2	24	327	137	165	25	. . .
Fayette	4	0	0	0	4	136	34	95	7	1
Fisher	6	0	2	0	4	76	16	55	5	1
Floyd	2	0	0	0	2	5	0	4	1	1
Foard	0	0	0	0	0	8	4	4	0	0
Franklin	7	0	0	0	7	143	71	68	4	1
Freestone	15	1	0	1	13	107	28	71	8	0
Frio	3	0	0	0	3	66	34	31	1	0
Gaines	2	0	0	1	1	47	17	24	6	0
Garza	9	1	2	0	6	91	25	62	4	4
Gillespie	4	0	0	0	4	120	33	83	4	2
Glasscock	0	0	0	0	0	0	0	0	0	0
Gonzales	16	0	0	0	16	122	45	73	4	0
Gray	11	3	0	0	8	94	30	59	5	0
Grimes	32	1	0	3	28	384	161	206	17	0
Hale	0	0	0	0	0	106	33	62	11	1
Hall	2	0	0	1	1	13	10	3	0	0
Hamilton	11	1	0	1	9	108	54	49	5	0
Hansford	2	0	1	0	1	21	7	14	0	0
Hardeman	2	0	1	0	1	19	9	8	2	0
Harrison	96	1	0	5	90	873	344	487	42	9
Hartley	1	0	0	1	0	22	8	13	1	0
Haskell	5	0	0	0	5	32	12	17	3	0
Hemphill	6	0	0	0	6	51	14	33	4	0
Henderson	274	2	2	12	258	1 148	477	559	112	1
Hill	12	1	4	4	3	408	148	230	30	6
Hockley	24	1	4	1	18	98	48	38	12	1
Hood	45	0	4	4	37	827	211	557	59	3
Hopkins	20	0	3	1	16	237	104	116	17	0
Houston	7	0	1	0	6	117	57	56	4	0
Howard	9	0	0	1	8	93	40	47	6	0
Hudspeth	7	1	0	1	5	41	16	20	5	0
Hutchinson	4	0	0	0	4	66	27	35	4	0
Jack	5	0	2	0	3	40	15	22	3	0
Jackson	16	0	1	2	13	90	23	64	3	0
Jasper	78	1	7	1	69	370	133	220	17	0
Jeff Davis	6	0	0	0	6	10	5	4	1	0
Jim Hogg	6	0	0	0	6	68	31	34	3	0
Jim Wells	213	2	9	6	196	411	171	216	24	2
Karnes	11	0	0	0	11	102	37	60	5	1
Kenedy	2	0	1	0	1	2	1	0	1	0
Kent	1	0	0	0	1	19	6	11	2	2
Kerr	27	0	6	2	19	361	117	228	16	5
Kimble	0	0	0	0	0	18	5	10	3	0
King	0	0	0	0	0	0	0	0	0	0
Kinney	0	0	0	0	0	0	0	0	0	0
Kleberg	32	0	7	1	24	241	67	169	5	0
Knox	3	0	0	1	2	22	5	13	4	0
Lamar	42	1	4	2	35	383	190	185	8	0
Lamb	15	0	1	0	14	87	28	52	7	5
La Salle	13	2	2	0	9	86	32	54	0	0
Lavaca	6	0	4	1	1	71	22	42	7	1
Lee	21	0	3	1	17	102	36	58	8	0
Leon	53	2	3	1	47	189	80	99	10	0
Limestone	15	1	1	2	11	338	95	220	23	1
Lipscomb	1	0	0	0	1	11	3	8	0	1
Live Oak	5	0	0	0	5	61	32	27	2	1
Llano	30	2	8	1	19	240	80	148	12	1
Loving	0	0	0	0	0	6	0	5	1	0
Lynn	3	0	0	0	3	21	11	10	0	0
Madison	17	0	0	0	17	122	46	60	16	1
Marion	45	1	5	0	39	206	84	95	27	1
Martin	1	0	0	0	1	16	13	2	1	0
Mason	4	0	0	0	4	60	11	45	4	0
Matagorda	39	0	3	3	33	339	126	202	11	6
Maverick	146	0	0	3	143	565	199	346	20	0
McCulloch	3	0	0	0	3	23	14	9	0	1
McMullen	0	0	0	0	0	8	4	3	1	0
Menard	0	0	0	0	0	8	2	6	0	1
Milam	24	2	4	0	18	164	59	94	11	0
Mills	4	0	0	0	4	33	15	18	0	0
Mitchell	0	0	0	0	0	30	7	21	2	0
Montague	23	0	1	3	19	166	64	87	15	2
Moore	5	0	2	0	3	84	24	56	4	1
Morris	19	0	0	2	17	128	43	75	10	0
Motley	1	0	0	0	1	2	1	1	0	0
Nacogdoches	114	5	8	5	96	392	176	186	30	5

Note: The data shown in this table do not reflect county totals but are the number of offenses reported by the sheriff's office or county police department.

[1]The FBI does not publish arson data unless it receives data from either the agency or the state for all 12 months of the calendar year.
. . . = Not available.

Table 10. Offenses Known to Law Enforcement, by State Metropolitan and Nonmetropolitan Counties, 2005—*Continued*

(Number.)

County	Violent crime	Murder and nonnegligent manslaughter	Forcible rape	Robbery	Aggravated assault	Property crime	Burglary	Larceny-theft	Motor vehicle theft	Arson[1]
Navarro	33	1	6	2	24	597	191	371	35	1
Newton	33	1	4	1	27	150	45	91	14	2
Nolan	3	0	1	0	2	50	17	25	8	0
Ochiltree	8	0	1	0	7	51	16	30	5	0
Oldham	2	0	2	0	0	29	5	22	2	0
Palo Pinto	9	1	0	2	6	143	67	66	10	0
Panola	45	1	2	1	41	343	86	220	37	0
Parmer	1	0	0	0	1	31	15	14	2	0
Pecos	8	0	2	1	5	27	10	16	1	0
Polk	82	3	8	6	65	671	270	331	70	5
Presidio	0	0	0	0	0	0	0	0	0	0
Rains	9	0	0	0	9	154	51	84	19	0
Reagan	0	0	0	0	0	22	4	14	4	0
Real	2	0	0	0	2	38	22	16	0	0
Red River	10	0	1	1	8	87	36	44	7	2
Reeves	14	0	0	1	13	100	29	65	6	0
Refugio	14	0	0	0	14	60	23	34	3	1
Roberts	2	0	2	0	0	26	7	18	1	1
Runnels	1	0	0	0	1	30	15	15	0	0
Sabine	5	1	1	0	3	154	59	89	6	0
San Augustine	17	0	1	0	16	66	33	27	6	1
San Saba	4	0	1	0	3	41	17	20	4	0
Schleicher	0	0	0	0	0	5	1	2	2	0
Scurry	13	0	1	0	12	77	24	48	5	0
Shackelford	4	0	0	0	4	10	5	4	1	0
Shelby	51	2	17	5	27	247	103	122	22	0
Sherman	1	0	0	0	1	0	0	0	0	0
Somervell	12	2	1	0	9	141	33	97	11	1
Starr	50	8	5	7	30	337	175	95	67	0
Stephens	8	0	0	0	8	53	22	28	3	0
Sterling	0	0	0	0	0	7	3	4	0	0
Stonewall	2	0	0	0	2	8	5	3	0	0
Sutton	0	0	0	0	0	18	4	11	3	0
Swisher	2	0	0	0	2	20	0	19	1	0
Terrell	1	0	0	0	1	7	2	5	0	0
Terry	6	0	1	1	4	32	15	14	3	0
Throckmorton	4	0	0	0	4	4	0	4	0	0
Titus	92	1	18	3	70	278	113	133	32	2
Trinity	32	1	0	5	26	150	68	70	12	3
Tyler	38	1	6	2	29	206	124	70	12	1
Upton	2	0	0	0	2	24	7	17	0	0
Uvalde	45	1	0	0	44	172	74	86	12	1
Val Verde	6	0	1	3	2	128	53	66	9	0
Van Zandt	100	4	1	5	90	978	351	505	122	3
Walker	52	0	3	2	47	451	168	248	35	1
Ward	3	0	0	0	3	7	1	5	1	0
Washington	44	1	3	5	35	270	130	130	10	8
Wharton	68	1	0	8	59	433	180	214	39	4
Wheeler	4	0	0	0	4	31	11	18	2	0
Wilbarger	2	1	0	0	1	40	14	25	1	2
Willacy	26	1	0	1	24	175	72	92	11	0
Winkler	2	0	0	0	2	32	9	22	1	1
Wood	59	1	0	1	57	452	170	265	17	5
Yoakum	3	0	0	0	3	18	6	11	1	0
Young	15	0	2	0	13	63	35	26	2	1
Zapata	33	0	2	0	31	292	111	159	22	1
Zavala	13	0	0	0	13	56	26	27	3	0
UTAH										
Metropolitan Counties										
Cache	23	0	12	0	11	475	95	362	18	2
Davis	17	0	3	1	13	184	46	119	19	2
Salt Lake[5]	558	4	112	90	352	10 685	1 893	7 705	1 087	41
Summit	26	1	8	3	14	687	96	553	38	0
Tooele	10	0	3	1	6	203	50	141	12	3
Utah	34	1	12	1	20	393	110	247	36	14
Weber	44	0	6	3	35	1 272	222	963	87	7
Nonmetropolitan Counties										
Beaver	11	0	0	1	10	106	26	74	6	2
Box Elder	5	0	3	0	2	279	60	206	13	0
Carbon	19	1	4	0	14	168	68	84	16	2
Daggett	2	0	0	0	2	10	3	7	0	0
Duchesne	8	0	3	0	5	203	42	140	21	1
Emery	8	0	0	1	7	111	23	83	5	0
Grand	11	0	2	0	9	99	21	71	7	0
Iron	24	0	6	0	18	130	44	64	22	1
Kane	3	0	2	0	1	10	3	6	1	0
Millard	27	1	0	0	26	335	70	243	22	2

Note: The data shown in this table do not reflect county totals but are the number of offenses reported by the sheriff's office or county police department.

[1]The FBI does not publish arson data unless it receives data from either the agency or the state for all 12 months of the calendar year.
[5]Because of annexations, figures are not comparable to previous years' data.

Table 10. Offenses Known to Law Enforcement, by State Metropolitan and Nonmetropolitan Counties, 2005—*Continued*

(Number.)

County	Violent crime	Murder and nonnegligent manslaughter	Forcible rape	Robbery	Aggravated assault	Property crime	Burglary	Larceny-theft	Motor vehicle theft	Arson[1]
Rich	4	0	0	1	3	61	18	40	3	0
San Juan	1	0	0	0	1	28	5	20	3	0
Sanpete	8	0	2	0	6	96	39	52	5	0
Sevier	15	0	3	1	11	146	23	117	6	1
Uintah	33	0	8	1	24	336	128	177	31	4
VERMONT										
Metropolitan Counties										
Franklin	17	0	2	0	15	274	75	188	11	0
Grand Isle	2	0	0	0	2	65	26	39	0	0
Nonmetropolitan Counties										
Addison	0	0	0	0	0	0	0	0	0	0
Bennington	0	0	0	0	0	0	0	0	0	0
Lamoille	9	0	5	0	4	62	10	46	6	0
Orange	1	0	0	0	1	48	11	37	0	0
Rutland	0	0	0	0	0	123	8	113	2	0
Washington	0	0	0	0	0	0	0	0	0	0
Windsor	0	0	0	0	0	3	1	2	0	0
VIRGINIA										
Metropolitan Counties										
Albemarle County Police Department	149	2	31	26	90	2 031	268	1 646	117	24
Amelia[6]	9	1	4	0	4	. . .	23	63	. . .	0
Amherst	38	1	5	8	24	355	52	280	23	1
Appomattox	8	1	1	2	4	115	24	77	14	2
Arlington County Police Department	407	5	36	163	203	4 401	349	3 640	412	9
Bedford	61	1	10	5	45	730	139	558	33	5
Botetourt	27	2	1	1	23	433	40	365	28	2
Campbell	69	0	13	7	49	774	155	558	61	14
Chesterfield County Police Department	598	8	43	242	305	7 770	1 337	5 904	529	97
Clarke	41	0	3	0	38	184	23	152	9	0
Craig	3	1	0	0	2	11	0	7	4	0
Cumberland	13	2	1	0	10	78	27	41	10	1
Fauquier	68	1	13	5	49	681	102	541	38	10
Fluvanna	22	0	6	1	15	223	50	159	14	3
Franklin	40	0	6	7	27	657	99	508	50	1
Frederick	67	0	21	8	38	1 147	202	837	108	5
Giles	24	1	6	6	11	183	36	132	15	1
Gloucester	29	0	5	1	23	435	56	357	22	10
Greene	15	1	0	0	14	151	23	117	11	3
Hanover	64	4	7	16	37	1 125	127	957	41	9
Henrico County Police Department	673	14	35	281	343	9 599	1 383	7 583	633	83
King and Queen	9	1	1	0	7	44	11	31	2	2
King William	5	0	0	0	5	52	17	30	5	0
Loudoun	171	5	36	47	83	2 858	214	2 446	198	51
Louisa	23	1	7	3	12	465	92	359	14	1
Mathews	8	0	1	1	6	98	17	75	6	4
Montgomery	50	1	10	4	35	548	165	354	29	7
Nelson	19	1	2	1	15	267	54	202	11	1
New Kent	17	0	4	1	12	227	48	162	17	2
Powhatan	13	0	4	1	8	230	56	149	25	1
Prince George County Police Department	36	1	6	9	20	422	98	291	33	2
Prince William County Police Department	645	13	24	255	353	7 633	1 163	5 835	635	91
Pulaski	33	0	4	6	23	572	76	483	13	6
Roanoke County Police Department	212	1	21	12	178	1 124	256	802	66	19
Rockingham	24	0	10	1	13	330	110	209	11	1
Scott	33	1	5	5	22	376	88	258	30	1
Spotsylvania	182	1	22	20	139	2 003	91	1 825	87	23
Surry	11	0	0	1	10	68	33	34	1	2
Sussex	25	0	3	3	19	202	51	124	27	2
Warren	19	0	2	1	16	251	53	182	16	2
Washington	71	0	18	6	47	920	138	743	39	8
York	56	1	6	32	17	1 242	183	1 008	51	19
Nonmetropolitan Counties										
Accomack	57	2	5	14	36	439	92	299	48	3
Alleghany	3	0	0	0	3	73	22	46	5	1
Augusta	79	6	5	12	56	681	139	502	40	7
Bland	0	0	0	0	0	61	18	37	6	1
Brunswick	20	2	2	1	15	199	63	116	20	2
Buchanan	49	1	7	5	36	514	183	282	49	9
Buckingham	18	1	2	3	12	178	56	108	14	0
Carroll	38	1	4	6	27	421	144	232	45	4
Charlotte	16	0	2	1	13	69	29	28	12	0
Culpeper	23	1	4	4	14	227	43	171	13	3

Note: The data shown in this table do not reflect county totals but are the number of offenses reported by the sheriff's office or county police department.

[1]The FBI does not publish arson data unless it receives data from either the agency or the state for all 12 months of the calendar year.
[6]After examining the data and making inquiries, the FBI determined that the agency's offense count was inflated. Consequently, this figure is not included in this table.
. . . = Not available.

Table 10. Offenses Known to Law Enforcement, by State Metropolitan and Nonmetropolitan Counties, 2005—*Continued*

(Number.)

County	Violent crime	Murder and nonnegligent manslaughter	Forcible rape	Robbery	Aggravated assault	Property crime	Burglary	Larceny-theft	Motor vehicle theft	Arson[1]
Dickenson	24	4	2	1	17	270	81	184	5	7
Essex	13	0	0	0	13	91	25	54	12	2
Floyd	9	0	1	0	8	170	32	127	11	3
Grayson	17	2	2	1	12	155	67	76	12	4
Greensville	36	1	1	4	30	298	58	229	11	0
Halifax	17	0	4	5	8	247	85	146	16	5
Henry	176	6	17	27	126	1 204	246	878	80	5
King George	31	0	14	2	15	478	49	401	28	0
Lancaster	5	1	3	1	0	121	32	84	5	0
Lunenburg	5	0	0	1	4	51	12	34	5	2
Madison	9	0	0	0	9	110	20	83	7	0
Mecklenburg	56	1	6	7	42	421	107	277	37	5
Middlesex	14	0	3	0	11	132	18	102	12	1
Northampton	27	1	3	11	12	231	73	153	5	0
Northumberland	16	2	2	0	12	151	43	102	6	2
Nottoway	24	2	4	2	16	102	29	63	10	0
Orange	18	2	5	2	9	172	38	125	9	4
Page	19	0	2	1	16	275	81	180	14	6
Patrick	13	1	3	1	8	316	72	206	38	5
Prince Edward	21	1	1	4	15	34	15	19	0	2
Rappahannock	0	0	0	0	0	47	13	29	5	0
Richmond	26	0	1	0	25	57	12	40	5	2
Rockbridge	13	0	5	2	6	253	37	209	7	2
Russell	41	0	1	6	34	382	127	217	38	10
Shenandoah	17	0	1	0	16	216	15	179	22	3
Smyth	25	5	9	0	11	343	49	274	20	8
Southampton	27	0	3	4	20	319	63	227	29	5
Tazewell	49	1	10	6	32	598	198	352	48	7
Westmoreland	24	2	1	5	16	197	44	138	15	1
Wise	43	0	3	1	39	384	87	259	38	19
Wythe	19	0	1	1	17	161	29	111	21	1
WASHINGTON										
Metropolitan Counties										
Asotin	18	1	1	3	13	181	35	130	16	0
Benton	53	3	4	2	44	808	211	487	110	8
Chelan	47	1	16	2	28	1 199	198	955	46	3
Clark	308	4	86	69	149	5 190	1 219	3 313	658	25
Cowlitz	53	0	17	1	35	1 077	399	565	113	16
Douglas	32	0	3	2	27	644	190	414	40	1
Franklin	16	0	0	4	12	214	61	128	25	0
King	663	8	125	156	374	10 176	2 666	5 374	2 136	214
Kitsap	502	4	106	41	351	3 974	1 180	2 486	308	24
Pierce	1 105	11	94	200	800	11 052	2 899	6 113	2 040	75
Skagit	82	3	16	11	52	2 438	750	1 515	173	22
Skamania	18	1	4	2	11	294	65	214	15	1
Snohomish	594	9	148	111	326	9 092	2 362	4 280	2 450	74
Spokane	272	2	11	12	247	2 518	759	1 477	282	12
Thurston	321	0	18	26	277	3 216	889	1 974	353	27
Whatcom	128	2	29	16	81	1 985	702	1 083	200	23
Yakima	134	6	33	29	66	3 589	1 261	1 804	524	52
Nonmetropolitan Counties										
Adams	35	1	6	6	22	283	86	167	30	3
Clallam	75	0	26	5	44	820	216	514	90	13
Columbia	3	0	0	1	2	139	24	111	4	0
Ferry	3	0	0	0	3	28	14	13	1	0
Garfield	6	0	1	0	5	89	9	73	7	1
Grant	83	3	9	22	49	1 714	544	992	178	15
Grays Harbor	47	1	4	6	36	637	228	349	60	9
Island	47	1	25	7	14	1 544	494	917	133	3
Jefferson	55	0	15	0	40	619	255	332	32	6
Kittitas	14	0	1	1	12	583	220	329	34	1
Klickitat	9	1	0	1	7	204	156	26	22	3
Lewis	65	3	16	4	42	986	345	561	80	8
Lincoln	6	0	2	0	4	189	46	129	14	1
Mason	102	5	26	9	62	2 331	892	1 184	255	5
Okanogan	67	2	21	1	43	535	194	307	34	1
Pacific	30	2	2	2	24	664	248	375	41	1
Pend Oreille	9	0	3	0	6	404	125	244	35	0
San Juan	9	0	3	0	6	286	103	161	22	2
Stevens	45	1	15	7	22	773	293	410	70	2
Wahkiakum	8	0	1	0	7	43	16	20	7	0
Walla Walla	35	0	14	1	20	393	84	282	27	0
Whitman	10	1	6	0	3	96	30	56	10	5

Note: The data shown in this table do not reflect county totals but are the number of offenses reported by the sheriff's office or county police department.

[1] The FBI does not publish arson data unless it receives data from either the agency or the state for all 12 months of the calendar year.

Table 10. Offenses Known to Law Enforcement, by State Metropolitan and Nonmetropolitan Counties, 2005—*Continued*

(Number.)

County	Violent crime	Murder and nonnegligent manslaughter	Forcible rape	Robbery	Aggravated assault	Property crime	Burglary	Larceny-theft	Motor vehicle theft	Arson[1]
WEST VIRGINIA										
Metropolitan Counties										
Berkeley	34	2	0	3	29	191	9	153	29	1
Boone	45	1	2	2	40	216	60	130	26	0
Brooke	39	0	4	7	28	111	31	71	9	4
Hampshire	22	0	1	0	21	73	23	42	8	0
Kanawha	145	5	9	23	108	1 884	699	946	239	39
Marshall	8	0	0	1	7	168	43	112	13	0
Monongalia	78	0	3	6	69	428	95	314	19	2
Morgan	10	0	0	0	10	52	16	36	0	0
Ohio	40	0	0	1	39	49	25	22	2	0
Pleasants	0	0	0	0	0	2	2	0	0	0
Preston	17	0	0	0	17	77	37	28	12	1
Putnam	64	1	1	8	54	1 105	316	689	100	5
Wayne	3	1	1	0	1	183	88	75	20	0
Wirt	1	0	0	1	0	18	10	6	2	0
Nonmetropolitan Counties										
Barbour	3	0	1	0	2	50	27	19	4	0
Braxton	14	0	2	1	11	54	10	37	7	0
Calhoun	0	0	0	0	0	0	0	0	0	0
Fayette	48	0	10	5	33	264	114	135	15	4
Gilmer	1	0	0	0	1	28	9	14	5	3
Grant	4	0	0	0	4	48	27	15	6	0
Greenbrier	30	0	2	1	27	65	25	34	6	0
Hardy	9	0	0	0	9	15	9	5	1	0
Harrison	44	3	0	2	39	350	107	203	40	5
Jackson	14	0	0	0	14	61	21	20	20	0
Lewis	5	0	0	1	4	33	7	22	4	1
Logan	21	0	0	3	18	46	14	26	6	3
Marion	22	0	5	3	14	200	54	120	26	2
Mason	15	0	0	1	14	68	34	9	25	0
McDowell	24	1	0	2	21	113	42	50	21	2
Mercer	100	2	5	12	81	622	226	354	42	9
Mingo	2	0	0	0	2	0	0	0	0	0
Monroe	6	0	0	0	6	28	6	18	4	0
Nicholas	55	0	5	2	48	481	101	347	33	4
Pendleton	0	0	0	0	0	2	1	1	0	0
Pocahontas	2	0	0	0	2	42	20	22	0	0
Raleigh	106	1	5	13	87	1 206	208	909	89	14
Randolph	3	0	0	0	3	24	7	16	1	2
Ritchie	0	0	0	0	0	51	24	22	5	1
Roane	12	1	1	0	10	87	15	61	11	1
Summers	10	0	0	0	10	63	16	41	6	1
Taylor	0	0	0	0	0	6	1	4	1	0
Tucker	1	0	0	0	1	17	8	9	0	0
Tyler	0	0	0	0	0	0	0	0	0	0
Upshur	19	0	1	0	18	75	18	50	7	0
Wyoming	3	0	0	0	3	143	111	29	3	0
WISCONSIN										
Metropolitan Counties										
Brown	33	0	14	0	19	1 412	287	1 056	69	6
Calumet	2	0	0	0	2	155	35	110	10	0
Chippewa	10	0	3	1	6	353	69	256	28	0
Columbia	20	0	5	2	13	386	90	274	22	3
Douglas	3	1	1	1	0	329	135	159	35	1
Eau Claire	41	1	0	3	37	411	88	301	22	0
Fond du Lac	31	0	2	0	29	312	81	219	12	3
Iowa	10	0	0	0	10	139	41	90	8	3
Kenosha	22	1	4	1	16	677	196	428	53	1
Kewaunee	6	0	0	0	6	86	14	71	1	0
La Crosse	16	0	2	1	13	186	30	138	18	0
Marathon	47	0	6	1	40	528	130	374	24	1
Oconto	7	5	1	0	1	496	168	294	34	2
Outagamie	7	1	0	0	6	449	83	346	20	1
Ozaukee	14	0	1	0	13	148	29	112	7	3
Pierce	26	0	0	0	26	277	80	171	26	0
Racine	11	0	5	3	3	686	110	535	41	0
Rock	83	0	11	0	72	461	163	274	24	5
Sheboygan	49	0	1	0	48	529	81	436	12	1
St. Croix	20	0	6	0	14	494	115	353	26	0
Washington	19	1	4	3	11	608	149	420	39	5
Waukesha	20	0	6	1	13	492	86	382	24	8
Winnebago	30	0	3	0	27	394	92	278	24	2

Note: The data shown in this table do not reflect county totals but are the number of offenses reported by the sheriff's office or county police department.

[1]The FBI does not publish arson data unless it receives data from either the agency or the state for all 12 months of the calendar year.

Table 10. Offenses Known to Law Enforcement, by State Metropolitan and Nonmetropolitan Counties, 2005—*Continued*

(Number.)

County	Violent crime	Murder and nonnegligent manslaughter	Forcible rape	Robbery	Aggravated assault	Property crime	Burglary	Larceny-theft	Motor vehicle theft	Arson[1]
Nonmetropolitan Counties										
Adams	15	0	0	1	14	27	13	14	0	0
Ashland	20	0	1	0	19	65	21	42	2	1
Barron	22	0	0	3	19	326	140	172	14	1
Bayfield	40	0	2	0	38	176	51	103	22	0
Buffalo	7	0	0	0	7	101	29	68	4	0
Burnett	27	1	2	0	24	294	120	159	15	0
Clark	17	1	4	1	11	204	44	137	23	3
Dodge	22	0	4	0	18	236	75	140	21	1
Door	4	0	2	0	2	227	51	169	7	0
Dunn	30	0	3	0	27	270	73	164	33	0
Florence	5	0	0	0	5	134	62	69	3	0
Forest	27	0	0	0	27	181	63	97	21	0
Grant	39	1	0	1	37	171	74	84	13	2
Green	8	1	2	0	5	182	52	124	6	0
Green Lake	5	0	2	0	3	78	21	52	5	0
Iron	3	1	0	0	2	59	21	37	1	0
Jackson	12	0	6	2	4	232	49	154	29	0
Jefferson	52	0	14	1	37	402	79	290	33	3
Juneau	86	1	9	2	74	247	83	148	16	0
Lafayette	5	1	0	1	3	135	29	99	7	1
Langlade	14	0	0	1	13	258	108	137	13	0
Lincoln	19	0	0	0	19	161	81	68	12	0
Manitowoc	36	1	6	0	29	327	105	203	19	0
Marinette	13	0	5	1	7	369	159	189	21	1
Marquette	7	1	1	0	5	157	27	105	25	0
Menominee	1	0	0	1	0	31	12	19	0	0
Monroe	5	0	0	1	4	166	49	108	9	0
Oneida	25	0	5	0	20	289	61	207	21	2
Pepin	10	0	0	0	10	24	22	0	2	0
Polk	22	0	9	0	13	374	179	155	40	4
Portage	14	0	6	1	7	377	116	246	15	6
Price	18	0	0	0	18	71	28	42	1	1
Richland	35	0	0	0	35	114	28	77	9	1
Rusk	41	0	2	1	38	236	65	164	7	1
Sauk	14	0	5	0	9	548	113	407	28	0
Sawyer	4	0	1	0	3	361	107	206	48	0
Shawano	8	0	4	1	3	424	134	262	28	0
Taylor	13	0	0	0	13	139	55	79	5	0
Trempealeau	10	0	6	0	4	124	27	85	12	0
Vernon	5	0	0	0	5	136	44	83	9	0
Walworth	10	0	5	0	5	334	81	224	29	0
Washburn	12	0	4	1	7	190	93	92	5	1
Waupaca	19	0	6	1	12	509	133	341	35	2
Waushara	13	0	1	0	12	283	61	209	13	0
Wood	5	0	0	0	5	270	86	164	20	0
WYOMING										
Metropolitan Counties										
Laramie	52	1	15	4	32	509	97	371	41	0
Natrona	16	0	0	1	15	342	115	215	12	2
Nonmetropolitan Counties										
Albany	4	0	1	1	2	78	14	57	7	0
Campbell	37	2	1	1	33	255	36	205	14	0
Carbon	3	0	0	0	3	83	8	74	1	0
Converse	7	0	2	0	5	40	6	30	4	0
Crook	13	0	3	0	10	35	3	30	2	0
Fremont	16	0	3	0	13	242	49	172	21	0
Goshen	34	0	2	0	32	75	15	57	3	0
Hot Springs	1	0	0	0	1	26	2	23	1	3
Johnson	1	0	0	0	1	42	9	28	5	0
Lincoln	10	0	0	0	10	111	31	70	10	0
Niobrara	1	0	0	0	1	4	0	4	0	0
Park	43	0	4	2	37	92	32	57	3	1
Platte	7	0	0	1	6	37	15	22	0	1
Sheridan	11	0	0	0	11	89	19	63	7	0
Sublette	39	0	0	0	39	304	20	266	18	3
Teton	14	0	2	1	11	133	25	100	8	2
Uinta	6	0	1	1	4	146	9	131	6	0
Washakie	3	0	0	0	3	7	3	4	0	0
Weston	0	0	0	0	0	4	1	3	0	0

Note: The data shown in this table do not reflect county totals but are the number of offenses reported by the sheriff's office or county police department.

[1]The FBI does not publish arson data unless it receives data from either the agency or the state for all 12 months of the calendar year.

Table 11. Offenses Known to Law Enforcement, by State and Other Agencies, 2005

(Number.)

Agency	Violent crime	Murder and non-negligent man-slaughter	Forcible rape	Robbery	Aggravated assault	Property crime	Burglary	Larceny-theft	Motor vehicle theft	Arson[1]
Alabama–State Agencies										
Alabama Conservation Department Marine Police	0	0	0	0	0	1	0	1	0	. . .
Alabama Department of Mental Health	3	0	1	0	2	0	0	0	0	. . .
State Capitol Police	0	0	0	0	0	1	0	0	1	. . .
Alabama–Other Agencies										
2nd Judicial Circuit Drug Task Force	0	0	0	0	0	0	0	0	0	. . .
22nd Judicial Circuit Drug Task Force	0	0	0	0	0	0	0	0	0	. . .
24th Judicial Circuit Drug and Violent Crime Task Force	1	0	0	0	1	1	0	0	1	. . .
Marshall County Drug Enforcement	0	0	0	0	0	0	0	0	0	. . .
Alaska–State Agencies										
Alaska State Troopers	1 046	10	158	41	837	4 812	1 325	2 877	610	45
Alcohol Beverage Control Board	0	0	0	0	0	0	0	0	0	0
Alaska–Other Agencies										
Anchorage International Airport	0	0	0	0	0	117	7	88	22	0
Fairbanks International Airport	0	0	0	0	0	37	3	31	3	0
Arizona–State Agencies										
Arizona Department of Public Safety	4	0	0	0	4	5	0	5	0	0
Arizona State Capitol	10	0	0	2	8	67	3	59	5	1
Arkansas–State Agencies										
Camp Robinson	0	0	0	0	0	18	8	9	1	0
California–State Agencies										
Agnews Developmental Center	0	0	0	0	0	9	8	1	0	0
Atascadero State Hospital	20	0	0	0	20	0	0	0	0	0
California State Fair	5	0	0	0	5	71	5	62	4	0
Department of Parks and Recreation										
Angeles	0	0	0	0	0	8	0	8	0	0
Bay Area	0	0	0	0	0	3	2	1	0	0
Calaveras County	0	0	0	0	0	9	0	8	1	0
Capital	1	0	0	0	1	10	5	4	1	0
Channel Coast	7	0	0	0	7	42	7	35	0	0
Colorado	0	0	0	0	0	3	2	0	1	0
Four Rivers District	0	0	0	0	0	9	0	9	0	2
Gold Fields District	2	0	0	1	1	109	10	94	5	0
Hollister Hills	0	0	0	0	0	0	0	0	0	0
Hungry Valley	0	0	0	0	0	2	0	0	2	0
Inland Empire	0	0	0	0	0	5	1	2	2	0
Marin County	0	0	0	0	0	5	4	1	0	0
Mendocino Headquarters	1	0	0	0	1	17	0	17	0	0
Monterey County	0	0	0	0	0	72	1	69	2	0
North Coast Redwoods	1	0	0	0	1	75	48	27	0	0
Northern Buttes	0	0	0	0	0	18	1	17	0	0
Oceano Dunes	6	0	2	0	4	55	0	49	6	0
Ocotillo Wells	1	0	0	0	1	1	0	0	1	0
Orange Coast	0	0	0	0	0	34	8	25	1	0
Russian River	2	0	0	1	1	65	0	65	0	0
San Diego Coast	4	0	0	0	4	102	7	90	5	2
San Joaquin	0	0	0	0	0	4	3	1	0	0
San Luis Obispo Coast	0	0	0	0	0	17	0	17	0	0
Santa Cruz Mountains	4	0	1	0	3	65	2	63	0	0
Sierra	0	0	0	0	0	3	2	1	0	0
Silverado	0	0	0	0	0	26	0	26	0	0
Twin Cities	0	0	0	0	0	5	0	3	2	0
Fairview Developmental Center	7	0	0	0	7	20	8	12	0	0
Highway Patrol										
Alameda County	1	0	0	0	1	254	0	19	235	0
Alpine County	0	0	0	0	0	0	0	0	0	0
Amador County	2	0	0	1	1	41	0	0	41	0
Butte County	2	0	1	0	1	561	3	71	487	0
Calaveras County	0	0	0	0	0	146	0	12	134	0
Colusa County	0	0	0	0	0	29	0	3	26	0
Contra Costa County	1	0	0	0	1	1 401	1	62	1 338	0
Del Norte County	0	0	0	0	0	69	0	0	69	0
El Dorado County	0	0	0	0	0	441	0	71	370	0
Fresno County	1	0	0	1	0	332	0	27	305	1
Glenn County	0	0	0	0	0	31	0	8	23	0
Humboldt County	1	0	0	0	1	243	5	21	217	0
Imperial County	1	0	0	0	1	148	0	11	137	0
Inyo County	1	0	0	0	1	36	0	2	34	0
Kern County	1	0	0	0	1	378	0	55	323	0
Kings County	1	0	0	0	1	268	0	2	266	0
Lake County	0	0	0	0	0	91	0	19	72	0
Lassen County	0	0	0	0	0	24	0	6	18	0
Los Angeles County	43	0	0	0	43	436	2	66	368	0
Madera County	0	0	0	0	0	447	0	70	377	0

[1]The FBI does not publish arson data unless it receives data from either the agency or the state for all 12 months of the calendar year.
. . . = Not available.

Table 11. Offenses Known to Law Enforcement, by State and Other Agencies, 2005—*Continued*

(Number.)

Agency	Violent crime	Murder and non-negligent man-slaughter	Forcible rape	Robbery	Aggravated assault	Property crime	Burglary	Larceny-theft	Motor vehicle theft	Arson[1]
Marin County	0	0	0	0	0	137	0	3	134	0
Mariposa County	0	0	0	0	0	21	0	5	16	0
Mendocino County	1	0	0	0	1	131	1	39	91	0
Merced County	1	0	0	0	1	598	0	80	518	0
Modoc County	0	0	0	0	0	6	0	1	5	0
Mono County	0	0	0	0	0	0	0	0	0	0
Monterey County	0	0	0	0	0	428	0	19	409	0
Napa County	0	0	0	0	0	117	0	33	84	0
Nevada County	0	0	0	0	0	134	0	46	88	0
Orange County	16	0	0	0	16	56	3	9	44	0
Placer County	1	0	0	1	0	412	0	95	317	1
Plumas County	0	0	0	0	0	45	0	8	37	0
Riverside County	22	0	0	0	22	125	15	14	96	0
Sacramento County	1	0	0	0	1	7 140	16	688	6 436	0
San Benito County	0	0	0	0	0	38	0	4	34	0
San Bernardino County	6	0	0	0	6	38	0	2	36	0
San Diego County	19	0	0	2	17	139	11	32	96	0
San Francisco County	0	0	0	0	0	11	0	0	11	0
San Joaquin County	0	0	0	0	0	1 594	0	424	1 170	0
San Luis Obispo County	2	0	0	0	2	228	0	57	171	0
San Mateo County	1	0	0	0	1	39	0	2	37	0
Santa Barbara County	2	0	0	0	2	166	0	42	124	0
Santa Clara County	1	0	1	0	0	92	0	14	78	0
Santa Cruz County	3	0	0	0	3	572	0	116	456	0
Shasta County	4	0	0	1	3	326	0	40	286	0
Sierra County	0	0	0	0	0	5	0	1	4	0
Siskiyou County	1	0	0	0	1	31	1	6	24	0
Solano County	8	0	0	1	7	88	1	1	86	0
Sonoma County	0	0	0	0	0	476	0	128	348	0
Stanislaus County	1	0	0	0	1	620	0	29	591	0
Sutter County	0	0	0	0	0	88	0	15	73	0
Tehama County	0	0	0	0	0	121	0	10	111	0
Trinity County	0	0	0	0	0	68	0	1	67	0
Tulare County	1	0	0	0	1	1 623	0	380	1 243	0
Tuolumne County	0	0	0	0	0	199	0	21	178	0
Ventura County	0	0	0	0	0	59	0	14	45	0
Yolo County	1	0	0	0	1	60	3	1	56	0
Yuba County	1	0	1	0	0	280	0	12	268	0
Lanterman State Hospital	0	0	0	0	0	3	0	3	0	0
Napa State Hospital	2	0	2	0	0	3	0	3	0	1
Porterville Developmental Center	12	0	0	1	11	13	2	11	0	0
Sonoma Developmental Center	0	0	0	0	0	19	1	17	1	0
California–Other Agencies										
East Bay Municipal Utility	0	0	0	0	0	34	4	25	5	1
East Bay Regional Parks										
Alameda County	15	0	3	4	8	138	10	123	5	2
Contra Costa County	15	0	2	12	1	221	12	204	5	3
Fontana Unified School District	14	0	0	8	6	316	74	229	13	9
Grant Joint Union High School	41	0	1	7	33	105	67	18	20	2
Los Angeles County Metropolitan Transportation Authority	8	0	0	1	7	30	3	27	0	0
Los Angeles Transportation Services Bureau	561	0	3	350	208	806	23	575	208	3
Monterey Peninsula Airport	1	0	0	1	0	17	0	10	7	0
Port of San Diego Harbor	17	0	0	7	10	391	9	381	1	2
San Bernardino Unified School District	87	0	2	66	19	309	206	79	24	10
Santa Clara Transit District	16	0	1	8	7	76	2	62	12	0
Stockton Unified School District	115	0	0	15	100	409	111	293	5	20
Union Pacific Railroad										
Alameda County	11	0	0	0	11	349	336	13	0	0
Amador County	0	0	0	0	0	0	0	0	0	0
Butte County	2	0	0	0	2	8	4	4	0	1
Calaveras County	0	0	0	0	0	0	0	0	0	0
Colusa County	0	0	0	0	0	0	0	0	0	0
Contra Costa County	4	0	0	0	4	4	4	0	0	0
El Dorado County	0	0	0	0	0	0	0	0	0	0
Fresno County	0	0	0	0	0	10	9	1	0	0
Glenn County	0	0	0	0	0	0	0	0	0	0
Humboldt County	0	0	0	0	0	0	0	0	0	0
Imperial County	0	0	0	0	0	143	141	2	0	0
Inyo County	0	0	0	0	0	0	0	0	0	0
Kern County	0	0	0	0	0	13	13	0	0	0
Kings County	0	0	0	0	0	0	0	0	0	0
Lassen County	0	0	0	0	0	0	0	0	0	0
Los Angeles County	3	0	0	0	3	283	274	9	0	0
Madera County	0	0	0	0	0	1	1	0	0	0
Marin County	0	0	0	0	0	0	0	0	0	0
Mendocino County	0	0	0	0	0	0	0	0	0	0
Merced County	0	0	0	0	0	1	1	0	0	1

[1]The FBI does not publish arson data unless it receives data from either the agency or the state for all 12 months of the calendar year.

Table 11. Offenses Known to Law Enforcement, by State and Other Agencies, 2005—*Continued*

(Number.)

Agency	Violent crime	Murder and non-negligent man-slaughter	Forcible rape	Robbery	Aggravated assault	Property crime	Burglary	Larceny-theft	Motor vehicle theft	Arson[1]
Modoc County	0	0	0	0	0	0	0	0	0	0
Monterey County	0	0	0	0	0	0	0	0	0	0
Napa County	0	0	0	0	0	0	0	0	0	0
Nevada County	0	0	0	0	0	0	0	0	0	0
Orange County	0	0	0	0	0	0	0	0	0	0
Placer County	1	0	0	0	1	22	7	15	0	0
Plumas County	0	0	0	0	0	2	0	2	0	0
Riverside County	0	0	0	0	0	135	102	33	0	1
Sacramento County	17	0	0	0	17	19	15	4	0	0
San Benito County	0	0	0	0	0	0	0	0	0	0
San Bernardino County	2	0	0	0	2	92	77	15	0	0
San Francisco County	0	0	0	0	0	0	0	0	0	0
San Joaquin County	13	0	0	0	13	387	365	22	0	0
San Luis Obispo County	0	0	0	0	0	2	1	1	0	0
San Mateo County	0	0	0	0	0	0	0	0	0	0
Santa Barbara County	0	0	0	0	0	1	0	1	0	0
Santa Clara County	0	0	0	0	0	1	0	1	0	0
Santa Cruz County	0	0	0	0	0	1	0	1	0	0
Shasta County	2	0	0	0	2	3	1	2	0	0
Sierra County	0	0	0	0	0	0	0	0	0	0
Siskiyou County	0	0	0	0	0	0	0	0	0	0
Solano County	0	0	0	0	0	0	0	0	0	0
Sonoma County	0	0	0	0	0	0	0	0	0	0
Stanislaus County	3	0	0	0	3	4	1	3	0	0
Sutter County	1	0	0	0	1	4	0	4	0	0
Tehama County	0	0	0	0	0	0	0	0	0	0
Trinity County	0	0	0	0	0	0	0	0	0	0
Tulare County	0	0	0	0	0	1	0	1	0	0
Ventura County	0	0	0	0	0	0	0	0	0	0
Yolo County	4	0	0	0	4	2	0	2	0	0
Yuba County	3	0	0	0	3	13	3	10	0	0
Colorado–State Agencies										
Colorado Mental Health Institute	0	0	0	0	0	2	1	1	0	0
Colorado State Patrol	31	0	0	2	29	43	0	12	31	0
Connecticut–State Agencies										
Connecticut State Police	438	12	118	62	246	4 758	1 160	3 179	419	111
State Capitol Police	0	0	0	0	0	7	1	6	0	0
Delaware–State Agencies										
Division of Alcohol and Tobacco Enforcement	0	0	0	0	0	0	0	0	0	0
Environmental Control	0	0	0	0	0	0	0	0	0	0
Fish and Wildlife	6	0	0	0	6	27	1	26	0	0
Office of Narcotics and Dangerous Drugs	0	0	0	0	0	42	0	42	0	0
Park Rangers	3	0	0	0	3	60	6	54	0	0
River and Bay Authority	1	0	1	0	0	12	3	7	2	0
State Capitol Police	3	0	0	0	3	35	4	30	1	0
State Fire Marshal	22	0	0	0	22	19	16	3	0	288
State Police										
Kent County	461	2	47	35	377	1 555	498	936	121	1
New Castle County	719	3	20	305	391	5 542	830	4 275	437	6
Sussex County	687	8	67	52	560	3 062	933	1 930	199	5
Delaware–Other Agencies										
Amtrak Police	0	0	0	0	0	0	0	0	0	0
Wilmington Fire Department	0	0	0	0	0	0	0	0	0	4
District of Columbia–Other Agencies										
Metro Transit Police	316	0	1	198	117	923	4	666	253	0
Florida–State Agencies										
Capitol Police	0	0	0	0	0	18	0	18	0	0
Department of Agriculture	146	2	5	36	103	481	95	290	96	2
Department of Environmental Protection, Division of Law Enforcement										
Alachua County	0	0	0	0	0	0	0	0	0	0
Baker County	0	0	0	0	0	0	0	0	0	0
Bay County	0	0	0	0	0	3	1	2	0	0
Bradford County	0	0	0	0	0	0	0	0	0	0
Brevard County	0	0	0	0	0	3	0	3	0	0
Broward County	0	0	0	0	0	5	0	5	0	0
Charlotte County	0	0	0	0	0	1	0	1	0	0
Citrus County	0	0	0	0	0	0	0	0	0	0
Clay County	0	0	0	0	0	0	0	0	0	0
Collier County	0	0	0	0	0	1	1	0	0	0

[1]The FBI does not publish arson data unless it receives data from either the agency or the state for all 12 months of the calendar year.

Table 11. Offenses Known to Law Enforcement, by State and Other Agencies, 2005—*Continued*

(Number.)

Agency	Violent crime	Murder and non-negligent man-slaughter	Forcible rape	Robbery	Aggravated assault	Property crime	Burglary	Larceny-theft	Motor vehicle theft	Arson[1]
Columbia County	0	0	0	0	0	0	0	0	0	0
Dixie County	0	0	0	0	0	0	0	0	0	0
Duval County	0	0	0	0	0	4	0	4	0	0
Escambia County	0	0	0	0	0	0	0	0	0	0
Flagler County	0	0	0	0	0	0	0	0	0	0
Franklin County	0	0	0	0	0	0	0	0	0	0
Gilchrist County	0	0	0	0	0	0	0	0	0	0
Gulf County	0	0	0	0	0	0	0	0	0	0
Hamilton County	0	0	0	0	0	1	0	1	0	0
Hendry County	0	0	0	0	0	0	0	0	0	0
Hernando County	0	0	0	0	0	0	0	0	0	0
Highlands County	0	0	0	0	0	0	0	0	0	0
Hillsborough County	0	0	0	0	0	1	0	1	0	0
Holmes County	0	0	0	0	0	0	0	0	0	0
Indian River County	0	0	0	0	0	9	0	9	0	0
Lake County	1	0	0	0	1	0	0	0	0	0
Lee County	0	0	0	0	0	2	0	2	0	0
Leon County	0	0	0	0	0	1	0	1	0	0
Levy County	0	0	0	0	0	2	0	2	0	0
Madison County	0	0	0	0	0	0	0	0	0	0
Manatee County	0	0	0	0	0	0	0	0	0	0
Marion County	0	0	0	0	0	0	0	0	0	0
Martin County	0	0	0	0	0	6	0	6	0	0
Miami-Dade County	0	0	0	0	0	5	0	5	0	0
Monroe County	0	0	0	0	0	10	0	10	0	0
Nassau County	0	0	0	0	0	3	0	3	0	0
Okaloosa County	0	0	0	0	0	1	0	1	0	0
Okeechobee County	0	0	0	0	0	1	0	1	0	0
Orange County	0	0	0	0	0	3	0	3	0	0
Osceola County	0	0	0	0	0	0	0	0	0	0
Palm Beach County	0	0	0	0	0	1	0	1	0	0
Pasco County	0	0	0	0	0	0	0	0	0	0
Pinellas County	0	0	0	0	0	0	0	0	0	0
Polk County	0	0	0	0	0	0	0	0	0	0
Putnam County	0	0	0	0	0	0	0	0	0	0
Santa Rosa County	0	0	0	0	0	0	0	0	0	0
Sarasota County	0	0	0	0	0	3	0	3	0	0
Seminole County	0	0	0	0	0	3	0	3	0	0
St. Johns County	0	0	0	0	0	2	0	2	0	0
St. Lucie County	0	0	0	0	0	5	0	5	0	0
Suwannee County	0	0	0	0	0	0	0	0	0	0
Volusia County	0	0	0	0	0	7	0	7	0	0
Wakulla County	0	0	0	0	0	1	0	1	0	0
Walton County	0	0	0	0	0	0	0	0	0	0
Washington County	0	0	0	0	0	0	0	0	0	0
Department of Insurance										
Broward County	0	0	0	0	0	0	0	0	0	0
Duval County	0	0	0	0	0	0	0	0	0	0
Escambia County	0	0	0	0	0	0	0	0	0	2
Hillsboro County	0	0	0	0	0	0	0	0	0	0
Lee County	0	0	0	0	0	0	0	0	0	0
Miami-Dade County	0	0	0	0	0	0	0	0	0	0
Orange County	0	0	0	0	0	0	0	0	0	0
Palm Beach County	0	0	0	0	0	0	0	0	0	0
Department of Law Enforcement										
Duval County (Jacksonville)	0	0	0	0	0	0	0	0	0	0
Escambia County (Pensacola)	0	0	0	0	0	0	0	0	0	0
Hillsborough County (Tampa)	0	0	0	0	0	0	0	0	0	0
Lee County (Fort Myers)	0	0	0	0	0	0	0	0	0	0
Leon County (Tallahassee)	5	1	1	0	3	6	0	6	0	0
Miami-Dade County (Miami)	0	0	0	0	0	1	0	1	0	0
Orange County (Orlando)	0	0	0	0	0	0	0	0	0	0
Florida Game Commission										
Alachua County	0	0	0	0	0	0	0	0	0	0
Baker County	0	0	0	0	0	0	0	0	0	0
Bay County	0	0	0	0	0	0	0	0	0	0
Bradford County	0	0	0	0	0	0	0	0	0	0
Brevard County	0	0	0	0	0	0	0	0	0	0
Broward County	0	0	0	0	0	0	0	0	0	0
Calhoun County	0	0	0	0	0	0	0	0	0	0
Charlotte County	0	0	0	0	0	0	0	0	0	0
Citrus County	0	0	0	0	0	0	0	0	0	0
Clay County	0	0	0	0	0	0	0	0	0	0

[1]The FBI does not publish arson data unless it receives data from either the agency or the state for all 12 months of the calendar year.

Table 11. Offenses Known to Law Enforcement, by State and Other Agencies, 2005—*Continued*

(Number.)

Agency	Violent crime	Murder and non-negligent man-slaughter	Forcible rape	Robbery	Aggravated assault	Property crime	Burglary	Larceny-theft	Motor vehicle theft	Arson[1]
Collier County	0	0	0	0	0	0	0	0	0	0
Columbia County	0	0	0	0	0	0	0	0	0	0
DeSoto County	0	0	0	0	0	0	0	0	0	0
Dixie County	0	0	0	0	0	0	0	0	0	0
Duval County	0	0	0	0	0	0	0	0	0	0
Escambia County	0	0	0	0	0	0	0	0	0	0
Flagler County	0	0	0	0	0	0	0	0	0	0
Franklin County	0	0	0	0	0	0	0	0	0	0
Gadsden County	0	0	0	0	0	0	0	0	0	0
Gilchrist County	0	0	0	0	0	0	0	0	0	0
Glades County	0	0	0	0	0	0	0	0	0	0
Gulf County	0	0	0	0	0	0	0	0	0	0
Hamilton County	0	0	0	0	0	0	0	0	0	0
Hardee County	0	0	0	0	0	0	0	0	0	0
Hendry County	0	0	0	0	0	0	0	0	0	0
Hernando County	0	0	0	0	0	2	0	2	0	0
Highlands County	0	0	0	0	0	0	0	0	0	0
Hillsborough County	0	0	0	0	0	0	0	0	0	0
Holmes County	0	0	0	0	0	0	0	0	0	0
Indian River County	0	0	0	0	0	0	0	0	0	0
Jackson County	0	0	0	0	0	0	0	0	0	0
Jefferson County	0	0	0	0	0	0	0	0	0	0
Lafayette County	0	0	0	0	0	0	0	0	0	0
Lake County	0	0	0	0	0	0	0	0	0	0
Lee County	0	0	0	0	0	0	0	0	0	0
Leon County	0	0	0	0	0	0	0	0	0	0
Levy County	0	0	0	0	0	0	0	0	0	0
Liberty County	0	0	0	0	0	0	0	0	0	0
Madison County	0	0	0	0	0	0	0	0	0	0
Manatee County	0	0	0	0	0	0	0	0	0	0
Marion County	0	0	0	0	0	0	0	0	0	0
Martin County	0	0	0	0	0	0	0	0	0	0
Miami-Dade County	0	0	0	0	0	0	0	0	0	0
Monroe County	0	0	0	0	0	0	0	0	0	0
Nassau County	0	0	0	0	0	0	0	0	0	0
Okaloosa County	0	0	0	0	0	0	0	0	0	0
Okeechobee County	0	0	0	0	0	0	0	0	0	0
Orange County	0	0	0	0	0	0	0	0	0	0
Osceola County	0	0	0	0	0	0	0	0	0	0
Palm Beach County	0	0	0	0	0	0	0	0	0	0
Pasco County	0	0	0	0	0	0	0	0	0	0
Pinellas County	0	0	0	0	0	0	0	0	0	0
Polk County	0	0	0	0	0	0	0	0	0	0
Putnam County	0	0	0	0	0	0	0	0	0	0
Santa Rosa County	0	0	0	0	0	0	0	0	0	0
Sarasota County	0	0	0	0	0	0	0	0	0	0
Seminole County	0	0	0	0	0	0	0	0	0	0
St. Johns County	0	0	0	0	0	0	0	0	0	0
St. Lucie County	0	0	0	0	0	0	0	0	0	0
Sumter County	0	0	0	0	0	0	0	0	0	0
Suwannee County	0	0	0	0	0	0	0	0	0	0
Taylor County	0	0	0	0	0	0	0	0	0	0
Union County	0	0	0	0	0	0	0	0	0	0
Volusia County	0	0	0	0	0	0	0	0	0	0
Wakulla County	0	0	0	0	0	0	0	0	0	0
Walton County	0	0	0	0	0	0	0	0	0	0
Washington County	0	0	0	0	0	0	0	0	0	0
Highway Patrol										
Alachua County	1	0	0	0	1	0	0	0	0	0
Baker County	0	0	0	0	0	0	0	0	0	0
Bay County	0	0	0	0	0	0	0	0	0	0
Bradford County	0	0	0	0	0	0	0	0	0	0
Brevard County	1	0	0	0	1	0	0	0	0	0
Broward County	63	0	0	2	61	81	0	30	51	0
Calhoun County	0	0	0	0	0	0	0	0	0	0
Charlotte County	3	0	0	0	3	0	0	0	0	0
Citrus County	0	0	0	0	0	0	0	0	0	0
Clay County	1	0	0	0	1	1	0	0	1	0
Collier County	2	0	0	0	2	0	0	0	0	0
Columbia County	5	0	0	0	5	0	0	0	0	0
DeSoto County	0	0	0	0	0	0	0	0	0	0
Dixie County	1	0	0	0	1	0	0	0	0	0
Duval County	4	0	0	1	3	2	0	1	1	0
Escambia County	5	0	0	0	5	2	0	1	1	0
Flagler County	1	0	0	0	1	0	0	0	0	0
Franklin County	0	0	0	0	0	0	0	0	0	0
Gadsden County	1	0	0	0	1	0	0	0	0	0
Gilchrist County	0	0	0	0	0	0	0	0	0	0
Glades County	0	0	0	0	0	0	0	0	0	0
Gulf County	0	0	0	0	0	0	0	0	0	0
Hamilton County	0	0	0	0	0	0	0	0	0	0
Hardee County	0	0	0	0	0	0	0	0	0	0
Hendry County	0	0	0	0	0	0	0	0	0	0
Hernando County	2	0	0	0	2	0	0	0	0	0
Highlands County	0	0	0	0	0	0	0	0	0	0
Hillsborough County	26	0	0	0	26	3	0	3	0	0
Holmes County	1	0	0	0	1	0	0	0	0	0
Indian River County	0	0	0	0	0	0	0	0	0	0

[1]The FBI does not publish arson data unless it receives data from either the agency or the state for all 12 months of the calendar year.

Table 11. Offenses Known to Law Enforcement, by State and Other Agencies, 2005—*Continued*

(Number.)

Agency	Violent crime	Murder and non-negligent man-slaughter	Forcible rape	Robbery	Aggravated assault	Property crime	Burglary	Larceny-theft	Motor vehicle theft	Arson[1]
Jackson County	0	0	0	0	0	0	0	0	0	0
Jefferson County	0	0	0	0	0	0	0	0	0	0
Lafayette County	0	0	0	0	0	0	0	0	0	0
Lake County	1	0	0	0	1	0	0	0	0	0
Lee County	8	0	0	0	8	2	0	2	0	0
Leon County	5	0	0	0	5	2	0	2	0	0
Levy County	0	0	0	0	0	0	0	0	0	0
Liberty County	0	0	0	0	0	0	0	0	0	0
Madison County	0	0	0	0	0	0	0	0	0	0
Manatee County	1	0	0	0	1	0	0	0	0	0
Marion County	3	0	0	0	3	1	0	0	1	0
Martin County	1	0	0	0	1	1	0	1	0	0
Miami-Dade County	27	0	0	0	27	30	0	10	20	0
Monroe County	0	0	0	0	0	0	0	0	0	0
Nassau County	0	0	0	0	0	0	0	0	0	0
Okaloosa County	0	0	0	0	0	1	0	1	0	0
Okeechobee County	0	0	0	0	0	3	0	3	0	0
Orange County	22	0	0	1	21	7	0	5	2	0
Osceola County	7	0	0	0	7	3	0	3	0	0
Palm Beach County Turnpike Station	42	0	0	1	41	36	0	28	8	0
Pasco County	4	0	0	0	4	0	0	0	0	0
Pinellas County	6	0	0	0	6	2	0	1	1	0
Polk County	4	0	0	0	4	0	0	0	0	0
Putnam County	0	0	0	0	0	0	0	0	0	0
Santa Rosa County	0	0	0	0	0	0	0	0	0	0
Sarasota County	4	0	0	1	3	1	0	1	0	0
Seminole County	3	0	0	0	3	0	0	0	0	0
St. Johns County	2	0	0	0	2	0	0	0	0	0
St. Lucie County	9	0	0	0	9	10	0	8	2	0
Sumter County	3	0	0	0	3	1	0	1	0	0
Suwannee County	2	0	0	0	2	0	0	0	0	0
Taylor County	0	0	0	0	0	0	0	0	0	0
Union County	0	0	0	0	0	0	0	0	0	0
Volusia County	5	0	0	0	5	1	0	1	0	0
Wakulla County	0	0	0	0	0	0	0	0	0	0
Walton County	0	0	0	0	0	0	0	0	0	0
Washington County	1	0	0	0	1	0	0	0	0	0
State Treasurer's Office, Division of Insurance Fraud	0	0	0	0	0	0	0	0	0	0
Florida–Other Agencies										
Duval County Schools	101	1	4	23	73	750	123	591	36	7
Florida School for the Deaf and Blind	2	0	1	0	1	6	0	6	0	0
Fort Lauderdale Airport	7	0	1	0	6	241	2	219	20	0
Jacksonville Airport Authority	3	0	0	1	2	114	23	48	43	0
Lee County Port Authority	0	0	0	0	0	255	6	224	25	0
Melbourne International Airport	0	0	0	0	0	1	0	0	1	0
Miami-Dade County Public Schools	303	0	3	138	162	3 108	549	2 494	65	36
Miccosukee Tribal	22	0	0	1	21	79	27	45	7	0
Palm Beach County School District	97	0	6	17	74	711	192	508	11	10
Port Everglades	2	0	0	0	2	31	2	27	2	0
Sarasota-Bradenton International Airport	0	0	0	0	0	2	1	1	0	0
Seminole Tribal	79	0	7	22	50	598	64	463	71	2
St. Petersburg-Clearwater International Airport	0	0	0	0	0	10	2	6	2	0
Tampa International Airport	7	1	0	1	5	223	2	176	45	0
Volusia County Beach Management	13	0	0	9	4	167	1	162	4	0
Georgia–State Agencies										
Georgia Public Safety Training Center	0	0	0	0	0	0	0	0	0	0
Ports Authority, Savannah	0	0	0	0	0	6	0	5	1	0
Georgia–Other Agencies										
Augusta Board of Education	0	0	0	0	0	174	2	172	0	0
Bibb County Board of Education	20	0	0	0	20	161	33	127	1	2
Chatham County Board of Education	156	0	0	2	154	338	136	202	0	6
Cherokee County Marshal	0	0	0	0	0	0	0	0	0	0
Forsyth County Fire Investigation Unit	2	0	0	0	2	9	4	5	0	. . .
Fulton County Marshal	63	0	0	6	57	161	8	139	14	. . .
Gwinnett County Public Schools	6	0	0	0	6	363	31	330	2	8
Hartsfield-Jackson Atlanta International Airport	16	0	1	3	12	316	5	288	23	0
Metropolitan Atlanta Rapid Transit Authority	120	0	0	52	68	394	3	288	103	0
Richmond County Marshal	0	0	0	0	0	0	0	0	0	0
Twiggs County Board of Education	0	0	0	0	0	5	3	2	0	0
Indiana–State Agencies										
Northern Indiana Commuter Transportation District	1	0	0	1	0	103	0	88	15	0
State Police[2]										
Adams County	. . .	0	0	1	. . .	3	1	1	1	0
Allen County	. . .	0	0	2	. . .	45	3	39	3	0
Bartholomew County	. . .	0	0	1	. . .	8	0	6	2	0
Benton County	. . .	0	0	0	. . .	4	2	2	0	0
Blackford County	. . .	0	0	0	. . .	4	2	2	0	0
Boone County	. . .	0	0	0	. . .	2	1	1	0	0
Brown County	. . .	0	1	0	. . .	2	0	2	0	0
Carroll County	. . .	0	0	0	. . .	9	5	3	1	0
Cass County	. . .	0	1	0	. . .	25	8	16	1	1
Clark County	. . .	0	2	1	. . .	58	7	40	11	0

[1]The FBI does not publish arson data unless it receives data from either the agency or the state for all 12 months of the calendar year.
[2]After examining the data and making inquiries, the FBI determined that the agency was unable to report aggravated assaults according to the UCR definition. Consequently, this figure is not included in this table.
. . . = Not available.

Table 11. Offenses Known to Law Enforcement, by State and Other Agencies, 2005—*Continued*

(Number.)

Agency	Violent crime	Murder and non-negligent man-slaughter	Forcible rape	Robbery	Aggravated assault	Property crime	Burglary	Larceny-theft	Motor vehicle theft	Arson[1]
Clay County	...	0	0	1	...	35	10	21	4	0
Clinton County	...	0	0	0	...	11	0	11	0	0
Crawford County	...	0	5	0	...	24	7	15	2	0
Daviess County	...	0	0	0	...	16	4	11	1	0
Dearborn County	...	0	0	0	...	51	5	43	3	0
Decatur County	...	1	4	1	...	15	2	11	2	0
De Kalb County	...	1	1	0	...	12	1	9	2	0
Delaware County	...	0	1	1	...	21	3	18	0	0
Dubois County	...	0	0	0	...	46	0	44	2	0
Elkhart County	...	0	0	0	...	34	2	30	2	0
Fayette County	...	0	0	0	...	13	4	7	2	0
Floyd County	...	0	1	0	...	26	7	18	1	0
Fountain County	...	0	1	0	...	10	6	3	1	0
Franklin County	...	0	1	0	...	39	13	22	4	0
Fulton County	...	0	1	0	...	13	5	8	0	0
Gibson County	...	1	0	1	...	22	5	16	1	0
Grant County	...	0	1	0	...	8	1	7	0	1
Greene County	...	0	1	0	...	42	17	22	3	0
Hamilton County	...	0	0	0	...	7	0	7	0	0
Hancock County	...	0	0	0	...	10	0	10	0	0
Harrison County	...	1	2	3	...	47	14	31	2	0
Hendricks County	...	0	1	1	...	29	4	22	3	0
Henry County	...	0	0	0	...	23	1	19	3	0
Howard County	...	0	0	1	...	24	7	14	3	0
Huntington County	...	0	0	0	...	16	5	9	2	0
Jackson County	...	0	2	0	...	69	21	42	6	2
Jasper County	...	0	0	0	...	9	0	8	1	0
Jay County	...	0	1	0	...	7	4	2	1	0
Jefferson County	...	0	3	0	...	12	5	6	1	0
Jennings County	...	0	1	0	...	18	5	13	0	0
Johnson County	...	0	0	0	...	8	0	6	2	0
Knox County	...	0	3	1	...	16	2	12	2	1
Kosciusko County	...	0	1	0	...	23	9	14	0	1
LaGrange County	...	1	0	0	...	45	8	33	4	1
Lake County	...	0	1	0	...	112	5	72	35	0
La Porte County	...	2	0	1	...	34	0	32	2	0
Lawrence County	...	0	0	0	...	13	1	11	1	0
Madison County	...	0	0	0	...	24	3	18	3	0
Marion County	...	0	2	4	...	304	4	242	58	0
Marshall County	...	0	1	0	...	42	4	38	0	0
Martin County	...	4	2	1	...	11	3	4	4	0
Miami County	...	0	2	2	...	67	21	44	2	0
Monroe County	...	1	0	0	...	70	14	50	6	0
Montgomery County	...	0	0	0	...	18	3	14	1	0
Morgan County	...	0	0	0	...	32	6	23	3	0
Newton County	...	0	0	0	...	5	2	2	1	1
Noble County	...	0	1	0	...	40	12	25	3	0
Ohio County	...	0	0	0	...	7	0	7	0	0
Orange County	...	1	2	2	...	27	21	5	1	1
Owen County	...	1	0	0	...	8	2	5	1	0
Parke County	...	0	0	1	...	15	7	8	0	0
Perry County	...	1	3	0	...	45	16	29	0	1
Pike County	...	0	2	0	...	8	1	7	0	0
Porter County	...	0	0	3	...	21	0	18	3	0
Posey County	...	0	1	1	...	21	3	17	1	0
Pulaski County	...	0	1	0	...	6	1	4	1	0
Putnam County	...	0	0	0	...	27	8	17	2	0
Randolph County	...	0	0	1	...	5	1	3	1	0
Ripley County	...	0	5	0	...	143	49	86	8	1
Rush County	...	0	3	2	...	10	3	6	1	0
Scott County	...	0	2	0	...	29	8	16	5	3
Shelby County	...	0	0	0	...	7	3	2	2	0
Spencer County	...	0	2	2	...	26	8	18	0	0
Starke County	...	0	0	0	...	3	2	1	0	0
Steuben County	...	0	1	1	...	29	2	27	0	0
St. Joseph County	...	0	1	1	...	37	5	28	4	0
Sullivan County	...	0	0	0	...	16	3	11	2	0
Switzerland County	...	0	1	0	...	10	2	7	1	0
Tippecanoe County	...	0	3	0	...	58	8	46	4	0
Tipton County	...	0	1	0	...	7	2	5	0	1
Union County	...	0	0	0	...	18	5	11	2	1
Vanderburgh County	...	0	0	1	...	30	0	27	3	0
Vermillion County	...	0	0	0	...	15	3	12	0	0
Vigo County	...	0	1	0	...	90	18	60	12	0
Wabash County	...	1	0	0	...	10	5	4	1	1
Warren County	...	0	0	0	...	8	4	4	0	0
Warrick County	...	0	0	1	...	17	2	13	2	0
Washington County	...	0	0	1	...	5	2	3	0	1
Wayne County	...	0	0	2	...	28	3	23	2	0
Wells County	...	0	0	0	...	4	0	4	0	0
White County	...	0	1	0	...	28	4	23	1	0
Whitley County	...	0	0	0	...	27	8	19	0	0

[1]The FBI does not publish arson data unless it receives data from either the agency or the state for all 12 months of the calendar year.
. . . = Not available.

Table 11. Offenses Known to Law Enforcement, by State and Other Agencies, 2005—*Continued*

(Number.)

Agency	Violent crime	Murder and non-negligent man-slaughter	Forcible rape	Robbery	Aggravated assault	Property crime	Burglary	Larceny-theft	Motor vehicle theft	Arson[1]
Indiana–Other Agencies										
St. Joseph County Airport Authority	0	0	0	0	0	13	1	6	6	0
Kansas–State Agencies										
Kansas Alcoholic Beverage Control	0	0	0	0	0	0	0	0	0	0
Kansas Bureau of Investigation	5	1	2	0	2	0	0	0	0	0
Kansas Department of Wildlife and Parks	1	0	0	0	1	58	1	56	1	0
Kansas Highway Patrol	54	1	0	1	52	128	3	81	44	2
Kansas–Other Agencies										
Johnson County Park	1	0	0	0	1	44	3	41	0	3
Potawatomi Tribal	3	0	0	0	3	86	8	75	3	0
Shawnee Mission Public Schools	1	0	0	0	1	11	0	11	0	0
Unified School District										
Goddard	0	0	0	0	0	23	2	20	1	2
Topeka	11	0	0	0	11	53	6	47	0	1
Wyandotte County Parks and Recreation	0	0	0	0	0	20	0	19	1	1
Kentucky–State Agencies										
Alcohol Beverage Control	0	0	0	0	0	0	0	0	0	0
Kentucky Fairgrounds Security	0	0	0	0	0	80	0	76	4	0
Kentucky Horse Park	0	0	0	0	0	30	2	28	0	0
Motor Vehicle Enforcement	7	0	0	0	7	4	0	3	1	0
Park Security	0	0	0	0	0	29	3	25	1	1
South Central Kentucky Drug Task Force	2	0	0	1	1	3	0	3	0	0
State Police	1 274	73	432	136	633	7 015	3 000	3 256	759	266
Unlawful Narcotics Investigation, Treatment and Education	0	0	0	0	0	8	0	8	0	0
Kentucky–Other Agencies										
Buffalo Trace-Gateway Narcotics Task Force	0	0	0	0	0	0	0	0	0	0
Cincinnati-Northern Kentucky International Airport	0	0	0	0	0	133	1	81	51	0
Clark County School System	1	0	0	0	1	3	0	3	0	0
FIVCO Area Drug Task Force	0	0	0	0	0	0	0	0	0	0
Greater Hardin County Narcotics Task Force	2	0	0	1	1	2	0	2	0	0
Jefferson County Board of Education	80	0	0	5	75	173	88	84	1	2
Lake Cumberland Area Drug Enforcement Task Force	1	0	0	0	1	1	0	1	0	0
Lexington Bluegrass Airport	0	0	0	0	0	1	0	1	0	0
Louisville Regional Airport Authority	0	0	0	0	0	41	0	9	32	0
Nicholas County Schools	0	0	0	0	0	3	0	3	0	0
Northern Kentucky Narcotics Enforcement Unit	0	0	0	0	0	1	0	1	0	0
Pennyrile Narcotics Task Force	0	0	0	0	0	1	0	1	0	0
Louisiana–State Agencies										
Department of Public Safety, State Capitol Detail	4	0	0	2	2	35	2	31	2	0
Tensas Basin Levee District	0	0	0	0	0	6	0	6	0	11
Maine–State Agencies										
Drug Enforcement Agency										
Kennebec County	0	0	0	0	0	0	0	0	0	0
Knox County	0	0	0	0	0	0	0	0	0	0
Oxford County	0	0	0	0	0	0	0	0	0	0
Penobscot County	0	0	0	0	0	0	0	0	0	0
State Police										
Androscoggin County	2	0	0	0	2	150	45	85	20	0
Aroostook County	7	0	1	1	5	223	78	128	17	0
Cumberland County	3	0	1	0	2	159	38	112	9	0
Franklin County	5	0	2	2	1	97	45	42	10	0
Hancock County	2	0	1	0	1	270	77	170	23	0
Kennebec County	7	1	2	0	4	460	132	303	25	0
Knox County	3	0	0	0	3	70	15	52	3	0
Lincoln County	2	1	0	0	1	11	5	4	2	0
Oxford County	10	2	1	0	7	185	75	94	16	0
Penobscot County	13	0	1	3	9	318	113	190	15	1
Piscataquis County	1	1	0	0	0	4	1	2	1	0
Sagadahoc County	2	0	0	0	2	2	0	2	0	0
Somerset County	10	1	3	0	6	191	71	110	10	0
Waldo County	4	0	0	3	1	92	33	53	6	0
Washington County	5	0	1	0	4	214	66	140	8	0
York County	9	1	2	0	6	165	48	104	13	0
Maryland–State Agencies										
Comptroller of the Treasury, Field Enforcement Division	0	0	0	0	0	0	0	0	0	0
Department of Public Safety and Correctional Services, Internal Investigations Unit	191	3	0	0	188	0	0	0	0	0
General Services										
Annapolis, Anne Arundel County	1	0	0	0	1	16	0	14	2	0
Baltimore City	0	0	0	0	0	68	0	67	1	0
Maryland State Police Statewide	2	1	1	0	0	0	0	0	0	0
Natural Resources Police	0	0	0	0	0	125	0	125	0	86
Rosewood	12	0	0	0	12	12	0	12	0	0
Springfield Hospital	0	0	0	0	0	24	2	22	0	0
State Fire Marshal	0	0	0	0	0	0	0	0	0	0

[1]The FBI does not publish arson data unless it receives data from either the agency or the state for all 12 months of the calendar year.

Table 11. Offenses Known to Law Enforcement, by State and Other Agencies, 2005—*Continued*

(Number.)

Agency	Violent crime	Murder and non-negligent man-slaughter	Forcible rape	Robbery	Aggravated assault	Property crime	Burglary	Larceny-theft	Motor vehicle theft	Arson[1]
State Police										
Allegany County	47	0	8	3	36	467	87	360	20	8
Anne Arundel County	16	0	2	0	14	79	3	55	21	0
Baltimore City	18	0	0	1	17	0	0	0	0	0
Baltimore County	21	0	1	2	18	56	0	37	19	0
Calvert County	78	1	4	6	67	400	90	289	21	20
Caroline County	31	1	1	3	26	109	27	65	17	4
Carroll County	233	1	27	17	188	1 459	324	1 021	114	6
Cecil County	254	3	8	29	214	895	338	471	86	25
Charles County	7	0	0	1	6	56	1	50	5	24
Dorchester County	11	0	1	0	10	82	24	40	18	2
Frederick County	61	0	4	12	45	521	96	398	27	7
Garrett County	34	0	3	1	30	170	65	98	7	5
Harford County	161	0	6	21	134	499	117	308	74	26
Howard County	4	0	0	1	3	32	0	24	8	0
Kent County	14	1	0	2	11	43	16	22	5	0
Montgomery County	4	0	0	0	4	23	0	19	4	0
Prince George's County	12	0	0	1	11	157	1	75	81	0
Queen Anne's County	22	0	8	3	11	242	57	168	17	8
Somerset County	62	1	2	5	54	240	99	124	17	6
St. Mary's County	96	0	4	11	81	275	61	173	41	25
Talbot County	11	1	2	1	7	84	13	60	11	1
Washington County	59	0	5	11	43	441	77	327	37	41
Wicomico County	138	1	1	16	120	337	126	177	34	10
Worcester County	28	0	1	2	25	222	71	130	21	2
Transit Administration	0	0	0	0	0	0	0	0	0	0
Transportation Authority	11	0	0	1	10	311	0	255	56	0
Maryland–Other Agencies										
Maryland-National Capital Park Police										
Montgomery County	17	2	2	8	5	179	15	159	5	0
Prince George's County	65	1	8	32	24	250	20	192	38	7
Massachusetts–State Agencies										
State Police										
Barnstable County	4	0	0	0	4	1	0	1	0	0
Berkshire County	8	0	0	0	8	81	32	38	11	0
Dukes County	0	0	0	0	0	0	0	0	0	0
Essex County	0	0	0	0	0	0	0	0	0	0
Franklin County	7	0	1	0	6	2	0	1	1	0
Hampden County	21	0	2	1	18	66	16	9	41	0
Hampshire County	7	0	0	0	7	10	3	5	2	0
Middlesex County	5	0	1	0	4	3	0	2	1	0
Plymouth County	11	0	0	1	10	6	1	3	2	0
Worcester County	3	0	0	1	2	30	0	11	19	0
Michigan–State Agencies										
State Police										
Alcona County	7	0	7	0	0	22	11	9	2	0
Alger County	7	0	1	0	6	97	38	51	8	0
Allegan County	62	1	10	2	49	413	124	241	48	4
Alpena County	33	2	8	2	21	183	74	104	5	2
Antrim County	10	0	4	0	6	39	11	25	3	1
Arenac County	4	0	0	0	4	43	23	19	1	0
Baraga County	8	0	1	0	7	34	12	17	5	1
Barry County	92	0	32	1	59	466	154	283	29	5
Bay County	71	1	29	7	34	465	131	285	49	1
Benzie County	6	0	3	0	3	52	8	41	3	1
Berrien County	82	0	32	3	47	353	88	229	36	8
Branch County	45	1	11	0	33	239	85	126	28	4
Calhoun County	54	0	16	4	34	242	83	148	11	2
Cass County	12	0	3	1	8	107	36	60	11	3
Charlevoix County	4	0	2	0	2	15	4	10	1	1
Cheboygan County	26	0	10	0	16	106	42	62	2	2
Chippewa County	24	0	8	0	16	188	84	92	12	3
Clare County	25	0	12	1	12	23	8	13	2	0
Clinton County	11	0	6	0	5	43	14	25	4	0
Crawford County	8	0	3	0	5	27	13	13	1	2
Delta County	14	0	9	0	5	155	64	84	7	1
Dickinson County	4	0	2	0	2	42	16	24	2	1
Eaton County	22	0	15	0	7	179	61	100	18	3
Emmet County	19	0	9	0	10	208	58	142	8	2
Genesee County	83	0	25	11	47	307	99	175	33	6
Gladwin County	34	0	9	0	25	99	32	56	11	1
Gogebic County	18	0	11	0	7	31	15	15	1	1
Grand Traverse County	29	0	9	1	19	252	42	200	10	2
Gratiot County	48	0	10	2	36	157	55	94	8	3
Hillsdale County	20	0	8	1	11	199	91	94	14	5
Houghton County	7	0	1	0	6	158	40	110	8	0
Huron County	15	0	8	0	7	76	25	48	3	3
Ingham County	14	0	9	0	5	114	28	80	6	1
Ionia County	50	0	11	1	38	271	80	147	44	4
Iosco County	44	0	22	0	22	292	129	153	10	11
Iron County	11	0	4	0	7	54	23	28	3	1
Isabella County	42	0	25	5	12	316	100	201	15	1
Jackson County	87	0	28	5	54	506	161	305	40	8
Kalamazoo County	6	0	4	0	2	41	10	28	3	2
Kalkaska County	13	0	4	0	9	118	76	36	6	1

[1]The FBI does not publish arson data unless it receives data from either the agency or the state for all 12 months of the calendar year.

Table 11. Offenses Known to Law Enforcement, by State and Other Agencies, 2005—*Continued*

(Number.)

Agency	Violent crime	Murder and non-negligent man-slaughter	Forcible rape	Robbery	Aggravated assault	Property crime	Burglary	Larceny-theft	Motor vehicle theft	Arson[1]
Kent County	20	0	10	0	10	59	1	54	4	2
Lake County	15	0	6	0	9	11	3	7	1	1
Lapeer County	53	0	19	2	32	113	39	61	13	5
Leelanau County	4	0	4	0	0	18	4	14	0	0
Lenawee County	38	0	16	0	22	186	70	94	22	2
Livingston County	69	1	11	3	54	624	115	462	47	2
Luce County	16	0	8	0	8	79	31	42	6	1
Mackinac County	14	0	5	0	9	122	58	55	9	0
Macomb County	23	2	12	1	8	40	6	30	4	6
Manistee County	25	0	10	1	14	180	68	102	10	2
Marquette County	27	0	5	2	20	347	131	193	23	4
Mason County	8	0	3	0	5	103	37	65	1	8
Mecosta County	18	0	10	0	8	135	50	80	5	0
Menominee County	29	2	21	0	6	127	53	68	6	0
Midland County	9	0	8	0	1	38	13	24	1	1
Missaukee County	7	0	3	0	4	50	28	20	2	0
Monroe County	43	0	10	7	26	257	75	148	34	1
Montcalm County	57	0	29	2	26	377	151	209	17	6
Montmorency County	4	0	1	0	3	39	22	14	3	0
Muskegon County	58	0	18	3	37	371	128	217	26	2
Newaygo County	58	1	28	0	29	462	148	286	28	5
Oakland County	47	0	14	7	26	275	58	181	36	2
Oceana County	21	0	16	0	5	160	67	83	10	1
Ogemaw County	22	1	10	1	10	170	71	84	15	4
Ontonagon County	3	0	2	0	1	24	8	12	4	0
Osceola County	31	0	20	0	11	187	93	87	7	1
Oscoda County	7	0	2	0	5	13	7	6	0	0
Otsego County	38	0	13	0	25	213	85	117	11	2
Ottawa County	13	0	9	0	4	82	23	54	5	1
Presque Isle County	2	0	1	0	1	14	5	9	0	0
Roscommon County	24	0	6	0	18	177	48	115	14	0
Saginaw County	83	0	27	9	47	267	72	163	32	7
Sanilac County	26	0	4	1	21	199	85	100	14	5
Schoolcraft County	10	0	2	0	8	98	33	59	6	1
Shiawassee County	44	0	15	2	27	229	67	132	30	5
St. Clair County	40	0	9	1	30	185	62	104	19	8
St. Joseph County	49	0	8	1	40	286	87	181	18	19
Tuscola County	50	0	30	0	20	198	79	97	22	4
Van Buren County	120	0	31	4	85	447	165	233	49	16
Washtenaw County	33	0	9	1	23	296	151	116	29	8
Wayne County	62	1	19	6	36	184	9	101	74	2
Wexford County	26	0	7	0	19	169	48	117	4	1
Michigan–Other Agencies										
Wayne County Airport	5	0	0	1	4	227	2	180	45	0
Minnesota–State Agencies										
Capitol Security, St. Paul	0	0	0	0	0	32	1	31	0	0
Minnesota State Patrol	0	0	0	0	0	0	0	0	0	0
State Patrol										
Brainerd	0	0	0	0	0	0	0	0	0	0
Detroit Lakes	0	0	0	0	0	0	0	0	0	0
Duluth	0	0	0	0	0	0	0	0	0	0
Golden Valley	0	0	0	0	0	0	0	0	0	0
Mankato	0	0	0	0	0	0	0	0	0	0
Marshall	0	0	0	0	0	0	0	0	0	0
Oakdale	0	0	0	0	0	0	0	0	0	0
Rochester	0	0	0	0	0	0	0	0	0	0
St. Cloud	0	0	0	0	0	0	0	0	0	0
Thief River Falls	0	0	0	0	0	0	0	0	0	0
Virginia	0	0	0	0	0	0	0	0	0	0
Minnesota–Other Agencies										
Minneapolis-St. Paul International Airport	0	0	0	0	0	0	0	0	0	0
Three Rivers Park District	4	0	0	0	4	109	4	105	0	2
Missouri–Other Agencies										
Clay County Park Authority	2	0	1	0	1	16	1	15	0	1
Jackson County Park Rangers	0	0	0	0	0	0	0	0	0	0
Lambert-St. Louis International Airport	1	0	0	1	0	218	1	214	3	2
St. Charles County Park Rangers	0	0	0	0	0	0	0	0	0	0
Nebraska–State Agencies										
Nebraska State Patrol	8	0	3	0	5	4	0	4	0	0
State Patrol										
Adams County	0	0	0	0	0	0	0	0	0	0
Antelope County	0	0	0	0	0	1	0	0	1	0
Arthur County	0	0	0	0	0	0	0	0	0	0
Banner County	0	0	0	0	0	1	1	0	0	0
Blaine County	0	0	0	0	0	1	0	1	0	0
Boone County	0	0	0	0	0	0	0	0	0	0
Box Butte County	0	0	0	0	0	2	0	1	1	0
Boyd County	0	0	0	0	0	0	0	0	0	0
Brown County	0	0	0	0	0	0	0	0	0	0
Buffalo County	1	0	1	0	0	1	0	1	0	0

[1]The FBI does not publish arson data unless it receives data from either the agency or the state for all 12 months of the calendar year.

Table 11. Offenses Known to Law Enforcement, by State and Other Agencies, 2005—*Continued*

(Number.)

Agency	Violent crime	Murder and non-negligent man-slaughter	Forcible rape	Robbery	Aggravated assault	Property crime	Burglary	Larceny-theft	Motor vehicle theft	Arson[1]
Burt County	0	0	0	0	0	0	0	0	0	0
Butler County	2	0	1	0	1	0	0	0	0	0
Cass County	2	0	1	1	0	2	0	1	1	0
Cedar County	1	1	0	0	0	1	1	0	0	0
Chase County	1	0	1	0	0	1	0	1	0	0
Cherry County	0	0	0	0	0	0	0	0	0	0
Cheyenne County	1	0	1	0	0	0	0	0	0	0
Clay County	1	0	0	0	1	0	0	0	0	0
Colfax County	1	0	0	0	1	0	0	0	0	0
Cuming County	0	0	0	0	0	0	0	0	0	0
Custer County	3	0	2	0	1	3	1	2	0	0
Dakota County	0	0	0	0	0	0	0	0	0	0
Dawes County	8	0	3	0	5	2	2	0	0	0
Dawson County	1	0	0	0	1	1	0	0	1	0
Deuel County	0	0	0	0	0	0	0	0	0	0
Dixon County	0	0	0	0	0	0	0	0	0	0
Dodge County	0	0	0	0	0	1	0	1	0	0
Douglas County	0	0	0	0	0	6	0	1	5	0
Dundy County	0	0	0	0	0	0	0	0	0	0
Fillmore County	1	0	0	1	0	0	0	0	0	0
Franklin County	0	0	0	0	0	0	0	0	0	0
Frontier County	0	0	0	0	0	0	0	0	0	0
Furnas County	0	0	0	0	0	0	0	0	0	0
Gage County	0	0	0	0	0	0	0	0	0	0
Garden County	1	0	0	0	1	0	0	0	0	0
Garfield County	0	0	0	0	0	0	0	0	0	0
Gosper County	0	0	0	0	0	0	0	0	0	0
Grant County	0	0	0	0	0	0	0	0	0	0
Greeley County	0	0	0	0	0	0	0	0	0	0
Hall County	1	0	0	0	1	8	2	5	1	0
Hamilton County	0	0	0	0	0	0	0	0	0	0
Harlan County	0	0	0	0	0	0	0	0	0	0
Hayes County	0	0	0	0	0	0	0	0	0	0
Hitchcock County	1	0	0	0	1	0	0	0	0	0
Holt County	0	0	0	0	0	6	5	1	0	0
Hooker County	0	0	0	0	0	1	1	0	0	0
Howard County	1	0	1	0	0	1	0	0	1	0
Jefferson County	0	0	0	0	0	0	0	0	0	0
Johnson County	1	0	1	0	0	0	0	0	0	0
Kearney County	0	0	0	0	0	0	0	0	0	0
Keith County	1	0	1	0	0	1	0	1	0	0
Keya Paha County	0	0	0	0	0	1	0	1	0	0
Kimball County	0	0	0	0	0	3	2	1	0	0
Knox County	0	0	0	0	0	0	0	0	0	0
Lancaster County	5	0	2	0	3	7	2	3	2	0
Lincoln County	1	0	0	0	1	4	0	2	2	0
Logan County	1	0	0	0	1	0	0	0	0	0
Loup County	0	0	0	0	0	0	0	0	0	0
Madison County	6	0	0	0	6	9	5	4	0	0
McPherson County	0	0	0	0	0	0	0	0	0	0
Merrick County	0	0	0	0	0	0	0	0	0	0
Morrill County	0	0	0	0	0	0	0	0	0	0
Nance County	0	0	0	0	0	0	0	0	0	0
Nemaha County	0	0	0	0	0	0	0	0	0	0
Nuckolls County	1	0	1	0	0	0	0	0	0	0
Otoe County	1	0	1	0	0	0	0	0	0	0
Pawnee County	0	0	0	0	0	0	0	0	0	0
Perkins County	0	0	0	0	0	0	0	0	0	0
Phelps County	0	0	0	0	0	0	0	0	0	0
Pierce County	1	0	0	0	1	4	3	0	1	0
Platte County	1	0	0	0	1	0	0	0	0	0
Polk County	0	0	0	0	0	0	0	0	0	0
Red Willow County	1	0	1	0	0	0	0	0	0	0
Richardson County	0	0	0	0	0	0	0	0	0	0
Rock County	0	0	0	0	0	0	0	0	0	0
Saline County	0	0	0	0	0	0	0	0	0	0
Sarpy County	0	0	0	0	0	0	0	0	0	0
Saunders County	3	0	1	1	1	2	2	0	0	0
Scotts Bluff County	2	0	0	0	2	5	1	2	2	0
Seward County	0	0	0	0	0	2	0	1	1	0
Sheridan County	0	0	0	0	0	0	0	0	0	0
Sherman County	0	0	0	0	0	1	0	0	1	0
Sioux County	0	0	0	0	0	0	0	0	0	0
Stanton County	0	0	0	0	0	0	0	0	0	0
Thayer County	0	0	0	0	0	0	0	0	0	0
Thomas County	0	0	0	0	0	0	0	0	0	0
Thurston County	3	0	1	0	2	0	0	0	0	0
Valley County	0	0	0	0	0	0	0	0	0	0
Washington County	0	0	0	0	0	0	0	0	0	0
Wayne County	0	0	0	0	0	2	0	2	0	0
Webster County	0	0	0	0	0	0	0	0	0	0
Wheeler County	0	0	0	0	0	0	0	0	0	0
York County	0	0	0	0	0	0	0	0	0	0
Nevada–Other Agencies										
Washoe County School District	14	0	0	5	9	320	44	274	2	13

[1]The FBI does not publish arson data unless it receives data from either the agency or the state for all 12 months of the calendar year.

Table 11. Offenses Known to Law Enforcement, by State and Other Agencies, 2005—*Continued*

(Number.)

Agency	Violent crime	Murder and non-negligent man-slaughter	Forcible rape	Robbery	Aggravated assault	Property crime	Burglary	Larceny-theft	Motor vehicle theft	Arson[1]
New Hampshire–State Agencies										
Liquor Commission	1	0	0	0	1	5	1	4	0	0
New Jersey–State Agencies										
Hunterdon Developmental Center	0	0	0	0	0	6	0	6	0	0
New Jersey Transit Police	109	0	0	61	48	380	20	324	36	...
Palisades Interstate Parkway	13	0	0	0	13	9	5	4	0	0
Port Authority of New York and New Jersey[3]	61	0	0	25	36	701	17	625	59	0
State Police										
Atlantic County	51	0	2	12	37	656	68	550	38	4
Bergen County	9	0	0	1	8	157	0	126	31	0
Burlington County	52	0	1	8	43	473	94	330	49	4
Camden County	5	0	1	0	4	22	1	20	1	0
Cape May County	31	0	2	2	27	380	116	230	34	0
Cumberland County	79	0	0	8	71	663	203	396	64	14
Essex County	13	0	1	2	10	27	2	16	9	2
Gloucester County	1	0	0	0	1	12	2	5	5	3
Hudson County	7	1	0	0	6	19	0	16	3	0
Hunterdon County	14	0	0	2	12	197	37	138	22	2
Mercer County	7	0	1	2	4	162	2	154	6	0
Middlesex County	17	0	0	7	10	142	0	120	22	1
Monmouth County	27	0	1	2	24	170	37	118	15	3
Morris County	10	0	0	2	8	16	3	11	2	0
Ocean County	4	0	0	1	3	110	8	98	4	0
Passaic County	4	0	0	0	4	14	0	10	4	0
Salem County	21	2	2	4	13	383	152	204	27	9
Somerset County	3	0	0	1	2	8	2	4	2	0
Sussex County	40	0	3	0	37	480	86	357	37	2
Union County	6	0	0	1	5	28	0	25	3	0
Warren County	22	1	0	0	21	193	45	127	21	2
New Mexico–State Agencies										
New Mexico State Police	292	13	50	25	204	1 758	859	623	276	5
New Mexico–Other Agencies										
Acoma Tribal	27	0	0	0	27	30	4	20	6	0
Laguna Tribal	149	0	8	0	141	40	7	29	4	0
Taos Pueblo Tribal	22	0	0	1	21	14	1	12	1	0
New York–State Agencies										
State Park										
Albany County	0	0	0	0	0	4	0	4	0	...
Allegany County	0	0	0	0	0	0	0	0	0	...
Bronx County	3	0	0	3	0	22	0	22	0	...
Broome County	0	0	0	0	0	7	0	7	0	...
Cattaraugus County	0	0	0	0	0	21	6	15	0	...
Cayuga County	1	0	1	0	0	9	0	9	0	...
Chautauqua County	0	0	0	0	0	0	0	0	0	...
Chemung County	0	0	0	0	0	0	0	0	0	...
Chenango County	0	0	0	0	0	4	1	3	0	...
Clinton County	0	0	0	0	0	1	0	1	0	...
Cortland County	0	0	0	0	0	0	0	0	0	...
Delaware County	0	0	0	0	0	0	0	0	0	...
Erie County	2	0	0	1	1	20	1	19	0	...
Franklin County	0	0	0	0	0	0	0	0	0	...
Fulton County	0	0	0	0	0	0	0	0	0	...
Genesee County	0	0	0	0	0	2	0	2	0	...
Greene County	0	0	0	0	0	0	0	0	0	...
Herkimer County	0	0	0	0	0	0	0	0	0	...
Jefferson County	0	0	0	0	0	6	0	6	0	...
Kings County	0	0	0	0	0	0	0	0	0	...
Lewis County	0	0	0	0	0	0	0	0	0	...
Livingston County	1	0	0	0	1	7	0	7	0	...
Madison County	0	0	0	0	0	0	0	0	0	...
Monroe County	1	0	0	0	1	20	1	19	0	...
Montgomery County	0	0	0	0	0	0	0	0	0	...
Nassau County	10	0	0	0	10	104	2	101	1	...
New York County	0	0	0	0	0	91	0	91	0	...
Niagara County	4	0	0	2	2	18	0	18	0	...
Oneida County	0	0	0	0	0	4	0	4	0	...
Onondaga County	0	0	0	0	0	5	0	5	0	...
Ontario County	0	0	0	0	0	0	0	0	0	...
Orange County	0	0	0	0	0	6	1	5	0	...
Orleans County	0	0	0	0	0	4	0	4	0	...
Oswego County	0	0	0	0	0	7	2	5	0	...
Otsego County	0	0	0	0	0	2	0	2	0	...
Queens County	0	0	0	0	0	0	0	0	0	...
Rensselaer County	0	0	0	0	0	8	1	7	0	...
Richmond County	0	0	0	0	0	0	0	0	0	...
Rockland County	1	0	0	0	1	32	3	29	0	...
Saratoga County	11	0	0	1	10	21	3	16	2	...

[1]The FBI does not publish arson data unless it receives data from either the agency or the state for all 12 months of the calendar year.
[3]Figures reported are the number of crimes that occurred in New Jersey.
. . . = Not available.

Table 11. Offenses Known to Law Enforcement, by State and Other Agencies, 2005—*Continued*

(Number.)

Agency	Violent crime	Murder and non-negligent man-slaughter	Forcible rape	Robbery	Aggravated assault	Property crime	Burglary	Larceny-theft	Motor vehicle theft	Arson[1]
Schenectady County	0	0	0	0	0	0	0	0	0	. . .
Schoharie County	0	0	0	0	0	0	0	0	0	. . .
Schuyler County	0	0	0	0	0	13	1	12	0	. . .
Seneca County	0	0	0	0	0	9	0	9	0	. . .
Steuben County	0	0	0	0	0	3	0	3	0	. . .
St. Lawrence County	0	0	0	0	0	19	0	19	0	. . .
Suffolk County	5	0	0	0	5	62	4	56	2	. . .
Sullivan County	0	0	0	0	0	0	0	0	0	. . .
Tioga County	0	0	0	0	0	0	0	0	0	. . .
Tompkins County	0	0	0	0	0	30	4	26	0	. . .
Ulster County	0	0	0	0	0	1	0	1	0	. . .
Washington County	0	0	0	0	0	0	0	0	0	. . .
Wayne County	0	0	0	0	0	1	0	1	0	. . .
Wyoming County	1	0	0	0	1	7	0	7	0	. . .
Yates County	0	0	0	0	0	2	0	2	0	. . .
State Police										
Albany County	31	1	2	5	23	217	27	187	3	. . .
Allegany County	78	0	32	4	42	474	163	299	12	. . .
Broome County	52	2	13	7	30	664	135	515	14	. . .
Cattaraugus County	47	0	13	0	34	473	102	353	18	. . .
Cayuga County	41	0	0	1	40	281	78	199	4	. . .
Chautauqua County	26	0	4	0	22	192	37	149	6	. . .
Chemung County	39	2	7	0	30	303	41	255	7	. . .
Chenango County	43	0	2	1	40	158	50	104	4	. . .
Clinton County	145	2	18	7	118	1 141	275	851	15	. . .
Columbia County	27	0	4	3	20	310	84	220	6	. . .
Cortland County	14	0	2	1	11	231	27	200	4	. . .
Delaware County	37	0	4	0	33	263	106	149	8	. . .
Dutchess County	123	1	26	14	82	669	150	498	21	. . .
Erie County	73	0	5	6	62	530	62	457	11	. . .
Essex County	38	1	7	1	29	326	95	228	3	. . .
Franklin County	116	1	13	0	102	343	188	138	17	. . .
Fulton County	32	0	8	0	24	133	36	90	7	. . .
Genesee County	14	0	2	0	12	102	13	88	1	. . .
Greene County	106	0	4	1	101	400	151	232	17	. . .
Hamilton County	2	0	0	0	2	41	17	24	0	. . .
Herkimer County	18	0	5	0	13	214	95	112	7	. . .
Jefferson County	102	4	25	3	70	613	125	472	16	. . .
Lewis County	19	0	7	0	12	80	43	34	3	. . .
Livingston County	15	1	2	1	11	104	18	84	2	. . .
Madison County	30	0	12	0	18	223	74	145	4	. . .
Monroe County	26	0	2	0	24	27	4	21	2	. . .
Montgomery County	20	0	2	0	18	92	21	69	2	. . .
Nassau County	6	0	0	0	6	8	0	8	0	. . .
New York County	2	0	1	0	1	54	0	54	0	. . .
Niagara County	18	0	6	4	8	227	28	192	7	. . .
Oneida County	68	1	9	5	53	699	160	517	22	. . .
Onondaga County	62	0	10	7	45	650	151	488	11	. . .
Ontario County	19	0	6	1	12	274	41	225	8	. . .
Orange County	151	1	40	30	80	903	170	658	75	. . .
Orleans County	24	0	3	0	21	72	16	52	4	. . .
Oswego County	62	0	7	4	51	721	203	503	15	. . .
Otsego County	45	2	5	6	32	480	106	367	7	. . .
Putnam County	34	0	5	7	22	145	19	121	5	. . .
Rensselaer County	66	0	14	4	48	539	141	369	29	. . .
Rockland County	13	0	1	1	11	29	6	18	5	. . .
Saratoga County	111	0	21	9	81	691	123	531	37	. . .
Schenectady County	8	0	2	1	5	56	12	41	3	. . .
Schoharie County	25	0	7	1	17	154	29	123	2	. . .
Schuyler County	9	0	1	0	8	35	5	28	2	. . .
Seneca County	11	0	7	0	4	130	35	93	2	. . .
Steuben County	73	0	29	5	39	529	146	358	25	. . .
St. Lawrence County	91	3	11	1	76	449	161	274	14	. . .
Suffolk County	10	0	2	2	6	25	9	12	4	. . .
Sullivan County	90	0	10	7	73	552	218	300	34	. . .
Tioga County	13	1	3	1	8	164	38	121	5	. . .
Tompkins County	37	0	3	1	33	250	38	202	10	. . .
Ulster County	229	2	25	7	195	447	128	284	35	. . .
Warren County	32	0	3	3	26	251	23	228	0	. . .
Washington County	22	0	5	1	16	152	48	95	9	. . .
Wayne County	63	0	19	5	39	500	154	320	26	. . .
Westchester County	81	2	8	17	54	472	84	357	31	. . .
Wyoming County	24	0	1	0	23	24	4	19	1	. . .
Yates County	5	0	2	0	3	19	2	17	0	. . .
New York–Other Agencies										
Board of Water										
Delaware County	1	0	0	0	1	2	0	2	0	. . .
Ulster County	2	0	0	0	2	6	0	6	0	. . .
Westchester County	0	0	0	0	0	22	0	21	1	. . .
Broome County Special Investigations Task Force	0	0	0	0	0	2	0	1	1	. . .

[1]The FBI does not publish arson data unless it receives data from either the agency or the state for all 12 months of the calendar year.
. . . = Not available.

Table 11. Offenses Known to Law Enforcement, by State and Other Agencies, 2005—*Continued*

(Number.)

Agency	Violent crime	Murder and non-negligent man-slaughter	Forcible rape	Robbery	Aggravated assault	Property crime	Burglary	Larceny-theft	Motor vehicle theft	Arson[1]
CSX Transportation										
Albany County	0	0	0	0	0	10	0	10	0	. . .
Bronx County	0	0	0	0	0	21	0	21	0	. . .
Cattaraugus County	0	0	0	0	0	0	0	0	0	. . .
Cayuga County	0	0	0	0	0	0	0	0	0	. . .
Chautauqua County	0	0	0	0	0	0	0	0	0	. . .
Columbia County	0	0	0	0	0	1	0	1	0	. . .
Dutchess County	0	0	0	0	0	0	0	0	0	. . .
Erie County	0	0	0	0	0	16	1	15	0	. . .
Genesee County	0	0	0	0	0	0	0	0	0	. . .
Greene County	0	0	0	0	0	0	0	0	0	. . .
Herkimer County	0	0	0	0	0	1	0	1	0	. . .
Jefferson County	0	0	0	0	0	0	0	0	0	. . .
Madison County	0	0	0	0	0	0	0	0	0	. . .
Monroe County	0	0	0	0	0	1	0	1	0	. . .
Montgomery County	0	0	0	0	0	4	0	4	0	. . .
Niagara County	0	0	0	0	0	0	0	0	0	. . .
Oneida County	0	0	0	0	0	0	0	0	0	. . .
Onondaga County	0	0	0	0	0	4	0	4	0	. . .
Ontario County	0	0	0	0	0	0	0	0	0	. . .
Orange County	0	0	0	0	0	1	0	1	0	. . .
Orleans County	0	0	0	0	0	0	0	0	0	. . .
Oswego County	0	0	0	0	0	0	0	0	0	. . .
Queens County	0	0	0	0	0	0	0	0	0	. . .
Rensselaer County	0	0	0	0	0	0	0	0	0	. . .
Rockland County	0	0	0	0	0	1	0	1	0	. . .
Schenectady County	0	0	0	0	0	3	0	3	0	. . .
Seneca County	0	0	0	0	0	0	0	0	0	. . .
St. Lawrence County	0	0	0	0	0	2	0	2	0	. . .
Ulster County	0	0	0	0	0	0	0	0	0	. . .
Wayne County	0	0	0	0	0	1	0	1	0	. . .
Westchester County	0	0	0	0	0	0	0	0	0	. . .
New York City Metropolitan Transportation Authority										
Bronx County	8	0	0	8	0	20	0	20	0	. . .
Dutchess County	1	0	0	0	1	26	0	26	0	. . .
Kings County	6	0	0	6	0	13	1	12	0	. . .
Nassau County	11	0	0	7	4	43	1	41	1	. . .
New York County	14	0	1	4	9	265	15	250	0	. . .
Orange County	0	0	0	0	0	7	0	7	0	. . .
Putnam County	1	0	0	1	0	10	0	10	0	. . .
Queens County	13	0	0	8	5	31	0	30	1	. . .
Richmond County	0	0	0	0	0	0	0	0	0	. . .
Rockland County	1	0	0	0	1	3	0	3	0	. . .
Suffolk County	11	0	0	8	3	51	1	50	0	. . .
Westchester County	16	0	0	13	3	61	5	53	3	. . .
Onondaga County Parks	0	0	0	0	0	27	5	22	0	. . .
Staten Island Rapid Transit	17	0	0	10	7	3	0	3	0	. . .
Suffolk County Parks	2	0	0	0	2	44	3	40	1	. . .
North Carolina–State Agencies										
Department of Human Resources	0	0	0	0	0	6	0	6	0	0
Department of Wildlife	2	0	0	0	2	0	0	0	0	0
Division of Alcohol Law Enforcement	0	0	0	0	0	0	0	0	0	0
State Capitol Police	3	0	0	1	2	80	15	60	5	0
State Park Rangers										
Cliffs of the Neuse	0	0	0	0	0	1	0	1	0	0
Crowders Mountain	0	0	0	0	0	1	0	1	0	0
Fort Fisher	0	0	0	0	0	0	0	0	0	0
Gorges	0	0	0	0	0	0	0	0	0	0
Hammocks Beach	0	0	0	0	0	0	0	0	0	0
Jones Lake	0	0	0	0	0	0	0	0	0	0
Lake James	0	0	0	0	0	0	0	0	0	0
Morrow Mountain	0	0	0	0	0	2	0	2	0	0
Mt. Mitchell	0	0	0	0	0	0	0	0	0	0
New River-Mount Jefferson	0	0	0	0	0	0	0	0	0	0
Stone Mountain	0	0	0	0	0	0	0	0	0	0
North Carolina–Other Agencies										
Raleigh-Durham International Airport	0	0	0	0	0	93	0	88	5	0
Ohio–State Agencies										
Ohio State Highway Patrol	302	3	13	19	267	567	23	427	117	16
Ohio–Other Agencies										
Cleveland Metropolitan Park District	12	0	0	4	8	195	6	181	8	3
Greater Cleveland Regional Transit Authority	35	0	1	26	8	62	1	30	31	0
Hamilton County Park District	1	0	1	0	0	41	4	36	1	0
Port Columbus International Airport	2	0	0	1	1	112	1	95	16	0
Oklahoma–State Agencies										
Capitol Park Police	2	0	0	0	2	33	4	28	1	0
Oklahoma–Other Agencies										
Jenks Public Schools	0	0	0	0	0	21	6	15	0	0
Madill Public Schools	0	0	0	0	0	1	0	1	0	0
Norman Public Schools	1	0	0	0	1	39	1	38	0	0
Putnam City Campus	2	0	0	0	2	87	5	80	2	0

[1]The FBI does not publish arson data unless it receives data from either the agency or the state for all 12 months of the calendar year.
. . . = Not available.

Table 11. Offenses Known to Law Enforcement, by State and Other Agencies, 2005—*Continued*

(Number.)

Agency	Violent crime	Murder and non-negligent man-slaughter	Forcible rape	Robbery	Aggravated assault	Property crime	Burglary	Larceny-theft	Motor vehicle theft	Arson[1]
Oregon–State Agencies										
State Police										
Baker County	2	0	1	0	1	13	1	10	2	0
Benton County	4	0	0	2	2	215	27	175	13	2
Clackamas County	13	0	1	1	11	29	2	17	10	15
Clatsop County	2	1	0	0	1	12	0	8	4	17
Columbia County	6	0	1	0	5	11	1	5	5	4
Coos County	5	0	0	0	5	10	3	5	2	10
Crook County	1	0	0	0	1	1	0	0	1	2
Curry County	1	0	0	0	1	16	0	16	0	1
Deschutes County	11	0	7	0	4	11	1	7	3	6
Douglas County	7	0	2	1	4	19	1	14	4	12
Gilliam County	0	0	0	0	0	3	0	3	0	1
Grant County	1	0	1	0	0	4	2	2	0	0
Harney County	0	0	0	0	0	0	0	0	0	0
Hood River County	2	0	1	0	1	7	0	7	0	1
Jackson County	6	1	4	0	1	22	0	18	4	14
Jefferson County	2	0	0	0	2	4	0	3	1	0
Josephine County	4	0	2	0	2	11	1	8	2	12
Klamath County	22	0	2	1	19	32	6	22	4	6
Lake County	0	0	0	0	0	0	0	0	0	. . .
Lane County	20	0	5	0	15	89	9	68	12	32
Lincoln County	5	0	0	0	5	35	2	29	4	3
Linn County	5	0	0	2	3	16	0	12	4	3
Malheur County	30	0	1	1	28	4	0	4	0	0
Marion County	96	0	9	3	84	101	3	61	37	28
Morrow County	0	0	0	0	0	0	0	0	0	0
Multnomah County	9	0	4	0	5	35	0	22	13	4
Polk County	0	0	0	0	0	7	0	7	0	2
Sherman County	1	0	1	0	0	3	0	2	1	0
Tillamook County	1	0	0	0	1	12	6	4	2	4
Umatilla County	26	0	3	0	23	35	11	17	7	8
Union County	3	0	1	1	1	12	0	6	6	1
Wallowa County	0	0	0	0	0	2	2	0	0	1
Wasco County	3	0	0	0	3	15	3	8	4	2
Washington County	5	0	0	0	5	10	0	5	5	4
Wheeler County	0	0	0	0	0	0	0	0	0	0
Yamhill County	1	0	0	0	1	5	1	2	2	1
Oregon–Other Agencies										
Port of Portland	4	0	1	2	1	360	7	325	28	1
Pennsylvania–State Agencies										
Bureau of Forestry										
Berks County	0	0	0	0	0	0	0	0	0	4
Carbon County	0	0	0	0	0	0	0	0	0	. . .
Centre County	0	0	0	0	0	0	0	0	0	13
Chester County	0	0	0	0	0	0	0	0	0	5
Clearfield County	0	0	0	0	0	0	0	0	0	. . .
Clinton County	0	0	0	0	0	0	0	0	0	12
Cumberland County	0	0	0	0	0	0	0	0	0	2
Delaware County	0	0	0	0	0	0	0	0	0	2
Fayette County	0	0	0	0	0	0	0	0	0	7
Huntingdon County	0	0	0	0	0	0	0	0	0	1
Lackawanna County	0	0	0	0	0	0	0	0	0	8
Lehigh County	0	0	0	0	0	0	0	0	0	. . .
Luzerne County	0	0	0	0	0	0	0	0	0	30
Lycoming County	0	0	0	0	0	0	0	0	0	. . .
Mifflin County	0	0	0	0	0	0	0	0	0	1
Monroe County	0	0	0	0	0	0	0	0	0	3
Pike County	0	0	0	0	0	0	0	0	0	15
Schuylkill County	0	0	0	0	0	0	0	0	0	9
Snyder County	0	0	0	0	0	0	0	0	0	3
Susquehanna County	0	0	0	0	0	0	0	0	0	3
Tioga County	0	0	0	0	0	0	0	0	0	4
Union County	0	0	0	0	0	0	0	0	0	1
Wyoming County	0	0	0	0	0	0	0	0	0	2
Bureau of Narcotics										
Adams County	0	0	0	0	0	0	0	0	0	0
Allegheny County	0	0	0	0	0	0	0	0	0	0
Bedford County	0	0	0	0	0	0	0	0	0	0
Berks County	0	0	0	0	0	2	0	2	0	0
Blair County	0	0	0	0	0	0	0	0	0	0
Bradford County	0	0	0	0	0	0	0	0	0	0
Bucks County	0	0	0	0	0	0	0	0	0	0
Cambria County	0	0	0	0	0	0	0	0	0	0
Cameron County	0	0	0	0	0	0	0	0	0	0
Carbon County	0	0	0	0	0	0	0	0	0	0
Centre County	0	0	0	0	0	0	0	0	0	0
Chester County	0	0	0	0	0	0	0	0	0	0
Clearfield County	0	0	0	0	0	0	0	0	0	0
Clinton County	0	0	0	0	0	0	0	0	0	0
Columbia County	0	0	0	0	0	0	0	0	0	0
Crawford County	0	0	0	0	0	0	0	0	0	0
Cumberland County	0	0	0	0	0	0	0	0	0	0
Dauphin County	0	0	0	0	0	2	0	2	0	0
Delaware County	0	0	0	0	0	0	0	0	0	0
Elk County	0	0	0	0	0	0	0	0	0	0

[1] The FBI does not publish arson data unless it receives data from either the agency or the state for all 12 months of the calendar year.
. . . = Not available.

Table 11. Offenses Known to Law Enforcement, by State and Other Agencies, 2005—*Continued*

(Number.)

Agency	Violent crime	Murder and non-negligent man-slaughter	Forcible rape	Robbery	Aggravated assault	Property crime	Burglary	Larceny-theft	Motor vehicle theft	Arson[1]
Erie County	0	0	0	0	0	0	0	0	0	0
Fayette County	0	0	0	0	0	0	0	0	0	0
Forest County	0	0	0	0	0	0	0	0	0	0
Franklin County	0	0	0	0	0	0	0	0	0	0
Fulton County	0	0	0	0	0	0	0	0	0	0
Greene County	0	0	0	0	0	0	0	0	0	0
Huntingdon County	0	0	0	0	0	0	0	0	0	0
Juniata County	0	0	0	0	0	0	0	0	0	0
Lackawanna County	0	0	0	0	0	0	0	0	0	0
Lancaster County	0	0	0	0	0	0	0	0	0	0
Lebanon County	0	0	0	0	0	0	0	0	0	0
Lehigh County	0	0	0	0	0	0	0	0	0	. . .
Luzerne County	0	0	0	0	0	0	0	0	0	0
Lycoming County	0	0	0	0	0	0	0	0	0	0
McKean County	0	0	0	0	0	0	0	0	0	0
Mifflin County	0	0	0	0	0	0	0	0	0	0
Monroe County	0	0	0	0	0	0	0	0	0	0
Montgomery County	0	0	0	0	0	0	0	0	0	0
Montour County	0	0	0	0	0	0	0	0	0	0
Northampton County	0	0	0	0	0	0	0	0	0	0
Northumberland County	0	0	0	0	0	0	0	0	0	0
Perry County	0	0	0	0	0	0	0	0	0	0
Philadelphia County	0	0	0	0	0	0	0	0	0	0
Pike County	0	0	0	0	0	0	0	0	0	0
Potter County	0	0	0	0	0	0	0	0	0	0
Schuylkill County	0	0	0	0	0	0	0	0	0	0
Snyder County	0	0	0	0	0	0	0	0	0	0
Somerset County	0	0	0	0	0	0	0	0	0	0
Sullivan County	0	0	0	0	0	0	0	0	0	0
Susquehanna County	0	0	0	0	0	0	0	0	0	0
Tioga County	0	0	0	0	0	0	0	0	0	0
Union County	0	0	0	0	0	0	0	0	0	0
Venango County	0	0	0	0	0	0	0	0	0	0
Warren County	0	0	0	0	0	0	0	0	0	0
Washington County	0	0	0	0	0	0	0	0	0	0
Wayne County	0	0	0	0	0	0	0	0	0	0
Westmoreland County	0	0	0	0	0	0	0	0	0	0
Wyoming County	0	0	0	0	0	0	0	0	0	0
York County	0	0	0	0	0	1	0	1	0	0
Department of Environmental Resources	1	0	0	0	1	14	1	12	1	0
State Capitol Police	5	0	1	2	2	59	4	52	3	0
State Police										
Adams County	46	1	9	9	27	591	171	371	49	5
Allegheny County	30	1	1	2	26	48	12	34	2	0
Armstrong County	53	6	8	8	31	522	157	318	47	11
Beaver County	47	1	3	3	40	243	89	131	23	9
Bedford County	51	1	13	4	33	676	224	404	48	11
Berks County	138	0	5	10	123	729	177	488	64	7
Blair County	43	2	9	5	27	384	128	229	27	1
Bradford County	40	0	17	1	22	440	121	281	38	24
Bucks County	39	1	6	8	24	250	74	148	28	7
Butler County	60	1	10	1	48	846	239	561	46	7
Cambria County	63	1	14	4	44	362	135	196	31	8
Cameron County	8	0	4	0	4	95	41	51	3	0
Carbon County	52	1	0	2	49	223	68	139	16	6
Centre County	79	1	13	2	63	654	162	443	49	14
Chester County	119	1	14	25	79	1 081	366	608	107	30
Clarion County	45	2	20	3	20	506	130	352	24	11
Clearfield County	81	0	27	2	52	734	268	415	51	27
Clinton County	17	2	2	3	10	597	138	431	28	1
Columbia County	18	0	4	1	13	190	91	88	11	0
Crawford County	35	1	12	7	15	676	276	325	75	2
Cumberland County	68	0	19	9	40	627	141	447	39	4
Delaware County	70	1	3	19	47	807	149	603	55	14
Elizabethville County	75	0	20	9	46	763	142	581	40	11
Elk County	10	0	3	1	6	189	69	107	13	13
Erie County	121	1	23	21	76	1 367	339	913	115	12
Fayette County	262	5	31	77	149	2 140	659	1 232	249	97
Franklin County	117	0	21	14	82	1 205	276	850	79	35
Fulton County	24	0	8	5	11	198	73	106	19	2
Greene County	31	1	6	8	16	413	144	228	41	5
Huntingdon County	60	0	10	5	45	475	177	276	22	12
Indiana County	67	0	11	17	39	1 070	253	735	82	33
Jefferson County	28	1	9	2	16	388	148	206	34	8
Juniata County	17	0	5	7	5	185	76	95	14	6
Lackawanna County	28	2	12	0	14	205	83	99	23	38
Lancaster County	67	2	16	12	37	1 042	408	553	81	18
Lawrence County	67	2	17	8	40	741	209	459	73	93
Lebanon County	46	1	2	7	36	328	88	201	39	10
Lehigh County	74	0	6	19	49	928	156	722	50	30
Luzerne County	200	3	20	30	147	1 115	280	758	77	55
Lycoming County	45	0	11	2	32	645	182	426	37	9

[1]The FBI does not publish arson data unless it receives data from either the agency or the state for all 12 months of the calendar year.
. . . = Not available.

Table 11. Offenses Known to Law Enforcement, by State and Other Agencies, 2005—*Continued*

(Number.)

Agency	Violent crime	Murder and non-negligent man-slaughter	Forcible rape	Robbery	Aggravated assault	Property crime	Burglary	Larceny-theft	Motor vehicle theft	Arson[1]
McKean County	11	1	4	0	6	225	81	121	23	4
Mercer County	45	1	4	5	35	499	181	275	43	4
Mifflin County	17	0	5	1	11	159	52	96	11	2
Monroe County	278	3	22	21	232	1 051	331	624	96	22
Montour County	7	0	1	4	2	76	23	51	2	1
Northampton County	23	1	2	3	17	288	63	203	22	4
Northumberland County	73	0	3	2	68	278	79	179	20	2
Perry County	63	1	17	5	40	483	143	306	34	3
Philadelphia County	0	0	0	0	0	1	0	1	0	0
Pike County	78	2	12	6	58	676	292	339	45	23
Potter County	28	0	13	0	15	237	112	106	19	0
Schuylkill County	161	0	14	4	143	740	162	493	85	13
Skippack County	117	0	1	6	110	401	93	292	16	9
Snyder County	13	0	2	1	10	336	88	230	18	0
Somerset County	58	1	21	2	34	630	257	318	55	7
Sullivan County	8	0	4	0	4	122	51	61	10	1
Susquehanna County	35	0	12	5	18	406	98	274	34	17
Tioga County	16	0	3	1	12	290	94	181	15	2
Tionesta County	16	0	4	1	11	169	87	66	16	3
Union County	15	0	5	1	9	184	51	122	11	2
Venango County	42	0	6	6	30	499	172	299	28	5
Warren County	20	2	3	4	11	266	124	126	16	4
Washington County	83	0	6	18	59	720	250	390	80	27
Wayne County	52	0	14	2	36	553	190	319	44	11
Westmoreland County	177	2	22	48	105	2 222	551	1 510	161	39
Wyoming County	25	1	7	2	15	261	82	158	21	5
York County	180	0	17	14	149	642	188	383	71	14
Pennsylvania–Other Agencies										
Allegheny County Port Authority	52	0	1	20	31	181	2	152	27	0
County Detective										
Butler County	0	0	0	0	0	0	0	0	0	0
Dauphin County	9	0	2	0	7	33	1	32	0	1
Lebanon County	19	0	12	0	7	2	0	1	1	0
Lehigh County	0	0	0	0	0	0	0	0	0	0
York County	4	0	1	1	2	20	0	19	1	0
Delaware County District Attorney, Criminal Investigation Division	37	0	7	0	30	6	0	3	3	0
Harrisburg International Airport	0	0	0	0	0	15	0	6	9	0
Rhode Island–State Agencies[4]										
Department of Environmental Management	1	0	0	0	1	38	4	34	0	0
Rhode Island State Police Headquarters	18	2	5	2	9	73	2	28	43	1
State Police										
Chepachet	8	0	2	2	4	23	1	18	4	0
Hope Valley	11	0	2	2	7	130	30	78	22	0
Lincoln	12	0	0	2	10	81	7	47	27	1
Portsmouth	0	0	0	0	0	13	0	12	1	0
Wickford	2	0	1	0	1	26	5	15	6	0
South Carolina–State Agencies										
Bureau of Protective Services	6	0	0	4	2	43	1	35	7	0
Department of Mental Health	13	0	4	0	9	34	3	28	3	0
Department of Natural Resources										
Beaufort County	0	0	0	0	0	0	0	0	0	0
Richland County	0	0	0	0	0	0	0	0	0	0
Highway Patrol										
Abbeville County	0	0	0	0	0	0	0	0	0	0
Aiken County	0	0	0	0	0	0	0	0	0	0
Anderson County	0	0	0	0	0	0	0	0	0	0
Barnwell County	0	0	0	0	0	0	0	0	0	0
Berkeley County	0	0	0	0	0	2	0	1	1	0
Charleston County	0	0	0	0	0	1	0	0	1	0
Cherokee County	3	0	0	0	3	0	0	0	0	0
Clarendon County	0	0	0	0	0	0	0	0	0	0
Colleton County	0	0	0	0	0	0	0	0	0	0
Darlington County	0	0	0	0	0	0	0	0	0	0
Dorchester County	1	0	0	0	1	1	0	0	1	0
Fairfield County	1	0	0	0	1	0	0	0	0	0
Georgetown County	0	0	0	0	0	0	0	0	0	0
Greenville County	0	0	0	0	0	0	0	0	0	0
Greenwood County	0	0	0	0	0	1	0	0	1	0
Horry County	1	0	0	0	1	0	0	0	0	0
Kershaw County	0	0	0	0	0	2	0	0	2	0
Laurens County	0	0	0	0	0	1	0	0	1	0
Lee County	0	0	0	0	0	0	0	0	0	0
Lexington County	0	0	0	0	0	0	0	0	0	0

[1]The FBI does not publish arson data unless it receives data from either the agency or the state for all 12 months of the calendar year.
[4]Because of changes in the state/local agency's reporting practices, figures are not comparable to previous years' data.

Table 11. Offenses Known to Law Enforcement, by State and Other Agencies, 2005—*Continued*

(Number.)

Agency	Violent crime	Murder and non-negligent man-slaughter	Forcible rape	Robbery	Aggravated assault	Property crime	Burglary	Larceny-theft	Motor vehicle theft	Arson[1]
Marlboro County	0	0	0	0	0	0	0	0	0	0
Newberry County	0	0	0	0	0	0	0	0	0	0
Oconee County	0	0	0	0	0	0	0	0	0	0
Orangeburg County	0	0	0	0	0	0	0	0	0	0
Pickens County	0	0	0	0	0	0	0	0	0	0
Richland County	0	0	0	0	0	0	0	0	0	0
Spartanburg County	0	0	0	0	0	0	0	0	0	0
Sumter County	0	0	0	0	0	0	0	0	0	0
Union County	0	0	0	0	0	0	0	0	0	0
York County	0	0	0	0	0	0	0	0	0	0
State Museum	0	0	0	0	0	2	0	2	0	0
United States Department of Energy, Savannah River Plant	0	0	0	0	0	30	0	30	0	0
South Carolina–Other Agencies										
Charleston County Aviation Authority	0	0	0	0	0	84	0	32	52	0
Columbia Metropolitan Airport	0	0	0	0	0	18	0	16	2	0
Greenville-Spartanburg International Airport	1	1	0	0	0	14	0	8	6	0
South Dakota–State Agencies										
Division of Criminal Investigation	19	4	2	1	12	11	1	7	3	0
Tennessee–State Agencies										
Alcoholic Beverage Commission	0	0	0	0	0	0	0	0	0	0
Department of Safety	22	0	0	0	22	33	0	13	20	0
State Fire Marshal	0	0	0	0	0	0	0	0	0	38
State Park Rangers										
Bicentennial Capitol Mall	0	0	0	0	0	1	0	1	0	0
Big Hill Pond	0	0	0	0	0	0	0	0	0	0
Big Ridge	0	0	0	0	0	0	0	0	0	0
Bledsoe Creek	0	0	0	0	0	4	0	4	0	0
Booker T. Washington	0	0	0	0	0	0	0	0	0	0
Burgess Falls Natural Area	0	0	0	0	0	1	0	1	0	0
Cedars of Lebanon	0	0	0	0	0	3	0	3	0	0
Chickasaw	0	0	0	0	0	0	0	0	0	0
Cove Lake	0	0	0	0	0	0	0	0	0	0
Cumberland Mountain	0	0	0	0	0	0	0	0	0	0
Cumberland Trail	0	0	0	0	0	2	0	1	1	0
David Crockett	0	0	0	0	0	0	0	0	0	0
David Crockett Birthplace	0	0	0	0	0	0	0	0	0	0
Dunbar Cave Natural Area	0	0	0	0	0	0	0	0	0	0
Edgar Evins	0	0	0	0	0	0	0	0	0	0
Fall Creek Falls	0	0	0	0	0	0	0	0	0	0
Fort Loudon State Historic Area	0	0	0	0	0	0	0	0	0	0
Fort Pillow State Historic Park	0	0	0	0	0	0	0	0	0	0
Frozen Head Natural Area	0	0	0	0	0	0	0	0	0	0
Harrison Bay	0	0	0	0	0	4	2	2	0	0
Henry Horton	0	0	0	0	0	1	0	1	0	0
Hiwassee/Ocoee Rivers	0	0	0	0	0	1	0	1	0	0
Indian Mountain	0	0	0	0	0	1	0	1	0	0
Johnsonville State Historic Area	0	0	0	0	0	0	0	0	0	0
Long Hunter	0	0	0	0	0	4	0	4	0	0
Meeman-Shelby Forest	0	0	0	0	0	0	0	0	0	1
Montgomery Bell	1	0	0	0	1	0	0	0	0	0
Mousetail Landing	0	0	0	0	0	0	0	0	0	0
Natchez Trace	0	0	0	0	0	0	0	0	0	0
Nathan Bedford Forrest	0	0	0	0	0	0	0	0	0	0
Norris Dam	0	0	0	0	0	0	0	0	0	0
Old Stone Fort State Archaeological Area	0	0	0	0	0	0	0	0	0	0
Panther Creek	0	0	0	0	0	1	0	1	0	0
Paris Landing	0	0	0	0	0	2	0	2	0	0
Pickett	0	0	0	0	0	0	0	0	0	0
Pickwick Landing	0	0	0	0	0	2	0	2	0	0
Pinson Mounds State Archaeological Area	0	0	0	0	0	0	0	0	0	0
Radnor Lake Natural Area	0	0	0	0	0	2	0	2	0	0
Red Clay State Historic Park	0	0	0	0	0	1	1	0	0	0
Reelfoot Lake	0	0	0	0	0	0	0	0	0	0
Roan Mountain	0	0	0	0	0	0	0	0	0	0
Rock Island	0	0	0	0	0	4	0	4	0	0
Sgt. Alvin C. York	0	0	0	0	0	0	0	0	0	0
South Cumberland Recreation Area	0	0	0	0	0	4	0	4	0	0
Standing Stone	0	0	0	0	0	0	0	0	0	0
Sycamore Shoals State Historic Area	0	0	0	0	0	0	0	0	0	0
Tim's Ford	0	0	0	0	0	2	0	2	0	0
T.O. Fuller	0	0	0	0	0	0	0	0	0	0
Warrior's Path	0	0	0	0	0	3	0	3	0	0
Tennessee Bureau of Investigation	1	0	1	0	0	2	1	1	0	0
Tennessee Department of Revenue, Special Investigations Unit	0	0	0	0	0	0	0	0	0	0
Wildlife Resources Agency										
Region 1	0	0	0	0	0	1	0	1	0	0
Region 2	0	0	0	0	0	0	0	0	0	0
Region 3	0	0	0	0	0	1	0	1	0	0
Region 4	0	0	0	0	0	1	0	1	0	0

[1]The FBI does not publish arson data unless it receives data from either the agency or the state for all 12 months of the calendar year.

Table 11. Offenses Known to Law Enforcement, by State and Other Agencies, 2005—*Continued*

(Number.)

Agency	Violent crime	Murder and non-negligent man-slaughter	Forcible rape	Robbery	Aggravated assault	Property crime	Burglary	Larceny-theft	Motor vehicle theft	Arson[1]
Tennessee–Other Agencies										
Chattanooga Metropolitan Airport	0	0	0	0	0	2	1	0	1	0
Drug Task Force										
1st Judicial District	0	0	0	0	0	0	0	0	0	0
2nd Judicial District	0	0	0	0	0	0	0	0	0	0
3rd Judicial District	1	1	0	0	0	0	0	0	0	0
4th Judicial District	0	0	0	0	0	1	0	1	0	0
5th Judicial District	0	0	0	0	0	1	0	1	0	0
8th Judicial District	0	0	0	0	0	0	0	0	0	0
9th Judicial District	0	0	0	0	0	0	0	0	0	0
10th Judicial District	3	0	0	0	3	1	0	0	1	0
12th Judicial District	0	0	0	0	0	1	0	1	0	0
13th Judicial District	0	0	0	0	0	0	0	0	0	0
14th Judicial District	0	0	0	0	0	0	0	0	0	0
15th Judicial District	0	0	0	0	0	0	0	0	0	0
17th Judicial District	0	0	0	0	0	0	0	0	0	0
18th Judicial District	0	0	0	0	0	0	0	0	0	0
19th Judicial District	0	0	0	0	0	2	0	2	0	0
21st Judicial District	1	0	0	0	1	0	0	0	0	0
22nd Judicial District	0	0	0	0	0	1	0	0	1	0
24th Judicial District	0	0	0	0	0	1	0	1	0	0
27th Judicial District	0	0	0	0	0	0	0	0	0	0
31st Judicial District	3	1	1	0	1	1	0	1	0	0
Knoxville Metropolitan Airport	0	0	0	0	0	20	0	19	1	0
Memphis International Airport	2	0	0	0	2	185	4	174	7	0
Metropolitan Board of Parks and Recreation, Nashville-Davidson	8	1	0	3	4	120	11	105	4	3
Nashville International Airport	2	0	0	0	2	86	1	78	7	0
Tri-Cities Regional Airport	0	0	0	0	0	4	0	4	0	0
West Tennessee Violent Crime Task Force	0	0	0	0	0	3	0	2	1	0
Texas–Other Agencies										
Amarillo International Airport	0	0	0	0	0	4	1	3	0	0
Cameron County Park Rangers	7	0	2	0	5	57	6	47	4	2
Dallas-Fort Worth International Airport	5	0	0	0	5	404	19	359	26	0
Hospital District										
Dallas County	2	0	0	1	1	524	8	511	5	0
Tarrant County	7	0	0	2	5	98	2	95	1	0
Houston Metropolitan Transit Authority	1	0	0	1	0	45	0	35	10	0
Independent School District										
Aldine	4	0	0	3	1	171	18	138	15	2
Alvin	2	0	0	0	2	84	4	80	0	1
Angleton	0	0	0	0	0	7	0	7	0	0
Austin	42	0	2	8	32	680	50	621	9	21
Bay City	2	0	0	0	2	64	9	55	0	1
Brownsville	45	0	0	4	41	428	83	332	13	11
Cedar Hill	3	0	0	0	3	67	7	60	0	0
Conroe	11	0	0	0	11	227	12	213	2	7
Corpus Christi	43	0	0	3	40	305	22	281	2	7
Ector County	0	0	0	0	0	251	0	251	0	0
El Paso	29	0	0	1	28	488	26	461	1	1
Fort Bend	17	0	1	3	13	342	28	306	8	10
Hempstead	1	0	0	0	1	13	2	11	0	0
Humble	3	0	0	1	2	55	11	43	1	2
Judson	32	0	0	1	31	16	0	16	0	3
Katy	18	0	3	2	13	370	14	352	4	1
Killeen	5	0	0	0	5	110	2	108	0	4
Klein	5	0	0	1	4	174	8	166	0	3
Mexia	1	0	0	0	1	10	3	7	0	1
Midland	0	0	0	0	0	50	11	39	0	0
North East	11	0	0	0	11	374	14	360	0	0
Pasadena	10	0	5	0	5	174	27	138	9	0
Raymondville	0	0	0	0	0	11	5	6	0	1
Socorro	8	0	0	0	8	118	2	116	0	1
Spring	28	0	0	1	27	165	3	157	5	3
Spring Branch	4	0	0	1	3	219	15	197	7	0
Taft	1	0	0	0	1	13	1	12	0	1
Tyler	3	0	0	2	1	221	24	196	1	0
United	4	0	0	0	4	132	9	120	3	0
Utah–State Agencies										
Parks and Recreation	1	0	0	0	1	74	0	71	3	0
Utah–Other Agencies										
Cache-Rich Drug Task Force	0	0	0	0	0	2	1	1	0	0
Granite School District	27	0	0	1	26	95	20	74	1	8
Utah County Major Crime Task Force	0	0	0	0	0	3	0	3	0	0

[1] The FBI does not publish arson data unless it receives data from either the agency or the state for all 12 months of the calendar year.

Table 11. Offenses Known to Law Enforcement, by State and Other Agencies, 2005—*Continued*

(Number.)

Agency	Violent crime	Murder and non-negligent man-slaughter	Forcible rape	Robbery	Aggravated assault	Property crime	Burglary	Larceny-theft	Motor vehicle theft	Arson[1]
Vermont–State Agencies										
Attorney General	0	0	0	0	0	11	0	11	0	0
Fish and Wildlife Department, Law Enforcement Division	1	0	0	0	1	2	0	2	0	0
State Police										
Bethel	18	0	6	0	12	251	112	118	21	4
Bradford	16	0	7	1	8	198	83	103	12	2
Brattleboro	8	1	1	0	6	68	34	23	11	2
Derby	11	0	3	0	8	232	87	131	14	5
Middlebury	8	0	5	0	3	227	74	133	20	1
Middlesex	4	0	0	0	4	335	133	202	0	0
Rockingham	16	1	3	0	12	188	67	95	26	0
Rutland	13	0	3	2	8	460	149	283	28	4
Shaftsbury	5	0	1	0	4	113	46	56	11	2
St. Albans	54	1	20	1	32	682	219	397	66	15
St. Johnsbury	23	0	3	2	18	318	95	184	39	2
Williston	18	2	4	0	12	281	98	162	21	9
Vermont State Police	0	0	0	0	0	0	0	0	0	0
Virginia–State Agencies										
Alcoholic Beverage Control Commission	2	0	0	1	1	38	2	36	0	0
Department of Conservation and Recreation	0	0	0	0	0	14	0	14	0	0
Southside Virginia Training Center	4	0	3	0	1	27	0	26	1	0
State Police										
Accomack County	1	0	0	1	0	11	2	8	1	1
Albemarle County	4	0	1	0	3	2	0	2	0	0
Alexandria	0	0	0	0	0	4	0	1	3	0
Alleghany County	0	0	0	0	0	4	0	3	1	0
Amelia County	0	0	0	0	0	1	0	1	0	0
Amherst County	0	0	0	0	0	2	0	1	1	0
Appomattox County	1	0	0	0	1	1	0	1	0	0
Augusta County	3	0	3	0	0	4	1	2	1	2
Bath County	0	0	0	0	0	4	0	4	0	0
Bedford	0	0	0	0	0	0	0	0	0	0
Bedford County	5	0	0	0	5	5	0	1	4	0
Bland County	3	0	1	0	2	19	2	17	0	0
Botetourt County	7	0	0	1	6	13	0	12	1	0
Bristol	0	0	0	0	0	3	0	2	1	0
Brunswick County	0	0	0	0	0	2	0	2	0	0
Buchanan County	3	0	2	1	0	3	0	3	0	1
Buckingham County	0	0	0	0	0	8	0	3	5	2
Buena Vista	0	0	0	0	0	0	0	0	0	0
Campbell County	1	0	0	0	1	11	1	8	2	0
Caroline County	1	0	1	0	0	6	0	4	2	0
Carroll County	0	0	0	0	0	29	0	19	10	0
Charlotte County	0	0	0	0	0	2	0	0	2	0
Charlottesville	0	0	0	0	0	0	0	0	0	0
Chesapeake	1	0	0	0	1	0	0	0	0	0
Chesterfield County	2	0	0	0	2	5	0	2	3	0
Clarke County	0	0	0	0	0	0	0	0	0	0
Clifton Forge	0	0	0	0	0	0	0	0	0	0
Colonial Heights	0	0	0	0	0	0	0	0	0	0
Covington	0	0	0	0	0	0	0	0	0	0
Craig County	0	0	0	0	0	0	0	0	0	0
Culpeper County	2	0	0	0	2	7	1	5	1	0
Cumberland County	0	0	0	0	0	2	0	1	1	1
Dickenson County	0	0	0	0	0	0	0	0	0	0
Dinwiddie County	2	0	0	1	1	0	0	0	0	0
Emporia	1	0	0	0	1	0	0	0	0	1
Essex County	0	0	0	0	0	0	0	0	0	0
Fairfax County	12	0	3	1	8	12	0	6	6	0
Falls Church	0	0	0	0	0	0	0	0	0	0
Fauquier County	2	0	0	0	2	13	0	13	0	0
Floyd County	0	0	0	0	0	0	0	0	0	0
Fluvanna County	0	0	0	0	0	1	0	1	0	0
Franklin County	2	0	0	0	2	5	0	3	2	0
Frederick County	1	0	0	0	1	16	0	12	4	0
Fredericksburg	0	0	0	0	0	2	0	1	1	0
Galax	0	0	0	0	0	0	0	0	0	0
Giles County	0	0	0	0	0	2	0	1	1	1
Gloucester County	0	0	0	0	0	0	0	0	0	0
Goochland County	0	0	0	0	0	0	0	0	0	0
Grayson County	2	1	0	0	1	9	0	2	7	0
Greene County	0	0	0	0	0	2	0	2	0	0
Greensville County	2	0	0	0	2	1	0	0	1	0
Halifax County	0	0	0	0	0	8	0	5	3	0
Hampton	4	0	0	0	4	8	0	4	4	0
Hanover County	0	0	0	0	0	2	0	1	1	0
Henrico County	0	0	0	0	0	1	0	0	1	0
Henry County	1	0	0	0	1	14	0	8	6	0
Highland County	0	0	0	0	0	1	0	1	0	0
Hopewell	0	0	0	0	0	1	0	1	0	0
Isle of Wight County	0	0	0	0	0	2	0	1	1	0
James City County	0	0	0	0	0	0	0	0	0	0

[1]The FBI does not publish arson data unless it receives data from either the agency or the state for all 12 months of the calendar year.

Table 11. Offenses Known to Law Enforcement, by State and Other Agencies, 2005—*Continued*

(Number.)

Agency	Violent crime	Murder and non-negligent man-slaughter	Forcible rape	Robbery	Aggravated assault	Property crime	Burglary	Larceny-theft	Motor vehicle theft	Arson[1]
King and Queen County	0	0	0	0	0	1	0	1	0	0
King George County	0	0	0	0	0	1	0	1	0	0
Lancaster County	0	0	0	0	0	0	0	0	0	0
Lee County	0	0	0	0	0	14	0	6	8	5
Loudoun County	0	0	0	0	0	15	2	8	5	0
Louisa County	0	0	0	0	0	3	0	3	0	0
Lunenburg County	0	0	0	0	0	0	0	0	0	0
Lynchburg	0	0	0	0	0	1	0	1	0	0
Madison County	0	0	0	0	0	0	0	0	0	0
Manassas County	0	0	0	0	0	0	0	0	0	0
Martinsville	0	0	0	0	0	1	0	1	0	0
Mathews County	0	0	0	0	0	1	0	1	0	0
Mecklenburg County	1	0	0	0	1	5	1	1	3	0
Middlesex County	0	0	0	0	0	0	0	0	0	0
Montgomery County	2	0	0	0	2	8	1	5	2	0
Nelson County	1	0	0	0	1	4	0	4	0	0
New Kent County	0	0	0	0	0	2	0	1	1	0
Newport News	4	0	0	0	4	2	0	1	1	0
Norfolk	5	0	0	0	5	5	0	4	1	1
Northampton County	1	0	1	0	0	4	0	4	0	0
Northumberland County	0	0	0	0	0	0	0	0	0	0
Norton	0	0	0	0	0	0	0	0	0	0
Nottoway County	0	0	0	0	0	6	0	6	0	1
Orange County	0	0	0	0	0	1	0	1	0	0
Page County	0	0	0	0	0	3	0	2	1	0
Patrick County	0	0	0	0	0	2	1	0	1	0
Petersburg	0	0	0	0	0	1	0	1	0	0
Pittsylvania County	1	0	0	0	1	37	2	11	24	0
Portsmouth	0	0	0	0	0	0	0	0	0	0
Powhatan County	5	0	0	0	5	1	0	1	0	0
Prince Edward County	0	0	0	0	0	0	0	0	0	0
Prince George County	0	0	0	0	0	1	0	0	1	0
Prince William County	8	0	0	0	8	19	0	11	8	0
Pulaski County	2	0	0	0	2	11	2	9	0	0
Rappahannock County	0	0	0	0	0	0	0	0	0	0
Richmond County	0	0	0	0	0	1	0	1	0	0
Roanoke	0	0	0	0	0	2	0	1	1	1
Roanoke County	0	0	0	0	0	3	0	1	2	0
Rockbridge County	5	0	0	0	5	36	0	34	2	1
Rockingham County	0	0	0	0	0	2	0	2	0	0
Russell County	1	0	0	0	1	10	0	6	4	1
Salem	0	0	0	0	0	1	0	1	0	0
Scott County	1	0	0	0	1	15	2	3	10	5
Shenandoah County	1	0	0	0	1	28	0	27	1	0
Smyth County	0	0	0	0	0	23	2	21	0	1
Southampton County	0	0	0	0	0	1	0	1	0	0
Spotsylvania County	2	0	1	0	1	10	1	7	2	0
Stafford County	0	0	0	0	0	10	0	6	4	0
Staunton	0	0	0	0	0	0	0	0	0	0
Suffolk	0	0	0	0	0	2	0	2	0	0
Surry County	1	0	0	0	1	1	1	0	0	0
Sussex County	1	0	0	0	1	2	1	1	0	0
Tazewell County	0	0	0	0	0	27	8	15	4	3
Virginia Beach	4	0	0	0	4	9	0	5	4	0
Warren County	1	0	0	0	1	0	0	0	0	0
Washington County	1	0	0	0	1	14	0	10	4	1
Waynesboro	1	0	0	0	1	0	0	0	0	0
Westmoreland County	2	0	2	0	0	0	0	0	0	0
Winchester	0	0	0	0	0	1	0	1	0	0
Wise County	0	0	0	0	0	14	2	10	2	2
Wythe County	3	1	0	0	2	75	1	72	2	0
York County	0	0	0	0	0	1	1	0	0	0
Virginia State Capitol	0	0	0	0	0	66	1	65	0	0
Virginia–Other Agencies										
Norfolk Airport Authority	0	0	0	0	0	50	0	50	0	0
Port Authority, Norfolk	0	0	0	0	0	1	0	1	0	0
Reagan National Airport	5	0	0	0	5	422	3	306	113	1
Richmond International Airport	0	0	0	0	0	27	0	14	13	0
Washington–Other Agencies										
Lummi Tribal	58	0	2	5	51	397	114	259	24	2
Nisqually Tribal	2	0	0	0	2	24	3	19	2	1
Nooksack Tribal	7	0	0	0	7	58	16	42	0	0
Port of Seattle	7	0	1	0	6	912	31	791	90	0
Swinomish Tribal	4	0	1	1	2	129	25	95	9	0
West Virginia–State Agencies										
Department of Natural Resources										
Berkeley County	0	0	0	0	0	0	0	0	0	0
Boone County	0	0	0	0	0	0	0	0	0	0
Braxton County	0	0	0	0	0	0	0	0	0	0
Brooke County	0	0	0	0	0	0	0	0	0	0
Cabell County	0	0	0	0	0	0	0	0	0	0
Calhoun County	0	0	0	0	0	0	0	0	0	0
Clay County	0	0	0	0	0	0	0	0	0	0
Doddridge County	0	0	0	0	0	0	0	0	0	0
Fayette County	0	0	0	0	0	0	0	0	0	0
Gilmer County	0	0	0	0	0	0	0	0	0	0

[1]The FBI does not publish arson data unless it receives data from either the agency or the state for all 12 months of the calendar year.

Table 11. Offenses Known to Law Enforcement, by State and Other Agencies, 2005—*Continued*

(Number.)

Agency	Violent crime	Murder and non-negligent man-slaughter	Forcible rape	Robbery	Aggravated assault	Property crime	Burglary	Larceny-theft	Motor vehicle theft	Arson[1]
Grant County	0	0	0	0	0	0	0	0	0	0
Greenbrier County	0	0	0	0	0	0	0	0	0	1
Hampshire County	0	0	0	0	0	0	0	0	0	0
Hancock County	0	0	0	0	0	0	0	0	0	0
Hardy County	0	0	0	0	0	0	0	0	0	0
Harrison County	0	0	0	0	0	0	0	0	0	0
Jackson County	0	0	0	0	0	0	0	0	0	0
Jefferson County	0	0	0	0	0	0	0	0	0	0
Kanawha County	0	0	0	0	0	0	0	0	0	0
Lewis County	0	0	0	0	0	0	0	0	0	0
Lincoln County	0	0	0	0	0	0	0	0	0	0
Logan County	0	0	0	0	0	0	0	0	0	0
Marion County	0	0	0	0	0	0	0	0	0	0
Marshall County	0	0	0	0	0	0	0	0	0	0
Mason County	0	0	0	0	0	0	0	0	0	0
McDowell County	0	0	0	0	0	0	0	0	0	0
Mercer County	0	0	0	0	0	0	0	0	0	0
Mineral County	0	0	0	0	0	0	0	0	0	0
Mingo County	0	0	0	0	0	0	0	0	0	0
Monongalia County	0	0	0	0	0	0	0	0	0	0
Morgan County	0	0	0	0	0	0	0	0	0	0
Nicholas County	0	0	0	0	0	0	0	0	0	0
Ohio County	0	0	0	0	0	0	0	0	0	0
Pendleton County	0	0	0	0	0	0	0	0	0	0
Pleasants County	0	0	0	0	0	0	0	0	0	0
Pocahontas County	0	0	0	0	0	0	0	0	0	0
Preston County	0	0	0	0	0	0	0	0	0	0
Putnam County	0	0	0	0	0	0	0	0	0	0
Raleigh County	0	0	0	0	0	0	0	0	0	0
Randolph County	0	0	0	0	0	0	0	0	0	0
Ritchie County	0	0	0	0	0	0	0	0	0	0
Roane County	0	0	0	0	0	0	0	0	0	0
Summers County	0	0	0	0	0	0	0	0	0	0
Taylor County	0	0	0	0	0	0	0	0	0	0
Tucker County	0	0	0	0	0	0	0	0	0	0
Tyler County	0	0	0	0	0	0	0	0	0	0
Upshur County	0	0	0	0	0	0	0	0	0	0
Wayne County	0	0	0	0	0	0	0	0	0	0
Webster County	0	0	0	0	0	0	0	0	0	0
Wetzel County	0	0	0	0	0	0	0	0	0	0
Wirt County	0	0	0	0	0	0	0	0	0	0
Wood County	0	0	0	0	0	0	0	0	0	0
Wyoming County	0	0	0	0	0	0	0	0	0	0
State Fire Marshal										
Barbour County	0	0	0	0	0	0	0	0	0	0
Berkeley County	0	0	0	0	0	0	0	0	0	0
Boone County	0	0	0	0	0	0	0	0	0	0
Braxton County	0	0	0	0	0	0	0	0	0	0
Brooke County	0	0	0	0	0	0	0	0	0	1
Cabell County	0	0	0	0	0	0	0	0	0	6
Calhoun County	0	0	0	0	0	0	0	0	0	0
Clay County	0	0	0	0	0	0	0	0	0	0
Doddridge County	0	0	0	0	0	0	0	0	0	0
Fayette County	0	0	0	0	0	0	0	0	0	1
Gilmer County	0	0	0	0	0	0	0	0	0	0
Grant County	0	0	0	0	0	0	0	0	0	0
Greenbrier County	0	0	0	0	0	0	0	0	0	0
Hampshire County	0	0	0	0	0	0	0	0	0	3
Hancock County	0	0	0	0	0	0	0	0	0	4
Hardy County	0	0	0	0	0	0	0	0	0	0
Harrison County	0	0	0	0	0	0	0	0	0	2
Jackson County	0	0	0	0	0	0	0	0	0	3
Jefferson County	0	0	0	0	0	0	0	0	0	1
Kanawha County	0	0	0	0	0	0	0	0	0	11
Lewis County	0	0	0	0	0	0	0	0	0	1
Lincoln County	0	0	0	0	0	0	0	0	0	3
Logan County	0	0	0	0	0	0	0	0	0	3
Marion County	0	0	0	0	0	0	0	0	0	0
Mason County	0	0	0	0	0	0	0	0	0	3
McDowell County	0	0	0	0	0	0	0	0	0	10
Mercer County	0	0	0	0	0	0	0	0	0	5
Mineral County	0	0	0	0	0	0	0	0	0	8
Mingo County	0	0	0	0	0	0	0	0	0	3
Monongalia County	0	0	0	0	0	0	0	0	0	2
Monroe County	0	0	0	0	0	0	0	0	0	0
Nicholas County	0	0	0	0	0	0	0	0	0	1
Ohio County	0	0	0	0	0	0	0	0	0	0
Pendleton County	0	0	0	0	0	0	0	0	0	0
Pleasants County	0	0	0	0	0	0	0	0	0	0
Pocahontas County	0	0	0	0	0	0	0	0	0	0
Preston County	0	0	0	0	0	0	0	0	0	0
Putnam County	0	0	0	0	0	0	0	0	0	1
Raleigh County	0	0	0	0	0	0	0	0	0	2
Randolph County	0	0	0	0	0	0	0	0	0	0

[1]The FBI does not publish arson data unless it receives data from either the agency or the state for all 12 months of the calendar year.

Table 11. Offenses Known to Law Enforcement, by State and Other Agencies, 2005—*Continued*

(Number.)

Agency	Violent crime	Murder and non-negligent man-slaughter	Forcible rape	Robbery	Aggravated assault	Property crime	Burglary	Larceny-theft	Motor vehicle theft	Arson[1]
Ritchie County	0	0	0	0	0	0	0	0	0	0
Roane County	0	0	0	0	0	0	0	0	0	0
Summers County	0	0	0	0	0	0	0	0	0	0
Taylor County	0	0	0	0	0	0	0	0	0	0
Tucker County	0	0	0	0	0	0	0	0	0	0
Tyler County	0	0	0	0	0	0	0	0	0	0
Upshur County	0	0	0	0	0	0	0	0	0	0
Wayne County	0	0	0	0	0	0	0	0	0	4
Webster County	0	0	0	0	0	0	0	0	0	0
Wetzel County	0	0	0	0	0	0	0	0	0	0
Wirt County	0	0	0	0	0	0	0	0	0	0
Wood County	0	0	0	0	0	0	0	0	0	0
Wyoming County	0	0	0	0	0	0	0	0	0	0
State Police										
Beckley	44	3	1	4	36	418	88	267	63	3
Berkeley Springs	5	0	0	2	3	126	52	58	16	0
Bridgeport	15	0	1	0	14	220	43	152	25	1
Buckeye	15	1	0	1	13	77	31	44	2	0
Buckhannon	13	1	4	0	8	128	25	96	7	3
Clay	11	2	1	1	7	83	34	42	7	3
Danville	15	0	1	1	13	299	57	222	20	2
Elizabeth	9	2	0	0	7	66	25	34	7	2
Elkins	34	1	0	1	32	234	51	171	12	1
Fairmont	18	0	4	0	14	140	23	103	14	0
Franklin	6	0	1	2	3	44	17	26	1	1
Gauley Bridge	2	0	0	0	2	61	16	38	7	0
Gilbert	13	0	0	2	11	97	26	63	8	0
Glenville	3	0	1	0	2	32	3	26	3	0
Grafton	3	0	0	0	3	21	3	17	1	0
Grantsville	3	0	1	0	2	47	29	13	5	0
Hamlin	46	0	4	4	38	490	126	294	70	5
Harrisville	19	0	2	0	17	65	16	43	6	1
Hinton	11	0	0	2	9	63	20	38	5	1
Hundred	10	0	1	0	9	35	11	20	4	1
Huntington	18	0	1	4	13	771	97	624	50	2
Jesse	2	0	0	0	2	69	21	43	5	0
Kearneysville	22	0	4	1	17	356	97	219	40	2
Keyser	35	0	2	5	28	196	71	105	20	3
Kingwood	16	0	3	1	12	159	82	61	16	1
Lewisburg	7	0	1	0	6	97	17	73	7	0
Logan	84	1	5	12	66	959	246	596	117	5
Martinsburg	85	1	3	13	68	897	193	626	78	3
Moorefield	17	0	4	0	13	69	23	37	9	1
Morgantown	28	2	0	7	19	573	138	398	37	0
Moundsville	5	0	0	0	5	31	11	19	1	0
New Cumberland	2	0	0	0	2	23	4	18	1	0
Oak Hill	12	1	0	1	10	144	31	97	16	2
Paden City	8	1	0	0	7	43	11	26	6	1
Parkersburg	10	0	2	0	8	254	52	181	21	3
Parsons	3	0	0	0	3	55	20	31	4	0
Philippi	12	0	2	1	9	77	19	52	6	0
Point Pleasant	11	0	0	0	11	92	33	52	7	3
Princeton	57	0	0	2	55	423	113	272	38	1
Quincy	15	0	1	3	11	383	101	232	50	10
Rainelle	6	0	0	1	5	58	16	39	3	0
Richwood	6	0	0	0	6	39	11	26	2	1
Ripley	6	0	1	0	5	65	12	40	13	1
Romney	26	1	3	0	22	186	58	102	26	1
South Charleston	37	1	1	3	32	1 008	107	833	68	2
Spencer	8	1	0	0	7	51	16	25	10	2
St. Marys	2	0	0	0	2	13	3	9	1	0
Summersville	2	0	0	0	2	97	21	70	6	0
Sutton	9	1	1	1	6	145	18	113	14	1
Union	14	0	1	0	13	61	21	32	8	0
Upperglade	11	0	0	0	11	84	31	44	9	1
Wayne	26	2	0	2	22	375	98	228	49	1
Welch	18	0	0	2	16	52	21	24	7	1
Wellsburg	2	0	0	0	2	9	2	6	1	0
Weston	6	0	1	1	4	102	7	88	7	1
West Union	4	0	0	0	4	25	7	15	3	0
Wheeling	9	0	1	0	8	57	6	45	6	0
Whitesville	8	0	0	0	8	102	20	73	9	2
Williamson	26	0	3	1	22	187	52	109	26	2
Winfield	19	0	5	1	13	166	24	128	14	2
State Police, Bureau of Criminal Investigation										
Beckley	0	0	0	0	0	0	0	0	0	0
Buckhannon	0	0	0	0	0	0	0	0	0	0
Charleston	0	0	0	0	0	0	0	0	0	0
Fairmont	0	0	0	0	0	0	0	0	0	0
State Police, Parkway Authority										
Fayette County	0	0	0	0	0	1	0	1	0	0
Kanawha County	0	0	0	0	0	3	1	2	0	0
Mercer County	0	0	0	0	0	1	0	1	0	0
Raleigh County	1	0	0	1	0	7	0	7	0	0

[1]The FBI does not publish arson data unless it receives data from either the agency or the state for all 12 months of the calendar year.

Table 11. Offenses Known to Law Enforcement, by State and Other Agencies, 2005—*Continued*

(Number.)

Agency	Violent crime	Murder and non-negligent man-slaughter	Forcible rape	Robbery	Aggravated assault	Property crime	Burglary	Larceny-theft	Motor vehicle theft	Arson[1]
West Virginia–Other Agencies										
Central West Virginia Drug Task Force	2	0	2	0	0	1	0	1	0	0
Greenbrier County Drug and Violent Crime Task Force	0	0	0	0	0	0	0	0	0	0
Harrison County Drug and Violent Crime Task Force	0	0	0	0	0	0	0	0	0	0
Huntington Drug and Violent Crime Task Force	0	0	0	0	0	0	0	0	0	0
Kanawha County Parks and Recreation	0	0	0	0	0	2	1	1	0	0
Logan County Drug and Violent Crime Task Force	0	0	0	0	0	0	0	0	0	0
Metropolitan Drug Enforcement Network Team	0	0	0	0	0	0	0	0	0	0
Mon Valley Drug Task Force	0	0	0	0	0	0	0	0	0	0
Ohio Valley Drug and Violent Crime Task Force	0	0	0	0	0	0	0	0	0	0
Southern Regional Drug and Violent Crime Task Force	0	0	0	0	0	0	0	0	0	0
Three Rivers Drug and Violent Crime Task Force	0	0	0	0	0	0	0	0	0	0
Tri-Lateral Drug Enforcement Network Team	0	0	0	0	0	0	0	0	0	0
Wisconsin–State Agencies										
Capitol Police	3	0	0	3	0	156	4	152	0	0
Department of Natural Resources	0	0	0	0	0	0	0	0	0	0
Wisconsin State Patrol	0	0	0	0	0	0	0	0	0	0
Wisconsin–Other Agencies										
Lac du Flambeau Tribal	8	0	3	0	5	264	34	209	21	1
Menominee Tribal	31	1	4	3	23	91	11	48	32	3
Oneida Tribal	7	0	5	0	2	122	8	103	11	0
Outlying Areas										
American Samoa	123	5	16	2	100	228	159	65	4	2
Federal Agencies										
National Institutes of Health	4	0	0	0	4	192	2	189	1	0
Department of the Interior										
Bureau of Indian Affairs	3 568	61	219	147	3 141	8 208	2 013	4 826	1 369	551
Bureau of Land Management	12	3	0	0	9	559	22	483	54	71
Bureau of Reclamation	8	0	0	0	8	15	3	3	9	0
Fish and Wildlife Service	58	6	2	41	9	268	62	130	76	121
National Park Service	355	13	49	68	225	4 306	436	3 696	174	83

[1]The FBI does not publish arson data unless it receives data from either the agency or the state for all 12 months of the calendar year.

Table 12. Crime Trends, by Population Group, 2004–2005

(Number, percent change.)

Population group and year	Estimated population, 2005	Number of agencies	Violent crime	Murder and non-negligent man-slaughter	Forcible rape	Robbery	Aggravated assault	Property crime	Burglary	Larceny-theft	Motor vehicle theft	Arson
ALL AGENCIES												
2004			1 242 275	15 023	84 608	380 740	761 904	9 420 361	1 954 079	6 300 090	1 166 192	65 868
2005	266 142 177	13 052	1 273 754	15 625	83 312	397 356	777 461	9 277 285	1 966 159	6 143 800	1 167 326	64 062
Percent change			2.5	4.0	-1.5	4.4	2.0	-1.5	0.6	-2.5	0.1	-3.0
All Cities												
2004			989 444	11 694	62 616	335 637	579 497	7 448 682	1 443 472	5 062 434	942 776	48 188
2005	178 931 386	9 283	1 015 579	12 362	61 666	349 047	592 504	7 321 880	1 457 027	4 924 744	940 109	47 168
Percent change			2.6	5.7	-1.5	4.0	2.2	-1.7	0.9	-2.7	-0.3	-2.1
Group I (all cities 250,000 and over)												
2004			467 868	6 547	21 328	190 117	249 876	2 594 174	514 028	1 616 790	463 356	20 279
2005	53 583 154	70	482 899	6 779	20 950	197 991	257 179	2 537 521	518 045	1 557 575	461 901	19 437
Percent change			3.2	3.5	-1.8	4.1	2.9	-2.2	0.8	-3.7	-0.3	-4.2
1,000,000 and over												
2004			200 986	2 875	7 201	93 100	97 810	996 170	187 227	625 397	183 546	6 499
2005	24 885 884	10	200 225	2 891	7 093	94 309	95 932	963 317	184 430	598 587	180 300	6 727
Percent change			-0.4	0.6	-1.5	1.3	-1.9	-3.3	-1.5	-4.3	-1.8	3.5
500,000 to 999,999												
2004			139 055	2 060	7 105	51 118	78 772	866 158	179 717	532 598	153 843	7 140
2005	15 331 041	23	151 803	2 135	6 958	56 353	86 357	851 735	181 568	516 344	153 823	6 388
Percent change			9.2	3.6	-2.1	10.2	9.6	-1.7	1.0	-3.1	0.0	-10.5
250,000 to 499,999												
2004			127 827	1 612	7 022	45 899	73 294	731 846	147 084	458 795	125 967	6 640
2005	13 366 229	37	130 871	1 753	6 899	47 329	74 890	722 469	152 047	442 644	127 778	6 322
Percent change			2.4	8.7	-1.8	3.1	2.2	-1.3	3.4	-3.5	1.4	-4.8
Group II (100,000 to 249,999)												
2004			163 542	2 002	10 641	55 101	95 798	1 312 244	258 761	878 205	175 278	7 799
2005	27 597 669	184	169 574	2 250	10 295	57 168	99 861	1 277 844	260 122	845 581	172 141	7 974
Percent change			3.7	12.4	-3.3	3.8	4.2	-2.6	0.5	-3.7	-1.8	2.2
Group III (50,000 to 99,999)												
2004			130 907	1 191	9 785	38 908	81 023	1 111 214	220 603	767 847	122 764	6 516
2005	28 195 726	413	132 761	1 322	9 585	40 614	81 240	1 092 987	223 622	747 316	122 049	6 319
Percent change			1.4	11.0	-2.0	4.4	0.3	-1.6	1.4	-2.7	-0.6	-3.0
Group IV (25,000 to 49,999)												
2004			88 179	822	7 999	23 994	55 364	872 496	164 414	629 745	78 337	5 250
2005	24 124 825	696	90 392	855	7 871	25 160	56 506	868 768	167 103	621 934	79 731	5 185
Percent change			2.5	4.0	-1.6	4.9	2.1	-0.4	1.6	-1.2	1.8	-1.2
Group V (10,000 to 24,999)												
2004			75 270	666	7 159	17 372	50 073	837 342	155 825	621 022	60 495	4 401
2005	25 225 550	1 592	75 533	660	7 190	17 790	49 893	829 194	157 096	610 489	61 609	4 358
Percent change			0.3	-0.9	0.4	2.4	-0.4	-1.0	0.8	-1.7	1.8	-1.0
Group VI (under 10,000)												
2004			63 678	466	5 704	10 145	47 363	721 212	129 841	548 825	42 546	3 943
2005	20 204 462	6 328	64 420	496	5 775	10 324	47 825	715 566	131 039	541 849	42 678	3 895
Percent change			1.2	6.4	1.2	1.8	1.0	-0.8	0.9	-1.3	0.3	-1.2
Metropolitan Counties												
2004			200 368	2 397	15 900	41 237	140 834	1 544 274	371 003	984 308	188 963	13 692
2005	62 213 302	1 542	204 903	2 386	15 316	44 414	142 787	1 531 141	372 925	966 736	191 480	13 120
Percent change			2.3	-0.5	-3.7	7.7	1.4	-0.9	0.5	-1.8	1.3	-4.2
Nonmetropolitan Counties[1]												
2004			52 463	932	6 092	3 866	41 573	427 405	139 604	253 348	34 453	3 988
2005	24 997 489	2 227	53 272	877	6 330	3 895	42 170	424 264	136 207	252 320	35 737	3 774
Percent change			1.5	-5.9	3.9	0.8	1.4	-0.7	-2.4	-0.4	3.7	-5.4
Suburban Areas[2]												
2004			338 151	3 514	27 839	76 236	230 562	3 076 368	643 725	2 110 522	322 121	22 306
2005	111 066 865	6 873	344 503	3 538	27 182	80 280	233 503	3 056 118	651 416	2 078 266	326 436	21 631
Percent change			1.9	0.7	-2.4	5.3	1.3	-0.7	1.2	-1.5	1.3	-3.0

[1] Includes state police agencies that report aggregately for the entire state.
[2] Suburban areas include law enforcement agencies in cities with fewer than 50,000 inhabitants and county law enforcement agencies within metropolitan statistical areas. They exclude all metropolitan agencies associated with a principal city. The agencies associated with suburban areas also appear in other groups within this table.

Table 13. Crime Trends, by Suburban and Nonsuburban Cities and Population Group, 2004–2005

(Number, percent change.)

Population group and year	Estimated population, 2005	Number of agencies	Violent crime	Murder and non-negligent man-slaughter	Forcible rape	Robbery	Aggravated assault	Property crime	Burglary	Larceny-theft	Motor vehicle theft	Arson
All Suburban Cities												
2004			137 783	1 117	11 939	34 999	89 728	1 532 094	272 722	1 126 214	133 158	8 614
2005	48 853 563	5 331	139 600	1 152	11 866	35 866	90 716	1 524 977	278 491	1 111 530	134 956	8 511
Percent change			1.3	3.1	-0.6	2.5	1.1	-0.5	2.1	-1.3	1.4	-1.2
Group IV (25,000 to 49,999)												
2004			51 906	462	4 288	15 344	31 812	541 493	99 532	384 491	57 470	3 315
2005	17 719 580	517	53 109	477	4 220	15 940	32 472	542 655	102 711	381 506	58 438	3 220
Percent change			2.3	3.2	-1.6	3.9	2.1	0.2	3.2	-0.8	1.7	-2.9
Group V (10,000 to 24,999)												
2004			49 678	424	4 455	12 684	32 115	543 817	98 974	398 458	46 385	2 841
2005	18 908 700	1 184	49 840	430	4 479	12 723	32 208	539 392	100 417	391 913	47 062	2 835
Percent change			0.3	1.4	0.5	0.3	0.3	-0.8	1.5	-1.6	1.5	-0.2
Group VI (under 10,000)												
2004			36 199	231	3 196	6 971	25 801	446 784	74 216	343 265	29 303	2 458
2005	12 225 283	3 630	36 651	245	3 167	7 203	26 036	442 930	75 363	338 111	29 456	2 456
Percent change			1.2	6.1	-0.9	3.3	0.9	-0.9	1.5	-1.5	0.5	-0.1
All Nonsuburban Cities												
2004			89 344	837	8 923	16 512	63 072	898 956	177 358	673 378	48 220	4 980
2005	20 701 274	3 285	90 745	859	8 970	17 408	63 508	888 551	176 747	662 742	49 062	4 927
Percent change			1.6	2.6	0.5	5.4	0.7	-1.2	-0.3	-1.6	1.7	-1.1
Group IV (25,000 to 49,999)												
2004			36 273	360	3 711	8 650	23 552	331 003	64 882	245 254	20 867	1 935
2005	6 405 245	179	37 283	378	3 651	9 220	24 034	326 113	64 392	240 428	21 293	1 965
Percent change			2.8	5.0	-1.6	6.6	2.0	-1.5	-0.8	-2.0	2.0	1.6
Group V (10,000 to 24,999)												
2004			25 592	242	2 704	4 688	17 958	293 525	56 851	222 564	14 110	1 560
2005	6 316 850	408	25 693	230	2 711	5 067	17 685	289 802	56 679	218 576	14 547	1 523
Percent change			0.4	-5.0	0.3	8.1	-1.5	-1.3	-0.3	-1.8	3.1	-2.4
Group VI (under 10,000)												
2004			27 479	235	2 508	3 174	21 562	274 428	55 625	205 560	13 243	1 485
2005	7 979 179	2 698	27 769	251	2 608	3 121	21 789	272 636	55 676	203 738	13 222	1 439
Percent change			1.1	6.8	4.0	-1.7	1.1	-0.7	0.1	-0.9	-0.2	-3.1

Note: Suburban cities include law enforcement agencies in cities with fewer than 50,000 inhabitants that are within metropolitan statistical areas. They exclude all metropolitan agencies associated with a principal city. Nonsuburban cities include law enforcement agencies in cities with fewer than 50,000 inhabitants that are not associated with metropolitan statistical areas.

Table 14. Crime Trends, by Metropolitan and Nonmetropolitan Counties and Population Group, 2004–2005

(Number, percent change.)

Population group and year	Estimated population, 2005	Number of agencies	Violent crime	Murder and non-negligent man-slaughter	Forcible rape	Robbery	Aggravated assault	Property crime	Burglary	Larceny-theft	Motor vehicle theft	Arson
Metropolitan Counties												
100,000 and over												
2004			143 345	1 592	9 584	35 264	96 905	1 036 868	232 732	673 335	130 801	9 256
2005	37 232 565	140	147 231	1 703	9 207	38 211	98 110	1 026 415	235 724	658 799	131 892	8 739
Percent change			2.7	7.0	-3.9	8.4	1.2	-1.0	1.3	-2.2	0.8	-5.6
25,000 to 99,999												
2004			42 116	597	4 775	4 348	32 396	382 558	109 046	241 615	31 897	2 875
2005	20 715 284	405	42 784	541	4 503	4 543	33 197	382 282	109 355	239 410	33 517	2 945
Percent change			1.6	-9.4	-5.7	4.5	2.5	-0.1	0.3	-0.9	5.1	2.4
Under 25,000												
2004			14 880	208	1 541	1 623	11 508	124 483	29 145	69 100	26 238	1 561
2005	4 243 777	996	14 843	142	1 597	1 657	11 447	122 026	27 771	68 219	26 036	1 436
Percent change			-0.2	-31.7	3.6	2.1	-0.5	-2.0	-4.7	-1.3	-0.8	-8.0
Nonmetropolitan Counties												
25,000 and over												
2004			22 394	347	2 264	2 009	17 774	192 005	63 168	114 074	14 763	1 567
2005	10 670 399	271	22 936	335	2 437	2 005	18 159	191 481	62 723	113 505	15 253	1 554
Percent change			2.4	-3.5	7.6	-0.2	2.2	-0.3	-0.7	-0.5	3.3	-0.8
10,000 to 24,999												
2004			16 172	247	1 649	968	13 308	127 406	42 835	74 895	9 676	1 061
2005	9 020 045	558	16 472	265	1 673	984	13 550	126 297	42 044	74 332	9 921	983
Percent change			1.9	7.3	1.5	1.7	1.8	-0.9	-1.8	-0.8	2.5	-7.4
Under 10,000												
2004			8 820	166	1 372	323	6 959	64 957	20 913	38 289	5 755	1 033
2005	3 880 111	1 247	8 665	138	1 287	331	6 909	64 212	19 802	38 486	5 924	893
Percent change			-1.8	-16.9	-6.2	2.5	-0.7	-1.1	-5.3	0.5	2.9	-13.6

Note: Metropolitan counties include sheriffs and county law enforcement agencies associated with a metropolitan statistical area. Nonmetropolitan counties include sheriffs and county law enforcement agencies not associated with a metropolitan statistical area. Offenses from state police agencies are not included in this table.

Table 15. Offenses Known, by Population, 2004–2005

(Number, percent change.)

Population group and year	Esitmated population, 2005	Number of agencies	Forcible rape		Robbery				Aggravated assault			
			Rape by force	Assault to rape attempts	Firearm	Knife or cutting instrument	Other weapon	Strong-arm	Firearm	Knife or cutting instrument	Other weapon	Hands, fists, feet, etc.
ALL AGENCIES												
2004			72 625	6 591	126 145	28 365	29 912	129 841	128 657	126 999	243 453	176 603
2005	247 500 172	12 974	71 835	6 484	135 444	29 485	30 321	131 878	139 994	130 113	241 384	175 641
Percent change			-1.1	-1.6	7.4	3.9	1.4	1.6	8.8	2.5	-0.8	-0.5
All Cities												
2004			53 085	4 992	108 166	24 568	25 381	114 338	98 651	98 249	176 672	122 809
2005	162 399 127	9 251	52 299	5 057	115 375	25 691	25 609	115 928	107 698	100 837	175 902	121 339
Percent change			-1.5	1.3	6.7	4.6	0.9	1.4	9.2	2.6	-0.4	-1.2
Group I (all cities 250,000 and over)												
2004			16 127	2 033	57 108	11 476	11 646	53 792	46 581	36 392	67 307	28 804
2005	39 810 525	63	15 936	1 988	62 037	12 024	11 298	53 850	52 325	37 141	65 540	28 307
Percent change			-1.2	-2.2	8.6	4.8	-3.0	0.1	12.3	2.1	-2.6	-1.7
1,000,000 and over												
2004			4 910	863	23 863	5 141	4 185	19 626	14 476	10 660	17 613	6 998
2005	13 896 753	8	4 856	825	25 025	5 256	4 241	19 101	15 658	10 570	17 132	6 679
Percent change			-1.1	-4.4	4.9	2.2	1.3	-2.7	8.2	-0.8	-2.7	-4.6
500,000 to 999,999												
2004			5 322	651	16 570	3 284	3 670	14 710	15 034	12 621	22 500	9 415
2005	13 202 512	20	5 370	596	18 850	3 543	3 393	15 833	17 988	13 226	21 464	9 566
Percent change			0.9	-8.4	13.8	7.9	-7.5	7.6	19.6	4.8	-4.6	1.6
250,000 to 499,999												
2004			5 895	519	16 675	3 051	3 791	19 456	17 071	13 111	27 194	12 391
2005	12 711 260	35	5 710	567	18 162	3 225	3 664	18 916	18 679	13 345	26 944	12 062
Percent change			-3.1	9.2	8.9	5.7	-3.4	-2.8	9.4	1.8	-0.9	-2.7
Group II (100,000 to 249,999)												
2004			8 728	789	20 279	4 423	4 605	19 574	18 289	17 633	33 307	16 366
2005	25 188 117	169	8 445	799	20 761	4 688	4 994	19 960	19 605	18 691	33 828	16 858
Percent change			-3.2	1.3	2.4	6.0	8.4	2.0	7.2	6.0	1.6	3.0
Group III (50,000 to 99,999)												
2004			8 932	689	13 211	3 858	3 669	17 473	13 499	15 784	29 002	21 020
2005	28 007 923	410	8 741	665	13 979	3 921	3 839	18 096	14 342	16 151	28 609	20 470
Percent change			-2.1	-3.5	5.8	1.6	4.6	3.6	6.2	2.3	-1.4	-2.6
Group IV (25,000 to 49,999)												
2004			7 441	501	8 073	2 241	2 629	10 917	8 248	10 868	18 586	17 405
2005	23 998 926	693	7 279	555	8 550	2 451	2 743	11 313	8 929	11 053	19 190	17 112
Percent change			-2.2	10.8	5.9	9.4	4.3	3.6	8.3	1.7	3.2	-1.7
Group V (10,000 to 24,999)												
2004			6 667	485	6 025	1 670	1 766	7 907	6 789	9 681	15 796	17 798
2005	25 206 502	1 591	6 649	536	6 411	1 653	1 763	7 960	6 997	9 585	15 966	17 342
Percent change			-0.3	10.5	6.4	-1.0	-0.2	0.7	3.1	-1.0	1.1	-2.6
Group VI (under 10,000)												
2004			5 190	495	3 470	900	1 066	4 675	5 245	7 891	12 674	21 416
2005	20 187 134	6 325	5 249	514	3 637	954	972	4 749	5 500	8 216	12 769	21 250
Percent change			1.1	3.8	4.8	6.0	-8.8	1.6	4.9	4.1	0.7	-0.8
Metropolitan Counties												
2004			13 957	1 143	16 426	3 435	4 023	14 072	22 792	22 648	54 546	37 925
2005	60 129 356	1 523	13 687	976	18 640	3 383	4 166	14 456	25 275	23 199	53 183	37 666
Percent change			-1.9	-14.6	13.5	-1.5	3.6	2.7	10.9	2.4	-2.5	-0.7
Nonmetropolitan Counties												
2004			5 583	456	1 553	362	508	1 431	7 214	6 102	12 235	15 869
2005	24 971 689	2 200	5 849	451	1 429	411	546	1 494	7 021	6 077	12 299	16 636
Percent change			4.8	-1.1	-8.0	13.5	7.5	4.4	-2.7	-0.4	0.5	4.8
Suburban Areas[1]												
2004			25 015	1 966	28 876	6 551	7 696	29 763	33 910	38 201	83 254	72 003
2005	108 886 972	6 849	24 571	1 918	31 561	6 614	7 820	30 459	37 231	39 229	82 729	70 710
Percent change			-1.8	-2.4	9.3	1.0	1.6	2.3	9.8	2.7	-0.6	-1.8

[1]Suburban areas include law enforcement agencies in cities with fewer than 50,000 inhabitants and county law enforcement agencies within metropolitan statistical areas. They exclude all metropolitan agencies associated with a principal city. The agencies associated with suburban areas also appear in other groups within this table.

Table 15. Offenses Known, by Population, 2004–2005—*Continued*

(Number, percent change.)

Population group and year	Burglary			Motor vehicle theft			Arson		
	Forcible entry	Unlawful entry	Attempted forcible entry	Automobiles	Trucks and buses	Other vehicles	Structure	Mobile	Other
ALL AGENCIES									
2004	1 102 724	594 513	112 970	762 424	189 795	93 947	26 009	18 391	15 503
2005	1 105 250	599 631	113 877	765 835	191 273	94 242	25 610	17 368	16 242
Percent change	0.2	0.9	0.8	0.4	0.8	0.3	-1.5	-5.6	4.8
All Cities									
2004	800 777	432 379	86 281	624 865	148 521	62 521	19 525	12 539	10 967
2005	807 738	434 425	87 817	626 437	148 913	62 727	19 300	12 088	11 798
Percent change	0.9	0.5	1.8	0.3	0.3	0.3	-1.2	-3.6	7.6
Group I (all cities 250,000 and over)									
2004	285 148	118 763	23 805	266 765	83 683	24 652	7 338	6 272	2 765
2005	286 513	118 434	24 580	271 003	82 838	24 813	7 122	6 096	3 429
Percent change	0.5	-0.3	3.3	1.6	-1.0	0.7	-2.9	-2.8	24.0
1,000,000 and over									
2004	93 746	36 545	6 408	94 246	37 082	8 347	2 004	2 696	1 017
2005	92 544	36 896	6 466	93 184	37 905	8 334	2 217	2 545	1 283
Percent change	-1.3	1.0	0.9	-1.1	2.2	-0.2	10.6	-5.6	26.2
500,000 to 999,999									
2004	100 123	41 717	10 067	82 005	22 295	10 753	2 337	1 338	853
2005	99 940	40 581	10 072	86 085	20 898	10 812	2 005	1 476	1 190
Percent change	-0.2	-2.7	0.0	5.0	-6.3	0.5	-14.2	10.3	39.5
250,000 to 499,999									
2004	91 279	40 501	7 330	90 514	24 306	5 552	2 997	2 238	895
2005	94 029	40 957	8 042	91 734	24 035	5 667	2 900	2 075	956
Percent change	3.0	1.1	9.7	1.3	-1.1	2.1	-3.2	-7.3	6.8
Group II (100,000 to 249,999)									
2004	137 896	73 606	15 189	123 793	25 139	10 114	3 125	2 111	1 733
2005	139 247	72 194	15 810	120 137	25 340	10 066	3 302	1 974	1 964
Percent change	1.0	-1.9	4.1	-3.0	0.8	-0.5	5.7	6.5	13.3
Group III (50,000 to 99,999)									
2004	126 068	74 109	16 285	95 286	16 832	8 789	2 732	1 664	1 979
2005	128 085	75 119	16 267	93 877	17 464	8 912	2 681	1 564	1 926
Percent change	1.6	1.4	-0.1	-1.5	3.8	1.4	-1.9	-6.0	-2.7
Group IV (25,000 to 49,999)									
2004	94 157	57 294	12 060	61 383	9 534	7 105	2 247	1 075	1 820
2005	95 258	58 851	12 168	63 019	9 396	7 079	2 193	1 042	1 845
Percent change	1.2	2.7	0.9	2.7	-1.4	-0.4	-2.4	-3.1	1.4
Group V (10,000 to 24,999)									
2004	87 341	57 831	10 353	46 375	7 940	6 113	2 034	848	1 432
2005	88 113	58 198	10 400	46 948	8 408	6 191	2 056	829	1 379
Percent change	0.9	0.6	0.5	1.2	5.9	1.3	1.1	-2.2	-3.7
Group VI (under 10,000)									
2004	70 167	50 776	8 589	31 263	5 393	5 748	2 049	569	1 238
2005	70 522	51 629	8 583	31 453	5 467	5 666	1 946	583	1 255
Percent change	0.5	1.7	-0.1	0.6	1.4	-1.4	-5.0	2.5	1.4
Metropolitan Counties									
2004	214 445	116 730	20 270	117 079	35 447	23 378	4 539	4 876	3 637
2005	212 183	120 803	19 850	117 835	36 184	23 611	4 522	4 448	3 451
Percent change	-1.1	3.5	-2.1	0.6	2.1	1.0	-0.4	-8.8	-5.1
Nonmetropolitan Counties									
2004	87 502	45 404	6 419	20 480	5 827	8 048	1 945	976	899
2005	85 329	44 403	6 210	21 563	6 176	7 904	1 788	832	993
Percent change	-2.5	-2.2	-3.3	5.3	6.0	-1.8	-8.1	-14.8	10.5
Suburban Areas[1]									
2004	362 906	220 341	40 392	220 499	51 903	36 393	8 309	6 565	6 620
2005	363 806	226 956	40 105	222 950	52 793	36 614	8 287	5 997	6 472
Percent change	0.2	3.0	-0.7	1.1	1.7	0.6	-0.3	-8.7	-2.2

[1]Suburban areas include law enforcement agencies in cities with fewer than 50,000 inhabitants and county law enforcement agencies within metropolitan statistical areas. They exclude all metropolitan agencies associated with a principal city. The agencies associated with suburban areas also appear in other groups within this table.

Table 16. Crime Per 100,000 Population, by Population Group, 2005

(Number, rate.)

Population group	Estimated population, 2005	Number of agencies	Violent crime		Murder and nonnegligent manslaughter		Forcible rape		Robbery	
			Number	Rate	Number	Rate	Number	Rate	Number	Rate
ALL AGENCIES	262 596 173	12 618	1 287 981	490.5	15 495	5.9	84 524	32.2	395 974	150.8
All Cities	177 338 654	8 958	1 028 872	580.2	12 265	6.9	62 754	35.4	347 710	196.1
Group I (250,000 and over)	52 235 624	67	491 646	941.2	6 585	12.6	21 300	40.8	195 446	374.2
1,000,000 and over	24 885 884	10	217 527	874.1	2 891	11.6	8 019	32.2	94 309	379.0
500,000 to 999,999	14 801 594	22	146 755	991.5	2 080	14.1	6 580	44.5	54 668	369.3
250,000 to 499,999	12 548 146	35	127 364	1 015.0	1 614	12.9	6 701	53.4	46 469	370.3
Group II (100,000 to 249,999)	27 675 027	184	170 530	616.2	2 275	8.2	10 739	38.8	57 649	208.3
Group III (50,000 to 99,999)	28 443 673	416	134 946	474.4	1 371	4.8	9 772	34.4	41 276	145.1
Group IV (25,000 to 49,999)	24 511 015	708	91 699	374.1	875	3.6	7 977	32.5	25 207	102.8
Group V (10,000 to 24,999)	24 967 155	1 577	75 675	303.1	662	2.7	7 159	28.7	17 831	71.4
Group VI (under 10,000)	19 506 160	6 006	64 376	330.0	497	2.5	5 807	29.8	10 301	52.8
Metropolitan Counties	60 897 351	1 531	205 817	338.0	2 353	3.9	15 398	25.3	44 325	72.8
Nonmetropolitan Counties[1]	24 360 168	2 129	53 292	218.8	877	3.6	6 372	26.2	3 939	16.2
Suburban Areas[2]	109 385 350	6 681	345 997	316.3	3 524	3.2	27 257	24.9	80 112	73.2

Population group	Aggravated assault		Property crime		Burglary		Larceny-theft		Motor vehicle theft	
	Number	Rate	Number	Rate	Number	Rate	Number	Rate	Number	Rate
ALL AGENCIES	791 988	301.6	9 283 808	3 535.4	1 969 907	750.2	6 151 484	2 342.6	1 162 417	442.7
All Cities	606 143	341.8	7 330 956	4 133.9	1 456 606	821.4	4 938 679	2 784.9	935 671	527.6
Group I (250,000 and over)	268 315	513.7	2 504 191	4 794.0	508 754	974.0	1 542 661	2 953.3	452 776	866.8
1,000,000 and over	112 308	451.3	963 317	3 870.9	184 430	741.1	598 587	2 405.3	180 300	724.5
500,000 to 999,999	83 427	563.6	840 078	5 675.6	176 438	1 192.0	516 344	3 488.4	147 296	995.1
250,000 to 499,999	72 580	578.4	700 796	5 584.9	147 886	1 178.5	427 730	3 408.7	125 180	997.6
Group II (100,000 to 249,999)	99 867	360.9	1 286 452	4 648.4	261 840	946.1	850 933	3 074.7	173 679	627.6
Group III (50,000 to 99,999)	82 527	290.1	1 107 923	3 895.1	227 646	800.3	756 768	2 660.6	123 509	434.2
Group IV (25,000 to 49,999)	57 640	235.2	890 406	3 632.7	170 680	696.3	638 267	2 604.0	81 459	332.3
Group V (10,000 to 24,999)	50 023	200.4	830 854	3 327.8	157 266	629.9	611 747	2 450.2	61 841	247.7
Group VI (under 10,000)	47 771	244.9	711 130	3 645.7	130 420	668.6	538 303	2 759.7	42 407	217.4
Metropolitan Counties	143 741	236.0	1 528 167	2 509.4	377 001	619.1	960 087	1 576.6	191 079	313.8
Nonmetropolitan Counties[1]	42 104	172.8	424 685	1 743.4	136 300	559.5	252 718	1 037.4	35 667	146.4
Suburban Areas[2]	235 104	214.9	3 063 460	2 800.6	658 151	601.7	2 077 882	1 899.6	327 427	299.3

[1]Includes state police agencies that report aggregately for the entire state.
[2]Suburban areas include law enforcement agencies in cities with fewer than 50,000 inhabitants and county law enforcement agencies that are within metropolitan statistical areas. They exclude all metropolitan agencies associated with a principal city. Agencies associated with suburban areas also appear in other groups within this table.

Table 17. Crime Per 100,000 Population, by Suburban and Nonsuburban Cities and Population Group, 2005

(Number, rate.)

Population group	Estimated population, 2005	Number of agencies	Violent crime		Murder and nonnegligent manslaughter		Forcible rape		Robbery	
			Number	Rate	Number	Rate	Number	Rate	Number	Rate
All Suburban Cities	48 487 999	5 150	140 180	289.1	1 171	2.4	11 859	24.0	35 787	73.8
Group IV (25,000 to 49,999)	18 007 058	526	54 007	299.9	493	2.7	4 256	23.0	15 944	88.5
Group V (10,000 to 24,999)	18 657 883	1 170	49 818	267.0	430	2.3	4 457	23.0	12 733	68.2
Group VI (under 10,000)	11 823 058	3 454	36 355	307.5	248	2.1	3 146	26.0	7 110	60.1
All Nonsuburban Cities	20 496 331	3 141	91 570	446.8	863	4.2	9 084	44.0	17 552	85.6
Group IV (25,000 to 49,999)	6 503 957	182	37 692	579.5	382	5.9	3 721	57.0	9 263	142.4
Group V (10,000 to 24,999)	6 309 272	407	25 857	409.8	232	3.7	2 702	42.0	5 098	80.8
Group VI (under 10,000)	7 683 102	2 552	28 021	364.7	249	3.2	2 661	34.0	3 191	41.5

Population group	Aggravated assault		Property crime		Burglary		Larceny-theft		Motor vehicle theft	
	Number	Rate	Number	Rate	Number	Rate	Number	Rate	Number	Rate
All Suburban Cities	91 363	188.4	1 535 293	3 166.0	281 150	579.8	1 117 795	2 305.3	136 348	281.2
Group IV (25,000 to 49,999)	33 314	185.0	558 108	3 099.0	105 563	586.2	392 602	2 180.3	59 943	332.9
Group V (10,000 to 24,999)	32 198	172.6	539 180	2 889.0	100 589	539.1	391 391	2 097.7	47 200	253.0
Group VI (under 10,000)	25 851	218.6	438 005	3 704.0	74 998	634.3	333 802	2 823.3	29 205	247.0
All Nonsuburban Cities	64 071	312.6	897 097	4 376.0	177 216	864.6	670 522	3 271.4	49 359	240.8
Group IV (25,000 to 49,999)	24 326	374.0	332 298	5 109.0	65 117	1 001.0	245 665	3 777.2	21 516	330.8
Group V (10,000 to 24,999)	17 825	282.5	291 674	4 622.0	56 677	898.3	220 356	3 492.6	14 641	232.1
Group VI (under 10,000)	21 920	285.3	273 125	3 554.0	55 422	721.3	204 501	2 661.7	13 202	171.8

Note: Suburban cities include law enforcement agencies in cities with fewer than 50,000 inhabitants that are within metropolitan statistical areas. They exclude all metropolitan agencies associated with a principal city. Nonsuburban cities include law enforcement agencies in cities with fewer than 50,000 inhabitants that are not associated with metropolitan statistical areas.

Table 18. Crime Per 100,000 Population, by Metropolitan and Nonmetropolitan Counties and Population Group, 2005

(Number, rate.)

Population group	Estimated population, 2005	Number of agencies	Violent crime		Murder and nonnegligent manslaughter		Forcible rape		Robbery	
			Number	Rate	Number	Rate	Number	Rate	Number	Rate
Metropolitan Counties										
100,000 and over	36 418 757	140	147 094	403.9	1 649	4.5	9 217	25.3	37 696	103.5
25,000 to 99,999	20 517 831	401	43 022	209.7	554	2.7	4 571	22.3	4 613	22.5
Under 25,000	3 960 763	990	15 701	396.4	150	3.8	1 610	40.6	2 016	50.9
Nonmetropolitan Counties										
25,000 and over	10 470 877	266	23 039	220.0	335	3.2	2 446	23.4	2 043	19.5
10,000 to 24,999	8 741 871	537	15 864	181.5	259	3.0	1 651	18.9	944	10.8
Under 10,000	3 585 374	1 175	8 473	236.3	135	3.8	1 276	35.6	325	9.1

Population group	Aggravated assault		Property crime		Burglary		Larceny-theft		Motor vehicle theft	
	Number	Rate	Number	Rate	Number	Rate	Number	Rate	Number	Rate
Metropolitan Counties										
100,000 and over	98 532	270.6	1 011 581	2 777.6	236 347	649.0	644 662	1 770.1	130 572	358.5
25,000 to 99,999	33 284	162.2	389 699	1 899.3	112 257	547.1	243 390	1 186.2	34 052	166.0
Under 25,000	11 925	301.1	126 887	3 203.6	28 397	717.0	72 035	1 818.7	26 455	667.9
Nonmetropolitan Counties										
25,000 and over	18 215	174.0	193 953	1 852.3	63 438	605.9	115 049	1 098.8	15 466	147.7
10,000 to 24,999	13 010	148.8	122 801	1 404.7	40 837	467.1	72 363	827.8	9 601	109.8
Under 10,000	6 737	187.9	62 409	1 740.7	19 412	541.4	37 238	1 038.6	5 759	160.6

Note: Metropolitan counties include sheriffs and county law enforcement agencies associated with metropolitan statistical areas. Nonmetropolitan counties include sheriffs and county law enforcement agencies not associated with metropolitan statistical areas. Offenses from state police agencies are not included in this table.

Table 19. Crime Per 100,000 Population, Selected Known Offenses, by Population Group, 2005

(Number, rate.)

Population group	Estimated population, 2005	Number of agencies	Forcible rape		Robbery			
			Rape by force	Assault-to-rape attempts	Firearms	Knives or cutting instruments	Other weapons	Strong-arm
ALL AGENCIES								
Number of known offenses	245 653 447	12 537	72 800	6 515	142 471	29 789	31 650	134 200
Rate			29.6	2.7	58.0	12.1	12.9	54.6
All Cities								
Number of known offenses	161 942 164	8 922	52 973	5 108	121 358	25 943	26 685	118 115
Rate			32.7	3.2	74.9	16.0	16.5	72.9
Group I (all cities 250,000 and over)								
Number of known offenses	39 950 427	62	16 143	2 035	67 327	12 225	12 218	55 718
Rate			40.4	5.1	168.5	30.6	30.6	139.5
1,000,000 and over								
Number of known offenses	13 896 753	8	4 856	825	25 025	5 256	4 241	19 101
Rate			34.9	5.9	180.1	37.8	30.5	137.4
500,000 to 999,999								
Number of known offenses	14 160 497	21	5 768	650	24 691	3 807	4 347	17 913
Rate			40.7	4.6	174.4	26.9	30.7	126.5
250,000 to 499,999								
Number of known offenses	11 893 177	33	5 519	560	17 611	3 162	3 630	18 704
Rate			46.4	4.7	148.1	26.6	30.5	157.3
Group II (100,000 to 249,999)								
Number of known offenses	25 000 562	167	8 571	803	21 073	4 718	5 021	19 971
Rate			34.3	3.2	84.3	18.9	20.1	79.9
Group III (50,000 to 99,999)								
Number of known offenses	28 194 534	412	8 950	694	14 351	3 943	3 883	18 429
Rate			31.7	2.5	50.9	14.0	13.8	65.4
Group IV (25,000 to 49,999)								
Number of known offenses	24 389 990	705	7 418	545	8 569	2 444	2 850	11 300
Rate			30.4	2.2	35.1	10.0	11.7	46.3
Group V (10,000 to 24,999)								
Number of known offenses	24 916 218	1 574	6 612	515	6 407	1 655	1 747	7 960
Rate			26.5	2.1	25.7	6.6	7.0	31.9
Group VI (under 10,000)								
Number of known offenses	19 490 433	6 002	5 279	516	3 631	958	966	4 737
Rate			27.1	2.6	18.6	4.9	5.0	24.3
Metropolitan Counties								
Number of known offenses	59 393 097	1 514	13 927	968	19 652	3 443	4 420	14 587
Rate			23.4	1.6	33.1	5.8	7.4	24.6
Nonmetropolitan Counties								
Number of known offenses	24 318 186	2 101	5 900	439	1 461	403	545	1 498
Rate			24.3	1.8	6.0	1.7	2.2	6.2
Suburban Areas[1]								
Number of known offenses	107 737 126	6 658	24 842	1 881	32 554	6 663	8 084	30 531
Rate			23.1	1.7	30.2	6.2	7.5	28.3

[1] Suburban areas include law enforcement agencies in cities with fewer than 50,000 inhabitants and county law enforcement agencies within metropolitan statistical areas. They exclude all metropolitan agencies associated with a principal city. The agencies associated with suburban areas also appear in other groups within this table.

Table 19. Crime Per 100,000 Population, Selected Known Offenses, by Population Group, 2005—*Continued*

(Number, rate.)

Population group	Aggravated assault				Burglary			Motor vehicle theft		
	Firearms	Knives or cutting instruments	Other weapons	Hands, fists, feet, etc.	Forcible entry	Unlawful entry	Attempted forcible entry	Autos	Trucks and buses	Other vehicles
ALL AGENCIES										
Number of known offenses	151 118	136 496	252 887	180 261	1 127 547	606 532	118 121	793 863	191 078	97 061
Rate	61.5	55.6	102.9	73.4	459.0	246.9	48.1	323.2	77.8	39.5
All Cities										
Number of known offenses	118 154	106 474	186 365	126 362	823 305	439 250	90 963	649 962	148 472	65 287
Rate	73.0	65.7	115.1	78.0	508.4	271.2	56.2	401.4	91.7	40.3
Group I (all cities 250,000 and over)										
Number of known offenses	61 844	41 964	75 146	32 701	297 284	119 287	27 302	289 824	82 282	27 239
Rate	154.8	105.0	188.1	81.9	744.1	298.6	68.3	725.5	206.0	68.2
1,000,000 and over										
Number of known offenses	21 424	13 833	21 653	9 505	92 544	36 896	6 466	93 184	37 905	8 334
Rate	154.2	99.5	155.8	68.4	665.9	265.5	46.5	670.5	272.8	60.0
500,000 to 999,999										
Number of known offenses	22 834	15 313	27 004	11 369	113 601	42 577	12 922	106 764	20 877	13 443
Rate	161.3	108.1	190.7	80.3	802.2	300.7	91.3	754.0	147.4	94.9
250,000 to 499,999										
Number of known offenses	17 586	12 818	26 489	11 827	91 139	39 814	7 914	89 876	23 500	5 462
Rate	147.9	107.8	222.7	99.4	766.3	334.8	66.5	755.7	197.6	45.9
Group II (100,000 to 249,999)										
Number of known offenses	19 763	18 785	33 863	16 903	140 111	72 531	15 848	121 561	25 386	9 884
Rate	79.1	75.1	135.4	67.6	560.4	290.1	63.4	486.2	101.5	39.5
Group III (50,000 to 99,999)										
Number of known offenses	14 890	16 474	28 821	20 941	130 884	77 013	16 459	95 466	17 599	9 191
Rate	52.8	58.4	102.2	74.3	464.2	273.1	58.4	338.6	62.4	32.6
Group IV (25,000 to 49,999)										
Number of known offenses	9 156	11 376	19 593	17 454	97 088	60 582	12 310	64 684	9 398	7 184
Rate	37.5	46.6	80.3	71.6	398.1	248.4	50.5	265.2	38.5	29.5
Group V (10,000 to 24,999)										
Number of known offenses	7 007	9 646	15 970	17 349	88 045	58 180	10 405	47 095	8 400	6 161
Rate	28.1	38.7	64.1	69.6	353.4	233.5	41.8	189.0	33.7	24.7
Group VI (under 10,000)										
Number of known offenses	5 494	8 229	12 972	21 014	69 893	51 657	8 639	31 332	5 407	5 628
Rate	28.2	42.2	66.6	107.8	358.6	265.0	44.3	160.8	27.7	28.9
Metropolitan Counties										
Number of known offenses	25 901	23 904	54 092	37 545	218 329	123 384	20 953	122 262	36 475	23 962
Rate	43.6	40.2	91.1	63.2	367.6	207.7	35.3	205.9	61.4	40.3
Nonmetropolitan Counties										
Number of known offenses	7 063	6 118	12 430	16 354	85 913	43 898	6 205	21 639	6 131	7 812
Rate	29.0	25.2	51.1	67.3	353.3	180.5	25.5	89.0	25.2	32.1
Suburban Areas[1]										
Number of known offenses	38 006	40 134	83 900	70 631	371 014	230 585	41 371	228 758	53 069	36 937
Rate	35.3	37.3	77.9	65.6	344.4	214.0	38.4	212.3	49.3	34.3

[1] Suburban areas include law enforcement agencies in cities with fewer than 50,000 inhabitants and county law enforcement agencies within metropolitan statistical areas. They exclude all metropolitan agencies associated with a principal city. The agencies associated with suburban areas also appear in other groups within this table.

Table 20. Murder, by State and Type of Weapon, 2005

(Number.)

State	Total murders[1]	Total firearms	Handguns	Rifles	Shotguns	Firearms (type unknown)	Knives or cutting instruments	Other weapons	Hands, fists, feet, etc.[2]
Alabama	326	223	206	4	12	1	25	62	16
Alaska	32	19	15	1	1	2	4	6	3
Arizona	440	334	270	22	19	23	43	34	29
Arkansas	176	120	74	3	15	28	26	21	9
California	2 503	1 845	1 493	83	76	193	288	237	133
Colorado	170	109	64	4	3	38	32	23	6
Connecticut	91	47	27	0	2	18	14	20	10
Delaware	37	23	15	0	0	8	8	2	4
Georgia	516	370	312	12	13	33	68	73	5
Hawaii	20	2	0	1	0	1	9	4	5
Idaho	34	23	10	1	5	7	1	6	4
Illinois[3]	448	339	328	4	2	5	51	37	21
Indiana	331	238	171	20	7	40	24	52	17
Iowa	38	21	13	1	2	5	5	5	7
Kansas	95	52	20	8	4	20	16	20	7
Kentucky	177	124	94	8	11	11	15	24	14
Louisiana	399	309	261	21	14	13	46	34	10
Maine	19	7	6	1	0	0	4	4	4
Maryland	551	418	394	4	15	5	68	47	18
Massachusetts	171	94	48	1	1	44	39	31	7
Michigan	614	421	195	38	20	168	52	118	23
Minnesota	115	73	63	7	2	1	16	15	11
Mississippi	163	113	77	13	8	15	25	15	10
Missouri	401	281	113	10	18	140	48	63	9
Montana	17	5	3	1	0	1	5	5	2
Nebraska	13	5	0	1	0	4	1	3	4
Nevada	205	124	84	6	5	29	26	41	14
New Hampshire	16	6	3	0	0	3	5	4	1
New Jersey	417	276	260	1	3	12	62	41	38
New Mexico	133	66	48	3	7	8	28	22	17
New York	868	500	428	10	10	52	188	107	73
North Carolina	566	353	241	20	34	58	66	96	51
North Dakota	7	1	0	0	0	1	1	5	0
Ohio	549	313	198	13	14	88	58	125	53
Oklahoma	187	129	100	14	9	6	19	22	17
Oregon	79	48	19	5	2	22	11	17	3
Pennsylvania	734	528	392	15	16	105	88	97	21
Rhode Island	34	16	6	1	0	9	5	7	6
South Carolina	312	217	168	8	14	27	37	36	22
South Dakota	14	6	3	0	1	2	3	3	2
Tennessee	428	301	203	8	30	60	48	50	29
Texas	1 406	946	767	48	67	64	205	173	82
Utah	56	27	11	0	7	9	12	10	7
Vermont	8	5	1	2	2	0	1	1	1
Virginia	459	318	149	6	18	145	51	68	22
Washington	205	126	103	8	11	4	40	19	20
West Virginia	72	40	18	0	6	16	3	19	10
Wisconsin	194	132	63	4	11	54	23	27	12
Wyoming	14	7	6	1	0	0	1	3	3

[1]Number of murders for which supplemental homicide data were received.
[2]Includes murders committed by pushing.
[3]Limited supplemental homicide data.

Table 21. Robbery, by State and Type of Weapon, 2005

(Number.)

State	Total population	Number of agencies	Total robberies[1]	Firearms	Knives or cutting instruments	Other weapons	Strong-arm
Alabama	2 612 774	263	2 263	1 208	160	190	705
Alaska	650 601	33	533	180	62	50	241
Arizona	4 751 564	81	6 675	3 655	686	479	1 855
Arkansas	2 365 406	177	2 433	1 162	164	253	854
California	35 804 748	716	63 273	21 896	6 213	5 943	29 221
Colorado	4 493 672	194	3 869	1 640	416	365	1 448
Connecticut	3 257 161	95	3 117	1 033	355	370	1 359
Delaware	843 524	50	1 306	550	109	118	529
District of Columbia	550 521	2	3 700	1 782	162	108	1 648
Florida	17 758 612	602	30 076	11 946	2 229	2 990	12 911
Georgia	5 882 872	249	10 751	6 286	554	1 042	2 869
Hawaii	1 048 094	2	915	103	63	92	657
Idaho	1 160 229	88	214	70	17	43	84
Indiana	4 948 152	172	6 478	3 367	468	356	2 287
Iowa	2 733 190	192	1 145	230	99	144	672
Kansas	1 323 938	216	330	103	39	34	154
Kentucky	3 444 023	283	3 444	1 607	306	458	1 073
Louisiana	2 927 488	125	3 497	1 908	224	340	1 025
Maine	1 307 115	149	322	59	39	43	181
Maryland	4 956 278	148	10 468	5 715	865	513	3 375
Massachusetts	5 308 070	285	6 352	1 655	1 298	754	2 645
Michigan	9 573 458	533	13 032	6 339	671	1 359	4 663
Minnesota	4 154 209	301	1 240	338	101	351	450
Mississippi	1 801 076	107	1 737	918	106	282	431
Missouri	5 677 517	526	7 141	3 412	434	604	2 691
Montana	728 656	67	167	37	24	40	66
Nebraska	1 604 496	216	1 031	453	100	89	389
Nevada	2 410 942	33	4 674	1 988	521	422	1 743
New Hampshire	1 079 375	130	332	75	44	58	155
New Jersey	8 717 925	517	13 215	4 397	1 403	944	6 471
Now Mexico	1 425 388	55	1 733	777	255	135	566
New York	10 145 688	618	9 071	3 148	1 139	1 102	4 482
North Carolina	7 951 544	367	11 639	6 222	1 004	1 003	3 410
North Dakota	541 802	62	42	1	5	6	30
Ohio	8 272 962	359	17 153	6 115	950	1 877	8 211
Oklahoma	3 493 881	294	3 224	1 450	328	218	1 228
Oregon	3 576 873	153	2 451	579	259	265	1 348
Pennsylvania	10 646 715	798	17 913	7 657	1 361	1 203	7 692
Rhode Island	983 008	44	733	194	108	151	280
South Carolina	4 101 068	274	5 547	2 903	452	509	1 683
South Dakota	315 246	51	52	12	9	4	27
Tennessee	5 771 658	428	9 900	5 608	783	795	2 714
Texas	22 803 084	979	35 771	16 029	3 619	3 364	12 759
Utah	2 147 551	98	1 035	304	123	106	502
Vermont	546 576	65	50	17	8	9	16
Virginia	6 093 394	356	7 061	3 784	559	776	1 942
Washington	5 711 284	241	4 884	1 110	516	532	2 726
West Virginia	1 504 736	345	728	216	79	94	339
Wisconsin	5 254 892	337	4 516	2 220	288	653	1 355
Wyoming	490 411	61	77	13	12	14	38

[1]Number of robberies for which breakdowns by type of weapon were received from agencies that submitted 12 months of data in 2005.

Table 22. Aggravated Assault, by State and Type of Weapon, 2005

(Number.)

State	Total population	Number of agencies	Total aggravated assaults[1]	Firearms	Knives or cutting instruments	Other weapons	Personal weapons
Alabama	2 612 774	263	5 616	1 520	885	1 159	2 052
Alaska	650 601	33	3 035	582	696	749	1 008
Arizona	4 751 564	81	15 104	3 892	2 476	4 953	3 783
Arkansas	2 365 406	177	9 946	2 550	1 579	2 731	3 086
California	35 804 748	716	113 655	23 182	18 607	41 540	30 326
Colorado	4 493 672	194	12 002	2 688	2 639	3 070	3 605
Connecticut	3 257 161	95	3 888	492	887	1 561	948
Delaware	843 524	50	3 612	731	833	1 737	311
District of Columbia	550 521	2	3 971	829	1 053	1 629	460
Florida	17 758 612	602	88 141	15 057	15 680	39 668	17 736
Georgia	5 882 872	249	16 160	4 358	3 415	5 290	3 097
Hawaii	1 048 094	2	1 629	154	417	591	467
Idaho	1 160 229	88	2 268	412	466	862	528
Indiana	4 948 152	172	9 679	1 584	1 376	2 769	3 950
Iowa	2 733 190	192	6 461	601	1 021	1 601	3 238
Kansas	1 323 938	216	2 825	461	514	1 171	679
Kentucky	3 444 023	283	5 202	1 063	789	1 880	1 470
Louisiana	2 927 488	125	14 116	3 460	2 588	4 204	3 864
Maine	1 307 115	149	809	32	163	246	368
Maryland	4 956 278	148	16 266	2 540	3 744	6 156	3 826
Massachusetts	5 308 070	285	16 567	1 734	3 653	8 353	2 827
Michigan	9 573 458	533	35 674	8 839	6 848	13 228	6 759
Minnesota	4 154 209	301	4 011	518	824	1 590	1 079
Mississippi	1 801 076	107	2 506	779	535	796	396
Missouri	5 677 517	526	20 834	5 153	2 855	6 350	6 476
Montana	728 656	67	1 727	270	276	469	712
Nebraska	1 604 496	216	3 275	451	595	1 629	600
Nevada	2 410 942	33	8 619	1 763	1 844	3 673	1 339
New Hampshire	1 079 375	130	825	112	286	220	207
New Jersey	8 717 925	517	16 079	2 449	3 333	5 122	5 175
New Mexico	1 425 388	55	7 800	1 639	1 351	2 457	2 353
New York	10 145 688	618	16 888	2 099	4 265	5 070	5 454
North Carolina	7 951 544	367	22 988	6 628	4 825	6 251	5 284
North Dakota	541 802	62	368	18	53	108	189
Ohio	8 272 962	359	13 702	3 223	2 694	4 359	3 426
Oklahoma	3 493 881	294	13 059	2 546	2 063	4 838	3 612
Oregon	3 576 873	153	6 325	780	1 186	2 245	2 114
Pennsylvania	10 646 715	798	25 800	5 678	3 876	6 411	9 835
Rhode Island	983 008	44	1 439	225	328	465	421
South Carolina	4 101 068	274	23 796	5 780	4 367	6 759	6 890
South Dakota	315 246	51	369	37	99	86	147
Tennessee	5 771 658	428	31 609	9 972	6 716	10 873	4 048
Texas	22 803 084	979	75 285	17 514	16 858	27 017	13 896
Utah	2 147 551	98	3 246	529	838	1 168	711
Vermont	546 576	65	379	46	74	82	177
Virginia	6 093 394	356	10 943	2 367	2 343	3 411	2 822
Washington	5 711 284	241	10 902	1 541	1 972	3 590	3 799
West Virginia	1 504 736	345	3 172	833	612	692	1 035
Wisconsin	5 254 892	337	7 274	1 327	921	1 731	3 295
Wyoming	490 411	61	916	80	178	277	381

[1]Number of aggravated assaults for which breakdowns by type of weapon were received from agencies that submitted 12 months of data in 2005.

Table 23. Offense Analysis, by Classification and Value, 2004–2005

(Number, percent, dollars.)

Classification	Number of offenses, 2005	Percent change, 2004–2005	Percent distribution	Average value (dollars)
Murder	12 068	3.9	X	X
Forcible Rape	70 472	-1.7	X	X
Robbery				
Total	298 403	4.6	100.0	1 230
Robbery by location				
Street/highway	131 666	5.8	44.1	1 005
Commercial house	42 672	3.5	14.3	1 670
Gas or service station	8 499	9.1	2.8	1 104
Convenience store	17 029	-0.3	5.7	625
Residence	42 324	9.7	14.2	1 335
Bank	6 266	-8.9	2.1	4 169
Miscellaneous	49 947	1.3	16.7	1 217
Burglary				
Total	1 612 683	0.8	100.0	1 725
Burglary by location				
Residence (dwelling)	1 060 513	1.1	65.8	1 745
Residence, night	301 431	1.2	18.7	1 331
Residence, day	500 972	2.6	31.1	1 877
Residence, unknown	258 110	-1.9	16.0	1 971
Nonresidence (store, office, etc.)	552 170	0.2	34.2	1 683
Nonresidence, night	228 743	-0.1	14.2	1 485
Nonresidence, day	165 487	2.6	10.3	1 583
Nonresidence, unknown	157 940	-1.6	9.8	2 076
Larceny-Theft (Except Motor Vehicle Theft)				
Total	5 036 548	-2.1	100.0	764
Larceny-theft by type				
Pocket-picking	21 696	-6.0	0.4	346
Purse-snatching	31 214	-5.2	0.6	377
Shoplifting	698 233	-5.3	13.9	163
Items from motor vehicles (except accessories)	1 301 026	-1.4	25.8	691
Motor vehicle accessories	514 703	-5.4	10.2	457
Bicycles	184 722	-2.3	3.7	268
Items from buildings	632 933	-0.7	12.6	1 155
Items from coin-operated machines	30 356	-10.5	0.6	233
All other	1 621 665	-0.4	32.2	1 106
Larceny-theft by value				
Under $50	1 889 335	-4.2	37.5	19
$50 to $200	1 130 650	-2.6	22.4	111
Over $200	2 016 563	0.2	40.0	1 828
Motor Vehicle Theft	973 451	0.2	X	6 173

X = Not applicable.

Table 24. Property Stolen and Recovered, by Type and Value, 2005

(Dollars, percent.)

Type of property	Value of property (dollars)		Percent recovered
	Stolen	Recovered	
Total	13 075 382 963	4 359 583 231	33.3
Currency, notes, etc.	979 345 861	32 177 230	3.3
Jewelry and precious metals	1 030 082 045	46 562 582	4.5
Clothing and furs	215 948 745	28 866 408	13.4
Locally stolen motor vehicles	6 186 522 823	3 839 499 496	62.1
Office equipment	530 721 906	20 331 812	3.8
Televisions, radios, stereos, etc.	792 464 592	30 390 889	3.8
Firearms	93 487 243	8 107 822	8.7
Household goods	219 147 349	10 741 009	4.9
Consumable goods	95 776 212	12 408 529	13.0
Livestock	18 726 081	2 209 729	11.8
Miscellaneous	2 913 160 106	328 287 725	11.3

SECTION III:
OFFENSES CLEARED

OFFENSES CLEARED

Figure 3-1. Percent of Crimes Cleared by Arrest or Exceptional Means, 2005

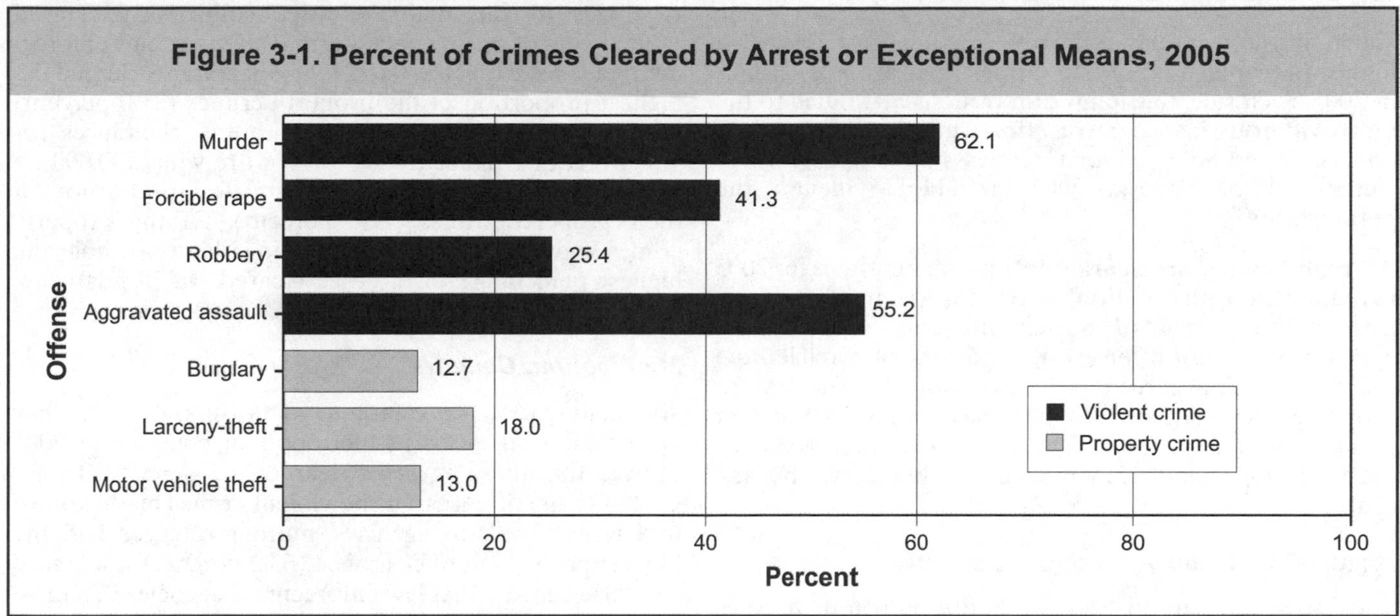

Law enforcement agencies that report crime to the Federal Bureau of Investigation (FBI) can clear, or "close," offenses in one of two ways: by arrest or by exceptional means. However, the administrative closing of a case by a local law enforcement agency does not necessarily mean that the agency can clear an offense for UCR purposes. To clear an offense within the program's guidelines, the reporting agency must adhere to certain criteria, which are outlined in this section. (*Note*: The UCR Program does not distinguish between offenses cleared by arrest and those cleared by exceptional means in its data presentations. The distinction is made solely for the purpose of a definition and not for data collection and publication.) See Appendix I for information on the UCR Program's statistical methodology.

Cleared by Arrest

In the UCR Program, a law enforcement agency reports that an offense is cleared by arrest, or solved for crime reporting purposes, when at least one person is arrested, charged with the commission of the offense, and turned over to the court for prosecution (whether following arrest, court summons, or police notice). To qualify as a clearance, all of these conditions must be met.

In its calculations, the UCR Program counts the number of offenses that are cleared, not the number of arrestees. Therefore, the arrest of one person may clear several crimes, and the arrest of many persons may clear only one offense. In addition, some clearances recorded by an agency during a particular calendar year, such as 2005, may pertain to offenses that occurred in previous years.

Cleared by Exceptional Means

In certain situations, elements beyond law enforcement's control prevent the agency from arresting and formally charging the offender. When this occurs, the agency can clear the offense *exceptionally*. There are four UCR Program requirements that law enforcement must meet in order to clear an offense by exceptional means. The agency must have:

- Identified the offender
- Gathered enough evidence to support an arrest, make a charge, and turn over the offender to the court for prosecution
- Identified the offender's exact location so that the suspect could be taken into custody immediately
- Encountered a circumstance outside the control of law enforcement that prohibits the agency from arresting, charging, and prosecuting the offender

Examples of exceptional clearances include, but are not limited to, the death of the offender (e.g., suicide or justifiably killed by a law enforcement officer or a citizen), the victim's refusal to cooperate with the prosecution after the offender has been identified, or the denial of extradition because the offender committed a crime in another jurisdiction and is being prosecuted for that offense. In the UCR Program, the recovery of property does not clear an offense.

National Clearances

A review of the data for 2005 revealed law enforcement agencies in the United States cleared 45.5 percent of violent crimes (murder, forcible rape, robbery, and aggravated assault) and 16.3 percent of property crimes (burglary, larceny-theft, and motor vehicle theft) brought to their attention. In addition, law enforcement cleared 17.9 percent of arson offenses, which are reported in a slightly different manner than the other property crimes. (More details concerning this offense are furnished in the property crime text in this section.)

As in most years, law enforcement agencies cleared a higher percentage of violent crimes than property crimes in 2005. As a rule, this long-term trend is attributed to the more vigorous investigative efforts put forth for violent crimes. In addition, violent crimes more often involve victims and/or witnesses who are able to identify the perpetrators.

A breakdown of the clearances for violent crimes for 2005 revealed that the nation's law enforcement agencies cleared 62.1 percent of murder offenses, 55.2 percent of aggravated assault offenses, 41.3 percent of forcible rape offenses, and 25.4 percent of robbery offenses. The data for property crimes showed that agencies cleared 18.0 percent of larceny-theft offenses, 13.0 percent of motor vehicle theft offenses, and 12.7 percent of burglary offenses. (Table 25)

Regional Clearances

The UCR Program divides the nation into four regions: the Northeast, the Midwest, the South, and the West. (See Appendix III for further details.) A review of clearance data for 2005 by region showed that agencies in the Northeast cleared the greatest proportion of their violent crime offenses (48.6 percent). Law enforcement agencies in the South cleared 47.1 percent of their violent crimes, while agencies in the West and Midwest cleared 44.7 percent and 39.9 percent, respectively.

Clearance data for 2005 showed that, among the regions, law enforcement agencies in the Northeast cleared the highest percentage of their property crimes (19.7 percent). Agencies in the South and Midwest cleared 16.8 percent and 15.8 percent, respectively. Agencies in the West cleared 14.3 percent of their property crimes. (Table 26)

Clearances by Population Groups

The UCR Program uses the following population group designations in its data presentations: cities (grouped according to population size) and counties (classified as either metropolitan or nonmetropolitan counties). (A breakdown of these classifications is furnished in Appendix III.)

Cities

In 2005, the clearance data collected showed that law enforcement agencies in the nation's cities cleared 42.9 percent of their violent crime offenses. Agencies in the smallest cities, those with populations under 10,000 inhabitants, cleared the greatest proportion of their violent crime offenses (58.6 percent), and law enforcement in cities with 500,000 to 999,999 inhabitants cleared the smallest proportion of their violent crime offenses (33.8 percent). The clearance data for murder, an offense of particular interest to law enforcement, showed that cities with populations of 10,000 to 24,999 inhabitants cleared the greatest percentage of their murders (74.2 percent), Law enforcement agencies in cities with 500,000 to 999,999 inhabitants cleared the lowest percentage of their murders (54.1 percent).

Agencies in the nation's cities collectively cleared 16.2 percent of their property crime offenses. Law enforcement in cities with 10,000 to 24,999 inhabitants cleared the highest proportion of the property crimes (21.0 percent) brought to their attention; as with the clearances for violent crime, agencies in cities with with 500,000 to 999,999 inhabitants cleared the smallest proportion of their property crimes (11.6 percent). Of the property crimes known to law enforcement in cities as a whole, the highest percentage of offenses cleared was for larceny-theft at 18.0 percent. (Table 25)

Metropolitan Counties

An examination of clearance data submitted by law enforcement agencies in metropolitan counties in 2005 showed that these agencies cleared 53.1 percent of their violent crime offenses. Of the violent crimes made known to law enforcement agencies, murder offenses had the highest proportion of clearance (63.2 percent). Clearance data also showed that law enforcement agencies in metropolitan counties cleared 16.0 percent of their total property crimes. (Table 25)

Nonmetropolitan Counties

Clearance figures for nonmetropolitan counties showed that agencies collectively cleared a greater proportion of their violent crimes than did the nation as a whole in 2005. Agencies in nonmetropolitan counties cleared 61.6 percent of their violent crime offenses. Law enforcement in nonmetropolitan counties had the highest number of clearances for murder (76.7 percent). The clearance data also showed that law enforcement agencies in nonmetropolitan counties cleared 18.0 percent of their property crime offenses. The highest percentage of offenses cleared was for motor vehicle theft at 26.0 percent. In addition, law enforcement in these counties cleared 17.8 percent of their larceny-theft offenses. (Table 25)

Clearances and Juveniles

When an offender under 18 years of age is cited to appear in juvenile court or before other juvenile authorities, the UCR Program considers the incident for which the juvenile is being held responsible to be cleared by arrest, although a physical arrest may not have occurred. In addition, according to program definitions, clearances that include both adult and juvenile offenders are classified as clearances for crimes committed by adults. Therefore, the figures in this publication should not be used to present a definitive picture of juvenile involvement in crime.

Of the clearances for violent crimes in 2005, 12.4 percent involved only juveniles, up from 12.1 percent in 2004. In addition, 17.9 percent of clearances for property crime in 2005 involved only juveniles, down from 18.9 percent in 2004. Clearances for murder offenses had the lowest percentage of involvement by juveniles only (4.9 percent), while clearances for arson offenses had the highest percentage of involvement by juveniles only (42.2 percent).

VIOLENT CRIME

National Clearances

In 2005, 45.5 percent of violent crime offenses in the nation was cleared by arrest or exceptional means. Murder had the highest percentage of offenses cleared (62.1 percent). Law enforcement agencies also cleared 55.2 percent of aggravated assaults, 41.3 percent of forcible rapes, and 25.4 percent of robberies. (Table 25)

Regional Clearances

A comparison of clearance data by region showed that law enforcement agencies in the Northeast cleared 48.6 percent of the violent crime reported to them, followed by the South (47.1 percent), the West (44.7 percent), and the Midwest (39.9 percent). For murder, the South cleared 69.1 percent of offenses, followed by the Northeast (64.1 percent), and the Midwest and West (53.9 percent each). Forcible rape offenses were cleared 47.3 percent of the time in the Northeast, 45.4 percent of the time in the South, 38.6 percent of the time in the West, and 33.6 percent of the time in the Midwest. For robbery, the Northeast cleared 28.2 percent of offenses, followed by the South (25.7 percent), the West (25.4 percent), and the Midwest (21.7 percent). The Northeast also had the highest proportion of clearances for aggravated assault (61.1 percent), followed by the South (55.8 percent), the West (54.4 percent), and the Midwest (49.8 percent). (Table 26)

Clearances by Population Groups

Cities

In the nation's cities, law enforcement agencies collectively cleared 42.9 percent of violent crimes reported to them. The nation's smallest cities—those with under 10,000 inhabitants—had the highest percentage of violent crimes cleared (58.6 percent). Cities with 500,000 to 999,999 inhabitants had the lowest percentage of violent offenses cleared, 33.8 percent. Cities with 10,000 to 24,999 inhabitants cleared the highest percentage of their murder offenses (74.2 percent), while cities with 500,000 to 999,999 inhabitants cleared the lowest percentage of murder offenses (54.1 percent). For forcible rape, cities with under 10,000 inhabitants cleared the largest percentage of offenses at 43.8 percent; cities with 500,000 to 999,999 inhabitants cleared the lowest percentage of offenses at 35.6 percent. Cities with under 10,000 inhabitants also cleared the greatest percentage of their robbery offenses at 36.0 percent, and cities with 500,000 to 999,999 inhabitants cleared the lowest percentage of their robbery offenses at 18.9 percent. For aggravated assault, cities with under 10,000 inhabitants cleared the highest proportion of offenses (65.1 percent); cities with 500,000 to 999,999 inhabitants cleared the lowest percentage of offenses (43.0 percent). (Table 25)

Metropolitan and Nonmetropolitan Counties

Law enforcement agencies in the nation's metropolitan counties cleared 53.1 percent of their violent crimes, with 63.2 percent of murders, 45.1 percent of forcible rapes, 27.1 percent of robberies, and 61.8 percent of aggravated assaults being cleared. Agencies in nonmetropolitan counties cleared 61.6 percent of their violent crime offenses, with 76.7 percent of murders, 46.0 percent of forcible rapes, 41.7 percent of robberies, and 65.5 of aggravated assaults being cleared. (Table 25)

Clearances by Classifiction Group and Type

For forcible rape, by classification group and type, law enforcement agencies cleared 42.9 percent of assault to rape attempts and 40.3 percent of rapes by force in 2005. Cleared robbery offenses included 29.9 percent of offenses involving strong-arm tactics, 28.4 percent of offenses involving knives or other cutting instruments, 19.9 percent of offenses involving firearms, and 27.0 percent of offenses involving other weapons. For aggravated assault, agencies cleared 63.2 percent of offenses involving hands, feet, fists, etc.; 61.2 percent of offenses involving knives or other cutting instruments; 38.6 percent of offenses involving firearms; and 55.5 percent of offenses involving other weapons. (Table 27)

Clearances and Juveniles

When an individual under 18 years of age (a juvenile) is cited to appear before juvenile authorities, the incident is cleared by arrest despite the lack of a physical arrest. In addition, the UCR Program considers any clearance that involves both adults (those age 18 years or over) and juveniles as an adult clearance. Therefore, the juvenile clearance data are limited to those clearances involving juveniles only, and the figures in this publication should not be used to present a definitive picture of juvenile involvement in crime.

In 2005, 12.4 percent of violent crime clearances in the United States exclusively involved juveniles. In the nation's cities, collectively, 12.6 percent of violent crime clearances involved only juveniles, with juveniles in cities exclusively involved in 5.2 percent of murder clearances, 10.7 percent of forcible rape clearances, 15.3 percent of robbery clearances, and 12.3 percent of aggravated assault clearances. Of the nation's city population groups, cities with 25,000 to 49,999 inhabitants had the highest percentage of overall clearances for violent crime only involving juveniles (14.0 percent); cities with 1,000,000 or more inhabitants had the lowest percentage (11.0 percent). Law enforcement agencies in metropolitan counties reported that 12.5 percent of their violent crime clearances—including 4.4 of their murder clearances, 12.8 percent of their forcible rape clearances, 14.5 percent of their robbery clearances, and 12.3 percent of their aggravated assault clearances—involved only juveniles. Agencies in nonmetropolitan counties reported that 9.3 percent of their clearances for violent crime involved only juveniles, including 3.1 of their murder clearances, 14.2 percent of their forcible rape clearances, 8.6 percent of their robbery clearances, and 9.0 percent of their aggravated assault clearances. (Table 28)

PROPERTY CRIME

National Clearances

Law enforcement agencies throughout the nation collectively cleared 16.3 percent of property crime offenses in 2005, including 12.7 percent of burglary offenses, 18.0 percent of larceny-theft offenses, 13.0 percent of motor vehicle theft offenses, and 17.9 percent of arson offenses. (Table 25)

Regional Clearances

By region in 2005, agencies in the Northeast cleared the highest percentage of property crimes at 19.7 percent, followed by the South at 16.8 percent, the Midwest at 15.8 percent, and the West at 14.3 percent. Agencies in the Northeast also cleared the highest percentage of burglary offenses at 16.2 percent, followed by the South at 13.2 percent, the West at 11.6 percent, and the Midwest at 11.0 percent. For larceny-theft, the Northeast (21.5 percent) was followed by the South (18.2 percent), the Midwest (17.7 percent), and the West (16.4 percent). The South, at 15.7 percent, cleared the greatest percentage of their motor vehicle theft offenses, followed by the Northeast at 14.2 percent, the Midwest at 12.7 percent, and the West at 10.3 percent. The Northeast cleared the greatest percentage of their arson offenses (21.6 percent), followed by the South (19.1 percent), the Midwest (17.4 percent), and the West (15.5 percent). (Table 26)

Clearances by Population Group

Cities

Law enforcement agencies in cities cleared 16.2 percent of property crimes, 12.2 percent of burglaries, 18.3 percent of larceny-thefts, 11.9 percent of motor vehicle thefts, and 17.3 percent of arsons in 2005. (Table 25)

Agencies in cities with populations of 10,000 to 24,999 cleared the largest percentage of their property crimes (21.0 percent), while agencies in cities with populations of 500,000 to 999,999 cleared the smallest percentage of their property crimes (11.6 percent). For burglaries, cities with under 10,000 inhabitants cleared the largest percentage of their offenses, at 16.4 percent, while cities with 500,000 to 999,999 inhabitants cleared the smallest percentage of their offenses, at 9.2 percent. Cities with 10,000 to 24,999 inhabitants cleared the greatest percentage of their larceny-theft offenses (22.5 percent), and cities with 500,000 to 999,999 inhabitants cleared the lowest percentage of their larceny-theft offenses (13.1 percent). For motor vehicle theft and arson, cities with under 10,000 inhabitants cleared the highest percentages of their offenses, at 23.9 percent and 27.0 percent, respectively; cities with 1,000,000 or more inhabitants cleared the lowest percentages of their offenses, at 8.2 percent and 8.9 percent, respectively. (Table 25)

Metropolitan Counties and Nonmetropolitan Counties

Metropolitan county law enforcement agencies reported that 16.0 percent of their property crimes, 13.5 percent of their burglaries, 17.0 percent of their larceny-thefts, 15.5 percent of their motor vehicle thefts, and 18.0 percent of their arsons were cleared by arrest or exceptional means. Agencies in nonmetropolitan counties reported clearing 18.0 percent of their property crimes, 16.3 percent of their burglaries, 17.8 percent of their larceny-thefts, 26.0 percent of their motor vehicle thefts, and 24.7 percent of their arsons. (Table 25)

Clearances by Classification and Type

For property crime clearances grouped by classification and type, data for 2005 showed that the highest percentage of burglary clearances in the nation in 2005 (13.9 percent) were of offenses that involved unlawful entry of structures. Law enforcement agencies cleared 12.2 percent of burglaries in which force was used to enter structures and 10.5 percent of attempted burglary offenses. For motor vehicle theft, agencies cleared 13.3 percent of motor vehicle theft offenses involving automobiles, 11.1 percent of motor vehicle theft offenses involving trucks and buses, and 10.6 percent of motor vehicle theft offenses involving other vehicles. (Table 27)

Data from the 12,816 agencies that provided supplemental information concerning arsons showed that clearances occurred for 22.4 percent of structural arson offenses, 7.5 percent of mobile arson offenses, and 21.2 percent of other arsons.

Clearances and Juveniles

When an offender under 18 years of age is cited to appear in juvenile court or before other juvenile authorities, the UCR Program considers the incident for which the juvenile is being held responsible to be cleared by arrest, although a physical arrest may not have occurred. In addition, clearances that include both adult and juvenile offenders are classified as clearances for crimes committed by adults.

In 2005, 17.9 percent of property crime clearances, 15.6 percent of burglary clearances, 18.8 percent of larceny-theft clearances, 15.2 percent of motor vehicle theft clearances, and 42.2 percent of arson clearances nationwide exclusively involved juveniles. (Table 28) Clearances of juveniles for arson were proportionally higher than those for any other crime.

In cities collectively, 18.6 percent of the clearances for property crime, 15.8 percent of clearances for burglary, 19.5 percent of clearances for larceny-theft, 15.6 percent of clearances for motor vehicle theft, and 45.5 percent of clearances for arson involved juveniles only. Law enforcement agencies in metropolitan counties cleared 15.7 percent of their property crimes; nonmetropolitan counties cleared 13.3 percent of their property crimes. (Table 28)

Of clearances for structural arsons, 39.2 percent involved only juveniles. Of these structural arsons, 74.6 percent involved community or public buildings, such as churches, jails, and schools. Approximately 21.1 percent of clearances for mobile arsons and 52.6 percent of other property type arsons involved only juveniles. (Unpublished Expanded Arson Table 2; see Appendix I for more information)

Table 25. Offenses Cleared by Arrest or Exceptional Means, by Population Group, 2005

(Number, percent.)

Population group	Violent crime	Murder and non-negligent man-slaughter	Forcible rape	Robbery	Aggravated assault	Property crime	Burglary	Larceny-theft	Motor vehicle theft	Arson[1]	Number of agencies	Estimated population, 2005
ALL AGENCIES												
Offenses known	1 197 089	14 430	82 118	353 050	747 491	8 935 714	1 906 980	5 915 843	1 112 891	64 231	13 441	255 115 278
Percent cleared	45.5	62.1	41.3	25.4	55.2	16.3	12.7	18.0	13.0	17.9		
All Cities												
Offenses known	934 954	11 125	60 170	304 134	559 525	6 961 634	1 392 315	4 683 212	886 107	46 897	9 618	167 119 985
Percent cleared	42.9	60.7	39.8	24.9	52.7	16.2	12.2	18.3	11.9	17.3		
Group I (all cities 250,000 and over)												
Offenses known	408 875	5 783	19 367	156 850	226 875	2 206 861	464 882	1 326 142	415 837	18 801	67	41 685 502
Percent cleared	36.2	56.5	39.0	21.2	45.8	12.5	10.2	14.2	9.4	12.6		
1,000,000 and over												
Offenses known	127 623	1 904	5 681	53 623	66 415	669 625	135 906	394 296	139 423	6 045	8	13 896 753
Percent cleared	34.9	61.1	43.5	21.7	44.1	12.2	10.4	14.2	8.2	8.9		
500,000 to 999,999												
Offenses known	149 233	2 120	6 724	55 512	84 877	809 352	175 359	486 968	147 025	6 122	22	14 422 520
Percent cleared	33.8	54.1	35.6	18.9	43.0	11.6	9.2	13.1	9.6	16.9		
250,000 to 499,999												
Offenses known	132 019	1 759	6 962	47 715	75 583	727 884	153 617	444 878	129 389	6 634	37	13 366 229
Percent cleared	40.2	54.5	38.7	23.4	50.6	13.6	11.2	15.4	10.4	11.8		
Group II (100,000 to 249,999)												
Offenses known	158 668	1 970	9 759	53 201	93 738	1 192 615	239 579	788 916	164 120	7 603	173	25 983 746
Percent cleared	41.8	63.5	39.7	25.0	51.1	15.0	11.0	17.1	10.7	15.8		
Group III (50,000 to 99,999)												
Offenses known	133 966	1 362	9 855	40 637	82 112	1 107 071	226 543	758 923	121 605	6 596	416	28 490 290
Percent cleared	46.0	58.1	38.3	28.3	55.5	17.3	12.2	19.7	11.8	18.3		
Group IV (25,000 to 49,999)												
Offenses known	90 994	835	7 926	25 096	57 137	886 669	169 837	637 075	79 757	5 348	714	24 684 401
Percent cleared	49.7	69.2	38.9	31.2	59.0	18.7	12.7	20.6	15.5	20.0		
Group V (10,000 to 24,999)												
Offenses known	75 281	643	7 218	17 675	49 745	828 044	155 566	611 433	61 045	4 405	1 597	25 289 898
Percent cleared	54.0	74.2	42.0	33.8	62.7	21.0	15.6	22.5	19.1	26.4		
Group VI (under 10,000)												
Offenses known	67 170	532	6 045	10 675	49 918	740 374	135 908	560 723	43 743	4 144	6 651	20 986 148
Percent cleared	58.6	72.7	43.8	36.0	65.1	19.7	16.4	20.2	23.9	27.0		
Metropolitan Counties												
Offenses known	208 839	2 422	15 576	45 051	145 790	1 551 069	378 400	981 519	191 150	13 365	1 598	63 038 742
Percent cleared	53.1	63.2	45.1	27.1	61.8	16.0	13.5	17.0	15.5	18.0		
Nonmetropolitan Counties												
Offenses known	53 296	883	6 372	3 865	42 176	423 011	136 265	251 112	35 634	3 969	2 225	24 956 551
Percent cleared	61.6	76.7	46.0	41.7	65.5	18.0	16.3	17.8	26.0	24.7		
Suburban Areas[2]												
Offenses known	350 472	3 581	27 650	81 090	238 151	3 099 019	660 524	2 112 131	326 364	22 067	6 688	109 688 618
Percent cleared	52.9	65.0	43.6	29.0	61.9	17.4	13.8	18.8	15.8	20.0		

[1]Not all agencies submit reports for arson to the FBI. Thus, the number of reports used to compute the percent of offenses cleared for arson is less than the number used to compute the percent of offenses cleared for all other offenses.

[2]Suburban areas include law enforcement agencies in cities with fewer than 50,000 inhabitants and county law enforcement agencies within metropolitan statistical areas. They exclude all metropolitan agencies associated with a principal city. The agencies associated with suburban areas also appear in other groups within this table.

Table 26. Offenses Cleared by Arrest or Exceptional Means, by Region and Geographic Division, 2005

(Number, percent.)

Region	Violent crime	Murder and non-negligent man-slaughter	Forcible rape	Robbery	Aggravated assault	Property crime	Burglary	Larceny-theft	Motor vehicle theft	Arson[1]	Number of agencies	Estimated population, 2005
ALL AGENCIES												
Offenses known	1 197 089	14 430	82 118	353 050	747 491	8 935 714	1 906 980	5 915 843	1 112 891	64 231	13 441	255 115 278
Percent cleared	45.5	62.1	41.3	25.4	55.2	16.3	12.7	18.0	13.0	17.9		
Northeast												
Offenses known	148 627	1 784	9 802	52 664	84 377	1 002 214	192 139	706 196	103 879	7 063	2 807	43 165 366
Percent cleared	48.6	64.1	47.3	28.2	61.1	19.7	16.2	21.5	14.2	21.6		
New England												
Offenses known	39 578	319	3 199	11 177	24 883	302 563	60 178	210 215	32 170	1 714	791	12 887 457
Percent cleared	46.7	53.0	34.1	25.0	58.0	15.2	13.1	16.4	11.1	21.0		
Middle Atlantic												
Offenses known	109 049	1 465	6 603	41 487	59 494	699 651	131 961	495 981	71 709	5 349	2 016	30 277 909
Percent cleared	49.2	66.5	53.7	29.0	62.4	21.7	17.5	23.6	15.6	21.8		
Midwest												
Offenses known	188 682	2 274	17 901	56 478	112 029	1 596 229	328 166	1 095 967	172 096	12 963	3 285	47 290 797
Percent cleared	39.9	53.9	33.6	21.7	49.8	15.8	11.0	17.7	12.7	17.4		
East North Central												
Offenses known	119 145	1 562	11 410	40 699	65 474	965 852	210 382	643 680	111 790	8 296	1 488	28 465 120
Percent cleared	34.8	49.2	30.6	20.1	44.3	14.5	10.3	16.5	11.2	16.6		
West North Central												
Offenses known	69 537	712	6 491	15 779	46 555	630 377	117 784	452 287	60 306	4 667	1 797	18 825 677
Percent cleared	48.7	64.3	38.8	25.8	57.5	17.7	12.2	19.4	15.5	18.9		
South												
Offenses known	552 487	6 573	33 266	152 310	360 338	3 902 700	898 300	2 613 661	390 739	23 994	5 469	99 921 080
Percent cleared	47.1	69.1	45.4	25.7	55.8	16.8	13.2	18.2	15.7	19.1		
South Atlantic												
Offenses known	307 591	3 543	16 083	88 060	199 905	2 023 522	458 816	1 343 997	220 709	11 752	2 734	53 498 221
Percent cleared	48.9	67.1	49.5	26.1	58.6	17.9	15.0	19.1	16.4	20.2		
East South Central												
Offenses known	69 746	874	4 947	18 024	45 901	506 844	124 804	338 157	43 883	2 717	1 110	14 022 972
Percent cleared	45.4	69.8	37.1	25.8	53.5	16.6	12.0	18.4	16.2	19.1		
West South Central												
Offenses known	175 150	2 156	12 236	46 226	114 532	1 372 334	314 680	931 507	126 147	9 525	1 625	32 399 887
Percent cleared	44.5	72.2	43.4	24.9	51.9	15.3	11.2	16.9	14.3	17.9		
West												
Offenses known	307 293	3 799	21 149	91 598	190 747	2 434 571	488 375	1 500 019	446 177	20 211	1 880	64 738 035
Percent cleared	44.7	53.9	38.6	25.4	54.4	14.3	11.6	16.4	10.3	15.5		
Mountain												
Offenses known	85 359	1 045	7 626	20 345	56 343	781 759	155 490	500 382	125 887	4 915	749	19 061 511
Percent cleared	43.6	56.9	32.8	21.6	52.7	15.6	11.3	18.1	11.1	20.2		
Pacific												
Offenses known	221 934	2 754	13 523	71 253	134 404	1 652 812	332 885	999 637	320 290	15 296	1 131	45 676 524
Percent cleared	45.1	52.7	41.9	26.5	55.1	13.7	11.8	15.6	10.0	13.9		

[1]Not all agencies submit reports for arson to the FBI. Thus, the number of reports used to compute the percent of offenses cleared for arson is less than the number used to compute the percent of offenses cleared for all other offenses.

Table 27. Offenses Cleared by Arrest or Exceptional Means, Additional Information on Selected Offenses, by Population Group, 2005

(Number, percent.)

Population group	Forcible rape		Robbery				Aggravated assault			
	Rape by force	Assault to rape attempts	Firearm	Knife or cutting instrument	Other weapon	Strongarm	Firearm	Knife or cutting instrument	Other weapon	Hands, fists, feet, etc.
ALL AGENCIES										
Offenses known	67 493	6 222	132 031	27 935	29 011	121 805	138 849	122 687	215 803	164 511
Percent cleared	40.3	42.9	19.9	28.4	27.0	29.9	38.6	61.2	55.5	63.2
All Cities										
Offenses known	50 545	4 940	114 236	24 762	25 078	109 155	111 839	98 831	167 195	118 729
Percent cleared	39.3	42.3	19.8	27.8	26.6	29.4	35.5	59.9	53.8	62.3
Group I (all cities 250,000 and over)										
Offenses known	15 972	2 049	65 852	11 994	11 964	53 377	60 985	40 164	69 620	31 109
Percent cleared	38.4	39.0	17.2	24.0	21.3	25.3	29.6	55.4	48.4	56.4
1,000,000 and over										
Offenses known	4 856	825	25 025	5 256	4 241	19 101	21 424	13 833	21 653	9 505
Percent cleared	43.7	42.5	16.8	21.9	22.9	27.7	27.3	51.1	46.4	66.4
500,000 to 999,999										
Offenses known	5 685	688	24 149	3 775	4 367	17 058	22 362	14 611	25 572	11 358
Percent cleared	34.3	33.6	15.0	23.5	19.9	21.3	28.6	53.9	43.9	45.2
250,000 to 499,999										
Offenses known	5 431	536	16 678	2 963	3 356	17 218	17 199	11 720	22 395	10 246
Percent cleared	37.9	40.7	21.1	28.1	21.2	26.5	33.9	62.4	55.3	59.5
Group II (100,000 to 249,999)										
Offenses known	7 697	721	18 842	4 398	4 633	18 096	17 897	16 996	29 612	15 717
Percent cleared	39.1	39.4	20.3	28.5	27.0	29.5	35.7	60.1	53.5	57.9
Group III (50,000 to 99,999)										
Offenses known	8 365	615	12 659	3 609	3 455	10 053	13 217	14 753	24 876	19 069
Percent cleared	38.3	45.5	22.7	30.3	30.0	32.9	39.6	62.1	58.1	62.2
Group IV (25,000 to 49,999)										
Offenses known	6 892	517	7 570	2 235	2 516	9 848	8 130	10 218	16 733	15 811
Percent cleared	37.9	43.1	25.4	33.1	31.2	34.7	45.3	63.6	58.2	64.8
Group V (10,000 to 24,999)										
Offenses known	6 284	512	5 754	1 570	1 570	7 150	6 213	8 659	13 907	15 852
Percent cleared	41.6	45.7	27.9	37.5	40.8	37.4	53.0	65.1	61.2	68.0
Group VI (under 10,000)										
Offenses known	5 335	526	3 559	956	940	4 631	5 397	8 041	12 447	21 171
Percent cleared	42.8	50.8	28.9	36.1	42.8	39.8	55.6	67.7	61.8	68.2
Metropolitan Counties										
Offenses known	11 346	853	16 449	2 799	3 430	11 307	20 508	18 398	37 300	30 464
Percent cleared	42.3	46.1	18.8	30.8	28.7	33.4	48.0	65.9	61.3	64.8
Nonmetropolitan Counties										
Offenses known	5 602	429	1 346	374	503	1 343	6 502	5 458	11 308	15 318
Percent cleared	45.5	44.3	38.1	48.1	39.4	44.8	63.0	68.3	62.5	66.6
Suburban Areas[1]										
Offenses known	21 614	1 758	27 926	5 779	6 586	25 282	30 978	32 837	62 661	61 279
Percent cleared	41.5	47.1	21.1	31.9	32.4	34.9	48.2	65.6	61.2	66.0

[1]Suburban areas include law enforcement agencies in cities with fewer than 50,000 inhabitants and county law enforcement agencies within metropolitan statistical areas. They exclude all metropolitan agencies associated with a principal city. The agencies associated with suburban areas also appear in other groups within this table.

Table 27. Offenses Cleared by Arrest or Exceptional Means, Additional Information on Selected Offenses, by Population Group, 2005—*Continued*

(Number, percent.)

Population group	Burglary			Motor vehicle theft			Arson[2]			Number of agencies	Estimated population, 2005
	Forcible entry	Unlawful entry	Attempted forcible entry	Autos	Trucks and buses	Other vehicles	Structure	Mobile	Other		
ALL AGENCIES											
Offenses known	1 036 237	554 943	107 005	745 304	174 409	88 159	25 494	17 189	16 422	12 816	233 548 794
Percent cleared	12.2	13.9	10.5	13.3	11.1	10.6	22.4	7.5	21.2		
All Cities											
Offenses known	773 221	410 804	83 648	617 641	139 395	60 826	19 238	12 012	12 109	9 275	155 939 999
Percent cleared	11.7	13.6	10.2	12.3	10.2	9.5	21.8	6.8	21.0		
Group I (all cities 250,000 and over)											
Offenses known	285 613	114 774	25 315	281 872	80 786	26 488	7 341	6 135	3 697	60	38 622 134
Percent cleared	9.6	11.3	9.1	9.9	7.6	6.2	16.9	4.4	17.0		
1,000,000 and over											
Offenses known	92 544	36 896	6 466	93 184	37 905	8 334	2 217	2 545	1 283	8	13 896 753
Percent cleared	9.8	11.7	11.8	9.8	5.0	5.7	15.8	3.0	8.7		
500,000 to 999,999											
Offenses known	106 593	40 277	12 153	102 407	20 597	12 873	2 330	1 605	1 226	20	12 986 164
Percent cleared	8.8	9.0	7.4	9.7	9.7	4.4	23.2	6.9	21.8		
250,000 to 499,999											
Offenses known	86 476	37 601	6 696	86 281	22 284	5 281	2 794	1 985	1 188	32	11 739 217
Percent cleared	10.4	13.6	9.7	10.3	10.2	11.6	12.5	4.4	21.1		
Group II (100,000 to 249,999)											
Offenses known	127 387	65 229	13 802	112 774	22 662	8 943	3 103	1 907	1 880	153	22 995 788
Percent cleared	10.8	12.3	8.9	10.8	10.7	9.1	19.3	6.0	20.9		
Group III (50,000 to 99,999)											
Offenses known	119 718	70 579	14 884	88 349	15 423	7 927	2 636	1 572	1 913	386	26 419 259
Percent cleared	11.8	13.5	10.3	11.9	11.6	9.6	23.3	7.1	20.6		
Group IV (25,000 to 49,999)											
Offenses known	88 647	56 037	11 294	59 186	8 051	6 317	2 150	1 004	1 910	676	23 326 602
Percent cleared	11.9	14.0	10.2	15.4	16.6	11.3	23.4	9.6	21.2		
Group V (10,000 to 24,999)											
Offenses known	81 678	53 034	9 685	44 359	7 304	5 664	1 970	805	1 400	1 523	24 125 328
Percent cleared	15.5	16.6	12.1	19.5	18.2	14.9	30.2	13.4	29.1		
Group VI (under 10,000)											
Offenses known	70 178	51 151	8 668	31 101	5 169	5 487	2 038	589	1 309	6 477	20 450 888
Percent cleared	16.7	16.7	12.7	25.3	22.4	18.3	31.3	19.7	24.1		
Metropolitan Counties											
Offenses known	180 714	102 538	17 313	106 607	29 311	19 888	4 287	4 358	3 295	1 423	53 580 983
Percent cleared	12.8	14.4	11.3	15.7	12.7	11.3	23.3	7.7	20.5		
Nonmetropolitan Counties											
Offenses known	82 302	41 601	6 044	21 056	5 703	7 445	1 969	819	1 018	2 118	24 027 812
Percent cleared	16.5	15.8	13.4	28.3	25.3	17.9	26.5	16.2	25.3		
Suburban Areas[1]											
Offenses known	320 813	199 988	36 066	205 354	43 637	31 725	7 910	5 849	6 384	6 682	100 648 330
Percent cleared	13.2	14.9	11.3	16.0	13.8	12.1	25.2	8.8	22.0		

[1]Suburban areas include law enforcement agencies in cities with fewer than 50,000 inhabitants and county law enforcement agencies within metropolitan statistical areas. They exclude all metropolitan agencies associated with a principal city. The agencies associated with suburban areas also appear in other groups within this table.

[2]Not all agencies submit reports for arson to the FBI. Thus, the number of reports used to compute the percent of offenses cleared for arson is less than the number used to compute the percent of offenses cleared for all other offenses.

Table 28. Percent of Clearances Involving Persons Under 18 Years of Age, by Population Group, 2005

(Number, percent.)

Population group	Violent crime	Murder and non-negligent man-slaughter	Forcible rape	Robbery	Aggravated assault	Property crime	Burglary	Larceny-theft	Motor vehicle theft	Arson[1]	Number of agencies	Estimated population, 2005
ALL AGENCIES												
Total clearances	452 474	7 720	28 864	75 689	340 201	1 258 838	206 502	929 087	123 249	10 444	12 523	226 239 464
Percent under 18 years	12.4	4.9	11.4	15.1	12.0	17.9	15.6	18.8	15.2	42.2		
All Cities												
Total clearances	346 499	5 848	21 168	65 784	253 699	1 006 002	148 963	763 999	93 040	7 508	9 087	151 688 470
Percent under 18 years	12.6	5.2	10.7	15.3	12.3	18.6	15.8	19.5	15.6	45.5		
Group I (all cities 250,000 and over)												
Total clearances	125 020	2 740	6 563	28 770	86 947	241 619	40 691	166 378	34 550	2 055	58	37 271 309
Percent under 18 years	11.3	5.9	7.8	15.2	10.5	16.2	13.9	16.7	16.2	45.6		
1,000,000 and over												
Total clearances	44 544	1 164	2 473	11 632	29 275	81 431	14 179	55 802	11 450	538	8	13 896 753
Percent under 18 years	11.0	6.1	8.2	15.0	9.8	14.4	11.5	15.4	13.3	40.1		
500,000 to 999,999												
Total clearances	36 104	740	1 813	7 513	26 038	73 189	11 771	50 142	11 276	827	18	11 635 339
Percent under 18 years	11.7	6.4	7.2	15.4	11.1	16.1	14.7	15.9	18.0	51.4		
250,000 to 499,999												
Total clearances	44 372	836	2 277	9 625	31 634	86 999	14 741	60 434	11 824	690	32	11 739 217
Percent under 18 years	11.3	5.1	7.9	15.3	10.5	18.0	15.7	18.7	17.4	42.9		
Group II (100,000 to 249,999)												
Total clearances	56 155	1 077	3 218	11 431	40 429	152 277	22 355	114 985	14 937	1 110	149	22 382 393
Percent under 18 years	12.4	5.4	9.9	15.7	11.9	19.6	16.1	20.7	16.2	47.0		
Group III (50,000 to 99,999)												
Total clearances	53 935	711	3 348	10 016	39 860	169 971	24 376	132 863	12 732	1 132	378	25 953 754
Percent under 18 years	13.7	4.4	12.1	16.3	13.3	20.8	15.7	22.2	15.8	47.2		
Group IV (25,000 to 49,999)												
Total clearances	39 868	511	2 812	6 801	29 744	150 274	19 190	120 184	10 900	1 007	662	22 887 459
Percent under 18 years	14.0	4.9	12.4	16.7	13.7	20.4	17.2	21.4	15.9	49.9		
Group V (10,000 to 24,999)												
Total clearances	35 334	442	2 741	5 270	26 881	156 919	21 791	124 793	10 335	1 121	1 460	23 184 349
Percent under 18 years	13.5	4.8	13.0	13.1	13.8	18.4	15.8	19.2	14.1	44.7		
Group VI (under 10,000)												
Total clearances	36 187	367	2 486	3 496	29 838	134 942	20 560	104 796	9 586	1 083	6 380	20 009 206
Percent under 18 years	13.6	1.6	13.3	13.6	13.8	17.2	17.8	17.4	13.7	38.8		
Metropolitan Counties												
Total clearances	77 740	1 257	5 065	8 529	62 889	185 194	37 918	125 432	21 844	2 013	1 378	51 626 291
Percent under 18 years	12.5	4.4	12.8	14.5	12.3	15.7	15.6	16.0	14.1	37.1		
Nonmetropolitan Counties												
Total clearances	28 235	615	2 631	1 376	23 613	67 642	19 621	39 656	8 365	923	2 058	22 924 703
Percent under 18 years	9.3	3.1	14.2	8.6	9.0	13.3	13.9	12.9	13.6	26.0		
Suburban Areas[2]												
Total clearances	141 465	1 965	9 544	18 184	111 772	444 658	72 835	330 764	41 059	3 918	6 517	97 257 307
Percent under 18 years	13.5	4.3	13.1	15.3	13.4	17.4	16.6	18.0	14.0	42.7		

[1]Not all agencies submit reports for arson to the FBI. Thus, the number of reports used to compute the percent of offenses cleared for arson is less than the number used to compute the percent of offenses cleared for all other offenses.

[2]Suburban areas include law enforcement agencies in cities with fewer than 50,000 inhabitants and county law enforcement agencies within metropolitan statistical areas. They exclude all metropolitan agencies associated with a principal city. The agencies associated with suburban areas also appear in other groups within this table.

SECTION IV:
PERSONS ARRESTED

PERSONS ARRESTED

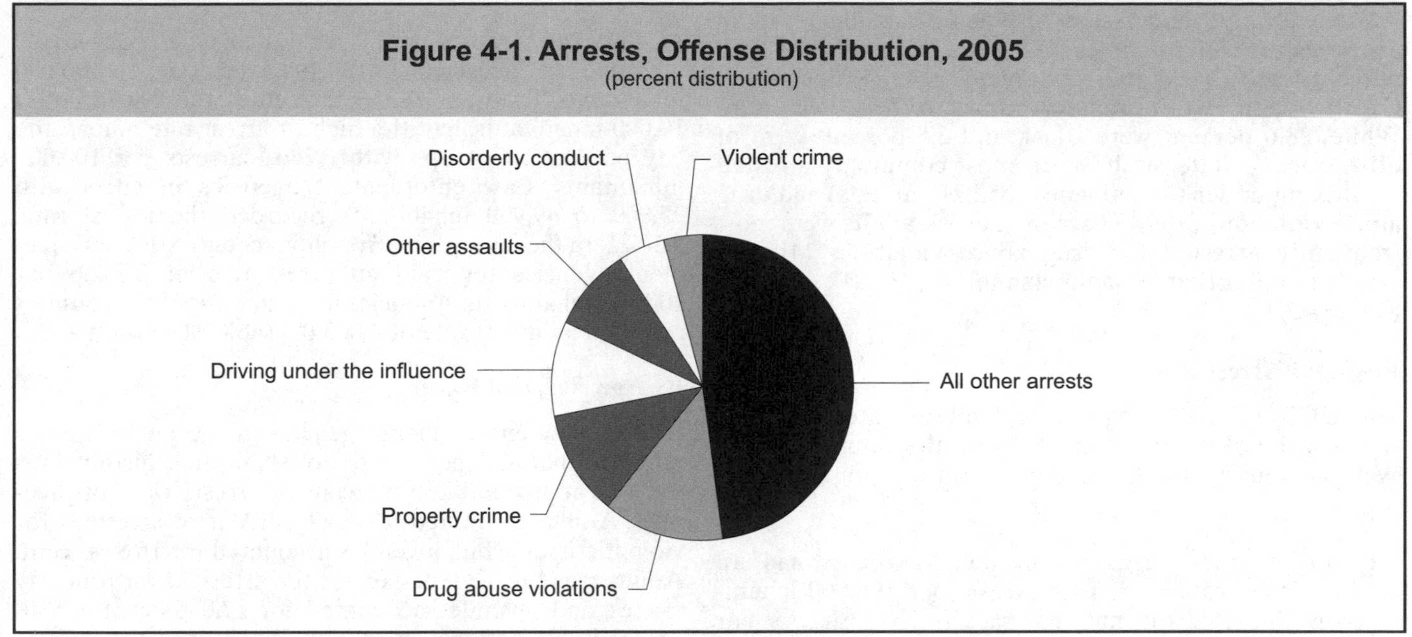

In the Uniform Crime Reporting (UCR) Program, one arrest is counted for each separate instance in which an individual is arrested, cited, or summoned for criminal acts in Part I and Part II crimes. (See Appendix II for additional information concerning Part I and Part II crimes.) One person may be arrested multiple times during the year; as a result, the arrest figures in this section should not be taken as the total number of individuals arrested. Instead, it provides the number of arrest occurrences reported by law enforcement. Information regarding the UCR Program's statistical methodology and table construction can be found in Appendix I.

National Volume, Trends, and Rates

In 2005, the UCR Program estimated that there were over 14 million (14,094,186) arrests in the United States for all criminal offenses (except traffic violations). Law enforcement made an estimated 1.6 million arrests (11.4 percent of all arrests) for property crimes and 603,503 arrests (4.3 percent of all arrests) for violent crimes. More arrests were made for drug abuse violations (an estimated 1.8 million arrests and 13.1 percent of all arrests) than for any other offense. (Table 29)

The estimated overall arrest rate of in the nation in 2005 was 4,761.6 arrests per 100,000 inhabitants. Arrests for violent crimes were measured at a rate of 204.8 arrests per 100,000 inhabitants; for property crimes, the arrest rate was 549.1. (Table 30)

A comparison of arrest figures from 2004 to 2005 revealed a 0.2 percent increase. Arrests for violent crimes rose 1.7 percent, while arrests for property crimes fell 2.9 percent during the 2-year period. An examination of the 5-year and 10-year arrest trends showed that the total number of arrests in 2005 rose 3.4 percent from the 2001 total. Arrests for violent crimes showed a 0.5 percent decrease from 2001 to 2005, while property crimes showed a 1.0 percent increase. In the 10-year trend data (1996 to 2005), the number of arrests showed a steeper decline (4.4 percent). For property crimes, the number of arrests fell 22.1 percent, but while arrests for violent crimes fell 12.2 percent. (Tables 32, 34, and 36)

By Age, Sex, and Race

Law enforcement agencies that contributed arrest data to the UCR Program reported information on the age, sex, and race of the persons they arrested. According to the 2005 data, adults accounted for 84.7 percent of arrestees nationally. (Table 38)

A review of arrest data by age from 2004 to 2005 showed that arrests of adults increased 0.9 percent during this period. Arrests of adults for property crimes fell 0.9 percent, while arrests of adults for violent crimes increased 1.6 percent over the same time span. In contrast to the 2-year arrest trend of adults, the arrest total for juveniles (those under 18 years of age) in 2005 decreased 3.1 percent from the 2004 figure. However, over the same 2-year period, arrests of juveniles for violent crimes rose 2.0 percent; juvenile arrests property crimes dropped 8.1 percent. (Table 36)

By gender, 76.2 percent of arrests in 2005 were of males. Males accounted for 82.1 percent of the total number of arrestees for violent crimes and 68.0 percent of the total number of arrestees for property crimes. Females accounted for 23.8 percent of all arrestees, 17.9 percent of violent crime arrestees, and 32.0 percent of property crime arrestees. (Table 42)

A review of the 2005 arrest data by race indicated that 69.8 percent of arrestees were White, 27.8 percent were Black, and 2.3 percent were of other races (American Indian or Alaskan Native and Asian or Pacific Islander). Of all arrestees for violent crimes, 59.0 percent were White, 38.8 percent were Black, and 2.3 percent were of other races. Of all arrestees for property crimes, 68.8 percent were White, 28.6 percent were Black and 2.5 percent were of other races. White adults were most commonly arrested for driving under the influence (852,211 arrests) and drug abuse violations (765,438 arrests). Black adults were most frequently arrested for drug abuse violations (410,299 arrests) and other assaults (simple) (233,912 arrests). (Table 43)

Regional Arrest Rates

The UCR Program divides the United States into four regions: the Northeast, the Midwest, the South, and the West. (Appendix III provides more information about the regions.)

Law enforcement agencies in the Northeast had an overall arrest rate of 3,761.9 arrests per 100,000 inhabitants, well below the national rate (4,761.6 arrests per 100,000 inhabitants). In this region, the arrest rate for violent crimes was 169.6 arrests per 100,000 inhabitants, and for property crime, the arrest rate was 432.8 arrests per 100,000 inhabitants. In the Midwest, law enforcement agencies reported an arrest rate of 4,782.3 arrests per 100,000 inhabitants. The arrest rate for violent crimes was 169.8 and the arrest rate for property crime was 538.4. Law enforcement agencies in the South, the nation's most populous region, reported an arrest rate of 5,435.7 per 100,000 inhabitants. Arrests for violent crime occurred at a rate of 200.0 arrests per 100,000 residents, and for property crime, the arrest rate was 600.8 arrests per 100,000 inhabitants. In the Western states, law enforcement agencies reported an overall arrest rate of 4,640.3 arrests per 100,000 inhabitants. The region's violent crime arrest rate was 255.4, while its property crime arrest rate was 573.0. (Table 30)

Population Groups: Trends and Rates

The national UCR Program aggregates data by various population groups, which include cities, metropolitan counties, and nonmetropolitan counties. A definition of these groups can be found in Appendix III. The total number of arrests in U.S. cities fell 0.2 percent from 2004 to 2005. The number of arrests for property crimes fell 3.3 percent during the 2-year time frame; however, arrests for violent crimes in cities increased 2.3 percent. (Table 44)

In 2005, law enforcement agencies in cities collectively recorded an arrest rate of 5,194.5 arrests per 100,000 inhabitants. The nation's smallest cities, those with under 10,000 inhabitants, had the highest arrest rate among the city population groups with 6,246.3 arrests per 100,000 inhabitants. Law enforcement agencies in cities with 25,000 to 49,999 inhabitants recorded the lowest rate, 4,582.1. In the nation's metropolitan counties, law enforcement agencies reported an arrest rate of 3,752.6 per 100,000 inhabitants. Agencies in nonmetropolitan counties reported an arrest rate of 4,003.0. (Table 31)

By Age, Sex, and Race

In 2005, law enforcement agencies in the nation's cities reported that 83.2 percent of arrests in their jurisdictions were of adults and 16.8 percent of arrests were of juveniles. Adults accounted for 83.2 percent of arrestees for violent crimes, while juveniles accounted for 16.8 percent. Adults made up 73.0 percent of the arrestees for property crimes, and juveniles accounted for 27.0 percent. Of all arrests in the nation's cities in 2005, 46.0 percent were of individuals under 25 years of age. In metropolitan counties, 88.2 percent of arrests were of adults, and 11.8 percent of arrests were of juveniles. In nonmetropolitan counties, 8.8 percent of persons arrested were adults and 91.2 percent were juveniles. (Tables 46, 47, 53, and 59)

A breakdown of arrests by gender showed that males accounted for 75.9 percent and females accounted for 24.1 percent of arrestees in the nation's cities in 2005. In both metropolitan and nonmetropolitan counties, males composed 77.0 percent and females composed 23.0 percent of all arrestees. (Tables 48, 54, and 60)

By race, 67.3 percent of arrestees in the Nation's cities in 2005 were White, 30.2 percent were Black, and 2.5 percent were of other races (American Indian or Alaska Native and Asian or Pacific Islander). Whites accounted for 75.2 percent of arrestees in metropolitan counties in 2005, Blacks made up 23.5 percent of arrestees, and persons of other races made up 1.3 percent of the total. In nonmetropolitan counties, Whites made up 82.4 percent of arrestees, Blacks accounted for 13.6 percent of arrestees, and other races made up 4.0 percent of the total. (Tables 49, 55, and 61)

VIOLENT CRIME

Of the estimated 603,503 arrests for violent crime in the United States in 2005, 449,297 (74.4 percent) were for aggravated assault, 114,616 (19.0 percent) were for robbery, 25,528 (4.2 percent) were for forcible rape, and 14,062 (2.3 percent) were for murder. (Table 29)

Arrest Trends

A look at 2-year, 5-year, and 10-year trend data showed that the number of arrests for violent crime increased 1.7 percent from 2004 to 2005, decreased 0.5 percent from 2001 to 2005, and declined 12.2 percent from 1996 to 2005. The number of adults arrested for violent crime (arrestees age 18 years and over) increased 1.6 percent from 2004 to 2005, decreased 0.6 percent from 2001 to 2005, and decreased 9.3 percent from 1996 to 2005. The number of juveniles arrested for violent crime (arrestees under 18 years of age) increased 2.0 percent from 2004 to 2005, decreased 0.3 percent from 2001 to 2005, and decreased 25.2 percent from 1996 to 2005. (Tables 32, 34, and 36)

The trend data for murder showed that the number of arrests for this offense increased 7.3 percent from 2004 to 2005, increased 7.5 percent from 2001 to 2005, and decreased 16.5 percent from 1996 to 2005. The number of adults arrested for murder rose 6.2 percent from 2004 to 2005, rose 6.8 percent from 2001 to 2005, and fell 11.3 percent from 1996 to 2005. The number of juveniles arrested for murder rose 19.9 percent from 2004 to 2005, rose 15.7 percent from 2001 to 2005, and fell 46.8 percent from 1996 to 2005. (Tables 32, 34, and 36)

For forcible rape, the 2-year trend data showed that arrests declined 2.9 percent from 2004 to 2005, with adult arrests dropping 1.3 percent and juvenile arrests dropping 11.3 percent. The 5-year trend data showed that arrests declined 5.2 percent from 2001 to 2005; adult arrests dropped 3.1 percent and juvenile arrests declined 15.3 percent during this period. The 10-year trend data showed that forcible rape arrests dropped 19.3 percent from 1996 to 2005, with adult arrests falling 18.1 percent and juvenile arrests falling 25.3 percent. (Tables 32, 34, and 36)

For robbery, the 2-year trend data showed that arrests increased 3.4 percent from 2004 to 2005, with adult arrests rising 1.1 percent and juvenile arrests increasing 11.4 percent. The 5-year trend data showed that total robbery arrests rose 6.2 percent from 2001 to 2005; adult arrests rose 4.1 percent and juvenile arrests rose 13.5 percent during this period. The 10-year trend data showed that arrests dropped 16.2 percent from 1996 to 2005, with adult arrests dropping 8.3 percent and juvenile arrests dropping 33.7 percent. (Tables 32, 34, and 36)

The aggravated assault trend data showed that the number of arrests for this offense rose 1.4 percent from 2004 to 2005, fell 2.0 percent from 2001 to 2005, and fell 10.6 percent from 1996 to 2005. The number of adults arrested for aggravated assault percent increased 1.8 percent from 2004 to 2005, declined 1.5 percent from 2001 to 2005, and declined 9.0 percent from 1996 to 2005. The number of juveniles arrested for aggravated assault dropped 0.8 percent from 2004 to 2005, dropped 4.6 percent from 2001 to 2005, and dropped 19.9 percent from 1996 to 2005. (Tables 32, 34, and 36)

Arrest Rates

Law enforcement agencies throughout the nation reported 204.8 violent crime arrests, 4.7 murder arrests, 8.6 forcible rape arrests, 39.2 robbery arrests, and 152.2 aggravated assault arrests per 100,000 inhabitants in 2005. By region, agencies reported violent crime arrest rates of 169.6 in the Northeast, 169.8 in the Midwest, 200.0 in the South, and 255.4 in the West. The regional murder arrest rates were 3.2 in the Northeast, 3.8 in the Midwest, 6.2 in the South, and 4.7 in the West. For forcible rape, the regional arrest rates were 8.0 in the Northeast, 9.8 in the Midwest, 9.5 in the South, and 7.3 in the West. Regional arrest rates for robbery were 43.7 in the Northeast, 33.0 in the Midwest, 39.7 in the South, and 39.9 in the West. For aggravated assault, the regional arrest rates were 114.7 in the Northeast, 123.2 in the Midwest, 144.6 in the South, and 203.6 in the West. (Table 30)

By population group, law enforcement agencies in the nation's cities collectively reported 230.2 violent crime arrests per 100,000 inhabitants in 2005. In the city population groups, cities with 250,000 or more inhabitants reported the highest violent crime arrest rate (323.9) and cities with 10,000 to 24,999 inhabitants reported the lowest violent crime arrest rate (154.7). (Table 31)

By Age, Sex, and Race

In 2005, most arrestees for violent crime (84.2 percent) were over 18 years of age. By sex, males accounted for 82.1 percent of arrestees for violent crime, 89.0 percent of arrestees for murder, 98.5 percent of arrestees for forcible rape, 88.9 percent of arrestees for robbery, and 79.2 percent of arrestees for aggravated assault. Females accounted for 17.9 percent of violent crime arrestees, 11.0 percent of murder arrestees, 1.5 percent of forcible rape arrestees, 11.1 percent of robbery arrestees, and 20.8 percent of aggravated assault arrestees. (Tables 38 and 42)

By race, 59.0 percent of arrestees for violent crime were White, 38.8 percent were Black, and 2.3 percent were of other races (American Indian or Alaska Native and Asian or Pacific Islander). For murder, 49.1 percent of arresteeswere White, 48.6 percent were Black, and 2.3 percent were of other races. For forcible rape, 65.1 percent of arrestees were White, 32.7 percent were Black, and 2.2 percent were of other races. For robbery, 42.2 percent of arrestees were White, 56.3 percent of arrestees were Black, and 1.5 percent were of other races. For aggravated assault, 63.3 percent of arrestees were White, 34.3 percent of arrestees were Black, and 2.4 percent were of other races. (Table 43)

PROPERTY CRIME

Of the estimated 1,609,327 arrests for property crimes in 2005, 1,146,696 (71.3 percent) were for larceny-theft, 298,835 (18.6 percent) were for burglary, 147,459 (9.2 percent) were for motor vehicle theft, and 16,337 (1.0 percent) were for arson. (Table 29)

Arrest Trends

The 2-year, 5-year, and 10-year trend data showed that the number of arrests for property crime dropped 2.9 percent from 2004 to 2005, increased 1.0 percent from 2001 to 2005, and declined 22.1 percent from 1996 to 2005. The number of adults arrested for property crime offenses (arrestees age 18 years and over) decreased 0.9 percent from 2004 to 2005, increased 8.4 percent from 2001 to 2005, and decreased 9.5 percent from 1996 to 2005. The number of juveniles arrested for property crime (arrestees under 18 years of age) dropped 8.1 percent from 2004 to 2005, decreased 15.3 percent from 2001 to 2005, and decreased 43.8 percent from 1996 to 2005. (Tables 32, 34, and 36)

The trend data for burglary showed that the number of arrests for this offense increased 0.6 percent from 2004 to 2005, increased 5.5 percent from 2001 to 2005, and decreased 18.0 percent from 1996 to 2005. The number of adults arrested for burglary rose 2.9 percent from 2004 to 2005, rose 13.9 percent from 2001 to 2005, and fell 1.5 percent from 1996 to 2005. The number of juveniles arrested for burglary fell 5.1 percent from 2004 to 2005, decreased 12.9 percent from 2001 to 2005, and fell 44.4 percent from 1996 to 2005. (Tables 32, 34, and 36)

For larceny-theft, the 2-year trend data showed that arrests dropped 3.9 percent from 2004 to 2005, with adult arrests decreasing 2.0 percent and juvenile arrests dropping 8.9 percent. The 5-year trend data showed that total larceny-theft arrests declined less than one-tenth of percent from 2001 to 2005; adult arrests increased 6.6 percent and juvenile arrests declined 14.9 percent during this period. The 10-year trend data showed that larceny-theft arrests dropped 23.6 percent from 1996 to 2005, with adult arrests falling 13.1 percent and juvenile arrests falling 42.7 percent. (Tables 32, 34, and 36)

For motor vehicle theft, the 2-year trend data showed that arrests declined 2.1 percent from 2004 to 2005, with adult arrests increasing 0.5 percent and juvenile arrests decreasing 9.3 percent. The 5-year trend data showed that total motor vehicle theft arrests rose 1.4 percent from 2001 to 2005; adult arrests rose 13.4 percent and juvenile arrests fell 24.3 percent during this period. The 10-year trend data showed that arrests dropped 18.1 percent from 1996 to 2005, with juvenile arrests dropping 54.0 percent. However, adult arrests increased 8.8 percent during this period. (Tables 32, 34, and 36)

The arson trend data showed that the number of arrests for this offense increased 3.5 percent from 2004 to 2005, fell 8.2 percent from 2001 to 2005, and fell 16.2 percent from 1996 to 2005. The number of adults arrested for arson rose 5.9 percent from 2004 to 2005, declined 4.2 percent from 2001 to 2005, and declined 5.7 percent from 1996 to 2005. The number of juveniles arrested for arson increased 1.2 percent from 2004 to 2005, dropped 11.7 percent from 2001 to 2005, and dropped 24.5 percent from 1996 to 2005. (Tables 32, 34, and 36)

Arrest Rates

Law enforcement agencies throughout the nation reported 549.1 property crime arrests, 101.2 burglary arrests, 392.6 larceny-theft arrests, 49.7 motor vehicle theft arrests, and 5.5 arson arrests per 100,000 inhabitants in 2005. By region, agencies reported property crime arrest rates of 432.8 in the Northeast, 538.4 in the Midwest, 600.8 in the South, and 573.0 in the West. The regional burglary arrest rates were 75.3 in the Northeast, 79.0 in the Midwest, 112.3 in the South, and 120.2 in the West. For larceny-theft, the regional arrest rates were 325.2 in the Northeast, 400.5 in the Midwest, 445.3 in the South, and 372.3 in the West. Regional arrest rates for motor vehicle theft were 27.1 in the Northeast, 53.9 in the Midwest, 37.7 in the South, and 74.5 in the West. For arson, the regional arrest rates were 5.2 in the Northeast, 5.0 in the Midwest, 5.6 in the South, and 6.0 in the West. (Table 30)

By population group, law enforcement agencies in the nation's cities collectively reported 648.8 property crime arrests per 100,000 inhabitants in 2005. (Table 31)

By Age, Sex, and Race

In 2005, most arrestees for property crime (74.0 percent) were over 18 years of age. By sex, males accounted for 68 percent of arrestees for property crime, 85.5 percent of arrestees for burglary, 61.4 percent of arrestees for larceny-theft, 82.4 percent of arrestees for motor vehicle theft, and 83.4 percent of arrestees for arson. Females accounted for 32.0 percent of property crime arrestees, 14.5 percent of burglary arrestees, 38.6 percent of larceny-theft arrestees, 17.6 percent of motor vehicle theft arrestees, and 16.6 percent of arson arrestees. (Tables 38 and 42)

By race, 68.8 percent of arrestees for property crime were White, 28.6 percent were Black, and 2.5 percent were of other races (American Indian or Alaska Native and Asian or Pacific Islander). For burglary, 69.6 percent of arrestees were White, 28.5 percent were Black, and 1.9 percent were of other races. For larceny-theft, 69.3 percent of arrestees were White, 28.0 percent were Black, and 2.7 percent were of other races. For motor vehicle theft, 62.8 percent of arrestees were White, 34.8 percent of arrestees were Black, and 2.3 percent were of other races. For arson, 76.6 percent of arrestees were White, 21.2 percent of arrestees were Black, and 2.3 percent were of other races. (Table 43)

Table 29. Estimated Number of Arrests, 2005

(Number.)

Offense	Arrests
Total[1]	14 094 186
Violent crime	603 503
Murder and nonnegligent manslaughter	14 062
Forcible rape	25 528
Robbery	114 616
Aggravated assault	449 297
Property crime	1 609 327
Burglary	298 835
Larceny-theft	1 146 696
Motor vehicle theft	147 459
Arson	16 337
Other assaults	1 301 392
Forgery and counterfeiting	118 455
Fraud	321 521
Embezzlement	18 970
Stolen property; buying, receiving, and possessing	133 856
Vandalism	279 562
Weapons; carrying and possessing, etc.	193 469
Prostitution and commercialized vice	84 891
Sex offenses, except forcible rape and prostitution	91 625
Drug abuse violations	1 846 351
Gambling	11 180
Offenses against the family and children	129 128
Driving under the influence	1 371 919
Liquor laws	597 838
Drunkenness	556 167
Disorderly conduct	678 231
Vagrancy	33 227
All other offenses, except traffic	3 863 785
Suspicion	3 764
Curfew and loitering law violations	140 835
Runaways	108 954

[1]Does not include suspicion.

Table 30. Arrests, by Geographic Region, 2005

(Number, rate per 100,000 population.)

Offense	United States (10,974 agencies; population 217,722,329)		Northeast (2,675 agencies; population 40,559,934)		Midwest (2,510 agencies; population 42,539,925)		South (4,115 agencies; population 70,401,054)		West (1,674 agencies; population 64,221,416)	
	Total	Rate	Total	Rate	Total	Rate	Total	Rate	Total	Rate
Total[1]	10 367 072	4 761.6	1 525 807	3 761.9	2 034 396	4 782.3	3 826 789	5 435.7	2 980 080	4 640.3
Violent crime	445 846	204.8	68 790	169.6	72 221	169.8	140 805	200.0	164 030	255.4
Murder and nonnegligent manslaughter	10 335	4.7	1 305	3.2	1 621	3.8	4 388	6.2	3 021	4.7
Forcible rape	18 733	8.6	3 226	8.0	4 184	9.8	6 666	9.5	4 657	7.3
Robbery	85 309	39.2	17 737	43.7	14 027	33.0	27 936	39.7	25 609	39.9
Aggravated assault	331 469	152.2	46 522	114.7	52 389	123.2	101 815	144.6	130 743	203.6
Property crime	1 195 560	549.1	175 541	432.8	229 055	538.4	422 975	600.8	367 989	573.0
Burglary	220 391	101.2	30 551	75.3	33 600	79.0	79 035	112.3	77 205	120.2
Larceny-theft	854 856	392.6	131 882	325.2	170 377	400.5	313 490	445.3	239 107	372.3
Motor vehicle theft	108 301	49.7	10 989	27.1	22 945	53.9	26 539	37.7	47 828	74.5
Arson	12 012	5.5	2 119	5.2	2 133	5.0	3 911	5.6	3 849	6.0
Other assaults	958 477	440.2	150 353	370.7	184 713	434.2	399 246	567.1	224 165	349.1
Forgery and counterfeiting	87 346	40.1	12 624	31.1	13 984	32.9	37 328	53.0	23 410	36.5
Fraud	231 721	106.4	34 093	84.1	34 501	81.1	140 271	199.2	22 856	35.6
Embezzlement	14 097	6.5	1 186	2.9	1 975	4.6	7 526	10.7	3 410	5.3
Stolen property; buying, receiving, and possessing	99 173	45.6	17 383	42.9	19 942	46.9	27 175	38.6	34 673	54.0
Vandalism	206 351	94.8	41 028	101.2	43 166	101.5	54 172	76.9	67 985	105.9
Weapons; carrying and possessing, etc.	142 878	65.6	18 682	46.1	24 755	58.2	50 062	71.1	49 379	76.9
Prostitution and commercialized vice	62 663	28.8	8 005	19.7	13 698	32.2	16 618	23.6	24 342	37.9
Sex offenses, except forcible rape and prostitution	67 072	30.8	11 046	27.2	13 096	30.8	18 935	26.9	23 995	37.4
Drug abuse violations	1 357 841	623.7	201 493	496.8	244 073	573.8	467 610	664.2	444 665	692.4
Gambling	8 101	3.7	908	2.2	3 710	8.7	2 545	3.6	938	1.5
Offenses against the family and children	93 172	42.8	22 420	55.3	23 924	56.2	32 409	46.0	14 419	22.5
Driving under the influence	997 338	458.1	133 116	328.2	227 267	534.2	294 074	417.7	342 881	533.9
Liquor laws	437 923	201.1	52 069	128.4	152 210	357.8	115 753	164.4	117 891	183.6
Drunkenness	412 930	189.7	32 470	80.1	32 585	76.6	243 432	345.8	104 443	162.6
Disorderly conduct	501 129	230.2	118 973	293.3	140 448	330.2	161 144	228.9	80 564	125.4
Vagrancy	24 372	11.2	4 222	10.4	1 271	3.0	9 476	13.5	9 403	14.6
All other offenses, except traffic	2 837 806	1 303.4	378 494	933.2	527 586	1 240.2	1 130 317	1 605.5	801 409	1 247.9
Suspicion	2 747	1.3	151	0.4	424	1.0	1 838	2.6	334	0.5
Curfew and loitering law violations	104 054	47.8	34 930	86.1	13 719	32.2	23 444	33.3	31 961	49.8
Runaways	81 222	37.3	7 981	19.7	16 497	38.8	31 472	44.7	25 272	39.4

[1]Does not include suspicion.

Table 31. Arrests, by Population Group, 2005

(Number, rate per 100,000 population.)

Offense	Total (10,974 agencies; population 217,722,329)		Cities: Total cities (7,911 cities; population 148,665,653)		Cities: Group I (54 cities, 250,000 and over; population 38,667,664)		Cities: Group II (148 cities, 100,000 to 249,999; population 22,470,281)		Cities: Group III (366 cities, 50,000 to 99,999; population 25,128,823)		Cities: Group IV (640 cities, 25,000 to 49,999; population 22,131,570)	
	Total	Rate	Total	Rate	Total	Rate	Total	Rate	Total	Rate	Total	Rate
Total[1]	10 367 072	4 761.6	7 722 488	5 194.5	2 124 271	5 493.7	1 131 790	5 036.8	1 238 300	4 927.8	1 014 090	4 582.1
Violent crime	445 846	204.8	342 217	230.2	125 252	323.9	59 355	264.1	53 887	214.4	38 624	174.5
Murder and nonnegligent manslaughter	10 335	4.7	7 379	5.0	3 340	8.6	1 508	6.7	930	3.7	644	2.9
Forcible rape	18 733	8.6	13 193	8.9	3 953	10.2	2 009	8.9	1 990	7.9	1 746	7.9
Robbery	85 309	39.2	72 073	48.5	30 543	79.0	13 174	58.6	11 216	44.6	7 396	33.4
Aggravated assault	331 469	152.2	249 572	167.9	87 416	226.1	42 664	189.9	39 751	158.2	28 838	130.3
Property crime	1 195 560	549.1	964 499	648.8	257 976	667.2	156 382	696.0	170 148	677.1	135 150	610.7
Burglary	220 391	101.2	159 661	107.4	43 844	113.4	28 009	124.6	28 415	113.1	19 511	88.2
Larceny-theft	854 856	392.6	712 539	479.3	171 679	444.0	114 309	508.7	129 828	516.6	107 490	485.7
Motor vehicle theft	108 301	49.7	83 941	56.5	40 592	105.0	12 897	57.4	10 295	41.0	6 891	31.1
Arson	12 012	5.5	8 358	5.6	1 861	4.8	1 167	5.2	1 610	6.4	1 258	5.7
Other assaults	958 477	440.2	710 869	478.2	187 180	484.1	116 033	516.4	112 767	448.8	96 598	436.5
Forgery and counterfeiting	87 346	40.1	64 874	43.6	14 762	38.2	9 253	41.2	11 253	44.8	9 897	44.7
Fraud	231 721	106.4	120 631	81.1	16 272	42.1	13 639	60.7	19 629	78.1	17 562	79.4
Embezzlement	14 097	6.5	10 341	7.0	1 838	4.8	1 886	8.4	2 251	9.0	1 668	7.5
Stolen property; buying, receiving, and possessing	99 173	45.6	75 620	50.9	21 642	56.0	12 550	55.9	13 998	55.7	10 546	47.7
Vandalism	206 351	94.8	160 608	108.0	39 338	101.7	23 747	105.7	26 187	104.2	22 304	100.8
Weapons; carrying and possessing, etc.	142 878	65.6	112 585	75.7	40 712	105.3	18 862	83.9	17 163	68.3	12 709	57.4
Prostitution and commercialized vice	62 663	28.8	59 411	40.0	42 477	109.9	8 266	36.8	4 838	19.3	2 574	11.6
Sex offenses, except forcible rape and prostitution	67 072	30.8	47 261	31.8	17 894	46.3	6 369	28.3	7 209	28.7	5 327	24.1
Drug abuse violations	1 357 841	623.7	1 025 810	690.0	367 968	951.6	154 703	688.5	154 090	613.2	115 265	520.8
Gambling	8 101	3.7	6 969	4.7	5 012	13.0	488	2.2	524	2.1	236	1.1
Offenses against the family and children	93 172	42.8	42 192	28.4	5 048	13.1	5 621	25.0	8 372	33.3	6 870	31.0
Driving under the influence	997 338	458.1	629 620	423.5	125 904	325.6	78 605	349.8	92 655	368.7	91 105	411.7
Liquor laws	437 923	201.1	348 779	234.6	51 940	134.3	41 817	186.1	55 965	222.7	44 757	202.2
Drunkenness	412 930	189.7	349 468	235.1	74 107	191.7	56 789	252.7	58 086	231.2	49 682	224.5
Disorderly conduct	501 129	230.2	430 347	289.5	99 720	257.9	54 137	240.9	67 930	270.3	54 348	245.6
Vagrancy	24 372	11.2	20 815	14.0	11 965	30.9	1 751	7.8	2 846	11.3	1 672	7.6
All other offenses, except traffic	2 837 806	1 303.4	2 038 271	1 371.0	546 409	1 413.1	293 097	1 304.4	331 624	1 319.7	281 209	1 270.6
Suspicion	2 747	1.3	1 208	0.8	0	0.0	184	0.8	159	0.6	159	0.7
Curfew and loitering law violations	104 054	47.8	99 936	67.2	56 754	146.8	6 432	28.6	13 879	55.2	7 146	32.3
Runaways	81 222	37.3	61 365	41.3	14 101	36.5	12 008	53.4	12 999	51.7	8 841	39.9

[1]Does not include suspicion.

Table 31. Arrests, by Population Group, 2005—*Continued*

(Number, rate per 100,000 population.)

Offense	Cities				Counties				Suburban area[3] (5,928 agencies; population 96,092,270)	
	Group V (1,418 cities, 10,000 to 24,999; population 22,456,518)		Group VI (5,285 cities, under 10,000; population 17,810,797)		Metropolitan counties[2] (1,225 agencies; population 47,831,303)		Nonmetropolitan counties (1,838 agencies; population 21,225,373)			
	Total	Rate	Total	Rate	Total	Rate	Total	Rate	Total	Rate
Total[1]	1 101 524	4 905.1	1 112 513	6 246.3	1 794 929	3 752.6	849 655	4 003.0	4 064 164	4 229.4
Violent crime	34 746	154.7	30 353	170.4	76 891	160.8	26 738	126.0	152 125	158.3
Murder and nonnegligent manslaughter	531	2.4	426	2.4	2 011	4.2	945	4.5	3 086	3.2
Forcible rape	1 800	8.0	1 695	9.5	3 526	7.4	2 014	9.5	7 065	7.4
Robbery	5 973	26.6	3 771	21.2	11 077	23.2	2 159	10.2	24 422	25.4
Aggravated assault	26 442	117.7	24 461	137.3	60 277	126.0	21 620	101.9	117 552	122.3
Property crime	138 342	616.0	106 501	598.0	169 285	353.9	61 776	291.0	436 872	454.6
Burglary	21 175	94.3	18 707	105.0	40 365	84.4	20 365	95.9	81 652	85.0
Larceny-theft	109 064	485.7	80 169	450.1	108 150	226.1	34 167	161.0	317 087	330.0
Motor vehicle theft	6 889	30.7	6 377	35.8	18 274	38.2	6 086	28.7	32 926	34.3
Arson	1 214	5.4	1 248	7.0	2 496	5.2	1 158	5.5	5 207	5.4
Other assaults	99 677	443.9	98 614	553.7	168 453	352.2	79 155	372.9	368 110	383.1
Forgery and counterfeiting	10 423	46.4	9 286	52.1	14 944	31.2	7 528	35.5	34 552	36.0
Fraud	23 848	106.2	29 681	166.6	70 881	148.2	40 209	189.4	115 295	120.0
Embezzlement	1 629	7.3	1 069	6.0	2 653	5.5	1 103	5.2	5 524	5.7
Stolen property; buying, receiving, and possessing	9 343	41.6	7 541	42.3	17 045	35.6	6 508	30.7	38 651	40.2
Vandalism	25 118	111.9	23 914	134.3	31 202	65.2	14 541	68.5	80 480	83.8
Weapons; carrying and possessing, etc.	11 166	49.7	11 973	67.2	22 277	46.6	8 016	37.8	49 537	51.6
Prostitution and commercialized vice	642	2.9	614	3.4	3 067	6.4	185	0.9	6 550	6.8
Sex offenses, except forcible rape and prostitution	5 344	23.8	5 118	28.7	12 431	26.0	7 380	34.8	23 541	24.5
Drug abuse violations	114 734	510.9	119 050	668.4	228 042	476.8	103 989	489.9	485 119	504.8
Gambling	235	1.0	474	2.7	620	1.3	512	2.4	1 304	1.4
Offenses against the family and children	8 884	39.6	7 397	41.5	35 523	74.3	15 457	72.8	50 259	52.3
Driving under the influence	115 714	515.3	125 637	705.4	233 753	488.7	133 965	631.2	471 481	490.7
Liquor laws	61 646	274.5	92 654	520.2	50 876	106.4	38 268	180.3	183 381	190.8
Drunkenness	53 649	238.9	57 155	320.9	40 311	84.3	23 151	109.1	145 410	151.3
Disorderly conduct	73 551	327.5	80 661	452.9	44 432	92.9	26 350	124.1	189 368	197.1
Vagrancy	790	3.5	1 791	10.1	3 288	6.9	269	1.3	6 371	6.6
All other offenses, except traffic	295 091	1 314.1	290 841	1 632.9	550 036	1 149.9	249 499	1 175.5	1 169 912	1 217.5
Suspicion	413	1.8	293	1.6	1 353	2.8	186	0.9	1 958	2.0
Curfew and loitering law violations	8 462	37.7	7 263	40.8	3 414	7.1	704	3.3	20 435	21.3
Runaways	8 490	37.8	4 926	27.7	15 505	32.4	4 352	20.5	29 887	31.1

[1]Does not include suspicion.
[2]Includes only metropolitan county law enforcement agencies.
[3]Suburban areas include law enforcement agencies in cities with fewer than 50,000 inhabitants and county law enforcement agencies within metropolitan statistical areas. They exclude all metropolitan agencies associated with a principal city. The agencies associated with suburban areas also appear in other groups within this table.

Table 32. Arrests, Ten-Year Trends, by Age, 1996 and 2005

(Number, percent change; 8,009 total agencies; 1996 estimated population 159,290,470; 2005 estimated population 178,017,991.)

Offense	Total, all ages			Under 18 years			18 years and over		
	1996	2005	Percent change	1996	2005	Percent change	1996	2005	Percent change
Total[1]	8 619 699	8 244 321	-4.4	1 703 500	1 278 948	-24.9	6 916 199	6 965 373	0.7
Violent crime	424 694	372 962	-12.2	76 032	56 889	-25.2	348 662	316 073	-9.3
Murder and nonnegligent manslaughter	9 564	7 989	-16.5	1 388	739	-46.8	8 176	7 250	-11.3
Forcible rape	18 745	15 129	-19.3	3 202	2 392	-25.3	15 543	12 737	-18.1
Robbery	80 980	67 841	-16.2	25 318	16 791	-33.7	55 662	51 050	-8.3
Aggravated assault	315 405	282 003	-10.6	46 124	36 967	-19.9	269 281	245 036	-9.0
Property crime	1 238 677	965 442	-22.1	453 872	254 899	-43.8	784 805	710 543	-9.5
Burglary	220 798	180 973	-18.0	85 248	47 416	-44.4	135 550	133 557	-1.5
Larceny-theft	905 963	692 593	-23.6	319 161	182 813	-42.7	586 802	509 780	-13.1
Motor vehicle theft	100 318	82 160	-18.1	42 957	19 755	-54.0	57 361	62 405	8.8
Arson	11 598	9 716	-16.2	6 506	4 915	-24.5	5 092	4 801	-5.7
Other assaults	756 129	737 475	-2.5	137 850	142 957	3.7	618 279	594 518	-3.8
Forgery and counterfeiting	72 103	70 738	-1.9	5 433	2 600	-52.1	66 670	68 138	2.2
Fraud	255 162	193 539	-24.2	6 947	4 779	-31.2	248 215	188 760	-24.0
Embezzlement	10 152	12 087	19.1	880	751	-14.7	9 272	11 336	22.3
Stolen property; buying, receiving, and possessing	91 832	82 771	-9.9	26 647	13 902	-47.8	65 185	68 869	5.7
Vandalism	190 069	168 366	-11.4	87 907	63 697	-27.5	102 162	104 669	2.5
Weapons; carrying and possessing, etc.	123 016	112 054	-8.9	31 067	26 834	-13.6	91 949	85 220	-7.3
Prostitution and commercialized vice	48 936	41 641	-14.9	723	870	20.3	48 213	40 771	-15.4
Sex offenses, except forcible rape and prostitution	56 484	52 410	-7.2	10 620	10 437	-1.7	45 864	41 973	-8.5
Drug abuse violations	830 684	1 034 844	24.6	117 400	106 150	-9.6	713 284	928 694	30.2
Gambling	6 352	3 446	-45.7	563	395	-29.8	5 789	3 051	-47.3
Offenses against the family and children	84 459	72 623	-14.0	4 839	3 067	-36.6	79 620	69 556	-12.6
Driving under the influence	877 727	816 243	-7.0	11 000	10 550	-4.1	866 727	805 693	-7.0
Liquor laws	364 792	348 974	-4.3	95 686	76 756	-19.8	269 106	272 218	1.2
Drunkenness	446 767	335 730	-24.9	14 821	9 094	-38.6	431 946	326 636	-24.4
Disorderly conduct	420 232	379 439	-9.7	112 697	116 422	3.3	307 535	263 017	-14.5
Vagrancy	16 424	17 376	5.8	1 998	1 395	-30.2	14 426	15 981	10.8
All other offenses, except traffic	2 062 908	2 269 707	10.0	264 418	220 050	-16.8	1 798 490	2 049 657	14.0
Suspicion	4 025	2 569	-36.2	1 453	360	-75.2	2 572	2 209	-14.1
Curfew and loitering law violations	119 407	87 658	-26.6	119 407	87 658	-26.6	X	X	X
Runaways	122 693	68 796	-43.9	122 693	68 796	-43.9	X	X	X

[1]Does not include suspicion.
X = Not applicable.

Table 33. Arrests, Ten-Year Trends, by Age and Sex, 1996 and 2005

(Number, percent change; 8,009 total agencies; 1996 estimated population 159,290,470; 2005 estimated population 178,017,991.)

Offense	Male						Female					
	Total			Under 18 years			Total			Under 18 years		
	1996	2005	Percent change	1996	2005	Percent change	1996	2005	Percent change	1996	2005	Percent change
Total[1]	6 773 900	6 261 672	-7.6	1 258 168	897 305	-28.7	1 845 799	1 982 649	7.4	445 332	381 643	-14.3
Violent crime	360 745	306 214	-15.1	64 377	46 426	-27.9	63 949	66 748	4.4	11 655	10 463	-10.2
Murder and nonnegligent manslaughter	8 572	7 114	-17.0	1 290	664	-48.5	992	875	-11.8	98	75	-23.5
Forcible rape	18 512	14 924	-19.4	3 153	2 332	-26.0	233	205	-12.0	49	60	22.4
Robbery	73 192	60 096	-17.9	22 962	15 118	-34.2	7 788	7 745	-0.6	2 356	1 673	-29.0
Aggravated assault	260 469	224 080	-14.0	36 972	28 312	-23.4	54 936	57 923	5.4	9 152	8 655	-5.4
Property crime	886 798	651 352	-26.6	330 753	167 587	-49.3	351 879	314 090	-10.7	123 119	87 312	-29.1
Burglary	195 124	153 888	-21.1	76 490	41 672	-45.5	25 674	27 085	5.5	8 758	5 744	-34.4
Larceny-theft	595 297	421 828	-29.1	212 281	105 513	-50.3	310 666	270 765	-12.8	106 880	77 300	-27.7
Motor vehicle theft	86 405	67 522	-21.9	36 188	16 172	-55.3	13 913	14 638	5.2	6 769	3 583	-47.1
Arson	9 972	8 114	-18.6	5 794	4 230	-27.0	1 626	1 602	-1.5	712	685	-3.8
Other assaults	597 763	554 044	-7.3	99 610	95 555	-4.1	158 366	183 431	15.8	38 240	47 402	24.0
Forgery and counterfeiting	45 250	43 068	-4.8	3 388	1 768	-47.8	26 853	27 670	3.0	2 045	832	-59.3
Fraud	137 874	104 201	-24.4	4 536	3 065	-32.4	117 288	89 338	-23.8	2 411	1 714	-28.9
Embezzlement	5 545	5 979	7.8	486	419	-13.8	4 607	6 108	32.6	394	332	-15.7
Stolen property; buying, receiving, and possessing	78 156	66 459	-15.0	23 140	11 540	-50.1	13 676	16 312	19.3	3 507	2 362	-32.6
Vandalism	163 890	139 529	-14.9	78 226	54 939	-29.8	26 179	28 837	10.2	9 681	8 758	-9.5
Weapons; carrying and possessing, etc.	113 685	103 184	-9.2	28 657	24 052	-16.1	9 331	8 870	-4.9	2 410	2 782	15.4
Prostitution and commercialized vice	20 524	14 615	-28.8	303	202	-33.3	28 412	27 026	-4.9	420	668	59.0
Sex offenses, except forcible rape and prostitution	52 296	48 112	-8.0	9 829	9 437	-4.0	4 188	4 298	2.6	791	1 000	26.4
Drug abuse violations	688 006	832 707	21.0	100 568	86 895	-13.6	142 678	202 137	41.7	16 832	19 255	14.4
Gambling	5 541	2 942	-46.9	528	378	-28.4	811	504	-37.9	35	17	-51.4
Offenses against the family and children	68 211	55 393	-18.8	3 089	1 894	-38.7	16 248	17 230	6.0	1 750	1 173	-33.0
Driving under the influence	745 658	658 705	-11.7	9 191	8 187	-10.9	132 069	157 538	19.3	1 809	2 363	30.6
Liquor laws	286 425	255 746	-10.7	66 537	49 116	-26.2	78 367	93 228	19.0	29 149	27 640	-5.2
Drunkenness	391 721	284 892	-27.3	12 156	6 999	-42.4	55 046	50 838	-7.6	2 665	2 095	-21.4
Disorderly conduct	324 503	279 714	-13.8	83 418	78 552	-5.8	95 729	99 725	4.2	29 279	37 870	29.3
Vagrancy	12 893	13 752	6.7	1 654	1 082	-34.6	3 531	3 624	2.6	344	313	-9.0
All other offenses, except traffic	1 651 922	1 751 008	6.0	201 228	159 156	-20.9	410 986	518 699	26.2	63 190	60 894	-3.6
Suspicion	3 209	2 211	-31.1	1 118	254	-77.3	816	358	-56.1	335	106	-68.4
Curfew and loitering law violations	84 194	61 069	-27.5	84 194	61 069	-27.5	35 213	26 589	-24.5	35 213	26 589	-24.5
Runaways	52 300	28 987	-44.6	52 300	28 987	-44.6	70 393	39 809	-43.4	70 393	39 809	-43.4

[1]Does not include suspicion.

Table 34. Arrests, Five-Year Trends, by Age, 2001 and 2005

(Number, percent change; 8,815 total agencies; 2001 estimated population 178,385,937; 2005 estimated population 185,294,195.)

Offense	Total, all ages			Under 18 years			18 years and over		
	2001	2005	Percent change	2001	2005	Percent change	2001	2005	Percent change
Total[1]	8 288 959	8 573 824	3.4	1 385 876	1 303 278	-6.0	6 903 083	7 270 546	5.3
Violent crime	375 575	373 631	-0.5	56 909	56 742	-0.3	318 666	316 889	-0.6
Murder and nonnegligent manslaughter	7 605	8 176	7.5	629	728	15.7	6 976	7 448	6.8
Forcible rape	16 327	15 483	-5.2	2 762	2 340	-15.3	13 565	13 143	-3.1
Robbery	63 773	67 748	6.2	14 495	16 445	13.5	49 278	51 303	4.1
Aggravated assault	287 870	282 224	-2.0	39 023	37 229	-4.6	248 847	244 995	-1.5
Property crime	993 208	1 003 251	1.0	309 409	262 047	-15.3	683 799	741 204	8.4
Burglary	179 626	189 547	5.5	56 207	48 941	-12.9	123 419	140 606	13.9
Larceny-theft	720 880	720 730	0.0	221 373	188 291	-14.9	499 507	532 439	6.6
Motor vehicle theft	81 860	83 025	1.4	26 007	19 675	-24.3	55 853	63 350	13.4
Arson	10 842	9 949	-8.2	5 822	5 140	-11.7	5 020	4 809	-4.2
Other assaults	790 255	808 673	2.3	143 353	156 493	9.2	646 902	652 180	0.8
Forgery and counterfeiting	71 796	71 517	-0.4	3 807	2 629	-30.9	67 989	68 888	1.3
Fraud	213 970	197 736	-7.6	5 506	4 779	-13.2	208 464	192 957	-7.4
Embezzlement	13 706	12 763	-6.9	1 317	796	-39.6	12 389	11 967	-3.4
Stolen property; buying, receiving, and possessing	75 415	83 855	11.2	16 633	13 963	-16.1	58 782	69 892	18.9
Vandalism	167 182	171 439	2.5	66 826	64 660	-3.2	100 356	106 779	6.4
Weapons; carrying and possessing, etc.	95 711	114 538	19.7	21 702	26 844	23.7	74 009	87 694	18.5
Prostitution and commercialized vice	39 139	43 308	10.7	687	841	22.4	38 452	42 467	10.4
Sex offenses, except forcible rape and prostitution	52 520	50 378	-4.1	10 945	9 733	-11.1	41 575	40 645	-2.2
Drug abuse violations	919 547	1 062 638	15.6	117 577	109 552	-6.8	801 970	953 086	18.8
Gambling	4 396	3 661	-16.7	312	426	36.5	4 084	3 235	-20.8
Offenses against the family and children	87 150	78 901	-9.5	5 652	3 401	-39.8	81 498	75 500	-7.4
Driving under the influence	847 303	829 098	-2.1	12 289	10 699	-12.9	835 014	818 399	-2.0
Liquor laws	386 431	358 417	-7.2	88 779	76 849	-13.4	297 652	281 568	-5.4
Drunkenness	412 931	373 325	-9.6	13 363	10 570	-20.9	399 568	362 755	-9.2
Disorderly conduct	359 245	367 634	2.3	102 717	117 123	14.0	256 528	250 511	-2.3
Vagrancy	15 720	19 886	26.5	1 532	3 202	109.0	14 188	16 684	17.6
All other offenses, except traffic	2 201 664	2 396 884	8.9	240 466	219 638	-8.7	1 961 198	2 177 246	11.0
Suspicion	2 240	2 386	6.5	786	295	-62.5	1 454	2 091	43.8
Curfew and loitering law violations	80 326	80 029	-0.4	80 326	80 029	-0.4	X	X	X
Runaways	85 769	72 262	-15.7	85 769	72 262	-15.7	X	X	X

[1]Does not include suspicion.
X = Not applicable.

Table 35. Arrests, Five-Year Trends, by Age and Sex, 2001 and 2005

(Number, percent change; 8,815 total agencies; 2001 estimated population 178,385,937; 2005 estimated population 185,294,195.)

Offense	Male						Female					
	Total, all ages			Under 18 years			Total, all ages			Under 18 years		
	2001	2005	Percent change	2001	2005	Percent change	2001	2005	Percent change	2001	2005	Percent change
Total[1]	6 399 891	6 506 200	1.7	986 957	913 169	-7.5	1 889 068	2 067 624	9.5	398 919	390 109	-2.2
Violent crime	310 781	306 511	-1.4	46 544	46 256	-0.6	64 794	67 120	3.6	10 365	10 486	1.2
Murder and nonnegligent manslaughter	6 585	7 250	10.1	563	649	15.3	1 020	926	-9.2	66	79	19.7
Forcible rape	16 145	15 300	-5.2	2 724	2 306	-15.3	182	183	0.5	38	34	-10.5
Robbery	57 233	60 085	5.0	13 223	14 875	12.5	6 540	7 663	17.2	1 272	1 570	23.4
Aggravated assault	230 818	223 876	-3.0	30 034	28 426	-5.4	57 052	58 348	2.3	8 989	8 803	-2.1
Property crime	686 811	676 647	-1.5	210 738	172 047	-18.4	306 397	326 604	6.6	98 671	90 000	-8.8
Burglary	154 572	160 826	4.0	49 339	43 043	-12.8	25 054	28 721	14.6	6 868	5 898	-14.1
Larceny-theft	454 670	439 286	-3.4	134 816	108 418	-19.6	266 210	281 444	5.7	86 557	79 873	-7.7
Motor vehicle theft	68 342	68 145	-0.3	21 393	16 116	-24.7	13 518	14 880	10.1	4 614	3 559	-22.9
Arson	9 227	8 390	-9.1	5 190	4 470	-13.9	1 615	1 559	-3.5	632	670	6.0
Other assaults	603 381	606 705	0.6	98 286	104 432	6.3	186 874	201 968	8.1	45 067	52 061	15.5
Forgery and counterfeiting	42 879	43 241	0.8	2 424	1 792	-26.1	28 917	28 276	-2.2	1 383	837	-39.5
Fraud	114 367	105 797	-7.5	3 597	3 061	-14.9	99 603	91 939	-7.7	1 909	1 718	-10.0
Embezzlement	6 913	6 255	-9.5	752	442	-41.2	6 793	6 508	-4.2	565	354	-37.3
Stolen property; buying, receiving, and possessing	61 656	67 082	8.8	13 839	11 610	-16.1	13 759	16 773	21.9	2 794	2 353	-15.8
Vandalism	140 283	141 823	1.1	58 080	55 657	-4.2	26 899	29 616	10.1	8 746	9 003	2.9
Weapons; carrying and possessing, etc.	87 988	105 428	19.8	19 453	23 991	23.3	7 723	9 110	18.0	2 249	2 853	26.9
Prostitution and commercialized vice	14 185	13 883	-2.1	219	191	-12.8	24 954	29 425	17.9	468	650	38.9
Sex offenses, except forcible rape and prostitution	49 210	47 050	-4.4	10 145	8 981	-11.5	3 310	3 328	0.5	800	752	-6.0
Drug abuse violations	752 614	854 368	13.5	98 127	89 890	-8.4	166 933	208 270	24.8	19 450	19 662	1.1
Gambling	3 797	3 081	-18.9	299	408	36.5	599	580	-3.2	13	18	38.5
Offenses against the family and children	67 753	60 033	-11.4	3 586	2 050	-42.8	19 397	18 868	-2.7	2 066	1 351	-34.6
Driving under the influence	704 313	670 011	-4.9	10 099	8 322	-17.6	142 990	159 087	11.3	2 190	2 377	8.5
Liquor laws	293 767	264 279	-10.0	59 822	49 449	-17.3	92 664	94 138	1.6	28 957	27 400	-5.4
Drunkenness	356 632	317 209	-11.1	10 549	8 094	-23.3	56 299	56 116	-0.3	2 814	2 476	-12.0
Disorderly conduct	270 901	269 402	-0.6	71 782	78 232	9.0	88 344	98 232	11.2	30 935	38 891	25.7
Vagrancy	12 495	15 612	24.9	1 218	2 319	90.4	3 225	4 274	32.5	314	883	181.2
All other offenses, except traffic	1 728 473	1 844 968	6.7	176 706	159 130	-9.9	473 191	551 916	16.6	63 760	60 508	-5.1
Suspicion	1 694	2 084	23.0	508	218	-57.1	546	302	-44.7	278	77	-72.3
Curfew and loitering law violations	55 839	56 266	0.8	55 839	56 266	0.8	24 487	23 763	-3.0	24 487	23 763	-3.0
Runaways	34 853	30 549	-12.3	34 853	30 549	-12.3	50 916	41 713	-18.1	50 916	41 713	-18.1

[1]Does not include suspicion.

Table 36. Arrest Trends, by Age, 2004 and 2005

(Number, percent change; 9,869 total agencies; 2004 estimated population 193,248,637; 2005 estimated population 194,973,254.)

Offense	Total, all ages			Under 15 years			Under 18 years			18 years and over		
	2004	2005	Percent change	2004	2005	Percent change	2004	2005	Percent change	2004	2005	Percent change
Total[1]	8 975 704	8 997 831	0.2	451 098	417 492	-7.4	1 403 555	1 360 641	-3.1	7 572 149	7 637 190	0.9
Violent crime	362 701	368 812	1.7	17 350	17 049	-1.7	54 733	55 853	2.0	307 968	312 959	1.6
Murder and nonnegligent manslaughter	7 698	8 259	7.3	72	71	-1.4	593	711	19.9	7 105	7 548	6.2
Forcible rape	16 485	16 004	-2.9	1 050	867	-17.4	2 743	2 434	-11.3	13 742	13 570	-1.3
Robbery	63 691	65 841	3.4	3 319	3 462	4.3	14 099	15 713	11.4	49 592	50 128	1.1
Aggravated assault	274 827	278 708	1.4	12 909	12 649	-2.0	37 298	36 995	-0.8	237 529	241 713	1.8
Property crime	1 081 721	1 050 692	-2.9	109 689	95 228	-13.2	301 174	276 804	-8.1	780 547	773 888	-0.9
Burglary	193 032	194 273	0.6	18 667	16 715	-10.5	53 508	50 756	-5.1	139 524	143 517	2.9
Larceny-theft	794 116	763 239	-3.9	82 359	70 698	-14.2	220 493	200 866	-8.9	573 623	562 373	-2.0
Motor vehicle theft	84 554	82 811	-2.1	5 469	4 633	-15.3	22 012	19 960	-9.3	62 542	62 851	0.5
Arson	10 019	10 369	3.5	3 194	3 182	-0.4	5 161	5 222	1.2	4 858	5 147	5.9
Other assaults	838 946	843 739	0.6	68 546	65 257	-4.8	160 251	158 891	-0.8	678 695	684 848	0.9
Forgery and counterfeiting	80 636	76 353	-5.3	503	324	-35.6	3 312	2 792	-15.7	77 324	73 561	-4.9
Fraud	217 421	209 228	-3.8	909	881	-3.1	5 089	4 991	-1.9	212 332	204 237	-3.8
Embezzlement	12 613	12 820	1.6	39	47	20.5	739	797	7.8	11 874	12 023	1.3
Stolen property; buying, receiving, and possessing	85 034	86 393	1.6	4 327	3 827	-11.6	15 616	14 635	-6.3	69 418	71 758	3.4
Vandalism	179 999	180 332	0.2	30 146	28 456	-5.6	68 840	68 010	-1.2	111 159	112 322	1.0
Weapons; carrying and possessing, etc.	107 676	115 803	7.5	9 010	9 253	2.7	25 062	26 859	7.2	82 614	88 944	7.7
Prostitution and commercialized vice	41 761	40 686	-2.6	102	99	-2.9	859	759	-11.6	40 902	39 927	-2.4
Sex offenses, except forcible rape and prostitution	53 672	52 464	-2.3	6 005	5 318	-11.4	11 610	10 573	-8.9	42 062	41 891	-0.4
Drug abuse violations	1 054 785	1 097 989	4.1	20 648	19 044	-7.8	117 095	114 888	-1.9	937 690	983 101	4.8
Gambling	3 758	3 450	-8.2	66	84	27.3	324	398	22.8	3 434	3 052	-11.1
Offenses against the family and children	81 769	83 428	2.0	1 273	1 096	-13.9	3 734	3 463	-7.3	78 035	79 965	2.5
Driving under the influence	926 335	904 976	-2.3	280	205	-26.8	13 003	11 824	-9.1	913 332	893 152	-2.2
Liquor laws	408 373	392 438	-3.9	9 177	8 180	-10.9	88 603	86 328	-2.6	319 770	306 110	-4.3
Drunkenness	381 585	374 847	-1.8	1 422	1 264	-11.1	11 470	10 576	-7.8	370 115	364 271	-1.6
Disorderly conduct	414 172	416 240	0.5	56 253	53 780	-4.4	132 445	131 174	-1.0	281 727	285 066	1.2
Vagrancy	17 154	17 413	1.5	976	1 027	5.2	3 135	3 173	1.2	14 019	14 240	1.6
All other offenses, except traffic	2 484 175	2 531 124	1.9	68 157	63 253	-7.2	245 043	239 249	-2.4	2 239 132	2 291 875	2.4
Suspicion	1 514	1 710	12.9	119	76	-36.1	410	337	-17.8	1 104	1 373	24.4
Curfew and loitering law violations	60 682	62 171	2.5	17 730	17 645	-0.5	60 682	62 171	2.5	X	X	X
Runaways	80 736	76 433	-5.3	28 490	26 175	-8.1	80 736	76 433	-5.3	X	X	X

[1]Does not include suspicion.
X = Not applicable.

Table 37. Arrest Trends, by Age and Sex, 2004 and 2005

(Number, percent change; 9,869 total agencies; 2004 estimated population 193,248,637; 2005 estimated population 194,973,254.)

Offense	Male						Female					
	Total, all ages			Under 18 years			Total, all ages			Under 18 years		
	2004	2005	Percent change	2004	2005	Percent change	2004	2005	Percent change	2004	2005	Percent change
Total[1]	6 804 493	6 810 923	0.1	975 521	949 070	-2.7	2 171 211	2 186 908	0.7	428 034	411 571	-3.8
Violent crime	298 249	303 078	1.6	44 588	45 595	2.3	64 452	65 734	2.0	10 145	10 258	1.1
Murder and nonnegligent manslaughter	6 766	7 308	8.0	534	638	19.5	932	951	2.0	59	73	23.7
Forcible rape	16 223	15 797	-2.6	2 669	2 382	-10.8	262	207	-21.0	74	52	-29.7
Robbery	56 576	58 357	3.1	12 768	14 264	11.7	7 115	7 484	5.2	1 331	1 449	8.9
Aggravated assault	218 684	221 616	1.3	28 617	28 311	-1.1	56 143	57 092	1.7	8 681	8 684	0.0
Property crime	729 891	706 862	-3.2	197 358	181 503	-8.0	351 830	343 830	-2.3	103 816	95 301	-8.2
Burglary	164 985	165 487	0.3	47 135	44 861	-4.8	28 047	28 786	2.6	6 373	5 895	-7.5
Larceny-theft	486 722	464 908	-4.5	127 742	115 818	-9.3	307 394	298 331	-2.9	92 751	85 048	-8.3
Motor vehicle theft	69 725	67 721	-2.9	17 974	16 279	-9.4	14 829	15 090	1.8	4 038	3 681	-8.8
Arson	8 459	8 746	3.4	4 507	4 545	0.8	1 560	1 623	4.0	654	677	3.5
Other assaults	630 965	633 168	0.3	106 844	106 036	-0.8	207 981	210 571	1.2	53 407	52 855	-1.0
Forgery and counterfeiting	48 227	45 891	-4.8	2 142	1 885	-12.0	32 409	30 462	-6.0	1 170	907	-22.5
Fraud	116 223	111 433	-4.1	3 187	3 176	-0.3	101 198	97 795	-3.4	1 902	1 815	-4.6
Embezzlement	6 184	6 301	1.9	453	450	-0.7	6 429	6 519	1.4	286	347	21.3
Stolen property; buying, receiving, and possessing	68 849	69 105	0.4	12 981	12 143	-6.5	16 185	17 288	6.8	2 635	2 492	-5.4
Vandalism	149 852	149 341	-0.3	58 953	58 543	-0.7	30 147	30 991	2.8	9 887	9 467	-4.2
Weapons; carrying and possessing, etc.	98 976	106 595	7.7	22 415	24 148	7.7	8 700	9 208	5.8	2 647	2 711	2.4
Prostitution and commercialized vice	13 237	12 896	-2.6	252	169	-32.9	28 524	27 790	-2.6	607	590	-2.8
Sex offenses, except forcible rape and prostitution	50 157	49 297	-1.7	10 667	9 696	-9.1	3 515	3 167	-9.9	943	877	-7.0
Drug abuse violations	848 607	880 766	3.8	95 060	93 769	-1.4	206 178	217 223	5.4	22 035	21 119	-4.2
Gambling	3 138	2 859	-8.9	306	381	24.5	620	591	-4.7	18	17	-5.6
Offenses against the family and children	62 114	63 097	1.6	2 307	2 076	-10.0	19 655	20 331	3.4	1 427	1 387	-2.8
Driving under the influence	750 943	728 842	-2.9	10 242	9 192	-10.3	175 392	176 134	0.4	2 761	2 632	-4.7
Liquor laws	301 585	287 331	-4.7	57 195	55 239	-3.4	106 788	105 107	-1.6	31 408	31 089	-1.0
Drunkenness	324 364	317 481	-2.1	8 822	8 063	-8.6	57 221	57 366	0.3	2 648	2 513	-5.1
Disorderly conduct	305 263	306 679	0.5	89 050	88 170	-1.0	108 909	109 561	0.6	43 395	43 004	-0.9
Vagrancy	13 511	13 660	1.1	2 225	2 298	3.3	3 643	3 753	3.0	910	875	-3.8
All other offenses, except traffic	1 910 357	1 942 440	1.7	176 673	172 737	-2.2	573 818	588 684	2.6	68 370	66 512	-2.7
Suspicion	1 173	1 363	16.2	307	253	-17.6	341	347	1.8	103	84	-18.4
Curfew and loitering law violations	40 652	41 889	3.0	40 652	41 889	3.0	20 030	20 282	1.3	20 030	20 282	1.3
Runaways	33 149	31 912	-3.7	33 149	31 912	-3.7	47 587	44 521	-6.4	47 587	44 521	-6.4

[1]Does not include suspicion.

Table 38. Arrests, Distribution by Age, 2005

(Number, percent; 10,974 total agencies; 2005 estimated population 217,722,329.)

Offense	Total, all ages	Under 15 years	Under 18 years	18 years and over	Under 10 years	10–12 years	13–14 years	15 years	16 years	17 years
Total	10 369 819	479 926	1 582 068	8 787 751	13 710	101 751	364 465	316 362	374 605	411 175
Total percent distribution[1]	100.0	4.6	15.3	84.7	0.1	1.0	3.5	3.1	3.6	4.0
Violent crime	445 846	21 606	70 482	375 364	642	4 743	16 221	13 904	16 789	18 183
Violent crime percent distribution[1]	100.0	4.8	15.8	84.2	0.1	1.1	3.6	3.1	3.8	4.1
Murder and nonnegligent manslaughter	10 335	97	929	9 406	0	10	87	149	239	444
Forcible rape	18 733	1 055	2 888	15 845	12	284	759	490	588	755
Robbery	85 309	4 986	21 515	63 794	73	751	4 162	4 640	5 712	6 177
Aggravated assault	331 469	15 468	45 150	286 319	557	3 698	11 213	8 625	10 250	10 807
Property crime	1 195 560	106 381	310 887	884 673	3 103	24 200	79 078	63 415	69 610	71 481
Property crime percent distribution[1]	100.0	8.9	26.0	74.0	0.3	2.0	6.6	5.3	5.8	6.0
Burglary	220 391	19 135	57 506	162 885	697	4 343	14 095	11 798	12 756	13 817
Larceny-theft	854 856	77 340	219 881	634 975	2 014	18 052	57 274	44 014	48 718	49 809
Motor vehicle theft	108 301	6 443	27 666	80 635	79	699	5 665	6 593	7 396	7 234
Arson	12 012	3 463	5 834	6 178	313	1 106	2 044	1 010	740	621
Other assaults	958 477	74 377	182 578	775 899	2 296	19 176	52 905	36 274	37 426	34 501
Forgery and counterfeiting	87 346	370	3 096	84 250	18	57	295	415	829	1 482
Fraud	231 721	1 033	5 882	225 839	72	140	821	800	1 521	2 528
Embezzlement	14 097	49	856	13 241	3	12	34	35	255	517
Stolen property; buying, receiving, and possessing	99 173	4 202	16 501	82 672	82	722	3 398	3 313	4 279	4 707
Vandalism	206 351	31 925	76 817	129 534	1 690	8 746	21 489	14 450	15 465	14 977
Weapons; carrying and possessing, etc.	142 878	11 246	33 069	109 809	336	2 642	8 268	6 439	7 284	8 100
Prostitution and commercialized vice	62 663	163	1 204	61 459	11	10	142	177	322	542
Sex offenses, except forcible rape and prostitution	67 072	6 052	12 196	54 876	303	1 682	4 067	2 106	2 042	1 996
Drug abuse violations	1 357 841	22 596	141 035	1 216 806	256	2 405	19 935	25 154	38 656	54 629
Gambling	8 101	199	1 464	6 637	1	17	181	272	395	598
Offenses against the family and children	93 172	1 230	3 901	89 271	90	261	879	774	878	1 019
Driving under the influence	997 338	236	12 956	984 382	71	17	148	522	3 162	9 036
Liquor laws	437 923	8 706	92 556	345 367	115	570	8 021	14 504	26 314	43 032
Drunkenness	412 930	1 393	11 816	401 114	56	108	1 229	1 945	2 802	5 676
Disorderly conduct	501 129	59 395	148 795	352 334	1 187	14 042	44 166	31 437	30 563	27 400
Vagrancy	24 372	1 082	3 416	20 956	5	155	922	846	960	528
All other offenses, except traffic	2 837 806	70 131	266 885	2 570 921	2 246	12 545	55 340	54 737	65 892	76 125
Suspicion	2 747	97	400	2 347	2	17	78	79	93	131
Curfew and loitering law violations	104 054	29 382	104 054	X	440	5 019	23 923	23 859	28 398	22 415
Runaways	81 222	28 075	81 222	X	685	4 465	22 925	20 905	20 670	11 572

[1]Percentages may not add to 100 because of rounding.
X = Not applicable.

Table 38. Arrests, Distribution by Age, 2005—*Continued*

(Number, percent; 10,974 total agencies; 2005 estimated population 217,722,329.)

Offense	18 years	19 years	20 years	21 years	22 years	23 years	24 years	25–29 years
Total	471 203	498 428	468 687	424 470	403 011	380 521	360 496	1 404 925
Total percent distribution[1]	4.5	4.8	4.5	4.1	3.9	3.7	3.5	13.5
Violent crime	20 630	20 382	18 670	18 151	17 453	16 800	15 989	63 475
Violent crime percent distribution[1]	4.6	4.6	4.2	4.1	3.9	3.8	3.6	14.2
Murder and nonnegligent manslaughter	630	681	624	623	557	571	514	1 747
Forcible rape	930	930	837	780	705	621	643	2 435
Robbery	7 000	6 128	4 827	4 011	3 470	3 080	2 884	10 010
Aggravated assault	12 070	12 643	12 382	12 737	12 721	12 528	11 948	49 283
Property crime	71 634	61 606	50 001	42 949	38 723	35 914	33 284	130 082
Property crime percent distribution[1]	6.0	5.2	4.2	3.6	3.2	3.0	2.8	10.9
Burglary	15 330	13 431	10 565	9 051	7 949	7 203	6 705	25 546
Larceny-theft	48 731	41 440	33 886	28 993	26 264	24 466	22 659	89 471
Motor vehicle theft	7 074	6 374	5 262	4 616	4 263	4 025	3 700	14 203
Arson	499	361	288	289	247	220	220	862
Other assaults	30 603	30 951	31 240	33 464	32 883	32 489	31 659	132 842
Forgery and counterfeiting	3 032	3 947	4 170	3 629	3 696	3 874	3 727	16 325
Fraud	5 287	7 476	8 408	8 148	8 592	8 700	8 939	39 430
Embezzlement	919	1 029	877	747	695	586	511	2 030
Stolen property; buying, receiving, and possessing	5 952	5 757	4 953	4 539	4 077	3 788	3 754	14 186
Vandalism	12 818	10 443	8 924	8 300	7 164	6 370	5 914	20 486
Weapons; carrying and possessing, etc.	9 165	8 654	7 390	7 167	6 718	5 972	5 514	19 318
Prostitution and commercialized vice	1 887	2 475	2 291	2 297	2 173	2 065	2 132	8 959
Sex offenses, except forcible rape and prostitution	2 493	2 499	2 335	2 028	1 900	1 746	1 619	6 864
Drug abuse violations	79 223	80 966	74 882	67 521	63 081	58 960	55 436	204 626
Gambling	583	504	534	396	351	316	263	910
Offenses against the family and children	1 829	2 021	2 122	2 439	2 785	2 860	3 255	15 541
Driving under the influence	22 666	31 732	35 923	49 288	50 229	47 891	45 444	169 866
Liquor laws	69 594	76 502	63 803	11 810	8 431	6 656	5 510	19 054
Drunkenness	11 626	13 367	13 326	18 902	17 474	16 040	14 427	55 206
Disorderly conduct	22 515	20 510	19 037	22 016	19 659	17 211	15 250	53 762
Vagrancy	803	656	575	543	510	526	529	2 160
All other offenses, except traffic	97 781	116 781	119 081	120 001	116 304	111 661	107 273	429 401
Suspicion	163	170	145	135	113	96	67	402
Curfew and loitering law violations	X	X	X	X	X	X	X	X
Runaways	X	X	X	X	X	X	X	X

[1]Percentages may not add to 100 because of rounding.
X = Not applicable.

Table 38. Arrests, Distribution by Age, 2005—*Continued*

(Number, percent; 10,974 total agencies; 2005 estimated population 217,722,329.)

Offense	30–34 years	35–39 years	40–44 years	45–49 years	50–54 years	55–59 years	60–64 years	65 years and over
Total	1 070 773	1 000 602	951 520	679 789	363 229	171 677	75 165	63 255
Total percent distribution[1]	10.3	9.6	9.2	6.6	3.5	1.7	0.7	0.6
Violent crime	48 288	43 645	39 019	26 489	13 812	6 622	3 035	2 904
Violent crime percent distribution[1]	10.8	9.8	8.8	5.9	3.1	1.5	0.7	0.7
Murder and nonnegligent manslaughter	1 003	724	619	511	255	155	73	119
Forcible rape	2 140	1 889	1 651	1 071	600	287	162	164
Robbery	6 811	6 058	4 875	2 817	1 197	421	119	86
Aggravated assault	38 334	34 974	31 874	22 090	11 760	5 759	2 681	2 535
Property crime	103 708	101 961	92 471	63 479	32 712	14 513	6 192	5 444
Property crime percent distribution[1]	8.7	8.5	7.7	5.3	2.7	1.2	0.5	0.5
Burglary	18 413	17 766	15 196	9 436	4 049	1 409	497	339
Larceny-theft	74 300	74 875	70 217	49 940	26 951	12 451	5 421	4 910
Motor vehicle theft	10 305	8 649	6 383	3 559	1 411	495	199	117
Arson	690	671	675	544	301	158	75	78
Other assaults	107 152	99 719	91 383	61 860	31 385	14 951	6 897	6 421
Forgery and counterfeiting	13 122	11 044	8 506	5 184	2 378	1 050	342	224
Fraud	36 088	32 368	26 766	17 692	9 229	4 752	2 070	1 894
Embezzlement	1 592	1 495	1 186	811	403	203	107	50
Stolen property; buying, receiving, and possessing	10 545	9 421	7 584	4 641	2 147	796	324	208
Vandalism	13 910	11 945	10 317	6 792	3 278	1 549	655	669
Weapons; carrying and possessing, etc.	11 425	8 725	7 639	5 583	3 151	1 733	872	783
Prostitution and commercialized vice	9 011	9 848	8 718	5 244	2 376	1 026	501	456
Sex offenses, except forcible rape and prostitution	6 347	6 798	7 286	5 022	3 264	2 022	1 214	1 439
Drug abuse violations	141 013	126 616	119 795	82 461	39 509	15 209	4 800	2 708
Gambling	562	488	451	344	282	266	192	195
Offenses against the family and children	15 632	14 803	12 431	7 780	3 348	1 406	569	450
Driving under the influence	121 775	108 585	108 578	84 796	52 919	29 014	14 013	11 663
Liquor laws	14 630	15 301	18 572	16 040	10 135	5 270	2 387	1 672
Drunkenness	43 805	45 906	54 289	46 108	27 606	13 196	5 787	4 049
Disorderly conduct	37 291	35 222	36 502	26 623	14 285	6 717	3 043	2 691
Vagrancy	2 105	2 754	3 323	3 138	1 930	885	330	189
All other offenses, except traffic	332 502	313 703	296 496	209 551	109 004	50 441	21 811	19 130
Suspicion	270	255	208	151	76	56	24	16
Curfew and loitering law violations	X	X	X	X	X	X	X	X
Runaways	X	X	X	X	X	X	X	X

[1]Percentages may not add to 100 because of rounding.
X = Not applicable.

Table 39. Male Arrests, Distribution by Age, 2005

(Number, percent; 10,974 total agencies, 2005 estimated population 217,722,329.)

Offense	Total, all ages	Under 15 years	Under 18 years	18 years and over	Under 10 years	10–12 years	13–14 years	15 years	16 years	17 years
Total	7 897 516	328 712	1 116 368	6 781 148	11 116	74 176	243 420	214 652	265 953	307 051
Total percent distribution[1]	100.0	4.2	14.1	85.9	0.1	0.9	3.1	2.7	3.4	3.9
Violent crime	366 028	17 225	57 525	308 503	558	3 882	12 785	11 132	13 846	15 322
Violent crime percent distribution[1]	100.0	4.7	15.7	84.3	0.2	1.1	3.5	3.0	3.8	4.2
Murder and nonnegligent manslaughter	9 200	84	839	8 361	0	8	76	132	215	408
Forcible rape	18 458	1 024	2 821	15 637	11	275	738	477	574	746
Robbery	75 819	4 447	19 492	56 327	65	672	3 710	4 171	5 242	5 632
Aggravated assault	262 551	11 670	34 373	228 178	482	2 927	8 261	6 352	7 815	8 536
Property crime	812 773	70 786	206 350	606 423	2 452	16 831	51 503	41 565	45 938	48 061
Property crime percent distribution[1]	100.0	8.7	25.4	74.6	0.3	2.1	6.3	5.1	5.7	5.9
Burglary	188 348	16 666	50 891	137 457	600	3 787	12 279	10 450	11 386	12 389
Larceny-theft	525 123	45 918	127 474	397 649	1 493	11 489	32 936	24 903	27 724	28 929
Motor vehicle theft	89 279	5 190	22 951	66 328	68	572	4 550	5 370	6 199	6 192
Arson	10 023	3 012	5 034	4 989	291	983	1 738	842	629	551
Other assaults	722 249	49 896	122 000	600 249	1 931	13 930	34 035	23 360	24 832	23 912
Forgery and counterfeiting	52 662	265	2 122	50 540	12	41	212	293	594	970
Fraud	126 310	657	3 808	122 502	34	94	529	521	1 015	1 615
Embezzlement	7 049	43	482	6 567	3	12	28	24	150	265
Stolen property; buying, receiving, and possessing	79 843	3 457	13 760	66 083	69	594	2 794	2 775	3 594	3 934
Vandalism	170 878	27 352	66 292	104 586	1 512	7 504	18 336	12 543	13 433	12 964
Weapons; carrying and possessing, etc.	131 393	9 771	29 536	101 857	320	2 318	7 133	5 646	6 593	7 526
Prostitution and commercialized vice	21 056	39	314	20 742	4	4	31	38	78	159
Sex offenses, except forcible rape and prostitution	61 511	5 515	11 066	50 445	270	1 544	3 701	1 887	1 831	1 833
Drug abuse violations	1 098 479	17 380	117 197	981 282	219	1 812	15 349	20 515	32 608	46 694
Gambling	7 372	194	1 429	5 943	1	17	176	263	388	584
Offenses against the family and children	70 441	742	2 363	68 078	60	175	507	441	529	651
Driving under the influence	805 461	182	10 099	795 362	56	16	110	394	2 446	7 077
Liquor laws	322 810	4 395	59 232	263 578	85	289	4 021	8 324	16 821	29 692
Drunkenness	349 830	916	9 006	340 824	50	79	787	1 348	2 125	4 617
Disorderly conduct	371 884	39 006	100 500	271 384	960	9 909	28 137	20 402	21 001	20 091
Vagrancy	19 248	747	2 497	16 751	3	111	633	605	719	426
All other offenses, except traffic	2 191 362	48 620	193 985	1 997 377	1 772	9 147	37 701	38 056	48 329	58 980
Suspicion	2 358	63	286	2 072	1	13	49	57	70	96
Curfew and loitering law violations	72 400	19 513	72 400	X	340	3 422	15 751	16 194	20 250	16 443
Runaways	34 119	11 948	34 119	X	404	2 432	9 112	8 269	8 763	5 139

[1]Percentages may not add to 100 because of rounding.
X = Not applicable.

Table 39. Male Arrests, Distribution by Age, 2005—*Continued*

(Number, percent; 10,974 total agencies, 2005 estimated population 217,722,329.)

Offense	18 years	19 years	20 years	21 years	22 years	23 years	24 years	25–29 years
Total	366 245	387 777	363 996	334 036	316 640	297 365	280 700	1 089 033
Total percent distribution[1]	4.6	4.9	4.6	4.2	4.0	3.8	3.6	13.8
Violent crime	17 759	17 394	15 573	15 144	14 568	13 926	13 187	52 063
Violent crime percent distribution[1]	4.9	4.8	4.3	4.1	4.0	3.8	3.6	14.2
Murder and nonnegligent manslaughter	584	630	582	561	503	524	483	1 565
Forcible rape	916	919	830	773	696	614	635	2 392
Robbery	6 461	5 554	4 358	3 591	3 138	2 726	2 546	8 744
Aggravated assault	9 798	10 291	9 803	10 219	10 231	10 062	9 523	39 362
Property crime	50 122	43 127	34 309	29 767	26 875	24 510	22 486	87 831
Property crime percent distribution[1]	6.2	5.3	4.2	3.7	3.3	3.0	2.8	10.8
Burglary	13 553	11 845	9 137	7 825	6 823	6 066	5 611	21 282
Larceny-theft	30 017	25 595	20 526	17 842	16 330	14 972	13 730	54 416
Motor vehicle theft	6 093	5 371	4 394	3 862	3 514	3 288	2 977	11 436
Arson	459	316	252	238	208	184	168	697
Other assaults	22 053	22 465	23 105	25 295	25 058	24 846	24 557	103 978
Forgery and counterfeiting	1 936	2 436	2 519	2 252	2 247	2 298	2 181	9 624
Fraud	3 191	4 267	4 680	4 430	4 614	4 728	4 823	20 346
Embezzlement	454	485	408	353	346	266	246	1 007
Stolen property; buying, receiving, and possessing	4 948	4 742	4 079	3 642	3 249	2 949	2 930	11 094
Vandalism	11 076	8 757	7 376	6 866	5 868	5 128	4 773	16 237
Weapons; carrying and possessing, etc.	8 660	8 171	6 985	6 746	6 317	5 598	5 159	18 002
Prostitution and commercialized vice	344	496	532	681	650	667	680	3 316
Sex offenses, except forcible rape and prostitution	2 231	2 216	2 062	1 820	1 726	1 585	1 437	6 266
Drug abuse violations	67 509	68 514	63 192	56 612	52 514	48 798	45 672	167 319
Gambling	567	482	501	377	339	305	247	842
Offenses against the family and children	1 333	1 414	1 394	1 735	1 919	2 005	2 271	11 390
Driving under the influence	18 140	25 675	29 173	39 262	40 305	38 740	37 069	140 706
Liquor laws	49 459	56 287	47 225	9 528	6 911	5 414	4 476	15 592
Drunkenness	9 759	11 342	11 313	16 378	15 224	14 034	12 530	47 687
Disorderly conduct	17 301	15 771	14 669	17 457	15 690	13 703	11 932	41 740
Vagrancy	687	529	450	438	416	429	404	1 701
All other offenses, except traffic	78 575	93 055	94 329	95 132	91 711	87 353	83 582	331 931
Suspicion	141	152	122	121	93	83	58	361
Curfew and loitering law violations	X	X	X	X	X	X	X	X
Runaways	X	X	X	X	X	X	X	X

[1]Percentages may not add to 100 because of rounding.
X = Not applicable.

Table 39. Male Arrests, Distribution by Age, 2005—*Continued*

(Number, percent; 10,974 total agencies, 2005 estimated population 217,722,329.)

Offense	30–34 years	35–39 years	40–44 years	45–49 years	50–54 years	55–59 years	60–64 years	65 years and over
Total	808 314	743 432	715 014	528 735	293 299	141 686	62 804	52 072
Total percent distribution[1]	10.2	9.4	9.1	6.7	3.7	1.8	0.8	0.7
Violent crime	38 921	34 882	31 091	21 545	11 589	5 662	2 626	2 573
Violent crime percent distribution[1]	10.6	9.5	8.5	5.9	3.2	1.5	0.7	0.7
Murder and nonnegligent manslaughter	853	606	537	419	212	133	64	105
Forcible rape	2 087	1 866	1 637	1 064	597	286	161	164
Robbery	5 756	5 178	4 181	2 460	1 076	374	105	79
Aggravated assault	30 225	27 232	24 736	17 602	9 704	4 869	2 296	2 225
Property crime	69 438	69 745	64 045	44 640	22 736	9 553	3 895	3 344
Property crime percent distribution[1]	8.5	8.6	7.9	5.5	2.8	1.2	0.5	0.4
Burglary	14 995	14 543	12 597	7 976	3 378	1 163	394	269
Larceny-theft	45 620	47 683	45 788	33 252	17 899	7 817	3 255	2 907
Motor vehicle theft	8 259	7 021	5 142	3 011	1 221	451	183	105
Arson	564	498	518	401	238	122	63	63
Other assaults	83 133	76 758	70 830	49 266	25 472	12 289	5 760	5 384
Forgery and counterfeiting	7 453	6 385	5 156	3 285	1 596	748	255	169
Fraud	18 366	16 989	15 083	10 193	5 516	2 885	1 284	1 107
Embezzlement	817	728	615	419	200	112	80	31
Stolen property; buying, receiving, and possessing	8 265	7 354	6 099	3 789	1 797	676	285	185
Vandalism	10 989	9 258	7 961	5 340	2 630	1 267	541	519
Weapons; carrying and possessing, etc.	10 488	7 833	6 805	5 037	2 917	1 601	815	723
Prostitution and commercialized vice	3 021	2 800	2 580	1 942	1 337	814	447	435
Sex offenses, except forcible rape and prostitution	5 744	6 236	6 712	4 689	3 137	1 970	1 193	1 421
Drug abuse violations	110 809	95 077	89 320	63 899	32 329	13 090	4 241	2 387
Gambling	496	396	352	270	223	208	168	170
Offenses against the family and children	11 776	11 357	10 059	6 559	2 861	1 176	473	356
Driving under the influence	100 202	86 113	83 375	66 327	43 296	24 635	12 139	10 205
Liquor laws	11 632	11 931	14 856	13 283	8 757	4 643	2 135	1 449
Drunkenness	36 891	37 339	44 198	38 845	24 296	11 858	5 360	3 770
Disorderly conduct	27 827	25 695	27 090	20 743	11 444	5 549	2 549	2 224
Vagrancy	1 629	2 073	2 573	2 590	1 623	770	278	161
All other offenses, except traffic	250 182	234 255	226 030	165 935	89 475	42 130	18 257	15 445
Suspicion	235	228	184	139	68	50	23	14
Curfew and loitering law violations	X	X	X	X	X	X	X	X
Runaways	X	X	X	X	X	X	X	X

[1]Percentages may not add to 100 because of rounding.
X = Not applicable.

Table 40. Female Arrests, Distribution by Age, 2005

(Number, percent; 10,974 total agencies; 2005 estimated population 217,722,329.)

Offense	Total, all ages	Under 15 years	Under 18 years	18 years and over	Under 10 years	10–12 years	13–14 years	15 years	16 years	17 years
Total	2 472 303	151 214	465 700	2 006 603	2 594	27 575	121 045	101 710	108 652	104 124
Total percent distribution[1]	100.0	6.1	18.8	81.2	0.1	1.1	4.9	4.1	4.4	4.2
Violent crime	79 818	4 381	12 957	66 861	84	861	3 436	2 772	2 943	2 861
Violent crime percent distribution[1]	100.0	5.5	16.2	83.8	0.1	1.1	4.3	3.5	3.7	3.6
Murder and nonnegligent manslaughter	1 135	13	90	1 045	0	2	11	17	24	36
Forcible rape	275	31	67	208	1	9	21	13	14	9
Robbery	9 490	539	2 023	7 467	8	79	452	469	470	545
Aggravated assault	68 918	3 798	10 777	58 141	75	771	2 952	2 273	2 435	2 271
Property crime	382 787	35 595	104 537	278 250	651	7 369	27 575	21 850	23 672	23 420
Property crime percent distribution[1]	100.0	9.3	27.3	72.7	0.2	1.9	7.2	5.7	6.2	6.1
Burglary	32 043	2 469	6 615	25 428	97	556	1 816	1 348	1 370	1 428
Larceny-theft	329 733	31 422	92 407	237 326	521	6 563	24 338	19 111	20 994	20 880
Motor vehicle theft	19 022	1 253	4 715	14 307	11	127	1 115	1 223	1 197	1 042
Arson	1 989	451	800	1 189	22	123	306	168	111	70
Other assaults	236 228	24 481	60 578	175 650	365	5 246	18 870	12 914	12 594	10 589
Forgery and counterfeiting	34 684	105	974	33 710	6	16	83	122	235	512
Fraud	105 411	376	2 074	103 337	38	46	292	279	506	913
Embezzlement	7 048	6	374	6 674	0	0	6	11	105	252
Stolen property; buying, receiving, and possessing	19 330	745	2 741	16 589	13	128	604	538	685	773
Vandalism	35 473	4 573	10 525	24 948	178	1 242	3 153	1 907	2 032	2 013
Weapons; carrying and possessing, etc.	11 485	1 475	3 533	7 952	16	324	1 135	793	691	574
Prostitution and commercialized vice	41 607	124	890	40 717	7	6	111	139	244	383
Sex offenses, except forcible rape and prostitution	5 561	537	1 130	4 431	33	138	366	219	211	163
Drug abuse violations	259 362	5 216	23 838	235 524	37	593	4 586	4 639	6 048	7 935
Gambling	729	5	35	694	0	0	5	9	7	14
Offenses against the family and children	22 731	488	1 538	21 193	30	86	372	333	349	368
Driving under the influence	191 877	54	2 857	189 020	15	1	38	128	716	1 959
Liquor laws	115 113	4 311	33 324	81 789	30	281	4 000	6 180	9 493	13 340
Drunkenness	63 100	477	2 810	60 290	6	29	442	597	677	1 059
Disorderly conduct	129 245	20 389	48 295	80 950	227	4 133	16 029	11 035	9 562	7 309
Vagrancy	5 124	335	919	4 205	2	44	289	241	241	102
All other offenses, except traffic	646 444	21 511	72 900	573 544	474	3 398	17 639	16 681	17 563	17 145
Suspicion	389	34	114	275	1	4	29	22	23	35
Curfew and loitering law violations	31 654	9 869	31 654	X	100	1 597	8 172	7 665	8 148	5 972
Runaways	47 103	16 127	47 103	X	281	2 033	13 813	12 636	11 907	6 433

[1]Percentages may not add to 100 because of rounding.
X = Not applicable.

Table 40. Female Arrests, Distribution by Age, 2005—*Continued*

(Number, percent; 10,974 total agencies; 2005 estimated population 217,722,329.)

Offense	18 years	19 years	20 years	21 years	22 years	23 years	24 years	25–29 years
Total	104 958	110 651	104 691	90 434	86 371	83 156	79 796	315 892
Total percent distribution[1]	4.2	4.5	4.2	3.7	3.5	3.4	3.2	12.8
Violent crime	2 871	2 988	3 097	3 007	2 885	2 874	2 802	11 412
Violent crime percent distribution[1]	3.6	3.7	3.9	3.8	3.6	3.6	3.5	14.3
Murder and nonnegligent manslaughter	46	51	42	62	54	47	31	182
Forcible rape	14	11	7	7	9	7	8	43
Robbery	539	574	469	420	332	354	338	1 266
Aggravated assault	2 272	2 352	2 579	2 518	2 490	2 466	2 425	9 921
Property crime	21 512	18 479	15 692	13 182	11 848	11 404	10 798	42 251
Property crime percent distribution[1]	5.6	4.8	4.1	3.4	3.1	3.0	2.8	11.0
Burglary	1 777	1 586	1 428	1 226	1 126	1 137	1 094	4 264
Larceny-theft	18 714	15 845	13 360	11 151	9 934	9 494	8 929	35 055
Motor vehicle theft	981	1 003	868	754	749	737	723	2 767
Arson	40	45	36	51	39	36	52	165
Other assaults	8 550	8 486	8 135	8 169	7 825	7 643	7 102	28 864
Forgery and counterfeiting	1 096	1 511	1 651	1 377	1 449	1 576	1 546	6 701
Fraud	2 096	3 209	3 728	3 718	3 978	3 972	4 116	19 084
Embezzlement	465	544	469	394	349	320	265	1 023
Stolen property; buying, receiving, and possessing	1 004	1 015	874	897	828	839	824	3 092
Vandalism	1 742	1 686	1 548	1 434	1 296	1 242	1 141	4 249
Weapons; carrying and possessing, etc.	505	483	405	421	401	374	355	1 316
Prostitution and commercialized vice	1 543	1 979	1 759	1 616	1 523	1 398	1 452	5 643
Sex offenses, except forcible rape and prostitution	262	283	273	208	174	161	182	598
Drug abuse violations	11 714	12 452	11 690	10 909	10 567	10 162	9 764	37 307
Gambling	16	22	33	19	12	11	16	68
Offenses against the family and children	496	607	728	704	866	855	984	4 151
Driving under the influence	4 526	6 057	6 750	10 026	9 924	9 151	8 375	29 160
Liquor laws	20 135	20 215	16 578	2 282	1 520	1 242	1 034	3 462
Drunkenness	1 867	2 025	2 013	2 524	2 250	2 006	1 897	7 519
Disorderly conduct	5 214	4 739	4 368	4 559	3 969	3 508	3 318	12 022
Vagrancy	116	127	125	105	94	97	125	459
All other offenses, except traffic	19 206	23 726	24 752	24 869	24 593	24 308	23 691	97 470
Suspicion	22	18	23	14	20	13	9	41
Curfew and loitering law violations	X	X	X	X	X	X	X	X
Runaways	X	X	X	X	X	X	X	X

[1]Percentages may not add to 100 because of rounding.
X = Not applicable.

Table 40. Female Arrests, Distribution by Age, 2005—*Continued*

(Number, percent; 10,974 total agencies; 2005 estimated population 217,722,329.)

Offense	30–34 years	35–39 years	40–44 years	45–49 years	50–54 years	55–59 years	60–64 years	65 years and over
Total	262 159	257 170	236 506	151 054	69 930	29 991	12 361	11 183
Total percent distribution[1]	10.6	10.4	9.6	6.1	2.8	1.2	0.5	0.5
Violent crime	9 367	8 763	7 928	4 944	2 223	960	409	331
Violent crime percent distribution[1]	11.7	11.0	9.9	6.2	2.8	1.2	0.5	0.4
Murder and nonnegligent manslaughter	150	118	82	92	43	22	9	14
Forcible rape	53	23	14	7	3	1	1	0
Robbery	1 055	880	694	357	121	47	14	7
Aggravated assault	8 109	7 742	7 138	4 488	2 056	890	385	310
Property crime	34 270	32 216	28 426	18 839	9 976	4 960	2 297	2 100
Property crime percent distribution[1]	9.0	8.4	7.4	4.9	2.6	1.3	0.6	0.5
Burglary	3 418	3 223	2 599	1 460	671	246	103	70
Larceny-theft	28 680	27 192	24 429	16 688	9 052	4 634	2 166	2 003
Motor vehicle theft	2 046	1 628	1 241	548	190	44	16	12
Arson	126	173	157	143	63	36	12	15
Other assaults	24 019	22 961	20 553	12 594	5 913	2 662	1 137	1 037
Forgery and counterfeiting	5 669	4 659	3 350	1 899	782	302	87	55
Fraud	17 722	15 379	11 683	7 499	3 713	1 867	786	787
Embezzlement	775	767	571	392	203	91	27	19
Stolen property; buying, receiving, and possessing	2 280	2 067	1 485	852	350	120	39	23
Vandalism	2 921	2 687	2 356	1 452	648	282	114	150
Weapons; carrying and possessing, etc.	937	892	834	546	234	132	57	60
Prostitution and commercialized vice	5 990	7 048	6 138	3 302	1 039	212	54	21
Sex offenses, except forcible rape and prostitution	603	562	574	333	127	52	21	18
Drug abuse violations	30 204	31 539	30 475	18 562	7 180	2 119	559	321
Gambling	66	92	99	74	59	58	24	25
Offenses against the family and children	3 856	3 446	2 372	1 221	487	230	96	94
Driving under the influence	21 573	22 472	25 203	18 469	9 623	4 379	1 874	1 458
Liquor laws	2 998	3 370	3 716	2 757	1 378	627	252	223
Drunkenness	6 914	8 567	10 091	7 263	3 310	1 338	427	279
Disorderly conduct	9 464	9 527	9 412	5 880	2 841	1 168	494	467
Vagrancy	476	681	750	548	307	115	52	28
All other offenses, except traffic	82 320	79 448	70 466	43 616	19 529	8 311	3 554	3 685
Suspicion	35	27	24	12	8	6	1	2
Curfew and loitering law violations	X	X	X	X	X	X	X	X
Runaways	X	X	X	X	X	X	X	X

[1]Percentages may not add to 100 because of rounding.
X = Not applicable.

Table 41. Arrests of Persons Under 15, 18, 21, and 25 Years of Age, 2005

(Number, percent; 10,974 total agencies; 2005 estimated population 217,722,329.)

Offense	Total, all ages	Number of persons arrested				Percent of total all ages			
		Under 15 years	Under 18 years	Under 21 years	Under 25 years	Under 15 years	Under 18 years	Under 21 years	Under 25 years
Total	10 369 819	479 926	1 582 068	3 020 386	4 588 884	4.6	15.3	29.1	44.3
Violent crime	445 846	21 606	70 482	130 164	198 557	4.8	15.8	29.2	44.5
Murder and nonnegligent manslaughter	10 335	97	929	2 864	5 129	0.9	9.0	27.7	49.6
Forcible rape	18 733	1 055	2 888	5 585	8 334	5.6	15.4	29.8	44.5
Robbery	85 309	4 986	21 515	39 470	52 915	5.8	25.2	46.3	62.0
Aggravated assault	331 469	15 468	45 150	82 245	132 179	4.7	13.6	24.8	39.9
Property crime	1 195 560	106 381	310 887	494 128	644 998	8.9	26.0	41.3	53.9
Burglary	220 391	19 135	57 506	96 832	127 740	8.7	26.1	43.9	58.0
Larceny-theft	854 856	77 340	219 881	343 938	446 320	9.0	25.7	40.2	52.2
Motor vehicle theft	108 301	6 443	27 666	46 376	62 980	5.9	25.5	42.8	58.2
Arson	12 012	3 463	5 834	6 982	7 958	28.8	48.6	58.1	66.3
Other assaults	958 477	74 377	182 578	275 372	405 867	7.8	19.0	28.7	42.3
Forgery and counterfeiting	87 346	370	3 096	14 245	29 171	0.4	3.5	16.3	33.4
Fraud	231 721	1 033	5 882	27 053	61 432	0.4	2.5	11.7	26.5
Embezzlement	14 097	49	856	3 681	6 220	0.3	6.1	26.1	44.1
Stolen property; buying, receiving, and possessing	99 173	4 202	16 501	33 163	49 321	4.2	16.6	33.4	49.7
Vandalism	206 351	31 925	76 817	109 002	136 750	15.5	37.2	52.8	66.3
Weapons; carrying and possessing, etc.	142 878	11 246	33 069	58 278	83 649	7.9	23.1	40.8	58.5
Prostitution and commercialized vice	62 663	163	1 204	7 857	16 524	0.3	1.9	12.5	26.4
Sex offenses, except forcible rape and prostitution	67 072	6 052	12 196	19 523	26 816	9.0	18.2	29.1	40.0
Drug abuse violations	1 357 841	22 596	141 035	376 106	621 104	1.7	10.4	27.7	45.7
Gambling	8 101	199	1 464	3 085	4 411	2.5	18.1	38.1	54.5
Offenses against the family and children	93 172	1 230	3 901	9 873	21 212	1.3	4.2	10.6	22.8
Driving under the influence	997 338	236	12 956	103 277	296 129	0.0	1.3	10.4	29.7
Liquor laws	437 923	8 706	92 556	302 455	334 862	2.0	21.1	69.1	76.5
Drunkenness	412 930	1 393	11 816	50 135	116 978	0.3	2.9	12.1	28.3
Disorderly conduct	501 129	59 395	148 795	210 857	284 993	11.9	29.7	42.1	56.9
Vagrancy	24 372	1 082	3 416	5 450	7 558	4.4	14.0	22.4	31.0
All other offenses, except traffic	2 837 806	70 131	266 885	600 528	1 055 767	2.5	9.4	21.2	37.2
Suspicion	2 747	97	400	878	1 289	3.5	14.6	32.0	46.9
Curfew and loitering law violations	104 054	29 382	104 054	104 054	104 054	28.2	100.0	100.0	100.0
Runaways	81 222	28 075	81 222	81 222	81 222	34.6	100.0	100.0	100.0

Table 42. Arrests, Distribution by Sex, 2005

(Number, percent; 10,974 total agencies; 2005 estimated population 217,722,329.)

Offense	Number of persons arrested			Percent male	Percent female	Percent distribution[1]		
	Total	Male	Female			Total	Male	Female
Total	10 369 819	7 897 516	2 472 303	76.2	23.8	100.0	100.0	100.0
Violent crime	445 846	366 028	79 818	82.1	17.9	4.3	4.6	3.2
Murder and nonnegligent manslaughter	10 335	9 200	1 135	89.0	11.0	0.1	0.1	0.0
Forcible rape	18 733	18 458	275	98.5	1.5	0.2	0.2	0.0
Robbery	85 309	75 819	9 490	88.9	11.1	0.8	1.0	0.4
Aggravated assault	331 469	262 551	68 918	79.2	20.8	3.2	3.3	2.8
Property crime	1 195 560	812 773	382 787	68.0	32.0	11.5	10.3	15.5
Burglary	220 391	188 348	32 043	85.5	14.5	2.1	2.4	1.3
Larceny-theft	854 856	525 123	329 733	61.4	38.6	8.2	6.6	13.3
Motor vehicle theft	108 301	89 279	19 022	82.4	17.6	1.0	1.1	0.8
Arson	12 012	10 023	1 989	83.4	16.6	0.1	0.1	0.1
Other assaults	958 477	722 249	236 228	75.4	24.6	9.2	9.1	9.6
Forgery and counterfeiting	87 346	52 662	34 684	60.3	39.7	0.8	0.7	1.4
Fraud	231 721	126 310	105 411	54.5	45.5	2.2	1.6	4.3
Embezzlement	14 097	7 049	7 048	50.0	50.0	0.1	0.1	0.3
Stolen property; buying, receiving, and possessing	99 173	79 843	19 330	80.5	19.5	1.0	1.0	0.8
Vandalism	206 351	170 878	35 473	82.8	17.2	2.0	2.2	1.4
Weapons; carrying and possessing, etc.	142 878	131 393	11 485	92.0	8.0	1.4	1.7	0.5
Prostitution and commercialized vice	62 663	21 056	41 607	33.6	66.4	0.6	0.3	1.7
Sex offenses, except forcible rape and prostitution	67 072	61 511	5 561	91.7	8.3	0.6	0.8	0.2
Drug abuse violations	1 357 841	1 098 479	259 362	80.9	19.1	13.1	13.9	10.5
Gambling	8 101	7 372	729	91.0	9.0	0.1	0.1	0.0
Offenses against the family and children	93 172	70 441	22 731	75.6	24.4	0.9	0.9	0.9
Driving under the influence	997 338	805 461	191 877	80.8	19.2	9.6	10.2	7.8
Liquor laws	437 923	322 810	115 113	73.7	26.3	4.2	4.1	4.7
Drunkenness	412 930	349 830	63 100	84.7	15.3	4.0	4.4	2.6
Disorderly conduct	501 129	371 884	129 245	74.2	25.8	4.8	4.7	5.2
Vagrancy	24 372	19 248	5 124	79.0	21.0	0.2	0.2	0.2
All other offenses, except traffic	2 837 806	2 191 362	646 444	77.2	22.8	27.4	27.7	26.1
Suspicion	2 747	2 358	389	85.8	14.2	0.0	0.0	0.0
Curfew and loitering law violations	104 054	72 400	31 654	69.6	30.4	1.0	0.9	1.3
Runaways	81 222	34 119	47 103	42.0	58.0	0.8	0.4	1.9

[1]Percentages may not add to 100 because of rounding,

Table 43. Arrests, Distribution by Race, 2005

(Number, percent; 10,971 total agencies; 2005 estimated population 217,692,433.)

Offense	Total, all ages					Percent distribution[1]				
	Total	White	Black	American Indian or Alaskan Native	Asian or Pacific Islander	Total	White	Black	American Indian or Alaskan Native	Asian or Pacific Islander
Total	10 189 691	7 117 040	2 830 778	135 877	105 996	100.0	69.8	27.8	1.3	1.0
Violent crime	442 520	260 984	171 675	5 180	4 681	100.0	59.0	38.8	1.2	1.1
Murder and nonnegligent manslaughter	10 083	4 955	4 898	109	121	100.0	49.1	48.6	1.1	1.2
Forcible rape	18 405	11 980	6 015	222	188	100.0	65.1	32.7	1.2	1.0
Robbery	84 785	35 796	47 700	512	777	100.0	42.2	56.3	0.6	0.9
Aggravated assault	329 247	208 253	113 062	4 337	3 595	100.0	63.3	34.3	1.3	1.1
Property crime	1 183 491	814 754	338 635	14 755	15 347	100.0	68.8	28.6	1.2	1.3
Burglary	217 894	151 757	62 045	2 196	1 896	100.0	69.6	28.5	1.0	0.9
Larceny-theft	846 213	586 393	236 608	11 332	11 880	100.0	69.3	28.0	1.3	1.4
Motor vehicle theft	107 604	67 578	37 489	1 103	1 434	100.0	62.8	34.8	1.0	1.3
Arson	11 780	9 026	2 493	124	137	100.0	76.6	21.2	1.1	1.2
Other assaults	944 820	615 268	305 398	13 529	10 625	100.0	65.1	32.3	1.4	1.1
Forgery and counterfeiting	83 747	59 221	23 104	471	951	100.0	70.7	27.6	0.6	1.1
Fraud	217 650	149 618	65 424	1 243	1 365	100.0	68.7	30.1	0.6	0.6
Embezzlement	13 730	9 201	4 262	97	170	100.0	67.0	31.0	0.7	1.2
Stolen property; buying, receiving, and possessing	97 075	62 215	33 184	748	928	100.0	64.1	34.2	0.8	1.0
Vandalism	203 578	152 621	45 807	3 095	2 055	100.0	75.0	22.5	1.5	1.0
Weapons; carrying and possessing, etc.	141 286	83 830	55 168	1 011	1 277	100.0	59.3	39.0	0.7	0.9
Prostitution and commercialized vice	62 501	34 436	26 104	612	1 349	100.0	55.1	41.8	1.0	2.2
Sex offenses, except forcible rape and prostitution	64 395	47 392	15 647	687	669	100.0	73.6	24.3	1.1	1.0
Drug abuse violations	1 330 802	861 645	451 375	8 600	9 182	100.0	64.7	33.9	0.6	0.7
Gambling	8 064	2 087	5 731	24	222	100.0	25.9	71.1	0.3	2.8
Offenses against the family and children	89 170	61 122	25 834	1 683	531	100.0	68.5	29.0	1.9	0.6
Driving under the influence	976 797	863 955	88 656	13 682	10 504	100.0	88.4	9.1	1.4	1.1
Liquor laws	430 992	367 991	46 769	11 916	4 316	100.0	85.4	10.9	2.8	1.0
Drunkenness	399 059	334 158	53 709	8 976	2 216	100.0	83.7	13.5	2.2	0.6
Disorderly conduct	493 708	316 467	165 850	7 712	3 679	100.0	64.1	33.6	1.6	0.7
Vagrancy	24 359	14 452	9 364	412	131	100.0	59.3	38.4	1.7	0.5
All other offenses, except traffic	2 794 372	1 881 076	842 609	39 022	31 665	100.0	67.3	30.2	1.4	1.1
Suspicion	2 744	1 840	885	12	7	100.0	67.1	32.3	0.4	0.3
Curfew and loitering law violations	103 886	64 881	36 928	876	1 201	100.0	62.5	35.5	0.8	1.2
Runaways	80 945	57 826	18 660	1 534	2 925	100.0	71.4	23.1	1.9	3.6

[1]Percentages may not add to 100 because of rounding.

Table 43. Arrests, Distribution by Race, 2005—*Continued*

(Number, percent; 10,971 total agencies; 2005 estimated population 217,692,433.)

Offense	Under 18 years					Percent distribution[1]				
	Total	White	Black	American Indian or Alaskan Native	Asian or Pacific Islander	Total	White	Black	American Indian or Alaskan Native	Asian or Pacific Islander
Total	1 570 282	1 059 742	469 382	20 490	20 668	100.0	67.5	29.9	1.3	1.3
Violent crime	70 080	33 780	34 897	632	771	100.0	48.2	49.8	0.9	1.1
Murder and nonnegligent manslaughter	924	397	499	18	10	100.0	43.0	54.0	1.9	1.1
Forcible rape	2 851	1 834	969	31	17	100.0	64.3	34.0	1.1	0.6
Robbery	21 460	6 598	14 487	96	279	100.0	30.7	67.5	0.4	1.3
Aggravated assault	44 845	24 951	18 942	487	465	100.0	55.6	42.2	1.1	1.0
Property crime	308 723	207 414	92 089	4 153	5 067	100.0	67.2	29.8	1.3	1.6
Burglary	57 054	38 287	17 663	565	539	100.0	67.1	31.0	1.0	0.9
Larceny-theft	218 383	149 754	61 407	3 176	4 046	100.0	68.6	28.1	1.5	1.9
Motor vehicle theft	27 499	14 798	11 943	349	409	100.0	53.8	43.4	1.3	1.5
Arson	5 787	4 575	1 076	63	73	100.0	79.1	18.6	1.1	1.3
Other assaults	181 114	105 684	71 486	2 063	1 881	100.0	58.4	39.5	1.1	1.0
Forgery and counterfeiting	3 051	2 259	725	18	49	100.0	74.0	23.8	0.6	1.6
Fraud	5 796	3 723	1 981	32	60	100.0	64.2	34.2	0.6	1.0
Embezzlement	849	532	293	8	16	100.0	62.7	34.5	0.9	1.9
Stolen property; buying, receiving, and possessing	16 305	8 941	7 019	146	199	100.0	54.8	43.0	0.9	1.2
Vandalism	76 096	59 349	14 961	955	831	100.0	78.0	19.7	1.3	1.1
Weapons; carrying and possessing, etc.	32 949	20 154	12 161	253	381	100.0	61.2	36.9	0.8	1.2
Prostitution and commercialized vice	1 200	501	670	9	20	100.0	41.8	55.8	0.8	1.7
Sex offenses, except forcible rape and prostitution	11 979	8 534	3 226	110	109	100.0	71.2	26.9	0.9	0.9
Drug abuse violations	139 776	96 207	41 076	1 301	1 192	100.0	68.8	29.4	0.9	0.9
Gambling	1 463	106	1 349	0	8	100.0	7.2	92.2	0.0	0.5
Offenses against the family and children	3 850	3 042	714	80	14	100.0	79.0	18.5	2.1	0.4
Driving under the influence	12 584	11 744	502	223	115	100.0	93.3	4.0	1.8	0.9
Liquor laws	91 800	84 107	4 322	2 535	836	100.0	91.6	4.7	2.8	0.9
Drunkenness	11 401	10 122	951	230	98	100.0	88.8	8.3	2.0	0.9
Disorderly conduct	147 976	87 640	57 331	1 889	1 116	100.0	59.2	38.7	1.3	0.8
Vagrancy	3 416	2 702	676	12	26	100.0	79.1	19.8	0.4	0.8
All other offenses, except traffic	264 643	190 241	67 221	3 429	3 752	100.0	71.9	25.4	1.3	1.4
Suspicion	400	253	144	2	1	100.0	63.3	36.0	0.5	0.3
Curfew and loitering law violations	103 886	64 881	36 928	876	1 201	100.0	62.5	35.5	0.8	1.2
Runaways	80 945	57 826	18 660	1 534	2 925	100.0	71.4	23.1	1.9	3.6

[1]Percentages may not add to 100 because of rounding.

Table 43. Arrests, Distribution by Race, 2005—*Continued*

(Number, percent; 10,971 total agencies; 2005 estimated population 217,692,433.)

Offense	18 years and over					Percent distribution[1]				
	Total	White	Black	American Indian or Alaskan Native	Asian or Pacific Islander	Total	White	Black	American Indian or Alaskan Native	Asian or Pacific Islander
Total	8 619 409	6 057 298	2 361 396	115 387	85 328	100.0	70.3	27.4	1.3	1.0
Violent crime	372 440	227 204	136 778	4 548	3 910	100.0	61.0	36.7	1.2	1.0
Murder and nonnegligent manslaughter	9 159	4 558	4 399	91	111	100.0	49.8	48.0	1.0	1.2
Forcible rape	15 554	10 146	5 046	191	171	100.0	65.2	32.4	1.2	1.1
Robbery	63 325	29 198	33 213	416	498	100.0	46.1	52.4	0.7	0.8
Aggravated assault	284 402	183 302	94 120	3 850	3 130	100.0	64.5	33.1	1.4	1.1
Property crime	874 768	607 340	246 546	10 602	10 280	100.0	69.4	28.2	1.2	1.2
Burglary	160 840	113 470	44 382	1 631	1 357	100.0	70.5	27.6	1.0	0.8
Larceny-theft	627 830	436 639	175 201	8 156	7 834	100.0	69.5	27.9	1.3	1.2
Motor vehicle theft	80 105	52 780	25 546	754	1 025	100.0	65.9	31.9	0.9	1.3
Arson	5 993	4 451	1 417	61	64	100.0	74.3	23.6	1.0	1.1
Other assaults	763 706	509 584	233 912	11 466	8 744	100.0	66.7	30.6	1.5	1.1
Forgery and counterfeiting	80 696	56 962	22 379	453	902	100.0	70.6	27.7	0.6	1.1
Fraud	211 854	145 895	63 443	1 211	1 305	100.0	68.9	29.9	0.6	0.6
Embezzlement	12 881	8 669	3 969	89	154	100.0	67.3	30.8	0.7	1.2
Stolen property; buying, receiving, and possessing	80 770	53 274	26 165	602	729	100.0	66.0	32.4	0.7	0.9
Vandalism	127 482	93 272	30 846	2 140	1 224	100.0	73.2	24.2	1.7	1.0
Weapons; carrying and possessing, etc.	108 337	63 676	43 007	758	896	100.0	58.8	39.7	0.7	0.8
Prostitution and commercialized vice	61 301	33 935	25 434	603	1 329	100.0	55.4	41.5	1.0	2.2
Sex offenses, except forcible rape and prostitution	52 416	38 858	12 421	577	560	100.0	74.1	23.7	1.1	1.1
Drug abuse violations	1 191 026	765 438	410 299	7 299	7 990	100.0	64.3	34.4	0.6	0.7
Gambling	6 601	1 981	4 382	24	214	100.0	30.0	66.4	0.4	3.2
Offenses against the family and children	85 320	58 080	25 120	1 603	517	100.0	68.1	29.4	1.9	0.6
Driving under the influence	964 213	852 211	88 154	13 459	10 389	100.0	88.4	9.1	1.4	1.1
Liquor laws	339 192	283 884	42 447	9 381	3 480	100.0	83.7	12.5	2.8	1.0
Drunkenness	387 658	324 036	52 758	8 746	2 118	100.0	83.6	13.6	2.3	0.5
Disorderly conduct	345 732	228 827	108 519	5 823	2 563	100.0	66.2	31.4	1.7	0.7
Vagrancy	20 943	11 750	8 688	400	105	100.0	56.1	41.5	1.9	0.5
All other offenses, except traffic	2 529 729	1 690 835	775 388	35 593	27 913	100.0	66.8	30.7	1.4	1.1
Suspicion	2 344	1 587	741	10	6	100.0	67.7	31.6	0.4	0.3
Curfew and loitering law violations	X	X	X	X	X	0.0	0.0	0.0	0.0	0.0
Runaways	X	X	X	X	X	0.0	0.0	0.0	0.0	0.0

[1]Percentages may not add to 100 because of rounding.
X = Not applicable.

Table 44. City Arrest Trends, 2004 and 2005

(Number, percent change; 7,140 total agencies; 2004 estimated population 127,417,958; 2005 estimated population 128,599,977.)

Offense	Total, all ages			Under 18 years			18 years and over		
	2004	2005	Percent change	2004	2005	Percent change	2004	2005	Percent change
Total[1]	6 531 523	6 518 328	-0.2	1 124 985	1 091 479	-3.0	5 406 538	5 426 849	0.4
Violent crime	263 387	269 528	2.3	42 235	43 530	3.1	221 152	225 998	2.2
Murder and nonnegligent manslaughter	5 196	5 614	8.0	430	547	27.2	4 766	5 067	6.3
Forcible rape	10 925	10 850	-0.7	1 858	1 690	-9.0	9 067	9 160	1.0
Robbery	51 856	53 592	3.3	11 843	13 171	11.2	40 013	40 421	1.0
Aggravated assault	195 410	199 472	2.1	28 104	28 122	0.1	167 306	171 350	2.4
Property crime	862 666	834 257	-3.3	248 930	228 903	-8.0	613 736	605 354	-1.4
Burglary	135 889	136 861	0.7	38 771	37 319	-3.7	97 118	99 542	2.5
Larceny-theft	658 734	630 817	-4.2	189 720	172 771	-8.9	469 014	458 046	-2.3
Motor vehicle theft	60 973	59 327	-2.7	16 494	14 931	-9.5	44 479	44 396	-0.2
Arson	7 070	7 252	2.6	3 945	3 882	-1.6	3 125	3 370	7.8
Other assaults	607 690	608 126	0.1	120 518	119 010	-1.3	487 172	489 116	0.4
Forgery and counterfeiting	61 437	57 432	-6.5	2 635	2 103	-20.2	58 802	55 329	-5.9
Fraud	114 580	108 217	-5.6	3 882	3 840	-1.1	110 698	104 377	-5.7
Embezzlement	9 287	9 372	0.9	570	615	7.9	8 717	8 757	0.5
Stolen property; buying, receiving, and possessing	64 724	65 903	1.8	13 201	12 335	-6.6	51 523	53 568	4.0
Vandalism	136 711	137 265	0.4	53 891	53 732	-0.3	82 820	83 533	0.9
Weapons; carrying and possessing, etc.	81 241	87 482	7.7	19 957	21 475	7.6	61 284	66 007	7.7
Prostitution and commercialized vice	38 544	37 726	-2.1	772	713	-7.6	37 772	37 013	-2.0
Sex offenses, except forcible rape and prostitution	36 634	35 668	-2.6	8 110	7 373	-9.1	28 524	28 295	-0.8
Drug abuse violations	763 229	795 053	4.2	90 820	89 551	-1.4	672 409	705 502	4.9
Gambling	2 637	2 415	-8.4	280	363	29.6	2 357	2 052	-12.9
Offenses against the family and children	37 407	37 411	0.0	2 632	2 383	-9.5	34 775	35 028	0.7
Driving under the influence	568 583	559 912	-1.5	8 680	7 999	-7.8	559 903	551 913	-1.4
Liquor laws	325 590	310 425	-4.7	67 361	65 736	-2.4	258 229	244 689	-5.2
Drunkenness	319 291	314 807	-1.4	9 796	9 161	-6.5	309 495	305 646	-1.2
Disorderly conduct	351 548	353 401	0.5	114 693	113 498	-1.0	236 855	239 903	1.3
Vagrancy	15 105	15 094	-0.3	2 844	2 829	-0.5	12 291	12 265	-0.2
All other offenses, except traffic	1 753 752	1 763 315	0.5	195 728	190 811	-2.5	1 558 024	1 572 504	0.0
Suspicion	1 285	1 105	-14.0	298	242	-18.8	987	863	-12.6
Curfew and loitering law violations	56 753	57 777	1.8	56 753	57 777	1.8	X	X	X
Runaways	60 697	57 742	-4.9	60 697	57 742	-4.9	X	X	X

[1]Does not include suspicion.
X = Not applicable.

Table 45. City Arrest Trends, by Age and Sex, 2004 and 2005

(Number, percent change; 7,140 total agencies; 2004 estimated population 127,417,958; 2005 estimated population 128,599,977.)

Offense	Male						Female					
	Total, all ages			Under 18 years			Total, all ages			Under 18 years		
	2004	2005	Percent change	2004	2005	Percent change	2004	2005	Percent change	2004	2005	Percent change
Total[1]	4 917 723	4 902 752	-0.3	776 151	756 306	-2.6	1 613 800	1 615 576	0.1	348 834	335 173	-3.9
Violent crime	215 550	220 508	2.3	34 342	35 534	3.5	47 837	49 020	2.5	7 893	7 996	1.3
Murder and nonnegligent manslaughter	4 622	5 021	8.6	399	501	25.6	574	593	3.3	31	46	48.4
Forcible rape	10 757	10 725	-0.3	1 806	1 656	-8.3	168	125	-25.6	52	34	-34.6
Robbery	45 939	47 438	3.3	10 690	11 969	12.0	5 917	6 154	4.0	1 153	1 202	4.2
Aggravated assault	154 232	157 324	2.0	21 447	21 408	-0.2	41 178	42 148	2.4	6 657	6 714	0.9
Property crime	568 894	548 010	-3.7	158 779	146 075	-8.0	293 772	286 247	-2.6	90 151	82 828	-8.1
Burglary	115 350	115 869	0.4	33 877	32 701	-3.5	20 539	20 992	2.2	4 894	4 618	-5.6
Larceny-theft	397 497	377 716	-5.0	108 009	97 845	-9.4	261 237	253 101	-3.1	81 711	74 926	-8.3
Motor vehicle theft	50 083	48 366	-3.4	13 439	12 192	-9.3	10 890	10 961	0.7	3 055	2 739	-10.3
Arson	5 964	6 059	1.6	3 454	3 337	-3.4	1 106	1 193	7.9	491	545	11.0
Other assaults	455 322	454 905	-0.1	79 705	79 073	-0.8	152 368	153 221	0.6	40 813	39 937	-2.1
Forgery and counterfeiting	36 496	34 594	-5.2	1 689	1 395	-17.4	24 941	22 838	-8.4	946	708	-25.2
Fraud	63 809	60 093	-5.8	2 441	2 464	0.9	50 771	48 124	-5.2	1 441	1 376	-4.5
Embezzlement	4 471	4 560	2.0	344	344	0.0	4 816	4 812	-0.1	226	271	19.9
Stolen property; buying, receiving, and possessing	52 038	52 293	0.5	10 937	10 202	-6.7	12 686	13 610	7.3	2 264	2 133	-5.8
Vandalism	113 342	113 458	0.1	45 934	46 160	0.5	23 369	23 807	1.9	7 957	7 572	-4.8
Weapons; carrying and possessing, etc.	74 560	80 527	8.0	17 908	19 372	8.2	6 681	6 955	4.1	2 049	2 103	2.6
Prostitution and commercialized vice	11 739	11 398	-2.9	198	154	-22.2	26 805	26 328	-1.8	574	559	-2.6
Sex offenses, except forcible rape and prostitution	33 989	33 284	-2.1	7 398	6 711	-9.3	2 645	2 384	-9.9	712	662	-7.0
Drug abuse violations	615 000	639 435	4.0	73 879	73 228	-0.9	148 229	155 618	5.0	16 941	16 323	-3.6
Gambling	2 255	2 079	-7.8	264	350	32.6	382	336	-12.0	16	13	-18.8
Offenses against the family and children	25 050	24 904	-0.6	1 610	1 411	-12.4	12 357	12 507	1.2	1 022	972	-4.9
Driving under the influence	456 842	446 606	-2.2	6 792	6 179	-9.0	111 741	113 306	1.4	1 888	1 820	-3.6
Liquor laws	240 705	227 665	-5.4	43 547	42 109	-3.3	84 885	82 760	-2.5	23 814	23 627	-0.8
Drunkenness	272 267	267 352	-1.8	7 561	6 996	-7.5	47 024	47 455	0.9	2 235	2 165	-3.1
Disorderly conduct	258 902	260 397	0.6	76 925	76 086	-1.1	92 646	93 004	0.4	37 768	37 412	-0.9
Vagrancy	11 992	11 970	-0.2	2 020	2 056	1.8	3 143	3 124	-0.6	824	773	-6.2
All other offenses, except traffic	1 341 442	1 345 715	0.3	140 820	137 408	-2.4	412 310	417 600	1.3	54 908	53 403	-2.7
Suspicion	988	878	-11.1	219	179	-18.3	297	227	-23.6	79	63	-20.3
Curfew and loitering law violations	38 116	39 048	2.4	38 116	39 048	2.4	18 637	18 729	0.5	18 637	18 729	0.5
Runaways	24 942	23 951	-4.0	24 942	23 951	-4.0	35 755	33 791	-5.5	35 755	33 791	-5.5

[1]Does not include suspicion.

Table 46. City Arrests, Distribution by Age, 2005

(Number, percent; 7,911 total agencies; 2005 estimated population 148,665,653.)

Offense	Total, all ages	Under 15 years	Under 18 years	18 years and over	Under 10 years	10–12 years	13–14 years	15 years	16 years	17 years
Total	7 723 696	401 038	1 294 505	6 420 101	10 905	85 234	304 899	261 293	304 728	327 536
Total percent distribution[1]	100.0	5.2	16.8	83.2	0.1	1.1	3.9	3.4	3.9	4.2
Violent crime	342 217	17 680	57 535	284 682	478	3 847	13 355	11 446	13 732	14 677
Violent crime percent distribution[1]	100.0	5.2	16.8	83.2	0.1	1.1	3.9	3.3	4.0	4.3
Murder and nonnegligent manslaughter	7 379	78	739	6 640	0	6	72	116	186	359
Forcible rape	13 193	746	2 080	11 113	3	207	536	343	435	556
Robbery	72 073	4 393	18 771	53 302	62	663	3 668	4 096	4 979	5 303
Aggravated assault	249 572	12 463	35 945	213 627	413	2 971	9 079	6 891	8 132	8 459
Property crime	964 499	91 090	260 214	704 285	2 620	20 820	67 650	53 250	57 793	58 081
Property crime percent distribution[1]	100.0	9.4	27.0	73.0	0.3	2.2	7.0	5.5	6.0	6.0
Burglary	159 661	14 980	43 387	116 274	544	3 398	11 038	9 020	9 496	9 891
Larceny-theft	712 539	68 211	190 200	522 339	1 757	16 003	50 451	38 138	41 832	42 019
Motor vehicle theft	83 941	5 270	22 331	61 610	59	567	4 644	5 348	5 968	5 745
Arson	8 358	2 629	4 296	4 062	260	852	1 517	744	497	426
Other assaults	710 869	58 238	140 227	570 642	1 722	15 101	41 415	27 846	28 366	25 777
Forgery and counterfeiting	64 874	277	2 319	62 555	14	40	223	311	619	1 112
Fraud	120 631	825	4 594	116 037	48	112	665	643	1 217	1 909
Embezzlement	10 341	43	678	9 663	3	10	30	25	197	413
Stolen property; buying, receiving, and possessing	75 620	3 715	13 982	61 638	69	649	2 997	2 814	3 638	3 815
Vandalism	160 608	26 061	61 693	98 915	1 312	7 127	17 622	11 732	12 302	11 598
Weapons; carrying and possessing, etc.	112 585	9 192	27 339	85 246	264	2 086	6 842	5 403	6 064	6 680
Prostitution and commercialized vice	59 411	153	1 151	58 260	11	9	133	167	308	523
Sex offenses, except forcible rape and prostitution	47 261	4 340	8 659	38 602	210	1 216	2 914	1 478	1 472	1 369
Drug abuse violations	1 025 810	18 605	113 876	911 934	190	1 966	16 449	20 799	31 367	43 105
Gambling	6 969	186	1 424	5 545	1	16	169	263	385	590
Offenses against the family and children	42 192	823	2 552	39 640	65	164	594	500	590	639
Driving under the influence	629 620	165	8 739	620 881	53	11	101	369	2 108	6 097
Liquor laws	348 779	6 932	70 807	277 972	101	468	6 363	11 314	20 073	32 488
Drunkenness	349 468	1 186	10 118	339 350	39	93	1 054	1 647	2 390	4 895
Disorderly conduct	430 047	52 100	120 002	301 345	1 008	12 446	38 646	27 172	26 178	23 552
Vagrancy	20 815	997	3 007	17 808	4	145	848	778	862	370
All other offenses, except traffic	2 038 271	58 160	215 075	1 823 196	1 776	10 443	45 941	44 743	52 741	59 431
Suspicion	1 208	69	303	905	1	11	57	63	74	97
Curfew and loitering law violations	99 936	28 362	99 936	X	426	4 891	23 045	22 924	27 065	21 585
Runaways	61 365	21 839	61 365	X	490	3 563	17 786	15 606	15 187	8 733

[1]Percentages may not add to 100 because of rounding.
X = Not applicable.

Table 46. City Arrests, Distribution by Age, 2005—*Continued*

(Number, percent; 7,911 total agencies; 2005 estimated population 148,665,653.)

Offense	18 years	19 years	20 years	21 years	22 years	23 years	24 years	25–29 years
Total	361 690	380 426	354 529	317 719	299 677	280 535	263 324	1 018 059
Total percent distribution[1]	4.7	4.9	4.6	4.1	3.9	3.6	3.4	13.2
Violent crime	15 983	15 943	14 649	14 090	13 575	13 032	12 276	48 883
Violent crime percent distribution[1]	4.7	4.7	4.3	4.1	4.0	3.8	3.6	14.3
Murder and nonnegligent manslaughter	476	514	461	479	421	432	361	1 246
Forcible rape	646	649	595	569	529	446	449	1 769
Robbery	5 757	5 061	3 990	3 325	2 869	2 587	2 374	8 286
Aggravated assault	9 104	9 719	9 603	9 717	9 756	9 567	9 092	37 582
Property crime	56 518	48 199	39 452	33 617	30 488	28 215	26 139	101 827
Property crime percent distribution[1]	5.9	5.0	4.1	3.5	3.2	2.9	2.7	10.6
Burglary	10 387	9 012	7 337	6 235	5 616	4 987	4 736	18 104
Larceny-theft	40 295	34 077	27 886	23 670	21 457	20 017	18 385	72 446
Motor vehicle theft	5 525	4 886	4 043	3 523	3 242	3 081	2 867	10 716
Arson	311	224	186	189	173	130	151	561
Other assaults	22 947	23 428	23 894	25 769	25 300	24 974	24 134	100 400
Forgery and counterfeiting	2 358	3 119	3 221	2 733	2 812	2 878	2 785	11 963
Fraud	3 571	4 616	5 019	4 656	4 840	4 725	4 707	20 110
Embezzlement	743	828	686	605	548	468	392	1 466
Stolen property; buying, receiving, and possessing	4 604	4 403	3 776	3 481	3 024	2 815	2 758	10 523
Vandalism	9 755	7 974	6 760	6 459	5 559	4 976	4 676	15 929
Weapons; carrying and possessing, etc.	7 558	7 123	5 950	5 708	5 394	4 710	4 394	15 183
Prostitution and commercialized vice	1 822	2 370	2 188	2 209	2 090	1 973	2 036	8 496
Sex offenses, except forcible rape and prostitution	1 677	1 735	1 672	1 450	1 371	1 275	1 172	4 988
Drug abuse violations	60 701	61 582	56 069	50 311	47 063	43 850	41 010	151 936
Gambling	555	463	477	360	325	296	234	804
Offenses against the family and children	1 216	1 329	1 350	1 460	1 587	1 567	1 741	7 228
Driving under the influence	14 778	20 746	23 566	32 295	32 803	30 979	29 174	109 155
Liquor laws	54 197	61 212	51 535	9 590	6 752	5 278	4 316	14 983
Drunkenness	9 589	11 006	11 053	16 156	14 882	13 615	12 070	46 489
Disorderly conduct	19 353	17 862	16 741	19 565	17 332	15 045	13 289	46 451
Vagrancy	679	527	451	433	408	401	414	1 684
All other offenses, except traffic	73 016	85 886	85 958	86 719	83 465	79 426	75 568	299 396
Suspicion	70	75	62	53	59	37	39	165
Curfew and loitering law violations	X	X	X	X	X	X	X	X
Runaways	X	X	X	X	X	X	X	X

[1]Percentages may not add to 100 because of rounding.
X = Not applicable.

Table 46. City Arrests, Distribution by Age, 2005—*Continued*

(Number, percent; 7,911 total agencies; 2005 estimated population 148,665,653.)

Offense	30–34 years	35–39 years	40–44 years	45–49 years	50–54 years	55–59 years	60–64 years	65 years and over
Total	762 594	715 894	685 620	498 194	267 527	125 037	53 655	44 621
Total percent distribution[1]	9.9	9.3	8.9	6.5	3.5	1.6	0.7	0.6
Violent crime	36 273	32 671	28 926	19 485	10 131	4 684	2 094	1 987
Violent crime percent distribution[1]	10.6	9.5	8.5	5.7	3.0	1.4	0.6	0.6
Murder and nonnegligent manslaughter	680	481	386	332	161	95	44	71
Forcible rape	1 517	1 333	1 129	724	386	167	99	106
Robbery	5 704	5 185	4 181	2 400	1 052	355	101	75
Aggravated assault	28 372	25 672	23 230	16 029	8 532	4 067	1 850	1 735
Property crime	82 187	81 754	74 867	52 257	27 182	12 041	5 086	4 456
Property crime percent distribution[1]	8.5	8.5	7.8	5.4	2.8	1.2	0.5	0.5
Burglary	13 223	13 169	11 405	7 212	3 166	1 072	386	227
Larceny-theft	60 657	61 482	58 115	41 970	22 756	10 504	4 514	4 108
Motor vehicle theft	7 836	6 666	4 888	2 716	1 049	359	135	78
Arson	471	437	459	359	211	106	51	43
Other assaults	78 249	71 440	64 895	43 996	22 113	10 416	4 578	4 109
Forgery and counterfeiting	9 641	8 032	6 262	3 842	1 754	749	249	157
Fraud	17 406	15 871	13 216	8 816	4 481	2 275	952	776
Embezzlement	1 139	1 037	778	538	248	118	40	29
Stolen property; buying, receiving, and possessing	7 763	6 895	5 578	3 510	1 569	571	224	144
Vandalism	10 582	8 880	7 722	5 126	2 500	1 129	432	456
Weapons; carrying and possessing, etc.	8 603	6 457	5 587	4 050	2 165	1 214	605	545
Prostitution and commercialized vice	8 571	9 326	8 246	4 956	2 205	928	447	397
Sex offenses, except forcible rape and prostitution	4 515	4 842	4 752	3 622	2 389	1 421	779	942
Drug abuse violations	104 653	95 135	89 864	62 560	30 292	11 457	3 583	1 868
Gambling	423	357	322	236	193	198	145	157
Offenses against the family and children	6 383	5 810	4 567	2 961	1 361	597	241	242
Driving under the influence	76 664	67 139	66 269	51 762	32 169	17 652	8 483	7 247
Liquor laws	11 683	12 398	15 507	13 712	8 782	4 610	2 029	1 388
Drunkenness	36 677	38 619	46 077	39 578	23 778	11 223	5 054	3 484
Disorderly conduct	31 445	29 286	30 470	22 312	12 031	5 520	2 461	2 182
Vagrancy	1 719	2 349	2 904	2 787	1 779	809	299	165
All other offenses, except traffic	227 907	217 517	208 748	152 039	80 386	37 412	15 866	13 887
Suspicion	111	79	63	49	19	13	8	3
Curfew and loitering law violations	X	X	X	X	X	X	X	X
Runaways	X	X	X	X	X	X	X	X

[1]Percentages may not add to 100 because of rounding.
X = Not applicable.

Table 47. City Arrests of Persons Under 15, 18, 21, and 25 Years of Age, 2005

(Number, percent; 7,911 total agencies; 2005 estimated population 148,665,653.)

Offense	Total, all ages	Number of persons arrested				Percent of total all ages			
		Under 15 years	Under 18 years	Under 21 years	Under 25 years	Under 15 years	Under 18 years	Under 21 years	Under 25 years
Total	7 723 696	401 038	1 294 595	2 391 240	3 552 495	5.2	16.8	31.0	46.0
Violent crime	342 217	17 680	57 535	104 110	157 083	5.2	16.8	30.4	45.9
Murder and nonnegligent manslaughter	7 379	78	739	2 190	3 883	1.1	10.0	29.7	52.6
Forcible rape	13 193	746	2 080	3 970	5 963	5.7	15.8	30.1	45.2
Robbery	72 073	4 393	18 771	33 579	44 734	6.1	26.0	46.6	62.1
Aggravated assault	249 572	12 463	35 945	64 371	102 503	5.0	14.4	25.8	41.1
Property crime	964 499	91 090	260 214	404 383	522 842	9.4	27.0	41.9	54.2
Burglary	159 661	14 980	43 387	70 123	91 697	9.4	27.2	43.9	57.4
Larceny-theft	712 539	68 211	190 200	292 458	375 987	9.6	26.7	41.0	52.8
Motor vehicle theft	83 941	5 270	22 331	36 785	49 498	6.3	26.6	43.8	59.0
Arson	8 358	2 629	4 296	5 017	5 660	31.5	51.4	60.0	67.7
Other assaults	710 869	58 238	140 227	210 496	310 673	8.2	19.7	29.6	43.7
Forgery and counterfeiting	64 874	277	2 319	11 017	22 225	0.4	3.6	17.0	34.3
Fraud	120 631	825	4 594	17 800	36 728	0.7	3.8	14.8	30.4
Embezzlement	10 341	43	678	2 935	4 948	0.4	6.6	28.4	47.8
Stolen property; buying, receiving, and possessing	75 620	3 715	13 982	26 765	38 843	4.9	18.5	35.4	51.4
Vandalism	160 608	26 061	61 693	86 182	107 852	16.2	38.4	53.7	67.2
Weapons; carrying and possessing, etc.	112 585	9 192	27 339	47 970	68 176	8.2	24.3	42.6	60.6
Prostitution and commercialized vice	59 411	153	1 151	7 531	15 839	0.3	1.9	12.7	26.7
Sex offenses, except forcible rape and prostitution	47 261	4 340	8 659	13 743	19 011	9.2	18.3	29.1	40.2
Drug abuse violations	1 025 810	18 605	113 876	292 228	474 462	1.8	11.1	28.5	46.3
Gambling	6 969	186	1 424	2 919	4 134	2.7	20.4	41.9	59.3
Offenses against the family and children	42 192	823	2 552	6 447	12 802	2.0	6.0	15.3	30.3
Driving under the influence	629 620	165	8 739	67 829	193 080	0.0	1.4	10.8	30.7
Liquor laws	348 779	6 932	70 807	237 751	263 687	2.0	20.3	68.2	75.6
Drunkenness	349 468	1 186	10 118	41 766	98 489	0.3	2.9	12.0	28.2
Disorderly conduct	430 347	52 100	129 002	182 958	248 189	12.1	30.0	42.5	57.7
Vagrancy	20 815	997	3 007	4 664	6 320	4.8	14.4	22.4	30.4
All other offenses, except traffic	2 038 271	58 160	215 075	459 935	785 113	2.9	10.6	22.6	38.5
Suspicion	1 208	69	303	510	698	5.7	25.1	42.2	57.8
Curfew and loitering law violations	99 936	28 362	99 936	99 936	99 936	28.4	100.0	100.0	100.0
Runaways	61 365	21 839	61 365	61 365	61 365	35.6	100.0	100.0	100.0

Table 48. City Arrests, Distribution by Sex, 2005

(Number, percent; 7,911 total agencies; 2005 estimated population 148,665,653.)

Offense	Number of persons arrested			Percent male	Percent female	Percent distribution[1]		
	Total	Male	Female			Total	Male	Female
Total	7 723 696	5 859 492	1 864 204	75.9	24.1	100.0	100.0	100.0
Violent crime	342 217	279 853	62 364	81.8	18.2	4.4	4.8	3.3
Murder and nonnegligent manslaughter	7 379	6 632	747	89.9	10.1	0.1	0.1	0.0
Forcible rape	13 193	13 031	162	98.8	1.2	0.2	0.2	0.0
Robbery	72 073	64 032	8 041	88.8	11.2	0.9	1.1	0.4
Aggravated assault	249 572	196 158	53 414	78.6	21.4	3.2	3.3	2.9
Property crime	964 499	643 664	320 835	66.7	33.3	12.5	11.0	17.2
Burglary	159 661	135 844	23 817	85.1	14.9	2.1	2.3	1.3
Larceny-theft	712 539	431 647	280 892	60.6	39.4	9.2	7.4	15.1
Motor vehicle theft	83 941	69 238	14 703	82.5	17.5	1.1	1.2	0.8
Arson	8 358	6 935	1 423	83.0	17.0	0.1	0.1	0.1
Other assaults	710 869	534 579	176 290	75.2	24.8	9.2	9.1	9.5
Forgery and counterfeiting	64 874	39 436	25 438	60.8	39.2	0.8	0.7	1.4
Fraud	120 631	69 497	51 134	57.6	42.4	1.6	1.2	2.7
Embezzlement	10 341	5 099	5 242	49.3	50.7	0.1	0.1	0.3
Stolen property; buying, receiving, and possessing	75 620	60 376	15 244	79.8	20.2	1.0	1.0	0.8
Vandalism	160 608	132 695	27 913	82.6	17.4	2.1	2.3	1.5
Weapons; carrying and possessing, etc.	112 585	103 526	9 059	92.0	8.0	1.5	1.8	0.5
Prostitution and commercialized vice	59 411	19 463	39 948	32.8	67.2	0.8	0.3	2.1
Sex offenses, except forcible rape and prostitution	47 261	42 669	4 592	90.3	9.7	0.6	0.7	0.2
Drug abuse violations	1 025 810	834 053	191 757	81.3	18.7	13.3	14.2	10.3
Gambling	6 969	6 516	453	93.5	6.5	0.1	0.1	0.0
Offenses against the family and children	42 192	28 338	13 854	67.2	32.8	0.5	0.5	0.7
Driving under the influence	629 620	504 372	125 248	80.1	19.9	8.2	8.6	6.7
Liquor laws	348 779	257 745	91 034	73.9	26.1	4.5	4.4	4.9
Drunkenness	349 468	296 973	52 495	85.0	15.0	4.5	5.1	2.8
Disorderly conduct	430 347	319 765	110 582	74.3	25.7	5.6	5.5	5.9
Vagrancy	20 815	16 674	4 141	80.1	19.9	0.3	0.3	0.2
All other offenses, except traffic	2 038 271	1 568 194	470 077	76.9	23.1	26.4	26.8	25.2
Suspicion	1 208	944	264	78.1	21.9	0.0	0.0	0.0
Curfew and loitering law violations	99 936	69 720	30 216	69.8	30.2	1.3	1.2	1.6
Runaways	61 365	25 341	36 024	41.3	58.7	0.8	0.4	1.9

[1]Percentages may not add to 100 because of rounding.

Table 49. City Arrests, Distribution by Race, 2005

(Number, percent; 7,910 total agencies; 2005 estimated population 148,664,155.)

Offense	Total arrests					Percent distribution[1]				
	Total	White	Black	American Indian or Alaskan Native	Asian or Pacific Islander	Total	White	Black	American Indian or Alaskan Native	Asian or Pacific Islander
Total	7 652 725	5 153 928	2 310 786	99 507	88 504	100.0	67.3	30.2	1.3	1.2
Violent crime	340 729	190 582	142 729	3 395	4 023	100.0	55.9	41.9	1.0	1.2
Murder and nonnegligent manslaughter	7 340	3 244	3 958	49	89	100.0	44.2	53.9	0.7	1.2
Forcible rape	13 091	7 870	4 947	115	159	100.0	60.1	37.8	0.9	1.2
Robbery	71 815	29 548	41 177	389	701	100.0	41.1	57.3	0.5	1.0
Aggravated assault	248 483	149 920	92 647	2 842	3 074	100.0	60.3	37.3	1.1	1.2
Property crime	957 742	645 677	286 523	12 100	13 442	100.0	67.4	29.9	1.3	1.4
Burglary	158 662	105 001	50 672	1 408	1 581	100.0	66.2	31.9	0.9	1.0
Larceny-theft	707 109	485 287	201 425	9 839	10 558	100.0	68.6	28.5	1.4	1.5
Motor vehicle theft	83 684	49 209	32 507	777	1 191	100.0	58.8	38.8	0.9	1.4
Arson	8 287	6 180	1 919	76	112	100.0	74.6	23.2	0.9	1.4
Other assaults	705 138	436 403	249 824	9 785	9 126	100.0	61.9	35.4	1.4	1.3
Forgery and counterfeiting	63 592	43 998	18 511	356	727	100.0	69.2	29.1	0.6	1.1
Fraud	118 583	78 296	38 619	666	1 002	100.0	66.0	32.6	0.6	0.8
Embezzlement	10 252	6 762	3 282	79	129	100.0	66.0	32.0	0.8	1.3
Stolen property; buying, receiving, and possessing	74 806	45 471	28 034	514	787	100.0	60.8	37.5	0.7	1.1
Vandalism	159 235	116 364	38 623	2 394	1 854	100.0	73.1	24.3	1.5	1.2
Weapons; carrying and possessing, etc.	111 875	63 529	46 647	639	1 060	100.0	56.8	41.7	0.6	0.9
Prostitution and commercialized vice	59 273	32 230	25 274	588	1 181	100.0	54.4	42.6	1.0	2.0
Sex offenses, except forcible rape and prostitution	46 724	32 695	13 002	452	575	100.0	70.0	27.8	1.0	1.2
Drug abuse violations	1 015 021	620 182	381 697	5 666	7 476	100.0	61.1	37.6	0.6	0.7
Gambling	6 959	1 416	5 411	14	118	100.0	20.3	77.8	0.2	1.7
Offenses against the family and children	40 949	29 748	9 998	832	371	100.0	72.6	24.4	2.0	0.9
Driving under the influence	621 981	545 099	60 532	8 590	7 760	100.0	87.6	9.7	1.4	1.2
Liquor laws	345 766	290 530	41 434	10 034	3 768	100.0	84.0	12.0	2.9	1.1
Drunkenness	341 671	283 064	48 780	7 885	1 942	100.0	82.8	14.3	2.3	0.6
Disorderly conduct	426 354	267 931	148 760	6 359	3 304	100.0	62.8	34.9	1.5	0.8
Vagrancy	20 807	12 034	8 280	384	109	100.0	57.8	39.8	1.8	0.5
All other offenses, except traffic	2 023 130	1 307 222	663 215	26 740	25 953	100.0	64.6	32.8	1.3	1.3
Suspicion	1 208	786	412	5	5	100.0	65.1	34.1	0.4	0.4
Curfew and loitering law violations	99 772	61 666	36 225	775	1 106	100.0	61.8	36.3	0.8	1.1
Runaways	61 158	42 243	14 974	1 255	2 686	100.0	69.1	24.5	2.1	4.4

[1]Percentages may not add to 100 because of rounding.

Table 49. City Arrests, Distribution by Race, 2005—*Continued*

(Number, percent; 7,910 total agencies; 2005 estimated population 148,664,155.)

Offense	Under 18 years					Percent distribution[1]				
	Total	White	Black	American Indian or Alaskan Native	Asian or Pacific Islander	Total	White	Black	American Indian or Alaskan Native	Asian or Pacific Islander
Total	1 287 063	853 064	399 467	15 962	18 570	100.0	66.3	31.0	1.2	1.4
Violent crime	57 249	26 240	29 903	421	685	100.0	45.8	52.2	0.7	1.2
Murder and nonnegligent manslaughter	738	291	427	11	9	100.0	39.4	57.9	1.5	1.2
Forcible rape	2 059	1 197	830	17	15	100.0	58.1	40.3	0.8	0.7
Robbery	18 725	5 706	12 692	67	260	100.0	30.5	67.8	0.4	1.4
Aggravated assault	35 727	19 046	15 954	326	401	100.0	53.3	44.7	0.9	1.1
Property crime	258 635	172 092	78 379	3 569	4 595	100.0	66.5	30.3	1.4	1.8
Burglary	43 136	27 756	14 543	384	453	100.0	64.3	33.7	0.9	1.1
Larceny-theft	188 992	129 793	52 572	2 890	3 737	100.0	68.7	27.8	1.5	2.0
Motor vehicle theft	22 245	11 200	10 448	254	343	100.0	50.3	47.0	1.1	1.5
Arson	4 262	3 343	816	41	62	100.0	78.4	19.1	1.0	1.5
Other assaults	139 308	79 717	56 345	1 574	1 672	100.0	57.2	40.4	1.1	1.2
Forgery and counterfeiting	2 301	1 660	589	12	40	100.0	72.1	25.6	0.5	1.7
Fraud	4 561	2 817	1 665	30	49	100.0	61.8	36.5	0.7	1.1
Embezzlement	675	437	215	7	16	100.0	64.7	31.9	1.0	2.4
Stolen property; buying, receiving, and possessing	13 861	7 235	6 334	108	184	100.0	52.2	45.7	0.8	1.3
Vandalism	61 184	47 154	12 486	771	773	100.0	77.1	20.4	1.3	1.3
Weapons; carrying and possessing, etc.	27 242	16 600	10 128	174	340	100.0	60.9	37.2	0.6	1.2
Prostitution and commercialized vice	1 147	469	650	8	20	100.0	40.9	56.7	0.7	1.7
Sex offenses, except forcible rape and prostitution	8 585	5 804	2 627	57	97	100.0	67.6	30.6	0.7	1.1
Drug abuse violations	113 156	74 921	36 284	985	966	100.0	66.2	32.1	0.9	0.9
Gambling	1 423	90	1 327	0	6	100.0	6.3	93.3	0.0	0.4
Offenses against the family and children	2 534	1 942	547	39	6	100.0	76.6	21.6	1.5	0.2
Driving under the influence	8 615	8 015	372	140	88	100.0	93.0	4.3	1.6	1.0
Liquor laws	70 345	63 944	3 690	1 999	712	100.0	90.9	5.2	2.8	1.0
Drunkenness	9 892	8 751	862	190	89	100.0	88.5	8.7	1.9	0.9
Disorderly conduct	128 467	76 519	49 428	1 485	1 035	100.0	59.6	38.5	1.2	0.8
Vagrancy	3 007	2 346	633	10	18	100.0	78.0	21.1	0.3	0.6
All other offenses, except traffic	213 643	152 200	55 706	2 351	3 386	100.0	71.2	26.1	1.1	1.6
Suspicion	303	202	98	2	1	100.0	66.7	32.3	0.7	0.3
Curfew and loitering law violations	99 772	61 666	36 225	775	1 106	100.0	61.8	36.3	0.8	1.1
Runaways	61 158	42 243	14 974	1 255	2 686	100.0	69.1	24.5	2.1	4.4

[1]Percentages may not add to 100 because of rounding.

Table 49. City Arrests, Distribution by Race, 2005—*Continued*

(Number, percent; 7,910 total agencies; 2005 estimated population 148,664,155.)

Offense	18 years and over					Percent distribution[1]				
	Total	White	Black	American Indian or Alaskan Native	Asian or Pacific Islander	Total	White	Black	American Indian or Alaskan Native	Asian or Pacific Islander
Total	6 365 662	4 300 864	1 911 319	83 545	69 934	100.0	67.6	30.0	1.3	1.1
Violent crime	283 480	164 342	112 826	2 974	3 338	100.0	58.0	39.8	1.0	1.2
Murder and nonnegligent manslaughter	6 602	2 953	3 531	38	80	100.0	44.7	53.5	0.6	1.2
Forcible rape	11 032	6 673	4 117	98	144	100.0	60.5	37.3	0.9	1.3
Robbery	53 090	23 842	28 485	322	441	100.0	44.9	53.7	0.6	0.8
Aggravated assault	212 756	130 874	76 693	2 516	2 673	100.0	61.5	36.0	1.2	1.3
Property crime	699 107	473 585	208 144	8 531	8 847	100.0	67.7	29.8	1.2	1.3
Burglary	115 526	77 245	36 129	1 024	1 128	100.0	66.9	31.3	0.9	1.0
Larceny-theft	518 117	355 494	148 853	6 949	6 821	100.0	68.6	28.7	1.3	1.3
Motor vehicle theft	61 439	38 009	22 059	523	848	100.0	61.9	35.9	0.9	1.4
Arson	4 025	2 837	1 103	35	50	100.0	70.5	27.4	0.9	1.2
Other assaults	565 830	356 686	193 479	8 211	7 454	100.0	63.0	34.2	1.5	1.3
Forgery and counterfeiting	61 291	42 338	17 922	344	687	100.0	69.1	29.2	0.6	1.1
Fraud	114 022	75 479	36 954	636	953	100.0	66.2	32.4	0.6	0.8
Embezzlement	9 577	6 325	3 067	72	113	100.0	66.0	32.0	0.8	1.2
Stolen property; buying, receiving, and possessing	60 945	38 236	21 700	406	603	100.0	62.7	35.6	0.7	1.0
Vandalism	98 051	69 210	26 137	1 623	1 081	100.0	70.6	26.7	1.7	1.1
Weapons; carrying and possessing, etc.	84 633	46 929	36 519	465	720	100.0	55.5	43.1	0.5	0.9
Prostitution and commercialized vice	58 126	31 761	24 624	580	1 161	100.0	54.6	42.4	1.0	2.0
Sex offenses, except forcible rape and prostitution	38 139	26 891	10 375	395	478	100.0	70.5	27.2	1.0	1.3
Drug abuse violations	901 865	545 261	345 413	4 681	6 510	100.0	60.5	38.3	0.5	0.7
Gambling	5 536	1 326	4 084	14	112	100.0	24.0	73.8	0.3	2.0
Offenses against the family and children	38 415	27 806	9 451	793	365	100.0	72.4	24.6	2.1	1.0
Driving under the influence	613 366	537 084	60 160	8 450	7 672	100.0	87.6	9.8	1.4	1.3
Liquor laws	275 421	226 586	37 744	8 035	3 056	100.0	82.3	13.7	2.9	1.1
Drunkenness	331 779	274 313	47 918	7 695	1 853	100.0	82.7	14.4	2.3	0.6
Disorderly conduct	297 887	191 412	99 332	4 874	2 269	100.0	64.3	33.3	1.6	0.8
Vagrancy	17 800	9 688	7 647	374	91	100.0	54.4	43.0	2.1	0.5
All other offenses, except traffic	1 809 487	1 155 022	607 509	24 389	22 567	100.0	63.8	33.6	1.3	1.2
Suspicion	905	584	314	3	4	100.0	64.5	34.7	0.3	0.4
Curfew and loitering law violations	X	X	X	X	X	X	X	X	X	X
Runaways	X	X	X	X	X	X	X	X	X	X

[1]Percentages may not add to 100 because of rounding.
X = Not applicable.

Table 50. Arrest Trends for Metropolitan Counties, 2004 and 2005

(Number, percent change; 1,091 total agencies; 2004 estimated population 46,302,195; 2005 estimated population 46,765,819.)

Offense	Total, all ages			Under 18 years			18 years and over		
	2004	2005	Percent change	2004	2005	Percent change	2004	2005	Percent change
Total[1]	1 697 178	1 726 746	1.7	208 826	201 651	-3.4	1 488 352	1 525 095	2.5
Violent crime	75 040	74 948	-0.1	10 141	9 895	-2.4	64 899	65 053	0.2
Murder and nonnegligent manslaughter	1 784	1 941	8.8	123	130	5.7	1 661	1 811	9.0
Forcible rape	3 680	3 370	-8.4	588	457	-22.3	3 092	2 913	-5.8
Robbery	10 085	10 416	3.3	2 062	2 313	12.2	8 023	8 103	1.0
Aggravated assault	59 491	59 221	-0.5	7 368	6 995	-5.1	52 123	52 226	0.2
Property crime	164 562	160 988	-2.2	40 439	36 870	-8.8	124 123	124 118	0.0
Burglary	38 887	38 746	-0.4	10 341	9 366	-9.4	28 546	29 380	2.9
Larceny-theft	105 545	102 285	-3.1	25 065	22 767	-9.2	80 480	79 518	-1.2
Motor vehicle theft	18 080	17 775	-1.7	4 101	3 702	-9.7	13 979	14 073	0.7
Arson	2 050	2 182	6.4	932	1 035	11.1	1 118	1 147	2.6
Other assaults	160 311	163 200	1.8	30 927	30 788	-0.4	129 384	132 412	2.3
Forgery and counterfeiting	13 975	13 601	-2.7	456	497	9.0	13 519	13 104	-3.1
Fraud	65 496	64 429	-1.6	863	815	-5.6	64 633	63 614	-1.6
Embezzlement	2 489	2 616	5.1	156	158	1.3	2 333	2 458	5.4
Stolen property; buying, receiving, and possessing	15 416	15 489	0.5	1 833	1 685	-8.1	13 583	13 804	1.6
Vandalism	30 170	29 860	-1.0	10 891	10 343	-5.0	19 279	19 517	1.2
Weapons; carrying and possessing, etc.	19 697	21 253	7.9	4 250	4 535	6.7	15 447	16 718	8.2
Prostitution and commercialized vice	3 031	2 808	-7.4	77	41	-46.8	2 954	2 767	-6.3
Sex offenses, except forcible rape and prostitution	11 805	11 612	-1.6	2 399	2 240	-6.6	9 406	9 372	-0.4
Drug abuse violations	203 879	215 099	5.5	19 794	19 170	-3.2	184 085	195 929	6.4
Gambling	662	552	-16.6	32	31	-3.1	630	521	-17.3
Offenses against the family and children	32 576	33 749	3.6	591	667	12.9	31 985	33 082	3.4
Driving under the influence	231 030	226 329	-2.0	2 463	2 279	-7.5	228 567	224 050	-2.0
Liquor laws	48 755	48 760	0.0	12 784	12 428	-2.8	35 971	36 332	1.0
Drunkenness	42 718	41 247	-3.4	1 188	1 003	-15.6	41 530	40 244	-3.1
Disorderly conduct	41 055	41 357	0.7	12 777	12 811	0.3	28 278	28 546	0.9
Vagrancy	1 658	2 119	27.8	262	325	24.0	1 396	1 794	28.5
All other offenses, except traffic	513 672	538 402	4.8	37 322	36 742	-1.6	476 350	501 660	5.3
Suspicion	81	463	471.6	37	50	35.1	44	413	838.6
Curfew and loitering law violations	3 332	3 767	13.1	3 332	3 767	13.1	X	X	X
Runaways	15 849	14 561	-8.1	15 849	14 561	-8.1	X	X	X

[1]Does not include suspicion.
X = Not applicable.

Table 51. Arrest Trends for Metropolitan Counties, by Age and Sex, 2004 and 2005

(Number, percent change; 1,091 total agencies; 2004 estimated population 46,302,195; 2005 estimated population 46,765,819.)

Offense	Male						Female					
	Total, all ages			Under 18 years			Total, all ages			Under 18 years		
	2004	2005	Percent change	2004	2005	Percent change	2004	2005	Percent change	2004	2005	Percent change
Total[1]	1 310 131	1 329 442	1.5	148 764	143 786	-3.3	387 047	397 304	2.7	60 062	57 865	-3.7
Violent crime	62 233	62 200	-0.1	8 347	8 098	-3.0	12 807	12 748	-0.5	1 794	1 797	0.2
Murder and nonnegligent manslaughter	1 543	1 682	9.0	109	108	-0.9	241	259	7.5	14	22	57.1
Forcible rape	3 638	3 318	-8.8	582	450	-22.7	42	52	23.8	6	7	16.7
Robbery	9 066	9 320	2.8	1 905	2 090	9.7	1 019	1 096	7.6	157	223	42.0
Aggravated assault	47 986	47 880	-0.2	5 751	5 450	-5.2	11 505	11 341	-1.4	1 617	1 545	-4.5
Property crime	118 563	115 927	-2.2	29 090	26 594	-8.6	45 999	45 061	-2.0	11 349	10 276	-9.5
Burglary	33 692	33 395	-0.9	9 242	8 434	-8.7	5 195	5 351	3.0	1 099	932	-15.2
Larceny-theft	68 058	65 902	-3.2	15 649	14 156	-9.5	37 487	36 383	-2.9	9 416	8 611	-8.5
Motor vehicle theft	15 075	14 744	-2.2	3 398	3 078	-9.4	3 005	3 031	0.9	703	624	-11.2
Arson	1 738	1 886	8.5	801	926	15.6	312	296	-5.1	131	109	-16.8
Other assaults	121 575	123 414	1.5	21 047	20 690	-1.7	38 736	39 786	2.7	9 880	10 098	2.2
Forgery and counterfeiting	8 627	8 281	-4.0	309	351	13.6	5 348	5 320	-0.5	147	146	-0.7
Fraud	33 807	33 246	-1.7	545	507	-7.0	31 689	31 183	-1.6	318	308	-3.1
Embezzlement	1 332	1 328	-0.3	99	92	-7.1	1 157	1 288	11.3	57	66	15.8
Stolen property; buying, receiving, and possessing	12 733	12 642	-0.7	1 566	1 411	-9.9	2 683	2 847	6.1	267	274	2.6
Vandalism	25 454	24 914	-2.1	9 456	8 936	-5.5	4 716	4 946	4.9	1 435	1 407	-2.0
Weapons; carrying and possessing, etc.	18 182	19 577	7.7	3 747	4 020	7.3	1 515	1 676	10.6	503	515	2.4
Prostitution and commercialized vice	1 391	1 416	1.8	48	12	-75.0	1 640	1 392	-15.1	29	29	0.0
Sex offenses, except forcible rape and prostitution	11 202	11 112	-0.8	2 235	2 103	-5.9	603	500	-17.1	164	137	-16.5
Drug abuse violations	163 844	172 134	5.1	16 046	15 706	-2.1	40 035	42 965	7.3	3 748	3 464	-7.6
Gambling	494	416	-15.8	32	29	-9.4	168	136	-19.0	0	2	0.0
Offenses against the family and children	27 610	28 351	2.7	399	433	8.5	4 966	5 398	8.7	192	234	21.9
Driving under the influence	190 284	185 034	-2.8	1 970	1 792	-9.0	40 746	41 295	1.3	493	487	-1.2
Liquor laws	35 999	35 280	-2.0	8 250	7 893	-4.3	12 756	13 480	5.7	4 534	4 535	0.0
Drunkenness	35 819	34 484	-3.7	902	756	-16.2	6 899	6 763	-2.0	286	247	-13.6
Disorderly conduct	30 446	30 505	0.2	8 721	8 809	1.0	10 609	10 852	2.3	4 056	4 002	-1.3
Vagrancy	1 244	1 539	23.7	176	231	31.3	414	580	40.1	86	94	9.3
All other offenses, except traffic	400 679	419 037	4.6	27 166	26 718	-1.6	112 993	119 365	5.6	10 156	10 024	-1.3
Suspicion	57	372	552.6	24	38	58.3	24	91	279.2	13	12	-7.7
Curfew and loitering law violations	2 175	2 458	13.0	2 175	2 458	13.0	1 157	1 309	13.1	1 157	1 309	13.1
Runaways	6 438	6 147	-4.5	6 438	6 147	-4.5	9 411	8 414	-10.6	9 411	8 414	-10.6

[1]Does not include suspicion.

Table 52. Arrests in Metropolitan Counties, Distribution by Age, 2005

(Number, percent; 1,225 total agencies; 2005 estimated population 47,831,303.)

Offense	Total, all ages	Under 15 years	Under 18 years	18 years and over	Under 10 years	10–12 years	13–14 years	15 years	16 years	17 years
Total	1 796 282	60 387	212 364	1 583 918	1 851	12 644	45 892	41 834	50 978	59 165
Total percent distribution[1]	100.0	3.4	11.8	88.2	0.1	0.7	2.6	2.3	2.8	3.3
Violent crime	76 891	3 131	10 286	66 605	113	712	2 306	2 017	2 389	2 749
Violent crime percent distribution[1]	100.0	4.1	13.4	86.6	0.1	0.9	3.0	2.6	3.1	3.6
Murder and nonnegligent manslaughter	2 011	14	144	1 867	0	2	12	27	37	66
Forcible rape	3 526	187	499	3 027	6	44	137	88	92	132
Robbery	11 077	557	2 491	8 586	10	84	463	501	657	776
Aggravated assault	60 277	2 373	7 152	53 125	97	582	1 694	1 401	1 603	1 775
Property crime	169 285	11 848	38 798	130 487	292	2 589	8 967	7 880	9 022	10 048
Property crime percent distribution[1]	100.0	7.0	22.9	77.1	0.2	1.5	5.3	4.7	5.3	5.9
Burglary	40 365	2 963	9 734	30 631	82	666	2 215	1 965	2 228	2 578
Larceny-theft	108 150	7 394	23 966	84 184	172	1 634	5 588	4 792	5 547	6 233
Motor vehicle theft	18 274	832	3 912	14 362	6	90	736	910	1 063	1 107
Arson	2 496	659	1 186	1 310	32	199	428	213	184	130
Other assaults	168 453	12 831	32 594	135 859	435	3 266	9 130	6 562	6 797	6 404
Forgery and counterfeiting	14 944	71	556	14 388	3	17	51	80	148	257
Fraud	70 881	141	919	69 962	14	18	109	112	213	453
Embezzlement	2 653	4	154	2 499	0	1	3	8	50	92
Stolen property; buying, receiving, and possessing	17 045	343	1 824	15 221	7	54	282	383	443	655
Vandalism	31 202	4 148	10 838	20 364	227	1 102	2 819	2 022	2 280	2 388
Weapons; carrying and possessing, etc.	22 277	1 752	4 819	17 458	57	471	1 224	888	1 031	1 148
Prostitution and commercialized vice	3 067	9	48	3 019	0	1	8	10	13	16
Sex offenses, except forcible rape and prostitution	12 431	1 165	2 377	10 054	48	332	785	438	383	391
Drug abuse violations	228 042	3 120	20 213	207 829	36	331	2 753	3 379	5 389	8 325
Gambling	620	12	35	585	0	1	11	7	10	6
Offenses against the family and children	35 523	203	702	34 821	8	53	142	138	154	207
Driving under the influence	233 753	40	2 392	231 361	8	5	27	77	580	1 695
Liquor laws	50 876	997	12 806	38 070	7	59	931	1 899	3 610	6 300
Drunkenness	40 311	135	1 066	39 245	5	10	120	201	253	477
Disorderly conduct	44 432	5 336	14 016	30 416	105	1 158	4 073	3 056	3 047	2 577
Vagrancy	3 288	84	480	2 808	1	10	73	65	93	148
All other offenses, except traffic	550 036	9 188	38 562	511 474	307	1 615	7 266	7 676	9 760	11 938
Suspicion	1 353	11	50	1 303	1	2	8	7	9	23
Curfew and loitering law violations	3 414	809	3 414	X	13	103	693	781	1 124	700
Runaways	15 505	5 009	15 505	X	164	734	4 111	4 140	4 180	2 168

[1]Percentages may not add to 100 because of rounding.
X = Not applicable.

Table 52. Arrests in Metropolitan Counties, Distribution by Age, 2005—*Continued*

(Number, percent; 1,225 total agencies; 2005 estimated population 47,831,303.)

Offense	18 years	19 years	20 years	21 years	22 years	23 years	24 years	25–29 years
Total	72 912	79 005	76 270	72 389	70 454	67 918	65 944	262 000
Total percent distribution[1]	4.1	4.4	4.2	4.0	3.9	3.8	3.7	14.6
Violent crime	3 622	3 363	2 968	3 007	2 855	2 808	2 710	10 765
Violent crime percent distribution[1]	4.7	4.4	3.9	3.9	3.7	3.7	3.5	14.0
Murder and nonnegligent manslaughter	124	121	123	100	96	105	106	339
Forcible rape	171	181	150	145	125	111	117	432
Robbery	1 095	889	679	562	479	398	415	1 386
Aggravated assault	2 232	2 172	2 016	2 200	2 155	2 194	2 072	8 608
Property crime	10 656	9 637	7 519	6 730	5 859	5 499	5 023	20 142
Property crime percent distribution[1]	6.3	5.7	4.4	4.0	3.5	3.2	3.0	11.9
Burglary	3 124	2 890	2 146	1 840	1 509	1 468	1 268	4 815
Larceny-theft	6 224	5 543	4 384	3 984	3 523	3 256	3 092	12 493
Motor vehicle theft	1 191	1 126	927	841	775	712	624	2 643
Arson	117	78	62	65	52	63	39	191
Other assaults	5 197	5 083	4 930	5 056	5 086	4 998	4 985	21 373
Forgery and counterfeiting	457	579	639	583	578	596	630	2 874
Fraud	986	1 691	2 125	2 224	2 401	2 525	2 713	12 334
Embezzlement	154	155	152	110	104	92	84	377
Stolen property; buying, receiving, and possessing	971	993	839	765	762	738	725	2 629
Vandalism	2 007	1 680	1 453	1 245	1 062	884	798	3 063
Weapons; carrying and possessing, etc.	1 281	1 205	1 116	1 119	1 001	945	841	3 055
Prostitution and commercialized vice	63	102	100	87	79	89	91	443
Sex offenses, except forcible rape and prostitution	479	472	422	360	333	311	288	1 229
Drug abuse violations	12 746	13 464	13 052	11 848	11 043	10 351	9 930	36 067
Gambling	14	19	21	12	10	6	16	54
Offenses against the family and children	358	448	474	619	809	853	1 011	5 730
Driving under the influence	4 838	6 792	7 869	11 205	11 847	11 494	10 919	40 881
Liquor laws	8 981	8 849	7 122	1 276	890	728	629	2 181
Drunkenness	1 303	1 515	1 378	1 794	1 680	1 599	1 547	5 514
Disorderly conduct	1 976	1 658	1 423	1 518	1 435	1 304	1 156	4 392
Vagrancy	118	120	108	100	95	119	105	441
All other offenses, except traffic	16 619	21 096	22 483	22 655	22 480	21 928	21 717	88 251
Suspicion	86	84	77	76	45	51	26	205
Curfew and loitering law violations	X	X	X	X	X	X	X	X
Runaways	X	X	X	X	X	X	X	X

[1]Percentages may not add to 100 because of rounding.
X = Not applicable.

Table 52. Arrests in Metropolitan Counties, Distribution by Age, 2005—*Continued*

(Number, percent; 1,225 total agencies; 2005 estimated population 47,831,303.)

Offense	30–34 years	35–39 years	40–44 years	45–49 years	50–54 years	55–59 years	60–64 years	65 years and over
Total	208 085	193 017	178 484	121 102	62 924	29 496	13 100	10 818
Total percent distribution[1]	11.0	10.7	9.9	6.7	3.5	1.6	0.7	0.6
Violent crime	8 780	8 030	7 347	5 137	2 614	1 314	634	651
Violent crime percent distribution[1]	11.4	10.4	9.6	6.7	3.4	1.7	0.8	0.8
Murder and nonnegligent manslaughter	218	144	130	124	58	32	18	29
Forcible rape	396	364	338	217	136	71	35	38
Robbery	890	713	563	339	112	42	15	9
Aggravated assault	7 276	6 809	6 316	4 457	2 308	1 169	566	575
Property crime	15 621	14 940	13 145	8 279	4 114	1 826	812	685
Property crime percent distribution[1]	9.2	8.8	7.8	4.9	2.4	1.1	0.5	0.4
Burglary	3 461	3 076	2 638	1 430	592	225	68	81
Larceny-theft	10 171	10 223	9 232	6 128	3 206	1 469	689	567
Motor vehicle theft	1 854	1 484	1 145	609	266	102	40	23
Arson	135	157	130	112	50	30	15	14
Other assaults	19 138	18 857	17 634	11 710	6 090	2 907	1 462	1 353
Forgery and counterfeiting	2 309	1 950	1 567	925	389	216	54	42
Fraud	11 875	10 586	8 822	5 732	3 141	1 514	651	642
Embezzlement	303	323	258	195	99	59	22	12
Stolen property; buying, receiving, and possessing	2 032	1 848	1 446	810	398	159	66	40
Vandalism	2 232	2 059	1 775	1 082	506	262	137	119
Weapons; carrying and possessing, etc.	1 985	1 501	1 301	958	576	300	148	126
Prostitution and commercialized vice	410	474	446	279	156	92	52	56
Sex offenses, except forcible rape and prostitution	1 230	1 276	1 220	897	599	373	254	311
Drug abuse violations	24 492	21 524	20 183	13 377	6 201	2 335	735	481
Gambling	70	87	66	63	48	44	32	23
Offenses against the family and children	6 513	6 415	5 641	3 607	1 423	589	216	115
Driving under the influence	29 529	26 154	25 669	19 926	12 251	6 579	3 071	2 337
Liquor laws	1 534	1 585	1 644	1 275	740	351	168	117
Drunkenness	4 457	4 560	5 168	4 214	2 513	1 225	451	327
Disorderly conduct	3 363	3 439	3 550	2 524	1 345	733	328	272
Vagrancy	356	370	387	315	136	66	31	22
All other offenses, except traffic	71 709	66 876	61 082	39 700	19 531	8 510	3 761	3 076
Suspicion	147	154	133	97	54	42	15	11
Curfew and loitering law violations	X	X	X	X	X	X	X	X
Runaways	X	X	X	X	X	X	X	X

[1]Percentages may not add to 100 because of rounding.
X = Not applicable.

Table 53. Arrests in Metropolitan Counties of Persons Under 15, 18, 21, and 25 Years of Age, 2005

(Number, percent; 1,225 total agencies; 2005 estimated population 47,831,303.)

Offense	Total, all ages	Number of persons arrested				Percent of total all ages			
		Under 15 years	Under 18 years	Under 21 years	Under 25 years	Under 15 years	Under 18 years	Under 21 years	Under 25 years
Total	1 796 282	60 387	212 364	440 551	717 256	3.4	11.8	24.5	39.9
Violent crime	76 891	3 131	10 286	20 239	31 619	4.1	13.4	26.3	41.1
Murder and nonnegligent manslaughter	2 011	14	144	512	919	0.7	7.2	25.5	45.7
Forcible rape	3 526	187	499	1 001	1 499	5.3	14.2	28.4	42.5
Robbery	11 077	557	2 491	5 154	7 008	5.0	22.5	46.5	63.3
Aggravated assault	60 277	2 373	7 152	13 572	22 193	3.9	11.9	22.5	36.8
Property crime	169 285	11 848	38 798	66 610	89 721	7.0	22.9	39.3	53.0
Burglary	40 365	2 963	9 734	17 894	23 979	7.3	24.1	44.3	59.4
Larceny-theft	108 150	7 394	23 966	40 117	53 972	6.8	22.2	37.1	49.9
Motor vehicle theft	18 274	832	3 912	7 156	10 108	4.6	21.4	39.2	55.3
Arson	2 496	659	1 186	1 443	1 662	26.4	47.5	57.8	66.6
Other assaults	168 453	12 831	32 594	47 804	67 929	7.6	19.3	28.4	40.3
Forgery and counterfeiting	14 944	71	556	2 231	4 618	0.5	3.7	14.9	30.9
Fraud	70 881	141	919	5 721	15 584	0.2	1.3	8.1	22.0
Embezzlement	2 653	4	154	615	1 005	0.2	5.8	23.2	37.9
Stolen property; buying, receiving, and possessing	17 045	343	1 824	4 627	7 617	2.0	10.7	27.1	44.7
Vandalism	31 202	4 148	10 838	15 978	19 967	13.3	34.7	51.2	64.0
Weapons; carrying and possessing, etc.	22 277	1 752	4 819	8 421	12 327	7.9	21.6	37.8	55.3
Prostitution and commercialized vice	3 067	9	48	313	659	0.3	1.6	10.2	21.5
Sex offenses, except forcible rape and prostitution	12 431	1 165	2 377	3 750	5 042	9.4	19.1	30.2	40.6
Drug abuse violations	228 042	3 120	20 213	59 475	102 647	1.4	8.9	26.1	45.0
Gambling	620	12	35	89	133	1.9	5.6	14.4	21.5
Offenses against the family and children	35 523	203	702	1 982	5 274	0.6	2.0	5.6	14.8
Driving under the influence	233 753	40	2 392	21 891	67 356	0.0	1.0	9.4	28.8
Liquor laws	50 876	997	12 806	37 758	41 281	2.0	25.2	74.2	81.1
Drunkenness	40 311	135	1 066	5 262	11 882	0.3	2.6	13.1	29.5
Disorderly conduct	44 432	5 336	14 016	19 073	24 486	12.0	31.5	42.9	55.1
Vagrancy	3 288	84	390	736	1 155	2.6	11.9	22.4	35.1
All other offenses, except traffic	550 036	9 188	38 562	98 760	187 540	1.7	7.0	18.0	34.1
Suspicion	1 353	11	50	297	495	0.8	3.7	22.0	36.6
Curfew and loitering law violations	3 414	809	3 414	3 414	3 414	23.7	100.0	100.0	100.0
Runaways	15 505	5 009	15 505	15 505	15 505	32.3	100.0	100.0	100.0

Table 54. Arrests in Metropolitan Counties, Distribution by Sex, 2005

(Number, percent; 1,225 total agencies; 2005 estimated population 47,831,303.)

Offense	Number of persons arrested			Percent male	Percent female	Percent distribution[1]		
	Total	Male	Female			Total	Male	Female
Total	1 796 282	1 383 730	412 552	77.0	23.0	100.0	100.0	100.0
Violent crime	76 891	63 819	13 072	83.0	17.0	4.3	4.6	3.2
Murder and nonnegligent manslaughter	2 011	1 750	261	87.0	13.0	0.1	0.1	0.1
Forcible rape	3 526	3 467	59	98.3	1.7	0.2	0.3	0.0
Robbery	11 077	9 899	1 178	89.4	10.6	0.6	0.7	0.3
Aggravated assault	60 277	48 703	11 574	80.8	19.2	3.4	3.5	2.8
Property crime	169 285	121 621	47 664	71.8	28.2	9.4	8.8	11.6
Burglary	40 365	34 799	5 566	86.2	13.8	2.2	2.5	1.3
Larceny-theft	108 150	69 587	38 563	64.3	35.7	6.0	5.0	9.3
Motor vehicle theft	18 274	15 136	3 138	82.8	17.2	1.0	1.1	0.8
Arson	2 496	2 099	397	84.1	15.9	0.1	0.2	0.1
Other assaults	168 453	127 472	40 981	75.7	24.3	9.4	9.2	9.9
Forgery and counterfeiting	14 944	9 159	5 785	61.3	38.7	0.8	0.7	1.4
Fraud	70 881	36 646	34 235	51.7	48.3	3.9	2.6	8.3
Embezzlement	2 653	1 363	1 290	51.4	48.6	0.1	0.1	0.3
Stolen property; buying, receiving, and possessing	17 045	14 028	3 017	82.3	17.7	0.9	1.0	0.7
Vandalism	31 202	26 047	5 155	83.5	16.5	1.7	1.9	1.2
Weapons; carrying and possessing, etc.	22 277	20 501	1 776	92.0	8.0	1.2	1.5	0.4
Prostitution and commercialized vice	3 067	1 490	1 577	48.6	51.4	0.2	0.1	0.4
Sex offenses, except forcible rape and prostitution	12 431	11 858	573	95.4	4.6	0.7	0.9	0.1
Drug abuse violations	228 042	182 727	45 315	80.1	19.9	12.7	13.2	11.0
Gambling	620	474	146	76.5	23.5	0.0	0.0	0.0
Offenses against the family and children	35 523	29 788	5 735	83.9	16.1	2.0	2.2	1.4
Driving under the influence	233 753	191 251	42 502	81.8	18.2	13.0	13.8	10.3
Liquor laws	50 876	36 825	14 051	72.4	27.6	2.8	2.7	3.4
Drunkenness	40 311	33 704	6 607	83.6	16.4	2.2	2.4	1.6
Disorderly conduct	44 432	32 772	11 660	73.8	26.2	2.5	2.4	2.8
Vagrancy	3 288	2 366	922	72.0	28.0	0.2	0.2	0.2
All other offenses, except traffic	550 036	429 413	120 623	78.1	21.9	30.6	31.0	29.2
Suspicion	1 353	1 262	91	93.3	6.7	0.1	0.1	0.0
Curfew and loitering law violations	3 414	2 254	1 160	66.0	34.0	0.2	0.2	0.3
Runaways	15 505	6 890	8 615	44.4	55.6	0.9	0.5	2.1

[1]Percentages may not add to 100 because of rounding.

Table 55. Arrests in Metropolitan Counties, Distribution by Race, 2005

(Number, percent; 1,225 total agencies; 2005 estimated population 47,831,303.)

Offense	Total arrests					Percent distribution[1]				
	Total	White	Black	American Indian or Alaskan Native	Asian or Pacific Islander	Total	White	Black	American Indian or Alaskan Native	Asian or Pacific Islander
Total	1 772 196	1 332 869	415 986	12 779	10 562	100.0	75.2	23.5	0.7	0.6
Violent crime	76 490	51 872	23 562	553	503	100.0	67.8	30.8	0.7	0.7
Murder and nonnegligent manslaughter	1 995	1 215	737	14	29	100.0	60.9	36.9	0.7	1.5
Forcible rape	3 484	2 634	797	34	19	100.0	75.6	22.9	1.0	0.5
Robbery	10 981	5 136	5 755	44	46	100.0	46.8	52.4	0.4	0.4
Aggravated assault	60 030	42 887	16 273	461	409	100.0	71.4	27.1	0.8	0.7
Property crime	167 843	121 209	44 399	949	1 286	100.0	72.2	26.5	0.6	0.8
Burglary	40 030	30 906	8 736	191	197	100.0	77.2	21.8	0.5	0.5
Larceny-theft	107 183	74 733	30 825	643	982	100.0	69.7	28.8	0.6	0.9
Motor vehicle theft	18 156	13 612	4 359	95	90	100.0	75.0	24.0	0.5	0.5
Arson	2 474	1 958	479	20	17	100.0	79.1	19.4	0.8	0.7
Other assaults	166 824	120 811	43 849	1 150	1 014	100.0	72.4	26.3	0.7	0.6
Forgery and counterfeiting	14 453	10 485	3 733	59	176	100.0	72.5	25.8	0.4	1.2
Fraud	65 975	45 465	20 068	186	256	100.0	68.9	30.4	0.3	0.4
Embezzlement	2 589	1 699	856	8	26	100.0	65.6	33.1	0.3	1.0
Stolen property; buying, receiving, and possessing	16 818	12 418	4 176	117	107	100.0	73.8	24.8	0.7	0.6
Vandalism	30 796	24 695	5 738	209	154	100.0	80.2	18.6	0.7	0.5
Weapons; carrying and possessing, etc.	22 142	14 606	7 252	124	160	100.0	66.0	32.8	0.6	0.7
Prostitution and commercialized vice	3 055	2 068	805	16	166	100.0	67.7	26.4	0.5	5.4
Sex offenses, except forcible rape and prostitution	12 175	9 878	2 156	69	72	100.0	81.1	17.7	0.6	0.6
Drug abuse violations	225 439	167 561	55 690	1 112	1 076	100.0	74.3	24.7	0.5	0.5
Gambling	618	420	161	6	31	100.0	68.0	26.1	1.0	5.0
Offenses against the family and children	34 485	21 322	12 944	130	89	100.0	61.8	37.5	0.4	0.3
Driving under the influence	232 082	207 656	21 359	1 522	1 545	100.0	89.5	9.2	0.7	0.7
Liquor laws	50 372	45 331	4 088	584	369	100.0	90.0	8.1	1.2	0.7
Drunkenness	39 533	35 462	3 485	399	187	100.0	89.7	8.8	1.0	0.5
Disorderly conduct	43 769	30 247	13 012	320	190	100.0	69.1	29.7	0.7	0.4
Vagrancy	3 283	2 268	986	11	18	100.0	69.1	30.0	0.3	0.5
All other offenses, except traffic	543 223	391 918	143 249	5 087	2 969	100.0	72.1	26.4	0.9	0.5
Suspicion	1 353	931	414	6	2	100.0	68.8	30.6	0.4	0.1
Curfew and loitering law violations	3 410	2 699	667	16	28	100.0	79.1	19.6	0.5	0.8
Runaways	15 469	11 848	3 337	146	138	100.0	76.6	21.6	0.9	0.9

[1]Percentages may not add to 100 because of rounding.

Table 55. Arrests in Metropolitan Counties, Distribution by Race, 2005—*Continued*

(Number, percent; 1,225 total agencies; 2005 estimated population 47,831,303.)

Offense	Under 18 years					Percent distribution[1]				
	Total	White	Black	American Indian or Alaskan Native	Asian or Pacific Islander	Total	White	Black	American Indian or Alaskan Native	Asian or Pacific Islander
Total	211 129	147 563	60 672	1 521	1 373	100.0	69.9	28.7	0.7	0.7
Violent crime	10 244	5 645	4 456	79	64	100.0	55.1	43.5	0.8	0.6
Murder and nonnegligent manslaughter	144	78	64	1	1	100.0	54.2	44.4	0.7	0.7
Forcible rape	495	381	105	7	2	100.0	77.0	21.2	1.4	0.4
Robbery	2 486	769	1 694	9	14	100.0	30.9	68.1	0.4	0.6
Aggravated assault	7 119	4 417	2 593	62	47	100.0	62.0	36.4	0.9	0.7
Property crime	38 608	25 784	12 317	182	325	100.0	66.8	31.9	0.5	0.8
Burglary	9 684	7 033	2 555	38	58	100.0	72.6	26.4	0.4	0.6
Larceny-theft	23 846	15 321	8 174	113	238	100.0	64.2	34.3	0.5	1.0
Motor vehicle theft	3 895	2 499	1 354	21	21	100.0	64.2	34.8	0.5	0.5
Arson	1 183	931	234	10	8	100.0	78.7	19.8	0.8	0.7
Other assaults	32 447	19 028	13 071	196	152	100.0	58.6	40.3	0.6	0.5
Forgery and counterfeiting	552	425	119	2	6	100.0	77.0	21.6	0.4	1.1
Fraud	903	635	262	0	6	100.0	70.3	29.0	0.0	0.7
Embezzlement	152	77	74	1	0	100.0	50.7	48.7	0.7	0.0
Stolen property; buying, receiving, and possessing	1 805	1 212	562	21	10	100.0	67.1	31.1	1.2	0.6
Vandalism	10 788	8 576	2 108	54	50	100.0	79.5	19.5	0.5	0.5
Weapons; carrying and possessing, etc.	4 810	2 908	1 828	35	39	100.0	60.5	38.0	0.7	0.8
Prostitution and commercialized vice	48	29	18	1	0	100.0	60.4	37.5	2.1	0.0
Sex offenses, except forcible rape and prostitution	2 359	1 822	522	7	8	100.0	77.2	22.1	0.3	0.3
Drug abuse violations	20 127	15 740	4 109	123	155	100.0	78.2	20.4	0.6	0.8
Gambling	35	13	22	0	0	100.0	37.1	62.9	0.0	0.0
Offenses against the family and children	697	588	108	1	0	100.0	84.4	15.5	0.1	0.0
Driving under the influence	2 364	2 262	73	21	8	100.0	95.7	3.1	0.9	0.3
Liquor laws	12 720	12 022	481	140	77	100.0	94.5	3.8	1.1	0.6
Drunkenness	1 042	951	71	12	8	100.0	91.3	6.8	1.2	0.8
Disorderly conduct	13 888	7 360	6 402	81	45	100.0	53.0	46.1	0.6	0.3
Vagrancy	390	345	41	0	4	100.0	88.5	10.5	0.0	1.0
All other offenses, except traffic	38 221	27 573	9 995	403	250	100.0	72.1	26.2	1.1	0.7
Suspicion	50	21	29	0	0	100.0	42.0	58.0	0.0	0.0
Curfew and loitering law violations	3 410	2 699	667	16	28	100.0	79.1	19.6	0.5	0.8
Runaways	15 469	11 848	3 337	146	138	100.0	76.6	21.6	0.9	0.9

[1]Percentages may not add to 100 because of rounding.

Table 55. Arrests in Metropolitan Counties, Distribution by Race, 2005—*Continued*

(Number, percent; 1,225 total agencies; 2005 estimated population 47,831,303.)

Offense	18 years and over					Percent distribution[1]				
	Total	White	Black	American Indian or Alaskan Native	Asian or Pacific Islander	Total	White	Black	American Indian or Alaskan Native	Asian or Pacific Islander
Total	1 561 067	1 185 306	355 314	11 258	9 189	100.0	75.9	22.8	0.7	0.6
Violent crime	66 246	46 227	19 106	474	439	100.0	69.8	28.8	0.7	0.7
Murder and nonnegligent manslaughter	1 851	1 137	673	13	28	100.0	61.4	36.4	0.7	1.5
Forcible rape	2 989	2 253	692	27	17	100.0	75.4	23.2	0.9	0.6
Robbery	8 495	4 367	4 061	35	32	100.0	51.4	47.8	0.4	0.4
Aggravated assault	52 911	38 470	13 680	399	362	100.0	72.7	25.9	0.8	0.7
Property crime	129 235	95 425	32 082	767	961	100.0	73.8	24.8	0.6	0.7
Burglary	30 346	23 873	6 181	153	139	100.0	78.7	20.4	0.5	0.5
Larceny-theft	83 337	59 412	22 651	530	744	100.0	71.3	27.2	0.6	0.9
Motor vehicle theft	14 261	11 113	3 005	74	69	100.0	77.9	21.1	0.5	0.5
Arson	1 291	1 027	245	10	9	100.0	79.6	19.0	0.8	0.7
Other assaults	134 377	101 783	30 778	954	862	100.0	75.7	22.9	0.7	0.6
Forgery and counterfeiting	13 901	10 060	3 614	57	170	100.0	72.4	26.0	0.4	1.2
Fraud	65 072	44 830	19 806	186	250	100.0	68.9	30.4	0.3	0.4
Embezzlement	2 437	1 622	782	7	26	100.0	66.6	32.1	0.3	1.1
Stolen property; buying, receiving, and possessing	15 013	11 206	3 614	96	97	100.0	74.6	24.1	0.6	0.6
Vandalism	20 008	16 119	3 630	155	104	100.0	80.6	18.1	0.8	0.5
Weapons; carrying and possessing, etc.	17 332	11 698	5 424	89	121	100.0	67.5	31.3	0.5	0.7
Prostitution and commercialized vice	3 007	2 039	787	15	166	100.0	67.8	26.2	0.5	5.5
Sex offenses, except forcible rape and prostitution	9 816	8 056	1 634	62	64	100.0	82.1	16.6	0.6	0.7
Drug abuse violations	205 312	151 821	51 581	989	921	100.0	73.9	25.1	0.5	0.4
Gambling	583	407	139	6	31	100.0	69.8	23.8	1.0	5.3
Offenses against the family and children	33 788	20 734	12 836	129	89	100.0	61.4	38.0	0.4	0.3
Driving under the influence	229 718	205 394	21 286	1 501	1 537	100.0	89.4	9.3	0.7	0.7
Liquor laws	37 652	33 309	3 607	444	292	100.0	88.5	9.6	1.2	0.8
Drunkenness	38 491	34 511	3 414	387	179	100.0	89.7	8.9	1.0	0.5
Disorderly conduct	29 881	22 887	6 610	239	145	100.0	76.6	22.1	0.8	0.5
Vagrancy	2 893	1 923	945	11	14	100.0	66.5	32.7	0.4	0.5
All other offenses, except traffic	505 002	364 345	133 254	4 684	2 719	100.0	72.1	26.4	0.9	0.5
Suspicion	1 303	910	385	6	2	100.0	69.8	29.5	0.5	0.2
Curfew and loitering law violations	X	X	X	X	X	X	X	X	X	X
Runaways	X	X	X	X	X	X	X	X	X	X

[1]Percentages may not add to 100 because of rounding.
X = Not applicable.

Table 56. Arrest Trends for Nonmetropolitan Counties, 2004 and 2005

(Number, percent change; 1,638 total agencies; 2004 estimated population 19,528,484; 2005 estimated population 19,607,458.)

Offense	Total, all ages			Under 18 years			18 years and over		
	2004	2005	Percent change	2004	2005	Percent change	2004	2005	Percent change
Total[1]	747 003	752 757	0.8	69 744	67 511	-3.2	677 259	685 246	1.2
Violent crime	24 274	24 336	0.3	2 357	2 428	3.0	21 917	21 908	0.0
Murder and nonnegligent manslaughter	718	704	-1.9	40	34	-15.0	678	670	-1.2
Forcible rape	1 880	1 784	-5.1	297	287	-3.4	1 583	1 497	-5.4
Robbery	1 750	1 833	4.7	194	229	18.0	1 556	1 604	3.1
Aggravated assault	19 926	20 015	0.4	1 826	1 878	2.8	18 100	18 137	0.2
Property crime	54 493	55 447	1.8	11 805	11 031	-6.6	42 688	44 416	4.0
Burglary	18 256	18 666	2.2	4 396	4 071	-7.4	13 860	14 595	5.3
Larceny-theft	29 837	30 137	1.0	5 708	5 328	-6.7	24 129	24 809	2.8
Motor vehicle theft	5 501	5 709	3.8	1 417	1 327	-6.4	4 084	4 382	7.3
Arson	899	935	4.0	284	305	7.4	615	630	2.4
Other assaults	70 945	72 413	2.1	8 806	9 093	3.3	62 139	63 320	1.9
Forgery and counterfeiting	5 224	5 320	1.8	221	192	-13.1	5 003	5 128	2.5
Fraud	37 345	36 582	-2.0	344	336	-2.3	37 001	36 246	-2.0
Embezzlement	837	832	-0.6	13	24	84.6	824	808	-1.9
Stolen property; buying, receiving, and possessing	4 894	5 001	2.2	582	615	5.7	4 312	4 386	1.7
Vandalism	13 118	13 207	0.7	4 058	3 935	-3.0	9 060	9 272	2.3
Weapons; carrying and possessing, etc.	6 738	7 068	4.9	855	849	-0.7	5 883	6 219	5.7
Prostitution and commercialized vice	186	152	-18.3	10	5	-50.0	176	147	-16.5
Sex offenses, except forcible rape and prostitution	5 233	5 184	-0.9	1 101	960	-12.8	4 132	4 224	2.2
Drug abuse violations	87 677	87 837	0.2	6 481	6 167	-4.8	81 196	81 670	0.6
Gambling	459	483	5.2	12	4	-66.7	447	479	7.2
Offenses against the family and children	11 786	12 268	4.1	511	413	-19.2	11 275	11 855	5.1
Driving under the influence	126 722	118 735	-6.3	1 860	1 546	-16.9	124 862	117 189	-6.1
Liquor laws	34 028	33 253	-2.3	8 458	8 164	-3.5	25 570	25 089	-1.9
Drunkenness	19 576	18 793	-4.0	486	412	-15.2	19 090	18 381	-3.7
Disorderly conduct	21 569	21 482	-0.4	4 975	4 865	-2.2	16 594	16 617	0.1
Vagrancy	361	200	-44.6	29	19	-34.5	332	181	-45.5
All other offenses, except traffic	216 751	229 407	5.8	11 993	11 696	-2.5	204 758	217 711	6.3
Suspicion	148	142	-4.1	75	45	-40.0	73	97	32.9
Curfew and loitering law violations	597	627	5.0	597	627	5.0	X	X	X
Runaways	4 190	4 130	-1.4	4 190	4 130	-1.4	X	X	X

[1]Does not include suspicion.
X = Not applicable.

Table 57. Arrest Trends for Nonmetropolitan Counties, by Age and Sex, 2004 and 2005

(Number, percent change; 1,638 total agencies; 2004 estimated population 19,528,484; 2005 estimated population 19,607,458.)

Offense	Male						Female					
	Total, all ages			Under 18 years			Total, all ages			Under 18 years		
	2004	2005	Percent change	2004	2005	Percent change	2004	2005	Percent change	2004	2005	Percent change
Total[1]	576 639	578 729	0.4	50 606	48 978	-3.2	170 364	174 028	2.2	19 138	18 533	-3.2
Violent crime	20 466	20 370	-0.5	1 899	1 963	3.4	3 808	3 966	4.1	458	465	1.5
Murder and nonnegligent manslaughter	601	605	0.7	26	29	11.5	117	99	-15.4	14	5	-64.3
Forcible rape	1 828	1 754	-4.0	281	276	-1.8	52	30	-42.3	16	11	-31.3
Robbery	1 571	1 599	1.8	173	205	18.5	179	234	30.7	21	24	14.3
Aggravated assault	16 466	16 412	-0.3	1 419	1 453	2.4	3 460	3 603	4.1	407	425	4.4
Property crime	42 434	42 925	1.2	9 489	8 834	-6.9	12 059	12 522	3.8	2 316	2 197	-5.1
Burglary	15 943	16 223	1.8	4 016	3 726	-7.2	2 313	2 443	5.6	380	345	-9.2
Larceny-theft	21 167	21 290	0.6	4 084	3 817	-6.5	8 670	8 847	2.0	1 624	1 511	-7.0
Motor vehicle theft	4 567	4 611	1.0	1 137	1 009	-11.3	934	1 098	17.6	280	318	13.6
Arson	757	801	5.8	252	282	11.9	142	134	-5.6	32	23	-28.1
Other assaults	54 068	54 849	1.4	6 092	6 273	3.0	16 877	17 564	4.1	2 714	2 820	3.9
Forgery and counterfeiting	3 104	3 016	-2.8	144	139	-3.5	2 120	2 304	8.7	77	53	-31.2
Fraud	18 607	18 094	-2.8	201	205	2.0	18 738	18 488	-1.3	143	131	-8.4
Embezzlement	381	413	8.4	10	14	40.0	456	419	-8.1	3	10	233.3
Stolen property; buying, receiving, and possessing	4 078	4 170	2.3	478	530	10.9	816	831	1.8	104	85	-18.3
Vandalism	11 056	10 969	-0.8	3 563	3 447	-3.3	2 062	2 238	8.5	495	488	-1.4
Weapons; carrying and possessing, etc.	6 234	6 491	4.1	760	756	-0.5	504	577	14.5	95	93	-2.1
Prostitution and commercialized vice	107	82	-23.4	6	3	-50.0	79	70	-11.4	4	2	-50.0
Sex offenses, except forcible rape and prostitution	4 966	4 901	-1.3	1 034	882	-14.7	267	283	6.0	67	78	16.4
Drug abuse violations	69 763	69 197	-0.8	5 135	4 835	-5.8	17 914	18 640	4.1	1 346	1 332	-1.0
Gambling	389	364	-6.4	10	2	-80.0	70	119	70.0	2	2	0.0
Offenses against the family and children	9 454	9 842	4.1	298	232	-22.1	2 332	2 426	4.0	213	181	-15.0
Driving under the influence	103 817	97 202	-6.4	1 480	1 221	-17.5	22 905	21 533	-6.0	380	325	-14.5
Liquor laws	24 881	24 386	-2.0	5 398	5 237	-3.0	9 147	8 867	-3.1	3 060	2 927	-4.3
Drunkenness	16 278	15 645	-3.9	359	311	-13.4	3 298	3 148	-4.5	127	101	-20.5
Disorderly conduct	15 915	15 777	-0.9	3 404	3 275	-3.8	5 654	5 705	0.9	1 571	1 590	1.2
Vagrancy	275	151	-45.1	29	11	-62.1	86	49	-43.0	0	8	X
All other offenses, except traffic	168 236	177 688	5.6	8 687	8 611	-0.9	48 515	51 719	6.6	3 306	3 085	-6.7
Suspicion	128	113	-11.7	64	36	-43.8	20	29	45.0	11	9	-18.2
Curfew and loitering law violations	361	383	6.1	361	383	6.1	236	244	3.4	236	244	3.4
Runaways	1 769	1 814	2.5	1 769	1 814	2.5	2 421	2 316	-4.3	2 421	2 316	-4.3

[1]Does not include suspicion.
X = Not applicable.

Table 58. Arrests in Nonmetropolitan Counties, Distribution by Age, 2005

(Number, percent; 1,838 total agencies; 2005 estimated population 21,225,373.)

Offense	Total, all ages	Under 15 years	Under 18 years	18 years and over	Under 10 years	10–12 years	13–14 years	15 years	16 years	17 years
Total	840 841	18 501	75 109	774 732	954	3 873	13 674	13 235	18 899	24 474
Total percent distribution[1]	100.0	2.2	8.8	91.2	0.1	0.5	1.6	1.6	2.2	2.9
Violent crime	26 738	795	2 661	24 077	51	184	560	441	668	757
Violent crime percent distribution[1]	100.0	3.0	10.0	90.0	0.2	0.7	2.1	1.6	2.5	2.8
Murder and nonnegligent manslaughter	945	5	46	899	0	2	3	6	16	19
Forcible rape	2 014	122	309	1 705	3	33	86	59	61	67
Robbery	2 159	36	253	1 906	1	4	31	43	76	98
Aggravated assault	21 620	632	2 053	19 567	47	145	440	333	515	573
Property crime	61 776	3 443	11 875	49 901	191	791	2 461	2 285	2 795	3 352
Property crime percent distribution[1]	100.0	5.6	19.2	80.8	0.3	1.3	4.0	3.7	4.5	5.4
Burglary	20 365	1 192	4 385	15 980	71	279	842	813	1 032	1 348
Larceny-theft	34 167	1 735	5 715	28 452	85	415	1 235	1 084	1 339	1 557
Motor vehicle theft	6 086	341	1 423	4 663	14	42	285	335	365	382
Arson	1 158	175	352	806	21	55	99	53	59	65
Other assaults	79 155	3 308	9 757	69 398	139	809	2 360	1 866	2 263	2 320
Forgery and counterfeiting	7 528	22	221	7 307	1	0	21	24	62	113
Fraud	40 209	67	369	39 840	10	10	47	45	91	166
Embezzlement	1 103	2	24	1 079	0	1	1	2	8	12
Stolen property; buying, receiving, and possessing	6 508	144	695	5 813	6	19	119	116	198	237
Vandalism	14 541	1 716	4 286	10 255	151	517	1 048	696	883	991
Weapons; carrying and possessing, etc.	8 016	302	911	7 105	15	85	202	148	189	272
Prostitution and commercialized vice	185	1	5	180	0	0	1	0	1	3
Sex offenses, except forcible rape and prostitution	7 380	547	1 160	6 220	45	134	368	190	187	236
Drug abuse violations	103 989	871	6 946	97 043	30	108	733	976	1 900	3 199
Gambling	512	1	5	507	0	0	1	2	0	2
Offenses against the family and children	15 457	204	647	14 810	17	44	143	136	134	173
Driving under the influence	133 965	31	1 825	132 140	10	1	20	76	474	1 244
Liquor laws	38 268	777	8 943	29 325	7	43	727	1 291	2 631	4 244
Drunkenness	23 151	72	632	22 519	12	5	55	97	159	304
Disorderly conduct	26 350	1 959	5 777	20 573	74	438	1 447	1 209	1 338	1 271
Vagrancy	269	1	19	250	0	0	1	3	5	10
All other offenses, except traffic	249 499	2 783	13 248	236 251	163	487	2 133	2 318	3 391	4 756
Suspicion	186	17	47	139	0	4	13	9	10	11
Curfew and loitering law violations	704	211	704	X	1	25	185	154	209	130
Runaways	4 352	1 227	4 352	X	31	168	1 028	1 151	1 303	671

[1]Percentages may not add to 100 because of rounding.
X = Not applicable.

Table 58. Arrests in Nonmetropolitan Counties, Distribution by Age, 2005—*Continued*

(Number, percent; 1,838 total agencies; 2005 estimated population 21,225,373.)

Offense	18 years	19 years	20 years	21 years	22 years	23 years	24 years	25–29 years
Total	36 601	38 997	37 888	34 362	32 880	32 068	31 228	124 866
Total percent distribution[1]	4.3	4.6	4.5	4.0	3.9	3.8	3.7	14.7
Violent crime	1 025	1 076	1 053	1 054	1 023	960	1 003	3 827
Violent crime percent distribution[1]	3.8	4.0	3.9	3.9	3.8	3.6	3.8	14.3
Murder and nonnegligent manslaughter	30	46	40	44	40	34	47	162
Forcible rape	113	100	92	66	51	64	77	234
Robbery	148	178	158	124	122	95	95	338
Aggravated assault	734	752	763	820	810	767	784	3 093
Property crime	4 460	3 770	3 030	2 602	2 376	2 200	2 122	8 113
Property crime percent distribution[1]	7.2	6.1	4.9	4.2	3.8	3.6	3.4	13.1
Burglary	1 819	1 529	1 082	976	824	748	701	2 627
Larceny-theft	2 212	1 820	1 616	1 339	1 284	1 193	1 182	4 532
Motor vehicle theft	358	362	292	252	246	232	209	844
Arson	71	59	40	35	22	27	30	110
Other assaults	2 459	2 440	2 416	2 639	2 497	2 517	2 540	11 069
Forgery and counterfeiting	217	249	310	313	306	400	312	1 488
Fraud	730	1 169	1 264	1 268	1 351	1 450	1 519	6 986
Embezzlement	22	46	39	32	43	26	35	187
Stolen property; buying, receiving, and possessing	377	361	338	293	291	235	271	1 034
Vandalism	1 056	789	711	596	543	510	440	1 494
Weapons; carrying and possessing, etc.	326	326	324	340	323	317	279	1 080
Prostitution and commercialized vice	2	3	3	1	4	3	5	20
Sex offenses, except forcible rape and prostitution	337	292	241	218	196	160	159	647
Drug abuse violations	5 776	5 920	5 761	5 362	4 975	4 759	4 496	16 623
Gambling	14	22	36	24	16	14	13	52
Offenses against the family and children	255	244	298	360	389	440	503	2 583
Driving under the influence	3 050	4 194	4 488	5 788	5 579	5 418	5 351	19 830
Liquor laws	6 416	6 441	5 146	944	789	650	565	1 890
Drunkenness	734	846	895	952	912	826	810	3 203
Disorderly conduct	1 186	990	873	933	892	862	805	2 919
Vagrancy	6	9	16	10	7	6	10	35
All other offenses, except traffic	8 146	9 799	10 640	10 627	10 359	10 307	9 988	41 754
Suspicion	7	11	6	6	9	8	2	32
Curfew and loitering law violations	X	X	X	X	X	X	X	X
Runaways	X	X	X	X	X	X	X	X

[1]Percentages may not add to 100 because of rounding.
X = Not applicable.

Table 58. Arrests in Nonmetropolitan Counties, Distribution by Age, 2005—*Continued*

(Number, percent; 1,838 total agencies; 2005 estimated population 21,225,373.)

Offense	30–34 years	35–39 years	40–44 years	45–49 years	50–54 years	55–59 years	60–64 years	65 years and over
Total	100 094	91 691	87 416	60 493	32 778	17 144	8 410	7 816
Total percent distribution[1]	11.8	10.8	10.3	7.1	3.9	2.0	1.0	0.9
Violent crime	3 235	2 944	2 746	1 867	1 067	624	307	266
Violent crime percent distribution[1]	12.1	11.0	10.3	7.0	4.0	2.3	1.1	1.0
Murder and nonnegligent manslaughter	105	99	103	55	36	28	11	19
Forcible rape	227	192	184	130	78	49	28	20
Robbery	217	160	131	78	33	24	3	2
Aggravated assault	2 686	2 493	2 328	1 604	920	523	265	225
Property crime	5 900	5 267	4 459	2 943	1 416	646	294	303
Property crime percent distribution[1]	9.6	8.5	7.2	4.8	2.3	1.0	0.5	0.5
Burglary	1 729	1 521	1 153	794	291	112	43	31
Larceny-theft	3 472	3 170	2 870	1 842	989	478	218	235
Motor vehicle theft	615	499	350	234	96	34	24	16
Arson	84	77	86	73	40	22	9	21
Other assaults	9 765	9 422	8 854	6 154	3 182	1 628	857	959
Forgery and counterfeiting	1 172	1 062	677	417	235	85	39	25
Fraud	6 807	5 911	4 728	3 144	1 607	963	467	476
Embezzlement	150	135	150	78	56	26	45	9
Stolen property; buying, receiving, and possessing	750	678	560	321	180	66	34	24
Vandalism	1 096	1 006	820	584	272	158	86	94
Weapons; carrying and possessing, etc.	837	767	751	575	410	219	119	112
Prostitution and commercialized vice	30	48	26	9	15	6	2	3
Sex offenses, except forcible rape and prostitution	602	680	1 314	503	276	228	181	186
Drug abuse violations	11 868	9 957	9 748	6 524	3 016	1 417	482	359
Gambling	69	44	63	45	41	24	15	15
Offenses against the family and children	2 736	2 578	2 223	1 212	564	220	112	93
Driving under the influence	15 582	15 292	16 640	13 108	8 499	4 783	2 459	2 079
Liquor laws	1 413	1 318	1 421	1 053	613	309	190	167
Drunkenness	2 671	2 727	3 044	2 316	1 315	748	282	238
Disorderly conduct	2 483	2 497	2 482	1 787	909	464	254	237
Vagrancy	30	26	32	36	15	10	0	2
All other offenses, except traffic	32 886	29 310	26 666	17 812	9 087	4 519	2 184	2 167
Suspicion	12	22	12	5	3	1	1	2
Curfew and loitering law violations	X	X	X	X	X	X	X	X
Runaways	X	X	X	X	X	X	X	X

[1]Percentages may not add to 100 because of rounding.
X = Not applicable.

Table 59. Arrests in Nonmetropolitan Counties of Persons Under 15, 18, 21, and 25 Years of Age, 2005

(Number, percent; 1,838 total agencies; 2005 estimated population 21,225,373.)

Offense	Total, all ages	Number of persons arrested				Percent of total all ages			
		Under 15 years	Under 18 years	Under 21 years	Under 25 years	Under 15 years	Under 18 years	Under 21 years	Under 25 years
Total	849 841	18 501	75 109	188 595	319 133	2.2	8.8	22.2	37.6
Violent crime	26 738	795	2 661	5 815	9 855	3.0	10.0	21.7	36.9
Murder and nonnegligent manslaughter	945	5	46	162	327	0.5	4.9	17.1	34.6
Forcible rape	2 014	122	309	614	872	6.1	15.3	30.5	43.3
Robbery	2 159	36	253	737	1 173	1.7	11.7	34.1	54.3
Aggravated assault	21 620	632	2 053	4 302	7 483	2.9	9.5	19.9	34.6
Property crime	61 776	3 443	11 875	23 135	32 435	5.6	19.2	37.4	52.5
Burglary	20 365	1 192	4 385	8 815	12 064	5.9	21.5	43.3	59.2
Larceny-theft	34 167	1 735	5 715	11 363	16 361	5.1	16.7	33.3	47.9
Motor vehicle theft	6 086	341	1 423	2 435	3 374	5.6	23.4	40.0	55.4
Arson	1 158	175	352	522	636	15.1	30.4	45.1	54.9
Other assaults	79 155	3 308	9 757	17 072	27 265	4.2	12.3	21.6	34.4
Forgery and counterfeiting	7 528	22	221	997	2 328	0.3	2.9	13.2	30.9
Fraud	40 209	67	369	3 532	9 120	0.2	0.9	8.8	22.7
Embezzlement	1 103	2	24	131	267	0.2	2.2	11.9	24.2
Stolen property; buying, receiving, and possessing	6 508	144	695	1 771	2 861	2.2	10.7	27.2	44.0
Vandalism	14 541	1 716	4 286	6 842	8 931	11.8	29.5	47.1	61.4
Weapons; carrying and possessing, etc.	8 016	302	911	1 887	3 146	3.8	11.4	23.5	39.2
Prostitution and commercialized vice	185	1	5	13	26	0.5	2.7	7.0	14.1
Sex offenses, except forcible rape and prostitution	7 380	547	1 160	2 030	2 763	7.4	15.7	27.5	37.4
Drug abuse violations	103 989	871	6 946	24 403	43 995	0.8	6.7	23.5	42.3
Gambling	512	1	5	77	144	0.2	1.0	15.0	28.1
Offenses against the family and children	15 457	204	647	1 444	3 136	1.3	4.2	9.3	20.3
Driving under the influence	133 965	31	1 825	13 557	35 693	0.0	1.4	10.1	26.6
Liquor laws	38 268	777	8 943	26 946	29 894	2.0	23.4	70.4	78.1
Drunkenness	23 151	72	632	3 107	6 607	0.3	2.7	13.4	28.5
Disorderly conduct	26 350	1 959	5 777	8 826	12 318	7.4	21.9	33.5	46.7
Vagrancy	269	1	19	50	83	0.4	7.1	18.6	30.9
All other offenses, except traffic	249 499	2 783	13 248	41 833	83 114	1.1	5.3	16.8	33.3
Suspicion	186	17	47	71	96	9.1	25.3	38.2	51.6
Curfew and loitering law violations	704	211	704	704	704	30.0	100.0	100.0	100.0
Runaways	4 352	1 227	4 352	4 352	4 352	28.2	100.0	100.0	100.0

Table 60. Arrests in Nonmetropolitan Counties, Distribution by Sex, 2005

(Number, percent; 1,838 total agencies; 2005 estimated population 21,225,373.)

Offense	Number of persons arrested			Percent male	Percent female	Percent distribution[1]		
	Total	Male	Female			Total	Male	Female
Total	849 841	654 294	195 547	77.0	23.0	100.0	100.0	100.0
Violent crime	26 738	22 356	4 382	83.6	16.4	3.1	3.4	2.2
Murder and nonnegligent manslaughter	945	818	127	86.6	13.4	0.1	0.1	0.1
Forcible rape	2 014	1 960	54	97.3	2.7	0.2	0.3	0.0
Robbery	2 159	1 888	271	87.4	12.6	0.3	0.3	0.1
Aggravated assault	21 620	17 690	3 930	81.8	18.2	2.5	2.7	2.0
Property crime	61 776	47 488	14 288	76.9	23.1	7.3	7.3	7.3
Burglary	20 365	17 705	2 660	86.9	13.1	2.4	2.7	1.4
Larceny-theft	34 167	23 889	10 278	69.9	30.1	4.0	3.7	5.3
Motor vehicle theft	6 086	4 905	1 181	80.6	19.4	0.7	0.7	0.6
Arson	1 158	989	169	85.4	14.6	0.1	0.2	0.1
Other assaults	79 155	60 198	18 957	76.1	23.9	9.3	9.2	9.7
Forgery and counterfeiting	7 528	4 067	3 461	54.0	46.0	0.9	0.6	1.8
Fraud	40 209	20 167	20 042	50.2	49.8	4.7	3.1	10.2
Embezzlement	1 103	587	516	53.2	46.8	0.1	0.1	0.3
Stolen property; buying, receiving, and possessing	6 508	5 439	1 069	83.6	16.4	0.8	0.8	0.5
Vandalism	14 541	12 136	2 405	83.5	16.5	1.7	1.9	1.2
Weapons; carrying and possessing, etc.	8 016	7 366	650	91.9	8.1	0.9	1.1	0.3
Prostitution and commercialized vice	185	103	82	55.7	44.3	0.0	0.0	0.0
Sex offenses, except forcible rape and prostitution	7 380	6 984	396	94.6	5.4	0.9	1.1	0.2
Drug abuse violations	103 989	81 699	22 290	78.6	21.4	12.2	12.5	11.4
Gambling	512	382	130	74.6	25.4	0.1	0.1	0.1
Offenses against the family and children	15 457	12 315	3 142	79.7	20.3	1.8	1.9	1.6
Driving under the influence	133 965	109 838	24 127	82.0	18.0	15.8	16.8	12.3
Liquor laws	38 268	28 240	10 028	73.8	26.2	4.5	4.3	5.1
Drunkenness	23 161	19 153	3 998	82.7	17.3	2.7	2.9	2.0
Disorderly conduct	26 350	19 347	7 003	73.4	26.6	3.1	3.0	3.6
Vagrancy	269	208	61	77.3	22.7	0.0	0.0	0.0
All other offenses, except traffic	249 499	193 755	55 744	77.7	22.3	29.4	29.6	28.5
Suspicion	186	152	34	81.7	18.3	0.0	0.0	0.0
Curfew and loitering law violations	704	426	278	60.5	39.5	0.1	0.1	0.1
Runaways	4 352	1 888	2 464	43.4	56.6	0.5	0.3	1.3

[1]Percentages may not add to 100 because of rounding.

Table 61. Arrests in Nonmetropolitan Counties, Distribution by Race, 2005

(Number, percent; 1,836 total agencies; 2005 estimated population 21,196,975.)

Offense	Total arrests					Percent distribution[1]				
	Total	White	Black	American Indian or Alaskan Native	Asian or Pacific Islander	Total	White	Black	American Indian or Alaskan Native	Asian or Pacific Islander
Total	764 770	630 243	104 006	23 591	6 930	100.0	82.4	13.6	3.1	0.9
Violent crime	25 301	18 530	5 384	1 232	155	100.0	73.2	21.3	4.9	0.6
Murder and nonnegligent manslaughter	748	496	203	46	3	100.0	66.3	27.1	6.1	0.4
Forcible rape	1 830	1 476	271	73	10	100.0	80.7	14.8	4.0	0.5
Robbery	1 989	1 112	768	79	30	100.0	55.9	38.6	4.0	1.5
Aggravated assault	20 734	15 446	4 142	1 034	112	100.0	74.5	20.0	5.0	0.5
Property crime	57 906	47 868	7 713	1 706	619	100.0	82.7	13.3	2.9	1.1
Burglary	19 202	15 850	2 637	597	118	100.0	82.5	13.7	3.1	0.6
Larceny-theft	31 921	26 373	4 358	850	340	100.0	82.6	13.7	2.7	1.1
Motor vehicle theft	5 764	4 757	623	231	153	100.0	82.5	10.8	4.0	2.7
Arson	1 019	888	95	28	8	100.0	87.1	9.3	2.7	0.8
Other assaults	72 858	58 054	11 725	2 594	485	100.0	79.7	16.1	3.6	0.7
Forgery and counterfeiting	5 702	4 738	860	56	48	100.0	83.1	15.1	1.0	0.8
Fraud	33 092	25 857	6 737	391	107	100.0	78.1	20.4	1.2	0.3
Embezzlement	889	740	124	10	15	100.0	83.2	13.9	1.1	1.7
Stolen property; buying, receiving, and possessing	5 451	4 326	974	117	34	100.0	79.4	17.9	2.1	0.6
Vandalism	13 547	11 562	1 446	492	47	100.0	85.3	10.7	3.6	0.3
Weapons; carrying and possessing, etc.	7 269	5 695	1 269	248	57	100.0	78.3	17.5	3.4	0.8
Prostitution and commercialized vice	173	138	25	8	2	100.0	79.8	14.5	4.6	1.2
Sex offenses, except forcible rape and prostitution	5 496	4 819	489	166	22	100.0	87.7	8.9	3.0	0.4
Drug abuse violations	90 342	73 902	13 988	1 822	630	100.0	81.8	15.5	2.0	0.7
Gambling	487	251	159	4	73	100.0	51.5	32.6	0.8	15.0
Offenses against the family and children	13 736	10 052	2 892	721	71	100.0	73.2	21.1	5.2	0.5
Driving under the influence	122 734	111 200	6 765	3 570	1 199	100.0	90.6	5.5	2.9	1.0
Liquor laws	34 854	32 130	1 247	1 298	179	100.0	92.2	3.6	3.7	0.5
Drunkenness	17 855	15 632	1 444	692	87	100.0	87.5	8.1	3.9	0.5
Disorderly conduct	23 585	18 289	4 078	1 033	185	100.0	77.5	17.3	4.4	0.8
Vagrancy	269	150	98	17	4	100.0	55.8	36.4	6.3	1.5
All other offenses, except traffic	228 019	181 936	36 145	7 195	2 743	100.0	79.8	15.9	3.2	1.2
Suspicion	183	123	59	1	0	100.0	67.2	32.2	0.5	0.0
Curfew and loitering law violations	704	516	36	85	67	100.0	73.3	5.1	12.1	9.5
Runaways	4 318	3 735	349	133	101	100.0	86.5	8.1	3.1	2.3

[1]Percentages may not add to 100 because of rounding.

Table 61. Arrests in Nonmetropolitan Counties, Distribution by Race, 2005—*Continued*

(Number, percent; 1,836 total agencies; 2005 estimated population 21,196,975.)

Offense	Under 18 years					Percent distribution[1]				
	Total	White	Black	American Indian or Alaskan Native	Asian or Pacific Islander	Total	White	Black	American Indian or Alaskan Native	Asian or Pacific Islander
Total	72 090	59 115	9 243	3 007	725	100.0	82.0	12.8	4.2	1.0
Violent crime	2 587	1 895	538	132	22	100.0	73.3	20.8	5.1	0.9
Murder and nonnegligent manslaughter	42	28	8	6	0	100.0	66.7	19.0	14.3	0.0
Forcible rape	297	256	34	7	0	100.0	86.2	11.4	2.4	0.0
Robbery	249	123	101	20	5	100.0	49.4	40.6	8.0	2.0
Aggravated assault	1 999	1 488	395	99	17	100.0	74.4	19.8	5.0	0.9
Property crime	11 480	9 538	1 393	402	147	100.0	83.1	12.1	3.5	1.3
Burglary	4 234	3 498	565	143	28	100.0	82.6	13.3	3.4	0.7
Larceny-theft	5 545	4 640	661	173	71	100.0	83.7	11.9	3.1	1.3
Motor vehicle theft	1 359	1 099	141	74	45	100.0	80.9	10.4	5.4	3.3
Arson	342	301	26	12	3	100.0	88.0	7.6	3.5	0.9
Other assaults	9 359	6 939	2 070	293	57	100.0	74.1	22.1	3.1	0.6
Forgery and counterfeiting	198	174	17	4	3	100.0	87.9	8.6	2.0	1.5
Fraud	332	271	54	2	5	100.0	81.6	16.3	0.6	1.5
Embezzlement	22	18	4	0	0	100.0	81.8	18.2	0.0	0.0
Stolen property; buying, receiving, and possessing	639	494	123	17	5	100.0	77.3	19.2	2.7	0.8
Vandalism	4 124	3 619	367	130	8	100.0	87.8	8.9	3.2	0.2
Weapons; carrying and possessing, etc.	897	646	205	44	2	100.0	72.0	22.9	4.9	0.2
Prostitution and commercialized vice	5	3	2	0	0	100.0	60.0	40.0	0.0	0.0
Sex offenses, except forcible rape and prostitution	1 035	908	77	46	4	100.0	87.7	7.4	4.4	0.4
Drug abuse violations	6 493	5 546	683	193	71	100.0	85.4	10.5	3.0	1.1
Gambling	5	3	0	0	2	100.0	60.0	0.0	0.0	40.0
Offenses against the family and children	619	512	59	40	8	100.0	82.7	9.5	6.5	1.3
Driving under the influence	1 605	1 467	57	62	19	100.0	91.4	3.6	3.9	1.2
Liquor laws	8 735	8 141	151	396	47	100.0	93.2	1.7	4.5	0.5
Drunkenness	467	420	18	28	1	100.0	89.9	3.9	6.0	0.2
Disorderly conduct	5 621	3 761	1 501	323	36	100.0	66.9	26.7	5.7	0.6
Vagrancy	19	11	2	2	4	100.0	57.9	10.5	10.5	21.1
All other offenses, except traffic	12 779	10 468	1 520	675	116	100.0	81.9	11.9	5.3	0.9
Suspicion	47	30	17	0	0	100.0	63.8	36.2	0.0	0.0
Curfew and loitering law violations	704	516	36	85	67	100.0	73.3	5.1	12.1	9.5
Runaways	4 318	3 735	349	133	101	100.0	86.5	8.1	3.1	2.3

[1]Percentages may not add to 100 because of rounding.

Table 61. Arrests in Nonmetropolitan Counties, Distribution by Race, 2005—*Continued*

(Number, percent; 1,836 total agencies; 2005 estimated population 21,196,975.)

Offense	18 years and over					Percent distribution[1]				
	Total	White	Black	American Indian or Alaskan Native	Asian or Pacific Islander	Total	White	Black	American Indian or Alaskan Native	Asian or Pacific Islander
Total	692 680	571 128	94 763	20 584	6 205	100.0	82.5	13.7	3.0	0.9
Violent crime	22 714	16 635	4 846	1 100	133	100.0	73.2	21.3	4.8	0.6
Murder and nonnegligent manslaughter	706	468	195	40	3	100.0	66.3	27.6	5.7	0.4
Forcible rape	1 533	1 220	237	66	10	100.0	79.6	15.5	4.3	0.7
Robbery	1 740	989	667	59	25	100.0	56.8	38.3	3.4	1.4
Aggravated assault	18 735	13 958	3 747	935	95	100.0	74.5	20.0	5.0	0.5
Property crime	46 426	38 330	6 320	1 304	472	100.0	82.6	13.6	2.8	1.0
Burglary	14 968	12 352	2 072	454	90	100.0	82.5	13.8	3.0	0.6
Larceny-theft	26 376	21 733	3 697	677	269	100.0	82.4	14.0	2.6	1.0
Motor vehicle theft	4 405	3 658	482	157	108	100.0	83.0	10.9	3.6	2.5
Arson	677	587	69	16	5	100.0	86.7	10.2	2.4	0.7
Other assaults	63 499	51 115	9 655	2 301	428	100.0	80.5	15.2	3.6	0.7
Forgery and counterfeiting	5 504	4 564	843	52	45	100.0	82.9	15.3	0.9	0.8
Fraud	32 760	25 586	6 683	389	102	100.0	78.1	20.4	1.2	0.3
Embezzlement	867	722	120	10	15	100.0	83.3	13.8	1.2	1.7
Stolen property; buying, receiving, and possessing	4 812	3 832	851	100	29	100.0	79.6	17.7	2.1	0.6
Vandalism	9 423	7 943	1 079	362	39	100.0	84.3	11.5	3.8	0.4
Weapons; carrying and possessing, etc.	6 372	5 049	1 064	204	55	100.0	79.2	16.7	3.2	0.9
Prostitution and commercialized vice	168	135	23	8	2	100.0	80.4	13.7	4.8	1.2
Sex offenses, except forcible rape and prostitution	4 461	3 911	412	120	18	100.0	87.7	9.2	2.7	0.4
Drug abuse violations	83 849	68 356	13 305	1 629	559	100.0	81.5	15.9	1.9	0.7
Gambling	482	248	159	4	71	100.0	51.5	33.0	0.8	14.7
Offenses against the family and children	13 117	9 540	2 833	681	63	100.0	72.7	21.6	5.2	0.5
Driving under the influence	121 129	109 733	6 708	3 508	1 180	100.0	90.6	5.5	2.9	1.0
Liquor laws	26 119	23 989	1 096	902	132	100.0	91.8	4.2	3.5	0.5
Drunkenness	17 388	15 212	1 426	664	86	100.0	87.5	8.2	3.8	0.5
Disorderly conduct	17 964	14 528	2 577	710	149	100.0	80.9	14.3	4.0	0.8
Vagrancy	250	139	96	15	0	100.0	55.6	38.4	6.0	0.0
All other offenses, except traffic	215 240	171 468	34 625	6 520	2 627	100.0	79.7	16.1	3.0	1.2
Suspicion	136	93	42	1	0	100.0	68.4	30.9	0.7	0.0
Curfew and loitering law violations	X	X	X	X	X	X	X	X	X	X
Runaways	X	X	X	X	X	X	X	X	X	X

[1]Percentages may not add to 100 because of rounding.
X = Not applicable.

Table 62. Arrest Trends for Suburban Areas, 2004 and 2005

(Number, percent change; 5,269 total agencies; 2004 estimated population 87,701,281; 2005 estimated population 88,632,388.)

Offense	Total, all ages			Under 18 years			18 years and over		
	2004	2005	Percent change	2004	2005	Percent change	2004	2005	Percent change
Total[1]	3 524 695	3 555 112	0.9	554 937	536 725	-3.3	2 969 758	3 018 387	1.6
Violent crime	134 450	134 816	0.3	20 900	20 691	-1.0	113 550	114 125	0.5
Murder and nonnegligent manslaughter	2 519	2 706	7.4	173	210	21.4	2 346	2 496	6.4
Forcible rape	6 425	6 129	-4.6	1 077	949	-11.9	5 348	5 180	-3.1
Robbery	20 307	20 741	2.1	4 530	4 902	8.2	15 777	15 839	0.4
Aggravated assault	105 199	105 240	0.0	15 120	14 630	-3.2	90 079	90 610	0.6
Property crime	386 714	377 080	-2.5	106 240	97 470	-8.3	280 474	279 610	-0.3
Burglary	72 997	72 895	-0.1	21 028	19 575	-6.9	51 969	53 320	2.6
Larceny-theft	278 533	269 644	-3.2	75 083	68 479	-8.8	203 450	201 165	-1.1
Motor vehicle theft	30 695	30 087	-2.0	7 711	6 985	-9.4	22 984	23 102	0.5
Arson	4 489	4 454	-0.8	2 418	2 431	0.5	2 071	2 023	-2.3
Other assaults	316 128	320 497	1.4	67 328	66 501	-1.2	248 800	253 996	2.1
Forgery and counterfeiting	30 317	28 822	-4.9	1 296	1 097	-15.4	29 021	27 725	-4.5
Fraud	105 353	103 713	-1.6	2 027	2 024	-0.1	103 326	101 689	-1.6
Embezzlement	4 653	4 889	5.1	282	289	2.5	4 371	4 600	5.2
Stolen property; buying, receiving, and possessing	33 442	33 069	-1.1	5 721	5 056	-11.6	27 721	28 013	1.1
Vandalism	70 507	69 993	-0.7	28 897	28 201	-2.4	41 610	41 792	0.4
Weapons; carrying and possessing, etc.	40 940	43 307	5.8	10 453	10 935	4.6	30 487	32 372	6.2
Prostitution and commercialized vice	5 169	4 788	-7.4	132	90	-31.8	5 037	4 698	-6.7
Sex offenses, except forcible rape and prostitution	21 075	20 352	-3.4	4 731	4 356	-7.9	16 344	15 996	-2.1
Drug abuse violations	405 093	424 905	4.9	50 975	49 125	-3.6	354 118	375 780	6.1
Gambling	1 295	1 084	-16.3	129	132	2.3	1 166	952	-18.4
Offenses against the family and children	44 661	45 166	1.1	1 626	1 588	-2.3	43 035	43 578	1.3
Driving under the influence	431 311	424 709	-1.5	5 859	5 487	-6.3	425 452	419 222	-1.5
Liquor laws	163 332	159 659	-2.2	40 007	39 234	-1.9	123 325	120 425	-2.4
Drunkenness	126 673	124 137	-2.0	5 065	4 378	-13.6	121 608	119 759	-1.5
Disorderly conduct	158 541	157 456	-0.7	55 248	54 227	-1.8	103 293	103 229	-0.1
Vagrancy	3 862	4 343	12.5	584	554	-5.1	3 278	3 789	15.6
All other offenses, except traffic	997 128	1 028 466	3.1	103 386	101 429	-1.9	893 742	927 037	3.7
Suspicion	686	964	40.5	120	142	18.3	566	822	45.2
Curfew and loitering law violations	16 870	18 047	7.0	16 870	18 047	7.0	X	X	X
Runaways	27 181	25 814	-5.0	27 181	25 814	-5.0	X	X	X

Note: Suburban areas include law enforcement agencies in cities with fewer than 50,000 inhabitants and county law enforcement agencies within metropolitan statistical areas. They exclude all metropolitan agencies associated with a principal city.

[1]Does not include suspicion.
X = Not applicable.

Table 63. Arrest Trends for Suburban Areas, by Age and Sex, 2004 and 2005

(Number, percent change; 5,269 total agencies; 2004 estimated population 87,701,281; 2005 estimated population 88,632,388.)

Offense	Male						Female					
	Total, all ages			Under 18 years			Total, all ages			Under 18 years		
	2004	2005	Percent change	2004	2005	Percent change	2004	2005	Percent change	2004	2005	Percent change
Total[1]	2 689 726	2 707 223	0.7	394 743	382 109	-3.2	834 969	847 889	1.5	160 194	154 616	-3.5
Violent crime	111 176	111 454	0.3	17 139	16 927	-1.2	23 274	23 362	0.4	3 761	3 764	0.1
Murder and nonnegligent manslaughter	2 188	2 330	6.5	155	172	11.0	331	376	13.6	18	38	111.1
Forcible rape	6 333	6 043	-4.6	1 055	927	-12.1	92	86	-6.5	22	22	0.0
Robbery	18 214	18 525	1.7	4 172	4 482	7.4	2 093	2 216	5.9	358	420	17.3
Aggravated assault	84 441	84 556	0.1	11 757	11 346	-3.5	20 758	20 684	-0.4	3 363	3 284	-2.3
Property crime	266 457	259 659	-2.6	72 895	67 038	-8.0	120 257	117 421	-2.4	33 345	30 432	-8.7
Burglary	63 182	62 817	-0.6	18 803	17 523	-6.8	9 815	10 078	2.7	2 225	2 052	-7.8
Larceny-theft	174 055	168 272	-3.3	45 705	41 686	-8.8	104 478	101 372	-3.0	29 378	26 793	-8.8
Motor vehicle theft	25 392	24 741	-2.6	6 286	5 676	-9.7	5 303	5 346	0.8	1 425	1 309	-8.1
Arson	3 828	3 829	0.0	2 101	2 153	2.5	661	625	-5.4	317	278	-12.3
Other assaults	237 823	240 642	1.2	45 692	45 141	-1.2	78 305	79 855	2.0	21 636	21 360	-1.3
Forgery and counterfeiting	18 392	17 442	-5.2	871	734	-15.7	11 925	11 380	-4.6	425	363	-14.6
Fraud	55 167	54 119	-1.9	1 260	1 272	1.0	50 186	49 594	-1.2	767	752	-2.0
Embezzlement	2 357	2 425	2.9	163	184	12.9	2 296	2 464	7.3	119	105	-11.8
Stolen property; buying, receiving, and possessing	27 300	26 561	-2.7	4 818	4 220	-12.4	6 142	6 508	6.0	903	836	-7.4
Vandalism	59 636	58 739	-1.5	24 938	24 363	-2.3	10 871	11 254	3.5	3 959	3 838	-3.1
Weapons; carrying and possessing, etc.	37 662	39 760	5.6	9 336	9 748	4.4	3 278	3 547	8.2	1 117	1 187	6.3
Prostitution and commercialized vice	2 284	2 258	-1.1	62	35	-43.5	2 885	2 530	-12.3	70	55	-21.4
Sex offenses, except forcible rape and prostitution	19 926	19 433	-2.5	4 363	4 057	-7.0	1 149	919	-20.0	368	299	-18.8
Drug abuse violations	325 747	340 747	4.6	41 088	39 916	-2.9	79 346	84 158	6.1	9 887	9 209	-6.9
Gambling	1 004	849	-15.4	119	128	7.6	291	235	-19.2	10	4	-60.0
Offenses against the family and children	36 192	36 443	0.7	1 050	988	-5.9	8 469	8 723	3.0	576	600	4.2
Driving under the influence	349 185	341 635	-2.2	4 628	4 261	-7.9	82 126	83 074	1.2	1 231	1 226	-0.4
Liquor laws	118 728	114 826	-3.3	25 748	24 958	-3.1	44 604	44 833	0.5	14 259	14 276	0.1
Drunkenness	106 189	103 987	-2.1	3 869	3 371	-12.9	20 484	20 150	-1.6	1 196	1 007	-15.8
Disorderly conduct	117 687	116 406	-1.1	38 606	37 588	-2.6	40 854	41 050	0.5	16 642	16 639	0.0
Vagrancy	3 068	3 380	10.2	442	421	-4.8	794	963	21.3	142	133	-6.3
All other offenses, except traffic	771 239	793 485	2.9	75 149	73 786	-1.8	225 889	234 981	4.0	28 237	27 643	-2.1
Suspicion	532	778	46.2	93	110	18.3	154	186	20.8	27	32	18.5
Curfew and loitering law violations	11 398	12 115	6.3	11 398	12 115	6.3	5 472	5 932	8.4	5 472	5 932	8.4
Runaways	11 109	10 858	-2.3	11 109	10 858	-2.3	16 072	14 956	-6.9	16 072	14 956	-6.9

Note: Suburban areas include law enforcement agencies in cities with fewer than 50,000 inhabitants and county law enforcement agencies within metropolitan statistical areas. They exclude all metropolitan agencies associated with a principal city.

[1]Does not include suspicion.

Table 64. Arrests in Suburban Areas, Distribution by Age, 2005

(Number, percent; 5,928 total agencies; 2005 estimated population 96,092,270.)

Offense	Total, all ages	Under 15 years	Under 18 years	18 years and over	Under 10 years	10–12 years	13–14 years	15 years	16 years	17 years
Total	4 066 122	184 044	616 776	3 449 346	5 264	39 232	139 548	121 807	145 261	165 664
Total percent distribution[1]	100.0	4.5	15.2	84.8	0.1	1.0	3.4	3.0	3.6	4.1
Violent crime	152 125	7 332	23 718	128 407	237	1 667	5 428	4 718	5 498	6 170
Violent crime percent distribution[1]	100.0	4.8	15.6	84.4	0.2	1.1	3.6	3.1	3.6	4.1
Murder and nonnegligent manslaughter	3 086	26	249	2 837	0	3	23	41	61	121
Forcible rape	7 065	422	1 105	5 960	6	105	311	183	233	267
Robbery	24 422	1 273	5 795	18 627	15	204	1 054	1 228	1 518	1 776
Aggravated assault	117 552	5 611	16 569	100 983	216	1 355	4 040	3 266	3 686	4 006
Property crime	436 872	37 533	114 237	322 635	985	8 360	28 188	23 348	25 760	27 596
Property crime percent distribution[1]	100.0	8.6	26.1	73.9	0.2	1.9	6.5	5.3	5.9	6.3
Burglary	81 652	6 951	21 975	59 677	205	1 555	5 191	4 539	4 994	5 491
Larceny-theft	317 087	27 158	81 602	235 485	662	6 082	20 414	16 431	18 287	19 726
Motor vehicle theft	32 926	1 786	7 851	25 075	21	202	1 563	1 882	2 099	2 084
Arson	5 207	1 638	2 809	2 398	97	521	1 020	496	380	295
Other assaults	368 110	31 404	76 536	291 574	965	8 311	22 128	15 298	15 570	14 264
Forgery and counterfeiting	34 552	159	1 302	33 250	9	28	122	176	333	634
Fraud	115 295	397	2 646	112 649	32	47	318	332	675	1 242
Embezzlement	5 524	21	325	5 199	2	10	9	11	95	198
Stolen property; buying, receiving, and possessing	38 651	1 435	5 978	32 673	30	264	1 141	1 212	1 517	1 814
Vandalism	80 480	12 892	32 098	48 382	635	3 481	8 776	6 068	6 644	6 494
Weapons; carrying and possessing, etc.	49 537	4 486	12 445	37 092	150	1 106	3 230	2 433	2 653	2 873
Prostitution and commercialized vice	6 550	20	116	6 434	1	1	18	25	35	36
Sex offenses, except forcible rape and prostitution	23 541	2 478	4 950	18 591	111	700	1 667	867	801	804
Drug abuse violations	485 119	8 908	55 500	429 619	106	941	7 861	9 596	14 926	22 070
Gambling	1 304	40	152	1 152	1	7	32	31	34	47
Offenses against the family and children	50 259	523	1 757	48 502	26	123	374	353	410	471
Driving under the influence	471 481	93	6 163	465 318	29	9	55	206	1 462	4 402
Liquor laws	183 381	3 831	44 143	139 238	49	242	3 540	6 782	12 585	20 945
Drunkenness	145 410	582	4 970	140 440	20	36	526	862	1 232	2 294
Disorderly conduct	189 368	25 144	62 754	126 614	461	5 850	18 833	13 109	13 033	11 468
Vagrancy	6 371	167	665	5 706	1	26	140	127	152	219
All other offenses, except traffic	1 169 912	30 979	115 798	1 054 114	1 080	5 789	24 110	23 505	28 206	33 108
Suspicion	1 958	50	201	1 757	2	8	40	44	44	63
Curfew and loitering law violations	20 435	5 697	20 435	X	60	806	4 831	4 947	5 817	3 974
Runaways	29 887	9 873	29 887	X	272	1 420	8 181	7 757	7 779	4 478

Note: Suburban areas include law enforcement agencies in cities with fewer than 50,000 inhabitants and county law enforcement agencies within metropolitan statistical areas. They exclude all metropolitan agencies associated with a principal city.

[1]Percentages may not add to 100 because of rounding.
X = Not applicable.

Table 64. Arrests in Suburban Areas, Distribution by Age, 2005—*Continued*

(Number, percent; 5,928 total agencies; 2005 estimated population 96,092,270.)

Offense	18 years	19 years	20 years	21 years	22 years	23 years	24 years	25–29 years
Total	199 115	206 848	190 720	168 658	159 604	150 532	142 924	549 400
Total percent distribution[1]	4.9	5.1	4.7	4.1	3.9	3.7	3.5	13.5
Violent crime	7 373	6 926	6 166	6 118	5 766	5 541	5 288	20 995
Violent crime percent distribution[1]	4.8	4.6	4.1	4.0	3.8	3.6	3.5	13.8
Murder and nonnegligent manslaughter	195	171	180	161	158	155	151	511
Forcible rape	380	370	326	330	281	225	225	862
Robbery	2 200	1 927	1 441	1 157	1 022	868	846	2 973
Aggravated assault	4 598	4 458	4 219	4 470	4 305	4 293	4 066	16 649
Property crime	27 737	23 860	19 075	16 436	14 650	13 403	12 318	47 516
Property crime percent distribution[1]	6.3	5.5	4.4	3.8	3.4	3.1	2.8	10.9
Burglary	6 167	5 465	4 186	3 505	3 011	2 762	2 510	9 281
Larceny-theft	19 204	16 289	13 152	11 361	10 201	9 353	8 606	33 384
Motor vehicle theft	2 150	1 948	1 625	1 451	1 332	1 193	1 127	4 514
Arson	216	158	112	119	106	95	75	337
Other assaults	12 219	11 748	11 419	11 884	11 630	11 409	11 280	47 138
Forgery and counterfeiting	1 213	1 548	1 659	1 404	1 384	1 427	1 503	6 446
Fraud	2 427	3 481	3 993	3 897	4 139	4 292	4 425	19 514
Embezzlement	372	387	346	274	264	226	194	793
Stolen property; buying, receiving, and possessing	2 461	2 349	2 002	1 762	1 665	1 568	1 487	5 613
Vandalism	5 468	4 338	3 529	3 113	2 589	2 247	2 051	7 314
Weapons; carrying and possessing, etc.	3 219	2 939	2 495	2 383	2 180	1 949	1 831	6 229
Prostitution and commercialized vice	170	226	212	231	229	188	216	914
Sex offenses, except forcible rape and prostitution	979	895	880	709	668	593	552	2 303
Drug abuse violations	32 744	32 786	29 233	25 376	23 445	21 453	20 181	71 863
Gambling	35	49	55	32	27	20	29	107
Offenses against the family and children	780	919	907	1 104	1 295	1 387	1 574	8 079
Driving under the influence	10 858	14 983	17 034	23 146	23 868	22 813	21 593	79 394
Liquor laws	34 686	35 619	28 249	4 635	3 001	2 390	1 953	6 603
Drunkenness	4 990	5 526	5 020	7 167	6 508	6 005	5 322	19 179
Disorderly conduct	9 328	8 087	7 232	8 002	7 094	6 123	5 407	18 614
Vagrancy	312	260	232	209	197	217	201	772
All other offenses, except traffic	41 625	49 802	50 871	50 684	48 933	47 216	45 476	179 720
Suspicion	119	120	111	92	72	65	43	294
Curfew and loitering law violations	X	X	X	X	X	X	X	X
Runaways	X	X	X	X	X	X	X	X

Note: Suburban areas include law enforcement agencies in cities with fewer than 50,000 inhabitants and county law enforcement agencies within metropolitan statistical areas. They exclude all metropolitan agencies associated with a principal city.

[1]Percentages may not add to 100 because of rounding.
X = Not applicable.

Table 64. Arrests in Suburban Areas, Distribution by Age, 2005—*Continued*

(Number, percent; 5,928 total agencies; 2005 estimated population 96,092,270.)

Offense	30–34 years	35–39 years	40–44 years	45–49 years	50–54 years	55–59 years	60–64 years	65 years and over
Total	421 185	392 042	365 979	253 530	132 970	62 886	28 234	24 719
Total percent distribution[1]	10.4	9.6	9.0	6.2	3.3	1.5	0.7	0.6
Violent crime	16 576	15 211	13 750	9 359	4 735	2 369	1 101	1 133
Violent crime percent distribution[1]	10.9	10.0	9.0	6.2	3.1	1.6	0.7	0.7
Murder and nonnegligent manslaughter	322	227	213	196	80	48	25	44
Forcible rape	752	689	630	409	234	114	58	75
Robbery	1 961	1 654	1 343	783	301	96	32	23
Aggravated assault	13 541	12 641	11 564	7 971	4 120	2 111	986	991
Property crime	37 744	36 450	32 038	21 327	10 879	4 963	2 208	2 031
Property crime percent distribution[1]	8.6	8.3	7.3	4.9	2.5	1.1	0.5	0.5
Burglary	6 682	6 081	5 123	2 883	1 273	451	155	142
Larceny-theft	27 534	27 396	24 673	17 174	9 079	4 295	1 958	1 826
Motor vehicle theft	3 276	2 698	1 992	1 073	428	163	70	35
Arson	252	275	250	197	99	54	25	28
Other assaults	40 134	39 004	36 158	24 029	12 259	5 842	2 806	2 615
Forgery and counterfeiting	5 234	4 400	3 447	2 023	893	441	139	89
Fraud	18 159	16 386	13 890	8 951	4 826	2 355	1 008	906
Embezzlement	601	580	501	359	165	89	31	17
Stolen property; buying, receiving, and possessing	4 165	3 694	2 930	1 734	746	284	134	79
Vandalism	4 920	4 420	3 712	2 423	1 161	555	262	280
Weapons; carrying and possessing, etc.	3 771	3 079	2 641	1 972	1 141	643	318	302
Prostitution and commercialized vice	844	995	917	612	298	178	102	102
Sex offenses, except forcible rape and prostitution	2 228	2 214	2 166	1 617	1 047	698	460	582
Drug abuse violations	47 955	42 084	38 788	25 604	11 749	4 298	1 278	782
Gambling	124	143	130	109	87	84	69	52
Offenses against the family and children	8 682	8 437	7 333	4 762	1 922	807	305	209
Driving under the influence	56 869	51 577	51 847	40 797	25 170	13 664	6 469	5 236
Liquor laws	4 552	4 387	4 772	3 853	2 303	1 169	589	477
Drunkenness	15 115	15 855	18 422	15 134	8 856	4 134	1 885	1 322
Disorderly conduct	13 022	12 642	12 864	8 961	4 829	2 279	1 070	1 060
Vagrancy	628	722	780	604	300	154	63	55
All other offenses, except traffic	139 651	129 567	118 724	79 179	39 538	17 831	7 919	7 378
Suspicion	211	195	169	121	66	49	18	12
Curfew and loitering law violations	X	X	X	X	X	X	X	X
Runaways	X	X	X	X	X	X	X	X

Note: Suburban areas include law enforcement agencies in cities with fewer than 50,000 inhabitants and county law enforcement agencies within metropolitan statistical areas. They exclude all metropolitan agencies associated with a principal city.

[1]Percentages may not add to 100 because of rounding.
X = Not applicable.

Table 65. Arrests in Suburban Areas of Persons Under 15, 18, 21, and 25 Years of Age, 2005

(Number, percent; 5,928 total agencies; 2005 estimated population 96,092,270.)

Offense	Total, all ages	Number of persons arrested				Percent of total all ages			
		Under 15 years	Under 18 years	Under 21 years	Under 25 years	Under 15 years	Under 18 years	Under 21 years	Under 25 years
Total	4 066 122	184 044	616 776	1 213 459	1 835 177	4.5	15.2	29.8	45.1
Violent crime	152 125	7 332	23 718	44 183	66 896	4.8	15.6	29.0	44.0
Murder and nonnegligent manslaughter	3 086	26	249	795	1 420	0.8	8.1	25.8	46.0
Forcible rape	7 065	422	1 105	2 181	3 242	6.0	15.6	30.9	45.9
Robbery	24 422	1 273	5 795	11 363	15 256	5.2	23.7	46.5	62.5
Aggravated assault	117 552	5 611	16 569	29 844	46 978	4.8	14.1	25.4	40.0
Property crime	436 872	37 533	114 237	184 909	241 716	8.6	26.1	42.3	55.3
Burglary	81 652	6 951	21 975	37 793	49 581	8.5	26.9	46.3	60.7
Larceny-theft	317 087	27 158	81 602	130 247	169 768	8.6	25.7	41.1	53.5
Motor vehicle theft	32 926	1 786	7 851	13 574	18 677	5.4	23.8	41.2	56.7
Arson	5 207	1 638	2 809	3 295	3 690	31.5	53.9	63.3	70.9
Other assaults	368 110	31 404	76 536	111 922	158 125	8.5	20.8	30.4	43.0
Forgery and counterfeiting	34 552	159	1 302	5 722	11 440	0.5	3.8	16.6	33.1
Fraud	115 295	397	2 646	12 547	29 300	0.3	2.3	10.9	25.4
Embezzlement	5 524	21	325	1 430	2 388	0.4	5.9	25.9	43.2
Stolen property; buying, receiving, and possessing	38 651	1 435	5 978	12 790	19 272	3.7	15.5	33.1	49.9
Vandalism	80 480	12 892	32 098	45 433	55 433	16.0	39.9	56.5	68.9
Weapons; carrying and possessing, etc.	49 537	4 486	12 445	21 098	29 441	9.1	25.1	42.6	59.4
Prostitution and commercialized vice	6 550	20	116	724	1 588	0.3	1.8	11.1	24.2
Sex offenses, except forcible rape and prostitution	23 541	2 478	4 950	7 704	10 226	10.5	21.0	32.7	43.4
Drug abuse violations	485 119	8 908	55 500	150 263	240 718	1.8	11.4	31.0	49.6
Gambling	1 304	40	152	291	399	3.1	11.7	22.3	30.6
Offenses against the family and children	50 259	523	1 757	4 363	9 723	1.0	3.5	8.7	19.3
Driving under the influence	471 481	93	6 163	49 038	140 458	0.0	1.3	10.4	29.8
Liquor laws	183 381	3 831	44 143	142 697	154 676	2.1	24.1	77.8	84.3
Drunkenness	145 410	582	4 970	20 506	45 508	0.4	3.4	14.1	31.3
Disorderly conduct	189 368	25 144	62 754	87 401	114 027	13.3	33.1	46.2	60.2
Vagrancy	6 371	167	665	1 469	2 293	2.6	10.4	23.1	36.0
All other offenses, except traffic	1 169 912	30 979	115 798	258 096	450 405	2.6	9.9	22.1	38.5
Suspicion	1 958	50	201	551	823	2.6	10.3	28.1	42.0
Curfew and loitering law violations	20 435	5 697	20 435	20 435	20 435	27.9	100.0	100.0	100.0
Runaways	29 887	9 873	29 887	29 887	29 887	33.0	100.0	100.0	100.0

Note: Suburban areas include law enforcement agencies in cities with fewer than 50,000 inhabitants and county law enforcement agencies within metropolitan statistical areas. They exclude all metropolitan agencies associated with a principal city.

Table 66. Arrests in Suburban Areas, Distribution by Sex, 2005

(Number, percent; 5,928 total agencies; 2005 estimated population 96,092,270.)

Offense	Number of persons arrested			Percent male	Percent female	Percent distribution[1]		
	Total	Male	Female			Total	Male	Female
Total	4 066 122	3 094 852	971 270	76.1	23.9	100.0	100.0	100.0
Violent crime	152 125	125 733	26 392	82.7	17.3	3.7	4.1	2.7
Murder and nonnegligent manslaughter	3 086	2 677	409	86.7	13.3	0.1	0.1	0.0
Forcible rape	7 065	6 966	99	98.6	1.4	0.2	0.2	0.0
Robbery	24 422	21 812	2 610	89.3	10.7	0.6	0.7	0.3
Aggravated assault	117 552	94 278	23 274	80.2	19.8	2.9	3.0	2.4
Property crime	436 872	298 461	138 411	68.3	31.7	10.7	9.6	14.3
Burglary	81 652	70 437	11 215	86.3	13.7	2.0	2.3	1.2
Larceny-theft	317 087	196 581	120 506	62.0	38.0	7.8	6.4	12.4
Motor vehicle theft	32 926	27 042	5 884	82.1	17.9	0.8	0.9	0.6
Arson	5 207	4 401	806	84.5	15.5	0.1	0.1	0.1
Other assaults	368 110	276 208	91 902	75.0	25.0	9.1	8.9	9.5
Forgery and counterfeiting	34 552	20 880	13 672	60.4	39.6	0.8	0.7	1.4
Fraud	115 295	62 133	53 162	53.9	46.1	2.8	2.0	5.5
Embezzlement	5 524	2 751	2 773	49.8	50.2	0.1	0.1	0.3
Stolen property; buying, receiving, and possessing	38 651	31 246	7 405	80.8	19.2	1.0	1.0	0.8
Vandalism	80 480	67 472	13 008	83.8	16.2	2.0	2.2	1.3
Weapons; carrying and possessing, etc.	49 537	45 449	4 088	91.7	8.3	1.2	1.5	0.4
Prostitution and commercialized vice	6 550	2 803	3 747	42.8	57.2	0.2	0.1	0.4
Sex offenses, except forcible rape and prostitution	23 541	22 373	1 168	95.0	5.0	0.6	0.7	0.1
Drug abuse violations	485 119	389 157	95 962	80.2	19.8	11.9	12.6	9.9
Gambling	1 304	1 043	261	80.0	20.0	0.0	0.0	0.0
Offenses against the family and children	50 259	40 209	10 050	80.0	20.0	1.2	1.3	1.0
Driving under the influence	471 481	379 193	92 288	80.4	19.6	11.6	12.3	9.5
Liquor laws	183 381	132 392	50 989	72.2	27.8	4.5	4.3	5.2
Drunkenness	145 410	122 051	23 359	83.9	16.1	3.6	3.9	2.4
Disorderly conduct	189 300	140 110	49 240	74.0	26.0	4.7	4.5	5.1
Vagrancy	6 371	4 888	1 483	76.7	23.3	0.2	0.2	0.2
All other offenses, except traffic	1 169 912	901 845	268 067	77.1	22.9	28.8	29.1	27.6
Suspicion	1 958	1 735	223	88.6	11.4	0.0	0.0	0.0
Curfew and loitering law violations	20 435	13 825	6 610	67.7	32.3	0.5	0.4	0.7
Runaways	29 887	12 886	17 001	43.1	56.9	0.7	0.4	1.8

Note: Suburban areas include law enforcement agencies in cities with fewer than 50,000 inhabitants and county law enforcement agencies within metropolitan statistical areas. They exclude all metropolitan agencies associated with a principal city.

[1]Percentages may not add to 100 because of rounding.

Table 67. Arrests in Suburban Areas, Distribution by Race, 2005

(Number, percent; 5,927 total agencies; 2005 estimated population 96,090,772.)

Offense	Total arrests					Percent distribution[1]				
	Total	White	Black	American Indian or Alaskan Native	Asian or Pacific Islander	Total	White	Black	American Indian or Alaskan Native	Asian or Pacific Islander
Total	4 016 468	3 065 121	888 620	33 432	29 295	100.0	76.3	22.1	0.8	0.7
Violent crime	151 159	102 090	46 433	1 343	1 293	100.0	67.5	30.7	0.9	0.9
Murder and nonnegligent manslaughter	3 060	1 827	1 168	19	46	100.0	59.7	38.2	0.6	1.5
Forcible rape	6 991	5 117	1 742	67	65	100.0	73.2	24.9	1.0	0.9
Robbery	24 224	11 837	12 133	99	155	100.0	48.9	50.1	0.4	0.6
Aggravated assault	116 884	83 309	31 390	1 158	1 027	100.0	71.3	26.9	1.0	0.9
Property crime	432 997	317 147	108 292	3 311	4 247	100.0	73.2	25.0	0.8	1.0
Burglary	80 969	62 060	17 987	417	505	100.0	76.6	22.2	0.5	0.6
Larceny-theft	314 159	226 412	81 648	2 621	3 478	100.0	72.1	26.0	0.8	1.1
Motor vehicle theft	32 705	24 459	7 778	245	223	100.0	74.8	23.8	0.7	0.7
Arson	5 164	4 216	879	28	41	100.0	81.6	17.0	0.5	0.8
Other assaults	364 613	265 351	93 228	3 168	2 866	100.0	72.8	25.6	0.9	0.8
Forgery and counterfeiting	33 547	24 675	8 387	126	359	100.0	73.6	25.0	0.4	1.1
Fraud	109 581	76 109	32 535	333	604	100.0	69.5	29.7	0.3	0.6
Embezzlement	5 431	3 646	1 704	24	57	100.0	67.1	31.4	0.4	1.0
Stolen property; buying, receiving, and possessing	38 099	27 030	10 541	241	287	100.0	70.9	27.7	0.6	0.8
Vandalism	79 474	64 806	13 489	635	544	100.0	81.5	17.0	0.8	0.7
Weapons; carrying and possessing, etc.	49 129	33 501	15 002	257	369	100.0	68.2	30.5	0.5	0.8
Prostitution and commercialized vice	6 506	4 508	1 685	34	279	100.0	69.3	25.9	0.5	4.3
Sex offenses, except forcible rape and prostitution	23 156	18 730	4 092	133	201	100.0	80.9	17.7	0.6	0.9
Drug abuse violations	478 666	362 145	111 358	2 467	2 696	100.0	75.7	23.3	0.5	0.6
Gambling	1 301	797	425	9	70	100.0	61.3	32.7	0.7	5.4
Offenses against the family and children	48 719	32 213	15 873	441	192	100.0	66.1	32.6	0.9	0.4
Driving under the influence	466 753	419 975	39 403	3 596	3 779	100.0	90.0	8.4	0.8	0.8
Liquor laws	181 465	162 743	13 887	2 950	1 885	100.0	89.7	7.7	1.6	1.0
Drunkenness	141 814	126 079	13 779	1 249	707	100.0	88.9	9.7	0.9	0.5
Disorderly conduct	187 229	135 933	48 452	1 600	1 244	100.0	72.6	25.9	0.9	0.7
Vagrancy	6 362	4 125	2 186	18	33	100.0	64.8	34.4	0.3	0.5
All other offenses, except traffic	1 158 338	843 010	297 139	11 008	7 181	100.0	72.8	25.7	1.0	0.6
Suspicion	1 958	1 359	585	7	7	100.0	69.4	29.9	0.4	0.4
Curfew and loitering law violations	20 355	16 198	3 926	92	139	100.0	79.6	19.3	0.5	0.7
Runaways	29 816	22 951	6 219	390	256	100.0	77.0	20.9	1.3	0.9

Note: Suburban areas include law enforcement agencies in cities with fewer than 50,000 inhabitants and county law enforcement agencies within metropolitan statistical areas. They exclude all metropolitan agencies associated with a principal city.

[1] Percentages may not add to 100 because of rounding.

Table 67. Arrests in Suburban Areas, Distribution by Race, 2005—*Continued*

(Number, percent; 5,927 total agencies; 2005 estimated population 96,090,772.)

Offense	Under 18 years					Percent distribution[1]				
	Total	White	Black	American Indian or Alaskan Native	Asian or Pacific Islander	Total	White	Black	American Indian or Alaskan Native	Asian or Pacific Islander
Total	612 972	454 097	149 111	4 790	4 974	100.0	74.1	24.3	0.8	0.8
Violent crime	23 581	13 407	9 806	179	189	100.0	56.9	41.6	0.8	0.8
Murder and nonnegligent manslaughter	249	132	114	2	1	100.0	53.0	45.8	0.8	0.4
Forcible rape	1 096	798	277	14	7	100.0	72.8	25.3	1.3	0.6
Robbery	5 775	2 082	3 618	22	53	100.0	36.1	62.6	0.4	0.9
Aggravated assault	16 461	10 395	5 797	141	128	100.0	63.1	35.2	0.9	0.8
Property crime	113 487	80 114	31 166	881	1 326	100.0	70.6	27.5	0.8	1.2
Burglary	21 850	16 198	5 395	115	142	100.0	74.1	24.7	0.5	0.6
Larceny-theft	81 036	56 542	22 745	665	1 084	100.0	69.8	28.1	0.8	1.3
Motor vehicle theft	7 802	5 092	2 548	87	75	100.0	65.3	32.7	1.1	1.0
Arson	2 799	2 282	478	14	25	100.0	81.5	17.1	0.5	0.9
Other assaults	76 132	48 987	26 090	543	512	100.0	64.3	34.3	0.7	0.7
Forgery and counterfeiting	1 292	1 011	261	5	15	100.0	78.3	20.2	0.4	1.2
Fraud	2 620	1 698	893	6	23	100.0	64.8	34.1	0.2	0.9
Embezzlement	322	199	118	1	4	100.0	61.8	36.6	0.3	1.2
Stolen property; buying, receiving, and possessing	5 910	3 690	2 120	47	53	100.0	62.4	35.9	0.8	0.9
Vandalism	31 806	26 360	5 046	185	215	100.0	82.9	15.9	0.6	0.7
Weapons; carrying and possessing, etc.	12 410	8 382	3 845	76	107	100.0	67.5	31.0	0.6	0.9
Prostitution and commercialized vice	116	70	45	1	0	100.0	60.3	38.8	0.9	0.0
Sex offenses, except forcible rape and prostitution	4 918	3 778	1 104	13	23	100.0	76.8	22.4	0.3	0.5
Drug abuse violations	55 118	44 819	9 502	374	423	100.0	81.3	17.2	0.7	0.8
Gambling	152	59	92	0	1	100.0	38.8	60.5	0.0	0.7
Offenses against the family and children	1 742	1 414	314	12	2	100.0	81.2	18.0	0.7	0.1
Driving under the influence	6 100	5 812	206	47	35	100.0	95.3	3.4	0.8	0.6
Liquor laws	43 883	41 049	1 817	641	376	100.0	93.5	4.1	1.5	0.9
Drunkenness	4 887	4 513	292	47	35	100.0	92.3	6.0	1.0	0.7
Disorderly conduct	62 415	40 739	20 904	327	445	100.0	65.3	33.5	0.5	0.7
Vagrancy	665	550	110	0	5	100.0	82.7	16.5	0.0	0.8
All other offenses, except traffic	115 044	88 198	25 135	922	789	100.0	76.7	21.8	0.8	0.7
Suspicion	201	99	100	1	1	100.0	49.3	49.8	0.5	0.5
Curfew and loitering law violations	20 355	16 198	3 926	92	139	100.0	79.6	19.3	0.5	0.7
Runaways	29 816	22 951	6 219	390	256	100.0	77.0	20.9	1.3	0.9

Note: Suburban areas include law enforcement agencies in cities with fewer than 50,000 inhabitants and county law enforcement agencies within metropolitan statistical areas. They exclude all metropolitan agencies associated with a principal city.

[1]Percentages may not add to 100 because of rounding.

Table 67. Arrests in Suburban Areas, Distribution by Race, 2005—*Continued*

(Number, percent; 5,927 total agencies; 2005 estimated population 96,090,772.)

Offense	18 years and over					Percent distribution[1]				
	Total	White	Black	American Indian or Alaskan Native	Asian or Pacific Islander	Total	White	Black	American Indian or Alaskan Native	Asian or Pacific Islander
Total	3 403 496	2 611 024	739 509	28 642	24 321	100.0	76.7	21.7	0.8	0.7
Violent crime	127 578	88 683	36 627	1 164	1 104	100.0	69.5	28.7	0.9	0.9
Murder and nonnegligent manslaughter	2 811	1 695	1 054	17	45	100.0	60.3	37.5	0.6	1.6
Forcible rape	5 895	4 319	1 465	53	58	100.0	73.3	24.9	0.9	1.0
Robbery	18 449	9 755	8 515	77	102	100.0	52.9	46.2	0.4	0.6
Aggravated assault	100 423	72 914	25 593	1 017	899	100.0	72.6	25.5	1.0	0.9
Property crime	319 510	237 033	77 126	2 430	2 921	100.0	74.2	24.1	0.8	0.9
Burglary	59 119	45 862	12 592	302	363	100.0	77.6	21.3	0.5	0.6
Larceny-theft	233 123	169 870	58 903	1 956	2 394	100.0	72.9	25.3	0.8	1.0
Motor vehicle theft	24 903	19 367	5 230	158	148	100.0	77.8	21.0	0.6	0.6
Arson	2 365	1 934	401	14	16	100.0	81.8	17.0	0.6	0.7
Other assaults	288 481	216 364	67 138	2 625	2 354	100.0	75.0	23.3	0.9	0.8
Forgery and counterfeiting	32 255	23 664	8 126	121	344	100.0	73.4	25.2	0.4	1.1
Fraud	106 961	74 411	31 642	327	581	100.0	69.6	29.6	0.3	0.5
Embezzlement	5 109	3 447	1 586	23	53	100.0	67.5	31.0	0.5	1.0
Stolen property; buying, receiving, and possessing	32 189	23 340	8 421	194	234	100.0	72.5	26.2	0.6	0.7
Vandalism	47 668	38 446	8 443	450	329	100.0	80.7	17.7	0.9	0.7
Weapons; carrying and possessing, etc.	36 719	25 119	11 157	181	262	100.0	68.4	30.4	0.5	0.7
Prostitution and commercialized vice	6 390	4 438	1 640	33	279	100.0	69.5	25.7	0.5	4.4
Sex offenses, except forcible rape and prostitution	18 238	14 952	2 988	120	178	100.0	82.0	16.4	0.7	1.0
Drug abuse violations	423 548	317 326	101 856	2 093	2 273	100.0	74.9	24.0	0.5	0.5
Gambling	1 149	738	333	9	69	100.0	64.2	29.0	0.8	6.0
Offenses against the family and children	46 977	30 799	15 559	429	190	100.0	65.6	33.1	0.9	0.4
Driving under the influence	460 653	414 163	39 197	3 549	3 744	100.0	89.9	8.5	0.8	0.8
Liquor laws	137 582	121 694	12 070	2 309	1 509	100.0	88.5	8.8	1.7	1.1
Drunkenness	136 927	121 566	13 487	1 202	672	100.0	88.8	9.8	0.9	0.5
Disorderly conduct	124 814	95 194	27 548	1 273	799	100.0	76.3	22.1	1.0	0.6
Vagrancy	5 697	3 575	2 076	18	28	100.0	62.8	36.4	0.3	0.5
All other offenses, except traffic	1 043 294	754 812	272 004	10 086	6 392	100.0	72.3	26.1	1.0	0.6
Suspicion	1 757	1 260	485	6	6	100.0	71.7	27.6	0.3	0.3
Curfew and loitering law violations	X	X	X	X	X	X	X	X	X	X
Runaways	X	X	X	X	X	X	X	X	X	X

Note: Suburban areas include law enforcement agencies in cities with fewer than 50,000 inhabitants and county law enforcement agencies within metropolitan statistical areas. They exclude all metropolitan agencies associated with a principal city.

[1]Percentages may not add to 100 because of rounding.
X = Not applicable.

Table 68. Police Disposition of Juvenile Offenders Taken Into Custody, by Population Group, 2005

(Number, percent.)

Population group	Estimated population, 2005	Number of agencies	Total juvenile offenders[1]	Handled within department and released	Referred to juvenile court jurisdiction	Referred to welfare agency	Referred to other police agency	Referred to criminal or adult court
ALL AGENCIES								
Number	120 999 116	5 138	660 974	133 664	467 288	2 461	8 808	48 753
Percent			100.0	20.2	70.7	0.4	1.3	7.4
Total Cities								
Number	85 869 567	3 926	553 741	116 983	389 513	1 903	6 330	39 012
Percent			100.0	21.1	70.3	0.3	1.1	7.0
Group I (250,000 and over)								
Number	22 983 307	30	133 474	42 044	90 205	143	453	629
Percent			100.0	31.5	67.6	0.1	0.3	0.5
Group II (100,000 to 249,999)								
Number	13 382 824	90	75 918	14 152	55 947	132	2 020	3 667
Percent			100.0	18.6	73.7	0.2	2.7	4.8
Group III (50,000 to 99,999)								
Number	15 306 602	227	101 901	20 675	72 643	656	1 477	6 450
Percent			100.0	20.3	71.3	0.6	1.4	6.3
Group IV (25,000 to 49,999)								
Number	12 452 163	356	77 522	13 613	56 157	347	1 282	6 123
Percent			100.0	17.6	72.4	0.4	1.7	7.9
Group V (10,000 to 24,999)								
Number	12 789 350	799	90 272	14 592	63 233	360	482	11 605
Percent			100.0	16.2	70.0	0.4	0.5	12.9
Group VI (under 10,000)								
Number	8 955 321	2 424	74 654	11 907	51 328	265	616	10 538
Percent			100.0	15.9	68.8	0.4	0.8	14.1
Metropolitan Counties								
Number	26 400 332	566	83 412	12 923	61 531	369	2 187	6 402
Percent			100.0	15.5	73.8	0.4	2.6	7.7
Nonmetropolitan Counties								
Number	8 729 217	646	23 821	3 758	16 244	189	291	3 339
Percent			100.0	15.8	68.2	0.8	1.2	14.0
Suburban Areas[2]								
Number	59 655 663	3 136	286 787	50 915	200 494	1 499	3 737	30 142
Percent			100.0	17.8	69.9	0.5	1.3	10.5

Note: Percentages may not add to 100 because of rounding.

[1] Includes all offenses, except traffic and neglect cases.
[2] Suburban areas include law enforcement agencies in cities with fewer than 50,000 inhabitants and county law enforcement agencies within metropolitan statistical areas. They exclude all metropolitan agencies associated with a principal city. The agencies associated with suburban areas also appear in other groups within this table.

Table 69. Total Arrests, by State, 2005

(Number.)

State and age group	Total, all classes[1]	Violent crime[2]	Property crime[2]	Murder and non-negligent man-slaughter	Forcible rape	Robbery	Aggravated assault	Burglary	Larceny-theft
Alabama									
Under 18 years	11 484	461	2 561	16	16	159	270	506	1 899
Total, all ages	178 684	5 357	17 455	284	359	1 325	3 389	2 932	13 377
Alaska									
Under 18 years	4 532	205	1 359	1	12	23	169	223	1 016
Total, all ages	37 227	1 721	4 271	28	67	144	1 482	549	3 265
Arizona									
Under 18 years	50 371	1 548	10 416	21	36	271	1 220	1 375	7 720
Total, all ages	302 339	8 459	38 498	244	215	1 501	6 499	4 636	28 513
Arkansas									
Under 18 years	12 380	477	3 054	13	21	78	365	560	2 409
Total, all ages	142 878	4 698	13 871	131	251	631	3 685	2 409	10 860
California									
Under 18 years	217 158	15 266	45 337	186	239	5 291	9 550	12 468	25 902
Total, all ages	1 506 819	122 875	173 561	1 953	2 095	18 150	100 677	51 086	89 779
Colorado									
Under 18 years	46 030	1 059	8 911	6	87	203	763	898	7 244
Total, all ages	249 404	6 336	29 857	95	456	855	4 930	3 132	24 382
Connecticut									
Under 18 years	20 811	1 071	3 878	7	54	267	743	793	2 668
Total, all ages	122 966	5 297	16 034	104	262	1 219	3 712	2 636	12 154
Delaware									
Under 18 years	7 449	517	1 398	3	25	158	331	300	986
Total, all ages	37 332	2 421	4 984	16	140	461	1 804	941	3 803
District of Columbia[3]									
Under 18 years	347	30	53	0	0	23	7	1	35
Total, all ages	4 504	80	82	0	0	42	38	1	58
Florida[4]									
Under 18 years	120 082	8 660	33 503	78	290	2 037	6 255	8 311	21 571
Total, all ages	1 055 052	50 929	122 426	728	2 058	8 696	39 447	24 763	85 457
Georgia									
Under 18 years	28 429	1 316	5 478	34	42	464	776	1 163	3 520
Total, all ages	216 627	9 493	24 021	229	244	2 060	6 960	4 101	17 481
Hawaii									
Under 18 years	8 261	232	1 243	3	7	104	118	75	1 029
Total, all ages	43 632	994	4 599	29	85	299	581	415	3 356
Idaho									
Under 18 years	9 864	170	2 001	2	8	10	150	269	1 602
Total, all ages	44 193	924	4 617	20	68	48	788	634	3 725
Illinois									
Under 18 years	37 470	3 565	6 141	44	95	1 314	2 112	1 026	2 616
Total, all ages	196 878	9 694	24 849	383	543	3 081	5 687	2 809	14 896
Indiana									
Under 18 years	34 293	1 589	7 013	21	27	216	1 325	926	5 402
Total, all ages	229 883	11 428	26 128	248	256	1 600	9 324	3 855	20 023
Iowa									
Under 18 years	19 926	802	5 205	0	23	119	660	726	4 170
Total, all ages	116 089	4 385	13 643	17	99	374	3 895	2 144	10 727
Kansas									
Under 18 years	6 555	177	1 069	1	16	6	154	171	780
Total, all ages	48 182	1 073	3 705	10	82	68	913	614	2 766
Kentucky									
Under 18 years	13 857	595	3 137	8	27	182	378	700	2 177
Total, all ages	210 113	4 493	17 367	269	299	1 108	2 817	3 724	12 477
Louisiana									
Under 18 years	23 806	1 052	4 575	18	49	164	821	1 140	3 189
Total, all ages	163 410	7 326	19 824	256	274	972	5 824	4 480	14 221
Maine									
Under 18 years	7 112	109	2 052	0	19	27	63	361	1 587
Total, all ages	49 931	723	6 553	0	106	181	436	1 034	5 207

Note: Because the number of agencies submitting arrest data varies from year to year, caution should be exercised when making direct comparisons between 2005 arrest totals and those from previous years. Arrest figures may vary widely from state to state because some offenses listed in Part II are not considered crimes in every state.

[1]Does not include traffic arrests.
[2]Violent crimes include murder, forcible rape, robbery, and aggravated assault. Property crimes include burglary, larceny-theft, motor vehicle theft, and arson.
[3]Includes arrests reported by the Metro Transit Police.
[4]The arrest category "all other offenses" also includes the arrest counts for offenses against the family and children, drunkenness, disorderly conduct, vagrancy, suspicion, curfew and loitering law violations, and runaways.

Table 69. Total Arrests, by State, 2005—*Continued*

(Number.)

State and age group	Motor vehicle theft	Arson	Other assaults	Forgery and counterfeiting	Fraud	Embezzlement	Stolen property; buying, receiving, and possessing	Vandalism	Weapons; carrying and possessing, etc.
Alabama									
Under 18 years	135	21	2 053	42	41	0	130	300	98
Total, all ages	1 051	95	24 141	2 001	8 060	10	1 901	2 179	1 148
Alaska									
Under 18 years	109	11	453	12	21	0	5	235	68
Total, all ages	392	65	4 036	130	181	7	29	981	397
Arizona									
Under 18 years	1 125	196	5 064	78	122	46	226	3 147	506
Total, all ages	5 062	287	23 542	2 773	1 985	284	1 586	10 306	3 322
Arkansas									
Under 18 years	73	12	1 259	48	72	0	97	390	160
Total, all ages	524	78	8 899	1 812	5 314	12	1 267	1 328	1 476
California									
Under 18 years	5 980	987	21 776	381	601	142	3 003	13 603	9 146
Total, all ages	30 967	1 729	86 613	10 755	10 258	2 042	21 770	29 940	32 968
Colorado									
Under 18 years	579	190	2 392	90	133	13	222	1 879	740
Total, all ages	2 036	307	15 236	2 051	2 175	127	1 548	5 964	2 359
Connecticut									
Under 18 years	305	112	4 345	37	68	14	146	1 071	444
Total, all ages	933	311	20 556	872	1 603	192	760	2 772	1 490
Delaware									
Under 18 years	54	58	1 659	14	91	28	96	319	137
Total, all ages	158	82	7 456	460	2 010	243	373	1 008	391
District of Columbia[3]									
Under 18 years	17	0	41	1	1	0	0	11	12
Total, all ages	23	0	121	1	2	1	10	22	30
Florida[4]									
Under 18 years	3 413	208	19 149	187	590	93	333	3 254	2 766
Total, all ages	11 741	465	06 502	5 382	16 006	1 251	3 051	0 650	8 532
Georgia									
Under 18 years	577	218	3 607	95	384	2	577	756	778
Total, all ages	1 953	486	17 452	3 083	8 400	193	3 470	2 417	4 541
Hawaii									
Under 18 years	124	15	792	10	5	1	18	330	33
Total, all ages	797	31	4 009	294	228	38	145	729	200
Idaho									
Under 18 years	90	40	773	16	37	12	46	479	120
Total, all ages	203	55	4 099	218	359	57	231	899	384
Illinois									
Under 18 years	2 455	44	7 080	13	167	0	0	1 837	1 182
Total, all ages	7 011	133	27 858	213	1 663	0	0	5 130	4 502
Indiana									
Under 18 years	593	92	3 129	31	74	2	1 187	1 230	200
Total, all ages	2 019	231	13 796	1 512	2 230	42	5 830	2 624	1 845
Iowa									
Under 18 years	221	88	2 472	49	62	8	39	1 454	107
Total, all ages	619	153	10 226	960	1 416	113	171	3 065	519
Kansas									
Under 18 years	85	33	937	15	15	3	40	415	55
Total, all ages	264	61	5 548	268	1 102	26	230	1 100	239
Kentucky									
Under 18 years	228	32	1 413	69	90	0	463	707	154
Total, all ages	927	239	14 461	4 251	14 890	349	3 023	2 753	1 878
Louisiana									
Under 18 years	208	38	4 475	29	21	7	217	891	295
Total, all ages	988	135	22 322	1 048	1 966	113	1 473	3 119	1 582
Maine									
Under 18 years	80	24	906	23	16	1	33	465	44
Total, all ages	263	49	6 243	367	845	27	211	1 574	333

Note: Because the number of agencies submitting arrest data varies from year to year, caution should be exercised when making direct comparisons between 2005 arrest totals and those from previous years. Arrest figures may vary widely from state to state because some offenses listed in Part II are not considered crimes in every state.

[3]Includes arrests reported by the Metro Transit Police.

[4]The arrest category "all other offenses" also includes the arrest counts for offenses against the family and children, drunkenness, disorderly conduct, vagrancy, suspicion, curfew and loitering law violations, and runaways.

Table 69. Total Arrests, by State, 2005—*Continued*

(Number.)

State and age group	Prostitution and commercialized vice	Sex offenses, except forcible rape and prostitution	Drug abuse violations	Gambling	Offenses against the family and children	Driving under the influence	Liquor laws	Drunkenness[5]
Alabama								
Under 18 years	0	17	1 034	7	9	93	662	83
Total, all ages	124	455	15 704	49	981	11 621	4 895	8 562
Alaska								
Under 18 years	3	49	335	0	16	85	305	34
Total, all ages	123	213	1 885	2	494	4 754	1 580	124
Arizona								
Under 18 years	36	316	5 304	4	376	501	4 630	0
Total, all ages	1 611	1 740	35 722	23	3 666	34 437	21 809	0
Arkansas								
Under 18 years	2	54	980	1	9	160	249	262
Total, all ages	301	306	12 009	25	456	9 983	3 143	7 734
California								
Under 18 years	561	2 416	21 791	93	7	1 447	4 351	3 566
Total, all ages	13 911	15 378	305 745	672	466	181 243	21 311	96 308
Colorado								
Under 18 years	10	327	3 747	1	69	434	4 941	13
Total, all ages	869	1 154	19 743	30	3 265	24 444	14 505	247
Connecticut								
Under 18 years	1	171	1 842	5	82	117	327	1
Total, all ages	493	710	14 480	80	1 194	9 323	1 183	9
Delaware								
Under 18 years	0	59	751	3	4	0	480	13
Total, all ages	140	180	5 018	12	195	200	2 464	429
District of Columbia[3]								
Under 18 years	0	1	17	0	0	0	6	0
Total, all ages	0	3	68	0	0	16	1 107	61
Florida[4]								
Under 18 years	81	442	14 065	43	0	361	1 305	. . .
Total, all ages	5 715	3 979	160 595	425	0	57 528	33 134	. . .
Georgia								
Under 18 years	25	356	2 502	31	90	161	575	38
Total, all ages	1 681	3 292	29 513	216	2 003	13 680	10 659	2 905
Hawaii								
Under 18 years	4	42	335	2	4	45	87	0
Total, all ages	341	203	2 132	114	55	4 346	808	0
Idaho								
Under 18 years	0	70	568	0	6	142	1 154	14
Total, all ages	3	207	3 231	1	252	6 150	3 654	97
Illinois								
Under 18 years	57	110	8 514	872	15	46	311	0
Total, all ages	4 931	1 552	58 093	3 069	358	6 045	880	0
Indiana								
Under 18 years	3	252	2 502	2	343	213	2 879	474
Total, all ages	1 809	1 548	24 698	17	2 098	27 569	13 196	16 799
Iowa								
Under 18 years	1	90	1 151	0	24	230	2 000	243
Total, all ages	215	322	9 740	6	1 009	13 781	10 764	8 651
Kansas								
Under 18 years	0	44	568	0	7	183	1 041	1
Total, all ages	8	164	4 569	0	146	9 092	5 114	220
Kentucky								
Under 18 years	6	200	1 988	0	33	389	376	568
Total, all ages	509	2 684	35 313	38	4 759	21 992	5 388	18 919
Louisiana								
Under 18 years	9	155	1 841	27	71	98	346	41
Total, all ages	447	852	22 323	102	1 358	8 800	6 570	2 666
Maine								
Under 18 years	5	48	582	1	9	124	958	4
Total, all ages	18	263	4 730	3	440	6 404	3 852	22

Note: Because the number of agencies submitting arrest data varies from year to year, caution should be exercised when making direct comparisons between 2005 arrest totals and those from previous years. Arrest figures may vary widely from state to state because some offenses listed in Part II are not considered crimes in every state.

[3]Includes arrests reported by the Metro Transit Police.
[4]The arrest category "all other offenses" also includes the arrest counts for offenses against the family and children, drunkenness, disorderly conduct, vagrancy, suspicion, curfew and loitering law violations, and runaways.
[5]Drunkenness is not considered a crime in some states; therefore, figures for drunkenness vary widely from state to state.
. . . = Not available.

Table 69. Total Arrests, by State, 2005—*Continued*

(Number.)

State and age group	Disorderly conduct	Vagrancy	All other offenses, except traffic	Suspicion	Curfew and loitering law violations	Runaways	Number of agencies	Estimated population, 2005
Alabama								
Under 18 years	1 827	14	1 554	0	76	422	. . .	. . .
Total, all ages	4 675	297	68 569	2	76	422	255	3 227 681
Alaska								
Under 18 years	127	0	927	3	6	284	. . .	. . .
Total, all ages	1 040	2	14 961	6	6	284	32	643 085
Arizona								
Under 18 years	3 583	19	5 559	0	3 748	5 142	. . .	. . .
Total, all ages	16 738	961	85 987	0	3 748	5 142	84	5 350 364
Arkansas								
Under 18 years	1 024	13	2 643	10	884	532	. . .	. . .
Total, all ages	3 163	1 255	64 230	180	884	532	156	2 154 095
California								
Under 18 years	12 579	407	39 734	0	16 474	4 477	. . .	. . .
Total, all ages	17 195	5 738	337 119	0	16 474	4 477	627	35 908 932
Colorado								
Under 18 years	4 417	3	10 073	8	2 975	3 573	. . .	. . .
Total, all ages	17 980	568	94 387	11	2 975	3 573	185	4 304 012
Connecticut								
Under 18 years	3 821	4	3 167	0	149	50	. . .	. . .
Total, all ages	15 958	73	29 688	0	149	50	91	3 084 326
Delaware								
Under 18 years	1 089	0	710	0	81	0	. . .	. . .
Total, all ages	2 768	608	5 891	0	81	0	50	843 524
District of Columbia[3]								
Under 18 years	52	0	120	0	2	0	. . .	. . .
Total, all ages	132	198	2 568	0	2	0	1	. . .
Florida[4]								
Under 18 years	. . .	. . .	35 250	. . .	. . .	. . .	. . .	. . .
Total, all ages	. . .	. . .	480 948	. . .	. . .	. . .	602	17 758 612
Georgia								
Under 18 years	3 348	103	5 089	73	583	2 462	. . .	. . .
Total, all ages	19 112	1 932	54 519	1 000	583	2 462	179	3 341 353
Hawaii								
Under 18 years	80	6	1 865	0	254	2 873	. . .	. . .
Total, all ages	611	6	20 653	0	254	2 873	2	1 048 094
Idaho								
Under 18 years	284	0	2 244	0	395	1 333	. . .	. . .
Total, all ages	1 491	5	15 586	0	395	1 333	71	906 893
Illinois								
Under 18 years	3 520	0	4 040	0	0	0	. . .	. . .
Total, all ages	19 223	0	28 818	0	0	0	1	2 873 441
Indiana								
Under 18 years	2 864	12	6 171	30	332	3 761	. . .	. . .
Total, all ages	8 960	29	63 431	201	332	3 761	158	4 680 394
Iowa								
Under 18 years	2 019	0	2 727	0	771	472	. . .	. . .
Total, all ages	5 776	37	30 047	0	771	472	190	2 640 488
Kansas								
Under 18 years	362	0	749	0	0	874	. . .	. . .
Total, all ages	1 674	0	13 030	0	0	874	219	1 296 042
Kentucky								
Under 18 years	1 000	0	2 289	0	137	243	. . .	. . .
Total, all ages	7 817	506	48 343	0	137	243	198	2 677 931
Louisiana								
Under 18 years	4 130	56	4 119	35	601	715	. . .	. . .
Total, all ages	16 478	368	43 277	80	601	715	105	2 450 103
Maine								
Under 18 years	162	0	1 383	0	98	89	. . .	. . .
Total, all ages	1 687	1	15 448	0	98	89	149	1 302 517

Note: Because the number of agencies submitting arrest data varies from year to year, caution should be exercised when making direct comparisons between 2005 arrest totals and those from previous years. Arrest figures may vary widely from state to state because some offenses listed in Part II are not considered crimes in every state.

[3]Includes arrests reported by the Metro Transit Police.
[4]The arrest category "all other offenses" also includes the arrest counts for offenses against the family and children, drunkenness, disorderly conduct, vagrancy, suspicion, curfew and loitering law violations, and runaways.
. . . = Not available.

Table 69. Total Arrests, by State, 2005—*Continued*

(Number.)

State and age group	Total, all classes[1]	Violent crime[2]	Property crime[2]	Murder and non-negligent man-slaughter	Forcible rape	Robbery	Aggravated assault	Burglary	Larceny-theft
Maryland									
Under 18 years	49 297	3 187	11 636	34	55	1 316	1 782	2 411	7 067
Total, all ages	302 456	11 827	34 741	333	415	3 528	7 551	6 936	22 856
Massachusetts									
Under 18 years	14 841	1 329	2 545	6	32	234	1 057	641	1 664
Total, all ages	112 437	7 109	12 077	37	253	909	5 910	2 436	8 774
Michigan									
Under 18 years	45 934	2 396	11 472	15	144	544	1 693	1 649	8 262
Total, all ages	344 114	14 852	37 023	229	785	2 403	11 435	6 200	26 392
Minnesota									
Under 18 years	46 818	1 279	8 649	22	136	404	717	953	6 942
Total, all ages	204 004	6 168	25 385	89	699	1 302	4 078	3 256	19 915
Mississippi									
Under 18 years	11 372	164	2 214	3	20	66	75	519	1 590
Total, all ages	101 737	2 107	9 299	140	209	459	1 299	2 041	6 785
Missouri									
Under 18 years	26 874	1 440	5 477	49	62	386	943	970	3 589
Total, all ages	229 077	11 029	26 797	294	397	1 715	8 623	4 254	19 251
Montana									
Under 18 years	6 493	111	1 683	0	9	8	94	113	1 449
Total, all ages	25 130	773	4 177	11	33	56	673	251	3 644
Nebraska									
Under 18 years	15 219	185	3 413	1	8	59	117	299	2 901
Total, all ages	95 377	1 757	9 799	39	155	321	1 242	928	8 391
Nevada									
Under 18 years	15 749	498	3 616	37	28	181	252	575	2 701
Total, all ages	149 978	4 212	18 379	205	197	1 189	2 621	4 772	11 439
New Hampshire									
Under 18 years	8 417	96	1 193	0	13	22	61	112	995
Total, all ages	46 351	519	3 182	6	56	123	334	402	2 588
New Jersey									
Under 18 years	59 154	3 266	7 908	28	60	1 428	1 750	1 572	5 760
Total, all ages	375 719	14 244	30 653	278	485	4 180	9 301	5 784	23 409
New Mexico									
Under 18 years	9 696	406	1 864	11	22	45	328	234	1 415
Total, all ages	83 276	3 319	6 691	95	114	372	2 738	1 039	4 830
New York									
Under 18 years	48 377	3 223	11 459	27	95	1 292	1 809	2 469	7 931
Total, all ages	335 353	16 026	50 045	350	748	4 248	10 680	7 945	38 780
North Carolina									
Under 18 years	47 488	2 508	10 838	50	79	742	1 637	2 793	7 492
Total, all ages	446 154	22 031	58 337	666	720	4 105	16 540	15 302	40 798
North Dakota									
Under 18 years	6 599	51	948	0	6	3	42	49	787
Total, all ages	27 248	223	2 181	4	32	16	171	195	1 782
Ohio									
Under 18 years	41 082	1 203	7 824	12	133	481	577	1 543	5 450
Total, all ages	251 917	7 107	31 505	227	623	2 561	3 696	5 977	23 230
Oklahoma									
Under 18 years	19 813	682	4 723	9	37	115	521	790	3 531
Total, all ages	145 946	5 551	15 497	167	329	681	4 374	2 867	11 244
Oregon									
Under 18 years	28 107	728	6 613	22	23	160	523	874	5 125
Total, all ages	142 649	4 355	26 635	130	291	955	2 979	3 171	20 550
Pennsylvania									
Under 18 years	101 608	5 107	12 609	41	211	1 811	3 044	2 242	8 573
Total, all ages	437 305	23 804	52 624	510	1 199	6 720	15 375	9 448	37 848
Rhode Island									
Under 18 years	5 286	203	1 000	0	11	58	134	224	654
Total, all ages	32 875	742	3 102	9	59	151	523	630	2 199
South Carolina									
Under 18 years	27 736	1 634	5 877	24	95	305	1 210	1 355	4 225
Total, all ages	221 852	10 880	25 092	287	533	1 558	8 502	5 054	18 747

Note: Because the number of agencies submitting arrest data varies from year to year, caution should be exercised when making direct comparisons between 2005 arrest totals and those from previous years. Arrest figures may vary widely from state to state because some offenses listed in Part II are not considered crimes in every state.

[1]Does not include traffic arrests.
[2]Violent crimes include murder, forcible rape, robbery, and aggravated assault. Property crimes include burglary, larceny-theft, motor vehicle theft, and arson.

Table 69. Total Arrests, by State, 2005—*Continued*

(Number.)

State and age group	Motor vehicle theft	Arson	Other assaults	Forgery and counterfeiting	Fraud	Embezzlement	Stolen property; buying, receiving, and possessing	Vandalism	Weapons; carrying and possessing, etc.
Maryland									
Under 18 years	1 809	349	8 881	67	79	39	33	2 433	1 646
Total, all ages	4 376	573	32 588	1 104	3 098	343	275	4 490	4 464
Massachusetts									
Under 18 years	192	48	1 743	21	23	3	198	763	190
Total, all ages	765	102	13 269	558	937	74	888	2 194	761
Michigan									
Under 18 years	1 419	142	4 353	52	355	63	661	1 586	953
Total, all ages	4 076	355	31 596	1 237	6 413	1 406	2 739	4 203	5 337
Minnesota									
Under 18 years	655	99	4 419	109	164	1	541	2 234	780
Total, all ages	2 038	176	20 123	2 639	3 364	9	2 313	5 163	2 265
Mississippi									
Under 18 years	83	22	1 298	21	35	15	161	295	183
Total, all ages	389	84	10 853	796	1 336	557	773	1 162	730
Missouri									
Under 18 years	808	110	4 577	61	44	16	193	1 744	477
Total, all ages	2 995	297	24 885	2 635	3 008	85	1 733	6 507	3 149
Montana									
Under 18 years	95	26	599	11	12	2	3	393	41
Total, all ages	240	42	3 386	146	184	17	24	893	117
Nebraska									
Under 18 years	131	82	2 031	24	57	3	168	1 083	167
Total, all ages	355	125	9 741	788	1 727	76	1 106	2 886	1 153
Nevada									
Under 18 years	265	75	1 459	17	49	33	173	642	192
Total, all ages	2 046	122	17 424	558	2 493	441	1 852	1 688	1 897
New Hampshire									
Under 18 years	56	30	1 066	11	104	6	94	424	33
Total, all ages	140	52	5 550	238	1 180	32	385	1 214	147
New Jersey									
Under 18 years	358	218	5 492	50	173	5	1 410	3 371	1 966
Total, all ages	1 092	368	28 190	1 983	5 387	80	5 198	7 113	6 287
New Mexico									
Under 18 years	79	136	978	15	25	9	71	246	285
Total, all ages	446	376	5 458	382	455	172	702	575	704
New York									
Under 18 years	863	196	4 743	244	358	7	1 242	3 872	988
Total, all ages	2 855	465	29 226	4 808	10 180	203	6 238	12 719	4 505
North Carolina									
Under 18 years	376	177	8 212	93	520	83	853	2 300	1 545
Total, all ages	1 844	393	56 641	3 422	30 503	1 937	6 379	9 073	7 931
North Dakota									
Under 18 years	103	9	445	16	16	4	38	324	40
Total, all ages	192	12	1 820	122	1 034	13	113	558	190
Ohio									
Under 18 years	612	219	5 442	76	87	4	996	1 890	532
Total, all ages	1 913	385	26 420	1 699	3 529	22	4 598	4 598	2 990
Oklahoma									
Under 18 years	254	148	1 218	19	61	27	346	472	322
Total, all ages	1 102	284	9 818	1 079	2 435	516	2 405	1 327	2 306
Oregon									
Under 18 years	460	154	2 166	74	91	12	81	1 651	331
Total, all ages	2 665	249	14 889	1 943	1 704	78	680	4 598	2 041
Pennsylvania									
Under 18 years	1 496	298	7 923	111	366	29	693	4 462	1 689
Total, all ages	4 647	681	42 373	3 573	12 547	397	3 298	11 896	4 839
Rhode Island									
Under 18 years	65	57	661	6	23	8	76	446	139
Total, all ages	199	74	3 634	138	908	153	272	1 190	308
South Carolina									
Under 18 years	220	77	4 859	74	165	27	322	1 357	899
Total, all ages	1 094	197	24 279	2 565	24 630	504	2 701	4 140	2 773

Note: Because the number of agencies submitting arrest data varies from year to year, caution should be exercised when making direct comparisons between 2005 arrest totals and those from previous years. Arrest figures may vary widely from state to state because some offenses listed in Part II are not considered crimes in every state.

Table 69. Total Arrests, by State, 2005—*Continued*

(Number.)

State and age group	Prostitution and commercialized vice	Sex offenses, except forcible rape and prostitution	Drug abuse violations	Gambling	Offenses against the family and children	Driving under the influence	Liquor laws	Drunkenness[5]
Maryland								
Under 18 years	38	301	7 666	80	56	289	1 298	0
Total, all ages	1 861	1 280	52 472	387	2 332	23 072	5 889	1
Massachusetts								
Under 18 years	12	78	1 785	4	117	140	757	248
Total, all ages	672	369	14 496	9	1 596	11 195	3 557	6 963
Michigan								
Under 18 years	15	361	3 792	20	18	823	5 326	15
Total, all ages	1 776	1 293	33 492	100	3 392	46 732	25 610	626
Minnesota								
Under 18 years	66	261	3 064	7	12	724	7 216	0
Total, all ages	2 133	1 313	20 001	47	520	30 699	27 086	0
Mississippi								
Under 18 years	0	46	912	11	162	114	231	177
Total, all ages	63	331	13 953	345	2 628	9 371	2 605	6 085
Missouri								
Under 18 years	4	419	2 526	5	99	274	1 008	7
Total, all ages	1 271	2 530	29 685	261	3 522	21 003	7 172	936
Montana								
Under 18 years	0	16	356	0	29	70	925	0
Total, all ages	2	74	1 662	2	307	3 128	2 722	0
Nebraska								
Under 18 years	4	127	1 158	2	23	295	1 563	0
Total, all ages	148	585	11 181	26	1 639	14 257	9 342	3
Nevada								
Under 18 years	82	131	745	5	33	73	1 255	96
Total, all ages	4 633	1 336	11 267	53	1 672	9 746	7 254	147
New Hampshire								
Under 18 years	1	46	718	2	6	91	1 081	354
Total, all ages	74	209	3 209	4	193	5 035	4 876	4 120
New Jersey								
Under 18 years	21	357	6 341	33	49	363	2 711	2
Total, all ages	2 342	1 886	53 846	283	14 872	24 694	7 265	16
New Mexico								
Under 18 years	0	16	1 169	4	57	184	773	18
Total, all ages	300	113	6 439	7	1 134	11 240	3 872	729
New York								
Under 18 years	21	892	5 816	17	346	285	1 134	0
Total, all ages	1 743	4 530	54 613	198	2 763	29 062	4 974	0
North Carolina								
Under 18 years	11	172	3 387	8	94	392	1 521	0
Total, all ages	1 370	1 632	38 775	452	8 324	28 720	14 565	0
North Dakota								
Under 18 years	0	18	232	0	72	66	1 208	7
Total, all ages	1	68	1 785	4	210	4 116	5 816	541
Ohio								
Under 18 years	9	226	3 052	11	956	237	2 320	88
Total, all ages	1 282	1 123	33 643	157	9 217	20 126	12 937	4 375
Oklahoma								
Under 18 years	3	48	1 593	4	29	255	383	716
Total, all ages	456	700	21 468	19	998	15 884	2 957	21 167
Oregon								
Under 18 years	19	198	2 267	6	8	173	4 226	0
Total, all ages	635	1 279	20 532	9	512	14 901	14 734	0
Pennsylvania								
Under 18 years	13	635	6 306	30	36	537	7 097	332
Total, all ages	2 552	2 881	51 944	320	935	41 464	24 985	21 315
Rhode Island								
Under 18 years	1	48	503	0	70	18	128	1
Total, all ages	110	136	2 863	11	134	2 313	638	17
South Carolina								
Under 18 years	5	207	3 044	5	36	71	761	186
Total, all ages	742	809	29 837	130	751	8 645	9 588	11 170

Note: Because the number of agencies submitting arrest data varies from year to year, caution should be exercised when making direct comparisons between 2005 arrest totals and those from previous years. Arrest figures may vary widely from state to state because some offenses listed in Part II are not considered crimes in every state.

[5]Drunkenness is not considered a crime in some states; therefore, figures for drunkenness vary widely from state to state.

Table 69. Total Arrests, by State, 2005—*Continued*

(Number.)

State and age group	Disorderly conduct	Vagrancy	All other offenses, except traffic	Suspicion	Curfew and loitering law violations	Runaways	Number of agencies	Estimated population, 2005
Maryland								
Under 18 years	2 489	14	7 724	67	497	777	. . .	. . .
Total, all ages	6 769	202	113 524	463	497	777	138	5 524 635
Massachusetts								
Under 18 years	1 138	0	3 407	28	17	295	. . .	. . .
Total, all ages	5 605	23	29 623	150	17	295	298	4 927 398
Michigan								
Under 18 years	1 555	0	8 445	0	2 031	1 642	. . .	. . .
Total, all ages	9 656	382	112 576	0	2 031	1 642	536	9 807 849
Minnesota								
Under 18 years	5 865	11	5 762	0	2 908	2 746	. . .	. . .
Total, all ages	15 075	298	33 749	0	2 908	2 746	329	4 836 926
Mississippi								
Under 18 years	2 029	1	2 476	2	443	382	. . .	. . .
Total, all ages	7 636	110	30 090	82	443	382	98	1 460 530
Missouri								
Under 18 years	1 976	17	3 785	0	947	1 778	. . .	. . .
Total, all ages	11 974	288	67 882	0	947	1 778	168	3 655 659
Montana								
Under 18 years	586	0	793	0	465	398	. . .	. . .
Total, all ages	2 193	10	4 450	0	465	398	68	776 834
Nebraska								
Under 18 years	860	2	3 201	0	507	346	. . .	. . .
Total, all ages	4 208	58	24 043	1	507	346	214	1 590 291
Nevada								
Under 18 years	173	24	1 997	20	2 994	1 442	. . .	. . .
Total, all ages	1 774	1 491	57 064	161	2 994	1 442	32	2 410 942
New Hampshire								
Under 18 years	305	5	2 386	0	25	370	. . .	. . .
Total, all ages	1 450	32	14 307	0	25	370	131	1 081 410
New Jersey								
Under 18 years	5 253	46	9 009	1	6 326	5 001	. . .	. . .
Total, all ages	21 601	1 714	136 737	1	6 326	5 001	540	8 389 085
New Mexico								
Under 18 years	497	0	2 485	1	47	546	. . .	. . .
Total, all ages	2 525	104	37 716	46	47	546	52	1 429 002
New York								
Under 18 years	2 545	117	11 068	0	0	0	. . .	. . .
Total, all ages	15 291	1 374	86 855	0	0	0	561	9 800 300
North Carolina								
Under 18 years	6 497	0	7 166	0	26	1 262	. . .	. . .
Total, all ages	18 175	90	136 509	0	26	1 262	348	7 455 705
North Dakota								
Under 18 years	710	0	1 369	0	334	701	. . .	. . .
Total, all ages	1 641	2	5 775	0	334	701	63	549 686
Ohio								
Under 18 years	3 230	6	9 822	8	2 043	1 020	. . .	. . .
Total, all ages	17 976	83	65 392	75	2 043	1 020	342	6 557 771
Oklahoma								
Under 18 years	1 029	0	2 373	0	2 082	3 428	. . .	. . .
Total, all ages	2 961	0	32 892	0	2 082	3 428	281	3 345 709
Oregon								
Under 18 years	1 266	0	3 482	0	2 368	2 347	. . .	. . .
Total, all ages	6 878	2	21 529	0	2 368	2 347	153	3 431 463
Pennsylvania								
Under 18 years	15 858	70	7 374	0	28 307	2 024	. . .	. . .
Total, all ages	54 107	1 004	50 116	0	28 307	2 024	796	10 564 202
Rhode Island								
Under 18 years	679	0	1 117	0	8	151	. . .	. . .
Total, all ages	2 518	1	13 528	0	8	151	45	871 688
South Carolina								
Under 18 years	3 759	0	3 890	0	46	512	. . .	. . .
Total, all ages	14 597	980	46 481	0	46	512	264	3 865 027

Note: Because the number of agencies submitting arrest data varies from year to year, caution should be exercised when making direct comparisons between 2005 arrest totals and those from previous years. Arrest figures may vary widely from state to state because some offenses listed in Part II are not considered crimes in every state.

. . . = Not available.

Table 69. Total Arrests, by State, 2005—*Continued*

(Number.)

State and age group	Total, all classes[1]	Violent crime[2]	Property crime[2]	Murder and non-negligent man-slaughter	Forcible rape	Robbery	Aggravated assault	Burglary	Larceny-theft
South Dakota									
Under 18 years	3 096	42	537	0	8	2	32	53	457
Total, all ages	16 299	265	1 277	5	46	10	204	173	1 045
Tennessee									
Under 18 years	34 316	1 596	6 343	36	60	448	1 052	1 264	4 425
Total, all ages	268 770	13 953	32 305	338	352	2 636	10 627	5 436	24 132
Texas									
Under 18 years	173 568	5 062	30 771	76	362	1 244	3 380	5 359	23 471
Total, all ages	1 057 731	32 382	120 156	906	2 183	6 481	22 812	18 246	93 279
Utah									
Under 18 years	26 481	360	5 626	2	67	52	239	365	4 985
Total, all ages	116 880	1 751	15 852	45	200	329	1 177	1 351	13 856
Vermont									
Under 18 years	1 599	38	364	1	6	1	30	85	227
Total, all ages	13 021	326	1 271	11	58	6	251	236	923
Virginia									
Under 18 years	32 980	1 061	5 552	16	33	430	582	1 068	4 029
Total, all ages	277 579	6 509	24 449	312	303	1 683	4 211	3 715	19 129
Washington									
Under 18 years	35 315	1 329	10 557	14	128	401	786	1 795	7 854
Total, all ages	241 635	7 734	38 178	152	801	1 676	5 105	5 835	29 569
West Virginia									
Under 18 years	3 033	106	743	2	4	22	78	101	582
Total, all ages	52 854	1 697	5 495	54	55	206	1 382	850	4 243
Wisconsin									
Under 18 years	69 037	882	10 981	6	135	172	569	1 270	8 952
Total, all ages	275 752	4 240	26 763	76	467	576	3 121	3 195	21 959
Wyoming									
Under 18 years	6 548	69	971	1	3	4	61	78	845
Total, all ages	37 252	577	2 674	14	35	35	493	334	2 199

Note: Because the number of agencies submitting arrest data varies from year to year, caution should be exercised when making direct comparisons between 2005 arrest totals and those from previous years. Arrest figures may vary widely from state to state because some offenses listed in Part II are not considered crimes in every state.

[1]Does not include traffic arrests.
[2]Violent crimes include murder, forcible rape, robbery, and aggravated assault. Property crimes include burglary, larceny-theft, motor vehicle theft, and arson.

Table 69. Total Arrests, by State, 2005—*Continued*

(Number.)

State and age group	Motor vehicle theft	Arson	Other assaults	Forgery and counterfeiting	Fraud	Embezzlement	Stolen property; buying, receiving, and possessing	Vandalism	Weapons; carrying and possessing, etc.
South Dakota									
Under 18 years	20	7	231	3	2	2	26	79	51
Total, all ages	50	9	1 252	66	267	36	102	211	88
Tennessee									
Under 18 years	562	92	5 710	100	194	28	130	1 331	724
Total, all ages	2 522	215	27 889	3 402	10 770	733	1 076	3 879	3 102
Texas									
Under 18 years	1 617	324	23 146	350	374	53	150	5 108	1 897
Total, all ages	7 896	735	102 596	9 557	16 388	544	737	12 303	13 688
Utah									
Under 18 years	201	75	2 243	78	80	1	161	1 658	394
Total, all ages	525	120	9 812	1 055	1 114	7	915	3 599	1 251
Vermont									
Under 18 years	46	6	212	6	19	0	20	124	11
Total, all ages	95	17	1 312	87	506	28	133	356	12
Virginia									
Under 18 years	336	119	4 612	73	95	67	144	1 229	650
Total, all ages	1 333	272	32 275	2 212	8 971	1 365	906	3 917	3 605
Washington									
Under 18 years	702	206	5 506	117	45	10	603	2 240	688
Total, all ages	2 328	446	32 592	2 960	1 541	133	5 117	6 996	3 537
West Virginia									
Under 18 years	54	6	493	13	12	6	29	186	41
Total, all ages	359	43	7 455	535	1 498	106	406	1 055	417
Wisconsin									
Under 18 years	651	108	2 484	128	224	14	336	3 013	869
Total, all ages	1 413	196	11 448	1 845	8 748	147	1 007	7 121	2 478
Wyoming									
Under 18 years	40	8	750	3	9	0	4	342	67
Total, all ages	121	20	3 069	145	179	7	74	817	202

Note: Because the number of agencies submitting arrest data varies from year to year, caution should be exercised when making direct comparisons between 2005 arrest totals and those from previous years. Arrest figures may vary widely from state to state because some offenses listed in Part II are not considered crimes in every state.

Table 69. Total Arrests, by State, 2005—*Continued*

(Number.)

State and age group	Prostitution and commercialized vice	Sex offenses, except forcible rape and prostitution	Drug abuse violations	Gambling	Offenses against the family and children	Driving under the influence	Liquor laws	Drunkenness[5]
South Dakota								
Under 18 years	0	30	92	1	19	55	511	4
Total, all ages	3	73	979	3	68	2 041	2 585	424
Tennessee								
Under 18 years	24	127	3 131	50	35	169	1 297	390
Total, all ages	2 025	657	34 286	319	1 219	22 279	7 784	17 177
Texas								
Under 18 years	88	805	14 503	88	143	1 211	5 137	3 350
Total, all ages	5 999	4 616	124 214	377	4 904	90 919	26 855	117 264
Utah								
Under 18 years	3	372	1 328	0	88	145	2 572	196
Total, all ages	344	892	8 215	0	1 872	6 577	10 429	5 015
Vermont								
Under 18 years	1	16	159	0	2	50	229	4
Total, all ages	1	62	1 312	0	293	3 626	739	8
Virginia								
Under 18 years	2	189	2 255	11	17	155	1 359	204
Total, all ages	737	957	26 954	72	1 376	22 279	9 255	24 979
Washington								
Under 18 years	35	232	2 729	0	12	519	3 508	1
Total, all ages	1 567	1 254	24 809	6	417	36 848	11 291	3
West Virginia								
Under 18 years	0	10	347	0	0	44	214	26
Total, all ages	163	181	5 703	2	125	6 613	2 029	4 313
Wisconsin								
Under 18 years	2	1 020	3 231	11	84	578	7 996	3
Total, all ages	121	2 525	16 207	20	1 745	31 806	31 708	10
Wyoming								
Under 18 years	1	15	476	0	19	88	1 133	36
Total, all ages	3	152	3 283	19	307	5 067	3 922	1 773

Note: Because the number of agencies submitting arrest data varies from year to year, caution should be exercised when making direct comparisons between 2005 arrest totals and those from previous years. Arrest figures may vary widely from state to state because some offenses listed in Part II are not considered crimes in every state.

[5]Drunkenness is not considered a crime in some states; therefore, figures for drunkenness vary widely from state to state.

Table 69. Total Arrests, by State, 2005—*Continued*

(Number.)

State and age group	Disorderly conduct	Vagrancy	All other offenses, except traffic	Suspicion	Curfew and loitering law violations	Runaways	Number of agencies	Estimated population, 2005
South Dakota								
Under 18 years	136	0	1 104	0	43	128	. . .	. . .
Total, all ages	643	13	5 731	1	43	128	47	281 739
Tennessee								
Under 18 years	3 967	0	4 827	0	1 693	2 450	. . .	. . .
Total, all ages	10 802	33	70 937	0	1 693	2 450	374	4 642 765
Texas								
Under 18 years	22 275	1 983	29 137	14	13 641	14 282	. . .	. . .
Total, all ages	38 811	2 756	304 711	31	13 641	14 282	965	22 040 153
Utah								
Under 18 years	2 316	436	5 842	4	1 830	748	. . .	. . .
Total, all ages	6 014	467	39 117	4	1 830	748	85	2 096 365
Vermont								
Under 18 years	154	0	189	0	0	1	. . .	. . .
Total, all ages	756	0	2 192	0	0	1	64	539 008
Virginia								
Under 18 years	1 571	0	7 213	0	2 588	3 933	. . .	. . .
Total, all ages	6 154	100	93 986	0	2 588	3 933	356	5 825 978
Washington								
Under 18 years	616	1	4 730	0	18	1 819	. . .	. . .
Total, all ages	4 775	20	60 014	6	18	1 819	221	5 417 774
West Virginia								
Under 18 years	41	0	586	0	64	72	. . .	. . .
Total, all ages	1 094	41	13 790	0	64	72	347	1 545 865
Wisconsin								
Under 18 years	12 833	33	17 454	29	3 803	3 029	. . .	. . .
Total, all ages	43 642	81	77 112	146	3 803	3 029	243	3 769 639
Wyoming								
Under 18 years	299	13	1 509	67	387	290	. . .	. . .
Total, all ages	1 350	29	12 826	100	387	290	62	497 656

Note: Because the number of agencies submitting arrest data varies from year to year, caution should be exercised when making direct comparisons between 2005 arrest totals and those from previous years. Arrest figures may vary widely from state to state because some offenses listed in Part II are not considered crimes in every state.

. . . = Not available.

SECTION V:
LAW ENFORCEMENT PERSONNEL

LAW ENFORCEMENT PERSONNEL

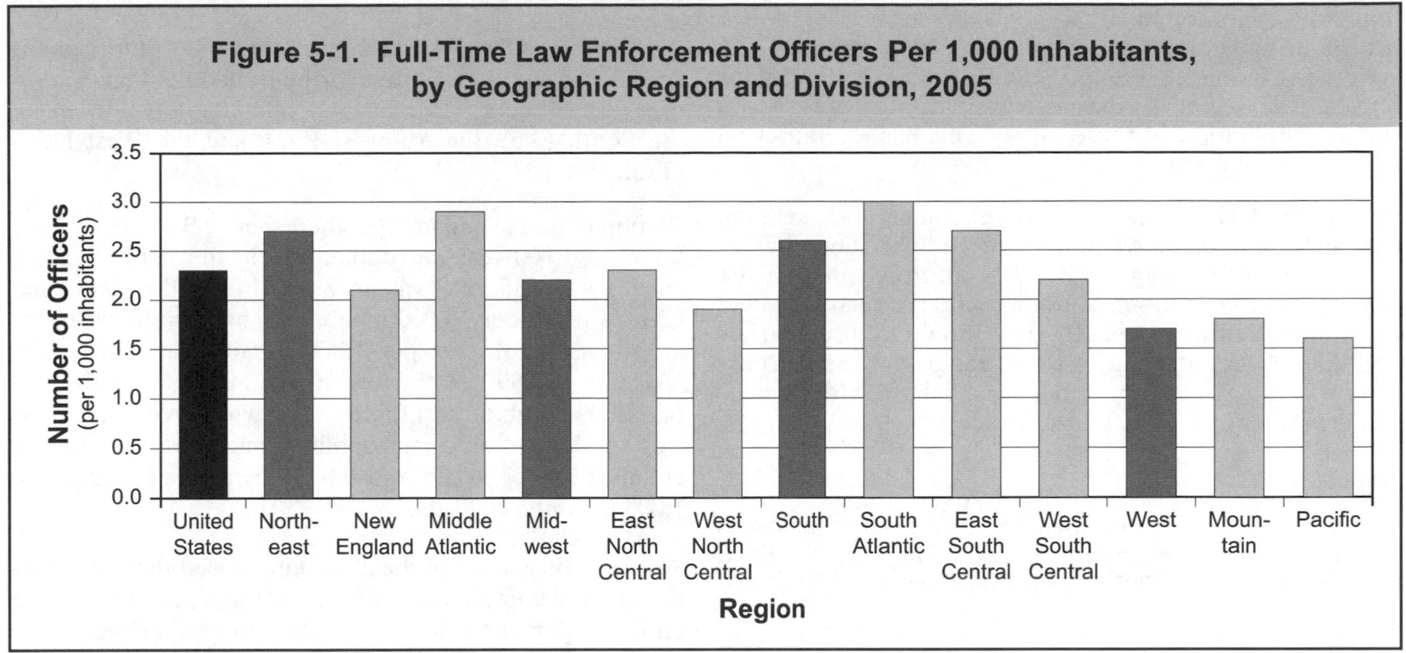

Because of differing service requirements and functions, caution should be used when drawing comparisons between and among the staffing levels of law enforcement agencies. What follows is not intended as recommended or preferred officer strength; the data should only be used as a guide.

Each year, UCR Program staff ask law enforcement agencies across the United States to report the total number of sworn law enforcement officers and civilians employed in their agencies as of October 31. This section of *Crime in the United States* presents those data as the number and rate of law enforcement officers and civilian employees throughout the United States. In 2005, 14,291 state, city, university and college, metropolitan and nonmetropolitan county, and other law enforcement agencies employed 673,146 sworn officers and 295,924 civilians, who provided law enforcement services to more than 279 million people nationwide. (Table 74)

The data in this section are broken down by geographic region and division, population group, state, city, university and college, metropolitan and nonmetropolitan county, and other law enforcement agencies. (Information about geographic regions and divisions and population groups can be found in Appendix III.) UCR Program staff compute the rate of sworn officers and law enforcement employees by taking the number of employees (sworn officers only or in combination with civilians), dividing by the population for which the agency provides law enforcement service, and multiplying by 1,000.

Tables 70 and 71 present the number and rate of law enforcement personnel per 1,000 inhabitants collectively employed by agencies, broken down by geographic region and division by population group.

Tables 72 and 73 provide a count of law enforcement agencies by population group, based on the employment rate ranges for sworn officer and civilian employees per 1,000 inhabitants.

Table 74 provides the number and percentage of male and female sworn officers and civilian employees by population group.

Table 75 lists the percentage of full-time civilian law enforcement employees by population group.

Table 76 breaks down by state the number of sworn law enforcement officers and civilians employed by state law enforcement agencies.

Tables 78 to 80 list the number of law enforcement employees for cities, universities and colleges, and metropolitan and nonmetropolitan counties.

Table 81 supplies employee data for those law enforcement agencies that serve the nation's transit systems, parks and forests, schools and school districts, hospitals, etc.

The demographic traits and characteristics of a jurisdiction affect its requirements for law enforcement service. For instance, a village between two large cities may require more law enforcement than a community of the same size with no urban center nearby. A town with legal gambling may have different law enforcement needs than a town near a military base. A city largely made up of college students may have different law enforcement needs than a city whose residents are mainly retirees.

Similarly, the functions of law enforcement agencies are diverse. Employees of these agencies patrol local streets and major highways, protect citizens in the nation's smallest towns and largest cities, and conduct investigations on offenses at the local and state level. State police in one area may enforce traffic laws on state highways and interstates; in another area, they may be responsible for investigating violent crimes. Sheriff's departments may collect tax monies, serve as the enforcement authority for local and state courts, administer jail facilities, or carry out some combination of these duties. This has an impact on an agency's staffing levels.

Because of the differing service requirements and functions, care should be taken when drawing comparisons between and among the staffing levels of law enforcement agencies. The data in this section are not intended as recommended or preferred officer strength; they should be used merely as guides. Adequate staffing levels can be determined only after careful study of the conditions that affect the service requirements in a particular jurisdiction.

Rate

The national rate of full-time law enforcement employees was 3.5 per 1,000 inhabitants in 2005. This rate remained unchanged from the 2004 rate. (Table 74)

Among the nation's four regions, law enforcement agencies in the Northeast had the highest rate of law enforcement employees in 2005, with 3.5 per 1,000 inhabitants. Agencies in the South had 3.4 law enforcement employees per 1,000 inhabitants, followed by the Midwest (2.7) and the West (2.4). (Table 70)

An examination of the 2005 law enforcement employee data by population group showed that the nation's cities had a collective rate of 3.0 law enforcement employees per 1,000 inhabitants. Cities with under 10,000 inhabitants had the highest rate of law enforcement employees, with 4.2 per 1,000 inhabitants. Cities with 25,000 to 49,999 inhabitants and cities with 50,000 to 99,999 inhabitants had the lowest rate of law enforcement employees (2.3 per 1,000 in population). (Table 70) Law enforcement agencies in the nation's metropolitan counties averaged 4.4 employees per 1,000 inhabitants; agencies in the nation's nonmetropolitan counties averaged 4.6 law enforcement personnel for each 1,000 inhabitants. (Table 74)

Sworn Personnel

The UCR Program defines law enforcement officers as individuals who ordinarily carry a firearm and a badge, have full arrest powers, and are paid from government funds set aside specifically for sworn law enforcement representatives.

An analysis of the 2005 data showed that law enforcement agencies in the cities in the Northeast had the highest rate of sworn officers—2.7 per 1,000 inhabitants, followed by the South (2.6), the Midwest (2.2), and the West (1.7). (Table 71)

By population group in 2005, there were 2.3 sworn officers for each 1,000 resident population in the nation's cities collectively. This rate was unchanged from the 2004 data. Cities with under 10,000 inhabitants had the highest rate at 3.3 sworn officers per 1,000 inhabitants. Cities with 50,000 to 99,999 had the lowest rate at 1.7 sworn officers per 1,000 inhabitants. (Table 71) Law enforcement agencies in the nation's metropolitan and nonmetropolitan counties averaged 2.6 and 2.8 officers, respectively, per 1,000 inhabitants. (Table 74)

A review by gender of the 2005 data howed that, 88.4 percent of law enforcement officers in the nation were male and 11.6 percent were female. In cities collectively, 88.3 percent of sworn officers were male and 11.7 percent were female. In metropolitan counties, 86.8 percent of officers were male and 13.2 percent were female; in nonmetropolitan counties, 92.3 percent of officers were male and 7.7 percent were female. (Table 74)

Civilian Employees

Civilian employees provide a myriad of services to the nation's law enforcement and criminal justice agencies. Among other duties, they dispatch officers, provide administrative and record-keeping support, and query local, state, and national databases.

In 2005, 30.5 percent of all law enforcement employees in the nation were civilians. In cities, civilians made up 23.2 percent of law enforcement agencies employees Civilians made up 41.2 percent of law enforcement employees in metropolitan counties and 39.6 percent of law enforcement employees in nonmetropolitan counties. Of the civilians working in law enforcement agencies throughout the nation, 61.8 percent were female and 38.2 percent were male. (Tables 74 and 75)

Table 70. Full-Time Law Enforcement Employees, by Geographic Region, Division, and Population Group, 2005

(Number, rate per 1,000 population; 2005 estimated population 279,200,617; total city and county agencies 14,291.)

Region	Estimated city population, 2005	Total city agencies	Total (10,832 cities; population 187,432,928)	Group I (70 cities, 250,000 and over; population 53,583,154)	Group II (180 cities, 100,000 to 249,999; population 27,066,683)	Group III (411 cities, 50,000 to 99,999; population 28,032,707)	Group IV (769 cities, 25,000 to 49,999; population 26,455,091)	Group V (1,791 cities, 10,000 to 24,999; population 28,385,387)	Group VI (7,611 cities, under 10,000; population 23,909,906)	County[1] (3,459 agencies; population 91,767,689)	Suburban area[2] (7,354 agencies; population 118,418,670)
ALL AGENCIES											
Number	187 432 928	10 832	561 844	202 230	66 461	63 134	61 199	68 958	99 862	407 226	438 747
Rate	. . .	. . .	3.0	3.8	2.5	2.3	2.3	2.4	4.2	4.4	3.7
Northeast											
Number	42 405 056	2 308	146 430	66 624	9 907	14 948	17 778	19 578	17 595	. . .	. . .
Rate	. . .	. . .	3.5	6.0	3.3	2.5	2.4	2.2	2.9	. . .	. . .
New England											
Number	12 586 682	772	32 921	2 663	4 660	5 957	6 669	7 421	5 551	. . .	. . .
Rate	. . .	. . .	2.6	4.7	3.2	2.4	2.3	2.2	3.1	. . .	. . .
Middle Atlantic											
Number	29 818 374	1 536	113 509	63 961	5 247	8 991	11 109	12 157	12 044	. . .	. . .
Rate	. . .	. . .	3.8	6.1	3.3	2.6	2.5	2.2	2.9	. . .	. . .
Midwest											
Number	44 574 925	3 224	120 861	37 075	10 221	14 533	15 682	19 825	23 525	. . .	. . .
Rate	. . .	. . .	2.7	4.0	2.3	2.0	2.1	2.2	3.2	. . .	. . .
East North Central											
Number	31 800 191	2 032	89 276	29 620	6 858	10 702	11 967	14 749	15 380	. . .	. . .
Rate	. . .	. . .	2.8	4.2	2.4	2.1	2.1	2.3	3.2	. . .	. . .
West North Central											
Number	12 774 734	1 192	31 585	7 455	3 363	3 831	3 715	5 076	8 145	. . .	. . .
Rate	. . .	. . .	2.5	3.4	2.2	1.7	2.0	2.2	3.1	. . .	. . .
South											
Number	54 093 278	3 960	183 984	50 010	27 170	19 332	17 832	22 785	46 855	. . .	. . .
Rate	. . .	. . .	3.4	3.2	2.8	2.7	2.8	3.0	5.9	. . .	. . .
South Atlantic											
Number	22 428 114	1 723	88 179	21 355	13 919	10 404	8 813	11 011	22 677	. . .	. . .
Rate	. . .	. . .	3.9	4.4	3.0	3.0	3.0	3.3	7.2	. . .	. . .
East South Central											
Number	9 108 421	948	31 940	6 255	4 895	1 994	3 843	5 048	9 905	. . .	. . .
Rate	. . .	. . .	3.5	2.9	3.3	3.1	2.8	3.1	5.3	. . .	. . .
West South Central											
Number	22 556 743	1 289	63 865	22 400	8 356	6 934	5 176	6 726	14 273	. . .	. . .
Rate	. . .	. . .	2.8	2.6	2.4	2.3	2.4	2.6	5.0	. . .	. . .
West											
Number	46 359 669	1 340	110 569	48 521	19 163	14 321	9 907	6 770	11 887	. . .	. . .
Rate	. . .	. . .	2.4	2.7	1.9	1.9	2.0	2.2	4.6	. . .	. . .
Mountain											
Number	14 397 412	582	37 913	15 654	6 594	4 004	3 372	2 672	5 617	. . .	. . .
Rate	. . .	. . .	2.6	2.9	2.2	2.0	2.2	2.5	4.3	. . .	. . .
Pacific											
Number	31 962 257	758	72 656	32 867	12 569	10 317	6 535	4 098	6 270	. . .	. . .
Rate	. . .	. . .	2.3	2.6	1.8	1.8	1.9	2.0	4.8	. . .	. . .

Note: Full-time law enforcement employees include civilians.

[1]The designation "county" is a combination of both metropolitan and nonmetropolitan counties.
[2]Suburban areas include law enforcement agencies in cities with fewer than 50,000 inhabitants and county law enforcement agencies within metropolitan statistical areas. They exclude all metropolitan agencies associated with a principal city. The agencies associated with suburban areas also appear in other groups within this table.
. . . = Not available.

Table 71. Full-Time Law Enforcement Officers, by Geographic Region, Division, and Population Group, 2005

(Number, rate per 1,000 population; 2005 estimated population 279,200,617; total city and county agencies 14,291.)

Region	Estimated city population, 2005	Total city agencies	Total (10,832 cities; population 187,432,928)	Group I (70 cities, 250,000 and over; population 53,583,154)	Group II (180 cities, 100,000 to 249,999; population 27,066,683)	Group III (411 cities, 50,000 to 99,999; population 28,032,707)	Group IV (769 cities, 25,000 to 49,999; population 26,455,091)	Group V (1,791 cities, 10,000 to 24,999; population 28,385,387)	Group VI (7,611 cities, under 10,000; population 23,909,906)	County[1] (3,459 agencies; population 91,767,689)	Suburban area[2] (7,354 agencies; population 118,418,670)
ALL AGENCIES											
Number	187 432 928	10 832	431 590	151 870	50 111	48 687	48 052	54 925	77 945	241 556	288 835
Rate	...	...	2.3	2.8	1.9	1.7	1.8	1.9	3.3	2.6	2.4
Northeast											
Number	42 405 056	2 308	114 314	47 584	8 210	12 485	14 830	16 403	14 802	...	...
Rate	...	...	2.7	4.3	2.7	2.1	2.0	1.8	2.5	...	...
New England											
Number	12 586 682	772	26 997	2 075	3 904	5 109	5 515	6 013	4 381	...	...
Rate	...	...	2.1	3.7	2.7	2.0	1.9	1.8	2.4	...	...
Middle Atlantic											
Number	29 818 374	1 536	87 317	45 509	4 306	7 376	9 315	10 390	10 421	...	...
Rate	...	...	2.9	4.3	2.7	2.1	2.1	1.9	2.5	...	...
Midwest											
Number	44 574 925	3 224	97 841	30 654	8 291	11 546	12 315	15 748	19 287	...	...
Rate	...	...	2.2	3.3	1.9	1.6	1.6	1.8	2.6	...	...
East North Central											
Number	31 800 191	2 032	73 140	25 283	5 639	8 501	9 410	11 687	12 620	...	...
Rate	...	...	2.3	3.6	2.0	1.7	1.7	1.8	2.6	...	...
West North Central											
Number	12 774 734	1 192	24 701	5 371	2 652	3 045	2 905	4 061	6 667	...	...
Rate	...	...	1.9	2.4	1.8	1.4	1.5	1.7	2.5	...	...
South											
Number	54 093 278	3 960	140 537	38 672	20 361	14 662	13 854	17 706	35 282	...	...
Rate	...	...	2.6	2.5	2.1	2.0	2.2	2.4	4.5	...	...
South Atlantic											
Number	22 428 114	1 723	67 073	15 854	10 401	7 835	6 929	8 649	17 405	...	...
Rate	...	...	3.0	3.3	2.2	2.3	2.4	2.6	5.6	...	...
East South Central											
Number	9 108 421	948	24 765	4 878	3 681	1 529	3 061	3 906	7 710	...	...
Rate	...	...	2.7	2.3	2.5	2.4	2.3	2.4	4.1	...	...
West South Central											
Number	22 556 743	1 289	48 699	17 940	6 279	5 298	3 864	5 151	10 167	...	...
Rate	...	...	2.2	2.1	1.8	1.7	1.8	2.0	3.6	...	...
West											
Number	46 359 669	1 340	78 898	34 960	13 249	9 994	7 053	5 068	8 574	...	...
Rate	...	...	1.7	2.0	1.3	1.3	1.4	1.6	3.3	...	...
Mountain											
Number	14 397 412	582	26 438	10 456	4 620	2 879	2 374	2 010	4 099	...	...
Rate	...	...	1.8	1.9	1.5	1.5	1.6	1.9	3.1	...	...
Pacific											
Number	31 962 257	758	52 460	24 504	8 629	7 115	4 679	3 058	4 475	...	...
Rate	...	...	1.6	2.0	1.2	1.3	1.3	1.5	3.5	...	...

[1]The designation "county" is a combination of both metropolitan and nonmetropolitan counties.
[2]Suburban areas include law enforcement agencies in cities with fewer than 50,000 inhabitants and county law enforcement agencies within metropolitan statistical areas. They exclude all metropolitan agencies associated with a principal city. The agencies associated with suburban areas also appear in other groups within this table.
. . . = Not available.

Table 72. Agencies With Full-Time Law Enforcement Employees, by Range of Rate, 2005

(Number, rate per 1,000 population.)

Rate range	Total cities[1] (9,915 cities; population 187,432,928)	Group I (70 cities, 250,000 and over; population 53,583,154)	Group II (180 cities, 100,000 to 249,999; population 27,066,683)	Group III (411 cities, 50,000 to 99,999; population 28,032,707)	Group IV (769 cities, 25,000 to 49,999; population 26,455,091)	Group V (1,791 cities, 10,000 to 24,999; population 28,385,387)	Group VI (6,694 cities, under 10,000; population 23,909,906)
TOTAL							
Number	9 915	70	180	411	769	1 791	6 694
Percent[2]	100.0	100.0	100.0	100.0	100.0	100.0	100.0
0.1–0.5							
Number	92	0	0	1	1	8	82
Percent	0.9	0.0	0.0	0.2	0.1	0.4	1.2
0.6–1.0							
Number	408	0	0	5	15	35	353
Percent	4.1	0.0	0.0	1.2	2.0	2.0	5.3
1.1–1.5							
Number	1 045	0	12	51	85	167	730
Percent	10.5	0.0	6.7	12.4	11.1	9.3	10.9
1.6–2.0							
Number	1 923	9	57	134	205	401	1 117
Percent	19.4	12.9	31.7	32.6	26.7	22.4	16.7
2.1–2.5							
Number	1 966	15	44	112	223	481	1 091
Percent	19.8	21.4	24.4	27.3	29.0	26.9	16.3
2.6–3.0							
Number	1 471	20	27	60	133	343	888
Percent	14.8	28.6	15.0	14.6	17.3	19.2	13.3
3.1–3.5							
Number	927	8	24	22	64	180	629
Percent	9.3	11.4	13.3	5.4	8.3	10.1	9.4
3.6–4.0							
Number	596	2	10	12	23	93	456
Percent	6.0	2.9	5.6	2.9	3.0	5.2	6.8
4.1–4.5							
Number	389	6	2	5	14	39	323
Percent	3.9	8.6	1.1	1.2	1.8	2.2	4.8
4.6–5.0							
Number	295	3	4	7	2	23	256
Percent	3.0	4.3	2.2	1.7	0.3	1.3	3.8
5.1 and over							
Number	803	7	0	2	4	21	769
Percent	8.1	10.0	0.0	0.5	0.5	1.2	11.5

Note: Full-time law enforcement employees include civilians.

[1]The number of agencies used to compile these figures differs from other law enforcement employee tables because agencies with no resident population are excluded from this table. These agencies include those associated with universities and colleges (see Table 79) and other agencies (see Table 81), as well as some state agencies that have concurrent jurisdiction with other local law enforcement.

[2]Percentages may not add to 100 because of rounding.

Table 73. Agencies With Full-Time Law Enforcement Officers, by Range of Rate, 2005

(Number, rate per 1,000 population.)

Rate range	Total cities[1] (9,915 cities; population 187,432,928)	Group I (70 cities, 250,000 and over; population 53,583,154)	Group II (180 cities, 100,000 to 249,999; population 27,066,683)	Group III (411 cities, 50,000 to 99,999; population 28,032,707)	Group IV (769 cities, 25,000 to 49,999; population 26,455,091)	Group V (1,791 cities, 10,000 to 24,999; population 28,385,387)	Group VI (6,694 cities, under 10,000; population 23,909,906)
TOTAL							
Number	9 915	70	180	411	769	1 791	6 694
Percent[2]	100.0	100.0	100.0	100.0	100.0	100.0	100.0
0.1–0.5							
Number	99	0	0	1	2	8	88
Percent	1.0	0.0	0.0	0.2	0.3	0.4	1.3
0.6–1.0							
Number	576	1	9	34	42	83	407
Percent	5.8	1.4	5.0	8.3	5.5	4.6	6.1
1.1–1.5							
Number	1 868	9	68	139	235	382	1 035
Percent	18.8	12.9	37.8	33.8	30.6	21.3	15.5
1.6–2.0							
Number	2 627	24	41	143	274	656	1 489
Percent	26.5	34.3	22.8	34.8	35.6	36.6	22.2
2.1–2.5							
Number	1 839	13	35	59	122	383	1 227
Percent	18.5	18.6	19.4	14.4	15.9	21.4	18.3
2.6–3.0							
Number	1 048	9	17	16	65	170	771
Percent	10.6	12.9	9.4	3.9	8.5	9.5	11.5
3.1–3.5							
Number	646	3	9	13	23	65	533
Percent	6.5	4.3	5.0	3.2	3.0	3.6	8.0
3.6–4.0							
Number	352	5	1	4	3	30	309
Percent	3.6	7.1	0.6	1.0	0.4	1.7	4.6
4.1–4.5							
Number	206	2	0	1	1	5	197
Percent	2.1	2.9	0.0	0.2	0.1	0.3	2.9
4.6–5.0							
Number	179	3	0	0	0	4	172
Percent	1.8	4.3	0.0	0.0	0.0	0.2	2.6
5.1 and over							
Number	475	1	0	1	2	5	466
Percent	4.8	1.4	0.0	0.2	0.3	0.3	7.0

[1]The number of agencies used to compile these figures differs from other law enforcement employee tables because agencies with no resident population are excluded from this table. These agencies include those associated with universities and colleges (see Table 79) and other agencies (see Table 81), as well as some state agencies that have concurrent jurisdiction with other local law enforcement.

[2]Percentages may not add to 100 because of rounding.

Table 74. Full-Time Law Enforcement Employees, by Population Group, 2005

(Number, percent.)

Population group	Estimated population, 2005	Number of agencies	Total law enforcement employees	Percent law enforcement employees		Total officers	Percent officers		Total civilians	Percent civilians	
				Male	Female		Male	Female		Male	Female
ALL AGENCIES	279 200 617	14 291	969 070	73.1	26.9	673 146	88.4	11.6	295 924	38.2	61.8
All Cities	187 432 928	10 832	561 844	74.9	25.1	431 590	88.3	11.7	130 254	30.6	69.4
Group I (250,000 and over)	53 583 154	70	202 230	70.4	29.6	151 870	83.0	17.0	50 360	32.6	67.4
1,000,000 and over	24 885 884	10	110 340	69.0	31.0	81 899	81.8	18.2	28 441	32.0	68.0
500,000 to 999,999	15 331 041	23	52 384	73.2	26.8	40 358	83.9	16.1	12 026	37.4	62.6
250,000 to 499,999	13 366 229	37	39 506	70.8	29.2	29 613	84.8	15.2	9 893	28.8	71.2
Group II (100,000 to 249,999)	27 066 683	180	66 461	73.3	26.7	50 111	88.7	11.3	16 350	26.1	73.9
Group III (50,000 to 99,999)	28 032 707	411	63 134	76.1	23.9	48 687	90.8	9.2	14 447	26.4	73.6
Group IV (25,000 to 49,999)	26 455 091	769	61 199	77.9	22.1	48 052	91.5	8.5	13 147	28.0	72.0
Group V (10,000 to 24,999)	28 385 387	1 791	68 958	79.3	20.7	54 925	92.7	7.3	14 033	26.9	73.1
Group VI (under 10,000)	23 909 906	7 611	99 862	79.4	20.6	77 945	91.6	8.4	21 917	36.2	63.8
Metropolitan Counties	63 938 833	1 264	280 410	69.7	30.3	165 011	86.8	13.2	115 399	45.4	54.6
Nonmetropolitan Counties	27 828 856	2 195	126 816	72.1	27.9	76 545	92.3	7.7	50 271	41.5	58.5
Suburban Areas	118 418 670	7 354	438 747	73.1	26.9	288 835	88.9	11.1	149 912	42.7	57.3

Note: Suburban areas include law enforcement agencies in cities with fewer than 50,000 inhabitants and county law enforcement agencies within metropolitan statistical areas. They exclude all metropolitan agencies associated with a principal city.

Table 75. Full-Time Civilian Law Enforcement Employees, by Population Group, 2005

(Number, percent.)

Population group	Estimated population, 2005	Number of agencies	Percent civilian employees
ALL AGENCIES	279 200 617	14 291	30.5
All Cities	187 432 928	10 832	23.2
Group I (250,000 and over)	53 583 154	70	24.9
1,000,000 and over	24 885 884	10	25.8
500,000 to 999,999	15 331 041	23	23.0
250,000 to 499,999	13 366 229	37	25.0
Group II (100,000 to 249,999)	27 066 683	180	24.6
Group III (50,000 to 99,999)	28 032 707	411	22.9
Group IV (25,000 to 49,999)	26 455 091	769	21.5
Group V (10,000 to 24,999)	28 385 387	1 791	20.4
Group VI (under 10,000)	23 909 906	7 611	21.9
Metropolitan Counties	63 938 833	1 264	41.2
Nonmetropolitan Counties	27 828 856	2 195	39.6
Suburban Areas	118 418 670	7 354	34.2

Note: Suburban areas include law enforcement agencies in cities with fewer than 50,000 inhabitants and county law enforcement agencies within metropolitan statistical areas. They exclude all metropolitan agencies associated with a principal city.

Table 76. Full-time Law Enforcement Employees, by State Agency, 2005

(Number.)

State and agency	Total law enforcement employees	Total officers		Total civilians	
		Male	Female	Male	Female
Alabama					
Other state agencies	154	121	5	3	25
Alaska					
State Troopers	551	322	16	80	133
Other state agencies	10	1	0	6	3
Arizona					
Department of Public Safety	1 939	1 062	73	320	484
Other state agencies	62	27	2	22	11
Arkansas					
Other state agencies	51	33	3	9	6
California					
Highway Patrol	9 978	6 296	657	1 304	1 721
Other state agencies	1 050	728	207	41	74
Colorado					
State Patrol	966	656	49	78	183
Other state agencies	58	15	2	24	17
Connecticut					
State Police	1 688	1 112	78	212	286
Other state agencies	32	23	1	5	3
Delaware					
State Police	895	582	70	111	132
Other state agencies	628	267	93	65	203
Florida					
Highway Patrol	2 192	1 475	188	178	351
Other state agencies	3 106	1 267	166	627	1 046
Georgia					
Department of Public Safety	918	739	22	97	60
Other state agencies	1 074	286	64	247	477
Idaho					
State Police	334	245	11	14	64
Illinois					
State Police	3 477	1 788	195	588	906
Other state agencies	405	231	27	94	53
Indiana					
State Police	1 759	1 062	63	226	408
Other state agencies	8	7	0	0	1
Iowa					
Department of Public Safety	854	535	36	120	163
Kansas					
Highway Patrol	806	515	18	94	179
Other state agencies[1]	496	278	13	76	129
Kentucky					
State Police	1 672	897	30	381	364
Other state agencies	560	439	12	50	59
Louisiana					
State Police	1 646	1 099	44	122	381
Other state agencies	51	37	5	0	9
Maine					
State Police	441	277	21	52	91
Other state agencies[1]	49	18	1	19	11
Maryland					
State Police	2 302	1 373	123	453	353
Other state agencies	1 618	901	143	283	291
Massachusetts					
State Police	2 736	2 066	193	223	254
Other state agencies	253	214	26	4	9
Michigan					
State Police	2 542	1 579	218	236	509
Minnesota					
State Patrol	807	510	47	152	98
Mississippi					
Highway Safety Patrol	984	493	10	154	327
Missouri					
State Highway Patrol	1 985	886	35	469	595
Other state agencies[1]	471	403	23	9	36
Montana					
Highway Patrol	247	183	9	14	41
Other state agencies	20	17	0	0	3

Note: Caution should be used when comparing data from state to state. The responsibilities of state police, highway patrol, and department of public safety agencies range from full law enforcement duties to only traffic patrol and vary by state, which can impact the level of employment for agencies and the ratio of sworn officers to civilians employed. Comparisons must take these factors and other identified variables affecting crime into consideration.

[1]The total employee count includes employees from agencies not represented in other law enforcement employee tables.

Table 76. Full-time Law Enforcement Employees, by State Agency, 2005—*Continued*

(Number.)

State and agency	Total law enforcement employees	Total officers		Total civilians	
		Male	Female	Male	Female
Nebraska					
State Patrol	677	452	26	72	127
Nevada					
Highway Patrol	796	428	75	111	182
New Hampshire					
State Police	412	261	27	43	81
Other state agencies	29	17	3	3	6
New Jersey					
State Police	4 375	2 765	107	706	797
Other state agencies	447	343	29	45	30
Port Authority of New York and New Jersey[2]	920	770	73	20	57
New Mexico					
State Police	755	582	23	53	97
New York					
State Police	5 698	4 231	389	464	614
North Carolina					
Highway Patrol	2 168	1 618	44	293	213
Other state agencies	1 172	704	161	89	218
North Dakota					
Highway Patrol	184	131	5	19	29
Ohio					
State Highway Patrol	2 679	1 404	143	537	595
Oklahoma					
Department of Public Safety	1 404	742	14	295	353
Other state agencies	70	38	4	17	11
Oregon					
State Police	1 153	549	61	210	333
Pennsylvania					
State Police	6 012	4 135	185	785	907
Other state agencies	804	652	71	15	66
Rhode Island					
State Police	274	201	21	33	19
Other state agencies	44	31	4	7	2
South Carolina					
Highway Patrol	1 043	813	26	68	136
Other state agencies[1]	1 306	805	131	154	216
South Dakota					
Highway Patrol	237	155	2	58	22
Other state agencies	143	41	4	37	61
Tennessee					
Department of Safety	1 807	891	44	199	673
Other state agencies	978	537	70	122	249
Texas					
Department of Public Safety	7 855	3 285	211	1 408	2 951
Utah					
Highway Patrol	501	414	17	26	44
Other state agencies	149	135	10	0	4
Vermont					
State Police	451	292	24	42	93
Other state agencies	110	83	6	4	17
Virginia					
State Police	2 567	1 806	97	207	457
Other state agencies	506	277	42	77	110
Washington					
State Patrol	2 175	1 063	94	483	535
West Virginia					
State Police	974	616	18	117	223
Other state agencies	188	162	1	2	23
Wisconsin					
State Patrol	675	432	60	80	103
Other state agencies	535	434	58	20	23
Wyoming					
Highway Patrol	206	175	7	3	21

Note: Caution should be used when comparing data from state to state. The responsibilities of state police, highway patrol, and department of public safety agencies range from full law enforcement duties to only traffic patrol and vary by state, which can impact the level of employment for agencies and the ratio of sworn officers to civilians employed. Comparisons must take these factors and other identified variables affecting crime into consideration.

[1]The total employee count includes employees from agencies not represented in other law enforcement employee tables.
[2]Data reported are the number of law enforcement employees for the state of New Jersey.

Table 77. Full-time Law Enforcement Employees, by State, 2005

(Number.)

State	Estimated population, 2005	Number of agencies	Total law enforcement employees	Total officers		Total civilians	
				Male	Female	Male	Female
Alabama	3 984 466	282	12 786	8 058	689	1 524	2 515
Alaska	662 033	41	1 838	1 058	116	201	463
Arizona	5 815 860	99	20 560	10 364	1 208	4 091	4 897
Arkansas	2 779 961	265	8 172	4 871	564	1 030	1 707
California	31 138 193	451	111 062	63 540	9 313	13 579	24 630
Colorado	4 397 035	227	15 449	9 245	1 338	1 519	3 347
Connecticut	3 510 297	101	9 628	7 138	692	677	1 121
Delaware	843 524	53	3 183	2 020	287	323	553
District of Columbia	550 521	3	4 811	3 210	957	260	384
Florida	17 661 970	402	71 146	36 447	5 995	10 747	17 957
Georgia	8 209 878	459	28 811	17 924	2 872	2 730	5 285
Hawaii	1 275 194	4	3 568	2 547	275	212	534
Idaho	1 426 766	107	3 679	2 362	161	193	963
Illinois	12 720 852	761	51 390	30 964	5 572	7 003	7 851
Indiana	6 043 427	244	16 701	9 839	778	2 813	3 271
Iowa	2 966 334	234	7 557	4 641	368	914	1 634
Kansas	2 698 592	342	10 412	6 471	614	1 264	2 063
Kentucky	4 167 174	395	10 219	7 317	589	871	1 442
Louisiana	3 713 890	179	16 901	11 067	2 555	873	2 406
Maine	1 320 239	131	2 886	2 084	129	285	388
Maryland	5 599 201	148	19 745	12 885	2 047	1 854	2 959
Massachusetts	6 213 692	331	19 579	14 940	1 346	1 363	1 930
Michigan	10 006 482	617	26 634	17 001	2 681	2 951	4 001
Minnesota	4 992 123	317	12 795	7 367	941	1 751	2 736
Mississippi	2 441 159	178	8 502	4 718	418	1 357	2 009
Missouri	5 607 484	526	18 588	11 671	1 248	2 241	3 428
Montana	933 609	109	2 796	1 505	108	471	712
Nebraska	1 687 588	156	4 613	3 017	369	313	914
Nevada	2 414 807	36	8 538	4 445	521	1 345	2 227
New Hampshire	1 124 982	139	3 098	2 175	173	213	537
New Jersey	8 447 923	532	40 810	29 346	2 531	3 217	5 716
New Mexico	1 809 415	95	5 537	3 672	364	456	1 045
New York	17 905 562	409	83 625	52 544	8 351	7 380	15 350
North Carolina	8 586 228	509	30 132	18 656	2 417	4 012	5 047
North Dakota	634 904	96	1 591	1 079	95	132	285
Ohio	10 491 311	554	31 100	19 889	2 383	3 420	5 408
Oklahoma	3 547 884	298	10 957	6 454	538	1 672	2 293
Oregon	3 321 523	152	7 454	4 726	536	524	1 668
Pennsylvania	8 268 941	786	27 474	20 451	2 613	1 695	2 715
Rhode Island	1 069 926	43	3 206	2 372	179	308	347
South Carolina	4 185 868	373	15 164	9 832	1 208	1 584	2 540
South Dakota	774 216	151	2 271	1 310	85	406	470
Tennessee	5 958 488	445	24 188	13 680	1 481	3 736	5 291
Texas	22 763 951	1 003	80 720	44 446	5 236	13 472	17 566
Utah	2 468 942	126	7 283	4 268	373	1 195	1 447
Vermont	371 547	69	1 562	1 066	92	139	265
Virginia	7 566 489	279	22 316	15 406	1 927	1 386	3 597
Washington	6 278 257	247	14 144	9 152	978	1 305	2 709
West Virginia	1 800 849	353	4 096	3 122	98	332	544
Wisconsin	5 535 323	369	18 001	11 223	1 847	1 690	3 241
Wyoming	505 737	65	1 792	1 194	111	98	389

Table 78. Law Enforcement Employees, by City, 2005

(Number.)

City	Total law enforcement employees	Total officers	Total civilians
Alabama			
Adamsville	30	18	12
Addison	3	3	0
Alabaster	70	55	15
Albertville	56	37	19
Alexander City	63	46	17
Aliceville	13	9	4
Andalusia	36	27	9
Anniston	128	93	35
Arab	32	24	8
Ardmore	11	7	4
Argo	3	3	0
Ashford	10	6	4
Ashville	5	5	0
Athens	55	43	12
Atmore	28	24	4
Attalla	27	22	5
Auburn	98	93	5
Autaugaville	2	2	0
Bay Minette	31	23	8
Bayou La Batre	18	13	5
Bear Creek	1	1	0
Birmingham	1 095	813	282
Boaz	32	22	10
Brantley	5	4	1
Brent	5	5	0
Brewton	22	16	6
Bridgeport	9	5	4
Brundidge	12	8	4
Calera	31	24	7
Camden	9	8	1
Carrollton	3	3	0
Castleberry	1	1	0
Cedar Bluff	5	5	0
Centre	9	8	1
Centreville	4	4	0
Cherokee	5	4	1
Chickasaw	23	19	4
Clanton	24	23	1
Clayhatchee	1	1	0
Clayton	4	4	0
Cleveland	2	2	0
Clio	4	4	0
Collinsville	8	4	4
Columbia	2	2	0
Coosada	3	3	0
Cordova	6	5	1
Cottonwood	3	3	0
Courtland	4	4	0
Creola	11	7	4
Crossville	9	3	6
Cullman	66	47	19
Dadeville	12	12	0
Daleville	25	19	6
Daphne	69	40	29
Dauphin Island	13	9	4
Decatur	148	126	22
Demopolis	23	20	3
Dothan	213	146	67
Double Springs	5	5	0
Eclectic	10	6	4
Elba	26	17	9
Elberta	7	6	1
Enterprise	73	53	20
Eufaula	48	32	16
Evergreen	18	13	5
Excel	1	1	0
Fairfield	42	30	12
Fairhope	41	28	13
Fayette	13	13	0
Florala	9	9	0
Florence	119	95	24
Fort Payne	41	37	4
Frisco City	2	2	0
Fultondale	23	17	6
Gadsden	125	96	29
Gardendale	35	26	9
Geraldine	2	2	0
Gordo	4	4	0
Grant	4	4	0
Graysville	11	6	5
Greenville	43	34	9
Grove Hill	6	6	0
Gulf Shores	42	31	11
Guntersville	39	31	8
Gurley	4	4	0
Hamilton	13	12	1
Hanceville	15	10	5
Harpersville	8	8	0
Hartford	14	10	4
Hartselle	38	29	9
Headland	13	10	3
Helena	26	21	5
Henagar	10	5	5
Hillsboro	1	1	0
Hobson City	8	4	4
Hokes Bluff	7	4	3
Homewood	101	71	30
Hoover	205	146	59
Huntsville	469	365	104
Jacksonville	30	24	6
Jasper	68	44	24
Jemison	11	10	1
Killen	5	5	0
Kimberly	5	4	1
Kinsey	3	2	1
Lafayette	16	15	1
Lanett	25	19	6
Leeds	26	21	5
Leighton	2	2	0
Level Plains	6	3	3
Lincoln	21	16	5
Linden	7	7	0
Littleville	8	5	3
Livingston	11	7	4
Louisville	4	4	0
Loxley	13	7	6
Luverne	14	10	4
Madison	75	54	21
Maplesville	5	5	0
Marion	13	9	4
McIntosh	6	6	0
McKenzie	2	2	0
Midland City	9	6	3
Millbrook	31	23	8
Millry	2	2	0
Mobile	671	519	152
Montevallo	20	15	5
Montgomery	618	463	155
Moody	19	18	1
Morris	7	6	1
Moundville	6	5	1
Mountain Brook	62	49	13
Muscle Shoals	43	34	9
Napier Field	1	1	0
New Brockton	2	2	0
New Hope	5	5	0
Northport	73	56	17
Notasulga	7	3	4
Odenville	6	4	2
Ohatchee	6	6	0
Oneonta	19	18	1
Opp	27	21	6
Orange Beach	56	36	20
Owens Crossroads	3	3	0
Oxford	60	49	11
Ozark	43	37	6
Pelham	80	65	15
Pell City	34	32	2
Phenix City	95	75	20
Phil Campbell	2	2	0
Pinckard	2	2	0
Pine Hill	5	5	0
Pleasant Grove	23	18	5
Prattville	86	77	9
Priceville	4	4	0
Ragland	7	3	4
Rainsville	15	11	4
Ranburne	2	2	0
Reform	5	5	0
Riverside	6	5	1

Table 78. Law Enforcement Employees, by City, 2005

(Number.)

City	Total law enforcement employees	Total officers	Total civilians
Roanoke	27	22	5
Robertsdale	19	10	9
Rockford	2	1	1
Russellville	28	23	5
Samson	6	5	1
Saraland	45	35	10
Sardis City	4	4	0
Satsuma	18	14	4
Scottsboro	63	44	19
Selma	84	59	25
Sheffield	39	34	5
Shorter	9	5	4
Silas	2	1	1
Silverhill	4	3	1
Skyline	2	1	1
Slocomb	7	6	1
Somerville	3	3	0
Southside	15	9	6
Spanish Fort	13	12	1
Springville	9	9	0
Steele	2	2	0
Stevenson	7	5	2
Sulligent	6	6	0
Sumiton	11	6	5
Sylacauga	48	38	10
Sylvania	2	2	0
Talladega	63	46	17
Tallassee	25	18	7
Tarrant City	28	22	6
Thomasville	20	15	5
Thorsby	5	5	0
Town Creek	4	4	0
Triana	2	1	1
Trinity	5	5	0
Troy	64	47	17
Tuscaloosa	310	236	74
Tuscumbia	25	25	0
Union Springs	17	10	7
Vance	4	4	0
Vestavia Hills	70	68	2
Warrior	19	14	5
Weaver	9	6	3
Wedowee	7	7	0
Wetumpka	35	27	8
Wilton	1	1	0
Winfield	11	10	1
Woodstock	4	4	0
York	11	5	6
Alaska			
Anchorage	495	345	150
Bethel	19	12	7
Bristol Bay Borough	9	3	6
Cordova	8	5	3
Craig	10	5	5
Dillingham	21	8	13
Fairbanks	58	42	16
Haines	10	5	5
Homer	19	12	7
Hoonah	5	4	1
Houston	3	3	0
Juneau	76	44	32
Kake	4	2	2
Kenai	26	17	9
Ketchikan	32	22	10
Kodiak	34	18	16
Kotzebue	16	7	9
Nome	16	10	6
North Pole	10	9	1
North Slope Borough	56	31	25
Palmer	27	13	14
Petersburg	14	7	7
Sand Point	4	3	1
Seldovia	1	1	0
Seward	14	8	6
Sitka	35	19	16
Skagway	7	3	4
Soldotna	15	13	2
St. Paul	6	3	3
Togiak	1	1	0

City	Total law enforcement employees	Total officers	Total civilians
Unalaska	25	12	13
Valdez	20	10	10
Wasilla	43	22	21
Whittier	3	3	0
Wrangell	11	6	5
Arizona			
Apache Junction	75	46	29
Avondale	118	74	44
Benson	19	12	7
Bisbee	22	15	7
Buckeye	53	39	14
Bullhead City	118	73	45
Camp Verde	32	20	12
Casa Grande	91	63	28
Chandler	441	297	144
Chino Valley	36	24	12
Clarkdale	10	8	2
Clifton	8	6	2
Colorado City	7	5	2
Coolidge	37	26	11
Cottonwood	43	27	16
Douglas	45	33	12
Eagar	12	8	4
El Mirage	53	45	8
Eloy	47	30	17
Flagstaff	147	94	53
Florence	29	19	10
Fredonia	3	3	0
Gilbert	284	187	97
Glendale	485	365	120
Globe	32	22	10
Goodyear	103	70	33
Hayden	7	6	1
Holbrook	21	13	8
Huachuca City	10	5	5
Jerome	4	4	0
Kearny	8	5	3
Kingman	78	53	25
Lake Havasu City	99	74	25
Mammoth	10	7	3
Marana	85	64	21
Mesa	1 340	801	539
Miami	11	7	4
Nogales	83	64	19
Oro Valley	110	85	25
Page	31	21	10
Paradise Valley	45	35	10
Parker	15	13	2
Patagonia	2	2	0
Payson	42	29	13
Peoria	230	159	71
Phoenix	3 782	2 898	884
Pima	4	4	0
Pinetop-Lakeside	22	14	8
Prescott	111	62	49
Prescott Valley	56	45	11
Quartzsite	11	9	2
Safford	22	20	2
Sahuarita	25	22	3
San Luis	44	34	10
Scottsdale	615	389	226
Sedona	31	23	8
Show Low	39	26	13
Sierra Vista	80	49	31
Snowflake-Taylor	19	12	7
Somerton	23	16	7
South Tucson	32	22	10
Springerville	10	8	2
St. Johns	12	9	3
Superior	12	7	5
Surprise	126	95	31
Tempe	540	329	211
Thatcher	11	10	1
Tolleson	32	25	7
Tombstone	7	6	1
Tucson	1 369	1 008	361

Table 78. Law Enforcement Employees, by City, 2005

(Number.)

City	Total law enforcement employees	Total officers	Total civilians
Wellton	4	4	0
Wickenburg	18	11	7
Willcox	17	9	8
Williams	19	10	9
Winslow	36	23	13
Youngtown	15	13	2
Yuma	229	152	77
Arkansas			
Alma	16	8	8
Altheimer	3	3	0
Arkadelphia	27	21	6
Ashdown	13	11	2
Ash Flat	3	3	0
Atkins	7	6	1
Augusta	6	6	0
Austin	1	1	0
Bald Knob	8	5	3
Barling	8	8	0
Bay	3	3	0
Bearden	2	2	0
Beebe	17	10	7
Benton	60	51	9
Bentonville	73	48	25
Berryville	12	10	2
Blytheville	61	43	18
Booneville	12	8	4
Bradford	5	4	1
Brinkley	15	11	4
Bryant	37	29	8
Bull Shoals	3	3	0
Cabot	44	32	12
Caddo Valley	3	3	0
Camden	33	22	11
Cammack Village	5	4	1
Caraway	3	3	0
Carlisle	10	6	4
Cave Springs	4	3	1
Centerton	9	9	0
Charleston	4	4	0
Cherokee Village	7	6	1
Clarksville	22	18	4
Clinton	9	8	1
Conway	134	96	38
Corning	11	7	4
Crossett	24	15	9
Danville	6	5	1
Dardanelle	13	9	4
Decatur	6	6	0
Dell	1	1	0
De Queen	16	13	3
Dermott	13	7	6
Des Arc	4	4	0
De Witt	14	9	5
Diaz	3	2	1
Dierks	3	3	0
Dover	6	3	3
Dumas	22	11	11
Earle	10	7	3
El Dorado	65	48	17
England	10	5	5
Etowah	1	1	0
Eudora	11	6	5
Eureka Springs	16	10	6
Fairfield Bay	13	7	6
Farmington	10	9	1
Fayetteville	176	116	60
Flippin	17	8	9
Fordyce	12	7	5
Foreman	4	4	0
Forrest City	44	34	10
Fort Smith	197	158	39
Gassville	4	4	0
Gentry	10	8	2
Glenwood	3	3	0
Gosnell	8	8	0
Gould	21	8	13
Gravette	8	7	1
Greenbrier	14	9	5
Green Forest	8	7	1
Greenland	4	4	0
Greenwood	20	18	2
Greers Ferry	3	3	0
Gurdon	4	3	1
Hamburg	7	6	1
Hampton	4	3	1
Harrisburg	4	3	1
Harrison	39	28	11
Hazen	6	5	1
Heber Springs	21	13	8
Helena	15	10	5
Hermitage	3	3	0
Highland	3	3	0
Hope	37	26	11
Horseshoe Bend	5	5	0
Hot Springs	131	98	33
Hoxie	5	4	1
Huntsville	7	6	1
Jacksonville	84	72	12
Jonesboro	132	122	10
Keiser	1	1	0
Kensett	3	3	0
Lake City	4	4	0
Lakeview	2	2	0
Lake Village	14	9	5
Leachville	5	4	1
Lepanto	8	4	4
Lewisville	2	2	0
Lincoln	6	5	1
Little Rock	622	505	117
Lonoke	17	12	5
Lowell	20	13	7
Luxora	3	3	0
Magnolia	28	21	7
Malvern	25	22	3
Marianna	16	11	5
Marion	20	18	2
Marked Tree	12	8	4
Marmaduke	4	4	0
Marvell	5	2	3
Maumelle	32	22	10
Mayflower	6	5	1
McCrory	6	5	1
McGehee	16	8	8
McRae	2	1	1
Mena	14	13	1
Mineral Springs	4	4	0
Monticello	25	21	4
Morrilton	31	20	11
Mountain Home	34	25	9
Mountain Pine	3	3	0
Mountain View	8	7	1
Mulberry	3	3	0
Murfreesboro	3	3	0
Nashville	15	14	1
Newport	22	15	7
North Little Rock	228	195	33
Ola	2	2	0
Osceola	38	22	16
Ozark	9	8	1
Pangburn	2	2	0
Paragould	49	42	7
Paris	13	8	5
Pea Ridge	6	6	0
Perryville	4	4	0
Piggott	8	7	1
Pine Bluff	150	128	22
Plainview	2	1	1
Plummerville	4	3	1
Pocahontas	14	13	1
Pottsville	4	4	0
Prairie Grove	8	7	1
Prescott	8	7	1
Quitman	4	4	0
Redfield	5	4	1
Rison	3	3	0
Rogers	116	82	34
Rose Bud	2	2	0
Russellville	57	49	8

Table 78. Law Enforcement Employees, by City, 2005

(Number.)

City	Total law enforcement employees	Total officers	Total civilians
Salem	3	3	0
Searcy	55	42	13
Sheridan	23	12	11
Sherwood	80	56	24
Siloam Springs	43	24	19
Smackover	5	4	1
Springdale	146	100	46
Star City	5	4	1
Stuttgart	30	21	9
Sulphur Springs	2	2	0
Swifton	1	1	0
Texarkana	116	79	37
Trumann	22	15	7
Tuckerman	6	5	1
Van Buren	59	44	15
Vilonia	7	7	0
Waldron	9	8	1
Walnut Ridge	8	7	1
Ward	6	5	1
Warren	23	14	9
Weiner	1	1	0
West Fork	7	6	1
West Helena	20	12	8
West Memphis	97	79	18
White Hall	13	11	2
Wynne	18	16	2
California			
Alameda	144	99	45
Albany	37	27	10
Alhambra	126	81	45
Alturas	10	9	1
Anaheim	559	396	163
Anderson	29	18	11
Antioch	169	111	58
Arcadia	98	65	33
Arcata	31	21	10
Arroyo Grande	36	27	9
Arvin	17	11	6
Atascadero	38	29	9
Atherton	25	20	5
Atwater	37	28	9
Auburn	34	23	11
Azusa	81	59	22
Bakersfield	461	315	146
Baldwin Park	102	76	26
Banning	51	36	15
Barstow	53	34	19
Bear Valley	16	8	8
Beaumont	37	27	10
Bell	49	38	11
Bell Gardens	74	54	20
Belmont	41	29	12
Belvedere	8	7	1
Benicia	47	34	13
Berkeley	294	181	113
Beverly Hills	195	134	61
Bishop	17	11	6
Blue Lake	5	5	0
Blythe	38	25	13
Brawley	40	28	12
Brea	130	103	27
Brentwood	65	50	15
Brisbane	20	17	3
Broadmoor	11	10	1
Buena Park	139	91	48
Burbank	243	155	88
Burlingame	58	40	18
Calexico	61	42	19
California City	19	14	5
Calipatria	6	6	0
Calistoga	15	11	4
Campbell	66	45	21
Capitola	31	19	12
Carlsbad	145	105	40
Carmel	18	11	7
Cathedral City	74	50	24
Ceres	63	42	21
Chico	140	88	52
Chino	145	100	45
Chowchilla	23	17	6
Chula Vista	336	221	115
City of Angels	10	9	1
Claremont	63	39	24
Clayton	14	11	3
Clearlake	33	25	8
Cloverdale	21	14	7
Clovis	145	99	46
Colma	23	18	5
Colton	99	73	26
Colusa	10	9	1
Concord	215	155	60
Corcoran	26	16	10
Corning	20	13	7
Corona	250	162	88
Coronado	61	42	19
Costa Mesa	228	158	70
Cotati	20	13	7
Covina	89	57	32
Crescent City	12	11	1
Culver City	167	119	48
Cypress	75	57	18
Daly City	154	115	39
Davis	93	56	37
Delano	55	39	16
Del Rey Oaks	6	6	0
Desert Hot Springs	32	25	7
Dinuba	36	27	9
Dixon	29	24	5
Dos Palos	5	5	0
Downey	149	104	45
East Palo Alto	46	37	9
El Cajon	203	136	67
El Centro	70	49	21
El Cerrito	48	37	11
El Monte	227	161	66
El Segundo	90	60	30
Emeryville	49	34	15
Escalon	14	11	3
Escondido	222	163	59
Etna	2	1	1
Eureka	67	41	26
Exeter	17	15	2
Fairfax	15	10	5
Fairfield	177	114	63
Farmersville	15	14	1
Ferndale	4	4	0
Firebaugh	15	11	4
Folsom	112	81	31
Fontana	219	153	66
Fort Bragg	21	16	5
Fortuna	23	15	8
Foster City	53	36	17
Fountain Valley	75	57	18
Fowler	9	8	1
Fremont	288	181	107
Fresno	1 177	798	379
Fullerton	218	153	65
Galt	38	27	11
Gardena	96	76	20
Garden Grove	232	161	71
Gilroy	98	59	39
Glendale	383	270	113
Glendora	87	53	34
Gonzales	14	13	1
Grass Valley	37	25	12
Greenfield	17	14	3
Gridley	22	17	5
Grover Beach	24	16	8
Guadalupe	15	12	3
Gustine	11	9	2
Half Moon Bay	23	18	5
Hanford	66	49	17
Hawthorne	155	99	56
Hayward	303	190	113
Healdsburg	29	18	11
Hemet	115	83	32
Hercules	27	24	3

Table 78. Law Enforcement Employees, by City, 2005

(Number.)

City	Total law enforcement employees	Total officers	Total civilians
Hermosa Beach	49	38	11
Hillsborough	33	24	9
Hollister	34	29	5
Holtville	8	6	2
Hughson	7	6	1
Huntington Beach	345	211	134
Huntington Park	105	64	41
Huron	15	10	5
Imperial	16	14	2
Indio	98	61	37
Inglewood	281	202	79
Ione	7	6	1
Irvine	224	157	67
Irwindale	34	26	8
Isleton	5	5	0
Jackson	13	10	3
Kensington	10	9	1
Kerman	19	16	3
King City	16	13	3
Kingsburg	20	15	5
Laguna Beach	85	49	36
La Habra	104	68	36
Lakeport	14	12	2
Lake Shastina	5	4	1
La Mesa	82	59	23
La Palma	31	25	6
La Verne	63	45	18
Lemoore	34	28	6
Lincoln	32	27	5
Lindsay	20	13	7
Livermore	133	86	47
Livingston	25	19	6
Lodi	113	76	37
Lompoc	72	50	22
Long Beach	1 344	896	448
Los Alamitos	28	24	4
Los Altos	46	31	15
Los Angeles	12 420	9 355	3 065
Los Banos	59	37	22
Los Gatos	59	44	15
Madera	77	60	17
Mammoth Lakes	25	20	5
Manhattan Beach	87	61	26
Manteca	89	66	23
Marina	38	30	8
Martinez	55	39	16
Marysville	34	23	11
Maywood	55	37	18
Menlo Park	65	46	19
Merced	125	87	38
Millbrae	25	18	7
Mill Valley	27	22	5
Milpitas	115	89	26
Modesto	368	260	108
Monrovia	77	54	23
Montclair	80	56	24
Montebello	113	77	36
Monterey	79	53	26
Monterey Park	109	76	33
Moraga	12	11	1
Morgan Hill	52	34	18
Morro Bay	21	17	4
Mountain View	145	96	49
Mount Shasta	17	9	8
Murrieta	97	68	29
Napa	116	68	48
National City	126	87	39
Nevada City	12	11	1
Newark	80	54	26
Newman	14	12	2
Newport Beach	233	147	86
Novato	72	52	20
Oakdale	36	27	9
Oakland	1 019	730	289
Oceanside	277	187	90
Ontario	314	218	96
Orange	216	150	66
Orland	11	10	1
Oroville	35	24	11
Oxnard	346	226	120

City	Total law enforcement employees	Total officers	Total civilians
Pacifica	49	38	11
Pacific Grove	31	24	7
Palm Springs	147	86	61
Palo Alto	157	87	70
Palos Verdes Estates	34	24	10
Paradise	41	26	15
Parlier	17	14	3
Pasadena	365	239	126
Paso Robles	52	40	12
Patterson	16	14	2
Petaluma	96	69	27
Piedmont	26	19	7
Pinole	38	26	12
Pismo Beach	34	23	11
Pittsburg	98	70	28
Placentia	71	54	17
Placerville	29	18	11
Pleasant Hill	62	42	20
Pleasanton	116	83	33
Pomona	317	180	137
Porterville	69	47	22
Port Hueneme	32	24	8
Red Bluff	38	24	14
Redding	162	113	49
Redlands	170	97	73
Redondo Beach	160	105	55
Redwood City	144	92	52
Reedley	38	27	11
Rialto	151	111	40
Richmond	219	156	63
Ridgecrest	41	30	11
Rio Dell	6	6	0
Rio Vista	13	10	3
Ripon	33	24	9
Riverbank	20	17	3
Riverside	541	371	170
Rocklin	75	48	27
Rohnert Park	109	74	35
Roseville	190	124	66
Ross	8	8	0
Sacramento	1 013	668	345
Salinas	217	164	53
San Anselmo	24	18	6
San Bernardino	462	302	160
San Bruno	66	45	21
San Carlos	45	32	13
Sand City	11	10	1
San Diego	2 823	2 070	753
San Fernando	51	35	16
San Francisco	2 553	2 193	360
San Gabriel	69	54	15
Sanger	35	27	8
San Jacinto	36	31	5
San Jose	1 715	1 349	366
San Leandro	129	89	40
San Luis Obispo	81	57	24
San Marino	30	24	6
San Mateo	148	109	39
San Pablo	63	49	14
San Rafael	98	72	26
Santa Ana	652	355	297
Santa Barbara	201	132	69
Santa Clara	206	132	74
Santa Cruz	118	90	28
Santa Maria	149	106	43
Santa Monica	380	198	182
Santa Paula	42	33	9
Santa Rosa	244	153	91
Sausalito	22	17	5
Scotts Valley	28	20	8
Seal Beach	39	29	10
Seaside	54	41	13
Sebastopol	21	14	7
Selma	44	29	15
Shafter	27	21	6
Sierra Madre	21	17	4
Signal Hill	44	32	12
Simi Valley	190	123	67
Soledad	16	14	2
Sonora	19	15	4

Table 78. Law Enforcement Employees, by City, 2005

(Number.)

City	Total law enforcement employees	Total officers	Total civilians
South Gate	129	87	42
South Lake Tahoe	60	40	20
South Pasadena	47	36	11
South San Francisco	103	72	31
Stallion Springs	4	4	0
St. Helena	17	13	4
Stockton	598	388	210
Suisun City	32	22	10
Sunnyvale	285	220	65
Susanville	20	18	2
Sutter Creek	6	6	0
Taft	19	9	10
Tiburon	17	14	3
Torrance	318	230	88
Tracy	116	77	39
Trinidad	3	3	0
Truckee	26	21	5
Tulare	82	59	23
Tulelake	3	3	0
Turlock	95	63	32
Tustin	135	92	43
Twin Cities	43	33	10
Ukiah	35	26	9
Union City	105	77	28
Upland	117	76	41
Vacaville	160	102	58
Vallejo	198	141	57
Ventura	179	127	52
Vernon	75	56	19
Visalia	170	116	54
Walnut Creek	115	78	37
Watsonville	85	64	21
Weed	17	10	7
West Covina	162	118	44
Westminster	138	95	43
West Sacramento	104	69	35
Wheatland	6	6	0
Whittier	178	125	53
Williams	9	8	1
Willits	18	12	6
Willows	12	10	2
Winters	13	11	2
Woodlake	15	13	2
Woodland	87	60	27
Yreka	21	15	6
Yuba City	73	50	23
Colorado			
Alamosa	29	24	5
Arvada	203	131	72
Aspen	37	27	10
Ault	6	6	0
Aurora	719	586	133
Avon	16	14	2
Basalt	11	8	3
Bayfield	4	4	0
Berthoud	8	7	1
Black Hawk	38	25	13
Boulder	250	166	84
Breckenridge	27	22	5
Brighton	65	52	13
Broomfield	178	98	80
Brush	15	12	3
Buena Vista	9	7	2
Burlington	10	9	1
Calhan	3	3	0
Canon City	45	33	12
Carbondale	17	14	3
Castle Rock	62	45	17
Cedaredge	7	5	2
Center	6	5	1
Central City	6	6	0
Cherry Hills Village	22	20	2
Collbran	1	1	0
Colorado Springs	993	675	318
Columbine Valley	6	6	0
Commerce City	100	77	23
Cortez	51	28	23
Craig	27	22	5
Crested Butte	7	6	1
Cripple Creek	23	14	9
Dacono	12	10	2
De Beque	10	10	0
Del Norte	6	5	1
Delta	19	17	2
Denver	1 792	1 460	332
Dillon	10	9	1
Durango	59	50	9
Eagle	10	8	2
Eaton	9	8	1
Edgewater	19	15	4
Elizabeth	6	4	2
Empire	1	1	0
Englewood	96	68	28
Erie	21	19	2
Estes Park	24	15	9
Evans	32	28	4
Federal Heights	36	24	12
Firestone	21	16	5
Florence	18	7	11
Fort Collins	242	155	87
Fort Lupton	21	17	4
Fort Morgan	34	28	6
Fountain	46	33	13
Fowler	2	2	0
Frederick	19	17	2
Frisco	13	12	1
Fruita	16	14	2
Georgetown	3	3	0
Gilcrest	3	3	0
Glendale	36	23	13
Glenwood Springs	31	25	6
Golden	61	42	19
Grand Junction	137	82	55
Greeley	231	124	107
Green Mountain Falls	2	2	0
Greenwood Village	81	61	20
Gunnison	28	15	13
Haxtun	2	2	0
Hayden	5	5	0
Holyoke	4	4	0
Hotchkiss	3	3	0
Hugo	3	3	0
Idaho Springs	9	7	2
Ignacio	7	7	0
Johnstown	14	12	2
Kersey	4	4	0
Kiowa	2	2	0
Kremmling	4	4	0
Lafayette	51	40	11
Lakeside	5	5	0
Lakewood	386	259	127
Lamar	31	21	10
La Salle	6	6	0
Las Animas	7	6	1
La Veta	4	3	1
Leadville	10	8	2
Limon	6	5	1
Littleton	90	66	24
Lochbuie	18	16	2
Log Lane Village	2	2	0
Lone Tree	26	23	3
Longmont	146	112	34
Louisville	38	33	5
Loveland	126	82	44
Mancos	4	3	1
Manitou Springs	15	14	1
Manzanola	1	1	0
Meeker	5	4	1
Milliken	10	9	1
Minturn	2	2	0
Monte Vista	13	9	4
Montrose	49	33	16
Monument	13	12	1
Morrison	3	2	1
Mountain View	5	4	1
Mount Crested Butte	6	5	1
New Castle	7	7	0

Table 78. Law Enforcement Employees, by City, 2005

(Number.)

City	Total law enforcement employees	Total officers	Total civilians
Northglenn	75	63	12
Oak Creek	2	2	0
Olathe	4	4	0
Ouray	5	5	0
Pagosa Springs	8	8	0
Palisade	8	6	2
Palmer Lake	5	4	1
Paonia	5	5	0
Parachute	6	6	0
Parker	66	49	17
Platteville	8	7	1
Pueblo	246	191	55
Rangely	11	6	5
Ridgway	3	3	0
Rifle	20	16	4
Rocky Ford	11	9	2
Salida	16	15	1
Sheridan	32	22	10
Silt	7	6	1
Silverthorne	20	16	4
Simla	2	2	0
Snowmass Village	13	9	4
South Fork	3	3	0
Springfield	3	3	0
Steamboat Springs	35	23	12
Sterling	24	21	3
Stratton	1	1	0
Telluride	15	10	5
Thornton	174	143	31
Trinidad	29	21	8
Vail	58	26	32
Victor	5	4	1
Walsenburg	19	10	9
Walsh	1	1	0
Westminster	252	175	77
Wheat Ridge	89	64	25
Wiggins	1	1	0
Windsor	20	17	3
Woodland Park	27	19	8
Wray	8	7	1
Yuma	8	7	1
Connecticut			
Ansonia	50	43	7
Avon	42	35	7
Berlin	50	40	10
Bethel	45	35	10
Bloomfield	55	45	10
Branford	59	46	13
Bridgeport	528	420	108
Bristol	142	119	23
Brookfield	39	30	9
Canton	20	15	5
Cheshire	56	47	9
Clinton	28	25	3
Coventry	18	13	5
Cromwell	32	24	8
Danbury	146	140	6
Darien	52	46	6
Derby	27	27	0
East Hampton	19	15	4
East Hartford	166	128	38
East Haven	51	48	3
Easton	18	15	3
East Windsor	33	26	7
Enfield	114	94	20
Fairfield	112	106	6
Farmington	59	44	15
Glastonbury	73	57	16
Granby	19	14	5
Greenwich	172	156	16
Groton	37	31	6
Groton Long Point	7	6	1
Groton Town	68	64	4
Guilford	46	38	8
Hamden	126	103	23
Hartford	475	416	59
Madison	31	23	8
Manchester	147	115	32
Meriden	130	118	12
Middlebury	18	12	6
Middletown	117	100	17
Milford	115	100	15
Monroe	50	39	11
Naugatuck	67	54	13
New Britain	154	144	10
New Canaan	49	45	4
New Haven	508	422	86
Newington	57	45	12
New London	90	75	15
New Milford	63	47	16
Newtown	50	44	6
North Branford	28	23	5
North Haven	54	45	9
Norwalk	188	171	17
Norwich	94	79	15
Old Saybrook	30	21	9
Orange	45	35	10
Plainfield	20	16	4
Plainville	40	33	7
Plymouth	20	20	0
Portland	11	10	1
Putnam	19	15	4
Redding	19	14	5
Ridgefield	47	42	5
Rocky Hill	45	34	11
Seymour	42	40	2
Shelton	60	53	7
Simsbury	44	35	9
Southington	76	60	16
South Windsor	54	40	14
Stamford	363	300	63
Stonington	48	36	12
Stratford	116	105	11
Suffield	23	18	5
Thomaston	15	12	3
Torrington	84	75	9
Trumbull	80	69	11
Vernon	61	48	13
Wallingford	93	71	22
Waterbury	336	278	58
Waterford	52	45	7
Watertown	47	36	11
West Hartford	141	121	20
West Haven	131	118	13
Weston	16	15	1
Westport	83	66	17
Wethersfield	55	45	10
Willimantic	46	41	5
Wilton	47	43	4
Winchester	29	23	6
Windsor	62	51	11
Windsor Locks	31	25	6
Wolcott	35	24	11
Woodbridge	33	25	8
Delaware			
Bethany Beach	11	9	2
Blades	2	2	0
Bridgeville	5	5	0
Camden	16	14	2
Cheswold	3	3	0
Clayton	5	5	0
Dagsboro	2	2	0
Delaware City	3	3	0
Delmar	10	9	1
Dewey Beach	11	8	3
Dover	121	90	31
Ellendale	2	2	0
Elsmere	12	11	1
Felton	4	4	0
Fenwick Island	6	6	0
Georgetown	20	18	2
Greenwood	5	4	1
Harrington	11	10	1
Laurel	13	12	1
Lewes	14	13	1
Milford	39	29	10
Millsboro	14	13	1
Milton	9	8	1
Newark	75	59	16
New Castle	19	17	2
Newport	8	8	0
Ocean View	8	7	1
Rehoboth Beach	26	18	8
Seaford	33	24	9
Selbyville	7	6	1

Table 78. Law Enforcement Employees, by City, 2005

(Number.)

City	Total law enforcement employees	Total officers	Total civilians
Smyrna	26	21	5
South Bethany	6	6	0
Wilmington	358	272	86
Wyoming	5	4	1
District of Columbia			
Washington	4 278	3 757	521
Florida			
Alachua	27	19	8
Altamonte Springs	119	98	21
Altha	1	1	0
Apalachicola	9	8	1
Apopka	86	77	9
Arcadia	24	20	4
Astatula	5	5	0
Atlantic Beach	39	28	11
Atlantis	17	12	5
Auburndale	44	31	13
Aventura	109	76	33
Avon Park	41	26	15
Baldwin	13	8	5
Bal Harbour Village	37	28	9
Bartow	74	47	27
Bay Harbor Island	30	23	7
Belleair	15	10	5
Belleair Bluffs	3	3	0
Belleview	16	14	2
Biscayne Park	12	11	1
Blountstown	12	8	4
Boca Raton	271	181	90
Bonifay	5	4	1
Bowling Green	6	6	0
Boynton Beach	200	148	52
Bradenton	146	121	25
Bradenton Beach	10	10	0
Brooksville	29	19	10
Bunnell	13	11	2
Bushnell	10	9	1
Cape Coral	276	171	105
Carrabelle	5	5	0
Casselberry	89	57	32
Cedar Grove	7	6	1
Cedar Key	5	5	0
Center Hill	3	3	0
Chattahoochee	10	9	1
Chiefland	11	8	3
Chipley	13	12	1
Clearwater	371	247	124
Clermont	53	38	15
Clewiston	27	19	8
Cocoa	76	69	7
Cocoa Beach	52	34	18
Coconut Creek	125	84	41
Cooper City	70	52	18
Coral Gables	259	178	81
Coral Springs	292	191	101
Cottondale	3	3	0
Crescent City	10	9	1
Cross City	5	5	0
Crystal River	18	16	2
Dade City	29	21	8
Dania	76	66	10
Davenport	8	7	1
Davie	223	167	56
Daytona Beach	279	230	49
Daytona Beach Shores	42	33	9
Deerfield Beach	143	119	24
De Funiak Springs	15	13	2
Deland	71	53	18
Delray Beach	218	145	73
Doral	76	73	3
Dundee	13	8	5
Dunedin	30	30	0
Dunnellon	11	8	3
Eagle Lake	4	4	0
Eatonville	14	12	2
Edgewater	37	33	4
Edgewood	10	9	1
El Portal	8	8	0
Eustis	52	38	14
Fellsmere	9	8	1
Fernandina Beach	44	35	9
Flagler Beach	18	15	3
Florida City	37	26	11
Fort Lauderdale	658	459	199
Fort Meade	18	13	5
Fort Myers	250	174	76
Fort Pierce	154	115	39
Fort Walton Beach	66	52	14
Frostproof	14	9	5
Fruitland Park	12	11	1
Gainesville	354	276	78
Golden Beach	18	17	1
Graceville	10	8	2
Greenacres City	64	43	21
Green Cove Springs	24	18	6
Greensboro	1	1	0
Gretna	9	9	0
Groveland	18	12	6
Gulf Breeze	26	19	7
Gulfport	41	31	10
Gulf Stream	11	11	0
Haines City	57	42	15
Hallandale	120	87	33
Hampton	1	1	0
Havana	13	9	4
Hialeah	462	341	121
Hialeah Gardens	37	28	9
Highland Beach	14	13	1
High Springs	18	13	5
Hillsboro Beach	16	14	2
Holly Hill	33	29	4
Hollywood	510	331	179
Holmes Beach	20	13	7
Homestead	129	95	34
Howey-In-the-Hills	6	6	0
Hypoluxo	4	4	0
Indialantic	18	12	6
Indian Creek Village	15	11	4
Indian Harbour Beach	25	18	7
Indian River Shores	22	21	1
Indian Rocks Beach	6	6	0
Indian Shores	12	11	1
Inglis	6	5	1
Interlachen	4	4	0
Jacksonville	2 746	1 566	1 180
Jacksonville Beach	76	56	20
Jasper	8	8	0
Jennings	1	1	0
Juno Beach	17	13	4
Jupiter	131	99	32
Jupiter Inlet Colony	5	5	0
Jupiter Island	20	16	4
Kenneth City	16	14	2
Key Biscayne	40	28	12
Key Colony Beach	6	6	0
Key West	122	86	36
Kissimmee	192	126	66
Lady Lake	37	22	15
Lake Alfred	15	10	5
Lake City	55	41	14
Lake Clarke Shores	11	11	0
Lake Hamilton	7	6	1
Lake Helen	15	7	8
Lakeland	367	228	139
Lake Mary	49	34	15
Lake Park	20	19	1
Lake Placid	11	9	2
Lake Wales	58	42	16
Lake Worth	121	87	34
Lantana	40	31	9
Largo	185	134	51
Lauderdale-by-the-Sea	23	22	1
Lauderdale Lakes	64	53	11
Lauderhill	138	110	28
Lawtey	1	1	0
Leesburg	96	73	23
Lighthouse Point	42	34	8

Table 78. Law Enforcement Employees, by City, 2005

(Number.)

City	Total law enforcement employees	Total officers	Total civilians
Live Oak	21	17	4
Longboat Key	28	20	8
Longwood	44	38	6
Lynn Haven	36	27	9
Madeira Beach	6	6	0
Madison	15	14	1
Maitland	50	41	9
Manalapan	15	10	5
Mangonia Park	15	14	1
Marco Island	31	29	2
Margate	176	108	68
Marianna	25	17	8
Mascotte	11	10	1
Medley	42	32	10
Melbourne	223	162	61
Melbourne Beach	10	9	1
Melbourne Village	5	5	0
Mexico Beach	8	6	2
Miami	1 363	1 012	351
Miami Gardens	167	144	23
Miami Lakes	48	47	1
Miami Shores	42	31	11
Miami Springs	54	42	12
Milton	29	21	8
Miramar	221	166	55
Monticello	13	9	4
Mount Dora	45	32	13
Mulberry	18	13	5
Naples	103	65	38
Neptune Beach	27	18	9
New Port Richey	45	34	11
New Smyrna Beach	65	55	10
Niceville	22	18	4
North Bay Village	31	25	6
North Lauderdale	70	61	9
North Miami	166	130	36
North Miami Beach	143	106	37
North Palm Beach	40	30	10
North Port	79	61	18
Oak Hill	8	8	0
Oakland	10	9	1
Oakland Park	95	85	10
Ocala	259	157	102
Ocean Ridge	18	13	5
Ocoee	68	60	8
Okeechobee	26	20	6
Oldsmar	5	5	0
Opa Locka	39	31	8
Orange City	22	19	3
Orange Park	27	22	5
Orlando	961	693	268
Ormond Beach	98	67	31
Oviedo	76	58	18
Pahokee	17	15	2
Palatka	39	33	6
Palm Bay	210	141	69
Palm Beach	130	76	54
Palm Beach Gardens	145	110	35
Palm Beach Shores	16	11	5
Palmetto	42	33	9
Palmetto Bay	43	39	4
Palm Springs	48	37	11
Panama City	131	92	39
Panama City Beach	62	46	16
Parker	10	9	1
Parkland	33	30	3
Pembroke Park	13	13	0
Pembroke Pines	299	234	65
Pensacola	213	160	53
Perry	24	22	2
Pinellas Park	131	101	30
Plantation	272	185	87
Plant City	88	66	22
Pompano Beach	300	222	78
Ponce Inlet	17	11	6
Port Orange	100	84	16
Port Richey	17	13	4
Port St. Joe	12	10	2
Port St. Lucie	247	189	58
Punta Gorda	51	34	17
Quincy	39	27	12
Redington Beaches	3	3	0
Riviera Beach	140	95	45
Rockledge	63	43	20
Royal Palm Beach	68	52	16
Safety Harbor	7	7	0
Sanford	134	113	21
Sanibel	42	24	18
Sarasota	253	187	66
Satellite Beach	28	21	7
Sea Ranch Lakes	11	7	4
Sebastian	49	33	16
Sebring	42	30	12
Seminole	11	11	0
Sewall's Point	10	9	1
Shalimar	4	4	0
Sneads	9	5	4
South Bay	10	8	2
South Daytona	33	25	8
South Miami	58	49	9
South Palm Beach	9	9	0
South Pasadena	6	6	0
Southwest Ranches	12	12	0
Springfield	21	15	6
Starke	27	19	8
St. Augustine	60	49	11
St. Augustine Beach	16	14	2
St. Cloud	75	50	25
St. Pete Beach	41	29	12
St. Petersburg	754	520	234
Stuart	62	44	18
Sunny Isles Beach	59	47	12
Sunrise	223	165	58
Surfside	33	20	13
Sweetwater	28	21	7
Tallahassee	474	344	130
Tamarac	86	70	16
Tampa	1 311	985	326
Tarpon Springs	64	48	16
Tavares	25	23	2
Temple Terrace	72	51	21
Tequesta	23	18	5
Titusville	120	82	38
Treasure Island	24	17	7
Trenton	3	2	1
Umatilla	10	9	1
Valparaiso	14	10	4
Venice	75	57	18
Vero Beach	81	58	23
Village of Pinecrest	70	51	19
Virginia Gardens	5	3	2
Waldo	8	7	1
Wauchula	19	14	5
Webster	2	2	0
Welaka	1	1	0
Wellington	53	49	4
West Melbourne	41	32	9
West Miami	21	16	5
Weston	89	60	29
West Palm Beach	378	277	101
White Springs	6	6	0
Wildwood	22	16	6
Williston	20	10	10
Wilton Manors	32	25	7
Windermere	13	12	1
Winter Garden	65	51	14
Winter Haven	109	74	35
Winter Park	112	87	25
Winter Springs	82	62	20
Zephyrhills	42	30	12
Zolfo Springs	1	1	0
Georgia			
Acworth	47	33	14
Adairsville	15	13	2
Adel	21	17	4
Adrian	2	2	0
Alapaha	2	1	1
Albany	190	160	30
Alma	12	10	2
Alpharetta	119	87	32
Americus	45	36	9
Aragon	9	5	4

Table 78. Law Enforcement Employees, by City, 2005

(Number.)

City	Total law enforcement employees	Total officers	Total civilians
Arcade	8	8	0
Arlington	4	3	1
Athens-Clarke County	282	223	59
Atlanta	2 260	1 672	588
Auburn	21	16	5
Austell	32	25	7
Avondale Estates	9	9	0
Bainbridge	47	42	5
Baldwin	12	8	4
Ball Ground	3	3	0
Barnesville	17	15	2
Bartow	2	1	1
Barwick	2	1	1
Baxley	13	11	2
Berlin	4	3	1
Blairsville	7	6	1
Bloomingdale	15	13	2
Blythe	2	1	1
Bowdon	11	7	4
Braselton	13	12	1
Braswell	9	9	0
Broxton	4	4	0
Brunswick	72	65	7
Buchanan	8	7	1
Buena Vista	8	6	2
Byron	17	14	3
Cairo	23	20	3
Calhoun	48	42	6
Camilla	21	18	3
Canon	2	1	1
Canton	48	41	7
Carrollton	75	63	12
Cartersville	57	49	8
Cave Spring	5	5	0
Cedartown	28	26	2
Centerville	21	17	4
Chamblee	45	31	14
Chatsworth	16	13	3
Clarkesville	6	5	1
Claxton	9	8	1
Clayton	11	10	1
Cleveland	11	11	0
Cochran	16	15	1
College Park	137	102	35
Collins	1	1	0
Colquitt	11	10	1
Columbus	464	362	102
Conyers	58	45	13
Coolidge	1	1	0
Cordele	33	27	6
Cornelia	19	17	2
Covington	63	53	10
Crawfordville	1	1	0
Cumming	17	12	5
Cuthbert	8	4	4
Dallas	17	12	5
Dalton	102	86	16
Danielsville	2	2	0
Darien	5	5	0
Davisboro	1	1	0
Dawson	18	13	5
Decatur	58	42	16
Demorest	6	4	2
Dillard	3	3	0
Doerun	6	4	2
Donalsonville	12	8	4
Doraville	61	40	21
Douglas	47	37	10
Douglasville	89	72	17
Dublin	56	47	9
Duluth	70	53	17
Eastman	14	13	1
Elberton	23	20	3
Ellaville	5	5	0
Emerson	9	7	2
Enigma	2	2	0
Ephesus	2	1	1
Eton	3	3	0
Fairburn	29	26	3
Fairmount	3	3	0
Fayetteville	43	38	5
Fitzgerald	33	29	4
Folkston	6	5	1
Forest Park	86	64	22
Forsyth	23	17	6
Fort Gaines	5	5	0
Fort Oglethorpe	32	26	6
Fort Valley	28	22	6
Franklin	9	7	2
Gainesville	119	99	20
Garden City	40	36	4
Garfield	1	1	0
Glennville	17	12	5
Greensboro	19	17	2
Greenville	6	5	1
Grovetown	30	17	13
Hagan	3	2	1
Hahira	5	4	1
Hamilton	1	1	0
Hampton	16	14	2
Hapeville	52	39	13
Harlem	12	7	5
Hartwell	24	19	5
Hawkinsville	11	10	1
Hazlehurst	13	11	2
Helen	12	9	3
Helena	2	2	0
Hephzibah	5	5	0
Hiawassee	5	4	1
Hinesville	90	75	15
Hiram	12	11	1
Hoboken	3	2	1
Hogansville	17	12	5
Holly Springs	16	15	1
Hoschton	7	6	1
Irwinton	1	1	0
Ivey	3	3	0
Jackson	17	14	3
Jefferson	20	26	2
Jeffersonville	4	4	0
Jonesboro	20	17	3
Kennesaw	69	43	26
Kingsland	38	34	4
Lafayette	22	19	3
LaGrange	97	83	14
Lake City	16	15	1
Lakeland	8	7	1
Lake Park	2	2	0
Lavonia	15	14	1
Lawrenceville	75	58	17
Leary	1	1	0
Leesburg	11	10	1
Lenox	2	1	1
Leslie	2	2	0
Lilburn	35	25	10
Lincolnton	5	5	0
Lithonia	7	5	2
Locust Grove	21	19	2
Lookout Mountain	7	7	0
Louisville	7	7	0
Ludowici	10	6	4
Lumber City	5	3	2
Lumpkin	4	4	0
Luthersville	4	3	1
Madison	14	13	1
Manchester	16	11	5
Marietta	156	125	31
Marshallville	3	2	1
McCaysville	4	4	0
McIntyre	5	5	0
McRae	9	7	2
Meigs	5	4	1
Metter	12	11	1
Milledgeville	62	40	22
Millen	7	7	0
Monroe	40	35	5
Montezuma	13	11	2
Monticello	12	11	1
Morrow	31	28	3
Morven	2	2	0

Table 78. Law Enforcement Employees, by City, 2005

(Number.)

City	Total law enforcement employees	Total officers	Total civilians
Moultrie	43	38	5
Mount Airy	2	1	1
Mount Vernon	5	5	0
Nashville	18	13	5
Newington	1	1	0
Newnan	76	65	11
Newton	3	3	0
Nicholls	6	5	1
Norcross	39	30	9
Oakwood	10	8	2
Ocilla	13	12	1
Omega	4	4	0
Oxford	4	4	0
Palmetto	14	12	2
Patterson	2	2	0
Pavo	6	5	1
Peachtree City	59	55	4
Pearson	5	4	1
Pelham	10	9	1
Pembroke	9	7	2
Pendergrass	4	4	0
Perry	41	37	4
Pinehurst	2	1	1
Pine Mountain	7	6	1
Pineview	1	1	0
Plains	6	6	0
Pooler	28	24	4
Porterdale	7	7	0
Port Wentworth	20	18	2
Powder Springs	38	31	7
Quitman	18	12	6
Reidsville	8	7	1
Reynolds	5	5	0
Richland	3	3	0
Richmond Hill	29	23	6
Rincon	14	12	2
Ringgold	7	7	0
Riverdale	43	37	6
Roberta	3	3	0
Rockmart	18	16	2
Rome	109	95	14
Rossville	10	9	1
Roswell	195	129	66
Royston	17	14	3
Sale City	1	1	0
Sandersville	22	19	3
Sardis	2	2	0
Savannah-Chatham Metropolitan	711	542	169
Senoia	10	9	1
Smyrna	129	84	45
Snellville	52	42	10
Springfield	8	7	1
Statesboro	70	57	13
Statham	5	5	0
Stillmore	3	2	1
St. Marys	36	33	3
Stone Mountain	18	17	1
Summerville	20	19	1
Suwanee	38	30	8
Swainsboro	22	19	3
Sycamore	1	1	0
Sylvania	15	10	5
Sylvester	23	17	6
Talbotton	4	4	0
Tallapoosa	15	14	1
Tallulah Falls	2	2	0
Temple	9	8	1
Tennille	8	8	0
Thomaston	25	22	3
Thomasville	62	56	6
Thunderbolt	11	10	1
Tifton	60	50	10
Toccoa	33	27	6
Trenton	7	7	0
Trion	8	8	0
Tunnel Hill	3	2	1
Tybee Island	27	18	9
Tyrone	15	14	1
Union City	43	39	4
Union Point	7	6	1
Valdosta	138	118	20
Varnell	7	3	4
Vidalia	38	30	8
Villa Rica	41	34	7
Wadley	7	6	1
Warm Springs	2	1	1
Warner Robins	140	109	31
Warrenton	7	7	0
Warwick	3	3	0
Watkinsville	6	6	0
Waverly Hall	3	3	0
Waycross	61	49	12
Waynesboro	23	17	6
West Point	19	14	5
Whigham	3	3	0
Whitesburg	5	5	0
Willacoochee	3	3	0
Winder	44	38	6
Winterville	4	4	0
Woodbury	16	10	6
Woodstock	48	44	4
Wrens	11	6	5
Zebulon	6	6	0
Hawaii			
Honolulu	2 476	2 005	471
Idaho			
Aberdeen	8	5	3
American Falls	9	8	1
Bellevue	4	3	1
Blackfoot	28	25	3
Boise	337	267	70
Bonners Ferry	8	8	0
Buhl	10	8	2
Caldwell	67	52	15
Cascade	5	4	1
Challis	1	1	0
Chubbuck	26	16	10
Coeur d'Alene	77	63	14
Cottonwood	1	1	0
Emmett	14	13	1
Filer	5	5	0
Fruitland	9	8	1
Garden City	34	27	7
Gooding	8	7	1
Grangeville	6	6	0
Hagerman	1	1	0
Hailey	14	12	2
Heyburn	6	5	1
Homedale	6	6	0
Idaho City	1	1	0
Idaho Falls	122	88	34
Jerome	19	17	2
Kellogg	8	7	1
Ketchum	27	12	15
Kimberly	6	6	0
Lewiston	65	45	20
McCall	8	6	2
Meridian	74	61	13
Montpelier	6	6	0
Moscow	41	34	7
Mountain Home	26	22	4
Nampa	136	104	32
Orofino	6	5	1
Osburn	2	2	0
Parma	4	4	0
Payette	13	11	2
Pinehurst	5	2	3
Pocatello	125	88	37
Ponderay	5	4	1
Post Falls	53	33	20
Preston	6	5	1
Rathdrum	12	9	3
Rexburg	41	34	7
Rigby	7	7	0
Rupert	15	14	1
Salmon	8	7	1

Table 78. Law Enforcement Employees, by City, 2005

(Number.)

City	Total law enforcement employees	Total officers	Total civilians
Sandpoint	22	17	5
Shelley	7	7	0
Shoshone	4	4	0
Soda Springs	8	7	1
Spirit Lake	5	5	0
St. Anthony	7	7	0
St. Maries	5	5	0
Sun Valley	10	9	1
Twin Falls	87	59	28
Weiser	12	10	2
Wendell	6	5	1
Wilder	2	2	0
Illinois			
Abingdon	3	3	0
Addison	103	66	37
Albany	1	1	0
Albers	1	1	0
Albion	3	3	0
Aledo	6	5	1
Algonquin	54	41	13
Alorton	4	3	1
Alsip	53	41	12
Altamont	5	5	0
Alton	89	65	24
Amboy	3	3	0
Anna	8	8	0
Annawan	1	1	0
Antioch	38	25	13
Arcola	6	5	1
Argenta	2	2	0
Arlington Heights	149	112	37
Arthur	5	5	0
Ashland	1	1	0
Assumption	1	1	0
Astoria	1	1	0
Athens	2	2	0
Atkinson	1	1	0
Atlanta	1	1	0
Atwood	3	3	0
Auburn	10	6	4
Augusta	1	1	0
Aurora	365	282	83
Aviston	1	1	0
Bannockburn	7	7	0
Barrington	42	34	8
Barrington Hills	26	18	8
Barry	1	1	0
Bartlett	69	51	18
Bartonville	15	10	5
Batavia	55	43	12
Beardstown	13	9	4
Beckemeyer	1	1	0
Bedford Park	43	37	6
Beecher	9	8	1
Belleville	98	80	18
Bellwood	51	38	13
Belvidere	40	37	3
Benld	4	4	0
Bensenville	42	34	8
Benton	9	8	1
Berkeley	20	16	4
Berwyn	116	92	24
Bethalto	23	16	7
Bloomingdale	64	48	16
Bloomington	140	120	20
Blue Island	58	39	19
Blue Mound	2	2	0
Bolingbrook	144	101	43
Bourbonnais	27	20	7
Bradley	38	30	8
Braidwood	22	15	7
Breese	6	6	0
Bridgeport	3	3	0
Bridgeview	46	43	3
Brighton	6	4	2
Broadview	41	34	7
Brookfield	38	31	7
Brooklyn	5	5	0
Buffalo Grove	84	70	14
Bull Valley	2	2	0
Bunker Hill	6	4	2
Burbank	71	52	19
Burnham	14	9	5
Burr Ridge	31	27	4
Byron	7	6	1
Cahokia	46	33	13
Cairo	14	9	5
Calumet City	112	81	31
Calumet Park	26	21	5
Cambridge	1	1	0
Camp Point	2	2	0
Canton	32	23	9
Carbondale	78	60	18
Carlinville	18	13	5
Carlyle	8	7	1
Carmi	10	9	1
Carol Stream	85	62	23
Carpentersville	78	64	14
Carrier Mills	2	2	0
Carrollton	6	6	0
Carterville	7	7	0
Carthage	4	4	0
Cary	33	29	4
Casey	8	7	1
Caseyville	14	10	4
Catlin	1	1	0
Central City	4	4	0
Centralia	34	25	9
Centreville	15	12	3
Chadwick	1	1	0
Champaign	160	128	32
Channahon	21	18	3
Charleston	36	33	3
Chatham	18	13	5
Chenoa	3	3	0
Cherry Valley	14	14	0
Chester	10	10	0
Chicago	14 442	13 267	1 175
Chicago Heights	108	79	29
Chicago Ridge	35	31	4
Chillicothe	14	10	4
Christopher	4	4	0
Cicero	164	144	20
Clarendon Hills	16	15	1
Clinton	14	13	1
Coal City	10	9	1
Coal Valley	7	6	1
Cobden	3	3	0
Colfax	1	1	0
Collinsville	53	38	15
Colona	12	10	2
Columbia	19	13	6
Cordova	2	2	0
Cortland	3	3	0
Coulterville	2	2	0
Country Club Hills	43	31	12
Countryside	35	28	7
Crest Hill	30	27	3
Crestwood	2	2	0
Crete	19	17	2
Creve Coeur	8	6	2
Crystal Lake	71	61	10
Cuba	2	2	0
Dallas City	1	1	0
Danvers	1	1	0
Danville	78	61	17
Darien	53	38	15
Decatur	191	161	30
Deerfield	54	39	15
De Kalb	73	60	13
De Pue	2	2	0
De Soto	3	3	0
Des Plaines	126	102	24
Divernon	2	2	0
Dixmoor	15	10	5
Dixon	29	26	3
Dolton	60	43	17
Downers Grove	114	80	34
Dupo	6	6	0
Du Quoin	14	10	4
Durand	1	1	0
Dwight	10	9	1
Earlville	2	2	0

Table 78. Law Enforcement Employees, by City, 2005

(Number.)

City	Total law enforcement employees	Total officers	Total civilians
East Alton	17	12	5
East Carondelet	1	1	0
East Dubuque	7	7	0
East Dundee	16	14	2
East Hazel Crest	12	10	2
East Moline	47	37	10
East Peoria	50	39	11
East St. Louis	91	59	32
Edwardsville	50	36	14
Effingham	34	21	13
Elburn	10	9	1
Eldorado	10	7	3
Elgin	244	177	67
Elizabeth	1	1	0
Elk Grove Village	106	93	13
Elmhurst	91	69	22
Elmwood	1	1	0
Elmwood Park	41	35	6
El Paso	5	5	0
Elwood	7	7	0
Energy	4	4	0
Erie	3	3	0
Eureka	6	6	0
Evanston	202	152	50
Evergreen Park	69	58	11
Fairbury	7	7	0
Fairfield	17	13	4
Fairmont City	9	7	2
Fairview	1	1	0
Fairview Heights	47	37	10
Farmer City	6	3	3
Farmington	5	5	0
Fisher	2	2	0
Flora	16	11	5
Flossmoor	23	18	5
Ford Heights	9	8	1
Forest Park	54	39	15
Forest View	11	8	3
Fox Lake	25	22	3
Fox River Grove	10	10	0
Frankfort	33	28	5
Franklin Park	68	49	19
Freeburg	10	9	1
Freeport	72	54	18
Fulton	8	7	1
Galena	12	9	3
Galesburg	78	50	28
Galva	4	4	0
Geneseo	21	14	7
Geneva	48	37	11
Genoa	10	10	0
Georgetown	4	4	0
Germantown	1	1	0
Gibson City	10	5	5
Gifford	1	1	0
Gilberts	9	8	1
Gillespie	10	7	3
Gilman	2	2	0
Girard	3	3	0
Glasford	1	1	0
Glen Carbon	25	18	7
Glencoe	45	35	10
Glendale Heights	80	53	27
Glen Ellyn	45	37	8
Glenview	106	78	28
Glenwood	25	21	4
Golf	4	4	0
Grafton	4	4	0
Granite City	61	50	11
Grant Park	4	4	0
Granville	2	2	0
Grayslake	46	32	14
Grayville	7	3	4
Greenfield	2	2	0
Greenup	4	4	0
Greenville	14	10	4
Gridley	1	1	0
Gurnee	86	57	29
Hamilton	4	4	0
Hampshire	10	10	0
Hampton	4	4	0
Hanover	1	1	0
Hanover Park	71	50	21
Harrisburg	15	14	1
Hartford	5	4	1
Harvard	21	15	6
Harvey	86	54	32
Harwood Heights	38	27	11
Havana	14	10	4
Hawthorn Woods	14	13	1
Hazel Crest	34	27	7
Hebron	5	5	0
Henry	3	3	0
Herrin	22	15	7
Herscher	2	2	0
Hickory Hills	37	29	8
Highland	28	20	8
Highland Park	81	59	22
Highwood	14	13	1
Hillsboro	8	8	0
Hillside	34	24	10
Hinckley	3	3	0
Hinsdale	37	28	9
Hodgkins	21	19	2
Hoffman Estates	114	97	17
Homer	1	1	0
Hometown	5	1	4
Homewood	47	35	12
Hoopeston	17	11	6
Hopedale	2	2	0
Hopkins Park	1	1	0
Huntley	28	24	4
Hutsonville	1	1	0
Indian Head Park	12	9	3
Irving	1	1	0
Island Lake	20	14	6
Itasca	35	27	8
Jacksonville	50	40	10
Jerome	8	8	0
Jerseyville	21	14	7
Johnsburg	10	9	1
Johnston City	5	5	0
Joliet	363	281	82
Jonesboro	3	3	0
Justice	33	28	5
Kankakee	85	69	16
Kenilworth	14	11	3
Kewanee	28	21	7
Kildeer	23	22	1
Kincaid	1	1	0
Kirkland	3	3	0
Knoxville	4	4	0
Lacon	3	3	0
La Grange	38	29	9
La Grange Park	24	20	4
Lake Bluff	22	16	6
Lake Forest	61	43	18
Lake in the Hills	55	41	14
Lakemoor	8	8	0
Lake Villa	19	17	2
Lakewood	9	8	1
Lake Zurich	54	34	20
La Moille	1	1	0
Lanark	3	3	0
Lansing	81	63	18
La Salle	25	20	5
Lebanon	10	10	0
Leland	1	1	0
Leland Grove	6	6	0
Lemont	34	32	2
Le Roy	6	6	0
Lewistown	3	3	0
Lexington	3	3	0
Libertyville	58	41	17
Lincoln	25	24	1
Lincolnshire	35	25	10
Lincolnwood	44	33	11
Lindenhurst	16	14	2
Lisle	54	41	13
Litchfield	24	16	8

Table 78. Law Enforcement Employees, by City, 2005

(Number.)

City	Total law enforcement employees	Total officers	Total civilians
Livingston	2	2	0
Lockport	42	35	7
Lombard	89	73	16
Loves Park	36	27	9
Lynwood	23	17	6
Lyons	34	27	7
Machesney Park	23	22	1
Mackinaw	2	2	0
Macomb	29	26	3
Madison	16	12	4
Mahomet	8	7	1
Manhattan	8	8	0
Manito	3	3	0
Manteno	16	15	1
Maple Park	1	1	0
Marengo	20	14	6
Marion	36	26	10
Marissa	5	5	0
Markham	40	30	10
Maroa	2	2	0
Marquette Heights	5	5	0
Marseilles	13	9	4
Marshall	12	11	1
Martinsville	2	2	0
Maryville	16	11	5
Mascoutah	14	13	1
Mason City	5	5	0
Matteson	46	36	10
Mattoon	55	42	13
Maywood	76	55	21
McCook	20	16	4
McCullom Lake	2	2	0
McHenry	66	49	17
McLean	1	1	0
McLeansboro	5	5	0
Melrose Park	89	73	16
Mendota	20	15	5
Meredosia	2	2	0
Metamora	4	4	0
Metropolis	20	16	4
Midlothian	30	24	6
Milan	16	12	4
Milledgeville	2	2	0
Millstadt	6	6	0
Minier	2	2	0
Minonk	2	2	0
Minooka	17	15	2
Mokena	33	30	3
Moline	109	83	26
Momence	8	8	0
Monee	12	11	1
Monmouth	26	17	9
Montgomery	29	21	8
Monticello	7	6	1
Morris	35	26	9
Morrison	6	6	0
Morton	29	22	7
Morton Grove	60	46	14
Mound City	1	1	0
Mount Carmel	17	13	4
Mount Carroll	3	3	0
Mount Morris	5	4	1
Mount Olive	6	4	2
Mount Prospect	107	84	23
Mount Pulaski	3	3	0
Mount Sterling	9	4	5
Mount Vernon	58	46	12
Mount Zion	10	8	2
Moweaqua	2	2	0
Mundelein	67	47	20
Murphysboro	19	12	7
Naperville	285	179	106
Nashville	8	7	1
Nauvoo	2	2	0
Neoga	3	3	0
New Athens	5	5	0
New Baden	5	5	0
New Lenox	37	34	3
Newman	1	1	0
Newton	7	6	1
Niles	73	59	14
Nokomis	6	5	1
Normal	86	76	10
Norridge	55	39	16
North Aurora	27	25	2
Northbrook	88	61	27
North Chicago	71	54	17
Northfield	28	19	9
Northlake	46	33	13
North Pekin	3	3	0
North Riverside	35	26	9
Oak Brook	61	43	18
Oakbrook Terrace	22	19	3
Oak Forest	53	40	13
Oak Lawn	150	100	50
Oak Park	139	124	15
Oblong	2	2	0
O'Fallon	57	43	14
Oglesby	13	9	4
Okawville	3	3	0
Olney	19	13	6
Olympia Fields	20	19	1
Oregon	9	8	1
Orion	3	3	0
Orland Hills	15	14	1
Orland Park	124	92	32
Oswego	50	44	6
Ottawa	45	34	11
Palatine	134	107	27
Palestine	3	3	0
Palos Heights	27	26	1
Palos Hills	35	33	2
Palos Park	12	11	1
Pana	12	8	4
Paris	25	18	7
Park City	15	11	4
Park Forest	47	38	9
Park Ridge	73	59	14
Pawnee	10	6	4
Paxton	7	7	0
Pecatonica	3	3	0
Pekin	61	54	7
Peoria	279	239	40
Peoria Heights	15	11	4
Peotone	10	9	1
Peru	28	21	7
Petersburg	5	5	0
Phoenix	8	6	2
Pinckneyville	8	7	1
Piper City	1	1	0
Pittsfield	6	6	0
Plainfield	61	46	15
Plano	19	17	2
Polo	4	4	0
Pontiac	24	22	2
Pontoon Beach	18	13	5
Port Barrington	1	1	0
Port Byron	2	2	0
Posen	13	12	1
Potomac	1	1	0
Princeton	16	15	1
Prophetstown	4	3	1
Prospect Heights	29	26	3
Quincy	91	76	15
Rantoul	38	29	9
Raymond	1	1	0
Red Bud	6	6	0
Richmond	5	4	1
Richton Park	31	27	4
Ridge Farm	2	2	0
Ridgway	3	3	0
Riverdale	48	35	13
River Forest	34	31	3
River Grove	31	23	8
Riverside	25	19	6
Robbins	11	4	7
Robinson	14	13	1
Rochelle	27	20	7
Rochester	7	7	0
Rockdale	5	4	1

Table 78. Law Enforcement Employees, by City, 2005

(Number.)

City	Total law enforcement employees	Total officers	Total civilians
Rock Falls	26	19	7
Rockford	332	301	31
Rock Island	108	80	28
Rockton	14	13	1
Rolling Meadows	80	54	26
Romeoville	74	56	18
Roodhouse	4	4	0
Roscoe	15	13	2
Roselle	51	37	14
Rosemont	93	74	19
Rossville	2	2	0
Round Lake	25	20	5
Round Lake Beach	49	41	8
Round Lake Heights	5	5	0
Round Lake Park	14	12	2
Roxana	6	5	1
Royalton	2	2	0
Rushville	5	5	0
Salem	21	14	7
Sandwich	19	13	6
Sauget	15	15	0
Sauk Village	30	22	8
Savanna	8	8	0
Schaumburg	200	131	69
Schiller Park	38	32	6
Seneca	8	4	4
Sesser	6	5	1
Shawneetown	4	4	0
Shelbyville	8	7	1
Sheridan	3	3	0
Sherman	6	6	0
Shiloh	12	12	0
Shorewood	27	23	4
Silvis	21	14	7
Skokie	137	105	32
Sleepy Hollow	7	6	1
Smithton	5	5	0
Somonauk	4	4	0
South Barrington	18	15	3
South Beloit	15	13	2
South Chicago Heights	13	9	4
South Elgin	40	31	9
Southern View	3	3	0
South Holland	51	40	11
South Jacksonville	6	5	1
South Pekin	2	2	0
South Roxana	5	5	0
Sparta	17	12	5
Springfield	314	268	46
Spring Grove	11	9	2
Spring Valley	14	11	3
St. Anne	3	3	0
Staunton	9	6	3
St. Charles	70	56	14
Steger	22	16	6
Sterling	40	27	13
St. Francisville	1	1	0
Stickney	21	15	6
Stockton	3	3	0
Stone Park	24	18	6
Stonington	1	1	0
Streamwood	70	59	11
Streator	30	23	7
Sugar Grove	14	13	1
Sullivan	9	7	2
Summit	37	31	6
Sumner	2	2	0
Swansea	26	19	7
Sycamore	27	25	2
Taylorville	28	22	6
Thomasboro	1	1	0
Thomson	1	1	0
Thornton	10	8	2
Tilton	3	3	0
Tinley Park	102	73	29
Tolono	4	4	0
Tremont	3	3	0
Trenton	4	4	0
Troy	22	16	6
Tuscola	8	7	1
University Park	18	14	4
Urbana	65	51	14
Valmeyer	1	1	0
Vandalia	18	13	5
Venice	6	4	2
Vernon Hills	69	48	21
Vienna	3	3	0
Villa Grove	5	4	1
Villa Park	54	39	15
Virden	10	6	4
Virginia	1	1	0
Wamac	4	4	0
Warren	4	3	1
Warrensburg	3	3	0
Warrenville	35	28	7
Warsaw	4	3	1
Washburn	2	2	0
Washington	27	19	8
Washington Park	11	8	3
Waterloo	16	14	2
Waterman	2	2	0
Watseka	10	9	1
Wauconda	35	23	12
Waukegan	222	165	57
Wayne	5	5	0
Westchester	50	35	15
West Chicago	60	46	14
West City	8	4	4
West Dundee	25	22	3
Western Springs	27	21	6
West Frankfort	19	11	8
Westmont	59	44	15
West Salem	1	1	0
Westville	3	3	0
Wheaton	92	68	24
Wheeling	93	65	28
White Hall	7	4	3
Williamsfield	2	2	0
Williamsville	2	2	0
Willowbrook	29	25	4
Willow Springs	19	14	5
Wilmette	64	46	18
Wilmington	16	11	5
Winchester	4	4	0
Winfield	24	22	2
Winnebago	6	6	0
Winnetka	34	26	8
Winthrop Harbor	16	11	5
Witt	1	1	0
Wood Dale	49	33	16
Woodhull	1	1	0
Woodridge	80	55	25
Wood River	25	19	6
Woodstock	50	37	13
Worden	2	2	0
Worth	26	24	2
Yates City	1	1	0
Yorkville	26	23	3
Zeigler	4	4	0
Zion	61	47	14
Indiana			
Alexandria	17	13	4
Anderson	148	127	21
Angola	20	16	4
Attica	6	6	0
Auburn	30	22	8
Aurora	14	10	4
Austin	6	6	0
Bargersville	6	5	1
Bedford	42	32	10
Beech Grove	39	28	11
Berne	8	7	1
Bicknell	10	7	3
Bloomington	115	81	34
Bluffton	32	20	12
Boonville	13	12	1
Brazil	16	12	4
Bremen	16	12	4
Brownsburg	54	39	15
Burns Harbor	4	3	1
Carmel	107	88	19

Table 78. Law Enforcement Employees, by City, 2005

(Number.)

City	Total law enforcement employees	Total officers	Total civilians
Cedar Lake	21	16	5
Charlestown	20	15	5
Chesterfield	7	6	1
Chesterton	26	21	5
Clarksville	44	36	8
Clinton	9	7	2
Columbia City	20	18	2
Columbus	91	84	7
Connersville	33	31	2
Corydon	7	7	0
Covington	6	6	0
Crawfordsville	43	28	15
Crown Point	43	34	9
Culver	4	4	0
Danville	26	19	7
Decatur	21	17	4
Delphi	11	7	4
Dyer	33	26	7
East Chicago	125	108	17
Edinburgh	14	9	5
Elkhart	140	111	29
Elwood	21	16	5
Evansville	316	279	37
Fairmount	9	5	4
Fishers	75	68	7
Fort Wayne	471	433	38
Frankfort	42	31	11
Franklin	52	36	16
Garrett	17	13	4
Gary	337	272	65
Gas City	14	10	4
Georgetown	4	4	0
Goshen	61	56	5
Greencastle	16	13	3
Greendale	15	11	4
Greenfield	43	33	10
Greensburg	27	18	9
Greenwood	73	51	22
Griffith	38	30	8
Hagerstown	5	5	0
Hammond	267	212	55
Hartford City	14	13	1
Hebron	8	7	1
Highland	51	44	7
Hobart	71	55	16
Huntingburg	11	10	1
Huntington	44	35	9
Indianapolis	2 813	1 603	1 210
Jasonville	5	5	0
Jasper	28	20	8
Jeffersonville	62	54	8
Kendallville	26	17	9
Kingsford Heights	3	3	0
Knox	7	7	0
Kokomo	142	104	38
Kouts	4	4	0
Lafayette	152	117	35
Lake Station	27	22	5
La Porte	53	45	8
Lawrenceburg	25	20	5
Lebanon	29	28	1
Ligonier	10	9	1
Linton	17	10	7
Logansport	51	41	10
Long Beach	7	5	2
Loogootee	6	4	2
Lowell	18	13	5
Madison	35	27	8
Marion	86	72	14
Martinsville	27	20	7
Merrillville	66	54	12
Michigan City	106	88	18
Mishawaka	135	103	32
Monticello	17	12	5
Mooresville	27	21	6
Mount Vernon	16	15	1
Muncie	124	115	9
Munster	50	39	11
Nappanee	21	15	6
New Albany	69	66	3
New Castle	39	36	3
New Chicago	6	2	4
New Whiteland	12	7	5
Noblesville	73	63	10
North Liberty	4	4	0
North Manchester	15	11	4
North Vernon	21	18	3
Oakland City	5	5	0
Peru	33	30	3
Plainfield	60	39	21
Plymouth	29	23	6
Portage	75	56	19
Portland	17	13	4
Princes Lakes	4	4	0
Princeton	17	16	1
Rensselaer	14	9	5
Richmond	92	78	14
Rushville	18	13	5
Salem	18	12	6
Schererville	60	48	12
Scottsburg	13	13	0
Seymour	53	38	15
Shelbyville	52	41	11
South Bend	335	262	73
South Whitley	4	4	0
Speedway	37	28	9
St. John	22	17	5
Sullivan	8	7	1
Tell City	22	14	8
Terre Haute	152	129	23
Tipton	14	12	2
Trail Creek	4	4	0
Union City	12	7	5
Valparaiso	62	46	16
Vincennes	42	37	5
Wabash	32	26	6
Walkerton	12	7	5
Warsaw	42	35	7
Washington	22	17	5
Waterloo	7	6	1
Westfield	33	28	5
West Lafayette	61	45	16
West Terre Haute	10	9	1
Westville	3	3	0
Whiting	25	18	7
Winchester	17	13	4
Winona Lake	5	5	0
Iowa			
Adel	8	7	1
Albia	7	6	1
Algona	13	9	4
Altoona	23	21	2
Ames	70	48	22
Anamosa	8	7	1
Ankeny	49	40	9
Atlantic	13	11	2
Audubon	3	3	0
Belle Plaine	2	2	0
Belmond	5	5	0
Bettendorf	57	44	13
Bloomfield	5	5	0
Boone	17	16	1
Burlington	54	40	14
Camanche	7	7	0
Carlisle	5	5	0
Carroll	16	15	1
Carter Lake	9	9	0
Cedar Falls	46	43	3
Cedar Rapids	228	192	36
Centerville	16	11	5
Chariton	7	6	1
Charles City	18	13	5
Cherokee	9	8	1
Clarinda	11	10	1
Clarion	7	6	1
Clear Lake	18	14	4
Clinton	50	41	9
Clive	24	21	3
Coralville	32	28	4
Council Bluffs	121	105	16
Cresco	7	7	0
Creston	16	12	4
Davenport	203	159	44
Decorah	18	12	6
Denison	17	12	5
Des Moines	493	374	119
De Witt	9	9	0
Dubuque	98	93	5
Dyersville	11	6	5
Eagle Grove	7	7	0
Eldora	6	6	0
Eldridge	7	7	0
Emmetsburg	7	6	1
Estherville	12	12	0
Evansdale	8	7	1
Fairfield	19	13	6
Forest City	8	8	0
Fort Dodge	40	37	3

Table 78. Law Enforcement Employees, by City, 2005

(Number.)

City	Total law enforcement employees	Total officers	Total civilians
Fort Madison	28	18	10
Garner	5	5	0
Glenwood	10	9	1
Grinnell	16	14	2
Grundy Center	4	4	0
Hampton	12	7	5
Harlan	9	8	1
Hawarden	4	4	0
Hiawatha	13	12	1
Humboldt	7	7	0
Independence	12	10	2
Indianola	19	17	2
Iowa City	98	70	28
Iowa Falls	15	11	4
Jefferson	7	7	0
Johnston	20	19	1
Keokuk	33	24	9
Knoxville	13	11	2
Le Claire	8	7	1
Le Mars	16	14	2
Leon	3	3	0
Manchester	13	9	4
Maquoketa	16	10	6
Marion	47	38	9
Marshalltown	59	43	16
Mason City	64	49	15
Missouri Valley	6	6	0
Monticello	7	6	1
Mount Pleasant	15	13	2
Mount Vernon	6	6	0
Muscatine	41	38	3
Nevada	9	8	1
New Hampton	8	7	1
Newton	33	27	6
North Liberty	5	5	0
Norwalk	13	11	2
Oelwein	15	11	4
Ogden	3	3	0
Onawa	6	6	0
Orange City	7	7	0
Osage	5	5	0
Osceola	11	10	1
Oskaloosa	19	17	2
Ottumwa	41	35	6
Pella	18	14	4
Perry	20	13	7
Pleasant Hill	15	14	1
Polk City	6	6	0
Red Oak	10	9	1
Rock Rapids	2	2	0
Rock Valley	3	3	0
Sac City	4	4	0
Sergeant Bluff	8	7	1
Sheldon	7	7	0
Shenandoah	8	5	3
Sioux Center	7	7	0
Sioux City	151	120	31
Spencer	29	20	9
Spirit Lake	10	9	1
St. Ansgar	1	1	0
State Center	1	1	0
Storm Lake	22	18	4
Story City	5	5	0
Tama	5	5	0
Tipton	6	6	0
Urbandale	48	44	4
Vinton	7	7	0
Washington	11	10	1
Waterloo	132	123	9
Waukee	10	9	1
Waukon	7	7	0
Waverly	16	15	1
Webster City	23	14	9
West Burlington	11	10	1
West Des Moines	77	63	14
West Liberty	7	6	1
West Union	4	4	0
Williamsburg	6	6	0
Wilton	4	4	0
Windsor Heights	14	13	1
Winterset	8	8	0
Kansas			
Abilene	16	14	2
Altamont	2	2	0
Andale	1	1	0
Andover	20	14	6
Anthony	5	5	0
Argonia	1	1	0
Arkansas City	40	25	15
Arma	4	4	0
Atchison	24	23	1
Attica	1	1	0
Atwood	2	2	0
Augusta	31	23	8
Baldwin City	9	8	1
Basehor	8	7	1
Baxter Springs	14	9	5
Bel Aire	12	11	1
Belle Plaine	5	5	0
Belleville	5	5	0
Beloit	9	8	1
Blue Rapids	1	1	0
Bonner Springs	26	24	2
Burden	1	1	0
Burlingame	2	2	0
Burlington	9	7	2
Burrton	2	2	0
Caldwell	4	4	0
Caney	9	5	4
Canton	1	1	0
Cawker City	1	1	0
Chanute	24	20	4
Chapman	3	3	0
Cheney	4	4	0
Cherryvale	7	6	1
Cimarron	3	3	0
Claflin	2	2	0
Clay Center	8	7	1
Clearwater	6	6	0
Coffeyville	30	23	7
Colby	16	11	5
Columbus	10	9	1
Colwich	3	3	0
Concordia	14	8	6
Conway Springs	3	3	0
Council Grove	7	6	1
Derby	49	37	12
Dodge City	63	48	15
Eastborough	7	7	0
Edwardsville	19	18	1
El Dorado	27	26	1
Elkhart	3	3	0
Ellinwood	5	5	0
Ellis	5	5	0
Ellsworth	6	5	1
Elwood	5	5	0
Emporia	68	45	23
Enterprise	4	3	1
Erie	3	3	0
Eskridge	1	1	0
Eudora	11	9	2
Fairway	11	9	2
Florence	2	2	0
Fort Scott	25	18	7
Fredonia	6	5	1
Frontenac	9	6	3
Galena	11	6	5
Galva	1	1	0
Garden City	83	52	31
Garden Plain	3	3	0
Gardner	29	27	2
Garnett	12	8	4
Girard	8	7	1
Goddard	5	5	0
Goodland	12	10	2
Grandview Plaza	5	5	0
Great Bend	32	28	4
Halstead	5	4	1
Harper	3	3	0
Haven	3	3	0
Hays	42	27	15
Haysville	30	21	9

Table 78. Law Enforcement Employees, by City, 2005

(Number.)

City	Total law enforcement employees	Total officers	Total civilians
Herington	10	5	5
Hesston	7	6	1
Hiawatha	8	7	1
Hill City	4	4	0
Hillsboro	5	5	0
Hoisington	9	7	2
Holcomb	4	3	1
Holton	12	8	4
Hope	1	1	0
Horton	9	4	5
Hoxie	1	1	0
Hugoton	8	6	2
Humboldt	6	6	0
Hutchinson	92	69	23
Independence	29	20	9
Inman	2	2	0
Iola	22	12	10
Junction City	64	46	18
Kanopolis	1	1	0
Kansas City	475	354	121
Kechi	4	4	0
Kingman	7	7	0
Kinsley	5	4	1
Kiowa	2	2	0
La Crosse	3	3	0
La Cygne	2	2	0
La Harpe	2	2	0
Lake Quivira	3	3	0
Lansing	17	14	3
Larned	12	8	4
Lawrence	169	133	36
Leavenworth	87	63	24
Leawood	76	54	22
Lebo	1	1	0
Lenexa	125	83	42
Le Roy	1	1	0
Lewis	1	1	0
Liberal	51	37	14
Lindsborg	7	6	1
Linn Valley	1	1	0
Little River	1	1	0
Louisburg	10	10	0
Lyndon	3	3	0
Lyons	8	7	1
Macksville	1	1	0
Maize	8	7	1
Marion	5	5	0
Marquette	1	1	0
Marysville	8	7	1
McLouth	1	1	0
McPherson	32	27	5
Meade	3	3	0
Medicine Lodge	6	5	1
Merriam	30	26	4
Minneapolis	5	5	0
Mission	29	28	1
Moran	1	1	0
Moundridge	3	3	0
Mount Hope	2	2	0
Mulberry	1	1	0
Mulvane	18	12	6
Neodesha	8	7	1
Newton	34	30	4
Nickerson	4	4	0
North Newton	2	2	0
Norton	5	5	0
Norwich	1	1	0
Oberlin	3	3	0
Olathe	193	154	39
Osage City	6	6	0
Osawatomie	16	10	6
Osborne	4	4	0
Oswego	5	5	0
Ottawa	34	28	6
Overbrook	2	2	0
Overland Park	295	245	50
Oxford	3	3	0
Paola	21	15	6
Park City	19	17	2
Parsons	26	21	5
Peabody	3	3	0
Perry	1	1	0
Pittsburg	50	35	15
Plainville	4	4	0
Pleasanton	2	2	0
Prairie Village	53	42	11
Pratt	21	15	6
Quinter	1	1	0
Richmond	2	1	1
Roeland Park	16	14	2
Rolla	1	1	0
Rose Hill	9	8	1
Rossville	3	3	0
Russell	19	8	11
Sabetha	5	5	0
Salina	105	76	29
Scott City	11	6	5
Scranton	1	1	0
Sedan	3	3	0
Sedgwick	2	2	0
Seneca	4	4	0
Shawnee	108	88	20
Silver Lake	2	2	0
Smith Center	3	3	0
South Hutchinson	9	7	2
Spearville	1	1	0
Spring Hill	10	9	1
Stafford	4	4	0
Sterling	5	5	0
St. Francis	5	4	1
St. George	1	1	0
St. John	4	4	0
St. Marys	5	5	0
Stockton	5	5	0
Tonganoxie	9	8	1
Topeka	340	285	55
Towanda	2	2	0
Troy	1	1	0
Udall	3	3	0
Valley Center	12	9	3
Valley Falls	2	2	0
Victoria	2	2	0
Wa Keeney	4	4	0
Wakefield	1	1	0
Wamego	12	7	5
Waterville	1	1	0
Wathena	2	2	0
Weir	1	1	0
Wellington	20	16	4
Wichita	802	634	168
Wilson	29	11	18
Winfield	29	22	7
Yates Center	3	3	0
Kentucky			
Adairville	1	1	0
Albany	10	9	1
Alexandria	15	12	3
Anchorage	14	10	4
Ashland	51	43	8
Auburn	2	2	0
Audubon Park	9	8	1
Augusta	3	3	0
Barbourville	17	14	3
Bardstown	28	22	6
Bardwell	1	1	0
Beattyville	7	5	2
Beaver Dam	6	6	0
Bellefonte	2	2	0
Bellevue	11	10	1
Benham	2	2	0
Benton	9	7	2
Berea	33	26	7
Bloomfield	1	1	0
Booneville	3	3	0

Table 78. Law Enforcement Employees, by City, 2005

(Number.)

City	Total law enforcement employees	Total officers	Total civilians
Bowling Green	123	93	30
Brandenburg	3	3	0
Brodhead	1	1	0
Brooksville	1	1	0
Brownsville	3	3	0
Burkesville	10	5	5
Burnside	3	3	0
Butler	1	1	0
Cadiz	9	8	1
Calhoun	1	1	0
Calvert City	7	6	1
Campbellsburg	1	1	0
Campbellsville	23	19	4
Campton	1	1	0
Caneyville	1	1	0
Carlisle	8	4	4
Carrollton	12	11	1
Catlettsburg	8	8	0
Cave City	6	6	0
Central City	12	11	1
Clarkson	2	2	0
Clay	2	2	0
Clay City	2	2	0
Clinton	4	4	0
Cloverport	2	2	0
Cold Spring	11	11	0
Columbia	10	10	0
Corbin	29	21	8
Covington	129	115	14
Crab Orchard	1	1	0
Crescent Springs	8	8	0
Crofton	1	1	0
Cumberland	7	5	2
Cynthiana	16	15	1
Danville	33	31	2
Dawson Springs	9	5	4
Dayton	7	7	0
Earlington	2	2	0
Eddyville	5	5	0
Edgewood	12	12	0
Edmonton	7	7	0
Elizabethtown	58	42	16
Elkhorn City	5	4	1
Elkton	8	8	0
Elsmere	12	11	1
Eminence	7	7	0
Erlanger	43	36	7
Eubank	1	1	0
Evarts	4	4	0
Falmouth	8	7	1
Flatwoods	11	10	1
Fleming-Neon	3	2	1
Flemingsburg	7	7	0
Florence	56	52	4
Forest Hills	1	1	0
Fort Mitchell	13	13	0
Fort Thomas	22	21	1
Fort Wright	11	10	1
Frankfort	73	68	5
Franklin	23	22	1
Fulton	13	9	4
Gamaliel	1	1	0
Georgetown	55	49	6
Glasgow	42	33	9
Glencoe	1	1	0
Graymoor-Devondale	4	4	0
Grayson	10	10	0
Greensburg	6	6	0
Greenup	3	3	0
Greenville	9	9	0
Guthrie	4	4	0
Hardinsburg	4	4	0
Harlan	14	11	3
Harrodsburg	25	15	10
Hartford	6	6	0
Hawesville	1	1	0
Hazard	24	18	6
Henderson	77	56	21
Hickman	7	4	3
Highland Heights	10	10	0
Hillview	12	12	0
Hindman	1	1	0
Hodgenville	8	8	0
Hopkinsville	84	76	8
Horse Cave	4	4	0
Hustonville	1	1	0
Hyden	4	4	0
Independence	29	28	1
Indian Hills	7	7	0
Inez	2	2	0
Irvine	6	6	0
Irvington	4	4	0
Jackson	13	11	2
Jamestown	5	5	0
Jeffersontown	59	50	9
Jenkins	6	5	1
Junction City	3	3	0
La Center	2	2	0
La Grange	11	11	0
Lakeside Park-Crestview Hills	11	10	1
Lancaster	7	7	0
Lawrenceburg	22	14	8
Lebanon	24	17	7
Lebanon Junction	5	5	0
Leitchfield	15	14	1
Lewisburg	1	1	0
Lewisport	3	3	0
Lexington	653	511	142
Liberty	5	5	0
Livermore	2	2	0
London	34	31	3
Lone Oak	3	2	1
Louisa	7	7	0
Louisville Metro	1 399	1 148	251
Loyall	1	1	0
Ludlow	11	10	1
Lynch	2	2	0
Lynnview	1	1	0
Madisonville	55	42	13
Manchester	12	12	0
Marion	8	8	0
Martin	3	3	0
Mayfield	32	24	8
Maysville	30	24	6
McKee	1	1	0
Middlesboro	25	21	4
Millersburg	2	2	0
Monticello	9	9	0
Morehead	29	19	10
Morganfield	13	8	5
Morgantown	4	4	0
Mortons Gap	1	1	0
Mount Olivet	1	1	0
Mount Sterling	25	23	2
Mount Vernon	8	8	0
Mount Washington	17	16	1
Muldraugh	3	3	0
Munfordville	4	4	0
Murray	37	32	5
New Castle	1	1	0
New Haven	1	1	0
Newport	56	51	5
Nicholasville	56	50	6
Nortonville	1	1	0
Oak Grove	18	14	4
Olive Hill	6	6	0
Owensboro	134	104	30
Owenton	4	4	0
Owingsville	7	7	0
Paducah	88	74	14
Paintsville	12	12	0
Paris	34	24	10
Park City	1	1	0
Park Hills	6	6	0
Pembroke	2	1	1
Perryville	1	1	0
Pewee Valley	1	1	0
Pikeville	27	19	8
Pineville	8	8	0
Pioneer Village	5	5	0

Table 78. Law Enforcement Employees, by City, 2005

(Number.)

City	Total law enforcement employees	Total officers	Total civilians
Pippa Passes	1	1	0
Pleasureville	1	1	0
Powderly	1	1	0
Prestonsburg	16	16	0
Princeton	17	16	1
Prospect	9	8	1
Providence	7	7	0
Raceland	5	5	0
Radcliff	52	37	15
Ravenna	2	2	0
Richmond	84	60	24
Russell	12	12	0
Russell Springs	8	7	1
Russellville	26	24	2
Sadieville	1	1	0
Salyersville	1	1	0
Scottsville	21	13	8
Sebree	1	1	0
Shelbyville	21	20	1
Shepherdsville	20	19	1
Shively	24	19	5
Silver Grove	1	1	0
Somerset	38	35	3
Southgate	7	7	0
South Shore	2	2	0
Springfield	12	7	5
Stamping Ground	1	1	0
Stanford	7	7	0
Stanton	8	8	0
St. Matthews	36	30	6
Sturgis	4	4	0
Taylor Mill	10	9	1
Taylorsville	4	4	0
Tompkinsville	10	7	3
Uniontown	2	2	0
Vanceburg	6	6	0
Versailles	47	37	10
Villa Hills	9	8	1
Vine Grove	7	7	0
Wallins	1	1	0
Warsaw	4	4	0
Wayland	1	1	0
West Buechel	7	7	0
West Liberty	11	5	6
West Point	3	3	0
Wheelwright	1	1	0
Whitesburg	5	5	0
Wilder	7	7	0
Williamsburg	11	10	1
Williamstown	6	5	1
Wilmore	10	9	1
Winchester	49	34	15
Wingo	1	1	0
Worthington	4	4	0
Wurtland	1	1	0
Louisiana			
Abbeville	41	39	2
Addis	7	6	1
Alexandria	186	151	35
Baldwin	8	7	1
Ball	6	5	1
Basile	11	7	4
Baton Rouge	773	611	162
Bernice	5	5	0
Berwick	10	10	0
Blanchard	4	4	0
Bogalusa	60	38	22
Bossier City	238	197	41
Breaux Bridge	21	21	0
Broussard	21	17	4
Brusly	8	7	1
Church Point	16	16	0
Clinton	4	4	0
Coushatta	6	6	0
Covington	41	32	9
Crowley	37	36	1
Cullen	3	3	0
Delhi	15	10	5
Denham Springs	35	27	8
De Quincy	14	14	0
De Ridder	28	23	5
Dixie Inn	2	2	0
Elton	5	5	0
Erath	10	7	3
Eunice	42	35	7
Farmerville	12	12	0
Ferriday	19	18	1
Folsom	3	3	0
Franklin	23	22	1
Franklinton	18	13	5
French Settlement	2	2	0
Glenmora	1	1	0
Golden Meadow	5	5	0
Gonzales	31	31	0
Grambling	15	10	5
Gretna	110	84	26
Harahan	30	30	0
Haughton	7	7	0
Haynesville	6	5	1
Homer	9	9	0
Houma	81	69	12
Independence	8	8	0
Iowa	14	10	4
Jackson	6	6	0
Jeanerette	11	11	0
Jena	7	6	1
Jennings	35	26	9
Jonesboro	17	13	4
Kaplan	19	19	0
Kenner	216	168	48
Kentwood	9	9	0
Kinder	18	18	0
Krotz Springs	6	4	2
Lafayette	300	228	72
Lake Arthur	8	8	0
Lake Charles	192	176	16
Lake Providence	11	11	0
Lecompte	3	3	0
Leesville	29	29	0
Mamou	14	14	0
Mandeville	49	36	13
Mansfield	16	16	0
Many	21	16	5
Marksville	21	16	5
McNary	1	1	0
Minden	31	29	2
Morgan City	53	50	3
Napoleonville	2	2	0
Natchitoches	63	48	15
New Orleans	1 925	1 671	254
Olla	4	4	0
Opelousas	60	54	6
Patterson	18	18	0
Pearl River	13	8	5
Pineville	61	53	8
Plaquemine	33	31	2
Pollock	1	1	0
Ponchatoula	25	22	3
Port Allen	20	16	4
Port Barre	15	9	6
Port Vincent	3	3	0
Rayne	25	25	0
Rayville	10	10	0
Richwood	16	9	7
Ruston	48	41	7
Shreveport	616	534	82
Sicily Island	2	1	1
Simmesport	7	7	0
Springhill	16	15	1
Sterlington	9	8	1
St. Gabriel	14	14	0
St. Joseph	4	4	0
St. Martinville	19	13	6
Stonewall	2	2	0
Sulphur	60	43	17
Tallulah	13	13	0

Table 78. Law Enforcement Employees, by City, 2005

(Number.)

City	Total law enforcement employees	Total officers	Total civilians
Thibodaux	63	55	8
Tickfaw	7	7	0
Ville Platte	22	16	6
Vinton	15	15	0
Vivian	15	10	5
Washington	7	7	0
Waterproof	2	2	0
Welsh	14	14	0
Westlake	25	19	6
West Monroe	79	74	5
Westwego	38	37	1
Winnfield	23	19	4
Woodworth	7	5	2
Youngsville	10	8	2
Zachary	39	36	3
Maine			
Ashland	1	1	0
Auburn	55	49	6
Augusta	56	41	15
Baileyville	7	7	0
Bangor	92	75	17
Bar Harbor	14	10	4
Bath	24	19	5
Belfast	15	13	2
Berwick	12	11	1
Bethel	4	4	0
Biddeford	70	47	23
Boothbay Harbor	7	6	1
Brewer	22	20	2
Bridgton	12	8	4
Brunswick	51	35	16
Bucksport	11	7	4
Buxton	14	9	5
Calais	12	8	4
Camden	16	11	5
Cape Elizabeth	16	12	4
Caribou	16	15	1
Carrabassett Valley	1	1	0
Clinton	3	3	0
Cumberland	12	11	1
Damariscotta	6	5	1
Dexter	6	5	1
Dixfield	4	4	0
Dover-Foxcroft	5	5	0
East Millinocket	4	4	0
Eastport	4	4	0
Eliot	9	8	1
Ellsworth	19	15	4
Fairfield	13	12	1
Falmouth	23	16	7
Farmington	15	14	1
Fort Fairfield	4	4	0
Fort Kent	9	5	4
Freeport	17	12	5
Fryeburg	5	4	1
Gardiner	12	11	1
Gorham	22	20	2
Gouldsboro	1	1	0
Greenville	3	2	1
Hallowell	3	3	0
Hampden	12	11	1
Holden	2	2	0
Houlton	18	13	5
Jay	11	7	4
Kennebunk	25	19	6
Kennebunkport	13	12	1
Kittery	27	20	7
Lewiston	95	81	14
Lincoln	7	6	1
Lisbon	22	16	6
Livermore Falls	10	6	4
Machias	4	4	0
Madawaska	7	6	1
Madison	8	7	1
Mechanic Falls	5	5	0
Mexico	5	5	0
Milbridge	3	3	0
Millinocket	9	9	0
Milo	3	3	0
Monmouth	3	3	0
Mount Desert	10	6	4
Newport	5	5	0
North Berwick	9	8	1
Norway	6	5	1
Oakland	10	9	1
Ogunquit	12	10	2
Old Orchard Beach	26	17	9
Old Town	18	15	3
Orono	15	13	2
Oxford	6	5	1
Paris	8	7	1
Phippsburg	1	1	0
Pittsfield	6	6	0
Portland	212	153	59
Presque Isle	23	19	4
Rangeley	3	3	0
Richmond	4	4	0
Rockland	21	18	3
Rockport	8	7	1
Rumford	17	14	3
Sabattus	8	7	1
Saco	43	32	11
Sanford	51	37	14
Scarborough	47	32	15
Searsport	3	3	0
Skowhegan	13	13	0
South Berwick	12	8	4
South Portland	67	51	16
Southwest Harbor	6	6	0
Swan's Island	1	1	0
Thomaston	5	5	0
Topsham	15	13	2
Van Buren	4	4	0
Veazie	5	5	0
Waldoboro	7	6	1
Washburn	2	2	0
Waterville	39	30	9
Wells	31	23	8
Westbrook	46	32	14
Wilton	5	5	0
Windham	35	25	10
Winslow	10	9	1
Winter Harbor	1	1	0
Winthrop	14	10	4
Wiscasset	6	5	1
Yarmouth	18	11	7
York	39	28	11
Maryland			
Aberdeen	48	39	9
Annapolis	166	119	47
Baltimore	3 663	3 034	629
Baltimore City Sheriff	156	134	22
Bel Air	41	29	12
Berlin	19	14	5
Berwyn Heights	7	6	1
Bladensburg	24	16	8
Boonsboro	2	2	0
Brunswick	13	11	2
Cambridge	58	46	12
Capitol Heights	7	5	2
Centreville	7	6	1
Chestertown	14	13	1
Cheverly	15	13	2
Cottage City	6	6	0
Crisfield	15	11	4
Cumberland	53	50	3
Delmar	10	9	1
Denton	11	10	1

Table 78. Law Enforcement Employees, by City, 2005

(Number.)

City	Total law enforcement employees	Total officers	Total civilians
District Heights	13	10	3
Easton	63	49	14
Edmonston	6	5	1
Elkton	41	31	10
Fairmount Heights	4	4	0
Federalsburg	9	8	1
Forest Heights	4	3	1
Frederick	159	124	35
Frostburg	13	9	4
Fruitland	15	14	1
Glenarden	5	4	1
Greenbelt	68	54	14
Greensboro	4	4	0
Hagerstown	116	95	21
Hampstead	9	7	2
Hancock	4	3	1
Havre de Grace	38	29	9
Hurlock	8	7	1
Hyattsville	37	27	10
Landover Hills	5	4	1
La Plata	10	9	1
Laurel	68	54	14
Luke	1	1	0
Manchester	5	5	0
Morningside	7	6	1
Mount Rainier	16	13	3
North East	8	7	1
Oakland	6	5	1
Ocean City	112	97	15
Ocean Pines	20	15	5
Oxford	5	5	0
Perryville	2	1	1
Pocomoke City	20	14	6
Preston	1	1	0
Princess Anne	11	10	1
Ridgely	5	5	0
Rising Sun	7	6	1
Riverdale Park	22	16	6
Rock Hall	4	4	0
Salisbury	109	85	24
Seat Pleasant	17	15	2
Smithsburg	3	2	1
Snow Hill	8	7	1
St. Michaels	8	7	1
Sykesville	8	7	1
Takoma Park	53	37	16
Taneytown	11	10	1
Thurmont	10	9	1
University Park	8	8	0
Upper Marlboro	2	2	0
Westernport	2	2	0
Westminster	58	44	14
Massachusetts			
Abington	30	28	2
Acton	43	33	10
Acushnet	18	16	2
Adams	21	16	5
Agawam	60	52	8
Amesbury	40	32	8
Amherst	56	50	6
Andover	70	52	18
Aquinnah	3	3	0
Arlington	77	59	18
Ashburnham	14	9	5
Ashby	5	5	0
Ashfield	2	2	0
Ashland	31	26	5
Athol	23	17	6
Attleboro	88	75	13
Auburn	38	28	10
Avon	20	15	5
Ayer	22	17	5
Barnstable	127	105	22
Barre	14	10	4
Becket	2	2	0
Bedford	35	27	8
Belchertown	22	17	5
Bellingham	36	29	7
Belmont	59	40	19
Berkley	7	6	1
Berlin	11	7	4
Bernardston	2	2	0
Beverly	71	68	3
Billerica	85	63	22
Blackstone	20	17	3
Bolton	14	9	5
Boston	2 663	2 075	588
Bourne	40	34	6
Boxborough	11	10	1
Boxford	13	13	0
Boylston	12	9	3
Braintree	82	74	8
Brewster	23	18	5
Bridgewater	35	34	1
Brockton	217	191	26
Brookfield	2	2	0
Brookline	160	140	20
Buckland	2	2	0
Burlington	66	59	7
Cambridge	279	248	31
Canton	44	43	1
Carlisle	9	9	0
Carver	29	17	12
Charlton	22	18	4
Chatham	23	19	4
Chelmsford	70	55	15
Chelsea	91	82	9
Chicopee	131	127	4
Clinton	33	28	5
Cohasset	23	17	6
Concord	41	34	7
Dalton	14	12	2
Danvers	59	46	13
Dartmouth	72	58	14
Dedham	63	60	3
Deerfield	7	6	1
Dennis	49	40	9
Dighton	8	8	0
Douglas	18	13	5
Dover	17	16	1
Dracut	43	38	5
Dudley	17	13	4
Dunstable	6	6	0
Duxbury	33	26	7
East Bridgewater	26	24	2
East Brookfield	3	3	0
Eastham	18	12	6
Easthampton	33	26	7
East Longmeadow	23	22	1
Easton	35	30	5
Edgartown	16	15	1
Egremont	2	2	0
Erving	4	4	0
Essex	9	8	1
Everett	101	91	10
Fairhaven	36	31	5
Fall River	278	222	56
Falmouth	79	66	13
Fitchburg	108	89	19
Foxborough	28	24	4
Framingham	119	109	10
Franklin	53	43	10
Freetown	17	17	0
Gardner	40	31	9
Georgetown	15	11	4
Gill	3	3	0
Gloucester	64	60	4
Goshen	2	2	0
Grafton	22	17	5
Granby	11	9	2
Granville	1	1	0
Great Barrington	14	13	1
Groton	21	15	6
Groveland	13	8	5
Hadley	15	11	4
Halifax	15	11	4
Hamilton	16	15	1
Hampden	10	7	3
Hanover	33	30	3
Hanson	25	21	4
Hardwick	3	3	0
Harwich	36	31	5
Hatfield	1	1	0

Table 78. Law Enforcement Employees, by City, 2005

(Number.)

City	Total law enforcement employees	Total officers	Total civilians
Haverhill	96	86	10
Hingham	54	45	9
Hinsdale	1	1	0
Holbrook	20	19	1
Holden	24	23	1
Holliston	24	23	1
Holyoke	142	124	18
Hopedale	16	12	4
Hopkinton	25	20	5
Hubbardston	9	5	4
Hudson	37	31	6
Ipswich	30	25	5
Kingston	32	24	8
Lakeville	20	16	4
Lancaster	11	10	1
Lanesboro	6	6	0
Lawrence	186	155	31
Lee	12	11	1
Leicester	22	17	5
Lenox	10	10	0
Leverett	2	2	0
Lexington	55	42	13
Lincoln	17	13	4
Littleton	19	15	4
Longmeadow	32	27	5
Lowell	317	243	74
Ludlow	34	29	5
Lunenburg	13	13	0
Lynn	198	179	19
Lynnfield	26	20	6
Malden	111	101	10
Manchester-by-the-Sea	16	14	2
Mansfield	44	32	12
Marblehead	38	30	8
Marion	14	14	0
Marlborough	69	58	11
Marshfield	47	44	3
Mashpee	40	32	8
Maynard	23	20	3
Medfield	25	19	6
Medford	114	109	5
Medway	22	21	1
Melrose	45	42	3
Mendon	18	13	5
Merrimac	8	6	2
Methuen	92	77	15
Middleboro	48	42	6
Middleton	13	12	1
Milford	50	45	5
Millbury	24	19	5
Millis	18	14	4
Millville	7	4	3
Milton	72	55	17
Monson	15	11	4
Montague	20	15	5
Monterey	2	2	0
Nahant	13	12	1
Nantucket	41	34	7
Natick	65	53	12
Needham	56	43	13
New Bedford	328	274	54
New Braintree	1	1	0
Newbury	14	13	1
Newburyport	34	33	1
Newton	176	149	27
Norfolk	19	17	2
Northampton	55	50	5
North Andover	53	40	13
North Attleboro	63	50	13
Northborough	25	18	7
Northbridge	27	22	5
North Brookfield	6	6	0
Northfield	4	3	1
North Reading	32	31	1
Norton	26	25	1
Norwell	32	23	9
Norwood	69	58	11
Oak Bluffs	16	14	2
Orange	14	13	1
Orleans	27	21	6
Oxford	24	19	5
Palmer	26	20	6
Paxton	11	10	1
Peabody	111	94	17
Pembroke	28	26	2
Pepperell	18	17	1
Petersham	2	2	0
Phillipston	1	1	0
Pittsfield	108	84	24
Plainville	20	15	5
Plymouth	114	95	19
Plympton	6	6	0
Princeton	8	5	3
Provincetown	25	17	8
Quincy	232	203	29
Randolph	56	55	1
Raynham	34	25	9
Reading	47	38	9
Rehoboth	26	21	5
Revere	102	93	9
Rochester	10	10	0
Rockland	41	32	9
Rockport	18	16	2
Rowley	17	15	2
Royalston	1	1	0
Rutland	7	6	1
Salem	91	82	9
Salisbury	17	12	5
Sandwich	34	33	1
Saugus	72	55	17
Scituate	37	31	6
Seekonk	38	33	5
Sharon	30	26	4
Sheffield	6	6	0
Shelburne	2	2	0
Sherborn	14	14	0
Shirley	16	11	5
Shrewsbury	54	40	14
Somerset	38	31	7
Somerville	137	112	25
Southampton	7	7	0
Southborough	17	15	2
Southbridge	39	36	3
South Hadley	30	25	5
Southwick	20	15	5
Spencer	21	17	4
Springfield	527	447	80
Sterling	10	9	1
Stockbridge	6	6	0
Stoneham	45	36	9
Stoughton	61	54	7
Stow	16	11	5
Sturbridge	20	15	5
Sudbury	33	27	6
Sunderland	4	4	0
Sutton	20	15	5
Swampscott	35	33	2
Swansea	37	31	6
Taunton	117	113	4
Templeton	9	8	1
Tisbury	14	13	1
Topsfield	14	10	4
Townsend	18	16	2
Truro	17	12	5
Tyngsboro	31	24	7
Upton	13	13	0
Uxbridge	21	17	4
Wakefield	40	39	1
Walpole	45	40	5
Waltham	179	146	33
Ware	17	17	0
Wareham	59	48	11
Warren	11	6	5
Watertown	75	63	12
Wayland	20	19	1
Webster	31	26	5
Wellesley	54	40	14
Wellfleet	18	13	5
Wenham	11	10	1
Westborough	35	28	7

Table 78. Law Enforcement Employees, by City, 2005

(Number.)

City	Total law enforcement employees	Total officers	Total civilians
West Boylston	18	13	5
West Bridgewater	20	19	1
West Brookfield	6	6	0
Westfield	87	76	11
Westford	47	38	9
Westminster	16	12	4
West Newbury	11	7	4
Weston	29	23	6
Westport	32	28	4
West Springfield	88	80	8
Westwood	33	25	8
Weymouth	110	96	14
Whately	2	2	0
Whitman	27	26	1
Wilbraham	29	28	1
Williamsburg	1	1	0
Williamstown	15	12	3
Wilmington	48	46	2
Winchendon	18	13	5
Winchester	46	38	8
Winthrop	34	33	1
Woburn	79	73	6
Worcester	496	448	48
Wrentham	21	19	2
Yarmouth	64	54	10
Michigan			
Adrian	38	33	5
Adrian Township	1	1	0
Albion	31	24	7
Algonac	9	8	1
Allegan	11	10	1
Allen Park	53	48	5
Alma	14	13	1
Almont	9	9	0
Alpena	20	18	2
Ann Arbor	223	152	71
Argentine Township	8	7	1
Armada	1	1	0
Auburn	3	2	1
Auburn Hills	71	56	15
Augusta	5	4	1
Bad Axe	10	9	1
Bancroft	1	1	0
Bangor	6	6	0
Baraga	3	3	0
Bath Township	11	10	1
Battle Creek	133	114	19
Bay City	74	66	8
Beaverton	1	1	0
Belding	11	9	2
Bellaire	2	2	0
Belleville	12	10	2
Bellevue	3	3	0
Benton Harbor	44	31	13
Benton Township	35	26	9
Berkley	34	28	6
Berrien Springs-Oronoko Township	9	8	1
Beverly Hills	30	25	5
Big Rapids	19	18	1
Birch Run	7	6	1
Birmingham	53	35	18
Blackman Township	27	26	1
Blissfield	6	6	0
Bloomfield Hills	26	22	4
Bloomfield Township	97	73	24
Bloomingdale	1	1	0
Boyne City	8	7	1
Breckenridge	3	3	0
Bridgman	4	4	0
Brighton	16	14	2
Bronson	5	5	0
Brooklyn/Columbia	4	4	0
Brown City	2	2	0
Brownstown Township	55	41	14
Buchanan	10	9	1
Buena Vista Township	15	13	2
Burr Oak	1	1	0
Burton	41	36	5
Cadillac	19	16	3
Calumet	1	1	0
Cambridge Township	3	3	0
Canton Township	113	80	33
Capac	4	4	0
Carleton	4	3	1
Caro	9	8	1
Carrollton Township	8	7	1
Carson City	2	2	0
Caseville	2	2	0
Caspian	1	1	0
Cass City	3	3	0
Cassopolis	5	5	0
Cedar Springs	7	7	0
Center Line	30	27	3
Central Lake	1	1	0
Charlevoix	7	7	0
Charlotte	19	18	1
Cheboygan	10	9	1
Chelsea	13	9	4
Chesterfield Township	61	46	15
Chikaming Township	5	4	1
Chocolay Township	4	4	0
Clare	9	8	1
Clarkston	2	2	0
Clawson	20	18	2
Clayton Township	8	7	1
Clay Township	19	14	5
Clinton	4	4	0
Clinton Township	135	105	30
Clio	5	5	0
Coldwater	19	18	1
Coleman	2	2	0
Coloma Township	10	8	2
Colon	3	3	0
Concord	2	2	0
Constantine	6	5	1
Corunna	3	3	0
Covert Township	6	6	0
Croswell	6	6	0
Crystal Falls	4	4	0
Davison	9	8	1
Davison Township	19	17	2
Dearborn	203	185	18
Dearborn Heights	109	87	22
Decatur	4	4	0
Deckerville	1	1	0
Denmark Township	1	1	0
Denton Township	4	4	0
Detroit	3 695	3 327	368
Dewitt	7	6	1
Dewitt Township	14	13	1
Douglas	9	8	1
Dowagiac	16	15	1
Dryden Township	3	3	0
Durand	6	6	0
East Grand Rapids	33	30	3
East Jordan	5	4	1
East Lansing	92	62	30
Eastpointe	55	50	5
East Tawas	7	6	1
Eaton Rapids	11	10	1
Edmore	2	2	0
Elk Rapids	5	5	0
Elkton	2	2	0
Elsie	2	2	0
Emmett Township	20	18	2
Erie Township	7	6	1
Escanaba	45	33	12
Essexville	8	8	0
Evart	3	3	0
Farmington	29	22	7
Farmington Hills	163	113	50
Fenton	21	16	5
Ferndale	56	47	9
Flat Rock	32	26	6
Flint	275	244	31
Flint Township	44	37	7

Table 78. Law Enforcement Employees, by City, 2005

(Number.)

City	Total law enforcement employees	Total officers	Total civilians
Flushing	14	13	1
Flushing Township	11	10	1
Forsyth Township	8	7	1
Fowlerville	5	5	0
Frankenmuth	8	8	0
Frankfort	3	3	0
Franklin	9	9	0
Fraser	56	44	12
Fremont	9	8	1
Frost Township	1	1	0
Fruitport	9	8	1
Gagetown	1	1	0
Galesburg	3	2	1
Garden City	47	38	9
Gaylord	13	11	2
Genesee Township	30	26	4
Gerrish Township	7	7	0
Gibraltar	10	9	1
Gladstone	12	11	1
Gladwin	5	5	0
Grand Beach	4	4	0
Grand Blanc Township	52	44	8
Grand Haven	37	32	5
Grand Ledge	16	15	1
Grand Rapids	395	331	64
Grandville	33	27	6
Grant	1	1	0
Grayling	6	6	0
Green Oak Township	16	14	2
Greenville	19	16	3
Grosse Ile Township	23	17	6
Grosse Pointe	27	25	2
Grosse Pointe Farms	44	35	9
Grosse Pointe Park	50	44	6
Grosse Pointe Shores	26	19	7
Grosse Pointe Woods	52	39	13
Hamburg Township	15	14	1
Hampton Township	11	10	1
Hamtramck	42	42	0
Hancock	7	7	0
Harbor Beach	4	4	0
Harbor Springs	7	6	1
Harper Woods	37	33	4
Hart	4	4	0
Hartford	7	7	0
Hastings	16	14	2
Hesperia	3	3	0
Hillsdale	17	15	2
Holland	75	62	13
Holly	16	11	5
Homer	3	3	0
Home Township	1	1	0
Hopkins	3	3	0
Houghton	7	7	0
Howard City	3	3	0
Howell	21	19	2
Hudson	3	3	0
Hudsonville	8	8	0
Huntington Woods	18	17	1
Huron Township	30	25	5
Imlay City	9	8	1
Inkster	70	59	11
Ionia	22	19	3
Iron Mountain	14	14	0
Iron River	8	7	1
Ironwood	16	14	2
Ishpeming	11	10	1
Ishpeming Township	1	1	0
Ithaca	4	4	0
Jackson	90	68	22
Jonesville	5	5	0
Kalamazoo	288	234	54
Kalamazoo Township	41	33	8
Kalkaska	6	5	1
Keego Harbor	6	5	1
Kentwood	86	69	17
Kingsford	19	19	0
Kingston	1	1	0
Kinross Township	3	3	0
Laingsburg	3	3	0
Lake Angelus	1	1	0
Lake Linden	2	2	0
Lake Odessa	4	4	0
Lake Orion	8	4	4
Lakeview	2	2	0
L'anse	4	4	0
Lansing	335	243	92
Lansing Township	17	16	1
Lapeer	23	20	3
Lapeer Township	1	1	0
Lathrup Village	8	8	0
Laurium	4	4	0
Lawton	6	6	0
Lennon	1	1	0
Leoni Township	2	1	1
Leslie	3	3	0
Lexington	3	3	0
Lincoln Park	62	51	11
Lincoln Township	13	11	2
Linden	5	5	0
Livonia	175	150	25
Lowell	9	7	2
Ludington	16	15	1
Luna Pier	3	3	0
Mackinac Island	12	10	2
Mackinaw City	5	5	0
Madison Heights	72	59	13
Madison Township	2	2	0
Mancelona	3	3	0
Manistee	16	14	2
Manistique	8	8	0
Manton	1	1	0
Marenisco Township	1	1	0
Marine City	9	8	1
Marion	1	1	0
Marlette	4	4	0
Marquette	40	34	6
Marshall	20	15	5
Marysville	18	15	3
Mason	14	13	1
Mattawan	5	5	0
Mayville	3	3	0
Melvindale	25	22	3
Memphis	2	2	0
Mendon	2	2	0
Menominee	18	16	2
Meridian Township	49	43	6
Michiana	3	3	0
Midland	52	49	3
Milan	17	12	5
Milford	26	19	7
Millington	1	1	0
Monroe	53	46	7
Montague	5	5	0
Montrose Township	11	11	0
Morenci	4	4	0
Morrice	2	2	0
Mount Morris	9	8	1
Mount Morris Township	37	34	3
Mount Pleasant	39	32	7
Mundy Township	22	19	3
Munising	5	5	0
Muskegon	87	78	9
Muskegon Heights	24	21	3
Muskegon Township	16	15	1
Napoleon Township	3	3	0
Nashville	2	2	0
Negaunee	9	8	1
Newaygo	5	4	1
New Baltimore	21	17	4
Newberry	2	2	0
New Buffalo	7	6	1
New Haven	8	7	1
Niles	29	20	9
North Branch	2	2	0
Northfield Township	13	10	3
North Muskegon	7	7	0
Northville	16	15	1
Northville Township	44	32	12
Norton Shores	29	27	2

Table 78. Law Enforcement Employees, by City, 2005

(Number.)

City	Total law enforcement employees	Total officers	Total civilians
Norvell Township	2	2	0
Norway	6	6	0
Novi	99	70	29
Oakley-Brady	3	3	0
Oak Park	77	65	12
Olivet	3	3	0
Onaway	1	1	0
Ontwa Township-Edwardsburg	8	7	1
Orchard Lake	9	8	1
Oscoda Township	12	11	1
Otisville	1	1	0
Otsego	8	7	1
Ovid	3	3	0
Owosso	23	21	2
Oxford	8	5	3
Parchment	4	3	1
Parma-Sandstone	2	2	0
Paw Paw	11	9	2
Pentwater	2	2	0
Perry	7	6	1
Petoskey	22	20	2
Pigeon	2	2	0
Pinckney	4	4	0
Pinconning	3	3	0
Pittsfield Township	48	36	12
Plainwell	10	9	1
Pleasant Ridge	5	5	0
Plymouth	16	15	1
Plymouth Township	47	31	16
Pontiac	166	138	28
Portage	74	57	17
Port Austin	1	1	0
Port Huron	72	52	20
Portland	7	7	0
Port Sanilac	1	1	0
Potterville	3	3	0
Prairieville Township	3	3	0
Raisin Township	3	3	0
Reading	1	1	0
Redford Township	79	65	14
Reed City	4	4	0
Reese	2	2	0
Richfield Township (Genesee County)	11	9	2
Richfield Township (Roscommon County)	5	5	0
Richland	2	2	0
Richland Township	4	4	0
Richmond	11	8	3
River Rouge	23	20	3
Riverview	32	28	4
Rochester	28	21	7
Rockford	12	10	2
Rockwood	10	8	2
Rogers City	7	7	0
Romeo	12	8	4
Romulus	75	60	15
Roosevelt Park	11	10	1
Rose City	1	1	0
Roseville	96	84	12
Royal Oak	101	83	18
Saginaw	105	94	11
Saginaw Township	47	43	4
Saline	19	14	5
Sandusky	7	6	1
Sault Ste. Marie	27	25	2
Schoolcraft	3	3	0
Scottville	3	3	0
Sebewaing	4	4	0
Shelby	3	3	0
Shelby Township	91	70	21
Shepherd	2	2	0
Somerset Township	2	2	0
Southfield	162	149	13
Southgate	49	40	9
South Haven	25	19	6
South Lyon	20	18	2
South Rockwood	2	2	0
Sparta	7	6	1
Spaulding Township	1	1	0
Spring Arbor Township	2	2	0
Springfield	16	15	1
Spring Lake-Ferrysburg	10	9	1
Springport Township	1	1	0
Stanton	2	2	0
St. Charles	3	3	0
St. Clair	12	10	2
St. Clair Shores	101	85	16
Sterling Heights	225	170	55
St. Ignace	6	6	0
St. Johns	12	10	2
St. Joseph	25	18	7
St. Joseph Township	13	12	1
St. Louis	11	10	1
Sturgis	24	19	5
Sumpter Township	16	15	1
Suttons Bay	2	2	0
Swartz Creek	9	8	1
Sylvan Lake	5	5	0
Taylor	129	100	29
Tecumseh	17	15	2
Thomas Township	8	7	1
Three Oaks	3	3	0
Three Rivers	20	16	4
Tittabawassee Township	4	4	0
Traverse City	36	33	3
Trenton	42	41	1
Troy	193	134	59
Tuscarora Township	8	7	1
Ubly	3	2	1
Unadilla Township	3	3	0
Union City	4	4	0
Utica	22	17	5
Van Buren Township	46	35	11
Vassar	6	6	0
Vernon	3	3	0
Vicksburg	8	7	1
Walker	47	38	9
Walled Lake	19	14	5
Warren	280	239	41
Waterford Township	101	77	24
Waterloo Township	2	2	0
Watertown Township	1	1	0
Watervliet	3	3	0
Wayland	6	5	1
Wayne	55	42	13
West Bloomfield Township	103	78	25
West Branch	6	5	1
Westland	127	100	27
White Cloud	2	2	0
Whitehall	8	8	0
White Lake Township	34	25	9
White Pigeon	4	4	0
Williamston	7	7	0
Wixom	25	21	4
Woodhaven	35	31	4
Woodstock Township	1	1	0
Wyandotte	49	37	12
Wyoming	114	88	26
Yale	4	4	0
Ypsilanti	48	36	12
Zeeland	9	8	1
Zilwaukee	2	2	0
Minnesota			
Albany	4	4	0
Albert Lea	39	29	10
Alexandria	21	17	4
Annandale	5	5	0
Anoka	34	27	7
Appleton	4	4	0
Apple Valley	69	47	22
Austin	34	31	3
Avon	3	3	0
Babbitt	4	4	0
Baxter	14	13	1
Bayport	5	5	0
Becker	6	5	1
Belgrade	2	2	0
Belle Plaine	7	6	1
Bemidji	31	28	3
Benson	7	6	1
Big Lake	14	12	2
Biwabik	7	7	0
Blackduck	3	3	0

Table 78. Law Enforcement Employees, by City, 2005

(Number.)

City	Total law enforcement employees	Total officers	Total civilians
Blaine	61	50	11
Blooming Prairie	3	3	0
Bloomington	147	116	31
Blue Earth	6	6	0
Brainerd	33	26	7
Breckenridge	9	6	3
Brooklyn Center	56	42	14
Brooklyn Park	110	85	25
Browns Valley	2	2	0
Brownton	1	1	0
Buffalo	20	17	3
Burnsville	88	70	18
Caledonia	6	5	1
Cambridge	13	11	2
Cannon Falls	7	7	0
Centennial Lakes	19	17	2
Champlin	33	24	9
Chaska	28	23	5
Chisholm	12	11	1
Cloquet	20	19	1
Cold Spring	7	6	1
Columbia Heights	30	23	7
Coon Rapids	74	63	11
Corcoran	6	6	0
Cottage Grove	54	39	15
Crookston	17	15	2
Crosby	10	8	2
Crystal	38	27	11
Dawson	3	3	0
Dayton	6	5	1
Deephaven-Woodland	8	7	1
Detroit Lakes	16	14	2
Dilworth	7	6	1
Duluth	168	141	27
Eagan	94	68	26
Eagle Lake	3	3	0
East Grand Forks	22	20	2
Eden Prairie	89	63	26
Edina	67	50	17
Elk River	37	29	8
Elmore	1	1	0
Ely	8	7	1
Eveleth	11	10	1
Fairmont	20	17	3
Faribault	34	26	8
Farmington	23	20	3
Fergus Falls	27	21	6
Floodwood	3	3	0
Forest Lake	25	22	3
Fridley	42	37	5
Gilbert	5	5	0
Glencoe	12	11	1
Glenwood	4	4	0
Golden Valley	38	29	9
Goodview	4	4	0
Grand Rapids	20	16	4
Granite Falls	4	4	0
Hallock	1	1	0
Hastings	28	25	3
Hermantown	14	12	2
Hibbing	30	27	3
Hokah	1	1	0
Hopkins	38	26	12
Houston	1	1	0
Hoyt Lakes	5	5	0
Hutchinson	33	22	11
International Falls	13	12	1
Inver Grove Heights	37	31	6
Jackson	7	6	1
Janesville	4	4	0
Jordan	10	8	2
Kasson	9	8	1
Kimball	2	2	0
La Crescent	8	7	1
Lake City	10	9	1
Lake Crystal	3	3	0
Lakefield	3	3	0
Lakes Area	14	12	2
Lakeville	65	48	17
Lester Prairie	3	3	0
Le Sueur	8	7	1
Lewiston	2	2	0
Lino Lakes	28	25	3
Litchfield	10	9	1
Little Falls	13	11	2
Long Prairie	6	6	0
Madison	3	3	0
Mankato	60	48	12
Maple Grove	69	57	12
Maplewood	65	50	15
Marshall	23	21	2
Medina	10	9	1
Melrose	6	5	1
Mendota Heights	17	16	1
Milaca	6	5	1
Minneapolis	1 046	798	248
Minnetonka	75	56	19
Minnetrista	12	11	1
Montevideo	11	10	1
Montgomery	7	6	1
Moorhead	58	46	12
Moose Lake	4	4	0
Mora	7	6	1
Morris	9	8	1
Mound	16	13	3
Mounds View	21	19	2
Mountain Lake	4	4	0
New Brighton	30	28	2
New Hope	33	27	6
Newport	7	7	0
New Prague	11	9	2
New Richland	2	2	0
New Ulm	23	20	3
North Branch	13	11	2
Northfield	28	22	6
North Mankato	13	12	1
North St. Paul	16	14	2
Oakdale	38	30	8
Oak Park Heights	10	9	1
Olivia	5	5	0
Orono	23	21	2
Ortonville	4	4	0
Osseo	6	5	1
Owatonna	31	29	2
Park Rapids	9	8	1
Paynesville	4	4	0
Plainview	5	5	0
Plymouth	79	67	12
Princeton	11	9	2
Prior Lake	25	22	3
Proctor	8	7	1
Ramsey	25	20	5
Red Wing	32	26	6
Redwood Falls	13	11	2
Richfield	56	43	13
Richmond	2	2	0
Robbinsdale	27	21	6
Rochester	165	120	45
Roseau	6	5	1
Rosemount	22	19	3
Roseville	54	47	7
Sartell	15	13	2
Sauk Centre	7	6	1
Sauk Rapids	14	13	1
Savage	32	27	5
Shakopee	47	38	9
Silver Bay	5	5	0
Silver Lake	2	2	0
Slayton	4	4	0
Sleepy Eye	6	6	0
South Lake Minnetonka	16	14	2
South St. Paul	27	25	2
Springfield	3	3	0
Spring Grove	2	2	0
Spring Lake Park	13	11	2
St. Anthony	22	20	2
Staples	5	5	0
St. Charles	3	3	0
St. Cloud	117	92	25
Stewart	2	2	0

Table 78. Law Enforcement Employees, by City, 2005

(Number.)

City	Total law enforcement employees	Total officers	Total civilians
St. Francis	11	9	2
Stillwater	26	22	4
St. James	8	7	1
St. Joseph	8	7	1
St. Louis Park	69	51	18
St. Paul	746	572	174
St. Paul Park	8	8	0
St. Peter	19	14	5
Thief River Falls	17	16	1
Tracy	4	4	0
Two Harbors	8	7	1
Virginia	22	21	1
Wabasha	7	6	1
Wadena	8	7	1
Waite Park	15	12	3
Warroad	6	5	1
Waseca	15	13	2
Wayzata	11	9	2
Wells	4	4	0
West Hennepin	11	9	2
West St. Paul	30	25	5
Wheaton	4	3	1
White Bear Lake	33	26	7
Willmar	35	32	3
Windom	9	8	1
Winnebago	2	2	0
Winona	44	38	6
Winsted	4	4	0
Woodbury	62	53	9
Worthington	31	23	8
Wyoming	7	7	0
Zumbrota	6	6	0
Mississippi			
Aberdeen	25	20	5
Amory	25	19	6
Baldwyn	12	11	1
Batesville	45	36	9
Bay St. Louis	35	25	10
Belzoni	16	10	6
Booneville	31	25	6
Brandon	50	33	17
Brookhaven	35	26	9
Bruce	6	6	0
Byhalia	13	8	5
Canton	34	26	8
Clarksdale	50	36	14
Cleveland	53	41	12
Coldwater	2	2	0
Collins	15	11	4
Columbia	32	20	12
Columbus	79	68	11
Como	4	4	0
Crystal Springs	20	14	6
Edwards	1	1	0
Eupora	8	7	1
Fayette	8	4	4
Florence	13	10	3
Flowood	45	34	11
Fulton	11	11	0
Gloster	7	5	2
Greenville	129	94	35
Greenwood	64	55	9
Grenada	45	40	5
Gulfport	247	177	70
Hattiesburg	178	106	72
Hazlehurst	14	14	0
Heidelberg	6	5	1
Hollandale	10	6	4
Holly Springs	25	19	6
Horn Lake	65	53	12
Houston	11	7	4
Indianola	32	25	7
Inverness	6	5	1
Itta Bena	8	4	4
Iuka	12	9	3
Jackson	685	483	202
Kosciusko	19	19	0
Laurel	80	55	25
Leakesville	5	2	3
Leland	22	16	6
Lexington	11	6	5
Long Beach	50	34	16
Lucedale	18	12	6
Madison	58	44	14
Magee	17	13	4
Magnolia	5	5	0
Marks	5	5	0
McComb	65	36	29
McLain	2	1	1
Mendenhall	9	6	3
Meridian	110	92	18
Moorhead	5	5	0
Morton	14	10	4
Moss Point	28	20	8
Mound Bayou	8	7	1
Natchez	76	51	25
New Albany	26	24	2
Newton	14	9	5
Ocean Springs	47	37	10
Okolona	10	10	0
Olive Branch	58	55	3
Oxford	59	49	10
Pascagoula	89	59	30
Pass Christian	27	21	6
Pearl	60	45	15
Pelahatchie	8	6	2
Petal	32	25	7
Philadelphia	30	22	8
Picayune	63	40	23
Pickens	9	9	0
Poplarville	11	10	1
Port Gibson	13	7	6
Purvis	9	6	3
Quitman	8	8	0
Raymond	5	5	0
Richland	39	28	11
Ridgeland	84	57	27
Ripley	15	14	1
Rolling Fork	6	5	1
Rosedale	6	5	1
Ruleville	12	8	4
Sandersville	4	3	1
Senatobia	17	15	2
Shelby	7	3	4
Southaven	106	84	22
Starkville	54	47	7
Stonewall	7	1	6
Summit	8	7	1
Sunflower	3	3	0
Tchula	4	4	0
Tupelo	124	110	14
Tylertown	7	6	1
Utica	6	6	0
Vaiden	5	5	0
Verona	6	6	0
Vicksburg	98	72	26
Water Valley	11	11	0
Waynesboro	16	13	3
West Point	34	25	9
Wiggins	14	11	3
Winona	13	11	2
Yazoo City	40	25	15
Missouri			
Adrian	2	2	0
Advance	3	3	0
Alton	2	2	0
Anderson	4	4	0
Appleton City	2	2	0
Arbyrd	1	1	0
Archie	2	2	0
Arnold	60	48	12
Ash Grove	4	3	1
Ashland	5	5	0
Aurora	22	15	7
Ava	10	8	2
Ballwin	66	51	15
Bates City	2	2	0
Battlefield	5	5	0
Bella Villa	2	2	0
Bellefontaine Neighbors	30	29	1
Bellflower	1	1	0
Bel-Nor	10	9	1
Bel-Ridge	18	16	2

Table 78. Law Enforcement Employees, by City, 2005

(Number.)

City	Total law enforcement employees	Total officers	Total civilians
Belton	61	41	20
Berkeley	58	47	11
Bernie	10	5	5
Bethany	6	6	0
Beverly Hills	5	2	3
Billings	3	3	0
Birch Tree	1	1	0
Bismarck	3	3	0
Bland	3	2	1
Bloomfield	3	3	0
Blue Springs	105	77	28
Bolivar	21	16	5
Boonville	28	21	7
Bourbon	7	7	0
Bowling Green	13	8	5
Branson	53	39	14
Branson West	6	6	0
Breckenridge Hills	16	15	1
Brentwood	34	25	9
Bridgeton	63	51	12
Brookfield	17	10	7
Bucklin	1	1	0
Buckner	3	2	1
Buffalo	9	8	1
Butler	38	21	17
Byrnes Mill	5	5	0
Cabool	10	6	4
California	7	6	1
Camdenton	14	11	3
Cameron	26	20	6
Canton	6	5	1
Cape Girardeau	104	76	28
Carl Junction	18	13	5
Carrollton	6	5	1
Carterville	6	5	1
Carthage	37	28	9
Caruthersville	21	20	1
Cassville	9	9	0
Centralia	13	8	5
Chaffee	10	6	4
Charlack	8	8	0
Charleston	22	16	6
Chesterfield	91	81	10
Chillicothe	21	16	5
Clarkton	3	3	0
Claycomo	13	12	1
Clayton	61	52	9
Clever	2	2	0
Clinton	21	20	1
Cole Camp	3	3	0
Columbia	171	137	34
Concordia	6	6	0
Conway	1	1	0
Cool Valley	11	10	1
Cooter	2	1	1
Cottleville	12	11	1
Country Club Hills	9	9	0
Crane	4	4	0
Crestwood	39	33	6
Creve Coeur	57	46	11
Crocker	3	3	0
Crystal City	21	16	5
Cuba	13	12	1
De Soto	19	14	5
Des Peres	48	38	10
Dexter	22	16	6
Diamond	2	2	0
Dixon	10	6	4
Doniphan	12	9	3
Drexel	2	2	0
Duenweg	4	4	0
Duquesne	8	5	3
East Lynne	1	1	0
East Prairie	11	7	4
Edina	4	3	1
Edmundson	8	7	1
Eldon	12	11	1
El Dorado Springs	12	8	4
Ellington	2	2	0
Ellisville	21	20	1
Ellsinore	1	1	0
Eminence	1	1	0
Eureka	27	23	4
Excelsior Springs	27	18	9
Fair Grove	3	3	0
Fair Play	1	1	0
Farmington	34	26	8
Fayette	8	8	0
Ferguson	61	52	9
Ferrelview	1	1	0
Festus	37	26	11
Florissant	104	83	21
Foley	1	1	0
Forsyth	7	6	1
Fredericktown	6	5	1
Freeman	1	1	0
Frontenac	27	21	6
Fulton	31	24	7
Gainesville	3	3	0
Gallatin	1	1	0
Garden City	4	4	0
Gerald	5	5	0
Gideon	2	2	0
Gilman City	1	1	0
Gladstone	42	42	0
Glasgow	4	4	0
Glendale	14	11	3
Golden City	1	1	0
Goodman	2	2	0
Gower	2	2	0
Grain Valley	22	18	4
Granby	4	4	0
Grandin	1	1	0
Grandview	62	49	13
Greenfield	3	3	0
Greenwood	6	6	0
Hallsville	3	3	0
Hamilton	3	3	0
Hannibal	49	36	13
Harrisonville	27	19	8
Hartville	2	2	0
Hawk Point	1	1	0
Hayti	9	8	1
Hayti Heights	1	1	0
Hazelwood	81	67	14
Henrietta	1	1	0
Herculaneum	11	10	1
Hermann	12	7	5
Higbee	1	1	0
Higginsville	15	9	6
Highlandville	2	2	0
Hillsboro	8	8	0
Hillsdale	14	13	1
Holcomb	2	2	0
Holden	9	8	1
Hollister	14	9	5
Holt	1	1	0
Holts Summit	9	8	1
Houston	5	5	0
Humansville	1	1	0
Huntsville	2	2	0
Iberia	3	3	0
Independence	279	197	82
Indian Point	1	1	0
Iron Mountain Lake	1	1	0
Ironton	6	4	2
Jackson	30	22	8
JASCO Metropolitan	5	4	1
Jefferson City	109	82	27
Jennings	47	43	4
Joplin	87	76	11
Kahoka	3	3	0
Kansas City	1 998	1 272	726
Kearney	13	12	1
Kennett	26	21	5
Keytesville	1	1	0
Kimberling City	9	6	3
Kirksville	28	25	3
Kirkwood	63	53	10
Knob Noster	11	7	4

Table 78. Law Enforcement Employees, by City, 2005

(Number.)

City	Total law enforcement employees	Total officers	Total civilians
Ladue	33	27	6
La Grange	8	7	1
Lake Lotawana	10	8	2
Lake Ozark	16	10	6
Lakeshire	4	4	0
Lake St. Louis	33	25	8
Lake Tapawingo	1	1	0
Lake Waukomis	1	1	0
Lake Winnebago	4	4	0
Lamar	11	10	1
La Monte	2	2	0
Lanagan	1	1	0
La Plata	3	3	0
Lathrop	4	4	0
Laurie	6	6	0
Lawson	7	6	1
Leadwood	3	3	0
Lebanon	38	28	10
Lee's Summit	155	105	50
Lexington	9	8	1
Liberal	2	2	0
Liberty	55	38	17
Licking	4	4	0
Lilbourn	3	3	0
Lincoln	3	3	0
Linn	3	3	0
Linn Creek	3	3	0
Lockwood	2	2	0
Lone Jack	5	5	0
Louisiana	14	9	5
Lowry City	1	1	0
Macon	15	13	2
Malden	13	11	2
Manchester	38	35	3
Mansfield	4	4	0
Maplewood	31	28	3
Marble Hill	3	3	0
Marceline	9	6	3
Marionville	4	4	0
Marquand	1	1	0
Marshall	35	23	12
Marshfield	10	10	0
Marston	1	1	0
Marthasville	1	1	0
Maryland Heights	94	78	16
Maryville	27	21	6
Matthews	1	1	0
Maysville	1	1	0
Memphis	4	4	0
Merriam Woods	1	1	0
Mexico	37	34	3
Milan	4	4	0
Miller	2	1	1
Miner	12	7	5
Moberly	45	33	12
Moline Acres	7	7	0
Monett	28	19	9
Monroe City	7	6	1
Montgomery City	6	6	0
Morehouse	1	1	0
Mosby	2	2	0
Mound City	2	2	0
Mountain Grove	14	9	5
Mountain View	7	6	1
Mount Vernon	9	9	0
Napoleon	2	2	0
Naylor	1	1	0
Neosho	28	25	3
Nevada	35	23	12
New Florence	1	1	0
New Franklin	2	1	1
New Haven	7	7	0
New London	2	2	0
New Madrid	7	6	1
New Melle	2	2	0
Nixa	31	22	9
Noel	4	4	0
Norborne	1	1	0
North Kansas City	60	46	14
Northmoor	2	2	0
Northwoods	20	18	2
Oak Grove	14	13	1
Oakview Village	5	4	1
Odessa	11	11	0
O'Fallon	128	101	27
Olympian Village	2	2	0
Oran	2	2	0
Orrick	2	2	0
Osage Beach	35	22	13
Osceola	2	2	0
Overland	56	43	13
Owensville	9	8	1
Ozark	32	28	4
Pacific	23	16	7
Pagedale	20	15	5
Park Hills	14	13	1
Parkville	16	15	1
Parma	3	2	1
Pasadena Park	34	22	12
Peculiar	11	10	1
Perryville	26	25	1
Pevely	19	14	5
Piedmont	6	6	0
Pierce City	4	4	0
Pilot Grove	1	1	0
Pilot Knob	1	1	0
Pineville	4	4	0
Platte City	12	12	0
Platte Woods	2	2	0
Plattsburg	5	5	0
Pleasant Hill	15	11	4
Pleasant Hope	1	1	0
Pleasant Valley	11	7	4
Polo	1	1	0
Poplar Bluff	53	43	10
Portageville	13	9	4
Potosi	14	12	2
Puxico	2	2	0
Randolph	2	2	0
Raymore	33	24	9
Raytown	74	56	18
Reeds Spring	2	2	0
Republic	27	20	7
Rich Hill	7	3	4
Richland	5	4	1
Richmond	14	9	5
Richmond Heights	41	40	1
Risco	1	1	0
Riverside	21	16	5
Riverview	10	10	0
Rockaway Beach	2	2	0
Rock Hill	9	8	1
Rock Port	2	2	0
Rogersville	6	6	0
Rolla	53	36	17
Salem	19	14	5
Salisbury	5	4	1
Sarcoxie	2	2	0
Savannah	5	5	0
Scott City	16	11	5
Sedalia	56	44	12
Senath	3	3	0
Seneca	6	6	0
Seymour	6	6	0
Shelbina	4	4	0
Shrewsbury	20	18	2
Sikeston	81	69	12
Silex	1	1	0
Slater	7	3	4
Smithville	15	14	1
Southwest City	3	3	0
Sparta	3	3	0
Springfield	409	331	78
St. Ann	51	38	13
St. Clair	14	12	2
Steele	9	9	0
St. George	4	4	0
St. James	6	6	0
St. John	25	23	2
St. Joseph	155	115	40

Table 78. Law Enforcement Employees, by City, 2005

(Number.)

City	Total law enforcement employees	Total officers	Total civilians
St. Louis	1 909	1 320	589
St. Marys	1	1	0
Stover	3	3	0
St. Peters	104	83	21
Strafford	6	6	0
Sturgeon	1	1	0
Sugar Creek	21	15	6
Sullivan	25	17	8
Summersville	1	1	0
Sunset Hills	31	24	7
Sweet Springs	3	3	0
Tarkio	3	3	0
Thayer	11	7	4
Theodosia	1	1	0
Tipton	3	3	0
Town and Country	41	34	7
Tracy	1	1	0
Trenton	19	12	7
Trimble	1	1	0
Troy	23	22	1
Truesdale	2	1	1
Union	21	19	2
Unionville	4	4	0
University City	98	77	21
Uplands Park	10	9	1
Van Buren	2	2	0
Vandalia	8	5	3
Velda City	12	9	3
Verona	2	2	0
Versailles	10	10	0
Viburnum	1	1	0
Vienna	1	1	0
Vinita Park	13	12	1
Walnut Grove	2	2	0
Wardell	1	1	0
Warrensburg	34	31	3
Warrenton	19	16	3
Warsaw	7	7	0
Warson Woods	8	7	1
Washburn	1	1	0
Washington	31	28	3
Waynesville	8	7	1
Weatherby Lake	3	3	0
Webb City	26	20	6
Webster Groves	46	43	3
Wellsville	4	4	0
Weston	4	4	0
West Plains	26	22	4
Wheaton	2	1	1
Willard	10	9	1
Willow Springs	7	6	1
Windsor	6	6	0
Winfield	3	2	1
Winona	4	4	0
Wood Heights	1	1	0
Woodson Terrace	20	17	3
Wright City	9	8	1
Montana			
Baker	3	3	0
Belgrade	16	12	4
Billings	145	124	21
Boulder	2	2	0
Bozeman	52	46	6
Bridger	2	2	0
Chinook	4	4	0
Colstrip	13	6	7
Columbia Falls	15	9	6
Columbus	5	4	1
Conrad	5	5	0
Cut Bank	9	7	2
Dillon	7	6	1
Ennis	1	1	0
Eureka	3	3	0
Fort Benton	4	3	1
Glasgow	8	7	1
Glendive	15	9	6
Great Falls	113	77	36
Hamilton	16	14	2
Havre	27	18	9
Helena	68	46	22
Hot Springs	1	1	0
Joliet	2	2	0
Kalispell	45	34	11
Laurel	19	12	7
Lewistown	23	14	9
Libby	5	5	0
Livingston	13	13	0
Manhattan	3	3	0
Miles City	18	12	6
Missoula	115	96	19
Pinesdale	3	3	0
Plains	3	3	0
Plentywood	5	4	1
Polson	12	10	2
Poplar	5	4	1
Red Lodge	6	6	0
Ronan City	5	4	1
Sidney	10	9	1
Stevensville	3	3	0
St. Ignatius	2	2	0
Thompson Falls	4	4	0
Three Forks	4	3	1
Troy	3	3	0
West Yellowstone	10	5	5
Whitefish	19	15	4
Whitehall	3	2	1
Wolf Point	7	6	1
Nebraska			
Albion	3	3	0
Alliance	23	17	6
Ashland	6	5	1
Auburn	7	7	0
Aurora	7	7	0
Bayard	3	3	0
Beatrice	33	22	11
Bellevue	93	81	12
Blair	17	15	2
Bridgeport	2	2	0
Broken Bow	7	6	1
Central City	6	5	1
Chadron	19	13	6
Columbus	52	34	18
Crete	15	10	5
David City	6	5	1
Elkhorn	15	14	1
Fairbury	9	8	1
Falls City	13	9	4
Fremont	44	38	6
Gering	19	16	3
Gothenburg	9	5	4
Grand Island	84	76	8
Hastings	47	33	14
Holdrege	16	10	6
Imperial	4	4	0
Kearney	62	48	14
Kimball	6	5	1
La Vista	32	28	4
Lexington	17	15	2
Lincoln	414	315	99
Lyons	1	1	0
Madison	4	4	0
McCook	20	16	4
Milford	5	5	0
Minden	5	5	0
Mitchell	3	3	0
Nebraska City	15	14	1
Neligh	2	2	0
Norfolk	61	41	20
North Platte	66	41	25
Ogallala	11	10	1
Omaha	954	775	179
O'Neill	8	7	1
Ord	4	4	0
Papillion	35	31	4
Pierce	3	3	0
Plainview	2	2	0
Plattsmouth	18	16	2
Ralston	14	13	1

Table 78. Law Enforcement Employees, by City, 2005

(Number.)

City	Total law enforcement employees	Total officers	Total civilians
Schuyler	9	7	2
Scottsbluff	32	27	5
Scribner	1	1	0
Seward	12	11	1
Sidney	15	13	2
South Sioux City	28	27	1
St. Paul	4	4	0
Syracuse	2	2	0
Tecumseh	4	3	1
Valentine	4	3	1
Valley	5	5	0
Wahoo	6	6	0
Wayne	12	7	5
West Point	8	7	1
Wilber	4	4	0
Wymore	3	3	0
York	20	14	6
Nevada			
Boulder City	40	29	11
Carlin	6	5	1
Elko	41	36	5
Fallon	34	22	12
Henderson	406	295	111
Las Vegas Metropolitan Police Department	4 310	2 053	2 257
Lovelock	7	6	1
Mesquite	40	29	11
North Las Vegas	382	245	137
Reno	441	355	86
Sparks	152	106	46
West Wendover	22	15	7
Winnemucca	18	15	3
Yerington	7	6	1
New Hampshire			
Alstead	2	2	0
Alton	13	11	2
Amherst	23	18	5
Andover	1	1	0
Antrim	4	4	0
Auburn	9	7	2
Barnstead	6	6	0
Barrington	9	8	1
Bartlett	4	4	0
Bedford	41	30	11
Belmont	14	12	2
Bennington	2	2	0
Berlin	30	22	8
Bethlehem	4	4	0
Boscawen	7	6	1
Bow	17	11	6
Brentwood	5	5	0
Bristol	9	7	2
Campton	6	5	1
Candia	7	6	1
Canterbury	2	2	0
Carroll	4	4	0
Charlestown	8	5	3
Chester	3	2	1
Claremont	26	21	5
Colebrook	8	5	3
Concord	96	74	22
Conway	29	20	9
Danville	3	3	0
Deerfield	9	8	1
Deering	2	2	0
Derry	75	60	15
Dover	68	56	12
Dublin	4	3	1
Dunbarton	2	2	0
Durham	22	19	3
Enfield	7	6	1
Epping	14	12	2
Epsom	6	5	1
Exeter	33	23	10
Farmington	14	12	2
Fitzwilliam	4	3	1
Franconia	3	3	0
Franklin	21	14	7
Freedom	2	2	0
Fremont	3	3	0
Gilford	23	17	6
Gilmanton	6	5	1
Goffstown	40	29	11
Gorham	10	7	3
Grantham	4	4	0
Greenland	7	7	0
Hampstead	7	7	0
Hampton	41	34	7
Hancock	3	3	0
Hanover	32	18	14
Haverhill	8	7	1
Henniker	10	8	2
Hillsborough	16	10	6
Hinsdale	8	7	1
Hooksett	34	25	9
Hopkinton	9	7	2
Hudson	59	44	15
Jaffrey	12	11	1
Keene	57	42	15
Kingston	10	9	1
Laconia	46	34	12
Lancaster	8	7	1
Lebanon	48	35	13
Lee	8	7	1
Lincoln	12	7	5
Lisbon	3	3	0
Litchfield	12	10	2
Littleton	16	13	3
Londonderry	58	43	15
Loudon	7	6	1
Madison	2	2	0
Manchester	263	202	61
Marlborough	3	3	0
Meredith	17	13	4
Merrimack	50	37	13
Middleton	3	3	0
Milford	30	26	4
Milton	6	5	1
Mont Vernon	2	2	0
Moultonborough	15	11	4
Nashua	217	162	55
New Boston	5	4	1
New Durham	5	4	1
Newfields	3	3	0
New Hampton	3	3	0
Newington	11	10	1
New Ipswich	5	4	1
Newmarket	19	13	6
Newport	16	12	4
Newton	8	5	3
Northfield	11	10	1
North Hampton	13	12	1
Northwood	5	4	1
Nottingham	7	6	1
Ossipee	9	8	1
Pelham	26	19	7
Pembroke	13	11	2
Peterborough	13	11	2
Pittsfield	8	7	1
Plaistow	24	16	8
Plymouth	17	10	7
Portsmouth	88	67	21
Raymond	26	18	8
Rindge	10	8	2
Rochester	67	50	17
Rollinsford	4	4	0
Rye	10	9	1
Sandown	6	6	0
Sandwich	2	2	0
Seabrook	36	28	8
Strafford	3	3	0
Stratham	11	10	1
Thornton	5	4	1
Tilton	15	13	2

Table 78. Law Enforcement Employees, by City, 2005

(Number.)

City	Total law enforcement employees	Total officers	Total civilians
Troy	4	4	0
Tuftonboro	3	3	0
Wakefield	10	9	1
Walpole	4	3	1
Warner	5	4	1
Washington	1	1	0
Waterville Valley	6	5	1
Weare	11	10	1
Wilton	7	6	1
Winchester	7	6	1
Windham	19	18	1
Wolfeboro	15	11	4
Woodstock	5	5	0
New Jersey			
Aberdeen Township	41	34	7
Absecon	35	26	9
Allendale	19	14	5
Allenhurst	13	9	4
Allentown	6	6	0
Alpine	13	13	0
Andover Township	16	10	6
Asbury Park	97	79	18
Atlantic City	544	392	152
Atlantic Highlands	20	15	5
Audubon	24	22	2
Avalon	32	20	12
Avon-by-the-Sea	19	12	7
Barnegat Township	45	36	9
Barrington	16	15	1
Bay Head	9	8	1
Bayonne	281	230	51
Beach Haven	15	10	5
Beachwood	20	18	2
Bedminster Township	18	17	1
Belleville	121	112	9
Bellmawr	26	24	2
Belmar	28	21	7
Belvidere	7	6	1
Bergenfield	51	42	9
Berkeley Heights Township	32	25	7
Berkeley Township	90	69	21
Berlin	19	18	1
Berlin Township	21	19	2
Bernards Township	41	37	4
Bernardsville	24	18	6
Beverly	8	7	1
Blairstown Township	8	7	1
Bloomfield	150	132	18
Bloomingdale	16	15	1
Bogota	20	15	5
Boonton	26	21	5
Boonton Township	12	12	0
Bordentown	13	11	2
Bordentown Township	27	22	5
Bound Brook	27	22	5
Bradley Beach	19	15	4
Branchburg Township	28	26	2
Brick Township	161	126	35
Bridgeton	85	72	13
Bridgewater Township	93	77	16
Brielle	16	15	1
Brigantine	49	38	11
Brooklawn	7	7	0
Buena	15	9	6
Burlington	37	33	4
Burlington Township	54	45	9
Butler	22	17	5
Byram Township	16	15	1
Caldwell	23	22	1
Califon	2	2	0
Camden	500	416	84
Cape May	28	22	6
Carlstadt	32	32	0
Carney's Point Township	27	21	6
Carteret	70	60	10
Cedar Grove Township	35	32	3
Chatham	30	24	6
Chatham Township	30	24	6
Cherry Hill Township	169	136	33
Chesilhurst	11	10	1
Chester	9	8	1
Chesterfield Township	9	9	0
Chester Township	17	16	1
Cinnaminson Township	37	32	5
Clark Township	50	40	10
Clayton	21	18	3
Clementon	18	16	2
Cliffside Park	58	48	10
Clifton	183	154	29
Clinton	10	10	0
Clinton Township	24	21	3
Closter	27	21	6
Collingswood	35	31	4
Colts Neck Township	23	22	1
Cranbury Township	18	17	1
Cranford Township	68	52	16
Cresskill	29	24	5
Deal	20	16	4
Delanco Township	11	10	1
Delaware Township	8	7	1
Delran Township	37	32	5
Demarest	13	13	0
Denville Township	42	33	9
Deptford Township	75	69	6
Dover	41	36	5
Dover Township	193	157	36
Dumont	41	33	8
Dunellen	21	17	4
Eastampton Township	18	17	1
East Brunswick Township	121	93	28
East Greenwich Township	21	19	2
East Hanover Township	40	33	7
East Newark	7	5	2
East Orange	300	258	42
East Rutherford	38	34	4
East Windsor Township	61	47	14
Eatontown	45	36	9
Edgewater	31	30	1
Edgewater Park Township	14	13	1
Edison Township	266	211	55
Egg Harbor City	23	14	9
Egg Harbor Township	122	96	26
Elizabeth	445	342	103
Elk Township	12	12	0
Elmer	1	1	0
Elmwood Park	43	41	2
Emerson	22	19	3
Englewood	95	82	13
Englewood Cliffs	28	27	1
Englishtown	8	8	0
Essex Fells	13	13	0
Evesham Township	84	75	9
Ewing Township	97	79	18
Fairfield Township	44	38	6
Fair Haven	16	12	4
Fair Lawn	70	59	11
Fairview	35	32	3
Fanwood	22	21	1
Far Hills	6	6	0
Flemington	15	14	1
Florence Township	32	26	6
Florham Park	38	32	6
Fort Lee	128	108	20
Franklin	14	13	1
Franklin Lakes	27	22	5
Franklin Township (Gloucester County)	31	28	3
Franklin Township (Hunterdon County)	6	6	0
Franklin Township (Somerset County)	127	106	21
Freehold	42	34	8
Freehold Township	86	70	16
Frenchtown	2	2	0
Galloway Township	80	67	13
Garfield	64	57	7
Garwood	19	16	3
Gibbsboro	7	7	0
Glassboro	50	44	6
Glen Ridge	34	29	5
Glen Rock	22	21	1
Gloucester City	32	29	3
Gloucester Township	130	110	20
Green Brook Township	28	22	6
Greenwich Township (Gloucester County)	23	18	5
Greenwich Township (Warren County)	11	10	1
Guttenberg	29	22	7

Table 78. Law Enforcement Employees, by City, 2005

(Number.)

City	Total law enforcement employees	Total officers	Total civilians
Hackensack	134	111	23
Hackettstown	22	21	1
Haddonfield	27	25	2
Haddon Heights	18	17	1
Haddon Township	32	30	2
Haledon	21	17	4
Hamburg	10	9	1
Hamilton Township, Atlantic County	84	68	16
Hamilton Township, Mercer County	211	181	30
Hammonton	42	31	11
Hanover Township	39	32	7
Harding Township	16	15	1
Hardyston Township	27	19	8
Harrington Park	11	11	0
Harrison	70	50	20
Harrison Township	16	16	0
Harvey Cedars	8	8	0
Hasbrouck Heights	34	32	2
Haworth	13	12	1
Hawthorne	38	33	5
Hazlet Township	55	47	8
Helmetta	3	3	0
High Bridge	6	6	0
Highland Park	35	28	7
Highlands	18	14	4
Hightstown	18	13	5
Hillsborough Township	69	56	13
Hillsdale	22	20	2
Hillside Township	89	73	16
Hi-Nella	5	5	0
Hoboken	176	161	15
Ho-Ho-Kus	18	16	2
Holland Township	7	6	1
Holmdel Township	53	43	10
Hopatcong	37	28	9
Hopewell Township	41	33	8
Howell Township	114	95	19
Independence Township	10	9	1
Interlaken	6	6	0
Irvington	218	186	32
Island Heights	10	5	5
Jackson Township	102	84	18
Jamesburg	18	13	5
Jefferson Township	46	39	7
Jersey City	1 025	838	187
Keansburg	35	29	6
Kearny	129	120	9
Kenilworth	31	30	1
Keyport	25	19	6
Kinnelon	16	15	1
Lacey Township	58	43	15
Lake Como	9	9	0
Lakehurst	10	9	1
Lakewood Township	139	112	27
Lambertville	13	11	2
Laurel Springs	7	7	0
Lavallette	16	12	4
Lawnside	11	10	1
Lawrence Township	85	70	15
Lebanon Township	10	9	1
Leonia	24	19	5
Lincoln Park	29	25	4
Linden	138	128	10
Lindenwold	44	41	3
Linwood	24	20	4
Little Egg Harbor Township	53	42	11
Little Falls Township	27	23	4
Little Ferry	29	26	3
Little Silver	21	15	6
Livingston Township	85	74	11
Lodi	51	42	9
Logan Township	19	18	1
Long Beach Township	51	40	11
Long Branch	125	100	25
Long Hill Township	37	29	8
Longport	19	14	5
Lopatcong Township	15	14	1
Lower Alloways Creek Township	17	12	5
Lower Township	59	45	14
Lumberton Township	33	29	4
Lyndhurst Township	53	49	4
Madison	38	35	3
Magnolia	11	11	0
Mahwah Township	65	56	9
Manalapan Township	79	64	15
Manasquan	24	18	6
Manchester Township	85	67	18
Mansfield Township, Burlington County	13	11	2
Mansfield Township, Warren County	15	14	1
Mantoloking	9	8	1
Mantua Township	28	26	2
Manville	28	22	6
Maple Shade Township	43	34	9
Maplewood Township	78	63	15
Margate City	45	34	11
Marlboro Township	95	75	20
Matawan	21	19	2
Maywood	28	24	4
Medford Lakes	10	9	1
Medford Township	47	41	6
Mendham	14	12	2
Mendham Township	17	15	2
Merchantville	16	14	2
Metuchen	34	28	6
Middlesex	33	31	2
Middle Township	65	51	14
Middletown Township	130	103	27
Midland Park	14	13	1
Millburn Township	64	54	10
Milltown	18	15	3
Millville	88	75	13
Monmouth Beach	11	10	1
Monroe Township, Gloucester County	79	67	12
Monroe Township, Middlesex County	61	46	15
Montclair	140	117	26
Montgomery Township	43	31	12
Montvale	24	22	2
Montville Township	48	42	6
Moonachie	20	17	3
Moorestown Township	49	39	10
Morris Plains	21	17	4
Morristown	68	60	8
Morris Township	52	43	9
Mountain Lakes	19	14	5
Mountainside	27	22	5
Mount Arlington	13	12	1
Mount Ephraim	14	12	2
Mount Holly Township	29	26	3
Mount Laurel Township	86	72	14
Mount Olive Township	61	51	10
Mullica Township	15	14	1
National Park	7	7	0
Neptune City	21	16	5
Neptune Township	94	74	20
Netcong	12	9	3
Newark	1 550	1 314	236
New Brunswick	173	143	30
Newfield	5	5	0
New Hanover Township	5	4	1
New Milford	38	35	3
New Providence	32	26	6
Newton	31	23	8
North Arlington	37	29	8
North Bergen Township	125	108	17
North Brunswick Township	100	84	16
North Caldwell	21	16	5
Northfield	25	24	1
North Haledon	23	18	5
North Hanover Township	10	9	1
North Plainfield	51	46	5
Northvale	15	14	1
North Wildwood	37	29	8
Norwood	14	13	1
Nutley Township	80	66	14
Oakland	34	28	6
Oaklyn	16	15	1
Ocean City	78	62	16
Ocean Gate	8	7	1
Oceanport	19	14	5
Ocean Township (Monmouth County)	72	60	12

Table 78. Law Enforcement Employees, by City, 2005

(Number.)

City	Total law enforcement employees	Total officers	Total civilians
Ocean Township (Ocean County)	31	18	13
Ogdensburg	7	7	0
Old Bridge Township	140	105	35
Old Tappan	14	13	1
Oradell	24	22	2
Orange	135	114	21
Oxford Township	5	4	1
Palisades Park	41	33	8
Palmyra	19	17	2
Paramus	112	92	20
Park Ridge	19	18	1
Parsippany-Troy Hills Township	131	105	26
Passaic	209	179	30
Paterson	545	444	101
Paulsboro	22	20	2
Peapack and Gladstone	9	8	1
Pemberton	6	5	1
Pemberton Township	66	58	8
Pennington	7	6	1
Pennsauken Township	122	93	29
Penns Grove	21	16	5
Pennsville Township	25	23	2
Pequannock Township	33	28	5
Perth Amboy	167	131	36
Phillipsburg	42	35	7
Pine Beach	7	6	1
Pine Hill	24	22	2
Pine Valley	5	4	1
Piscataway Township	111	92	19
Pitman	16	15	1
Plainfield	183	152	31
Plainsboro Township	45	32	13
Pleasantville	72	59	13
Plumsted Township	11	10	1
Pohatcong Township	13	12	1
Point Pleasant	41	33	8
Point Pleasant Beach	33	26	7
Pompton Lakes	29	25	4
Princeton	42	32	10
Princeton Township	45	35	10
Prospect Park	16	15	1
Rahway	94	81	13
Ramsey	40	34	6
Randolph Township	49	38	11
Raritan	23	18	5
Raritan Township	40	37	3
Readington Township	26	24	2
Red Bank	48	40	8
Ridgefield	33	30	3
Ridgefield Park	37	29	8
Ridgewood	47	43	4
Ringwood	28	23	5
Riverdale	22	17	5
River Edge	26	22	4
Riverside Township	13	13	0
Riverton	7	6	1
River Vale Township	22	21	1
Rochelle Park Township	25	20	5
Rockaway	15	14	1
Rockaway Township	69	56	13
Roseland	33	27	6
Roselle	67	57	10
Roselle Park	42	34	8
Roxbury Township	54	47	7
Rumson	21	17	4
Runnemede	22	20	2
Rutherford	48	43	5
Saddle Brook Township	35	34	1
Saddle River	22	17	5
Salem	23	22	1
Sayreville	109	91	18
Scotch Plains Township	51	44	7
Sea Bright	12	11	1
Sea Girt	16	12	4
Sea Isle City	24	21	3
Seaside Heights	34	22	12
Seaside Park	19	15	4
Secaucus	67	59	8
Ship Bottom	12	11	1
Shrewsbury	21	16	5
Somerdale	14	13	1
Somers Point	32	26	6
Somerville	36	30	6
South Amboy	31	26	5
South Bound Brook	14	13	1
South Brunswick Township	104	77	27
South Hackensack Township	19	18	1
South Harrison Township	5	5	0
South Orange	64	56	8
South Plainfield	72	55	17
South River	39	31	8
South Toms River	12	11	1
Sparta Township	47	39	8
Spotswood	23	19	4
Springfield	45	41	4
Springfield Township	10	9	1
Spring Lake	17	14	3
Spring Lake Heights	15	12	3
Stafford Township	75	53	22
Stanhope	8	7	1
Stillwater Township	4	4	0
Stone Harbor	23	17	6
Stratford	15	15	0
Summit	57	48	9
Surf City	8	8	0
Swedesboro	8	7	1
Teaneck Township	113	98	15
Tenafly	39	34	5
Tewksbury Township	13	12	1
Tinton Falls	42	41	1
Totowa	31	28	3
Trenton	412	359	53
Tuckerton	9	9	0
Union Beach	20	16	4
Union City	221	171	50
Union Township	191	139	52
Upper Saddle River	25	19	6
Ventnor City	51	39	12
Vernon Township	45	35	10
Verona	34	29	5
Vineland	167	145	22
Voorhees Township	67	52	15
Waldwick	24	19	5
Wallington	27	25	2
Wall Township	84	70	14
Wanaque	26	22	4
Warren Township	35	28	7
Washington	14	13	1
Washington Township (Bergen County)	25	24	1
Washington Township (Gloucester County)	93	84	9
Washington Township (Mercer County)	35	27	8
Washington Township (Morris County)	47	34	13
Washington Township (Warren County)	14	13	1
Watchung	35	28	7
Waterford Township	27	24	3
Wayne Township	145	118	27
Weehawken Township	63	58	5
Wenonah	6	6	0
Westampton Township	24	21	3
West Amwell Township	6	5	1
West Caldwell Township	32	27	5
West Deptford Township	45	40	5
Westfield	72	59	13
West Long Branch	25	20	5
West Milford Township	53	46	7
West New York	133	122	11
West Orange	131	115	16
West Paterson	30	25	5
Westville	11	10	1
West Wildwood	5	5	0
West Windsor Township	58	46	12
Westwood	30	26	4
Wharton	23	21	2
Wildwood	59	47	12
Wildwood Crest	29	22	7
Willingboro Township	83	73	10
Winfield Township	10	10	0
Winslow Township	97	80	17
Woodbine	1	1	0
Woodbridge Township	246	196	50

Table 78. Law Enforcement Employees, by City, 2005

(Number.)

City	Total law enforcement employees	Total officers	Total civilians
Woodbury	30	27	3
Woodbury Heights	8	7	1
Woodcliff Lake	19	18	1
Woodlynne	8	7	1
Wood-Ridge	24	21	3
Woodstown	10	9	1
Woolwich Township	18	17	1
Wyckoff Township	32	24	8
New Mexico			
Alamogordo	108	59	49
Albuquerque	1 349	975	374
Angel Fire	5	4	1
Artesia	44	27	17
Aztec	18	14	4
Bayard	5	5	0
Belen	30	18	12
Bloomfield	20	14	6
Bosque Farms	11	10	1
Capitan	3	3	0
Carlsbad	77	55	22
Carrizozo	6	3	3
Cimarron	2	2	0
Clayton	16	6	10
Cloudcroft	3	3	0
Clovis	67	51	16
Corrales	22	19	3
Cuba	6	5	1
Deming	43	38	5
Dexter	6	4	2
Espanola	45	37	8
Estancia	5	4	1
Eunice	12	7	5
Farmington	140	92	48
Grants	28	19	9
Hobbs	122	76	46
Hurley	5	4	1
Jal	10	5	5
Las Cruces	241	166	75
Las Vegas	57	39	18
Lordsburg	13	10	3
Los Alamos	59	30	29
Los Lunas	37	28	9
Lovington	26	19	7
Mesilla	4	4	0
Milan	12	7	5
Moriarty	11	9	2
Portales	39	24	15
Questa	2	1	1
Raton	23	16	7
Red River	8	3	5
Rio Rancho	170	111	59
Ruidoso	36	22	14
Ruidoso Downs	16	11	5
Santa Clara	6	5	1
Santa Fe	178	137	41
Santa Rosa	13	8	5
Silver City	35	30	5
Socorro	32	20	12
Springer	3	3	0
Sunland Park	25	23	2
Taos	37	19	18
Taos Ski Valley	3	3	0
Tatum	7	3	4
Texico	4	4	0
Truth or Consequences	17	15	2
Tularosa	11	7	4
New York			
Addison Town and Village	2	2	0
Akron Village	2	2	0
Albany	456	334	122
Albion Village	13	13	0
Alexandria Bay Village	2	2	0
Alfred Village	6	6	0
Allegany Village	2	2	0
Altamont Village	1	1	0
Amherst Town	187	154	33
Amity Town and Belmont Village	2	2	0

City	Total law enforcement employees	Total officers	Total civilians
Amityville Village	28	25	3
Amsterdam	36	36	0
Angola Village	3	3	0
Arcade Village	6	6	0
Ardsley Village	19	19	0
Asharoken Village	3	3	0
Attica Village	5	5	0
Auburn	79	71	8
Avon Village	5	5	0
Baldwinsville Village	17	14	3
Ballston Spa Village	11	7	4
Batavia	39	33	6
Bath Village	15	12	3
Beacon	39	37	2
Bedford Town	50	45	5
Bethlehem Town	61	42	19
Binghamton	158	148	10
Blooming Grove Town	19	17	2
Bolivar Village	1	1	0
Boonville Village	3	3	0
Brant Town	1	1	0
Briarcliff Manor Village	18	18	0
Brighton Town	47	41	6
Brockport Village	13	12	1
Bronxville Village	22	20	2
Buchanan Village	6	6	0
Buffalo	932	783	149
Caledonia Village	3	3	0
Cambridge Village	4	4	0
Camden Village	3	3	0
Camillus Town and Village	26	23	3
Canajoharie Village	5	5	0
Canandaigua	29	26	3
Canastota Village	8	7	1
Canton Village	11	9	2
Carmel Town	41	33	8
Carthage Village	4	4	0
Cayuga Heights Village	7	6	1
Centre Island Village	8	8	0
Chatham Village	4	3	1
Chester Town	10	10	0
Chester Village	16	14	2
Chittenango Village	7	6	1
Cicero Town	9	8	1
Clarkstown Town	195	169	26
Clayton Village	3	3	0
Clay Town	24	19	5
Clifton Springs Village	2	2	0
Clyde Village	5	4	1
Cobleskill Village	12	11	1
Coeymans Town	11	7	4
Cohoes	47	34	13
Colchester Town	2	2	0
Cold Spring Village	1	1	0
Colonie Town	155	109	46
Cooperstown Village	4	3	1
Corinth Village	5	4	1
Corning	26	21	5
Cornwall-on-Hudson Village	5	5	0
Cornwall Town	14	10	4
Cortland	46	43	3
Croton-on-Hudson Village	20	19	1
Cuba Town	4	4	0
Dansville Village	12	9	3
Deerpark Town	3	3	0
Delhi Village	4	4	0
Depew Village	36	29	7
Dewitt Town	39	35	4
Dobbs Ferry Village	26	24	2
Dolgeville Village	4	4	0
Dryden Village	6	6	0
Dunkirk	36	35	1
East Aurora-Aurora Town	21	17	4
Eastchester Town	55	48	7
East Fishkill Town	40	31	9
East Greenbush Town	32	24	8
East Hampton Village	30	26	4
East Rochester Village	9	8	1
East Syracuse Village	12	10	2
Eden Town	5	4	1

Table 78. Law Enforcement Employees, by City, 2005

(Number.)

City	Total law enforcement employees	Total officers	Total civilians
Ellenville Village	12	10	2
Ellicott Town	13	12	1
Ellicottville	3	3	0
Elmira Heights Village	11	11	0
Elmira Town	4	4	0
Elmsford Village	16	16	0
Endicott Village	39	35	4
Evans Town	27	22	5
Fairport Village	11	10	1
Fallsburg Town	24	20	4
Floral Park Village	45	35	10
Florida Village	1	1	0
Fort Edward Village	5	5	0
Fort Plain Village	4	4	0
Frankfort Town	1	1	0
Frankfort Village	2	2	0
Franklinville Village	2	2	0
Fredonia Village	18	14	4
Freeville Village	1	1	0
Fulton City	37	35	2
Garden City Village	66	53	13
Gates Town	40	32	8
Geddes Town	18	16	2
Geneseo Village	8	8	0
Geneva	41	36	5
Glen Cove	57	53	4
Glens Falls	36	31	5
Glenville Town	40	26	14
Gloversville	33	31	2
Goshen Town	12	11	1
Goshen Village	19	17	2
Gouverneur Village	11	8	3
Granville Village	6	6	0
Great Neck Estates Village	16	13	3
Greece Town	101	93	8
Greene Village	3	2	1
Green Island Village	4	3	1
Greenwich Village	2	2	0
Greenwood Lake Village	9	6	3
Groton Village	2	1	1
Guilderland Town	52	36	16
Hamburg Village	16	14	2
Hammondsport Village	1	1	0
Harriman Village	7	7	0
Harrison Town	84	75	9
Hastings-on-Hudson Village	21	21	0
Haverstraw Village	26	25	1
Hempstead Village	146	116	30
Herkimer Village	22	21	1
Highland Falls Village	13	9	4
Hoosick Falls Village	4	2	2
Hornell	23	22	1
Horseheads Village	14	11	3
Hudson Falls Village	16	12	4
Hunter Town	1	1	0
Huntington Bay Village	6	6	0
Hyde Park Town	18	15	3
Ilion Village	19	17	2
Inlet Town	3	2	1
Irondequoit Town	70	57	13
Irvington Village	25	23	2
Ithaca	86	71	15
Jamestown	79	65	14
Johnson City Village	47	40	7
Kenmore Village	24	24	0
Kensington Village	6	6	0
Kent Town	26	21	5
Kings Point Village	25	23	2
Kingston	84	78	6
Kirkland Town	5	5	0
Lackawanna	65	45	20
Lake Placid Village	18	15	3
Lake Success Village	23	20	3
Lancaster Town	61	47	14
Le Roy Village	13	10	3
Lewisboro Town	2	2	0
Lewiston Town and Village	11	10	1
Liberty Village	19	16	3
Little Falls	13	11	2
Liverpool Village	6	5	1
Lloyd Harbor Village	12	11	1
Lloyd Town	13	10	3
Lockport	51	48	3
Long Beach	91	76	15
Lowville Village	6	6	0
Lyons Village	11	9	2
Macedon Town and Village	5	5	0
Malone Village	15	15	0
Malverne Village	26	26	0
Mamaroneck Town	41	40	1
Mamaroneck Village	58	52	6
Manlius Town	44	37	7
Marcellus Village	1	1	0
Marlborough Town	10	8	2
Massena Village	26	21	5
Maybrook Village	2	2	0
Mechanicville	12	11	1
Medina Village	12	11	1
Menands Village	13	10	3
Middleport Village	2	2	0
Mohawk Village	4	4	0
Monroe Village	23	18	5
Montgomery Town	11	10	1
Monticello Village	27	25	2
Moravia Village	1	1	0
Moriah Town	2	2	0
Mount Kisco Village	37	34	3
Mount Morris Village	4	4	0
Mount Pleasant Town	54	45	9
Nassau Village	1	1	0
Newark Village	16	15	1
New Berlin Town	1	1	0
Newburgh	109	96	13
Newburgh Town	70	57	13
New Castle Town	46	42	4
New Hartford Town and Village	32	21	11
New Paltz Town and Village	24	20	4
New Rochelle	249	181	68
New Windsor Town	50	38	12
New York	53 035	35 896	17 139
Niagara Falls	155	138	17
Niagara Town	7	6	1
Niskayuna Town	43	32	11
Nissequogue Village	3	3	0
North Castle Town	41	38	3
North Greenbush Town	19	18	1
Northport Village	19	15	4
North Syracuse Village	16	14	2
North Tonawanda	59	48	11
Ocean Beach Village	2	2	0
Ogdensburg	34	29	5
Old Brookville Village	50	39	11
Old Westbury Village	30	25	5
Olean	44	37	7
Oneida	26	23	3
Oneonta City	30	26	4
Orangetown Town	94	84	10
Orchard Park Town	36	32	4
Ossining Town	19	16	3
Ossining Village	63	57	6
Oxford Village	1	1	0
Oyster Bay Cove Village	11	11	0
Painted Post Village	4	4	0
Palmyra Village	6	5	1
Peekskill	72	57	15
Pelham Manor Village	29	28	1
Pelham Village	28	25	3
Penn Yan Village	14	13	1
Perry Village	13	12	1
Piermont Village	8	8	0
Plattsburgh City	62	52	10
Pleasantville Village	28	26	2
Port Chester Village	62	59	3
Port Dickinson Village	5	4	1
Port Jervis	33	32	1
Portville Village	1	1	0
Port Washington	67	60	7
Poughkeepsie	136	103	33
Poughkeepsie Town	96	87	9
Pound Ridge Town	1	1	0

Table 78. Law Enforcement Employees, by City, 2005

(Number.)

City	Total law enforcement employees	Total officers	Total civilians
Pulaski Village	3	3	0
Quogue Village	14	14	0
Ramapo Town	141	118	23
Ravena Village	3	2	1
Rensselaer City	31	24	7
Riverhead Town	95	79	16
Rochester	845	676	169
Rockville Centre Village	62	52	10
Rome	79	75	4
Rosendale Town	5	4	1
Rotterdam Town	67	43	24
Rouses Point Village	2	2	0
Rye	45	41	4
Rye Brook Village	29	28	1
Sands Point Village	22	22	0
Saranac Lake Village	13	12	1
Saratoga Springs	86	71	15
Saugerties Town	20	15	5
Saugerties Village	11	11	0
Scarsdale Village	43	39	4
Schodack Town	12	10	2
Schoharie Village	1	1	0
Scotia Village	14	13	1
Seneca Falls Village	21	16	5
Shawangunk Town	4	4	0
Sherrill	4	4	0
Sidney Village	9	9	0
Silver Creek Village	6	5	1
Skaneateles Village	6	6	0
Sleepy Hollow Village	24	24	0
Sodus Village	1	1	0
Solvay Village	14	14	0
Southampton Town	140	101	39
South Glens Falls Village	6	6	0
South Nyack Village	6	6	0
Southport Town	1	1	0
Spring Valley Village	69	61	8
Stony Point Town	31	30	1
Suffern Village	32	27	5
Syracuse	550	487	63
Tarrytown Village	42	35	7
Ticonderoga Town	10	7	3
Tonawanda	34	29	5
Tonawanda Town	157	105	52
Troy	131	115	16
Tuckahoe Village	28	25	3
Tupper Lake Village	11	11	0
Tuxedo Park Village	5	3	2
Tuxedo Town	14	12	2
Ulster Town	27	24	3
Utica	185	167	18
Vernon Village	1	1	0
Wallkill Town	38	33	5
Walton Village	6	5	1
Wappingers Falls Village	5	3	2
Warsaw Village	6	6	0
Warwick Town	41	34	7
Washingtonville Village	18	16	2
Waterford Town and Village	11	8	3
Waterloo Village	8	7	1
Watertown	64	60	4
Watervliet	29	25	4
Watkins Glen Village	4	4	0
Waverly Village	11	10	1
Wayland Village	2	2	0
Webster Town and Village	37	31	6
Wellsville Village	15	11	4
Westfield Village	6	6	0
Westhampton Beach Village	17	15	2
West Seneca Town	79	65	14
Whitehall Village	4	4	0
White Plains	267	218	49
Whitesboro Village	7	7	0
Whitestown Town	5	5	0
Windham Town	3	3	0
Wolcott Village	1	1	0
Woodbury Town	26	22	4
Yonkers	685	612	73
Yorktown Town	63	53	10
North Carolina			
Abordoon	24	22	2
Ahoskie	22	17	5
Albemarle	56	50	6
Andrews	6	6	0
Angier	11	10	1
Apex	56	45	11
Archdale	28	23	5
Asheboro	73	67	6
Asheville	220	175	45
Atlantic Beach	21	16	5
Aulander	1	1	0
Aurora	1	1	0
Ayden	21	17	4
Badin	5	5	0
Bailey	3	3	0
Bald Head Islands	12	11	1
Banner Elk	7	7	0
Beaufort	16	15	1
Beech Mountain	14	10	4
Belhaven	13	9	4
Belmont	38	32	6
Benson	16	15	1
Bethel	5	5	0
Beulaville	5	5	0
Biltmore Forest	13	12	1
Biscoe	9	8	1
Black Creek	2	2	0
Black Mountain	22	18	4
Bladenboro	6	6	0
Blowing Rock	15	11	4
Boiling Spring Lakes	7	6	1
Boiling Springs	7	7	0
Bolton	4	2	2
Boone	43	35	8
Brevard	30	24	6
Broadway	4	4	0
Brookford	1	1	0
Bryson City	6	6	0
Bunn	2	2	0
Burgaw	10	9	1
Burlington	147	106	41
Burnsville	8	8	0
Butner	44	39	5
Cameron	1	1	0
Candor	5	5	0
Canton	17	12	5
Cape Carteret	5	5	0
Carolina Beach	28	25	3
Carrboro	35	32	3
Carthage	9	9	0
Cary	173	143	30
Caswell Beach	4	4	0
Catawba	2	2	0
Chadbourn	9	8	1
Chapel Hill	135	105	30
Charlotte-Mecklenburg[1]	1 946	1 513	433
Cherryville	21	16	5
China Grove	11	11	0
Chocowinity	3	3	0
Claremont	9	8	1
Clayton	43	37	6
Cleveland	4	4	0
Clinton	35	32	3
Clyde	4	4	0
Coats	6	6	0
Columbus	6	6	0
Concord	154	129	25
Conover	25	24	1
Conway	1	1	0
Cooleemee	3	3	0
Cornelius	51	37	14
Cramerton	10	10	0
Creedmoor	15	10	5
Dallas	16	12	4
Davidson	20	18	2
Denton	6	6	0
Dobson	4	4	0
Drexel	5	5	0
Dunn	52	38	14
Durham	583	435	148

[1]The employee data presented in this table for Charlotte-Mecklenburg represent only Charlotte-Mecklenburg Police Department employees and exclude Mecklenburg County Sheriff's Office employees.

Table 78. Law Enforcement Employees, by City, 2005

(Number.)

City	Total law enforcement employees	Total officers	Total civilians
East Bend	2	2	0
East Spencer	6	5	1
Eden	55	47	8
Edenton	17	15	2
Elizabeth City	58	45	13
Elizabethtown	15	14	1
Elkin	21	17	4
Elon	15	14	1
Emerald Isle	21	16	5
Enfield	12	11	1
Erwin	9	8	1
Fair Bluff	1	1	0
Fairmont	13	10	3
Faison	2	2	0
Farmville	20	15	5
Fayetteville	473	315	158
Fletcher	15	14	1
Forest City	36	30	6
Four Oaks	6	6	0
Foxfire Village	2	2	0
Franklin	18	16	2
Franklinton	8	7	1
Fremont	3	3	0
Fuquay-Varina	34	29	5
Garland	3	3	0
Garner	58	52	6
Garysburg	2	2	0
Gaston	2	2	0
Gastonia	186	162	24
Gibsonville	16	14	2
Glen Alpine	2	2	0
Goldsboro	113	103	10
Graham	35	32	3
Granite Falls	14	12	2
Granite Quarry	4	4	0
Greensboro	627	511	116
Greenville	206	162	44
Grifton	7	7	0
Hamlet	22	18	4
Havelock	33	27	6
Haw River	8	8	0
Henderson	61	53	8
Hendersonville	44	34	10
Hertford	8	7	1
Hickory	131	105	26
Highlands	11	10	1
High Point	267	231	36
Hillsborough	29	26	3
Holden Beach	8	8	0
Holly Ridge	6	6	0
Holly Springs	31	24	7
Hope Mills	40	29	11
Hot Springs	1	1	0
Hudson	12	11	1
Huntersville	63	56	7
Indian Beach	4	4	0
Jackson	2	1	1
Jacksonville	121	99	22
Jefferson	3	3	0
Jonesville	11	10	1
Kannapolis	94	71	23
Kenansville	4	4	0
Kenly	9	9	0
Kernersville	79	62	17
Kill Devil Hills	31	25	6
King	20	18	2
Kings Mountain	39	32	7
Kingstown	1	1	0
Kinston	84	73	11
Kitty Hawk	17	15	2
Knightdale	20	19	1
Kure Beach	10	9	1
La Grange	8	8	0
Lake Lure	10	9	1
Lake Royale	5	5	0
Lake Waccamaw	3	3	0
Landis	10	9	1
Laurel Park	6	6	0
Laurinburg	43	37	6
Leland	19	16	3
Lenoir	67	51	16
Lexington	75	64	11
Liberty	11	10	1
Lilesville	1	1	0
Lillington	12	11	1
Lincolnton	31	26	5
Littleton	2	2	0
Locust	6	6	0
Longview	15	15	0
Louisburg	13	12	1
Lowell	8	8	0
Lucama	2	2	0
Lumberton	81	69	12
Madison	14	13	1
Maggie Valley	7	6	1
Magnolia	2	2	0
Maiden	16	15	1
Manteo	9	8	1
Marion	25	20	5
Marshall	2	2	0
Mars Hill	5	5	0
Marshville	8	8	0
Matthews	63	52	11
Maxton	15	10	5
Mayodan	15	13	2
Maysville	2	2	0
McAdenville	4	3	1
Mebane	20	17	3
Middlesex	5	5	0
Mint Hill	27	25	2
Mocksville	18	16	2
Monroe	86	76	10
Montreat	3	3	0
Mooresville	61	49	12
Morehead City	45	36	9
Morganton	93	62	31
Morrisville	30	28	2
Mount Airy	51	38	13
Mount Gilead	5	5	0
Mount Holly	41	34	7
Mount Olive	16	15	1
Murfreesboro	13	9	4
Murphy	14	10	4
Nags Head	22	20	2
Nashville	14	13	1
Navassa	3	3	0
New Bern	122	85	37
Newland	7	6	1
Newport	7	7	0
Newton	44	36	8
Newton Grove	3	3	0
Norlina	5	5	0
North Topsail Beach	12	11	1
Northwest	2	2	0
North Wilkesboro	27	23	4
Norwood	8	7	1
Oakboro	4	4	0
Oak Island	28	24	4
Ocean Isle Beach	12	12	0
Old Fort	6	5	1
Oxford	37	31	6
Parkton	3	3	0
Pembroke	16	12	4
Pikeville	2	2	0
Pilot Mountain	10	9	1
Pinebluff	3	3	0
Pinehurst	28	23	5
Pine Knoll Shores	8	8	0
Pine Level	4	4	0
Pinetops	8	6	2
Pineville	46	36	10
Pink Hill	1	1	0
Pittsboro	11	10	1
Plymouth	11	11	0
Princeton	4	4	0
Raeford	14	13	1
Raleigh	809	681	128
Ramseur	8	8	0
Randleman	12	12	0
Ranlo	7	7	0

Table 78. Law Enforcement Employees, by City, 2005

(Number.)

City	Total law enforcement employees	Total officers	Total civilians
Red Springs	21	16	5
Reidsville	50	41	9
Richlands	4	4	0
Rich Square	2	2	0
River Bend	5	5	0
Roanoke Rapids	43	40	3
Robbins	6	6	0
Robersonville	6	6	0
Rockingham	35	30	5
Rockwell	4	4	0
Rocky Mount	189	147	42
Rolesville	7	7	0
Roseboro	3	3	0
Rose Hill	4	4	0
Rowland	7	6	1
Roxboro	36	32	4
Rutherfordton	14	14	0
Salemburg	1	1	0
Salisbury	94	76	18
Saluda	4	4	0
Sanford	100	79	21
Scotland Neck	8	7	1
Selma	29	24	5
Seven Devils	5	5	0
Shallotte	11	10	1
Sharpsburg	9	8	1
Shelby	82	67	15
Siler City	23	18	5
Smithfield	40	36	4
Southern Pines	36	30	6
Southern Shores	11	10	1
Southport	10	9	1
Sparta	6	6	0
Spencer	14	13	1
Spindale	13	13	0
Spring Hope	6	6	0
Spring Lake	21	16	5
Spruce Pine	10	10	0
Stanfield	3	3	0
Stanley	16	12	4
Stantonsburg	5	5	0
Star	4	4	0
Statesville	86	67	19
Stoneville	4	4	0
St. Pauls	18	13	5
Sugar Mountain	5	5	0
Sunset Beach	12	12	0
Surf City	14	13	1
Swansboro	6	6	0
Sylva	13	12	1
Tabor City	9	8	1
Tarboro	34	28	6
Taylorsville	11	11	0
Taylortown	1	1	0
Thomasville	74	67	7
Topsail Beach	8	7	1
Trent Woods	4	4	0
Troutman	7	7	0
Troy	10	9	1
Tryon	10	7	3
Valdese	13	12	1
Vanceboro	2	2	0
Vass	3	3	0
Wadesboro	23	18	5
Wagram	2	2	0
Wake Forest	46	39	7
Wallace	16	13	3
Walnut Cove	6	6	0
Walnut Creek	2	2	0
Warrenton	5	4	1
Warsaw	14	10	4
Washington	46	36	10
Waxhaw	16	14	2
Waynesville	36	31	5
Weaverville	12	11	1
Weldon	7	7	0
Wendell	18	15	3
West Jefferson	8	8	0
Whispering Pines	8	7	1
Whitakers	4	4	0
White Lake	5	5	0
Whiteville	25	21	4
Wilkesboro	23	21	2
Williamston	21	20	1
Wilmington	282	241	41
Wilson	128	109	19
Windsor	8	8	0
Wingate	7	7	0
Winston-Salem	605	457	148
Winterville	17	16	1
Winton	1	1	0
Woodfin	11	11	0
Woodland	1	1	0
Wrightsville Beach	26	21	5
Yadkinville	12	11	1
Yanceyville	5	5	0
Youngsville	9	8	1
Zebulon	19	18	1
North Dakota			
Beulah	6	5	1
Bismarck	111	87	24
Bowman	4	3	1
Carrington	4	4	0
Cavalier	4	4	0
Crosby	2	2	0
Devils Lake	18	16	2
Dickinson	36	24	12
Emerado	2	1	1
Fargo	146	128	18
Fessenden	1	1	0
Grafton	11	10	1
Grand Forks	93	78	15
Harvey	3	3	0
Hazen	4	4	0
Hillsboro	2	2	0
Jamestown	32	28	4
Lamoure	2	2	0
Larimore	2	2	0
Lincoln	2	2	0
Lisbon	3	3	0
Mandan	37	28	9
Mayville	3	3	0
Minot	82	60	22
Napoleon	1	1	0
Northwood	2	2	0
Oakes	3	3	0
Powers Lake	1	1	0
Rolla	4	3	1
Rugby	4	4	0
South Heart	1	1	0
Steele	1	1	0
Thompson	1	1	0
Valley City	18	13	5
Wahpeton	16	14	2
Watford City	4	4	0
West Fargo	40	28	12
Williston	29	21	8
Wishek	2	2	0
Ohio			
Ada	11	8	3
Akron	512	469	43
Alliance	55	42	13
Amberley Village	20	16	4
Amherst	26	20	6
Ansonia	2	2	0
Arcanum	4	4	0
Archbold	10	9	1
Arlington Heights	4	4	0
Ashland	36	28	8
Ashtabula	38	33	5
Athens	29	22	7
Aurora	33	25	8
Austintown	47	37	10
Avon	31	25	6
Avon Lake	34	29	5
Bainbridge Township	28	20	8
Baltimore	1	1	0
Barberton	54	41	13
Barnesville	11	7	4

Table 78. Law Enforcement Employees, by City, 2005

(Number.)

City	Total law enforcement employees	Total officers	Total civilians
Bath Township (Summit County)	29	20	9
Bay Village	27	25	2
Bazetta Township	11	11	0
Beach City	2	2	0
Beachwood	54	41	13
Beavercreek	65	48	17
Beaver Township	16	12	4
Bedford	41	32	9
Bedford Heights	67	34	33
Bellaire	11	11	0
Bellbrook	17	12	5
Bellefontaine	28	23	5
Bellevue	18	14	4
Bellville	5	5	0
Belpre	14	9	5
Bentleyville Village	5	5	0
Berea	39	31	8
Bethel	5	4	1
Bethesda	1	1	0
Beverly	2	2	0
Bexley	35	28	7
Blanchester	7	7	0
Blendon Township	12	11	1
Blue Ash	47	37	10
Bluffton	6	6	0
Boardman	84	63	21
Bowling Green	58	43	15
Bradford	2	2	0
Brecksville	36	29	7
Brewster	4	4	0
Brimfield Township	13	12	1
Broadview Heights	41	31	10
Brookfield Township	10	9	1
Brooklyn	40	33	7
Brooklyn Heights	17	17	0
Brook Park	52	44	8
Brookville	16	11	5
Brunswick	54	40	14
Bryan	26	19	7
Buckeye Lake	4	4	0
Buckland	1	1	0
Bucyrus	24	19	5
Burton	3	3	0
Butler Township	17	16	1
Cadiz	6	6	0
Cambridge	28	22	6
Campbell	14	14	0
Canal Fulton	11	10	1
Canfield	21	15	6
Canton	202	167	35
Carey	11	7	4
Carlisle	8	7	1
Carrollton	8	8	0
Celina	22	16	6
Centerville	53	40	13
Chagrin Falls	19	11	8
Chardon	16	10	6
Chester Township	15	14	1
Cheviot	10	10	0
Chillicothe	48	43	5
Cincinnati	1 331	1 080	251
Circleville	29	21	8
Clayton	13	13	0
Clearcreek Township	13	12	1
Cleveland	1 998	1 615	383
Cleveland Heights	118	109	9
Cleves	3	3	0
Clinton Township	10	9	1
Clyde	18	14	4
Coitsville Township	2	2	0
Coldwater	6	6	0
Columbiana	16	12	4
Columbus	2 136	1 792	344
Conneaut	24	18	6
Copley Township	27	20	7
Cortland	10	10	0
Covington	6	5	1
Crestline	12	8	4
Creston	4	3	1
Crooksville	4	3	1
Cuyahoga Falls	115	95	20
Dalton	1	1	0
Danville	2	2	0
Dayton	509	414	95
Deer Park	15	11	4
Defiance	28	25	3
Delaware	60	44	16
Delhi Township	30	27	3
Delphos	18	14	4
Delta	6	6	0
Donnelsville	2	2	0
Dover	23	22	1
Doylestown	7	6	1
Dublin	91	68	23
East Cleveland	53	51	2
Eastlake	49	36	13
East Liverpool	24	19	5
East Palestine	8	6	2
Eaton	21	14	7
Elmwood Place	3	3	0
Englewood	26	20	6
Euclid	144	94	50
Evendale	22	20	2
Fairborn	53	37	16
Fairfax	9	8	1
Fairfield	81	61	20
Fairfield Township	16	15	1
Fairlawn	34	22	12
Fairport Harbor	8	7	1
Fairview Park	29	28	1
Fayette	2	2	0
Findlay	92	73	19
Forest	2	2	0
Forest Park	40	32	8
Fort Recovery	2	2	0
Fort Shawnee	4	4	0
Franklin	32	25	7
Franklin Township	15	11	4
Frazeysburg	1	1	0
Fredericktown	4	4	0
Fremont	39	32	7
Gahanna	68	55	13
Galion	20	15	5
Gallipolis	13	12	1
Garfield Heights	81	63	18
Gates Mills	16	12	4
Geneva	16	12	4
Geneva-on-the-Lake	5	5	0
Genoa	4	4	0
Genoa Township	26	23	3
Georgetown	8	8	0
Germantown	16	11	5
German Township, Montgomery County	5	5	0
Gibsonburg	4	4	0
Glendale	7	7	0
Gnadenhutten	2	2	0
Goshen Township, Clermont County	11	10	1
Goshen Township, Mahoning County	9	8	1
Grandview Heights	22	18	4
Granville	14	10	4
Greenfield	15	12	3
Greenhills	8	8	0
Greenville	29	22	7
Greenwich	4	4	0
Grove City	76	58	18
Hamilton	163	137	26
Hamler-Marion Township	1	1	0
Harrison	23	21	2
Hartville	7	7	0
Heath	24	17	7
Hebron	11	10	1
Hicksville	9	8	1
Highland Heights	30	23	7
Highland Hills	10	10	0
Hilliard	63	51	12
Hillsboro	20	16	4
Holgate	1	1	0
Holland	7	7	0
Howland Township	20	19	1
Hubbard	19	15	4

Table 78. Law Enforcement Employees, by City, 2005

(Number.)

City	Total law enforcement employees	Total officers	Total civilians
Hubbard Township	8	7	1
Hudson	38	30	8
Hunting Valley	9	9	0
Huron	19	14	5
Independence	51	37	14
Indian Hill	25	20	5
Ironton	18	13	5
Jackson	23	17	6
Jackson Center	3	3	0
Jackson Township (Stark County)	43	35	8
Jefferson	6	5	1
Johnstown	14	10	4
Kent	53	39	14
Kenton	16	16	0
Kettering	111	81	30
Kirtland	14	9	5
Kirtland Hills	10	9	1
Lagrange	6	6	0
Lakemore	7	7	0
Lake Township	15	14	1
Lakewood	108	87	21
Lancaster	84	64	20
Lawrence Township	5	5	0
Lebanon	35	26	9
Leipsic	3	3	0
Lexington	13	9	4
Liberty Township	26	21	5
Lima	104	83	21
Lincoln Heights	9	9	0
Lisbon	10	6	4
Lockland	14	13	1
Logan	20	18	2
London	20	15	5
Lorain	120	102	18
Lordstown	12	8	4
Loudonville	10	6	4
Louisville	10	10	0
Loveland	20	18	2
Lyndhurst	41	31	10
Macedonia	27	22	5
Madeira	13	12	1
Madison Township (Lake County)	18	16	2
Magnolia	2	2	0
Malvern	1	1	0
Manchester	2	2	0
Mansfield	125	86	39
Mariemont	11	10	1
Marietta	39	32	7
Marion	80	63	17
Marlboro Township	5	4	1
Martins Ferry	18	14	4
Marysville	35	29	6
Mason	41	37	4
Massillon	47	45	2
Maumee	60	44	16
Mayfield Heights	47	37	10
Mayfield Village	24	16	8
McComb	3	3	0
McConnelsville	5	4	1
Mechanicsburg	3	3	0
Medina	51	37	14
Medina Township	6	6	0
Mentor	111	80	31
Mentor-on-the-Lake	16	11	5
Miamisburg	50	40	10
Miami Township	40	37	3
Middleburg Heights	39	32	7
Middlefield	11	7	4
Middleport	6	4	2
Middletown	127	86	41
Milford	17	15	2
Millersburg	9	9	0
Minerva	15	9	6
Minerva Park	5	5	0
Mingo Junction	10	9	1
Minster	6	6	0
Mogadore	8	8	0
Monroe	23	18	5
Monroeville	5	5	0
Montgomery	23	21	2
Montpelier	9	8	1
Montville Township	10	10	0
Moraine	42	32	10
Moreland Hills	15	14	1
Mount Gilead	6	6	0
Mount Healthy	11	11	0
Mount Orab	6	6	0
Mount Sterling	8	5	3
Mount Vernon	29	26	3
Munroe Falls	7	7	0
Napoleon	22	17	5
Navarre	5	5	0
Nelsonville	7	7	0
New Albany	21	15	6
New Boston	12	8	4
Newburgh Heights	6	4	2
Newcomerstown	12	7	5
New Concord	4	4	0
New Lebanon	7	7	0
New Lexington	12	8	4
New Middletown	3	3	0
New Paris	1	1	0
New Philadelphia	26	22	4
New Richmond	5	5	0
Newton Falls	11	7	4
Newton Township	2	2	0
Newtown	6	6	0
Niles	42	36	6
North Baltimore	6	6	0
North Canton	33	25	8
North College Hill	15	14	1
North Kingsville	5	5	0
North Olmsted	74	57	17
North Randall	16	14	2
North Ridgeville	44	35	9
North Royalton	70	41	29
Northwood	28	21	7
Norton	21	16	5
Norwalk	32	24	8
Norwood	58	50	8
Oak Harbor	6	4	2
Oakwood	37	31	6
Oberlin	21	16	5
Olmsted Falls	17	11	6
Olmsted Township	22	19	3
Ontario	23	17	6
Oregon	60	46	14
Orrville	19	14	5
Ottawa	8	8	0
Ottawa Hills	11	11	0
Oxford	38	25	13
Painesville	41	37	4
Parma	147	91	56
Parma Heights	40	34	6
Pataskala	17	16	1
Paulding	5	4	1
Payne	1	1	0
Pepper Pike	27	20	7
Perkins Township	32	25	7
Perrysburg	39	31	8
Perry Township (Franklin County)	10	9	1
Perry Township (Montgomery County)	4	4	0
Perry Township (Stark County)	27	21	6
Pierce Township	16	15	1
Piqua	39	33	6
Plain City	9	9	0
Poland Township	14	12	2
Poland Village	6	6	0
Port Clinton	18	13	5
Portsmouth	42	38	4
Powell	18	17	1
Powhatan Point	4	3	1
Ravenna	30	22	8
Reading	24	19	5
Reminderville	7	5	2
Reynoldsburg	65	51	14
Richfield	24	17	7
Richland Township	2	2	0
Richmond Heights	30	22	8
Richwood	6	6	0

Table 78. Law Enforcement Employees, by City, 2005

(Number.)

City	Total law enforcement employees	Total officers	Total civilians
Rittman	12	8	4
Riverside	25	24	1
Rockford	2	2	0
Rossford	17	16	1
Ross Township	1	1	0
Russell Township	8	7	1
Salem	26	25	1
Salineville	3	3	0
Sandusky	61	51	10
Seaman	3	2	1
Sebring	11	7	4
Seven Hills	19	18	1
Seville	9	8	1
Shadyside	9	6	3
Shaker Heights	96	69	27
Sharon Township	9	9	0
Sharonville	48	38	10
Shawnee Township	15	9	6
Sheffield Lake	16	12	4
Shelby	19	15	4
Silverton	13	10	3
Smith Township	5	4	1
Smithville	6	6	0
Solon	74	46	28
South Charleston	2	2	0
South Euclid	50	39	11
South Russell	9	9	0
South Zanesville	3	3	0
Spencerville	4	4	0
Springboro	29	23	6
Springdale	45	36	9
Springfield	144	124	20
Springfield Township (Hamilton County)	51	44	7
Springfield Township (Mahoning County)	6	6	0
Springfield Township (Summit County)	18	16	2
St. Bernard	15	14	1
Steubenville	55	45	10
St. Henry	2	2	0
St. Marys	19	15	4
Stow	47	38	9
St. Paris	4	4	0
Strasburg	4	4	0
Streetsboro	32	24	8
Strongsville	97	76	21
Sunbury	11	10	1
Sylvania	38	31	7
Sylvania Township	65	48	17
Tallmadge	37	26	11
Terrace Park	6	5	1
Tiffin	41	29	12
Tipp City	21	18	3
Toledo	785	677	108
Toronto	10	10	0
Trenton	18	13	5
Trotwood	51	47	4
Troy	49	43	6
Twinsburg	46	33	13
Uhrichsville	8	8	0
Union City	4	4	0
Uniontown	9	7	2
Union Township (Clermont County)	59	46	13
Union Township (Licking County)	2	2	0
University Heights	34	29	5
Upper Arlington	61	48	13
Urbana	24	20	4
Valley View	20	18	2
Vandalia	36	29	7
Van Wert	31	23	8
Vermilion	24	19	5
Village of Leesburg	2	2	0
Wadsworth	37	28	9
Waite Hill	6	6	0
Walbridge	5	4	1
Walton Hills	20	15	5
Wapakoneta	19	14	5
Warren	95	77	18
Warrensville Heights	50	36	14
Warren Township	8	8	0
Washington Court House	27	21	6
Waterville	13	12	1
Waterville Township	5	5	0
Wauseon	16	14	2
Waverly	15	12	3
Waynesville	4	4	0
Wellington	8	6	2
Wellston	16	12	4
Wellsville	7	7	0
West Carrollton	31	24	7
West Chester Township	102	79	23
Westerville	82	69	13
West Jefferson	14	10	4
Westlake	69	50	19
West Union	6	4	2
Whitehall	53	43	10
Wickliffe	49	31	18
Willard	16	13	3
Williamsburg	5	5	0
Willoughby	59	44	15
Willoughby Hills	26	18	8
Willowick	35	25	10
Wilmington	25	24	1
Windham	6	4	2
Wintersville	9	8	1
Woodlawn	16	15	1
Woodsfield	6	6	0
Woodville	5	5	0
Wooster	43	38	5
Worthington	48	34	14
Wyoming	19	15	4
Xenia	68	45	23
Yellow Springs	11	8	3
Youngstown	229	189	40
Oklahoma			
Achille	4	3	1
Ada	38	32	6
Agra	1	1	0
Altus	56	40	16
Alva	12	7	5
Anadarko	20	14	6
Antlers	10	6	4
Apache	3	3	0
Ardmore	65	54	11
Arkoma	7	3	4
Atoka	15	14	1
Barnsdall	5	4	1
Bartlesville	75	49	26
Beaver	3	3	0
Beggs	7	4	3
Bethany	36	25	11
Bixby	31	22	9
Blackwell	24	15	9
Blanchard	11	8	3
Boise City	3	3	0
Boley	1	1	0
Bristow	13	9	4
Broken Arrow	164	116	48
Broken Bow	17	12	5
Buffalo	3	3	0
Caddo	3	3	0
Calera	8	7	1
Carnegie	7	4	3
Catoosa	16	15	1
Chandler	12	7	5
Checotah	14	10	4
Chelsea	9	6	3
Cherokee	7	3	4
Chickasha	42	31	11
Choctaw	15	13	2
Chouteau	7	6	1
Claremore	50	36	14
Clayton	6	3	3
Cleveland	5	5	0
Clinton	24	14	10
Coalgate	7	6	1
Colbert	2	2	0
Collinsville	14	9	5
Comanche	4	4	0
Cordell	6	5	1
Coweta	21	14	7
Crescent	7	4	3
Cushing	23	16	7
Davenport	2	2	0
Davis	13	8	5

Table 78. Law Enforcement Employees, by City, 2005

(Number.)

City	Total law enforcement employees	Total officers	Total civilians
Del City	32	26	6
Dewey	9	8	1
Drumright	5	5	0
Duncan	46	41	5
Durant	42	31	11
Edmond	120	98	22
Elk City	30	20	10
El Reno	37	26	11
Enid	120	91	29
Erick	2	2	0
Eufaula	13	10	3
Fairfax	8	4	4
Fairview	8	8	0
Fort Gibson	14	11	3
Frederick	12	11	1
Geary	10	6	4
Glenpool	20	14	6
Goodwell	3	3	0
Granite	2	2	0
Grove	26	19	7
Guthrie	25	18	7
Guymon	27	16	11
Harrah	11	10	1
Hartshorne	13	5	8
Haskell	6	6	0
Healdton	7	3	4
Heavener	12	8	4
Henryetta	17	12	5
Hinton	4	4	0
Hobart	15	9	6
Holdenville	14	10	4
Hollis	9	5	4
Hominy	10	5	5
Hooker	4	4	0
Hugo	16	14	2
Hulbert	4	3	1
Hydro	2	2	0
Idabel	24	18	6
Inola	7	4	3
Jay	12	7	5
Jenks	20	14	6
Jones	4	4	0
Kingfisher	10	8	2
Kingston	7	7	0
Konawa	6	3	3
Krebs	4	4	0
Lawton	201	146	55
Lexington	12	6	6
Lindsay	13	8	5
Locust Grove	10	5	5
Lone Grove	9	6	3
Luther	10	4	6
Madill	13	11	2
Mangum	10	6	4
Mannford	10	7	3
Marietta	6	5	1
Marlow	13	10	3
Maysville	4	3	1
McAlester	59	46	13
McLoud	10	6	4
Meeker	5	5	0
Miami	43	31	12
Midwest City	115	92	23
Minco	4	4	0
Moore	69	64	5
Mooreland	2	2	0
Morris	4	4	0
Mountain View	3	3	0
Muldrow	17	11	6
Muskogee	115	88	27
Mustang	25	19	6
Newcastle	19	13	6
Newkirk	7	6	1
Nichols Hills	20	16	4
Nicoma Park	5	5	0
Noble	14	9	5
Norman	165	114	51
Nowata	8	6	2
Oilton	4	4	0
Okemah	11	7	4
Oklahoma City	1 232	989	243
Okmulgee	30	29	1
Oologah	4	4	0
Owasso	54	40	14
Pauls Valley	20	14	6
Pawhuska	12	6	6
Pawnee	6	6	0
Perkins	6	6	0
Perry	21	14	7
Piedmont	10	8	2
Pocola	13	6	7
Ponca City	66	54	12
Porum	2	2	0
Poteau	33	26	7
Prague	11	5	6
Pryor	28	20	8
Purcell	18	18	0
Ringling	1	1	0
Roland	12	8	4
Rush Springs	4	4	0
Sallisaw	33	21	12
Sand Springs	44	30	14
Sapulpa	57	46	11
Sayre	11	6	5
Seiling	3	3	0
Seminole	18	12	6
Shawnee	68	50	18
Skiatook	19	12	7
Snyder	5	5	0
Spencer	10	8	2
Spiro	4	4	0
Stigler	13	8	5
Stillwater	102	69	33
Stilwell	19	12	7
Stratford	3	3	0
Stringtown	7	6	1
Stroud	13	9	4
Sulphur	15	11	4
Tahlequah	40	28	12
Talihina	9	5	4
Tecumseh	15	10	5
The Village	25	21	4
Tishomingo	7	6	1
Tonkawa	13	8	5
Tulsa	926	803	123
Tushka	3	3	0
Tuttle	15	10	5
Valliant	4	4	0
Vian	5	5	0
Vinita	21	15	6
Wagoner	19	13	6
Walters	4	4	0
Warner	3	3	0
Warr Acres	29	22	7
Watonga	11	8	3
Waukomis	3	3	0
Waurika	2	2	0
Waynoka	4	4	0
Weatherford	28	17	11
Westville	11	7	4
Wetumka	5	5	0
Wewoka	12	8	4
Wilburton	7	6	1
Wilson	4	4	0
Woodward	29	20	9
Wright City	4	3	1
Wynnewood	5	4	1
Yale	6	3	3
Yukon	48	32	16
Oregon			
Albany	87	59	28
Amity	3	3	0
Ashland	38	30	8
Astoria	25	15	10
Athena	2	2	0
Aumsville	5	4	1
Aurora	2	2	0
Baker City	17	15	2
Bandon	8	7	1
Beaverton	149	120	29

Table 78. Law Enforcement Employees, by City, 2005

(Number.)

City	Total law enforcement employees	Total officers	Total civilians
Bend	105	81	24
Black Butte	7	6	1
Boardman	6	5	1
Brookings	20	13	7
Burns	4	4	0
Canby	28	24	4
Cannon Beach	9	8	1
Carlton	4	3	1
Central Point	27	23	4
Clatskanie	6	5	1
Coburg	6	5	1
Columbia City	2	2	0
Condon	2	1	1
Coos Bay	32	22	10
Coquille	7	6	1
Corvallis	77	53	24
Dallas	19	18	1
Eagle Point	12	10	2
Elgin	3	3	0
Eugene	295	181	114
Fairview	13	12	1
Florence	23	15	8
Forest Grove	32	29	3
Gearhart	3	3	0
Gervais	2	2	0
Gladstone	18	16	2
Gold Beach	5	4	1
Grants Pass	68	40	28
Gresham	153	115	38
Hermiston	34	23	11
Hillsboro	147	110	37
Hines	3	3	0
Hood River	17	15	2
Hubbard	6	5	1
Independence	16	14	2
Jacksonville	5	4	1
John Day	9	4	5
Junction City	15	10	5
Keizer	47	39	8
King City	5	5	0
Klamath Falls	42	38	4
La Grande	33	18	15
Lake Oswego	70	43	27
Lakeview	6	6	0
Lebanon	31	22	9
Lincoln City	30	20	10
Madras	9	8	1
Malin	2	1	1
Manzanita	3	3	0
McMinnville	40	32	8
Medford	149	95	54
Merrill	2	1	1
Milton-Freewater	17	11	6
Milwaukie	36	32	4
Molalla	15	12	3
Monmouth	14	12	2
Mount Angel	6	5	1
Myrtle Creek	9	7	2
Myrtle Point	7	6	1
Newberg	39	26	13
Newport	24	20	4
North Bend	24	17	7
North Plains	3	2	1
Nyssa	7	7	0
Oakridge	10	5	5
Ontario	29	22	7
Oregon City	38	31	7
Philomath	9	8	1
Phoenix	12	9	3
Pilot Rock	3	3	0
Portland	1 259	989	270
Powers	1	1	0
Prairie City	1	1	0
Prineville	28	17	11
Rainier	7	6	1
Redmond	45	33	12
Reedsport	15	10	5
Rockaway Beach	3	3	0
Rogue River	6	5	1
Roseburg	40	36	4
Salem	315	186	129
Sandy	11	10	1
Scappoose	10	9	1
Shady Cove	3	3	0
Sherwood	26	23	3
Silverton	14	13	1
Springfield	102	68	34
Stanfield	4	4	0
Stayton	18	15	3
St. Helens	19	17	2
Sunriver	12	11	1
Sutherlin	16	13	3
Sweet Home	21	14	7
Talent	10	8	2
The Dalles	21	19	2
Tigard	75	59	16
Tillamook	10	9	1
Troutdale	24	20	4
Tualatin	42	36	6
Turner	3	3	0
Umatilla	11	9	2
Vernonia	5	5	0
Warrenton	9	8	1
West Linn	32	27	5
Weston	1	1	0
Winston	8	7	1
Woodburn	40	31	9
Yamhill	2	2	0
Pennsylvania			
Abington Township	114	90	24
Adams Township (Butler County)	4	4	0
Akron	4	4	0
Albion	1	1	0
Alburtis	4	4	0
Aldan	4	4	0
Aliquippa	18	18	0
Allegheny Township (Blair County)	5	5	0
Allegheny Township (Westmoreland County)	9	8	1
Allentown	247	168	79
Altoona	75	67	8
Ambler	14	12	2
Ambridge	13	13	0
Amity Township	13	12	1
Annville Township	5	4	1
Arnold	12	11	1
Ashland	5	5	0
Ashley	2	2	0
Aspinwall	7	6	1
Aston Township	18	16	2
Athens	3	2	1
Avalon	6	6	0
Baldwin Borough	33	29	4
Baldwin Township	5	5	0
Bally	2	2	0
Bangor	10	9	1
Barrett Township	7	7	0
Beaver	10	8	2
Beaver Falls	19	18	1
Bedford	5	5	0
Bedminster Township	5	4	1
Bell Acres	4	4	0
Bellefonte	10	8	2
Bellevue	16	13	3
Bellwood	2	2	0
Bensalem Township	107	83	24
Berks-Lehigh Regional	24	23	1
Bern Township	11	11	0
Berwick	14	13	1
Bessemer	1	1	0
Bethel Park	44	38	6
Bethel Township (Berks County)	2	2	0
Bethlehem	163	141	22
Bethlehem Township	31	29	2
Biglerville	2	2	0
Birdsboro	7	6	1
Birmingham Township	4	4	0
Blairsville	5	5	0
Blair Township	4	4	0
Blakely	3	3	0

Table 78. Law Enforcement Employees, by City, 2005

(Number.)

City	Total law enforcement employees	Total officers	Total civilians
Blawnox	3	3	0
Bloomsburg Town	19	15	4
Boyertown	8	7	1
Brackenridge	4	4	0
Bradford	22	22	0
Bradford Township	5	5	0
Brandywine Regional	19	17	2
Brecknock Township (Berks County)	6	6	0
Brecknock Township (Lancaster County)	3	3	0
Brentwood	20	15	5
Bridgeport	10	9	1
Bridgeville	10	9	1
Bridgewater	2	2	0
Brighton Township	6	6	0
Bristol	15	13	2
Bristol Township	79	65	14
Brockway	2	2	0
Brookhaven	8	7	1
Brookville	6	5	1
Brownsville	3	3	0
Bryn Athyn	5	5	0
Buckingham Township	23	21	2
Buffalo Township	5	5	0
Bushkill Township	12	10	2
Butler	24	23	1
Butler Township (Butler County)	23	21	2
Butler Township (Luzerne County)	9	8	1
California	8	7	1
Caln Township	21	19	2
Cambria Township	4	4	0
Cambridge Springs	3	3	0
Camp Hill	11	10	1
Canonsburg	16	15	1
Carbondale	15	15	0
Carlisle	37	32	5
Carnegie	14	13	1
Carrolltown	1	1	0
Carroll Township (Washington County)	3	3	0
Carroll Township (York County)	11	11	0
Carroll Valley	5	4	1
Castle Shannon	13	12	1
Catawissa	3	3	0
Center Township	26	26	0
Centerville	3	3	0
Central Berks Regional	12	11	1
Chalfont	7	6	1
Charleroi	8	6	2
Chartiers Township	11	11	0
Cheltenham Township	96	85	11
Chester	106	96	10
Chester Township	10	9	1
Cheswick	3	3	0
Chippewa Township	8	7	1
Churchill	9	9	0
Clairton	9	9	0
Clarion	9	8	1
Claysville	2	2	0
Clay Township	3	3	0
Clearfield	7	7	0
Cleona	4	4	0
Clifton Heights	9	8	1
Coaldale	4	4	0
Cochranton	1	1	0
Colebrookdale District	10	9	1
Collegeville	9	8	1
Collier Township	12	11	1
Collingdale	10	8	2
Colonial Regional	24	22	2
Columbia	23	20	3
Colwyn	3	3	0
Conemaugh Township (Cambria County)	2	2	0
Conemaugh Township (Somerset County)	8	7	1
Conewago Township	8	7	1
Conewango Township	4	4	0
Conneaut Lake Regional	3	3	0
Conneautville	1	1	0
Connellsville	19	18	1
Conshohocken	21	19	2
Conway	3	3	0
Conyngham	2	2	0
Coopersburg	6	6	0
Coraopolis	12	0	3
Cornwall	8	7	1
Corry	16	12	4
Coudersport	4	4	0
Covington Township	2	2	0
Cranberry Township	27	24	3
Crescent Township	3	3	0
Cresson	1	1	0
Cresson Township	2	2	0
Croyle Township	1	1	0
Cumberland Township (Adams County)	6	6	0
Cumru Township	28	25	3
Dallas	4	4	0
Dallas Township	7	7	0
Decatur Township	1	1	0
Derry Township (Dauphin County)	44	37	7
Dickson City	8	8	0
Donegal Township	2	2	0
Dormont	16	15	1
Downingtown	19	16	3
Doylestown	20	15	5
Doylestown Township	23	21	2
Dublin Borough	2	2	0
Du Bois	13	13	0
Duboistown	1	1	0
Duncannon	2	2	0
Dunmore	8	8	0
Duquesne	15	14	1
East Bethlehem Township	2	2	0
East Buffalo Township	8	8	0
East Cocalico Township	23	23	0
East Conemaugh	2	2	0
East Coventry Township	6	6	0
East Earl Township	7	7	0
Eastern Adams Regional	8	8	0
East Fallowfield Township	8	7	1
East Franklin Township	2	2	0
East Hempfield Township	33	29	4
East Lampeter Township	43	39	4
East McKeesport	2	2	0
East Norriton Township	31	28	3
East Pennsboro Township	20	19	1
East Pikeland Township	8	7	1
Easttown Township	15	14	1
East Vincent Township	7	7	0
East Washington	1	1	0
East Whiteland Township	21	19	2
Ebensburg	4	4	0
Economy	13	12	1
Eddystone	10	9	1
Edgewood	10	10	0
Edgeworth	6	4	2
Edinboro	9	8	1
Edwardsville	4	4	0
Elizabeth	2	2	0
Elizabethtown	18	16	2
Elizabeth Township	16	15	1
Emmaus	17	16	1
Emporium	2	2	0
Emsworth	9	8	1
Ephrata	35	30	5
Erie	206	178	28
Etna	7	6	1
Evans City	2	2	0
Exeter	5	4	1
Exeter Township (Berks County)	33	32	1
Fairview Township (York County)	17	15	2
Falls Township (Bucks County)	60	52	8
Fawn Township	4	4	0
Ferguson Township	18	16	2
Ferndale	1	1	0
Findlay Township	23	16	7
Fleetwood	6	6	0
Folcroft	9	9	0
Ford City	4	4	0
Forest City	2	2	0
Forest Hills	14	11	3
Forks Township	19	18	1
Forty Fort	5	5	0

Table 78. Law Enforcement Employees, by City, 2005

(Number.)

City	Total law enforcement employees	Total officers	Total civilians
Foster Township	5	5	0
Fountain Hill	9	9	0
Fox Chapel	11	11	0
Frackville	6	6	0
Franconia Township	13	12	1
Franklin Park	10	9	1
Franklin Township (Carbon County)	4	4	0
Gallitzin	1	1	0
Gettysburg	16	14	2
Gilpin Township	1	1	0
Girard	4	4	0
Glenolden	10	9	1
Granville Township	7	6	1
Greencastle	3	3	0
Greensburg	37	27	10
Green Tree	12	11	1
Greenwood Township	1	1	0
Grove City	10	9	1
Hamburg	8	7	1
Hamiltonban Township	1	1	0
Hanover Township (Luzerne County)	15	15	0
Harmar Township	8	8	0
Harmony Township	4	4	0
Harrisburg	230	179	51
Harrison Township	16	12	4
Hatboro	18	14	4
Hatfield Township	32	26	6
Haverford Township	87	70	17
Heidelberg	3	3	0
Hellam Township	10	10	0
Hellertown	11	10	1
Hemlock Township	4	4	0
Hempfield Township (Mercer County)	7	6	1
Highspire	6	6	0
Hilltown Township	21	18	3
Hollidaysburg	11	7	4
Homestead	12	12	0
Honesdale	9	9	0
Honey Brook Township	2	2	0
Hooversville	1	1	0
Horsham Township	49	40	9
Hummelstown	7	7	0
Huntingdon	12	12	0
Indiana	28	21	7
Indiana Township	10	10	0
Ingram	4	4	0
Irwin	5	5	0
Jackson Township (Butler County)	6	6	0
Jackson Township (Cambria County)	2	2	0
Jackson Township (Luzerne County)	4	4	0
Jefferson Hills Borough	18	17	1
Jenkins Township	2	2	0
Jenkintown	10	9	1
Jermyn	1	1	0
Jersey Shore	8	7	1
Johnstown	57	50	7
Kane	3	3	0
Kennedy Township	15	11	4
Kidder Township	8	8	0
Kingston	24	19	5
Kingston Township	12	11	1
Kittanning	9	8	1
Kline Township	1	1	0
Koppel	1	1	0
Kutztown	11	10	1
Laflin Borough	3	3	0
Lake City	3	3	0
Lancaster	214	172	42
Lancaster Township (Butler County)	2	2	0
Lansdale	27	21	6
Larksville	4	4	0
Laureldale	4	4	0
Lawrence Township	10	9	1
Lebanon	50	47	3
Leetsdale	4	4	0
Leet Township	10	5	5
Lehighton	8	7	1
Lehigh Township, Northampton County	12	11	1
Lehman Township	2	2	0
Lewisburg	8	7	1
Liberty Township, Adams County	2	2	0
Ligonier Township	3	3	0
Limerick Township	18	16	2
Lincoln	2	2	0
Linesville	1	1	0
Lititz	16	13	3
Littlestown	8	7	1
Locust Township	5	5	0
Logan Township	18	16	2
Lower Allen Township	21	18	3
Lower Burrell	17	17	0
Lower Gwynedd Township	19	18	1
Lower Heidelberg Township	7	6	1
Lower Makefield Township	35	31	4
Lower Moreland Township	28	23	5
Lower Paxton Township	60	54	6
Lower Pottsgrove Township	15	13	2
Lower Providence Township	35	29	6
Lower Salford Township	21	19	2
Lower Saucon Township	16	14	2
Lower Southampton Township	33	30	3
Lower Swatara Township	11	10	1
Lower Windsor Township	11	10	1
Luzerne Township	1	1	0
Macungie	4	4	0
Madison Township	1	1	0
Mahoning Township (Carbon County)	5	5	0
Mahoning Township (Montour County)	7	6	1
Malvern	5	4	1
Manheim	8	7	1
Manheim Township	67	50	17
Mansfield	5	5	0
Marion Township	1	1	0
Marlborough Township	4	4	0
Marple Township	38	32	6
Martinsburg	2	2	0
Masontown	5	5	0
Mayfield	1	1	0
McCandless	29	27	2
McDonald Borough	3	3	0
McKeesport	47	44	3
McKees Rocks	8	7	1
McSherrystown	4	4	0
Mechanicsburg	16	15	1
Media	21	14	7
Mercer	4	4	0
Mercersburg	2	2	0
Meyersdale	1	1	0
Middletown	16	15	1
Middletown Township	57	51	6
Midland	5	5	0
Mifflin County Regional	27	25	2
Milford	2	2	0
Millcreek Township	74	57	17
Millersburg	4	4	0
Millersville	14	12	2
Millville	1	1	0
Milton	10	9	1
Minersville	6	6	0
Mohnton	4	4	0
Monaca	8	8	0
Monessen	12	12	0
Monongahela	10	9	1
Monroeville	56	51	5
Montgomery Township	43	34	9
Moon Township	36	30	6
Moore Township	9	8	1
Moosic	9	9	0
Morris-Cooper Township	2	2	0
Morrisville	12	11	1

Table 78. Law Enforcement Employees, by City, 2005

(Number.)

City	Total law enforcement employees	Total officers	Total civilians
Morton	4	4	0
Moscow	3	3	0
Mount Carmel	9	8	1
Mount Joy	14	12	2
Mount Oliver	8	6	2
Mount Union	5	5	0
Muhlenberg Township	32	29	3
Munhall	24	20	4
Murrysville	25	20	5
Myerstown	4	4	0
Nanticoke	13	12	1
Narberth	6	6	0
Neshannock Township	7	7	0
Nesquehoning	4	4	0
Nether Providence Township	17	15	2
Neville Township	5	3	2
Newberry Township	18	16	2
New Bethlehem	1	1	0
New Britain	3	2	1
New Britain Township	13	11	2
New Cumberland	9	8	1
New Hanover Township	9	8	1
New Holland	13	12	1
New Hope	11	9	2
Newport	2	2	0
Newport Township	1	1	0
New Sewickley Township	11	10	1
Newtown	2	2	0
Newtown Township (Delaware County)	18	16	2
Newville	2	2	0
New Wilmington	4	4	0
Norristown	67	58	9
Northampton	14	12	2
Northampton Township	46	40	6
North Apollo	1	1	0
North Cornwall Township	10	9	1
North Coventry Township	13	12	1
North East	7	6	1
Northeastern Regional	11	10	1
Northern Berks Regional	15	14	1
Northern York Regional	49	45	4
North Fayette Township	23	18	5
North Franklin Township	5	5	0
North Huntingdon Township	35	28	7
North Lebanon Township	10	9	1
North Londonderry Township	8	7	1
North Middleton Township	9	8	1
North Strabane Township	20	19	1
Northumberland	5	5	0
North Versailles Township	22	19	3
North Wales	7	6	1
Northwest Lawrence Regional	2	2	0
Northwest Regional	16	15	1
Norwood	7	7	0
Oakmont	7	7	0
O'Hara Township	14	13	1
Ohio Township	9	8	1
Ohioville	2	2	0
Oil City	23	18	5
Old Lycoming Township	11	10	1
Olyphant	5	5	0
Orangeville Area	1	1	0
Orwigsburg	4	4	0
Oxford	12	11	1
Paint Township	5	4	1
Palmerton	9	8	1
Palmyra	10	9	1
Parkesburg	9	9	0
Patton	2	2	0
Patton Township	17	15	2
Paxtang	3	3	0
Pen Argyl	5	5	0
Penbrook	6	6	0
Penn Hills	58	53	5
Pennridge Regional	23	15	8
Penn Township (Butler County)	4	3	1
Penn Township (Lancaster County)	9	8	1
Penn Township (Westmoreland County)	22	20	2
Penn Township (York County)	22	20	2
Perkasie	19	17	2
Peters Township	22	20	2
Philadelphia	7 501	6 636	865
Phoenixville	31	29	2
Pine-Marshall-Bradford Woods	20	18	2
Pittsburgh	943	880	63
Pittston	10	10	0
Plainfield Township	11	11	0
Plains Township	16	15	1
Pleasant Hills	21	17	4
Plum	30	24	6
Plumstead Township	17	15	2
Plymouth	1	1	0
Plymouth Township (Montgomery County)	55	46	9
Pocono Mountain Regional	43	38	5
Point Township	5	5	0
Portage	2	2	0
Port Allegany	2	2	0
Pottstown	57	43	14
Pottsville	29	28	1
Prospect Park	9	9	0
Punxsutawney	11	8	3
Pymatuning Township	3	3	0
Quakertown	23	15	8
Radnor Township	57	47	10
Rankin	1	1	0
Reading	235	208	27
Reynoldsville	2	2	0
Rice Township	4	4	0
Richland Township (Bucks County)	11	10	1
Richland Township (Cambria County)	20	19	1
Ridgway	6	5	1
Ridley Park	14	10	4
Ridley Township	38	30	8
Rimersburg	3	3	0
Riverside	3	3	0
Roaring Spring	3	3	0
Robesonia	2	2	0
Robeson Township	6	5	1
Robinson Township (Allegheny County)	26	21	5
Rochester	13	11	2
Rochester Township	4	4	0
Rockledge	5	5	0
Rosslyn Farms	2	2	0
Ross Township	44	42	2
Rostraver Township	15	14	1
Rush Township	3	3	0
Salisbury Township	13	11	2
Sandy Lake	1	1	0
Sandy Township	8	7	1
Saxton	1	1	0
Sayre	11	9	2
Schuylkill Haven	7	7	0
Schuylkill Township (Chester County)	11	10	1
Scottdale	7	7	0
Scott Township (Allegheny County)	20	19	1
Scranton	170	150	20
Selinsgrove	6	5	1
Seward	1	1	0
Sewickley	9	8	1
Shaler Township	29	28	1

Table 78. Law Enforcement Employees, by City, 2005

(Number.)

City	Total law enforcement employees	Total officers	Total civilians
Shamokin	18	13	5
Sharon Hill	8	7	1
Sharpsburg	7	7	0
Shenandoah	7	6	1
Shenango Township (Lawrence County)	6	6	0
Shillington	8	8	0
Shippingport	2	2	0
Shiremanstown	2	2	0
Shohola Township	1	1	0
Silver Lake Township	1	1	0
Sinking Spring	5	5	0
Slatington	6	6	0
Slippery Rock	3	3	0
Smethport	2	2	0
Solebury Township	14	13	1
South Abington Township	11	10	1
South Beaver Township	4	4	0
South Buffalo Township	2	2	0
South Centre Township	4	4	0
South Coatesville	4	2	2
Southern Regional (Lancaster County)	9	9	0
Southern Regional (York County)	12	11	1
South Fayette Township	17	16	1
South Fork	1	1	0
South Greensburg	2	2	0
South Heidelberg Township	6	6	0
South Lebanon Township	8	7	1
South Londonderry Township	6	6	0
South Park Township	17	16	1
South Pymatuning Township	2	2	0
South Waverly	3	1	2
Southwestern Regional	13	13	0
Southwest Greensburg	2	2	0
Southwest Mercer County Regional	20	19	1
Southwest Regional	1	1	0
South Whitehall Township	38	35	3
South Williamsport	8	7	1
Spring City	4	3	1
Springdale	1	1	0
Springettsbury Township	33	30	3
Springfield Township (Bucks County)	4	4	0
Springfield Township (Delaware County)	41	35	6
Springfield Township (Montgomery County)	30	29	1
Spring Garden Township	20	18	2
Spring Township (Berks County)	25	24	1
Spring Township (Centre County)	7	6	1
State College	79	63	16
St. Clair Boro	7	7	0
St. Clair Township	1	1	0
Steelton	9	8	1
Stewartstown	6	5	1
Stowe Township	7	6	1
Strasburg	4	4	0
Stroud Area Regional	58	53	5
Sugarcreek	6	6	0
Sugarloaf Township (Luzerne County)	4	4	0
Summerhill Township	3	3	0
Summit Hill	3	3	0
Sunbury	19	15	4
Susquehanna Township (Dauphin County)	41	39	2
Swarthmore	9	9	0
Swatara Township	35	33	2
Swissvale	14	14	0
Swoyersville	7	7	0
Sykesville	1	1	0
Tamaqua	11	9	2
Taylor	8	8	0
Telford	8	7	1
Tidioute	1	1	0
Tinicum Township (Bucks County)	5	5	0
Tinicum Township (Delaware County)	16	15	1
Titusville	16	16	0
Towamencin Township	34	22	12
Towanda	7	7	0
Trainer	7	7	0
Tredyffrin Township	60	51	9
Troy	3	3	0
Tullytown	4	3	1
Tunkhannock	5	5	0
Tunkhannock Township (Wyoming County)	4	4	0
Union City	1	1	0
Uniontown	17	17	0
Union Township (Lawrence County)	1	1	0
Upland	1	1	0
Upper Chichester Township	24	22	2
Upper Darby Township	137	127	10
Upper Dublin Township	45	39	6
Upper Makefield Township	12	11	1
Upper Merion Township	82	62	20
Upper Moreland Township	48	38	10
Upper Nazareth Township	4	3	1
Upper Perkiomen	9	8	1
Upper Pottsgrove Township	9	9	0
Upper Providence Township (Delaware County)	13	12	1
Upper Providence Township (Montgomery County)	20	18	2
Upper Saucon Township	18	17	1
Upper Southampton Township	23	20	3
Upper St. Clair Township	35	28	7
Upper Uwchlan Township	10	10	0
Upper Yoder Township	5	5	0
Uwchlan Township	26	24	2
Vandergrift	8	8	0
Vernon Township	3	3	0
Verona	2	2	0
Walnutport	4	4	0
Warminster Township	58	50	8
Warren	23	15	8
Warrington Township	33	30	3
Warwick Township (Bucks County)	21	19	2
Warwick Township (Lancaster County)	18	17	1
Washington (Washington County)	31	29	2
Washington Township (Fayette County)	3	3	0
Washington Township (Franklin County)	14	13	1
Washington Township (Northampton County)	3	3	0
Washington Township (Westmoreland County)	8	8	0
Watsontown	3	3	0
Waynesboro	20	18	2
Waynesburg	9	8	1
Weatherly	4	4	0
Wellsboro	8	5	3
Wernersville	2	2	0
Wesleyville	5	5	0
West Alexander	2	2	0
West Brandywine Township	8	7	1
West Carroll Township	1	1	0
West Conshohocken	10	9	1
West Earl Township	6	6	0
West Fallowfield Township	1	1	0
Westfall Township	6	6	0
West Goshen Township	33	26	7

Table 78. Law Enforcement Employees, by City, 2005

(Number.)

City	Total law enforcement employees	Total officers	Total civilians
West Hempfield Township	21	19	2
West Hills Regional	12	11	1
West Homestead	7	7	0
West Kittanning	1	1	0
West Lampeter Township	14	13	1
West Lebanon Township	10	9	1
West Manchester Township	29	26	3
West Manheim Township	7	7	0
West Mifflin	41	35	6
West Norriton Township	32	27	5
West Pikeland Township	3	3	0
West Pittston	3	3	0
West Pottsgrove Township	9	8	1
West Reading	14	12	2
West Sadsbury Township	3	2	1
West Shore Regional	11	9	2
West View	10	9	1
West Whiteland Township	31	29	2
West Wyoming	2	2	0
West York	5	5	0
Whitehall	25	20	5
Whitehall Township	56	47	9
White Haven Borough	2	2	0
Whitpain Township	36	29	7
Wilkes-Barre	92	83	9
Wilkes-Barre Township	17	15	2
Wilkinsburg	27	24	3
Wilkins Township	12	12	0
Williamsport	57	53	4
Willistown Township	18	16	2
Windber	3	2	1
Wyoming	6	6	0
Wyomissing	27	22	5
Yardley	2	2	0
Yeadon	17	15	2
York	111	99	12
York Area Regional	53	48	5
York Springs-Latimore Township	2	2	0
Youngsville	2	2	0
Zelienople	10	9	1
Rhode Island			
Barrington	31	24	7
Bristol	51	40	11
Burrillville	35	25	10
Central Falls	53	41	12
Charlestown	26	21	5
Coventry	67	55	12
Cranston	178	144	34
Cumberland	58	47	11
East Greenwich	42	33	9
East Providence	119	97	22
Foster	9	5	4
Glocester	19	14	5
Hopkinton	21	16	5
Jamestown	18	14	4
Johnston	94	75	19
Lincoln	41	33	8
Little Compton	13	9	4
Middletown	42	38	4
Narragansett	52	40	12
Newport	105	84	21
New Shoreham	11	5	6
North Kingstown	61	48	13
North Providence	94	71	23
North Smithfield	27	22	5
Pawtucket	188	153	35
Portsmouth	36	33	3
Providence	568	480	88
Richmond	16	12	4
Scituate	23	17	6
Smithfield	53	40	13
South Kingstown	70	52	18
Tiverton	39	27	12
Warren	27	22	5
Warwick	228	180	48
Westerly	58	47	11
West Greenwich	17	11	6
West Warwick	69	58	11
Woonsocket	115	98	17
South Carolina			
Abbeville	19	17	2
Aiken	103	80	23
Allendale	9	8	1
Anderson	114	86	28
Andrews	11	10	1
Aynor	11	4	7
Bamberg	12	10	2
Barnwell	15	13	2
Batesburg-Leesville	25	20	5
Beaufort	52	46	6
Bennettsville	37	33	4
Bethune	1	1	0
Bishopville	13	11	2
Blacksburg	15	14	1
Blackville	8	6	2
Bluffton	17	17	0
Bonneau	2	2	0
Bowman	3	3	0
Branchville	3	2	1
Brunson	3	3	0
Burnettown	4	3	1
Calhoun Falls	11	10	1
Camden	28	25	3
Cameron	1	1	0
Campobello	6	5	1
Cayce	74	61	13
Central	11	11	0
Chapin	6	6	0
Charleston	492	356	136
Cheraw	32	26	6
Chesnee	6	6	0
Chester	31	28	3
Chesterfield	6	5	1
Clemson	34	26	8
Clinton	34	29	5
Clio	5	4	1
Clover	15	11	4
Columbia	339	301	38
Conway	63	48	15
Cottageville	4	4	0
Coward	1	1	0
Darlington	29	26	3
Denmark	9	6	3
Dillon	23	18	5
Due West	6	6	0
Duncan	13	13	0
Easley	45	33	12
Eastover	4	4	0
Edgefield	9	9	0
Edisto Beach	5	5	0
Ehrhardt	5	4	1
Elgin	4	4	0
Elloree	5	4	1
Estill	8	7	1
Eutawville	2	2	0
Fairfax	9	8	1
Florence	118	103	15
Folly Beach	20	13	7
Forest Acres	33	25	8
Fort Lawn	3	3	0
Fort Mill	31	25	6
Fountain Inn	27	20	7
Gaffney	44	40	4
Georgetown	40	31	9
Goose Creek	69	54	15
Greeleyville	2	2	0
Greenville	221	177	44
Greenwood	52	44	8
Greer	66	53	13
Hampton	10	10	0
Hanahan	34	26	8
Hardeeville	18	15	3
Harleyville	3	3	0
Hartsville	39	36	3
Hemingway	7	4	3
Holly Hill	8	8	0
Honea Path	14	13	1
Inman	7	7	0
Irmo	21	19	2
Isle of Palms	27	17	10
Iva	6	5	1
Jackson	5	4	1
Jamestown	3	2	1
Johnsonville	5	4	1
Johnston	6	6	0
Jonesville	3	3	0
Kingstree	23	21	2
Lake View	4	4	0
Lamar	5	5	0
Lancaster	45	33	12

Table 78. Law Enforcement Employees, by City, 2005

(Number.)

City	Total law enforcement employees	Total officers	Total civilians
Landrum	9	8	1
Lane	2	2	0
Latta	10	10	0
Laurens	35	28	7
Lexington	38	33	5
Liberty	15	10	5
Lincolnville	2	2	0
Lyman	8	7	1
Lynchburg	4	4	0
Manning	18	16	2
Marion	25	21	4
Mauldin	44	35	9
McBee	3	2	1
McColl	8	8	0
McCormick	5	5	0
Moncks Corner	27	24	3
Mount Pleasant	165	125	40
Mullins	21	19	2
Myrtle Beach	243	183	60
Newberry	29	25	4
New Ellenton	7	7	0
Nichols	3	3	0
Ninety Six	6	5	1
North	4	3	1
North Augusta	63	47	16
North Charleston	358	279	79
North Myrtle Beach	144	79	65
Norway	8	7	1
Orangeburg	96	74	22
Pacolet	4	4	0
Pageland	16	12	4
Pawleys Island	4	3	1
Pelion	3	3	0
Pendleton	11	10	1
Pickens	13	12	1
Pine Ridge	2	1	1
Port Royal	19	17	2
Prosperity	4	4	0
Ridgeland	12	11	1
Ridge Spring	2	2	0
Ridgeville	2	2	0
Ridgeway	2	2	0
Rock Hill	150	107	43
Salem	2	2	0
Salley	3	1	2
Saluda	10	9	1
Santee	15	9	6
Scranton	2	1	1
Seneca	43	33	10
Simpsonville	48	38	10
Society Hill	7	7	0
South Congaree	8	6	2
Spartanburg	141	121	20
Springdale	9	8	1
Springfield	1	1	0
St. Matthews	7	7	0
Sullivans Island	9	8	1
Summerton	11	10	1
Summerville	83	66	17
Sumter	148	109	39
Surfside Beach	23	17	6
Swansea	7	7	0
Tega Cay	17	13	4
Timmonsville	8	7	1
Travelers Rest	21	15	6
Turbeville	3	3	0
Union	35	32	3
Vance	1	1	0
Wagener	3	3	0
Walhalla	16	14	2
Walterboro	31	22	9
Ware Shoals	9	8	1
Wellford	6	6	0
West Columbia	56	45	11
Westminster	10	10	0
West Pelzer	4	4	0
West Union	1	1	0
Whitmire	5	4	1
Williston	9	8	1
Winnsboro	27	26	1
Woodruff	13	11	2
Yemassee	4	4	0
York	33	26	7
South Dakota			
Aberdeen	46	38	8
Alcester	2	2	0
Armour	1	1	0
Avon	1	1	0
Belle Fourche	9	8	1
Beresford	8	4	4
Box Elder	9	7	2
Brandon	11	10	1
Bridgewater	1	1	0
Brookings	36	27	9
Burke	1	1	0
Canistota	1	1	0
Canton	4	4	0
Centerville	1	1	0
Chamberlain	5	5	0
Chancellor-Marion	4	4	0
Clark	2	2	0
Colman	1	1	0
Corsica	1	1	0
Deadwood	13	10	3
Eagle Butte	3	3	0
Elk Point	3	3	0
Estelline	1	1	0
Eureka	2	2	0
Faith	2	1	1
Flandreau	7	6	1
Freeman	2	2	0
Garretson	1	1	0
Gettysburg	2	2	0
Gregory	3	3	0
Groton	3	3	0
Highmore	1	1	0
Hot Springs	8	7	1
Hoven	1	1	0
Hurley	1	1	0
Huron	29	24	5
Jefferson	1	1	0
Kadoka	1	1	0
Kimball	1	1	0
Lead	6	5	1
Lemmon	4	4	0
Lennox	3	3	0
Leola	2	2	0
Madison	12	11	1
Martin	6	5	1
McIntosh	1	1	0
McLaughlin	4	3	1
Menno	1	1	0
Milbank	5	5	0
Miller	4	4	0
Mitchell	30	27	3
Mobridge	13	7	6
Montrose	1	1	0
Murdo	1	1	0
New Effington	1	1	0
North Sioux City	7	5	2
Parkston	1	1	0
Philip	2	2	0
Pierre	36	24	12
Platte	2	2	0
Rapid City	132	103	29
Rosholt	1	1	0
Salem	1	1	0
Scotland	1	1	0
Selby	1	1	0
Sioux Falls	237	205	32
Sisseton	8	8	0
Spearfish	25	18	7
Springfield	2	2	0
Sturgis	18	15	3
Tea	4	4	0
Tyndall	1	1	0
Vermillion	18	17	1
Viborg	1	1	0
Wagner	4	4	0
Watertown	42	31	11
Waubay	1	1	0
Webster	5	5	0
Whitewood	2	2	0
Winner	29	9	20
Worthing	1	1	0
Yankton	45	26	19

Table 78. Law Enforcement Employees, by City, 2005

(Number.)

City	Total law enforcement employees	Total officers	Total civilians
Tennessee			
Adamsville	9	6	3
Alamo	3	3	0
Alcoa	45	39	6
Alexandria	3	3	0
Algood	9	9	0
Ardmore	11	7	4
Ashland City	14	13	1
Athens	28	26	2
Atoka	10	10	0
Baileyton	2	2	0
Bartlett	113	86	27
Baxter	4	4	0
Bean Station	7	7	0
Belle Meade	19	15	4
Bells	5	5	0
Benton	9	7	2
Berry Hill	17	13	4
Bethel Springs	3	1	2
Big Sandy	2	2	0
Blaine	4	4	0
Bluff City	9	9	0
Bolivar	25	20	5
Bradford	3	2	1
Brentwood	66	53	13
Brighton	4	3	1
Bristol	88	63	25
Brownsville	40	33	7
Bruceton	4	4	0
Burns	2	2	0
Calhoun	2	2	0
Camden	18	13	5
Carthage	11	7	4
Caryville	5	5	0
Celina	6	4	2
Centerville	19	13	6
Chapel Hill	5	5	0
Charleston	3	3	0
Chattanooga	605	433	172
Church Hill	9	8	1
Clarksville	282	229	53
Cleveland	100	88	12
Clifton	6	6	0
Clinton	29	28	1
Collegedale	20	20	0
Collierville	122	83	39
Collinwood	3	3	0
Columbia	93	84	9
Cookeville	87	65	22
Coopertown	11	11	0
Copperhill	3	3	0
Cornersville	4	3	1
Covington	30	29	1
Cowan	4	4	0
Cross Plains	3	3	0
Crossville	40	36	4
Crump	2	2	0
Cumberland City	3	3	0
Cumberland Gap	1	1	0
Dandridge	10	9	1
Dayton	18	16	2
Decatur	5	5	0
Decaturville	2	1	1
Decherd	13	11	2
Dickson	48	43	5
Dover	7	6	1
Dresden	9	8	1
Dunlap	10	9	1
Dyer	6	6	0
Dyersburg	77	54	23
Eagleville	2	1	1
East Ridge	42	33	9
Elizabethton	41	37	4
Elkton	1	1	0
Englewood	4	3	1
Erin	7	6	1
Erwin	12	12	0
Estill Springs	6	6	0
Ethridge	2	1	1
Etowah	14	10	4
Fairview	17	16	1
Fayetteville	25	23	2
Franklin	137	115	22
Friendship	1	1	0
Gainesboro	5	5	0
Gallatin	67	51	16
Gallaway	9	9	0
Gates	3	3	0
Gatlinburg	55	45	10
Germantown	99	76	23
Gibson	2	2	0
Gleason	5	5	0
Goodlettsville	50	37	13
Gordonsville	5	5	0
Grand Junction	3	3	0
Graysville	4	3	1
Greenbrier	12	11	1
Greeneville	46	44	2
Greenfield	8	7	1
Halls	5	5	0
Harriman	22	21	1
Henderson	15	14	1
Hendersonville	92	69	23
Henning	4	4	0
Henry	4	3	1
Hohenwald	14	13	1
Hollow Rock	2	2	0
Hornbeak	1	1	0
Humboldt	31	25	6
Huntingdon	16	12	4
Huntland	4	4	0
Jacksboro	5	5	0
Jackson	226	185	41
Jamestown	10	9	1
Jasper	8	8	0
Jefferson City	21	19	2
Jellico	9	8	1
Johnson City	176	149	27
Jonesborough	20	15	5
Kenton	5	5	0
Kimball	10	9	1
Kingsport	142	101	41
Kingston	12	11	1
Kingston Springs	6	5	1
Knoxville	470	376	94
Lafayette	24	16	8
La Follette	28	21	7
La Grange	1	1	0
Lake City	10	7	3
Lakewood	5	5	0
La Vergne	62	45	17
Lawrenceburg	40	34	6
Lebanon	86	69	17
Lenoir City	19	18	1
Lewisburg	35	28	7
Lexington	29	24	5
Livingston	22	16	6
Lookout Mountain	21	16	5
Loretto	4	4	0
Loudon	15	14	1
Lynnville	1	1	0
Madisonville	16	14	2
Manchester	34	30	4
Martin	35	27	8
Maryville	54	44	10
Mason	5	5	0
Maynardville	4	4	0
McEwen	4	3	1
McKenzie	20	15	5
McMinnville	40	36	4
Medina	7	7	0
Memphis	2 657	1 975	682
Middleton	3	3	0
Milan	30	25	5
Millersville	15	12	3
Millington	41	32	9
Minor Hill	3	2	1
Monteagle	12	6	6
Monterey	8	8	0
Morristown	83	77	6
Moscow	4	4	0
Mountain City	9	9	0
Mount Carmel	8	8	0
Mount Juliet	39	30	9
Mount Pleasant	13	12	1
Munford	12	11	1
Murfreesboro	212	167	45
Nashville	1 546	1 244	302
Newbern	18	13	5
New Hope	1	1	0
New Johnsonville	3	3	0
New Market	1	1	0
Newport	35	24	11
New Tazewell	10	10	0
Niota	3	3	0
Nolensville	5	5	0
Norris	7	7	0
Oakland	15	13	2
Oak Ridge	70	59	11
Obion	3	3	0
Oliver Springs	16	12	4

Table 78. Law Enforcement Employees, by City, 2005

(Number.)

City	Total law enforcement employees	Total officers	Total civilians
Oneida	19	14	5
Paris	37	26	11
Parsons	7	7	0
Petersburg	2	2	0
Pigeon Forge	64	53	11
Pikeville	4	4	0
Pittman Center	2	2	0
Pleasant View	4	4	0
Portland	28	22	6
Powells Crossroads	2	2	0
Pulaski	29	26	3
Puryear	2	2	0
Red Bank	23	22	1
Red Boiling Springs	5	5	0
Ridgely	6	5	1
Ridgetop	6	5	1
Ripley	31	25	6
Rockwood	16	15	1
Rogersville	19	14	5
Rossville	4	4	0
Rutherford	5	5	0
Rutledge	6	4	2
Savannah	26	16	10
Scotts Hill	2	2	0
Selmer	18	17	1
Sevierville	63	49	14
Sewanee	11	7	4
Sharon	1	1	0
Shelbyville	50	39	11
Signal Mountain	14	13	1
Smithville	11	10	1
Smyrna	88	66	22
Sneedville	1	1	0
Soddy-Daisy	28	23	5
Somerville	13	13	0
South Carthage	4	4	0
South Fulton	7	6	1
South Pittsburg	11	7	4
Sparta	16	15	1
Spencer	3	3	0
Spring City	8	7	1
Springfield	50	36	14
Spring Hill	34	27	7
St. Joseph	1	1	0
Surgoinsville	3	3	0
Sweetwater	20	18	2
Tazewell	7	6	1
Tellico Plains	5	5	0
Tiptonville	7	7	0
Toone	1	1	0
Townsend	3	3	0
Tracy City	4	4	0
Trenton	23	17	6
Trezevant	1	1	0
Trimble	1	1	0
Troy	4	4	0
Tullahoma	40	35	5
Tusculum	2	2	0
Union City	44	37	7
Vonore	9	8	1
Wartburg	3	3	0
Wartrace	1	1	0
Watertown	6	4	2
Waverly	13	12	1
Waynesboro	9	8	1
Westmoreland	10	6	4
White Bluff	3	3	0
White House	29	20	9
White Pine	9	8	1
Whiteville	8	8	0
Whitwell	8	4	4
Winchester	25	24	1
Winfield	3	3	0
Woodbury	9	8	1
Texas			
Abernathy	4	4	0
Abilene	235	177	58
Addison	75	56	19
Alamo	36	27	9
Alamo Heights	30	20	10
Alice	48	37	11
Allen	115	86	29
Alpine	14	9	5
Alto	4	4	0
Alton	14	10	4
Alvarado	18	12	6
Alvin	70	43	27
Amarillo	379	291	88
Andrews	20	14	6
Angleton	47	36	11
Anna	4	4	0
Anson	4	4	0
Anthony	10	9	1
Anton	1	1	0
Aransas Pass	28	20	8
Arcola	6	5	1
Argyle	7	7	0
Arlington	721	544	177
Arp	4	4	0
Athens	35	26	9
Atlanta	19	15	4
Austin	1 835	1 361	474
Azle	28	22	6
Baird	2	2	0
Balch Springs	52	36	16
Balcones Heights	20	14	6
Ballinger	8	6	2
Bangs	3	3	0
Bartlett	5	5	0
Bastrop	20	17	3
Bay City	45	33	12
Bayou Vista	5	5	0
Baytown	175	121	54
Beaumont	313	255	58
Bedford	114	68	46
Beeville	28	23	5
Bellaire	55	42	13
Bellmead	24	17	7
Bellville	9	8	1
Belton	36	27	9
Benbrook	47	36	11
Bertram	3	3	0
Beverly Hills	14	9	5
Big Sandy	6	5	1
Big Spring	64	45	19
Bishop	9	5	4
Blanco	4	4	0
Blue Mound	11	7	4
Boerne	39	24	15
Bogata	3	3	0
Bonham	25	17	8
Borger	33	23	10
Bovina	2	2	0
Bowie	19	14	5
Brady	15	8	7
Brazoria	10	6	4
Breckenridge	18	11	7
Bremond	2	2	0
Brenham	32	29	3
Bridge City	18	12	6
Bridgeport	20	12	8
Brookshire	13	8	5
Brookside Village	5	5	0
Brownfield	26	19	7
Brownsville	298	231	67
Brownwood	52	34	18
Bruceville-Eddy	3	3	0
Bryan	160	118	42
Bullard	5	4	1
Bulverde	11	11	0
Burkburnett	24	19	5
Burleson	63	42	21
Burnet	14	12	2
Caldwell	11	10	1
Calvert	4	4	0
Cameron	14	10	4
Caney City	2	2	0
Canton	18	13	5
Canyon	22	19	3
Carrollton	215	151	64
Carthage	21	14	7
Castle Hills	27	21	6
Castroville	11	9	2
Cedar Hill	67	54	13
Cedar Park	73	52	21
Celina	6	6	0
Center	23	15	8
Childress	14	9	5
Chillicothe	3	2	1
Cibolo	17	15	2
Cisco	9	7	2
Clarksville	6	6	0
Cleburne	67	50	17
Cleveland	32	21	11
Clifton	6	5	1

Table 78. Law Enforcement Employees, by City, 2005

(Number.)

City	Total law enforcement employees	Total officers	Total civilians
Clint	1	1	0
Clute	31	22	9
Clyde	7	6	1
Cockrell Hill	17	12	5
Coffee City	2	2	0
Coleman	14	9	5
College Station	143	100	43
Colleyville	39	30	9
Collinsville	2	2	0
Colorado City	12	6	6
Columbus	11	10	1
Comanche	3	3	0
Combes	7	6	1
Commerce	23	18	5
Conroe	125	94	31
Converse	29	26	3
Coppell	71	55	16
Copperas Cove	63	46	17
Corinth	29	28	1
Corpus Christi	579	409	170
Corrigan	12	7	5
Corsicana	55	42	13
Cottonwood Shores	2	2	0
Crane	11	7	4
Crockett	19	16	3
Crowell	1	1	0
Crowley	29	22	7
Crystal City	15	10	5
Cuero	14	13	1
Cuney	4	2	2
Daingerfield	8	7	1
Dalhart	18	15	3
Dallas	3 518	2 970	548
Dalworthington Gardens	14	13	1
Danbury	1	1	0
Dayton	22	14	8
Decatur	22	17	5
Deer Park	70	49	21
De Kalb	8	6	2
De Leon	5	5	0
Del Rio	91	67	24
Denison	53	42	11
Denton	192	138	54
Denver City	12	7	5
DeSoto	74	67	7
Devine	11	9	2
Diboll	19	14	5
Dickinson	37	29	8
Dilley	7	6	1
Dimmitt	8	7	1
Donna	31	23	8
Double Oak	5	5	0
Driscoll	4	2	2
Dublin	9	6	3
Dumas	28	24	4
Duncanville	74	62	12
Eagle Lake	9	8	1
Eagle Pass	83	68	15
Early	8	7	1
Earth	1	1	0
Eastland	11	9	2
East Mountain	1	1	0
Edcouch	15	10	5
Eden	4	4	0
Edgewood	4	4	0
Edinburg	128	94	34
Edna	11	9	2
El Campo	35	25	10
Electra	12	7	5
Elgin	18	13	5
El Paso	1 428	1 097	331
Elsa	20	13	7
Ennis	39	34	5
Euless	116	81	35
Everman	18	13	5
Fairfield	10	10	0
Fair Oaks Ranch	11	11	0
Falfurrias	15	14	1
Farmers Branch	100	71	29
Farmersville	7	7	0
Farwell	1	1	0
Ferris	13	9	4
Flatonia	4	4	0
Florence	4	4	0
Floresville	22	21	1
Flower Mound	93	66	27
Floydada	7	7	0
Forest Hill	29	24	5
Forney	26	15	11
Fort Stockton	24	16	8
Fort Worth	1 727	1 342	385
Frankston	5	4	1
Fredericksburg	30	26	4
Freeport	36	27	9
Freer	9	5	4
Friendswood	64	48	16
Friona	10	6	4
Frisco	113	85	28
Gainesville	57	42	15
Galena Park	23	17	6
Galveston	210	168	42
Ganado	4	3	1
Garland	431	304	127
Gatesville	21	16	5
Georgetown	84	56	28
Giddings	18	12	6
Gilmer	20	17	3
Gladewater	19	14	5
Glenn Heights	21	14	7
Godley	3	3	0
Gonzales	13	13	0
Gorman	5	4	1
Graham	22	21	1
Granbury	30	24	6
Grand Prairie	299	200	99
Grand Saline	7	7	0
Granger	3	3	0
Grapeland	3	2	1
Grapevine	133	97	36
Greenville	71	48	23
Gregory	3	3	0
Groesbeck	8	8	0
Groves	20	19	1
Gruver	2	2	0
Gun Barrel City	18	14	4
Hale Center	4	3	1
Hallettsville	7	6	1
Hallsville	4	4	0
Haltom City	88	64	24
Hamlin	8	4	4
Harker Heights	48	40	8
Harlingen	158	123	35
Hart	2	2	0
Haskell	4	4	0
Hawk Cove	1	1	0
Hawkins	6	6	0
Hawley	2	2	0
Hearne	17	12	5
Heath	15	14	1
Hedwig Village	24	17	7
Helotes	15	14	1
Hemphill	3	3	0
Hempstead	15	13	2
Henderson	42	32	10
Hereford	28	22	6
Hewitt	30	22	8
Hickory Creek	9	9	0
Hidalgo	41	29	12
Highland Park	67	54	13
Highland Village	32	25	7
Hill Country Village	10	10	0
Hillsboro	30	22	8
Hitchcock	15	10	5
Holland	1	1	0
Holliday	3	3	0
Hollywood Park	10	10	0
Hondo	18	16	2
Hooks	5	5	0
Horizon City	11	10	1
Horseshoe Bay	12	11	1
Houston	6 027	4 779	1 248
Howe	6	6	0
Hubbard	5	5	0
Hudson	4	4	0
Hudson Oaks	12	12	0
Humble	76	59	17
Huntington	6	5	1
Huntsville	53	47	6
Hurst	111	68	43
Hutchins	18	13	5
Hutto	11	10	1
Idalou	3	3	0
Ingleside	24	17	7
Ingram	7	6	1
Iowa Park	17	11	6
Irving	468	320	148
Italy	7	6	1
Itasca	6	6	0
Jacinto City	22	18	4
Jacksboro	15	9	6

Table 78. Law Enforcement Employees, by City, 2005

(Number.)

City	Total law enforcement employees	Total officers	Total civilians
Jacksonville	34	27	7
Jamaica Beach	6	5	1
Jasper	27	20	7
Jefferson	8	7	1
Jersey Village	32	22	10
Johnson City	4	4	0
Jones Creek	4	3	1
Jonestown	7	6	1
Joshua	13	12	1
Jourdanton	6	6	0
Junction	5	5	0
Karnes City	7	6	1
Katy	57	40	17
Kaufman	24	18	6
Keene	15	11	4
Keller	67	47	20
Kemah	23	19	4
Kemp	6	6	0
Kenedy	9	6	3
Kennedale	27	21	6
Kermit	16	9	7
Kerrville	68	52	16
Kilgore	37	28	9
Killeen	229	159	70
Kingsville	65	48	17
Kirby	17	12	5
Kirbyville	5	5	0
Knox City	1	1	0
Kountze	6	6	0
Kress	1	1	0
Kyle	26	17	9
Lacy-Lakeview	22	14	8
La Feria	16	12	4
Lago Vista	18	11	7
La Grange	8	8	0
Laguna Vista	3	3	0
La Joya	17	11	6
Lake Dallas	21	13	8
Lake Jackson	58	43	15
Lakeside	5	5	0
Lakeview	16	12	4
Lakeway	29	23	6
Lake Worth	34	26	8
La Marque	34	27	7
Lamesa	24	17	7
Lampasas	22	16	6
Lancaster	69	52	17
La Porte	98	72	26
Laredo	479	407	72
La Vernia	5	4	1
La Villa	5	5	0
Lavon	6	5	1
League City	121	85	36
Leander	36	25	11
Leon Valley	31	23	8
Levelland	30	21	9
Lewisville	180	127	53
Lexington	4	4	0
Liberty	19	11	8
Lindale	17	13	4
Linden	5	4	1
Little Elm	23	20	3
Littlefield	21	13	8
Live Oak	40	27	13
Livingston	21	14	7
Llano	9	7	2
Lockhart	35	26	9
Lockney	3	3	0
Lone Star	6	5	1
Longview	165	147	18
Lorena	6	5	1
Lorenzo	1	1	0
Los Fresnos	19	14	5
Lubbock	472	359	113
Lufkin	94	73	21
Luling	23	14	9
Lumberton	18	15	3
Lytle	6	6	0
Madisonville	13	11	2
Magnolia	9	8	1
Malakoff	5	5	0
Manor	14	12	2
Mansfield	145	75	70
Manvel	10	8	2
Marble Falls	31	21	10
Marfa	3	3	0
Marion	4	3	1
Marlin	21	16	5
Marshall	68	52	16
Mart	4	3	1
Martindale	5	5	0
Mathis	15	7	8
McAllen	398	262	136
McGregor	15	9	6
McKinney	133	103	30
Meadows Place	16	15	1
Melissa	9	8	1
Memorial Villages	39	32	7
Memphis	3	3	0
Mercedes	31	24	7
Meridian	3	2	1
Merkel	4	4	0
Mesquite	282	209	73
Mexia	26	18	8
Midland	209	161	48
Midlothian	32	24	8
Milford	8	8	0
Mineola	8	7	1
Mineral Wells	34	27	7
Mission	150	111	39
Missouri City	81	61	20
Monahans	16	10	6
Mont Belvieu	15	10	5
Montgomery	7	7	0
Morgans Point Resort	8	7	1
Mount Pleasant	38	28	10
Muleshoe	13	8	5
Munday	2	2	0
Mustang Ridge	2	2	0
Nacogdoches	71	54	17
Naples	3	3	0
Nash	8	8	0
Nassau Bay	14	13	1
Navasota	21	16	5
Nederland	31	20	11
Needville	6	6	0
New Boston	12	9	3
New Braunfels	100	80	20
New Deal	3	2	1
Nocona	9	6	3
Nolanville	5	5	0
Northlake	7	7	0
North Richland Hills	140	98	42
Oak Ridge	4	2	2
Oak Ridge North	16	16	0
Odessa	195	150	45
O'Donnell	1	1	0
Olmos Park	12	12	0
Olney	9	5	4
Olton	2	2	0
Onalaska	6	6	0
Orange	56	42	14
Orange Grove	7	7	0
Ore City	4	4	0
Overton	9	5	4
Ovilla	8	8	0
Oyster Creek	9	5	4
Paducah	7	2	5
Palacios	20	15	5
Palestine	46	36	10
Palmer	8	7	1
Pampa	33	21	12
Panhandle	3	3	0
Pantego	18	12	6
Paris	76	55	21
Parker	7	7	0
Pasadena	332	253	79
Pearland	121	91	30
Pearsall	11	9	2
Pecos	41	19	22
Pelican Bay	3	3	0
Penitas	8	5	3
Perryton	14	7	7
Pflugerville	62	46	16
Pharr	132	98	34
Pilot Point	6	6	0
Pinehurst	10	6	4
Pineland	2	2	0
Pittsburg	13	10	3
Plainview	40	32	8
Plano	468	328	140
Pleasanton	23	17	6
Point Comfort	1	1	0
Ponder	2	2	0
Port Aransas	20	12	8
Port Arthur	143	110	33
Port Isabel	23	19	4
Portland	30	21	9
Port Lavaca	25	19	6
Port Neches	21	18	3

Table 78. Law Enforcement Employees, by City, 2005

(Number.)

City	Total law enforcement employees	Total officers	Total civilians
Poteet	8	6	2
Pottsboro	4	4	0
Premont	5	5	0
Presidio	5	4	1
Primera	6	5	1
Princeton	10	9	1
Progreso	11	9	2
Prosper	7	6	1
Quanah	4	4	0
Queen City	4	4	0
Quinlan	2	2	0
Quitman	6	6	0
Ranger	5	5	0
Ransom Canyon	3	3	0
Raymondville	22	12	10
Red Oak	27	17	10
Refugio	13	9	4
Reno	5	4	1
Richardson	220	133	87
Richland Hills	21	15	6
Richmond	40	31	9
Richwood	7	6	1
Riesel	3	3	0
Rio Grande City	30	22	8
Rising Star	1	1	0
River Oaks	23	18	5
Roanoke	29	22	7
Robinson	21	14	7
Robstown	31	23	8
Rockdale	16	11	5
Rockport	24	22	2
Rockwall	68	52	16
Rollingwood	7	7	0
Roma	29	23	6
Roman Forest	6	6	0
Ropesville	1	1	0
Roscoe	1	1	0
Rosebud	3	3	0
Rose City	2	1	1
Rosenberg	79	61	18
Rowlett	90	63	27
Royse City	14	13	1
Runaway Bay	5	5	0
Rusk	13	11	2
Sabinal	4	4	0
Sachse	40	27	13
Saginaw	33	28	5
Salado	4	4	0
San Angelo	178	148	30
San Antonio	2 482	1 975	507
San Augustine	7	6	1
San Benito	55	48	7
San Diego	8	7	1
Sanger	13	12	1
San Juan	44	35	9
San Marcos	107	81	26
San Saba	5	4	1
Sansom Park Village	15	11	4
Santa Anna	3	3	0
Santa Fe	24	18	6
Santa Rosa	5	5	0
Schertz	50	36	14
Seabrook	33	28	5
Seadrift	2	2	0
Seagoville	29	20	9
Seagraves	4	3	1
Sealy	14	12	2
Seguin	61	46	15
Selma	21	19	2
Seminole	13	11	2
Seven Points	12	9	3
Seymour	10	7	3
Shallowater	5	5	0
Shamrock	9	3	6
Shavano Park	13	12	1
Shenandoah	23	22	1
Sherman	84	59	25
Silsbee	20	15	5
Sinton	12	11	1
Slaton	16	10	6
Smithville	16	10	6
Snyder	17	15	2
Socorro	30	22	8
Somerset	1	1	0
Somerville	4	4	0
Sonora	6	5	1
Sour Lake	6	5	1
South Houston	39	31	8
Southlake	70	56	14
South Padre Island	34	25	9
Southside Place	11	8	3
Spearman	4	4	0
Springtown	14	10	4
Spring Valley	21	16	5
Spur	2	2	0
Stafford	48	34	14
Stamford	10	7	3
Stanton	5	5	0
Stephenville	43	32	11
Stinnett	2	2	0
Stratford	4	4	0
Sugar Land	159	113	46
Sullivan City	10	8	2
Sulphur Springs	40	29	11
Sunrise Beach Village	2	2	0
Sunset Valley	10	10	0
Surfside Beach	6	5	1
Sweeny	7	7	0
Sweetwater	27	22	5
Taft	7	7	0
Tahoka	4	4	0
Tatum	4	3	1
Taylor	33	22	11
Teague	7	6	1
Temple	144	120	24
Terrell	51	35	16
Terrell Hills	13	13	0
Texarkana	104	92	12
Texas City	103	83	20
The Colony	58	42	16
Thorndale	2	2	0
Thrall	4	4	0
Three Rivers	7	6	1
Tioga	2	2	0
Tomball	50	39	11
Tool	7	7	0
Trinity	10	6	4
Trophy Club	19	18	1
Troup	5	5	0
Tulia	15	8	7
Tye	4	4	0
Tyler	220	170	50
Universal City	38	28	10
University Park	49	36	13
Uvalde	39	30	9
Valley View	2	2	0
Van	5	5	0
Van Alstyne	14	9	5
Vernon	30	23	7
Victoria	132	95	37
Vidor	28	21	7
Waco	318	222	96
Waelder	3	3	0
Wake Village	6	5	1
Waller	8	7	1
Wallis	3	3	0
Watauga	41	31	10
Waxahachie	62	48	14
Weatherford	71	52	19
Webster	57	41	16
Weimar	8	7	1
Wells	1	1	0
Weslaco	96	68	28
West	6	6	0
West Columbia	15	8	7
West Lake Hills	19	13	6
West Orange	10	9	1
Westover Hills	14	11	3
West Tawakoni	7	6	1
West University Place	29	21	8
Westworth	14	9	5
Wharton	33	23	10
Whitehouse	21	16	5
White Oak	17	13	4
Whitesboro	11	7	4
White Settlement	42	26	16
Whitney	12	7	5
Wichita Falls	273	185	88
Willis	14	12	2
Willow Park	11	10	1
Wills Point	11	9	2
Wilmer	17	12	5
Windcrest	22	16	6
Wink	1	1	0
Winnsboro	13	9	4
Winters	4	4	0
Wolfforth	7	7	0
Woodville	7	6	1
Woodway	35	25	10
Wortham	6	5	1

Table 78. Law Enforcement Employees, by City, 2005

(Number.)

City	Total law enforcement employees	Total officers	Total civilians
Wylie	36	33	3
Yoakum	17	10	7
Yorktown	4	4	0
Utah			
Alpine/Highland	17	16	1
Alta	8	3	5
American Fork	38	33	5
Big Water	1	1	0
Blanding	6	5	1
Bountiful	45	34	11
Brian Head	5	5	0
Brigham City	30	25	5
Cedar City	37	31	6
Centerville	20	17	3
Clearfield	47	33	14
Clinton	18	15	3
Draper	35	28	7
East Carbon	4	4	0
Ephraim	5	5	0
Fairview	1	1	0
Farmington	14	12	2
Garland	4	4	0
Grantsville	11	9	2
Gunnison	2	2	0
Harrisville	7	6	1
Heber	17	13	4
Helper	6	6	0
Hildale	6	5	1
Hurricane	19	15	4
Kamas	2	2	0
Kanab	7	5	2
Kaysville	20	18	2
La Verkin	4	4	0
Layton	100	74	26
Lehi	30	27	3
Logan	87	54	33
Mantua	1	1	0
Mapleton	7	6	1
Midvale	49	44	5
Minersville	1	1	0
Moab	16	12	4
Monticello	4	4	0
Moroni	1	1	0
Mount Pleasant	6	5	1
Murray	95	72	23
Naples	5	4	1
Nephi	11	9	2
North Ogden	20	17	3
North Park	8	7	1
North Salt Lake	15	13	2
Ogden	159	132	27
Orem	118	86	32
Park City	37	28	9
Parowan	3	3	0
Payson	19	17	2
Perry	4	4	0
Pleasant Grove/Lindon	38	31	7
Pleasant View	7	6	1
Price	18	16	2
Provo	143	91	52
Richfield	14	12	2
Riverdale	24	20	4
Roosevelt	11	9	2
Roy	45	39	6
Salem	7	7	0
Salina	7	6	1
Salt Lake City	564	409	155
Sandy	141	105	36
Santaquin/Genola	7	7	0
Smithfield	8	7	1
South Jordan	49	43	6
South Ogden	28	24	4
South Salt Lake	66	53	13
Spanish Fork	26	24	2
Springville	32	24	8
St. George	114	87	27
Stockton	1	1	0
Sunset	9	8	1
Syracuse	16	14	2
Taylorsville City	57	49	8
Tooele	32	28	4
Tremonton	10	9	1
Vernal	21	17	4
Wellington	4	4	0
Wendover	5	4	1
West Bountiful	10	9	1
West Jordan	128	95	33
West Valley	223	178	45
Willard	2	2	0
Woods Cross	13	11	2
Vermont			
Barre	25	18	7
Barre Town	9	8	1
Bellows Falls	13	9	4
Bennington	31	24	7
Berlin	8	7	1
Bradford	1	1	0
Brandon	7	6	1
Brattleboro	43	28	15
Bristol	4	4	0
Burlington	137	99	38
Castleton	3	3	0
Chester	6	5	1
Colchester	31	24	7
Dover	5	4	1
Essex	32	26	6
Fair Haven	3	3	0
Hardwick	7	6	1
Hartford	27	20	7
Hinesburg	3	3	0
Ludlow	9	5	4
Lyndonville	2	2	0
Manchester	12	8	4
Middlebury	14	13	1
Milton	14	13	1
Montpelier	24	16	8
Morristown	9	9	0
Newport	12	10	2
Northfield	6	5	1
Norwich	5	4	1
Randolph	6	6	0
Richmond	5	5	0
Rutland	50	39	11
Shelburne	17	11	6
South Burlington	44	37	7
Springfield	19	14	5
St. Albans	24	16	8
St. Johnsbury	16	11	5
Stowe	14	13	1
Swanton	5	4	1
Vergennes	4	4	0
Vernon	4	3	1
Waterbury	4	4	0
Weathersfield	1	1	0
Williston	15	13	2
Wilmington	5	4	1
Windsor	12	7	5
Winhall	6	5	1
Winooski	23	15	8
Woodstock	6	5	1
Virginia			
Abingdon	24	22	2
Alexandria	435	313	122
Altavista	11	11	0
Amherst	5	5	0
Appalachia	6	6	0
Ashland	24	21	3
Bedford	32	28	4
Berryville	9	8	1
Big Stone Gap	17	15	2
Blacksburg	72	56	16
Blackstone	18	13	5
Bluefield	21	16	5
Boykins	1	1	0
Bridgewater	8	8	0
Bristol	77	57	20
Broadway	4	4	0
Brookneal	4	4	0
Buena Vista	15	14	1
Burkeville	1	1	0
Cape Charles	5	5	0
Cedar Bluff	3	3	0
Charlottesville	138	111	27
Chase City	11	10	1
Chatham	4	4	0
Chesapeake	504	364	140
Chilhowie	5	5	0
Chincoteague	13	10	3
Christiansburg	62	47	15
Clarksville	8	7	1
Clifton Forge	16	10	6
Clinchco	1	1	0
Clintwood	3	3	0
Coeburn	8	7	1
Colonial Beach	15	10	5
Colonial Heights	49	45	4
Courtland	3	1	2
Covington	23	14	9
Crewe	5	5	0
Culpeper	45	38	7
Damascus	6	6	0

Table 78. Law Enforcement Employees, by City, 2005

(Number.)

City	Total law enforcement employees	Total officers	Total civilians
Danville	138	128	10
Dayton	6	6	0
Dublin	10	9	1
Dumfries	17	15	2
Edinburg	1	1	0
Elkton	9	8	1
Emporia	35	25	10
Exmore	7	7	0
Fairfax City	79	65	14
Falls Church	43	29	14
Farmville	38	24	14
Franklin	38	26	12
Fredericksburg	86	64	22
Fries	1	1	0
Front Royal	44	35	9
Galax	39	24	15
Gate City	5	5	0
Glade Spring	4	4	0
Glasgow	1	1	0
Glen Lyn	1	1	0
Gordonsville	6	6	0
Gretna	4	3	1
Grottoes	6	6	0
Grundy	5	5	0
Halifax	5	5	0
Hampton	376	270	106
Harrisonburg	93	80	13
Haymarket	6	5	1
Haysi	2	2	0
Herndon	67	54	13
Hillsville	12	11	1
Honaker	5	4	1
Hopewell	66	47	19
Hurt	1	1	0
Independence	2	2	0
Jonesville	2	2	0
Kenbridge	8	8	0
Kilmarnock	4	4	0
La Crosse	3	3	0
Lawrenceville	5	5	0
Lebanon	13	12	1
Leesburg	85	67	18
Lexington	15	13	2
Louisa	4	4	0
Luray	14	12	2
Lynchburg	214	135	79
Manassas	110	86	24
Manassas Park	32	24	8
Marion	20	18	2
Martinsville	59	53	6
McKenney	1	1	0
Middleburg	3	3	0
Middletown	3	3	0
Mount Jackson	4	4	0
Narrows	4	4	0
New Market	5	5	0
Newport News	517	386	131
Norfolk	822	699	123
Norton	24	18	6
Occoquan	1	1	0
Onancock	4	4	0
Onley	3	3	0
Orange	17	14	3
Parksley	3	3	0
Pearisburg	8	7	1
Pembroke	2	2	0
Pennington Gap	6	6	0
Petersburg	131	95	36
Pocahontas	1	1	0
Poquoson	24	20	4
Portsmouth	334	242	92
Pound	4	4	0
Pulaski	36	28	8
Purcellville	12	11	1
Quantico	3	2	1
Radford	49	35	14
Rich Creek	1	1	0
Richlands	19	15	4
Richmond	890	696	194
Roanoke	308	254	54
Rocky Mount	19	17	2
Rural Retreat	1	1	0
Salem	89	63	26
Saltville	7	6	1
Shenandoah	4	4	0
Smithfield	26	21	5
South Boston	31	29	2
South Hill	25	20	5
Stanley	4	4	0
Staunton	60	49	11
Stephens City	3	3	0
St. Paul	5	5	0
Strasburg	19	17	2
Suffolk	213	171	42
Tappahannock	11	10	1
Tazewell	13	12	1
Timberville	3	3	0
Victoria	6	5	1
Vienna	49	40	9
Vinton	31	20	11
Virginia Beach	951	786	165
Warrenton	20	18	2
Warsaw	4	3	1
Waverly	13	8	5
Waynesboro	56	49	7
Weber City	4	4	0
West Point	10	9	1
Williamsburg	47	33	14
Winchester	83	70	13
Wise	14	13	1
Woodstock	14	13	1
Wytheville	36	24	12
Washington			
Aberdeen	49	36	13
Airway Heights	12	11	1
Algona	8	6	2
Anacortes	32	24	8
Arlington	29	25	4
Asotin	3	3	0
Auburn	115	85	30
Bainbridge Island	28	22	6
Battle Ground	22	20	2
Bellevue	259	172	87
Bellingham	156	104	52
Black Diamond	11	11	0
Blaine	15	13	2
Bonney Lake	29	24	5
Bothell	78	53	25
Bremerton	75	62	13
Brewster	7	5	2
Brier	9	7	2
Buckley	8	8	0
Burien	32	31	1
Burlington	27	21	6
Camas	27	22	5
Castle Rock	6	5	1
Centralia	36	29	7
Chehalis	21	17	4
Cheney	18	13	5
Chewelah	6	5	1
Clarkston	14	13	1
Cle Elum	8	6	2
Clyde Hill	8	7	1
Colfax	6	6	0
College Place	15	13	2
Colton	1	1	0
Colville	13	11	2
Connell	6	6	0
Cosmopolis	6	5	1
Coulee City	1	1	0
Coulee Dam	8	8	0
Coupeville	5	5	0
Covington	10	10	0
Des Moines	50	39	11
Dupont	9	8	1
Duvall	14	13	1
East Wenatchee	18	15	3
Eatonville	7	6	1
Edgewood	8	8	0
Edmonds	70	53	17
Ellensburg	31	23	8
Elma	8	7	1
Enumclaw	29	22	7
Ephrata	16	13	3
Everett	211	172	39
Everson	5	5	0
Federal Way	146	111	35
Ferndale	18	15	3
Fife	43	23	20
Fircrest	10	9	1
Forks	15	8	7
Garfield	1	1	0
Gig Harbor	17	14	3

Table 78. Law Enforcement Employees, by City, 2005

(Number.)

City	Total law enforcement employees	Total officers	Total civilians
Goldendale	11	10	1
Grand Coulee	7	7	0
Grandview	24	18	6
Granger	12	9	3
Granite Falls	6	5	1
Hoquiam	20	18	2
Issaquah	54	28	26
Kalama	4	4	0
Kelso	31	27	4
Kenmore	11	11	0
Kennewick	105	87	18
Kent	169	116	53
Kettle Falls	6	5	1
Kirkland	100	63	37
Kittitas	2	2	0
La Center	8	7	1
Lacey	60	46	14
Lake Forest Park	26	22	4
Lake Stevens	12	10	2
Lakewood	117	97	20
Langley	3	3	0
Liberty Lake	7	7	0
Long Beach	7	6	1
Longview	64	52	12
Lynden	18	14	4
Lynnwood	95	67	28
Mabton	4	3	1
Maple Valley	10	10	0
Marysville	61	41	20
Mattawa	2	2	0
McCleary	3	3	0
Medical Lake	7	6	1
Medina	11	9	2
Mercer Island	33	28	5
Mill Creek	22	17	5
Milton	11	9	2
Monroe	43	31	12
Montesano	10	8	2
Morton	3	2	1
Moses Lake	34	27	7
Mountlake Terrace	40	31	9
Mount Vernon	57	45	12
Moxee	2	2	0
Mukilteo	25	23	2
Napavine	3	2	1
Newcastle	7	7	0
Newport	4	3	1
Normandy Park	13	12	1
North Bend	5	5	0
North Bonneville	1	1	0
Oakesdale	1	1	0
Oak Harbor	40	27	13
Oakville	1	1	0
Ocean Shores	15	13	2
Odessa	2	2	0
Olympia	96	68	28
Omak	14	11	3
Oroville	6	5	1
Orting	8	8	0
Othello	21	15	6
Pacific	12	10	2
Palouse	2	2	0
Pasco	67	56	11
Pe Ell	1	1	0
Port Angeles	55	29	26
Port Orchard	21	19	2
Port Townsend	17	14	3
Poulsbo	20	17	3
Prosser	17	9	8
Pullman	39	27	12
Puyallup	72	51	21
Quincy	13	11	2
Raymond	6	5	1
Reardan	2	2	0
Redmond	103	71	32
Renton	128	88	40
Republic	3	3	0
Richland	62	53	9
Ridgefield	8	7	1
Ritzville	4	4	0
Rosalia	1	1	0
Roy	3	3	0
Royal City	3	3	0
Ruston	2	2	0
Sammamish	21	20	1
SeaTac	36	33	3
Seattle	1 762	1 281	481
Sedro Woolley	19	14	5
Selah	14	13	1
Sequim	18	15	3
Shelton	33	18	15
Shoreline	44	42	2
Snohomish	22	18	4
Snoqualmie	15	13	2
Soap Lake	4	4	0
South Bend	4	3	1
Spokane	386	281	105
Spokane Valley	101	100	1
Springdale	1	1	0
Stanwood	13	11	2
Steilacoom	13	12	1
Sultan	10	9	1
Sumas	6	6	0
Sumner	33	19	14
Sunnyside	41	23	18
Tacoma	408	372	36
Tenino	4	4	0
Tieton	3	2	1
Toledo	1	1	0
Tonasket	5	4	1
Toppenish	24	17	7
Tukwila	81	67	14
Tumwater	30	25	5
Union Gap	21	16	5
University Place	29	25	4
Vader	1	1	0
Vancouver	226	195	31
Walla Walla	71	44	27
Wapato	20	12	8
Warden	5	4	1
Washougal	19	17	2
Wenatchee	51	40	11
Westport	8	7	1
West Richland	17	14	3
White Salmon	8	8	0
Wilbur	2	2	0
Winlock	2	2	0
Winthrop	1	1	0
Woodinville	8	8	0
Woodland	10	8	2
Yakima	166	120	46
Yelm	13	11	2
Zillah	8	7	1
West Virginia			
Alderson	2	2	0
Ansted	1	1	0
Barboursville	19	17	2
Barrackville	2	2	0
Beckley	64	44	20
Belington	2	2	0
Belle	4	4	0
Benwood	6	5	1
Berkeley Springs	3	2	1
Bethlehem	4	4	0
Bluefield	28	23	5
Bradshaw	2	2	0
Bramwell	1	1	0
Bridgeport	22	20	2
Buckhannon	8	7	1
Cameron	4	4	0
Capon Bridge	2	2	0
Cedar Grove	2	2	0
Ceredo	9	6	3
Chapmanville	5	5	0
Charleston	204	177	27
Charles Town	18	15	3
Chesapeake	4	4	0
Chester	5	5	0
Clarksburg	47	39	8
Clendenin	4	4	0
Danville	3	3	0
Delbarton	2	2	0
Dunbar	16	12	4
East Bank	4	4	0
Eleanor	1	1	0
Elkins	11	8	3
Fairmont	40	34	6
Fairview	1	1	0
Farmington	1	1	0
Fayetteville	8	7	1
Follansbee	7	7	0
Fort Gay	2	2	0
Gassaway	1	1	0
Gauley Bridge	7	5	2

Table 78. Law Enforcement Employees, by City, 2005

(Number.)

City	Total law enforcement employees	Total officers	Total civilians
Gilbert	4	4	0
Glasgow	2	2	0
Glen Dale	8	5	3
Glenville	4	3	1
Grafton	8	7	1
Grantsville	1	1	0
Grant Town	1	1	0
Granville	1	1	0
Hamlin	2	2	0
Handley	1	1	0
Harpers Ferry/Bolivar	4	3	1
Harrisville	2	2	0
Henderson	1	1	0
Hinton	8	7	1
Huntington	93	87	6
Hurricane	14	12	2
Iaeger	1	1	0
Kenova	13	9	4
Kermit	2	2	0
Keyser	12	8	4
Keystone	4	2	2
Kimball	1	1	0
Kingwood	3	3	0
Lewisburg	13	11	2
Logan	11	5	6
Lumberport	2	2	0
Mabscott	4	4	0
Madison	6	5	1
Man	4	4	0
Mannington	4	4	0
Marlinton	1	1	0
Marmet	5	5	0
Martinsburg	43	35	8
Mason	4	4	0
Masontown	4	2	2
Matewan	1	1	0
Matoaka	2	1	1
McMechen	2	2	0
Mitchell Heights	1	1	0
Monongah	1	1	0
Montgomery	7	6	1
Moorefield	6	6	0
Morgantown	67	57	10
Moundsville	21	17	4
Mount Hope	6	5	1
Mullens	4	4	0
New Cumberland	3	3	0
New Martinsville	14	10	4
Nitro	18	17	1
Northfork	3	3	0
Nutter Fort	6	6	0
Oak Hill	15	13	2
Oceana	4	4	0
Paden City	4	3	1
Parkersburg	75	64	11
Parsons	1	1	0
Pennsboro	1	1	0
Petersburg	2	2	0
Philippi	6	6	0
Piedmont	1	1	0
Pineville	5	5	0
Point Pleasant	11	10	1
Pratt	3	3	0
Princeton	20	16	4
Rainelle	4	4	0
Ranson	12	11	1
Ravenswood	10	9	1
Reedsville	1	1	0
Richwood	3	3	0
Ridgeley	3	3	0
Ripley	9	8	1
Rivesville	1	1	0
Romney	4	3	1
Ronceverte	5	5	0
Rowlesburg	1	1	0
Salem	2	2	0
Shepherdstown	5	3	2
Shinnston	6	6	0
Sistersville	4	4	0
Smithers	8	7	1
Sophia	3	3	0
South Charleston	41	37	4
Spencer	7	7	0
St. Albans	22	18	4
Star City	6	5	1
St. Marys	4	4	0
Stonewood	3	3	0
Summersville	17	15	2
Sutton	3	2	1
Terra Alta	2	2	0
Triadelphia	2	1	1
Vienna	20	16	4
War	4	4	0
Wardensville	2	2	0
Webster Springs	2	2	0
Weirton	44	40	4
Welch	8	7	1
Wellsburg	7	6	1
West Logan	1	1	0
Weston	7	6	1
Westover	9	9	0
West Union	1	1	0
Wheeling	84	82	2
White Sulphur Springs	7	6	1
Whitesville	2	2	0
Williamson	10	9	1
Williamstown	6	5	1
Winfield	4	4	0
Wisconsin			
Algoma	5	5	0
Altoona	12	11	1
Amery	8	7	1
Antigo	19	16	3
Appleton	131	103	28
Arcadia	5	5	0
Ashland	21	19	2
Ashwaubenon	58	48	10
Bangor	3	3	0
Baraboo	30	24	6
Barron	7	7	0
Bayfield	4	4	0
Bayside	21	14	7
Beaver Dam	39	29	10
Belleville	4	4	0
Beloit	94	77	17
Beloit Town	11	10	1
Berlin	13	12	1
Black River Falls	8	7	1
Blair	3	3	0
Blanchardville	1	1	0
Bloomer	7	6	1
Bloomfield	8	7	1
Boscobel	6	6	0
Brillion	6	6	0
Brodhead	11	7	4
Brookfield	81	63	18
Brookfield Township	12	11	1
Brown Deer	36	31	5
Burlington	27	21	6
Burlington Town	9	9	0
Butler	9	7	2
Caledonia	36	28	8
Campbellsport	2	2	0
Campbell Township	5	5	0
Cedarburg	29	20	9
Chenequa	8	8	0
Chetek	6	5	1
Chilton	6	6	0
Chippewa Falls	32	25	7
Cleveland	3	2	1
Clinton	6	6	0
Clintonville	15	11	4
Colby-Abbotsford	7	6	1
Columbus	18	12	6
Combined Locks	5	5	0
Cornell	3	3	0
Cottage Grove	12	11	1
Crandon	3	2	1
Cross Plains	4	4	0
Cuba City	5	4	1
Cudahy	42	29	13
Cumberland	5	5	0
Darien	7	6	1
Darlington	5	5	0
Deerfield	3	3	0
Deforest	16	13	3
Delafield	16	14	2
Delavan	22	17	5
Delavan Town	11	10	1
Denmark	2	2	0
De Pere	38	32	6
Dodgeville	10	9	1
Durand	4	4	0
Eagle River	6	6	0
Eagle Village	1	1	0
East Troy	8	7	1
Eau Claire	131	99	32
Edgar	1	1	0
Edgerton	12	11	1

Table 78. Law Enforcement Employees, by City, 2005

(Number.)

City	Total law enforcement employees	Total officers	Total civilians
Eleva	1	1	0
Elkhart Lake	3	3	0
Elkhorn	19	16	3
Elk Mound	2	2	0
Ellsworth	6	6	0
Elm Grove	23	16	7
Elroy	4	4	0
Evansville	9	8	1
Everest	27	24	3
Fennimore	5	5	0
Fitchburg	51	39	12
Fond du Lac	77	71	6
Fontana	6	5	1
Fort Atkinson	27	20	7
Fox Lake	4	3	1
Fox Point	16	15	1
Fox Valley	29	26	3
Franklin	76	58	18
Frederic	1	1	0
Geneva Town	8	6	2
Genoa City	6	5	1
Germantown	42	31	11
Glendale	49	45	4
Grafton	29	21	8
Grand Chute	30	26	4
Grand Rapids	3	3	0
Grantsburg	2	2	0
Green Bay	232	191	41
Greendale	35	27	8
Greenfield	78	58	20
Green Lake	4	4	0
Hales Corners	20	16	4
Hartford	29	25	4
Hartland	17	15	2
Hayward	7	6	1
Hazel Green	2	2	0
Hillsboro	3	3	0
Hobart-Lawrence	2	1	1
Holmen	9	8	1
Horicon	11	8	3
Hortonville	6	5	1
Hudson	24	21	3
Hurley	6	6	0
Independence	3	3	0
Iron Ridge	1	1	0
Jackson	12	11	1
Janesville	115	103	12
Jefferson	17	14	3
Juneau	5	4	1
Kaukauna	26	24	2
Kenosha	194	183	11
Kewaskum	7	7	0
Kewaunee	6	6	0
Kiel	7	6	1
Kohler	8	7	1
La Crosse	114	93	21
Ladysmith	10	9	1
Lake Delton	17	16	1
Lake Geneva	28	20	8
Lake Hallie	5	4	1
Lake Mills	13	11	2
Lancaster	8	7	1
Lodi	6	5	1
Luxemburg	2	2	0
Madison	475	390	85
Manitowoc	74	64	10
Maple Bluff	5	5	0
Marathon City	2	2	0
Marinette	29	24	5
Marion	3	3	0
Markesan	4	4	0
Marshall Village	9	8	1
Marshfield	50	38	12
Mauston	9	8	1
Mayville	11	9	2
McFarland	15	13	2
Medford	10	9	1
Menasha	36	30	6
Menomonee Falls	66	57	9
Menomonie	35	28	7
Mequon	43	36	7
Merrill	24	21	3
Middleton	40	32	8
Milton	10	9	1
Milwaukee	2 420	1 922	498
Mineral Point	6	6	0
Minocqua	14	11	3
Mondovi	4	4	0
Monona	24	19	5
Monroe	35	26	9
Mosinee	7	6	1
Mount Horeb	12	10	2
Mount Pleasant	45	35	10
Mukwonago	20	13	7
Muskego	46	36	10
Neenah	47	38	9
Neillsville	7	6	1
New Berlin	92	73	19
New Glarus	5	5	0
New Holstein	8	7	1
New Lisbon	4	4	0
New London	18	16	2
New Richmond	14	13	1
Niagara	5	5	0
North Fond du Lac	14	12	2
North Hudson	6	5	1
Oak Creek	76	55	21
Oconomowoc	26	20	6
Oconomowoc Town	13	11	2
Oconto	8	8	0
Oconto Falls	5	5	0
Omro	6	5	1
Onalaska	31	28	3
Oregon	14	13	1
Osceola	5	5	0
Oshkosh	115	98	17
Osseo	4	4	0
Palmyra	5	5	0
Park Falls	8	7	1
Pepin	1	1	0
Peshtigo	7	6	1
Pewaukee	19	16	3
Pewaukee Village	18	16	2
Phillips	5	5	0
Platteville	26	20	6
Pleasant Prairie	29	27	2
Plover	19	16	3
Plymouth	16	16	0
Portage	30	22	8
Port Washington	24	19	5
Poynette	6	5	1
Prairie du Chien	17	13	4
Prescott	9	8	1
Princeton	2	2	0
Pulaski	6	6	0
Racine	221	196	25
Reedsburg	23	16	7
Rhinelander	23	17	6
Rice Lake	22	21	1
Richland Center	13	11	2
Ripon	18	12	6
River Falls	25	22	3
River Hills	11	11	0
Rothschild	12	10	2
Sauk Prairie	15	13	2
Saukville	12	10	2
Shawano	21	19	2
Sheboygan	115	88	27
Sheboygan Falls	15	13	2
Shorewood	32	26	6
Shorewood Hills	6	5	1
Silver Lake	4	4	0
Siren	3	3	0
Slinger	9	8	1
Somerset	6	5	1
South Milwaukee	39	33	6
Sparta	18	16	2
Spencer	3	3	0
Spooner	6	5	1
Spring Green	4	3	1
Stanley	4	4	0
St. Croix Falls	4	4	0
Stevens Point	58	44	14
St. Francis	25	20	5
Stoughton	26	20	6
Strum	2	2	0
Sturgeon Bay	22	21	1
Sturtevant	13	7	6
Summit	8	8	0
Sun Prairie	68	44	24
Superior	64	58	6
Theresa	3	2	1
Thiensville	8	7	1
Three Lakes	4	4	0
Tomah	20	18	2
Tomahawk	8	7	1
Town of East Troy	7	6	1
Town of Madison	19	17	2
Town of Menasha	31	25	6
Trempealeau	2	2	0

Table 78. Law Enforcement Employees, by City, 2005

(Number.)

City	Total law enforcement employees	Total officers	Total civilians
Twin Lakes	17	12	5
Two Rivers	30	26	4
Valders	1	1	0
Verona	15	14	1
Viroqua	9	8	1
Walworth	7	6	1
Washburn	5	5	0
Waterloo	9	8	1
Watertown	52	38	14
Waukesha	148	112	36
Waunakee	18	16	2
Waupaca	18	14	4
Waupun	19	17	2
Wausau	72	65	7
Wautoma	6	5	1
Wauwatosa	112	88	24
West Allis	158	134	24
West Bend	75	56	19
Westby	3	3	0
West Milwaukee	21	18	3
West Salem	7	6	1
Whitefish Bay	27	24	3
Whitehall	4	4	0
Whitewater	36	23	13
Williams Bay	7	6	1
Winneconne	6	5	1
Wisconsin Dells	12	12	0
Wisconsin Rapids	47	37	10
Woodruff	6	5	1
Wyoming			
Afton	5	5	0
Baggs	2	2	0
Basin	3	3	0
Buffalo	18	10	8
Casper	105	88	17
Cheyenne	113	93	20
Cody	21	20	1
Diamondville	4	3	1
Douglas	19	14	5
Evanston	34	28	6
Evansville	10	8	2
Gillette	62	41	21
Glenrock	10	7	3
Green River	40	31	9
Guernsey	4	4	0
Hanna	6	2	4
Jackson	29	21	8
Kemmerer	9	8	1
La Barge	1	1	0
Lander	19	18	1
Laramie	73	45	28
Lovell	8	6	2
Lusk	4	4	0
Lyman	7	5	2
Mills	12	10	2
Moorcroft	5	4	1
Newcastle	16	9	7
Pine Bluffs	6	2	4
Powell	22	15	7
Rawlins	33	20	13
Riverton	32	22	10
Rock Springs	66	41	25
Saratoga	9	4	5
Sheridan	47	29	18
Sundance	4	4	0
Thermopolis	14	8	6
Torrington	21	15	6
Wheatland	11	10	1
Worland	10	10	0

Table 79. Full-Time Law Enforcement Employees, by State and University or College, 2005

(Number.)

School	Total law enforcement employees	Total officers	Total civilians
Alabama			
Alabama A&M University	23	13	10
Alabama State University	33	20	13
Faulkner University	15	15	0
Jacksonville State University	17	13	4
Talladega College	4	4	0
Troy University	9	7	2
University of Alabama			
Birmingham	144	68	76
Huntsville	16	12	4
Tuscaloosa	51	42	9
University of Montevallo	14	9	5
University of North Alabama	12	11	1
University of South Alabama	45	29	16
Alaska			
University of Alaska			
Anchorage	20	14	6
Fairbanks	18	11	7
Arizona			
Arizona State University, Main Campus	99	56	43
Arizona Western College	11	6	5
Central Arizona College	5	4	1
Northern Arizona University	23	15	8
Pima Community College	34	26	8
University of Arizona	77	47	30
Yavapai College	9	8	1
Arkansas			
Arkansas State University			
Beebe	18	17	1
Jonesboro	21	17	4
Arkansas Tech University	11	9	2
Henderson State University	8	7	1
Northwest Arkansas Community College	9	4	5
Southern Arkansas University	7	6	1
University of Arkansas			
Fayetteville	33	27	6
Little Rock	28	23	5
Medical Sciences	43	38	5
Monticello	7	6	1
Pine Bluff	18	15	3
University of Central Arkansas	29	23	6
California			
Allan Hancock College	21	6	15
California State Polytechnic University			
Pomona	26	16	10
San Luis Obispo	30	14	16
California State University			
Bakersfield	13	10	3
Channel Islands	19	14	5
Chico	24	16	8
East Bay	31	15	16
Fresno	21	15	6
Fullerton	30	22	8
Long Beach	32	26	6
Los Angeles	33	18	15
Monterey Bay	16	14	2
Northridge	33	20	13
Sacramento	23	18	5
San Bernardino	41	12	29
San Jose	62	28	34
San Marcos	18	12	6
Stanislaus	20	11	9
College of the Sequoias	6	5	1
Contra Costa Community College	29	19	10
Cuesta College	7	6	1
El Camino College	21	15	6
Foothill-De Anza College	17	9	8
Fresno Community College	17	13	4
Humboldt State University	20	11	9
Marin Community College	8	6	2
Pasadena Community College	14	8	6
Riverside Community College	24	19	5
San Bernardino Community College	15	8	7
San Diego State University	53	33	20
San Francisco State University	48	29	19
San Jose/Evergreen Community College	10	6	4
Santa Rosa Junior College	21	12	9
Solano Community College	7	6	1
Sonoma State University	21	10	11

Table 79. Full-Time Law Enforcement Employees, by State and University or College, 2005—*Continued*

(Number.)

School	Total law enforcement employees	Total officers	Total civilians
University of California			
Berkeley	128	66	62
Davis	69	40	20
Hastings College of Law	12	12	0
Irvine	38	27	11
Lawrence-Livermore Laboratory	9	2	7
Los Angeles	77	52	25
Riverside	34	24	10
San Diego	53	29	24
San Francisco	103	38	65
Santa Barbara	44	30	14
Santa Cruz	43	18	25
West Valley-Mission College	13	9	4
Colorado			
Adams State College	5	3	2
Arapahoe Community College	9	7	2
Auraria Higher Education Center	32	20	12
Colorado School of Mines	10	9	1
Colorado State University			
Fort Collins	38	30	8
Pueblo	3	2	1
Fort Lewis College	7	6	1
Pikes Peak Community College	17	15	2
Red Rocks Community College	1	1	0
University of Colorado			
Boulder	57	34	23
Colorado Springs	24	14	10
Health Sciences Center	58	28	30
University of Northern Colorado	19	13	6
Connecticut			
Central Connecticut State University	30	22	8
Eastern Connecticut State University	25	19	6
Southern Connecticut State University	34	27	7
University of Connecticut			
Health Center	22	15	7
Storrs, Avery Point, and Hartford	91	72	19
Western Connecticut State University	29	21	8
Yale University	84	70	14
Delaware			
Delaware State University	29	10	19
University of Delaware	76	39	37
Florida			
Florida A&M University	36	29	7
Florida Atlantic University	73	36	37
Florida Gulf Coast University	21	14	7
Florida International University	56	39	17
Florida State University			
Panama City	79	60	19
Tallahassee	76	58	18
New College of Florida	17	11	6
Pensacola Junior College	17	13	4
Santa Fe Community College	22	15	7
Tallahassee Community College	14	9	5
University of Central Florida	74	48	26
University of Florida	140	89	51
University of North Florida	36	27	9
University of South Florida			
St. Petersburg	18	11	7
Tampa	57	42	15
University of West Florida	27	20	7
Georgia			
Albany State University	26	13	13
Armstrong Atlantic State University	14	8	6
Augusta State University	18	15	3
Berry College	16	10	6
Clark Atlanta University	42	17	25
Clayton College and State University	22	13	9
Coastal Georgia Community College	9	9	0
Dalton State College	8	8	0
Emory University	47	30	17
Fort Valley State University	20	11	9
Georgia College and State University	17	12	5
Georgia Institute of Technology	82	54	28
Georgia Perimeter College	50	12	38
Georgia Southern University	33	27	6
Georgia Southwestern State University	11	10	1
Georgia State University	105	64	41
Kennesaw State University	41	23	18
Medical College of Georgia	46	36	10
Mercer University	34	25	9
Middle Georgia College	12	11	1
Morehouse College	37	11	26
Morris-Brown College	8	3	5
North Georgia College	12	7	5
Piedmont College	2	2	0
Southern Polytechnic State University	16	13	3

Table 79. Full-Time Law Enforcement Employees, by State and University or College, 2005—*Continued*

(Number.)

School	Total law enforcement employees	Total officers	Total civilians
South Georgia College	3	3	0
University of Georgia	83	62	21
University of West Georgia	25	19	6
Valdosta State University	24	16	8
Wesleyan College	4	4	0
Young Harris College	2	2	0
Illinois			
Black Hawk College	9	8	1
Chicago State University	27	24	3
College of DuPage	23	15	8
College of Lake County	17	10	7
Eastern Illinois University	26	23	3
Governors State University	11	9	2
Illinois State University	26	21	5
John A. Logan College	7	7	0
Joliet Junior College	16	8	8
Loyola University of Chicago	52	29	23
Moraine Valley Community College	15	10	5
Morton College	5	3	2
Northeastern Illinois University	21	15	6
Northern Illinois University	65	44	21
Northwestern University			
Chicago	19	15	4
Evanston	38	26	12
Oakton Community College	12	11	1
Parkland College	17	12	5
Rock Valley College	14	12	2
Southern Illinois University			
Carbondale	46	36	10
Edwardsville	41	33	8
School of Medicine	11	2	9
South Suburban College	14	10	4
Triton College	15	10	5
University of Illinois			
Chicago	123	74	49
Springfield	18	11	7
Urbana	70	55	15
Waubonsee College	2	2	0
Western Illinois University	30	25	5
William Rainey Harper College	15	11	4
Indiana			
Ball State University	34	27	7
DePauw University	12	9	3
Indiana State University	35	25	10
Indiana University			
Bloomington	55	43	12
Gary	13	10	3
Indianapolis	52	32	20
New Albany	8	7	1
Marian College	8	5	3
Purdue University	49	39	10
Iowa			
Iowa State University	41	33	8
University of Iowa	47	25	22
University of Northern Iowa	25	18	7
Kansas			
Emporia State University	9	9	0
Fort Hays State University	11	9	2
Kansas City Community College	11	10	1
Kansas State University	43	24	19
Pittsburg State University	16	13	3
University of Kansas			
Main Campus	48	29	19
Medical Center	57	31	26
Washburn University	17	13	4
Wichita State University	31	21	10
Kentucky			
Eastern Kentucky University	41	24	17
Kentucky State University	14	9	5
Morehead State University	26	15	11
Murray State University	22	16	6
Northern Kentucky University	24	16	8
University of Kentucky	51	41	10
University of Louisville	60	27	33
Western Kentucky University	33	24	9
Louisiana			
Delgado Community College	38	26	12
Grambling State University	25	14	11
Louisiana State University			
Baton Rouge	68	66	2
Health Sciences Center, New Orleans	34	34	0
Health Sciences Center, Shreveport	59	42	17
Shreveport	10	9	1

Table 79. Full-Time Law Enforcement Employees, by State and University or College, 2005—*Continued*

(Number.)

School	Total law enforcement employees	Total officers	Total civilians
Louisiana Tech University	21	19	2
McNeese State University	18	11	7
Nicholls State University	14	9	5
Northwestern State University	16	14	2
Southern University and A&M College			
Baton Rouge	27	18	9
New Orleans	7	7	0
Tulane University	47	35	12
University of Louisiana, Monroe	27	21	6
University of New Orleans	19	17	2
Maine			
University of Maine			
Farmington	4	4	0
Orono	32	21	11
University of Southern Maine	27	15	12
Maryland			
Bowie State University	29	15	14
Coppin State University	15	13	2
Frostburg State University	18	15	3
Morgan State University	39	31	8
Salisbury University	20	16	4
St. Mary's College	13	1	12
Towson University	55	36	19
University of Baltimore	42	12	30
University of Maryland			
Baltimore City	145	61	84
Baltimore County	36	26	10
College Park	103	74	29
Eastern Shore	11	8	3
Massachusetts			
Assumption College	18	12	6
Bentley College	33	24	9
Boston College	68	52	16
Boston University	59	47	12
Brandeis University	21	17	4
Bristol Community College	9	6	3
Clark University	14	12	2
Dean College	11	7	4
Emerson College	15	13	2
Fitchburg State College	15	13	2
Framingham State College	17	13	4
Harvard University	91	71	20
Holyoke Community College	11	11	0
Lasell College	19	14	5
Massachusetts College of Art	21	6	15
Massachusetts College of Liberal Arts	10	7	3
Massachusetts Institute of Technology	62	59	3
Massasoit Community College	14	12	2
Merrimack College	17	12	5
Mount Holyoke College	20	15	5
Northeastern University	77	55	22
North Shore Community College	21	19	2
Quinsigamond Community College	10	10	0
Salem State College	27	26	1
Springfield College	29	12	17
Tufts University, Medford	68	43	25
University of Massachusetts			
Amherst	68	53	15
Dartmouth	35	21	14
Harbor Campus, Boston	37	26	11
Medical Center, Worcester	25	20	5
Wellesley College	19	15	4
Wentworth Institute of Technology	17	11	6
Western New England College	21	12	9
Westfield State College	16	12	4
Michigan			
Central Michigan University	22	18	4
Delta College	7	5	2
Eastern Michigan University	31	25	6
Ferris State University	19	14	5
Grand Rapids Community College	13	11	2
Grand Valley State University	19	15	4
Lansing Community College	17	14	3
Macomb Community College	34	28	6
Michigan State University	100	64	36
Michigan Technological University	12	9	3
Mott Community College	3	3	0
Northern Michigan University	23	19	4
Oakland Community College	23	22	1
Oakland University	24	23	1
Saginaw Valley State University	9	7	2
University of Michigan			
Ann Arbor	93	53	40
Flint	19	7	12
Western Michigan University	59	28	31

Table 79. Full-Time Law Enforcement Employees, by State and University or College, 2005—*Continued*

(Number.)

School	Total law enforcement employees	Total officers	Total civilians
Minnesota			
University of Minnesota			
Duluth	10	9	1
Morris	6	3	3
Twin Cities	60	41	19
Mississippi			
Coahoma Community College	8	7	1
Hinds Community College	14	13	1
Itawamba Community College	11	10	1
Jackson State University	50	30	20
Mississippi State University	34	28	6
Missouri			
Central Missouri State University	22	18	4
Lincoln University	14	11	3
Missouri Western State University	12	10	2
Northwest Missouri State University	11	9	2
Southeast Missouri State University	23	17	6
St. Louis Community College, Meramec	12	9	3
Truman State University	11	9	2
University of Missouri			
Columbia	47	30	17
Kansas City	36	18	18
Rolla	16	7	9
St. Louis	22	18	4
Washington University	38	25	13
Montana			
Montana State University	29	14	15
University of Montana	19	13	6
Nebraska			
University of Nebraska			
Kearney	8	7	1
Lincoln	33	28	5
Nevada			
Truckee Meadows Community College	9	6	3
University of Nevada			
Las Vegas	47	34	13
Reno	31	27	4
New Jersey			
Brookdale Community College	19	12	7
Essex County College	59	17	42
Kean University of New Jersey	48	28	20
Middlesex County College	18	12	6
Monmouth University	34	20	14
Montclair State University	39	27	12
New Jersey Institute of Technology	60	26	34
Richard Stockton College	27	19	8
Rowan University	48	8	40
Rutgers University			
Camden	37	18	19
Newark	63	33	30
New Brunswick	123	50	73
Stevens Institute of Technology	21	10	11
The College of New Jersey	29	21	8
University of Medicine and Dentistry			
Camden	18	17	1
Newark	116	46	70
Piscataway	38	30	8
William Paterson University	44	27	17
New Mexico			
Eastern New Mexico University	9	8	1
New Mexico State University	28	16	12
University of New Mexico	51	31	20
Western New Mexico University	5	4	1
New York			
Cornell University	55	43	12
Ithaca College	26	16	10
State University of New York			
Binghamton	41	29	12
Buffalo	68	61	7
Maritime College	8	5	3
Stony Brook	129	52	77
State University of New York Agricultural and Technical College			
Alfred	15	10	5
Canton	12	11	1
Cobleskill	11	10	1
Farmingdale	21	17	4
Morrisville	12	11	1

Table 79. Full-Time Law Enforcement Employees, by State and University or College, 2005—*Continued*

(Number.)

School	Total law enforcement employees	Total officers	Total civilians
State University of New York College			
Brockport	19	17	2
Buffalo	32	27	5
Cortland	21	18	3
Environmental Science and Forestry	12	10	2
Fredonia	16	15	1
Geneseo	20	16	4
New Paltz	25	22	3
Old Westbury	24	20	4
Oneonta	24	17	7
Optometry	14	5	9
Oswego	25	20	5
Plattsburgh	16	14	2
Potsdam	14	12	2
Utica-Rome	16	11	5
North Carolina			
Appalachian State University	31	19	12
Beaufort County Community College	2	2	0
Belmont Abbey College	7	7	0
Davidson College	9	8	1
Duke University	135	58	77
East Carolina University	62	45	17
Elizabeth City State University	16	11	5
Elon University	12	11	1
Fayetteville State University	23	15	8
North Carolina Agricultural and Technical State University	51	28	23
North Carolina Central University	53	26	27
North Carolina School of the Arts	15	14	1
North Carolina State University, Raleigh	55	45	10
Queens University	7	5	2
Saint Augustine's College	23	5	18
University of North Carolina			
Asheville	18	10	8
Chapel Hill	72	48	24
Charlotte	41	33	8
Greensboro	47	31	16
Pembroke	15	12	3
Wilmington	35	22	13
Wake Forest University	34	11	23
Western Carolina University	20	16	4
Winston-Salem State University	25	15	10
North Dakota			
North Dakota State College of Science	3	3	0
North Dakota State University	11	9	2
University of North Dakota	16	12	4
Ohio			
Bowling Green State University	31	24	7
Central State University	13	12	1
Columbus State Community College	32	19	13
Cuyahoga Community College	32	26	6
Hocking College	7	7	0
Kent State University	33	26	7
Lakeland Community College	14	10	4
Marietta College	8	7	1
Miami University	36	25	11
Muskingum College	6	5	1
Ohio State University	61	48	13
Ohio University	30	24	6
Sinclair Community College	25	21	4
University of Akron	37	31	6
University of Cincinnati	134	57	77
University of Toledo	37	30	7
Wright State University	26	17	9
Youngstown State University	26	21	5
Oklahoma			
Cameron University	9	9	0
East Central University	5	5	0
Murray State College	1	1	0
Northeastern Oklahoma A&M College	10	7	3
Northeastern State University	15	13	2
Oklahoma State University			
Main Campus	35	28	7
Okmulgee	6	6	0
Tulsa	5	3	2
Rogers State University	4	4	0
Seminole State College	3	3	0
Southeastern Oklahoma State University	8	7	1
Southwestern Oklahoma State University	4	4	0
Tulsa Community College	16	10	6
University of Central Oklahoma	20	16	4
University of Oklahoma			
Health Sciences Center	52	41	11
Norman	54	31	23

Table 79. Full-Time Law Enforcement Employees, by State and University or College, 2005—*Continued*

(Number.)

School	Total law enforcement employees	Total officers	Total civilians
Pennsylvania			
California University	15	13	2
Cheyney University	13	12	1
Clarion University	16	11	5
Dickinson College	14	11	3
Edinboro University	15	14	1
Elizabethtown College	14	10	4
Indiana University	27	21	6
Kutztown University	20	14	6
Lehigh University	29	20	9
Lock Haven University	11	10	1
Mansfield University	11	11	0
Millersville University	17	15	2
Moravian College	13	9	4
Pennsylvania State University			
Altoona	11	9	2
Beaver	5	5	0
Behrend	9	6	3
Berks	9	8	1
Harrisburg	7	5	2
McKeesport	3	3	0
Mont Alto	5	4	1
University Park	61	45	16
Shippensburg University	20	17	3
Slippery Rock University	17	15	2
University of Pittsburgh			
Bradford	6	5	1
Pittsburgh	126	68	58
West Chester University	34	16	18
Rhode Island			
Brown University	61	31	30
University of Rhode Island	47	26	21
South Carolina			
Aiken Technical College	11	2	9
Benedict College	26	19	7
Bob Jones University	4	4	0
Clemson University	49	30	19
Coastal Carolina University	50	15	35
College of Charleston	48	24	24
Columbia College	9	8	1
Denmark Technical College	5	5	0
Erskine College	1	1	0
Francis Marion University	10	10	0
Lander University	12	10	2
Medical University of South Carolina	68	44	24
Midlands Technical College	6	6	0
Presbyterian College	8	7	1
South Carolina State University	32	19	13
The Citadel	11	11	0
Trident Technical College	23	21	2
University of South Carolina			
Aiken	8	8	0
Columbia	63	42	21
Upstate	10	10	0
Winthrop University	21	14	7
South Dakota			
South Dakota State University	20	12	8
Tennessee			
Austin Peay State University	20	12	8
East Tennessee State University	25	18	7
Middle Tennessee State University	31	26	5
Northeast State Technical Community College	7	5	2
Southwest Tennessee Community College	33	28	5
Tennessee State University	51	35	16
Tennessee Technological University	23	15	8
University of Memphis	33	27	6
University of Tennessee			
Chattanooga	22	16	6
Knoxville	81	52	29
Martin	14	11	3
Memphis	35	20	15
Vanderbilt University	101	75	26
Volunteer State Community College	6	5	1
Walters State Community College	7	7	0
Texas			
Abilene Christian University	10	9	1
Alamo Community College District	71	47	24
Alvin Community College	11	9	2
Amarillo College	16	14	2
Angelo State University	14	10	4
Austin College	8	7	1
Baylor Health Care System	137	48	89
Baylor University, Waco	35	23	12
Central Texas College	9	8	1

Table 79. Full-Time Law Enforcement Employees, by State and University or College, 2005—*Continued*

(Number.)

School	Total law enforcement employees	Total officers	Total civilians
College of the Mainland	6	6	0
Eastfield College	12	10	2
El Paso Community College	40	32	8
Grayson County College	4	3	1
Hardin-Simmons University	8	5	3
Houston Baptist University	13	10	3
Lamar University, Beaumont	32	17	15
Laredo Community College	22	21	1
McLennan Community College	13	6	7
Midwestern State University	12	8	4
Mountain View College	10	10	0
North Lake College	17	16	1
Paris Junior College	3	3	0
Prairie View A&M University	38	23	15
Rice University	41	25	16
Richland College	13	12	1
Southern Methodist University	24	17	7
South Plains College	6	6	0
Southwestern University	7	6	1
Stephen F. Austin State University	38	22	16
St. Mary's University	17	13	4
St. Thomas University	11	1	10
Sul Ross State University	9	7	2
Tarleton State University	15	13	2
Texas A&M International University	20	14	6
Texas A&M University			
College Station	119	52	67
Commerce	25	16	9
Corpus Christi	26	16	10
Galveston	7	6	1
Kingsville	18	12	6
Texas Christian University	35	20	15
Texas Southern University	58	37	21
Texas State Technical College			
Harlingen	13	9	4
Marshall	4	4	0
Waco	15	13	2
Texas State University, San Marcos	69	32	37
Texas Technological University, Lubbock	70	48	22
Texas Woman's University	31	16	15
Trinity University	26	14	12
Tyler Junior College	12	5	7
University of Houston			
Central Campus	89	42	47
Clearlake	21	13	8
Downtown Campus	27	16	11
University of Mary Hardin-Baylor	8	8	0
University of North Texas			
Denton	77	43	34
Health Science Center	22	9	13
University of Texas			
Arlington	75	31	44
Austin	121	52	69
Brownsville	32	15	17
Dallas	33	16	17
El Paso	55	21	34
Health Science Center, San Antonio	88	35	53
Health Science Center, Tyler	28	6	22
Houston	319	84	235
Medical Branch	103	38	65
Pan American	34	14	20
Permian Basin	11	7	4
San Antonio	73	38	35
Southwestern Medical School	100	36	64
Tyler	13	7	6
West Texas A&M University	14	10	4
Utah			
Brigham Young University	40	29	11
College of Eastern Utah	1	1	0
Southern Utah University	4	3	1
University of Utah	95	32	63
Utah State University	18	13	5
Utah Valley State College	9	7	2
Weber State University	10	9	1
Vermont			
University of Vermont	31	17	14
Virginia			
Christopher Newport University	20	15	5
College of William and Mary	22	17	5
Emory and Henry College	4	2	2
Ferrum College	6	6	0
George Mason University	60	43	17
Hampton University	37	20	17
James Madison University	27	22	5
Longwood College	20	13	7
Mary Washington College	22	13	9
Norfolk State University	46	29	17

Table 79. Full-Time Law Enforcement Employees, by State and University or College, 2005—*Continued*

(Number.)

School	Total law enforcement employees	Total officers	Total civilians
Northern Virginia Community College	38	38	0
Old Dominion University	46	36	10
Radford University	26	20	6
Thomas Nelson Community College	9	6	3
University of Richmond	32	16	16
University of Virginia	113	53	60
University of Virginia, College at Wise	8	7	1
Virginia Commonwealth University	158	72	86
Virginia Military Institute	6	6	0
Virginia Polytechnic Institute and State University	56	37	19
Virginia State University	33	19	14
Virginia Western Community College	8	6	2
Washington			
Central Washington University	14	12	2
Eastern Washington University	12	11	1
Evergreen State College	14	9	5
University of Washington	56	44	12
Washington State University			
Pullman	19	17	2
Vancouver	2	2	0
Western Washington University	20	14	6
West Virginia			
Bluefield State College	1	1	0
Concord University	8	6	2
Fairmont State University	7	4	3
Glenville State College	4	2	2
Marshall University	23	20	3
Potomac State College	5	5	0
Shepherd University	10	9	1
West Liberty State College	4	4	0
West Virginia State University	10	9	1
West Virginia Tech	3	3	0
West Virginia University	56	47	9
Wisconsin			
University of Wisconsin			
Eau Claire	10	8	2
Green Bay	11	5	6
La Crosse	10	8	2
Madison	110	61	49
Milwaukee	31	28	3
Oshkosh	12	10	2
Parkside	21	17	4
Platteville	8	7	1
Stevens Point	7	2	5
Stout	10	9	1
Superior	6	1	5
Whitewater	10	9	1
Wyoming			
Sheridan College	2	2	0
University of Wyoming	23	13	10

Table 80. Law Enforcement Employees by County, 2005

(Number.)

County	Total law enforcement employees	Total officers	Total civilians
ALABAMA			
Metropolitan Counties			
Autauga	59	22	37
Bibb	12	11	1
Blount	69	42	27
Calhoun	42	36	6
Chilton	51	24	27
Colbert	58	31	27
Elmore	71	30	41
Etowah	76	59	17
Geneva	13	11	2
Hale	9	7	2
Henry	23	9	14
Houston	79	51	28
Jefferson	655	523	132
Lauderdale	42	31	11
Lawrence	41	21	20
Lee	123	61	62
Limestone	93	36	57
Lowndes	37	9	28
Madison	273	106	167
Mobile	468	144	324
Montgomery	149	112	37
Morgan	123	48	75
Russell	87	31	56
Shelby	177	106	71
St. Clair	88	40	48
Nonmetropolitan Counties			
Baldwin	215	74	141
Chambers	48	17	31
Cherokee	38	16	22
Choctaw	13	5	8
Clay	11	9	2
Cleburne	25	10	15
Coffee	18	14	4
Coosa	19	7	12
Covington	48	22	26
Crenshaw	9	8	1
Cullman	119	73	46
Dale	21	17	4
Dallas	49	24	25
De Kalb	29	24	5
Escambia	46	23	23
Fayette	15	10	5
Jackson	76	33	43
Lamar	21	8	13
Macon	33	18	15
Marengo	29	12	17
Monroe	42	20	22
Perry	14	7	7
Pickens	21	7	14
Pike	18	14	4
Sumter	24	6	18
Talladega	93	36	57
Tallapoosa	54	22	32
Washington	16	9	7
Winston	23	10	13
ARIZONA			
Metropolitan Counties			
Coconino	203	60	143
Maricopa	3 331	744	2 587
Pima	1 248	471	777
Yavapai	349	108	241
Yuma	313	68	245
Nonmetropolitan Counties			
Apache	73	32	41
Cochise	190	87	103
Gila	120	46	74
Graham	55	22	33
Greenlee	31	14	17
Mohave	234	91	143
Navajo	130	42	88
Santa Cruz	70	39	31
ARKANSAS			
Metropolitan Counties			
Benton	168	92	76
Cleveland	11	6	5
Craighead	40	35	5
Crawford	56	23	33
Crittenden	156	35	121
Faulkner	89	39	50
Franklin	17	9	8
Garland	117	41	76
Grant	14	12	2
Jefferson	52	45	7
Lincoln	21	8	13
Lonoke	39	21	18
Madison	12	8	4
Miller	61	27	34
Perry	16	8	8
Poinsett	35	12	23
Pulaski	525	387	138
Saline	68	41	27
Sebastian	67	50	17
Washington	250	109	141
Nonmetropolitan Counties			
Arkansas	38	12	26
Ashley	28	15	13
Baxter	51	31	20
Boone	38	23	15
Bradley	5	4	1
Calhoun	11	6	5
Carroll	56	15	41
Chicot	7	6	1
Clark	29	15	14
Clay	24	9	15
Cleburne	12	2	10
Columbia	31	14	17
Conway	33	15	18
Cross	32	15	17
Dallas	28	6	22
Desha	9	7	2
Drew	28	10	18
Fulton	13	7	6
Greene	46	11	35
Hempstead	21	14	7
Hot Spring	26	15	11
Howard	22	10	12
Independence	73	47	26
Izard	12	10	2
Jackson	20	11	9
Johnson	34	13	21
Lafayette	16	7	9
Lawrence	21	10	11
Lee	7	5	2
Little River	19	8	11
Logan	25	12	13
Marion	21	13	8
Mississippi	78	24	54
Monroe	11	4	7
Montgomery	15	7	8
Nevada	16	6	10
Newton	10	6	4
Ouachita	31	14	17
Phillips	15	12	3
Pike	15	8	7
Polk	23	11	12
Pope	85	32	53
Prairie	15	7	8
Randolph	18	9	9
Scott	14	7	7
Searcy	14	7	7
Sevier	20	11	9
Sharp	21	11	10
St. Francis	28	11	17
Stone	19	8	11
Union	58	26	32
Van Buren	28	13	15
White	74	34	40
Woodruff	9	6	3
Yell	23	12	11
CALIFORNIA			
Metropolitan Counties			
Butte	234	94	140
Contra Costa	1 011	684	327
El Dorado	393	193	200
Fresno	1 127	475	652
Imperial	247	163	84
Kern	1 063	479	584
Kings	196	80	116
Los Angeles	13 939	8 188	5 751
Madera	100	66	34
Marin	316	209	107
Merced	237	187	50
Monterey	430	325	105
Napa	113	85	28
Orange	3 258	1 700	1 558
Placer	386	210	176
Riverside	3 033	1 641	1 392
Sacramento	2 165	1 482	683
San Benito	60	27	33
San Bernardino	2 930	1 573	1 357
San Diego	3 620	2 122	1 498

Table 80. Law Enforcement Employees by County, 2005

(Number.)

County	Total law enforcement employees	Total officers	Total civilians
San Francisco	929	796	133
San Joaquin	698	282	416
San Luis Obispo	332	144	188
Santa Barbara	625	265	360
Santa Clara	681	494	187
Santa Cruz	300	142	158
Solano	438	107	331
Sonoma	653	273	380
Stanislaus	590	233	357
Sutter	124	99	25
Tulare	640	451	189
Ventura	1 095	681	414
Yolo	232	82	150
Yuba	162	123	39
Nonmetropolitan Counties			
Alpine	15	12	3
Amador	83	44	39
Calaveras	104	58	46
Colusa	59	32	27
Del Norte	60	30	30
Glenn	61	28	33
Humboldt	225	176	49
Inyo	70	51	19
Lake	146	62	84
Lassen	87	66	21
Mariposa	68	54	14
Mendocino	155	120	35
Modoc	23	19	4
Mono	43	26	17
Nevada	186	69	117
Plumas	70	35	35
Sierra	15	10	5
Siskiyou	128	96	32
Tehama	106	78	28
Trinity	39	20	19
Tuolumne	131	69	62
COLORADO			
Metropolitan Counties			
Adams	484	340	144
Arapahoe	613	416	197
Boulder	343	207	136
Clear Creek	59	23	36
Douglas	402	268	134
Elbert	33	29	4
Gilpin	37	25	12
Jefferson	720	511	209
Larimer	396	165	231
Mesa	192	101	91
Park	74	29	45
Pueblo	254	137	117
Teller	89	70	19
Weld	244	105	139
Nonmetropolitan Counties			
Alamosa	38	29	9
Archuleta	45	13	32
Baca	10	4	6
Bent	7	6	1
Chaffee	43	18	25
Cheyenne	9	5	4
Conejos	20	17	3
Costilla	12	7	5
Crowley	10	7	3
Custer	19	9	10
Delta	52	20	32
Dolores	7	5	2
Eagle	81	43	38
Fremont	75	36	39
Garfield	100	33	67
Grand	46	21	25
Gunnison	26	12	14
Hinsdale	4	3	1
Huerfano	22	10	12
Jackson	8	4	4
Kiowa	3	2	1
Kit Carson	20	6	14
Lake	19	10	9
La Plata	106	86	20
Las Animas	36	16	20
Lincoln	18	5	13
Logan	50	21	29
Mineral	7	4	3
Moffat	36	18	18
Montezuma	47	37	10

County	Total law enforcement employees	Total officers	Total civilians
Montrose	96	48	48
Morgan	52	41	11
Otero	22	20	2
Ouray	7	6	1
Phillips	3	3	0
Pitkin	39	22	17
Prowers	30	9	21
Rio Blanco	22	13	9
Rio Grande	21	7	14
Routt	42	25	17
Saguache	17	8	9
San Juan	5	4	1
San Miguel	35	14	21
Sedgwick	10	5	5
Summit	72	56	16
Washington	44	13	31
Yuma	17	7	10
DELAWARE			
Metropolitan Counties			
New Castle County Police Department	451	336	115
FLORIDA			
Metropolitan Counties			
Alachua	715	261	454
Baker	47	40	7
Bay	276	197	79
Brevard	665	476	189
Broward	1 568	347	1 221
Charlotte	514	253	261
Clay	523	269	254
Collier	1 218	600	618
Escambia	754	390	364
Gadsden	122	64	58
Gilchrist	51	25	26
Hernando	351	234	117
Hillsborough	3 178	1 168	2 010
Indian River	416	186	230
Jefferson	30	19	11
Lake	382	256	126
Lee	898	580	318
Leon	609	327	282
Manatee	1 060	680	380
Marion	821	336	485
Martin	573	250	323
Miami-Dade	4 141	2 808	1 333
Nassau	208	142	66
Okaloosa	364	258	106
Orange	1 895	1 281	614
Osceola	484	335	149
Palm Beach	2 870	1 234	1 636
Pasco	948	501	447
Pinellas	2 606	833	1 773
Polk	1 448	547	901
Santa Rosa	280	181	99
Sarasota	946	423	523
Seminole	983	387	596
St. Johns	512	241	271
St. Lucie	563	241	322
Volusia	694	448	246
Wakulla	142	68	74
Nonmetropolitan Counties			
Bradford	37	22	15
Calhoun	26	15	11
Citrus	306	201	105
Columbia	179	82	97
DeSoto	109	49	60
Dixie	57	47	10
Flagler	131	91	40
Franklin	83	67	16
Glades	30	27	3
Gulf	45	30	15
Hamilton	57	19	38
Hardee	85	63	22
Hendry	118	60	58
Highlands	262	105	157
Holmes	38	20	18
Jackson	68	49	19
Lafayette	25	9	16
Levy	148	73	75
Liberty	22	18	4
Madison	30	27	3

Table 80. Law Enforcement Employees by County, 2005

(Number.)

County	Total law enforcement employees	Total officers	Total civilians
Monroe	518	240	278
Okeechobee	117	79	38
Putnam	214	122	92
Sumter	175	129	46
Suwannee	93	50	43
Taylor	48	32	16
Union	12	10	2
Walton	213	139	74
Washington	68	30	38
GEORGIA			
Metropolitan Counties			
Augusta-Richmond	696	628	68
Barrow	131	120	11
Bartow	229	172	57
Bibb	291	252	39
Brantley	22	15	7
Bryan	39	34	5
Butts	40	32	8
Carroll	184	102	82
Catoosa	125	63	62
Chattahoochee	10	5	5
Cherokee	327	284	43
Clarke	142	96	46
Clayton County Police Department	312	275	37
Cobb County Police Department	698	565	133
Columbia	305	246	59
Coweta	177	108	69
Crawford	27	12	15
Dade	26	26	0
Dawson	84	53	31
DeKalb	755	572	183
DeKalb County Police Department	1 322	966	356
Dougherty	251	237	14
Dougherty County Police Department	50	42	8
Douglas	292	198	94
Effingham	103	63	40
Fayette	213	127	86
Floyd County Police Department	73	67	6
Fulton	800	526	364
Fulton County Police Department	383	302	81
Glynn	127	41	86
Glynn County Police Department	125	112	13
Gwinnett County Police Department	820	561	259
Hall	338	295	43
Haralson	67	34	33
Harris	55	37	18
Heard	34	18	16
Henry	179	97	82
Henry County Police Department	207	179	28
Jasper	33	17	16
Jones	72	38	34
Lamar	52	27	25
Lee	76	37	39
Liberty	102	59	43
Long	16	15	1
Lowndes	208	180	28
Madison	71	31	40
Marion	10	4	6
McDuffie	42	14	28
McIntosh	52	28	24
Meriwether	46	29	17
Murray	63	36	27
Newton	190	93	97
Oconee	66	43	23
Oglethorpe	27	16	11
Paulding	232	155	77
Pickens	57	33	24
Pike	36	34	2
Rockdale	111	94	17
Spalding	162	84	78
Terrell	17	9	8
Twiggs	33	15	18
Walker	108	72	36
Whitfield	185	154	31
Nonmetropolitan Counties			
Atkinson	14	5	9
Baldwin	91	47	44
Ben Hill	46	25	21
Bleckley	29	14	15
Bulloch	78	41	37
Calhoun	15	6	9
Camden	122	63	59
Candler	18	7	11
Charlton	26	15	11
Chattooga	43	24	19
Clay	9	3	6
Clinch	14	12	2
Coffee	40	34	6
Colquitt	89	84	5
Cook	45	17	28
Crisp	66	44	22
Dodge	34	19	15
Dooly	60	20	40
Early	49	27	22
Emanuel	29	28	1
Fannin	29	20	9
Franklin	51	25	26
Glascock	3	2	1
Gordon	82	48	34
Grady	36	13	23
Greene	51	31	20
Habersham	27	26	1
Hancock	35	21	14
Hart	41	25	16
Irwin	14	8	6
Jackson	107	66	41
Jeff Davis	40	14	26
Jefferson	41	39	2
Johnson	10	6	4
Laurens	99	58	41
Lincoln	29	12	17
Lumpkin	74	37	37
Macon	11	10	1
Miller	23	10	13
Mitchell	45	19	26
Peach	58	28	30
Pierce	30	11	19
Polk	66	23	43
Polk County Police Department	33	30	3
Pulaski	18	11	7
Putnam	60	31	29
Quitman	6	5	1
Rabun	41	40	1
Randolph	17	7	10
Schley	6	4	2
Screven	21	9	12
Seminole	21	12	9
Stephens	47	30	17
Stewart	3	3	0
Taliaferro	12	7	5
Tattnall	36	15	21
Taylor	18	8	10
Telfair	21	11	10
Thomas	77	73	4
Tift	98	45	53
Towns	37	19	18
Treutlen	17	10	7
Troup	119	68	51
Upson	69	35	34
Ware	108	37	71
Ware County Police Department	15	1	14
Warren	4	4	0
Washington	34	20	14
Wayne	49	26	23
Webster	5	4	1
Wheeler	7	3	4
White	56	35	21
Wilkes	16	15	1
Wilkinson	22	12	10
Nonmetropolitan Counties			
Hawaii Police Department	514	378	136
Kauai Police Department	171	130	41
Maui Police Department	407	309	98
IDAHO			
Metropolitan Counties			
Ada	309	139	170
Bannock	70	40	30
Boise	18	12	6
Bonneville	81	55	26
Canyon	139	71	68
Franklin	14	11	3
Gem	23	13	10
Jefferson	28	18	10
Kootenai	109	69	40
Nez Perce	36	21	15
Owyhee	19	11	8
Power	17	10	7

Table 80. Law Enforcement Employees by County, 2005

(Number.)

County	Total law enforcement employees	Total officers	Total civilians
Nonmetropolitan Counties			
Adams	15	10	5
Bear Lake	11	5	6
Benewah	15	7	8
Bingham	47	27	20
Blaine	28	16	12
Bonner	70	45	25
Boundary	18	10	8
Butte	9	3	6
Camas	5	3	2
Caribou	21	15	6
Cassia	50	31	19
Clark	7	3	4
Clearwater	26	17	9
Custer	14	7	7
Elmore	50	21	29
Fremont	26	19	7
Gooding	16	10	6
Idaho	32	22	10
Jerome	16	12	4
Latah	33	25	8
Lemhi	7	6	1
Lewis	11	6	5
Lincoln	8	5	3
Madison	31	20	11
Minidoka	25	16	9
Oneida	10	6	4
Payette	31	16	15
Shoshone	32	19	13
Teton	16	9	7
Twin Falls	60	41	19
Valley	25	14	11
Washington	17	9	8
ILLINOIS			
Metropolitan Counties			
Bond	19	11	8
Boone	84	34	50
Calhoun	9	4	5
Champaign	59	53	6
Clinton	36	15	21
Cook	6 945	2 542	4 403
De Kalb	93	41	52
Du Page	553	431	122
Ford	23	7	16
Grundy	60	27	33
Henry	77	23	54
Jersey	28	13	15
Kane	303	96	207
Kankakee	189	63	126
Kendall	98	90	8
Lake	425	169	256
Macon	158	49	109
Macoupin	52	46	6
Madison	166	80	86
Marshall	16	7	9
McHenry	362	120	242
McLean	66	55	11
Menard	14	7	7
Mercer	23	10	13
Monroe	29	14	15
Peoria	191	60	131
Piatt	30	11	19
Rock Island	145	64	81
Sangamon	225	77	148
Stark	11	4	7
St. Clair	172	160	12
Tazewell	97	41	56
Vermilion	86	35	51
Will	501	260	241
Winnebago	282	110	172
Woodford	38	35	3
Nonmetropolitan Counties			
Adams	63	26	37
Alexander	9	8	1
Brown	6	5	1
Bureau	35	21	14
Carroll	21	8	13
Cass	8	7	1
Christian	35	18	17
Clark	16	9	7
Clay	14	8	6
Coles	44	25	19
Crawford	20	9	11
Cumberland	19	7	12
De Witt	42	16	26
Douglas	25	11	14
Edgar	19	8	11
Edwards	9	4	5
Effingham	44	18	26
Fayette	26	10	16
Franklin	39	17	22
Fulton	41	21	20
Gallatin	2	2	0
Greene	13	6	7
Hamilton	7	3	4
Hancock	22	10	12
Hardin	7	4	3
Henderson	15	8	7
Iroquois	31	18	13
Jackson	71	25	46
Jasper	19	9	10
Jefferson	56	24	32
Jo Daviess	38	19	19
Johnson	13	8	5
Knox	55	52	3
La Salle	98	46	52
Lawrence	15	4	11
Lee	41	20	21
Livingston	53	30	23
Logan	31	19	12
Marion	36	12	24
Mason	20	9	11
Massac	28	12	16
McDonough	25	13	12
Montgomery	25	13	12
Morgan	36	15	21
Moultrie	18	10	8
Ogle	62	43	19
Perry	33	11	22
Pike	28	11	17
Pope	3	3	0
Pulaski	14	10	4
Putnam	11	6	5
Randolph	26	11	15
Richland	19	7	12
Saline	45	10	35
Schuyler	4	4	0
Scott	7	3	4
Shelby	24	12	12
Stephenson	70	25	45
Union	16	9	7
Wabash	5	4	1
Warren	18	9	9
Washington	12	5	7
Wayne	22	11	11
White	9	8	1
Whiteside	63	24	39
Williamson	66	35	31
INDIANA			
Metropolitan Counties			
Allen	338	125	213
Bartholomew	69	37	32
Benton	20	6	14
Boone	55	25	30
Brown	39	13	26
Carroll	25	12	13
Clark	100	35	65
Dearborn	28	28	0
Delaware	111	47	64
Elkhart	177	67	110
Floyd	79	22	57
Franklin	12	10	2
Gibson	41	16	25
Greene	39	13	26
Hamilton	73	60	13
Hancock	76	38	38
Harrison	29	21	8
Hendricks	60	50	10
Howard	113	33	80
Jasper	45	21	24
Johnson	113	88	25
La Porte	149	57	92
Madison	118	50	68
Monroe	42	30	12
Morgan	65	22	43
Newton	47	15	32
Ohio	9	9	0
Owen	33	11	22
Porter	144	121	23
Posey	13	12	1

Table 80. Law Enforcement Employees by County, 2005

(Number.)

County	Total law enforcement employees	Total officers	Total civilians
Putnam	35	15	20
Shelby	79	26	53
St. Joseph	290	128	162
Tippecanoe	147	46	101
Vanderburgh	248	106	142
Vermillion	24	7	17
Vigo	99	36	63
Warrick	80	37	43
Washington	37	12	25
Wells	38	15	23
Nonmetropolitan Counties			
Adams	38	15	23
Blackford	28	8	20
Cass	55	18	37
Crawford	7	7	0
Daviess	57	14	43
Decatur	27	9	18
De Kalb	55	18	37
Dubois	36	16	20
Fayette	36	11	25
Fountain	19	8	11
Fulton	28	10	18
Grant	111	45	66
Henry	60	29	31
Huntington	40	14	26
Jackson	50	14	36
Jay	32	11	21
Jefferson	19	12	7
Jennings	40	14	26
Knox	28	12	16
Kosciusko	83	35	48
LaGrange	51	17	34
Lawrence	64	25	39
Marshall	52	21	31
Martin	15	7	8
Miami	35	15	20
Montgomery	42	17	25
Noble	74	21	53
Orange	28	8	20
Parke	38	12	26
Perry	17	7	10
Pike	26	9	17
Pulaski	39	9	30
Randolph	40	16	24
Ripley	11	11	0
Rush	23	10	13
Scott	25	9	16
Spencer	51	13	38
Starke	27	12	15
Steuben	62	21	41
Switzerland	25	9	16
Union	6	6	0
Wabash	35	14	21
Warren	20	7	13
Wayne	101	69	32
White	30	12	18
IOWA			
Metropolitan Counties			
Benton	23	9	14
Black Hawk	136	102	34
Bremer	28	12	16
Dallas	43	17	26
Dubuque	73	63	10
Grundy	16	12	4
Guthrie	11	5	6
Harrison	25	9	16
Johnson	86	59	27
Jones	23	10	13
Linn	170	112	58
Madison	13	6	7
Mills	28	11	17
Polk	325	166	159
Pottawattamie	148	46	102
Scott	162	44	118
Story	82	31	51
Warren	33	23	10
Washington	32	15	17
Woodbury	110	31	79
Nonmetropolitan Counties			
Adair	8	6	2
Adams	8	4	4
Allamakee	14	8	6
Appanoose	16	9	7
Audubon	8	4	4
Boone	23	10	13
Buchanan	28	11	17
Buena Vista	10	9	1
Butler	18	11	7
Calhoun	11	6	5

County	Total law enforcement employees	Total officers	Total civilians
Carroll	16	10	6
Cass	10	7	3
Cedar	36	11	25
Cerro Gordo	50	17	33
Cherokee	15	5	10
Chickasaw	13	8	5
Clarke	19	6	13
Clay	17	10	7
Clayton	25	12	13
Clinton	40	23	17
Crawford	12	10	2
Davis	10	5	5
Decatur	11	6	5
Delaware	11	10	1
Des Moines	42	21	21
Dickinson	17	8	9
Emmet	17	8	9
Fayette	27	10	17
Floyd	20	10	10
Franklin	11	8	3
Fremont	18	7	11
Greene	14	7	7
Hamilton	29	9	20
Hancock	10	8	2
Hardin	28	10	18
Henry	26	12	14
Howard	15	8	7
Humboldt	12	9	3
Ida	13	7	6
Iowa	21	11	10
Jackson	10	10	0
Jasper	43	14	29
Jefferson	27	8	19
Keokuk	9	6	3
Kossuth	24	9	15
Lee	28	15	13
Louisa	19	8	11
Lucas	13	5	8
Lyon	30	10	20
Mahaska	24	9	15
Marion	24	11	13
Marshall	54	18	36
Mitchell	16	6	10
Monona	18	8	10
Monroe	12	5	7
Montgomery	24	8	16
Muscatine	23	23	0
O'Brien	29	11	18
Osceola	13	8	5
Page	14	7	7
Palo Alto	15	8	7
Plymouth	27	10	17
Pocahontas	13	7	6
Poweshiek	18	11	7
Ringgold	11	6	5
Sac	14	6	8
Shelby	13	7	6
Sioux	35	13	22
Tama	21	12	9
Taylor	10	6	4
Union	11	5	6
Van Buren	11	5	6
Wapello	40	10	30
Wayne	10	5	5
Webster	33	16	17
Winnebago	13	5	8
Winneshiek	23	10	13
Worth	16	5	11
Wright	18	7	11
KANSAS			
Metropolitan Counties			
Butler	99	47	52
Doniphan	11	6	5
Douglas	129	80	49
Franklin	48	23	25
Harvey	35	15	20
Jackson	23	14	9
Jefferson	40	22	18
Johnson	528	438	90
Leavenworth	88	48	40
Linn	21	10	11
Miami	41	26	15
Osage	43	22	21
Sedgwick	495	162	333
Shawnee	146	111	35
Sumner	26	17	9
Wabaunsee	18	7	11
Wyandotte	146	117	29

Table 80. Law Enforcement Employees by County, 2005

(Number.)

County	Total law enforcement employees	Total officers	Total civilians
Nonmetropolitan Counties			
Allen	23	8	15
Anderson	17	16	1
Atchison	25	11	14
Barber	10	5	5
Barton	23	20	3
Bourbon	21	6	15
Brown	20	8	12
Chase	9	5	4
Chautauqua	8	3	5
Cherokee	43	16	27
Cheyenne	4	3	1
Clark	9	4	5
Cloud	12	7	5
Coffey	30	13	17
Cowley	36	20	16
Crawford	69	32	37
Decatur	3	3	0
Dickinson	26	14	12
Edwards	8	4	4
Elk	8	3	5
Ellis	26	16	10
Ellsworth	16	8	8
Finney	98	40	58
Ford	53	27	26
Geary	94	25	69
Gove	5	4	1
Graham	7	3	4
Grant	15	5	10
Gray	12	6	6
Greeley	6	3	3
Greenwood	22	14	8
Hamilton	12	6	6
Harper	9	3	6
Haskell	16	10	6
Hodgeman	8	4	4
Jewell	9	5	4
Kearny	18	10	8
Kingman	16	7	9
Kiowa	12	6	6
Labette	32	19	13
Lane	8	4	4
Lincoln	12	8	4
Logan	4	3	1
Lyon	34	20	14
Marion	9	8	1
Marshall	16	8	8
McPherson	33	15	18
Meade	14	4	10
Mitchell	15	7	8
Montgomery	33	22	11
Morris	12	7	5
Morton	10	5	5
Nemaha	17	7	10
Neosho	38	13	25
Ness	12	6	6
Norton	9	4	5
Osborne	15	10	5
Ottawa	20	5	15
Pawnee	15	7	8
Phillips	13	9	4
Pottawatomie	31	23	8
Pratt	15	8	7
Rawlins	5	3	2
Reno	80	68	12
Republic	13	7	6
Rice	6	5	1
Riley County Police Department	167	94	73
Rooks	5	4	1
Rush	8	3	5
Russell	18	10	8
Saline	92	42	50
Scott	4	3	1
Seward	36	11	25
Sheridan	7	4	3
Sherman	11	5	6
Smith	8	3	5
Stafford	9	4	5
Stanton	13	5	8
Stevens	18	9	9
Thomas	15	10	5
Trego	3	3	0
Wallace	3	2	1
Washington	5	5	0
Wichita	9	4	5
Wilson	29	11	18
Woodson	11	7	4
KENTUCKY			
Metropolitan Counties			
Boone	143	133	10
Bourbon	6	5	1
Boyd	23	19	4
Boyd County Police Department	5	4	1
Bracken	4	3	1
Bullitt	42	36	6
Campbell	13	10	3
Campbell County Police Department	32	31	1
Christian	22	17	5
Christian County Police Department	8	7	1
Clark	16	13	3
Daviess	65	40	25
Edmonson	5	3	2
Fayette	73	41	32
Gallatin	7	5	2
Gallatin County Police Department	1	1	0
Grant	19	17	2
Greenup	13	12	1
Hancock	7	6	1
Hardin	36	34	2
Henderson	21	17	4
Henry	6	6	0
Jefferson	278	229	49
Jessamine	26	20	6
Kenton	29	24	5
Kenton County Police Department	65	39	26
Larue	5	4	1
McLean	8	6	2
McLean County Police Department	1	1	0
Meade	11	9	2
Nelson	29	23	6
Oldham	17	16	1
Oldham County Police Department	33	30	3
Pendleton	7	6	1
Scott	31	29	2
Shelby	24	23	1
Spencer	7	6	1
Trigg	7	7	0
Trimble	3	2	1
Warren	59	42	17
Webster	7	5	2
Woodford	7	7	0
Nonmetropolitan Counties			
Adair	5	3	2
Allen	12	10	2
Anderson	12	11	1
Ballard	11	11	0
Barren	14	12	2
Bath	5	4	1
Bell	11	8	3
Boyle	10	10	0
Breathitt	2	2	0
Breckinridge	8	6	2
Butler	4	2	2
Caldwell	7	5	2
Calloway	23	17	6
Carlisle	2	1	1
Carroll	5	4	1
Carter	8	6	2
Casey	7	7	0
Clay	7	5	2
Clinton	5	4	1
Crittenden	4	3	1
Cumberland	5	4	1
Elliott	3	2	1
Elliott County Police Department	4	3	1
Estill	3	2	1
Fleming	11	11	0
Floyd	16	8	8
Franklin	19	18	1
Fulton	4	4	0
Garrard	6	4	2
Graves	14	10	4
Grayson	10	8	2
Green	4	3	1
Harlan	15	12	3
Harrison	8	8	0
Hart	6	5	1
Hickman	3	3	0
Hopkins	25	18	7
Jackson	6	4	2
Johnson	14	10	4
Knott	8	5	3

Table 80. Law Enforcement Employees by County, 2005

(Number.)

County	Total law enforcement employees	Total officers	Total civilians
Knox	14	6	8
Laurel	29	24	5
Lawrence	8	6	2
Lee	3	2	1
Leslie	9	6	3
Letcher	13	6	7
Lewis	7	5	2
Lincoln	9	9	0
Livingston	7	7	0
Logan	19	19	0
Lyon	5	5	0
Madison	17	15	2
Magoffin	5	3	2
Marion	7	6	1
Marshall	20	17	3
Martin	7	5	2
Mason	11	9	2
McCracken	37	37	0
McCreary	6	5	1
Menifee	6	6	0
Mercer	10	9	1
Metcalfe	4	3	1
Monroe	4	3	1
Montgomery	15	12	3
Morgan	8	3	5
Muhlenberg	11	11	0
Nicholas	2	1	1
Ohio	22	19	3
Owen	7	5	2
Owsley	5	4	1
Perry	13	12	1
Pike	23	13	10
Powell	8	6	2
Pulaski	35	26	9
Robertson	1	1	0
Rockcastle	10	8	2
Rowan	13	10	3
Russell	10	9	1
Simpson	14	11	3
Taylor	13	10	3
Todd	4	3	1
Union	0	8	1
Washington	5	5	0
Wayne	9	7	2
Whitley	11	9	2
Wolfe	3	2	1
LOUISIANA			
Metropolitan Counties			
Ascension	232	197	35
Bossier	297	261	36
Cameron	69	69	0
De Soto	86	77	9
East Baton Rouge	817	701	116
East Feliciana	34	20	14
Iberville	132	63	69
Jefferson	1 325	904	421
Lafourche	325	244	81
Livingston	196	196	0
Ouachita	357	357	0
Plaquemines	192	192	0
Pointe Coupee	82	82	0
St. Charles	343	242	101
St. Helena	49	32	17
St. John the Baptist	210	206	4
St. Tammany	595	482	113
Terrebonne	315	315	0
Union	43	32	11
West Feliciana	69	42	27
Nonmetropolitan Counties			
Allen	44	23	21
Assumption	73	42	31
Beauregard	67	52	15
Bienville	44	38	6
Catahoula	92	21	71
Claiborne	30	26	4
East Carroll	215	191	24
Franklin	80	80	0
Jackson	37	37	0
Jefferson Davis	46	35	11
Lincoln	59	41	18
Madison	66	66	0
Morehouse	140	36	104
Natchitoches	62	60	2
Red River	45	38	7
Richland	139	120	19
Sabine	102	74	28
St. Mary	152	125	27
Tangipahoa	247	171	76
Tensas	132	31	101

County	Total law enforcement employees	Total officers	Total civilians
Vermilion	99	55	44
Vernon	142	140	2
Washington	110	110	0
Webster	127	127	0
West Carroll	18	18	0
Winn	24	24	0
MAINE			
Metropolitan Counties			
Androscoggin	27	18	9
Cumberland	52	48	4
Penobscot	28	24	4
Sagadahoc	19	17	2
York	27	23	4
Nonmetropolitan Counties			
Aroostook	25	19	6
Franklin	26	15	11
Hancock	19	17	2
Kennebec	55	45	10
Knox	20	18	2
Lincoln	24	21	3
Oxford	16	15	1
Piscataquis	17	7	10
Somerset	17	15	2
Waldo	18	16	2
Washington	23	13	10
MARYLAND			
Metropolitan Counties			
Allegany	25	23	2
Anne Arundel	91	64	27
Anne Arundel County Police Department	876	657	219
Baltimore County	87	70	17
Baltimore County Police Department	2 154	1 816	338
Calvert	108	93	15
Carroll	76	59	17
Cecil	98	87	11
Charles	396	254	142
Frederick	210	157	53
Harford	307	254	53
Howard	64	37	27
Howard County Police Department	513	368	145
Montgomery	157	128	29
Montgomery County Police Department	1 633	1 193	440
Prince George's	282	183	99
Prince George's County Police Department	1 634	1 403	231
Queen Anne's	47	44	3
Somerset	22	19	3
Washington	201	77	124
Wicomico	95	73	22
Nonmetropolitan Counties			
Caroline	28	26	2
Dorchester	31	27	4
Garrett	49	28	21
Kent	23	21	2
St. Mary's	225	122	103
Talbot	25	23	2
Worcester	47	40	7
MICHIGAN			
Metropolitan Counties			
Barry	55	31	24
Bay	88	38	50
Berrien	168	72	96
Calhoun	182	73	109
Cass	72	35	37
Clinton	59	26	33
Eaton	131	72	59
Genesee	271	142	129
Ingham	214	127	87
Ionia	54	22	32
Jackson	140	52	88
Kalamazoo	207	160	47
Kent	554	209	345
Lapeer	82	48	34
Livingston	128	68	60
Macomb	504	251	253
Monroe	202	96	106
Muskegon	117	49	68
Newaygo	64	26	38
Oakland	1 038	857	181
Ottawa	211	117	94
Saginaw	135	75	60
St. Clair	170	67	103
Van Buren	93	49	44
Washtenaw	278	135	143
Wayne	1 291	920	371

Table 80. Law Enforcement Employees by County, 2005

(Number.)

County	Total law enforcement employees	Total officers	Total civilians
Nonmetropolitan Counties			
Alcona	26	15	11
Alger	13	10	3
Allegan	106	62	44
Alpena	27	13	14
Antrim	46	20	26
Arenac	13	11	2
Baraga	13	6	7
Benzie	50	16	34
Branch	50	26	24
Charlevoix	37	18	19
Cheboygan	36	18	18
Chippewa	33	15	18
Clare	24	20	4
Crawford	26	14	12
Delta	31	15	16
Dickinson	33	14	19
Emmet	43	23	20
Gladwin	39	18	21
Gogebic	18	12	6
Grand Traverse	121	64	57
Gratiot	37	19	18
Hillsdale	41	26	15
Huron	38	23	15
Iosco	25	6	19
Iron	20	8	12
Isabella	50	24	26
Kalkaska	36	17	19
Keweenaw	6	6	0
Lake	56	15	41
Leelanau	40	22	18
Lenawee	102	47	55
Luce	4	3	1
Mackinac	18	7	11
Manistee	29	13	16
Marquette	49	20	29
Mason	40	19	21
Mecosta	47	24	23
Menominee	32	16	16
Midland	65	42	23
Missaukee	27	13	14
Montcalm	56	25	31
Montmorency	24	11	13
Oceana	35	19	16
Ogemaw	28	14	14
Ontonagon	12	9	3
Osceola	33	16	17
Oscoda	17	11	6
Otsego	26	13	13
Presque Isle	26	13	13
Roscommon	43	28	15
Sanilac	53	26	27
Schoolcraft	13	4	9
Shiawassee	61	30	31
St. Joseph	48	26	22
Tuscola	44	20	24
Wexford	50	24	26
MINNESOTA			
Metropolitan Counties			
Anoka	217	112	105
Benton	66	26	40
Carlton	44	21	23
Carver	136	71	65
Chisago	95	41	54
Clay	61	30	31
Dakota	157	75	82
Dodge	32	22	10
Hennepin	734	315	419
Houston	23	11	12
Isanti	54	18	36
Olmsted	128	50	78
Polk	28	23	5
Ramsey	401	239	162
Scott	117	36	81
Sherburne	206	57	149
Stearns	141	49	92
St. Louis	172	87	85
Wabasha	31	16	15
Washington	218	85	133
Wright	177	111	66

County	Total law enforcement employees	Total officers	Total civilians
Nonmetropolitan Counties			
Aitkin	46	18	28
Becker	53	21	32
Beltrami	68	27	41
Big Stone	8	5	3
Blue Earth	60	23	37
Brown	35	9	26
Cass	59	33	26
Chippewa	17	7	10
Clearwater	16	6	10
Cook	17	11	6
Cottonwood	19	8	11
Crow Wing	102	38	64
Douglas	70	29	41
Faribault	21	10	11
Fillmore	31	18	13
Freeborn	52	21	31
Goodhue	104	37	67
Grant	11	6	5
Hubbard	34	13	21
Itasca	69	63	6
Jackson	18	7	11
Kanabec	30	13	17
Kandiyohi	110	34	76
Kittson	10	5	5
Koochiching	17	9	8
Lac qui Parle	9	5	4
Lake	27	14	13
Lake of the Woods	12	7	5
Le Sueur	25	15	10
Lincoln	10	4	6
Lyon	35	12	23
Mahnomen	18	11	7
Marshall	18	12	6
Martin	29	10	19
McLeod	59	22	37
Meeker	38	14	24
Mille Lacs	60	21	39
Morrison	46	16	30
Mower	48	20	28
Murray	11	6	5
Nicollet	25	11	14
Nobles	30	10	20
Norman	8	5	3
Otter Tail	75	31	44
Pennington	34	7	27
Pine	73	27	46
Pipestone	25	10	15
Pope	12	6	6
Red Lake	9	5	4
Redwood	22	11	11
Renville	17	10	7
Rice	48	22	26
Rock	16	11	5
Roseau	20	10	10
Sibley	22	10	12
Steele	25	18	7
Stevens	10	4	6
Swift	13	6	7
Todd	31	14	17
Traverse	7	4	3
Wadena	18	7	11
Waseca	25	12	13
Watonwan	21	9	12
Wilkin	9	6	3
Winona	61	19	42
Yellow Medicine	19	7	12
MISSISSIPPI			
Metropolitan Counties			
Copiah	45	18	27
Desoto	192	81	111
George	17	12	5
Harrison	370	130	240
Hinds	431	97	334
Jackson	135	74	61
Madison	112	48	64
Marshall	43	25	18
Perry	18	9	9
Rankin	149	72	77

Table 80. Law Enforcement Employees by County, 2005

(Number.)

County	Total law enforcement employees	Total officers	Total civilians
Simpson	33	13	20
Stone	16	12	4
Tate	33	16	17
Tunica	143	70	73
Nonmetropolitan Counties			
Adams	50	25	25
Attala	13	8	5
Chickasaw	21	13	8
Choctaw	10	5	5
Claiborne	27	12	15
Clay	31	10	21
Coahoma	44	16	28
Covington	12	5	7
Greene	13	5	8
Grenada	14	11	3
Humphreys	15	8	7
Itawamba	21	11	10
Jefferson	57	9	48
Jones	58	54	4
Kemper	12	5	7
Lauderdale	130	47	83
Lawrence	24	11	13
Lee	126	41	85
Leflore	33	22	11
Lincoln	48	23	25
Lowndes	49	41	8
Marion	31	31	0
Monroe	40	14	26
Montgomery	7	6	1
Neshoba	17	16	1
Newton	17	9	8
Noxubee	10	4	6
Oktibbeha	25	22	3
Panola	52	17	35
Pike	45	23	22
Pontotoc	36	20	16
Prentiss	27	13	14
Quitman	8	7	1
Scott	46	15	31
Sharkey	12	7	5
Smith	14	8	6
Sunflower	36	10	26
Tallahatchie	26	11	15
Tippah	24	9	15
Tishomingo	21	10	11
Union	38	27	11
Walthall	18	11	7
Warren	47	37	10
Washington	52	31	21
Wayne	20	9	11
Webster	9	6	3
Winston	9	8	1
Yalobusha	13	9	4
Yazoo	13	10	3
MISSOURI			
Metropolitan Counties			
Andrew	16	11	5
Bates	29	12	17
Boone	136	65	71
Buchanan	86	62	24
Caldwell	51	9	42
Callaway	25	23	2
Cass	86	68	18
Christian	68	47	21
Clay	173	105	68
Clinton	23	16	7
Cole	45	35	10
Dallas	21	16	5
De Kalb	9	5	4
Franklin	119	97	22
Greene	258	133	125
Howard	12	8	4
Jackson	134	87	47
Jasper	115	74	41
Jefferson	225	151	74
Lafayette	39	28	11
Lincoln	88	79	9
McDonald	23	12	11
Moniteau	14	11	3
Newton	64	32	32
Osage	10	9	1
Platte	119	85	34
Polk	35	23	12
Ray	34	12	22
St. Charles	210	150	60
St. Louis County Police Department	949	713	236
Warren	52	31	21
Washington	33	18	15
Webster	27	17	10
Nonmetropolitan Counties			
Adair	28	10	18
Atchison	8	4	4
Audrain	28	28	0
Barry	36	20	16
Barton	15	6	9
Benton	24	17	7
Bollinger	13	9	4
Butler	38	21	17
Camden	51	36	15
Cape Girardeau	64	40	24
Carroll	11	7	4
Carter	8	3	5
Cedar	19	12	7
Chariton	16	11	5
Clark	19	11	8
Cooper	11	9	2
Crawford	35	24	11
Dade	11	6	5
Daviess	6	5	1
Dent	19	14	5
Douglas	11	7	4
Dunklin	20	8	12
Gasconade	10	9	1
Gentry	8	7	1
Grundy	8	4	4
Harrison	13	5	8
Henry	24	16	8
Hickory	11	7	4
Holt	7	4	3
Howell	38	28	10
Iron	12	7	5
Johnson	37	33	4
Knox	5	2	3
Laclede	18	18	0
Lawrence	33	22	11
Lewis	10	4	6
Linn	7	6	1
Livingston	17	9	8
Macon	15	12	3
Madison	11	9	2
Maries	7	7	0
Marion	40	15	25
Mercer	8	3	5
Miller	18	14	4
Mississippi	43	11	32
Monroe	8	8	0
Montgomery	14	13	1
Morgan	43	22	21
New Madrid	21	12	9
Oregon	10	6	4
Ozark	16	7	9
Pemiscot	38	15	23
Perry	28	17	11
Pettis	43	27	16
Phelps	58	25	33
Pike	30	10	20
Pulaski	30	18	12
Putnam	6	3	3
Randolph	35	22	13
Ripley	10	7	3
Saline	31	18	13
Schuyler	8	3	5
Scotland	6	2	4
Scott	39	22	17
Shannon	6	2	4
Shelby	9	4	5
Ste. Genevieve	55	42	13
St. Francois	75	63	12
Stoddard	18	9	9
Stone	52	41	11
Sullivan	6	5	1
Taney	67	35	32
Texas	12	6	6
Vernon	20	11	9
Wayne	9	5	4
Worth	3	2	1
Wright	13	5	8
MONTANA			
Metropolitan Counties			
Carbon	15	8	7
Cascade	119	31	88
Missoula	170	49	121
Yellowstone	198	53	145

Table 80. Law Enforcement Employees by County, 2005

(Number.)

County	Total law enforcement employees	Total officers	Total civilians
Nonmetropolitan Counties			
Beaverhead	7	7	0
Big Horn	27	11	16
Blaine	15	10	5
Broadwater	9	8	1
Carter	3	3	0
Chouteau	16	9	7
Custer	14	6	8
Daniels	12	3	9
Dawson	52	5	47
Deer Lodge	22	15	7
Fallon	4	2	2
Fergus	20	8	12
Flathead	112	50	62
Gallatin	82	45	37
Garfield	4	3	1
Glacier	19	12	7
Golden Valley	2	2	0
Granite	10	5	5
Hill	28	12	16
Jefferson	20	10	10
Judith Basin	5	4	1
Lake	50	21	29
Lewis and Clark	71	40	31
Liberty	8	4	4
Lincoln	28	19	9
Madison	13	8	5
McCone	11	4	7
Meagher	12	4	8
Mineral	13	7	6
Musselshell	7	7	0
Park	14	13	1
Petroleum	1	1	0
Phillips	13	6	7
Pondera	16	9	7
Powder River	10	3	7
Powell	16	9	7
Prairie	4	3	1
Ravalli	59	29	30
Richland	13	7	6
Roosevelt	29	11	18
Rosebud	27	14	13
Sanders	17	10	7
Sheridan	7	5	2
Silver Bow	86	36	50
Stillwater	14	7	7
Sweet Grass	10	5	5
Teton	14	9	5
Toole	19	12	7
Treasure	2	2	0
Valley	16	7	9
Wheatland	12	5	7
Wibaux	3	3	0
NEBRASKA			
Metropolitan Counties			
Cass	75	41	34
Dakota	24	14	10
Dixon	10	7	3
Douglas	187	126	61
Lancaster	91	73	18
Sarpy	184	127	57
Seward	22	12	10
Washington	43	22	21
Nonmetropolitan Counties			
Arthur	1	1	0
Banner	1	1	0
Blaine	1	1	0
Boone	12	5	7
Box Butte	7	6	1
Boyd	4	4	0
Brown	10	6	4
Burt	10	5	5
Butler	22	8	14
Cedar	9	4	5
Chase	7	3	4
Cherry	11	5	6
Cheyenne	8	7	1
Clay	11	6	5
Colfax	9	6	3
Cuming	6	5	1
Custer	7	6	1
Dawes	9	3	6
Deuel	5	4	1
Dodge	24	17	7
Dundy	9	5	4
Fillmore	11	6	5
Franklin	7	3	4
Frontier	8	5	3
Furnas	14	9	5
Gage	23	11	12
Garden	8	4	4
Garfield	2	2	0
Gosper	5	4	1
Grant	1	1	0
Greeley	4	3	1
Hall	35	28	7
Hamilton	17	8	9
Harlan	8	4	4
Hayes	2	2	0
Hitchcock	7	4	3
Holt	4	3	1
Hooker	1	1	0
Howard	8	4	4
Jefferson	7	6	1
Johnson	9	4	5
Kearney	12	7	5
Keith	15	8	7
Keya Paha	1	1	0
Kimball	9	3	6
Knox	11	5	6
Lincoln	29	24	5
Logan	2	2	0
Loup	1	1	0
Madison	17	14	3
McPherson	1	1	0
Merrick	10	6	4
Morrill	8	3	5
Nance	10	6	4
Nemaha	5	5	0
Nuckolls	7	4	3
Otoe	21	11	10
Pawnee	4	3	1
Perkins	8	4	4
Phelps	8	6	2
Pierce	9	4	5
Platte	61	18	43
Polk	11	7	4
Red Willow	7	5	2
Richardson	11	6	5
Rock	8	3	5
Saline	10	10	0
Scotts Bluff	26	18	8
Sherman	6	5	1
Stanton	8	7	1
Thayer	11	7	4
Thomas	1	1	0
Thurston	11	5	6
Valley	6	3	3
Wayne	6	5	1
Webster	10	6	4
Wheeler	2	2	0
York	22	9	13
NEVADA			
Metropolitan Counties			
Carson City	141	96	45
Storey	21	13	8
Washoe	724	401	323
Nonmetropolitan Counties			
Churchill	45	37	8
Douglas	112	86	26
Elko	63	51	12
Esmeralda	15	11	4
Eureka	18	11	7
Humboldt	41	29	12
Lander	28	19	9
Lincoln	17	14	3
Lyon	103	73	30
Mineral	23	17	6
Nye	141	102	39
Pershing	20	13	7
White Pine	27	22	5
NEW HAMPSHIRE			
Metropolitan Counties			
Rockingham	78	50	28

Table 80. Law Enforcement Employees by County, 2005

(Number.)

County	Total law enforcement employees	Total officers	Total civilians
Nonmetropolitan Counties			
Carroll	26	12	14
Cheshire	19	10	9
Merrimack	30	17	13
NEW JERSEY			
Metropolitan Counties			
Atlantic	120	90	30
Bergen	514	439	75
Bergen County Police Department	146	90	56
Burlington	94	74	20
Camden	196	170	26
Cape May	133	117	16
Cumberland	57	49	8
Essex	463	385	78
Essex County Police Department	36	36	0
Gloucester	80	69	11
Hudson	227	173	54
Hunterdon	27	22	5
Mercer	157	121	36
Middlesex	235	195	40
Monmouth	666	455	211
Morris	353	254	99
Ocean	209	112	97
Passaic	861	667	194
Salem	153	134	19
Somerset	219	177	42
Sussex	152	125	27
Union	212	167	45
Warren	22	19	3
NEW MEXICO			
Metropolitan Counties			
Bernalillo	320	256	64
Dona Ana	162	131	31
Sandoval	49	42	7
San Juan	107	83	24
Santa Fe	91	69	22
Torrance	13	10	3
Valencia	44	34	10
Nonmetropolitan Counties			
Catron	10	6	4
Chaves	57	39	18
Cibola	21	13	8
Colfax	10	8	2
Curry	19	14	5
Grant	32	30	2
Guadalupe	5	4	1
Harding	2	2	0
Hidalgo	28	9	19
Lea	54	38	16
Lincoln	26	17	9
Luna	29	26	3
McKinley	40	33	7
Mora	7	5	2
Otero	38	26	12
Quay	7	7	0
Rio Arriba	23	20	3
Roosevelt	16	11	5
San Miguel	12	10	2
Sierra	17	15	2
Socorro	16	14	2
Taos	21	15	6
Union	4	3	1
NEW YORK			
Metropolitan Counties			
Albany	148	109	39
Broome	72	53	19
Chemung	39	32	7
Livingston	62	44	18
Madison	38	31	7
Monroe	296	257	39
Nassau	3 537	2 722	815
Niagara	133	109	24
Oneida	122	91	31
Onondaga	275	235	40
Ontario	98	67	31
Orange	113	101	12
Orleans	38	24	14
Oswego	70	63	7
Rensselaer	40	32	8
Rockland	83	74	9
Saratoga	124	89	35
Schenectady	19	12	7
Schoharie	27	16	11
Suffolk	387	254	133
Suffolk County Police Department	3 354	2 765	589
Tioga	54	35	19
Tompkins	44	39	5
Ulster	68	59	9
Warren	107	72	35
Washington	38	32	6
Wayne	64	52	12
Westchester Public Safety	312	246	66
Nonmetropolitan Counties			
Allegany	40	28	12
Cayuga	37	32	5
Chautauqua	117	75	42
Clinton	25	20	5
Columbia	53	44	9
Cortland	47	30	17
Delaware	22	14	8
Essex	26	23	3
Franklin	7	3	4
Fulton	49	31	18
Genesee	57	39	18
Greene	29	27	2
Jefferson	46	37	9
Lewis	25	15	10
Montgomery	35	21	14
Otsego	17	14	3
Schuyler	40	36	4
Seneca	45	28	17
St. Lawrence	40	36	4
Sullivan	53	42	11
Wyoming	39	28	11
Yates	40	21	19
NORTH CAROLINA			
Metropolitan Counties			
Alamance	197	97	100
Alexander	43	27	16
Anson	31	27	4
Brunswick	127	95	32
Buncombe	301	188	113
Burke	104	80	24
Cabarrus	168	162	6
Caldwell	112	73	39
Catawba	113	104	9
Chatham	83	66	17
Cumberland	534	292	242
Currituck	84	54	30
Davie	58	31	27
Durham	411	159	252
Edgecombe	118	50	68
Forsyth	494	208	286
Franklin	97	41	56
Gaston[1]	205	115	90
Gaston County Police Department[1]	218	133	85
Greene	40	23	17
Guilford	470	231	239
Haywood	83	49	34
Henderson	168	130	38
Hoke	66	43	23
Johnston	175	99	76
Madison	30	19	11
Mecklenburg[2]	1 274	328	946
Nash	125	67	58
New Hanover	367	278	89
Onslow	148	101	47
Orange	113	102	11
Pender	81	48	33
Person	66	38	28
Pitt	241	108	133
Randolph	213	147	66
Rockingham	129	88	41
Stokes	61	41	20
Union	200	159	41
Wake	679	333	346
Wayne	146	83	63
Yadkin	56	33	23

[1]The employee data are listed separately for Gaston County, North Carolina, and the Gaston County, North Carolina, Police Department. However, Gaston County and the Gaston County Police Department report combined crime figures; these can be found in Table 10 under "Gaston County Police Department" (in the North Carolina data).

[2]The employee data presented in this table for Mecklenburg, North Carolina, represent only Mecklenburg County Sheriff's Office employees and exclude Charlotte-Mecklenburg Police Department employees.

Table 80. Law Enforcement Employees by County, 2005

(Number.)

County	Total law enforcement employees	Total officers	Total civilians
Nonmetropolitan Counties			
Alleghany	26	10	16
Ashe	37	19	18
Avery	29	21	8
Beaufort	68	43	25
Bertie	30	21	9
Bladen	77	48	29
Camden	17	15	2
Carteret	83	41	42
Caswell	39	25	14
Cherokee	44	23	21
Chowan	35	17	18
Clay	19	11	8
Cleveland	125	83	42
Columbus	101	61	40
Craven	117	59	58
Dare	139	58	81
Davidson	181	122	59
Duplin	80	60	20
Gates	16	10	6
Graham	10	9	1
Granville	74	39	35
Halifax	73	47	26
Harnett	143	94	49
Hertford	55	21	34
Hyde	18	13	5
Iredell	187	143	44
Jackson	57	38	19
Jones	15	8	7
Lee	69	38	31
Lenoir	77	52	25
Lincoln	145	76	69
Martin	30	27	3
McDowell	62	42	20
Mitchell	14	13	1
Montgomery	41	29	12
Moore	106	67	39
Northampton	46	22	24
Pamlico	19	13	6
Pasquotank	40	37	3
Perquimans	10	9	1
Polk	38	24	14
Richmond	71	44	27
Robeson	207	104	103
Rowan	168	110	58
Rutherford	102	66	36
Sampson	92	64	28
Scotland	55	32	23
Stanly	64	45	19
Surry	92	51	41
Swain	16	15	1
Transylvania	57	42	15
Tyrrell	13	7	6
Vance	83	41	42
Warren	51	24	27
Washington	32	15	17
Watauga	69	36	33
Wilson	117	71	46
Yancey	23	13	10
NORTH DAKOTA			
Metropolitan Counties			
Burleigh	63	37	26
Cass	123	64	59
Grand Forks	30	24	6
Morton	32	19	13
Nonmetropolitan Counties			
Adams	4	4	0
Barnes	7	6	1
Benson	4	4	0
Billings	4	3	1
Bottineau	13	9	4
Bowman	2	2	0
Burke	4	3	1
Cavalier	12	5	7
Dickey	5	4	1
Divide	3	3	0
Dunn	3	2	1
Eddy	5	5	0
Emmons	3	3	0
Foster	4	3	1
Golden Valley	5	4	1
Grant	3	3	0
Griggs	4	4	0
Hettinger	4	4	0
Kidder	3	2	1
Lamoure	5	4	1
Logan	2	2	0
McHenry	8	7	1
McIntosh	2	2	0
McKenzie	10	5	5
McLean	26	20	6
Mercer	22	9	13
Mountrail	10	5	5
Nelson	5	4	1
Oliver	3	2	1
Pembina	13	9	4
Pierce	7	3	4
Ramsey	5	4	1
Ransom	5	4	1
Renville	5	5	0
Richland	32	15	17
Rolette	12	10	2
Sargent	4	3	1
Sheridan	3	3	0
Sioux	1	1	0
Slope	1	1	0
Stark	12	9	3
Steele	3	3	0
Stutsman	10	8	2
Towner	3	2	1
Traill	10	5	5
Walsh	17	11	6
Ward	41	20	21
Wells	3	3	0
Williams	20	19	1
OHIO			
Metropolitan Counties			
Allen	154	73	81
Brown	40	27	13
Butler	295	156	139
Carroll	19	17	2
Clark	151	123	28
Clermont	204	89	115
Cuyahoga	1 028	168	860
Delaware	145	75	70
Erie	74	36	38
Fairfield	123	95	28
Franklin	847	625	222
Fulton	30	18	12
Geauga	115	51	64
Greene	160	120	40
Lake	189	54	135
Lawrence	42	34	8
Licking	185	127	58
Lorain	240	76	164
Madison	32	32	0
Mahoning	217	204	13
Miami	136	50	86
Montgomery	443	212	231
Morrow	55	31	24
Ottawa	59	58	1
Portage	130	52	78
Preble	62	18	44
Richland	115	51	64
Stark	231	132	99
Summit	479	387	92
Trumbull	116	47	69
Warren	158	85	73
Washington	41	31	10
Wood	111	78	33
Nonmetropolitan Counties			
Adams	30	21	9
Ashland	61	41	20
Ashtabula	78	41	37
Athens	27	23	4
Auglaize	52	20	32
Champaign	28	20	8
Clinton	63	35	28
Columbiana	28	21	7
Coshocton	53	46	7
Crawford	64	18	46
Darke	64	40	24
Defiance	37	21	16
Fayette	38	28	10
Gallia	29	19	10
Guernsey	40	21	19
Hancock	87	35	52
Hardin	23	17	6
Harrison	18	14	4
Henry	25	24	1
Highland	55	55	0

Table 80. Law Enforcement Employees by County, 2005

(Number.)

County	Total law enforcement employees	Total officers	Total civilians
Hocking	21	18	3
Holmes	49	35	14
Huron	71	24	47
Jackson	43	15	28
Knox	72	54	18
Logan	103	38	65
Marion	40	28	12
Mercer	34	27	7
Monroe	18	15	3
Morgan	15	11	4
Muskingum	123	83	40
Noble	16	6	10
Paulding	24	12	12
Perry	17	13	4
Pike	17	14	3
Putnam	53	32	21
Ross	93	58	35
Scioto	66	52	14
Seneca	73	18	55
Shelby	69	33	36
Tuscarawas	92	33	59
Van Wert	25	19	6
Vinton	15	12	3
Williams	24	20	4
OKLAHOMA			
Metropolitan Counties			
Canadian	56	29	27
Cleveland	101	52	49
Comanche	31	27	4
Creek	64	33	31
Grady	15	13	2
Le Flore	16	11	5
Lincoln	36	14	22
Logan	26	13	13
McClain	23	11	12
Oklahoma	695	165	530
Okmulgee	13	12	1
Osage	69	30	39
Pawnee	18	10	8
Rogers	63	24	39
Sequoyah	18	14	4
Tulsa	504	184	320
Wagoner	44	13	31
Nonmetropolitan Counties			
Adair	31	10	21
Alfalfa	9	4	5
Atoka	10	5	5
Beaver	12	7	5
Beckham	22	6	16
Blaine	13	6	7
Bryan	15	12	3
Caddo	33	18	15
Carter	22	19	3
Cherokee	31	18	13
Choctaw	18	7	11
Cimarron	8	4	4
Coal	5	4	1
Cotton	11	5	6
Craig	17	9	8
Custer	30	13	17
Delaware	44	19	25
Dewey	11	4	7
Ellis	12	4	8
Garfield	42	17	25
Garvin	23	11	12
Grant	10	5	5
Greer	7	3	4
Harmon	3	3	0
Harper	8	4	4
Haskell	17	8	9
Hughes	10	4	6
Jackson	33	10	23
Jefferson	13	6	7
Johnston	24	7	17
Kay	28	14	14
Kingfisher	14	7	7
Kiowa	10	4	6
Latimer	16	6	10
Love	22	6	16
Major	11	4	7
Marshall	24	6	18
Mayes	35	18	17
McCurtain	20	17	3
McIntosh	20	12	8
Murray	8	5	3
Muskogee	92	32	60
Noble	10	5	5
Nowata	20	10	10
Okfuskee	12	5	7
Ottawa	32	18	14
Payne	53	22	31
Pittsburg	30	19	11
Pontotoc	18	11	7
Pottawatomie	25	17	8
Pushmataha	17	6	11
Roger Mills	13	8	5
Seminole	17	12	5
Stephens	35	10	25
Texas	37	11	26
Tillman	11	5	6
Washington	34	16	18
Washita	15	6	9
Woods	5	4	1
Woodward	16	8	8
OREGON			
Metropolitan Counties			
Benton	35	31	4
Deschutes	94	79	15
Jackson	81	57	24
Lane	127	70	57
Marion	106	85	21
Multnomah	126	93	33
Polk	28	23	5
Washington	281	208	73
Yamhill	44	34	10
Nonmetropolitan Counties			
Clatsop	30	26	4
Coos	49	30	19
Crook	17	13	4
Curry	28	19	9
Douglas	111	71	40
Gilliam	6	5	1
Grant	6	5	1
Harney	11	5	6
Hood River	34	18	16
Jefferson	21	11	10
Josephine	57	33	24
Klamath	38	32	6
Lake	8	7	1
Lincoln	32	28	4
Linn	101	67	34
Morrow	26	16	10
Sherman	6	5	1
Tillamook	27	25	2
Umatilla	35	16	19
Union	11	9	2
Wallowa	13	8	5
Wasco	19	16	3
Wheeler	12	5	7
PENNSYLVANIA			
Metropolitan Counties			
Allegheny	174	145	29
Allegheny County Police Department	233	187	46
Beaver	29	24	5
Centre	16	14	2
Cumberland	31	27	4
Lancaster	47	38	9
Pike	21	17	4
Washington	27	23	4
York	95	84	11
Nonmetropolitan Counties			
Adams	10	9	1
Clarion	8	5	3
Elk	6	5	1
Franklin	16	13	3
Greene	8	7	1
Jefferson	4	3	1
Snyder	5	5	0
Union	7	6	1
Warren	49	20	29

Table 80. Law Enforcement Employees by County, 2005

(Number.)

County	Total law enforcement employees	Total officers	Total civilians
SOUTH CAROLINA			
Metropolitan Counties			
Aiken	220	107	113
Anderson	220	182	38
Berkeley	185	114	71
Calhoun	23	21	2
Charleston	697	254	443
Darlington	66	60	6
Dorchester	192	96	96
Edgefield	53	49	4
Fairfield	47	45	2
Florence	229	117	112
Greenville	432	350	82
Horry	216	37	179
Horry County Police Department	239	221	18
Kershaw	68	55	13
Laurens	107	56	51
Lexington	376	214	162
Pickens	132	92	40
Richland	490	453	37
Saluda	50	19	31
Spartanburg	316	288	28
Sumter	121	112	9
York	262	125	137
Nonmetropolitan Counties			
Abbeville	54	26	28
Allendale	12	10	2
Bamberg	13	11	2
Barnwell	38	25	13
Beaufort	197	178	19
Cherokee	90	42	48
Chesterfield	65	43	22
Clarendon	53	30	23
Colleton	123	63	60
Dillon	84	33	51
Georgetown	127	70	57
Greenwood	112	71	41
Jasper	33	28	5
Lancaster	100	68	32
Lee	30	25	5
Marion	38	32	6
Marlboro	25	21	4
McCormick	25	13	12
Newberry	94	46	48
Oconee	133	80	53
Orangeburg	108	75	33
Union	33	29	4
Williamsburg	64	31	33
SOUTH DAKOTA			
Metropolitan Counties			
Lincoln	15	14	1
McCook	4	3	1
Meade	55	17	38
Minnehaha	181	72	109
Pennington	168	55	113
Turner	5	4	1
Union	18	5	13
Nonmetropolitan Counties			
Aurora	4	3	1
Beadle	23	6	17
Bennett	9	6	3
Bon Homme	7	2	5
Brookings	20	11	9
Brown	50	15	35
Brule	11	3	8
Buffalo	1	1	0
Butte	11	5	6
Campbell	2	2	0
Charles Mix	9	6	3
Clark	2	2	0
Clay	11	8	3
Codington	9	6	3
Corson	3	2	1
Custer	11	10	1
Davison	25	6	19
Day	6	3	3
Deuel	8	4	4
Dewey	2	2	0
Douglas	2	2	0
Edmunds	6	4	2
Fall River	16	6	10
Faulk	8	3	5
Grant	8	3	5
Gregory	4	3	1
Haakon	2	2	0
Hamlin	3	3	0
Hand	3	2	1
Hanson	2	2	0
Harding	3	2	1
Hughes	24	6	18
Hutchinson	3	3	0
Hyde	1	1	0
Jackson	1	1	0
Jerauld	2	2	0
Jones	2	2	0
Kingsbury	5	4	1
Lake	10	9	1
Lawrence	43	16	27
Lyman	5	4	1
Marshall	11	6	5
McPherson	1	1	0
Mellette	3	2	1
Miner	4	3	1
Moody	10	5	5
Perkins	4	3	1
Potter	3	2	1
Roberts	8	4	4
Sanborn	3	2	1
Shannon	1	1	0
Spink	13	8	5
Stanley	6	5	1
Sully	3	3	0
Todd	1	1	0
Tripp	5	4	1
Walworth	10	2	8
Yankton	10	9	1
Ziebach	2	2	0
TENNESSEE			
Metropolitan Counties			
Anderson	114	41	73
Blount	301	256	45
Bradley	212	98	114
Cannon	19	8	11
Carter	79	71	8
Cheatham	64	29	35
Chester	23	11	12
Dickson	113	52	61
Fayette	58	33	25
Grainger	36	16	20
Hamblen	67	31	36
Hamilton	357	137	220
Hartsville-Trousdale	32	17	15
Hawkins	60	38	22
Hickman	36	23	13
Jefferson	57	36	21
Knox	1 033	477	556
Loudon	62	35	27
Macon	47	21	26
Madison	210	63	147
Marion	47	17	30
Montgomery	287	243	44
Polk	36	18	18
Robertson	103	40	63
Rutherford	338	165	173
Sequatchie	25	16	9
Shelby	1 986	487	1 499
Smith	43	16	27
Stewart	32	13	19
Sullivan	221	101	120
Sumner	230	63	167
Tipton	68	37	31
Unicoi	38	19	19
Union	40	18	22
Washington	185	87	98
Williamson	108	93	15
Wilson	143	82	61
Nonmetropolitan Counties			
Bedford	90	25	65
Benton	40	13	27
Bledsoe	18	11	7
Campbell	54	27	27
Carroll	35	17	18
Claiborne	46	23	23
Clay	15	8	7
Cocke	64	30	34
Coffee	68	65	3
Crockett	28	11	17
Cumberland	84	41	43
Decatur	15	9	6
DeKalb	35	14	21
Dyer	66	24	42
Fentress	26	15	11
Franklin	55	30	25
Gibson	61	32	29
Giles	54	20	34
Greene	143	53	90
Grundy	23	10	13

Table 80. Law Enforcement Employees by County, 2005

(Number.)

County	Total law enforcement employees	Total officers	Total civilians
Hancock	39	16	23
Hardeman	36	18	18
Hardin	26	17	9
Haywood	39	16	23
Henderson	37	25	12
Henry	60	28	32
Houston	20	9	11
Humphreys	27	14	13
Jackson	23	14	9
Johnson	40	16	24
Lake	19	9	10
Lauderdale	55	19	36
Lawrence	59	45	14
Lewis	26	12	14
Lincoln	54	22	32
Marshall	46	20	26
Maury	113	58	55
McMinn	67	35	32
McNairy	30	15	15
Meigs	18	8	10
Monroe	60	55	5
Moore	24	12	12
Morgan	43	11	32
Obion	56	24	32
Overton	50	19	31
Perry	25	11	14
Pickett	10	6	4
Putnam	115	52	63
Rhea	49	29	20
Roane	56	30	26
Scott	38	30	8
Sevier	136	81	55
Van Buren	13	7	6
Warren	78	38	40
Wayne	32	13	19
Weakley	42	21	21
White	56	22	34
TEXAS			
Metropolitan Counties			
Aransas	61	25	36
Archer	12	7	5
Armstrong	7	3	4
Atascosa	69	26	43
Austin	45	27	18
Bandera	46	26	20
Bastrop	133	51	82
Bell	250	90	160
Bexar	1 713	482	1 231
Bowie	44	39	5
Brazoria	279	164	115
Brazos	176	85	91
Burleson	31	15	16
Caldwell	78	27	51
Calhoun	56	22	34
Callahan	11	6	5
Cameron	346	94	252
Carson	14	6	8
Chambers	77	35	42
Clay	19	10	9
Collin	441	117	324
Comal	215	103	112
Coryell	56	20	36
Crosby	17	6	11
Dallas	1 677	419	1 258
Delta	18	10	8
Denton	517	204	313
Ector	196	87	109
Ellis	190	74	116
El Paso	1 057	245	812
Fort Bend	536	353	183
Galveston	297	208	89
Goliad	25	10	15
Grayson	126	55	71
Gregg	183	84	99
Guadalupe	183	62	121
Hardin	62	32	30
Harris	3 563	2 537	1 026
Hays	234	97	137
Hidalgo	708	229	479
Hunt	111	34	77
Irion	7	3	4
Jefferson	346	145	201
Johnson	197	75	122
Jones	20	9	11
Kaufman	192	68	124
Kendall	53	38	15
Lampasas	32	15	17
Liberty	61	43	18
Lubbock	259	114	145
McLennan	293	105	188
Medina	56	21	35
Midland	174	81	93
Montgomery	448	286	162
Nueces	300	93	207
Orange	130	57	73
Parker	119	67	52
Potter	200	98	102
Randall	147	70	77
Robertson	29	11	18
Rockwall	102	30	72
Rusk	64	39	25
San Jacinto	32	15	17
San Patricio	83	40	43
Smith	255	112	143
Tarrant	1 226	477	749
Taylor	171	75	96
Tom Green	161	60	101
Travis	1 352	656	696
Upshur	67	34	33
Victoria	155	88	67
Waller	57	35	22
Webb	274	145	129
Wichita	166	40	126
Williamson	430	174	256
Wilson	68	24	44
Wise	125	63	62
Nonmetropolitan Counties			
Anderson	78	34	44
Andrews	29	13	16
Angelina	105	56	49
Bailey	17	5	12
Baylor	8	2	6
Bee	41	20	21
Blanco	16	9	7
Borden	3	2	1
Bosque	33	18	15
Brewster	19	10	9
Briscoe	3	2	1
Brown	61	23	38
Burnet	72	46	26
Camp	18	7	11
Cass	39	14	25
Castro	18	8	10
Cherokee	64	26	38
Childress	15	6	9
Cochran	12	6	6
Coke	6	5	1
Coleman	11	5	6
Collingsworth	9	5	4
Colorado	40	18	22
Comanche	30	9	21
Concho	5	5	0
Cooke	53	18	35
Cottle	2	1	1
Crane	11	6	5
Crockett	17	12	5
Culberson	12	6	6
Dallam	14	4	10
Dawson	17	6	11
Deaf Smith	33	12	21
Dewitt	28	10	18
Dickens	6	2	4
Dimmit	27	10	17
Donley	8	5	3
Duval	34	15	19
Eastland	24	8	16
Edwards	10	4	6
Erath	47	22	25
Falls	23	9	14
Fannin	40	17	23
Fayette	38	19	19
Fisher	9	5	4
Floyd	8	3	5
Foard	4	3	1
Franklin	18	8	10
Freestone	37	15	22
Frio	21	12	9
Gaines	23	11	12
Garza	14	8	6
Gillespie	30	20	10
Glasscock	6	3	3
Gonzales	42	18	24
Gray	39	14	25
Grimes	53	26	27
Hale	68	27	41
Hall	9	3	6
Hamilton	24	13	11

Table 80. Law Enforcement Employees by County, 2005

(Number.)

County	Total law enforcement employees	Total officers	Total civilians
Hansford	9	4	5
Hardeman	9	5	4
Harrison	87	53	34
Hartley	4	4	0
Haskell	9	3	6
Hemphill	15	8	7
Henderson	113	71	42
Hill	55	21	34
Hockley	24	13	11
Hood	106	35	71
Hopkins	53	27	26
Houston	29	19	10
Howard	29	13	16
Hudspeth	34	14	20
Hutchinson	28	10	18
Jack	32	11	21
Jackson	24	14	10
Jasper	42	15	27
Jeff Davis	3	3	0
Jim Hogg	36	19	17
Jim Wells	57	27	30
Karnes	17	8	9
Kenedy	15	10	5
Kent	5	3	2
Kerr	90	46	44
Kimble	18	11	7
King	2	2	0
Kinney	14	5	9
Kleberg	66	45	21
Knox	7	3	4
Lamar	76	25	51
Lamb	27	15	12
La Salle	15	13	2
Lavaca	22	12	10
Lee	16	10	6
Leon	36	18	18
Limestone	52	19	33
Lipscomb	9	5	4
Live Oak	26	11	15
Llano	45	25	20
Loving	3	2	1
Lynn	19	6	13
Madison	23	9	14
Marion	13	12	1
Martin	8	3	5
Mason	10	5	5
Matagorda	70	40	30
Maverick	80	41	39
McCulloch	15	8	7
McMullen	4	3	1
Menard	9	5	4
Milam	28	12	16
Mills	8	5	3
Mitchell	11	5	6
Montague	25	11	14
Moore	47	18	29
Morris	20	8	12
Motley	2	2	0
Nacogdoches	82	38	44
Navarro	107	56	51
Newton	19	11	8
Nolan	24	11	13
Ochiltree	19	8	11
Oldham	10	5	5
Palo Pinto	49	18	31
Panola	38	25	13
Parmer	19	6	13
Pecos	29	15	14
Polk	70	38	32
Presidio	26	5	21
Rains	23	9	14
Reagan	15	6	9
Real	7	3	4
Red River	30	13	17
Reeves	515	18	497
Refugio	32	10	22
Roberts	5	4	1
Runnels	21	6	15
Sabine	18	8	10
San Augustine	18	5	13
San Saba	9	4	5
Schleicher	10	5	5
Scurry	23	8	15
Shackelford	14	4	10
Shelby	32	12	20
Sherman	9	4	5
Somervell	38	18	20
Starr	97	29	68
Stephens	10	6	4
Sterling	4	4	0
Stonewall	7	2	5
Sutton	14	5	9
Swisher	10	5	5
Terrell	11	4	7
Terry	41	9	32
Throckmorton	6	2	4
Titus	48	21	27
Trinity	14	8	6
Tyler	28	19	9
Upton	15	8	7
Uvalde	45	29	16
Val Verde	48	33	15
Van Zandt	72	28	44
Walker	63	30	33
Ward	30	14	16
Washington	54	31	23
Wharton	67	37	30
Wheeler	11	6	5
Wilbarger	16	6	10
Willacy	35	14	21
Winkler	25	11	14
Wood	64	27	37
Yoakum	20	9	11
Young	29	14	15
Zapata	109	42	67
Zavala	28	10	18
UTAH			
Metropolitan Counties			
Cache	137	105	32
Davis	228	183	45
Juab	24	22	2
Morgan	13	11	2
Salt Lake	1 191	314	877
Summit	91	42	49
Tooele	67	26	41
Utah	305	217	88
Washington	164	125	39
Weber	372	120	252
Nonmetropolitan Counties			
Beaver	45	13	32
Box Elder	87	28	59
Carbon	41	18	23
Daggett	31	10	21
Duchesne	52	16	36
Emery	42	27	15
Garfield	26	6	20
Grand	32	17	15
Iron	74	27	47
Kane	25	17	8
Millard	52	23	29
Piute	2	2	0
Rich	10	4	6
San Juan	35	27	8
Sanpete	20	19	1
Sevier	63	51	12
Uintah	45	36	9
Wasatch	41	19	22
Wayne	5	5	0
VERMONT			
Metropolitan Counties			
Chittenden	13	10	3
Franklin	28	19	9
Grand Isle	3	2	1
Nonmetropolitan Counties			
Addison	17	9	8
Bennington	19	14	5
Caledonia	9	7	2
Essex	4	3	1
Lamoille	15	8	7
Orange	2	2	0
Orleans	7	5	2
Rutland	23	19	4
Washington	12	10	2
Windham	26	20	6
Windsor	10	8	2
VIRGINIA			
Metropolitan Counties			
Albemarle County Police Department	133	111	22
Amelia	19	11	8
Amherst	70	64	6
Appomattox	33	30	3
Arlington County Police Department	434	355	79
Bedford	73	71	2
Botetourt	82	65	17
Campbell	59	56	3
Caroline	47	39	8
Charles City	16	10	6

Table 80. Law Enforcement Employees by County, 2005

(Number.)

County	Total law enforcement employees	Total officers	Total civilians
Chesterfield County Police Department	530	436	94
Clarke	28	17	11
Craig	13	0	5
Cumberland	19	12	7
Dinwiddie	43	35	8
Fairfax County Police Department	1 609	1 339	270
Fauquier	110	95	15
Fluvanna	36	23	13
Franklin	94	77	17
Frederick	103	94	9
Giles	35	24	11
Gloucester	104	83	21
Goochland	33	26	7
Greene	26	19	7
Hanover	206	187	19
Henrico County Police Department	701	516	185
Isle of Wight	42	35	7
James City County Police Department	81	76	5
King and Queen	16	10	6
King William	32	20	12
Loudoun	458	381	77
Louisa	48	38	10
Mathews	19	13	6
Montgomery	118	104	14
Nelson	21	16	5
New Kent	36	26	10
Pittsylvania	128	70	58
Powhatan	49	34	15
Prince George County Police Department	61	46	15
Prince William County Police Department	594	495	99
Pulaski	48	40	8
Roanoke County Police Department	170	127	43
Rockingham	163	53	110
Scott	26	24	2
Spotsylvania	155	121	34
Stafford	193	138	55
Surry	21	12	9
Sussex	43	38	5
Warren	87	72	15
Washington	69	51	18
York	97	92	5
Nonmetropolitan Counties			
Accomack	65	56	9
Alleghany	59	43	16
Augusta	131	59	72
Bath	19	19	0
Bland	18	10	8
Brunswick	50	37	13
Buchanan	36	30	6
Buckingham	24	17	7
Carroll	33	28	5
Charlotte	34	31	3
Culpeper	97	80	17
Dickenson	23	21	2
Essex	20	20	0
Floyd	27	20	7
Grayson	24	18	6
Greensville	31	21	10
Halifax	43	35	8
Henry	122	108	14
Highland	12	8	4
King George	40	28	12
Lancaster	32	26	6
Lee	37	37	0
Lunenburg	21	14	7
Madison	28	15	13
Mecklenburg	49	47	2
Middlesex	15	15	0
Northampton	52	42	10
Northumberland	25	17	8
Nottoway	22	14	8
Orange	37	29	8
Page	53	47	6
Patrick	46	32	14
Prince Edward	25	25	0
Rappahannock	23	22	1
Richmond	19	11	8
Rockbridge	36	28	8
Russell	47	34	13
Shenandoah	70	60	10
Smyth	48	48	0
Southampton	76	63	13
Tazewell	50	43	7
Westmoreland	30	21	9
Wise	61	58	3
Wythe	47	40	7

County	Total law enforcement employees	Total officers	Total civilians
WASHINGTON			
Metropolitan Counties			
Asotin	14	12	2
Benton	87	56	31
Chelan	72	60	12
Clark	203	124	79
Cowlitz	54	42	12
Douglas	35	28	7
Franklin	25	22	3
King	828	519	309
Kitsap	154	121	33
Pierce	368	314	54
Skagit	111	56	55
Skamania	23	20	3
Snohomish	320	255	65
Spokane	190	135	55
Thurston	111	85	26
Whatcom	96	77	19
Yakima	98	71	27
Nonmetropolitan Counties			
Adams	27	17	10
Clallam	46	35	11
Columbia	14	9	5
Ferry	16	8	8
Garfield	12	7	5
Grant	55	42	13
Grays Harbor	75	37	38
Island	44	37	7
Jefferson	50	22	28
Kittitas	36	29	7
Klickitat	48	16	32
Lewis	58	41	17
Lincoln	26	13	13
Mason	57	41	16
Okanogan	37	32	5
Pacific	19	15	4
Pend Oreille	28	15	13
San Juan	31	20	11
Stevens	32	28	4
Wahkiakum	9	8	1
Walla Walla	31	25	6
Whitman	20	17	3
WEST VIRGINIA			
Metropolitan Counties			
Berkeley	67	45	22
Boone	24	21	3
Brooke	27	17	10
Cabell	60	41	19
Clay	5	4	1
Hampshire	15	12	3
Hancock	31	26	5
Jefferson	27	22	5
Kanawha	113	87	26
Lincoln	7	7	0
Marshall	27	24	3
Mineral	13	10	3
Monongalia	53	32	21
Morgan	11	10	1
Ohio	26	25	1
Pleasants	7	6	1
Preston	19	14	5
Putnam	43	37	6
Wayne	27	20	7
Wirt	2	2	0
Wood	67	36	31
Nonmetropolitan Counties			
Barbour	5	4	1
Braxton	9	8	1
Calhoun	2	2	0
Doddridge	2	2	0
Fayette	34	29	5
Gilmer	5	5	0
Grant	8	8	0
Greenbrier	29	25	4
Hardy	11	8	3
Harrison	40	38	2
Jackson	21	15	6
Lewis	14	12	2
Logan	23	16	7
Marion	33	23	10
Mason	24	17	7
McDowell	13	11	2
Mercer	35	28	7
Mingo	19	16	3
Monroe	8	8	0
Nicholas	27	23	4

Table 80. Law Enforcement Employees by County, 2005

(Number.)

County	Total law enforcement employees	Total officers	Total civilians
Pendleton	8	4	4
Pocahontas	13	7	6
Raleigh	64	49	15
Randolph	12	8	4
Ritchie	9	7	2
Roane	8	7	1
Summers	7	5	2
Taylor	11	7	4
Tucker	6	4	2
Tyler	5	4	1
Upshur	10	9	1
Webster	3	3	0
Wetzel	8	8	0
Wyoming	20	19	1
WISCONSIN			
Metropolitan Counties			
Brown	306	146	160
Calumet	45	22	23
Chippewa	67	53	14
Columbia	81	40	41
Dane	543	426	117
Douglas	81	74	7
Eau Claire	116	35	81
Fond du Lac	108	53	55
Iowa	42	20	22
Kenosha	307	103	204
Kewaunee	38	36	2
La Crosse	105	41	64
Marathon	170	64	106
Milwaukee	910	604	306
Oconto	64	26	38
Outagamie	206	74	132
Ozaukee	100	73	27
Pierce	49	45	4
Racine	268	187	81
Rock	178	91	87
Sheboygan	170	74	96
St. Croix	83	76	7
Washington	164	66	98
Waukesha	335	147	188
Winnebago	213	142	71
Nonmetropolitan Counties			
Adams	56	56	0
Ashland	35	28	7
Barron	66	48	18
Bayfield	41	22	19
Buffalo	21	10	11
Burnett	40	17	23
Clark	54	50	4
Crawford	27	26	1
Dodge	159	49	110
Door	62	46	16
Dunn	24	20	4
Florence	13	13	0
Forest	19	17	2
Grant	46	24	22
Green	52	44	8
Green Lake	44	20	24
Iron	19	19	0
Jackson	38	19	19
Jefferson	121	98	23
Juneau	58	46	12
Lafayette	24	13	11
Langlade	44	16	28
Lincoln	55	27	28
Manitowoc	105	59	46
Marinette	56	28	28
Marquette	37	35	2
Menominee	13	11	2
Monroe	25	22	3
Oneida	82	38	44
Pepin	18	17	1
Polk	72	26	46
Portage	88	44	44
Price	30	20	10
Richland	25	24	1
Rusk	32	32	0
Sauk	146	108	38
Sawyer	43	31	12
Shawano	58	39	19
Taylor	43	20	23
Trempealeau	49	24	25
Vernon	26	25	1
Vilas	71	34	37
Walworth	75	75	0
Washburn	29	13	16
Waupaca	83	34	49
Waushara	64	25	39
Wood	78	43	35
WYOMING			
Metropolitan Counties			
Laramie	64	49	15
Natrona	52	43	9
Nonmetropolitan Counties			
Albany	20	19	1
Big Horn	20	11	9
Campbell	56	40	16
Carbon	25	17	8
Converse	16	10	6
Crook	13	6	7
Fremont	36	32	4
Goshen	18	11	7
Hot Springs	13	7	6
Johnson	10	9	1
Lincoln	39	16	23
Niobrara	5	4	1
Park	47	19	28
Platte	11	8	3
Sheridan	25	19	6
Sublette	39	29	10
Sweetwater	42	30	12
Teton	40	19	21
Uinta	39	25	14
Washakie	9	8	1
Weston	8	7	1

Table 81. Full-Time Law Enforcement Employees, by State and Other Agencies, 2005

(Number.)

Agency	Total law enforcement employees	Total officers	Total civilians
Alabama–State Agencies			
Alabama Alcoholic Beverage Control Board	115	95	20
Alabama Department of Mental Health	4	0	1
Alabama Public Service Commission Enforcement Division	6	6	0
State Capitol Police	29	22	7
Alabama–Other Agencies			
22nd Judicial Circuit Drug Task Force	5	5	0
City of Montgomery, Housing Authority Investigative Unit	5	4	1
Huntsville International Airport	18	13	5
Madison-Morgan County Strategic Counterdrug Team	3	2	1
Alaska–State Agencies			
Alcohol Beverage Control Board	10	1	9
Alaska–Other Agencies			
Anchorage International Airport	60	57	3
Fairbanks International Airport	26	25	1
Arizona–State Agencies			
Arizona State Capitol	62	29	33
Arkansas–State Agencies			
Camp Robinson	28	17	11
State Capitol Police	23	19	4
California–State Agencies			
Atascadero State Hospital	145	133	12
California State Fair	8	5	3
Department of Parks and Recreation, Capital	797	703	94
Napa State Hospital	100	94	6
California–Other Agencies			
East Bay Regional Parks, Alameda County	80	58	22
Fontana Unified School District	25	18	7
Grant Joint Union High School	23	18	5
Monterey Peninsula Airport	8	7	1
Port of San Diego Harbor	160	133	27
San Bernardino Unified School District	85	24	61
San Francisco Bay Area Rapid Transit, Contra Costa County	277	186	91
Stockton Unified School District	20	16	4
Colorado–State Agencies			
Colorado Mental Health Institute	58	17	41
Connecticut–State Agencies			
State Capitol Police	32	24	8
Delaware–State Agencies			
Attorney General			
Kent County	56	31	25
New Castle County	256	119	137
Sussex County	50	29	21
Division of Alcohol and Tobacco Enforcement	18	14	4
Environmental Control	14	12	2
Fish and Wildlife	32	26	6
Office of Narcotics and Dangerous Drugs	5	5	0
Park Rangers	23	23	0
River and Bay Authority	60	44	16
State Capitol Police	60	37	23
State Fire Marshal	54	20	34
Delaware–Other Agencies			
Drug Enforcement Administration, Wilmington Resident Office	11	8	3
Wilmington Fire Department	184	180	4
District of Columbia–Other Agencies			
Metro Transit Police	502	379	123
National Zoological Park	31	31	0
Florida–State Agencies			
Capitol Police	89	65	24
Department of Environmental Protection, Division of Law Enforcement, Leon County	176	128	48
Department of Law Enforcement, Leon County, Tallahassee	1 812	428	1 384
Florida Game Commission, Leon County	858	684	174
State Treasurer's Office, Division of Insurance Fraud	171	128	43
Florida–Other Agencies			
Florida School for the Deaf and Blind	16	9	7
Fort Lauderdale Airport	144	92	52
Jacksonville Airport Authority	44	35	9
Lee County Port Authority	59	37	22
Melbourne International Airport	12	11	1
Miami-Dade County Public Schools	140	110	30
Miccosukee Tribal	60	46	14
Palm Beach County School District	233	157	76
Port Everglades	139	61	78
Sarasota-Bradenton International Airport	14	14	0
Seminole Tribal	156	119	37
Tampa International Airport	145	66	79
Volusia County Beach Management	66	62	4
Georgia–State Agencies			
Georgia Bureau of Investigation, Headquarters	826	264	562
Georgia Department of Transportation, Office of Investigation	3	3	0
Georgia Public Safety Training Center	160	26	134
Ports Authority, Savannah	85	57	28

Table 81. Full-Time Law Enforcement Employees, by State and Other Agencies, 2005—*Continued*

(Number.)

Agency	Total law enforcement employees	Total officers	Total civilians
Georgia–Other Agencies			
Augusta Board of Education	44	41	3
Chatham County Board of Education	46	37	9
Cherokee County Marshal	15	8	7
Cobb County Board of Education	36	34	2
Fayette County Marshal	10	9	1
Fulton County Marshal	61	57	4
Gwinnett County Marshal	1	1	0
Gwinnett County Public Schools	23	19	4
Metropolitan Atlanta Rapid Transit Authority	322	281	41
Muscogee City Marshal	15	14	1
Pickens County Board of Education	5	4	1
Richmond County Marshal	46	41	5
Troup County Marshal	4	4	0
Illinois–State Agencies			
Illinois Commerce Commission	16	9	7
Illinois Department of Natural Resources	167	152	15
Secretary of State Police, District 3	222	97	125
Illinois–Other Agencies			
Burlington Northern Santa Fe Railroad	20	17	3
Capitol Airport Authority	4	4	0
Cook County Forest Preserve	85	79	6
Crystal Lake Park District	3	3	0
CSX Transportation	21	21	0
Decatur Park District	9	9	0
Du Page County Forest Preserve	29	25	4
Elgin, Joliet and Eastern Railway	5	5	0
John H. Stroger Hospital	72	66	6
Lake County Forest Preserve	16	14	2
Norfolk Southern Railway	51	50	1
Pekin Park District	1	1	0
Rockford Park District	20	19	1
Springfield Park District	7	7	0
Will County Forest Preserve	12	11	1
Indiana–State Agencies			
Northern Indiana Commuter Transportation District	8	7	1
Indiana–Other Agencies			
St. Joseph County Airport Authority	17	17	0
Kansas–State Agencies			
Kansas Alcoholic Beverage Control	32	20	12
Kansas Bureau of Investigation	239	77	162
Kansas Department of Wildlife and Parks	166	165	1
Kansas Lottery Security Division	9	5	4
Securities Office, Investigation Section	31	8	23
Kansas–Other Agencies			
Blue Valley School District	8	6	2
Johnson County Park	16	15	1
Kickapoo Tribal	14	9	5
Metropolitan Topeka Airport Authority	26	20	6
Sac and Fox Tribal	11	9	2
Shawnee Mission Public Schools	11	11	0
Unified School District			
Auburn-Washburn	5	1	4
Goddard	4	4	0
Maize	3	3	0
Topeka	17	16	1
Wyandotte County Parks and Recreation	11	11	0
Kentucky–State Agencies			
Alcohol Beverage Control	39	37	2
Fish and Wildlife Enforcement	155	147	8
Kentucky Fairgrounds Security	2	1	1
Kentucky Horse Park	8	8	0
Motor Vehicle Enforcement	238	159	79
Park Security	66	66	0
South Central Kentucky Drug Task Force	2	1	1
Unlawful Narcotics Investigation, Treatment and Education	50	32	18
Kentucky–Other Agencies			
Barren County Drug Task Force	5	4	1
Buffalo Trace-Gateway Narcotics Task Force	3	3	0
Cincinnati-Northern Kentucky International Airport	71	55	16
Clark County School System	2	2	0
Clay County Schools	2	2	0
Fayette County Schools	29	25	4
FIVCO Area Drug Task Force	7	6	1
Greater Hardin County Narcotics Task Force	11	10	1
Jefferson County Board of Education	26	14	12
Lake Cumberland Area Drug Enforcement Task Force	6	5	1
Lexington Bluegrass Airport	82	65	17
Louisville Regional Airport Authority	18	18	0
McCracken County Public Schools	4	4	0
Northern Kentucky Narcotics Enforcement Unit	3	2	1
Pennyrile Narcotics Task Force	14	12	2
Louisiana–State Agencies			
Department of Public Safety, State Capitol Detail	48	40	8
Tensas Basin Levee District	3	2	1

Table 81. Full-Time Law Enforcement Employees, by State and Other Agencies, 2005—*Continued*

(Number.)

Agency	Total law enforcement employees	Total officers	Total civilians
Maryland–State Agencies			
Comptroller of the Treasury, Field Enforcement Division	88	26	62
Department of Public Safety and Correctional Services, Internal Investigations Unit	22	18	4
General Services			
Annapolis, Anne Arundel County	80	44	36
Baltimore City	96	44	52
Natural Resources Police	504	285	219
Rosewood	12	5	7
Springfield Hospital	13	4	9
State Fire Marshal	73	41	32
Transit Administration	163	148	15
Transportation Authority	567	429	138
Maryland–Other Agencies			
Maryland-National Capital Park Police			
Montgomery County	101	84	17
Prince George's County	111	81	30
Massachusetts–State Agencies			
Massachusetts Bay Transportation Authority, Suffolk County	253	240	13
Michigan–Other Agencies			
Bishop International Airport	7	7	0
Capitol Region Airport Authority	25	17	8
Huron-Clinton Metropolitan Authority	37	36	1
Wayne County Airport	160	141	19
Minnesota–Other Agencies			
Minneapolis-St. Paul International Airport	119	84	35
Three Rivers Park District	31	16	15
Missouri–State Agencies			
Capitol Police	36	29	7
Missouri–Other Agencies			
Clay County Park Authority	6	6	0
Jackson County Park Rangers	19	17	2
Lambert-St. Louis International Airport	103	87	16
St. Charles County Park Rangers	10	10	0
Montana–State Agencies			
Gambling Investigations Bureau	20	17	3
Nevada–Other Agencies			
Clark County School District	173	151	22
Washoe County School District	37	33	4
New Hampshire–State Agencies			
Liquor Commission	29	20	9
New Jersey–State Agencies			
Department of Human Resources	135	124	11
Human Services, Woodland Township	4	4	0
Hunterdon Development Center	10	9	1
New Jersey Transit Police	268	206	62
Palisades Interstate Parkway	30	29	1
New Jersey–Other Agencies			
Park Police			
Camden County	22	21	1
Morris County	31	30	1
Union County	375	330	45
Prosecutor			
Atlantic County	169	73	96
Bergen County	248	167	81
Burlington County	147	91	56
Camden County	258	173	85
Cape May County	61	21	40
Cumberland County	66	23	43
Essex County	407	284	123
Gloucester County	99	56	43
Hudson County	274	94	180
Hunterdon County	48	18	30
Mercer County	162	102	60
Middlesex County	207	132	75
Monmouth County	282	80	202
Morris County	167	72	95
Ocean County	162	76	86
Passaic County	218	89	129
Salem County	15	15	0
Somerset County	120	53	67
Sussex County	52	31	21
Union County	251	80	171
Warren County	61	35	26
New Mexico–Other Agencies			
Acoma Tribal	20	13	7
Laguna Tribal	40	23	17
Taos Pueblo Tribal	16	10	6
New York–Other Agencies			
Delaware and Hudson Railroad, Albany County	9	8	1
New York City Metropolitan Transportation Authority	691	636	55
Suffolk County Parks	44	41	3

Table 81. Full-Time Law Enforcement Employees, by State and Other Agencies, 2005—*Continued*

(Number.)

Agency	Total law enforcement employees	Total officers	Total civilians
North Carolina–State Agencies			
Department of Human Resources	6	6	0
Department of Wildlife	222	204	18
Division of Alcohol Law Enforcement	122	104	18
North Carolina Arboretum	4	4	0
North Carolina State Bureau of Investigation	538	333	205
State Capitol Police	61	50	11
State Fairgrounds	1	1	0
State Park Rangers			
Carolina Beach	6	4	2
Cliffs of the Neuse	5	5	0
Crowders Mountain	13	7	6
Eno River	8	5	3
Falls Lake Recreation Area	17	16	1
Fort Fisher	4	3	1
Fort Macon	5	4	1
Goose Creek	5	5	0
Gorges	3	3	0
Hammocks Beach	5	5	0
Hanging Rock	5	5	0
Jockey's Ridge	6	4	2
Jones Lake	8	5	3
Jordan Lake Recreation Area	17	13	4
Kerr Lake	14	12	2
Lake James	4	3	1
Lake Norman	8	4	4
Lake Waccamaw	4	3	1
Lumber River	8	6	2
Medoc Mountain	4	2	2
Merchants Millpond	7	4	3
Morrow Mountain	6	4	2
Mt. Mitchell	4	3	1
New River-Mount Jefferson	10	7	3
Pettigrew	2	2	0
Pilot Mountain	7	4	3
Raven Rock	4	3	1
Singletary Lake Group Camp	2	2	0
South Mountains	10	6	4
Stone Mountain	9	7	2
Weymouth Woods Sandhills Preserve	3	2	1
William B. Umstead	5	5	0
North Carolina–Other Agencies			
Asheville Regional Airport	17	16	1
Caswell Center Hospital	4	4	0
Cherokee Tribal	45	41	4
Durham County Alcohol Beverage Control Law Enforcement Office	3	3	0
Forsyth Municipal Alcohol Beverage Control Law Enforcement	7	6	1
Nash County Alcohol Beverage Control Enforcement	2	2	0
Piedmont Triad International Airport	28	18	10
Raleigh-Durham International Airport	29	27	2
Wilmington International Airport	14	10	4
Ohio–Other Agencies			
Cleveland Metropolitan Park District	80	69	11
Greater Cleveland Regional Transit Authority	104	90	14
Hamilton County Park District	38	35	3
Port Columbus International Airport	56	39	17
Toledo-Lucas County Port Authority	10	10	0
Wood County Park District	5	5	0
Oklahoma–State Agencies			
Capitol Park Police	70	42	28
Oklahoma–Other Agencies			
Jenks Public Schools	6	6	0
Madill Public Schools	1	1	0
Norman Public Schools	5	4	1
Putnam City Campus	12	8	4
Oregon–Other Agencies			
Port of Portland	65	51	14
Pennsylvania–State Agencies			
Bureau of Forestry			
Berks County	1	1	0
Centre County	1	1	0
Chester County	1	1	0
Clearfield County	1	1	0
Clinton County	1	1	0
Cumberland County	1	1	0
Delaware County	1	1	0
Fayette County	1	1	0
Huntingdon County	1	1	0
Indiana County	1	1	0

Table 81. Full-Time Law Enforcement Employees, by State and Other Agencies, 2005—*Continued*

(Number.)

Agency	Total law enforcement employees	Total officers	Total civilians
Lackawanna County	1	1	0
Lehigh County	1	1	0
Luzerne County	1	1	0
Lycoming County	1	1	0
Mifflin County	1	1	0
Monroe County	1	1	0
Northumberland County	1	1	0
Pike County	1	1	0
Schuylkill County	1	1	0
Snyder County	1	1	0
Susquehanna County	1	1	0
Tioga County	1	1	0
Union County	1	1	0
Bureau of Narcotics			
Adams County	11	9	2
Berks County	16	15	1
Blair County	16	14	2
Bucks County	16	15	1
Carbon County	16	15	1
Centre County	16	14	2
Chester County	32	32	0
Clearfield County	16	14	2
Clinton County	16	14	2
Cumberland County	15	13	2
Dauphin County	14	12	2
Delaware County	32	32	0
Erie County	15	13	2
Franklin County	14	12	2
Huntingdon County	16	14	2
Juniata County	16	14	2
Lancaster County	14	12	2
Lebanon County	14	12	2
Lehigh County	16	15	1
Luzerne County	23	17	6
Lycoming County	16	14	2
Mifflin County	16	14	2
Monroe County	16	15	1
Montgomery County	16	15	1
Montour County	16	14	2
Northampton County	16	15	1
Northumberland County	16	14	2
Perry County	14	12	2
Philadelphia County	32	32	0
Potter County	16	14	2
Schuylkill County	16	15	1
Snyder County	16	14	2
Tioga County	16	14	2
Union County	16	14	2
Westmoreland County	26	22	4
York County	14	12	2
Department of Environmental Resources	15	7	8
State Capitol Police	141	132	9
State Park Police, Pymatuning	3	3	0
Pennsylvania–Other Agencies			
Allegheny County Port Authority	69	45	24
County Detective			
Butler County	4	4	0
Cumberland County	8	7	1
Dauphin County	16	13	3
Lebanon County	7	6	1
Lehigh County	10	10	0
Westmoreland County	59	15	44
York County	11	10	1
Delaware County District Attorney, Criminal Investigation Division	39	33	6
Harrisburg International Airport	19	14	5
Rhode Island–State Agencies			
Department of Environmental Management	44	35	9
Rhode Island–Other Agencies			
Narragansett Tribal	6	6	0
South Carolina–State Agencies			
Bureau of Protective Services	66	62	4
Department of Mental Health	90	60	30
Department of Natural Resources			
Abbeville County	3	3	0
Aiken County	4	4	0
Allendale County	2	2	0
Anderson County	2	2	0
Bamberg County	3	3	0
Barnwell County	2	2	0
Beaufort County	5	5	0
Berkeley County	6	6	0
Calhoun County	2	2	0
Charleston County	16	13	3

Table 81. Full-Time Law Enforcement Employees, by State and Other Agencies, 2005—*Continued*

(Number.)

Agency	Total law enforcement employees	Total officers	Total civilians
Cherokee County	4	4	0
Chester County	2	2	0
Chesterfield County	2	2	0
Clarendon County	7	7	0
Colleton County	5	5	0
Darlington County	3	3	0
Dillon County	1	1	0
Dorchester County	5	5	0
Edgefield County	4	4	0
Fairfield County	3	3	0
Florence County	7	5	2
Georgetown County	9	8	1
Greenville County	3	3	0
Greenwood County	4	4	0
Hampton County	3	3	0
Horry County	5	5	0
Jasper County	2	2	0
Kershaw County	2	2	0
Lancaster County	2	2	0
Laurens County	2	2	0
Lee County	1	1	0
Lexington County	5	5	0
Marion County	3	3	0
Marlboro County	3	3	0
McCormick County	2	2	0
Newberry County	5	5	0
Oconee County	2	2	0
Orangeburg County	4	4	0
Pickens County	5	4	1
Richland County	7	6	1
Saluda County	4	4	0
Spartanburg County	3	3	0
Sumter County	2	2	0
Union County	3	3	0
Williamsburg County	4	4	0
York County	4	3	1
Employment Security Commission	3	3	0
Forestry Commission			
Aiken County	1	1	0
Bamberg County	1	1	0
Beaufort County	1	1	0
Berkeley County	2	2	0
Calhoun County	1	1	0
Charleston County	1	1	0
Chesterfield County	6	6	0
Colleton County	2	2	0
Darlington County	1	1	0
Fairfield County	2	2	0
Greenville County	2	2	0
Hampton County	1	1	0
Horry County	2	2	0
Jasper County	1	1	0
Kershaw County	3	3	0
Lee County	1	1	0
Oconee County	1	1	0
Orangeburg County	1	1	0
Pickens County	2	2	0
Richland County	3	3	0
Sumter County	2	2	0
Williamsburg County	1	1	0
York County	1	1	0
South Carolina School for the Deaf and Blind	1	1	0
State Museum	4	3	1
State Ports Authority	79	41	38
State Transport Police			
Abbeville County	10	10	0
Aiken County	47	30	17
Allendale County	11	11	0
Anderson County	19	15	4
Beaufort County	23	18	5
Chesterfield County	13	13	0
Darlington County	12	12	0
United States Department of Energy, Savannah River Plant	133	65	68
South Carolina–Other Agencies			
Charleston County Aviation Authority	37	26	11
Columbia Metropolitan Airport	18	17	1
Greenville-Spartanburg International Airport	22	17	5
Whitten Center	3	3	0
South Dakota–State Agencies			
Division of Criminal Investigation	143	45	98
Tennessee–State Agencies			
Alcoholic Beverage Commission	59	37	22
State Fire Marshal	31	26	5

Table 81. Full-Time Law Enforcement Employees, by State and Other Agencies, 2005—*Continued*

(Number.)

Agency	Total law enforcement employees	Total officers	Total civilians
State Park Rangers			
Bicentennial Capitol Mall	8	7	1
Big Hill Pond	4	1	3
Big Ridge	4	4	0
Bledsoe Creek	4	2	2
Booker T. Washington	7	3	4
Burgess Falls Natural Area	4	2	2
Cedars of Lebanon	15	4	11
Chickasaw	4	4	0
Cove Lake	12	4	8
Cumberland Mountain	4	4	0
Cumberland Trail	5	5	0
David Crockett	4	4	0
David Crockett Birthplace	6	3	3
Dunbar Cave Natural Area	2	2	0
Edgar Evins	4	4	0
Fall Creek Falls	8	8	0
Fort Loudon State Historic Area	4	4	0
Fort Pillow State Historic Park	1	1	0
Frozen Head Natural Area	7	3	4
Harpeth Scenic Rivers	2	2	0
Harrison Bay	5	5	0
Henry Horton	7	3	4
Hiwassee/Ocoee River	10	6	4
Indian Mountain	1	1	0
Johnsonville State Historic Area	2	1	1
Long Hunter	4	4	0
Meeman-Shelby Forest	6	6	0
Montgomery Bell	4	4	0
Mousetail Landing	3	3	0
Natchez Trace	5	5	0
Nathan Bedford Forrest	13	3	10
Norris Dam	4	4	0
Old Stone Fort State Archaeological Area	3	3	0
Panther Creek	2	2	0
Paris Landing	5	5	0
Pickett	3	3	0
Pickwick Landing	5	5	0
Pinson Mounds State Archaeological Area	1	1	0
Radnor Lake Natural Area	8	6	2
Red Clay State Historic Park	5	2	3
Reelfoot Lake	4	4	0
Hoan Mountain	4	4	0
Rock Island	4	4	0
Sgt. Alvin C. York	2	2	0
South Cumberland Recreation Area	6	6	0
Standing Stone	4	4	0
Sycamore Shoals State Historic Area	2	2	0
Tim's Ford	5	5	0
T.O. Fuller	4	4	0
Warrior's Path	5	5	0
Tennessee Bureau of Investigation	419	156	263
Tennessee Department of Revenue, Special Investigations Unit	32	22	10
Wildlife Resources Agency			
Region 1	40	39	1
Region 2	60	54	6
Region 3	44	43	1
Region 4	48	47	1
Tennessee–Other Agencies			
Chattanooga Metropolitan Airport	9	9	0
Drug Task Force			
3rd Judicial District	4	3	1
4th Judicial District	2	1	1
5th Judicial District	7	6	1
9th Judicial District	2	1	1
10th Judicial District	8	7	1
12th Judicial District	2	2	0
14th Judicial District	2	2	0
17th Judicial District	5	4	1
18th Judicial District	9	8	1
19th Judicial District	6	5	1
21st Judicial District	10	8	2
22nd Judicial District	2	2	0
23rd Judicial District	4	4	0
24th Judicial District	7	6	1
31st Judicial District	1	1	0
Knoxville Metropolitan Airport	44	26	18
Memphis International Airport	61	49	12
Metropolitan Board of Parks and Recreation, Nashville-Davidson	22	21	1
Nashville International Airport	79	63	16
TennCare Office of Inspector General	59	13	46
Tri-Cities Regional Airport	18	17	1
West Tennessee Violent Crime Task Force	7	6	1
Texas–Other Agencies			
Amarillo International Airport	14	14	0
Cameron County Park Rangers	10	10	0
Dallas-Fort Worth International Airport	398	272	126
Hospital District			
Dallas County	77	47	30
Tarrant County	44	29	15
Houston Metropolitan Transit Authority	225	161	64

Table 81. Full-Time Law Enforcement Employees, by State and Other Agencies, 2005—*Continued*

(Number.)

Agency	Total law enforcement employees	Total officers	Total civilians
Independent School District			
Aldine	45	36	9
Alvin	15	12	3
Angleton	4	3	1
Austin	92	63	29
Bay City	8	7	1
Brownsville	90	18	72
Cedar Hill	15	6	9
Conroe	60	43	17
Corpus Christi	55	31	24
East Central	10	9	1
Ector County	26	24	2
El Paso	41	35	6
Fort Bend	57	44	13
Hempstead	1	1	0
Humble	24	19	5
Judson	18	16	2
Katy	39	30	9
Killeen	10	10	0
Klein	42	28	14
Mexia	3	3	0
Midland	22	7	15
North East	42	36	6
Pasadena	36	28	8
Raymondville	4	4	0
Socorro	24	19	5
Spring	33	31	2
Spring Branch	38	29	9
Taft	2	2	0
Tyler	10	9	1
United	119	30	89
Utah–State Agencies			
Parks and Recreation	86	85	1
Wildlife Resources	63	60	3
Utah–Other Agencies			
Granite School District	24	14	10
Vermont–State Agencies			
Attorney General	4	4	0
Department of Liquor Control, Division of Enforcement and Licensing	21	17	4
Department of Motor Vehicles	45	30	15
Fish and Wildlife Department, Law Enforcement Division	40	38	2
Virginia–State Agencies			
Alcoholic Beverage Control Commission	175	132	43
Department of Conservation and Recreation	220	92	128
Southside Virginia Training Center	20	18	2
Virginia State Capitol	91	77	14
Virginia–Other Agencies			
Chesapeake Bay Bridge-Tunnel	87	45	42
Norfolk Airport Authority	40	33	7
Port Authority, Norfolk	83	76	7
Reagan National Airport	247	185	62
Richmond International Airport	34	33	1
Washington–Other Agencies			
Colville Tribal	35	23	12
Lummi Tribal	21	19	2
Nisqually Tribal	11	9	2
Nooksack Tribal	7	6	1
Port of Seattle	133	104	29
Skokomish Tribal	15	14	1
Swinomish Tribal	12	10	2
West Virginia–State Agencies			
Capitol Protective Services	27	23	4
Department of Natural Resources			
Barbour County	1	1	0
Berkeley County	2	2	0
Boone County	1	1	0
Braxton County	2	2	0
Brooke County	1	1	0
Cabell County	1	1	0
Calhoun County	2	2	0
Clay County	2	2	0
Doddridge County	1	1	0
Fayette County	3	3	0
Gilmer County	1	1	0
Grant County	2	2	0
Greenbrier County	2	2	0
Hampshire County	6	5	1
Hancock County	1	1	0
Hardy County	2	2	0
Harrison County	3	3	0
Jackson County	2	2	0
Jefferson County	1	1	0
Kanawha County	3	3	0

Table 81. Full-Time Law Enforcement Employees, by State and Other Agencies, 2005—*Continued*

(Number.)

Agency	Total law enforcement employees	Total officers	Total civilians
Lewis County	2	2	0
Logan County	2	2	0
Marion County	5	4	1
Marshall County	2	2	0
Mason County	1	1	0
McDowell County	2	2	0
Mercer County	2	2	0
Mineral County	2	2	0
Mingo County	1	1	0
Monongalia County	2	2	0
Monroe County	1	1	0
Morgan County	1	1	0
Nicholas County	2	2	0
Ohio County	1	1	0
Pendleton County	3	3	0
Pocahontas County	3	3	0
Preston County	3	3	0
Putnam County	6	5	1
Raleigh County	7	5	2
Randolph County	5	4	1
Ritchie County	1	1	0
Roane County	1	1	0
Summers County	3	3	0
Taylor County	1	1	0
Tucker County	2	2	0
Tyler County	1	1	0
Upshur County	2	2	0
Wayne County	1	1	0
Webster County	2	2	0
Wetzel County	1	1	0
Wirt County	1	1	0
Wood County	8	6	2
Wyoming County	2	2	0
State Fire Marshal			
Boone County	1	1	0
Cabell County	1	1	0
Fayette County	4	4	0
Harrison County	2	2	0
Jackson County	1	1	0
Jefferson County	1	1	0
Kanawha County	20	7	13
Lewis County	1	1	0
Marion County	1	1	0
Mercer County	1	1	0
Mineral County	1	1	0
Nicholas County	2	2	0
Ohio County	2	2	0
Putnam County	1	1	0
Randolph County	1	1	0
Wetzel County	1	1	0
Wood County	1	1	0
Wyoming County	1	1	0
West Virginia–Other Agencies			
Kanawha County Parks and Recreation	5	5	0
Wisconsin–State Agencies			
Capitol Police	64	50	14
Department of Natural Resources	471	442	29
Wisconsin–Other Agencies			
Lac du Flambeau Tribal	10	9	1
Menominee Tribal	22	20	2
Oneida Tribal	28	21	7
Puerto Rico and Other Outlying Areas			
Guam	368	271	97
Puerto Rico	21 021	19 106	1 915
Virgin Islands	541	415	126
Federal Agency			
National Institutes of Health	101	79	22

APPENDIXES

APPENDIX I — METHODOLOGY

Submitting Uniform Crime Reporting (UCR) Program data to the Federal Bureau of Investigation (FBI) is a collective effort on the part of city, county, state, tribal, and federal law enforcement agencies to present a nationwide view of crime. Law enforcement agencies in 46 states and the District of Columbia voluntarily contribute crime data to the UCR Program through their respective state UCR programs. For those states that do not have a state program, local agencies submit crime statistics directly to the FBI. The state UCR Programs function as liaisons between local agencies and the FBI. Many states have mandatory reporting requirements, and many state programs collect data beyond the scope of the UCR Program to address crime problems specific to their particular jurisdictions. In most cases, state programs also provide direct and frequent service to participating law enforcement agencies, make information readily available for statewide use, and help streamline the national program's operations.

The criteria that have been established for state programs ensure consistency and comparability in the data submitted to the national program, and also ensure regular and timely reporting. These criteria include the following: (1) The state program must conform to the national program's standards, definitions, and required information. (2) The state criminal justice agency must have a proven, effective, statewide program, and must have instituted acceptable quality control procedures. (3) The state crime reporting must cover a percentage of the population at least equal to that covered by the national program through direct reporting. (4) The state program must have adequate field staff assigned to conduct audits and to assist contributing agencies in record-keeping practices and crime-reporting procedures. (5) The state program must provide the FBI with all of the detailed data regularly collected by the FBI from individual agencies that report to the state program in the form of duplicate returns, computer printouts, and/or appropriate electronic media. (6) The state program must have the proven capability (tested over a period of time) to supply all the statistical data required in time to meet the publication deadlines of the national program.

The FBI, in order to fulfill its responsibilities in connection with the UCR Program, continues to edit and review individual agency reports for completeness and quality. National program staff members directly contact individual contributors within the state, when necessary, in connection with crime-reporting matters; staff members also coordinate such contact with the UCR Program. Upon request, they conduct training programs within the state on law enforcement record-keeping and crime-reporting procedures. The FBI conducts an audit of each state's UCR data collection procedures once every three years, in accordance with audit standards established by the federal government. Should circumstances develop in which the state program does not comply with the aforementioned requirements, the national program may institute a direct collection of Uniform Crime Reports from law enforcement agencies within the state.

Reporting Procedures

Based on records of all reports of crime received from victims, officers who discover infractions, and other sources, law enforcement agencies tabulate the number of Part I offenses brought to their attention and submit these data to the FBI every month, either directly or through their state UCR program. Part I offenses include murder, and nonnegligent manslaughter, forcible rape, robbery, aggravated assault, burglary, larceny-theft, motor vehicle theft, and arson. See Appendix II for definitions of these offenses.

Law enforcement's monthly submission to the FBI includes other important information. When, through investigation, an agency determines that complaints of crimes are unfounded or false, it eliminates that offense from its crime tally through an entry on the monthly report. The report also provides the total number of actual Part I offenses, the number of offenses cleared, and the number of clearances that involve only offenders under 18 years of age. (Law enforcement can clear crimes in one of two ways: by the arrest of at least one person who is charged and turned over to the court for prosecution, or by exceptional means, in which when some element beyond law enforcement's control precludes the arrest of a known offender.) Law enforcement agencies also submit monthly to the FBI the value of property stolen and recovered in connection with the offenses and detailed information pertaining to criminal homicide and arson. In addition, the FBI collects supplementary information about offenses, such as the locations of robberies, time of day of burglaries, and other analyses about the offenses.

The expanded homicide data (details about murders such as the age, sex, and race of both the victim and the offender, the weapon used in the homicide, the circumstances surrounding the offense, and the relationship of the victim to the offender) includes the UCR Program's *Supplementary Homicide Reports* (SHRs). SHRs provide information regarding the ages, sexes, and races of murder victims and offenders; the types of weapons used in murders; the victim-to-offender relationships; and the circumstances surrounding the incidents. Law enforcement agencies are asked to complete an SHR for each murder reported to the UCR Program. The UCR Program's expanded homicide data also provide information about jusitifable homicide (the killing of a felon by either a police officer in the line of duty or a private citizen). For more information, see <http://www.fbi.gov/ucr/05cius/offenses/expanded_information/murder_homicide.html>.

Expanded arson data include details about the types of structures involved in arsons and arson rates per population group. For more information, see

<http://www.fbi.gov/ucr/05cius/offenses/expanded_information/data/arsontable_01.html>and <http://www.fbi.gov/ucr/05cius/offenses/expanded_information/data/arsontable_02.html>.

The UCR Program also requires law enforcement agencies to report data regarding law enforcement employees. In addition to reporting monthly data on law enforcement officers killed or assaulted, agencies report anually on the number of full-time sworn and civilian law enforcement personnel employed as of October 31 of the reporting year.

Editing Procedures

The UCR Program thoroughly examines each report it receives for arithmetical accuracy and for deviations in crime data from month to month and from present to past years that may indicate errors. UCR staff members compare an agency's monthly reports with its previous submissions and with reports from similar agencies to identify any unusual fluctuations in the agency's crime count. Large variations in crime levels may indicate modified records procedures, incomplete reporting, or changes in the jurisdiction's geopolitical structure.

Data reliability is a high priority of the national UCR program, which brings any deviations or arithmetical adjustments to the attention of state UCR programs and other submitting agencies. Typically, staff members study the monthly reports to evaluate periodic trends prepared for individual reporting units. Any significant increase or decrease becomes the subject of a special inquiry. Changes in crime reporting procedures or annexations that affect an agency's jurisdiction can influence the level of reported crime. When this occurs, the UCR Program excludes the figures for specific crime categories or totals (if necessary) from the trend tabulations.

The final responsibility for data submissions rests with the individual contributing law enforcement agency. Although every effort is made to ensure the validity of the data, accuracy of the statistics depends primarily on the adherence of each contributor to the established standards of reporting.

Population Estimation

The FBI calculated 2005 state growth rates using revised 2004 state/national population estimates and 2005 provisional state/national population estimates provided by the U.S. Census Bureau. The FBI then estimated population figures for city and county jurisdictions by applying the 2005 state growth rate to the updated 2004 Census Bureau data.

Crime Trends

Trend statistics offer the data user an additional perspective from which to study crime by showing fluctuations from year to year. Percent change tabulations in this publication are computed only for the reporting agencies that provided comparable data for the periods under consideration. The program excludes all figures from the trend calculations, except those received for common months from common agencies. Also excluded are unusual fluctuations that the program determines are the result of variables such as improved records procedures, annexations, etc.

Caution to Users

Data users should exercise care in making any direct comparison between data in this publication and those in prior issues of *Crime in the United States*. Because of differing levels of participation from year to year and reporting problems that require the UCR Program to estimate crime counts for certain contributors, the data are not comparable from year to year.

2005 Arrest Data

Because of changes in state or local agency reporting practices (implementation of the National Incident-Based Reporting System), data are not comparable to previous years' data for Colorado (Denver), Michigan (Detroit), Montana, and Rhode Island. Limited arrest data were received from Illinois. No 2005 arrest data were received from the District of Columbia's Metropolitan Police Department; the only agency in the District of Columbia for which 12 months of arrest data were received (Metro Transit Police) have no attributable population. Twelve months of arrest figures for the New York City Police Department and law enforcement agencies in Florida were not available to be included in the arrest tables. However, arrest totals for these areas were estimated by the national UCR program and are included in Table 29, "Estimated Number of Arrests, United States, 2005."

Offense Estimation

Tables 1 through 5 and Table 7 of this publication contain statistics for the entire United States. Because not all law enforcement agencies provide data for complete reporting periods, the UCR Program includes estimated crime numbers in these presentations. The program estimates offenses that occur within three types of areas: metropolitan statistical areas (MSAs), cities outside MSAs, and nonmetropolitan counties. The national program computes estimates by using the known crime figures of similar areas within a state and assigning the same proportion of crime volumes to nonreporting agencies or agencies with missing data. The estimation process considers the following: population size of agency; type of jurisdiction, e.g., police department versus sheriff's office; and geographic location.

Various circumstances require the national program to estimate offense totals for certain states. For example, some states do not provide forcible rape figures in accordance with UCR guidelines, or reporting problems at the state level that resulted in no usable data.

APPENDIX II—OFFENSE DEFINITIONS

The Uniform Crime Reporting (UCR) Program divides offense into two groups. Contributing agencies submit information on the number of Part I offenses known to law enforcement; those offenses cleared by arrest or exceptional means; and the age, sex, and race of persons arrested for each of thse offenses. Contributors provide only arrest data for Part II offenses.

Part I offenses include murder, and nonnegligent manslaughter, forcible rape, robbery, aggravated assault, burglary, larceny-theft, motor vehicle theft, and arson.

Violent crime is composed of four offenses: murder and nonnegligent manslaughter, forcible rape, robbery, and aggravated assault. According to the UCR Program's definition, violent crimes involve force or threat of force.

Criminal homicide—a.) Murder and nonnegligent manslaughter: the willful (nonnegligent) killing of one human being by another. Deaths caused by negligence, attempts to kill, assaults to kill, suicides, and accidental deaths are excluded. The program classifies justifiable homicides separately and limits the definition to (1) the killing of a felon by a law enforcement officer in the line of duty; or (2) the killing of a felon, during the commission of a felony, by a private citizen. b.) Manslaughter by negligence: the killing of another person through gross negligence. Traffic fatalities are excluded.

Forcible rape—The carnal knowledge of a female forcibly and against her will. Assaults and attempts to commit rape by force or threat of force are also included. Statutory rape (no force used—female victim is under the age of consent) and other sex offenses are excluded. Sexual attacks on males are counted as aggravated assaults or sex offenses, depending on the circumstances and the extent of any injuries.

Robbery—The taking or attempted taking of anything of value from the care, custody, or control of a person or persons by force or threat of force or violence and/or by putting the victim in fear.

Aggravated assault—An unlawful attack by one person upon another for the purpose of inflicting severe or aggravated bodily injury. This type of assault usually is accompanied by the use of a weapon or by means likely to produce death or great bodily harm. Attempted aggravated assaults that involve the display of—or threat to use—a gun, knife, or other weapon is included in this crime category because serious personal injury would likely result if the assault were completed. When aggravated assault and larceny-theft occur together, the offense falls under the category of robbery. Simple assaults are excluded.

Property crime includes the offenses of burglary, larceny-theft, motor vehicle theft, and arson. The object of the theft-type offenses is the taking of money or property, but there is no force or threat of force against the victims. The property crime category includes arson because the offense involves the destruction of property; however, arson victims may be subjected to force.

Burglary (breaking or entering)—The unlawful entry of a structure to commit a felony or a theft. The use of force to gain entry need not have occurred. The Program has three subclassifications for burglary: forcible entry, unlawful entry where no force is used, and attempted forcible entry. The UCR definition of "structure" includes, for example, apartment, barn, house trailer or houseboat when used as a permanent dwelling, office, railroad car (but not automobile), stable, and vessel (i.e., ship).

Larceny-theft (except motor vehicle theft)—The unlawful taking, carrying, leading, or riding away of property from the possession or constructive possession of another. Examples are thefts of bicycles or automobile accessories, shoplifting, pocket-picking, or the stealing of any property or article that is not taken by force and violence or by fraud. Attempted larcenies are included. Embezzlement, confidence games, forgery, worthless checks, and the like, are excluded.

Motor vehicle theft—The theft or attempted theft of a motor vehicle. It includes the stealing of automobiles, trucks, buses, motorcycles, snowmobiles, and the like. The taking of a motor vehicle for temporary use by persons having lawful access is excluded from this definition. A motor vehicle is self-propelled and runs on land surface and not on rails. Motorboats, construction equipment, airplanes, and farming equipment are specifically excluded from this category.

Arson—Any willful or malicious burning or attempt to burn, with or without intent to defraud, a dwelling house, public building, motor vehicle, aircraft, personal property of another, and the like. Limited data are available for arson because of limited participation and varying collection procedures by local law enforcement agencies. Arson statistics are included in trend, clearance, and arrest tables throughout Crime in the United States, but they are not included in any estimated volume data.

In addition to reporting Part I offenses, law enforcement agencies provide the UCR Program with monthly data on persons arrested for all crimes except traffic violations. These arrest data include the age, sex, and race of arrestees for both Part I and Part II offenses. **Part II** offenses encompass all crimes, except traffic violations, that are not classified as Part I offenses, including:

Other assaults (simple)—Assaults and attempted assaults which are not of an aggravated nature and do not result in serious injury to the victim.

Forgery and counterfeiting—The altering, copying, or imitating of something, without authority or right, with the intent to deceive or defraud by passing the copy or thing altered or imitated as that which is original or genuine; or the selling, buying, or possession of an altered, copied, or imitated thing with the intent to deceive or defraud. Attempts are included.

Fraud—The intentional perversion of the truth for the purpose of inducing another person or other entity in reliance upon it to part with something of value or to surrender a legal right. Fraudulent conversion and obtaining of money or property by false pretenses. Confidence games and bad checks, except forgeries and counterfeiting, are included.

Embezzlement—The unlawful misappropriation or misapplication by an offender to his/her own use or purpose of money, property, or some other thing of value entrusted to his/her care, custody, or control.

Stolen property; buying, receiving, and possessing—Buying, receiving, possessing, selling, concealing, or transporting any property with the knowledge that it has been unlawfully taken, as by burglary, embezzlement, fraud, larceny, robbery, etc. Attempts are included.

Vandalism—To willfully or maliciously destroy, injure, disfigure, or deface any public or private property, real or personal, without the consent of the owner or person having custody or control by cutting, tearing, breaking, marking, painting, drawing, covering with filth, or any other such means as may be specified by local law. Attempts are included.

Weapons; carrying and possessing, etc.—The violation of laws or ordinances prohibiting the manufacture, sale, purchase, transportation, possession, concealment, or use of firearms, cutting instruments, explosives, incendiary devices, or other deadly weapons. Attempts are included.

Prostitution and commercialized vice—The unlawful promotion of or participation in sexual activities for profit, including attempts.

Sex offenses, except forcible rape, prostitution, and commercialized vice—Statutory rape, offenses against chastity, common decency, morals, and the like. Attempts are included.

Drug abuse violations—The violation of laws prohibiting the production, distribution, and/or use of certain controlled substances. The unlawful cultivation, manufacture, distribution, sale, purchase, use, possession, transportation, or importation of any controlled drug or narcotic substance. Arrests for violations of state and local laws, specifically those relating to the unlawful possession, sale, use, growing, manufacturing, and making of narcotic drugs. The following drug categories are specified: opium or cocaine and their derivatives (morphine, heroin, codeine); marijuana; synthetic narcotics/manufactured narcotics that can cause true addiction (demerol, methadone); and dangerous nonnarcotic drugs (barbiturates, benzedrine).

Gambling—To unlawfully bet or wager money or something else of value; assist, promote, or operate a game of chance for money or some other stake; possess or transmit wagering information; manufacture, sell, purchase, possess, or transport gambling equipment, devices, or goods; or tamper with the outcome of a sporting event or contest to gain a gambling advantage.

Offenses against the family and children—Unlawful nonviolent acts by a family member (or legal guardian) that threaten the physical, mental, or economic well-being or morals of another family member and that are not classifiable as other offenses, such as assault or sex offenses. Attempts are included.

Driving under the influence—Driving or operating a motor vehicle or common carrier while mentally or physically impaired as the result of consuming an alcoholic beverage or using a drug or narcotic.

Liquor laws—The violation of state or local laws or ordinances prohibiting the manufacture, sale, purchase, transportation, possession, or use of alcoholic beverages, not including driving under the influence and drunkenness. Federal violations are excluded.

Drunkenness—To drink alcoholic beverages to the extent that one's mental faculties and physical coordination are substantially impaired. Excludes driving under the influence.

Disorderly conduct—Any behavior that tends to disturb the public peace or decorum, scandalize the community, or shock the public sense of morality.

Vagrancy—The violation of a court order, regulation, ordinance, or law requiring the withdrawal of persons from the streets or other specified areas; prohibiting persons from remaining in an area or place in an idle or aimless manner; or prohibiting persons from going from place to place without visible means of support.

All other offenses—All violations of state or local laws not specifically identified as Part I or Part II offenses, except traffic violations.

Suspicion—Arrested for no specific offense and released without formal charges being placed.

Curfew and loitering laws (persons under 18 years of age)—Violations by juveniles of local curfew or loitering ordinances.

Runaways (persons under 18 years of age)—Limited to juveniles taken into protective custody under the provisions of local statutes.

APPENDIX III—GEOGRAPHIC AREA DEFINITIONS

The UCR Program collects crime data and supplemental information that make it possible to generate a variety of statistical compilations, including data presented by reporting areas. These statistics allow data users to analyze local crime data in conjunction with those for areas of similar geographic location or population size. The reporting areas that the UCR Program uses in its data breakdowns include community types, population groups, and regions and divisions. For community types, the UCR Program considers proximity to metropolitan areas using the designations created by the U.S. Office of Management and Budget (OMB). (Generally, sheriffs, county police, and state police report crimes within counties but outside of cities; local police report crimes within city limits.) The number of inhabitants living in a locale (based on the U.S. Census Bureau's figures) determines the population group into which the program places it. For its geographic breakdowns, the UCR Program divides the United States into regions, divisions, and states.

The 2005 state growth rates are calculated using revised 2004 state/national population estimates and 2005 provisional state/national population estimates provided by the Census Bureau. The population figures for city and county jurisdictions were estimated by applying the 2005 state growth rate to the updated 2004 Census Bureau data.

Regions and Divisions

Listed below are the four regions of the United States, along with their nine subdivisions as established by the Census Bureau. The UCR Program uses this widely recognized geographic organization when compiling the nation's crime data. The regions and divisions are as follows:

Northeast

New England—Connecticut, Maine, Massachusetts, New Hampshire, Rhode Island, and Vermont

Middle Atlantic—New York, New Jersey, and Pennsylvania

Midwest

East North Central—Illinois, Indiana, Michigan, Ohio, and Wisconsin

West North Central—Iowa, Kansas, Minnesota, Missouri, Nebraska, North Dakota, and South Dakota

South

South Atlantic—Delaware, District of Columbia, Florida, Georgia, Maryland, North Carolina, South Carolina, Virginia, and West Virginia

East South Central—Alabama, Kentucky, Mississippi, and Tennessee

West South Central—Arkansas, Louisiana, Oklahoma, and Texas

West

Mountain—Arizona, Colorado, Idaho, Montana, Nevada, New Mexico, Utah, and Wyoming

Pacific—Alaska, California, Hawaii, Oregon, and Washington

Community Types

To assist data users who wish to analyze and present uniform statistical data about metropolitan areas, the UCR Program uses reporting units that represent major population centers. The program compiles data for the following three types of communities:

Metropolitan statistical areas (MSAs)—Each MSA contains a principal city or urbanized area with a population of at least 50,000 inhabitants. MSAs include the principal city, the county in which the city is located, and other adjacent counties that have a high degree of economic and social integration with the principal city and county (as defined by the OMB), which is measured through commuting. In the UCR Program, counties within an MSA are considered metropolitan counties. In addition, MSAs may cross state boundaries.

In 2005, approximately 82.9 percent of the nation's population lived in MSAs. Some tables in this publication refer to suburban areas, which are subdivisions of MSAs that exclude the principal cities but include all the remaining cities (those with fewer than 50,000 inhabitants) and any unincorporated areas.

Because the elements that comprise MSAs, particularly the geographic compositions, are subject to change, the UCR Program discourages data users from making year-to-year comparisons of MSA data.

Cities Outside MSAs—Ordinarily, cities outside MSAs are incorporated areas. In 2005, cities outside MSAs made up 6.8 percent of the Nation's population.

Nonmetropolitan Counties Outside MSAs—Most nonmetropolitan counties are composed of unincorporated areas. In 2005, 10.3 percent of the population resided in nonmetropolitan counties.

Metropolitan and nonmetropolitan community types are further illustrated in the following table:

Metropolitan	Nonmetropolitan
Principal cities (50,000+ inhabitants) Suburban cities	Cities outside metropolitian areas
Metropolitan counties	Nonmetropolitan counties

Population Groups

The UCR Program uses the following population group designations:

Population Group	Political Label	Population Range
I	City	250,000 or more
II	City	100,000 to 249,999
III	City	50,000 to 99,999
IV	City	25,000 to 49,999
V	City	10,000 to 24,999
VI	City[1]	Fewer than 10,000
VIII (Nonmetropolitan county)	County[2]	N/A
IX (Metropolitan county)	County[2]	N/A

[1]Includes universities and colleges to which no population is attributed.

[2]Includes state police agencies to which no population is attributed.

Individual law enforcement agencies are the source of UCR data. The number of agencies included in each population group may vary from year to year because of population growth, geopolitical consolidation, municipal incorporation, etc. In noncensus years, the UCR Program estimates population figures for individual jurisdictions. (A more comprehensive explanation of population estimations can be found in Appendix I.)

The categories below show the number of agencies contributing to the UCR Program within each population group for 2005:

Population Group	Number of Agencies	Population Covered
I	70	53,583,154
II	187	28,055,458
III	451	30,837,315
IV	826	28,453,837
V	1,895	30,045,724
VI	8,862	26,316,456
VIII (Nonmetropolitan county)[2]	3,016	30,609,555
IX (Metropolitan county)[2]	2,149	68,508,905
Total	17,456	296,410,404

[1]Includes universities and colleges to which no population is attributed.

[2]Includes state police to which no population is attributed.

APPENDIX IV—THE NATION'S TWO CRIME MEASURES

The Department of Justice administers two statistical programs to measure the magnitude, nature, and impact of crime in the nation: the Uniform Crime Reporting (UCR) Program and the National Crime Victimization Survey (NCVS). Each of these programs produces valuable information about aspects of the nation's crime problem. Because the UCR and NCVS programs are conducted for different purposes, use different methods, and focus on somewhat different aspects of crime, the information they produce together provides a more comprehensive panorama of the nation's crime problem than either could produce alone.

Uniform Crime Reporting (UCR) Program

The UCR Program, administered by the Federal Bureau of Investigation (FBI), was created in 1929 and collects information on the following crimes reported to law enforcement authorities: murder and nonnegligent manslaughter, forcible rape, robbery, aggravated assault, burglary, larceny-theft, motor vehicle theft, and arson. Law enforcement agencies also report arrest data for 21 additional crime categories.

The UCR Program compiles data from monthly law enforcement reports and from individual crime incident records transmitted directly to the FBI or to centralized state agencies that report to the FBI. The program thoroughly examines each report it receives for reasonableness, accuracy, and deviations that may indicate errors. Large variations in crime levels may indicate modified records procedures, incomplete reporting, or changes in a jurisdiction's boundaries. To identify any unusual fluctuations in an agency's crime counts, the program compares monthly reports to previous submissions of the agency and to those for similar agencies.

In 2005, law enforcement agencies active in the UCR Program represented more than 296 million United States inhabitants—94.1 percent of the total population.

The FBI annually publishes its findings in a preliminary release in the spring of the following calendar year, followed by a detailed annual report, *Crime in the United States*, issued in the fall. (The printed copy of *Crime in the United States* is now published by Bernan Press.) In addition to crime counts and trends, this report includes data on crimes cleared, persons arrested (age, sex, and race), law enforcement personnel (including the number of sworn officers killed or assaulted), and the characteristics of homicides (including age, sex, and race of victims and offenders; victim-offender relationships; weapons used; and circumstances surrounding the homicides). Other periodic reports are also available from the UCR Program.

The state and local law enforcement agencies participating in the UCR Program are continually converting to the more comprehensive and detailed National Incident-Based Reporting System (NIBRS). The NIBRS provides detailed information about each criminal incident in 22 broad categories of offenses.

The UCR Program presents crime counts for the nation as a whole, as well as for regions, states, counties, cities, towns, tribal law enforcement areas, and colleges and universities. This allows for studies among neighboring jurisdictions and among those with similar populations and other common characteristics.

National Crime Victimization Survey

The NCVS, conducted by the Bureau of Justice Statistics (BJS), began in 1973. It provides a detailed picture of crime incidents, victims, and trends. After a substantial period of research, the BJS completed an intensive methodological redesign of the survey in 1993. It conducted this redesign to improve the questions used to uncover crime, update the survey methods, and broaden the scope of crimes measured. The redesigned survey collects detailed information on the frequency and nature of the crimes of rape, sexual assault, personal robbery, aggravated and simple assault, household burglary, theft, and motor vehicle theft. It does not measure homicide or commercial crimes (such as burglaries of stores).

Twice a year, Census Bureau personnel interview household members in a nationally representative sample of approximately 43,000 households (about 76,000 people). Approximately 150,000 interviews of individuals 12 years of age and over are conducted annually. Households stay in the sample for 3 years, and new households rotate into the sample on an ongoing basis.

The NCVS collects information on crimes suffered by individuals and households, whether or not those crimes were reported to law enforcement. It estimates the proportion of each crime type reported to law enforcement, and it summarizes the reasons that victims give for reporting or not reporting.

The survey provides information about victims (age, sex, race, ethnicity, marital status, income, and educational level); offenders (sex, race, approximate age, and victim-offender relationship); and crimes (time and place of occurrence, use of weapons, nature of injury, and economic consequences). Questions also cover victims' experiences with the criminal justice system, self-protective measures used by victims, and possible substance abuse by offenders. Supplements are added to the survey periodically to obtain detailed information on specific topics, such as school crime.

The BJS published the first data from the redesigned NCVS in a June 1995 bulletin. The publication of NCVS data includes *Criminal Victimization in the United States*, an annual report that covers the broad range of detailed information collected by the NCVS. The bureau also publishes detailed reports on topics such as crime against women, urban crime, and gun use in crime. The National Archive of Criminal Justice Data at the University of

Michigan archives the NCVS data files to help researchers perform independent analyses.

Comparing the UCR Program and the NCVS

Because the BJS designed the NCVS to complement the UCR Program, the two programs share many similarities. As much as their different collection methods permit, the two measure the same subset of serious crimes with the same definitions. Both programs cover rape, robbery, aggravated assault, burglary, theft, and motor vehicle theft; both define rape, robbery, theft, and motor vehicle theft virtually identically. (Although rape is defined analogously, the UCR Program measures the crime against women only, and the NCVS measures it against both sexes.)

There are also significant differences between the two programs. First, the two programs were created to serve different purposes. The UCR Program's primary objective is to provide a reliable set of criminal justice statistics for law enforcement administration, operation, and management. The BJS established the NCVS to provide previously unavailable information about crime (including crime not reported to police), victims, and offenders.

Second, the two programs measure an overlapping but nonidentical set of crimes. The NCVS includes crimes both reported and not reported to law enforcement. The NCVS excludes—but the UCR Program includes—homicide, arson, commercial crimes, and crimes committed against children under 12 years of age. The UCR Program captures crimes reported to law enforcement but collects only arrest data for simple assaults and sexual assaults other than forcible rape.

Third, because of methodology, the NCVS and UCR have different definitions of some crimes. For example, the UCR defines burglary as the unlawful entry or attempted entry of a structure to commit a felony or theft. The NCVS, not wanting to ask victims to ascertain offender motives, defines burglary as the entry or attempted entry of a residence by a person who had no right to be there.

Fourth, for property crimes (burglary, theft, and motor vehicle theft), the two programs calculate crime rates using different bases. The UCR Program rates for these crimes are per capita (number of crimes per 100,000 persons), whereas the NCVS rates for these crimes are per household (number of crimes per 1,000 households). Because the number of households may not grow at the same annual rate as the total population, trend data for rates of property crimes measured by the two programs may not be comparable.

In addition, some differences in the data from the two programs may result from sampling variation in the NCVS and from estimating for nonresponsiveness in the UCR Program. The BJS derives the NCVS estimates from interviewing a sample and are, therefore, subject to a margin of error. The bureau uses rigorous statistical methods to calculate confidence intervals around all survey estimates, and describes trend data in the NCVS reports as genuine only if there is at least a 90-percent certainty that the measured changes are not the result of sampling variation. The UCR Program bases its data on the actual counts of offenses reported by law enforcement agencies. In some circumstances, the UCR Program estimates its data for nonparticipating agencies or those reporting partial data.

Apparent discrepancies between statistics from the two programs can usually be accounted for by their definitional and procedural differences, or resolved by comparing NCVS sampling variations (confidence intervals) of crimes said to have been reported to police with UCR Program statistics.

For most types of crimes measured by both the UCR Program and the NCVS, analysts familiar with the programs can exclude those aspects of crime not common to both from analysis. Resulting long-term trend lines can be brought into close concordance. The impact of such adjustments is most striking for robbery, burglary, and motor vehicle theft, whose definitions most closely coincide.

With robbery, the BJS bases the NCVS victimization rates on only those robberies reported to the police. It is also possible to remove UCR Program robberies of commercial establishments, such as gas stations, convenience stores, and banks, from analysis. When users compare the resulting NCVS police-reported robbery rates and the UCR Program noncommercial robbery rates, the results reveal closely corresponding long-term trends.

Conclusion

Each program has unique strengths. The UCR Program provides a measure of the number of crimes reported to law enforcement agencies throughout the country. The program's *Supplementary Homicide Reports* provide the most reliable, timely data on the extent and nature of homicides in the nation. The NCVS is the primary source of information on the characteristics of criminal victimization and on the number and types of crimes not reported to law enforcement authorities.

By understanding the strengths and limitations of each program, it is possible to use the UCR Program and NCVS to achieve a greater understanding of crime trends and the nature of crime in the United States. For example, changes in police procedures, shifting attitudes towards crime and police, and other societal changes can affect the extent to which people report and law enforcement agencies record crime. NCVS and UCR Program data can be used in concert to explore why trends in reported and police-recorded crime may differ.

INDEX

INDEX